ACTIVE LEARNING EDITION
PSYCHOLOGY IN ACTION

Karen Huffman
Palomar College

Gary Piggrem
DeVry University

JOHN WILEY & SONS, INC.

ISBN 0-471-45307-2

Contents

SUPPLEMENTS

Psychology in Action Sixth Edition, is accompanied by a host of ancillary materials designed to facilitate the theme of this edition, "Eureka (Aha!): Discovering the Joy of Learning." Ordering information and policies may be obtained by contacting your local Wiley sales representative.

Instructor's Supplements

Computerized Test Bank

Wendy J. Hunter, Ph.D., prepared the Computerized Test Bank, a multiplatform CD-ROM, that fully supports graphics, prints tests, student answer sheets and answer keys. The software's advanced features allow you to create an exam to your exact specifications, within an easy-to-use interface. The test generation program has nearly 2,000 test items which include approximately 10 essay questions for each unit (with suggested answers) and a variety of multiple-choice questions. Each multiple-choice question has been linked to the student learning objective it pertains to, coded "Factual" or "Applied," the correct answer indicated, and page referenced to its source in the text. Also included are several "humorous questions" that can be inserted in tests to reduce test anxiety. In addition, the Computerized Test Bank includes questions from the Student Study Guide and the main text's "review questions." These can be easily added to the test to reinforce student efforts or simply for the professor's reference.

Instructor's Resource Guide (available in hard copy and electronic format — Microsoft Word files)

Prepared by Kathleen Weatherford, Trident Technical College, this comprehensive resource includes for each text unit: an outline, student learning objectives, outline/lecture organizer (page referenced to text), lecture lead-ins, supplemental lectures ("hot" topics), key terms (page referenced to text), unit summary/lecture organizer, discussion questions, suggested films and videos, activities section, three active learning/critical thinking exercises, and a writing project. This edition also includes a Cross-Cultural Focus (either an activity or a brief lecture) and numerous Active Learning Exercises specifically created for use with any size class.

Transparency Acetates

One hundred full-color overhead transparencies are created from text illustrations, resized with bold type for use in large lecture halls.

Videos

Please contact your Wiley sales representative for information on Videos that are available to adopters of the text, such as Roger Bingham's series on the brain, and many other titles.

Student's Supplements

Student Study and Review Guide (Sixth Edition)

Prepared by Karen Huffman and Richard Hosey, this valuable resource offers students an easy way to review the textbook material and ensures that they know it. For each textbook module students have numerous tools that help them master the material, including: unit outline, learning objectives, key terms, key term crossword puzzles, matching exercises, fill-in exercises, an additional Active Learning Exercise, and two Sample Tests (20 items each) with answers.

Take Note! Art Booklet

A student supplement with all of the transparency acetate images printed in a black-and-white lay-flat booklet. Images are the same size and quality as the transparency acetates. This supplement allows students to take notes and keep up with their instructor more easily during class.

Media Package: Web Site

An exciting new Web site has been created expressly for the Sixth Edition that will include both student and instructor materials. All of the assets can be accessed directly from the Web site.

The media package includes the following supplementary material: multimedia mini-modules to enhance teaching of complex topics such as conditioning; HTML-based exercises, homework assignments, and more; self-tests; Web Links; and In the News articles and discussion questions prepared by Jon Iuzzini, Texas A&M University. The package also includes additional free downloads, such as the following:

- *PowerPoint Files.* Prepared by Paul J. Wellman, Texas A&M, two sets of files will be available for both student and instructor use: art slides and lecture note slides. Students will be able to access the Power Point files on the Web, and instructors will have the files on the Instructor's Resource CD-Rom, as well as, on the Web.

- *Vocabulary Flash Cards.* Prepared by Marvin W. Lee, Shenandoah University, the vocabulary flash cards comprise an interactive module that allows students to test their knowledge of vocabulary terms. Students will also be able to take self-tests and monitor their progress.

- *Simulations.* These exciting and new interactive modules will help students understand introductory but complex concepts that are featured in the text. Each interactive simulation will include summaries and thought-provoking questions to help support the student's understanding of the module.

- *Online Guide.* Prepared by Paul J. Wellman, this guide offers information about how to use the Web for research, and how to best find the information you are seeking.

WebCT

In addition to the Web site, we also offer a WebCT course prepared by John Conklin, Camosun College, a Web course management system in the highly customizable WebCT format. The course includes: module overviews, module reviews for each section, assignments, Web links, discussion questions, self-tests, quiz questions and test questions, as well as all standard features of WebCT, such as bulletin board, calendar, e-mail and chat. A brief Instructor's Manual will be available (in electronic format only) to assist you in your use of this course.

Blackboard

Due to its popularity, we also offer a Web course management system in the popular Blackboard format. The course includes: module overviews, module reviews for each section, homework assignments, Web links, discussion questions, self-tests, quiz questions and test questions, as well as all standard features of Blackboard.

Preface to the Active Learning Edition

NOTE TO THE INSTRUCTOR

Have you ever asked yourself how other teachers "cover" a full-length introduction to psychology text? Do you want to assign parts of chapters and not others? Do you wish you had more flexibility in how you divided in-class coverage and outside reading? Would you like to have more coverage of applied psychology, demonstrating how psychology is used everyday, such as in the workplace? These and related questions led to the creation of this *Active Learning Edition* of *Psychology in Action*.

This edition of *Psychology in* has been designed to maximize the flexibility and "userfriendliness" of the sixth edition, while maintaining its rigor, readability, and extensive pedagogical tools. To increase instructor (and student) flexibility, we have organized this text into 57 separate, independent modules—rather than the traditional 16 to 18 chapters found in most texts. This format allows you, as the instructor, to pick and choose specific topics you wish to assign to your students, and easily omit others. For example, if you wish to talk about intelligence, but not thinking or language, you could assign Module 23 and skip Modules 21 and 22. Because each module is truly independent from the others, you also can safely skip from topic to topic and custom design your introductory psychology course. This modular format allows you to "mix and match" class coverage and outside readings in a flexible manner that better reflects your in-class presentations. This type of flexibility is not available with a traditional format.

In addition to the benefits of "customization" for the professor, the modular approach allows students the benefit of distributed versus massed practice. As research has shown, we all learn and retain information better when it is divided into smaller chunks (see modules 4, 19, and 20). Perceptually, students are more apt to read short assignments that appear manageable, than read 40–50 page chapters that can look overwhelming.

Perhaps the most important feature of this text is that it covers all the topics normally found in introductory texts, while also meeting the rigorous demands of the DeVry University's unique Psychology-110 curriculum. Recognizing that this 110 course combined two previous courses, Psychology 104 Human Relations and Psychology 105 General Psychology, we created five additional modules to meet the specific needs of this new, combination course. These modules (workplace motivation, leadership, conflict, groups, and communication) provide coverage for DeVry's Psychology-110 curriculum that is currently not found in any other introductory psychology text on the market.

This Active Learning Edition of *Psychology in Action* is the only text that covers *all* of the terminal objectives in the Psychology-110 course in a consistent, and seamless manner. Although these five modules have been custom designed for DeVry's Psychology- I 10 course, the information is timely and important to anyone teaching (or taking) a general psychology course-especially those who need an applied, businessoriented focus.

NOTE TO THE STUDENT

While reading a traditional college text with 40 or 50 page chapters, do you find it difficult to concentrate? Do you frequently count ahead to find out how many pages are left in the chapter until you reach the end? Do you find yourself looking at a chapter and deciding to read it some other time because it looks like too much to read at the moment? This edition of *Psychology in Action* was written to help you overcome these barriers to using your textbook effectively.

The modular approach used in this text breaks topic areas into smaller, specifically focused, and more manageable units that can be quickly read and more easily learned. To help you in learning the material, the text includes many Critical Thinking/Active Learning exercises, so you are *really learning* the material, not just memorizing it. There also are Try This Yourself exercises to help you apply what you've learned in a meaningful (and fun) way, Check and Review Sections (with brief summaries and practice test questions), Tools for Student Success (see Module 4), built in short Study Tips, Visual Summaries, and so on. All of these features are designed to enhance your learning experience and increase your mastery of the material in a practical and useful way.

To further increase your understanding and mastery of the material, this Modular version of *Psychology in Action* also includes a new, ACTIVE LEARNING WORKSHEET at the end of each module. Some worksheets test your comprehension with fun and quick crossword puzzles based on key terins within the module. Other worksheets involve personal applications, matching exercises, fill-in the blanks, and other engaging forms of self-testing. Immediate feedback is provided with sample answers found in Appendix A.

As a user of *Psychology in Action,* you have guaranteed access to John Wiley & Sons student resource Web site *http://www.wiley.com/college/huffman.* Most modules of the text contain specific website icons located near topics that have important website resources. The site also includes special online student tutorial quizzes and practice tests, active learning exercises, links to psychology related topics, Internet activities, as well as other valuable features and activities. Check us out!

If you have suggestions or comments, please write to us directly. We love to hear from our readers and other professors. The most convenient way to contact us is through email: Karen Huffman (khuffman@palomar.edu) and Gary Piggrem (gpiggrem@devrycols.edu). We truly hope that this edition of *Psychology in Action* will help you have an effective and enjoyable learning experience in your psychology class.

ACKNOWLEDGMENTS

A text such as this would be impossible to do without the assistance and cooperation of other dedicated professionals. It has been a group effort involving the input and support of our families, friends, and colleagues. To each person we offer our sincere thanks.

We would like to recognize the efforts of the following DeVry University professors and administrators who offered insightful, timely, and helpful comments during the development of the project:

Professor Susan Riley, Columbus DeVry
Professor Christina Halawa, Tinley Park DeVry

Professor Joe Deboni, Addison Devry
Professor Beth Rene Roepnack, Alpharetta DeVry
Professor David Langlotz, Ontario DeVry
Professor Jan Pascal, Kansas City DeVry
Professor Susan Henning, Alpharetta DeVry
Professor Andrea Meld, Seattle DeVry
Professor Joy Easton, Orlando DeVry
Professor Liz O'Shaunessey, Long Beach DeVry
Professor Kim Lamanna-Finn, North Brunswick DeVry
Bob Rossi, DeVry On-Line
Dean Sandra Graham, Addison DeVry
Dean Sandra Vance, Orlando DeVry
Dean Dale Burgess, Atlanta DeVry(s)
Dean Martin Gloege, Denver DeVry

We'd also like to personally thank some people who made this endeavor not just possible, but also enjoyable:

From Gary: I want to thank my colleague, Dr. Tony Obradovich for his unflinching support throughout this process. I also would like to thank Maris Roze for his encouragement, insight, and enthusiastic support.

Finally, we both would like to thank the folks at John Wiley & Sons. Mark Berrafato supplied us with editorial guidance, keeping the project focused and on schedule. Jay Beck and Wiley Custom Services for production and project management expertise; Jeanine Furino for her production editorieal magic; and of course all the Wiley DeVry Sales Representatives.

Sincerely,
Karen & Gary

Critical Thinking/Active Learning

This text's focus on active learning naturally contributes to the development of critical thinking. I believe that an active learner is by definition also a critical thinker. Critical thinking has many meanings and some books dedicate entire chapters to defining the term. The word *critical* comes from the Greek word kritikos, which means to question, makes sense of, be able to analyze. Thinking is the cognitive activity involved in making sense of the world around us. Critical thinking, therefore, is defined as thinking about and evaluating our thoughts, feelings, and behavior so that we can clarify and improve them (adapted from Chaffee, 1988, p. 29).

Critical thinking is a process. As a process — something you do — you can do it better. You can develop your critical thinking skills. Each unit of *Psychology in Action* (and corresponding units in the Student Study and Review Guide and Instructor's Resource Guide) includes a specific Active Learning Exercise devoted to improving one or more of the components of critical thinking. To learn more about each of these components, study the following three lists. They present the affective (emotional), cognitive (thinking), and behavioral (action) components of critical thinking. You will no doubt find that you already employ some of these skills. You will also no doubt recognize areas you could strengthen through practice.

I. Affective Components — the emotional foundation that either enables or limits critical thinking

- *Valuing truth above self-interest.* Critical thinkers hold themselves and those they agree with to the same intellectual standards to which they hold their opponents.

- *Accepting change.* Critical thinkers remain open to the need for adjustment and adaptation throughout the life cycle. Because critical thinkers fully trust the processes of reasoned inquiry, they are willing to use these skills to examine even their most deeply held values and beliefs, and to modify these beliefs when evidence and experience contradict them.

- *Emphathizing.* Critical thinkers appreciate and try to understand others' thoughts, feelings, and behaviors. Noncritical thinkers view everything and everyone in relation to the self.

- *Welcoming divergent views.* Critical thinkers value examining issues from every angle and know that it is especially important to explore and understand positions with which they disagree.

- *Tolerating ambiguity.* Although formal education often trains us to look for a single "right" answer, critical thinkers recognize that many issues are complex and subtle, and that complex issues may not have a "right" answer. They recognize and value qualifiers such as "probably," "highly likely," and "not very likely."

- *Recognizing personal biases.* Critical thinkers use their highest intellectual skills to detect personal biases and self-deceptive reasoning so they can design realistic plans for self-correction.

II. Cognitive Components — the thought processes actually involved in critical thinking

- *Thinking independently.* Critical thinking is independent thinking. Critical thinkers do not passively accept the beliefs of others and are not easily manipulated.

- *Defining problems accurately.* A critical thinker identifies the issues in clear and concrete terms, to prevent confusion and lay the foundation for gathering relevant information.

- *Analyzing data for value and content.* By carefully evaluating the nature of evidence and the credibility of the source, critical thinkers recognize illegitimate appeals to emotion, unsupported assumptions, and faulty logic. This enables them to discount sources of information that lack a record of honesty, contradict themselves on key questions, or have a vested interest in selling a product or idea.

- *Employing a variety of thinking processes in problem solving.* Among these thinking processes are inductive logic — reasoning that moves from the specific to the general; deductive logic — reasoning that moves from the general to the specific; dialogical thinking — thinking that involves an extended verbal exchange between differing points of view or frames of reference; and dialectical thinking — thinking that tests the strengths and weaknesses of opposing points of view.

- *Synthesizing.* Critical thinkers recognize that comprehension and understanding result from combining various elements into meaningful patterns.

- *Resisting overgeneralization.* Overgeneralization is the temptation to apply a fact or experience to situations that are only superficially similar.

- *Employing metacognition.* Metacognition, also known as reflective or recursive thinking, involves reviewing and analyzing your own mental processes — thinking about your own thinking.

III. Behavioral Components — the actions necessary for critical thinking

- *Delaying judgment until adequate data is available.* A critical thinker does not make snap judgments.

- *Employing precise terms.* Precise terms help critical thinkers identify issues clearly and concretely so they can be objectively defined and empirically tested.

- *Gathering data.* Collecting up-to-date, relevant information on all sides of an issue is a priority before making decisions.

- *Distinguishing fact from opinion.* Facts are statements that can be proven true. Opinions are statements that express how a person feels about an issue or what someone thinks is true.

- *Encouraging critical dialogue.* Critical thinkers are active questioners who challenge existing facts and opinions and welcome questions in return. Socratic questioning is an important type of critical dialogue in which the questioner deeply probes the meaning, justification, or logical strength of a claim, position, or line of reasoning.

- *Listening actively.* Critical thinkers fully engage their thinking skills when listening to another.

- *Modifying judgments in light of new information.* Critical thinkers are willing to abandon or modify their judgments if later evidence or experience contradicts them.

- *Applying knowledge to new situations.* When critical thinkers master a new skill or experience an insight, they transfer this information to new contexts. Noncritical thinkers can often provide correct answers, repeat definitions, and carry out calculations, yet be unable to transfer their knowledge to new situations because of a basic lack of understanding.

> A great many people think they are thinking when they are merely rearranging their prejudices.
>
> WILLIAM JAMES

PSYCHOLOGY
IN ACTION

Introduction and Research Methods

Core Learning Objectives

As you read Modules 1, 2, 3, and 4, keep the following questions in mind and answer them in your own words:

► What is psychology? What are its goals and main career specialties?

► What is the scientific method?

► How do psychologists conduct experiments?

► What are the advantages and disadvantages of non-experimental studies?

► What are the major research and ethical issues and biases?

► Who are the important contributors to psychology's past, and what are the primary perspectives that guide modern psychology?

LEARNING OBJECTIVES

Alongside the outline is a list of four to six questions that represent general questions you should be asking yourself as you read the modules. For reinforcement, they are repeated in the margins at the place where they are discussed. These questions are an important part of the SQ4R method described in the Preface and the Student Study and Review Guide that accompanies this text.

CHAPTER OUTLINE

Each section begins with an outline of major topics and subtopics that will be discussed in the following modules. The major topics are boldfaced. Under each are approximately three to five subtopics. This pattern of headings is repeated within each module. The section outline and the corresponding headings provide a mental scaffold to organize the new information you are learning.

MODULE 1
Understanding Psychology
What is Psychology?
Goals of Psychology
Careers in Psychology

MODULE 2
Doing Research in Psychology
The Scientific Method
Experiments
Nonexperimental Studies
Ethical Problems

■ CRITICAL THINKING/ACTIVE LEARNING
Becoming a Better Consumer of Scientific Research

■ RESEARCH HIGHLIGHT
An Elegant Study of Therapeutic Touch

MODULE 3
Perspectives in Psychology
Psychology's Past
Psychology's Present

✳ GENDER AND CULTURAL DIVERSITY
Are There Cultural Universals?

MODULE 4
Tools for Student Success

OPENING VIGNETTE

Every section begins with a short opening story that sets the stage for the following modules. These vignettes introduce interesting real-world examples and applications of the theories covered.

Imagine that you are Emily Rosa, a 9-year-old looking for a topic for your school's annual science fair. Like most fourth-graders, you turn to your parents for ideas. It so happens that your mom and stepfather have frequently discussed the controversial practice of therapeutic touch (TT) — an alternative nursing technique designed to treat many medical conditions by manipulating "human energy fields." Although acknowledging that massage or actual touch can help patients, your parents are highly skeptical that TT practitioners can cure illness by simply waving their hands above the patient's body. You've heard your parents complain that TT practitioners charge up to $70 an hour for their treatment, despite the lack of corroborating scientific evidence. Suddenly, it hits you! Why not design a science fair project that tests TT?

Emily Rosa

As it turns out, your simple but elegant scientific study so completely debunks TT that you're invited to publish your findings in the highly respected Journal of the American Medical Association (JAMA). As the youngest researcher to ever publish in a major medical journal, you are recognized by the **Guinness Book of World Records**, receive a $1,000 check from the Skeptics Society, and are invited to appear on several nationally televised news broadcasts.

Although this sounds like a fourth-grader's fantasy, the story is true. Nine-year-old Emily Rosa (almost) single-handedly debunked an entire medical treatment employed by over 100,000 trained practitioners. As JAMA editor George Lundberg stated in a television interview, "Age doesn't matter. It's good science that matters, and this is good science" (Lemonick, 1998).

Antonio R. Damasio

Now, think of yourself as Dr. Antonio Damasio, distinguished professor and head of the Department of Neurology at the University of Iowa College of Medicine in Iowa City. You are introduced to a tall, slender, and extremely pleasant young female patient, referred to as "S." Tests show that she has normal healthy sensory perceptions, language abilities, and intelligence. Shortly after being introduced, S hugs and touches you repeatedly. You discover that this same cheerful, touching behavior pervades all areas of her life. She makes friends and romantic attachments easily and is eager to interact with almost anyone. By all reports, S lives in an extremely pleasant world dominated by positive emotions.

So what's "wrong" with S? Can you diagnose her? The real Dr. Damasio discovered that a very small part of S's brain, the amygdala, is damaged, and she can't, therefore, recognize or respond to fear in a person's face. As a result, "she has not learned the telltale signs that announce possible danger and possible unpleasantness, especially as they show up in the face of another person..." (Damasio, 1999, p. 66).

Welcome to the world of psychology. As a new traveler in this territory, you may be expecting a tour focusing on abnormal behavior and psychotherapy. But as the introductory stories show, psychology is much more than mental disorders and their treatment. In the upcoming modules, we will introduce you to a broad range of topics in psychology. As your tour guides, we take our responsibilities seriously and promise to make your journey exciting, intellectually stimulating, rewarding, and practical. So let's get started!

Module 1 begins by defining psychology and examining its goals. Module 2 examines psychological research and its problems and ethics, as well as career opportunities in psychology. Module 3 explores psychology's past and present, and Module 4 concludes with *Tools for Student Success*, which will help you get the most out of your course in psychology and this text.

INTRODUCTORY PARAGRAPH

Following the vignette is a paragraph of commentary that presents the major topics to be discussed in the modules, reinforcing and setting the stage for the material that follows.

MODULE 1
UNDERSTANDING PSYCHOLOGY

What Is Psychology?

We began this section with two stories that demonstrate psychology's scientific foundation. Emily's skepticism and empirical approach, and Dr. Damasio's careful observation and treatment of his patient, exemplify that, at its core, **psychology** is a science — the *scientific* study of behavior and mental processes. Psychologists value *empirical evidence*, information acquired by direct observation and measurement using systematic scientific methods. By taking an empirical approach, psychologists can be reasonably confident that the results of their studies are not contaminated by factors unrelated to the behavior being studied.

Our introductory examples also demonstrate another core value of psychology, that of **critical thinking,** the process of objectively evaluating, comparing, analyzing, and synthesizing information. Learning to think critically is one of the most important and lasting benefits of a college education.

This text contains numerous "Critical Thinking/Active Learning" exercises designed to help you improve your critical thinking skills while you master specific concepts and key terms. You'll also find "Try This Yourself" activities sprinkled throughout the text that further boost your critical thinking. Would you like to try one right now? Answer true or false for each of the following statements:

Psychology *The scientific study of behavior and mental processes*

Critical Thinking *The process of objectively evaluating, comparing, analyzing, and synthesizing information. Critical thinking has three components: affective skills (e.g., empathy and tolerance for ambiguity), cognitive abilities (e.g., independent thinking and synthesizing), and behavioral traits (e.g., delaying judgment and applying knowledge to new situations).*

RUNNING GLOSSARY

Key terms and concepts are bold-faced in the text the first time they appear. They are also printed again in the margin and defined in a "running glossary." The running glossary provides a helpful way of reviewing key ideas before tests. If you want to check the meaning of a term from another module, use the end-of-book glossary.

TRY THIS
Yourself

TRY THIS YOURSELF ACTIVITIES · · · · · · · ·

In most modules you will find several opportunities to apply what you are learning. These "Try This Yourself" sections are clearly identified with a special heading shown above. These activities are brief and fun to do. Research shows that actively involving yourself in learning increases comprehension and retention.

_____ 1. Most people only use about 10 percent of their brain.

_____ 2. Brain activity almost stops during sleep.

_____ 3. Police departments often use psychics to help solve crimes.

_____ 4. Punishment is the most effective way to permanently change behavior.

_____ 5. Eyewitness testimony is often unreliable.

_____ 6. Most adults go through a stormy midlife crisis in middle age.

_____ 7. Polygraph ("lie detector") tests can accurately identify attempts to deceive.

_____ 8. People who threaten suicide seldom actually commit suicide.

_____ 9. People with schizophrenia have two or more distinct personalities.

_____ 10. Males are naturally more aggressive than females.

Answers: 1. False (Module 6). 2. False (Module 13). 3. False (Module 12). 4. False (Module 16). 5. True (Module 20). 6. False (Module 27). 7. False (Module 32). 8. False (Module 39). 9. False (Module 40). 10. It depends on how you define *aggression.* (Modules 29 and 48).

Beware of the pseudopsychologist. Only scientific psychological research enables us to reliably understand and predict behavior. Pseudopsychologists, such as astrologers and psychics, make many claims that do not meet scientific or critical thinking standards.

How did you do? If you missed some questions, your "common sense" may have led you astray. Dealing with human behavior every day, you may think you already know about psychology — after all, it's "just common sense." In addition, the media may have misled you. Many "pop psychology" findings readily accepted by the popular press are in fact bogus — they do not follow from *scientifically* collected data. The belief that people use only "10 percent of our brains" is an example of this type of misinformation. Furthermore, the media and public often fail to differentiate *scientific* psychology from *pseudopsychologies,* which give the appearance of science but are actually false. (*Pseudo* means "false.") Pseudopsychologies include claims made by psychics (who supposedly help police locate missing children and communicate with the dead), palmistry (reading people's character from the markings on the palms of their hands), psychometry (the ability to determine facts about an object by handling it), psychokinesis (the movement of objects by purely mental means), and astrology (the study of how the positions of the stars and planets influence people's personalities and affairs).

For some, pseudopsychologies are mere entertainment, but about half of all Americans say they believe in them, and some reportedly spend thousands of dollars and valuable time on useless calls to psychic hotlines and horoscope readings. It's important to recognize that after years of research, no one has ever produced a *single,* reproducible, scientifically valid demonstration of *any* pseudopsychology (Druckman & Swets, 1988; Kelly, 1998, 1999; Milton & Wiseman, 1999). In fact, James Randi ("The Amazing Randi") is a famous magician who has dedicated his life to educating the public about fraudulent pseudopsychologists, and for many years has offered $1.1 million to "anyone who proves a genuine psychic power under proper observing conditions" (Randi, 1997; Opinion Archive, 2001). Although some have tried, the money has never been collected. If you would like more information about James Randi (and his million dollar offer), visit his website at http://www.randi.org.

The "Amazing Randi." World-renowned magician, James Randi, has offered $1.1 million dollars for scientific proof of any ESP or paranormal phenomena. After many years, the offer still stands.

Goals of Psychology: To Describe, Explain, Predict, and Change Behavior and Mental Processes

In contrast to pseudopsychologies, which rely upon self-report, anecdotal evidence, and opinions, true psychology bases its findings on scientific research and critical thinking. Psychology has four basic goals: to describe, explain, predict, and change behavior and mental processes through the use of scientific methods.

Nature–Nurture Controversy *The long-standing dispute over the relative contributions of nature (heredity) and nurture (environment) to the development of behavior and mental processes*

Interaction *A process in which multiple factors mutually influence the outcome — as in the interaction between heredity and environment*

1. *Description.* Description tells "what" occurred. In some studies, psychologists attempt to *describe,* or name and classify, particular behaviors by making careful scientific observations. Description is usually the first step in understanding behavior. For example, if someone says, "Boys are more aggressive than girls," what does that mean? The speaker's definition of *aggression* may differ from yours. Science requires specificity.

2. *Explanation.* An explanation tells "why" a behavior occurred. In other words, *explaining* a behavior or mental process depends on discovering and understanding its causes. One of the most enduring debates in science is the **nature–nurture controversy** (Collins, 2000; McCrae et al., 2000). To what extent are behavior and mental processes *explained* by biological and genetic factors (the nature side) or by environment and learning (the nurture side)? As you will see throughout the text, however, psychology (like all sciences) generally avoids "either-or" positions and focuses instead on **interactions.** Today, almost all scientists agree that nature and nurture *interact* to produce most psychological traits and even most physical traits. For example, research on aggression suggests numerous interacting causes or explanations, including culture and learning, as well as genes, instincts, and higher levels of testosterone (Anderson & Dill, 2000; Gay, 1999; Pahlavan, Bonnet, & Duda, 2000; Zillman & Weaver, 1999).

3. *Prediction.* Once psychologists meet the goals of description and explanation (answering the "whats" and "whys"), they move on to the higher-level goal of *prediction,* specifying the conditions under which a behavior or event is likely to occur. For instance, knowing that alcohol leads to increased aggression (Goodwin, 2000), we can predict that more fights will erupt at sports matches where alcohol is sold than at those where alcohol isn't sold.

4. *Change.* For some people, "change" as a goal of psychology brings to mind evil politicians or cult leaders "brainwashing" unknowing victims. However, to psychologists, *change* means applying psychological knowledge to prevent unwanted outcomes or bring about desired goals. In almost all cases, change as a goal of psychology is positive. Psychologists help people improve their work environment, stop addictive behaviors, become less depressed, improve their family relationships, and so on. Furthermore, as you know from personal experience, it is very difficult (if not impossible) to change someone against her or his will. (*Question:* Do you know how many psychologists it takes to change a lightbulb? *Answer:* None. The lightbulb has to want to change itself.)

Basic Versus Applied Research

Basic Research *Research conducted to study theoretical questions without trying to solve a specific problem*

To meet these four goals, psychologists use two major forms of research — basic and applied. **Basic research** is usually conducted in universities or in research laboratories to explore new theories and advance general scientific understanding. Discoveries linking aggression to testosterone, instincts, genes, substance abuse, culture, and learning came primarily from basic research. Because basic research almost always leads to later applications of the findings, it may not have any immediate real-world uses. It is primarily conducted for the sheer joy of learning — knowledge for its own sake.

Applied Research *Research that uses the principles and discoveries of psychology for practical purposes, to solve real-world problems*

Basic research meets the first three goals of psychology (description, explanation, and prediction). When we want to apply the fourth goal of psychology, to change existing real-world problems, scientists conduct **applied research.** As you can see in Figure 1.1, applied research in *human factors* has generated important safety and design improvements in automobiles, airplanes, and even stovetop burner arrangements.

Keep in mind that basic and applied research often interact, with one leading to the other. For example, once basic research identifies specific factors that contribute to aggression, psychologists may conduct applied research to address problems related to aggressive behavior. Knowing that alcohol is linked to aggression, some

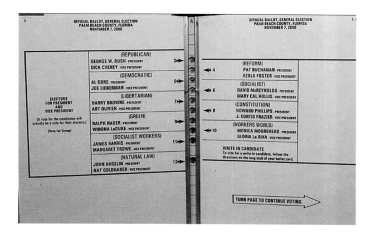

Basic and Applied Research. During the 2000 Presidential election, the U.S. watched while politicians heatedly debated the "butterfly ballot" in Palm Beach, Florida. Basic research on general cognitive processes and applied research on ballot design might have prevented this problem (Baron, Roediger, & Anderson, 2000).

sports stadiums now limit the sale of alcohol during the final quarter of football and the last two innings of baseball.

Careers in Psychology: What Psychologists Do

Knowing what psychology is and understanding its four major goals, would you consider a career in the field? Many students think of psychologists only as therapists,

(a) Spatial Correspondence

Poorly designed   Well-designed

····ILLUSTRATIONS

Don't skip over the photos, figures, and tables. They visually reinforce important concepts and often contain material that may appear on exams.

WEBSITE ICONS

Topics which have important website resources are marked with a special web icon as seen here. The student resource website at http:www.wiley.com/college/huffman includes online tutorial quizzes, practice tests, active learning exercises, internet links to psychology related topics, additional "check and review" questions, and other valuable features that will be updated regularly. Visit this site often.

(b) Visibility

Poorly designed   Well-designed

(c) Shape Indicates Function

Landing gear   Landing flap

Figure 1.1 *Human factors design and the real world.* Well-designed appliances and machinery are easily understood and operated. (a) The controls for stovetops should be arranged in a pattern that corresponds to the placement of the burners. (b) In an automobile, gauges for fuel, oil, and speed should be easily visible to the driver. (c) Controls and knobs are easier and safer to use if their shape corresponds to their function.

TABLE 1.1 SAMPLE SPECIALTIES IN PSYCHOLOGY

Biopsychology/ behavior neuroscience	Investigates the relationship between biology and and mental processes, including how physical and chemical processes affect the structure and function of the brain and nervous system
Clinical psychology	Specializes in the evaluation, diagnosis, and treatment of mental and behavioral disorders
Cognitive psychology	Examines "higher" mental processes, including thought, memory, intelligence, creativity, and language
Counseling psychology	Overlaps with clinical psychology but generally works with adjustment problems that are less severe, including marital, behavioral, or academic
Developmental psychology	Studies the course of human growth and development from conception until death
Educational and school psychology	Studies the process of education and works to promote the intellectual, social, and emotional development of children in the school environment
Experimental psychology	Examines processes such as learning, conditioning, motivation, emotion, sensation, and perception in humans and other animals (The term *experimental psychologist* is somewhat misleading because psychologists working in almost all areas of specialization also conduct experiments.)
Gender and/or cultural psychology	Investigates how males and females and different cultures differ from one another and how they are similar.
Industrial/organizational psychology	Applies the principles of psychology to the workplace, including personnel selection and evaluation, leadership, job satisfaction, employee motivation, and group processes within the organization
Social psychology	Investigates the role of social forces and interpersonal behavior, including aggression, prejudice, love, helping, conformity, and attitudes

Neuroscientist Candace Pert (and others) discovered the body's natural painkillers, called endorphins.

Psychologists often wear many hats. Dan Bellack teaches full-time at Trident Technical College, serves as Department Chair, and also works with faculty on teaching improvement.

For most people, this is the role they commonly associate with psychology — that of clinical or counseling psychologist.

Dr. Louis Herman's research with dolphins has provided important insight into both animal and human behavior.

but there are numerous career paths in psychology. Although many psychologists are employed as full-time therapists, a large percentage also work in academic, business, industrial, and government settings (Table 1.1).

Note that Table 1.1 is divided into several career specialties and that psychologists typically wear more than one hat. For example, your instructor may be an experimental psychologist by training but devote his or her entire professional life to teaching. Another experimental psychologist might teach, conduct research, and serve as an industrial consultant all at the same time. Similarly, a clinical psychologist might teach college courses while also being a full-time therapist.

What is the difference between a psychiatrist and a clinical or counseling psychologist? The joke answer would be "about $100 an hour." The serious answer is that psychiatrists are medical doctors. They have M.D. degrees with a specialization in psychiatry and are licensed to prescribe medications and drugs. In contrast, most clinical and counseling psychologists have received Ph.D., Psy.D., or Ed.D. degrees after intense study of human behavior and methods of therapy. Many clinical and counseling psychologists work with psychiatrists in a team approach to therapy.

Because of its diversity, psychology is currently one of the most popular career choices, and the U.S. Department of Labor expects that employment opportunities for psychologists will continue at least through the year 2005. To get an idea of the relative number of psychologists working in different fields of psychology, see Figure 1.2.

In this text, we will introduce many psychological fields of study and career options that may interest you. For example, Modules 5, 6, and 7 explore the world of neuroscience, and you may decide you would like the work of a neuroscientist/biopsychologist. Similarly, Module 8 discusses health psychology and the work of health psychologists, whereas Modules 37–45 examine problems in mental health and how therapists treat them. If you find a particular area of interest, ask your instructor and campus career counselors for further career guidance. We also encourage you to explore the APA home page (http://www.apa.org) or the APS home page (http://www.psychologicalscience.org). Psychology is always looking "for a few good men" — and women.

····**NARRATIVE QUESTIONS**
These embedded, narrative questions model for you the process of active learning and the questioning goal for the SQ4R method. This helps focus your reading and increases comprehension.

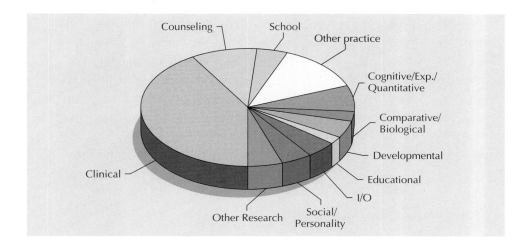

Figure 1.2 *Percentage of psychology degrees awarded by subfield.* Note that this is just a small sampling of the numerous specialty areas in psychology. The percentages shown here are based on data from the *American Psychological Association* (APA), the largest professional psychological organization. The other major organization is the *American Psychological Society* (APS). Source: *Graduate Studies in Psychology, 2000.*

Check & Review

UNDERSTANDING PSYCHOLOGY

Psychology is the scientific study of behavior and mental processes. It emphasizes the empirical approach and the value of **critical thinking.** Psychology is not the same as common sense, "pop psychology," or pseudopsychology. The goals of psychology are to *describe, explain, predict,* and *change* behavior and mental processes. To meet these goals, psychologists conduct either **basic research**, which studies theoretical issues, or **applied research**, which seeks to solve specific real-world problems.

There are many opportunities for a career in psychology. Some professional areas are grouped under the heading of basic research, including experimental, biopsychology or neuroscience, cognitive, gender and cultural, developmental, and social psychology. Applied areas include clinical, counseling, industrial/organizational, educational, and school psychology.

Questions

1. Psychology is the _____ study of _____ and _____.
2. What is the definition of *critical thinking*?
3. List and describe the four goals of psychology.
4. Name the subfield of psychology that studies each of the following topics:
   _____ a. The brain and nervous system
   _____ b. Growth and development from conception to death
   _____ c. Thinking, memory, and intelligence
   _____ d. Evaluation, diagnosis, and treatment of mental and behavioral disorders
   _____ e. Application of psychological principles to the workplace

Answers to Questions can be found in Appendix B.

CHECK & REVIEW

Each module concludes with an interim summary and four to six self-test questions that allow you to stop and check your understanding of the important concepts just discussed. These review questions give you feedback on whether you have fully mastered the major concepts in that section. Use these questions to review for exams, too. Answers for all questions are in Appendix B in the back of the text.

MODULE 1   ACTIVE LEARNING WORKSHEET

Enter the correct letter from Column A in the blank space in Column B, and then double-check your answers with those in Appendix B.

Column A
a. Applied Research
b. Clinical Psychology
c. Interaction
d. Nature–Nurture Controversy
e. Basic Research
f. Goals of Psychology
g. Developmental Psychology
h. Biopsychology
i. Cognitive Psychology
j. Industrial/Organizational Psychology

Column B
1.___ Multiple factors influence the outcome.
2.___ Describe, explain, predict, and change.
3.___ Focuses on solving real-world problems.
4.___ Applies psychology to the workplace.
5.___ Studies the biology of behavior.
6.___ Studies growth and development.
7.___ Concerned with "higher" mental processes.
8.___ Diagnoses and treats psychological disorders.
9.___ Interested in knowledge for its own sake.
10.___ Asks "Is it learned or innate?"

Answers can be found in Appendix B.

MODULE 2
DOING RESEARCH IN PSYCHOLOGY

Because psychology involves studying behavior and mental processes scientifically, psychologists approach research in the same way as scientists in biology, chemistry, or any other scientific field. First, they conduct an investigation and methodically collect data. They then piece together their findings, bit by bit, until they come to an objective conclusion. Throughout the entire process, psychologists follow standardized scientific procedures so that others — laypeople as well as scientists — can understand, interpret, and repeat their research. In this section, we will examine the *scientific method* in general, specific types of psychological research, and various research and ethical problems.

The Scientific Method: A Way of Discovering

Scientific investigations generally involve six basic steps, as summarized in Figure 2.1. Let's look at some of the key concepts associated with each step of the *scientific method*.

What is the scientific method?

Step 1: Reviewing the Literature of Existing Theories

Most research actually begins with informal questions. Emily Rosa asked about therapeutic touch. Students often ask about study methods for tests. Young parents question what to do about their small child who wants to sleep with them in their bed. If you asked 20 people, you might get 20 different answers to each of these questions. For example, one of the most popular beliefs about sleeping arrangements in our Western culture is that "children who regularly sleep in their parents' bed become too dependent on their parents and will never learn to sleep alone."

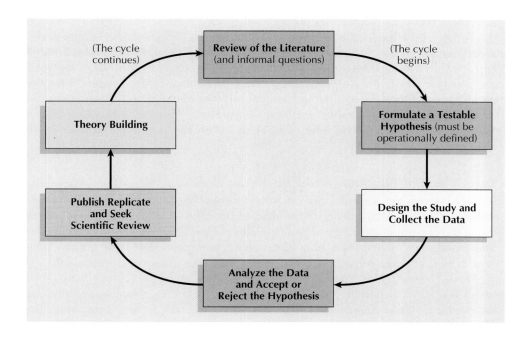

Figure 2.1 *The six steps of the scientific method.* A scientific investigation consists of six carefully planned steps, beginning with a review of the existing theories and ending with a return to theory building. Note that the steps are arranged in a circle to symbolize the circular, cumulative nature of science. One scientific study generally leads to additional and refined hypotheses, further studies and clarification of the results, and additions to the overall scientific knowledge base, known as *theories*.

Let's look at this "theory" more closely. How would you scientifically investigate it? The first official step in the scientific method would be to *review the literature*. That is, as a scientific researcher, you would carefully check this popular belief against what has been published in major professional, scientific journals (such as *Psychological Science, Journal of Cross Cultural Psychology,* and others). Scientific researchers do *not* rely on reports in the popular media (such as the *New York Times* or *Psychology Today*).

During this review, you might find several studies about children's sleeping arrangements, including cross-cultural studies noting that the "family bed," where the entire family sleeps in one bed, is a common arrangement in many parts of the world. In these cultures, shared sleeping arrangements are considered important to a child's social and emotional development (see Morelli, Rogoff, Oppenheim, & Goldsmith, 1999). You might also find *scientific* theories explaining why sleeping with parents may or may not be a good idea. (See Module 25 for a further discussion of theories of attachment.) Unlike casual, informal theories, scientific theories represent accumulated scientific knowledge developed from previous research and empirical observation. Contrary to common belief, theories are *not* just guesses or hunches or beliefs. A *scientific* **theory** is an interrelated set of concepts that explains a body of data.

Theory *A system of interrelated, accumulated research findings used to explain a set of observations and generate testable hypotheses*

Step 2: Formulate a Testable Hypothesis

As you just saw with the sleeping arrangement example, theories can come from many sources, including an investigator's personal observations, empirical findings from previous studies, or extensions from previous studies. Once the review of literature is completed, the researcher is in a position to begin testing the original theory or a revised theory based on findings from the literature. A cardinal rule of a scientific theory is that it must make testable *predictions* about *observable* behavior. That is, the theory must make predictions that can be objectively tested.

To test a theory, the researcher formulates a "testable hypothesis." A **hypothesis** is a specific prediction about how one variable is related to another. The *variables* in any given hypothesis are simply the factors that can vary or change. To test the theory about sleeping arrangements, a researcher might formulate this hypothesis: "Children who sleep with their parents on a regular basis will be more attached to their parents." Alternatively, such children "will be overly dependent." A hypothesis may or may not be correct; it is merely a possible explanation for a behavior that can be verified through scientific testing.

Hypothesis *A statement of a predicted relationship between two or more variables*

To be fully *testable*, a hypothesis must be formulated precisely (as opposed to vaguely or loosely), and the variables under study must be **operationally defined**, or stated in observable, measurable terms. With our previous hypothesis, how would you operationally define *sleeping arrangements*? What could you measure? One way might be to define *sleeping arrangements* as "one or more children sharing one bed for the majority of nights with one or more parents." This could be observed and measured as "the number of hours a week that a child sleeps alone or with one or more parents or caregivers."

Operational Definition *A precise description of how the variables in a study will be observed and measured; for example, drug abuse might be defined as "the number of missed work days due to excessive use of an addictive substance"*

Step 3: Design the Study and Collect the Data

The third step in the scientific method is to figure out how to put the hypothesis to an empirical test. As you will learn in the next section, there are various research methods to choose from, including naturalistic observation, case studies, surveys, experiments, and so on. The researcher considers the relative advantages and disadvantages of each method, then selects the one deemed most appropriate and practical.

Once the method is chosen, the researcher decides how to collect *data,* or the measurements of behaviors. For example, if you were testing sleeping arrangements and attachment, you might choose to use the survey method. To begin, you would first decide when to conduct your survey, how many people you needed to question, and where you would get your subjects or *participants* (the people or animals that are systematically observed and tested in a study.) In your sleeping and attachment survey, you might decide to mail 500 questionnaires to parents asking about their child's sleeping habits and attachment behaviors. Questions might include the following: "How many hours a day does your child sleep alone or with one or more parents?" "Does the child cry when you leave him or her in the care of another trusted adult?" "How does your child respond when you return after a brief (30-minute) separation?"

Step 4: Analyze the Data and Accept or Reject the Hypothesis

After the observations and measurements have been collected, the "raw data" must be analyzed so that you can decide whether they support or reject your initial hypothesis. To do such an analysis, researchers rely on *statistics,* mathematical methods used to organize, summarize, and interpret numerical data. Statistics play a vital role in the scientific method. If you are interested in learning more about statistical analysis, see Appendix A at the back of this book.

Step 5: Publish, Replicate, and Seek Scientific Review

To advance in any scientific discipline, researchers must share their work with one another and with the general public. Thus, the fifth step in the scientific method begins when the researcher writes up the study and its results and submits it to scientific journals for *publication*. Most journals ask other psychologists to critically evaluate material that is submitted for publication. On the basis of these peer reviews, the study may then be accepted for publication.

Throughout this text, you'll see *citations,* authors' names and publication dates, at the end of many sentences, like this: (Andreasen, 2000). This tells you that the material comes from reputable sources and is as up-to-date as possible. Complete publication information (title of article or chapter, author, journal name or book title, date, and page numbers) is provided in the References section at the back of this book. We hope you use these references as a starting point for research projects, for additional information on a topic of interest, and to "check up on us." As a critical thinker, never take the word of any one author or authors. Check their sources.

Once a study is published, other scientists interested in that topic attempt to replicate, or repeat, the study. *Replication* increases scientific confidence if the findings are the same. If not, researchers look for explanations and conduct further studies. As responsible scientists, psychologists almost never accept a theory on the basis of a single study; they wait for replication. The more times a study is replicated by other researchers using different participants in varied settings, the greater confidence psychologists have in the findings.

What if some replications find contradictory results? If the study can't be replicated or the findings are questionable, it is publicly criticized in follow-up journal articles. Also, researchers can average or combine the results of all such studies and reach conclusions about the overall weight of the evidence. Using a popular statistical technique, called **meta-analysis**, researchers can combine and analyze data from many studies, instead of assessing each study's results separately. For example, researchers Daniel Voyer, Susan Voyer, and M. P. Bryden (1995) used meta-analysis of almost 50 years of research on gender differences in spatial abilities. They found that males do better than females on some, but not all, tests of spatial ability. This meta-analysis also found that the differences have decreased in recent years, possibly owing to changes in educational practices. As you can see, with time the process of *scientific review* gradually discloses flaws and weeds out erroneous findings.

Meta-analysis *A statistical procedure for combining and analyzing data from many studies*

Step 6: Theory Building — The Cycle Continues

In steps 1 through 5, the researcher reviews the literature, formulates a hypothesis, conducts the research, analyzes the data, and publishes the findings so they can be replicated and reviewed. Now, the fun begins. In addition to explaining existing research findings, a good theory also generates *new* hypotheses and suggests new methods of inquiry. Thus, the research cycle continues. As Figure 1.3 shows, the scientific method is *circular* and *cumulative*.

Be forewarned. This ongoing, circular nature of theory building often frustrates students. In most modules, you will encounter numerous and sometimes conflicting hypotheses and theories about behavior and mental processes. You will be tempted to ask, "Which theory is right?" But remember that theories are never absolute. As we mentioned in the earlier discussion of the nature–nurture controversy, the "correct" answer is almost always *interactionism*. In most cases, multiple theories contribute to the full understanding of complex concepts.

> **How do psychologists conduct experiments?**

Experiment *A carefully controlled scientific procedure conducted to determine whether certain variables manipulated by the experimenter have a causal effect on other variables*

Experiments: Looking for the Causes

Now that you have a good basic understanding of the scientific method, we can examine two major types of psychological research — experimental research and nonexperimental studies. As Table 2.1 shows, both types of research have distinct advantages and disadvantages. We will discuss each approach separately, but keep in mind that most psychologists use several methods to study a single problem. In fact, when multiple methods are used and the findings are mutually supportive, scientists have an especially strong foundation for concluding that one variable does affect another in a particular way.

We begin our discussion with the single most powerful research method, the **experiment**, where an experimenter manipulates and controls the variables to deter-

TABLE 2.1 BASIC METHODS OF PSYCHOLOGICAL RESEARCH

Method	Basic Purpose	Advantages	Disadvantages
Experiment: manipulation and control of variables	Identify cause and effect	Allows researchers precise control over variables and to identify cause and effect	Ethical concerns, practical limitations, artificiality of lab conditions, uncontrolled variables may confound results, researcher and participant biases
Nonexperimental/ descriptive studies: naturalistic observation, surveys, case studies	Observe and record behavior and mental processes	Minimizes artificiality, easier to collect data	Little or no control over variables, researcher and participant biases, can't explain why certain behaviors occur
Nonexperimental/correlational studies: statistical analyses of relationships between variables	Identify relationships and how well one variable predicts another	Helps clarify relationships between variables that can't be examined by other methods and allows prediction	Does not allow researchers to identify cause and effect relationships

mine cause and effect. Only through an experiment can researchers isolate a single factor and examine the effect of that factor alone on a particular behavior (Ray, 2000). For example, in studying for an upcoming test, you probably use several methods — reading lecture notes, rereading highlighted sections of your textbook, and repeating key terms with their definitions over and over. Using multiple methods, however, makes it impossible to determine which study methods are effective or ineffective. The only way to discover which method is best is to isolate each one in an experiment. In fact, several experiments have been conducted to determine effective learning and study techniques (Son & Metcalfe, 2000). If you're interested in the results of this research or want to develop better study habits, refer to "Tools for Student Success" (Module 4) and other special sections throughout the text identified with this icon   .

An experiment has several critical components: independent variables, dependent variables, and experimental controls:

Independent and Dependent Variables

If a researcher chooses to use an experiment to test a hypothesis, he or she must then decide which variables to manipulate and which to examine for possible changes. The variables in an experiment are either independent or dependent. An **independent variable** (IV) (sometimes called the *treatment variable* or the *intervention variable*) is a factor that is selected and manipulated by the experimenter. It is hypothesized to have some effect on the dependent variable, and the experiment is conducted to verify this effect. In contrast, a **dependent variable** (DV) (or *outcome variable*) is a measurable behavior exhibited by the participant in the experiment. Because the IV is free to be selected and varied by the experimenter, it is called *independent*. The DV is called *dependent* because it is assumed to *depend* (at least is part) on manipulations of the IV.

If you were designing an experiment to discover whether watching violence on television causes aggressiveness in viewers, you might randomly assign groups of children to watch violent or nonviolent television programs (the IV) for one hour. Afterward, you could put a large plastic doll in front of each child and record the number of times the child hits, kicks, or punches the plastic doll in one hour (the DV).

Independent Variable *(IV) In an experiment, a variable that is manipulated by the experimenter to determine its causal effect on the dependent variable*

Dependent Variable *(DV) The variable that is observed and measured for change in an experiment; thought to be affected by (or dependent on) the manipulation of the independent variable*

Establishing a Control Group and One or More Experimental Groups

In addition to IVs and DVs, each experiment must have one control group and one or more *experimental conditions*, or ways of treating the subject/participants. Having at least two groups allows the performance of one group to be compared with that of another.

In the simplest experimental design, the researcher *randomly assigns* one group of participants to the *experimental group* and the other participants to the *control group* (Dehue, 2000). In the violence on TV and aggression example, one group, the **experimental group**, is exposed to the IV — in this case violent TV programs. The **control group** members would be treated exactly the same way as those in the experimental group, except that they would be assigned to a zero, or *control condition*, which means they are not exposed to any amount of the IV. They would watch a nonviolent TV program for the same amount of time.

We also could design the experiment with more than two *comparison groups* by using different levels of the independent variable. If one group watches 6 hours of violent TV whereas the comparison group watches 2 hours of violent TV and the control group watches no violent TV, then any observable difference in the DV (aggression) is logically caused by the IV.

Experimental Group *In a controlled experiment, the group of participants that receives the independent variable*

Control Group *In a controlled experiment, the group of participants that receives a zero level of the independent variable and that is used to assess the effects of the independent variable or treatment*

Extraneous Variables *Variables that are not directly related to the hypothesis under study and that the experimenter does not actively attempt to control (e.g., time of day and heating of room).*

While creating both control and comparison groups, experimenters also take care that all **extraneous variables** (those that are not being directly manipulated or measured) are held constant (the same). For example, time of day, heating, and lighting would need to be kept constant for all participants so that they do not affect participants' responses.

Experimental Safeguards

Every experiment is designed to answer essentially the same question: Does the IV *cause* the predicted change in the DV? To answer this question, the experimenter must establish several safeguards. In addition to the previously mentioned controls within the experiment itself (e.g., operational definitions, having a control group, and holding extraneous variables constant), a good scientific experiment also protects against potential sources of error from both the researcher and the participant. As we discuss these potential problems (and their possible solutions), you may want to refer several times to the summary in Table 2.2.

Researcher Problems

Researchers must guard against two particular problems — *experimenter bias* and *ethnocentrism*.

1. *Experimenter bias.* Experimenters, like everyone else, have their own personal beliefs and expectancies. The danger in research, however, is that these personal matters may produce a *self-fulfilling prophecy*: The researchers find what they expect to find. In collecting data, they may *inadvertently* give subtle cues or treat participants differently in accordance with their expectations. For example, an experimenter may breathe a sigh of relief when a participant gives a response supporting the researcher's hypothesis. This tendency of experimenters to influence the results in the expected direction is called **experimenter bias**.

Experimenter Bias *The tendency of experimenters to influence the results of a research study in the expected direction*

Scientists can prevent bias in several ways. One technique is to set up objective methods for recording data and enlist "blind observers" (neutral people other than the researcher) to collect the data without knowing what the researcher has predicted. In addition, researchers can arrange the experiment so that *either* the observer or the participant is unaware of which group received the experimental treatment. This is called a *single-blind study*. When *both* the experimenter and the participants are unaware, it is known as a **double-blind study**.

Double-Blind Study *A study in which neither the participant nor the experimenter knows which treatment is being given to the participant or to which group the participant has been assigned*

In a typical double-blind experiment testing a new drug, both the experimenter administering the drug and the participants taking the drug are unaware (or "blind") as to who is receiving a **placebo**, a fake pill or injection, and who is

Placebo [pluh-SEE-bo] *An inactive substance or fake treatment used as a control technique, usually in drug research, or given by a medical practitioner to a patient*

T A B L E 2 . 2   POTENTIAL RESEARCH PROBLEMS AND SOLUTIONS

	Problem	Solution
Researcher	Experimenter bias	Blind observers, single-blind and double-blind studies, placebos
	Ethnocentrism	Cross-cultural sampling
Participant	Sample bias	Random/representative sampling, random assignment
	Participant bias	Anonymity, confidentiality, deception (as well as single- and double-blind studies and placebos)

receiving the drug itself. Researchers use placebos because they have found that the mere act of taking a pill or receiving an injection can change the behavior of a participant. (The term *placebo* comes from the Latin verb *placere,* "to please.") Thus, to ensure that a particular effect is indeed due to the drug being tested and not to the *placebo effect,* control participants must be treated exactly as the experimental participants, even if this means faking the motions of giving them drugs or medications.

2. *Ethnocentrism.* Researchers cannot assume that just because a certain behavior is typical in their own culture, it is typical in all cultures. One way to avoid this type of **ethnocentrism** is to have two researchers, one from one culture and one from another, conduct the same research study two times, once with their own culture and once with at least one other culture. When using this kind of *cross-cultural sampling,* differences due to ethnocentrism can be isolated from actual differences in behavior between the two cultures.

Ethnocentrism *The belief that behavior in one's culture is typical of all cultures; also, viewing one's own ethnic group (or culture) as central and "correct" and then judging the rest of the world according to this standard*

Participant Problems

In addition to potential problems from the researcher, there are also several possibilities for error associated with participants, which can be grouped under the larger categories of *sample bias* and *participant bias.*

1. *Sample bias.* A *sample* is a group of research participants selected to represent a larger group, or *population.* When we do research, we obviously cannot measure the entire population, so we select and test a limited sample. However, using such a small group requires that the sample be reasonably similar to the composition of the population at large. If systematic differences exist among the groups being studied, known as **sample bias**, experimental results may not truly reflect the influence of the independent variable.

For example, much research has been done on heart disease, but it has been conducted almost exclusively with men. Unfortunately, physicians may apply findings from this research to the treatment of all their patients, both men and women. Because the purpose of conducting experiments is to apply, or *generalize,* the results to a wide population, it is extremely important that the sample represents the general population.

Sample Bias *The tendency for the sample of participants in a research study to be atypical of a larger population*

To safeguard against sample bias, research psychologists use random/representative sampling and random assignment:

- *Random/representative sampling.* Obviously, psychologists want their research findings to be applicable to more people than just those who took part in the study. For instance, critics have suggested that much psychological literature is biased because it is based primarily on white participants (see Robert Guthrie's 1998 book, *Even the Rat was White*). One way to ensure less bias and more relevance is to select participants who constitute a representative sample of the entire population of interest. Proper *random sampling* will likely produce a *representative,* unbiased sample.

- *Random assignment.* To ensure the validity of the results, participants must also be assigned to experimental groups using a chance, or *random,* system, such as a coin toss or drawing numbers out of a hat. This procedure of **random assignment** ensures that each participant is equally likely to be assigned to any particular group and that differences among the participants will be spread out across all experimental conditions.

Random Assignment *Occurs when participant's chances of being assigned to each group in an experiment are equal, thereby ensuring that any later differences between people in the experimental and control conditions must be the result of the treatment*

2. *Participant bias.* In addition to problems with initial sampling of participants, bias can also occur when participants try to present themselves in a good light (the *social desirability response*) or deliberately attempt to mislead the researcher. They may also be less than truthful when asked embarrassing questions or placed in awkward experimental conditions.

Researchers attempt to control for this type of participant bias by offering anonymous participation and other guarantees for privacy and confidentiality. Also, as mentioned above, single- and double-blind studies and placebos offer additional safeguards. If participants don't know which group they're in, or whether they're receiving the real drug or the "fake one," they won't try to overly please or deliberately mislead the experimenter.

Finally, one of the most effective, but controversial, ways to prevent participant bias is *deception*. Just like the unsuspecting subjects on the popular TV program *Candid Camera*, research participants will behave more naturally when they don't know they are part of a research project. However, many researchers consider the use of deception unethical — a topic we discuss in a later section.

Check & Review

SCIENTIFIC METHOD AND EXPERIMENTS

The scientific method consists of six carefully planned steps: (1) reviewing the literature for existing **theories**, (2) formulating a testable hypothesis, (3) designing the study and collecting the data, (4) analyzing the data and accepting or rejecting the **hypothesis**, (5) publishing followed by replication and scientific review, and (6) building further theory. The steps are arranged in a circle to show the circular, cumulative nature of science.

The experimental method is the only research method that can be used to identify cause-and-effect relationships. **Independent variables** (IVs) are the factors the experimenter manipulates, and **dependent variables** (DVs) are measur-

able behaviors of the participants. Experimental controls include having one control group and one or more experimental groups, and holding **extraneous variables** constant.

To safeguard against the researcher problem of **experimenter bias**, researchers employ blind observers, single-blind and **double-blind studies**, and **placebos**. To control for **ethnocentrism**, they use cross-cultural sampling. In addition, to offset participant problems with **sample bias**, researchers use random/representative sampling and **random assignment**. To control for participant bias, they rely on many of the same controls in place to prevent experimenter bias, such as double-blind studies. They also attempt to ensure anonymity and confidentiality and sometimes use deception.

Questions

1. What are the six steps of the scientific method?

2. Why is an experiment the only way we can determine the cause of behavior?

3. If researchers gave participants varying amounts of a new "memory" drug and then gave them a story to read and measured their scores on a quiz, the _____ would be the IV, and the _____ would be the DV. (a) response to the drug, amount of the drug; (b) experimental group, control group; (c) exposure to the drug, quiz scores; (d) researcher variables, extraneous variables.

4. What are the two primary sources of problems for both researchers and participants? What are the solutions?

What are the advantages and disadvantages of nonexperimental studies?

Nonexperimental Studies: Naturalistic Observation, Surveys, Case Studies, and Correlational Studies

Does drinking alcohol during pregnancy cause birth defects? Can stress cause cancer? Does smoking marijuana diminish motivation? Both the public and the scientific community would like answers to all these questions. However, only after performing carefully controlled experiments can we legitimately say that "A" *causes* "B."

But how could you experimentally discover if alcohol causes birth defects? You would need to administer large doses of disguised alcoholic drinks to pregnant women (the experimental group) while giving the same disguised drink without alcohol to another group of pregnant women (the control group). At the end of the pregnancy, you would carefully examine the newborns for increased levels of birth defects! Obviously, this kind of experiment could never be done on humans. It is *always* unethical to assign people to undergo research that may prove harmful. (Ethical problems associated with animal research are discussed in an upcoming section.)

When experiments cannot be used to determine cause and effect, scientists must rely on nonexperimental studies, such as naturalistic observation, surveys, individual case studies, and correlational studies. What distinguishes these nonexperimental methods is that the researcher cannot manipulate the variables under study. This lack of control means that none of these methods can be used to determine the *causes* of behavior. Nonetheless, nonexperimental studies are valuable for describing specifics about behavior, determining relationships between variables, and predicting behavior.

In this section, we will discuss four major nonexperimental methods: *naturalistic observation, surveys, case studies,* and *correlational studies*. As we discuss each of these methods, keep in mind that most of the problems and safeguards discussed with the experimental method also apply to the nonexperimental methods.

Naturalistic Observation

When using **naturalistic observation**, researchers systematically measure and record observable behavior of participants as it occurs in the real world, without interfering in any way. The purpose of most naturalistic observation is to gather descriptive information. Because of the popularity of researchers like Jane Goodall, most people picture naturalistic observation occurring in jungles, but supermarkets, libraries, subways, airports, museums, classrooms, assembly lines, and other settings also lend themselves to naturalistic observation.

Naturalistic Observation *The systematic recording of observable behavior in the participant's natural state or habitat with little or no experimenter intervention*

Imagine yourself as an educational psychologist who was asked, "Do smaller classes result in greater student achievement? If so, for what type of student?" A researcher who wanted to study these questions might not want to begin the investigation by bringing students and teachers into a controlled experimental laboratory setting. She or he might first go to several classrooms and observe how children and teachers behave in their natural setting.

In naturalistic observation, the researcher does not manipulate or control anything in the situation. The observer tries to be as unobtrusive as possible, to become, as they say, "like a fly on the wall." The researcher might conceal him- or herself in the background, stand behind a one-way mirror, or observe from a distance while the participants are (hopefully) unaware that they are being observed. If participants know someone is watching, their behavior becomes unnatural. For example, have you ever been driving down the street, singing along with the radio, and quickly stopped when you noticed the person in the next car was watching you? The same type of thing normally happens when participants in scientific studies realize they are being observed.

The chief advantage of naturalistic observation is that researchers can obtain data about a truly natural behavior, rather than about a behavior that is a reaction to an artificial experimental situation. If Jane Goodall had observed chimpanzees in a lab (or zoo), their behavior would probably be quite different from behavior in their natural habitat. On the downside, naturalistic observation can be difficult and time-consuming, and the lack of control by the researcher makes it difficult to conduct observations for behavior that occurs infrequently.

Naturalistic observation. Studying behavior in its natural environment allows behavior to unfold naturally (without interference).

Surveys

Surveys, tests, questionnaires, and interviews (we will refer to them all as "surveys") are similar techniques for sampling a wide variety of behaviors and attitudes. They

Survey *Nonexperimental research technique that assesses behaviors and attitudes of a sample or population*

Why not conduct your own sample survey? Station yourself at a conspicuous spot on campus, in your dorm, or some other place. Ask random passersby whether they consider themselves animal rights activists or nonactivists. Then read them the question in Table 1.4 and ask them to indicate their response next to the appropriate item. How do your survey results compare with those of Plous?

range from personality inventories that probe the makeup of individuals to public opinion surveys such as the well-known Gallup and Harris Polls.

The survey technique was used in a study conducted by S. Plous, who wanted a portrait of animal rights activists in the United States. At a big animal rights rally in Washington, D.C., in June 1990, he surveyed 574 people. After asking them whether they considered themselves animal rights activists (402 did) or nonactivists (172), he asked what they felt should be the agenda of the animal rights movement. Table 2.3 (Plous, 1991, 1998) shows a portion of the survey results. Just over half the activists felt that the single highest priority of the animal rights movement should be banning use of animals in research, whereas only one-quarter of the non-activists agreed.

Surveys are typically used to determine general opinions, attitudes, feelings, or behaviors related to a specific issue, such as voting preferences prior to state or national elections. One problem with surveys is that they rely on self-reported data, and not all participants are completely honest. In addition, survey techniques cannot, of course, be used to explain *causes* of behavior. But they can be helpful in predicting behavior. Plous, for example, could not pinpoint the causes of the activists' beliefs, but the results of his survey might be used to predict the attitudes and goals of some animal rights activists in the United States. As a critical thinker, can you see why his results are limited? Because he administered his survey only to participants at an animal rights rally, he lacked a *random/representative sampling*.

Case Studies

What if a researcher wants to investigate photophobia, fear of light? Most people are not afraid of light, so it would be next to impossible to gather enough participants to conduct an experiment or to use surveys or naturalistic observation. In the case of such rare disorders, researchers try to find someone who has the problem and study him or her intensively. Such an in-depth study of a single research participant is called a **case study**.

Case Study *An in-depth study of a single research participant*

TABLE 2.3 WHAT SHOULD THE ANIMAL RIGHTS MOVEMENT FOCUS ON MOST?

The Treatment of:	Activists[a]	Nonactivists
Animals used in research	54	26
Animals used for food	24	8
Animals used for clothing or fashion	12	22
Animals in the wild	5	30
Animals used in sports or entertainment	4	14
Animals used in education	1	0

[a] Figures indicate the percentage of respondents giving each answer.

In a case study, many aspects of a person's life are examined in detail to allow full description of the person's problem behavior and evaluation of any treatment. Dr. Damasio's (1999) study of patient "S," mentioned in this chapter's opening vignette, provides an excellent example of a case study. Damasio and his colleagues began with comprehensive evaluations of the patient's physical and mental health, intelligence, and personality. Results showed that S was in good health with normal sensory perception, language ability, and intelligence. She also had remarkable artistic and drafting skills. Her one problem was that she could not identify facial expressions of fear. She easily recognized other emotions and could mimic them with her own facial muscles. And, interestingly, she could draw finely detailed faces showing all emotions — except fear.

After extensive neurological tests and extensive interviews, Damasio and his staff discovered that S's inability to recognize fear in someone's face resulted from damage to her amygdala. They also found that S does not experience fear in the same way as others. She intellectually knows "what fear is supposed to be, what should cause it, and even what one may do in situations of fear, but little or none of that intellectual baggage, so to speak, is of any use to her in the real world" (Damasio, 1999, p. 66). Her inability to recognize fear in herself and others has led to poor social judgments and serious problems in social interactions.

At this time, there is no "happy ending" for S and others with similar damage, but case studies like this may eventually provide valuable clues that will lead to successful treatment. Keep in mind, however, that case studies have their research limits, including lack of generalizability, biased and inaccurate recall among participants, and so on.

Correlational Studies

Nonexperimental researchers sometimes want to determine the degree of relationship, or *correlation,* between two variables, so they turn to **correlational studies**. As the name implies, when any two variables are *correlated,* they are "related," and a change in one variable is accompanied by a concurrent change in the other.

Using the correlational method, researchers begin with their topic of interest, such as alcohol consumption during pregnancy. Then they select a group for study. In our previous example of drinking alcohol during pregnancy, the group under investigation would be pregnant women. After selecting the group, the variables of interest are measured for each participant in the study. In this case, the researchers might survey or interview the selected group of women about the amount and timing of any alcohol use during their pregnancies.

After the data are collected, the researchers analyze their results using a statistical formula that results in a *correlation coefficient,* a numerical value that indicates the degree and direction of the relationship between the two variables. (Note that there is an important distinction between correlational studies and correlation as a mathematical procedure. *Correlational studies* are a type of research methodology in which researchers set out to identify relationships between variables, whereas *correlation coefficients* are statistical procedures used in correlational studies, as well as with surveys and other research designs.)

A correlation coefficient can vary between 0 and +1.00 and 0 and −1.00. A perfect correlation (+1.00 or −1.00) would allow us to make completely accurate predictions. The sign (+ or −) tells whether the two variables vary in the same or opposite direction (Figure 2.2). The number indicates the relative strength. Thus, a correlation of −.45 or +.45 is higher (and more predictive) than a lower number like −.20 or +.20.

The Value of Correlations

Understanding correlational studies and correlation coefficients may be difficult, but it's worth the effort. Correlations help us make reliable and valuable predictions.

Correlational Study *A form of research that studies relationships between variables without the ability to infer causal relationships; correlational studies describe how strongly two variables are related and whether they are positively, negatively, or not at all (zero) correlated*

Figure 2.2 *Three types of possible correlation.* (a) *Positive correlation.* If both variables vary in the same direction — both go up or both go down — the relationship is described as positive. For instance, salary and years of education are *positively correlated.* As the number of years of education goes up, there is a concurrent upward movement in salary. Similarly, as the number of drunk drivers goes down, the number of car accidents also goes down. (b) *Negative correlation.* When two variables vary in the opposite direction — as one goes up, the other goes down — the relationship is negative. For example, the number of absences from class and scores on exams are *negatively correlated.* Students who miss a lot of class miss important information and tend to get lower grades on exams. (c) *Zero correlation.* Variables that are not at all related have a *zero correlation.* As one variable goes up, the other variable can go up or down because there is no relationship between the two. Shoe size and intelligence, for example, are not related. They have a zero correlation.

For example, correlational studies have repeatedly found high correlation coefficients between birth defects and a pregnant mother's use of alcohol, and between car accidents and the driver's use of cellular phones. This information enables us to reliably predict our relative risks and make informed decisions about our lives and behavior. If you would like additional information about correlations, see Appendix A at the back of the book.

Before we leave this topic, it's important to caution you that *correlation does not imply causation.* This is a logic error commonly associated with correlational studies. Although a high correlation allows us to predict one variable from another, it does not tell us whether a cause–effect relationship exists between the two variables. For example, what if we said there was a substantial positive correlation between the size of young children's feet and how fast they read? Would this mean that having small feet *causes* a child to be a slow reader? Obviously not! Nor do increases in reading speed *cause* increases in foot size. Instead, both are caused by a third variable — an increase in children's age. Although we can safely *predict* that as a child's foot size increases, his or her reading speed will also increase, this *correlation does not imply causation.*

We use this extreme example to make an important point about an all too common public reaction to research findings. People read media reports about *relationships* between stress and cancer or between family dynamics and homosexuality and then jump to the conclusion that "stress causes cancer" or that "withdrawn fathers and overly protective mothers cause their son's homosexuality." But they fail to realize that a third factor, perhaps genetics, may cause greater susceptibility to both cancer and increased rates of homosexuality.

Once again, as Figure 2.3 shows, a correlation between two variables does not mean that one variable *causes* another. Correlational studies do sometimes point to *possible* causes, like the correlation between alcohol and birth defects. However, only the experimental method manipulates the IV under controlled conditions and therefore can draw conclusions about cause and effect.

Ethical Problems: Protecting the Rights of Others

What are the major research and ethical issues and biases?

The APA, the largest professional organization of psychologists, recognizes the importance of maintaining high ethical standards in research, therapy, and all other areas of professional psychology. The preamble to their publication *Ethical Principles of Psychologists and Code of Conduct* (1992) admonishes psychologists to maintain their competence, to retain objectivity in applying their skills, and to preserve

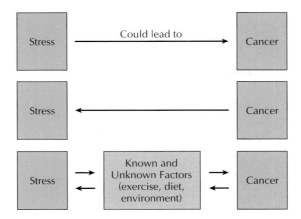

Figure 2.3 *Correlation is not causation.* Research has found a strong correlation between stress and cancer, however, this correlation does not tell us whether stress causes cancer, cancer causes stress, or whether other known and unknown factors could contribute to both stress and cancer.

CRITICAL THINKING/ACTIVE LEARNING EXERCISES

These special critical thinking/active learning exercises provide important insight into the module material and improve your basic critical thinking skills.

critical thinking ▶▶▶▶▶▶▶▶▶▶▶▶▶▶▶▶ *Active Learning*

Becoming a Better Consumer of Scientific Research

The news media, advertisers, politicians, teachers, close friends, and other individuals frequently use research findings in their attempts to change your attitudes and behavior. How can you tell whether their information is accurate and worthwhile?

The following exercise will improve your ability to critically evaluate sources of information. It is based on the concepts you learned in the previous discussion of psychological research techniques. Read each "research" report and decide what the primary problem or research limitation is. In the space provided, make one of the following marks:

CC = The report is misleading because correlation data are used to suggest causation.

CG = The report is inconclusive because there was no control group.

EB = The results of the research were unfairly influenced by experimenter bias.

SB = The results of the research are questionable because of sample bias.

_____ 1. A clinical psychologist strongly believes that touching is an important adjunct to successful therapy. For two months, he touches half his patients (Group A) and refrains from touching the other half (Group B). He then reports a noticeable improvement in Group A.

_____ 2. A newspaper reports that violent crime corresponds to phases of the moon. The reporter concludes that the gravitational pull of the moon controls human behavior.

_____ 3. A researcher interested in women's attitudes toward premarital sex sends out a lengthy survey to subscribers of *Vogue* and *Cosmopolitan* magazines.

_____ 4. An experimenter is interested in studying the effects of alcohol on driving ability. Prior to testing on an experimental driving course, Group A consumes 2 ounces of alcohol, Group B consumes 4 ounces of alcohol, and Group C consumes 6 ounces of alcohol. After the test drive, the researcher reports that alcohol consumption adversely affects driving ability.

_____ 5. After reading a scientific journal that reports higher divorce rates among couples living together before marriage, a college student decides to move out of the apartment she shares with her boyfriend.

_____ 6. A theater owner reports increased beverage sales following the brief flashing of a subliminal message to "Drink Coca-Cola" during the film showing.

Answers: 1. EB; 2. CC; 3. SB; 4. CG; 5. CC; 6. CG

Informed Consent *A participant's agreement to take part in a study after being told what to expect*

the dignity and best interests of their clients, colleagues, students, research participants, and society. In this section, we will discuss three important areas of ethical concern: human participants, animal rights, and clients in therapy.

Respecting the Rights of Human Participants

The APA has developed guidelines regulating research with human participants. These are the key issues:

- **Informed consent and voluntary participation.** One of the chief principles set forth in the APA document is that an investigator should obtain the participant's **informed consent** before initiating an experiment. The researcher should fully inform the participant as to the nature of the study, including significant factors that might influence a person's willingness to participate, such as physical risks, discomfort, or unpleasant emotional experiences. The researcher must also explain that participants are free to decline to participate or to withdraw from the research at any time.

RESEARCH HIGHLIGHT

An Elegant Study of Therapeutic Touch

Nine-year-old Emily Rosa, the child in our opening story, is a wonderful model of critical thinking and the scientific approach to everyday life. Therapeutic touch (TT) practitioners claim to heal or alleviate medical problems by passing their hands over the patient's body, supposedly realigning energy fields until they're "in balance" (Scheiber & Selby, 2000). This realignment reportedly stems disease and allows the patient's body to heal itself (Quinn & Strelkauskas, 1993). But rather than asking TT practitioners or their patients if their energy manipulations actually heal or relieve pain, Emily asked a more important question. She wanted to know whether *human energy fields* (HEF) even exist.

As you can see in Figure 2.4, Emily set up a small screen and then asked 21 TT practitioners to stick their hands, palms up, through the screen. The researcher (Emily) then held her hand over either the left or right hand of the practitioner — decided by a flip of coin. In 10 to 20 separate trials, the TT practitioners had to say which of his or her hands was nearer to the researcher's hand. Each participant was allowed to make any desired "mental preparations" ahead of time and to take as much time as necessary to make each determination. When the

results were analyzed, the TT practitioners performed no better than chance (Rosa, Rosa, Sarner, & Barrett, 1998)!

Not only did Emily's research bring her personal recognition and science fair honors but it also demonstrated the importance of scientifically analyzing therapeutic claims. This fourth-grader's "simple" study demonstrated that 21 practitioners failed to even *detect* her energy field — much less modify it. As our earlier discussion of the goals of psychology and the scientific method explained, therapeutic techniques must meet basic scientific standards. Given the lack of scientific support for TT's most fundamental claim, members of the medical and scientific community now question its continued use.

Needless to say, TT practitioners and supporters dispute the findings of Emily's study (Gorman, 1999). They say the research arrangement was unnatural, that

Figure 2.4 *Emily's clever design.* Nine-year-old Emily Rosa designed a clever scientific experiment to test whether therapeutic touch practitioners could sense her presence. The practitioners placed their hands through the holes in a screen. Then Emily tossed a coin and held one of her hands over the practitioner's left or right hand to see if they could detect her "energy field." They couldn't.

"our hands are moving, not stationary. You don't just walk into a room and perform — it's a whole process" (Lemonick, 1998, p. 67). TT practitioners who fully believe in their work can contact the James Randi Educational Foundation. As mentioned earlier, Randi offers $1.1 million to anyone who can demonstrate proof of any HEF or other pseudopsychology under scientifically controlled conditions. Despite extensive recruiting efforts, only one TT practitioner has attempted the test. She failed (Rosa, Rosa, Sarner, & Barrett, 1998).

- **The use of deception.** Participation in research should be voluntary and informed, but what if you're studying topics like persuasion techniques or attitude change? If participants know the true purpose behind some studies, they will almost certainly not respond naturally. Therefore, APA acknowledges the need for some *deception research*. When using deception, researchers are expected to follow strict guidelines, including **debriefing** participants at the end of the experiment. Debriefing involves explaining the reasons for conducting the research and clearing up any misconceptions or concerns on the part of the participant.

- **Confidentiality.** All information acquired about people during a study must be held confidential and not published in such a way that individual rights to privacy are compromised.

- **Students as research participants.** If research participation is a course requirement or an opportunity for extra credit, the student must be given the choice of an alternative activity of equal value.

Debriefing *A necessary and important aspect of deception research in which the participants are informed after the research about the purpose of the study, the nature of the anticipated results, and any deceptions used*

Respecting the Rights of Animal Participants

Most psychological research involves the use of human participants, but in some cases animals are used. For example, researchers sometimes study behavior continuously over months or years (longer than people are willing to participate), and occasionally they want to control aspects of life that people will not let them control and that would be unethical to control (such as who mates with whom or serious food restrictions). The relative simplicity of some animals' nervous systems also provides important advantages for research.

Keep in mind that the amount of animal research in psychology is relatively small. Only about 7 to 8 percent of all psychological research is done on animals, and 90 percent of that is done with rats and mice (American Psychological Association, 1984). In addition, most animal research involves naturalistic observation or learning experiments using rewards rather than punishments (Burgdorf, Knutson, & Panksepp, 2000; Neuringer, Deiss, & Olson, 2000). Furthermore, in all institutions where animal research is conducted, animal care committees are established to ensure proper treatment of research animals, to review projects, and to set guidelines that are in accordance with the APA standards for the care and treatment of research animals.

Finally, keep in mind that animal research has benefited both humans and other animals in many ways. Without animals in medical research, how would we test new drugs, surgical procedures, and methods for relieving pain? In psychology, research on learning in rats and pigeons led to the development of programmed learning materials, and teaching sign language to chimps and gorillas has led to a better understanding of the structure of human language. Animal research is also pursued for its potential benefit to animals themselves. As a result of psychological research, more natural environments have been created for zoo animals, successful breeding techniques have been developed for endangered species, and more effective training techniques have been developed for pets and wild animals in captivity. Despite the benefits of animal research, the use of animals in psychological research continues to be a controversial and ethical problem. While the controversy continues, psychologists take great care in the handling of research animals and actively search for new and better ways to protect them (Guidelines for the Treatment, 2000; Miller, 1991).

Respecting the Rights of Clients

Ethics are important in therapy, as well as in research. Successful psychotherapy requires that clients reveal their innermost thoughts and feelings during the course of treatment. It follows, then, that clients must trust their therapists. This places a

Is animal research ethical? Opinions are sharply divided on this question.

burden of responsibility on therapists to maintain the highest of ethical standards and uphold this trust.

Therapists are expected to conduct themselves in a moral and professional manner. They should remain objective while becoming sufficiently involved with the client's problems to know how to best help them. They should encourage their clients to become involved not only in deciding the type of treatment but also in the treatment process itself. Therapists are also expected to evaluate their clients' progress and report that progress to them.

All personal information and therapy records must be kept confidential, with records available only to authorized persons and with the client's permission. Such confidentiality can become an ethical issue when a client reveals something that might affect or possibly injure another person. For example, if you were a therapist, what would you do if a client revealed plans to commit murder? Would you alert the police or uphold your client's trust?

In cases of serious threat to others, the public's right to safety ethically outweighs the client's right to privacy. In fact, a therapist is legally required to break confidentiality if a client threatens violence to self or others, in cases involving suspected or actual child or elderly abuse, and in some other limited situations. In general, however, a counselor's primary obligation is to protect client disclosures (Corey, 2001).

A Final Note on Ethical Issues

After discussing ways research can be flawed and ethics can be violated, you may be unnecessarily concerned. Remember that guidelines exist to protect the rights of humans, animals, and therapy clients. Most importantly, a *human subjects committee* or *institutional review board* must first approve all research using human participants conducted at a college, university, or any reputable institution. This group ensures that every proposed study provides for informed consent, participants' confidentiality, and safe procedures. Similar committees also exist to oversee and protect the rights of animal participants.

Any member of APA who disregards these principles may be censured or expelled from the organization. Clinicians who violate ethical guidelines for working with clients risk severe sanctions and can permanently lose their license to practice. In addition, both researchers and clinicians are held professionally and legally responsible by their institutions, as well as by local and state agencies.

Check & Review

NONEXPERIMENTAL STUDIES/RESEARCH AND ETHICAL PROBLEMS

Unlike experiments, nonexperimental methods cannot determine the causes of behavior, but they can describe specifics, determine relationships, and help with prediction. **Naturalistic observation** is used to study and describe behavior in its natural habitat. **Surveys** use interviews or questionnaires to obtain information on a sample of participants. Individual

case studies are in-depth studies of a participant.

Correlational studies examine how strongly two variables are related (+1.00 to −1.00) and whether the relationship is positively, negatively, or not at all (zero) correlated. Correlational studies and the correlation coefficient provide important research findings and valuable predictions. However, it is important to remember that *correlation does not imply causation.*

Psychologists are expected to maintain high ethical standards in their relations

with human and animal research participants, as well as with clients in therapy. The APA has published guidelines detailing these ethical standards.

Questions

1. What is the major difference between naturalistic observations, surveys, and case studies?

2. Maria is thinking of running for student body president, but she wonders

whether her campaign should emphasize campus security, improved parking facilities, or increased health services. Which scientific method of research would you recommend she use to determine the focus of her campaign? (a) case study; (b) naturalistic observation; (c) an experiment; (d) a survey.

3. Which of the following correlation coefficients indicates the strongest relationship? (a) +.78; (b) −.84; (c) +.35; (d) 00.

4. A participant's agreement to take part in a study after being told what to expect is known as _____ (a) participant observer; (b) placebo effect; (c) informed consent; (d) debriefing.

Answers to Questions can be found in Appendix B.

ACTIVE LEARNING WORKSHEET   MODULE 2

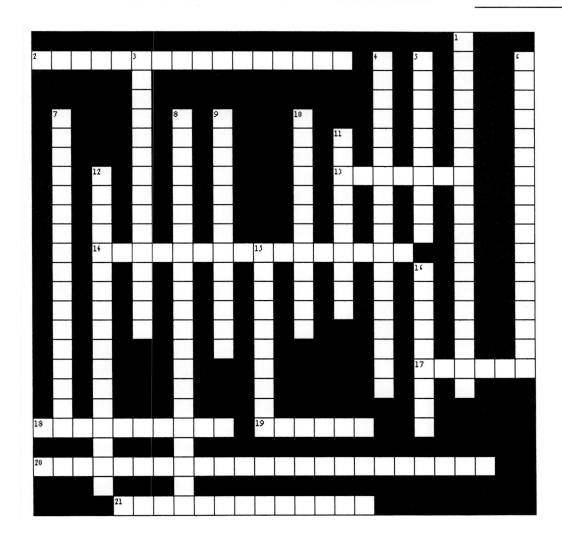

ACROSS

2. Experimenter influences the results of a research study in the expected direction.

13. An inactive substance or fake treatment used as a control technique in research.

14. Participant's chances of being assigned to each group in an experiment are equal.

17. Interrelated, accumulated research findings used to explain a set of observations and generate testable hypotheses.

18. Informing research participants about the purpose of the study, the nature of the anticipated results, and any deceptions used.

19. Nonexperimental research technique that assesses behaviors and attitudes of a sample or population.

20. Systematic recording of observable behavior in the participant's natural state or habitat with little or no experimenter intervention.

21. Believing behavior in your culture is typical of all cultures.

DOWN

1. Variables not directly related to the hypothesis under study and that the experimenter does not actively attempt to control.

3. Participant's agreement to take part in a study after being told what to expect.

4. Form of research that studies relationships between variables without the ability to infer causal relationships.

5. Statement of a predicted relationship between two or more variables.

6. Study in which neither the participant nor the experimenter knows which treatment is being given to the participant or to which group the participant has been assigned.

7. Variable that is observed and measured for change in an experiment.

8. Precise description of how the variables in a study will be observed and measured.

9. Statistical procedure for combining and analyzing data from many studies.

10. Research participants receiving a zero level of the independent variable.

11. Carefully controlled scientific procedure that determines whether certain variables manipulated by the experimenter have a causal effect on other variables.

12. Research participants receiving the independent variable.

15. Participants in a research study judged to be atypical of a larger population.

16. In-depth study of a single research participant.

Answers can be found in Appendix B.

MODULE 3
PERSPECTIVES IN PSYCHOLOGY

People have always been interested in human nature. Before psychology became a separate scientific discipline, the study of why people act as they do and how one person is different from another fell within the realm of philosophy. It was not until the first psychological laboratory was founded in 1879 that psychology as a science officially began. As interest in the new field grew, psychologists adopted various approaches to their research. Eventually, the different approaches and beliefs regarding the study of behavior came to be grouped into *schools of psychology*. In the next few pages, we will first explore those early schools in psychology's past and then briefly summarize the seven major approaches or *perspectives* in modern psychology.

Who are the important contributors to psychology's past, and what are the primary perspectives that guide modern psychology?

Psychology's Past: Important Pioneers

As you can see in Table 3.1, the early pioneers and approaches to psychology are grouped into six major schools: experimental psychology, structuralism, functionalism, psychoanalytic, behaviorism, and Gestalt.

Experimental Psychology

Wilhelm Wundt is generally known as the founder of experimental psychology. He established the first psychological laboratory at the University of Leipzig, Germany, in 1879, and wrote what is often considered the most important book in the history of psychology, *Principles of Physiological Psychology.*

In this laboratory, Wundt and his followers undertook the study of psychology, which to them consisted of the study of experience. They went about this study by trying to break down conscious experiences into basic elements. Their chief method was termed *introspection,* monitoring and reporting on the contents of conscious-

"Well, you don't look like an experimental psychologist to me."

TABLE 3.1 PSYCHOLOGY'S PAST — MAJOR SCHOOLS OF PSYCHOLOGY

School	Prominent Figures	Major Emphases	Study Techniques
Experimental psychology (1870s–1880s)	Wilhelm Wundt	Thought processes	Trained introspection
Structuralism (1890s)	Titchener	Thought processes, structure of the mind, and identification of the elements of thought	Trained introspection
Functionalism (1890s)	William James John Dewey	Applying psychological findings to practical situations and the function of mental processes in adapting to the environment	Introspection Experimental method Comparative method (humans and animals)
Psychoanalytic/ psychodynamic (1895–present)	Sigmund Freud Carl Jung Alfred Adler Karen Horney	Unconscious determinants of behavior, effect of early life experiences on later personality development	Individual case studies of patients
Behaviorism (1906–present)	Ivan Pavlov Edward Thorndike John B. Watson B. F. Skinner	Objective, observable behavior, stimulus–response, and effect of the environment on overt behavior	Experiments, primarily on learning and often done with animals
Gestalt psychology (1910s)	Max Wertheimer Wolfgang Kohler Kurt Koffka	Organization and context in the perception of meaningful wholes	Sensation and perception experiments

ness. If you were one of Wundt's participants trained in introspection, you might be presented with the sound of a clicking metronome. You would focus solely on the clicks and report only your immediate reactions to them — your basic sensations and feelings.

Structuralism

Edward Titchener, one of Wundt's followers, brought Wundt's ideas to the United States. Titchener established a psychological laboratory and coined the term *structuralism* to embody Wundt's ideas. Like Wundt, structuralists believed that, just as the elements hydrogen and oxygen combine to form the compound water, the "elements" of conscious experience combine to form the "compounds" of the mind. They sought to identify the elements of thought through introspection and then determine how these elements combined to form the whole of experience. Thus, their study focused on the investigation of thought processes and the structure of the mind.

Functionalism

Structuralists inaugurated psychology as a science and established the importance of studying mental processes. However, psychologists, especially those in the United States, became impatient with structuralism. They felt it was limited to only one area of behavior (e.g., introspection) and had few practical applications. These American psychologists, feeling the need for application of psychological findings to practical situations, began a new school of psychology known as *functionalism,* which stressed the importance of how behavior *functions* to allow people and animals to adapt to their environment.

By the end of the nineteenth century, Charles Darwin's theory of evolution was beginning to have a significant impact on psychology (Segerstrale, 2000). Of particular interest was his idea of the "survival of the fittest," which stressed the function of superior biological structures in adapting organisms to their environment. It was this idea that led several American psychologists to investigate the function of mental processes in adapting the individual to the environment — thus the name *functionalism.* Darwin's theory of evolution also suggested the possibility that mental processes of animals and people might be part of a continuum. Therefore, *functionalists* studied mental processes of both animals and humans to test their theories. Many then applied their research findings to practical situations.

William James was the leading force in the functionalist school. In keeping with structuralism, he viewed psychology as the study of consciousness, but James did not believe consciousness could be separated into distinct elements. He felt that mental activities form a unit of experience — that they are continually changing, while remaining interrelated, one thought flowing into another in a continuous "stream of consciousness."

Functionalism had a great impact on the development of psychology. It expanded the scope of psychology to include research on emotions and observable behaviors, initiated the psychological testing movement, changed the course of modern education, and extended psychology's influence to diverse areas in industry.

William James (1842–1910). James was a leading force in the Functionalist school of psychology, which stressed the adaptive and practical functions of human behavior.

Psychoanalytic

During the late 1800s and early 1900s, while functionalism was prominent in the United States, the *psychoanalytic* school was forming in Europe (Gay, 2000). Its founder, Sigmund Freud, was an Austrian physician who was fascinated by the way the mind influences behavior. After encountering several patients with ongoing physical complaints that seemed to have no physiological basis, Freud assumed that their complaints must be psychological. Further studies of these patients convinced Freud that such problems are caused by conflicts between what people believe to be acceptable behavior and their unacceptable motives, which are primarily of a sexual or aggressive nature. Freud believed these motives, the driving forces behind behavior, were hidden in the *unconscious,* the part of the mind that is outside of our awareness. Freud developed psychoanalytic theory to explain these conflicts and to provide a basis for a system of therapy known as *psychoanalysis.*

Isn't there a lot of criticism of Freud? Freud's nonscientific approach and emphasis on sexual and aggressive impulses have caused a great deal of controversy over the years. Even some of Freud's most ardent followers, Carl Jung, Alfred Adler, Karen Horney, and Erik Erikson, later broke away from their mentor — in large part because they wanted less emphasis on sex and aggression and more on social motives and relationships. Some also objected to possible sexist bias in his writings and theories. These early followers and their theories are now referred to as *neo-Freudians* (*neo* means "new" or "recent").

Today, there are few strictly Freudian psychoanalysts left, but the broad features of his theory remain in the modern approach known as *psychodynamic.* Although psychodynamic psychologists are making increasing use of experimental methods,

Sigmund Freud (1856–1939). Freud founded the Psychoanalytic perspective, an influential theory of personality, and a type of therapy known as psychoanalysis.

their primary method is the analysis of case studies, because their primary goal is to interpret complex meanings hypothesized to underlie people's actions.

In sum, the original psychoanalytic approach has had a profound impact on psychotherapy, psychiatry, and modern psychodynamic psychologists. Freud is generally credited with expanding the impact of psychology throughout the world.

Behaviorism

Ivan Pavlov (1849–1936). Pavlov earned Russia's first Nobel prize in 1904 for his study of digestion, but his lasting contribution to psychology was his accidental discovery of classical conditioning

In the early 1900s, another major school of thought appeared that dramatically shaped the course of psychology. Whereas structuralism, functionalism, and the psychoanalytic school looked at nonobservable mental forces, *behaviorism* emphasized objective, observable behaviors. Behaviorist John B. Watson strongly objected to the method of "introspection," the study of mental processes, and the influence of unconscious forces. Because he believed all behavior could be viewed as a response to a *stimulus* (an object or event, either internal or external, that stimulates or causes an organism to respond), Watson adopted Russian physiologist Ivan Pavlov's concept of conditioning to explain behavior as a result of *stimulus and response*. In Pavlov's famous experiment teaching a dog to salivate to the sound of a bell, the bell is the stimulus and the salivation is the response.

Because animals are ideal subjects for studying objective, overt behaviors, the majority of early behaviorist research was done with animals or with techniques developed through animal research. Using dogs, rats, pigeons, and other animals, behaviorists such as John Watson in the early 1900s and, more recently, B. F. Skinner focused primarily on learning — on how behaviors are acquired. They formulated a number of basic principles about learning that are explained in Module 16.

B. F. Skinner (1904–1990). Skinner was a prominent figure in Behaviorism and one of the most influential psychologists of the twentieth century.

It sounds like behaviorists are interested only in animals. Aren't any of them interested in humans? Yes, behaviorists *are* interested in people. One of the most well-known behaviorists, B. F. Skinner, was convinced that we could use behaviorist approaches to actually "shape" human behavior and thereby change the present negative course (as he perceived it) of humankind. He did considerable writing and lecturing to convince others of this position. Behaviorists have been most successful in treating people with overt (observable, behavioral) problems, such as phobias (irrational fears) and alcoholism (Modules 38 and 45).

Gestalt Psychology

Another early influence on psychology was the school of *Gestalt psychology*, founded by a group of German psychologists headed by Max Wertheimer in the early 1900s. Unlike behaviorism, Gestalt psychology assigned an important role to mental activities, which they believed organized sensations into meaningful perceptions.

Although Wundt and the structuralists were also interested in perception, the underlying philosophy of the Gestaltists was quite different. Gestaltists rejected the notion that experiences can be broken down into elements. Rather, they insisted that experience can be studied only as a whole — that the whole experience is qualitatively different from the sum of the distinct elements of that experience (*Gestalt* means roughly "organized whole" or "pattern" in German). As you will note in upcoming modules, Gestalt psychology remains an important contributor to modern studies of sensation, perception, personality, and a type of psychotherapy.

Women and Minorities

Before leaving the topic of "psychology's past," we need to explore the contributions of women and minorities. During the late 1800s and early 1900s, most colleges and universities provided little opportunity for women and minorities, either as students or faculty. Despite these early limitations, both women and minorities have made important contributions to psychology.

One of the first women to be recognized in the field was Mary Calkins. Calkins performed valuable research on memory and in 1905 served as the first female president of the APA. Her achievements are particularly noteworthy, considering the significant discrimination against women in those times. Even after completing all the requirements for a Ph.D. at Harvard and being described by William James as his brightest student, the university refused to grant the degree to a woman. The first woman to receive a Ph.D. in psychology was Margaret Floy Washburn (in 1894), who wrote several influential books and served as the second female president of APA.

Francis Cecil Sumner, without benefit of a formal high school education, became the first African American to earn a Ph.D. in psychology from Clark University in 1920. He translated over 3,000 articles from German, French, and Spanish and founded one of the country's leading psychology departments. One of Sumner's students at Clark University, Kenneth B. Clark, later (in 1971) became the first African American to be elected APA president. Along with his wife, Mamie, Kenneth Clark documented the harmful effects of prejudice. Their research had a direct effect on the Supreme Court's ultimate ruling against racial segregation in the schools.

Sumner and Clark, Calkins and Washburn, along with other important minorities and women, made important and lasting contributions to the developing science of psychology. In recent years, several programs have been developed to encourage people of color and women to pursue graduate degrees in psychology.

Mary Calkins (1863–1930). Calkins was the first woman president of the American Psychological Association, established a psychology laboratory at Wellesley College, and conducted important research on memory.

Kenneth Clark (1914 –). Clark was the first African-American president of the American Psychological Association. He and his wife, Mamie, also conducted research on prejudice that was cited in 1964 by the Supreme Court.

Psychology's Present: Seven Perspectives

In modern psychology, early schools like structuralism have almost entirely disappeared, whereas viewpoints like functionalism, psychoanalytic, and Gestalt have blended into newer, broader perspectives. In addition, rather than "schools of psychology," most psychologists today talk about different "perspectives." By this, they mean approaches that influence the topics psychologists study, how they conduct their research, and what information they consider important. Many modern psychologists also recognize the value of using several perspectives and that no one view has all the answers; this is referred to as an *eclectic approach*.

The rest of this book focuses on the current era in psychology, with occasional references to the history we've just described. Today, seven perspectives dominate: biopsychology or neuroscience, cognitive, behavioral, sociocultural, evolutionary, humanistic, and psychodynamic. Table 3.2 previews the major figures and emphases of these perspectives, and upcoming modules provide detailed descriptions.

A Final Note

One final note as you begin your study of psychology: You will learn a great deal about psychological functioning, but take care that you don't overestimate your expertise. Once friends and acquaintances know that you're taking a course in psychology, they may ask you to interpret their dreams, help them to discipline their children, or even offer your opinion on whether they should break up their relationships. It is a good idea, therefore, to remember that the ideas, philosophies, and even experimental findings of the science of psychology are continually being revised. As David L. Cole, a recipient of the APA Distinguished Teaching in Psychology Award, stated, "Undergraduate psychology can, and I believe should, seek to liberate the student from ignorance, but also the arrogance of believing we know more about ourselves and others than we really do" (1982).

At the same time, psychological findings and ideas developed through careful research and study can make important contributions to our lives. As Albert Einstein once said, "One thing I have learned in a long life: that all our science, measured against reality, is primitive and childlike — and yet, it is the most precious thing we have."

TABLE 3.2 PSYCHOLOGY'S PRESENT — SEVEN MAJOR PERSPECTIVES

Perspectives	Prominent Figures	Major Emphases
Psychoanalytic/psychodynamic (1895–present)	Sigmund Freud Carl Jung Alfred Adler Karen Horney	Unconscious determinants of behavior, effect of early life experiences on later personality development
Behaviorism (1906–present)	Ivan Pavlov Edward Thorndike John B. Watson B. F. Skinner	Objective, observable behavior; stimulus–response; and effect of the environment on overt behavior
Humanistic psychology (1950s–present)	Carl Rogers Abraham Maslow	Self-concept, free will, and human nature as naturally positive and growth-seeking
Cognitive psychology (1950s–present)	Jean Piaget Albert Ellis Albert Bandura Robert Sternberg Howard Gardener	Conscious thought, perception, and information processing
Neuroscience/biopsychology (1950s–present)	Johannes Müller Karl Lashley David Hubel James Olds Roger Sperry Candace Pert	Genetics and physiological processes occurring in the brain and nervous system
Evolutionary psychology (1980s–present)	Charles Darwin Konrad Lorenz E. O. Wilson David Buss	Natural selection, adaptation, and evolution of behavior patterns
Sociocultural psychology (1980s–present)	John Berry Patricia Greenfield Richard Brislin	Social interaction and the cultural determinants of behavior

GENDER & CULTURAL DIVERSITY

······GENDER AND
CULTURAL DIVERSITY
*These sections embedded
in the narrative are
identified with a separate
heading and a special
icon, as seen here. To
succeed in today's world, it
is important to be aware
of other cultures and
important gender issues.*

Are There Cultural Universals?

Psychology is a broad field with numerous subdisciplines and professions. Until recently, most psychologists worked and conducted research primarily in Europe and North America. Given this "one-sided" research, psychology's findings may not apply equally to people in other countries, or to minorities and women in Europe and North America, for that matter (Matsumoto, 2000; Shiraev & Levy, 2000). However, modern psychology, in particular *cultural psychology,* is working to correct this imbalance. Key research from cross-cultural and multiethnic studies is integrated throughout the text, in special "Gender & Cultural Diversity" sections with an icon in the margin that looks like this:

In this first gender and cultural diversity discussion, we explore a central question in cultural psychology: Are there *cultural universals*? That is, are there aspects of human behavior and mental processes that are true and *pancultural* or *universal* for all people of all cultures?

For many "universalists," emotions and facial recognition of emotions provide the clearest example of a possible cultural universal. Numerous studies conducted over many years with people from very different cultures suggests that everyone can easily identify facial expressions for at least six basic emotions: happiness, surprise, anger, sadness, fear, and disgust. All humans supposedly have this capacity whether they are shown the face of a child or an adult, a Western or non-Western person (Ekman, 1993; Ekman & Friesen, 1971; Hejmadi, Davidson, & Rozin, 2000; Matsumoto, 1992, 2000). Moreover, nonhuman primates and congenitally blind infants also display similarly recognizable facial signals. In other words, across cultures (and some species), a frown is recognized as a sign of displeasure, and a smile, as a sign of pleasure (Figure 3.1).

Critics of the universalist position emphasize problems with these studies. For example, how do you label and study the emotion described by Japanese as *hagaii* (feeling helpless anguish mixed with frustration). Particularly, if the Western psychologist has no experience with these emotions and no English equivalent words? Other critics argue that *if* cultural universals exist, it is because they are biological and innate — and they should be labeled as such. However, equating biology with

Figure 3.1 *Do you recognize these emotions?* The recognition and display of facial expressions of emotion may be true "culture universals."

universality has its own problem. Behaviors or mental processes that are universal may be so because of culture-constant learning rather than biological destiny (Matsumoto, 2000). For example, *if* we found that certain gender roles were expressed the same in all cultures, it might reflect shared cultural training beginning at birth and not an "anatomy is destiny" position.

As we discussed earlier, scientists avoid the tendency to compartmentalize behaviors into "either-or" categories. Like the nature–nurture controversy, the answer once again is an *interaction*. Emotions and their recognition may be both biological and culturally universal. As a beginning student in psychology, you will encounter numerous areas of conflict, with well-respected arguments and opponents on each side. Your job is to adopt an open-minded, critical-thinking approach to each of these debates.

In addition to building your critical thinking skills, hearing arguments from both sides also will develop your understanding and appreciation for diversity, both intellectual and cultural. It might even improve your personal and business interactions. Richard Brislin (1993) told the story of a Japanese businessman who was asked to give a speech to a Fortune 500 company in New York. He was aware that Americans typically begin speeches by telling an amusing story or a couple of jokes. In contrast, Japanese typically begin speeches by apologizing for the "inadequate" talk they are about to give. This savvy businessman began his speech: "I realize that Americans often begin by making a joke. In Japan, we frequently begin with an apology. I'll compromise by apologizing for not having a joke" (p. 9). By appreciating cultural diversity, we can, like the Japanese businessman, learn to interact successfully in other cultures.

Check & Review

SCHOOLS OF PSYCHOLOGY

Among the early schools of psychology, the experimentalists focused on the study of experience and the use of introspection, whereas the structuralists sought to identify elements of consciousness and how those elements formed the structure of the mind. Functionalists studied how mental processes help the individual adapt to the environment. A later pioneer in psychology, Sigmund Freud developed psychoanalytic theory to explain psychological problems developed from unconscious conflicts. Behaviorism emphasizes observable behaviors and stimulus–response relationships. The Gestalt school studied organizing principles of perceptual processes.

Seven major perspectives guide modern psychology: biopsychology or neuroscience, cognitive, behavioral, sociocultural, evolutionary, humanistic, and psychodynamic. These seven perspectives permeate the field of psychology and will be discussed in great detail in later modules.

Questions

1. The _____ school of psychology originated the method of introspection to examine thoughts and feelings.

2. _____ investigated the function of mental processes in adapting to the environment, and many applied their findings to real-world situations.

3. Why is Freud's theory so controversial?

4. Which of the following terms do not belong together? (a) structuralism, observable behavior; (b) behaviorism, stimulus–response; (c) psychoanalytic, unconscious conflict; (d) Gestalt; whole.

Answers to Questions can be found in Appendix B.

ACTIVE LEARNING WORKSHEET   MODULE 3

"What's My Line?"

Complete each statement with the correct psychological perspective (Experimental, Structuralism, Functionalism, Psychoanalytic/Psychodynamic, Behaviorism, Gestalt, Humanism, Cognitive, Neuroscience/biopsychology, Evolutionary, Sociocultural, Eclectic).

1. "As a(n) _____ psychologist, I believe that the whole experience is qualitatively different from the sum of the distinct elements."

2. "I believe that all behavior can be viewed as a response to a stimulus. My perspective is called _____."

3. "As a(n) _____ psychologist, I emphasize hidden forces within one's personality."

4. "I am concerned with conscious thought, perception, and information processing. My perspective is known as _____."

5. "As a(n) _____ psychologist, I emphasize natural selection, adaptation, and evolution of behavior patterns."

6. "I attempt to explain behavior and mental processes in terms of biological or physical mechanisms. My perspective is called _____."

7. "As a(n) _____ psychologist, I emphasize self-actualization, free will, and personal growth."

8. "I emphasize the application of psychological findings to practical situations. My perspective is known as _____."

9. "As a(n) _____ psychologist, I focus on social interaction and cultural determinants of behavior."

10. "I see value in using multiple perspectives because no one view has all the answers. My approach is known as _____."

Answers can be found in Appendix B.

MODULE 4
TOOLS FOR STUDENT SUCCESS

Congratulations! The fact that you are reading this section is an important first step to succeeding in college. We recognize that "student success skills" have a bad reputation and that many people reject such help because they think it's only for "nerds" or "problem students." But would these same individuals assume they could become top-notch musicians or athletes without mastering the "tools" of those trades? All students (even those who seem to get A's without much effort) can improve their "student tools."

In the next few pages, we offer specific, well-documented tips and strategies guaranteed to make you a more efficient and successful college student. You'll learn about active reading, time management, and improving your grades. Finally, we'll point you toward some important resources for college success. We will revisit these topics as appropriate throughout the book, specifically as related to issues such as learning, memory, thinking, motivation, and stress. The icon 💡 will help you identify these passages.

ACTIVE READING   How to Study (and Master) This Text

Have you ever read several pages of a text and then found you couldn't recall a single detail? Or have you read and believed you understood the text yet done poorly on an exam? Such problems generally reflect a lack of *active reading*. There are a number of ways to actively read a text. Let's begin with Step One.

STEP ONE *Familiarizing Yourself with the General Text*

Your textbook is the major tool for success in any course. Most instructors rely on it to present basic course material, reserving class time for clarifying and elaborating on important topics. You can be a more successful student (and test taker) if you take full advantage of all the special features offered in *Psychology in Action*. Here's how to use these features:

- *Preface.* If you have not already read the preface, do it now. It is a road map for the rest of the text.

- *Table of Contents.* Scan the table of contents for a bird's-eye view of what you will study in this course. Get the big picture from the module titles and the major topics within each section.

- *Individual Modules.* Each module of *Psychology in Action* contains numerous learning aids to help you master the material. There are section outlines, learning objectives, introductory vignettes, running glossaries, Check and Review (summaries and self-test questions), visual summaries, and more. These learning aids are highlighted and explained in the margins of Module 1, 2, 3, and 4.

- *Appendixes.* Two appendixes, A, *Statistics,* and B, *Answers to Review Questions and Activities,* present important information. The statistics appendix further discusses some of the concepts introduced in Module 2. It also explains how to read and interpret the graphs and tables found throughout the text. Appendix B contains answers to the Check and Review questions, Try This Yourself feature, Active Learning Worksheets, and various other activities found in the modules.

- *Glossary.* There are two glossaries in this text. A running glossary appears in the margins of each module to define key terms and concepts when they are first introduced. There is also an end-of-book glossary that gathers all the terms from the running module glossaries in one place. Use the end-of-book glossary to review terms from other modules.

- **References.** As you read each module, you will see references cited in parentheses, not in footnotes, as is common in other disciplines. For example, *(Ventner et al., 2001)* refers to an article written by Craig Ventner and his colleagues announcing the first successful mapping of the full human genome, which was published in 2001. All the references cited in the text are listed in alphabetical order (by the author's last name) in the References section at the back of the book.

  Note that instructors rarely (if ever) expect you to memorize these parenthetical citations. They are provided so you can look up the source of a study if you would like more information. At the same time, keep in mind that authors of certain key studies and famous psychologists *are* important to remember. Therefore, we emphasize these names in the text's discussion.

- **Name index and subject index.** If you are interested in learning more about a particular individual, look for his or her name in the name index. The page numbers refer you to every place in the text where the individual is mentioned. If you are interested in a specific subject (e.g., anorexia nervosa or stress), check the subject index for page references.

STEP TWO *How to Read Your Textbook*

Once you have a sense of the book as a whole, your next step to success is improving your general reading skills. The most important tool for college success is the ability to read and master the assigned class text. Many colleges offer instruction in reading efficiency, and we highly recommend that you take the course. All students can become faster and more efficient readers. In this section, we can offer only the highlights of a full-length course.

One of the best ways to read *actively* is to use the SQ4R method, developed by Francis Robinson (1970). The initials stand for six steps in effective reading: Survey, Question, Read, Recite, Review, and wRite. Robinson's technique helps you better understand and remember what you read. As you might have guessed, *Psychology in Action* was designed to incorporate each of these six steps.

- **Survey.** Each section of the text opens with an outline, Learning Objectives in question format, an introductory vignette, and a short commentary on the vignette. Together, they provide an overview, or *survey,* of the following modules. Knowing what to expect can help you focus on the main points when you read.

- **Question.** To maintain your attention and increase comprehension as you read, turn the heading of each section into a *question.* The Learning Objectives listed at the beginning of each section and repeated in the margins already do this for the main sections. Use them as models for turning the second- and third-level headings into questions. Also try to anticipate the questions your instructor might ask on an exam.

- **Read.** The first *R* in SQ4R refers to reading. Try to answer the questions you formed in the previous step as you read the module. Read carefully — in short, concentrated time periods.

- **Recite.** After you have read one small section, stop and *recite.* Try to summarize what you've just read — either silently to yourself or as written notes. Also, think of personal examples of major concepts and how you might apply a certain concept to real-life situations. This will greatly increase your retention of the material.

- **Review.** Read the Interim Reviews that conclude each major section and then answer the Review Questions. Write down your responses, before checking your answers in Appendix B. When you finish the entire module, look back over your answers, the module headings, and Interim Reviews. Before each class quiz or exam, repeat this review process.

- *wRite.* In addition to the writing you do in the above steps, take brief notes in the text margins. This helps keep you focused during your reading. (The Student Study Guide that accompanies this text teaches a special "marginal marking" technique that our students find extremely helpful.)

The SQ4R method may sound time consuming and difficult. However, once you've mastered the technique, it actually saves time. More importantly, it also greatly improves your reading comprehension — and exam grades!

TIME MANAGEMENT How to Succeed in College and Still Have a Life

Time management is not only desirable; it is also essential to college success. If you answer yes to each of the following, congratulate yourself and move on to the next section.

1. I have a good balance among work, college, and social activities.
2. I set specific, written goals and deadlines for achieving them.
3. I complete my assignments and papers on time and seldom stay up late to cram the night before an exam.
4. I am generally on time for classes, appointments, and work.
5. I am good at estimating how much time it will take to complete a task.
6. I recognize that I am less productive at certain times of the day (e.g., right after lunch), and I plan activities accordingly.
7. I am good at identifying and eliminating nonessential tasks from my schedule and delegate work whenever possible.
8. I prioritize my responsibilities and assign time accordingly.
9. I arrange my life to avoid unnecessary interruptions (visitors, meetings, telephone calls during study hours).
10. I am able to say no to unnecessary or unreasonable requests for my time.

If you cannot answer yes to each of these statements and need help with time management, here are four basic strategies:

1. *Establish a baseline.* To break any bad habit (poor time management, excessive TV watching, overeating), you must first establish a *baseline*, a characteristic level of performance for assessing changes in behavior. The first step in a successful weight loss program, for example, is to establish a caloric baseline. Before beginning a diet, dieters are asked to continue their normal eating patterns for 1 to 2 weeks while meticulously recording every meal, snack, and caloric drink. The total number of calories consumed each day, as well as trouble spots — times when the dieter is likely to overeat — constitute a baseline against which to judge future behavior.

   A similar strategy also works for time management. Before attempting any changes, simply record your day-to-day activities for 1 to 2 weeks (see the sample in Figure 4.1). Like most dieters who are shocked at their daily eating habits, most students are unpleasantly surprised when they recognize how poorly they manage their time.

2. *Set up a realistic activity schedule.* Once you realize how you normally spend your time each day, you can begin to manage it. Start by making a daily and weekly "to do" list. Be sure to include all required activities (class attendance, study time, work, etc.), as well as basic maintenance tasks like laundry, cooking, cleaning, and eating. Using this list, create a daily schedule of activities that

	Sunday	Monday	Tuesday	Wednesday	Thursday	Friday	Saturday
7:00		Breakfast		Breakfast		Breakfast	
8:00		History	Breakfast	History	Breakfast	History	
9:00		Psychology	Statistics	Psychology	Statistics	Psychology	
10:00		Review History & Psychology	Campus Job	Review History & Psychology	Statistics Lab	Review History & Psychology	
11:00		Biology		Biology		Biology	
12:00		Lunch / Study		Exercise	Lunch	Exercise	
1:00		Bio Lab	Lunch	Lunch	Study	Lunch	
2:00			Study	Study			

Figure 4.1 *Sample record of daily activities.* To help manage your time, draw a grid similar to this and record your daily activities in appropriate boxes. Then use it to fill in other necessities, such as extra study time and "down time."

includes time for each of these required activities and maintenance tasks. Also be sure to schedule a reasonable amount of "down time" for sports, movies, TV watching, and social activities with friends and family.

Try to be realistic. Some students try to replace all the hours they previously "wasted" watching TV or visiting friends with studying. Obviously, this approach inevitably fails. To make permanent time management changes, you must *shape* your behavior. That is, start small and build skills. For example, schedule 15 minutes increased study time for the first few days, then move to 30 minutes, 60 minutes, and so on.

3. *Reward yourself for good behavior.* The most efficient way to maintain good behavior is to reward it — the sooner, the better. But the rewards of college (a degree and/or job advancement) are generally years away. To get around this problem and improve your time management skills, give yourself immediate, tangible rewards for sticking with your daily schedule. Allow yourself a guilt-free call to a friend, for example, or time for a favorite TV program after studying for your set period of time.

4. *Maximize your time.* Time management experts, such as Alan Lakein (1998), suggest you should "work harder, not longer." Many students report that they're studying all the time, for example, but they're generally confusing "fret time" (worrying and complaining) and useless prep time (fiddling around getting ready to study) with real, concentrated study time.

Time experts also point out that people often overlook important "time opportunities." For example, if you ride the bus to class, you can use this time to review notes or read a textbook. If you drive yourself and waste time looking for parking spaces, go earlier and spend the extra time studying in your car or classroom. While waiting for doctor or dental appointments or to pick up your kids after school, take out your text and study for 10 to 20 minutes. These hidden moments count!

IMPROVING YOUR GRADES Note Taking, Study Habits, and General Test-Taking Strategies

- *Note taking.* Effective note taking depends on active listening. Find a seat in the front of the class and look directly at the instructor while he or she is talking. Focus your attention on what is being said by asking yourself, "What is the main idea?" Write down key ideas and supporting details and examples, including important names, dates, and new terms. Don't try to write down everything the instructor says, word for word. This is passive, rote copying, not active listening. Also, be sure to take extra notes if your professor says, "This is an important concept," or if he or she writes notes on the board. Finally, arrive in class on time and don't leave early — you may miss important notes and assignments.

- *Distributed study time.* The single most important key to improved grades may be *distributed* study time. Although it *does* help to intensively review before a quiz or exam, if this is your major method of studying, you are not likely to do well in any college course. One of the clearest findings in psychology is that spaced practice is a much more efficient way to study and learn than massed practice (Module 19). Just as you wouldn't wait until the night before a big basketball game to begin practicing your free throws, you shouldn't begin to study the night before an exam.

- *Overlearning.* Many students study just to the point where they can recite the immediate information. For best results, you should repeatedly review the material (using visualization and rehearsal) until it is firmly locked in place. This is particularly important if you suffer from test anxiety. For additional help on test anxiety and improving memory in general, see Modules 19, 20, and 44.

- *Psyche out your instructor.* Pay close attention to the lecture time spent on various topics. This is generally a good indication of what the instructor considers important (and what may appear on exams).

  Try, too, to understand the perspective (and personality) of your instructor. Recognize that most instructors went into education because they *love* the academic life. They were probably model students who attended class regularly, submitted work on time, and seldom missed an exam. Try your hardest to be in class for every exam. Remember that instructors have many students and hear lots of "dead grandmother" excuses for missing class and exams. Also bear in mind that most instructors actually enjoyed lectures during college and were trained under this system. *Never* say, "I missed last week's classes. Did I miss anything important?" This is guaranteed to upset the most even-tempered instructor.

- *General test taking.* Here are several strategies to improve your performance on multiple-choice exams:

  1. *Take your time.* Carefully read each question and each of the alternative answers. Do not choose the first answer that looks correct. There may be a better alternative farther down the list.

  2. *Be test smart.* If you're unsure of an answer, make a logical guess. Begin by eliminating any answer that you know is incorrect. If two answers both seem reasonable, try to recall specific information from the text or professor's lecture. Be sure to choose "all of the above" if you know that at least two of the options are correct. Similarly, if you are confident that one of the options is incorrect, *never* choose "all of the above."

  3. *Review your answers.* After you finish a test, go back and check your answers. Make sure you have responded to all the questions and recorded your answers correctly. Also, bear in mind that information relevant to one question is often given away in another test question. Don't hesitate to change

an answer if you get more information — or even if you simply have a hunch about another answer. Although many students (and faculty) believe "your first hunch is your best guess," research clearly shows this is bad advice (Johnston, 1978). Changing answers pays off! The popular myth of *not* changing answers probably persists because we tend to pay more attention to losses than successes. Think about what happens when you get a test back. Most students pay attention to only the items they got wrong and fail to note the number of times they changed from an incorrect to a correct answer.

4. **Practice your test taking.** Complete the Check and Review sections found throughout each module and check your answers in Appendix B. Make up questions from your lectures and text notes. Also, try the interactive quizzes on our website http://www.wiley.com/college/huffman. Each module of the text has its own sample quiz with individualized feedback. If you answer a question incorrectly, you get immediate feedback and further explanations that help you master the material.

RESOURCES FOR SUCCESS   Where Can I Get Additional Help?

In addition to college counselors and financial aid officers, there are several resources that students often overlook in their search for success:

1. **Instructors.** Get to know your instructor. It's up to you to seek out instructors for help during their scheduled office hours. If these times conflict with your schedule, ask for an alternative appointment or try to stop by right before or after class.

2. **Friends and Family.** Ask friends or family members to serve as your *conscience/coach* for improved time management and study skills. After completing your daily activity schedule (see page 41), set up weekly (or biweekly) appointments with a friend or family member to check your progress and act as your "conscience." You may think it would be easy to lie to your conscience/coach, but most people find it much harder to lie to another person than to lie to themselves (about calories, study time, TV watching, etc.). Encourage your conscience/coach to ask pointed questions about your *actual* study time versus your *fretting* and *prepping* time.

3. **Classmates and Roommates.** Your college roommate and friendly classmates can serve not only as your conscience/coach but also as potential study partners. Also, ask your classmates and roommates what tricks/techniques they use to maintain their attention and interest during lectures or while reading texts.

If you would like more information on student success skills, consult our *Psychology in Action* website http://www.wiley.com/college/huffman. In addition to the interactive tutorials and quizzes mentioned earlier, we also offer specific Internet links for student success and recommend books and articles on time management and the other topics discussed here. Best wishes for a successful course and college career!

A FINAL WORD   Your Attitude

Imagine for a moment that the toilet in your bathroom is overflowing and creating a horrible, smelly mess. Whom should you reward? The plumber who quickly and efficiently solves the problem? Or someone who "tries very hard"?

Some students seem to believe they can pass college courses by simply attending class and doing the homework — that this shows their great interest and effort. This might have worked for *some* students in *some* classes in high school, but it probably won't work in college. Most college professors seldom assign homework and may not notice if you skip class. They assume students are independent, self-motivated adult learners.

Professors also generally consider college a last stop on the way to the real world and believe grades should reflect knowledge and performance — not effort. Although points may be given in some classes for attendance, participation, and effort, the heaviest weight will almost always come from exams, papers, and projects. Did you fix the toilet or not?

ACTIVE LEARNING WORKSHEET   MODULE 4

You have just discovered 15 Tools for Student Success. To help you apply this material to your own study skills, place a "+" mark by those activities or skills you currently use, and a "–" by those you don't. Then review the items with a "–" mark, and decide how you can incorporate them into your study skills "toolbag."

_____ Familiarizing Myself with the General Text

_____ Using the SQ4R Method to Read the Chapter

_____ Establishing a Baseline for Time Management

_____ Setting up a Realistic Activity Schedule

_____ Rewarding Myself for Good Behavior

_____ Maximizing My Time

_____ Effective Note Taking Through Active Listening

_____ Distributed Study Time versus Cramming

_____ Overlearning

_____ Psyching out my Instructor

_____ Taking My Time on Tests

_____ Being Test Smart

_____ Reviewing My Test Answers

_____ Practicing My Test Taking Skills

_____ Seeking Help from Instructors, Family, Friends, and Classmates

Visual Summary for Modules 1, 2, 3, and 4 •---•••

Understanding Psychology

Psychology is the *scientific* study of behavior and mental processes. It values empierical evidence and **critical thinking,** unlike pseudopsychologies, which use nonscientific and nonverifiable methods.

Goals of Psychology

Describe, explain, predict, and change behavior and mental processes.

Careers or Specialties

Various areas, including biopsychology, clinical, cognitive, counseling, developmental, educational and school, experimental, gender and/or cultural, industrial/organizational, and social.

Types of Research

Basic research studies theoretical questions.
Applied research attempts to answer real-world problems.

Doing Research in Psychology

The Scientific Method

Six *basic steps*: 1) Review the literature, 2) Formulate the **hypothesis,** 3)Design the study and collect data, 4) Analyze the data and accept or reject the hypothesis, 5) Publish, replicate, and undergo scientific review, 6) Continue **theory** building.

Experimental Research

Distinguishing feature: establishes cause and effect.

Components:
- **Independent variables** (what the experimenter manipulates)
- **Dependent variables** (what the experimenter measures)
- Experimental controls (including **control group, experimental group, extraneous variables)**

Experimental Safeguards

Researcher Problems

Participant Problems

Experimenter bias is prevented through blind observers, single-blind and **double-blind** studies, and **placebos.** Cross-cultural sampling prevents **ethnocentrism.**

Sample bias is prevented through random/representative sampling and **random assignment.** Participant bias is prevented through anonymity, confidentiality, and deception.

VISUAL SUMMARY

At the end of each section of modules, the material is summarized in a visual format. This unique study tool visually summarizes and organizes the main concepts of each section in a clear, two-page layout that serves as a quick review after completing your reading. Relationships between topics can be clearly seen and understood.

Doing Research in Psychology (cont).

Nonexperimental Studies

Distinguishing feature: Describes specifics about behavior, determines relationships between variables, and helps with prediction.

Methods

Naturalistic Observation Systematic recording of observable behavior in the participant's natural habitat with little or no experimenter intervention.	**Surveys** Assesses behaviors and attitudes of a sample or population.	**Case studies** In-depth study of a single research participant.	**Correlational Studies** Statistical analyses of relationships between variables.

Ethical Problems

Human research participants have rights, including **informed consent** and voluntary participation, limited use of deception, **debriefing**, and confidentiality. Rights of animal participants and clients in therapy are protected through careful adherence to APA standards.

Perspectives in Psychology

Psychology's Past

- *Experimental psychology*: Studied experience through introspection.
- *Structuralism*: Focused on thought processes and the structure of the mind through introspection.
- *Functionalism*: Emphasized the function of mental processes in adapting to the environment and application of psychology to practical situations.
- *Psychoanalytic/Psychodynamic*: Emphasized unconscious processes and early life experiences.
- *Behaviorism*: Studied objective, observable behavior, and the effect of the environment.
- *Gestalt psychology*: Emphasized organization, context, and meaningful wholes.

Psychology's Present

- *Psychoanalytic/Psychodynamic*: Emphasizes unconscious processes and early life experiences.
- *Behaviorism*: Studies objective, observable, environmental influences.
- *Humanistic*: Focuses on self-concept, free will, and human nature as positive growth-seeking.
- *Cognitive*: Emphasizes conscious thought, perception, and information processing.
- *Neuroscience/Biopsychology*: Studies natural selection, adaptation, and evolution of behavior patterns.
- *Sociocultural*: Focuses on social interaction and cultural determinants of behavior.

Neuroscience and Biological Foundations

Core Learning Objectives

As you read Modules 5, 6, and 7, keep the following questions in mind and answer them in your own words:

▶ How is the nervous system organized?

▶ What are neurons, and how do they communicate information throughout the body?

▶ What are the best tools for studying the brain?

▶ What are the lower-level structures of the brain, and what are their roles in behavior and mental processes?

▶ How does the cortex control behavior and mental processes?

▶ How do the left and right hemispheres of the brain affect behavior and mental processes?

▶ How are heredity and evolution linked to human behavior?

In 1848, when the Rutland and Burlington Railroad was laying new track through Vermont, 25-year-old Phineas P. Gage was a foreman in charge of blasting through the rocky terrain. Blasting a boulder into smaller, more easily removed rocks was a dangerous job, but not very complicated. First, a hole was drilled into the boulder and partially filled with blasting powder. Then a fuse was run into the blasting powder that was carefully tamped down, and the hole was filled with sand. The sand was tamped again with a metal rod to remove any air pockets that might diminish the blast, the fuse was lit, and everyone ran for cover.

Gage had done this hundreds of times, but on September 13, 1848, he failed to notice that his assistant had not yet put sand into the hole. So when Gage put down the tamping rod, it scraped against the rock and created sparks that ignited the blasting powder. But instead of shattering the boulder, the blast turned the iron rod into a missile. The 13-pound metal rod, 1 1/4 inches in diameter and 3 1/2 feet long, rocketed out of the hole and shot through Gage's head. Entering under his left cheekbone, the rod slammed through his brain, exiting out the top of his skull into the air, and eventually landing 60 to 80 feet away. Portions of his brain's frontal lobes littered the ground and smeared the tamping iron. This should have been the end of the story, but it wasn't.

Gage was stunned and his extremities shook convulsively. But in just a few minutes, he was able to talk to his men, and he even walked with little or no assistance up a flight of stairs before receiving medical treatment 1 1/2 hours later. Although his mind was "clear" and Gage insisted he would be back at work in a day or two, the attending physician, John Harlow, doubted that he would recover and the town cabinetmaker even measured Gage so there would be a coffin "in readiness to use" (Harlow, 1848, 1868; Macmillan, 1986, 2000).

Gage did survive physically, but not psychologically. A serious personality transformation had occurred. Before the accident, Gage was "the most efficient and capable foreman," "a shrewd, smart business man," and very energetic and persistent in executing all his plans. After the accident, Gage "frequently changed what he proposed doing, and was, among

other things, fitful, capricious, impatient of advice, obstinate, and lacking in deference to his fellows" (Macmillan, 2000, p. 13). In the words of his friends and acquaintances, "Gage was no longer Gage" (Harlow, 1868). Following months of recuperation, Gage attempted to return to work but was refused his old job. The damage to his brain had changed him too profoundly.

According to historical records by his physician, Gage never again held a job equal to that of foreman. He supported himself with odd jobs and traveled around New England, exhibiting himself and the tamping iron, and for a time he did the same at Barnum Museum. He even lived in Chile for 7 years before ill health forced a return to the United States. Near the end of his life, Gage experienced numerous epileptic seizures of increasing severity and frequency. Despite the massive damage to his frontal lobes caused by the tamping iron, Phineas Gage lived on for another 11 1/2 years, eventually dying from the epileptic seizures.

How did Gage physically survive? What accounts for his radical change in personality? If the tamping iron had traveled through the brain at a slightly different angle, Gage would have immediately died. But as you can see in the photos above, the rod entered and exited the front part of the brain, a section unnecessary for physical survival but intimately involved in motivation, emotion, and a host of other cognitive activities.

Phineas Gage's injury and "recovery" is a classic example from the field of **neuroscience** and *biopsychology,* the scientific study of the *biology* of behavior and mental processes. Most beginning psychology students expect to study only abnormal behavior and are surprised by the amount of biology. Obviously, the brain is critical to survival, but have you thought about how it is also responsible for all your thoughts, fears, loves, and other behavior and mental processes? Your brain and nervous system control everything you do, feel, see, or think. *You are your brain.*

To help you fully understand and appreciate the wonders of your brain and nervous system, Modules 5, 6, and 7 provide a basic overview and lay the foundation for the biological processes discussed throughout the text. Module 5 presents a brief overview of the nervous system. Then we examine the *neuron,* or nerve cell, and the way neurons communicate with one another to produce thinking, feeling, and behavior. Module 6 explores the brain itself. Module 7 provides a look at heredity and evolutionary processes.

Neuroscience *An interdisciplinary field studying how biological processes, especially activity in the brain and nervous system, relate to behavior*

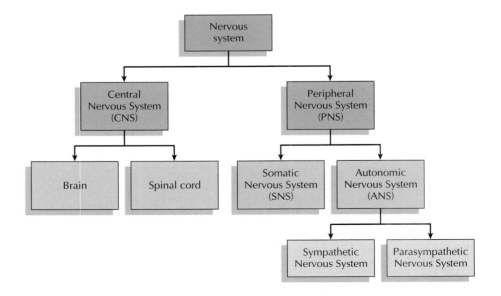

MODULE 5
BIOLOGICAL FOUNDATIONS

One of the many advantages of taking this psychology course is learning about yourself and how you learn. As you'll discover in Module 19, when you are introduced to a large set of new terms and concepts, the best way to master this material (and get it "permanently" stored in long-term memory) is through *organization*. A broad overview showing the "big picture" helps you organize and file specific details. Just as you would use a large globe of the world that shows all the continents to learn about individual countries, you need a "map" of the entire nervous system before studying the individual parts. Thus, we begin with this broad overview, followed by a close examination of the neuron itself, communication between neurons, and chemical messengers in the nervous system.

An Overview of the Nervous System: The Central Nervous System and Peripheral Nervous System

Have you heard the expression "Information is power?" Nowhere is this truer than in the human body. Without information we could not survive. Our brain and bodies must take in information from the outside world, decide what to do with the information, and then follow through. Just as the circulatory system handles blood, our nervous system handles information.

To fully comprehend the intricacies of the nervous system, it helps to know the names of its major parts and how they are interrelated. Take a look at Figure 5.1. The nervous system has two major divisions, the *Central Nervous System* (CNS), which processes and organizes information, and the *Peripheral Nervous System* (PNS), which serves primarily as a relay system getting information to and from the CNS.

Central Nervous System (CNS)

The **central nervous system (CNS)** consists of the *brain* and the *spinal cord*, both of which are surrounded by a protective bony structure — the skull and spinal column. Unlike neurons in the PNS that can regenerate and require less protection, serious

Neuroscience and you. All behavior and mental processes require a complex interaction between the brain, nervous system, and body.

How is the nervous system organized?

Central Nervous System (CNS)
The brain and spinal cord.

Figure 5.1 *The nervous system.*
Note how the nervous system is divided and subdivided into various subsystems according to their differing functions. Review this diagram often as you study upcoming sections.

damage to cells in the CNS is usually permanent. However, the brain may not be as "hard wired" as we once believed. As you will discover throughout this module, the brain changes with learning and experience. In response to environmental demands (and some injuries), the brain can reorganize its functions, rewire itself with new connections, possibly reroute neurons around damaged areas, and even generate new brain cells (Begley, 2000; Gage, 2000; Kempermann & Gage, 1999; Taub, Crago, & Uswatte, 1998; Taub & Uswatte, 2000; Travis, 2000; Vogel, 2000).

Because of its central importance for psychology and behavior, the brain is the major subject of this unit, but the spinal cord is also important. Beginning at the base of the brain and continuing down the back, the spinal cord contains nerve fibers that link the brain to other parts of the body. These fibers relay incoming sensory information to the brain and send messages from the brain to muscles and glands.

The spinal cord is also responsible for one of our simplest behavior patterns-the *reflex arc,* which occurs when a stimulus provokes an automatic response. Have you ever noticed that you automatically jerk your hand away from a hot pan *before* your brain has a chance to respond? Reflexes occur within the spinal cord, without any help from the brain (Figure 5.2). It is only later, when the spinal cord transfers the sensory information to the brain, that you actually experience the sensation called *pain.* If the top of your spinal cord were severed, you would not feel pain — or pleasure. As you will discover in Module 11, the brain receives and interprets sensory messages, while the independently operating spinal cord allows us to react automatically and protect ourselves.

Peripheral Nervous System (PNS)

The **peripheral nervous system (PNS)** is just what it sounds like — the part that involves nerves *peripheral* to (or outside of) the brain and spinal cord. The chief function of the PNS is to carry information to and from the CNS. It links the brain and spinal cord to the body's sense receptors, muscles, and glands.

Peripheral Nervous System (PNS) *All nerves and neurons outside the brain and spinal cord. Its major function is to connect the CNS to the rest of the body.*

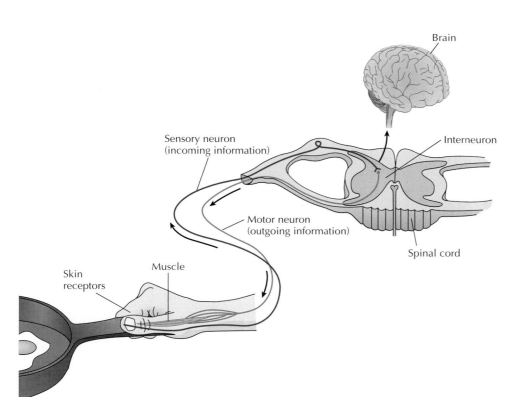

Brain

Sensory neuron (incoming information)

Interneuron

Motor neuron (outgoing information)

Spinal cord

Skin receptors

Muscle

Figure 5.2 *The workings of the spinal cord* In a simple reflex arc, a sensory receptor initiates a neural impulse that travels to the spinal cord. The signal then travels back to the appropriate muscle, which then contracts. Action is automatic and immediate in a reflex because the signal only travels as far as the spinal cord before action is initiated, not all the way to the brain. The brain is later "notified" of the action when the spinal cord sends along the message.

Somatic Nervous System (SNS)
A subdivision of the peripheral nervous system (PNS) that connects to sensory receptors and controls skeletal muscles.

Autonomic Nervous System (ANS)   *Subdivision of the peripheral nervous system (PNS) that controls involuntary functions, such as heart rate and digestion. It is further subdivided into the sympathetic nervous system, which arouses, and the parasympathetic nervous system, which calms.*

Sympathetic Nervous System
Subdivision of the autonomic nervous system (ANS) responsible for arousing the body and mobilizing its energy during times of stress; also called the "fight or flight" system.

Parasympathetic Nervous System
Subdivision of the autonomic nervous system (ANS) responsible for calming the body and conserving energy.

The PNS is subdivided into the somatic nervous system and the autonomic nervous system. The **somatic nervous system (SNS)** (also called the skeletal nervous system) consists of all the nerves that connect to sensory receptors and control skeletal muscles. The name comes from the term *soma*, which means "body," and the somatic nervous system plays a key role in communication throughout the entire *body*. In a kind of "two way street," the somatic nervous system first carries sensory information to the CNS, and then carries messages from the CNS to skeletal muscles. When you hear a question from your instructor and then raise your hand to volunteer an answer, it is chiefly due to your *somatic nervous system*.

Although the somatic system can help you respond to your college instructor's questions, it cannot make your pupils dilate or your heartbeat respond to the attractive classmate sitting beside you. For this, you need the other subdivision of the PNS known as the **autonomic** (or self-governing) **nervous system (ANS).** The ANS is responsible for *involuntary* tasks, such as heart rate, digestion, pupil dilation, and breathing. One function of the ANS is to maintain *homeostasis*, the body's steady state of normal functioning. It does this by regulating the endocrine glands, the heart muscle, and the smooth muscles of the blood vessels and internal organs

The autonomic nervous system is itself further divided into two branches, the **sympathetic** and **parasympathetic.** These tend to work in opposition to each other to regulate the functioning of such target organs as the heart, the intestines, and the lungs (Figure 5.3). A convenient, if somewhat oversimplified, distinction is that the sympathetic branch arouses the body for action (often called the "fight or flight" response), whereas the parasympathetic branch relaxes it. It's important to note, however, that these two systems are not an either/or arrangement. Like two children on a teeter-totter, one will be up while the other is down, but they essentially balance each other out. If either one of them truly took over, you would die. Your heart would either slow down and stop (parasympathetic complete dominance), or speed out of control and stop (sympathetic system complete dominance).

The *parasympathetic nervous system* dominates when you are in a relaxed, low-stress physical and mental state — when you calmly smell the roses in your garden. Its major task is to conserve energy by slowing your heart rate, lowering your blood pressure, and increasing your digestive and eliminative processes. It is definitely healthier to have the parasympathetic system dominant.

During stressful times, either mental or physical, the *sympathetic nervous system* dominates. If you noticed a dangerous snake coiled around the base of the rose bush,

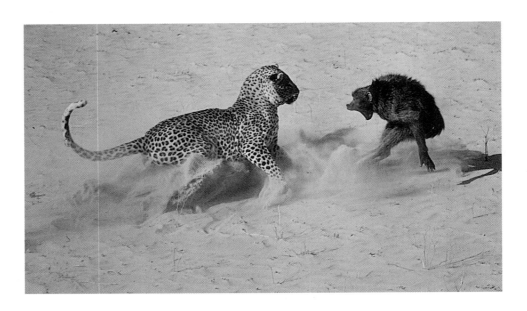

The fight-or-flight response of the sympathetic nervous system is activated in both of these animals.

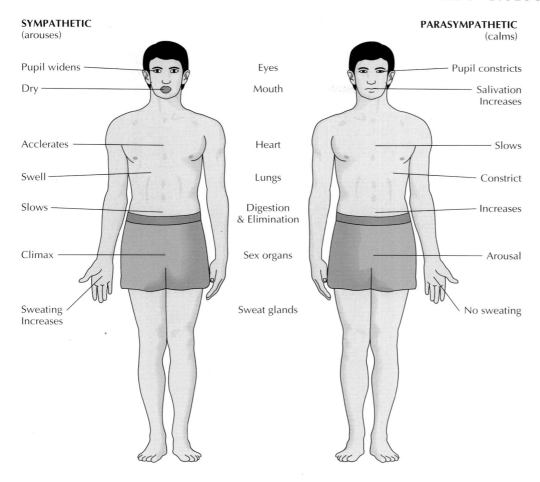

SYMPATHETIC
(arouses)

PARASYMPATHETIC
(calms)

Pupil widens	Eyes	Pupil constricts
Dry	Mouth	Salivation Increases
Acclerates	Heart	Slows
Swell	Lungs	Constrict
Slows	Digestion & Elimination	Increases
Climax	Sex organs	Arousal
Sweating Increases	Sweat glands	No sweating

Figure 5.3 *Actions of the autonomic nervous system (ANS).* This figure illustrates the chief functions of the parasympathetic and sympathetic branches of the ANS.

your sympathetic nervous system would increase your heart rate, respiration, and blood pressure, stop your digestive and eliminative processes, and cause several hormones, such as epinephrine and cortisol to be released into the bloodstream. The net result of sympathetic activation is to get more oxygenated blood and energy to the skeletal muscles, thus allowing you to cope with the stress-to "fight or flight." (Study tip: One way to differentiate the two subdivisions of the ANS is to imagine yourself jumping out of an airplane. When you initially jump, your *sympathetic* nervous system would be in charge. When your "para" chute opens, your "para"sympathetic nervous system also "opens" to help calm you and return normal functioning.)

Can you see how the fight-flight system provides an adaptive, evolutionary advantage? At the beginning of human evolution, when we faced a dangerous bear or aggressive human intruder, there were only two reasonable responses — fight or flight! The automatic mobilization of bodily resources and increased energy gained through activation of the sympathetic nervous system had significant survival value. Today, we have the same autonomic responses as our ancient ancestors, but our world is quite different. Now when we face stressful situations, we rarely respond by taking physical action. If our boss yells at us or makes unreasonable demands, we've learned not to fight or take flight. We have little use for the increased heart rate and stress hormones that are released into the bloodstream by the autonomic nervous system. In fact, the physiological changes caused by stress-activated sympathetic responses are actually detrimental to our health. We'll discuss stress and the fight-or-flight response in more detail in the modules related to Stress and Health Psychology.

Check & Review

AN OVERVIEW OF THE NERVOUS SYSTEM

Neuroscience is an interdisciplinary field that studies how biological processes, especially activity in the brain and nervous system, relate to behavior. The **central nervous system** is composed of the brain and the spinal cord. The spinal cord is the communications link between the brain and the rest of the body below the neck. It is involved in all voluntary and reflex responses of the body below the neck.

The **peripheral nervous system** includes all nerves going to and from the brain and spinal cord. Its two major subdivisions are the **somatic nervous system** and the **autonomic nervous system**.

The somatic nervous system includes all nerves carrying incoming sensory information and outgoing motor information to and from the sense organs and skeletal muscles. The autonomic nervous system includes the nerves outside the brain and spinal cord that maintain normal functioning of glands, heart muscle, and the smooth muscle of blood vessels and internal organs.

The autonomic nervous system is further divided into two branches, the **parasympathetic** and the **sympathetic**, which tend to work in opposition to one another. The parasympathetic nervous system normally dominates when a person is relaxed. The sympathetic nervous system dominates when a person is under physical or mental stress. It mobilizes the body for fight or flight by increasing heart rate and blood pressure and slowing digestive processes.

Questions

1. The nervous system is separated into two major divisions: the _____ nervous system, which consists of the brain and spinal cord, and the _____ nervous system, which consists of all the nerves going to and from the brain and spinal cord.

2. The autonomic nervous system is subdivided into two branches called the _____ and _____ systems. (a) automatic, semiautomatic; (b) somatic, peripheral; (c) afferent, efferent; (d) sympathetic, parasympathetic

3. If you are startled by the sound of a loud explosion, the _____ nervous system will become dominant. (a) peripheral; (b) somatic; (c) parasympathetic; (d) sympathetic

4. What is the major difference between the sympathetic and parasympathetic nervous systems?

Answers to Questions can be found in Appendix B.

Neurons as the Basic Building Blocks: We Are Our Neurons

What are neurons, and how do they convey information throughout the body?

Neuron *Individual nerve cell responsible for processing, storing, and transmitting information throughout the body.*

Glial Cells *Nervous system cells that provide structural, nutritional, and other support for the neuron; also called* glia *or* neuroglia.

Your brain and the rest of your nervous system essentially consist of **neurons**, individual cells that communicate information throughout the body, as well as within the brain. Each neuron is a tiny information processing system with thousands of connections for receiving and sending signals to other neurons. Although no one knows for sure, one well-educated guess is that a human has 100 billion to 150 billion neurons, about the same number as there are stars in our galaxy.

Neurons are held in place and supported by **glial cells** (from the Greek word for "glue"). They surround neurons, control their supply of chemicals, perform clean-up tasks, and even insulate one neuron from another so their neural messages do not get scrambled. Although glial cells greatly outnumber neurons and interact in ways that make information transfer and the brain more efficient, they are only supporting players. The "star" is the neuron. Most neuroscientists believe that all behavior — every move you make, every thought you have, and every heartbeat — ultimately depends on what happens at the level of the neuron.

Basic Parts of a Neuron

Just as no two people are alike, no two neurons are exactly alike, although most share three basic features: dendrites, the cell body, and an axon (Figure 5.4). Information from other cells normally enters the neuron via numerous dendrites, passes through the cell body, and is transmitted to other cells by the axon.

Dendrites receive information from other neurons and sensory receptors.

Nucleus provides energy for the neuron to carry out its functions.

Cell body the cell's life support center

Axon

Myelin sheath

Axon carries neuron's message to other body areas.

Myelin sheath covers the axon of some neurons and helps speed neural impulses.

Terminal branches of axon form junctions with other cells.

Figure 5.4 *The structure of a neuron.* Information enters the neuron through the dendrites, is integrated in the cell body, and then transmitted to other neurons via the axon. The myelin sheath is a fatty insulation wrapping around the axon that greatly increases the speed of the neural impulse.

Dendrites look like leafless branches of a tree; in fact, the word *dendrite* means "little tree" in Greek. Dendrites act like antennas, receiving electrochemical information from other neurons and transmitting it to the cell body. Current research suggests that dendrites not only send information to the cell body but also relay information from the cell body back down to the ends of the dendrites, which modifies the dendrites' responses to further signals (Sejnowski, 1997). Each neuron may have hundreds or thousands of dendrites.

From the many dendrites, information flows into the cell body and then to the axon. The **cell body**, or *soma*, contains the biochemical machinery that keeps the neuron alive. The **axon** (from the Greek word for "axle") is a long, tubelike structure specialized for carrying information away from the cell body, toward other neurons or to muscles and glands. The **myelin sheath**, a white, fatty coating derived from glial cells, surrounds the axons of some neurons, helping to insulate and speed neural messages. (Study tip: To remember how information travels through the neuron, think of the three parts in reverse alphabetical order: *dendrite, cell body, axon.*)

How Neurons Communicate: An Electrical and Chemical Language

The basic function of neurons is to transmit information throughout the nervous system. Neurons "speak" to each other or, in some cases, to muscles or glands, in a type of electrical and chemical language. We begin our discussion by looking at communication *within* the neuron itself. Then we explore how communication occurs *between* neurons.

Action Potential — How a Neuron "Talks" to Itself

The process of neural communication begins within the neuron itself, when messages are received by the dendrites and cell body. These messages are passed along the axon in the form of a neural impulse or **action potential** (Figure 5.5).

Because the neural impulse that travels down the axon is chemical, the axon does not transmit it in the same way a wire conducts an electrical current. The movement down the axon actually results from a change in the permeability of the

Dendrites *Branching neuron structures that receive neural impulses from other neurons and convey impulses toward the cell body*

Cell Body *The part of the neuron that contains the cell nucleus, as well as other structures that help the neuron carry out its functions.*

Axon *A long, tubelike structure that conveys impulses away from the neuron's cell body toward other neurons or to muscles or glands*

Myelin [MY-uh-lin] Sheath *A layer of fatty insulation wrapped around the axon of some neurons, which increases the rate at which nerve impulses travel along the axon.*

Action Potential *A neural impulse that carries information along the axon of a neuron. The action potential is generated when positively charged ions move in and out of channels in the axon's membrane.*

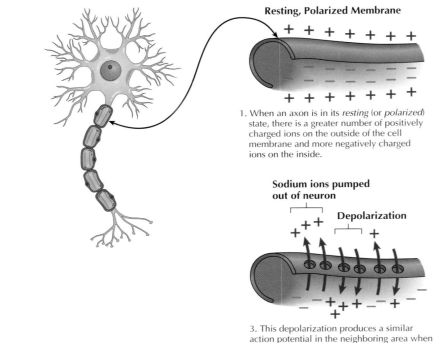

Resting, Polarized Membrane

1. When an axon is in its *resting* (or *polarized*) state, there is a greater number of positively charged ions on the outside of the cell membrane and more negatively charged ions on the inside.

Depolarization (sodium ions flow in)

2. An *action potential* begins when a small section of the axon adjacent to the cell body is adequately stimulated by an incoming message. Pores (or channels) in the membrane at the stimulated area open and allow positively charged sodium ions to move inside the cell membrane. This movement causes a *depolarization* at that spot on the membrane.

Sodium ions pumped out of neuron

Depolarization

3. This depolarization produces a similar action potential in the neighboring area when pores open and more positively charged sodium ions flow in. Meanwhile, the positively charged ions in the previous section are being "pumped" out.

Flow of depolarization

4. As the action potential continues down the axon, neighboring sections open and the process is repeated. Note that the first section has now completely recharged and is beginning the return to the resting state.

Figure 5.5 *The action potential — How a neuron "talks" to itself.*

cell membrane. Picture the axon as a tube of membranous tissue filled with chemicals. This tube is floating in a sea of still more chemicals. The chemicals both inside and outside the tube are *ions*, molecules that carry an electrical charge, either positive or negative.

When the neuron is inactive, or *resting*, it is said to be *polarized*. That is, the fluid inside has mostly negatively charged ions, whereas the fluid outside the axon is the "polar opposite" — primarily positive. When the neuron is activated by sufficient stimulation from other neurons or sensory receptors, the electrical potential between the inside and the outside of the cell changes. A sudden inflow of positive ions *depolarizes* that first, small section of the axon, so that it becomes "overly positive." This change then causes nearby ion channels to open and also become depolarized, and then the next channel, and the next. In short, a chemical chain reaction occurs. The neural impulse (or action potential) travels down the axon, one section at a time, until it reaches the end of the axon.

How fast does a neural impulse travel? Actually, a nerve impulse moves slowly, much more slowly than electricity through a wire. Because electricity travels by a purely physical process, it can move through a wire at 97 percent of the speed of light, approximately 300 million meters per second. A neural impulse, on the other hand, travels along a bare axon at only about 10 meters per second.

Some axons, however, are enveloped in fatty insulation, the myelin sheath, which greatly increases the speed of an action potential. The myelin blankets the axon, with the exception of periodic *nodes*, points at which the myelin is very thin or absent (see again Figure 5.4). In a myelinated axon, the speed of the nerve impulse increases because the action potential jumps from node to node rather than traveling point by point along the entire axon. An action potential in a myelinated axon moves about 10 times faster than in a bare axon, at over 100 meters per second. The importance of the myelin sheath becomes apparent when it is destroyed in certain diseases such as multiple sclerosis. The greatly slowed rate of conduction of action potentials affects the person's movement and coordination.

It is important to remember that once the action potential is started, it continues. There's no such thing as a "partial" action potential. Similar to the firing of a bullet from a gun, the action potential fires either completely or not at all. This is referred to as the *all-or-none law*. Immediately after a neuron fires, it enters a brief *refractory period* where it cannot fire again. During the refractory period, the neuron *repolarizes*: The resting balance is restored with negative ions inside and positive ions outside. Now the neuron is free to fire again.

Neurotransmitters — How Neurons "Talk" to One Another

Now that you understand the basic structure of the neuron and how the neuron communicates with itself (by passing electrochemical messages along its length), we can examine how neurons communicate with other neurons, which is primarily through neurotransmitters.

Communication between one neuron and the next begins at the junction between neurons, known as the **synapse**. This synaptic juncture includes the axon terminal of the sending neuron, the tiny space between neurons (the *synaptic gap*), and the covering membrane of the receiving neuron (Figure 5.6). When the action potential reaches the knoblike terminals at the axon's end, it causes tiny sacs, called *synaptic vesicles*, to open and release a few thousand molecules of a chemical substance known as a **neurotransmitter**. These molecules then flow across the synaptic gap. If the adjacent, receiving neuron receives sufficient neurotransmitter stimulation, a follow-up action potential is initiated along its membrane and communication is "successful."

Although communication is said to be successful when the neurotransmitter reaches its target cell, it is important to note that action potentials do not always occur in the receiving neuron. Neurotransmitters have either an *excitatory* or *inhibitory* effect on their target cells.

Think of the case of a sculptor welding the final touches on to her masterpiece. As the heat soaks through her glove, she almost drops the very expensive part. However, this excitation is counteracted by inhibition, supplied by her brain. Recognizing that dropping the piece would be a very costly mistake, her brain sends information to the spinal cord inhibiting the withdrawal reflex. When neurotransmitters are excitatory, they make the target neuron more likely to fire an action potential; when they are inhibitory, they make the target neuron less likely to fire. In short, neurotransmitters carry one of two messages — "fire" or "don't fire."

Both types of messages are critical to your survival. Just as driving a car requires both an accelerator and brakes, your body needs both "on" and "off" neural switches. Your nervous system manages an amazing balancing act between *overexcitation*, leading to seizures, and *underexcitation*, leading to coma and death. In fact, poisons, such as strychnine, work by disabling many inhibitory messages, leading to overexcitation and uncontrollable, possibly fatal convulsions.

Synapse [SIN-aps] *The junction between the axon tip of the sending neuron and the dendrite or cell body of the receiving neuron; during an action potential, chemicals called neurotransmitters are released and flow across the synaptic gap*

Neurotransmitter *Chemicals manufactured and released by neurons that alter activity in other neurons.*

Chemical Messengers in the Nervous System: Neurotransmitters, Endorphins, and Hormones

Our brains and nervous systems would be lifeless without communication. The major chemical messengers responsible for communication are the *neurotransmitters*, *endorphins*, and *hormones*.

Figure 5.6 *Neurotransmitters — How neurons "talk" to one another.* (a) In this schematic view of a synapse, neurotransmitter chemicals are stored in small synaptic vesicles at the end of the axon. When action potentials reach the axon terminal, they stimulate the release of neurotransmitter molecules into the synaptic gap. The neurotransmitter chemicals then travel across the synaptic gap, and bind to receptor sites on the dendrites or cell body of the receiving neuron. (b) If the receiving neuron is sufficiently stimulated, a new action potential is generated and communication is successful.

Neurotransmitters

Researchers have discovered hundreds of substances known or suspected to be neurotransmitters. Some neurotransmitters regulate the actions of glands and muscles; others promote sleep or stimulate mental and physical alertness; others affect learning and memory; and still others affect motivation, emotions, and psychological disorders, including schizophrenia and depression. Table 5.1 lists a few of the better-understood neurotransmitters and their known or suspected effects.

Neurotransmitters and Disease

One of the many advantages of studying your brain and its neurotransmitters is an increased understanding of your own or others' medical problems and their treatment. For example, do you remember why actor Michael J. Fox retired from his popular TV sitcom, *Spin City*? It was because of muscle tremors and movement problems related to a poorly understood condition called *Parkinson's disease* (PD). As Table 5.1 shows, the neurotransmitter *dopamine* is a suspected factor in PD, and its symptoms are reduced with L-dopa (levodopa), a drug that increases dopamine levels in the brain (Brundin et al., 2000; Diederich & Goetz, 2000).

Interestingly, when some Parkinson's patients are adjusting to L-dopa and higher levels of dopamine, they may experience symptoms that mimic schizo-

TABLE 5.1 HOW NEUROTRANSMITTERS AFFECT US

Neurotransmitter	Known or Suspected Effects
Serotonin	Affects mood, sleep, appetite, sensory perception, temperature regulation, pain suppression, impulsivity, and aggression; may play a role in some psychological disorders, such as depression
Acetylcholine (ACh)	Affects muscle action, cognitive functioning, memory, REM (rapid-eye-movement) sleep, emotion. Suspected role in Alzheimer's disease
Dopamine (DA)	Affects movement, attention, memory, learning, and emotion. Plays a role in both schizophrenia and Parkinson's disease.
Norepinephrine (NE) (or noradrenaline)	Affects learning, memory, dreaming, emotion, waking from sleep, eating, alertness, wakefulness, reactions to stress
Epinephrine (or adrenaline)	Affects emotional arousal, memory storage, and metabolism of glucose necessary for energy release
GABA (gamma aminobutyric acid)	Neural inhibition in the central nervous system; Tranquilizing drugs act on GABA to decrease anxiety

phrenia, a serious psychological disorder that disrupts thought processes and produces delusions and hallucination. Excessively high levels of *dopamine* are a suspected contributor to some forms of *schizophrenia*, and when patients take antipsychotic drugs that suppress dopamine, their symptoms are sometimes reduced or even eliminated (Laruelle, Abi-Dargham, Gil, Kegeles, & Innis, 1999; Reynolds, 1999). In sum, *decreased* levels of dopamine are associated with Parkinson's disease, whereas *increased* levels are related to some forms of schizophrenia.

Another neurotransmitter, *serotonin* (Table 5.1), may also be involved in the depression that often accompanies Parkinson's disease. Although some researchers believe Parkinson's patients become depressed in reaction to the motor disabilities of the disorder, others think the depression is directly related to lower levels of serotonin (Schapira, 1999). And popular antidepressant drugs, like *Prozac* and *Zoloft*, work by boosting levels of available serotonin (Margolis & Swartz, 2001; Tauscher et al., 1999; Wegerer et al., 1999). Even without medication, serotonin levels increase after successful psychotherapy for depression (Bransfod, 2000). (Recall from Module 2 that scientific research is "circular and cumulative" and basic and applied research often overlap. Research with Parkinson's disease demonstrates these principles.)

Neurotransmitters, Poisons, and Mind-Altering Drugs

An understanding of neurotransmitters explains not only the origin of certain diseases and their pharmaceutical drug treatments but also how poisons, such as snake venom, and mind-altering drugs, such as nicotine, alcohol, caffeine, and cocaine, affect the brain.

Most poisons and drugs act at the synapse by replacing, decreasing, or enhancing the amount of neurotransmitter. Given that transmission of messages *between* neurons is chemical, many chemicals that we ingest can significantly affect neurotransmission. They can do this because their molecules have shapes similar to various neurotransmitters.

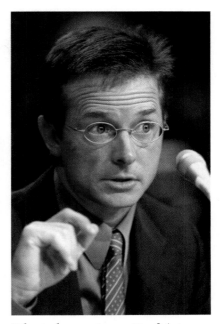

Why study neurotransmitters? Actor Michael J. Fox suffers from Parkinson's disease, which involves a decrease in cells that produce dopamine. In this photo, he is testifying before a U.S. subcommittee to urge increased funding for research on Parkinson's and other medical conditions.

Figure 5.7 *Receptor sites.* (a) Receptor sites on the dendrite recognize neurotransmitters because of their three-dimensional shape. (b) Molecules without the correct shape will not fit the receptors and therefore will not stimulate the dendrite. (c) Some *agonist* drugs, like nicotine, are similar enough in structure to a certain neurotransmitter (in this case, acetylcholine) that they mimic its effects on the receiving neuron. (d) Some *antagonist* drugs, like curare, block the action of neurotransmitters (again, acetylcholine) by filling a receptor site and thus not allowing the neurotransmitter to stimulate the receptor.

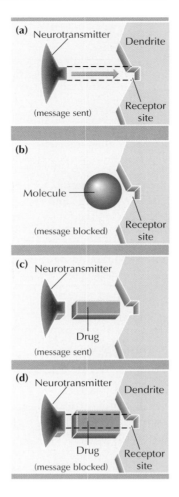

Neurotransmitters communicate with other neurons by binding to receptor sites in much the same way that a key fits into a lock. Just as different keys have distinct three-dimensional shapes, various chemical molecules, including neurotransmitters, have distinguishing three-dimensional characteristics. If a neurotransmitter has the proper shape, it will bind to the receptor site (Figure 5.7a and 5.7b) and thereby influence the firing of the receiving cell.

Some drugs, called *agonists* (from the Greek *agon*, meaning "contest, struggle"), mimic or enhance the action of neurotransmitters (Figure 5.7c). For example, both the poison in the black widow spider and the nicotine in cigarettes have a molecular shape similar enough to the neurotransmitter *acetylcholine* (*ACh*) that they can mimic its effect, including increasing the heart rate. Amphetamines have a similar excitatory effect by mimicking the neurotransmitter *norepinephrine*.

In contrast, *antagonist* drugs (from the Greek word meaning "a member of the opposing team"), work by opposing or blocking neurotransmitters (Figure 5.7d). Most snake venom and some poisons, like the lethal drug *curare* that South American hunters use, act as antagonists to ACh. Because ACh is vital in muscle action, blocking it paralyzes muscles, including those involved in breathing, which can be fatal.

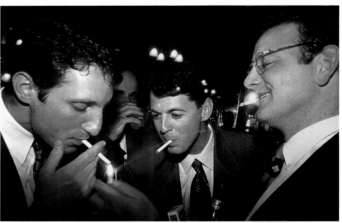

Neurotransmitters, poisons, and drugs. Most poisons and psychoactive drugs work by replacing, decreasing, or increasing the amount of certain neurotransmitters. The neurotransmitter acetylcholine (ACh) is responsible for muscular contraction, including the muscles responsible for breathing. The poison curare blocks the action of ACh and South American hunters sometimes apply it to the tips of blowgun darts or arrows to paralyze their prey. In contrast, nicotine in cigarettes increases the effects of ACh and smokers experience increased heart and respiration rates.

Endorphins

In addition to neurotransmitters, the body also has chemical messengers called *endogenous opioid peptides*, more commonly known as **endorphins**. These chemicals produce effects similar to those of opium-based drugs such as morphine — they reduce pain and promote pleasure. (Some endorphins work as neurotransmitters, but most act as *neuromodulators* that increase or decrease [modulate] the effects of neurotransmitters.)

Endorphins were discovered in the early 1970s, when Candace Pert and Soloman Snyder (1973) were doing research on morphine, a pain-relieving and mood-elevating opiate derived from opium, which is made from poppies. They found that the morphine was taken up by specialized receptors in areas of the brain linked with mood and pain sensations.

But why would the brain have special receptors for morphine — a powerfully addicting drug? Pert and Snyder reasoned that the brain must have its own internally produced, or *endogenous*, morphinelike chemicals. They later confirmed that such chemicals do exist and named them *endorphins* (a contraction of *endogenous* [self-produced] and *morphine*). The brain evidently produces its own naturally occurring chemical messengers that elevate mood and reduce pain, as well as affecting memory, learning, blood pressure, appetite, and sexual activity. Endorphins also help explain why soldiers and athletes continue to fight or play the game despite horrific injuries.

Hormones

The neural system communicates through the production and circulation of *neurotransmitters, endorphins*, and **hormones**. On receiving signals from the brain, glands within the **endocrine system** release these chemicals into the bloodstream, which circulates them throughout the body. Like neurotransmitters, hormones affect the nervous system, and sometimes the same chemical functions as both a hormone and a neurotransmitter. But unlike neurotransmitters that are released immediately adjacent to the cells they are to excite or inhibit, hormones are released into the blood, thus taking more time to diffuse throughout the body.

The nervous system and the endocrine system work hand in hand to direct our behavior and maintain our body's normal functioning. This interplay between the two systems is most evident in the fight-or-flight response of the sympathetic branch of the ANS, discussed earlier. The major functions of many endocrine glands, including the pituitary, the thyroid, the adrenals, and the pancreas (Figure 5.8), is to help the ANS respond to emergencies and maintain *homeostasis*, establishing a balance and normal functioning of bodily processes.

In times of emergency, chemical messengers travel along two paths — the ANS and the pituitary gland. The pituitary gland is sometimes referred to as the "master gland" because it releases a large variety of hormones throughout the body, which stimulate action in the other endocrine glands. In response to stressful situations, the pituitary sends messages to the adrenal glands (organs that are right above the kidneys). The adrenal glands then release *cortisol*, which boosts energy and blood sugar levels, *epinephrine* (commonly called *adrenaline*), and *norepinephrine*. When these adrenal hormones are released into your system, they activate the sympathetic branch of the ANS — thus preparing your body for "fight or flight."

Hormones produced by the endocrine system also help preserve *homeostasis* (or balance). They accomplish this by maintaining the tissue and blood levels of certain chemicals within a specific range. For example, sugar is a chemical that the body needs to function normally. But if too much sugar enters the bloodstream, the pancreas (an endocrine gland) secretes the hormone *insulin* to lower the blood sugar level to a more normal, safer level. When the insulin level is extremely low, as in people with diabetes, blood sugar levels may be three or more times higher than normal.

Endorphins [en-DOR-fins] *Chemical substances in the nervous system that are similar in structure and action to opiates and are involved in pain control, pleasure, and memory*

Hormones *Chemicals manufactured by endocrine glands and circulated in the bloodstream to produce bodily changes or maintain normal bodily functions*

Endocrine [EN-doh-krin] System *A system of glands located throughout the body that secrete hormones into the bloodstream*

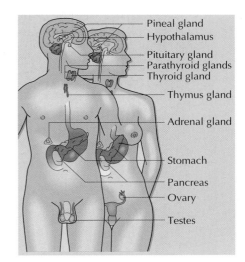

Figure 5.8 *The endocrine system.* The major endocrine glands are shown along with some internal organs to help you locate the glands.

Abnormally high levels of blood sugar can lead to dangerous changes in body tissues, including diabetes-related blindness.

Hormones also influence our growth, reproduction, moods, and response to stress. The amount of sex hormone (testosterone) present during prenatal development even determines whether the fetus develops a penis and scrotum or a clitoris and labia. Before closing, we want to emphasize that our discussion of neurotransmitters, endorphins, and hormones is greatly simplified. Diseases like Parkinson's, schizophrenia, depression, and diabetes are complex and involve interacting, multiple causes and treatment. Similarly, neurotransmitters, endorphins, and hormones all play multiple, overlapping roles. However, even this limited coverage gives you a foundation for understanding the brain and nervous system — topics in our upcoming section.

Check & Review

NEURONS, NEURAL COMMUNICATION, AND CHEMICAL MESSENGERS

Neurons are cells that transmit information throughout the body. They have three main parts: **dendrites**, which receive information from other neurons; the **cell body**, which provides nourishment and "decides" whether the axon should fire; and the **axon**, which sends along the neural information. **Glial cells** support and provide nutrients for neurons in the central nervous system (CNS).

The axon is specialized for transmitting neural impulses, or **action potentials**. During times when no action potential is moving down the axon, the axon is at rest. The neuron is activated, and an action potential occurs, when the charge within the neuron becomes more positive than the charge outside the cell's membrane. Action potentials travel more quickly down myelinated axons because the **myelin sheath** serves as insulation.

Information is transferred from one neuron to another at synapses by chemicals called **neurotransmitters**. Neurotransmitters bind to receptor sites much as a key fits into a lock, and their effects can be *excitatory* or *inhibitory*. Most psychoactive drugs affect the nervous system by acting directly on receptor sites for specific neurotransmitters or by increasing or decreasing the amount of neurotransmitter that crosses the **synapse**.

In addition to neurotransmitters, there are two other important chemical messengers — endorphins and hormones. Neuromodulators (such as **endorphins**) — increase or decrease the effects of neurotransmitters. **Hormones** are released from glands in the **endocrine system** directly into the bloodstream. They regulate levels of critical chemicals in the body.

Questions

1. Draw and label the three major parts of a neuron and the myelin sheath.

2. An impulse travels through the structures of the neuron in the following order: (a) cell body, axon, dendrites; (b) cell body, dendrites, axon; (c) dendrites, cell body, axon; (d) axon, cell body, dendrites

3. Chemical messengers that are released by axons and stimulate dendrites are called _____. (a) chemical messengers; (b) neurotransmitters; (c) synaptic transmitters; (d) neuromessengers

4. Explain how neurotransmitters, endorphins, and hormones carry messages throughout the body.

Answers to Questions can be found in Appendix B.

ACTIVE LEARNING WORKSHEET   MODULE 5

ACROSS

1. Junction between the axon tip of the sending neuron and the dendrite or cell body of the receiving neuron.

4. All nerves and neurons outside the brain and spinal cord.

7. Interdisciplinary field studying how biological processes, especially activity in the brain and nervous system, relate to behavior.

9. Chemicals manufactured by endocrine glands and circulated in the bloodstream to produce bodily changes or maintain normal bodily functions.

10. Long, tube-like structure that conveys impulses away from the neuron's cell body toward other neurons or to muscles or glands.

12. Layer of fatty insulation around the axon of some neurons that increases speed of neural impulse.

13. Subdivision of the ANS that arouses and mobilizes energy during times of stress.

14. Neural impulse that carries information along the axon of a neuron.

15. Brain and spinal cord.

DOWN

1. Subdivision of the PNS that connects to sensory receptors and controls skeletal muscles.

2. Chemicals manufactured and released by neurons that alter activity in other neurons.

3. Subdivision of the PNS that controls involuntary functions, which is further subdivided into the sympathetic nervous system and the parasympathetic nervous system.

5. Chemicals similar in structure and action to opiates and involved in pain control, pleasure, and memory.

6. Individual nerve cells responsible for processing, storing, and transmitting information throughout the body.

8. Branching neuron structures that receive neural impulses from other neurons and convey impulses toward the cell body.

11. Nervous system cells that provide structural, nutritional, and other support for the neuron.

Answers can be found in Appendix B.

A TOUR THROUGH THE BRAIN

Having covered basic, biological foundations (neurons, neurotransmitters, divisions of the neural system, and hormones), we come now to the "main event" of neuroscience — the brain itself. We began this unit with the tale of Phineas Gage and his horrible brain injury because it emphasized the vital importance of this relatively tiny three-pound organ that sits atop your shoulders. Who would you be without your brain? Without its lower-level structures, you would not be alive. Without your cortex, you would not be capable of thinking, speaking, or perceiving. And as we saw with Phineas Gage, when the cortex is damaged, we lose much of what we define as "self."

We begin our study of the brain with a look at the tools neural cartographers have used to study and map it. Then we start our exploration of the brain at the lower end, where the spinal cord joins the brainstem, and move upward toward the cerebral cortex. Note as we move from the brainstem to the cortex that the functions of brain structures change from regulating "lower," basic functions like survival to controlling "higher," more complex mental processes such as thinking.

Tools for Exploration: Mapping the Brain

What are the best tools for studying the brain?

The earliest explorers of the brain dissected the brains of deceased humans and conducted experiments on other animals using *lesioning techniques* (systematically destroying brain tissue to study the effects on behavior and mental processes) (Table 6.1). By the mid-1800s, this early research had produced a basic map of the peripheral nervous system and some areas of the brain. Early researchers also relied on clinical observations and case studies of living people. Tragic accidents, as in the case of Phineas Gage, and diseases or other brain disorders also offered valuable insights into brain functioning. The story of Phineas Gage might have ended with his death were it not for his doctor, John Harlow (1848), who wrote a detailed account of the accident. Years later, when he learned of Gage's death, he also petitioned Phineas's family to exhume the body and allow him to keep Phineas Gage's skull as a medical record. Today, both the skull and the tamping iron that had been buried with Gage are on display at Harvard University's Warren Anatomical Medical Museum.

Modern researchers still use dissection, lesioning, clinical observation, and case studies, but they also employ other techniques such as electrical recording and electrical brain stimulation. *Electrodes* (tiny electrified disks or wires) pasted to the skin or skull translate brain waves (electrical energy from the brain) to produce wavy lines on a moving piece of paper; this report is called an *electroencephalogram* (*electro-* means "electrical," *encephalon* means "brain," and *gram* means "record"). The electroencephalograph (EEG) is a major research tool for studying changes in brain waves during sleep and dreaming. For even more precise information, researchers can use *electrical stimulation of the brain* (ESB). Electrodes are inserted into the brain to record the naturally occurring electrical activity of neurons or to stimulate certain areas with weak electrical currents.

In recent years, advances in brain science have led to exciting, new techniques, including various types of brain-imaging scans (see again Table 6.1). Most of these methods are relatively *noninvasive*. That is, they are performed without breaking the skin or entering the body. They can be used both in clinical settings to examine suspected brain damage and disease, and in laboratory settings to study brain function during ordinary activities like sleeping, eating, reading, speaking, and so on (Goldman, Nahas, & George, 2000; Robertson et al., 2000). For example, computed tomography (CT) scans (a computer-enhanced series of X-rays of the brain) have been used to look for abnormalities in brain structures among people suffering from

TABLE 6.1 TOOLS FOR STUDYING THE BRAIN

Method	Description	Sample Results
Brain dissection	Careful cutting and study of a cadaver brain to reveal structural details	Brain dissections of Alzheimer's disease victims often show identifiable changes in various parts of the brain.
Ablation/lesions	Surgically removing parts of the brain (ablation), or destroying specific areas of the brain (lesioning), is followed by observation for changes in behavior or mental processes.	Lesioning specific parts of the rat's hypothalamus greatly affects its eating behavior.
Clinical observations/ case studies	Observing and recording changes in personality, behavior, or sensory capacity associated with brain diseases or injuries	Damage to one side of the brain often causes numbness or paralysis on the body's opposite side; also Phineas Gage's injury and subsequent changes.
Electrical recordings	Using electrodes attached to a person or animal's skin or scalp, brain activity is recorded to produce an electroencephalogram.	Reveals areas of the brain most active during a particular task or changes in mental states, like sleeping and hypnosis; also traces abnormal brain waves caused by brain malfunctions, like epilepsy or tumors
Electrical stimulation of the brain (ESB)	Using an electrode, a weak electric current stimulates specific areas or structures of the brain.	Penfield (1958) mapped the surface of the brain and found that different areas have different functions.

(Table continues)

Brain dissection. Structures of the brain can be examined by dissecting the brains of deceased people who donated their bodies for scientific study.

Electroencephalograph (EEG). Electrodes are attached to the patient's scalp, and the brain's electrical activity is displayed on a computer monitor or recorded on a paper chart.

TABLE 6.1 CONTINUED

Method	Description	Sample Results
Brain imaging	Studies intact, living brains by taking pictures	Reveals various brain structures, their functions, and changes associated with disease or injury
Types of images: • CT (computed tomography) scan	A computer that creates cross-sectional pictures of the brain reads X-rays directed through the brain at different angles; least expensive type of imaging and widely used in research	Reveals the effects of strokes, injuries, tumors, and other brain disorders
• PET (positron emission tomography) scan	Radioactive form of glucose is injected into the bloodstream; scanner records amount of glucose used in particularly active areas of the brain and produces computer-constructed picture of the brain	Originally designed to detect abnormalities, also used to identify brain areas active during ordinary activities (reading, singing, etc.)
• MRI (magnetic resonance imaging) scan	A high-frequency magnetic field is passed through the brain by means of electromagnets.	Produces high-resolution three-dimensional pictures of the brain useful for identifying abnormalities and mapping brain structures and function
• fMRI (functional magnetic resonance imaging) scan	A newer, faster version of the MRI that detects blood flow by picking up magnetic signals from blood that has given up its oxygen to activate brain cells	Indicates which areas of the brain are active or inactive during ordinary activities or responses (like reading or talking); also, shows changes associated with disorders

This false color CT scan used X rays to locate a brain tumor. The tumor is the deep purple mass at the top left.

PET scans and brain functions. In these two scans, the left one shows brain activity when the eyes are open, whereas the one on the right is with the eyes closed. Note the increased activity, red and yellow, in the occipital lobe (the top of the photo) when the eyes are open.

Magnetic resonance imaging (MRI). Note the fissures and internal structures of the cerebral cortex, as well as the cerebellum and the brain stem. The throat, nasal airways, and cerebrospinal fluid surrounding the brain are dark.

mental illness, whereas positron emission tomography (PET) scans map actual *activity* in the brain and can be used to pinpoint brain areas that handle various activities, such as singing or fist clenching, and even areas responsible for different emotions (Craik et al., 1999; Mayberg et al., 1999).

It is important to note that each method has its particular strengths and weaknesses, but all provide invaluable insights and information. We'll discuss findings from these research tools in upcoming modules.

Lower-Level Brain Structures: The Oldest Parts of the Brain

Brain size and complexity vary significantly from species to species. Lower species such as fish and reptiles have smaller, less complex brains than do higher species such as cats and dogs. The most complex brains belong to whales, dolphins, and higher primates such as chimps, gorillas, and humans. The billions of neurons that make up the human brain control much of what we think, feel, and do.

As we begin our tour of the brain, keep in mind that certain brain structures are specialized to perform certain tasks, a process known as **localization of function**. Don't, however, exaggerate the differences. Most parts of the brain perform integrating, overlapping functions. Figure 6.1 shows the major structures of the brain. You should refer to it as you read.

The Brainstem

You are sleeping. Your eyes dart back and forth as you begin your last dream of the night. Your heart rate, blood pressure, and respiration increase as the dream gets more exciting. But then your dream is shattered by a buzzing alarm clock. All your automatic behaviors and survival responses in this scenario have been either controlled by or influenced by parts of the brainstem. The **brainstem** looks like its name. The lower-end "stem" is a continuation of the spinal cord, and the higher end lies deep within the brain. Three structures generally are associated with the brainstem — the pons, the medulla, and the reticular formation.

Messages to and from upper-level brain structures pass through two major structures in the brainstem — the pons and medulla. The **pons**, located in the upper portion of the brainstem, is involved in respiration, movement, sleeping, waking, and dreaming (among other things). The **medulla** is below the pons, at the bottom of the brainstem and just above the spinal cord. Its functions are similar to those of the pons. Because the medulla is essentially an extension of the spinal cord, many nerve fibers pass through it carrying information to and from the brain. The medulla also contains many nerve fibers that control automatic bodily functions such as respiration and heart rate. Damage to the medulla can lead to failure of bodily functions and death. This is the area of the brain that was damaged when Senator Robert Kennedy was assassinated in 1968.

Running through the core of the brainstem and extending upward is the **reticular** (netlike) **formation** (RF). This dense, finger-shaped network of neurons filters incoming sensory information and arouses the higher centers of the brain when something happens that demands their attention. Basically, without your RF, you would not be alert or perhaps even conscious. Damage to this area can cause a coma.

The Cerebellum

The **cerebellum** ("little brain") is located at the base of the brain behind the brainstem. (Some say it looks like a cauliflower.) In evolutionary terms, it is a very old structure responsible for maintaining smooth movement and coordinating motor

---

What are the lower-level structures of the brain, and what are their roles in behavior and mental processes?

Localization of Function *Specialization of various parts of the brain for particular functions*

Brainstem *An area at the base of the brain in front of the cerebellum responsible for automatic, survival functions*

Pons *A structure at the top of the brainstem involved in respiration, movement, waking, sleep, and dreaming*

Medulla [muh-DUL-uh] *A structure at the base of the brainstem responsible for automatic body functions such as breathing and heart rate*

Reticular Formation (RF) *A diffuse set of neurons in the core of the brainstem that screens incoming information and arouses the cortex*

Cerebellum [sehr-uh-BELL-um] *Structure at the base of the brain, behind the brainstem, responsible for maintaining smooth movement, balance, and some aspects of perception and cognition*

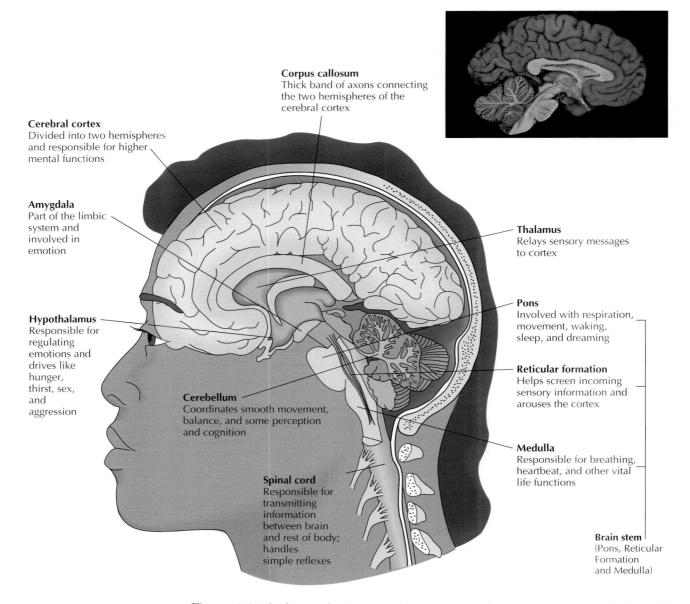

Corpus callosum
Thick band of axons connecting the two hemispheres of the cerebral cortex

Cerebral cortex
Divided into two hemispheres and responsible for higher mental functions

Amygdala
Part of the limbic system and involved in emotion

Hypothalamus
Responsible for regulating emotions and drives like hunger, thirst, sex, and aggression

Thalamus
Relays sensory messages to cortex

Pons
Involved with respiration, movement, waking, sleep, and dreaming

Reticular formation
Helps screen incoming sensory information and arouses the cortex

Cerebellum
Coordinates smooth movement, balance, and some perception and cognition

Medulla
Responsible for breathing, heartbeat, and other vital life functions

Spinal cord
Responsible for transmitting information between brain and rest of body; handles simple reflexes

Brain stem
(Pons, Reticular Formation and Medulla)

Figure 6.1 *The human brain.* If your brain were sliced down the center, lengthwise, it would look like the top right photo. Although you wouldn't be alive to read this, the drawing on the lower half of the page would depict what the inside surface of the left half of your brain would look like. It highlights key structures and some of their principal functions. As you read about each of these structures, you may find it helpful to keep this drawing in mind or to refer back to it as necessary.

activity. Although the actual commands for movement come from higher brain centers in the cortex, the cerebellum coordinates the muscles so that movement is smooth and precise. The cerebellum is also involved with the sense of balance. In fact, roadside tests for drunken driving are essentially testing the cerebellum, because it is one of the first structures depressed by alcohol.

Research suggests that the cerebellum does much more than just coordinate movement and maintain physical balance. It may also have a role in perception and cognition. Using magnetic resonance imaging (MRI), researchers have documented that parts of the cerebellum are very active during perceptual and cognitive activities that require the processing of sensory data (Luft, Skalej, Stefanou, Klose, & Voight, 1998).

The cerebellum at work. Can you see why the cerebellum might be important to this construction worker? It is responsible for coordinating movement and maintaining posture and balance.

The Thalamus

The **thalamus** lies at the top of the brainstem. Resembling two little footballs, one on each side of the brain, connected by a thin group of nerve fibers, it serves as the major sensory relay center for the brain. Like an air traffic control center that receives information from all aircraft, and then directs them to the appropriate landing or take off areas, the thalamus receives input from nearly all the sensory systems and then directs this information to the appropriate cortical areas. For example, while reading this page, your thalamus sends incoming visual signals to the visual area of your cortex. When your ears receive sound, the information is transferred to the auditory (or hearing) area of your cortex.

Thalamus [THAL-uh-muss] *A brain structure at the top of the brainstem that relays sensory messages to the cerebral cortex*

The thalamus plays an active role in integrating information from various senses and may be involved in learning and memory (Crosson, 1999). Injury to the thalamus can cause deafness, blindness, or loss of any other sense (except smell). This suggests that some analysis of sensory messages may occur here. Because the thalamus is the major sensory relay area to the cerebral cortex, damage or abnormalities also might cause the cortex to misinterpret or not receive vital sensory information. Other research using brain-imaging techniques links abnormalities in the thalamus to schizophrenia (Andreasen, 1999, 2000; Hazlett et al., 2000; Omori et al., 2000). Schizophrenia is a serious psychological disorder characterized by problems with sensory filtering and perception. Can you see how a defective thalamus might produce characteristics of schizophrenia, such as hallucinations and delusion?

The Hypothalamus

Beneath the thalamus lies the **hypothalamus** (*hypo-* means "under"). Although no larger than a kidney bean, it has been called the "master control center" for emotions and many basic motives such as hunger, thirst, sex, and aggression (Fulton, Woodside, & Shizgal; Meston & Frohlich, 2000). Its general function is *homeostasis*, including temperature control, which it accomplishes by regulating the endocrine system. Hanging down from the hypothalamus, the *pituitary gland* is usually considered the master endocrine gland because it releases hormones that activate the other endocrine glands. The hypothalamus influences the pituitary through direct neural connections and by releasing its own hormones into the blood supply of the pituitary.

Hypothalamus [hi-poh-THAL-uh-muss] *A small brain structure beneath the thalamus that maintains homeostasis and regulates emotions and drives, such as hunger, thirst, sex, and aggression*

Despite its relatively small size, the hypothalamus influences important aspects of behavior either *directly*, by generating some behaviors itself, or *indirectly* by controlling parts of the autonomic nervous system (ANS) and endocrine system. An example of its direct effects are found when animals exhibit increased or decreased eating and drinking patterns depending on what area of the hypothalamus is affected. The indirect effects of the hypothalamus are seen in the interaction of stress and the ANS.

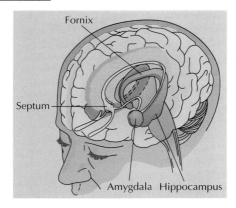

Fornix

Septum

Amygdala   Hippocampus

Figure 6.2 *The major brain structures associated with the limbic system.*

Limbic System *An interconnected group of lower-level brain structures involved with the arousal and regulation of emotion, motivation, memory, and many other aspects of behavior and mental processes*

Amygdala [uh-MIG-dull-uh] *An almond-shaped lower-level brain structure that is part of the limbic system and is involved in emotion*

The Limbic System

The **limbic system** is an interconnected group of structures located roughly along the border between the cerebral cortex and the lower-level brain structures (hence the term *limbic,* which means "edge" or "border"). The limbic system includes the *fornix*, the *hippocampus*, the *amygdala*, and the *septum* (Figure 6.2). Scientists disagree about which structures should be included in the limbic system, and many also include the hypothalamus, parts of the thalamus, and parts of the cerebral cortex.

Recent research studying the fornix and hippocampus suggests that they, along with the amygdala, are involved in the formation of new and short-term memories (Chin, 2000; Giovagnoli, 2001; McGaugh, 2000). However, the major focus of interest in the limbic system, and particularly the **amygdala**, has been its production and regulation of emotional behavior, particularly aggression and fear. Research on cats and rats shows that stimulating the amygdala increases aggressive behavior, and research on the human amygdala demonstrates its role in aggression and violence, as well as, the learning and expression of fear and the ability to recognize fear in the faces of others (Adolphs, Tranel, & Damasio, 1998; Cahill, Vazdarjanova, & Setlow, 2000; Davidson, Putnam, & Larson, 2000; Schmolck & Squire, 2001).

Perhaps one of the best-known functions of the limbic system is its role in pleasure or reward. James Olds and Peter Milner (1954) were the first to note that electrically stimulating certain areas of the limbic system caused a "pleasure" response in rats. The feeling was apparently so rewarding that the rats would cross electrified grids, swim through water (which they normally avoid), and press a lever thousands of times until they collapsed from exhaustion — just to have their brains stimulated. Follow-up studies found somewhat similar responses in other animals and even among human volunteers (Blum, Cull, Braverman, & Comings, 1996; Wise & Rompre, 1989). Modern research suggests that brain stimulation activates neurotransmitters or neuromodulators rather than discrete "pleasure centers."

Keep in mind that even though limbic system structures and neurotransmitters are instrumental in emotional behavior, emotion in humans is also tempered by the cerebral cortex, especially the frontal lobes. As the case of Phineas Gage shows, damage to the frontal lobes, which have neural connections to the amygdala and other parts of the limbic system, can permanently impair social and emotional behavior. This is yet another example of the inseparable interconnectivity of the entire brain.

Check & Review

TOOLS FOR EXPLORATION AND LOWER-LEVEL BRAIN STRUCTURES

Researchers study the brain through dissection of brains of cadavers, lesion techniques (which involve destroying part of an animal's brain to study resultant changes in behavior), and direct observation or case studies. Electrical recording techniques involve implanting electrodes into the brain or on its surface to study the brain's electrical activity. Computed tomography (CT), positron emission tomography (PET), magnetic resonance imaging (MRI),

and functional magnetic resonance imaging (fMRI) scans are sophisticated techniques for studying intact, living brains.

The most important lower-level brain structures are the brainstem, cerebellum, thalamus, hypothalamus, and limbic system. The **brainstem** controls automatic functions such as heartbeat and breathing; the cerebellum contributes to balance, muscle coordination, and some higher mental operations. Parts of the brain stem (the **pons** and **medulla**) are involved in sleeping, waking, dreaming, and control of automatic bodily functions, whereas the **retic-**

ular formation screens incoming information and arouses the cortex. The **cerebellum** maintains smooth movement, balance, and some aspects of perception and cognition. The **thalamus** is the major incoming sensory relay area of the brain. The **hypothalamus** is involved in emotion and in drives associated with survival, such as regulation of body temperature, thirst, hunger, sex, and aggression. The **limbic system** is a group of brain structures (including the **amygdala**) involved with emotional behavior and memory.

The Cerebral Cortex: The Center of "Higher" Processes

Above the lower-level brain structures, such as the brainstem, thalamus, and limbic system, lie the two *cerebral hemispheres*, the outer surface of which is called the **cerebral cortex**. (The word *cortex* means "bark," and the cerebral cortex surrounds most of the brain like the bark on a tree.) In general, the right hemisphere is in charge of the left side of the body, whereas the left hemisphere controls the right side of the body (Figure 6.3). We will later discuss how the two hemispheres have somewhat different tasks and special functions.

If you were able to open your skull and look inside at your own brain, you would note that the two hemispheres take up most of the room. They balloon out and cover most of the lower-level structures from view. The hemispheres together are slightly larger than two clenched fists. The thin surface layer of the cerebral hemispheres (the cortex) contains approximately 30 billion neurons and nine times as many glial cells. If the cortex of both hemispheres were spread out, they would cover an area almost the size of a standard newspaper page and be about a quarter of an inch thick. How does all this material fit inside our skull? Imagine crumpling the newspaper sheet into a loose ball. You would retain the same surface area but in a much smaller space. The cortex contains numerous "wrinkles" (called *convolutions*), which allow it to hold billions of neurons in the restricted space of the skull.

Each of the two cerebral hemispheres is divided into four areas, or *lobes*: frontal (behind your forehead), parietal (at the top and to the rear of your skull), temporal (in the "temple" region above your ears), and occipital (at the back of your head). Divisions of these lobes are marked by prominent folds, which provide convenient geographic landmarks (Figure 6.4). Like the lower-level brain parts discussed earlier, each lobe specializes in somewhat different tasks — another example of *localization of function*. At the same time, some functions overlap between lobes. As we describe each lobe and its functions, you may want to refer frequently to Figure 6.4.

The Frontal Lobes

By far the largest of the cortical lobes, the **frontal lobes** are located at the top front portion of the two brain hemispheres — right behind your forehead. The frontal lobes receive and coordinate messages from the other three lobes of the cortex and are responsible for at least three additional major functions:

1. *Motor control.* At the very back of the frontal lobes lies the *motor cortex,* which sends messages to the various muscles and glands in the body. All neural signals that instigate voluntary movement originate here. For instance, when you reach out to choose a candy bar from a vending machine, it is the motor control area of the frontal lobes that guides your hand in pulling the proper lever.

2. *Speech production.* In the *left* frontal lobe, on the surface of the brain near the bottom of the motor control area, lies *Broca's area,* which is known to play a crucial role in speech production. In 1865, French physician Paul Broca was the first to note that patients with damage to this area had great difficulty speaking but could comprehend written or spoken language. This type of aphasia (or impaired language ability) has come to be known as *Broca's aphasia.*

How does the cortex control behavior and mental processes?

Cerebral Cortex *The bumpy, convoluted area on the outside surface of the two cerebral hemispheres that regulates most complex behavior, including receiving sensations, motor control, and higher mental processes*

Frontal Lobes *Cortical lobes in front of the brain, which govern motor control, speech production, and higher functions, such as thinking, personality, emotion, and memory*

Figure 6.3 *Information crossover.* Information from left side of the body crosses over to the right brain.

"Whoa! That was a good one! Try it, Hobbs – just poke his brain right where my finger is."

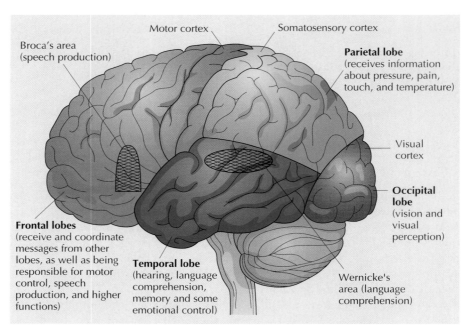

Figure 6.4 *The cerebral cortex.* This is a view of the left hemisphere with its four lobes, the frontal, parietal, temporal, and occipital, along with their major functions.

A modern day Phineas Gage? Construction worker Travis Bogumill was accidentally shot in the head with a nail gun. Like Phineas Gage, he was able to walk and talk immediately after the accident but also suffered some damage to his frontal lobes. The x-ray in the bottom photo shows the 3¼ inch nail that was removed from his brain.

3. *Higher functions.* Most functions that distinguish humans from other animals, such as thinking, personality, emotion, and memory, are controlled primarily by the frontal lobes. Abnormalities in the frontal lobes are often observed in patients with schizophrenia. And as we discovered in the story of Phineas Gage, damage to the frontal lobe affects motivation, drives, creativity, self-awareness, initiative, and the ability to plan ahead. Damage in this area also affects emotional behavior.

Using advanced research techniques, Hanna Damasio and her colleagues (1994) constructed computer images of Gage's brain, which showed the tamping iron most likely destroyed frontal lobe areas governing emotional control, social behavior, and decision-making. As Gage's case and other research indicates, what makes us uniquely human and what makes up our individual personalities is regulated by our frontal lobes.

A recent case reminiscent of Phineas Gage's experience also suggests that a person's short-term or "working memory" is located in the very front of the frontal lobes. In 1998, a construction worker named Travis Bogumill was accidentally shot in the head with a nail gun. The nail entered the right side of his brain near the rear of the frontal lobe. Like Gage, Bogumill was able to walk and talk after the accident. The nail was removed and, so far, Bogumill seems to be doing well. The only damage seems to be an impaired ability to perform complex mathematical problems in his head. Before the accident, Bogumill was able to easily multiply two-digit numbers in his head. After the accident, he was barely

Would you like a quick way to understand both your motor cortex and your sensory cortex?

1. *Motor cortex.* Try wiggling each of your fingers one at a time. Now try wiggling each of your toes. Note on Figure 6.5 how the area of your motor cortex is much larger for your fingers than for your toes, which correlates with your greater sensitivity and precise control in your fingers.

2. *Somatosensory cortex.* Ask a friend to close his or her eyes. Using a random number of fingers (one to four), press down on the skin of your friend's back for 1 or 2 seconds and ask your friend to report how many fingers you are using. Now repeat the same procedure on the palm or back of your friend's hand. Your friend should be much better at guessing when you're pressing on his or her hand than on his or her back. Again as in Figure 6.5, the area of the somatosensory cortex is much larger for the hands than for the back, which reflects more sensitivity and higher accuracy in detecting the finger pressure on the hand.

---

able to multiply two-digit numbers with a paper and pencil. This case supports other experimental research that shows that the frontal lobes and the working memory are responsible for reasoning, problem solving, mathematical calculation, and thinking about future rewards or actions (Giovagnoli, 2001; Hazlett, 2000; Koechlin, Basso, Pietrini, Panzer, & Grafman, 1999; O'Doherty, Kringelbach, Rolls, Hornak, & Andrews, 2001).

Parietal Lobes

At the top of the brain just behind the frontal lobes are the **parietal lobes**, the seat of body sensations and much of our memory about the environment. At the front of the parietal lobes is the *somatosensory cortex*, which receives information about pressure, pain, touch, and temperature. When you step on a sharp nail, you quickly (and reflexively) withdraw your foot because the messages travel directly to and from your spinal cord. However, you don't experience "pain" until the neural messages reach the parietal lobes of the brain.

As you can see in Figure 6.5, the more sensitive a body part is, the greater the area of sensory cortex devoted to it. Note how the face and hands receive the largest share of cortical tissue. These areas are much more sensitive than the rest of the body and require more precise control. Note also that the greater the area of motor cortex, the finer the motor control.

Parietal [puh-RYE-uh-tuhl] Lobes *Cortical lobes at the top of the brain where bodily sensations are interpreted.*

The Temporal Lobes

The **temporal lobes** (Latin for "pertaining to the temples") are found on the sides of the brain right above your ears. Their major functions are auditory perception (hearing), language comprehension, memory, and some emotional control. An area called the *auditory cortex* (which processes sound) is located at the top front of each temporal lobe. Incoming sensory information from the ears is processed in this area and then sent to the parietal lobes, where it is combined with visual and other body sensation information.

An area of the *left* temporal lobe, *Wernicke's area*, is involved in language comprehension. About a decade after Broca's discovery, German neurologist Carl Wernicke noted that patients with damage in this area could not understand what they read or heard, but they could speak quickly and easily. However, their speech was

Temporal Lobes *Cortical lobes above the ears involved in audition (hearing), language comprehension, memory, and some emotional control*

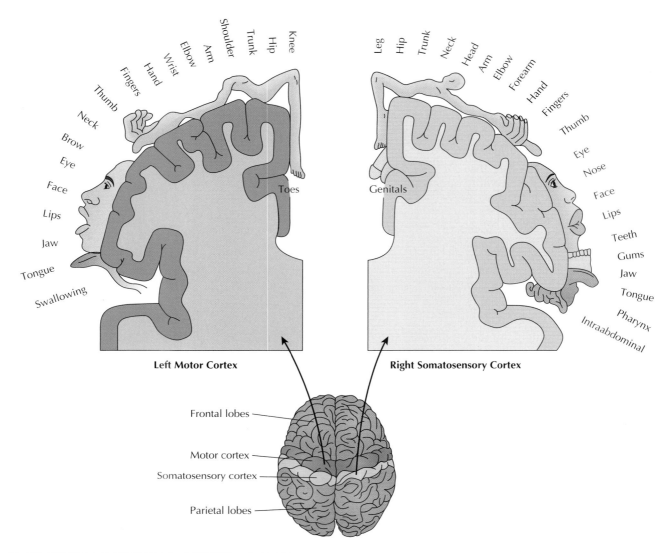

Left Motor Cortex

Right Somatosensory Cortex

Frontal lobes

Motor cortex

Somatosensory cortex

Parietal lobes

Figure 6.5 *Body representation on the motor cortex and somatosensory cortex.* This drawing represents a vertical cross-section taken from the left hemisphere's motor cortex and right hemisphere's somatosensory cortex. The amount of cortex devoted to a specific body part is depicted by the oddly shaped human figures draped around the outside edge of the cortex. (These figures are sometimes referred to as the "motor homunculus" and "somatosensory homunculus.") Note the disproportionate size of the hands and faces on each of these figures. The larger sizes reflect the larger cortical area necessary for the precise motor control and greater sensitivity of the hands and face.

The motor and somatosensory cortex. This fanciful representation of a human suggests the overriding importance of the hands and the mouth by the amount of cortex that is dedicated to them.

often unintelligible because it contained made-up words, like *chipecke*, sound substitutions (*girl* became *curl*), and word substitutions (*bread* became *cake*). This syndrome is now referred to as *Wernicke's aphasia*. (Study tip: Remember that *Broca's area* in the left frontal lobes is responsible for *speech* production, whereas *Wernicke's area* in the left temporal lobe is involved in *language* comprehension.)

David Hubel and Thorsten Wiesel received the Nobel Prize for their work in mapping visual areas in the occipital cortex of the brain.

Occipital Lobes

As the name implies, the **occipital lobes** (Latin for *oh*, "in back of," and *caput*, "head") are located at the lower back of the brain. Among other things, the occipital lobes are responsible for vision and visual perception. Damage to the occipital lobe can produce blindness, even though the eyes and their neural connection to the brain are perfectly healthy. The occipital lobes are also involved in shape, color, and motion perception.

Occipital [ahk-SIP-uh-tuhl] Lobes *Cortical lobes at the back of the brain responsible for vision and visual perception*

Association Areas

Thus far, we have focused on relatively small areas of the four lobes of the cortex that have specific functions. If a surgeon were to administer ESB to the parietal lobe area of your brain, you would most likely report physical sensations, such as feeling touch, pressure, and so on. On the other hand, if ESB were applied to your occipital lobe, you would see flashes of light or color.

Surprisingly, most areas of your cortex, if stimulated, produce nothing at all. These so-called quiet sections are not dormant, however. They are clearly involved in interpreting, integrating, and acting on information processed by other parts of the brain. Thus, these collective "quiet areas" are aptly called **association areas** because they *associate* various areas and functions of the brain. The association areas in the frontal lobe, for example, help in decision making and planning. Similarly, the association area right in front of the motor cortex is involved in the planning of voluntary movement.

Association Areas *So-called quiet areas in the cerebral cortex involved in interpreting, integrating, and acting on information processed by other parts of the brain*

As you recall from Module 1, one of the most popular myths in psychology is that we use only 10 percent of our brain. This myth might have begun with early research on association areas of the brain. Given that approximately three-fourths of the cortex is "uncommitted" (with no precise, specific function responsive to electrical brain stimulation), researchers might have mistakenly assumed that these areas were nonfunctional.

Two Brains in One? A House Divided

We mentioned earlier that the cerebral cortex is divided into two hemispheres that control opposite sides of the body. Each hemisphere also has separate areas of specialization. (This is another example of *localization of function*, yet it is technically referred to as **lateralization**.)

By the mid-1800s, early researchers had discovered that the left and right hemispheres carry out different tasks. In addition to mapping the brain and nervous system, they also noted that injury to one side of the brain produced paralysis or loss of sensation on the opposite side of the body. Also around this same time, case studies like Phineas Gage's documented that accidents, strokes, and tumors in the left hemisphere generally led to problems with language, reading, writing, speaking, arithmetic reasoning, and other higher mental processes. The "silent" right hemisphere came to be viewed as the "subordinate" or "nondominant" half, lacking special functions or abilities.

How do the left and right hemispheres of the brain affect behavior and mental processes?

Lateralization *Specialization of the left and right hemispheres of the brain for particular operations*

Split-Brain *A surgical separation of the brain's two hemispheres used medically to treat severe epilepsy; split-brain patients provide data on the functions of the two hemispheres*

Corpus Callosum [CORE-puss] [cah-LOH-suhm] *Bundle of nerve fibers connecting the brain's left and right hemispheres.*

Split-Brain Research

In the 1960s, this portrayal of the left and right hemispheres as dominant and subordinate players began to change as a result of landmark research with **split-brain** patients.

The two cerebral hemispheres are normally connected at several places, but the primary connection between the left and right halves is a thick, ribbonlike band of nerve fibers under the cortex called the **corpus callosum**. (See Figure 6.1 on page 68.) In some cases of *severe* epilepsy, surgeons cut the corpus callosum to stop the spread of epileptic seizures from the cortex of one hemisphere to the other. Given that brain surgery is a radical and permanent procedure, such an operation is always a last resort and is performed only when patients' conditions have not responded to other forms of treatment. However, the results are generally successful — epileptic seizures are reduced and sometimes disappear entirely.

Split-brain patients also provide an unintended, dramatic side benefit to scientific research. Because this operation cuts the only direct communication link between the two hemispheres, it reveals what each half of the brain can do when it is quite literally cut off from the other. Although relatively few split-brain operations have been conducted since 1961, the resulting research has profoundly improved our understanding of how the two halves of the brain function. In fact, in 1981 Roger Sperry received a Nobel Prize in physiology/medicine for his split-brain research.

How do these patients function after the split-brain surgery? The surgery does create a few unusual responses. For example, one split-brain patient reported that when he dressed himself, he sometimes pulled his pants down with his left hand and up with his right (Gazzaniga, 2000). However, patients generally show very few outward changes in their behavior, other than fewer epileptic seizures. If you met and talked with a split-brain patient, you probably wouldn't even know he or she had had the operation. In fact, one famous psychologist, Karl Lashley, joked that the only function of the corpus callosum seemed to be to keep the two hemispheres from sagging (Gazzaniga, 1995).

The subtle changes in split-brain patients normally appear with simple but specialized testing. For example, when a split-brain patient is asked to stare straight ahead while a photo of a fork is flashed to his left visual field, he cannot name it, although he can point to a similar photo with his left hand. Can you explain why?

To answer this question, you need to understand two major points about your brain. First, as you know, the left hemisphere receives and sends messages from and to the right side of the body, and vice versa. However, vision is different. Your eyes connect to your brain in such a way that, when you look straight ahead, the left half of your field of vision sends an image through both eyes to your right hemisphere (Figure 6.6). Likewise, the right side of your visual field is transmitted to your left hemisphere.

Assuming you don't have a split-brain, if information were presented only to your right hemisphere, it would be quickly sent to your left hemisphere — where the language center could name it. However, when the corpus callosum is split and experimenters present an image to only the left visual field, information cannot be transferred from the right hemisphere to the left. Thus, the patient cannot say what he saw, but he can point to a photo of the same object with his left hand. (Figure 6.7 offers a further example of split-brain testing.)

Keep in mind that split-brain surgery is a last resort medical treatment, which reduces the severity of epileptic seizures and generally has few effects on everyday functioning. An unexpected benefit of this surgery is that it has allowed researchers to demonstrate the functional specialization of each hemisphere (Schiffer, Zaidel, Bogen, & Chasan-Taber, 1998).

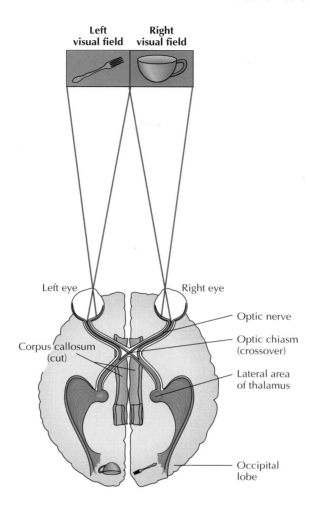

Figure 6.6 *Crisscrossing of visual information.* Imagine this as a drawing of your brain, and that you are being asked to stare straight ahead. Note how visual images from the left half of each eye connect only to the left half of your brain; whereas, images from the right half of each eye connect to the right half. The information received by either hemisphere is normally transmitted across your corpus callosum to the other side. When the corpus callosum is cut, however, the "split-brain" patient does not receive the shared information.

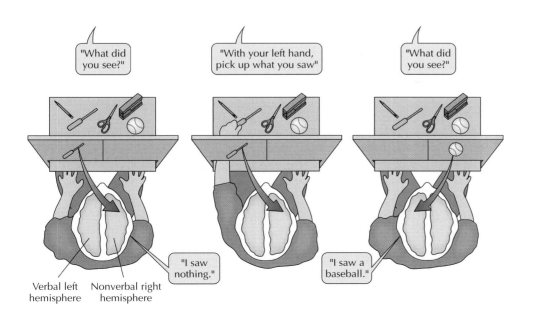

Figure 6.7 *Split-brain research.* When a split-brain patient stares straight ahead and a picture of a screw driver is flashed only to the left visual field, the information goes only to the nonverbal right hemisphere, and he cannot name what he saw. However, when asked to "pick up what you saw," his left hand can touch the items hidden behind the screen and easily identify the screwdriver. This shows that the right hemisphere received the photo image of the screwdriver, but the patient could not name it because the information did not travel across the severed corpus callosum to the left hemisphere where language is stored. Note when the image of a baseball is presented to the left hemisphere, the patient easily names it. Can you see why split-brain research is so important to brain researchers interested in studying the various functions of the two hemispheres?

Figure 6.8 *Functions of the left and right hemispheres.* The left hemisphere specializes in verbal and analytical functions, whereas the right hemisphere focuses on nonverbal abilities, such as spatiomanipulative skills, art and musical abilities, and visual recognition tasks.

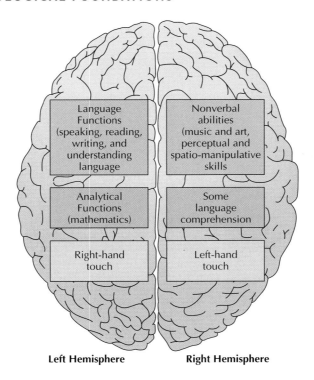

Left Hemisphere   Right Hemisphere

Hemispheric Specialization

Dozens of studies on split-brain patients, and newer research on people whose brains are intact, have documented several differences between the two brain hemispheres (summarized in Figure 6.8) (Franz, Waldie, & Smith, 2000; Gazzaniga, 1970, 1995, 2000; Robertson et al., 2000; Zaidel, 1985, 1998). In general, for roughly 95 percent of all adults, the left hemisphere is specialized not only for language functions (speaking, reading, writing, and understanding language) but also for analytical functions, such as mathematics (Dehaene, Spelke, Pinel, Stanescu, & Tsivkin, 1999). In contrast, the right hemisphere is specialized primarily for nonverbal abilities, including art and musical abilities and perceptual and spatiomanipulative skills, such as maneuvering through space, drawing or building geometric designs, working jigsaw puzzles, building model cars, painting pictures, and recognizing faces (Springer & Deutsch, 1998). However, recent research with fMRI imaging suggests that the right hemisphere may also contribute to complex language comprehension (Robertson et al., 2000).

In another study, a team of researchers led by Fredric Schiffer (1998) at McLean Hospital in Massachusetts reported that different aspects of personality appear in the different hemispheres. In one patient, the right hemisphere seemed more disturbed by childhood memories of being bullied than did the left. In another patient, the right hemisphere seemed to regard the patient more positively, while also feeling more negative emotions such as loneliness and sadness (Schiffer, Zaidel, Bogen, & Chasan-Taber, 1998).

Is this left and right brain specialization reversed in left-handed people?
Not necessarily. About 68 percent of left-handers (people who use their left hands to write, hammer a nail, and throw a ball) and 97 percent of right-handers have their language areas on the left hemisphere. This suggests that even though the right side of the brain is dominant for movement in left-handers, other types of skills are often localized in the same brain areas as for right-handers.

Would you like a demonstration of the specialized functions of your own two hemispheres? Some research suggests that the eyes tend to move to the right when a mental task involves the left hemisphere and to the left when the task involves the right hemisphere (see Kinsbourne, 1972). Read the following questions to a friend and record whether his or her eyes move to the right or to the left as he or she ponders the answers. Try to keep the monitoring of your friend's eye movements as natural as possible.

1. Define the word *neuroscience*.
2. What is a function of the corpus callosum?
3. What structure of the brain is located right above pituitary gland?

4. If you are on top of the brain and traveling straight down, what is directly below the parietal lobes?

The first two questions involve language skills and the left hemisphere, which should produce more eye movement to the right. Questions 3 and 4 require spatial reasoning and the right hemisphere, which should elicit more eye movement to the left.

Try the same test on at least four other friends or family members. You'll note two major points: (1) cerebral lateralization is a matter of degree — not all or nothing, and (2) individual differences do exist, especially among left-handers.

Although lefthanders are generally penalized for living in a right-handed world, there may be some benefits to being left-handed. For example, history shows that a disproportionate number of lefties have achieved greatness in art, music, sports, mathematics, and architecture, including Leonardo da Vinci, Michelangelo, Picasso, and M. C. Escher. Because the right hemisphere is superior at imagery and visualizing three-dimensional objects, it may help to use the left hand for drawing, painting, or drafting (Springer & Deutsch, 1998). Moreover, left-handers tend to recover better from strokes that damage the language areas in the brain, which may be because the nonspeech hemisphere in left-handers is better able to compensate (Geschwind, 1979).

The Myth of the "Neglected Right Brain"

Courses and books directed at "right-brain thinking" and "drawing on the right side of the brain" often promise to increase your intuition, creativity, and artistic abilities by waking up your neglected and underused right brain (e.g. Bragdon & Gamon, 1999; Edwards, 1999). This myth of the neglected right brain arose from popularized accounts of split-brain patients and exaggerated claims and unwarranted conclusions about differences between the left and right hemispheres.

The fact is that the two hemispheres work together in a coordinated, integrated way, with each making important contributions. If you are a married student with small children, you can easily understand this principle. Just as you and your partner often "specialize" in different jobs (one giving the kids their baths, the other washing the dinner dishes), the hemispheres also divide their workload. However, both parents and both hemispheres are generally aware of what the other "half" is doing.

In our tour of the nervous system, the principles of *localization of function* and *specialization* are common — dendrites receive information, the occipital lobe specializes in vision, and so on. However, it's important to remember that all parts of the brain and nervous system play overlapping and synchronized roles.

Check & Review

THE CEREBRAL CORTEX AND HEMISPHERIC SPECIALIZATION

The left and right cerebral hemispheres of the brain take up most of the room inside the skull. The outer covering of the hemispheres, the **cerebral cortex**, is divided into four lobes. The **frontal lobes** control movement and speech and are involved with self-awareness and planning ahead. The **parietal lobes** are the receiving area for sensory information. The **temporal lobes** are concerned with hearing and language. The occipital lobes are dedicated to vision and visual information processing.

The two hemispheres of the brain are linked by the **corpus callosum**, through which they communicate and coordinate. However, **split-brain** research shows that each hemisphere does perform somewhat separate functions. In most people, the left hemisphere is dominant in verbal skills, such as speaking and writing, and also for analytical tasks. The right hemisphere appears to excel at nonverbal tasks, such as spatio-manipulative skills, art and music, and visual recognition.

Recent research shows the brain can reorganize and change its structure and function throughout the lifespan (**neuroplasticity**), and create new nerve cells (**neurogenesis**) from **stem cells.**

Questions

1. The bumpy, convoluted area making up the outside surface of the brain is the _____.

2. You are giving a speech. Name the cortical lobes involved in the following behaviors:

    a. Identifying faces in the audience

    b. Hearing questions from the audience

    c. Remembering where your car is parked when you're ready to go home

    d. Noticing that your new shoes are too tight and hurting your feet

3. The case of Phineas Gage suggests that the _____ lobes regulate our personality and are largely responsible for much of what makes us uniquely human. (a) frontal; (b) temporal; (c) parietal; (d) occipital

4. Although the left and right hemispheres of the brain are specialized, they are normally in close communication through the _____. (a) reciprocating circuits; (b) thalamus; (c) corpus callosum; (d) cerebellum

Answers to Questions can be found in Appendix B.

critical thinking ▶▶▶▶▶▶▶▶▶▶▶▶▶▶▶▶ Active Learning

Understanding Central Nervous System Anatomy and Function

Being able to define a term or concept doesn't necessarily mean you fully comprehend it. The following exercise will help clarify your understanding of brain terminology and function. It also provides a model for the types of questions that lead to critical thinking.

Situation #1
A neurosurgeon is about to perform brain surgery. The surgeon stimulates (touches with an electrode) a tiny portion of the patient's brain, and the patient's right finger moves. After noting the reaction, the surgeon stimulates a portion of the brain a short distance away and the patient's right thumb moves.

Questions to Answer
1. What section of the brain has been stimulated? In which lobe of the brain is this section found?

2. Which hemisphere of the brain is being stimulated?

3. During this stimulation, would the patient experience pain? Why or why not?

Situation #2
The scene: An emergency room in a hospital. Two doctors are talking about a car crash victim who has just been wheeled in.

First Doctor: "Good grief! The whole cerebral cortex is severely damaged; we'll have to remove the entire area."

Second Doctor: "We can't do that. If we remove all that tissue, the patient will die in a matter of minutes."

First Doctor: "Where did you get your medical training — watching *General Hospital*? The patient won't die if we remove his whole cerebral cortex."

Second Doctor: "I resent your tone and insinuation. I went to one of the finest medical schools, and I'm telling you the patient will die if we remove his whole cerebral cortex."

Questions to Answer

1. If the whole cerebral cortex is removed, will the patient die? Explain your answer.

2. If the patient is kept alive without a cerebral cortex, what kinds of behaviors or responses would be possible? What changes would you expect in personality, memories, and emotions?

3. What behaviors could be expected with only the subcortex, medulla, and spinal cord intact? What if only the medulla and spinal cord were functioning? Only the spinal cord?

4. If a patient could be kept alive without a cerebral cortex, would life be worth living? How much of your brain would have to be removed before you would rather die?

RESEARCH HIGHLIGHT

Rewiring, Repairing, and Transplanting Brains and Spinal Cords

In 1989, President George Bush signed a resolution declaring the 1990s the "Decade of the Brain." The decade is over. What did we learn during those 10 years? Was it worth the thousands of research hours and millions of research dollars? You be the judge.

Imagine being completely paralyzed and unable to speak. Each year, thousands of people suffer serious brain and spinal cord injuries, and until recently, these injuries were considered permanent and beyond medical help. Scientists have long believed that after the first 2 or 3 years of life humans and most animals lack the capacity to repair or replace damaged neurons in the brain or spinal cord. Though nerves in the peripheral nervous system sometimes repair and regenerate themselves, it was accepted doctrine that this could not occur in the central nervous system.

Thanks in part to the "Decade of the Brain," this dogma has been overturned — the human brain is capable of lifelong *neuroplasticity* and *neurogenesis*. Let's begin with neuroplasticity. Rather than being a solid fixed organ, your brain is capable of changing its structure and function in response to changing environmental conditions (Beatty, 2001; Hata & Stryker, 1994; Tierney, Varga, Hosey, Grafman, & Braun, 2001). This process is termed **neuroplasticity**. Although the basic brain organization (cerebellum, cortex, and so on) is irreversibly established well before birth, the details are subject to revision. As you're learning a new sport or foreign language, for example, your brain changes and "rewires" itself. New synapses form and others disappear. Some dendrites grow longer and sprout new branches, whereas others are "pruned" away. This is what makes our brains so wonderfully adaptive (Begley, 2000; Hyman, 1999).

Can adult brains grow new neurons? Neuroscientists once believed that each of us was born with all the brain cells we would ever have, but Fred Gage and others have shown that neurons are renewed throughout our life span.

Remarkably, this rewiring has even helped "remodel" the brain following strokes. For example, psychologist Edward Taub and his colleagues (1998, 2000) have had success with constraint-induced (CI) movement therapy in stroke patients. Immobilizing the unaffected ("good") arm (or leg) of the patient has restored function in some patients as long as 21 years after their strokes. Rather than coddling the affected arm, Taub requires rigorous and repetitive exercise, which he believes causes intact parts of the brain to take over for the stroke-damaged areas. In effect, Taub "recruits" intact brain cells.

Other scientists researching Alzheimer's disease suggest "rerouting" neurons around damaged areas of the brain (Begley, 2000). This treatment would be analogous to an electrician's wiring a shunt around the damaged part of an electrical circuit. Obviously, there are limits to neuroplasticity. Even with the best "rewiring," most of us will never become another Tiger Woods or Albert Einstein. However, the fact that our brains continually reorganize themselves throughout our lives has enormous implications.

Perhaps the most dazzling find of the Decade of the Brain is **neurogenesis** — the production of nerve cells. Until very recently, it was believed that we are born with all the neurons we'll ever have. Life was a slow process of dying neurons and increasing loss of brain tissue. Today, however, we know that 80-year-olds have just as many neurons as 20-year-olds. Although we do lose hundreds of cells each day, our brains also replenish themselves with *new* cells that originate deep within the brain and migrate to become part of the brain's circuitry (Fuchs & Segre, 2000; Gage, 2000; Gould, Reeves, Graziano, & Gross, 1999; Kempermann & Gage, 1999; Vogel, 2000).

Even more exciting is the fact that the source of these newly created cells is neural **stem cells** — rare, precursor ("immature") cells that can grow and develop into any type of cell depending on the chemical

Stem cell research and Parkinson's disease. A fetal graft implanted in the brain of a Parkinson's patient ten years ago still produces significant levels of dopamine (the brain scan on the left). Note, however, that the activity of this area of the brain is still below that of the normal brain on the right.

Neuroplasticity *The brain's ability to reorganize and change its structure and function throughout the life span*

Neurogenesis [nue-roh-JEN-uh-sis] *The division of nonneuronal cells to produce neurons*

Stem Cell *Precursor (immature) cells that give birth to new specialized cells; a stem cell holds all the information it needs to make bone, blood, brain — any part of a human body — and can also copy itself to maintain a stock of stem cells*

signals they receive as they grow. Until now, physicians have used stem cells for bone marrow transplants, but many more clinical applications have already begun. For example, clinical trials using stem cells to repopulate or replace cells devastated by injury or disease have helped patients suffering from strokes, Alzheimer's, Parkinson's, epilepsy, stress, and depression (Diederich & Goetz, 2000; Park, 2000; Travis, 2000).

Does this mean that people paralyzed from spinal cord injuries might be able to walk again? At this point, neurogenesis in the brain and spinal cord is minimal, but one possible bridge might be *transplanting* embryonic stem cells in the damaged area of the spinal cord. In research with rats, researchers have transplanted mouse embryonic stem cells into a damaged rat spinal cord (McDonald et al., 1999). When the damaged spinal cord was viewed several weeks later, the implanted cells had survived and spread throughout the injured spinal cord area. More importantly, the transplant-rats also showed some movement in previously paralyzed parts of their bodies. Medical researchers have also begun human trials using nerve grafts to repair damaged spinal cords (Barker & Dunnett, 1999; Saltus, 2000).

Although it is unwise to raise false hopes, we are making remarkable breakthroughs in neuroscience. The rewiring, repairing, and transplanting we discussed in this section are just a small part of what was discovered in the last 10 years. It has been said the Decade of the Brain represents the human brain's first big step toward understanding itself. Can you imagine what the next step (or the next decade) might bring?

Is paralysis permanent? Findings from the "Decade of the Brain" may provide hope for actor Christopher Reeve who was paralyzed in a horse riding accident and for people with other serious medical conditions.

MODULE 6   ACTIVE LEARNING WORKSHEET

ACROSS

1. Specialization of various parts of the brain for particular functions.

4. Brain area responsible for maintaining smooth movement, balance, and some aspects of perception and cognition.

6. So-called "quiet areas" in the cerebral cortex involved in interpreting, integrating and acting on information processed by other parts of the brain.

16. Bundle of nerve fibers connecting the brain's left and right hemispheres.

18. Precursor (immature) cells that give birth to new specialized cells.

19. Almond-shaped lower-level brain structure that is part of the limbic system and involved in emotion.

20. Cortical lobes in the front of the brain that govern motor control, speech production, and higher functions.

21. Part of the brain that begins as a continuation of the spinal cord and ends deep within the cortex; it is responsible for automatic, survival functions.

22. A surgical separation of the brain's two hemispheres used medically to treat severe epilepsy.

DOWN

2. Bumpy, convoluted area on the outside surface of the two cerebral hemispheres that regulates most complex behavior.

3. Specialization of the left and right hemispheres of the brain for particular operations.

5. Cortical lobes above the ears involved in audition, language comprehension, memory, and some emotional control.

7. Brain's ability to reorganize and change its structure and function throughout the life span.

8. Interconnected group of lower-level brain structures involved with the arousal and regulation of emotion, motivation, memory, and many other aspects of behavior and mental processes.

9. Diffuse set of neurons in the core of the brain stem that screens incoming information and arouses the cortex.

10. Brain stem structure responsible for automatic body functions such as breathing and heart rate.

11. Tiny brain structure under the thalamus that regulates emotions and drives, such as hunger, thirst, sex, and aggression.

12. Cortical lobes at the top of the brain where bodily sensations are interpreted.

13. The division of nonneuronal cells to produce neurons.

14. Cortical lobes at the back of the brain responsible for vision and visual perception.

15. Area at the top of the brain stem involved with respiration, movement, waking, sleep, and dreaming.

17. Brain structure at the top of the brain stem that relays sensory messages to the cerebral cortex.

Behavioral Genetics *A new field that combines genetics and psychology to study genetic and environmental influences on behavior*

Chromosome *Threadlike strands of DNA (deoxyribonucleic acid) molecules that carry genetic information*

Gene *A segment of DNA (deoxyribonucleic acid) that occupies a specific place on a particular chromosome and carries the code for hereditary transmission*

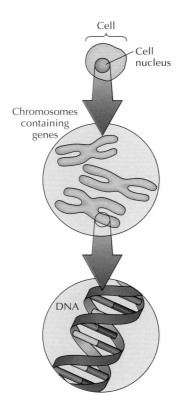

Figure 7.1 *DNA, genes, chromosomes, cell.*

MODULE 7
GENETICS AND EVOLUTION

We began Module 5 with a look at the smallest part of the nervous system — the neuron — and then toured the structures of the brain. Now, we go backward in time to the moment of your own conception to see how *behavioral genetics* helps to explain your present adult being. Then we close this section by going even further back in history to look at the role of *evolution*.

Behavioral Genetics: How Much Can We Blame Our Parents?

A relatively new field called **behavioral genetics** has greatly increased our understanding of the relative contributions of genetic and environmental influences on behavior. One of the oldest debates in psychology is the nature–nurture controversy, and throughout this text, you will find numerous examples of how both nature and nurture contribute to various behaviors and mental processes, such as intelligence, prenatal development, and mental disorders. To provide a foundation for these upcoming discussions, we will explore a few basic principles of genetics and the methods used to study behavioral genetics.

Basic Principles of Genetics

Every cell in your body contains lifelong *messages* from your parents — and you thought it was just their phone calls that bothered you! At the moment of your conception, your mother contributed one set of 23 **chromosomes** and another set of 23 came from your father. Each of these 46 chromosomes is composed of double-stranded molecules of *DNA (deoxyribonucleic acid)*, which, in turn, are made up of thousands of **genes** (Figure 7.1). Genes, the basic units of heredity, are themselves composed of small segments of DNA. We share many of the same genes with other animals and even insects and plants. But it's the genes we share with other humans that set us apart from gorillas, spiders, and tomatoes.

Have you ever wondered why some children have blond hair if both parents have brown hair? It depends on the particular combinations of gene types inherited by the child. For most characteristics, the child inherits two genes, one from each parent. If the inherited gene is *dominant*, the trait encoded in the gene will always be expressed. If the gene is *recessive*, the trait for that gene will be expressed only if the other gene in the pair is also a recessive gene. Because many people have single recessive genes that are not expressed, two brown-eyed parents, who both have recessive genes for blond hair, could produce a blond haired child.

Methods for Studying Behavioral Genetics

Beyond hair and eye color or vision, how much are you shaped by your genetic inheritance? Or by your environment? To answer these questions, researchers generally rely on four methods:

1. *Twin studies.* Because each of us receives a different combination of genes, each person is truly biologically unique. The only exception to this genetic uniqueness occurs with *identical (monozygotic) twins*, which result when a fertilized ovum divides and forms two identical separate cells. These cells go on to produce two complete individuals with identical genetic information. *Fraternal (dizygotic) twins*,

Can you curl your tongue lengthwise? This "ability" is one of the few traits that depends on only one dominant gene. You can increase your understanding of dominant versus recessive genes by doing a simple observation. If you can curl your tongue, one or both of your biological parents must also be able to curl his or her tongue — because this is a dominant trait. Conversely, if you cannot curl your tongue, both of your biological parents cannot curl their tongues.

on the other hand, result from the fertilization of two separate eggs by different sperm. These two "womb mates" are genetically no more alike than brothers and sisters born at different times.

The study of identical and fraternal twins offers a unique opportunity to evaluate the relative contributions of genetic and environmental forces in development (Segal & Bouchard, 2000). Identical twins who are separated at birth and reared apart are particularly important because they provide a limited form of control for the relative contributions of nature and nurture.

2. *Adoption studies.* Aside from studies of identical twins who may be adopted and reared apart, adoption studies compare two groups of relatives — biological parents and siblings ("blood relatives") and adoptive parents and siblings. If adopted children resemble their biological parents (and siblings), even though they were not raised in that family, then genetic factors probably had the greatest influence. On the other hand, if adopted children resemble their adoptive family, even though they do not share similar genes, then environmental factors may predominate.

3. *Family studies.* Researchers can also limit their studies to only blood relatives to see how much heredity has an influence. In these studies, the family history is explored in great detail. If a specific trait is inherited, there should be trait similarity among biological/blood relatives. Moreover, relatives who share more genes, like siblings, should exhibit more similarity than cousins. However, correlation does not prove causation! Remember that families share not only genes but also environments. Family studies can provide useful insights about the *possible*

"Virtual Twins" Julie (left) and Sara. Traditionally, biological twins have been "the gold standard" for genetic studies, but psychologist Nancy Segal has recently studied "virtual twins" (pairs of unrelated siblings of the same age, one or both adopted, who have been raised together since infancy). Segal suggests these twins provide unique information because they share a common family environment but no common genes.

Heritability *The proportion of observed variance in a particular trait (such as intelligence) that can be attributed to inherited genetic factors in contrast to environmental ones*

impact of heredity, but they can't be used to establish cause-and-effect relationships.

4. Genetic abnormalities. One type of research that can provide definitive evidence is the study of genetic abnormalities. For example, an extra twenty-first chromosome fragment almost always causes a condition called Down syndrome. People with Down syndrome often have distinctive round faces, with small folds of skin across the inner edge of the eyes, and impaired psychomotor and physical development, as well as mental retardation. Other disorders like Alzheimer's disease, involving brain deterioration and memory loss, and schizophrenia, a severe mental disorder characterized by loss of contact with reality, are suspected to be caused by abnormalities in several genes or chromosomes (Bailer et al., 2000; Berretini, 2000). We will discuss these disorders in detail in upcoming modules.

Findings from these four methods have allowed behavior geneticists to estimate the **heritability** of various traits. That is, the extent to which differences among individuals on psychological dimensions, such as intelligence and personality, are determined by genetic factors, as opposed to differences in environment. If genetics contributed *nothing* to the trait, it would have a heritability estimate of zero percent. If a trait were *completely* due to genetics, we would say it had a heritability estimate of 100 percent.

There are two important points to remember about heritability:

1. Heritability estimates do not apply to individuals. When people hear media reports that intelligence, musical abilities, or athletic talents are 30 to 50 percent inherited, they often mistakenly assume that this applies to them as individuals. Thus, if intelligence is 50 percent inherited, they believe that 50 percent is due to their parents and 50 percent to the environment. However, estimates of *heritability* are mathematical computations of the proportion of total variance in a trait that is explained by genetic variation within a *group*. In other words, these statistics *describe groups, not individuals*. Height, for example, has one of the highest heritability estimates — around 90 percent (Plomin, 1990). However, any one individual's personal height may be very different from his or her parents' or other blood relatives' height. We each inherit a unique combination of genes (unless we are identical twins). It is impossible to predict your individual height from a heritability estimate. You can estimate only for the group as a whole.

2. Genes and environment are inseparable. As first discussed in Module 1 (and throughout upcoming modules), nature and nurture interact — they play off each other and are inseparable (Casti, 2000; Gottlieb, 2000; Maccoby, 2000). Imagine your inherited genes as analogous to water, sugar, salt, flour, eggs, baking powder, and oil. When you mix these ingredients and pour them on a hot griddle (one environment), you get pancakes. Add more oil (a different combination of genes) and a waffle iron (a different environment), and you get waffles. With another set of ingredients and environments (different pans and an oven), you can have crepes, muffins, or cakes. How can you separate the effects of ingredients and cooking methods? You can't. Nature and nurture interact.

> With a good heredity, nature deals you a fine hand at cards; and with a good environment, you learn to play the hand well.
>
> Walter C. Alvarez

RESEARCH HIGHLIGHT

Breakthrough — The Human Genome is Mapped!

Since the 1980s, an exciting, ambitious, multibillion dollar international scientific effort called the *Human Genome Project (HGP)*, led by Francis Collins, and the *International Human Genome Sequencing Consortium (IHGSC)*, led by Craig Venter, have been creating "the human book of life." Working with new, high-tech methods, these two research teams set out to map all of the estimated 100,000 genes on the human chromosome. (The full set of genes for any organism is known as the *genome*—the total DNA blueprint of heritable traits contained in every cell of the body.)

On February 12, 2001, the journals *Science* and *Nature* published the breakthrough news that the mapping was complete, and that humans have only about 30,000 genes, which compares to around 19,000 for the roundworm and 13,000 for the fruit fly (International Human Genome, 2001; Venter et al., 2001). Although humans seem to have fewer genes than originally thought, their genes appear to be far more complex, and the completion of the analyses of the human genome is considered one of the most significant landmarks of all time, comparable to landing a man on the moon or splitting the atom. Francis Collins, leader of the HGP, described the genome as a "book of life" with three volumes:

"It's a history book—a narrative of the journey of our species through time. It's a shop manual, with an incredibly detailed blueprint for building every human cell. And it's a transformational textbook of medicine, with insights that will give healthcare providers immense new powers to treat, prevent, and cure disease" (cited in Sherrid, p. 48).

Cracking the genetic code. J. Craig Venter and Francis Collins, lead researchers for the Human Genome Project, received joint credit for mapping the human genome. Their work is considered a monumental milestone in genetic research. Can you explain why?

This enormous research venture has already produced important findings on genetic contributors to disease (Jegalian & Lahn, 2001; Lemonick, 2000; Seppa, 2000).

Evolutionary Psychology: Darwin Explains Behavior and Mental Processes

If you've traveled in many countries or taken courses in anthropology, your initial focus may have been on all the strange and unusual practices of other cultures. But over time, you also undoubtedly noted that people the world over seem to eat, work, play with their friends, care for their children, and fight with their enemies in remarkably similar ways. How do we explain this?

Evolutionary psychology suggests that many behavioral commonalities, from eating to fighting with our enemies, emerged and remain in human populations because they helped our ancestors (and ourselves) survive. This perspective is based on the writings of Charles Darwin (1859) who suggested that natural forces select traits that are adaptive to the organism's survival. This process of **natural selection** occurs when one particular genetic trait gives a person a reproductive advantage over others. Although some people mistakenly believe that natural selection means "survival of the fittest," what really matters is *reproduction* — the survival of the genome. Because of natural selection, the fastest or otherwise most fit organisms will be more likely than the less fit to live long enough to mate and thus pass on their genes to the next generation.

Imagine that you are camping alone in a remote area and see a large grizzly bear approaching. According to the principles of *natural selection*, your chances for survival depend on how quickly and smartly you respond to the threat. But what if your child and a group of strangers and their children are also camping in the same spot? Whom do you protect? Most parents would "naturally" choose to help their own child. Why? Why does this feel so "natural" and automatic? According to evolutionary psychologists, natural selection favors animals whose concern for kin is proportional to their

Evolutionary Psychology *A branch of psychology that studies evolutionary principles, like natural selection and genetic mutations, which affect adaptation to the environment and help explain commonalities in behavior*

Natural Selection *The driving mechanism behind evolution that allows individuals with genetically influenced traits that are adaptive in a particular environment to stay alive and produce offspring*

Evolution in Action? Similar behaviors in humans and other animals may suggest common evolutionary influences.

degree of biological relatedness. Thus, most people will devote more resources, protection, love and concern to close relatives. This helps ensure their "genetic survival."

In addition to natural selection, *genetic mutations* also help explain behavior. Given that each of us inherits over 100,000 genes, the probability is quite high that everyone carries at least one gene that has *mutated*, or changed from the original. The vast majority of mutated genes have no effect on behavior whatsoever. But, on occasion, a mutated gene will change an individual's behavior. It might cause someone to be more social, more risk taking, more shy, more careful. If the gene gives the person reproductive advantage, he or she will be more likely to pass on the gene to future generations. Another common misunderstanding is that evolution translates into continuing, long-term improvement. A genetic mutation can produce a population that is perfectly adapted to a current environment, but which may later perish if the environment changes.

Social and cultural factors can also affect evolution, as evidenced when the social or cultural factors influence the mating behavior of the people in a population (Segerstrale, 2000). For example, because the concept of beauty is culturally influenced, those who best fit their culture's concept of beauty may find it easier to acquire mates and have more offspring, to whom they pass on their physical and behavioral traits. Similarly, in cultures that arrange marriages according to social class or religious factors, different traits may be selected and passed along to succeeding generations.

Evolutionary psychology is one of the seven major perspectives in modern psychology and we will revisit this field many times throughout this text. For example, the unit on Stress and Health Psychology examines the role of stress over the course of evolution, whereas the section on Life Span Development I explores the role of evolution in infant reflexes, language development, and attachment. In the Gender and Human Sexuality section, we look at modern controversies surrounding evolution and gender role development and supposed differences in sexual behavior. Motivation and Emotion discusses the role of evolution in drives toward novelty and exploration and the universal recognition of facial expressions of emotion. Evidence of evolution in our helping and aggressive behaviors is discussed in the unit on Social Psychology.

In the following section, we explore biological differences between women and men that may have evolved from different gender-related adaptations.

GENDER & CULTURAL DIVERSITY

The Evolution of Sex Differences

Because of the way our species evolved, modern men and women have many abilities that helped our ancestors adapt to their environment and hence to survive and reproduce. For example, Figures 7.2 and 7.3 show that men tend to score higher on tests of mathematical reasoning and spatial relationships, whereas women score higher on tests involving mathematical calculation and tasks requiring perceptual speed. Men also tend to be more accurate in target-directed motor skills, whereas women tend to be more efficient in skills requiring fine motor coordination. What accounts for these differences?

One possible answer from evolutionary psychologists is that ancient societies typically assigned men the task of "hunters" and women as "gatherers." The man's superiority on many spatial tasks and target-directed motor skills, for example, may have evolved from the adaptive demands of hunting. Similarly, activities such as gathering, child-rearing, and domestic tool construction and manipulation may have contributed to the woman's language superiority (Farber, 2000; Joseph, 2000; Silverman & Phillips, 1998). Some critics, however, suggest that evolution progresses much too slowly to account for this type of behavioral adaptation. Furthermore, evolutionary explanations of sex differences are highly speculative and obviously difficult to test scientifically (Eagly & Wood, 1999).

A less controversial explanation of sex differences comes from well-established knowledge of hormonal effects. All women and men produce both estrogens and androgens (the principal classes of female and male hormones). It is the relative proportion of these hormones that accounts for sex differences. Even before birth, development of genital anatomy is largely due to the presence or absence of *testosterone* (one of the androgens secreted by the testes). Although genetic sex is determined at the moment of conception — an XX pairing produces a female zygote and an XY pairing produces a male — during the first 6 to 8 weeks after conception, the genital areas of both male and female embryos are essentially the same. Once the sex glands begin to produce differing levels of hormonal secretions (androgens and estrogens), their genital organs *differentiate.*

In some cases, however, endocrine disorders can lead to overproduction or underproduction of these hormones during prenatal development. In general, males exposed prenatally to abnormally low levels of androgens exhibit more femalelike behavior than other males. Conversely, females exposed prenatally to abnormally high levels of androgens tend to show more malelike behavior compared with other females.

For example, studies of girls with *congenital adrenal hyperplasia* (CAH), a rare genetic disorder with an excess amount of *androgens*, grow up to be more "tomboyish" and aggressive than nonaffected girls (Leveroni & Berenbaum, 1998). Moreover, girls with CAH tend to outperform nonaffected girls on cognitive tests of spatial ability on which males are known to excel, such as the mental rotation task shown in Figure 7.3 (Hampson, Rouet, & Altman, 1998; Nass & Baker, 1991). Although physiological effects resulting from CAH — the development of male genitals and the overproduction of androgens — can be surgically or medically corrected, the hormonal influence on brain development appears irreversible.

In addition to possible sex differences due to prenatal hormonal influences, there also may be differences in the anatomical structure of men and women's brains (Boone, 2000; Castle, 2000; Dorion et al., 2000; Amunts, Jaencke, Mohlberg, Steinmetz, & Zilles, 2000). For example, Mark Lumley and Kevin Sielky (2000) found an interesting gender difference in a disorder known as *alexithymia,* which involves difficulty identifying and describing feelings. The disorder seems to reflect deficiencies in right hemisphere function or interhemispheric transfer, but only for men. For women, poorer short-term memory is a better predictor. In another study, Ruben Gur and his colleagues (1999) found that women have a greater percentage of their brains dedicated to gray matter (neuron cell bodies) than do men. Considering that there is very little or no difference between men and women in overall intelligence,

Problem-Solving Tasks Favoring Women

Perceptual speed:
As quickly as possible identify matching items.

Displaced objects:
After looking at the middle picture, tell which item is missing from the the picture on the right.

Verbal fluency:
List words that begin with the same letter. (Women also tend to perform better in ideational fluency tests, for example, listing objects that are the same color.)

B – – –	Bat, big, bike, bang, bark, bank, bring, brand, broom, bright, brook bug, buddy, bunk

Precision manual tasks:
Place the pegs in the holes as quickly as possible.

Mathematical calculation:
Compute the answer.

72	6 (18+4)−78+^{36}/$_2$

Figure 7.2 *Problem solving tasks favoring women.*

Problem-Solving Tasks Favoring Men

Spatial tasks:
Mentally rotate the 3-d object to identify its match.

Spatial tasks:
Mentally manipulate the folded paper to tell where the holes will fall when it is unfolded.

Target-directed motor skills:
Hit the bulls eye.

Disembedding tests:
Find the simple shape on the left in the more complex figures.

Mathematical reasoning:
What is the answer?

5 $^1/_2$	If you bicycle 24 miles a day, how many days will it take to travel 132 miles?

Figure 7.3 *Problem solving tasks favoring men.*

the increased percentage of gray matter might just be an evolutionary adaptation to the smaller cranial size in women. Most women (and their brains) tend to be smaller than most men. Thus, some of the structural differences between male and female brains might reflect adaptations to differences in skull size (De Vries & Boyle, 1998).

Evolutionary psychology research emphasizes heredity and early biological processes in determining gender differences in cognitive behavior, but keep in mind that almost all sex differences are *correlational*. The mechanisms involved in the actual *cause* of certain human behaviors have yet to be determined. Furthermore, it is important to remember that all known variations *between* the two sexes are much smaller than differences *within* each sex. Finally, to repeat a theme discussed throughout this text, it is extremely difficult to separate the effects of biology (nature) from those of the environment (nurture) (Gottlieb, 2000; Maccoby, 2000).

Check & Review

GENETICS AND EVOLUTIONARY PSYCHOLOGY

Genes are strings of chemicals that hold the code for certain traits that are passed on from parent to child, and they can be dominant or recessive. Genes are found on long strands of DNA molecules called **chromosomes. Behavioral geneticists** use twin studies, adoption studies, family studies, and genetic abnormalities to explore genetic contributions to behavior and make estimates of **heritability.**

Evolutionary psychology is the branch of psychology that looks at evolutionary changes related to behavior. Several different processes, including **natural selection**, mutations, and social and cultural factors can affect evolution.

Questions

1. Evolutionary psychology is the branch of psychology that looks at
   a. How fossil discoveries affect behavior
   b. The relationship between genes and the environment
   c. The relationship between evolutionary changes and behavior
   d. The effect of culture change on behavior

2. What are the four chief methods used to study behavioral genetics?

3. According to evolutionary theorists, why are people more likely to help their family members than strangers?

4. How would evolutionary psychology explain why men tend to score higher on mathematical reasoning, spatial relationships, and target directed motor skills, whereas women score higher on mathematical calculation, tasks requiring perceptual speed, and fine motor coordination?

Answers to Questions can be found in Appendix B.

ACTIVE LEARNING WORKSHEET   MODULE 7

Respond to the following questions, and then compare your answers with those in Appendix B.

1. Imagine you are the parent of 3-year-old identical twins. Your friends and relatives frequently comment on how much the twins are alike in their size and temperament. Can you conclude that these similarities are primarily genetic? Can you think of other explanations?

2. Which of the following methods for studying behavioral genetics is most likely to provide definitive evidence? a) twin studies, b) adoption studies, c) family studies, d) genetic abnormalities

3. An evolutionary psychologist has just reported a study showing males are more talkative than females. What questions would you ask before trusting the research findings?

Visual Summary for Modules 5, 6, and 7

Biological Foundations

An Overview of the Nervous System

Central Nervous System (CNS)
→ Brain
→ Spinal Cord

Peripheral Nervous System (PNS)
→ Somatic Nervous System (SNS)
→ Autonomic Nervous System (ANS)
→ Parasympathetic
→ Sympathetic

Neurons as the Basic Building Blocks

Neurons: Individual nerve cells that transmit information throughout the body.
Glial cells: Provide structural, nutritional, and other support for neurons.

Key Features of a Neuron

- **Dendrites**: Receive information and send impulses to cell body.
- **Cell body**: Integrates incoming information and nourishes neuron.
- **Axon**: Carries information from cell body to other neurons.
(**Myelin Sheath**: Fatty insulation around some axons that speeds up action potential.)

How Neurons Communicate

- Communication *within the neuron* is through the **action potential**, a neural impulse that carries information along the axon.
- Communication *between neurons* occurs when an action potential reaches the axon terminal and stimulates the release of **neurotransmitters** into the **synapse**.

Chemical Messengers in the Nervous System

Three key chemical messengers:
1) **Neurotransmitters**: Chemicals manufactured and released by neurons that alter activity in other neurons, which thereby affects behavior and mental processes.
2) **Endorphins**: Chemicals that produce effects similar to those of opium based drugs like morphine.
3) **Hormones**: Chemicals released from the endocrine system into the bloodstream, which affect the nervous system.

A Tour Through the Brain

Tools for Exploration

Methods include brain dissection, ablation, lesioning, clinical observation, case studies, electrical recordings, electrical stimulation of the brain (ESB), brain imaging (such as CT, PET, MRI, fMRI).

A Tour Through the Brain (cont).

Lower-Level Brain Structures

Brain Stem

Group of structures including the **pons** (breathing, sleeping, waking, dreaming, etc.), **medulla** (breathing, heart rate, etc.), and **reticular formation** (screening incoming information and arousing the cortex).

Cerebellum

Responsible for smooth movement, balance, and aspects of perception and cognition.

Thalamus

Relays sensory messages to the cortex.

Hypothalamus

Maintains homeostasis and controls emotions and motives like hunger, thirst, sex, and aggression.

Limbic System

Group of interconnected structures responsible for arousal and regulation of emotion, motivation, memory, and learning. The **amygdala** is the structure most involved with emotion.

The Cerebral Cortex

The cerebral cortex is responsible for all higher mental processes and is divided into four lobes:

Frontal Lobes

Motor control, speech production, and higher functions (thinking, personality, emotion, and memory).

Parietal Lobes

Sensory processing (pressure, pain, touch, and temperature).

Temporal Lobes

Audition, language comprehension, memory, and some emotional control.

Occipital Lobes

Vision and visual perception.

(**Association areas**: Remaining areas of the cortex that interpret, integrate, and act on information from other parts of the brain.)

Two Brains in One

Splitting the **corpus callosum**, which transfers neural impulses between the brain's left and right hemispheres, is a treatment for some forms of epilepsy. **Split-brain research** on these patients shows:

Left hemisphere specializes in verbal and analytical functions.

Right hemisphere governs nonverbal abilities (spatio-manipulative skills, art, music, and visual recognition).

The brain can reorganize and change its structure and function throughout the lifespan (**neuroplasticity**), and create new nerve cells (**neurogenesis**) from **stem cells** (immature cells that produce specialized cells).

Genetics and Evolution

Behavioral Genetics

Each of the 46 human **chromosomes** is composed of DNA, which is made up of **genes**.

Genetics studies are done with twins, adopted children, families, and genetic abnormalities. Such studies allow estimates of **heritability**.

The Human Genome Project (HGP) and the International Human Genome Sequencing Consortium (IHGSC) have mapped all the genes on the human chromosome.

Evolutionary Psychology

Studies evolutionary principles, like **natural selection** and genetic mutations, which affect adaptation to the environment and help explain commonalities in behavior.

Stress and Health Psychology

Core Learning Objectives

As you read Modules 8, 9, and 10, keep the following questions in mind and answer them in your own words:

► What is health psychology? Can health psychologists help with problems related to smoking, binge drinking, and chronic pain?

► What is stress and what are its major sources and results?

► How is stress related to serious illnesses like cancer and coronary heart disease?

► What techniques and resources are available to help people cope with stress?

College Life Stress Inventory

Copy the "stress rating" number into the last column for any event you have experienced in the last year. Then add up the ratings for your total stress score.

Event	Stress Rating	Your Items
1. Being raped	100	_____
2. Finding out that you are HIV-positive	100	_____
3. Being accused of rape	98	_____
4. Death of a close friend	97	_____
5. Death of a close family member	97	_____
6. Contracting a sexually transmitted disease (other than AIDS)	94	_____
7. Concerns about being pregnant	91	_____
8. Finals week	90	_____
9. Concerns about your partner being pregnant	90	_____
10. Oversleeping for an exam	89	_____
11. Flunking a class	89	_____
12. Having a boyfriend or girlfriend cheat on you	85	_____
13. Ending a steady dating relationship	85	_____
14. Serious illness in a close friend or family member	85	_____
15. Financial difficulties	84	_____
16. Writing a major term paper	83	_____
17. Being caught cheating on a test	83	_____
18. Drunk driving	82	_____
19. Sense of overload in school or work	82	_____
20. Two exams in one day	80	_____
21. Cheating on your boyfriend or girlfriend	77	_____
22. Getting married	76	_____
23. Negative consequences of drinking or drug use	75	_____
24. Depression or crisis in your best friend	73	_____
24. Difficulties with parents	73	_____
25. Talking in front of a class	72	_____
26. Lack of sleep	69	_____
27. Change in housing situation (hassles, moves)	69	_____
28. Competing or performing in public	69	_____
29. Getting in a physical fight	66	_____
30. Difficulties with a roommate	66	_____
31. Job changes (applying, new job, work hassles)	65	_____
32. Declaring a major or concerns about future plans	65	_____
33. A class you hate	62	_____
34. Drinking or use of drugs	61	_____
35. Confrontations with professors	60	_____
36. Starting a new semester	58	_____
37. Going on a first date	57	_____
38. Registration	55	_____
39. Maintaining a steady dating relationship	55	_____
40. Commuting to campus or work, or both	54	_____
41. Peer pressures	53	_____
42. Being away from home for the first time	53	_____
43. Getting sick	52	_____
44. Concerns about your appearance	52	_____
45. Getting straight A's	51	_____
46. A difficult class that you love	48	_____
47. Making new friends; getting along with friends	47	_____
48. Fraternity or sorority rush	47	_____
49. Falling asleep in class	40	_____
50. Attending an athletic event (e.g., football game)	20	_____
Total		_____

From Renner & Mackin, 1998.

How did you do? Were you surprised that getting married or getting straight A's could be considered stressful? Michael Renner and Scott Mackin (1998) developed this scale on the basis of their research with college students, and they found that scores ranged between a low of 182 and a high of 2,571, with an average of 1,247. What was your total score? If you are a "typical" college student, 18 to 22 years of age, living on campus, and away from home for the first time, this scale may provide an accurate assessment of important stressors in your life. However, as an older returning student, a young student living at home, or a married person with small children, you have different stressors (such as divorce, unemployment, child care) and this scale would be inappropriate.

We use this scale as an introduction to the complex and fascinating world of health psychology. The topics of health and stress are a part of everyday conversation, with most people assuming that everyone shares the same definitions and life experiences. As you have just found with the college stress inventory, however, stress is highly individual. Stress is also a normal part of all our lives, but when it is chronic or severe, it can damage our health.

The well-established relationship between stress and physical illness takes us into a broader discussion of the psychology of health. In Module 8, we explore this field and three important health issues: smoking, binge drinking, and chronic pain. Module 9 examines the numerous causes and results of stress, the role of stress in cancer and heart disease, and how people cope with stress. Module 10 provides specific tips to help you stay healthy.

What is health psychology? Can health psychologists help with problems related to smoking, binge drinking, and chronic pain?

Health Psychology *The study of the relationship between psychological behavior and physical health and illness, with an emphasis on wellness and the prevention of illness.*

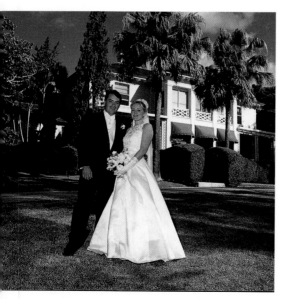

Marriage as a stressor? Getting married is normally a very happy occasion; nevertheless the changes it brings can be stressful.

MODULE 8
HEALTH PSYCHOLOGY IN ACTION

Throughout most of history, the relationship between mind and physical health had been a widely accepted fact. However, in the late 1800s, the discovery of physiological causes for infectious diseases such as typhoid and syphilis led scientists to intensify the search for physiological causes of disease. As a result, medicine and public health made marked advances. Over the last century, life expectancy for Americans of all races and genders has steadily increased, and for those born in 1997 it is an all-time high of 76.5 years (National Center for Health Statistics, 2001).

Interestingly, the major causes of death have shifted from contagious diseases (pneumonia, influenza, tuberculosis, measles, and typhoid fever) to noncontagious diseases (cancer, heart and cardiovascular disease, chronic lung disease) (National Center for Health Statistics, 2001). Can you see how today's key health problems are strongly related to behavior and lifestyle? Scientists and medical experts are now reemphasizing the close relationship between psychological behavior and physical health and illness, with an emphasis on wellness and the prevention of illness. This is the heart (and definition) of **health psychology** (Baum & Posluszny, 2001).

What Health Psychologists Do: Research and Practice

Health psychologists study how people's lifestyles and activities, emotional reactions, ways of interpreting events, and personality characteristics influence their physical health and well-being. Some health psychologists are involved primarily in research, whereas others work directly with physicians and other health professionals to implement research findings.

As researchers, they have been particularly interested in the relationship between stress and the immune system. A normally functioning immune system helps detect and defend against disease, and a suppressed immune system leaves the body susceptible to any number of diseases. Today we know that stress plays a role in suppressing the immune system and may make us more vulnerable to a host of modern illnesses and disease, including cancer, heart disease, AIDS (acquired immunodeficiency syndrome, and even the common cold (Cohen et al., 1998, 1999; Kiecolt-Glaser & Glaser, 2001; Leserman et al., 2000; Pratt et al., 1996). Until the 1970s, however, most experts believed the immune system was completely independent of the other body systems. As you will see in a later section, the scientific view of stress and the immune system has changed dramatically in the last few years.

As practitioners, health psychologists can work as independent clinicians or as consultants alongside physicians, physical and occupational therapists, and other health care workers. Their goal is to reduce psychological distress or unhealthy behaviors. They also help patients and families make critical decisions and prepare psychologically for surgery or other treatment.

In addition to their work as researchers and practitioners, health psychologists also educate the general public about health *maintenance*. They provide information about the effects of stress, smoking, alcohol, lack of exercise, and other health issues. In addition, health psychologists help people cope with chronic problems, such as pain, diabetes, and high blood pressure, as well as unhealthful behaviors, such as lack of assertiveness and anger expression (Davidson, MacGregor, Stuhr, Dixon, & MacLean, 2000; Haerenstam, Theorell, & Kaijser, 2000; Lepore, Ragan, & Jones, 2000). To illustrate the work of health psychologists, we begin this module with two of the most prevalent (and preventable) health problems in the United States — smoking and binge drinking.

Smoking: Hazardous to Your Health

> A custom loathsome to the eye, hateful to the nose, harmful to the brain, dangerous to the lungs, and in the black, stinking fume thereof, nearest resembling the horrible Stygian smoke of the pit that is bottomless.

This is what King James I wrote about smoking in 1604, shortly after Sir Walter Raleigh introduced tobacco to England from the Americas. Today, nearly 400 years later, many people would agree with the king's tirade against the practice.

According to the latest U.S. Public Health Service report, tobacco is the single most preventable cause of death and disease in the United States (Fiore, 2000). Smoking is a major risk factor for coronary heart disease and lung cancer and contributes to cancers of the mouth, larynx, throat, esophagus, bladder, and pancreas (Centers for Disease Control, 2001). Smoking also contributes to chronic bronchitis, emphysema, and ulcer disease. Moreover, smoking shortens life (Burns, 2000). This is true for both the smoker and those who breathe secondhand smoke.

What about all the new antismoking laws? Do they help? Ironically, the antismoking laws passed in the 1990s may have made quitting smoking even more difficult for some. First, the fact that smokers have to leave smoke-free environments and group together outdoors on the hottest summer days and the worst winter days to satisfy their habit creates a strong social bond: Together they will suffer the tyranny of nonsmoking laws. Cigarette companies play to this group loyalty (and the individual's "independence" and "perseverance") by showing smokers sitting high up on the ledges of office buildings and on the wings of airplanes in flight "going to any lengths" to have a cigarette. Second, when people cannot smoke in offices, on airplanes, in restaurants, or other public places, the interval between nicotine doses increases, which increases the severity of the withdrawal symptoms (Palfai, Monti, Ostafin, & Hutchinson, 2000). In effect, the smoker gets repeated previews of just how unpleasant quitting is going to be — and who wouldn't rather avoid something unpleasant?

Most people know that smoking is bad for their health and that the more they smoke, the more at risk they are. It is therefore not surprising that most health psychologists and medical professionals are concerned with preventing smoking in the first place and getting those who already smoke to stop.

Smoker's unite? Due to increased restrictions, many people are forced to go outside to smoke. Ironically, this may forge stronger bonds between smokers and make them even more resistant to quitting.

Smoking Prevention

The first puff on a cigarette is rarely pleasant. Why, then, do people ever start smoking? The answer is complex. First, smoking usually starts when people are young. The European School Survey Project on Alcohol and Other Drugs (ESPAD) (2001) reported that tobacco smoking was well established by the mid-teens in most European countries and showed few signs of diminishing since the previous ESPAD survey in 1995. A similar survey of U.S. middle schools, grades 6 to 8, found that one in eight students were experimenting with some form of tobacco, such as cigarettes, cigars, and chewing tobacco (Kaufman, 2000). There are many reasons people begin to smoke at such a young age, but peer pressure and imitation of role models (such as celebrities) are particularly strong factors. Young smokers want to look mature and be accepted by their social peers.

Secondly, regardless of the age at which a person begins smoking, once he or she begins to smoke, there is a biological need to continue because of the addictive effects of nicotine. The evidence clearly shows that nicotine is a powerful addictive drug, comparable to heroin, cocaine, and alcohol (Balfour & Ridley, 2000; Pahlavan, Bonnet, & Duda, 2000; Pich et al., 1997). In fact, when we inhale smoke, it takes only seconds for the nicotine to reach the brain, where it increases the release of the neurotransmitters acetylcholine and norepinephrine. Acetylcholine and norepi-

Smoking as a "pediatric disease."
Because many smokers take up the
habit as adolescents or preteens, health
psychologists recommend that anti-
smoking programs begin in elementary
school.

nephrine, in turn, increase alertness, concentration, memory, and feelings of pleasure (McGaughy, Decker, & Sarter, 1999; Picciotto, 1998; Quattrocki, Baird, &
Yurgelun-Todd, 2000). Several recent research projects have also indicated that
nicotine stimulates the release of dopamine, the neurotransmitter most closely
related to reward centers in the brain (Noble, 2000; Carboni, Bortone, Giua, &
DiChiara, 2000). These neurotransmitters also decrease the symptoms of nicotine
withdrawal, anxiety, tension, and pain, which come after a short period without
tobacco.

Finally, social pressures and physical addiction combine to create additional
benefits (Lazev, Herzog, & Brandon, 1999). For example, smokers learn to associate
smoking with pleasant things, such as good food, friends, sex, and, not least, the
high that nicotine gives them, so their smoking is rewarded. When smokers are
deprived of cigarettes, they go through physical withdrawal with extremely unpleasant symptoms. When they get their next puff, the nicotine relieves the symptoms, so
smoking is rewarded. It follows that the best way to reduce the number of smokers
is to prevent people from taking their first puff.

**If most people begin smoking during adolescence, shouldn't prevention be
aimed at this group?** Prevention programs for teens face a tough uphill battle. For
adolescents, the long-term health disadvantages of heart disease and cancer seem
totally irrelevant, whereas smoking itself provides immediate short-term rewards
from peers and the addictive, reinforcing properties of nicotine. Many smoking prevention programs therefore focus on immediate short-term problems with smoking,
such as bad breath and interference with athletic performance.

Through films and discussion groups, teens also are educated about peer pressure and the media's influence on smoking, given opportunities to role-play refusal
skills, taught general social and personal skills needed in decision making, and given
strategies for coping with the stresses of adolescence and daily life (Worden, Flynn,
Solomon, & Secker-Walker, 1996). Unfortunately, the research shows that the effect
of psychosocial prevention programs is small (Baum & Posluszny, 1999). To have
even a modest effect, these programs must begin early and continue for many years
(Eckhardt, Woodruff, & Elder, 1997).

To reduce the health risk and help fight peer pressure, many schools ban smoking in college buildings and offer more smoke-free dormitories. Another possible
deterrent to the college smoking trend results from expensive legal battles and settlements by the tobacco industry and the fact that these expenses are passed on to
consumers in the form of higher prices for cigarettes. This increase, added to state
and local taxes, brings the cost to over $4 per pack in most states. For a student who
smokes a pack of cigarettes a day, the annual cost is nearly $1,500 — more than
twice the cost of textbooks for an entire academic year.

Stopping Smoking

> To cease smoking is the easiest thing I ever did; I ought to know, for I have done it a thousand times.
>
> Mark Twain

Antismoking ads. Because Joe Camel was once a popular icon that reportedly encouraged young children to smoke, antismoking activists created a "Joe Chemo" image to advertise the dangers of smoking.

Unfortunately, Mark Twain was never able to quit for very long, and many ex-smokers say that stopping smoking was the most difficult thing they ever did. Although some people find the easiest way for them to cope with the physical withdrawal from nicotine is to suddenly and completely stop, the success rate for this "cold turkey" approach is extremely low. Even with medical aids, such as patches, gum, or pills, it is still very difficult to quit (Killen et al., 2000; Patten, 2000). Any program designed to help smokers break their habit must combat the social rewards of smoking as well as the physical addiction to nicotine.

Sometimes the best approach is a combination of cognitive and behavioral techniques and nicotine replacement therapy. Cognitively, smokers can learn to identify stimuli or situations that make them feel like smoking and then change or avoid them (Brandon, Collins, Juliano, & Lazev, 2000). They can also refocus their attention on something other than smoking or remind themselves of the benefits of not smoking (Taylor, Harris, Singleton, Moolchan, & Heishman, 2000). Behaviorally, they might cope with the urge to smoke by chewing gum, exercising, or chewing on a toothpick after a meal instead of lighting a cigarette.

No program to quit smoking will work without a tremendous amount of personal motivation, but the payoffs can be just as tremendous: a more enjoyable and longer life. (See Wetter et al., 1998, for the Agency for Health Care Policy and Research's "Smoking Cessation Clinical Practice Guidelines.")

A hidden cost of smoking. Would people continue to smoke if they could see what it does to their lungs? Compare the healthy tissue of the lung of a nonsmoker on the left to the blackened, unhealthy lung of the smoker on the right.

Check & Review

WHAT HEALTH PSYCHOLOGISTS DO AND SMOKING

Health psychology is the study of the relationship between psychological behavior and physical health and illness, with an emphasis on wellness and the prevention of illness. As researchers, health psychologists study psychological issues that affect physical health and find ways to help patients cope with medical procedures and health problems. As practitioners, health psychologists work with patients alongside health care professionals to help reduce psychological distress and unhealthy behaviors and educate the general public about health risks and health maintenance.

Because smoking is the single most preventable cause of death and disease in the United States, prevention and cessation of smoking are of primary importance to all

Health psychology in action. Your lifestyle and behavioral risk factors have a significant impact on your health and life expectancy (Gorman, 2001).

health practitioners, including health psychologists. Smoking prevention programs involve educating the public about short- and long-term consequences of smoking, trying to make smoking less socially acceptable, and helping nonsmokers resist social pressures to smoke. Most approaches to help people quit smoking include cognitive and behavioral techniques to aid smokers in their withdrawal and nicotine replacement therapy (using patches, gum, and pills).

Binge Drinking: A Growing Social Problem

Were you surprised by news reports of two freshmen at Massachusetts Institute of Technology who died from alcohol poisoning after binge drinking at fraternity parties? One of the students had a blood alcohol level of .5888 percent — the equivalent of more than 20 beers in 1 hour and over seven times the legal driving limit in most states. Unlike smoking, alcohol and other drugs can kill directly and immediately when they are taken in large amounts over a short period of time. They also impair the judgment and reaction times of the user, thus contributing to thousands of deaths and injuries from automobile accidents, rapes, and other assaults. (See Module 14 to review the short- and long-term health risks of alcohol.)

Binge drinking occurs when a man consumes five or more drinks in a row or a woman consumes four or more drinks at a time (Weingardt et al., 1998). Approximately 5.1 million Americans between the ages of 12 and 20 years are binge drinkers, and the greatest majority are college students (Wechsler, Lee, Kuo, & Lee, 2000). Binge drinking is a serious health problem for all college-age students, those who drink and those who don't.

What can be done about college binge drinking? Stopping students from binge drinking is very difficult. Students seem to think of it as part of the "college experience." Therefore, any real attack on binge drinking must approach the problem from many different directions. First, it is important to overcome the myths about college drinking and teach the facts. But just learning the facts does not stop people from drinking. The social rewards also must be reduced or removed.

So what are these misconceptions, and how do we reduce the social rewards? Henry Wechsler (1998), the first author of *The Harvard School of Public Health College Alcohol Study*, suggests the following:

* ***Students who binge tend to think that they are just average or moderate drinkers.*** We must make it clear to these students that binge drinking is not the norm. It is not normal or healthy to drink four or five drinks at a sitting, let alone to do that frequently.

* ***Many students believe that binge drinking is harmless to the drinker and to college society.*** But binge drinkers risk AIDS from unprotected sex and can be the victims or perpetrators of assault, rape, and car accident injuries.

* ***Many students think that it's okay to binge-drink because the college administration looks the other way.*** College administrations must enforce antidrinking rules and make a greater effort to help students who abuse alcohol. Strict penalties might help repeat offenders.

* ***Members of fraternities and sororities seem to think that drinking is part of the Greek life.*** College communities therefore have a responsibility to work with these organizations so that drinking is not central to social events.

Binge drinking can be fatal. *On many college campuses, it is a tradition to "drink your age" on your 21st birthday. Following this tradition, Bradley McCue, a University of Michigan Junior, drank 21 shots of alcohol plus three more to break his friends' record. He died on the morning of his 21st birthday from alcohol poisoning. For more information, contact www.BRAD.org.*

- *When students see alumni drinking at tailgate parties and hear their stories of partying until dawn, they think that drinking is what alumni expect them to do at college.* Any alcohol-control measures directed at students must also apply to visiting alumni. Sporting events should be alcohol free, and colleges should avoid alcohol-related sports promotions.

GENDER & CULTURAL DIVERSITY

Binge Drinking Around the World

After reading the above section on binge drinking, you may think it is a problem unique to college students in the United States. Unfortunately, binge drinking is a worldwide problem.

- The European School Survey Project (2001) found an overall increase in binge drinking since 1995, especially in Britain, Denmark, Ireland, and Poland. More than 30 percent of school children in those countries reported binge drinking three or more times in the last month.

- In Mexico, a study of drinking patterns at 16 religious fiestas and 13 nonreligious fiestas in the community of Santa María Atzompa found that nearly all the men qualified as binge drinkers at every fiesta. Furthermore, the binge drinking contributed to several outbreaks of violence at the fiestas (Perez, 2000).

- A study in Spain and South America found that young men who reported binge drinking were more likely than others to behave aggressively toward people outside their family (Orpinas, 1999).

- Scientists in Denmark compared the drinking patterns of 56,970 men and women who prefer drinking beer, wine, or spirits (Gronbaek, Tjonneland, Johansen, Stripp, & Overvad, 2000). Results showed that beer drinkers were the least likely of the different types of drinkers to binge, whereas wine drinkers were the most likely to binge.

- Research on alcohol consumption in Russia shows that 44 percent of men are binge drinkers (Bobak, McKee, Rose, & Marmot, 1999).

- The lower rate of binge drinking in Japan has been linked to a genetic mutation that makes it difficult for many Japanese, and other Asians, to metabolize alcohol. Nearly half of the Japanese population is sensitive to alcohol owing to this genetic mutation. Research shows that Japanese who do not carry the mutation are much more likely to be binge drinkers than those who do not carry the mutation (Takeshita & Morimoto, 1999; Tu & Israel, 1995).

Chronic Pain: The Role of Psychologists in Helping Patients Cope

Pain is the most common reason why people seek medical attention. It is the major symptom reported in over 80 percent of all visits to physicians (Turk, 1994). Although we try to avoid pain, it is necessary for our survival. Pain alerts us to dangerous or harmful situations, and pain forces us to rest and recover from injury (Watkins & Maier, 2000). But **chronic pain**, pain that continues long past the healing of a wound or pain that is associated with a chronic disease, does not serve a useful function.

Alcohol is a global problem. Like the Octoberfest in Munich, Germany, many cultures use alcohol as a common part of holiday celebrations.

Chronic Pain *Continuous or recurrent pain over a period of 6 months or more.*

Although psychological factors rarely are the source of chronic pain, they can encourage and intensify it, and increase the related anguish and disability (Affleck, Tennen, & Apter, 2001; Fruehwald, Loffler, Eher, Saletu, & Baumhackl, 2001; Snow-Turek, Norris, & Tan, 1996). To treat chronic pain, health psychologist use specific treatment methods, such as behavior modification, biofeedback, and relaxation.

Behavior Modification

Chronic pain is a serious problem with no simple solution. For example, exercise is known to produce an increase in *endorphins,* naturally produced chemicals that attach themselves to nerve cells in the brain and block the perception of pain. However, chronic pain patients tend to decrease their activity and exercise. In addition, well-meaning family members often ask chronic pain sufferers, "How are you feeling?" "Is the pain any better today?" Unfortunately, talking about pain focuses attention on it and increases its intensity (Harvey & McGuire, 2000). Furthermore, as the pain increases, anxiety increases, the anxiety itself then increases the pain, which further increases the anxiety, which further increases the pain!

To counteract these hidden personal and family problems and negative cycles, health psychologists may begin a behavior modification program for both the patient with chronic pain and his or her family. The effectiveness of such programs for treating chronic pain was first shown in the late 1970s (Cairns & Pasino, 1977). Researchers established individualized pain management programs, monitored each patient's adherence, and congratulated those who followed through with their pain treatment programs (daily exercise, use of relaxation techniques, and so on). Compared with a control group, patients who used these techniques experienced substantially reduced pain. Today, many pain control programs incorporate similar techniques for rewarding "well behaviors" (Kole-Snijders et al., 1999).

Biofeedback

In *biofeedback,* information about physiological functions, such as heart rate or blood pressure, is monitored, and the feedback helps the individual learn to control these functions. Such feedback about physiological processes helps reduce some types of chronic pain. Most biofeedback with chronic pain patients is done with the *electromyograph* (EMG). This device measures muscle tension by recording electrical activity in the skin. The EMG is most helpful when the pain involves extreme muscle tension, such as tension headache and lower back pain. Electrodes are attached to the site of the pain, and the patient is instructed to relax. When sufficient relaxation is achieved, the machine signals with a tone or a light. The signal serves as feedback to the patient.

Research shows that biofeedback is sometimes as effective as more expensive and lengthy forms of treatment (Newton-John, Spence, & Schotte, 1995). The reason for its success seems to be that it teaches patients to recognize patterns of emotional arousal and conflict that affect their physiological responses. This self-awareness, in turn, enables them to learn self-regulation skills that help control their pain (McKee, 1991).

Pain control through biofeedback. Using an electromyograph (EMG), muscular tension is recorded and the patient is taught specific relaxation techniques that reduce tension and help relieve chronic pain.

Relaxation Techniques

Because the pain always seems to be there, chronic pain sufferers tend to talk and think about their pain whenever they're not thoroughly engrossed in an activity. Watching TV shows or films, attending parties, or any activity that diverts attention from the pain seems to reduce discomfort. Attention might also be diverted with special *relaxation techniques* like those that are taught in so-called "natural childbirth" classes. These techniques focus the birthing mother's attention on breathing and relaxing the muscles, which helps distract her attention from the fear and pain of the birthing process. Similar techniques also can be helpful to chronic pain sufferers. Remember, though, that these techniques do not eliminate the pain; they merely allow the person to ignore it for a time. (Later in Module 10, you'll learn a relaxation technique that can be used for chronic pain and for everyday stress.)

Relaxation techniques. Massage is a healthy way to reduce stress and tension related pain.

Check & Review

BINGE DRINKING AND CHRONIC PAIN

Binge drinking is a serious problem that can lead to rape or assault, to death from alcohol poisoning, or automobile and other accidents. It occurs when a man has five or more drinks in a row and a woman has four or more. To reduce binge drinking, we must overcome the myths about drinking and teach the facts. We also must reduce or remove the social rewards.

Chronic pain is continuous or recurrent pain that persists over a period of six months or more.

Although psychological factors rarely are the source of chronic pain, they can encourage and intensify it. Increased activity, exercise, and dietary changes help to reduce chronic pain. Health psychologists also use behavior modification, biofeedback, and relaxation techniques to treat chronic pain.

Questions

1. What is binge drinking?

2. What are the 5 misconceptions about binge drinking, and how can we remove the social reinforcers?

3. Continuous or recurrent pain over a period of 6 months or more is known as _____.

4. An increase in activity and exercise levels benefits patients with pain because exercise increases the release of (a) endorphins; (b) insulin; (c) acetylcholine; (d) norepinephrine.

Answers to Questions can be found in Appendix B.

ACTIVE LEARNING WORKSHEET   MODULE 8

Complete the following, and then double-check your answers with those in Appendix B.

1. Health psychologists who work as researchers study the relationship between _____ and the_____.

2. When health psychologists work as _____, their goal is to reduce psychological distress or unhealthy behaviors.

3. According to the latest U.S. Public Health Service report, _____ is the single most preventable cause of death and disease in the United States.

4. You read a newspaper article claiming that the rate of birth defects is three times as high for mothers who drink alcohol than for those who do not drink alcohol. Can you conclude that this difference is directly attributable to alcohol consumption, or can you think of other plausible explanations?

5. Your friend avoids visiting his grandmother because "all she ever talks about is her aches and pains." Using information from this module, what advice would you offer your friend regarding his grandmother?

MODULE 9
STRESS AND ITS ROLE IN HEALTH

What is stress, and what are its major sources and results?

Stress *A nonspecific response of the body to any demand made on it; the arousal, both physical and mental, to situations or events that we perceive as threatening or challenging.*

Eustress *Pleasant, desirable stress*

Distress *Unpleasant, objectionable stress*

Hans Selye (1974), a physiologist renowned for his research and writing in the area of stress since the 1930s, defines **stress** as the nonspecific response of the body to any demand made on it. When you play two nonstop tennis matches in the middle of a heat wave, your body responds with a fast heartbeat, rapid breathing, and an outpouring of perspiration. When you find out 10 minutes before class starts that the term paper you just started is due today rather than next Friday, your body has the same physiological stress response to a very different stressor. Stress reactions can occur to either internal, cognitive stimuli or external, environmental stimuli (Baum & Posluszny, 1999).

The body is nearly always in some state of stress, whether pleasant or unpleasant, mild or severe. *Anything* placing a demand on the body can cause stress. When stress is beneficial, such as moderate exercise, it is called **eustress** and when it is objectionable, as from chronic illness, it is called **distress** (Selye, 1974). The total absence of stress would mean the total absence of external stimulation, which would eventually lead to death. Because health psychology has been chiefly concerned with the negative effects of stress, we will adhere to convention and use the word "stress" to refer primarily to harmful or unpleasant stress (Selye's *distress*), even though there are some forms of beneficial *eustress*.

Sources of Stress: From Major Life Changes to Minor Hassles

Although stress is pervasive in our lives, some things cause more stress than others. The major sources of stress are life changes, chronic stressors, hassles, burnout, frustration, and conflict.

THE FAR SIDE®   BY GARY LARSON

"The fuel light's on, Frank! We're all going to die! ... Wait, wait. ... Oh, my mistake— that's the intercom light."

Life Changes

The College Life Stress Inventory that you took at the beginning of this section was designed especially for college students. It is based on an earlier inventory developed for adults past college age by Thomas Holmes and Richard Rahe (1967) — the Social Readjustment Rating Scale (SRRS). The SRRS measures stress related to *life changes* brought about by major events, such as marriage, the death of a family member, moving to a new home, and getting (or losing) a job.

Such major changes disrupt our lives and cause more stress than normal. Holmes and Rahe believed that change, of any kind, that required some adjustment in behavior or lifestyle caused stress. Moreover, they believed that exposure to numerous stressful events within a short period of time could have a detrimental effect on health. Keep in mind, however, that Holmes and Rahe use the scientific definition of *stress*. Therefore, change can be anguishing, as with the loss of a parent or divorce, but it can also be joyous, as in the case of a marriage, or emotionally neutral, as with a change in work hours. The point is that all change causes stress. And too much stress can exceed the body's ability to cope, leading to moderate or serious illness.

In recent years, Mark Miller and Richard Rahe updated the original Holmes and Rahe SRRS. As you can see in Table 9.1, this scale is very similar to the one at the beginning of this section, but it is designed for older adults outside of college. These items are ranked according to their relative importance in contributing to health problems. Each event is assigned a numerical rating expressed in *life change units* (LCUs). To score yourself on this scale, add up the LCUs for all life events you have experienced during the last year and compare your score with the following standards: 0–150 = No significant problems, 150–199 = Mild life crisis (33 percent chance of illness), 200–299 = Moderate life crisis (50 percent chance of illness), 300 and above Major life crisis (80 percent chance of illness).

The SRRS scale is an easy and popular way to measure stress, and cross-cultural studies have shown that most people rank the magnitude of stressful events in similar ways (McAndrew, Akande, Turner, & Sharma, 1998). However, the SRRS is not foolproof. First, it only shows a *correlation* between stress and illness, and as you recall from Module 2, *correlation does not prove causation*. Like results on all correlational studies, stress could cause subsequent illnesses, but they could also be caused by other (yet unknown) factors.

In addition, as noted earlier, stress varies according to the individual. Any one event may be perceived as a stressful ordeal, a neutral occurrence, or an exciting opportunity. It depends on your personal interpretation and appraisal (Whelan & Kirkby, 2000). You might find moving to another state a terrible sacrifice and a tremendous stressor, whereas your friend might see the move as a wonderful opportunity and experience little or no stress. Furthermore, different people have differing abilities to deal with change, perhaps because of good coping skills, general physical health, healthier lifestyles, or even genetic predisposition.

Chronic Stressors

Not all stressful situations are single, short-term events such as a death or a birth. A bad marriage, poor working conditions, or an intolerable political climate can be *chronic stressors*. Even the stress of chronic aircraft noise is associated with measurable hormonal and cardiac changes (Evans et al., 1995). Our social lives also can be chronically stressful, because making and maintaining friendships involves considerable thought and energy (Griffith, Dubow, & Ippolito, 2000).

Perhaps the largest source of chronic stress is work. People often experience stress associated with keeping or changing jobs or with job performance (Steptoe, Cropley, & Joekes, 2000). However, the most stressful jobs are those that make great demands on performance and concentration but allow little creativity or opportunity for advancement (Parasuraman & Purohit, 2000). Assembly-line work ranks very high in this category.

Researchers have documented that stress at work can also cause serious

Chronic stress? Although assembly line work might seem stress-free, the lack of creativity and little opportunity for advancement make this a highly stressful job.

TABLE 9.1 SOCIAL READJUSTMENT RATING SCALE

Life Events	Life Change Units
Death of spouse	100
Divorce	73
Marital separation	65
Jail term	63
Death of a close family member	63
Personal injury or illness	53
Marriage	50
Fired at work	47
Marital reconciliation	45
Retirement	45
Change in health of family member	44
Pregnancy	40
Sex difficulties	39
Gain of a new family member	39
Business readjustment	39
Change in financial state	38
Death of a close friend	37
Change to different line of work	36
Change in number of arguments with spouse	35
Mortgage or loan for major purchase	31
Foreclosure on mortgage or loan	30
Change in responsibilities at work	29
Son or daughter leaving home	29
Trouble with in-laws	29
Outstanding personal achievement	28
Spouse begins or stops work	26
Begin or end school	26
Change in living conditions	25
Revision of personal habits	24
Trouble with boss	23
Change in work hours or conditions	20
Change in residence	20
Change in schools	20
Change in recreation	19
Change in church activities	19
Change in social activities	18
Mortgage or loan for lesser purchase (car, major appliance)	17
Change in sleeping habits	16
Change in number of family get-togethers	15
Change in eating habits	15
Vacation	13
Christmas	12
Minor violations of the law	11

Source: Holmes & Rahe (1967).

Is nursing a stressful career? People who think of their profession as a "calling" may lose their idealism when faced with the ongoing stresses and emotional turmoil. Over time they may suffer a type of mental and physical exhaustion known as "burn out."

Hassles *Little problems of daily living that are not significant in themselves but that accumulate and sometimes become a major source of stress*

Burnout *A state of physical, emotional, and mental exhaustion attributable to long-term involvement in emotionally demanding situations*

stress at home not only for workers but for other family members as well. And, of course, in our private lives, divorce, child and spouse abuse, alcoholism, and money problems can place severe stress on all members of a family (Grunberg, Moore, Anderson-Connolly, & Greenberg, 1999; Thompson & Kaslow, 2000; Tien, Sandler, & Zautra, 2000).

Hassles and Burnout

In addition to chronic stressors, a great deal of daily stress is in the form of **hassles**, little problems of daily living that are not significant in themselves but that pile up to become a major source of stress (Repetti, 1993). Some hassles tend to be shared by all: time pressures (getting to work or school on time, finding a parking place, fighting traffic jams), problems with family and coworkers (equitable sharing of work, scheduling conflicts, gossip), and financial concerns (competing demands for available funds, increasing prices). But our reactions to hassles may vary. For example, compared to women, men tend to have more impairment of their immune system and an increased heart rate in response to hassles (Delahanty et al., 2000; Scanlan, Vitaliano, Ochs, Savage, & Borson, 1998).

Some authorities believe hassles can be more significant than major life events in creating stress (Lazarus, 1999; Tien, Sandler, & Zautra, 2000). For example, divorce is extremely stressful, but it may so be because of the increased number of hassles — change in finances, child-care arrangements, longer working hours, and so on. Similarly, a move is a stressful life change, but preparing to move or having your house up for sale for an extended period of time can be more stressful than the actual move itself.

Persistent hassles in your work situation can lead to a form of physical, mental, and emotional exhaustion known as **burnout**. Although the term has become an overused buzzword, health psychologists use it to describe a specific syndrome that develops most commonly in idealistic people who are exposed to chronically stressful and emotionally draining professions (Alexander & Hegarty, 2000; Melamed et al., 1999). People who tend to think of their job as a "calling" tend to enter their careers with a high sense of motivation and commitment. But over

---

TRY THIS
Yourself

Kanner and others developed a *Hassles Scale* to assess those everyday events on the job, at school, and in interpersonal relations that annoy, frustrate, and anger us (Kanner, Coyne, Schaefer, & Lazarus, 1981). Write down the top 10 hassles you most commonly experience and then compare your answers to the following list:

The 10 Most Common Hassles for College Students

		Percentage of Times Checked
1.	Troubling thoughts about the future	76.6
2.	Not getting enough sleep	72.5
3.	Wasting time	71.1
4.	Inconsiderate smokers	70.7
5.	Physical appearance	69.9
6.	Too many things to do	69.2
7.	Misplacing or losing things	67.0
8.	Not enough time to do the things you need to do	66.3
9.	Concerns about meeting high standards	64.0
10.	Being lonely	60.8

Source: Kanner, A. D., Coyne, J. C., Schaefer, C., & Lazarus, R. S. (1981). Comparison of two modes of stress measurement: Daily hassles and uplifts versus major life events. *Journal of Behavioral Medicine, 4,* 1–39.

time, some become emotionally drained and disillusioned and feel a loss of personal accomplishment — they "burn out." The result may be increased absences from work, a sharp downturn in productivity, and an increased risk of physical problems. Police officers, nurses, social workers, and teachers are particularly vulnerable.

Frustration

Frustration is a negative emotional state generally associated with a blocked goal such as not being accepted for admission to your first-choice college. The more motivated we are, the more frustration we experience when our goals are blocked. After getting stuck in traffic and missing an important appointment, we may become very frustrated. On the other hand, if the same traffic jam causes us to be five minutes late to a painful medical appointment, we may experience little or no frustration.

Frustration *An unpleasant state of tension, anxiety, and heightened sympathetic activity resulting from a blocked goal*

Conflicts

A final source of stress is **conflict,** which arises when people are forced to make a choice between at least two incompatible alternatives. The amount of stress produced by a conflict depends on the complexity of the conflict itself, and the difficulty involved in resolving it. There are three basic types of conflict: *approach–approach, avoidance–avoidance,* and *approach–avoidance.*

Conflict *A negative emotional state caused by having to choose between two or more incompatible goals or impulses*

In an **approach–approach conflict,** a person must choose between two or more *favorable* alternatives. Thus, no matter what choice is made, the result will be desirable. At first it might seem that this type of conflict shouldn't create any stress, but consider this example. Suppose you have to choose between two summer jobs. One job is at a resort where you will meet interesting people and have a good time; the other will provide you with valuable experience and look impressive on your résumé. No matter which job you choose, you will benefit in some way. In fact, you would like to take both jobs, but you can't. The requirement to choose is the source of stress.

Approach–Approach Conflict *Conflict in which a person must choose between two or more alternatives that will lead to desirable results*

An **avoidance–avoidance conflict** involves making a choice between two or more unpleasant alternatives that will lead to negative results, no matter which choice is made. In the book (and film) *Sophie's Choice,* Sophie and her two children are sent to a German concentration camp. A soldier demands that she give up (apparently to be killed) either her daughter or her son, or they both will be killed. Obviously, neither alternative is acceptable; both will have tragic results. Although this is an extreme example, avoidance–avoidance conflicts can lead to intense stress.

Avoidance–Avoidance Conflict *Conflict in which a person must choose between two or more alternatives that will both lead to undesirable results*

An **approach–avoidance conflict** occurs when a person must choose between alternatives that will have both desirable and undesirable results. We have all been faced with such decisions as "I want to spend more time in a close relationship, but that means I won't be able to see as much of my old friends." This conflict thus leads to a great deal of ambivalence. In an approach–avoidance conflict, we experience both good and bad results from any alternative we choose.

Approach–Avoidance Conflict *Conflict in which a person must make a choice that will lead to both desirable and undesirable results*

The longer any conflict exists or the more important the decision, the more stress a person will experience. Generally, the approach–approach conflict is the easiest to resolve and produces the least stress. The avoidance–avoidance conflict, on the other hand, is usually the most difficult because all choices lead to unpleasant results. Approach–avoidance conflicts are somewhat less stressful than avoidance–avoidance conflicts and are usually moderately difficult to resolve.

One thing that seems to increase the hassles and frustration in our lives is the fact that technology is constantly changing. In their book *TechnoStress: Coping with technology @WORK @HOME @PLAY,* Michelle Weil and Larry Rosen (1997) discuss how emerging technologies can add stress to our lives.

Do any of the following situations sound familiar to you? Buying a new VCR that is (still!) impossible to program? Coming across yet another bug in your new word processing program that dumps your entire term paper? Playing endless phone tag with a professor whom you want to write a recommendation for you? Never getting your e-mail cleaned up because of endless ads and dumb jokes? Being stranded on the freeway because the computer that controls your car's engine malfunctions? These are examples of technostress.

Just as some handle generalized stress differently, people handle technostress in different ways. Weil and Rosen identify three techno-types. You can readily categorize yourself by answering the questions in the following techno-type quiz:

1. Suppose that for your birthday someone gives you a new electronic kitchen appliance (a coffeemaker, for example) that is completely computerized. Which of the following best describes how you would feel when you open the package?
   a. Thrilled, excited, and eager. Can't wait to give it a try.
   b. Hesitant and wondering if you really need it. The way you do it now works just fine. Maybe you'll just put it away for now.
   c. Upset, worried, or nervous. Unsure of your ability to use it correctly. Considering how you can return it for something a bit more practical.
2. When you want to record a TV show that airs while you are at work, what do you do?
   a. Quickly, confidently, and easily program the VCR to record the show.
   b. Ask your son, daughter, or spouse to set the VCR, or find the manual and try to figure out how to do it. You

know it's possible but are unsure that you'll be able to make it work.
   c. Squelch the thought, unless there is someone in the house to do it for you. After all, aren't VCRs just for playing rented movies?
3. Your friend calls and tells you that he just bought a new state-of-the-art, souped-up multimedia computer system and wants you to come see it. What's your response?
   a. Drop all your plans for the weekend, run right over, and play with the new toy for 8 hours.
   b. Murmur words of congratulations and promise to get over to see it as soon as your schedule clears.
   c. Pretend to listen, adding appropriately placed *oh*'s and *uh-huh*'s while clearly evading the request.

How did you do? If you answered *a* to two or three of the questions, chances are that you are what is called an *eager adopter.* If you mostly answered B, you, like most people, are most probably a *hesitant "prove it."* If you felt that *c* was the answer for you, you are a *resister.*

According to Weil and Rosen, eager adopters love technology. They make up only 10 to 15 percent of the population, but they consider technology fun and are the first to buy the latest gadget. Hesitant "prove its" account for one-half to two-thirds of the population, and they do not think technology is fun. They take a wait-and-see attitude, but once they are convinced that a new technology will make their life easier or is necessary, they will try to adopt it. Finally, the resisters avoid technology because they feel inadequate.

If you are an eager adopter, you are probably not stressed by technology. If you are one of the other types, consider this advice to relieve technostress: First, evaluate each new technology on its usefulness for you and your lifestyle. If something is useful, try to use it in the least stressful manner. Second, recognize that technology is here to stay, and you can learn to cope with technostress just as you do with other types of stress.

Check & Review

SOURCES OF STRESS

Stress is the body's arousal, both physical and mental, to situations or events that we perceive as threatening or challenging. A situation or event, either pleasant or unpleasant, that triggers arousal and causes stress is known as a stressor.

The major sources of stress are life changes, chronic stressors, hassles, burnout, frustration, and conflicts. Chronic stressors are ongoing events such as poor working conditions. **Hassles** are little everyday life problems that pile up to cause major stress. Persistent hassles and a loss of initial idealism in your work situation can lead to a form of physical, mental, and emotional exhaustion known as **burnout**. **Frustration** has to do with blocked goals, whereas **conflict** involves two or more competing goals. Conflicts can be classified as **approach–approach, avoidance–avoidance**, or **approach–avoidance**.

Questions

1. John was planning to ask Susan to marry him. When he saw Susan kissing another man at a party, he was quite upset. In this situation, John's seeing Susan kissing another man is _____, and it illustrates _____. (a) a stressor, distress; (b) eustress, a stressor; (c) distress, a stressor; (d) a stressor, eustress.

2. The Social Readjustment Rating Scale constructed by Holmes and Rahe measures the stress situation in a person's life on the basis of _____. (a) life changes; (b) stress tolerance; (c) daily hassles; (d) the balance between eustress and distress.

3. Frustration is a negative emotional state that is generally associated with _____, whereas _____ is a negative emotional state caused by an inability to choose between two or more incompatible goals or impulses.

4. Give an example for each of the 3 types of conflict: approach–approach, approach–avoidance, and avoidance–avoidance.

Answers to Questions can be found in Appendix B.

Results of Stress: How the Body Responds

When stressed either mentally or physically, your body undergoes several major and minor physiological changes, some of which we have already mentioned. The most significant changes are controlled by the autonomic nervous system and are particularly important because they can lower the body's resistance to disease.

Physiological Effects of Stress

Under normal, everyday low-stress conditions, the parasympathetic part of the autonomic nervous system tends to lower heart rate and blood pressure, while increasing muscle movement in the stomach and intestines. This allows the body to conserve energy, absorb nutrients, and maintain normal functioning. Under stressful conditions, the sympathetic part of the autonomic nervous system is dominant. It increases heart rate, blood pressure, respiration, and muscle tension; decreases the movement of stomach muscles; constricts blood vessels; and releases hormones such as epinephrine (adrenaline) and cortisol. These hormones in turn release fats and glucose into the bloodstream for energy.

Fight or Flight

There is a good reason for all this sympathetic activity. At the beginning of human evolutionary history, the autonomic nervous system served as the fight-or-flight system. Back then, when a person was under extreme stress — when she was confronted by a bear or he found big, strong strangers hunting in his territory — there were only two reasonable alternatives: fight or flight. Our ancestors, when faced with such stressors, needed the physiological boosts supplied by their sympathetic nervous system.

Today we have the same autonomic responses of our ancient ancestors, but our world is quite different. When we encounter stressful situations, we rarely jump into action. If we hear from our boss that we're being fired or that the stock market just dropped another 20 percent, we cannot "fight or flee." We have little need for the

Stress in ancient times. The automatic, "fight or flight" response was adaptive and necessary for early human survival. However, in modern society it occurs as a response to situations in which we cannot fight or flee, and is often detrimental to our health.

General Adaptation Syndrome *As described by Hans Selye, a generalized physiological reaction to severe stressors consisting of three phases: the alarm reaction, the resistance phase, and the exhaustion phase*

increased heart rate, blood pressure, and hormone levels produced by our autonomic nervous system. In fact, we are taught not to fight or to flee but to stay calm and resolve stressful situations rationally. When we comply with these cultural rules, we are left with all the arousal but no outlet for the physical changes caused by stressors. Thus, in modern times, the fight/flight response of the autonomic nervous system is less helpful than to our ancestors. It might even be maladaptive and dangerous (Arnsten, 1998).

Stress causes physiological changes that in the long run can be detrimental to health. Hans Selye, who was mentioned earlier, described a generalized physiological reaction to severe stressors that he called the **general adaptation syndrome** (GAS) (1936). Figure 9.1 shows the three phases of this reaction. In the initial phase, called the *alarm reaction,* the body reacts to the stressor by activating the sympathetic nervous system (with increases in heart rate, blood pressure, secretion of hormones, and so on). The body has abundant energy and is alert and ready to deal with the stressor but is in a lowered state of resistance to illness.

If the stressor remains, the body enters the *resistance phase.* Now the alarm reaction subsides and the body adapts to the stressor, with resistance to illness increasing above normal levels. However, this adaptation and resistance phase is very taxing, and long-term exposure to the stressor may eventually lead to the *exhaustion phase* if the resistance is not successful. During this final stage, the signs of the alarm reaction reappear, resistance to illness decreases, all adaptation energy becomes depleted, and our susceptibility to illness increases. In severe cases, long-term exposure to stressors can be life threatening because we become vulnerable to serious illness such as heart attacks, stroke, and cancer.

Figure 9.1 *The general adaptation syndrome (GAS).* According to Hans Selye, when the body is exposed to severe, prolonged stress, it goes through three phases. During the initial phase, the alarm reaction (A), the body is in a lowered state of resistance to illness. If the stress continues, the body enters the resistance phase (B), when it is in a heightened state of resistance. After prolonged exposure to stress, the body enters the exhaustion phase (C), when resistance to illness decreases. Eventually this can lead to death.

Stress and the Immune System

A relatively new field, **psychoneuroimmunology**, studies the interactions of psychological factors (*psycho-*), the nervous and endocrine systems (*neuro-*), and the immune system (*immunology*). This interdisciplinary research has shown that the sympathetic nervous system is *directly* linked to virtually every part of the immune system and that physiological changes caused by stress (such as bereavement, surgery, sleep deprivation, or divorce) can suppress immune system functioning (De Moranville et al., 2000; Leonard, 2000; Miller & Cohen, 2001). Normal functioning of the immune system includes detecting and defending against disease. Therefore, a suppressed immune system leaves the body susceptible to illness. Changes in immune function have been linked to high levels of such stress-related hormones as epinephrine, norepinephrine, and cortisol in the bloodstream. Apparently, increases in these hormones often precede suppressed immune system function and the appearance of disease.

But how does something psychological, like bereavement, affect the cells of the immune system? Psychological factors do not directly affect cells of the immune system. Rather, a psychological stressor (such as death of a loved one) activates the autonomic fight-or-flight response. Autonomic functioning mobilizes the body's energy resources for immediate survival by releasing hormones, such as cortisol, that put all the body's long-term processes — tissue repair, immunity, digestion, reproduction — on hold, thus making more energy available to the brain and muscles. If the emergency lasts only a few minutes, this is a good solution to the fight–flight problem, and immune functioning soon resumes. But when a person is under prolonged stress, such as a difficult final exam schedule or a bad marriage that lasts for years, he or she is constantly in a state of heightened autonomic activation and may have reduced immune system response for an extended period.

Does this mean that I might get a cold or the flu just because I've been under a lot of stress? Sheldon Cohen and his colleagues (1998, 1999) have conducted studies that show stress does indeed have a small to moderate effect both on becoming infected with the cold virus and on exhibiting full-blown cold symptoms. It seems that stress suppresses the body's defenses that normally prevent the cold virus from multiplying and spreading throughout the body.

Psychoneuroimmunology [sye-koh-NEW-roh-IM-you-NOLL-oh-gee] *An interdisciplinary field that studies the effects of psychological factors on the immune system*

RESEARCH HIGHLIGHT

Procrastination, Performance, and Health

If your professor assigned a term paper for this class, have you already started working on it? Or are you putting it off until the last minute? Have you ever wondered if working continuously on a term paper from the first day of class until the paper is due might ultimately be more stressful than putting off the paper until the last minute?

To answer this question, Dianne Tice and Roy Baumeister (1997) at Case Western Reserve University assigned a term paper in their health psychology class at the beginning of the semester. Throughout the semester, they carefully monitored the stress, health, and procrastination levels of 44 student volunteers from the class. After the term papers were submitted at the end of the course, Tice and Baumeister found that procrastinators suffered significantly more stress and developed more health problems than nonprocrastinators. They were also more likely to turn in their papers late and earn lower grades on those papers.

As discussed in the Tools for Student Success (Module 4) research shows spaced practice rather than cramming the night before produces higher scores on exams. Now you have additional research showing that distributed work also produces better grades on term papers — as well as less stress. The bottom line is this: *Don't procrastinate.* It can be hazardous to your health, as well as your grades.

Check & Review

RESULTS OF STRESS

When stressed, the body undergoes physiological changes. The sympathetic branch of the autonomic nervous system is activated, increasing heart rate and blood pressure. This sympathetic activation is beneficial if people need to fight or flee, but in today's world, it generally has negative consequences.

Hans Selye described a generalized physiological reaction to severe stressors, which he called the **general adaptation syndrome** (GAS). It has three phases: the alarm reaction, the resistance phase, and the exhaustion phase. Prolonged stress can suppress the immune system, which can render the body susceptible to a number of diseases.

Questions

1. How does the autonomic nervous system respond to stress?

2. The GAS consists of three phases: the _____ reaction, the _____ phase, and the _____ phase.

3. As Michael watches his instructor pass out papers, he suddenly realizes this is the first major exam and he is totally unprepared. Which phase of the GAS is the most likely experiencing? (a) resistance; (b) alarm; (c) exhaustion; (d) phaseout.

4. Why do students tend to get sick with a cold or flu during midterms or finals?

Stress and Serious Illness: A Variety of Diseases

How is stress related to serious illnesses like cancer and coronary heart disease?

We now know that many diseases far more serious than the common cold are either caused by or made worse by stress. Some of these are heart disease, cancer, rheumatoid arthritis, bursitis, migraine headache, asthma, and gastrointestinal conditions such as ulcers and colitis (Kiecolt-Glaser & Glaser, 2001; Matuszek, 2000; Sapolsky, 1999; Wu et al., 2000). In this section, we will explore how stress is related to two of our main killers — *cancer* and *coronary heart disease*.

Cancer

The word *cancer* is frightening to nearly everyone, and for good reason: Cancer is among the leading causes of death for adults in the U.S. It occurs when a particular type of primitive body cell begins rapidly dividing, and then forms a tumor that invades healthy tissue. Unless destroyed or removed, the tumor eventually damages organs and causes death. To date, over 100 types of cancer have been identified. They appear to be caused by an interaction between environmental factors and inherited predispositions.

To understand how the environment contributes to cancer, it helps to know what normally happens to cancerous cells. Whenever cancer cells start to multiply, the immune system checks the uncontrolled growth by attacking the abnormal cells (see the accompanying photograph). This goes on constantly, with abnormal cells arising, and, in a healthy person, the immune system keeping cancer cells in check.

Something different happens when the body is stressed. As you read earlier, the stress response involves the release of adrenal hormones that suppress immune system functioning. The compromised immune system is less able to resist infection and cancer development. An experimental animal study found that stress inhibited immune system defenses against cancer and promoted tumor growth (Wu et al., 2000). Other research with humans suggests that stress can also directly affect lymphocytes, the main immune system cells that control cancer (Goebel & Mills, 2000).

The good news is that we can substantially reduce our risk of cancer by making changes that reduce our stress level and enhance our immune system. For example,

White blood cells and the immune system. The round structure near the left center of this photomicrograph is a T-lymphocyte, a type of white blood cell produced by the immune system. It has just killed a cancer cell, the sweet potato-shaped structure.

even mild sleep deprivation can affect the immune system. When researchers interrupted the sleep of 23 men and then measured their *natural killer cells* (a type of immune system cell), they found the killer cells were 28 percent below average (Irwin et al., 1994). Can you see how staying up late studying for an exam (or partying) can decrease the effectiveness of your immune system? Fortunately, these researchers also found that a normal night's sleep after the deprivation returned the killer cells to their normal levels.

Cardiovascular Disorders

Cardiovascular disorders are the cause of over half of all deaths in the United States (Centers for Disease Control, 2001). Understandably, then, health psychologists are concerned because stress is a major contributor to these deaths. *Heart disease* is a general term for all disorders that eventually affect the heart muscle and lead to heart failure. *Coronary heart disease* results from *atherosclerosis,* a thickening of the walls of the coronary arteries that reduces or blocks the blood supply to the heart. Atherosclerosis causes *angina* (chest pain due to insufficient blood supply to the heart) or *heart attack* (death of heart muscle tissue). Controllable factors that contribute to heart disease include stress, smoking, certain personality characteristics, obesity, a high-fat diet, and lack of exercise (American Heart Association, 2000; Tennant, 1999).

How does stress contribute to heart disease? Recall that one of the major autonomic nervous system fight–flight reactions is the release of epinephrine and cortisol into the bloodstream. These hormones increase heart rate and release fat from the body's stores to give muscles a quickly available source of energy.

If no physical action is taken (and this is most likely the case in our modern lives), the fat released into the bloodstream is not burned as fuel and may become fatty deposits on the walls of blood vessels (Figure 9.2). These fatty deposits are a major cause of blood supply blockage that causes heart attacks. In other words, if stress causes blocked arteries and blocked arteries cause heart attacks, then people who are continually under a lot of stress are prone to heart attacks.

Personality Types

The effects of stress on heart disease may be amplified if an individual tends to be hard driving, competitive, ambitious, impatient, and hostile. People with such **Type A personalities** are chronically on edge, tend to talk rapidly, feel intense time urgency, and are preoccupied with responsibilities. The antithesis of the Type

Type A Personality *Set of behavior characteristics that includes intense ambition, competition, drive, constant preoccupation with responsibilities, exaggerated time urgency, and a cynical, hostile outlook*

Figure 9.2 *Fatty deposits in arteries.* One major cause of heart disease is the blockage of arteries that supply blood to the heart. The artery at the left is normal; the one on the right is almost completely blocked. Reducing stress, exercising, and eating a low-fat diet can help prevent the buildup of fatty deposits in the arteries.

Type B Personality *Set of behavior characteristics consistent with a calm, patient, relaxed attitude toward life*

A personality is Type B. People with a **Type B personality** have a laid-back, calm, relaxed attitude toward life.

Two cardiologists, Meyer Friedman and Ray Rosenman (1959) were the first to identify and describe the Type A personality. The story goes that in the mid-1950s, an upholsterer who was recovering the waiting room chairs in Friedman's office noticed an odd wear pattern. He mentioned to Friedman that all the chairs looked like new except for the front edges, which were badly worn, as if all the patients sat only on the edges of the chairs. Initially, this didn't seem too important to Friedman. However, this chronic sense of time urgency and being literally "on the edge of your seat" was later believed to be a possible contributing factor to heart disease and the hallmark of the Type A personality.

Initial research into Type A behavior suggested Friedman and Rosenman were right, but more recent research has been less supportive. When researchers examined the relationship between characteristics of the Type A behavior pattern and heart disease, they found that the critical component and strongest predictor of heart disease was *hostility* (Fredrikson, Wik, & Fischer, 1999; Miller, Smith, Turner, Guijarro, & Hallet, 1996).

Actually, *cynical* hostility appears to be the most important factor in the Type A relationship to heart disease. Having a negative attitude toward the world means cynical people always expect problems. They are constantly alert and "on watch," trying to foresee problems and possibly avert them. This attitude produces a nearly constant state of stress, which translates physiologically into higher blood pressure, heart rate, and production of stress-related hormones. In addition, because of their hostile, suspicious, argumentative, and competitive style, these people tend to have more interpersonal conflicts (Friedman, Hawley, and Tucker, 1994). Constant interpersonal conflicts can lead to a loss of social support and heightened autonomic activation, which can then lead to increased risk of cardiovascular disease (Sher, 2000; Tennant, 1999).

Can people with a Type A personality change their behavior? Health psychologists have developed two types of behavior modification to help people with Type A personality — the *shotgun approach* and the *target behavior approach*. The *shotgun approach* aims to change all the behaviors that relate to the Type A personality. Friedman and his colleagues (1986) use the shotgun approach in their Recurrent Coronary Prevention Program. The program provides individual counseling, dietary advice, exercise, drugs, and group therapy to eliminate or modify Type A behaviors. Type A's are specifically encouraged to slow down and perform tasks incompatible with their personalities. For example, they might try to listen to other people without interrupting or stand in the longest supermarket line on purpose. The major criticism of the shotgun approach is that it eliminates desirable (ambitiousness and drive) as well as undesirable Type A traits (cynicism and hostility).

The alternative approach, the *target behavior approach*, focuses on only those Type A behaviors that are likely to cause heart disease — namely, cynical hostility. By modifying target behaviors, the person will likely reduce his or her risk of heart disease.

Hardiness

In addition to Type A and Type B personalities, there may be other personality patterns that affect the way we respond to stress. Have you ever wondered how some people survive in the face of great stress (repeated personal tragedies, demanding jobs, and even a poor home life) but others do not? Suzanne Kobasa was among the first to study this question (Kobasa, 1979, Pengilly & Dowd, 2000). Examining male executives with high levels of stress, she found that some people are more resistant to stress than others because of a personality factor called **hardiness**, a resilient type of optimism that comes from three distinctive attitudes:

1. *Commitment.* Hardy people feel a strong sense of commitment to both their work and personal life. They also make intentional commitments to purposeful activity and problem solving.

2. *Control.* These people also see themselves not as victims of whatever life brings but as personally in control.

3. *Challenge.* Finally, hardy people look at change as an opportunity for growth and improvement — not as a threat. Hardy people welcome challenges.

The important lesson from this research is that hardiness is a *learned behavior* — not luck or genetics. If you're not one of the *hardy* souls, you can develop the trait. The next time you face a bad stressor, such as four exams in one week, try using the 3 C's: "I am fully *committed* to my college education." "I can *control* the number of tests by taking one or two of them earlier than scheduled, or I can rearrange my work schedule." "I welcome this *challenge* as a final motivation to enroll in those reading improvement and college success courses I've always planned to take."

Before we go on, it's also important to note that Type A personality and lack of hardiness are not the only controllable risk factors associated with heart disease. Smoking, obesity, and lack of exercise are very important factors. Smoking restricts blood circulation, and obesity stresses the heart by causing it to pump more blood to the excess body tissue. A high-fat diet, especially one high in cholesterol, contributes to the fatty deposits that clog blood vessels. Lack of exercise contributes to weight gain and prevents the body from obtaining important exercise benefits, including strengthening heart muscle, increasing heart efficiency, and releasing hormones such as serotonin that alleviate stress and promote well-being.

Hardiness *A resilient personality characteristic based on three qualities: a commitment to personal goals, control over life, and viewing change as a challenge rather than a threat.*

Check & Review

STRESS AND SERIOUS ILLNESS

Cancer appears to result from an interaction of heredity, environmental insults (such as smoking), and immune system deficiency. Stress may be an importnat cause of decreased immunity. During times of stress, the body may be less able to check cancerous tissue growth because the immune system is suppressed.

The leading cause of death in the United States is heart disease. Risk factors in heart disease include smoking, stress, obesity, a high-fat diet, lack of exercise, and **Type A personality** (if it includes cynical hostil-

ity). The two main approaches to modifying Type A behavior are the shotgun approach and the target behavior approach. People with psychological **hardiness** are less vulnerable to stress because of three distinctive personality characteristics — commitment, control, and challenge.

Questions

1. Stress can contribute to heart disease by releasing the hormones _____ and _____, which increase the level of fat in the blood.

2. Which of the following is *not* among

the characteristics associated with Type A personality? (a) time urgency; (b) patience; (c) competition; (d) hostility.

3. The two major approaches to modifying Type A behavior are the _____ approach and the _____ approach. Which one do you think would work best for you, and why?

4. Explain how the three characteristics of the hardy personality help reduce stress.

Answers to Questions can be found in Appendix B.

MODULE 9   ACTIVE LEARNING WORKSHEET

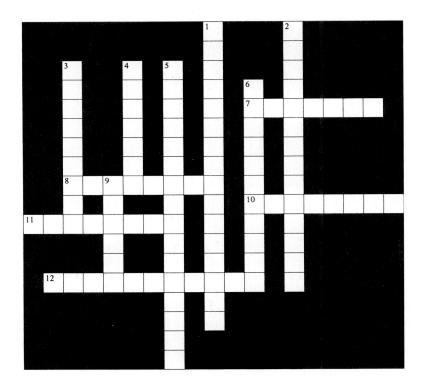

ACROSS

7. Little problems of daily living that are not significant in themselves, but they accumulate and sometimes become a major source of stress.

8. Pleasant, desirable stress.

10. A negative emotional state caused by an inability to choose between two or more incompatible goals or impulses.

11. Unpleasant, objectionable stress.

12. An unpleasant state of tension, anxiety, and heightened sympathetic activity resulting from a blocked goal.

DOWN

1. Set of behavior characteristics consistent with a calm, patient, relaxed attitude toward life.

2. A person's belief about whether the results of their successes or failures are under their personal control (internal) or outside their control (external).

3. A resilient personality characteristic based on three qualities: a commitment to personal goals, control over life, and viewing change as a challenge rather than a threat.

4. A state of physical, emotional, and mental exhaustion attributable to long-term involvement in emotionally demanding situations.

5. Set of behavior characteristics that includes intense ambition, competition, drive, constant preoccupation with responsibilities, exaggerated time urgency, and a cynical, hostile outlook.

6. Continuous or recurrent pain over a period of six months or more.

9. A nonspecific response of the body to any demand made on it; the arousal, both physical and mental, to situations or events that we perceive as threatening or challenging.

Answers can be found in Appendix B.

MODULE 10
COPING WITH STRESS

It would be helpful if we could avoid all negative stressful situations, but this is impossible. Everyone encounters pressure at work, long lines at the bank, and the death of a family member. Because we can't escape stress, we need to learn how to effectively cope with it. Lazarus and Folkman (1984) defined *coping* as "constantly changing cognitive and behavioral efforts to manage specific external and/or internal demands that are appraised as taxing or exceeding the resource of the person." In simpler terms, coping is an attempt to manage stress in some effective way. It is not one single act but a process that allows us to deal with various stressors. The coping process can focus on the emotional effects of the stressor or on solving the problem causing the stress.

What techniques and resources are available to help people cope with stress?

Emotion-Focused Forms of Coping: Reappraising the Situation

Emotion-focused forms of coping are emotional or cognitive strategies that change how we view a stressful situation. Suppose you are refused a highly desirable job or rejected by a desired lover. You might reappraise the situation and decide that the job or lover might not have been the right match for you or that you weren't really qualified or ready for that specific job or relationship.

One of the most common forms of emotion-focused coping is the use of **defense mechanisms**, unconscious strategies that protect the ego and avoid anxiety by distorting reality. The use of defense mechanisms reduces anxiety and often helps us cope with unavoidable stress. For instance, *fantasizing* about what you will do once you graduate from college can motivate you to study for exams.

On the other hand, defense mechanisms can sometimes be destructive. You might decide you didn't get the job or the lover because you didn't have the right "connections" or "the perfect body." This is known as *rationalization,* fabricating excuses when frustrated in attaining particular goals. Not seeing the situation more clearly and realistically might prevent you from developing skills or qualities that could get you a desirable job or lover in the future.

In sum, emotion-focused forms of coping that are accurate reappraisals of stressful situations and do not distort reality may alleviate stress in some situations (Burke & Greenglass, 2000; Gold & Friedman, 2000). Many times, however, it is necessary and more effective to confront the stressor directly.

Emotion-Focused Forms of Coping *Coping strategies based on changing one's perceptions of stressful situations*

Defense Mechanisms *Unconscious strategies used to distort reality and relieve anxiety and guilt*

Problem-Focused Forms of Coping: Putting Problem-Solving Skills to Work

Problem-focused forms of coping deal directly with the situation or the stressor to eventually decrease or eliminate it (Bond & Bunce, 2000). Generally, these approaches are the same as problem-solving strategies discussed in Module 21. Thus, the better a person is at solving problems, the more likely he or she will develop effective strategies. These strategies include identifying the stressful problem, generating possible solutions, selecting the appropriate solution, and applying the solution to the problem — thus eliminating the stress.

To illustrate the difference between the two forms of coping, let's suppose that you are flying to Denver to be in your best friend's wedding. You have an exam that lets out at 10:00 and your plane leaves at noon; the wedding is at 4:00. It will be tight, but you can make it. Unfortunately, on the way to the airport, the taxi has a

Problem-Focused Forms of Coping *Coping strategies based on using problem-solving strategies to decrease or eliminate the source of stress*

critical thinking ▶▶▶▶▶▶▶▶▶▶▶▶▶▶▶▶ Active Learning

Is Your Job Stressful?

An important component of critical thinking is the ability to *define problems accurately*. By carefully identifying the problem in clear and concrete terms, critical thinkers prevent confusion and lay the foundation for gathering relevant information. Health psychologists (and industrial/organizational psychologists) have studied numerous factors in job-related stress. Their findings suggest that one way to prevent these stresses is to gather lots of information before making a career decision.

If you would like to apply this to your own career plans, start by identifying what you like and do not like about your current (and past) jobs. With this information in hand, you are then prepared to research jobs that will better suit your interests, needs, and abilities and avoid the stress caused by jobs failing to meet this criteria. To help your analysis, answer yes or no to these questions:

1. Is there a sufficient amount of laughter and sociability in your workplace?

2. Does your boss notice and appreciate your work?

3. Is your boss understanding and friendly?

4. Are you embarrassed by the physical conditions of your workplace?

5. Do you feel safe and comfortable in your place of work?

6. Do you like the location of your job?

7. If you won the lottery and were guaranteed a lifetime income, would you feel truly sad if you also had to quit your job?

8. Do you watch the clock, daydream, take long lunches, and leave work as soon as possible?

9. Do you frequently feel stressed and overwhelmed by the demands of your job?

10. Compared to others with your qualifications, are you being paid what you are worth?

11. Are promotions made in a fair and just manner?

12. Given the demands of your job, are you fairly compensated for your work?

Now score your answers. Give yourself one point for each answer that matches the following: 1. No; 2. No; 3. No; 4. Yes; 5. No; 6. No; 7. No; 8. Yes; 9. Yes; 10. No; 11. No; 12. No.

The questions you just answered are based on four factors that research shows are conducive to increased job satisfaction and reduced stress: supportive colleagues, supportive working conditions, mentally challenging work, and equitable rewards (Robbins, 1996). Your total score reveals your overall level of dissatisfaction, whereas a look at specific questions can help identify which of these four factors is most important to your job satisfaction — and most lacking in your current job.

Supportive colleagues (items 1, 2, 3): For most employees, work fills important social needs. Therefore, having friendly and supportive colleagues and superiors leads to increased satisfaction.

Supportive working conditions (items 4, 5, 6): Not surprisingly, studies find most employees prefer working in safe, clean, and relatively modern facilities. They also prefer jobs close to home.

Mentally challenging work (items 7, 8, 9): Jobs with too little challenge create boredom and apathy, whereas too much challenge creates frustration and feelings of failure.

Equitable rewards (items 10, 11, 12): Employees want pay and promotions based on job demands, individual skill levels, and community pay standards.

---

flat tire. You can cognitively evaluate the situation and tell yourself that because this is your best friend, he'll understand that you did everything you could to be there; it wasn't your fault that the taxi had a flat (emotion-focused approach). Or, you could ask the driver to immediately call for another taxi to come and take you to the airport (problem-centered approach).

In general, the better a person is at solving problems, the more likely he or she will develop effective problem-focused coping strategies, including identifying the stressful problem, generating possible solutions, selecting the appropriate solution, and applying the solution to the problem.

Can people use both forms of coping strategies at once? Yes, most stressful situations are complex, and people often combine problem-focused and emotion-focused coping strategies. Furthermore, as you know from your own life, stressful situations change and the type of strategy we use depends not only on the stressor but also the changing nature of the stressor. In some situations, we may first need to use an emotion-focused strategy, which allows a step back from an especially overwhelming problem. Then, later on, when we have our emotional strength and our feet on the ground, we can reappraise the situation and use the problem-solving approach to look for solutions.

We may also use one coping strategy to prepare us to use the other. For example, humor is an emotion-focused coping strategy that is highly effective in altering negative moods. Also, in many situations, dealing with emotions helps us problem-solve (Keltner & Bonanno, 1997; Moran & Massam, 1999). Imagine that you are about to take your first exam in a difficult course. You are naturally very anxious: To calm yourself, you can first take an emotion-focused approach. You might say to yourself, "Relax and take a deep breath; it can't be as bad as you imagine." With reduced anxiety, you can then use problem-focused coping techniques and concentrate on answering the questions on the test.

Resources for Effective Coping: From Good Health to Money

A person's ability to cope effectively depends on the stressor itself — its complexity, intensity, and duration — and on the type of coping strategy used. It also depends on available resources. Researchers have identified several important coping resources:

1. *Health and energy*. All stressors cause physiological changes. Therefore, an individual's health significantly affects his or her ability to cope. Look again at Figure 9.1 (p. 110) on the GAS: The resistance stage is the coping stage. The stronger and healthier people are, the better they cope and the longer they stay in the resistance stage without entering the exhaustion stage.

2. *Positive beliefs*. A positive self-image and a positive attitude can be especially significant coping resources. Research shows that even temporarily raising self-esteem reduces the amount of anxiety caused by stressful events (Greenberg et al., 1993). Also, hope can sustain a person in the face of severe odds, as is often documented in news reports of people who have triumphed over seemingly unbeatable circumstances. According to Lazarus and Folkman, hope can come from a belief in oneself, which can enable us to devise our own coping strategies; a belief in others, such as medical doctors who we feel can effect positive outcomes; or a belief in a just and helpful God.

3. *Social skills*. Social situations — meetings, discussion groups, dates, parties, and so on — are often a source of pleasure, but they can also be a source of stress. Merely meeting someone new and trying to find something to talk about can be very stressful for some people. Therefore, people who acquire social skills (know appropriate behaviors for certain situations, have conversation-starters "up their sleeves," and express themselves well) suffer less anxiety than people who do not. In fact, people lacking social skills are more at risk for developing illness (Cohen & Williamson, 1991).

Social skills help us not only interact with others but also communicate our needs and desires, enlist help when we need it, and decrease hostility in tense situations. If you have weak social skills, you may find it worth the effort to learn how to act in a variety of social situations. Observe others and ask people with good social skills for advice. You can also practice your new skills by role-playing before applying them in real life.

4. *Social support*. Having the support of others helps offset the stressful effects of divorce, loss of a loved one, chronic illness, pregnancy, stressful work training, job loss, and work overload (Frazier, 2000; Gold & Friedman, 2000). When we are faced with stressful circumstances, our friends and family often help us take care of our health, listen and "hold our hand," make us feel important, and provide stability to offset the changes in our lives (D'Imperio, Dubow, & Ippolito, 2000; Lohman & Jarvis, 2000).

People need people. *These recently widowed women realize that an important resource for coping with stress is social support from friends, families, and support groups.*

For people with specific problems, support and self-help groups can be very helpful. There are groups for alcoholics and families of alcoholics, for former drug addicts, for divorced people, for single parents, for cancer patients, for parents who have had a young child die, and so on. Support groups help people cope not only because they provide other people to lean on but also because people can learn techniques for coping from others with similar problems (see Chapter 15).

5. *Material resources.* We've all heard the saying "Money isn't everything," but when it comes to coping with stress, money and the things that money can buy can be very real resources. Money increases the number of options available to eliminate sources of stress or reduce the effects of stress. When they are faced with the minor hassles of everyday living, with chronic stressors, or with major catastrophes, people with money who have the skills to effectively use that money generally fare much better and experience much less stress than people without money (Chi & Chou, 1999; Ennis, Hobfoll, & Schroeder, 2000).

6. *Personal control.* Do you believe that what happens to you is primarily the result of your own actions? That success is mostly a matter of hard work versus luck? Our sense of controlling our environment, rather than feeling helpless, is an important resource in effective coping. This perception of personal **locus of control** over the events in one's life tends to make people more sensitive to health messages and more likely to take actions to improve their health. It also buffers the negative effects of stress. In fact, one of the greatest threats to well-being occurs when people feel caught in a situation and unable to control their circumstances.

People with an *external locus of control* are more likely to believe in bad luck or fate. They feel powerless to change their circumstances and are less likely to make healthy changes, follow treatment programs, or positively cope with the situation. Conversely, people with an *internal locus of control* believe they are in charge of their own destiny and tend to adopt more positive coping strategies. For example, internals who believe their heart attacks happened because of their unhealthy choices, such as smoking or having a stressful job, are more likely to change their unhealthy behaviors and recover more quickly (Ewart & Fitzgerald, 1994). Studies in China (Hamid & Chan, 1998), Taiwan, and the UK (Lu, Kao, Cooper, & Spector, 2000) found that those who had a higher internal locus of control experienced less psychological stress than did those with a higher external locus of control.

Locus of Control *The belief that life's circumstances are under personal, internal control or outside, external factors*

Active Coping Strategies: Taking Action Against Stress

In addition to coping styles and resources that rely primarily on cognitive and emotional strategies, there are other more direct, action-oriented approaches. Active coping methods "provide more direct and deliberate means of controlling and reducing the impact of stress ... [and] prepare us to deal with unexpected stress and keep us in stress-ready condition" (Gill, 1983, p. 84). The two major active methods are exercise and relaxation.

Exercise

If you exercise and keep yourself physically fit, you will probably experience less anxiety, depression, and tension than do people who do not exercise or who are less fit. Moreover, researchers have found that people engaging in strenuous exercise experienced greater reductions in anxiety than did those in moderate programs (Hong, 2000; Katula, Blissmer, & McAuley, 1999; McEntee & Halgin, 1999).

Exercise reduces the negative effects of stress in several ways. First, it uses up the hormones secreted into the bloodstream during stress, thereby helping the immune system return to normal functioning sooner. Second, exercise can help work out tension that has built up in muscles. Third, exercise increases strength, flexibility, and stamina for encountering future stressors and increases the efficiency of the cardiovascular system. The best exercise for all these purposes is aerobic exercise — regular strenuous activity that heightens cardiovascular functioning, such as brisk walking, jogging, bicycling, swimming, dancing, and so on.

Relaxation

One of the most effective means of dealing with physical stress reactions is to make a conscious decision to relax during the stressful situation (Matuszek, 2000; Robert-McComb, 2001). There are a variety of relaxation techniques. Earlier, we discussed the use of biofeedback with chronic pain, but it is also extremely helpful in teaching people to relax and manage their stress. Progressive relaxation is also very helpful in reducing or relieving the muscular tension commonly associated with stress. Using this technique, patients first tense and then relax specific muscles, such as in the neck, shoulders, and arms. This technique teaches people to recognize the feel of tense and relaxed muscles.

A Final Note

You are the one who is ultimately responsible for your own health and well-being. Although doctors, nurses, and other health professionals are there for you if you become ill, it is best to do all you can to prevent disease in the first place. By minimizing the harmful effects of stress in our lives, we help our bodies stay well and fight off disease.

Coping with stress. Exercise and friends are important resources for effective stress reduction. "I get by with a little help from my friends." John Lennon and Paul McCartney, Sgt. Pepper's Lonely Hearts Club Band, 1967.

TRY THIS *Yourself*

You can use the following progressive relaxation technique anytime and anywhere you feel stressed, such as while waiting for an exam to begin. Here's how:

1. Sit in a comfortable position, with your head supported.
2. Start breathing slowly and deeply.
3. Let your entire body go limp — let go of all tension. Try to visualize your body getting more and more relaxed.
4. Systematically tense and release each part of your body, beginning with your toes. Focus your attention on your toes and try to visualize what they are doing. Curl them tightly, while counting to 10, then release them and feel the difference between the tense state and the relaxed state. Next, tense your feet to the count of 10, then relax them and feel the difference between the two states. Continue with your calves, thighs, buttocks, abdomen, back muscles, shoulders, upper arms, forearms, hands and fingers, neck, jaws, facial muscles, and forehead.

Try practicing progressive relaxation twice a day for about 15 minutes. You will be surprised at how quickly you can learn to relax — even in the most stressful situations.

Check & Review

COPING WITH STRESS

The two major forms of coping with stress are **emotion-focused** and **problem-focused**. Emotion-focused coping change how we view stressful situations. Problem-focused coping deal directly with the situation or the factor causing the stress so as to decrease or eliminate it. The ability to cope with a stressor also depends on the resources available to a person. Resources include health and energy, positive beliefs, social skills, social support, material resources, and personal control. Exercise and relaxation are active methods people can use to cope with stress.

Questions

1. Which form of coping is being used in the following reactions to forgetting your best friend's birthday? (a) "I can't be expected to remember everyone's birthday"; (b) "I'd better put Cindy's birthday on my calendar so this won't happen again."

2. What are two common defense mechanisms, and why should people avoid using them?

3. People with a(n) _____ locus of control are better able to cope with stress.

4. What are the six major resources for coping with stress? Which resource is most helpful for you? Least helpful?

Answers to Questions can be found in Appendix B.

ACTIVE LEARNING WORKSHEET   MODULE 10

This activity will help you review important concepts, as well as help you improve your coping responses to stress.

- Briefly describe a recent time when you experienced significant stress. _____
  _____
  _____

- Did you use an emotion-focused form of coping? If so, briefly describe it. _____
  _____
  _____

- Did you use a problem-focused form of coping? If so, briefly describe it. _____
  _____
  _____

- Your book describes several resources for coping with stress. Place a "+" mark by those activities or skills you currently use and a "–" by those you don't. Then review the items with a "–" mark, and decide how you can incorporate them into your daily life.

  _____ health and energy

  _____ positive beliefs

  _____ social skills

  _____ social support

  _____ material resources

  _____ personal control

  _____ exercise

  _____ relaxation

Visual Summary for Modules 8, 9, and 10

Health Psychology in Action

Health Psychology: Studies relationship between psychological behavior and physical health and illness.

What Health Psychologists Do

- Research issues that affect physical health and methods for improving health.
- Work in the health field to reduce distress and unhealthy behaviors.

Smoking

- *Why do people smoke?* Peer pressure; imitation of role models; addiction (nicotine increases release of neurotransmitters that increase alertness, memory, and well being and decrease anxiety, tension, and pain); learned associations with positive results.
- *Prevention?* Educate about short- and long- term con-sequences, make smoking less socially acceptable, and help nonsmokers resist social pressures.
- *Stopping?* Use cognitive and behavioral techniques to deal with withdrawal; supplement with nicotine replacement therapy (patches, gum, and pills).

Binge Drinking

Binge drinking: When a man consumes 5 or more drinks in a row, or a woman consumes 4 or more.
How to reduce?
- Overcome the myths and teach facts.
- Reduce or remove social rewards.

Chronic Pain

Chronic pain: Pain lasting over 6 months.
How to reduce?
- Increase activity, exercise, and dietary changes.
- Use behavior modification strategies to reinforce changes.
- Employ *biofeedback* with *electromyograph (EMG)* to reduce muscle tension.
- Use relaxation techniques and practice distraction.

Stress and Its Role in Health

Stress: Body's nonspecific response to any demand made on it.

Sources of Stress

- *Life changes*: Holmes and Rahe Scale measures stress caused by adaptations to important life events.
- *Chronic stressors*: Ongoing, long term stress related to political world, family, work, etc.
- **Hassles:** Small, everyday problems that accumulate.
- **Burnout:** Exhaustion resulting from emotionally demanding situations.
- **Frustration:** Negative emotional state from blocked goals.
- **Conflict:** Negative emotional state from 2 or more incompatible goals.

There are 3 types of conflict

Approach-approach conflict: Two or more desirable goals

Avoidance-avoidance conflict: Two or more undesirable goals

Approach-avoidance conflict: Both desirable and undesirable goals

Stress and Its Role in Health (cont).

Results of Stress

- *Sympathetic nervous system activation* increases heart rate, blood pressure, respiration, and muscle tension and releases stress hormones.
- *Fight/flight system* frequently engaged but generally overused and harmful in modern times.
- *Suppressed immune system* leaves body vulnerable to disease.

- **General adaptation syndrome** is a 3-phase generalized physiological that develops in response to severe stressors:
1. Alarm reaction ➡ 2. Resistance phase ➡ 3. Exhaustion

Stress and Serious Illness

Cancer
- Occurs when cells replicate beyond control.
- Caused by hereditary dispositions and environmental factors that lead to changes in body chemistry and the immune system

Cardiovascular Disorders
Heart disease: All disorders that affect the heart muscle and lead to heart failure.
Contributing Factors:

Stress related hormones, which release fat into bloodstream that later attaches to the walls of blood vessels.	**Type A personality** with high ambition, time worries, anger, and hostility is at increased risk; whereas, the personality factor of **hardiness** decreases risk.	Behaviors such as smoking, stress, lack of exercise, obesity, and high-fat diet.

Coping with Stress

Emotion-Focused Forms of Coping	Problem-Focused Forms of Coping	Resources for Effective Coping	Active Coping Strategies
Emotional and cognitive strategies that change how one appraises a stressful situation. **Defense mechanisms** are unconscious strategies that protect the ego and avoid anxiety by distorting reality.	Strategies that deal directly with the stressful situation by applying problem-solving techniques to decrease or eliminate it.	Good health, energy, positive beliefs, social skills, social support, material resources, and personal control (e.g., internal **locus of control**) all reduce stress.	Exercise and relaxation techniques directly reduce stress.

Sensation and Perception

I have just touched my dog. He was rolling on the grass, with pleasure in every muscle and limb. I wanted to catch a picture of him in my fingers, and I touched him as lightly as I would cobwebs. ... He pressed close to me, as if he were fain to crowd himself into my hand. He loved it with his tail, with his paw, with his tongue. If he could speak, I believe he would say with me that paradise is attained by touch. [pp. 3–4]

Thus Helen Keller began her book *The World I Live In.* Her world was totally different from that of most people: She couldn't see it or hear it because she was blind and deaf, but she was as capable and as appreciative of life — if not more so — as any person with all five senses. This was because she made the most of the senses she did have. Excerpts from her book describe how she used these senses:

Through the sense of touch I know the faces of friends, the illimitable variety of straight and curved lines, all surfaces, the exuberance of the soil, the delicate shapes of flowers, the noble forms of trees, and the range of mighty winds. Besides objects, surfaces, and atmospherical changes, I perceive countless vibrations. ... Footsteps, I discover, vary tactually according to the age, the sex, and the manners of the walker. ... When a carpenter works in the house or in the barn near by, I know by the slanting, up-and-down, toothed vibration, and the ringing concussion of blow upon blow, that he is sawing or hammering...

In the evening quiet there are fewer vibrations than in the daytime, and then I rely more largely upon smell. ... Sometimes, when there is no wind, the odors are so grouped that I know the character of the country and can place a hayfield, a country store, a garden, a barn, a grove of pines, a farmhouse with the windows open. ... I know by smell the kind of house we enter. I have recognized an old-fashioned country house because it has several layers of odors, left by a succession of families, of plants, perfumes, and draperies. [pp. 43–44, 46, 68–69]

Helen Keller wasn't born deaf and blind. When she was 19 months old, she suffered a fever that left her without sight or hearing and thus virtually isolated from the world. Keller's parents realized they had to find help for their daughter, and after diligently searching, they found Anne Sullivan, a young teacher who was able to break through Keller's barrier of isolation by taking advantage of her sense of touch. One day, Sullivan took Keller to the pumphouse and, as Sullivan (1902) wrote,

I made Helen hold her mug under the spout while I pumped. As the cold water gushed forth, filling the mug, I spelled "w-a-t-e-r" in Helen's free hand. The word coming so close upon the sensation of cold water rushing over her hand seemed to startle her. She dropped the mug and stood as one transfixed. A new light came into her face. [p. 257]

That one moment, brought on by the sensation of cold water on her hand, was the impetus for a lifetime of learning about, understanding, and appreciating the world through her remaining senses. In 1904, Helen Keller graduated cum laude from Radcliffe College and went on to become a famous author and lecturer, inspiring physically limited people throughout the world.

Sensation *The process of receiving, translating, and transmitting raw sensory data from the external and internal environments to the brain*

Perception *The process of selecting, organizing, and interpreting sensory data into usable mental representations of the world*

Bottom-Up Processing *Information processing that begins "at the bottom" with raw sensory data that feed "up" to the brain; perceptual analysis that emphasizes characteristics of the stimulus itself rather than internal, cognitive processes*

Top-Down Processing *Information processing that starts "at the top" with the observer's thoughts, expectations, and knowledge and works down; perceptual analysis that emphasizes the perceiver's internal, cognitive processes rather than being driven by characteristics of the outside stimuli*

The story of Helen Keller has been told and retold as an example of how people can overcome sensory deficiencies by using their other senses to the optimum. It also provides a wonderful introduction to the two major topics of this section: **sensation,** the process of receiving, converting, and transmitting information from the outside world (outside the brain, not necessarily outside the body), and **perception,** the process of selecting, organizing, and interpreting raw sensory data into useful mental representations of the world.

As you can see in Figure 11.1, the basic function of sensation is *detection* of sensory stimuli, whereas perception generally involves *interpretation* of the same stimuli. Like the central nervous system (CNS) and peripheral nervous system (PNS), the basic functions of sensation and perception are somewhat different. But also like the CNS and PNS, the boundary between these two processes is not precise — there is considerable overlap.

We begin this section discussing how we receive sensory information and work our way upward to the top levels of perceptual processing. Psychologists refer to this type of information processing as **bottom-up processing**, taking sensory data in through the sensory receptors and sending it "upward" to the brain for analysis. In contrast, **top-down processing** begins with "higher," "top"-level processing involving thoughts, previous experiences, expectations, language, and cultural background and works down to the sensory level. When first learning to read, you used *bottom-up processing*. You initially learned that certain arrangements of lines and "squiggles" represented specific letters. Only later did you realize that these letters joined together to make up words. After years of experience and language training, you quickly perceive the words in this sentence before the individual letters — *top-down processing*. Although top-down processing is far superior for reading, both bottom-up and top-down processing are important to perception.

Our opening discussion of sensation covers not only what are commonly known as the five senses — vision, hearing, taste, smell, and touch — but also those senses that provide the brain with data from inside the body: the *vestibular sense* (the sense of balance) and *kinesthesis* (the sense of bodily position and movement). After we've covered sensation, Module 12 explores perception, where the focus is on how we select, organize, and interpret sensory data. In that module, you discover how we decide what to pay attention to, how we perceive distance, how we see different colors, and whether there is any scientific evidence to support subliminal perception and extrasensory perception (ESP).

What do you see — sensation or perception? *(a) When you stare at this drawing (known as the Necker cube), which area is the top, front, or back of the cube? In the process of sensation, your visual sensory system detects a collection of lines, angles, patterns of color, and so on. But at the perceptual level, you interpret these lines as a geometric shape called a cube. If you stare at it long enough, your perception/interpretation will change. (b) Now look at this drawing of a woman. Do you see a young woman looking back over her right shoulder or an older woman with her chin down on her chest? Although basic sensory input stays the same, your brain's attempt to interpret ambiguous stimuli creates a type of perceptual dance, shifting from one interpretation to another (Gaetz, Weinberg, Rzempoluck, & Jantzen, 1998).*

(a)

(b)

MODULE 11
SENSATION

How do our sensory organs gather sensory information and convert it into signals the brain can understand?

To experience sensations, we must have both a means of detecting stimuli and a means of converting them into a language the brain can understand. Let's take a closer look at how our sensory organs accomplish both tasks.

Experiencing Sensations: Detection and Conversion of Stimuli

Our eyes, ears, skin, and other sense organs all contain special cells called *receptors*, which receive and process sensory information from the environment. For each sense, these specialized cells respond to a distinct stimulus, such as sound waves or odor molecules.

Through a process called **transduction**, the receptors convert the stimulus into neural impulses, which are sent to the brain. In hearing, for example, tiny receptor cells in the inner ear convert mechanical vibrations (from sound waves) into electrochemical signals. These signals are carried by neurons to the brain. Each type of sensory receptor is designed to detect a wide variety of stimuli and a wide range of stimulation. However, also built into our sensory systems are structures that purposefully reduce the amount of stimuli we receive.

Transduction *The process by which a stimulus to a receptor is converted into neural impulses*

Why would we want to reduce the amount of sensory information we receive? Can you imagine what would happen if you did not have some natural filtering of stimuli? You would constantly hear blood rushing through your veins and continually feel your clothes brushing against your skin. Some level of filtering is needed so the brain is not overwhelmed with unnecessary information. It needs to be free to respond to those stimuli that have meaning for survival. Each of our senses is therefore custom-designed to respond to only a select range of potential sensory information.

All species have evolved selective receptors that suppress or amplify information to allow survival. For example, hawks have an acute sense of vision but a poor sense of smell. Similarly, we humans cannot sense many stimuli, such as ultraviolet light, microwaves, the ultrasonic sound of a dog whistle, or infrared heat patterns from warm-blooded animals (which rattlesnakes can). However, we can see a candle burning 30 miles away on a dark, clear night, hear the tick of a watch at 20 feet under quiet conditions, smell one drop of perfume in a six-room apartment, and taste 1 teaspoon of sugar dissolved in 2 gallons of water.

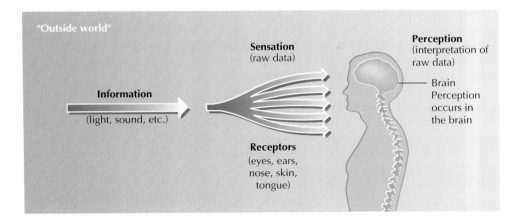

"Outside world"

Information
(light, sound, etc.)

Sensation
(raw data)

Receptors
(eyes, ears, nose, skin, tongue)

Perception
(interpretation of raw data)

Brain
Perception occurs in the brain

Figure 11.1 *Sensation and perception.* Sensation is the detection and conversion of raw data from the senses. Perception is the interpretation of these raw sensory data by the brain.

Figure 11.2 *Sensory areas of the brain.* Neural impulses travel from the sensory receptors to various parts of the brain.

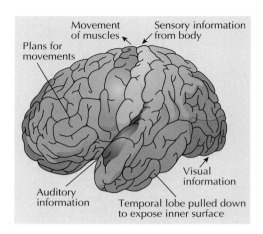

Plans for movements
Movement of muscles
Sensory information from body
Visual information
Auditory information
Temporal lobe pulled down to expose inner surface

Sensory Reduction *The process of filtering and analyzing incoming sensations that occurs before a neural impulse is sent to the cortex*

Coding *The three-part process that converts a particular sensory input into a specific sensation*

Psychophysics *The branch of psychology that studies the relation between attributes of the physical world and our psychological experience of them*

Absolute Threshold *The smallest magnitude of a certain stimulus energy that can be detected*

Difference Threshold *The smallest magnitude of difference in stimulus energy that a person can detect; also called the just noticeable difference*

In the process of **sensory reduction**, we not only filter incoming sensations, we also analyze the sensations sent through before a neural impulse is finally sent to the cortex of the brain. If cells in the reticular formation within the brainstem decide the information is important, it is passed on to the cerebral cortex. This explains why parents of a newborn can sleep through passing sirens and blaring stereos yet awaken to the slightest whimper of their baby.

How does the brain differentiate between various incoming sensations, such as sounds and smells? It depends on the number and type of sensory cells that are activated, on the precise nerve that is stimulated, and ultimately on the part of the brain that the nerve stimulates. Through a process known as **coding**, sounds and smells are interpreted as distinct sensations not because of the environmental stimuli that activate them but because their respective neural impulses travel by different routes and arrive at different parts of the brain. Figure 11.2 illustrates the parts of the brain involved in sensory reception.

Thresholds

How do we know that humans can hear a watch ticking at 20 feet or smell one drop of perfume in a six-room apartment? The answer comes from research in **psychophysics**, an area of psychology that examines how physical stimuli (such as sound and smell) are related to an individual's psychological reactions to those stimuli. Using knowledge from both physics and psychology, psychophysicists study how the strength or intensity of a stimulus affects an observer.

Suppose you are the parent of a school-age daughter who, like Helen Keller, has just suffered from a serious illness accompanied by high fever. During her period of recovery, you notice that she does not seem to hear as well as before her illness, so you take her to a hearing specialist.

In a test for hearing loss, the specialist uses a tone generator that produces sounds of differing pitches and intensities. Your daughter listens to the sounds over earphones and is asked to indicate the earliest point at which she can hear a tone. She thereby indicates her **absolute threshold**, or the smallest magnitude of sound she can detect. To test your daughter's **difference threshold**, or *just noticeable difference* (JND), the examiner presents a small change in volume and asks the child to respond when she notices a difference. By noting your daughter's thresholds and comparing them with thresholds of people with normal hearing, the specialist can determine whether your daughter has a hearing loss and, if so, the extent of the loss.

Sensory thresholds exist not only for hearing but also for vision, taste, smell, and the skin senses. In fact, much of the research done in all areas of sensation originally began with the study of various thresholds.

Do people's thresholds vary? People with sensory impairments obviously have thresholds that differ from the norm. But even among individuals with no sensory difficulties, there is a considerable range in sensitivities. Moreover, the sensitivity of an individual can vary from moment to moment, depending on his or her physiological state. Lack of food and certain drugs, for example, can change a person's normal threshold.

Adaptation

Your friends have invited you to come by to visit their beautiful new baby daughter. As they greet you at their front door, you are overwhelmed by the odor of a nearby diaper pail and even the baby herself. You wonder what's wrong. Why don't they do something about the smell? The answer is **sensory adaptation**: When a constant stimulus is presented for a length of time, sensation often fades or disappears. Receptors higher up in the sensory system get "tired" and actually fire less frequently.

Sensory adaptation makes sense from an evolutionary perspective. Basically, we can't afford to waste attention and time on unchanging, normally unimportant stimuli. "Turning down the volume" on repetitive information helps the brain cope with an overwhelming amount of sensory stimuli and allows time to pay attention to *change*. This helps your friends with their smelly baby, and if you stay long enough, your senses also will adapt — fortunately. Sometimes this adaptation, however, can be dangerous, as when we stop paying attention to that gas leak we noticed in the kitchen.

Although some senses adapt quickly, like smell and touch, we never completely adapt to visual stimuli or extremely intense stimuli, such as the odor of ammonia, the heat of the desert sun, or the pain of a burned hand. Again, from an evolutionary perspective, these limitations on sensory adaptation aid survival. They remind us to avoid strong odors and heat and to do something about the damaged tissue, such as put some ice on that burned hand.

If we don't adapt to pain, how do athletes keep playing despite painful injuries? In certain situations, the body releases natural painkillers called *endorphins*. Endorphins act in the same way as morphine to relieve pain by inhibiting pain perception. Both pleasant (the "runner's high," sexual activity) and unpleasant stimuli (injuries, fighting) can release endorphins. Pain relief through endorphins may also be the secret behind *acupuncture*, the ancient Chinese technique of gently twisting thin needles placed in the skin.

In addition to endorphin release, one of the most accepted explanations of pain perception is the **gate-control theory**, first proposed by Ronald Melzack and Patrick Wall (1965). According to this theory, the experience of pain depends partly on whether the neural message gets past a "gatekeeper" in the spinal cord that either blocks pain signals or allows them to pass on to the brain. Normally, the gate is kept shut, either by impulses coming down from the brain itself or by messages coming into the spinal cord from large-diameter fibers that conduct most sensory signals,

Sensory Adaptation *A sensory phenomenon in which the perceived intensity of a repeated stimulus decreases over time*

Gate-Control Theory of Pain *The idea that pain sensations are processed and altered by mechanisms within the spinal cord*

Childbirth and the gate-control theory of pain. Modern childbirth classes teach women to focus their attention away from the pain during childbirth, and the partner (or "labor coach) is encouraged to talk to her and gently massage the back and neck muscles. Can you see how the gate-control theory explains the effectiveness of these techniques?

such as touch and pressure. However, when body tissue is damaged, impulses from smaller pain fibers open the gate.

The gate-control theory helps explain why touch and pressure, such as rubbing your banged elbow, can reduce pain: The large fibers carry competing pressure messages. Messages from the brain itself can also control the pain gate, thus explaining how athletes and soldiers can carry on despite excruciating pain. When we are soothed by endorphins or distracted by competition or fear, our experience of pain can be greatly diminished. On the other hand, when we get anxious or dwell on our pain by talking about it constantly, we can intensify it (Sullivan, Tripp, & Santor, 1998).

Research also suggests that the pain gate may be chemically controlled, that a neurotransmitter called *substance P* opens the pain gate, and that endorphins close it (Cesaro & Ollat, 1997; Liu, Mantyh, & Basbaum, 1997). Other research finds that the brain not only responds to incoming signals from sensory nerves but also is capable of *generating* pain (and other sensations) entirely on its own (Melzack, 1999; Vertosick, 2000). Have you heard of *tinnitus*, the ringing-in-the-ears sensation that sometimes accompanies hearing loss? In the absence of normal sensory input, nerve cells send conflicting messages ("static") to the brain, and in this case the brain interprets the static as "ringing." A similar process happens with the strange phenomenon of *phantom pain*, wherein people continue to feel pain (and itching or tickling) long after a limb is amputated. The brain interprets the static as pain because it arises in the area of the spinal cord responsible for pain signaling (Vertosick, 2000).

Each of the sensory principles we've discussed thus far — reduction, transduction, coding, thresholds, and adaptation — applies to all the senses. Yet the way in which each sense is processed is uniquely different, as we shall see in the remainder of this module.

Check & Review

EXPERIENCING SENSATIONS

Sensation refers to the process of receiving, converting, and transmitting information from the outside world, whereas **perception** is the process of selecting, organizing, and interpreting raw sensory data into useful mental representations of the world.

Sensory processing includes transduction, reduction, and coding. **Transduction** converts stimuli into neural impulses that are sent to the brain, and we cope with the vast quantities of sensory stimuli through the process of **sensory reduction**. Each sensory system is specialized to **code** its stimuli into unique sets of neural impulses that the brain interprets as light, sound, touch, and so on.

The **absolute threshold** is the smallest magnitude of a stimulus we can detect. The **difference threshold** is the smallest change in a stimulus that we can detect. The process of **sensory adaptation** decreases our sensitivity to constant, unchanging stimuli.

Questions

1. The key functions of sensation and perception are, respectively, (a) stimulation and transduction; (b) transmission and coding; (b) reduction, and transduction; (c) detection and interpretation; (d) interpretation and transmission.

2. If a researcher were testing to determine the dimmest light a person could perceive, the researcher would be measuring the _____.

3. Why can't you smell your own perfume or aftershave after a few minutes?

4. The _____ theory of pain helps explain why it sometimes helps to rub or massage an injured thumb. (a) sensory adaptation; (b) gate-control; (c) just noticeable difference; (d) Lamaze.

Answers to Review Questions can be found in Appendix B.

How We See and Hear: Vision and Hearing

> How do our eyes and ears enable us to see and hear?

While on a long train trip, Helen Keller's aunt improvised a doll for 6-year-old Helen out of a few towels. It had no nose, no mouth, no ears, and no eyes — nothing to indicate a face. Helen found this disturbing. Most disturbing, though, was the lack of eyes. In fact, it agitated her so much that she was not content until she found

What does a butterfly see? The flower on the right was photographed under ultraviolet light. Because butterflies have ultraviolet receptors, this may be what it's like to see like a butterfly.

some beads and her aunt attached them for eyes. Uncomprehending as she was of the myriad sensations our eyes bring us, Helen still seemed to know the importance of having eyes.

Vision

To fully appreciate the marvels of sight, we first need to examine the properties of light, because without it, we wouldn't be able to see. We will then examine the structure and function of the eye, and finally, the way in which visual input is processed.

Waves of Light

Light is a form of electromagnetic energy that moves in waves similar to the movement of waves in the ocean. There are many different types of electromagnetic waves, from short X-rays to long radio waves. Together they form the *electromagnetic spectrum* (Figure 11.3). Most wavelengths are invisible to the human eye; only a small part of the spectrum, known as the *visible spectrum*, can be detected by our visual receptors.

As Table 11.1 shows, light waves vary in length, height, and range — each with a distinct effect on vision. The **wavelength**, the distance between the crest of one wave and the crest of the next, determines its **frequency** (in vision, its **hue** or color). Longer wavelengths produce reddish colors, whereas shorter wavelengths produce bluish colors. The **amplitude**, or height, of a light wave determines its *intensity* (in vision, its *brightness*). Higher waves produce brighter colors, and smaller waves produce dimmer colors. The range of waves — that is, the mixture of length and amplitude — determines its *complexity* (in vision, its *saturation*). The

Wavelength *The length of a light or sound wave, measured from the crest of one wave to the crest of the next*

Hue *The visual dimension seen as a particular color; determined by the length of a light wave*

Frequency *How often a light or sound wave cycles — that is, the number of complete wavelengths that pass a point in a given time (e.g., per second)*

Amplitude *The height of a light or sound wave; pertaining to light, it refers to brightness*

Figure 11.3 *The electromagnetic spectrum.* (a) Gamma radiation and X radiation have short wavelengths, visible light has medium wavelengths, and TV, radio, and AC (alternating current) circuits have long wavelengths. (b) The human eye can see only visible light, a small part of the full spectrum. Visible light with a short wavelength is perceived as blue, visible light with a medium wavelength is green or yellow, and visible light with a long wavelength is red.

TABLE 11.1 PROPERTIES OF VISION AND HEARING

Physical properties	**Wavelength:** The distance between successive peaks.	**Wave Amplitude:** The height from peak to trough.	**Range of Wavelengths:** The mixture of waves.
	Long wavelength/low frequency	*Low amplitude/low intensity*	*Low range/low complexity*
	Short wavelength/ high frequency	*High amplitude/ high intensity*	*High range/high complexity*
VISION (Light Waves)	**Hue:** Short wave lengths produce higher frequency and bluish colors; long wavelengths produce lower frequency and reddish colors.	**Brightness:** Great amplitude produces more intensity and bright colors; small amplitude produces less intensity and dim colors.	**Saturation:** Wider range produces more complex color; narrow range produces less complex color.
AUDITION (Sound Waves)	**Pitch:** Shorter wavelengths produce higher frequency and high pitched sounds; long wavelengths produce lower frequency and low-pitched sounds.	**Loudness:** Great amplitude produces loud sounds; small amplitude produces soft sounds.	**Timbre:** Pure tones produce only one frequency; complex tones produce multiple frequencies.

wider range produces more saturated (more varied and complex) color, whereas a narrow range produces less saturated color (less complex and varied; may be a single pure color).

Eye Anatomy and Function

The eye is uniquely designed to capture light and focus it on receptors at the back of the eyeball. The receptors, in turn, convert light energy into neural signals to be interpreted by the brain. Several structures in the eye are involved in the process. We will trace the path of light through these structures — the cornea, pupil, lens, and retina. As we do, please refer to Figure 11.4.

Light waves first enter the eye through a tough, transparent shield called the *cornea*, which is attached to the white, opaque outer wall of the eye. Light passes from the cornea through the *pupil*, an adjustable opening controlled by the *iris* (the colored part of the eye), and then on through the *lens*, a transparent elastic structure. Light waves eventually end up at the back of the eyeball on the *retina*, a group of light receptors, where they are transduced into neural messages and then carried by the *optic nerve* to the brain.

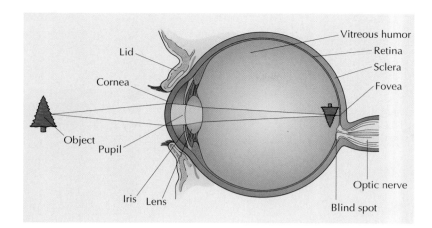

Figure 11.4 *The anatomy of the eye.* Note the path of light waves as they travel from the outside world, enter the eye at the cornea, and pass through the pupil and lens to the retina. In the retina, light waves are transduced (or changed) into neural impulses that move along the optic nerve upward to the brain.

Now that we have the big picture of eye anatomy, and how light information enters and travels to the brain, let's examine how the main structures function.

Cornea and Lens

The cornea protects the eye and does part of the focusing of incoming light rays. The lens further bends incoming rays of light to focus them on the retina. The focus is adjustable, like in a camera. But unlike a camera lens, which changes the focus for objects at different distances by moving relative to the film plane, the lens of the eye work by changing their shape. The lens become more or less curved to focus light from objects located at varying distances. This focusing process is known as **accommodation**. When you look at a faraway object, your lens accommodates by thinning and flattening to focus; when your glance shifts back to a near object, such as the book you're reading, your lens accommodates by thickening and curving.

Small abnormalities in the eye sometimes interfere with accommodation (Figure 11.5). If you have normal vision, your lens focuses the image of any object — near or far — on the retina at the back of your eye. If you are **nearsighted**, however, your eyeball is deeper than normal in relation to its lens, or your cornea may be too sharply curved. The light rays are focused at a point in front of the retina, and at the retina, the image is blurred. The opposite occurs if you are **farsighted**. Your eyeball is shorter than normal and the light is focused on a point beyond the retina, leading to an inability to focus on objects at close range. Nearsightedness *(myopia)* and farsightedness *(hyperopia)* can occur at any age; however, at about age 40, most people find that they need reading glasses. This is because the lenses start to lose elasticity and the ability to accommodate for near vision *(presbyopia)*. Both nearsightedness and farsightedness are easily remedied with corrective lenses. Advances in laser surgery now make it possible to change the shape of the cornea to correct some visual acuity problems.

Retina

Ultimately, incoming light waves end up on the **retina**. This is an area at the back of the eye that contains blood vessels and a network of neurons that transmit neural information to the occipital lobes of the brain. The retina also contains special light-sen-

Accommodation The process by which the lens changes shape to focus light on the retina; the lens thins and flattens to focus on distant objects and thickens and bulges to focus on a nearby object

Nearsightedness (Myopia) A visual acuity problem that occurs when the cornea and lens focus an image in front of the retina

Farsightedness (Hyperopia) A visual acuity problem that results when the cornea and lens focus an image behind the retina

In normal vision, an image is focused on the retina.

In nearsightedness (myopia), the image is focused in front of the retina.

In farsightedness (hyperopia), the image is focused behind the retina.

Figure 11.5 *Normal vision, nearsightedness, and farsightedness.*

Retina The light-sensitive inner surface of the back of the eye, which contains the receptor rods and cones plus other neurons that help in processing visual information

Figure 11.6 *Structures of the retina.* (a) The retina of the eye is a complicated structure with many different types of cells. The most important are the rods and cones. (b) In this photomicrograph, the two large yellow cone-shaped objects are retinal cones, and the long reddish rod-shaped objects are the retinal rods. The bipolar cells are located directly above the rods and cones.

(a)

(b)

Rods *Visual receptors in the retina that detect black, white, and gray and are responsible for peripheral vision; they are most sensitive in dim light*

Cones *Visual receptors concentrated near the center of the retina that are responsible for color vision and fine detail; they are most sensitive in brightly lit conditions*

sitive cells called **rods** and **cones**, so named for their distinctive shapes (Figure 11.6). There are about 6 million cones and 120 million rods tightly packed together at the back of the retina (Carlson, 1998).

The rods, besides being much more numerous, are also more sensitive to light than the cones. They enable us to see in dim light. This greater sensitivity, however, is achieved at the expense of fine detail and and color vision — the job of the cones.

Cones become more numerous toward the center of the retina, and in the center is the *fovea*, a tiny pit filled with cones, responsible for our sharpest vision. Cones function better in bright light and diminish in function as the light dims. Cones enable us not only to see things in fine detail but also to see in color. All cones are sensitive to many wavelengths, but each is maximally sensitive to one color — red, green, or blue. You may have noticed that it is impossible to see the color and fine detail of a flower in near-dark conditions, when only the rods are functioning.

Near the fovea lies an area that has no visual receptors at all and absolutely no vision. This aptly named "blind spot" is where blood vessels and nerve pathways enter and exit the eyeball. Normally, we are unaware of our blind spot because our eyes are always moving. We fill in the information missing from the blind spot with information from adjacent areas on the retina or with images from the other eye.

To experience your blind spot, hold the book about 1 foot in front of you, close your right eye, and stare at the X below with your left eye. Very slowly, move the book closer to you. You should see the worm disappear and the apple become whole.

When the brightness level suddenly changes, how do the rods "take over" from the cones, and vice versa? Think back to the last time you walked into a dark movie theater on a sunny afternoon. You were momentarily blinded. This happens because in bright light, the pigment inside the rods is bleached and they are temporarily nonfunctional. Going from a very light to a very dark setting requires a rapid shift from cones to rods. During the changeover, there is a second or two before the rods are functional enough for you to see. They continue to adjust for 20 to 30 minutes, until your maximum light sensitivity is reached. This process is known as **dark adaptation**. The visual adjustment that takes place when you leave the theater and go back into the sunlight — *light adaptation* — takes about 7 to 10 minutes and is the work of the cones. This adaptation process is particularly important to remember when driving your car from a brightly lit garage into a dark night.

Dark Adaptation *The process by which rods and cones adjust to allow vision in dim light*

Hearing

In this section, we examine **audition**, the sense of hearing, which we use nearly as much as our sense of vision. In fact, Helen Keller said she "found deafness to be a much greater handicap than blindness. … Blindness cuts people off from things. Deafness cuts people off from people." What is it about hearing that makes it so important? In discussing vision, we talked first about waves of light, then about the anatomy of the eye, and, finally, about problems with vision. We'll follow the same pattern with audition, starting here with waves of sound.

Audition *The sense of hearing*

Waves of Sound

Sound is the movement of air molecules in a particular wave pattern. The waves produced are called *sound waves*. They result from rapid changes in air pressure caused by vibrating objects, such as vocal cords or guitar strings.

Like light waves, sound waves vary in three basic ways (see again Table 11.1):

1. **Length**   Wavelengths in hearing correspond to **pitch** (wavelengths of light correspond to hue or color). Sounds of different frequencies are perceived as high or low. For instance, the faster a person's vocal cords vibrate (the more waves per second), the higher the pitch of the person's voice.

2. **Height**   The amplitude (or height) of the sound wave determines *loudness*, which is measured in units termed *decibels* (the height of light waves determines *brightness*). Figure 11.7 gives decibel ratings for various sounds.

3. **Range**   The range (or mixture) of sound waves determines *timbre*, or complexity of tone. Timbre is the quality of sound that allows us to know whether a note is being played by a violin, trumpet, or oboe.

Pitch *The highness or lowness of tones or sounds, depending on their frequency*

Ear Anatomy and Function

The ear has three major sections: the *outer ear*, the *middle ear*, and the *inner ear*. The outer ear gathers and delivers sound waves to the middle ear, which amplifies and concentrates the sounds. The inner ear contains the receptor cells that ultimately transduce the mechanical energy created by sounds into neural impulses. As we trace the path of sound waves through the ear, it will help to refer to Figure 11.8.

Sound waves are gathered and funneled into the outer ear by the *pinna*, the external, visible part of the ear that we automatically envision when we think of an ear. The pinna channels the sound waves into the *auditory canal*, a tubelike structure that focuses the sound. At the end of the auditory canal is a thin, tautly stretched membrane known as the *eardrum*, or *tympanic membrane*. As sound waves hit the eardrum, it vibrates. The vibrating eardrum causes the three tiniest bones in the body, the *malleus* (hammer), the *incus* (anvil), and the *stapes* (stirrup), to vibrate. (Together, these three bones are referred to as the *ossicles*.) The stapes presses on a membrane, known as the *oval window*, and causes it to vibrate.

Figure 11.7 *Loudness.* The loudness of a sound is measured in decibels. This figure lists some familiar sounds and their decibel levels. One decibel is the faintest sound a normal person can hear. Normal conversation takes place at about 60 decibels. Constant noise above about 90 decibels can cause permanent nerve damage to the ear.

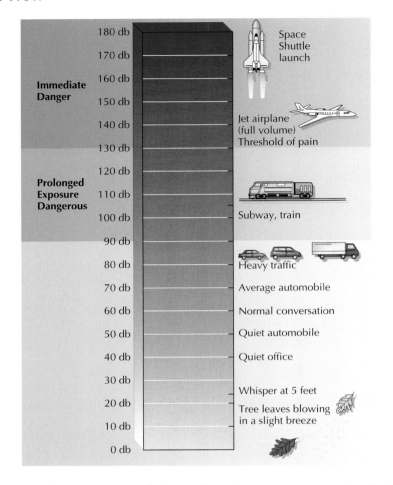

Cochlea [KOK-lee-uh] *The three-chambered, snail-shaped structure in the inner ear that contains the receptors for hearing*

The movement of the oval window creates waves in the fluid that fills the **cochlea**, a snail-shaped structure that contains the *basilar membrane*, on which are located the receptors for hearing. The hearing receptors are known as *hair cells*, and they do in fact resemble hairs. As the waves travel through the cochlear fluid, the hair cells bend from side to side. It is at this point that the mechanical energy of the wave is transduced into electrochemical impulses that are carried by the *auditory nerve* to the brain.

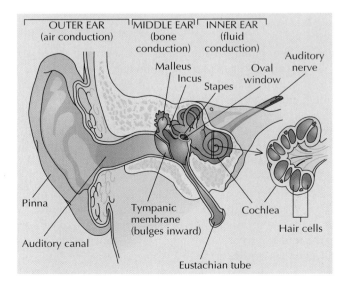

Figure 11.8 *Anatomy of the ear.* Sound waves enter the outer ear, are amplified and concentrated in the middle ear, and are transduced in the inner ear.

Pitch and Loudness

We hear different pitch and loudness levels by a combination of mechanisms, depending on the frequency of the sound. First, let's discuss how we hear various pitches of sounds. It seems that we hear high-pitched sounds according to the place along the *basilar membrane* that is most stimulated. When we hear a particular sound, it causes the eardrum, the ossicles, and the oval window to vibrate, which in turn produces a "traveling wave" through the fluid in the cochlea. This wave causes some bending of hair cells all along the basilar membrane, but there is a single point where the hair cells are maximally bent for each distinct pitch. This localized maximal bending is described by the **place theory**, which explains how we hear higher-pitched sounds.

How we hear lower-pitched sounds is explained by the **frequency theory**. According to this theory, we hear a particular low sound because it causes hair cells along the basilar membrane to bend and fire action potentials at the same rate as the frequency of that low sound. For example, a sound with a frequency of 90 hertz would produce 90 action potentials per second in the auditory nerve.

How we detect loudness levels also differs according to the frequency of the sounds. When a sound has a high pitch, we hear it as louder because the neurons fire at a faster rate. Louder sounds produce more intense vibrations, which result in a greater bending of the hair cells, a greater release of neurotransmitters, and consequently a higher firing rate of action potentials. However, there must be an alternate explanation for the perception of the loudness of low sounds, because as just described, rate of firing explains how we hear the pitch of a low sound. Most researchers think that the loudness of lower-pitched sounds is detected by the number of axons that are firing at any one time.

Is it true that loud music can damage your hearing? Yes. There are basically two types of deafness: (1) *conduction deafness*, or middle-ear deafness, which results from problems with the mechanical system that conducts sound waves to the inner ear, and (2) *nerve deafness*, or inner-ear deafness which involves damage to the cochlea, hair cells, or auditory nerve. Disease and biological changes associated with aging can cause nerve deafness. But the most common (and preventable) cause of nerve deafness is continuous exposure to loud sounds that damages the hair cells. If a noise is loud (150 decibels or more), such as stereos or headphones at full blast, jackhammers, or a jet airplane engine, even brief exposure can cause permanent deafness. Daily exposure to approximately 85 decibels (such as heavy traffic or

Place Theory *Theory that explains how we hear higher-pitched sounds; different high-pitched sounds bend the basilar membrane hair cells at different locations in the cochlea*

Frequency Theory *Theory that explains how we hear lower-pitched sounds; hair cells on the basilar membrane of the cochlea bend and fire action potentials at the same rate as the frequency of the low sound*

Loud noise and nerve deafness. Members of the Red Hot Chili Peppers (and their audience) are potential victims of noise-induced nerve deafness, which is irreversible.

RESEARCH HIGHLIGHT

Tracking Down the Genes for Deafness

Some people suffer hearing loss because of disease (as in Helen Keller's case), accident, or exposure to extremely loud noise. Others are born with a gene that causes deafness. Researchers trying to track down these genes have generally taken one of two approaches. One approach uses animals, such as mice, which have certain known genetic mutations that are naturally occurring or are experimentally induced by the researchers (Self et al., 1998; Wang et al., 1998). The second

approach is to study the genetics of human families that have a large percentage of members who are born deaf or become deaf later in life (Denoyelle et al., 1997; Lynch et al., 1997).

Together, the two approaches have located several human deafness gene mutations (Pennisi, 1997). These genes are responsible for producing a type of protein called *myosin*, which is, in turn, instrumental in the development of the auditory hair cells. The mutation alters the structure of the hair cells, causing the person to be deaf at birth or to go deaf several years after birth. But problems with myosin cannot be the only cause of genetic deafness. It is suspected that many more genetic mutations will be discovered in the next few years.

motorcycles) can also lead to permanent hearing loss. Obviously, if you cannot avoid such loud noises, earplugs will help reduce the damage. Pay attention to any change in your normal hearing threshold or if you experience *tinnitus*, a whistling or ringing sensation in your ears. These are often the first signs of hearing loss.

Because damage to the nerve or receptor cells is almost always irreversible, the only treatment for nerve deafness is a small electronic device called a *cochlear implant*. If the auditory nerve is intact, the implant bypasses hair cells and directly stimulates the nerve. At present, a cochlear implant produces only a crude approximation of hearing, but the technology is improving. The best bet is to protect your sense of hearing. That means avoiding exceptionally loud noises (rock concerts, jackhammers, stereo headphones at full blast), wearing earplugs when such situations cannot be avoided, and paying attention to bodily warnings. These warnings include a change in your normal hearing threshold and tinnitus.

Check & Review

HOW WE SEE AND HEAR

Light is a form of energy that is part of the electromagnetic spectrum. The **wavelength** of a light determines its **hue**, or color; the **amplitude**, or the height, of a light wave, determines its *intensity*. The range of light waves determines its *complexity*. The function of the eye is to capture light and focus it on visual receptors that convert light energy to neural impulses. Light enters through the pupil and lens to the retina, and then travels along the optic nerve to the brain. Cells in the **retina** called **rods** are specialized for night vision, whereas **cones** are specialized for color and fine detail.

The sense of hearing is known as **audition**. We hear sound via sound waves, which result from rapid changes in air pressure caused by vibrating objects. The wavelength of these sound waves is sensed as the **pitch** of the sound, whereas the amplitude of the waves is perceived as *loudness*. The range of sound waves is sensed as *timbre*, the purity or complexity of the tone. The outer ear conducts sound waves to the middle ear, which in turn conducts vibrations to the inner ear, where hair cells in the **cochlea** transduce mechanical energy into neural impulses. The neural message is then carried along the auditory nerve to the brain.

Questions

1. Trace the path of light as it enters the eye and leaves to go to the brain.
2. The lens of the eye focuses by _____ and _____. The focusing process is known as _____.
3. Trace the path of sound as it enters the ear and leaves to go to the brain.
4. Explain how place theory differs from frequency theory.

Answers to Questions can be found in Appendix B.

Our Other Senses: Smell, Taste, and Other Body Senses

Vision and audition may be the most prominent of our senses, but the others — taste, smell, and the body senses — are also important for gathering information about our environment. The enjoyment of a summer's day comes not only from the visual and auditory beauty of the world but also from the taste of a fresh garden tomato, the smell of honeysuckle, and the feel of a warm, gentle breeze.

Smell and Taste

Smell and taste are sometimes referred to as the *chemical senses* because they both involve *chemoreceptors* that are sensitive to certain chemical molecules rather than to electromagnetic or mechanical energy. Smell and taste receptors also are located near each other and often interact so closely that we have difficulty separating the sensations. Have you ever noticed how food seems bland when your nose is blocked by a cold and you cannot smell your food?

Olfaction

The sense of smell, or **olfaction**, results from stimulation of receptor cells in the nose (Figure 11.9). These receptors are embedded in a mucus-coated membrane called the *olfactory epithelium*. The olfactory receptors are actually modified neurons, with branched dendrites extending out into the epithelium. When chemical molecules in the air passing through the nose come in contact with the dendrites, they initiate a neural impulse. The impulse travels along the neuron's axon directly to the *olfactory bulb*, a structure just below the frontal lobes where most olfactory information is processed before being sent to other parts of the brain.

Figuring out how we distinguish different odors is complicated for many reasons, not least that we have over 1,000 types of receptors, and we can detect over 10,000 distinct smells (floral, musky, rotten, fruity, and so on). According to one prominent theory, each odor fits into only one type of olfactory receptor cell, like a key into a lock. This theory is, in fact, called the *lock-and-key theory of olfaction*. Another theory proposes that each olfactory receptor is sensitive to only part of a molecule's structure, and distinct odors activate unique combinations of receptor types (Malnic, Hirono, & Buck, 1999).

GENDER & CULTURAL DIVERSITY

Do Some People Smell Better Than Others?

No, we are not asking if some people smell like roses and others smell like rotten eggs. The question relates to differences in olfactory sensitivity between people. Research has shown that women and younger adults are better at identifying smells, smokers have a dulled sense of smell, and up to 35 percent of people have some form of *anosmia* (odor blindness) (Frye, Schwartz, & Doty, 1990; Gilbert & Wyslocki, 1987; Segal et al., 1995).

Interestingly, some research also finds possible ethnicity differences in smell sensitivity. Using international data from the 1986 National Geographic Smell Survey, C. E. Barber (1997) was able to compare the olfactory sensitivity of several different groups. He compared men to women, young to old, and African to American respondents on one particular odor — androstenone, which is produced by bacteria on the human body and is a component of sweat. Survey respondents included 19,219 Americans and 3,204 Africans of both genders and many different ages.

Barber's research supported earlier findings of increased sensitivity among women and young adults, but African respondents (both men and women) were better than

Olfaction *The sense of smell*

Figure 11.9 *Anatomy of the olfactory system.* (a) The nasal cavity showing the location of olfactory receptors. (b) All olfactory receptors that are sensitive to the same odor send their axons to the same area of the olfactory bulb.

> How do our other senses enable us to experience the world?

their American counterparts at detecting androstenone. There are many possibilities for the differences in sensitivity, including the environment. Because this was survey research, no one cause can be accurately determined, and the findings of this one study on androstenone cannot be generalized to other odors without further research.

Does smell affect sexual attraction? People have always been interested in increasing their sexual attractiveness. One popular means has been the use of perfumes and, today, aftershave lotions and men's cologne. Is there any scientific basis to such practices? One line of research has focused on **pheromones** — chemical odors we give off that are thought to affect the behavior of others, including their sexual behavior.

Pheromones have been found in a number of animal species and are used to mark trails to food, define territory, and increase sexual arousal and mating behaviors. Although some research supports the idea that pheromones increase sexual behaviors in humans (Cutler, 1999; Cutler, Friedmann, & McCoy, 1998), other findings question the results (Wysocki & Preti, 1998). Despite what the perfume ads might suggest, human sexuality is much more complex than that of other animals.

Nonetheless, human pheromones may explain several interesting phenomena other than sex. For example, researchers have documented an olfactory linkage behind the common belief that women who live together (in an apartment, military barracks, or sorority) eventually develop synchronized menstrual cycles (Stern & McClintock, 1998). Also, mothers and their babies can recognize each other solely on the basis of smell just a few hours after birth. Will other human pheromone phenomena be discovered? Only further study will tell.

Gustation

In modern times, **gustation** (the sense of taste) may be the least critical of our senses. In our primate past, however, it probably contributed to our survival. The major function of taste is to provide information about substances that are entering our digestive tract so that we can screen out those that may be harmful. This function is aided by the sense of smell.

When the sense of smell is eliminated, the enormous variety of tastes can be reduced to four: sweet, sour, salty, and bitter. Like smell receptors in the lock-and-key theory, taste receptors respond differentially to the varying shapes of food and liquid molecules. The major taste receptors (or *taste buds*) are clustered within little bumps called *papillae*. You can see these papillae on the surface of your tongue (Figure 11.10).

Why are children so picky about food? In young people, taste buds die and are replaced about every 7 days. As we age, however, the buds are replaced more slowly, so taste diminishes. Thus, children, who have abundant taste buds, often dislike foods with strong or unusual tastes (such as liver and spinach), but as they grow older and lose taste buds, they may come to like these foods.

Some pickiness is related to learning. Many food and taste preferences result from childhood experiences and cultural influences. For example, many Japanese children eat raw fish and some Chinese children eat chicken feet as part of their normal diet, whereas American children might consider these foods "yucky." Likewise, most American children love cheese, which children in some other cultures find repulsive.

Pickiness also relates to the fact that the sense of taste enables humans and animals to discriminate between foods that are safe to eat and foods that are poisonous. Because many plants that taste bitter contain toxic chemicals, an animal is more likely to survive if it avoids bitter-tasting plants (Guinard et al., 1996). On the other hand, humans and animals have a preference for sweet foods that are generally nonpoisonous and are good sources of energy.

Pheromones [FARE-oh-mones]
Airborne chemicals released from one individual that affect another individual's behavior, including recognition of family members, aggression, territorial marking, and sexual mating

Gustation *The sense of taste*

Figure 11.10 *The surface of the human tongue magnified 47 times.* When liquids enter the mouth or food is chewed and dissolved, the fluid runs over the papillae (the lavender circular areas) and into the pores to the taste buds, which contain the receptors for taste. This is why we should chew our food slowly and completely if we want maximum taste satisfaction.

The Body Senses

Imagine for a moment that you are an Olympic skier and you're anxiously awaiting the starting signal that will begin your once-in-a-lifetime race for the gold medal in the giant slalom. What senses will you need to manage the subtle and ever-changing balance adjustments required for Olympic-level skiing? How will you make your skis carve the cleanest, shortest, fastest line from start to finish? What will enable your arms, legs, and trunk to work in perfect harmony so that you can record the shortest time and win the gold? The senses that will allow you to do all this, and much more, are the body senses. The *body senses* tell the brain how the body is oriented, where and how the body is moving, the things it touches or is touched by, and so on. These senses include the skin senses, the vestibular sense, and the kinesthetic sense.

The Skin Senses

The skin senses are extremely vital. Skin not only protects the internal organs but also provides the brain with basic survival information. With nerve endings in the various layers of skin, our skin senses tell us when a pot is dangerously hot, when the weather is freezing cold, and when we have been hurt. Researchers have "mapped" the skin by applying probes to all areas of the body. Mapping shows there are three basic skin sensations: touch (or pressure), temperature, and pain. Receptors for these sensations occur in various concentrations and depths in the skin. For example, touch (pressure) receptors are maximally concentrated on the face and fingers and least in the back and legs. As your hands move over objects, pressure receptors register the indentations created in the skin, allowing perception of texture, and people who are blind learn to read the raised dots that constitute Braille.

The relationship between the types of receptors and the different sensations is not clear. It used to be thought that each receptor responded to only one type of stimulation, but we now know that some receptors respond to more than one. For example, pressure receptors also respond to certain sound waves. And itching, tickling, and vibrating sensations seem to be produced by light stimulation of both pressure and pain receptors.

In conducting studies on temperature receptors, researchers have found that the average square centimeter of skin contains about six cold spots where only cold can be sensed, and one or two warm spots where only warmth can be felt. Interestingly, we don't seem to have separate "hot" receptors. Instead, our cold receptors detect not only coolness but also extreme temperatures — both hot and cold (Craig & Bushnell, 1994). See Figure 11.11.

The Vestibular Sense

The *vestibular sense* is the sense of body orientation and position with respect to gravity and three-dimensional space (in other words, it is the sense of balance). Even the most routine activities — riding a bike, walking, or even sitting up — would be impossible without this sense. The vestibular apparatus is located in the inner ear and is composed of the vestibular sacs and the semicircular canals.

The **semicircular canals** provide the brain with balance information, particularly information about the rotation of the head. As the head moves, liquid in the canals moves and bends hair cell receptors. At the end of the semicircular canals are the *vestibular sacs*, which contain hair cells sensitive to the specific angle of the head — straight up and down or tilted. Information from the semicircular canals and the vestibular sacs is converted to neural impulses that are then carried to the appropriate section of the brain.

What causes motion sickness? Information from the vestibular sense is used by the eye muscles to maintain visual fixation and sometimes by the body to

Figure 11.11 *How do we experience "hot?"* Researchers use an instrument called a "heat grill" — two pipes twisted together, one containing warm water and the other cold. If you grasp both pipes, you experience intense heat because both warm and cold receptors are activated simultaneously. We do not have separate "hot" receptors.

Semicircular Canals *Three arching structures in the inner ear that contain hair receptors that respond to head movements to provide information on balance*

How do they do it? Without her finely tuned vestibular and kinesthetic senses to maintain her balance and coordination, US gymnast Amy Chow would be on her way to the hospital rather than the Olympics.

Kinesthesis *The sensory system that provides information on body posture and orientation*

change body orientation. If the vestibular sense gets overloaded or becomes confused by boat, airplane, or automobile motion, the result is often dizziness and nausea. Random versus expected movements also are more likely to produce motion sickness. Thus, automobile drivers are better prepared than passengers for upcoming movement and are less likely to feel sick (Rolnick & Lubow, 1991). Motion sickness seems to vary with age: Infants are generally immune, children between ages 2 and 12 years have the highest susceptibility, and the incidence declines in adulthood.

The Kinesthetic Sense

Kinesthesis (from the Greek word for "motion") is the sense that provides the brain with information about bodily posture and orientation, as well as bodily movement. Unlike the receptors for sight, hearing, smell, taste, and balance, which are clumped together in one organ or area, kinesthetic receptors are found throughout the muscles, joints, and tendons of the body. As we sit, walk, bend, lift, turn, and so on, our kinesthetic receptors respond by sending messages to the brain. They tell which muscles are being contracted and which relaxed, how our body weight is distributed, where our arms and legs are in relation to the rest of our body. Without these sensations, we would literally have to watch every step we make.

We rely on kinesthesis constantly yet seldom acknowledge it, because this sense is rarely disturbed in our everyday lives. In one study, an experimenter intentionally disturbed participants' wrist tendon receptors by producing certain vibrations. Participants reported sensations of having multiple forearms and impossible positions of their arms (Craske, 1977). But we don't have to go through experimental procedures to appreciate our kinesthetic sense. All we have to do is observe children learning new skills and remember when we were just learning to ride a bike or catch a football. During the learning process, we consciously move certain body parts and certain muscles, but gradually we learn to operate on "automatic pilot." Our kinesthetic sense needs training in recognizing how various postures and movements should feel.

Check & Review

OUR OTHER SENSES

The sense of smell (**olfaction**) and the sense of taste (**gustation**) are called the chemical senses and are closely interrelated. The receptors for olfaction are at the top of the nasal cavity. According to the lock-and-key theory, we can smell different odors because each three-dimensional odor molecule fits into only one type of receptor. The receptors for gustation are located on the tongue, and are sensitive to four basic tastes: salty, sweet, sour, and bitter.

The body senses are the skin senses, the vestibular sense, and the **kinesthetic** sense. The skin senses detect pressure, temperature, and pain. They protect the internal organs and provide basic survival information. The vestibular apparatus is located in the inner ear. The kinesthetic sense provides the brain with information about body posture and orientation, as well as body movement. The kinesthetic receptors are spread throughout the body in muscles, joints, and tendons.

Questions

1. The _____ theory of olfaction suggests that we cannot smell carbon monoxide because of the shape of the carbon monoxide molecule. (a) chemoreceptor; (b) lock-and-key; (c) geometric; (d) multidimensional.

2. The weightlessness experienced by space travelers as a result of zero gravity has its greatest effect on the _____ senses. (a) visceral; (b) reticular; (c) somasthetic; (d) vestibular.

3. Receptors located in the muscles, joints, and tendons of the body provide _____ information to maintain bodily posture, orientation, and movement.

4. The skin senses include _____. (a) pressure; (b) pain; (c) warmth and cold; (d) all of these

Answers to Questions can be found in Appendix B.

ACTIVE LEARNING WORKSHEET   MODULE 11

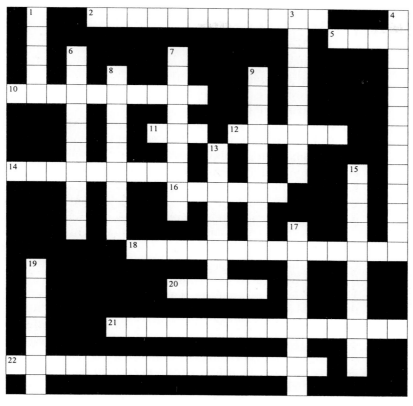

ACROSS

2. Process by which energy stimulating a receptor is converted into neural impulses.

5. Visual receptors in the retina that detect black, white, and gray and are responsible for peripheral vision.

10. Airborne chemicals released from one individual that affect another individual's behavior.

11. Visual dimension seen as a particular color; determined by the length of a light wave.

12. Light-sensitive inner surface of the back of the eye containing receptor rods and cones.

14. Sense of taste.

16. Three-part process that converts a particular sensory input into a specific sensation.

18. A visual acuity problem resulting from the cornea and lens focusing an image behind the retina.

20. Visual receptors concentrated near the center of the retina responsible for color vision and fine detail.

21. Theory explaining how we hear lower-pitched sounds.

22. Process of filtering and analyzing incoming sensations that occurs before a neural impulse is sent to the cortex.

DOWN

1. Highness or lowness of tones or sounds, depending on their frequency.

3. Sense of smell.

4. Branch of psychology that studies the relation between attributes of the physical world and our psychological experience of them.

6. Process of selecting, organizing, and interpreting sensory data into usable mental representations of the world.

7. How often a light or sound wave cycles.

8. Height of a light or sound wave.

9. Length of a light or sound wave.

13. Sense of hearing.

15. Theory explaining how we hear higher-pitched sounds.

17. Process of receiving, translating, and transmitting raw sensory data from the external and internal environments to the brain.

19. Three-chambered, snail-shaped structure containing receptors for hearing.

Answers can be found in Appendix B.

MODULE 12
PERCEPTION

At this point, we are ready to move from sensation and the major senses to perception. Keep in mind, however, that the boundary between the two is ambiguous. Look, for example, at Figure 12.1a. What do you see? Most people see splotches of light and dark, but they perceive no real pattern. If you stare long enough, your brain will try to organize the picture into recognizable shapes or objects, as it does when you lie on your back outdoors and gaze at the clouds on a summer's day. Have you seen the image in the photo yet? If not, try rotating the picture (so that the caption is at the top left). Now do you see it? If you still can't, look at Figure 12.1b on the facing page. Before you *perceived* the cow, you *sensed* only light and dark splotches. Only when you could select relevant splotches and organize them into a meaningful pattern were you able to interpret them as the face of a cow.

Normally, our perceptions agree with our sensations, but there are times when they do not. This results in an **illusion**. Illusions are false impressions of the physical world that can be produced by actual physical distortions, as in desert mirages, or by errors in the perceptual process, as in the illusions shown in Figures 12.2 and 12.3. Besides being amusing, illusions provide psychologists with a tool for studying the normal process of perception (e.g., Humphreys and Muller, 2000; Kramer, Hahn, Irwin, & Theeuwes, 2000). (Be careful not to confuse *illusion* with *hallucination* or *delusion*. *Hallucinations* are sensory perceptions that occur without an external stimulus, as in seeing "pulsating flowers" after using LSD [lysergic acid diethylamide] and other hallucinogenic drugs. *Delusions* refer to false beliefs, often of persecution or grandeur, which also may accompany drug or psychotic experiences.)

Perception consists of three basic processes: selection, organization, and interpretation of incoming sensations. We will examine how each process contributes to our perception of the world.

Selection: Extracting Important Messages

The first step in perception is *selection*: choosing where to direct our attention. Three major factors are involved in the decision to pay attention to some stimuli

Illusion *A false impression of the environment*

How do we decide what to pay attention to in our environment?

Figure 12.1a *What is it?*

Figure 12.1b *It's a cow!* Now go back to Figure 12.1a and you will easily perceive a cow.

in our environment and not to others: selective attention, feature detectors, and habituation.

Selective Attention

As you sit reading this text, you may be ignoring sounds from another room or the discomfort of the chair you're sitting on. In almost every situation, there is an excess of sensory information, but the brain manages to sort out the important messages and discard the rest (Folk & Remington, 1998; Kramer, Hahn, Irwin, & Theeuwes, 2000). When you are in a group of people, surrounded by various conversations, you can still select and attend to the voices of people you find interesting. This process is known as **selective attention**.

Feature Detectors

The second major factor in selection is the presence of specialized cells in the brain called **feature detectors** (or *feature analyzers*) that respond only to certain sensory information. In 1959, researchers discovered specialized nerve cells in the optic nerve of a frog, which they called "bug detectors" because they respond only to moving bugs (Lettvin, Maturana, McCulloch, & Pitts, 1959), and in the early 1960s, researchers found feature detectors in cats that respond to specific lines and angles (Hubel, 1963; Hubel & Wiesel, 1965, 1979). Similar studies with humans have found feature detectors in the temporal and frontal lobes that respond maximally to faces, and damage to these areas can produce a condition called *prosopagnosia* (*prospon* means "face" and *agnosia* means "failure to know") (O'Scalaidhe, Wilson, & Goldman-Rakic, 1997). Interestingly, people with this disorder can recognize that they are looking at a face, but cannot say whose face it is — even if it belongs to a relative or friend or is their own, reflected in a mirror.

Certain basic mechanisms for perceptual selection are thus built into the brain, but a certain amount of interaction with the environment is apparently necessary for feature detector cells to develop normally (Crair, Gillespie, & Stryker, 1998). One well-known study demonstrated that kittens raised in a cylinder with vertically or horizontally striped walls develop severe behavioral and neurological impairments (Blakemore & Cooper, 1970) (Figure 12.4). When "horizontal cats" — those raised with only horizontal lines in their environment — were removed from the cylinder and allowed to roam, they could easily jump onto horizontal surfaces but had great difficulty negotiating objects with vertical lines, such as chair legs. The reverse was true for the "vertical cats": They could easily avoid table and

Figure 12.2 *The horizontal–vertical illusion.* Which is longer, the horizontal or the vertical line? People living in areas where they can see long straight lines on the ground, such as roads and shadows of telephone poles, perceive the horizontal line as shorter because of the foreshortening effect.

Selective Attention *The process whereby the brain sorts out, and only attends to, the important messages from the senses*

Feature Detectors *Specialized cells in the brain that respond only to certain sensory information*

Figure 12.3 *The Müller–Lyer illusion.* Which vertical line is longer? Both are actually the same length, but people who live in urban environments normally see the vertical line on the right as longer than the line on the left. This is because they are used to making size and distance judgments from perspective cues created by right angles and horizontal and vertical lines of buildings and streets.

Figure 12.4 *Nature versus nurture.* Kittens reared in a vertical world failed to develop their "innate" ability to detect horizontal lines or objects, whereas the reverse is true for kittens restricted to only horizontal lines. This is because brain cells sensitive to these features deteriorated during the critical (and irreversible) period in visual development.

Habituation *The tendency of the brain to ignore environmental factors that remain constant*

chair legs but never attempted to jump onto horizontal structures. Examination of the visual cortex of these cats revealed that because of their restricted environment, they had failed to develop their potential feature detectors for either vertical or horizontal lines.

Habituation

Another physiological factor important in selecting sensory data is **habituation**, the tendency to ignore environmental factors that remain constant. The brain seems "prewired" to pay more attention to changes in the environment than to stimuli that remain constant. For example, when you buy a new CD, you initially listen carefully to all the songs. Over time, your attention declines and you can play the entire CD and not really notice it. This may not matter with CDs — we can always replace them when we become bored. But this same habituation phenomenon also applies to your friends and love life — and people aren't as easily replaced. Attention and compliments from a stranger are almost always more exciting and "valuable" than from long-time friends and lovers. Unfortunately, some people leave good relationships not realizing that they will soon *habituate* to the new person. (This knowledge is another payoff for studying psychology!)

How does habituation differ from sensory adaptation? Good question. Habituation is a perceptual process that occurs in the brain, whereas sensory adaptation occurs when sensory receptors (in the skin, eyes, ears, and so on) actually decrease the number of sensory messages they send to the brain. This is another example of bottom-up versus top-down processing. Sensory adaptation occurs when you first put on your shoes in the morning. Pressure/touch receptors in your feet send multiple messages to your brain, but with time they *adapt* and send fewer messages. You also habituate and your brain "chooses to ignore" the fact that you're wearing shoes. You only notice when something changes — when you break a buckle or shoelace or get a blister from new shoes.

When given a wide variety of stimuli to choose from, we automatically select stimuli that are *intense, novel, moving, contrasting,* and *repetitious.* Parents and teachers often use these same attention-getting principles, but advertisers and politicians have spent millions of dollars developing them to a fine art. The next time you're watching TV, notice the commercial and political ads. Are they louder or brighter than the regular program (intensity)? Do they use talking dogs, singing frogs, or politicians playing saxophones (novelty)? Is the promoted product or candidate set in *favorable* contrast to the competition? No need to ask about repetition. This is the foundation of all commercial and political ads. Surprisingly, obnoxious advertising does not always deter people from buying the advertised product (or candidate). For sheer volume of sales, the question of whether you like the ad is irrelevant. If they get your attention, that's all that matters.

Check & Review

SELECTION

The selection process allows us to choose which of the billions of separate sensory messages will eventually be processed. **Selective attention** allows us to direct our attention to the most important aspect of the environment at any one time.

Feature detectors are specialized cells in the brain that distinguish between different sensory inputs. The selection process is very sensitive to changes in the environment. We **habituate** to unchanging stimuli and pay attention when stimuli change in intensity, novelty, location, and so on.

Questions

1. Explain how *illusions* differ from *delusions* and *hallucinations.*

2. Specialized cells in the brain called _____ respond only to certain types of sensory information.

3. Explain why "horizontal cats" could jump onto only horizontal surfaces.

4. You write a reminder on a Post-it and stick it on the door, where you see it every day. A month later, you forget your appointment because of the tendency to ignore constant stimuli, which is known as _____. (a) sensory adaptation; (b) selective perception; (c) habituation; (d) selective attention

Answers to Questions can be found in Appendix B.

Organization: Form, Constancies, Depth, and Color

Having selected incoming information, we must organize it into patterns and principles that will help us understand the world. In other words, raw sensory data are like the parts of a watch — they must be assembled in a meaningful way before they are useful. We organize sensory data in terms of *form, constancy, depth,* and *color.*

Form Perception

Look at the first drawing in Figure 12.5. What do you see? Can you draw a similar object on a piece of paper? This is known as an "impossible figure," yet it clearly exists — on this page. The second part of the figure shows a painting by M. C. Escher, a Dutch painter who created striking examples of perceptual distortion. Although drawn to represent three-dimensional objects or situations, the parts don't assemble into logical wholes. Like the illusions studied earlier, impossible figures also help us understand perceptual principles — in this case, the principle of *form organization.*

Gestalt psychologists were among the first to study how the brain organizes sensory impressions. The German word *gestalt* means "whole" or "pattern." Accordingly, Gestaltists emphasized the importance of organization and patterning in enabling us to perceive the whole stimulus rather than perceiving its discrete parts as separate entities. The Gestaltists proposed laws of organization that specify how people perceive form. The most fundamental Gestalt principle or law of organization is that we tend to distinguish between **figure and ground**.

How do we organize stimuli in order to perceive form, constancies, depth, and color?

Figure and Ground *A Gestalt law of perceptual organization stating that our perceptions consist of two aspects: the figure, which stands out and has a definite contour or shape, and the ground, which is less distinct*

Figure 12.5 *Can you explain these "impossible figures?"* When you first glance at figure (a) and the famous painting by M.C. Escher in (b), you detect specific features of the stimuli and judge them as sensible (an example of *bottom-up* processing). But as you try to sort and organize the different elements into a stable, well-organized whole, you realize they don't add up — they're illogical or "impossible" (an example of *top-down processing*).

(a)

(b)

Figure 12.6 *Figure and ground.* What do you see? A vase or two faces looking at one another? Your answer depends on whether your perceptual expectations cause you to see the vase as figure or as ground.

For example, while you are reading this material, your eyes are receiving sensations of black lines and white paper, but your brain is organizing these sensations into letters and words that are perceived against a backdrop of white pages. The letters constitute the figure and the pages constitute the ground. The discrepancy between figure and ground is sometimes so vague that we have difficulty perceiving which is which, as can be seen in Figure 12.6. This is known as a *reversible figure*. The figure and ground and other basic Gestalt principles are summarized in Table 12.1. Although these examples are all visual, each law applies to other modes of perception as well.

Table 12.1 *Basic Gestalt principles of organization.* Figure–ground, proximity, continuity, closure, and similarity are shown here, but the Gestalt principle of contiguity cannot be shown because it involves nearness in time, not visual nearness. Top photo: Maria Martinez (1881(?)–1980), black-on-black jar. Jerry Jacka photography, Museum of New Mexico. Center cartoon: B. Kliban. "July" page from the 1977 Cat Calendar published by Workman Publishing. Copyright Judith Kamman Kliban. Bottom photo: Alexander Calder. The Hostess (1928), Wire construction, $11\frac{1}{2} \times 4\frac{1}{2} \times 11\frac{7}{8}$, The Museum of Modern Art, New York. Gift of Edward M. M. Marburg. Photograph © 1997 The Museum of Modern Art, New York.

GENDER & CULTURAL DIVERSITY

Are the Gestalt Laws Universally True?

Are the Gestalt laws of perception universally true for all people? The Gestalt psychologists conducted most of their work with formally educated people from urban European cultures, but A. R. Luria (1976) wondered whether their laws held true for all participants, regardless of their type of education and cultural setting. In what is now a classic study, Luria recruited a wide range of participants living in what was then the USSR, including Ichkeri women from remote villages (with no formal education), collective farm activists (who were semiliterate), and female students in a teachers' school (with years of formal education).

Luria found that when presented with the stimuli shown in Figure 12.7, the formally trained female students were the only ones who identified the shapes by their categorical names. That is, whether circles were made of solid lines, incomplete lines, or solid colors, they called them all circles. However, the other two groups named the shapes according to the objects they resembled. They called a circle a watch, plate, or moon, and referred to the square as a mirror, house, or apricot-drying board. When asked if items 12 and 13 from Figure 12.7 were alike, one woman answered, "No, they're not alike. This one's not like a watch, but that one's a watch because there are dots" (p. 37).

Apparently, the Gestalt laws of perceptual organization are valid only for people who have been schooled in geometrical concepts. But an alternative explanation for Luria's findings has also been suggested. Luria's study, as well as most research on visual perception and optical illusions, relies on two-dimensional presentations — either on a piece of paper or projected on a screen. It may be that experience with pictures and photographs (not formal education in geometrical concepts) is necessary for learning to interpret two-dimensional figures as portraying three-dimensional forms. Westerners who have had years of practice learning to interpret two-dimensional drawings of three-dimensional objects may not remember how much practice it took to learn the cultural conventions about judging the size and shape of objects drawn on paper (Matsumoto, 2000; Price & Crapo, 1999).

Figure 12.7 *Luria's stimuli.* When you see these shapes, you readily identify them as circles, triangles, and other geometric forms. According to cross-cultural research, this is due to your formal educational training. If you were from a culture without formal education, you would probably identify them as familiar objects in your environment — "the circle is like the moon."

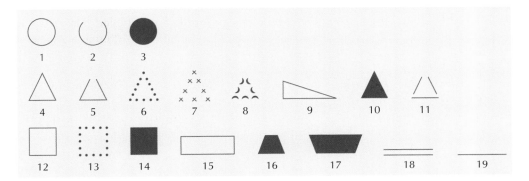

Perceptual Constancy *The tendency for the environment to be perceived as remaining the same even with changes in sensory input*

Perceptual Constancies

Now that we've seen how form perception contributes to organization, let's examine perceptual constancies. As noted earlier with sensory adaptation and habituation, we are particularly alert to change. However, we also manage to perceive a great deal of consistency in the environment. Without **perceptual constancy** our world would be totally chaotic. Things would seem to grow as we got closer to them, to change shape as our viewing angle changed, and to change color as light levels changed. The four best-known constancies are visual:

1. *Size constancy.* Most perceptual constancies are based on prior experience and learning. For example, preschoolers express wonder at the fact that the car parked down the street is only "this high" (as they show about 2 inches between their fingers), whereas the car they are standing next to is taller than they are. Their size judgment is mistaken because they haven't yet had the experiences necessary for learning size constancy. According to this principle, the perceived size of an object remains the same even though the size of its retinal image changes.

Anthropologist Colin Turnbull (1961) provided a now classic example of an adult who had never developed a sense of size constancy. While studying the Twa people living in the dense rain forest of the Congo River valley in Africa, Turnbull took a native named Kenge for a Jeep ride to the African plains. Kenge had lived his entire life in an area so dense with foliage that he had never seen distances farther than about 100 yards. Now he was suddenly able to see for almost 70 miles. Lacking perceptual experience with such wide-open spaces, Kenge had great difficulty judging sizes. When he first saw a herd of water buffalo in the distance, he thought they were insects. When Turnbull insisted they were buffalo that were very far away, Kenge was insulted and asked, "Do you think that I am ignorant?" To Kenge's surprise, as they drove toward the "insects," the creatures seemed to grow into buffalo. He concluded that witchcraft was being used to fool him, and after Turnbull showed him a lake so large that its opposite shore couldn't be seen, he asked to be taken back to his rain forest.

2. *Shape constancy.* Other constancies also develop through individual experience. When you look at a chair directly from the front or the back, it has a rectangular shape. When you look at it directly from the side, it has an h shape. Yet you still perceive the chair as having a single shape because your brain remembers past experiences with objects that only seemed to change shape as you moved but actually remained constant. This is known as *shape constancy.*

An ophthalmologist named Adelbert Ames demonstrated the power of shape and size constancies by creating what is now known as the Ames room (see photographs on next page). On examining this photograph, you might conclude that the person on the left is a midget and the person on the right is a giant. In actuality, both people are normal size. This illusion is based on the unusual construction of the room. As can be seen in the diagram in Figure 12.8, perspective tricks the observer into perceiving the room as square when it is actually shaped like a trapezoid. The illusion is so strong that when a person walks from the left corner to the right, the observer perceives the person to be "growing," even though that is not possible.

If we know the truth of this illusion, why does it still work? Our brain has had a lifetime of interaction with normally constructed rooms, and our desire to perceive the room according to our experience is so powerful that we overrule the truth. This is not a breakdown in perception but rather a result of trying to apply

The Ames room illusion. In the left photo, the woman on the right appears much taller than the boy on the left, but when they reverse positions (the right photo) the boy is taller. For an explanation of how this is possible, see Figure 12.8.

the standard perceptual processes of shape and size constancy to an unusual situation.

3. Color constancy and **4. Brightness constancy.** Other forms of constancy that add stability to our world are *color constancy* and *brightness constancy*. These enable us to perceive things as retaining the same color or brightness levels even though the amount of light may vary. For example, if you place a piece of gray paper in bright sunlight and a piece of white paper in shade, you will still perceive the white as lighter and the gray as darker. This is true regardless of the amount of reflected light actually coming from their surfaces. If you know an object from prior experience, you expect it will be the same color and the same relative brightness in bright light as in low light. That is, you expect it to be its "right" color.

As is the case with shape and size constancy, color constancy and brightness constancy are learned as a result of experience with familiar objects. If an object is unfamiliar, we determine its color and brightness by the actual wavelength of reflected light in combination with the color and brightness of the background.

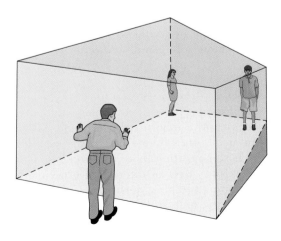

Figure 12.8 *Explanation for the Ames room illusion.* To the viewer peering through the peephole, the room appears perfectly normal. However, in this specially constructed room, the trapezoidal shape and sloping ceilings and floors provide misleading depth cues. Because the brain assumes the two people are the same distance away, it compensates for the differences in retinal size by making the person on the left appear much smaller.

Check & Review

ORGANIZATION — FORM AND CONSTANCIES

The Gestalt psychologists set forth laws explaining how people perceive form. The most fundamental principle is the distinction between **figure and ground**. Other principles include proximity, continuity, closure, contiguity, and similarity. Through the **perceptual constancies** of size, shape, color, and brightness, we are able to perceive a stable environment, even though the actual sensory information we receive may be constantly changing.

These constancies are based on our prior experiences and learning.

Questions

1. Name the Gestalt principle that is being described: (a) You see a black line on the concrete and realize that it is a single trail of ants. (b) You can read a sentence on a bulletin board even if someone is standing in front of a few words. (c) You see a circle even though part of its curve is erased in three spots.

2. The principle of _____ is at work when, as your brother walks away from you, you don't perceive him to be shrinking.

3. The principle of _____ allows us to see a white blouse as white both in sunlight and in shade.

4. As a flock of Canadian geese flies overhead in its familiar V formation, the geese are seen as _____ and the sky as _____. (a) continuity, a closure; (b) a sensation, perception; (c) figure; ground; (d) ground, figure

Answers to Questions can be found in Appendix B.

Depth Perception *By organizing perception in three-dimensions — even though the images that strike the retina are two-dimensional — we can perceive distance*

At first sight. In this love story, Val Kilmer stars as blind masseur who undergoes experimental surgery to have his sight restored. To the audience's surprise, Kilmer is not completely happy as a sighted person.

Depth Perception

The role of experience and learning in organizing perceptions is particularly clear in depth perception. **Depth perception** allows us to accurately estimate the distance of perceived objects and thereby perceive the world in three dimensions. It is possible to judge the distance of objects with nearly all senses. For example, if a person enters a dark room and walks toward you, his or her voice and footsteps get louder, and body smells grow stronger, and you may even be able to feel the slight movement of air from his or her approaching movement. However, in most cases, we rely most heavily on vision to perceive distance. When you add the ability to accurately perceive distance to the ability to judge the height and width of an object, you are able to perceive the world in three dimensions. But no matter which sense you use to perceive the three-dimensional world, perception of depth is primarily learned.

Take the classic example of a patient known as S. B., blind since the age of 10 months, whose sight was restored at age 52. Following the operation that removed cataracts from both eyes, S. B. had great difficulty learning to use his newly acquired vision for judging distance and depth. On one occasion, he was found trying to crawl out of the window of his hospital room. He thought he would be able to lower himself by his hands to the ground below, even though the window was on the fourth floor.

Didn't S. B. have some inborn depth and distance perception? The answer is not clear. As you know, one of the most enduring debates in psychology (and other sciences) is the question of "nature versus nurture," inborn versus learned. In this case, naturists argue that depth perception is inborn, whereas nurturists insist it is learned. Today, most scientists think there is some truth in both viewpoints.

Evidence for the innate position comes from a set of interesting experiments with an apparatus called the *visual cliff* (Figure 12.9). The apparatus consists of a tabletop with a slightly raised platform across the middle. On one side of the platform the tabletop is clear glass, with the red-and-white-checked pattern running down the side of the table and onto the floor several feet below the glass, simulating a steep cliff.

When an infant is placed on the platform and is coaxed by his or her mother to crawl to one side of the table, the infant will readily move to the "shallow" side but will hesitate or refuse to move to the "deep" side (Gibson & Walk, 1960). This reaction is given as evidence of innate depth perception — the infant's hesitation is attributed to fear of the apparent cliff.

Although some have argued that by the time infants are crawling and old enough to be tested they may have *learned* to perceive depth, research with babies at 2 months of age will show a change in heart rate when placed on the deep side of the cliff, but not on the shallow side (Banks & Salapatek, 1983). Similar research with baby chickens, goats, and lambs — animals that walk almost immediately after birth — supports the hypothesis that some depth perception is inborn, as these animals hesitate in stepping onto the steep side.

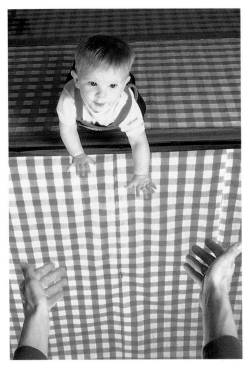

Figure 12.9 *The visual cliff.* Crawling infants generally refuse to move across this glass surface designed to look like the edge of an elevated platform—even when their mothers stood on the opposite side and coaxed them. This suggests they are able to perceive depth.

Once again, the nature–nurture debate continues. However, we all recognize that in our three-dimensional world, the ability to perceive depth and distance is essential. But how do we perceive a three-dimensional world with a two-dimensional receptor system? One mechanism is the interaction of both eyes to produce **binocular cues**; the other involves **monocular cues**, which work with each eye separately.

1. *Binocular cues.* One of the most important cues for depth perception comes from **retinal disparity**. Because our eyes are about $2^{1}/_{2}$ inches apart, each retina receives a slightly different view of the world. You can demonstrate this for yourself by pointing at some distant object across the room with your arm extended straight in front of you. Holding your pointing finger steady, close your left eye and then your right. You will notice that your finger seems to jump from one position to another as you change eyes, because of retinal disparity. The brain fuses the different images received by the two eyes into one overall visual image (Figure 12.10). Such *stereoscopic vision* provides important cues to depth.

As we move closer and closer to an object, a second binocular (and neuromuscular) cue, **convergence**, helps us judge depth. The closer the object, the more our eyes are turned inward, toward our noses (Figure 12.11). Hold your index finger at arm's length in front of you and watch it as you bring it closer and closer until it is right in front of your nose. The amount of strain in your eye muscles created by the convergence, or turning inward of the eyes, is used as a cue by your brain to interpret distance.

Knowing how convergence operates might help you improve your performance in athletic endeavors. Allen Souchek (1986) found that depth perception is better when looking directly at an object, rather than out of the corner of your eye. Thus, if you turn your body or your head so that you look straight at your tennis opponent or the pitcher, you will more accurately judge the distance of the ball and thereby more likely swing at the right time.

2. *Monocular cues.* Retinal disparity and convergence are inadequate in judging distances longer than the length of a football field. According to R. L. Gregory (1969), "we are effectively one-eyed for distances greater than perhaps 100 meters"

Binocular Cues *Visual input from two eyes that allows perception of depth or distance*

Monocular Cues *Visual input from a single eye alone that contributes to perception of depth or distance*

Retinal Disparity *A binocular cue to distance in which the separation of the eyes causes different images to fall on each retina*

Convergence *A binocular depth cue in which the closer the object, the more the eyes converge, or turn inward*

(a)

(b)

(c)

Figure 12.10 *Retinal disparity.* (a) Stare at your two index fingers a few inches in front of your eyes with their tips a half inch apart. Do you see the "floating finger?" Move it further away and the "finger" will shrink. Move it closer and it will enlarge. (b) Because of retinal disparity, objects at different distances (such as the "floating finger") project their images on different parts of the retina. Far objects project on the retinal area near the nose, whereas near objects project farther out, closer to the ears. (c) "Magic Eye" images take advantage of retinal disparity. Patiently stare at this image while focusing your eyes beyond it. Most people eventually see the three-dimensional image. © Magic Eye 1983 N. E. Thing Enterprises, Inc. Reproduced with permission of Andrews and McMeel. All rights reserved.

(p. 67). Luckily, we have several monocular cues available separately to each eye. Artists use these same monocular cues to create an illusion of depth on a flat canvas, a three-dimensional world on a two-dimensional surface. Figure 12.12 demonstrates six different monocular cues.

Two additional monocular cues — ones that cannot be used by artists — are *accommodation* of the lens of the eye and *motion parallax*. As you learned earlier, *accommodation* refers to changes in the shape of the lens of the eye in response to the distance of the object being focused. For near objects, the lens bulges; for far objects, it flattens. Information from the muscles that move the lens is sent to the brain, which interprets the signal and perceives the distance of the object.

Motion parallax (also known as *relative motion*) refers to the fact that when an observer is moving, objects at various distances move at different speeds across the retinal field. Close objects appear to whiz by, farther objects seem to move slowly, and very distant objects appear to remain stationary. This effect can easily be seen when traveling by car or train. Telephone poles and fences next to the road or track seem to move by very rapidly, houses and trees in the midground seem to move by relatively slowly, and the mountains in the distance seem not to move at all.

Color Perception

We humans may be able to discriminate among 7 million different hues. Is such color perception inborn and culturally universal? Research on many cultures with many different languages suggests that we all seem to see essentially the same colored world (Davies, 1998). Furthermore, studies of infants old enough to focus and move their eyes show that they are able to see color nearly as well as adults (Teller, Peeples, & Sekel, 1978; Werner & Wooten, 1979).

Figure 12.11 *Convergence.* (a) Your eyes turn in to view close objects and (b) turn out to view distant objects.

(a) Perspective

(b) Interposition

(c) Relative size

(d) Texture gradient

Figure 12.12 *Monocular depth cues.* Several monocular depth cues can be seen in this photograph. (a) *Linear perspective* results when parallel lines converge in the distance. (b) *Interposition* results when a close object obscures part of a distant object. (c) *Relative size* is the result of close objects projecting a larger retinal image than distant objects. (d) *Texture gradient* results from the change in perceived texture as the background recedes into the distance. (e) *Aerial perspective* means that faraway objects look fuzzy and blurred compared with near objects because of intervening particles of dust or haze in the atmosphere. (f) *Light and shadow* means that brighter objects are perceived as closer, whereas darker objects are perceived as farther away.

Figure 12.13 *Color-deficient vision.* People who suffer red–green deficiency have trouble perceiving the number within the design.

Trichromatic Theory *The theory first proposed by Thomas Young stating that color perception results from mixing three distinct color systems — red, green, and blue*

Opponent-Process Theory *The theory first proposed by Ewald Hering that color perception is based on three systems of color opposites — blue–yellow, red–green, and black–white*

Although we know color is produced by different wavelengths of light, the actual way in which we perceive color is a matter of scientific debate. Traditionally, there have been two theories of color vision, the trichromatic (three-color) theory and the opponent-process theory. The **trichromatic theory** (from the Greek *tri-*, "three," and *chroma*, "color") was first proposed by Thomas Young in the early nineteenth century and was later refined by Hermann von Helmholtz and others. It states that there are three "color systems," as they called them — one system that is maximally sensitive to blue, another maximally sensitive to green, and another maximally sensitive to red (Young, 1802). The proponents of this theory demonstrated that mixing lights of these three colors could yield the full spectrum of colors we perceive. Unfortunately, this theory has two major flaws. One is that it doesn't explain defects in color vision; the other is that it doesn't explain *color aftereffects*, a phenomenon you can experience in the Try This Yourself feature on this page.

The **opponent-process theory**, proposed by Ewald Hering later in the nineteenth century, also proposes three color systems, but with the stipulation that each is sensitive to two opposing colors — blue and yellow, red and green, black and white — in an "on–off" fashion. In other words, each color receptor responds either to blue or yellow or to red or green, with the black-or-white system responding to differences in brightness levels. This theory makes a lot of sense because when different colored lights are combined, people are unable to see reddish greens and bluish yellows; in fact, when red and green lights or blue and yellow lights are mixed in equal amounts, we see white. The opponent-process theory adequately explains color vision defects, because most people who have a color weakness are unable to see either red and green or blue and yellow.

Are you color-blind? Figure 12.13 provides one type of test. Actually, most color vision defects are weaknesses — color confusion rather than color blindness. Many people who have some color blindness are not even aware of it.

TRY THIS
Yourself

The opponent-process theory also accounts for the phenomenon of color aftereffects — images that are perceived after staring at a particular colored pattern for a period of time. Try staring at the color-distorted American flag for several minutes. Then stare at a plain sheet of white paper. You should get interesting color aftereffects — red in place of green, blue in place of yellow, and white in place of black, a "genuine" American flag.

What happened? As you stared at the figure, the green stripes stimulated only the green channel of the red–green opponent color cells. Several minutes of continuous stimulation fatigued the green channel, whereas the nonstimulated red channel was not fatigued. When you looked at the blank piece of paper, the white stimulated both the red and the green channels equally. Under normal viewing conditions, the red and green channels would have canceled each other out and you would have seen white. However, because the green channel was fatigued, the red channel fired at a higher rate and you therefore saw a red color aftereffect.

Two Correct Theories

Judging from the discussion so far, it would seem the opponent-process theory is the correct one. Actually, however, both theories are correct. In 1964, George Wald demonstrated that there are indeed three different types of cones in the retina, each with its own type of photopigment. One type of pigment is sensitive to blue light, one is sensitive to green light, and the third is sensitive to red light.

At nearly the same time that Wald was doing his research on cones, R. L. DeValois (1965) was studying electrophysiological recording of cells in the optic nerve and optic pathways to the brain. DeValois discovered cells that respond to color in an opponent fashion in the thalamus. Thus, it appears that both theories have been correct all along. Color is processed in a trichromatic fashion at the level of the retina (in the cones) and in an opponent fashion at the level of the optic nerve and the thalamus (in the brain).

Check & Review

ORGANIZATION — DEPTH AND COLOR

Depth perception allows us to accurately estimate the distance of perceived objects and thereby perceive the world in three dimensions. But how do we perceive a three-dimensional world with two-dimensional receptors called eyes? There are two major types of cues: **binocular cues**, which require two eyes, and monocular cues, which require only one eye. The binocular cues are **retinal disparity** and **convergence**. **Monocular cues** include linear perspective, aerial perspective, texture gradients, interposition, light and shadow, relative size, accommodation, and motion parallax.

Color perception is explained by a combination of two color theories. The **trichromatic theory** proposes three color systems maximally sensitive to blue, green, and red. The **opponent-process theory** also proposes three color systems but holds that each is sensitive to two opposing colors — blue and yellow, red and green, and black and white — and that they operate in an on–off fashion. The trichromatic system operates at the level of the retina, whereas the opponent-process system occurs in the brain.

Questions

1. The visual cliff is an apparatus designed to study _____ in young organisms. (a) color discrimination; (b) shape constancy; (c) depth perception; (d) monocular vision.

2. Since Jolly Roger, the pirate, lost one eye in a fight, he can no longer use _____ as a cue for the perception of depth and distance. (a) accommodation; (b) retinal disparity; (c) motion parallax; (d) aerial perspective.

3. After staring at a bright red rectangle for a period of time, a phenomenon known as _____ occurs, which means that if you look away and at a white background, you will see a _____.

4. Explain how the trichromatic theory of color perception differs from the opponent-process theory.

Answers to Questions can be found in Appendix B.

Interpretation: Explaining Our Perceptions

After selectively sorting through incoming sensory information and organizing it into patterns, the brain uses this information to explain and make judgments about the external world. This final stage of perception — interpretation — is influenced by several factors, including perceptual adaptation, perceptual set, individual motivation, and frame of reference.

1. *Perceptual adaptation.* What would it be like if your visual field was inverted and reversed? You would certainly have trouble getting around. Things that you expected to be on your right would be on your left, and things you expected to be above your head would be below your head. Do you think you could ever *adapt* to this distorted world?

To answer such a question, psychologist George Stratton (1897) wore special lenses for 8 days. For the first few days, Stratton had a great deal of difficulty navi-

What factors influence how we interpret sensations?

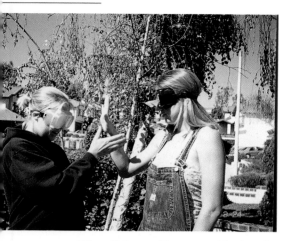

What if the world were upside down? The student on the right is wearing inverting lenses that literally turn the world upside down–the sky is down, the ground is up. The one on the left is wearing displacement goggles that shift the apparent location of objects 40 degrees to the left. Both have difficulty shaking hands. However, the human brain adapts to this type of distortion relatively quickly, and eventually the upside down world would appear normal.

Perceptual Set *A readiness to perceive in a particular manner, based on expectations*

gating in this environment and coping with everyday tasks. But by the third day, his experience had begun to change and he noted:

> Walking through the narrow spaces between pieces of furniture required much less care than hitherto. I could watch my hands as they wrote, without hesitating or becoming embarrassed thereby.

By the fifth day, Stratton had almost completely adjusted to his strange perceptual environment. His expectations of how the world should be arranged had changed.

2. *Perceptual set.* Our previous experiences, assumptions, and expectations also affect how we interpret and perceive the world. If a car backfires, runners at a track meet may jump the gun. People who believe that extraterrestrials occasionally visit the earth may interpret a weather balloon or an odd-shaped cloud as a spaceship. These mental predispositions, or **perceptual sets**, prepare us in a certain way and greatly influence our perception — in other words, we largely see what we expect to see. Studies that used the famous reversible figure of the young/old woman that you saw on page 128 found that when people are led to expect either a young woman or an old woman generally see the one they expect (Leeper, 1935). Perceptual set also explains why labels such as *mental patient*, *nerd*, *fag*, or *bitch* can lead to painful and dangerous forms of prejudice and discrimination.

3. *Individual motivation.* How we interpret what we perceive is also influenced by our personal interests and needs. Stephan, Berscheid, and Walster (1971) found that sexually aroused men judged photographs of women as more attractive than did nonaroused males, and this reaction was particularly strong when the men believed they would actually have dates with the women.

4. *Frame of reference.* Our perceptions of people, objects, or situations are also affected by their frame of reference, or context. A man might judge a woman's photograph attractive when seen by itself, but he might judge it unattractive if it is seen next to a photo of a Miss America.

Perceptual set. Do you notice anything unusual in this photo? What happens when you turn the book upside down? Despite the distortion, most people see the first photo as normal because of perceptual set.

Subliminal Perception and ESP: Are They for Real?

Does *subliminal perception* really exist? Can people really send and receive messages about the world by using *extrasensory perception* (ESP)? What are the facts?

Subliminal Perception

Several years ago, it was popular to believe that movie theaters were manipulating consumers by subliminally presenting messages like "Eat popcorn" and "Drink Coca-Cola." Similarly, record companies were supposedly embedding subliminal messages in rock music that encouraged violence and sex in listeners. The words on the movie screen and the messages in the music were allegedly presented so quickly that they were below the threshold for awareness. The public was both fascinated and outraged. Politicians rushed to pass laws against the "invisible sell" and the "moral corruption" of our youth. Were they right to be concerned?

There are two major issues surrounding *subliminal perception*. First, is it possible to perceive something without conscious awareness? The answer is clearly yes. Scientific research on **subliminal** (literally, "below the threshold") stimuli demonstrates that information processing does occur even when we are not aware of it (Bargh, 1999; Dimberg, Thunberg, & Elmehed, 2000; Greenwald & Banaji, 1995).

Experimental studies commonly use an instrument called a *tachistoscope* to flash images too quickly for conscious recognition but slowly enough to be registered. For example, in one study the experimenter flashed one of two pictures subliminally (either a happy or angry face) followed by a neutral face. They found this subliminal presentation evoked matching unconscious facial expressions in the participant's own facial muscles (Dimberg, Thunberg, & Elmehed, 2000). The fact that participants were unaware of the subliminal stimuli, as well as their own matching facial response, raises questions regarding our own emotional states. (For example, do we unconsciously become a little more "up" or "down" if we're exposed to good-natured, pleasant people or depressed and angry people?) This study also demonstrates that at least some behaviors can be influenced by subliminal stimuli.

Although subliminal perception *does* occur, the second — and more important — question is "Does it lead to *subliminal persuasion*?" The answer to this question is less clear. Subliminal stimuli are basically *weak* stimuli. At best, they have a modest (if any) effect on consumer behavior and absolutely *no effect* on the minds of youth listening to rock music or citizens' voting behavior (Begg, Needham, & Bookbinder, 1993; Trappey, 1996). If you're wondering about buying subliminal tapes promising to help you lose weight or relieve stress, save your money. Blank "placebo" tapes appear to be just as "effective" as subliminal tapes.

In sum, there is evidence that subliminal perception occurs, but the effect on actual behavior is uncertain. When it comes to commercials and self-help tapes, advertisers are better off using the loudest, clearest, and most attention getting

Can we be influenced by subliminal messages, and do some people have ESP?

Subliminal ads and politics? During the 2000 Presidential campaign, Republicans allegedly used subliminal ads (the word "RATS") to create negative perceptions of Democrat drug prescription plans.

Subliminal *Pertaining to any stimulus presented below the threshold of conscious awareness*

Zits

stimuli, and your money and time for self-improvement are better spent on the old-fashioned methods of exercise and diet.

Extrasensory Perception

Extrasensory Perception *Perceptual, or "psychic," abilities that supposedly go beyond the known senses, including telepathy, clairvoyance, precognition, and psychokinesis*

Extrasensory perception (ESP) is the alleged ability to perceive things that cannot be perceived with the normal five senses. People who claim to have ESP, so-called *psychics*, profess to be able to read other people's minds (*telepathy*), perceive objects or events that are inaccessible to their normal senses (*clairvoyance*), predict the future (*precognition*), or move or affect objects without touching them (*psychokinesis*). Popular tabloids are filled with accounts of psychics claiming to be able to find lost children, talk to the dead, or even predict the stock market (Jaroff, 2001; McDonald, 2001).

Scientific investigations of ESP began in the early 1900s with Joseph B. Rhine. Many of these early experiments, as well as those done by subsequent ESP researchers, involved Zener cards, a deck of 25 cards that bear five different symbols — a plus sign, a square, a star, a circle, and wavy lines. When experimenters want to study telepathy, for instance, they ask a "sender" to concentrate on a card; then they ask a "receiver" to try to "read the mind" of the sender. By chance alone, the receiver will guess the symbols on about five of the 25 cards correctly. A participant who consistently scores above "chance" is credited with having ESP.

Using Zener cards, Rhine apparently found a few people who scored somewhat better than chance, but his methodology has been severely criticized, particularly in the area of experimental control. In many early experiments, for example, the Zener cards were so cheaply printed that a faint outline of the symbol could be seen from the back. Also, because experimenters knew which cards were correct, they could unknowingly give participants cues through subtle facial gestures.

The most important criticism of both experimental and casual claims of ESP is their lack of stability and replicability — a core requirement for scientific acceptance. Findings in ESP are notoriously "fragile" (Hyman, 1996). A meta-analysis of 30 studies using scientific controls, such as double-blind procedures and maximum security and accuracy in recordkeeping, reported absolutely no evidence of ESP (Milton & Wiseman, 1999). As one critic pointed out, positive ESP results usually mean "Error Some Place" (Marks, 1990).

ESP and pizza. Can you label the supposed psychic ability of this pizza delivery person?

If ESP is so unreliable, why do so many people believe in it? Our fast-paced technological world and rapid scientific progress lead many people to believe that virtually anything is possible, and *possible* is often translated as *probable*. Because ESP is by nature subjective and extraordinary, people tend to accept it as an explanation for out-of-the-ordinary experiences. Moreover, as mentioned earlier, people's motivations and interests can influence their perceptions. Often, both research participants and researchers are strongly motivated to believe in ESP. They *selectively attend* to things they want to see or hear. In addition, people generally have difficulty processing and evaluating complex scientific information. In the case of psychic abilities, it is hard to distinguish chance and coincidental events from the multitude of experiences in daily life.

But the most important underlying reason for why people believe in ESP is that they want to. A quick glance at children's fairy tales, comic books, and popular movies finds an abundance of superhuman characters and violations of the laws of physics. It seems that release from natural law is one of the most common and satisfying human fantasies. When it comes to ESP, people eagerly engage in a process known as "the willing suspension of disbelief." We seem to have a hard time accepting our finiteness, and a belief in psychic phenomena offers an increased feeling of power and control.

A Final Note

Modules 11 and 12 discuss a number of internal and external factors that affect sensation as well as all three stages of perception — selection, organization, and interpretation. In upcoming modules, we will continue our study of perception by examining how incoming sensory information is processed and retrieved in the different types of memory, how perception develops in infants, and how we perceive ourselves and others.

Helen Keller recognized how crucial sensation and perception are to our lives. She learned to "see" and "hear" with her sense of touch and often recognized visitors by their smell or by vibrations from their walk. Despite the heightened sensitivity of her functioning senses, however, Keller professed a lifelong yearning to experience a normal sensory world. She gave this advice to those whose senses are "normal":

I who am blind can give one hint to those who see: use your eyes as if tomorrow you would be stricken blind. And the same method can be applied to the other senses. Hear the music of voices, the song of a bird, the mighty strains of an orchestra as if you would be stricken deaf tomorrow. Touch each object as if tomorrow your tactile sense would fail. Smell the perfume of flowers, taste with relish each morsel as if tomorrow you could never smell and taste again. Make the most of every sense; glory in all the facets of pleasure and beauty that the world reveals to you through the several means of contact which nature provides. [1962, p. 23]

Check & Review

INTERPRETATION, SUBLIMINAL PERCEPTION, AND ESP

Interpretation, the final stage of perception, can be influenced by perceptual adaptation, **perceptual set,** individual motivation, and frame of reference. **Subliminal** (below the threshold) messages can be perceived without our knowing awareness. However, there is little or no evidence of subliminal persuasion. **Extrasensory perception** (ESP) is the supposed ability to perceive things that go beyond the normal senses. ESP research has produced "fragile" results, and critics condemn its lack of experimental control and replicability.

Questions

1. George Stratton's research is important because it demonstrated _____. (a) the role of learning in perception; (b) innate factors in human perception; (c) the difference between sensation and perception; (d) the ability of the retina to invert images.

2. Experiments on subliminal perception have _____. (a) supported the existence of the phenomenon but it has little or no effect on persuasion; (b) shown that subliminal perception occurs only among children and some adolescents; (c) shown that subliminal messages affect only people who are highly suggestible; (d) failed to support the phenomenon.

3. The supposed ability to read other people's minds is called _____, perceiving objects or events that are inaccessible to the normal senses is known as _____, predicting the future is called _____, and moving or affecting objects without touching them is known as _____.

4. A major criticism of studies that indicate the existence of ESP is that they _____.

Answers to Questions can be found in Appendix B.

Problems with Believing in Extrasensory Perception

The subject of extrasensory perception (ESP) often generates not only great interest but also strong emotional responses. And when individuals feel strongly about an issue, they sometimes fail to recognize the faulty reasoning underlying their beliefs. Belief in ESP is particularly associated with illogical, noncritical thinking. This exercise gives you a chance to practice your critical thinking skills as they apply to ESP. Begin by studying the following types of faulty reasoning:

1. *Fallacy of positive instances:* Noting and remembering events that confirm personal expectations and beliefs (the "hits") and ignoring nonsupportive evidence (the "misses"). Remembering the time the palmist said you would receive a call in the middle of the night (a "hit") but ignoring that she also said that you had three children (a "miss").

2. *Innumeracy:* Failing to recognize chance occurrences for what they are owing to a lack of training in statistics and probabilities. Unusual events are misperceived as statistically impossible (such as predicting a president's illness), and extraordinary explanations, such as ESP, are seen as the logical alternative.

3. *Willingness to suspend disbelief:* Refusing to engage one's normal critical thinking skills because of a personal need for power and control. Although few people would attribute a foreign country's acquisition of top-secret information to ESP, some of these same individuals would willingly believe that a psychic could help them find their lost child.

4. *The "vividness" problem:* Human information processing and memory storage and retrieval are often based on the initial "vividness" of the information. Sincere personal testimonials, theatrical demonstrations, and detailed anecdotes easily capture our attention and tend to be remembered better than rational, scientific descriptions of events. This is the heart of most stories about extraterrestrial visitations.

Now decide which type of faulty reasoning *best* describes each of the following. Although more than one type may be applicable, enter only one number beside each report. Comparing your answers with your classmates' and friends' answers will further sharpen your critical thinking skills.

_____ John hadn't thought of Paula, his old high school sweetheart, for years. Yet one morning he woke up thinking about her. He was wondering what she looked like and whether she was married now, when suddenly the phone rang. For some strange reason, he felt sure the call was from Paula. He was right. John now cites this call as evidence for his personal experience with extrasensory perception.

_____ A psychic visits a class in introductory psychology. He predicts that out of this class of 23 students, 2 individuals will have birthdays on the same day. When a tally of birthdays is taken, his prediction is supported and many students leave class believing that the existence of ESP has been supported.

_____ A National League baseball player dreams of hitting a bases-loaded triple. Two months later, during the final game of the World Series, he gets this exact triple and wins the game. He informs the media of his earlier dream and the possibility that ESP exists.

_____ A mother is sitting alone in her office at work and suddenly sees a vivid image of her home on fire. She immediately calls home and awakens the sitter, who excitedly reports smoke coming under the door. The sitter successfully extinguishes the fire, and the mother later attributes her visual images to ESP.

ACTIVE LEARNING WORKSHEET MODULE 12

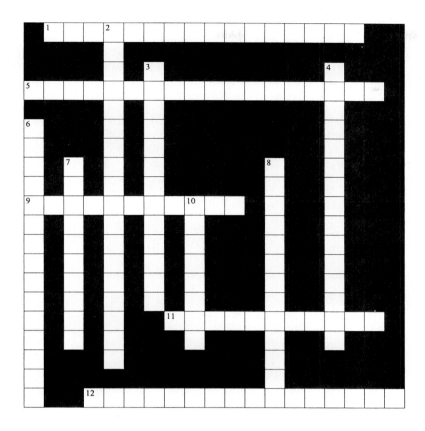

ACROSS

1. Specialized cells in the brain that respond only to certain sensory information.

5. The process whereby the brain sorts out and attends only to the important messages from the senses.

9. The tendency of the brain to ignore environmental factors that remain constant.

11. A binocular depth cue in which the closer the object, the more the eyes converge, or turn inward.

12. A binocular cue to distance in which the separation of the eyes causes different images to fall on each retina.

DOWN

2. The theory first proposed by Thomas Young stating that color perception results from mixing three distinct color systems — red, green, and blue.

3. Visual input from two eyes that allows perception of depth or distance.

4. A Gestalt law of perceptual organization stating that our perceptions consist of two aspects: the figure, which stands out and has a definite contour or shape, and the ground, which is more distinct.

6. By organizing perception in three-dimensions— even though the images that strike the retina are two-dimensional-we can perceive distance.

7. Pertaining to any stimulus presented below the threshold of conscious awareness.

8. Visual input from a single eye alone that contributes to perception of depth or distance.

10. A false impression of the environment.

Answers can be found in Appendix B.

Visual Summary for Modules 11 and 12

Experiencing Sensations

Sensation: Input of sensory information
Perception: Brain's interpretation of sensory input.

Processing

To process sensations, we need:
- **Receptors:** Body cells that detect and respond to stimulus energy.
- **Transduction:** A process of converting receptor energy into neural impulses the brain can understand.
- **Sensory reduction:** Filtering and analyzing of sensations before messages are sent to the brain.
- **Coding:** A three-part process that converts sensory input into specific sensations (sight, sound, touch, etc.).

Thresholds

Absolute threshold: Smallest *magnitude* of a stimulus we can detect
Difference threshold: Smallest *change* in a stimulus we can detect

Adaptation

Sensory adaptation: Decreased sensory response to continuous stimulation.

How We See and Hear

Vision

Light is a form of energy and part of the *electromagnetic spectrum*. Light waves vary in:

1) *Length* (the **wavelength** of a light determines **frequency**, which creates **hue**, or color)
2) *Height* (the **amplitude** determines intensity or brightness)
3) *Range* (the mixture of length and amplitude determines complexity or saturation)

Eye anatomy and function

The eye captures light and focuses it on visual receptors, which convert light energy to neural impulses sent along to the brain.

Parts of the Eye

- *Cornea:* Clear bulge at front of eye, where light enters.
- *Pupil:* Hole through which light passes into eye.
- *Iris:* Colored muscles that surround pupil.

- *Lens:* Elastic structure that bulges and flattens to focus an image on retina (a process called **accommodation**).
- **Retina:** Contains visual receptor cells, called **rods** (for night vision) and **cones** (for color vision and fine detail).

Hearing

Audition (or hearing) occurs via *sound waves*, which result from rapid changes in air pressure caused by vibrating objects. Sound waves vary in:

1) *Length* (the wavelength of a sound determines frequency, which corresponds to **pitch**)
2) *Height* (the amplitude of a sound determines loudness)
3) *Range* (the mixture of a sound wave determines timbre)

Ear anatomy and function

Outer ear conducts sound waves to *eardrum*, which vibrates tiny bones of middle ear that conduct sound vibrations to oval window. Movement of the oval window creates waves in **cochlea**, which contains *hair cells* (receptors for hearing) that convert sound energy to neural impulses sent along to the brain.

Our Other Senses

Smell and Taste

Olfaction (sense of smell) receptors are in the *olfactory epithelium* at the top of the nasal cavity. *Lock-and-key theory*: We smell different odors because each 3-D odor molecule fits only into one type of receptor.

Gustation (sense of taste) receptors are taste buds clustered within *papillae* of tongue. Four basic tastes: salty, sweet, sour, and bitter.

The Body Senses

Skin senses detect touch (pressure), temperature, and pain.

Vestibular sense (or sense of balance) results from receptors in inner ear.

Kinethesis (body posture, orientation, and body movement) results from receptors in muscles, joints, and tendons.

Perception

Selection

Three major factors:
1) **Selective attention**: The brain sorts out and only attends to most important sensory messages.
2) **Feature detectors**: Specialized brain cells that only respond to specific sensory information.
3) **Habituation**: Tendency of brain to ignore environmental factors that remain constant.

Organization

Four general attributes:
1) **Form**: Gestalt psychologists explain that we perceive form by looking at **figure and ground**, *reversible figure, proximity, continuity, closure, contiguity,* and *similarity*.
2) **Constancy**: Even though actual sensory data may be constantly changing, we perceive the world as stable due to *size constancy, shape constancy, color constancy,* and *brightness constancy*.
3) **Depth**: **Binocular** (2 eyes) **cues** involve **retinal disparity** and **convergence**. **Monocular** (one eye) **cues** include *linear perspective, interposition, relative size, texture gradient, aerial perspective, light and shadow, accomodation,* and *motion parallax*.
4) **Color**: Color perception is a combination of two theories: **trichromatic theory**, which says we have 3 color systems maximally sensitive to blue, green, and red. And **opponent-process theory**, which says we have 3 color systems but each is sensitive to two opposing colors (blue and yellow, red and green, black and white).

Interpretation

Four major factors:
1) *Perceptual adaptation*: The brain adapts to changed environment.
2) *Perceptual set*: A readiness to perceive in a particular manner based on expectations.
3) *Individual motivation*: Based on personal interests and needs and context.
4) *Frame of reference*: Based on context of situation.

Subliminal Perception and ESP

Subliminal stimuli occur below the threshold of our conscious awareness, but have a weak effect (if any) on behavior.

Extrasensory perception (ESP) is the supposed ability to perceive things through unknown senses, but research results are "fragile," lack experimental control, and are nonreplicable.

States of Consciousness

On September 4, 1974, an Eastern Airlines flight from Charleston, South Carolina, to Charlotte, North Carolina, crashed, killing the pilot, Captain James Reeves, all of his flight crew, and 68 passengers. The week before, Captain Reeves's hectic work schedule was filled with long flights, erratic start times, and work shifts that began anywhere from early morning to late night. Approximately 30 minutes before the crash, Captain Reeves checked in with the Charlotte control tower. Sounding tired and depressed, Reeves complained, "Rest. That's what I need is rest. I don't need all of this [expletive] flying" (cited in Coren, 1996, p. 227).

In October 1996, President Bill Clinton signed into law a bill adding an extra 20 years to a criminal's prison sentence if a certain drug was used to incapacitate the criminal's victim. This was the first time in U.S. history that using a drug was considered a weapon and classified as a crime. What is the drug? Rohypnol — also known as the "date rape drug." Colorless, odorless, and tasteless when dissolved in liquid, Rohypnol can easily be slipped into any drink. Unsuspecting victims have reported waking up naked in fraternity houses, on beaches, or in the homes of their dates, with no recall of the previous several hours (Tattersall, 2000). In addition to the horror of rape and the possibility of sexually transmitted diseases and pregnancy, Rohypnol can also lead to respiratory depression and death.

On March 13, 2000, Time magazine declared, "Americans are in love with Ecstasy" (Barnes, Graft, Reaves, & Shannon, 2000, p. 66). Once used for therapeutic purposes and then by elite club hoppers, Ecstasy, known scientifically as MDMA, is now flooding college dorms, rave parties, and high school campuses. Why? According to users, "it's fun." College students describe melting into "cuddle puddles," groups of writhing individuals massaging and embracing one another on the dance floor. They report that their skin feels "tremblingly alive when caressed." According to 23-year-old, "Katrina," "A

guy touching your skin with a cold drink. It's delicious." What do these three stories have in common? All the situations involve an altered state of consciousness: a fatigued pilot surrendering to much-needed sleep, unsuspecting dates slipping into unconsciousness and amnesia, and party-goers seeking out "cuddle puddles."

What do we mean by "altered consciousness?" And when does a change in consciousness become dangerous? In this section, we begin with a general look at the definition and description of **consciousness**, an organism's awareness of its own self and its surroundings (Damasio, 1999). Next, we examine changes in everyday, waking consciousness, known as *altered* or **alternate states of consciousness** (ASCs). ASCs include sleep and dreaming, chemically induced changes from psychoactive drugs, daydreaming, fantasies, hypnosis, and meditation. The section concludes by exploring why humans throughout history and across cultures have sought alternate states of consciousness.

Consciousness *An organism's awareness of its own self and surroundings (Damasio, 1999). Consciousness is always about something. It concerns perceptions (of objects and events), thoughts (including verbal thought and mental images, such as dreams and daydreams), feelings, and actions (Farthing, 1992).*

Alternate States of Consciousness *A mental state other than ordinary waking consciousness, found during sleep, dreaming, psychoactive drug use, hypnosis, and so on; distinct changes typically occur in perception, emotion, memory, time sense, thinking, self-control, and suggestibility*

CONSCIOUSNESS AND SLEEP AND DREAMS

How can we define and describe *consciousness*?

Understanding Consciousness: Definition and Description

How Do We Define It?

Our definition of *consciousness* is fairly simple and currently popular: an organism's awareness of its own self and surroundings. We could have chosen another, because psychologists have many definitions of consciousness. The problem is that the term is difficult to *scientifically* study and define. What, for example, do we mean by "awareness"? What would it be like to be "unaware"? How can we study the contents of our consciousness when the only tool of discovery is the object itself? How can the mind's awareness study itself? Consciousness is a fundamental concept in the field of psychology, yet it eludes simple definition (Damasio, 1999).

In the late nineteenth century, when psychology first became a scientific discipline separate from philosophy, it defined itself as "the study of human consciousness." But such a nebulous area of study eventually led to great dissatisfaction within the field. One group, the behaviorists, led by John Watson, believed that *behavior,* not consciousness, was the proper focus of the new science. In fact, he declared that "the time seems to have come when psychology must discard all references to consciousness; when it need no longer delude itself into thinking that it is making mental states the object of observation" (1913, p. 164).

In recent years, psychology has renewed its original interest in consciousness thanks to research in cognitive and cultural psychology. Also, advances in scientific technology, such as the electroencephalograph (EEG) and positron emission tomography (PET), allow scientific study of brain activity during various states of consciousness. Many neuroscientists believe consciousness will ultimately be linked to patterns of neural activity in the brain, although the precise location or functioning of this "seat of consciousness" has not yet been discovered (Johnson, 2000).

How Do We Describe It?

Consciousness may be easier to *describe* than to define. The first American psychologist, William James, likened consciousness to a stream that's constantly changing yet always the same. It meanders and flows, sometimes where the person wills and sometimes not. Through the process of *selective attention*, we control our consciousness by deliberate concentration and full attention. For example, at the present moment you are (we hope) fully awake and concentrating on the words on this page. At times, however, your control may weaken, and the stream of your consciousness may drift to thoughts of a computer you want to buy, your job, or that attractive classmate sitting nearby.

In line with James's metaphor, modern researchers have found that the "stream of consciousness" also varies in depth. Consciousness is not an all-or-nothing phenomenon — we are not simply conscious or unconscious. Instead, consciousness exists along a continuum, ranging from high awareness and sharp, focused alertness at one extreme, to middle levels of awareness such as daydreaming, to unconsciousness and coma at the other extreme (Table 13.1).

TABLE 13.1 LEVELS OF CONSCIOUSNESS

High level of awareness	Controlled processes	High level of awareness, focused attention required	
Middle level of awareness	Automatic processes	Awareness, but minimal attention required	
	Daydreaming	Low level of awareness and conscious effort, somewhere between active consciousness and dreaming while asleep	
Minimal or no awareness	Unconscious mind (Freudian)	Reservoir of unacceptable thoughts, feelings, and memories that are too painful or anxiety provoking to be admitted to consciousness	
	Unconscious (biologically based)	Lowest level of awareness due to head injuries, disease, anesthesia during surgery, or coma	

Levels of Consciousness. Consciousness is not an all-or-nothing phenomenon. Instead, it exists along a continuum, with highly focused awareness at one extreme and minimal or no awareness at the other.

Table 13.1 portrays Freud's concept of the unconscious mind as one step up from true, biological unconsciousness. Freud believed that this lowest level of awareness (the "unconscious") was a reservoir containing thoughts and emotions too embarrassing or threatening to be allowed into conscious awareness. (Freudian theory is discussed more fully in Module 35, and we'll cover daydreaming later in this section.)

Controlled Versus Automatic Processes

Controlled Processes *Mental activities found at one extreme of the continuum of awareness; they require focused attention and generally interfere with other ongoing activities*

Automatic Processes *Mental activities requiring minimal attention; other ongoing activities are generally not affected*

When you're working at a demanding task or learning something new, like how to drive a car, consciousness is at the high end of the continuum. **Controlled processes**, like these, demand focused attention and generally interfere with other ongoing activities. Have you ever been so absorbed during an exam that you completely forgot your surroundings until the instructor announced, "Time is up," and asked for your paper? This type of focused attention is the hallmark of controlled processes.

In contrast, **automatic processes** require minimal attention and generally do not interfere with other ongoing activities. Have you ever wondered why it was so difficult to learn to drive a car, yet now you can listen to the radio, think about your classes, and talk to fellow passengers all while driving? Learning a new task requires complete concentration and *controlled processing,* but once that task is well learned, you can relax and rely on your *automatic processes* (Fanz, Waldie, & Smith, 2000).

Automatic processes are generally helpful. However, there are times when we are on "automatic pilot" and don't want to be. Consider the problems of Novelist Colin Wilson (1967):

> When I learned to type, I had to do it painfully and with much nervous wear and tear. But at a certain stage a miracle occurred, and this complicated operation was "learned" by a useful robot that I conceal in my subconscious mind. Now I only have to think about what I want to say; my robot secretary does the typing. He is really very useful. He also drives the car for me, speaks French (not very well), and occasionally gives lectures at American universities. [My robot] is most annoying when I am tired, because then he tends to take over most of my functions without even asking me. I have even caught him making love to my wife. [p. 98]

Check & Review

UNDERSTANDING CONSCIOUSNESS

Most of our lives are spent in normal, waking **consciousness**, an organism's awareness of its own self and surroundings. However, we also spend considerable time in various **alternate states of consciousness** (ASCs), such as sleep and dreaming, daydreams, sexual fantasies, chemically induced changes from psychoactive drugs, hypnosis, and meditation.

Consciousness has always been difficult to study and define. William James described it as a "flowing stream." Modern researchers emphasize that consciousness exists along a continuum. **Controlled processes**, which require focused attention, are at the highest level of awareness. **Automatic processes**, which require minimal attention, are found in the middle of the continuum. Unconsciousness and coma are at the lowest level of awareness.

Questions

1. _____ is (are) best defined as our awareness of our environments and ourselves. (a) Alternate states of consciousness (ASCs); (b) Consciousness; (c) States of consciousness; (d) Selective attention

2. Why were early psychologists reluctant to study consciousness?

3. Controlled processes require _____ attention, whereas automatic processes need _____ attention.

4. As you read this text, you will likely do best if you _____ . (a) are in an alternate state of consciousness; (b) employ automatic processing; (c) let your stream of consciousness take charge; (d) employ controlled processing

Answers to Questions can be found in Appendix B.

What happens to consciousness while we sleep and dream

Sleep and Dreams: A Mysterious Realm

Having explored the definition and description of everyday, waking consciousness, we now turn to sleep and dreaming — the major forms of ASCs. Although each of us spends almost one-third of our life sleeping and dreaming, these ASCs are widely misunderstood.

Circadian Rhythms

Sleep has always been a welcome but mysterious and sometimes elusive guest in our lives. The ancient Greeks believed the god Morpheus granted — or refused — sleep to mortals. In other words, sleep was a gift.

To understand sleep, you first need to understand that sleep is an integral part of biological, circadian rhythms (Siegel, 2000). Each day, our planet cycles from light to dark and back again. Most animals have adapted to this change by developing a 24-hour cycle of activities, or **circadian rhythms** — in Latin, *circa* means "about" and *dies* means "day."

Although nocturnal animals, such as rats, sleep most of the day and stay awake at night, humans and most other animals are awake during the light times of the 24-hour period and asleep during the dark periods. For humans, circadian rhythms influence not only sleep and waking but also fluctuations in blood pressure, pulse rate, body temperature, blood sugar level, and cell growth (Siegel, 2000).

Circadian [ser-KAY-dee-an] Rhythms *Biological changes that occur on a 24-hour cycle (circa = about, and dies = day)*

TRY THIS
Yourself

Before reading on, test your personal knowledge of sleep and dreaming by reviewing the common myths below.

- **Myth:** *Everyone needs 8 hours of sleep a night to maintain sound mental and physical health.*

  Although most of us average 7.6 hours of sleep a night, some people get by on an incredible 15 to 30 minutes, whereas others need as much as 11 hours (Doghramji, 2000; Maas, 1999). Moreover, in the past 25 years, Americans have reduced their sleep time 20 percent and have added 1 month per year to our average work/commute time (National Sleep Foundation, 2000).

- **Myth:** *It is easy to learn complicated things, like a foreign language, while asleep.*

  Although some learning can occur during the lighter stages (1 and 2) of sleep, the processing and retention of this material is minimal (Aarons, 1976; Ogilvie, Wilkinson, & Allison, 1989). Wakeful learning is much more effective and efficient.

- **Myth:** *Some people never dream.*

  In rare cases, adults with certain brain injuries or disorders do not dream (Solms, 1997), but otherwise, adults regularly dream. Even people who firmly believe they never dream report dreams if they are repeatedly awakened during an overnight study in a sleep laboratory. Children also dream regularly. For example, between ages 3 and 8, they dream approximately 20 to 28 percent of their sleep time (Foulkes, 1982, 1993). Apparently, almost everyone dreams, but some people don't remember their dreams.

- **Myth:** *Dreams last only a few seconds.*

  Research shows that dreams seem to occur in "real time;" that is, a dream that seemed to last 20 minutes probably did last approximately 20 minutes (Dement & Wolpert, 1958).

- **Myth:** *When people experience genital arousal during sleep, it means they are having a sexual dream.*

  When sleepers are awakened during this time, they are no more likely to report sexual dreams than at other times (Rechtschaffen & Siegel, 2000).

- **Myth:** *Dreaming of dying can be fatal.*

  This is a good opportunity to exercise your critical thinking skills. Take time to critically evaluate this common belief. Where did this myth come from? Has anyone ever personally experienced and recounted a fatal dream? How would we scientifically prove or disprove this belief?

What controls these circadian rhythms and associated changes like sleep?
Recent research suggests that these changes are automatically regulated by structures in the brain called *biological clocks*. The "clock" is not a single mechanism but a complex set of interrelated physiological operations that may be dictated by our genetic inheritance (Bower, 2000; Dunlap, 1998). The biological "overseer" of this complex set of operations seems to be a group of cells in the hypothalamus, thalamus, and a tiny structure at the base of the brain (the suprachiasmatic nucleus) that are sensitive to the light and dark cycles of day and night (Rechtschaffen & Siegel, 2000).

Disrupted Circadian Rhythms and Sleep Deprivation

Changes in circadian rhythms help explain problems that arise from late-night study sessions and changing work shifts. In addition to meeting the demands of college life, many students also work full or part time and often on rotating shifts. Between studying and working, their sleep cycle changes frequently. Studies show that disruptions in circadian rhythms generally lead to increased fatigue, decreased concentration, sleep disorders, and other health problems (Boiven, Czeisler, & Waterhouse, 1997; Rechtschaffen & Siegel, 2000).

As a student, you may be comforted to know that others share your own complaints. Less comforting is the knowledge that physicians, nurses, police, and other workers also tend to work under less than optimal conditions. In fact, more than 20 percent of employees in the United States (primarily in the fields of health care, data processing, and transportation) have work schedules that change from day to day or week to week (Maas, 1999).

Although some people seem to function well despite these changes, studies do show that shift workers are generally less productive and more accident-prone while on the job (Dement & Vaughan, 1999; Lenne, Triggs, & Redman, 1998; National Sleep Foundation, 2000). In a major review of Japanese near-collision train incidents, 82 percent took place between midnight and morning (Charland, 1992).

Some of the worst recent disasters — including the Union Carbide chemical accident in Bhopal, India, the nuclear power plant disaster in Chernobyl, and the Alaskan oil spill from the *Exxon Valdez* — occurred during the night shift. And, as described in the section opener, official investigations of airline crashes often cite pilot shift work as a possible contributing factor. Although it's true that catastrophic accidents can be traced to unusual coincidences, a case could be made that the workers most directly involved were working against the circadian cycle and oriented toward sleep when full alertness was required.

Not only can rotating work schedules disrupt circadian cycles but so can flying across several time zones. Have you ever taken a long airline flight and felt fatigued, sluggish, and irritable for the first few days after arriving? If so, you experienced symptoms of *jet lag*. Like rotating shift work, jet lag correlates with decreased alertness, decreased mental agility, exacerbation of psychiatric disorders, and overall reduced efficiency (Iyer, 2001; Maas, 1999).

Is it true that jet lag is worse when you fly long distances eastward rather than westward? Transcontinental flights in either direction disrupt our circadian cycles, but traveling westward is easier because our bodies adjust more easily to *phase advances* (accelerations of circadian rhythms). Conversely, traveling eastward is harder because our bodies have trouble adjusting to *phase delays* (decelerations of circadian rhythms).

Why our bodies react differently to phase advances and phase delays is somewhat of a mystery. Scientists can only cite research with young adults isolated without daylight or clocks where participants generally move to a 25-hour day (a phase advance) (Moore, 1997). Studies also show that phase advances are less troublesome for women, night owls, extroverted people, and younger people (Kiester, 1997). But again, the reasons are not clear.

Disruptions in circadian cycles due to shift work and jet lag can have serious effects, but what about long-term sleep deprivation? History shows that over 2,000 years ago, during Roman times and in the Middle Ages, sleep deprivation was a form of torture. Today, armies use loud, blaring music and noise to disrupt their enemy's sleep.

Exploring the scientific effects of severe sleep loss is limited by obvious ethical concerns. We do know that after about 72 hours, research participants unwillingly slip into brief, repeated periods of "microsleep," lasting a few seconds at a time. To complicate things, sleep deprivation increases stress, making it difficult to identify what is cause and what is effect.

Despite these problems, sleep researchers have documented several hazards related to sleep deprivation — mood alterations, reduced concentration and motivation, increased irritability, lapses in attention, reduced motor skills, and increased cortisol levels (a sign of stress) (Lenne, Triggs, & Redman, 1998; Pilcher & Huffcutt,

Are you sleep deprived? Take the following two-part test and find out.

Part 1   A typical task used by sleep deprivation researchers is to ask people to trace a star using their nondominant hand while watching their hand in a mirror. Set up a small mirror next to the text and see if you can copy the star below. The task is difficult, and sleep-deprived people typically make many errors when tested at the low point in their circadian cycle.

Sleep deprivation. *Insufficient sleep can seriously affect your college grades—as well as your physical health, motor skills, and overall mood.*

Part 2   Now give yourself one point each time you answer yes to the following questions:

Do you often fall asleep...
watching TV?
during boring meetings or lectures or in warm rooms?
after heavy meals or after a small amount of alcohol?
while relaxing after dinner?
within five minutes of getting into bed?
In the morning, do you generally...
need an alarm clock to wake up at the right time?

struggle to get out of bed?
hit the snooze bar several times to get more sleep?

During the day, do you...
feel tired, irritable, and stressed out?
have trouble concentrating and remembering?
feel slow when it comes to critical thinking, problem solving, and being creative?
feel drowsy while driving?
need a nap to get through the day?
have dark circles around your eyes?

According to Cornell University psychologist James Maas (1999), if you answered yes to three or more items, you probably are not getting enough sleep.

Source: Quiz adapted and reprinted from Maas, 1999 with permission.

1996; Rechtschaffen & Siegel, 2000). Experiments with severe sleep deprivation in rats show even more serious side effects and sometimes death (Rechtschaffen, 1997; Rechtschaffen & Bergmann, 1995). But perhaps the greatest danger associated with sleep deprivation comes from pilots and other workers whose lapses in attention cost many lives (McCartt, Rohrbaugh, Hammer, & Fuller, 2000; Siegel, 2000).

It is interesting to note, however, that many physiological functions are not significantly disrupted by periods of sleep deprivation (Walsh & Lindblom, 1997). In fact, in 1965, a 17-year-old student named Randy Gardner, who wanted to earn a place in the *Guinness Book of World Records,* stayed awake for 264 consecutive hours. He did become irritable and had to remain active to stay awake, but he did not become incoherent or psychotic (Coren, 1996; Spinweber, 1993). Afterward, Randy slept a mere 14 hours and then returned to his usual 8-hour sleep cycle (Dement, 1992).

Stages of Sleep

Sleep is an important component of our circadian rhythms. Each night, we go through four to five cycles of distinct sleep stages, each with a rhythm of its own and corresponding changes in brain and behavior. How do we know this? How can scientists study private mental events like sleep? Surveys and interviews can provide some information about the nature of sleep, but perhaps the most important tool for sleep researchers is the EEG.

As we move from a waking state to deep sleep, our brains show complex and predictable changes in electrical activity. The EEG records these brain wave changes by means of small disklike electrodes placed on the scalp. The electrodes pick up electrical changes in the nerve cells of the cerebral cortex. The changes are then amplified and recorded on a long roll of paper or computer monitor. These recordings, or electroencephalograms, allow researchers to observe the brain's activity while its owner is asleep. Sleep researchers also use other recording devices, such as those seen in Figure 13.1.

Cycling Through the Stages of Sleep

Perhaps the best way to appreciate the methods and findings of sleep researchers is to pretend for a moment that you are a participant in a sleep experiment. When you arrive at the sleep lab, you are assigned one of several "bedrooms." The researcher hooks you up to various physiological recording devices, such as the EEG, EMG, and electrooculograph (EOG). If you are like other participants, you probably need a night or two to adapt to the equipment and return to a normal mode of sleeping.

Figure 13.1 *How sleep is studied.* Researchers in a sleep laboratory use sophisticated equipment to record physiological changes during sleep. Electroencephalograph (EEG) electrodes are taped to the scalp to measure brain wave activity. Electromyograph (EMG) electrodes are applied to the chin and mouth to measure muscular activity. Electrooculograph (EOG) electrodes are taped near the eyes to record eye movements. Other devices not shown in this photo record heart rate, respiration rate, and genital arousal.

Once adapted, you are ready for the researchers to monitor your typical night's sleep. As your eyes close and you begin to relax, the researcher in the next room notices that your EEG recordings have moved from the wave pattern associated with normal wakefulness, *beta waves*, to the slower *alpha waves*, which indicate drowsy relaxation (Figure 13.2). During this relaxed, "presleep" state, you may experience a *hypnagogic state*, which is characterized by feelings of floating, weightlessness, visual images (such as flashing lights or colors), or swift, jerky movements and a corresponding feeling of slipping or falling. Hypnagogic experiences are sometimes incorporated into fragmented dreams and remembered in the morning. They may also explain reported accounts of alien abduction. These alleged encounters typically occur while the victim is falling asleep, and many reports mention "strange flashes of light" and "floating off the bed."

As you continue relaxing, your brain's electrical activity slows even further. You are now in *Stage 1* sleep; your breathing becomes more regular, your heart rate slows, and your blood pressure decreases. At this stage, you could still be readily awakened. No one wakens you, though, so you relax more deeply and slide gently into *Stage 2* sleep. This stage is noted on your electroencephalograph by occasional short bursts of rapid, high-amplitude brain waves known as *sleep spindles*. During Stage 2 sleep, you become progressively more relaxed and less responsive to the external environment. Even deeper levels of sleep follow Stage 2 — *Stages 3 and 4*. As shown in Figure 13.3, these stages are marked by the appearance of slow, high-amplitude *delta waves*. It is very hard to awaken you in the deepest stages of sleep, even by shouting and shaking. (Can you see why it is difficult to learn foreign languages or other material from tapes while sound asleep [Wyatt & Bootzin, 1994]?) Stage 4 sleep is also the time when children are most likely to wet the bed and when sleepwalking occurs.

In about an hour, you progress through all four stages of sleep. Then the sequence begins to reverse itself (see again Figure 13.3). Although we don't necessarily go through all sleep stages in this sequence, during the course of a night people usually complete four to five cycles of light to deep sleep and back. Each cycle lasts about 90 minutes.

Figure 13.3 also shows an interesting phenomenon that occurs at the end of the first cycle. You go back through Stage 3, and then to Stage 2, but instead of reentering the calm, relaxed Stage 1, something totally different happens. Quite abruptly, your scalp recordings display a pattern of small-amplitude, fast wave activity similar in many ways to an awake, vigilant person's brain waves. Your breathing and pulse rates become fast and irregular, and your genitals very likely show signs of arousal (an erection or vaginal lubrication). Although your brain and body are giv-

Figure 13.2 *Electroencephalograph patterns during sleep.* As you move from being awake to deeply asleep, your brain waves decrease in frequency (cycles per second) and increase in amplitude (height). Note how the REM (rapid-eye-movement) sleep waves most closely resemble the pattern in the "presleep," hynagogic state. The brain is more aroused during REM sleep than it is in the lightest level of non-REM sleep, Stage 1.

Figure 13.3 *Stages in a typical night's sleep.* During a normal night's sleep, the sleeper moves in and out of various stages of sleep. Starting off alert, the sleeper gradually shifts downward into Stage 1, then Stages 2, 3, and 4. The sleep cycle then reverses. At the peak of the return trip, the sleeper spends some time in REM (rapid-eye-movement) sleep and then the cycle starts downward again. As the night continues, the sleeper repeats the general cycle four to five times. (The dashed lines indicate the boundaries of each cycle.) Note that the periods of Stage 4 and then Stage 3 sleep diminish during the night, whereas REM periods increase in duration. *Source:* Adapted from Julien, 2000, with permission.

ing many signs of active arousal, your musculature is deeply relaxed and unresponsive. This stage is often referred to as paradoxical sleep because it is in some ways the deepest sleep and in other ways the lightest. (The term *paradoxical* means "apparently self-contradictory.")

REM Sleep

Rapid-Eye-Movement (REM) Sleep *A stage of sleep marked by rapid eye movements, high-frequency brain waves, and dreaming*

During the paradoxical sleep stage, rapid eye movements occur under your closed lids. Thus, another — and more common — name for paradoxical sleep is **rapid-eye-movement (REM) sleep**. REM sleep often signals that dreaming is taking place. When researchers awaken participants to ask them whether they have been dreaming, REM awakenings produce dream recall about 80 to 90 percent of the time, whereas the other stages of sleep are accompanied by dream recall a smaller percentage of the time (Rechtschaffen & Siegel, 2000; Squier & Domhoff, 1998). The muscle "paralysis" that occurs during REM sleep may have evolved so that humans will not act out their dreams by running, fighting, or injuring themselves (Pressman & Orr, 1997).

What is the purpose of REM sleep? Although the exact function of REM sleep is unknown, we do know that it is the primary time for dreaming. At the same time, memory circuits of the brain are activated by self-generated brain waves primarily during REM sleep. This indicates that REM sleep may play an important role in consolidating new memories (Kavanau, 2000; Squier & Domhoff, 1998). It also plays a role in learning, because animals increase their REM sleep following learning sessions (Hennevin, Hars, Matio, & Bloch 1995). Further evidence of the importance of REM sleep in complex brain functions comes from the fact that it occurs only in mammals of higher intelligence and is absent in nonmammals such as reptiles (Rechtschaffen & Siegel, 2000). There is general agreement that it serves an important biological need. When researchers selectively deprive sleepers of REM sleep (by waking them each time they enter the state), most people experience *REM rebound*. That is, they try to "catch up" on REM sleep on subsequent occasions by spending more time than usual in this state (Dement & Vaughan, 1999).

Non-REM Sleep

Although REM sleep is important to our biological functioning, the need for non-REM sleep may be even greater. When people are deprived of *total* sleep, rather than just REM sleep, and then allowed their recovery sleep, their first uninterrupted night has a greater proportion of non-REM sleep (Borbely, 1982). It seems that

The sleep cycle in cats. *During non-REM (non–rapid-eye-movement) sleep, cats often sleep in an upright position. With the onset of REM sleep, postural muscles are deeply relaxed so the cat rolls over on its side.*

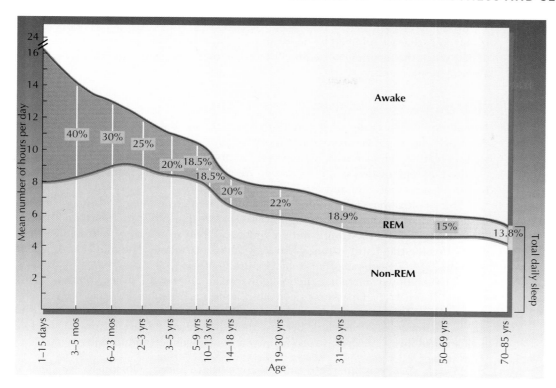

Figure 13.4 *Sleep and dreaming over the life span.* Notice that as you get older, the overall amount of sleep and the proportion of REM (rapid-eye-movement) sleep both decrease. The most dramatic changes occur during the first 2 to 3 years of life. As an infant, you spent almost 8 hours a day in REM sleep, but at age 70, you spend less than an hour.

nature's first need is for non-REM sleep. As you may remember from Figure 13.3, when you initially begin to sleep, you spend more time in Stage 1 sleep through Stage 4 sleep (non-REM). After this need has been satisfied, the latter parts of the night are devoted to more REM sleep.

The idea that nature first satisfies its need for non-REM sleep before going on to REM sleep is also supported by studies showing that adults who are "short sleepers" (5 or fewer hours each night) spend less time in REM sleep than do "long sleepers" (9 or more hours each night). Similarly, infants get more sleep and have a higher percentage of REM sleep than do adults (Figure 13.4). Apparently, the greater the total amount of sleep, the greater the percentage of REM sleep.

Check & Review

CIRCADIAN RHYTHMS AND STAGES OF SLEEP

Circadian rhythms affect our sleep and waking cycle so that disruptions due to shift work and jet lag can cause serious problems.

A typical night's sleep consists of four to five 90-minute cycles. The cycle begins in Stage 1 and then moves through Stages 2, 3, and 4. After reaching the deepest level of sleep, the cycle reverses up to the **REM** (rapid-eye-movement) state, in which the person often is dreaming.

Questions

1. Biological rhythms that occur on a daily basis are called _____ rhythms. (a) circuitous; (b) chronobiology; (c) calendrical; (d) circadian

2. Jet lag results from _____. (a) sleep deprivation; (b) disruption of the circadian rhythms; (c) the effect of light on the pineal gland; (d) disruption of brain wave patterns that occur at high altitudes.

3. The machine that measures the voltage (or brain waves) that the brain produces is the _____.

4. Just before sleep, brain waves move from _____ waves, indicating normal wakefulness, to _____ waves associated with drowsy relaxation. (a) beta, alpha; (b) theta, delta; (c) alpha, beta; (d) sigma, chi

Answers to Questions can be found in Appendix B.

Theories of Sleep and Dreaming

It's obvious that we all need to sleep, and for thousands of years humans have speculated about the meaning of dreams. In this section, we will discuss theories of sleep and dreaming.

Why Do We Sleep?

No one knows precisely what functions sleep serves, but there are two prominent theories. The **repair/restoration theory** suggests that sleep helps us recuperate from depleting, daily activities. Essential factors in our brain or body are apparently repaired or replenished while we sleep. We recover not only from physical fatigue but also from emotional and intellectual demands.

The **evolutionary/circadian theory** emphasizes the relationship of sleep to basic circadian rhythms. According to this view, sleep evolved so animals could conserve energy when they were not foraging for food or seeking mates. Sleep also serves to keep them still at times when predators are active (Hirshkowitz, Moore, & Minhoto, 1997; Rechtschaffen & Siegel, 2000).

The evolutionary/circadian theory helps explain differences in sleep patterns across species (Figure 13.5). Opossums sleep many hours each day because they are relatively safe in their environment and are able to easily find food and shelter. In comparison, sheep and horses sleep very little because their diets require constant foraging for food and because their only defense against predators is vigilance and running away.

Which theory is correct? Both theories have merit. Obviously, we need to repair and restore ourselves after a busy day. But bears don't hibernate all winter simply to recover from a busy summer. Like humans and other animals, they also need to conserve energy when the environment is hostile. It may be that sleep initially served to conserve energy and keep us out of trouble, and over time it has evolved to allow for repair and restoration.

Is there a known biological cause for sleep? Some researchers have looked for a specific neurotransmitter. But the answer is not that simple. For example, the neurotransmitter acetylcholine plays a complicated role in arousal. Have you ever noticed how coffee, tea, or colas wake you up when you're feeling tired? The caffeine in these drinks increases arousal by blocking the chemical that inhibits acetylcholine (Rainnie, Grunze, McCarley, & Greene, 1994). In other words, by inhibiting an inhibitor, the net effect is increased arousal. Both acetylcholine and other neurotransmitters, such as serotonin and norepinephrine, affect sleep (Hobson & Silvestri, 1999). In addition, pathways within the brain that contribute to arousal

Repair/Restoration Theory *The theory that sleep serves a recuperative function, allowing organisms to repair or replenish key factors in the brain or body that are depleted during daytime activities*

Evolutionary/Circadian Theory *The theory that sleep is a part of circadian rhythms and evolved as a means of conserving energy and protecting individuals from predators*

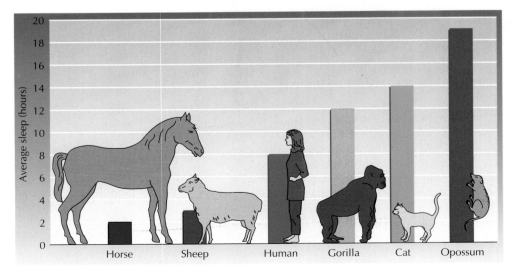

Figure 13.5 *Average daily hours of sleep for different mammals.* According to the evolutionary/circadian theory of sleep, animals that sleep the longest are least threatened by the environment and can easily find food and shelter. Note how the opossum and cat spend longer hours in sleep than the horse and sheep, presumably because of differences in diet and the number of predators.

use histamine as their neurotransmitter, which helps explain why allergy sufferers feel drowsy when they take antihistamine drugs (Lin, Hou, Sakai, & Jouvet, 1996). In short, no single neurotransmitter serves as a "sleeping pill."

Other researchers are studying the role of the brain in sleep. Many areas have been identified as having a role in producing or maintaining sleep, including the ventrolateral preoptic nucleus (VPN), the pons, the ascending reticular activating system (ARAS), the basal forebrain, the medulla, the thalamus, the hypothalamus, and the limbic system (Hobson & Silvestri, 1999; Rechtschaffen & Siegel, 2000). But there seems to be no single "Morpheus area" for sleep as there is a Broca's area for language (Module 6).

Why Do We Dream?

What do we dream about? Is there special meaning or information in our dreams? Why do we have bad dreams? Why do we dream at all? These questions have long fascinated writers and poets, as well as psychologists. This section begins with a look at gender and cultural diversity in dream content, followed by a discussion of the three major theoretical explanations for why we dream: psychoanalytic/psychodynamic, biological, and cognitive. We then examine nightmares and other sleep disorders.

Throughout the ages, humans have wondered about dreams. A Chinese Taoist of the third century B.C. spoke of the interplay of reality and dreams: "Suddenly I woke up and I was indeed Chuang Tzu. Did Chuang Tzu dream he was a butterfly? Or did the butterfly dream he was Chuang Tzu?"

GENDER & CULTURAL DIVERSITY

Variations and Similarities in Dreams

Research comparing men and women and their dream content generally finds that dreams reflect life events important to the dreamer. Although men and women tend to share many common dream themes, women are more likely to dream of children, family and familiar people, household objects, and indoor events. Men, on the other hand, more often dream about strangers, violence, weapons, sexual activity, achievement, and outdoor events (Domhoff, 1996; Hall et al., 1982; Murray, 1995). However, recent evidence suggests that as gender differences and stereotypes lessen, segregation of dream content by gender becomes less distinct (Bursik, 1998).

Likewise, researchers have found strong similarities and differences in dream content between cultures. For example, dreams involving basic human needs and fears (like sex, aggression, and death) seem to be found in all cultures. Children often dream about large, threatening, wild animals. People of all ages dream of falling, being chased, and being unable to do something they need to do. Dreams also typically include more misfortune than good fortune, and the dreamer is more often the victim of aggression than the cause of it (Domhoff, 1996, 1999; Hall & Van De Castle, 1996).

Yet there are also cultural differences. The Yir Yoront, an Australian hunting and gathering group, generally prefer marriage between a man and his mother's brother's daughter (Schneider & Sharp, 1969). Therefore, it is not uncommon (or surprising) that young, single men in the group often report recurrent dreams of aggression from their mother's brother (their future father-in-law) (Price & Crapo, 1999). Similarly, Americans often report embarrassing dreams of being naked in public, but these dreams are rare in cultures where few clothes are worn.

Interestingly, how people interpret dreams and their cultural value also varies across cultures (Matsumoto, 2000; Price & Crapo, 1999). The Iroquois of North America believe that one's spirit uses dreams to communicate unconscious wishes to the conscious mind (Wallace, 1958). They often share their dreams with religious leaders, who help them interpret and cope with their underlying psychic needs to prevent illness and even death. On the other hand, the Maya of Central America

Dream images. *Have you ever had a dream like this? How would you interpret this dream according to the theories discussed in the text?*

Manifest Content *The surface content of a dream, containing dream symbols that distort and disguise the true meaning of the dream, according to Freudian dream theory*

Latent Content *The true, unconscious meaning of a dream, according to Freudian dream theory*

Activation–Synthesis Hypothesis *The idea that dreams are by-products of random stimulation of brain cells; the brain attempts to combine (or synthesize) this spontaneous activity into coherent patterns, known as dreams*

shared their dreams and interpretations at communal gatherings as an important means of teaching cultural folk wisdom (Tedlock, 1992).

The Psychoanalytic/Psychodynamic View One of the oldest and most scientifically controversial explanations for why we dream is Freud's *psychoanalytic view.* His original theory suggested that dreams are disguised symbols of repressed desires and anxieties and that someone trained in dream interpretation must decipher the true meaning of the dream. In one of his first books, *The Interpretation of Dreams* (1900), Freud argued that dreams are "the royal road to the unconscious." Dreaming is a special state where forbidden and personally unacceptable desires rise to the surface of consciousness. (As a critical thinker, do you notice the close similarity between Freudian theory and the Iroquois concept of dreaming? Some historians believe that Freud borrowed many concepts from the Iroquois — without giving appropriate credit.)

According to Freud, dreams sometimes offer direct insight into the unconscious, as when a lonely person dreams of romance or an angry child dreams of getting even with the class bully. More often, though, the dream content is so threatening and anxiety-producing that it must be couched in symbols. A journey, for example, is often a symbol for death, horseback riding and dancing are symbols for sexual intercourse, and a cigar or a gun might represent a penis. Freud referred to these symbols (the journey, horseback riding, or the gun) as the **manifest content** (or the story line) of the dream and the underlying, true meaning (death, sex, penis) as the **latent content**.

How correct is Freud's theory? Modern psychodynamic theorists believe that latent content can be a wish, a fear, or anything that is emotionally important to the dreamer, but traditional Freudian ideas about how and why dreams happen have little or no scientific support (Fisher & Greenberg, 1996). After being confronted about the symbolic nature of his beloved cigars, Freud himself supposedly remarked, "Sometimes, a cigar is just a cigar."

The biological view. According to the **activation–synthesis hypothesis**, dreams are a by-product of random stimulation of brain cells and have no direct psychological meaning (Hobson, 1988, 1999). On the basis of research conducted on the brain activity of cats during REM sleep, Alan Hobson and Robert McCarley (1977) proposed that specific neurons in the brain stem fire spontaneously during REM sleep and that the cortex struggles to "synthesize" or make sense out of this random stimulation by manufacturing dreams.

Have you ever dreamed that you were trying to run away from a frightening situation but found that you cannot move? The activation–synthesis hypothesis might explain this dream as random stimulation of the amygdala and paralysis of major postural muscles during REM sleep. The amygdala is a specific brain area linked to strong emotions, especially fear, and research shows high activity in the amygdala during REM sleep (Rechtschaffen & Siegel, 2000). If the amygdala is randomly stimulated and the sleeper experiences fear, the brain may attempt to send messages telling the muscles to move, but there would be no movement, owing to the paralysis. The dreamer then struggles to make sense out of this limited, conflicting information by manufacturing a dream about running away and being unable to move.

This is *not* to say that dreams are totally meaningless. Hobson (1988, 1999) suggests that even if dreams begin with more-or-less random activity in various brain areas, the dreamer's interpretation of this activity depends on his or her personality, motivations, memories, and life experiences.

The Cognitive View. According to the cognitive view, dreams are an extension of everyday life — a form of thinking during sleep. Rather than seeing dreams as mysterious messages from the unconscious or the result of random brain stimulation, dreams are simply another type of *information processing:* They help us sift and sort our everyday experiences and thoughts. The brain periodically shuts out sensory input so it can process, assimilate, and update information — a type of *mental housecleaning* similar to disk defragmentation on your computer.

Interpreting Your Dreams

Television, movies, and other popular media often portray dreams as highly significant and easily interpreted. However, scientists are deeply divided about the meaning of dreams and their relative importance. These differences in scientific opinion provide an excellent opportunity for you to practice the critical thinking skill of *tolerance for ambiguity*.

To improve your tolerance for ambiguity (and learn a little more about your own dreams), begin by briefly jotting down a recent and vivid dream. This should be at least three or four paragraphs in length. Now analyze your dream using the following perspectives:

1. According to the psychoanalytic/psychodynamic view, what might be the forbidden, unconscious fears, drives or desires represented by your dream? Can you identify the manifest content versus the latent content?

2. How would the biological view, the activation–synthesis hypothesis, explain your dream? Can you identify a specific thought that might have been stimulated and then led to this particular dream?

3. Psychologists from the cognitive perspective believe dream analysis provides important information processing, helps us make needed changes in our life, and even suggests solutions to real-life problems. Do you agree or disagree? Does your dream provide an insight that increases your self-understanding?

Having analyzed your dream from each perspective, can you see how difficult it is to find the one right answer? Higher-level critical thinkers recognize that competing theories are akin to the story of the four blind men who are each exploring separate parts of an elephant. By listening to their description of the trunk, tail, leg, and so on, critical thinkers can synthesize the information and develop a greater understanding. But no one part — or single theory — reveals the whole picture.

As we discovered earlier, REM sleep increases following stress and intense learning periods, and other research reports strong similarities between dream content and waking thoughts, fears, and concerns (Domhoff, 1996, 1999; Hill, Diemer, & Heaton, 1997). For example, college students often report "examination-anxiety" dreams: You can't find your classroom, you're running out of time, your pen or pencil won't work, or you've completely forgotten a scheduled exam and show up totally unprepared (Van de Castle, 1995). (Sound familiar?)

In Sum. The psychoanalytic/psychodynamic, biological, and cognitive views of dreaming offer three perspectives, but numerous questions remain. How, for example, could a complex phenomenon like dreaming have evolved if it requires *expert* interpretation? Can the "random firing" of brain cells explain complicated, storylike dreams or recurrent dreams? How would they explain why human fetuses show REM patterns? Is the fetus working out suppressed wishes and anxieties in the womb? What does it have to dream about in response to random brain activity? Or could it be sifting and sorting its "waking" experiences? And how is it that the same dream can often be explained by many theories? To see this for yourself, try the Critical Thinking/Active Learning Exercise on this page.

Check & Review

THEORIES OF SLEEP AND DREAMING

The exact function of sleep is not known, but according to the **repair/restoration theory**, it is thought to be necessary for its restorative value, both physically and psychologically. According to **evolutionary/circadian theory**, it also has adaptive value. Sleep seems to be controlled by several neurotransmitters and by various areas of the brain.

Three major theories attempt to explain why we dream: The psychoanalytic/psychodynamic view says dreams are disguised symbols of repressed anxieties and desires. The biological (**activation–synthesis hypothesis**) perspective argues that dreams are simple by-products of random stimulation of brain cells. The cognitive view suggests that dreams are an important part of information processing of everyday experiences.

Questions

1. How does the repair/restoration theory of sleep differ from the evolutionary/circadian theory?

2. What are the basic gender and cultural similarities and differences in dreams?

3. Freud believed that dreams were the "royal road to the_____." (a) therapeutic alliance; (b) psyche; (c) latent content; (d) unconscious

4. _____ theory states that dreams are by-products of random stimulation of brain cells, whereas the _____ view suggests dreams serve an information processing function and help us sift and sort our everyday experiences and thoughts. (a) Biological, learning; (b) Cognitive, wish-fulfillment; (c) Activation–synthesis, cognitive; (d) Psychodynamic, infodynamic

Answers to Questions can be found in Appendix B.

Sleep Disorders

Are you one of the lucky people who take sleep for granted? If so, you may be surprised to discover the following facts (based on, Dement & Vaughan, 1999; Doghramji, 2000; Hobson & Silvestri, 1999; National Sleep Foundation, 2000):

- An estimated one-third of American adults suffers from sleep disorders, and about 25 percent of children under age 5 have a sleep disturbance. In adults over 60, about 30 percent have trouble getting to sleep, and 65 percent report difficulties staying asleep.

- Each year, Americans spend more than $98 million on over-the-counter sleep aids and another $50 million on caffeine tablets to keep them awake during the day.

- Twenty percent of all drivers have fallen asleep for a few seconds (microsleep) at the wheel.

The costs of sleep deprivation and sleep disorders are enormous, not only for the individual but also for the public. Psychologists and other mental health professionals divide sleep disorders into two major diagnostic categories: (1) *dyssomnias,* which involve problems in the amount, timing, and quality of sleep, and (2) *parasomnias,* which include abnormal disturbances occurring during sleep.

Dyssomnias

There are at least three prominent examples of dyssomnias:

1. *Insomnia.* The term *insomnia* literally means "lack of sleep." People with **insomnia** have persistent difficulty falling asleep or staying asleep, or they wake up too early. Many people think they have insomnia if they cannot sleep before an exciting event (this is normal) or because they wrongly assume that everyone must sleep 8 hours a night. Sometimes, too, people think they are not sleeping when they really are. However, a large percentage of the population (as much as 30 percent) genuinely suffers from this disorder, and nearly everybody has insomnia at some time (Doghramji, 2000; Ince, 1995). A telltale complaint of insomnia is that the person feels poorly rested the next day. Most people with serious insomnia have other medical or psychological disorders as well, such as alcohol and other drug abuse, anxiety disorders, and depression (Ohayon, 1997).

Unfortunately, the most popular treatment for insomnia is drugs — either over-the-counter pills such as Sominex or prescription tranquilizers and barbiturates. The problem with nonprescription pills is that they generally don't work. Prescription pills, on the other hand, do help you sleep, but they decrease Stage 4 and REM sleep, thereby seriously affecting the quality of sleep (Lord, 2000). Frequently prescribed drugs like Dalmane, Xanax, and Halcion are often helpful in treating sleeping problems related to anxiety and specific stressful situations, such as losing a loved one (Kuffer & Reynolds, 1997). However, people who regularly use over-the-counter or prescription sleeping pills experience significant sleep disturbances that may actually increase insomnia. Moreover, chronic users also run the risk of psychological and physical drug dependence (Jacobs, 1999; Rybacki & Long, 1999). Although sleeping pills may be useful for occasional, short-term (two to three nights) use, they generally create more problems than they solve.

Insomnia *A sleep disorder in which a person has persistent problems in falling asleep or staying asleep or awakens too early*

TABLE 13.2 METHODS FOR ENHANCING SLEEP

You can help yourself to a good night's sleep by preparing during the day and at bedtime. These suggestions come from the Better Sleep Council, a nonprofit education organization in Burtonsville, Maryland.

During the day:
Exercise. Daily physical activity works away tension. But don't exercise vigorously late, or you'll get fired up instead.
Keep regular hours. An erratic schedule can disrupt biological rhythms. Get up at the same time each day.
Avoid stimulants. Coffee, tea, soft drinks, chocolate, and some medications contain caffeine. Nicotine may be an even more potent sleep disrupter.
Avoid late meals. Heavy or spicy meals at bedtime keep you awake. Have light snacks.
Avoid heavy drinking. Overindulgence can shatter your normal sleep pattern.
Stop worrying. Focus on your problems at a set time earlier in the day. If you worry in bed, tell yourself you'll resolve the problems tomorrow.
Use presleep rituals. Follow the same routine every evening: listen to music, write in a diary, meditate.

In bed:
Use progressive muscle relaxation. Alternatively tense and relax various muscle groups.
Apply yoga. These gentle exercises help you relax.
Light a candle in your mind. Focus on the flame to get rid of distracting thoughts.
Try sandman's snacks. Eggs, tunafish, chicken, turkey, and soybeans contain L-tryptophan, an amino acid called "nature's sleeping pill."
Have a nightcap. Warm milk and herbal teas can promote sleep.
Use fantasies. Imagine yourself in a tranquil setting. Feel yourself relax.
Use deep breathing. Take deep breaths, telling yourself you're falling asleep.
Try a splashdown. A warm bath can induce drowsiness because it sends blood away from the brain to the skin surface.
Use mind games. Imagine you're writing 6-foot-high numbers. Start at 100 and count backward.
Count sheep. It works by relaxing both sides of the brain.

What is recommended instead of drugs? If you're having difficulty falling asleep at night, don't keep checking the clock and figuring how many hours and minutes before you have to get up. Instead, plan ahead by exercising during the day and avoiding alcohol and caffeine. When you're in bed, try some of the relaxation techniques listed in Table 13.2.

2. Sleep apnea. One of the many possible causes of insomnia is sleep apnea. *Apnea* literally means "no breathing." Many people have either irregular breathing or occasional periods of 10 seconds or less without breathing during their sleep. People with **sleep apnea**, however, may fail to breathe for a minute or longer and then wake up gasping for breath. When they do breathe during their sleep, they often snore. Repeated awakenings result in insomnia and leave the person feeling tired and sleepy during the day. However, people are often unaware of these frequent awakenings and may fail to recognize the reason for their daytime fatigue.

Sleep Apnea *A temporary cessation of breathing during sleep; one of the suspected causes of snoring, high blood pressure, and heart damage*

Sleep apnea seems to result from blocked upper airway passages or from the brain ceasing to send signals to the diaphragm, thus causing breathing to stop. If you or your sleeping partner snore loudly or have repeated awakenings followed by gasps for breath, you may be suffering from sleep apnea and should seek medical attention (Ulfbert, Carter, & Edling, 2000). Treatment depends partly on the severity of the sleep apnea. If the problem occurs only when you're sleeping on your back, sewing tennis balls on the back of your pajama top may help. Obstruction of the breathing passages is also related to obesity (Christensen, 2000), so dieting is often recommended. For others, surgery, dental appliances that reposition the tongue, or ventilating machines may be the answer.

For many years, researchers assumed that snoring (without the accompanying stoppages of breathing in sleep apnea) was a minor problem — except for bed partners. Recent findings, however, suggest that even this "simple snoring" can also

Narcolepsy [NAR-co-lep-see] *A disease marked by sudden and irresistible onsets of sleep during normal waking hours. (narco = numbness; lepsy = seizure)*

lead to heart disease and possible death (Peppard, Young, Palta, & Skatrud, 2000). Although occasional mild snoring remains somewhat normal, it is a possible "warning sign that should prompt people to seek help" (Christensen, 2000 p. 172).

3. *Narcolepsy.* A serious sleep disorder that is somewhat the opposite of insomnia is narcolepsy — excessive daytime sleepiness characterized by sudden and irresistible demands for sleep. Narcolepsy afflicts an estimated 135,000 people in the United States and generally runs in families (McClintock, 2000; Siegel, 2000). During an attack, REM-like sleep suddenly intrudes into the waking state of consciousness. Victims may experience sudden attacks of muscle weakness or paralysis (cataplexy). Such people may fall asleep while walking, talking, or driving a car. These attacks are obviously dramatic and can be incapacitating. Can you imagine what it would be like to be driving along the highway or walking across campus and suddenly have a narcoleptic attack?

Although long naps each day and stimulant or antidepressant drugs may help reduce the frequency of attacks, both the causes and cure of narcolepsy are still unknown. Stanford University's Sleep Disorders Center was among the first to selectively breed a group of narcoleptic dogs, which has increased our understanding of the genetics of this disorder (McClintock, 2000). Research on these specially bred dogs has found degenerated neurons in certain areas of the brain (Siegel, 2000). Whether human narcolepsy results from similar degeneration is a question for future research.

Parasomnias

The second category of sleep disorders, parasomnias, includes abnormal sleep disturbances such as nightmares and night terrors. **Nightmares**, or bad dreams, occur toward the end of the sleep cycle, during REM sleep. Less common but more frightening are **night terrors**, which occur early in the cycle, during Stage 3 or Stage 4 of non-REM sleep. The sleeper awakens suddenly, in a state of panic and with no recollection of any dream (Dement & Vaughan, 1999).

Sleepwalking, which tends to accompany night terrors, usually occurs during non-REM sleep (which explains why movement is possible). *Sleep talking*, on the other hand, occurs with about equal probability in REM and non-REM sleep. It can include single, indistinct words or long, articulate sentences. It is even possible to engage some sleep talkers in a limited conversation.

Nightmares, night terrors, sleepwalking, and sleep talking are all more common among young children, but they can also occur in adults, usually during times of stress or major life events (Hobson & Silvestri, 1999; Muris, Merckelbach, Gadet, & Moulaert, 2000). Patience and soothing reassurance at the time of the sleep disruption are the only treatment usually recommended for both children and adults.

Nightmares *Anxiety-arousing dreams that generally occur near the end of the sleep cycle, during REM sleep*

Night Terrors *Abrupt awakenings from non-REM (non–rapid-eye-movement) sleep accompanied by intense physiological arousal and feelings of panic*

Nightmare or night terror? *Can you explain the difference?*

Check & Review

SLEEP DISORDERS

Many people suffer from numerous sleep problems, which fall into two major diagnostic categories — *dyssomnias* (including insomnia, sleep apnea, and narcolepsy) and *parasomnias* (such as nightmares and night terrors).

People who have repeated difficulty falling or staying asleep or awakening too early experience **insomnia**. A person with **sleep apnea** temporarily stops breathing during sleep, causing loud snoring or poor-quality sleep. **Narcolepsy** is excessive day-time sleepiness characterized by sudden sleep attacks. **Nightmares** are bad dreams that occur during REM (rapid-eye-movement) sleep. **Night terrors** are abrupt awakenings with feelings of panic that occur during non-REM sleep.

Following are four descriptions of people suffering from sleep disorders. Label each type.

1. George awakens many times each night and feels fatigued and poorly rested the next day.

2. While sleeping, Joan often snores loudly and frequently stops breathing temporarily.

3. Tyler is a young child who often wakes up terrified and cannot describe what has happened. These episodes occur primarily during non-REM sleep.

4. Xavier complains to his physician about sudden and irresistible onsets of sleep during his normal workday.

Answers to Questions can be found in Appendix B.

ACTIVE LEARNING WORKSHEET   MODULE 13

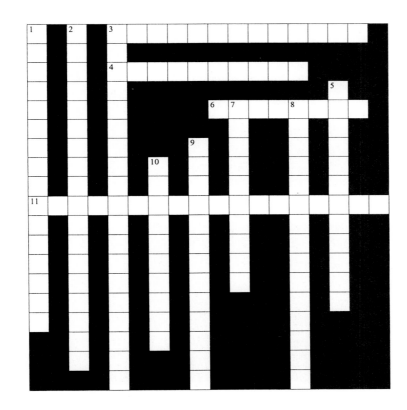

ACROSS

3. An organism's awareness of its own self and surroundings.

4. A disease marked by sudden and irresistible onsets of sleep during normal waking hours.

6. A sleep disorder in which a person has persistent problems in falling asleep or staying asleep or awakens too early.

11. A stage of sleep marked by rapid eye movements, high-frequency brain waves, and dreaming.

DOWN

1. Biological changes that occur on a 24-hour cycle.

2. Mental activities requiring minimal attention; other ongoing activities are generally not affected.

3. Mental activities found at one extreme of the continuum of awareness; they require focused attention and generally interfere with other ongoing activities.

5. Abrupt awakenings from non-REM sleep accompanied by intense physiological arousal and feelings of panic.

7. Anxiety-arousing dreams that generally occur near the end of the sleep cycle, during REM sleep.

8. The surface content of a dream, containing dream symbols that distort and disguise the true meaning of the dream, according to Freudian dream theory.

9. The true, unconscious meaning of a dream, according to Freudian dream theory.

10. A temporary cessation of breathing during sleep.

Answers can be found in Appendix B.

MODULE 14

DRUGS AND OTHER ROUTES TO ASCs

Since the beginning of civilization, people of all cultures have used — and abused — psychoactive drugs (Abadinsky, 2001; Hanson, Venturelli, & Fleckenstein, 2000). **Psychoactive drugs** are generally defined as chemicals that change conscious awareness or perception. Do you (or someone you know) use caffeine (in coffee, tea, chocolate, or cola) or nicotine (in cigarettes) as a pick-me-up, or alcohol (in beer, wine, and cocktails) to relax and lessen inhibitions? All three — caffeine, nicotine, and alcohol — are psychoactive drugs.

How use differs from abuse and how chemical alterations in consciousness affect a person both psychologically and physically are important topics in psychology. In this section, we begin by clarifying differences in terminology. We then go on to look at the four major categories of psychoactive drugs that affect our consciousness.

Psychoactive Drugs *Chemicals that affect the nervous system and cause a change in behavior, mental processes, and conscious experience*

Drugs That Influence Consciousness: Terminology and Classification

Have you noticed how difficult it is to have a logical, nonemotional discussion about drugs? In our society, where the drugs of choice are caffeine, tobacco, and ethyl alcohol, people often become defensive when these drugs are grouped with illicit drugs such as marijuana and heroin. Similarly, users of marijuana are disturbed that their drug of choice is grouped with "hard" drugs like heroin. Most psychologists believe that all psychoactive drugs can be abused. On the other hand, even addictive drugs like amphetamines and cocaine have legitimate medical uses. To facilitate our discussion and understanding of drugs, we need to clarify several confusing terms related to drugs.

> How do drugs affect consciousness?

Misconceptions and Important Terminology

Is drug abuse the same as drug addiction? The term **drug abuse** generally refers to drug taking that causes emotional or physical harm to the individual or others. The drug consumption is also typically compulsive and follows a high frequency, intense pattern. *Addiction* is a broad term referring to a condition in which a person feels compelled to use a specific drug. In recent times, the term *addiction* has been used to describe almost any type of compulsive activity (Doweiko, 1999; Orzack, 1999). People talk about being "addicted" to TV, work, physical exercise, and even the Internet.

Drug Abuse *Drug taking that causes emotional or physical harm to the drug user or others*

History of psychoactive drugs. Before the Food and Drug Administration (FDA) regulated the sale of drugs, heroin, opium and cocaine were commonly found in over-the-counter, non-prescription drugs.

Psychological Dependence *A desire or craving to achieve the effects produced by a drug*

Physical Dependence *A condition in which bodily processes have been so modified by repeated use of a drug that continued use is required to prevent withdrawal symptoms*

Withdrawal *Discomfort and distress, including physical pain and intense cravings, experienced after stopping the use of addictive drugs*

Tolerance *A decreased sensitivity to a drug brought about by its continuous use*

Because of problems associated with the terms *addiction* and *drug abuse*, many drug researchers use **psychological dependence** to refer to the mental desire or craving to achieve the effects produced by a drug. They use the term **physical dependence** to refer to changes in bodily processes that make a drug necessary for minimum daily functioning. Physical dependence is shown most clearly when the drug is withheld, and the user undergoes painful **withdrawal** reactions, including physical pain and intense cravings. **Tolerance** occurs when larger and more frequent doses of a drug are required to produce the initial desired effect. After repeated use of a drug, many of the body's physiological processes adjust to higher and higher levels of the drug.

Tolerance leads many users to escalate their drug use and to experiment with other drugs in an attempt to recreate the originally pleasurable altered state. In some cases, use of one drug increases tolerance for another. This is known as *cross-tolerance*. Despite the connotations of the words *tolerance* and *cross-tolerance*, it's important to remember that the brain, heart, liver, and other body organs can be seriously damaged.

Although psychological dependence is sometimes considered less dangerous than physical dependence, the effects on the drug user's life can be even more damaging. The craving in psychological dependence can be so strong that the user ingests the drug regularly and maintains a constant drug-induced state. In addition, the psychological aspects of drug taking are often so powerful that an "addict" will return to a drug habit even after all signs of physical dependence are removed. Psychological and physical dependence may or may not occur together, as Table 14.1 shows.

In the next section, we discuss specific groups of psychoactive drugs. For convenience, psychologists divide psychoactive drugs into four broad categories: depressants, stimulants, opiates, and hallucinogens (Table 14.1).

Before we go on, you may want to take the following test to help determine whether you may be physically or psychologically dependent on alcohol or other drugs.

1. Have you gotten into financial difficulties because of drinking or using other drugs?
2. Has drinking alcohol or using other drugs ever been behind your losing a job?
3. Has your efficiency or ambition decreased since drinking and using other drugs?
4. Is your drinking and drug use jeopardizing your academic performance?
5. Does drinking or using other drugs cause you to have difficulty sleeping?
6. Have you ever felt remorse after drinking and using other drugs?
7. Do you crave a drink or other drug at a definite time daily, or do you want a drink or other drug the next morning?
8. Have you ever had a complete or partial loss of memory because of drinking or using other drugs?
9. Have you ever been to a hospital or institution because of drinking or other drug use?

If you answered yes to these questions, you are more likely to be a substance abuser than someone who answered no.

Source: Bennett et al., "Identifying Young Adult Substance Abusers: The Rutgers Collegiate Substance Abuse Screening Test." *Journal of Studies on Alcohol* 54:522–527. Copyright 1993 Alcohol Research Documentation, Inc., Piscataway, NJ. Reprinted by permission. The RCSAST is to be used only as part of a complete assessment battery because more research needs to be done with this instrument.

Depressants

Depressants (sometimes called downers) depress the central nervous system, causing relaxation, sedation, loss of consciousness, and even death. This category includes ethyl alcohol, barbiturates like Seconal, and antianxiety drugs like Valium. Because tolerance and dependence (both physical and psychological) are rapidly acquired with these drugs, there is strong potential for abuse.

Next to tobacco, alcohol is the most widely used drug in Western society. It is primarily a depressant, but at low doses, it has stimulating effects, thus explaining its reputation as a "party drug." The first few drinks seem to relax the inhibitions and thus enliven a person at the same time. But as drinking increases, symptoms of drunkenness appear: Reactions slow, speech slurs, and skilled performance deteriorates (Table 14.2). At the highest doses, the depressant effects can leave the drinker "out of control" and incapable of voluntary action. If blood levels reach 0.5 percent, there is risk of coma and even death from respiratory depression (Doweiko, 1999). One college fraternity pledge, for example, died after a 7-hour drinking binge and approximately 24 drinks. His blood alcohol level was measured at 0.58, which was 6–7 times the legal limit (Cohen, 1997).

Why is mixing alcohol and barbiturates so dangerous? Alcohol should not be combined with *any* other drug, but combining alcohol and barbiturates — two depressants — is particularly dangerous. Together, they can relax the diaphragm muscles to such a degree that the person literally suffocates. Actress Judy Garland is among celebrities known to have died from a barbiturate-and-alcohol mixture.

It is also important to note that alcohol's effect is determined primarily by the amount that reaches the brain. Because the liver breaks down alcohol at the rate of about 1 ounce per hour, the number of drinks and the speed of consumption are both very important. High school and college students have died after drinking large amounts of alcohol in a short period. In addition, men's bodies are more efficient at breaking down alcohol. Even after accounting for differences in size and muscle-to-fat ratio, women have a higher blood alcohol level than men do following equal doses of alcohol.

Alcohol also plays a major role in our most serious social problems. Did you know, for example, that alcohol is a factor in nearly half of all murders, suicides, spousal abuse, and accidental deaths in the United States (Doweiko, 1999; Murphy & O'Farrell, 1996)? Or did you know that drinking drivers account for about one-half of all highway fatalities, and that medical authorities list alcohol as the third leading cause of birth defects (Butler, Joel, & Jeffries, 2000; Julien, 2000)?

Alcohol also seems to encourage aggressive tendencies (commonly referred to as "beer muscles") and sexual daring and desire (sometimes called "beer goggles") (Allgeier & Allgeier, 2000; Pihl et al., 1997). But it may be that alcohol only releases what's already there. People prone to aggression will become more aggressive, and people prone to being affectionate will become more affectionate. Moral judgments are less mature and attention is focused on the immediate situation rather than future consequences. Even those who believe (when sober) that drinking and driving is wrong will often drive home from a bar. Although the American Medical Association calls alcohol the most dangerous and physically damaging of all psychoactive drugs, drinking still enjoys wide social acceptance.

Stimulants

Whereas depressants are downers, **stimulants** are uppers. Stimulant drugs act on the central nervous system to increase its overall activity and responsiveness. Stimulant drugs, such as caffeine, nicotine, amphetamines, and cocaine, produce alertness, excitement, elevated mood, decreased fatigue, and sometimes increased motor activity.

Depressants *Psychoactive drugs that act on the central nervous system to suppress or slow bodily processes and reduce overall responsiveness*

Drunk driving. *Like this fatal car accident in Austin, Texas, drunk drivers are responsible for almost half of all highway related deaths in America.*

Stimulants *Drugs that act on the brain and nervous system to increase their overall activity and general responsiveness*

TABLE 14.1 EFFECTS OF THE MAJOR PSYCHOACTIVE DRUGS

	Category	Desired Effects	Undesirable Effects	Physical/ Psychological Dependence
Depressants	Alcohol, barbiturates, antianxiety drugs (Valium)	Tension reduction, euphoria, disinhibition, drowsiness	Anxiety, nausea, disorientation, impaired reflexes and motor functioning, loss of consciousness, shallow respiration, convulsions, coma, death	Yes/yes
Stimulants	Cocaine, amphetamines	Exhilaration, euphoria, high physical and mental energy, perceptions of power and sociability, loss of appetite	Irritability, anxiety, paranoia, hallucinations, psychosis, convulsions, death	Yes/yes
	Caffeine	Increased alertness	Insomnia, restlessness, increased pulse rate, sleep disruption, mild delirium, ringing in the ears, rapid heartbeat	Yes/yes
	Nicotine	Relaxation, increased alertness, sociability	Irritability, raised blood pressure, stomach pains, vomiting, dizziness, cancer, heart disease, emphysema, death	Yes/yes
Narcotics (Opiates)	Morphine, heroin, codeine	Euphoria, "rush" of pleasure, pain relief, prevention of withdrawal discomfort	Nausea, vomiting, constipation, painful withdrawal, shallow respiration, convulsions, coma, death	Yes/yes
Hallucinogens (Psychedelics)	LSD (lysergic acid diethylamide)	Delusions, hallucinations, distorted perceptions and sensations	Longer and more extreme delusions, hallucinations, and perceptual distortions ("bad trips"), psychosis, death	No/no
	Marijuana	Relaxation, mild euphoria, increased appetite	Perceptual and sensory distortions, hallucinations, fatigue, lack of motivation, paranoia, possible psychosis	No/yes

Source: Abadinsky, 2001; Hanson, Venturelli, & Fleckenstein, 2000; and Julien, 2000.

T A B L E   1 4 . 2   ALCOHOL'S EFFECT ON THE BODY AND BEHAVIOR

Blood Alcohol Content (%)	Effect
.05	Relaxed state; increased sociability
.08	Everyday stress lessened
.10[a]	Movements and speech become clumsy
.20	Very drunk; loud and difficult to understand; emotions unstable
.40	Difficult to wake up; incapable of voluntary action
.50	Coma and/or death

[a] Most states use .10 as the lowest indicator of driving while intoxicated. A few states use .08, whereas some go as high as .12.

Caffeine is now one of the world's most widely used drugs (Julien, 2000). It is found in coffee, tea, cola drinks, chocolate, and more than 100 prescription and nonprescription drugs. Table 14.3 lists the caffeine content in common foods and some over-the-counter drugs. Like depressants, stimulants — including caffeine — can be addictive (Schuh & Griffiths, 1997).

Nicotine

Nicotine in small doses stimulates the central nervous system at the same time that it relieves stress and improves mood. Like caffeine, it is also a widely used legal stimulant, but unlike caffeine it kills many of its users. A sad, ironic example of the dangers of nicotine is Wayne McLaren, the rugged Marlboro Man in cigarette ads, who died of lung cancer at age 51. But McLaren was only one of 400,000 who die from smoking related illnesses each year in the United States. In economically developed countries of the world, nicotine kills more than 4 million people yearly (CDC, 2001).

When smoking doesn't kill, it can result in chronic bronchitis, emphysema, and heart disease (CDC, 2001). Countless others are affected by secondhand smoke, by

T A B L E   1 4 . 3   COMMON SOURCES OF CAFFEINE

Source	Average Caffeine Content (milligrams)
Coffee (5-ounce cup)	
Drip	145
Percolated	108
Instant	64
Tea (5-ounce cup)	50
Soft drinks (12 ounces)	40
OTC[a] stimulants (per tablet)	
Vivarin	200
No-Doz	100
OTC analgesics (per tablet)	
Excedrin	65
Anacin, Midol, Vanquish	33
OTC cold remedies (per teaspoon)	
Coryban-D, Triaminicin	30

[a] OTC: over-the-counter.

THE FAR SIDE By GARY LARSON

The real reason dinosaurs became extinct

smoke-related fires, and by prenatal exposure to nicotine. The U.S. Public Health Service considers cigarette smoking the single most preventable cause of death and disease in the United States (Fiore et al., 2000).

As scientific evidence of the dangers of smoking accumulates and as social pressure from nonsmokers increases, many smokers are trying to kick the habit. But fewer than 1 in 10 actually succeeds (Parker-Pope, 2000). Researchers have found that nicotine activates the same brain areas (nucleus accumbens) as cocaine — a drug well known for its addictive potential (Pich et al., 1997). The reported pleasures of smoking (relaxation, increased alertness, diminished pain and appetite) are so powerfully reinforcing that some smokers continue to smoke — even after having a cancerous lung removed.

Cocaine

Sigmund Freud is often cited as a supporter of cocaine use, but few people know that in his later writings Freud called cocaine the "third scourge" of humanity, after alcohol and heroin. Cocaine is a powerful central nervous system stimulant extracted from the leaves of the coca plant. It can be sniffed as a white powder, injected intravenously, or smoked in the form of crack. Cocaine produces feelings of alertness, euphoria, well-being, power, energy, and pleasure.

Although cocaine was once considered a relatively harmless "recreational drug," its potential for physical damage and severe psychological dependence is now recognized (Hammer, Egilmez, & Emmett-Oglesby, 1997). Even small initial doses of cocaine can be fatal because cocaine interferes with the electrical system of the heart, causing irregular heartbeats and in some cases heart failure. It can also produce heart attacks and strokes by temporarily constricting blood vessels

(Kerfoot, Sakoulas, & Hyman, 1996). The most dangerous form of cocaine is the smokable, concentrated version known as crack or rock. Its lower price makes it affordable and attractive to a large audience, but its greater potency also makes it more quickly addictive and dangerous.

Opiates

Opiates (or narcotics), which include morphine and heroin, numb the senses and thus are used medically to relieve pain (Julien, 2000). The classification term *opiates* is used because the drugs are derived from (or are similar to those derived from) the opium poppy. They are attractive to people seeking an alternate state of consciousness because they produce feelings of relaxation and euphoria. They produce their effect by mimicking the brain's own natural painkillers and mood elevation, called *endorphins*. The word *endorphin* literally means "endogenous morphine.")

This mimicking of the body's natural endorphins creates a dangerous pathway to drug abuse. After repeated flooding with artificial opiates, the brain eventually reduces or stops the production of its own opiates. If the user attempts to stop, the brain lacks both the artificial and normal level of painkilling chemicals. The withdrawal can be excruciatingly painful. The euphoria, pain relief, and avoidance of withdrawal all contribute to make heroin extremely addictive, and, in fact, the recreational use of heroin has doubled since the mid-1980s (Friend, 1997; Leland, 1996). Interestingly, when opiates are used medically to relieve intense pain, they are very seldom habit-forming. However, when taken recreationally, they are strongly addictive (Butler, Joel, & Jeffries, 2000; Doweiko, 1999).

Opiates *Drugs that are derived from opium and function as an analgesic or pain reliever. The word opium derives from the Greek word meaning "juice."*

Hallucinogens

One of the most intriguing alterations of consciousness comes from **hallucinogens**, drugs that produce sensory or perceptual distortions, including visual, auditory, or kinesthetic hallucinations. According to some reports, colors are brighter and more luminous, patterns seem to pulsate and rotate, and senses may seem to fuse — that is, colors are "heard" or sounds "tasted."

Some cultures have used hallucinogens for religious purposes, as a way to experience "other realities" or to communicate with the supernatural. In Western societies, most people use hallucinogens for their reported "mind-expanding" potential. For example, hallucinogens are highly valued by some artists as a way of increasing creativity. But the experience is not always positive. Terror-filled "bad trips" can occur, and dangerous flashbacks may unpredictably recur long after the initial ingestion. The flashback experience may be brought on by stress, fatigue, marijuana use, illness, emerging from a dark room, and occasionally by intentional effort on the part of the individual (Doweiko, 1999).

Hallucinogens are also commonly referred to as *psychedelics* (from the Greek for "mind manifesting"). Hallucinogens include mescaline (derived from the peyote cactus), psilocybin (from mushrooms), phencyclidine (chemically derived), and LSD (lysergic acid diethylamide, derived from ergot, a rye mold). Marijuana (pot, grass, or hashish) is sometimes classified as a hallucinogen because in sufficient dosages, it can produce mental effects similar to the stronger hallucinogens. We will focus on LSD and marijuana in our discussion because they are the most widely used of these drugs.

Hallucinogens [hal-LOO-sin-oh-jenz] *Drugs that produce sensory distortions or perceptual distortions*

LSD

LSD, an odorless, tasteless, and colorless substance, is one of the most potent drugs known. As little as 10 micrograms of LSD can produce a measurable effect in one individual, whereas an amount the size of an aspirin is enough to produce effects in 3,000 people. In 1943 Albert Hofman, the Swiss chemist who first synthesized LSD in a laboratory, accidentally licked some of the drug off his finger and later recorded this in his journal:

Vision from an LSD trip?

Last Friday, April 16, 1943, I was forced to stop my work in the laboratory in the middle of the afternoon and to go home, as I was seized by a peculiar restlessness associated with a feeling of mild dizziness. Having reached home, I lay down and sank in a kind of drunkenness which was not unpleasant and which was characterized by extreme activity of imagination. As I lay in a dazed condition with my eyes closed (I experienced daylight as disagreeably bright) there surged upon me an uninterrupted stream of fantastic images of extraordinary plasticity and vividness and accompanied by an intense, kaleidoscope-like play of colors. This condition gradually passed off after about two hours.

HOFMAN (1968), PP. 184–185

Perhaps because the LSD experience is so powerful, few people actually "drop acid" on a regular basis, which may account for its relatively low reported abuse rate. However, a recent increase in LSD use by high school and college students has been reported (Connolly, 2000). LSD can be an extremely dangerous drug. Bad LSD trips can be terrifying and may lead to accidents, death, or suicide.

Marijuana

Although marijuana is generally classified as a hallucinogen, it has some of the properties of a depressant (including drowsiness and lethargy) and a narcotic (acting as a weak painkiller). In low doses, it also produces mild euphoria, whereas moderate doses lead to an intensification of sensory experiences and the illusion that time is passing very slowly. At the highest doses, marijuana may produce hallucinations, delusions, and distortions of body image (Hanson, Venturelli, & Fleckenstein, 2000). Regardless of its classification, it is one of the most popular of all illegal consciousness-altering drugs today.

The active ingredient in marijuana (cannabis) is THC, or tetrahydrocannabinol, which attaches to receptors that are abundant throughout the brain. The presence of these receptors implies that the brain produces some THC-like chemicals of its own. And, in fact, researchers have discovered a brain chemical (called anandamide) that binds to the same receptors that THC was previously found to use. In 1997, a second THC-like chemical (2-AG) was also discovered (Stella, Schweitzer, & Piomelli, 1997). At this point, no one knows the function of anandamide or 2-AG or why the brain has its own marijuana-like receptors.

With the exception of alcohol during the time of Prohibition, there has never been a drug more hotly debated than marijuana. On the positive side, some research has found marijuana therapeutic in the treatment of glaucoma (an eye disease), in alleviating the nausea and vomiting associated with chemotherapy, in increasing appetite, and in treating asthma, seizures, and anxiety (Abadinsky, 2001; Fackelmann, 1997; Julien, 2000; Lehrman, 1995).

But marijuana users also report impaired memory, attention, and learning — especially the first few times they use the drug. In addition, marijuana use can lead to throat and respiratory disorders, impaired lung functioning and immune response, declines in testosterone levels, reduced sperm count, disruption of the menstrual cycle and ovulation, and brain damage (Doweiko, 1999; Herkenham, 1992; Julien, 2000; O'Leary et al., 2000). Studies suggest that marijuana's effects on the brain are disturbingly similar to those produced by highly addictive drugs, such as heroin, cocaine, alcohol, and nicotine (Blum et al., 2000; Goldberg et al., 2000).

Marijuana can also be habit-forming, but few users experience the intense cravings associated with cocaine or opiates. Withdrawal symptoms are rare because the drug dissolves in the body's fats and leaves the body very slowly, which also explains why a marijuana user can test positive for days or weeks after the last use.

Arguments over the short-term and long-term dangers (and potential benefits) associated with marijuana use will undoubtedly continue for many years. In the meantime, it is important to stress that marijuana (like most psychoactive drugs) affects memory, motor coordination, perceptual skills, and reaction time necessary for safe driving and motor operation. Impaired decision making is also a serious problem with marijuana and most other psychoactive drugs. Just as "drinking and driving don't mix," psychoactive drug use may lead to risky sexual behaviors and increased risk of AIDS (acquired immunodeficiency syndrome) and other sexually transmitted diseases (Kingree, Braithwaite, & Woodring, 2000).

Explaining Drug Use

After an exploration of the four major categories of drugs, two basic questions remain: How do psychoactive drugs create alternate states of consciousness? And why do so many people use and abuse them?

How Drugs Work

Psychoactive drugs influence the nervous system in a variety of ways. Alcohol, for example, has a diffuse effect on neural membranes throughout the entire nervous system. Most psychoactive drugs, however, act in a more specific way: by changing the effect of neurotransmitters in the brain.

Drugs can alter the effect of neurotransmitters in two basic ways: They *enhance* the effect or *inhibit* it. Drugs that mimic the action of a particular neurotransmitter, and in so doing enhance the effectiveness of synaptic transmission, are called **agonists**. Drugs that block the action of specific neurotransmitters are called **antagonists** (Figure 14.1).

Agonist and antagonist drugs also act at one of four stages of neural transmission by (1) altering the production or synthesis of neurotransmitters, (2) changing the amount of neurotransmitter stored or released by a neuron, (3) altering the effect of neurotransmitters on the receptor sites of the receiving neuron, or (4) blocking inactivation of the neurotransmitter in the synapse (Figure 14.2).

Step 1: *Production or synthesis*. Patients with Parkinson's disease have decreased activity in cells that produce dopamine. Usually the treatment is the drug

Agonist *A chemical (or drug) that mimics the action of a specific neurotransmitter*

Antagonist *A chemical (or drug) that opposes or blocks the action of a neurotransmitter*

Figure 14.1 *How agonists and antagonists work.* (a) In normal neurotransmitter activation, the neurotransmitter fits nicely into the receptor and stimulates the receiving neuron. (b) If a drug is taken that contains the same molecular shape as a naturally occurring neurotransmitter, it mimics the neurotransmitter's message. This is known as an agonistic drug action. (c) Some psychoactive drugs contain a molecule that is similar enough in shape to a neurotransmitter that it partially fills a receptor site, but dissimilar enough that the receiving neuron does not receive its messages and will not fire. This is known as antagonistic drug action.

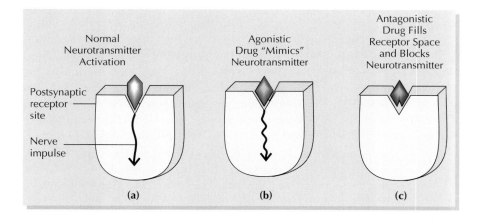

Antagonistic Drug Fills Receptor Space and Blocks Neurotransmitter

Normal Neurotransmitter Activation

Agonistic Drug "Mimics" Neurotransmitter

Postsynaptic receptor site

Nerve impulse

(a)   (b)   (c)

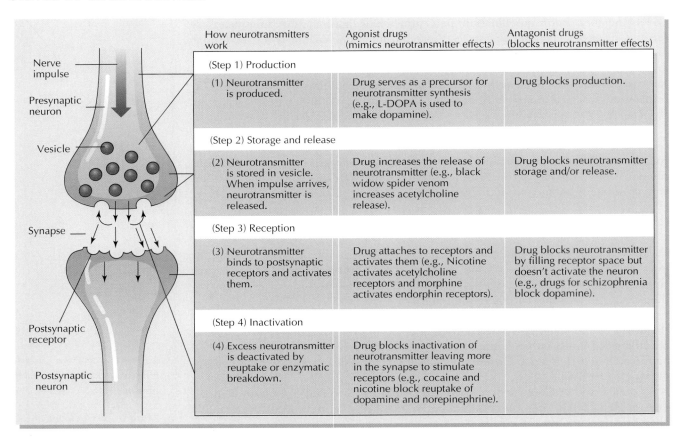

	How neurotransmitters work	Agonist drugs (mimics neurotransmitter effects)	Antagonist drugs (blocks neurotransmitter effects)
(Step 1) Production			
	(1) Neurotransmitter is produced.	Drug serves as a precursor for neurotransmitter synthesis (e.g., L-DOPA is used to make dopamine).	Drug blocks production.
(Step 2) Storage and release			
	(2) Neurotransmitter is stored in vesicle. When impulse arrives, neurotransmitter is released.	Drug increases the release of neurotransmitter (e.g., black widow spider venom increases acetylcholine release).	Drug blocks neurotransmitter storage and/or release.
(Step 3) Reception			
	(3) Neurotransmitter binds to postsynaptic receptors and activates them.	Drug attaches to receptors and activates them (e.g., Nicotine activates acetylcholine receptors and morphine activates endorphin receptors).	Drug blocks neurotransmitter by filling receptor space but doesn't activate the neuron (e.g., drugs for schizophrenia block dopamine).
(Step 4) Inactivation			
	(4) Excess neurotransmitter is deactivated by reuptake or enzymatic breakdown.	Drug blocks inactivation of neurotransmitter leaving more in the synapse to stimulate receptors (e.g., cocaine and nicotine block reuptake of dopamine and norepinephrine).	

Diagram labels: Nerve impulse; Presynaptic neuron; Vesicle; Synapse; Postsynaptic receptor; Postsynaptic neuron

Figure 14.2 *Psychoactive drugs and neurotransmitters.* Most psychoactive drugs produce their effects by disrupting the body's supply of neurotransmitters at one of the steps in transmission. Drugs can alter the production or synthesis of neurotransmitters (step 1), they can affect storage and release (step 2), or they can disrupt the reception by the next neuron (step 3). Once neurotransmitters carry a message across the synapse, the sending neuron normally reabsorbs (reuptakes) the excess neurotransmitters, or enzymes are released to destroy the excess neurotransmitter (step 4). Cocaine produces its effects primarily by blocking the reuptake. Because the extra neurotransmitters remain in the synapse, the adjacent neurons continue to fire and the stimulation effects are increased.

L-dopa (levodopa) because it is converted in the brain to dopamine. Producing what the brain itself cannot, the drug sometimes relieves the tremors, rigidity, and difficulty in movement characteristic of patients with Parkinson's disease. L-dopa can provide added years of nearly normal life, but the disease is progressive and the benefits decrease over time. Finding the early onset of Parkinson-like symptoms in young people, like actor Michael J. Fox, offers important research clues to a major degenerative disease of our aging population.

Step 2: Storage and release. As an example, venom from a black widow spider increases the release of the neurotransmitter acetylcholine. More acetylcholine available to the receiving neurons creates an exaggerated stimulant effect: extreme arousal, heightened anxiety, and dangerous increases in blood pressure and heart rate.

Step 3: Reception. Some drugs, called receptor *agonists,* have a molecular structure very similar to that of the body's own neurotransmitters (Figure 14.1). Nicotine is similar to the neurotransmitter acetylcholine, so when it fills the acetylcholine receptors, it produces similar effects (increased stimulation).

Other drugs are similar enough to occupy the same sites as the neurotransmitter but dissimilar enough that they do not cause a response in the receiving neuron. They are called receptor *antagonists*. The problem is that as long as they are attached to the receptors, they prevent the "real" neurotransmitter from getting its message through. As you will see in Module 40, many researchers believe an excess of dopamine causes schizophrenia, so it is often treated with drugs that act as receptor antagonists. These fill the sites and block the action of the excess dopamine, thus relieving the major symptoms of the disorder.

Step 4: Inactivation. After neurotransmitters carry their message across the synapse, the sending neuron normally removes the excess, or leftover neurotransmitter, in two ways: resorption (or reuptake) and enzymatic breakdown. If the excess is not removed, the receiving neurons continue to respond as if they were receiving fresh messages. Both nicotine and cocaine work by blocking the reuptake or breakdown of dopamine and other neurotransmitters (Fowler et al., 1996; Koob & Nestler, 1997; Landry, 1997). The normal mood-enhancing effects of these neurotransmitters are thereby increased.

Why People Use and Abuse Drugs

People use and abuse drugs for at least two major reasons: environment and biology.

1. Environmental factors. Drug use is often portrayed in movies, TV, and advertisements as an essential accompaniment to all good times — holidays, parties, and celebrations. Movie stars, athletes, and college students are shown drinking alcohol, smoking or chewing tobacco, and occasionally snorting cocaine.

In addition to seeing such positive portrayals of drug use, often by figures that serve as role models, drug users also learn that their drug of choice produces positive emotions. Cocaine induces strong feelings of power, security, and individual dynamism; alcohol and nicotine reduce stress and anxiety; amphetamines increase arousal.

Commonly abused drugs (like cocaine and alcohol) are also positively associated with sexual arousal and heightened sexual experiences. But both cocaine and alcohol actually reduce sexual performance (Allgeier & Allgeier, 2000). These drugs maintain their reputation as *aphrodisiacs,* substances that increase sexual desire, because they initially lower inhibition. Furthermore, if users believe cocaine or alcohol will improve their sexual performance and enjoyment, they may act in such a way that they will make this belief come true — at least in the beginning.

Individual and sociocultural reasons also explain why people use and abuse drugs. Some of these reasons include availability of drugs, economic deprivation, poor school performance (especially in junior high school), early first use, low value placed on achievement, inadequate parental warmth and support, lack of religious beliefs, family conflict, poor coping skills, and low social competence (Dimoff, 2000; Gruber & Machamer, 2000; Windle, 1999).

2. Biological forces. Drug use may begin because of positive associations and other environmental factors, but it is maintained and perpetuated primarily through biological pressures. For example, most natural reinforcers (eating, drinking, and sexual activity) have one thing in common with commonly abused drugs: They stimulate the brain's reward system (see the Research Highlight that follows).

Genetics may also influence individual differences in drug abuse. For example, certain gene variations may result in a "reward deficiency syndrome," which causes some people to get less pleasure from everyday experiences (Blum, Cull, Braverman, & Comings, 1996). In the past 30 years, a growing body of research has also suggested a biological predisposition toward alcohol/drug dependence (Fehr et al., 2000; Kendler, Gardner, & Prescott, 1997).

Once drug use is established, it is more likely to continue because removal or withholding of the drug leads to painful withdrawal symptoms. For example, someone who quits opiates after long-term use usually experiences physical symptoms such as rapid breathing, perspiration, tremors, and muscle twitches.

The brain produces chemicals closely resembling opiates (endorphins) and contains special receptor sites for them. As regular opiate use overloads the endorphin receptor sites, the brain soon stops producing these substances. When the drugs are

RESEARCH HIGHLIGHT

Addictive Drugs as the Brain's "Evil Tutor"

Have you ever wondered why alcoholics and other addicts continue to take drugs that are clearly destroying their lives? One explanation may be that the brain "learns" to be addicted. Scientists have long known that various neurotransmitters are key to all forms of normal learning. Now evidence suggests that addictive drugs (acting on certain neurotransmitters) teach the brain to want more and more of the destructive substances — whatever the cost. Drugs become the brain's "evil tutor" (Wickelgren, 1998, p. 2045.)

How does this happen? The neurotransmitter dopamine has been a primary focus of drug abuse research because of its well-known effect on a part of the brain's reward system known as the *nucleus accumbens* (Blum et al., 2000; DiChiara, 1997; Giros, Jaber, Jones, Wrightman, & Caron, 1996). Nicotine and amphetamines, for example, stimulate the release of dopamine, and cocaine blocks its uptake. Drugs that increase dopamine activity are most likely to result in physical dependence.

Recently, however, evidence points to the importance of another neurotransmitter, glutamate. Although surges in dopamine caused by drug use appear to activate the brain's reward system, glutamate may explain compulsive drug taking. Even after the initial effects of a drug disappear, glutamate-induced learning encourages the addict to want more and more of the drug and directs the body to get it. Glutamate apparently creates lasting memories of drug use by changing the nature of "conversations" between neurons. Changes in neuronal connections

"That is not one of the seven habits of highly effective people."

result whenever we learn something or store it in memory. But in this case, glutamate "teaches" the brain to be addicted.

Glutamate's lesson is rarely forgotten. Even when users are highly motivated to end the vicious cycle of drug abuse, glutamate related changes in the brain keep them "hooked." In addition to the well-known intense cravings and pain of withdrawal, the addicted brain also creates cravings at the mere sight of drug-related items. When 13 cocaine addicts and 5 controls watched films of people using both neutral objects and drug-associated items (such as glass pipes and razor blades), the addicts reported significant cravings. During this same time, positron emission tomography (PET) scans of the addicts' brains showed significant neural activity in brain regions known to release glutamate

(Grant et al., 1996). Apparently, activating the glutamate system — through drug use or some reminder of the drug — creates strong cravings, which helps explain the common problem of drug relapse.

As a critical thinker, are you wondering how this new research might help with drug abuse and relapse? Recalling earlier information about agonists and antagonists: What about developing and trying a glutamate antagonist? The good news is that this exact method seems to work. When shown drug-related objects, long-term drug addicts who received a glutamate antagonist reported a significant reduction in cravings and less drug-seeking behavior (Herman & O'Brien, 1997). Drugs that interfere with glutamate transmission are also being tested for the treatment of general drug abuse (Wickelgren, 1998).

no longer taken, neither opiates nor endorphins are available for regulating pain and discomfort, and the user experiences excruciating pains of withdrawal. Problems with withdrawal symptoms are also the primary reason people fail in their efforts to stop smoking.

A Concluding Note

Before we go on, we'd like to offer a brief warning about our presentation on drugs. Every attempt has been made to be as factual as possible, but space is obviously limited and information can quickly become dated. With all drug consumption, both prescription and "recreational," the consumer must assume responsibility for maintaining a complete and up-to-date drug education.

This warning is particularly important for illicit street drugs and **designer drugs**, illicitly manufactured variations on known recreational drugs. One of the best-known designer drugs is Ecstasy, the common name for MDMA, which possesses stimulant and hallucinogenic properties (Abadinsky, 2001). As discussed in the section opener, Ecstasy users report feeling warm, friendly, sensual, and alert. Keep in mind, however, that studies show the drug also causes heart arrhythmias, high blood pressure, and its long-term effects on the human brain are unknown (Burgess, O'Donohoe, & Gill, 2000).

Street and designer drugs are particularly dangerous for two reasons. First, they lack scientific study on their potential side effects, interaction with other drugs, and long-term risks. Second, there are no truth-in-packaging laws to protect illicit drug buyers from unscrupulous practices. Sellers often substitute unknown, cheaper, and possibly even more dangerous substances for the ones they claim to be selling. When you add in the risk of contracting deadly infectious diseases such as AIDS and hepatitis from sharing nonsterile needles, the dangers of drug use go far beyond the particular drug itself (Doweiko, 1999).

Designer Drugs *Illicitly manufactured variations on known recreational drugs*

Check & Review

DRUGS AND CONSCIOUSNESS

Psychoactive drugs change conscious awareness or perception. *Drug abuse* refers to drug taking that causes emotional or physical harm to the individual or others, whereas *addiction* is a broad term referring to a person's feeling of compulsion to use a specific drug. Psychoactive drug use can lead to psychological dependence or physical dependence or both. **Psychological dependence** is a desire or craving to achieve the effects produced by a drug. **Physical dependence** is a change in bodily processes due to continued drug use that results in **withdrawal** symptoms when the drug is withheld. **Tolerance** is a physiological process whereby the user needs larger and more frequent doses of a drug to produce the desired effect.

The major categories of psychoactive drugs are **depressants**, **stimulants**, **opiates**, and **hallucinogens**. Depressant drugs slow the central nervous system, whereas stimulants activate it. Opiates numb the senses and relieve pain, whereas hallucinogens produce sensory or perceptual distortions.

Drugs act primarily by changing the effect of neurotransmitters in the brain. Drugs that act as **agonists** mimic neurotransmitters, whereas **antagonists** oppose or block normal neurotransmitter functioning. There are many reasons for drug use and abuse, which fall into the two main categories of environment and biology.

Questions

1. Drugs that change behavior, mental processes, and conscious experience are called _____. (a) addictive; (b) hallucinogenic; (c) psychoactive; (d) mind altering

2. Drug-taking that causes emotional or physical harm to the drug user or others is known as _____. (a) addiction; (b) physical dependence; (c) psychological dependence; (d) drug abuse

3. How does physical dependence differ from psychological dependence?

4. Describe four ways psychoactive drugs act on neurotransmitters.

Answers to Questions can be found in Appendix B.

Additional Routes to Alternate States: Daydreams, Fantasies, Hypnosis, and Meditation

As we discovered earlier, ASCs may be reached through everyday activities such as sleep and dreaming or through the chemical means of drugs. In this section, we explore several additional routes for changing consciousness: daydreams and fantasies, hypnosis, and meditation.

> **How do alternate states of consciousness, like hypnosis, affect consciousness?**

Daydreams and Fantasies

In the mildest forms of altered consciousness, *daydreaming* and *fantasies*, attention shifts away from the external world to focus internally on memories, desires, and expectations. Scientists have found that during a typical 24-hour period, we spend as much as one-third of our waking hours daydreaming. And, over 95 percent of both men and women say they have had sexual fantasies. Men's sexual fantasies tend to have more visual images and explicit sexual behaviors, whereas women's fantasies include more touching and romance within a committed and caring relationship (Leitenberg & Henning, 1995; Renaud & Byers, 1999).

Can daydreams and sexual fantasies be dangerous? Daydreaming while sitting in a lecture or driving a car may be counterproductive and potentially dangerous, but under other circumstances, it can be helpful. Most people daydream during quiet, private moments when outside events are boring or automated, such as while waiting at bus stops or washing dishes. It appears that our consciousness responds to an unchanging external world by turning inward and creating more interesting thoughts and images. Daydreaming not only helps us escape and cope with boring tasks and difficult situations but also seems to allow mental and physical relaxation, improve intellectual functioning, and release creative abilities (Klinger, 1987).

Sexual fantasies also serve many purposes. They entertain and excite with no risk of embarrassment, pregnancy, or sexually transmitted diseases (Allgeier & Allgeier, 2000). Many sexual fantasies involve having sex with unavailable or multiple partners — behaviors we would not consider in real life. Such fantasies may lead to feelings of guilt, but thinking about something is not the same as doing it. This lack of distinction between thought and behavior may explain the negativism and uncertainty surrounding both daydreams and fantasies. However, just as parents accept that children often think about hitting others but do not accept the actual behavior, we can accept our daydreams about running away to Tahiti with a sexy stranger without the fear of actually doing it.

Hypnosis

"Relax … your body is so tired … your eyelids are so very heavy … your muscles are becoming more and more relaxed … your breathing is becoming deeper and deeper … relax … your eyes are closing and your whole body feels like lead … let go … relax." These are the types of suggestions most hypnotists use to begin hypnosis. Once hypnotized, some people can be convinced they are standing at the edge of the ocean listening to the sound of waves and feeling the ocean mist on their faces. Invited to eat a delicious apple that is actually an onion, the hypnotized person may relish the flavor. Told they are watching a very funny or sad movie, they may begin to laugh or cry at their self-created visions.

What is hypnosis? Scientific research has removed much of the mystery surrounding **hypnosis**. It is defined as an ASC characterized by one or more of the following: (1) narrowed, highly focused attention (the participant is able to "tune out" competing sensory stimuli); (2) increased use of imagination and hallucinations (in the case of visual hallucinations, a person may see things that aren't there or not see things that are); (3) a passive and receptive attitude; (4) decreased responsiveness to pain; (5) heightened suggestibility (a willingness to respond to proposed changes

Hypnosis *An alternate state of heightened suggestibility characterized by relaxation and intense focus*

in perception — "this onion is an apple") (Barber, 2000; Hilgard, 1986, 1992; Spiegel, 1999).

Hypnotism has been well researched, yet several myths and controversies persist.

1. *Forced hypnosis.* One of the most common misconceptions is that people can be hypnotized against their will. But hypnosis requires the person to make a conscious decision to relinquish control of his or her consciousness to someone else, so it is virtually impossible to hypnotize someone who is unwilling. As a matter of fact, about 8 to 9 percent of people cannot be hypnotized even when they are willing and trying very hard to cooperate. And the notion that people can be hypnotically brainwashed and turned into mindless robots is false. The best potential subjects are able to focus attention, are open to new experience, and are capable of imaginative involvement or fantasy (Barber, 2000; Ligett, 2000).

2. *Unethical behavior.* A related myth is that hypnosis can make a person behave immorally or take dangerous risks against his or her will. Generally, people will not go against their strongest and most basic values. Participants retain the ability to control their behavior during hypnosis. They are aware of their surroundings and can refuse to comply with the hypnotist's suggestions (Kirsch & Lynn, 1995).

3. *Exceptional memory.* Another myth is that hypnotized people can recall things they otherwise could not. Some research has found that recall memory for some information is occasionally improved under hypnosis because the participant is able to relax and focus intently. However, the number of errors also increases! Furthermore, when pressed to recreate details, hypnotized participants have more difficulty separating fact and fantasy and are more willing to guess (Perry, Orne, London, & Orne, 1996). As you will see in Module 20, all memory is ultimately a *reconstruction* rather than a *reproduction*. Therefore, because memory is normally filled with fabrication and distortion, hypnosis generally increases the potential for error (Baker, 1998; Perry, 1997). Consequently, a growing number of judges and state bar associations ban the use of hypnosis and the testimony of hypnotized individuals from the courtroom (Brown, Scheflin, & Hammond, 1997; McConkey, 1995).

4. *Superhuman strength.* It is also a misconception that under hypnosis, people can perform acts of special, superhuman strength. When nonhypnotized people are simply asked to try their hardest on tests of physical strength, they can generally do anything that a hypnotized person can (Druckman & Bjork, 1994).

5. *Fakery.* Are hypnosis participants faking it and simply playing along with the hypnotist? Or are they actually in a special state of consciousness that changes normal awareness and perception? Although most participants are not consciously faking hypnosis, some researchers believe the effects result from a blend of conformity, relaxation, obedience, suggestion, and role playing (Baker, 1996, 1998; Kirsch & Lynn, 1995; Lynn, 1997). According to this relaxation/*role-playing theory*, hypnosis is a normal mental state in which deeply relaxed, suggestible people allow the hypnotist to direct their fantasies and behavior.

In contrast, the *altered-state theorists* believe that hypnotic effects result from a special altered state of consciousness (Bowers & Woody, 1996; Hilgard, 1978, 1992). They doubt that relaxation, role playing, and suggestion explain instances in which patients endure complex surgeries without drug-induced anesthesia. As in other controversial areas of psychology, there is a group of "unified" theorists here; they suggest that hypnosis is a combination of both relaxation/role playing and a unique alternate state of consciousness.

Therapeutic Uses of Hypnosis

From the 1700s to modern times, hypnosis has been used (and abused) by entertainers and quacks, while also being employed as a respected clinical tool by physicians, dentists, and therapists. This curious dual existence began with Franz Anton Mesmer (1734–1815). Mesmer believed that all living bodies were filled with magnetic energy and claimed to use this "knowledge" to cure diseases. After lulling his

Stage hypnosis. Many people mistakenly believe that people can be hypnotized against their will. Stage hypnotists generally use eager volunteers who want to be hypnotized and willingly cooperate.

You can recreate a favorite trick that stage hypnotists promote as evidence of superhuman strength under hypnosis. Simply arrange two chairs as shown in the picture. You will see that hypnosis is not necessary — all that is needed is a highly motivated volunteer willing to stiffen his or her body.

patients into a deep state of relaxation and making them believe completely in his curative powers, Mesmer passed magnets over their bodies and told them their problems would go away. For some people, it worked — hence the term *mesmerized*.

Mesmer's theories were eventually discredited, but James Braid, a Scottish physician, later put people in this same trancelike state for surgery. Around the same time, however, powerful and reliable anesthetic drugs were discovered, and interest in Braid's technique dwindled. It was Braid who coined the term *hypnosis* in 1843, from the Greek word for sleep.

Today, hypnosis is frequently used in both medical and psychotherapy settings (Spiegel, 1999). Even with available anesthetics, it is occasionally used in surgery and for the treatment of chronic pain and severe burns (Chaves, 2000; Horton-ausknecht, Mitzdorf, & Melchart, 2000).

Hypnosis has found its best use, however, in medical areas in which patients have a high degree of anxiety, fear, and misinformation, such as dentistry and obstetrics. Because pain is strongly affected by tension and anxiety, any technique that helps the patient relax is medically useful.

In psychotherapy, hypnosis can help patients relax, remember painful memories, and reduce anxiety. It has had modest success in the treatment of phobias and in efforts to lose weight, stop smoking, and improve study habits (Ahijevych, Yerardi, & Nedilsky, 2000; Gemignani et al., 2000).

Many athletes use self-hypnosis techniques (mental imagery and focused attention) to improve performance. Long-distance runner Steve Ortiz, for example, mentally relives all his best races before a big meet. He says that by the time the race actually begins, "I'm almost in a state of self-hypnosis. I'm just floating along" (cited in Kiester, 1984, p. 23).

Meditation

Meditation A group of techniques designed to focus attention and produce a heightened state of awareness

Meditation refers to a group of techniques designed to focus attention and produce a heightened state of awareness. Success in meditation requires controlling the mind's natural tendency to wander.

Some meditation techniques involve body movements and postures, as in t'ai chi and hatha yoga. In other techniques, the meditator remains motionless, attending to a single focal point — gazing at a stimulus (such as a candle flame), observing the breath, or silently repeating a mantra. (A mantra is a special sound, word, or phrase used for mind concentration or spiritual worship.)

Meditation has only recently gained acceptance and popularity in the United States, primarily for its value in promoting relaxation and reducing anxiety. It has, however, been practiced in some parts of the world for centuries. Some believe meditation offers a higher and more enlightened form of consciousness, superior to all other levels, and that it allows meditators to have remarkable control over bodily processes (Epstein, 1998; Flora, 2000).

With sophisticated electronic equipment, researchers have verified that meditation can produce dramatic changes in basic physiological processes such as brain waves, heart rate, oxygen consumption, and sweat gland activity. For the one in four Americans who suffers from high blood pressure, it may be useful to know that meditation has proven somewhat successful in reducing stress and lowering blood pressure (Andreasen, 2000).

What does it feel like when you meditate? In the beginning stages of meditation, people often report a mellow type of relaxation, followed by a mild euphoria. With long practice, some advanced meditators report experiences of profound rapture and joy or strong hallucinations (Smith, 1982). A particularly vivid description is provided by Gopi Khrishna (1999):

Suddenly, with a roar like that of a waterfall, I felt a stream of liquid light entering my brain through the spinal cord. The illumination grew brighter and brighter, the

You can enjoy many of the experiences and benefits of meditation with a relaxation technique developed by Herbert Benson (1977):

1. Pick a focus word or short phrase that is calming and rooted in your personal value system (such as *love*; *peace*; *one*; *shalom*; *Hail, Mary, full of grace*).
2. Sit quietly in a comfortable position, close your eyes, and relax your muscles.
3. Focusing on your breathing, breathe through your nose, and as you breathe out, say your focus word or phrase silently to yourself. Continue for 10 to 20 minutes. You may open your eyes to check the time, but do not use an alarm. When you have finished, sit quietly for several minutes, at first with closed eyes and later with opened eyes.
4. Maintain a passive attitude throughout the exercise — permit relaxation to occur at its own pace. When distracting thoughts occur, ignore them and gently return to your repetition.
5. Practice the technique once or twice daily, but not within 2 hours after a meal — the digestive processes seem to interfere with a successful relaxation response.

roaring louder. I experienced a rocking sensation and then felt myself slipping out of my body, entirely enveloped in a halo of light. I felt the point of consciousness that was myself growing wider, surrounded by waves of light. [pp. 4–5]

GENDER & CULTURAL DIVERSITY

Consciousness Across Cultures

Throughout recorded history, people have sought ways to alter consciousness. As early as 2500 B.C., the Sumerians recorded their reactions to the drug opium with a symbol that archeologists translate as "joy" or "rejoicing," and the oldest known code of laws, from Hammurabi of Babylonia (ca. 1792–1750 B.C.), regulated the sale of wine.

In a survey of 488 societies in all parts of the world, 90 percent were found to practice institutionally recognized methods of changing consciousness (Bourguignon, 1973). These methods include taking drugs, ritualistic fasting, dancing, chanting, and inducing a trance. Such historical and cultural commonalities have led some researchers to suggest that there is a basic, inborn human need to experience nonordinary reality (Barr, 1999; Weil & Rosen, 1993).

Why Are People So Interested in Altering Their Consciousness?

Studies of *kava*, a drink made from the dried roots of a South Pacific Island plant, offer three possible answers to this question ("Hawaii high," 1998; Merlin, Lebot, & Lindstrom, 1992). Though other cultures use different substances or means, most attempts to achieve ASC serve the same functions as kava does for the Pacific Islanders:

1. ***Sacred rituals.*** Many cultures seek an alternate state of consciousness (ASC) as a pathway to spiritual enlightenment. The earliest use of kava was as a means of communicating with the gods. The islanders believed that the voices of their ancestors could be heard in the nonordinary reality induced by the kava. Similarly, tobacco has always been an integral part of Native American religions (Robicsek, 1992). It serves as a ritual fumigant, a goodwill offering, a sacrifice,

Alcohol or kava? *Americans often use alcohol, like the Pacific Islanders use kava, to celebrate special occasions.*

Alternate routes to alternate states. Meditation, drugs, and childhood experiences with swings are common ways of changing consciousness

and a sacrament. In addition to drug use, individuals in many cultures voluntarily undergo long fasts, isolation, chanting, whirling, and sensory deprivation in search of spiritual enlightenment.

2. *Social interactions.* ASCs are also an integral part of most cultures' social functions. Pacific Islanders often exchange large, elaborately decorated kava plants at festivals and weddings, and political meetings often start with a ritual cup of kava. In small amounts, the drink relaxes the muscles and produces a mild euphoria while leaving the mind alert ("Hawaii high," 1998). Thus, kava is favored both for celebrations and as a means of reducing the frictions of village life (Sahelian, 1998). In comparison, have you noticed how often champagne is used to celebrate weddings, births, and New Year's Eve? In our North American culture, alcohol is a prominent feature of many social interactions.

3. *Individual rewards.* In addition to spiritual and social functions, many ASCs are desirable on an individual level because they provide pleasure and escape from anxiety or stress. In New Guinea and Fiji, people commonly visit kava bars after work for a relaxing cup of kava. The stresses of the day are replaced with a sense of well-being. In Western societies, alcohol serves a similar purpose.

Check & Review

ADDITIONAL ROUTES TO ALTERNATE STATES

Daydreaming and sexual fantasies are common forms of mild alternate states of consciousness (ASCs). They serve many functions — primarily positive. **Hypnosis** is an alternate state of heightened suggestibility characterized by relaxation and intense focus. Hypnosis has been used to reduce pain and increase concentration and as an adjunct to psychotherapy. **Meditation** is a group of techniques designed to focus attention and produce heightened awareness. Meditation can produce dramatic changes in physiological processes, including heart rate and respiration.

Although the study of consciousness has waxed and waned among psychologists, the public has historically been very interested — particularly in ASCs. Among peoples of all cultures, ASCs (1) are part of sacred rituals, (2) serve social interaction needs, and (3) provide individual rewards.

Questions

1. Why do some people feel guilty or negative about daydreaming and sexual fantasies?

2. Why is it almost impossible to hypnotize an unwilling participant?

3. _____ is a group of techniques designed to focus attention and produce a heightened state of awareness. (a) Hypnosis; (b) Scientology; (c) Parapsychology; (d) Meditation

4. List three major functions served by ASCs in all cultures.

Answers to Questions can be found in Appendix B.

ACTIVE LEARNING WORKSHEET   MODULE 14

ACROSS

3. Chemicals that affect the nervous system and cause a change in behavior, mental processes, and conscious experience.

4. Drugs that are derived from opium and function as an analgesic or pain reliever.

9. A chemical (or drug) that opposes or blocks the action of a neurotransmitter.

12. Drug taking that causes emotional or physical harm to the drug user or others.

13. Psychoactive drugs that act on the central nervous system to suppress or slow bodily processes and reduce overall responsiveness.

14. Illicitly manufactured variations on known recreational drugs.

DOWN

1. An alternate state of heightened suggestibility characterized by relaxation and intense focus.

2. A condition in which bodily processes have been so modified by repeated use of a drug that continued use is required to prevent withdrawal symptoms.

5. A decreased sensitivity to a drug brought about by its continuous use.

6. Discomfort and distress, including physical pain and intense cravings, experienced after stopping the use of addictive drugs.

7. Drugs that act on the brain and nervous system, to increase their overall activity and general responsiveness.

8. Drugs that produce sensory distortions or perceptual distortions.

10. A chemical (or drug) that mimics the action of a specific neurotransmitter.

11. A group of techniques designed to focus attention and produce a heightened state of awareness.

Answers can be found in Appendix B.

Visual Summary for Modules 13 and 14

Understanding Consciousness

Consciousness: An organism's awareness of its own self and surroundings. **Alternate states of consciousness (ASCs)**: Mental states other than ordinary waking consciousness found in sleep, dreaming, drug use, hypnosis, and so on.

A Continuum of Awareness

Examples

• Top: **Controlled processes** requiring focused attention ➝ Taking an exam

• Middle: **Automatic processes** requiring minimal attention ➝ Brushing your teeth
Daydreams and fantasies

• Lowest: Minimal or no awareness ➝ Unconsciousness and coma

Sleep and Dreams

• *Sleep as a Biological Rhythm:* 24-hour cycles **(Circadian rhythms)** affect our sleep and waking cycle. Disruptions due to shift work, jet lag and sleep deprevation can cause serious problems.
• *Stages of Sleep:* Typical night's sleep has four to five 90-minute cycles. Non-REM cycle begins in Stage 1 and then moves through Stages 2, 3, and 4. After reaching deepest level, cycle reverses up to REM state.

non-REM Sleep – (Stages 1–4)

Function: Required for basic biological functioning.

REM Sleep (paradoxical sleep)

Function: Important for memory, learning, and basic biological functioning. Rapid eye movement often signals dreaming.

Theories of Sleep

1) **Repair/Restoration:** Allows recuperation from physical, emotional, and intellectual fatigue.
2) **Evolutionary/Circadian:** Sleep is part of circadian cycle, and evolved to conserve energy and protect from predators.

Theories of Dreaming

1) Psychoanalytic/psychodynamic view: Dreams are disguised symbols **(manifest and latent content)** of repressed desires and anxieties.
2) Biological view: Random stimulation of brain cells **(activation-synthesis hypothesis).**
3) Cognitive view: Dreams help sift and sort everyday experiences (information processing theory).

Sleep and Dreams (cont).

Sleep Disorders

Insomnia
Repeated difficulty falling or staying asleep or awakening too early.

Sleep Apnea
Temporary stopping of breathing during sleep; causing snoring and poor quality sleep.

Narcolepsy
Sudden and irresistible onsets of sleep during waking hours.

Nightmares
Bad dreams generally during REM sleep.

Night Terrors
Abrupt awakenings and panic during non-REM sleep.

Drugs and Consciousness

Psychoactive drugs: Chemicals that change conscious awareness or perception.

Important Terminology

Drug abuse: Drug taking that causes emotional or physical harm to the individual or others.
Addiction: Broad term referring to feelings of compulsion.
Psychological dependence: Desire or craving to achieve effects produced by a drug.
Physical dependence: Change in bodily processes due to continued drug use that results in withdrawal symptoms when the drug is withheld.
Tolerance: Larger and more frequent doses of drug are needed to produce desired effect.

Four Major Categories of Drugs

1) **Depressants** or "downers" (alcohol and barbiturates) slow down central nervous system (CNS).
2) **Stimulants** or "uppers" (caffeine, nicotine, and cocaine) activate CNS.
3) **Opiates** (heroin or morphine) numb senses and relieve pain.
4) **Hallucinogens** or psychedelics (LSD or marijuana) produce sensory or perceptual distortions.

Explaining Drug Use

"*How?*" Drugs that act as **agonists** mimic neurotransmitters, while **antagonists** oppose or block normal neurotransmitter functioning.

"*Why?*" Environmental factors (such as positive portrayals and positive emotions) and biological factors (such as stimulation of brain's reward system, genetics, and prevention of withdrawal symptoms).

Additional Routes to Alternate States

Daydreaming and Sexual Fantasies: Common forms of mild ASCs that serve mostly positive functions.

Hypnosis: Alternate state of heightened suggestibility characterized by relaxation and intense focus.

Myths and Controversies: 1) Forced hypnosis, 2) Unethical behavior, 3) Exceptional memories, 4) Superhuman strength, and 5) Fakery.

Uses: Reduce pain and anxiety, increase concentration, and as an adjunct to psychotherapy.

Meditation: Group of techniques designed to focus attention and produce a heightened awareness.

Uses: Can produce dramatic changes in physiological processes, including heart rate and respiration.

Consciousness Across Cultures: ASCs among peoples of all cultures 1) are part of sacred rituals, 2) serve social interaction needs, and 3) provide individual rewards.

Learning

During the 2000 presidential debates, George W. Bush mentioned the case of James Byrd and the death penalty conviction of his murderers as evidence of how Texas dealt with this particular "hate crime." Sadly, a follow-up national poll of likely voters found that many people did not know about (or could no longer remember) the brutal murder of James Byrd that happened only 2 years before.

Do you remember what happened on Sunday morning, June 28, 1998? James Byrd, a disabled 49-year-old African American, was hitchhiking home along Martin Luther King Boulevard in Jasper, Texas, when three young white men pulled up and offered him a ride. But they had no intention of taking him home. Instead, they chained Mr. Byrd by his ankles to the back of their rusted 1982 pickup and dragged him along an old logging road outside of town until his head and right arm ripped from his body.

James Byrd

The three men who committed this grisly murder were quickly captured and brought to justice. Two were sentenced to death and the third was given life imprisonment with-out the possibility of parole. During the trial, jurors recoiled in horror as they viewed photographs of Byrd's dismembered body. They seemed almost as stunned by the horrific tattoos on the body of one of his murderers (see the photo to the right). The swift arrest and conviction of James Byrd's murderers

John William "Bill" King. King was sentenced to death for the murder of James Byrd. Note the tattoos on his arm, which include a Satanic image of the Virgin Mary holding a horned baby Jesus, Nazi and racist prison gang insignias, Ku Klux Klan symbols, and the figure of a lynched Black man (Galloway, 1999).

brought a measure of comfort to his family, the residents of Jasper, and the nation as a whole.

But now as time has passed and the media spotlight has faded, we're left wondering what turns three young men into such callous, hate-filled monsters. Moreover, how do we explain the Imperial Wizard of the Ku Klux Klan who placed a KKK sticker on James Byrd's grave in March 2000? Despite the nation's collective outrage over this savage murder, hate crimes targeting groups solely on the basis of ethnicity, sexual orientation, gender, or religious preference continue to occur. Why? Where does such hatred come from? Is racism learned?

In the everyday sense, *learning* usually refers to classroom activities, such as math and reading, or motor skills, like riding a bike or playing the piano. But to psychologists, **learning** is much broader. It is formally defined as a relatively permanent change in behavior or behavioral potential as a result of practice or experience. Unlike that of fish, birds, and other animals that are driven primarily by innate, *instinctual* drives, human behavior results chiefly from learning. Our behavior is flexible and adaptive, rather than genetically programmed. Tragedies like the murder of James Byrd show us the dark side of human learning, but the very fact that racism and hatred are *learned* offers great hope. What is learned can be unlearned (or at least suppressed). Unlike salmon that are born with a predetermined, unchangeable instinct that drives them upstream to mate and die, humans are flexible and can learn new, more adaptive behaviors.

In this section, we will discover how we learn hatred, racism, phobias, and superstitions, as well as love and generosity. Much of the following modules focus on the most basic form of learning called *conditioning*, which is the process of learning associations between environmental stimuli and behavioral responses. We begin with two types of conditioning — classical and operant conditioning. (As you're reading through this section, it may help you organize and learn the material to repeatedly review the summary table provided in Table 15.1.) In Module 17, we also look at cognitive-social learning, and along the way, we discuss how learning theories and concepts can be used to improve your life. Module 18 provides an exploration of the neurological changes that take place during and after learning and then the evolutionary perspective.

Learning *A relatively permanent change in behavior or behavioral potential as a result of practice or experience*

MODULE 15
CLASSICAL CONDITIONING

Have you ever noticed that when you are hungry and see a large slice of chocolate cake or a juicy steak, your mouth starts to water? It seems natural that your mouth should water if you put food into it, but why do you salivate at just the sight of the food?

Understanding Classical Conditioning: Pavlov's and Watson's Contributions

What is classical conditioning, and how can I apply it in everyday life?

The answer to this question was accidentally discovered in the Leningrad laboratory of Ivan Pavlov (1849–1936). Pavlov was a Russian physiologist who was awarded the Nobel Prize for his work on the role of saliva in digestion. One of Pavlov's experiments involved salivary responses in dogs, where he attached a glass funnel to the experimental dogs' salivary glands to collect and measure the output (Figure 15.1). Pavlov wanted to determine whether dry food required more saliva than moist food and if nonfood objects required varying amounts of saliva, depending on how hard it was to spit them out.

Pavlov's (Accidental) Discovery

In the course of Pavlov's research, one of his students noticed that many dogs began to salivate at the sight of the food, the food dish, the smell of the food, or even the person who delivered the food — long *before* food was placed in their mouth. (This is the important, *accidental* part of the discovery, which might have gone unnoticed if the collection tubes had not been in place.) Although this "unscheduled" salivation interfered with Pavlov's research design and irritated him, it was also intriguing. Salivation is a *reflex response*, a largely, involuntary, automatic response to an external stimulus. Why were his dogs reflexively salivating *before* the food was even presented? Why did they salivate to extraneous stimuli other than food?

Ivan Pavlov (1849–1936), his assistants, and his famous "salivating dog." In 1903, Pavlov published the results from his first "conditioned reflex" (classical conditioning) study. Pavlov's dogs learned to salivate to many experimental stimuli, including a metronome, tuning fork, and bell. They also learned to salivate at the mere sight of the experimenter and the harness— unintentional conditioning!

TABLE 15.1 AN OVERVIEW OF CLASSICAL AND OPERANT CONDITIONING

	Classical Conditioning	Operant Conditioning
Other Names	Respondent conditioning Pavlovian conditioning	Instrumental conditioning Law of effect (Thorndike) Skinnerian conditioning
Pioneers	Ivan Pavlov John B. Watson	Edward Thorndike B. F. Skinner
Example	Sound of bell (CS) begins to produce salivation	Baby cries and parents pick up baby
Major Terms	Unconditioned stimulus (UCS) Conditioned stimulus (CS) Unconditioned response (UCR) Conditioned response (CR) Conditioned emotional response (CER)	Reinforcers (primary and secondary) Reinforcement (positive and negative) Punishment (positive and negative) Shaping Reinforcement schedules (continuous and partial)
Shared Terms	Extinction Spontaneous recovery Generalization Discrimination	Extinction Spontaneous recovery Generalization Discrimination
Major Differences	Involuntary (subject is passive)	Voluntary (subject is active)
Behavior Order	CS must come *before* the UCS	Reinforcement comes *after* the behavior

Harness to restrict movement by subject

Tube for collecting saliva from subject's mouth

Amount of saliva recorded here

Figure 15.1 *Pavlov's original classical conditioning apparatus.* During Pavlov's initial experiments, a tube was inserted into the dog's salivary gland to collect and measure the salivation produced under different experimental conditions.

Classical Conditioning *A basic form of learning in which an organism involuntarily learns to associate stimuli; a previously neutral stimulus is paired with an unconditioned stimulus to elicit a conditioned response that is identical or very similar to the unconditioned response (also known as respondent or Pavlovian conditioning)*

Unconditioned Stimulus (UCS) *Any stimulus that causes a reflex or emotional response without any learning or conditioning required*

Unconditioned Response (UCR) *The reflex response evoked by a stimulus without any learning required*

Conditioned Stimulus (CS) *A previously neutral stimulus that, through conditioning, now causes a classically conditioned response*

Conditioned Response (CR) *A learned response to a previously neutral stimulus that has been associated with the stimulus through repeated pairings*

Pavlov's scientific training helped him appreciate the significance of what had at first seemed annoying. A reflex (salivation) that occurred *before* the appropriate stimulus (food) was presented is clearly not inborn and biological. It had to have been acquired through experience — through *learning*. The type of learning that Pavlov described came to be known as **classical conditioning** (as in first [*classical*] learning [*conditioning*]). Classical conditioning (also known as *respondent* or *Pavlovian conditioning*) occurs when a previously neutral stimulus elicits a response through association with a stimulus that already elicits a similar or related response.

To understand this definition, you need to learn four basic terms describing each element of the classical conditioning process: *unconditioned stimulus* (UCS), *unconditioned response* (UCR), *conditioned stimulus* (CS), and *conditioned response* (CR).

Before Pavlov's dogs *learned* to salivate at something extraneous like the sight of the experimenter, the original salivary reflex was inborn and biological. It consisted of an **unconditioned stimulus** (UCS), food, and an **unconditioned response** (UCR), salivation.

Pavlov's discovery (and great contribution to psychology) was that learning occurs when a *neutral stimulus* (NS) (a stimulus that does not evoke a response) is regularly paired with an unconditioned stimulus. The neutral stimulus then becomes a **conditioned stimulus** (CS), which elicits a **conditioned response** (CR). (Study tip: If you're finding this confusing, note that *conditioning* is just another word for *learning*. When you see words like *unconditioned response*, mentally rearrange and think "unlearned response." It also helps to read through the diagram in Figure 15.2, which provides a visual organizer and detailed example from Pavlov's research.)

Does the neutral stimulus always come first? Researchers have investigated four different ways to pair stimuli (Table 15.2) and found that both the timing and the order in which the NS is presented are very important (Chromiak, Barber, & Kyler, 2000; Church & Kirkpatrick, 2001). Results show that *delayed conditioning* (the NS is presented before the UCS and remains until UCR begins) generally yields the fastest learning; whereas *backward conditioning* (the UCS is presented before the NS) is least effective. If you heard a fire alarm *after* you had already abandoned a building (backward conditioning), would you have the same association as if you heard the alarm first? No, because the sound of the fire alarm is the signal of the upcoming event (the fire), and hearing it afterward would lack real significance.

Watson's Contribution to Classical Conditioning

At this point, you may be wondering what dogs salivating to the sound of a bell has to do with your life — other than explaining why you salivate at the sight of delicious food. In fact, classical conditioning has been shown to be the most basic and fundamental way that all animals, including humans, learn most new responses, emotions, and attitudes. Your love for your parents (or significant other), the hatred and racism that led to the murder of James Byrd, and your drooling at the sight of chocolate cake are largely the result of classical conditioning.

In one of the most famous (and controversial) psychological studies, John Watson and Rosalie Rayner (1920, 2000) experimentally demonstrated how the emotion of fear could be classically conditioned. Albert, a healthy 11-month-old normal child, was brought to Watson's lab at Johns Hopkins University (Figure 15.3). Albert was first allowed to play with a white laboratory rat to find out if he was afraid of rats. Like most infants, "Little Albert" was curious and reached for the rat, showing

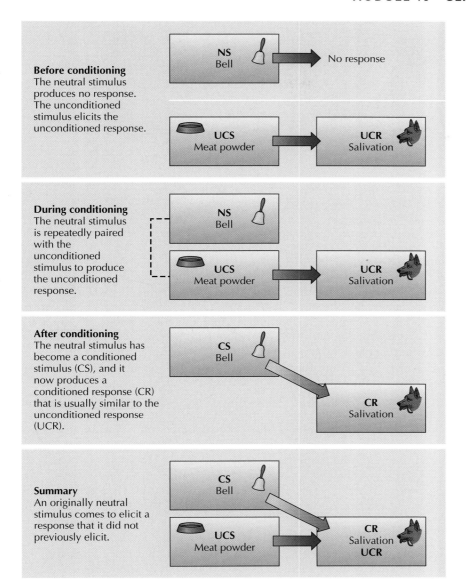

Figure 15.2 *Pavlov's classical conditioning paradigm.* Use this figure to help you visualize and organize the three major phases of classical conditioning and their associated key terms.

Before conditioning
The neutral stimulus produces no response. The unconditioned stimulus elicits the unconditioned response.

During conditioning
The neutral stimulus is repeatedly paired with the unconditioned stimulus to produce the unconditioned response.

After conditioning
The neutral stimulus has become a conditioned stimulus (CS), and it now produces a conditioned response (CR) that is usually similar to the unconditioned response (UCR).

Summary
An originally neutral stimulus comes to elicit a response that it did not previously elicit.

TABLE 15.2 CONDITIONING SEQUENCES

Delayed conditioning	NS presented before UCS and remains until UCR begins	Bell presented with food until dog begins to salivate
Simultaneous conditioning	NS presented at the same time as UCS	Bell and food presented simultaneously
Trace conditioning	NS presented and then taken away, or ends before UCS presented	Bell rung, but food presented only once the sound stops
Backward conditioning	UCS presented before NS	Food presented before the bell

NS = neutral stimulus; UCR = unconditioned response; UCS = unconditioned stimulus.

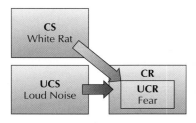

Figure 15.3 *Watson and Rayner.* This diagram shows how Little Albert's fear of rats was conditioned using a loud noise. In the photo, Watson and Rayner are shown with Little Albert who's crying from the loud noise.

Conditioned Emotional Response (CER) *Any classically conditioned emotional response to a previously neutral stimulus*

no fear. Using the fact that infants are naturally frightened (UCR) by loud noises (UCS), Watson stood behind Albert and again put the rat (NS) near him. When the infant reached for the rat, Watson banged a steel bar of Albert's crib with a hammer. As you might imagine, the loud noise frightened Albert and made him cry. The white rat (NS) was paired with the immediate loud noise (UCS) only seven times before the white rat alone produced a **conditioned emotional response** (CER), fear of the rat. Thus, Watson and Rayner's original hypothesis that fears are classically conditioned was confirmed.

For obvious reasons, Watson and Rayner's experiment could not be performed today because it violates several ethical guidelines for scientific research. Moreover, shortly after the experiment, Albert was adopted, and Watson and Rayner simply ended their experiment. They did not attempt to extinguish (remove) Albert's fear even though they believed that a CER could endure for a long period. This disregard for Albert's well-being is a serious criticism of Watson and Rayner's study. Their research methodology has also been criticized. Rather than objectively measuring Albert's fear, Watson and Rayner only subjectively evaluated it (Paul & Blumenthal, 1989).

Despite such criticisms, John B. Watson made important and lasting contributions to psychology. At the time he was conducting research, psychology's early founders were defining the field as the *scientific study of the mind*. Watson criticized psychology's study of subjective mental processes, insisting that it was "unscientific and a dead end." Instead, he focused on strictly observable behaviors and founded the new school or approach known as *behaviorism*, which believes that human behavior, though biologically influenced, is almost completely the result of conditioning and learning. His study of Little Albert has had legendary significance for many psychologists. He showed us that many of our likes, dislikes, prejudices, and fears are conditioned emotional responses.

Historical note: Shortly after the Little Albert experiment, Watson was fired from his academic position and no other university would hire him, despite his international fame as a scientist. His firing resulted from his scandalous and highly publicized affair with his graduate student Rosalie Rayner and subsequent divorce. Watson later married Rayner and became an influential advertising executive. He is credited with many successful ad campaigns based on classical conditioning, including ones for Johnson & Johnson baby powder, Maxwell House coffee, and Lucky Strike cigarettes (Angelo, 1998; Buckley, 1982, 1989; Hunt, 1993).

Check & Review

UNDERSTANDING CLASSICAL CONDITIONING

In **classical conditioning**, the type of learning investigated by Pavlov and Watson, an originally *neutral stimulus* (NS) is paired with an **unconditioned stimulus** (UCS) that causes a particular reflex or **unconditioned response** (UCR). After several pairings, the neutral stimulus becomes a **conditioned stimulus** (CS) that alone will produce a **conditioned response** (CR) or **conditioned emotional response** (CER) that is the same as the original reflex response.

There are four conditioning sequences: delayed conditioning, simultaneous conditioning, trace conditioning, and backward conditioning. Delayed conditioning is the most effective, and backward conditioning is the least effective.

Pavlov's work laid a foundation for Watson's insistence that psychology must be an objective science, studying only overt behavior, without considering internal, mental activity. Watson called this position *behaviorism,* demonstrated in his famous "Little Albert" study, that emotional responses can be classically conditioned.

Questions

1. Eli's grandma gives him a Tootsie roll every time she visits. When Eli sees his grandma arriving, his mouth begins to water. In this example the conditioned stimulus (CS) is _____ . (a) hunger; (b) Grandma; (c) the Tootsie roll; (d) the watering mouth

2. After conditioning, the _____ elicits the _____ .

3. In John Watson's demonstration of classical conditioning with little Albert, the unconditioned STIMULUS was _____ . (a) symptoms of fear; (b) a rat; (c) a bath towel; (d) a loud noise

4. A Vietnam War veteran experiences an intense emotional reaction to a clap of thunder. His emotional response is an example of a(n) _____. (a) CS; (b) UCS; (c) CER; (d) UCR

Answers to Questions can be found in Appendix B.

Principles of Classical Conditioning: Fine-Tuning the Process

Now that you understand the basics of classical conditioning and how they explain CERs, we can build on this foundation. In this section, we will discuss five important principles of classical conditioning: *stimulus generalization, stimulus discrimination, extinction, spontaneous recovery,* and *higher-order conditioning.*

Generalization and Discrimination

One of Pavlov's early experiments conditioned dogs to salivate at the sound of low-pitched tones. Pavlov and his students later demonstrated that the dogs also would salivate to higher-pitched tones. When objects or sounds that are similar to the originally conditioned stimulus (low-pitched tone) trigger the conditioned response (salivation), it is called **stimulus generalization**. The more the stimulus resembles the conditioned stimulus, the stronger the conditioned response (Hovland, 1937). Stimulus generalization also occurred in Watson's experiment with Albert. After conditioning, Albert feared rats, as well as a white rabbit, a white glove, cotton balls, and even a white beard on a Santa Claus mask.

Would Little Albert still be afraid of a Santa Claus mask as he grew older? Probably not. Through the process of **stimulus discrimination**, he would eventually learn to recognize differences between rats and other stimuli. Although stimulus generalization seems to naturally follow from initial classical conditioning, organisms only learn to distinguish (or *discriminate*) between an original CS and similar stimuli if they have enough experience with both. Just as you learn to discriminate between the sound of your cellular phone and the ringing of others, when Pavlov repeatedly presented food following a high-pitched tone, but not with a low-pitched tone, the dog gradually learned to distinguish between the two tones. Thus, both Little Albert and Pavlov's dog produced conditioned responses only to specific stimuli — *stimulus discrimination.*

Stimulus Generalization *The occurrence of a learned response not only to the original stimulus but also to other similar stimuli*

Stimulus Discrimination *The occurrence of a learned response to a specific stimulus but not to other, similar stimuli*

Figure 15.4 *The process of extinction.* In this hypothetical graph from a typical experiment demonstrating extinction, note how the response rate decreases over time and with additional extinction trials.

Extinction *The gradual suppression of a behavior or a response that occurs when a conditioned stimulus is repeatedly presented without the unconditioned stimulus with which it had been previously associated*

Spontaneous Recovery *The reappearance of a previously extinguished response after a period of time without exposure to the conditioned stimulus*

Higher-Order Conditioning *In classical conditioning, a procedure in which a neutral stimulus (NS) becomes a conditioned stimulus (CS) through association with an already established conditioned stimulus. A NS is paired with a previous CS_1, which then becomes a CS_2 and produces the same CR as CS_1*

Extinction and Spontaneous Recovery

Classical conditioning, like all learning, is only *relatively* permanent. Most behaviors that are learned through classical conditioning can be suppressed. The process is called **extinction**. Extinction occurs when the UCS is repeatedly withheld whenever the CS is presented, which weakens the previous association. For instance, when Pavlov sounded the tone again and again without presenting food, the dog's salivation gradually declined. Similarly, if you have a classically conditioned fear of the sound of a dentist's drill and later start to work as a dental assistant, your fear would gradually diminish (Figure 15.4).

Does extinction cause us to "unlearn" a classical conditioned response? No, extinction is not *unlearning* (Bouton, 1994). A behavior becomes extinct when the response rate decreases and the person or animal no longer responds to the stimulus. It does not mean the person or animal has "erased" the previous learned connection between the stimulus and the response. In fact, if the stimulus is reintroduced, the conditioning is much faster the second time. Furthermore, Pavlov found that if he allowed several hours to pass after the extinction procedure and then presented the tone again, the salivation would spontaneously reappear. The reappearance of a conditioned response after extinction, referred to as **spontaneous recovery**, helps explain why you suddenly feel excited at the sight of your old high school sweetheart. Even though years have passed (and extinction has occurred), some people (who haven't read this book and studied this phenomenon) might mislabel this excitement as "lasting love." You, on the other hand, would recognize it as possible *spontaneous recovery* (Figure 15.5).

Higher-Order Conditioning

Children are not born salivating to McDonald's golden arches. However, you've probably heard them begging to eat at a McDonald's restaurant after seeing this symbol. How did this happen? In Pavlov's original study, the NS was paired with a UCS. It was later learned that pairing a second, new stimulus with the already conditioned stimulus could make it also become a CS. This is known as **higher-order conditioning**.

If you wanted to demonstrate higher-order conditioning in Pavlov's dogs, you would first condition the dogs to salivate to the sound of the bell. Then you would pair the flash of light to the ringing of the bell. Eventually, the dog would salivate to the flash of light alone (Figure 15.6 a,b). In a similar fashion, children first learn to pair up the general McDonald's restaurant with food, and later learn that two golden arches are a symbol for McDonald's (Figure 15.6 c,d). Their salivation and begging to eat at the restaurant are a classic case of higher-order conditioning (and successful advertising).

Classical Conditioning in Real Life: From Prejudice to Advertisements

As you might expect, advertisers, politicians, film producers, music artists, and others have used classical conditioning to manipulate our purchases, votes, emotions, and motivation. It also has been used to our benefit (Woods & Ramsay, 2000). Let's examine several examples, good and bad, from everyday life.

Prejudice

In a classic study in the 1930s, Kenneth Clark and Mamie P. Clark (1939) studied children's reactions to black dolls and to white dolls. They found that given a choice, both black and white children preferred the white dolls. When asked which doll was good and which was bad, both groups of children also responded that the white doll

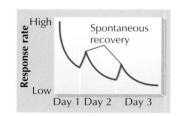

Figure 15.5 *Spontaneous recovery.* A hypothetical graph from a standard extinction experiment, but note that on occasion the extinguished response will "spontaneously reappear."

Figure 15.6 *How children learn to salivate for McDonald's.* As you can see in the top two boxes (a and b), *higher-order conditioning* is a two-stage process. In the first stage, a neutral stimulus (such as a bell) is paired with an unconditioned stimulus (such as meat powder) until it becomes a conditioned stimulus that elicits a conditioned response (salivation). During the second stage (higher order conditioning), a different neutral stimulus (such as a flashing light) is paired with the bell until it also becomes a conditioned stimulus. Now examine the bottom two boxes (c and d). Can you see how the same two-stage type of higher-order conditioning helps explain why children become so excited (and salivate) when they see the golden arches.

was good and nice and that the black doll was bad, dirty, and ugly. The Clarks reasoned that the children, as well as many others in the United States, had *learned* to associate inferior qualities with darker skin and positive qualities with light skin. The Clark study played a pivotal role in the famous *Brown v. Board of Education of Topeka* ruling in 1954 that segregation of public facilities was unconstitutional. (This was also the first time social science research was formally cited in a U.S. Supreme Court case to support a legal argument.)

If you're thinking this 1930 study no longer applies, follow-up research in the late 1980s found that 65 percent of the African American children and 74 percent of the white children still preferred the white doll (Powell-Hopson & Hopson, 1988). The Clark study provided important insights into the negative effects of prejudice on the victims — African American children. But what about the white children who also strongly preferred the white doll? Was their preference also due to classical conditioning? And did a similar type of classical conditioning contribute to the vicious murder of James Byrd? Although we can't be sure how the hatred and racism that took James Byrd's life originally started, prejudice of many types (racism, ageism, sexism, homophobia, and religious intolerance) can be classically conditioned, as Figure 15.7 shows.

Phobias

Do you know someone who "freaks out" at the sight of a cockroach? At some time during childhood, this person probably was conditioned to associate the NS (cockroach) with a UCS (perhaps seeing a parent flinch at the sight of a cockroach) until

Figure 15.7 *How prejudice may be acquired through classical conditioning.* (a) Before children are conditioned to be prejudiced, they show no response to a member of different group. (b) Given that children are naturally upset and fearful when they see their parents upset, they can learn to be upset and fearful (UCR) if the see their parents respond negatively (UCS) to a member of a disliked group (NS). (c) After several pairings of the person from this group with their parents' negative reactions, the sight of the other person becomes a conditioned stimulus (CS), and being upset and fearful becomes the conditioned response (CR). (d) A previously unbiased child has now learned to be prejudiced.

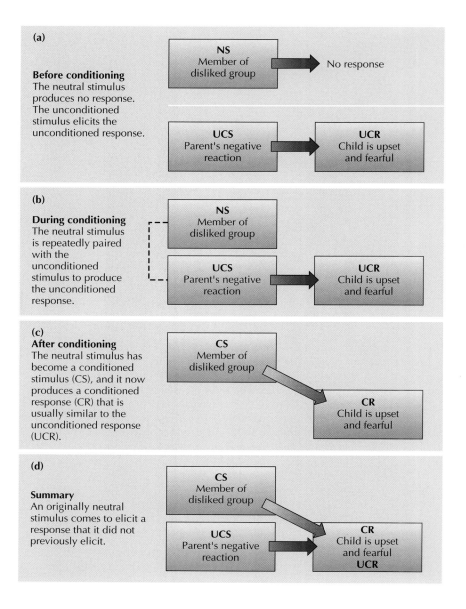

a CR (fear at the sight of a cockroach) was conditioned. Researchers have found that classically conditioned emotional responses explain most *phobias*, exaggerated and irrational fears of a specific object or situation (Evans & Rilling, 2000; Schneider et al., 1999). The good news is that extreme fear of cockroaches, hypodermic needles, spiders, closets, and even snakes can be effectively treated with *behavior modification* (Module 44).

Medical Treatments

Examples of classical conditioning are also found in the medical field. For instance, a program conducted by several hospitals in California gives an *emetic* (a nausea-producing drug) to their alcohol-addicted patients. But before the nausea begins, the patient gargles with his or her preferred alcoholic beverage to maximize the taste and odor cues paired with nausea. During conditioning, the smell and taste of various alcoholic drinks (NS) are paired with nausea (UCS), making the patient vomit or feel sick (UCR). Afterward, just the smell or taste of alcohol (CS) makes the person sick (CR). Some patients have found this treatment successful, but not all.

Although nausea is deliberately produced in this treatment for alcoholism, it is an unfortunate, unintended side effect of some cancer treatment. The nausea and vomiting produced by chemotherapy often generalize to other environmental cues, such as the hospital room color or odor (Stockhorst et al., 2000). Using their knowledge of classical conditioning to change associations, therapists can now help cancer patients control their nausea and vomiting response.

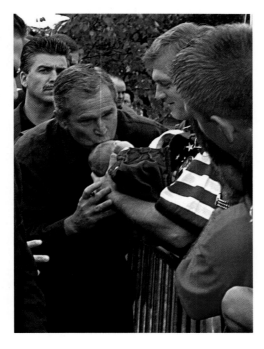

Classical conditioning in action. Have you ever wondered why politicians kiss babies? It's because they hope to become a favorable conditioned stimulus. They hope that by pairing themselves with positive stimuli (like babies or the American flag) you will have a favorable predisposition to vote for them (a conditioned emotional response).

Advertising

Beginning with John B. Watson in the 1920s, advertisers have employed numerous classical conditioning principles to market their products. For example, TV commercials, magazine ads, and business promotions often pair their products or company logo (NS) with pleasant images, such as attractive models and celebrities (UCS) that automatically trigger favorable responses (UCR). Advertisers hope that after repeated viewings, their products (CS) alone will elicit those same favorable responses (CR) and that we will buy their products or use their services. Researchers caution that these ads also help produce visual stimuli that trigger conditioned responses such as urges to smoke or drink alcohol, which makes addiction recovery more difficult (Dols, Willems, van den Hout, & Bittoun, 2000; Foltin & Haney, 2000).

TRY THIS
Yourself

If you'd like to see how classical conditioning affects your own life, try this:

1. Look through a popular magazine and find several advertisements. What images are used as the unconditioned stimulus (UCS)? Note how you react to these images.
2. While watching a movie or a favorite TV show, note what sounds and images are used as conditioned stimuli. (Hint: certain types of music are used to set the stage for happy stories, sad events,

and fearful situations.) What are your conditioned emotional responses (CERs)?
3. Read the words below and pay attention to your emotional response. Your reactions — positive, negative, or neutral — are a result of your own personal classical conditioning history. Can you trace back to the UCS?

> father   final exams   spinach
> Santa Claus   beer   mother

Check & Review

PRINCIPLES AND APPLICATIONS OF CLASSICAL CONDITIONING

In classical conditioning, **stimulus generalization** occurs when stimuli similar to the original conditioned stimulus (CS) elicit the conditioned response (CR). **Stimulus discrimination** takes place when only the CS elicits the CR. **Extinction** occurs when the unconditioned stimulus (UCS) is repeatedly withheld and the association between the CS and the UCS is broken. **Spontaneous recovery** happens when a CR that had been extinguished reappears with no prompting. In **higher-order conditioning**, the neutral stimulus (NS) is paired with a CS to which the participant has already been conditioned, rather than with a UCS.

Classical conditioning has many applications in everyday life. Through classical conditioning, we can learn negative attitudes toward groups of people — and unlearn those attitudes. It is also used in behavior modification programs, some medical treatments, and to help patients change associations and reduce undesirable conditioned behavior. In addition, classical conditioning is the basis for a great deal of advertising.

Questions

1. Like most college students, your heart rate and blood pressure greatly increase when the fire alarm sounds. If the fire alarm system was malfunctioning and rang every half hour, by the end of the day, your heart rate and blood pressure would no longer increase. Why?

2. A baby is bitten by a dog and then is afraid of all small animals. This is an example of (a) stimulus discrimination; (b) extinction; (c) reinforcement; (d) stimulus generalization.

3. When a conditioned stimulus is used to reinforce the learning of a second conditioned stimulus, _____ has occurred.

4. If you wanted to use higher order conditioning to get little Albert to fear Barbie dolls, you would present a Barbie doll with _____. (a) the loud noise; (b) the original unconditioned response; (c) the white rat; (d) the original conditioned response

Answers to Questions can be found in Appendix B.

ACTIVE LEARNING WORKSHEET   MODULE 15

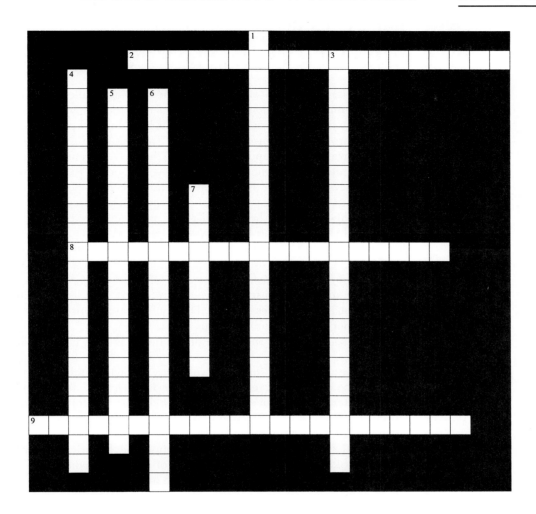

ACROSS

2. The reappearance of a previously extinguished response after a period of time without exposure to the conditioned stimulus.

8. A learned response to a previously neutral stimulus that has been associated with the stimulus.

9. The occurrence of a learned response not only to the original stimulus but also to other similar stimuli.

DOWN

1. The reflex response evoked by a stimulus without any learning required.

3. The occurrence of a learned response to a specific stimulus but not to other, similar stimuli.

4. A basic form of learning in which an organism involuntarily learns to associate stimuli.

5. A previously neutral stimulus that, through conditioning, now causes a classically conditioned response.

6. Any stimulus that causes a reflex or emotional response without any learning or conditioning required.

7. Occurs when the UCS is repeatedly withheld whenever the CS is presented.

Answers can be found in Appendix B.

MODULE 16
OPERANT CONDITIONING

What is operant conditioning, and how can I apply it in
everyday life?

Operant Conditioning *Learning*
based on consequences; behavior is
strengthened if followed by reinforce-
ment and diminished if followed by
punishment

Consequences are the heart of **operant conditioning** (also called *instrumental con-*
ditioning or *Skinnerian conditioning*). In classical conditioning, the consequences of
an animal or person's behavior are irrelevant. Pavlov's dog still got the meat powder
whether it salivated or not. However, in operant conditioning the *consequences* of an
organism's behavior are all important. Whether behavior is reinforced or punished
(consequences) determines whether the response will occur again. Stated in a different way, behaviors that are reinforced are more likely to be repeated, whereas
those that are punished are less likely to be repeated. If you receive praise and an A
on your term paper, you will be more likely to write another term paper, and the
reverse is true if you receive an F and critical comments.

Classical and operant conditioning also tend to differ in the types of responses
they generate. In classical conditioning, the organism's response is *passive* and *invol-*
untary. It "happens to" the organism when a UCS follows a CS. In operant conditioning, the organism's response is *active* and *voluntary*. The learner "operates" on
the environment and produces effects. These effects (or consequences), in turn,
influence whether the behavior will occur again.

It's important to mention that these distinctions between classical and operant
condition are *generally* true — but not *always* true. Technically speaking, classical
conditioning does sometimes influence voluntary behavior, and operant conditioning can influence involuntary, reflexive behavior. Furthermore, both forms of conditioning often interact to produce and maintain behavior. But for most purposes, the
distinction holds, and it's easier simply to remember that classical conditioning is
passive and operant conditioning is active.

In the sections that follow, we will examine the historical contributions of
Thorndike and Skinner, the general principles of operant conditioning, and several
interesting applications of operant conditioning to real life.

Understanding Operant Conditioning: Thorndike and Skinner

Edward Thorndike (1874–1949), the pioneer of operant conditioning, was among
the first to examine how voluntary behaviors are influenced by their consequences.
In one of his famous experiments, he put a cat inside a specially built *puzzle box*
(Figure 16.1). The only way the cat could get out was by pulling on a rope or stepping on a pedal, whereupon the door would open and the cat could get out to eat.
Eventually, through trial-and-error, the cat would accidentally pull on the rope or
step on the pedal that opened the door. With each additional trial, the cat's actions
became more purposeful and it soon learned to open the door immediately.

Thorndike concluded that the frequency of a behavior is modified by its consequences. He is credited with developing the *law of effect*: the probability of a action
being repeated *strengthens* if it is followed by a pleasant or satisfying consequence.
In short, rewarded behavior is more likely to reoccur (Thorndike, 1911). Thorndike's
law of effect was a first step in understanding how active, *voluntary* behaviors can
be modified by their consequences.

B. F. Skinner (1904–1990) extended Thorndike's law of effect to more complex
forms of behaviors. As a strict behaviorist, however, Skinner avoided terms like *pleas-*
ant, *desired*, and *voluntary* because they make assumptions about what an organism
feels and wants and because they imply that behavior is due to conscious choice or

Figure 16.1 *Thorndike box.* This is a
typical Thorndike box that was used in
Edward Thorndike's trial-and-error experiments with cats. When a cat stepped on
a pedal inside the box, the door latch was
released and a weight attached to the
door pulled it open so the cat could exit.
(From Thorndike, 1898).

intention. He argued that to understand behavior, we should consider only observable, external or environmental stimuli and responses. We should look outside the learner, not inside.

To test his theories, Skinner conducted systematic research. The typical Skinner experiment used an animal, usually a pigeon or a rat, and an apparatus that has come to be called a *Skinner box*. Skinner trained a rat to push a lever to receive a food pellet. The rat got a pellet each time it pushed the lever, and the number of responses made by the rat was recorded. Skinner used this basic experimental design to demonstrate a number of operant conditioning principles that are discussed in the next section.

Principles of Operant Conditioning: How It All Works

There are several important principles that you need to understand about operant conditioning. We begin with factors involved in *strengthening a response*, including primary and secondary reinforcers, positive and negative punishment, schedules of reinforcement, and shaping. We then explore those principles that *weaken a response*, including positive and negative punishment. We conclude this section with a look at the pros and cons of punishment and with a review of terms that are shared between classical and operant conditioning.

As we discuss these concepts, keep in mind that the effects or consequences of behavior result from either reinforcement or punishment. Specifically, **reinforcement** is any procedure that results in an increase in a response. Conversely, **punishment** is any procedure that results in a decrease in a response. The distinction between reinforcement and punishment is critical to understanding operant conditioning and applying its principles to your life.

Strengthening a Response

Earlier, we said that Skinner was a strict behaviorist who insisted that scientific observation be limited to that which can be observed. Therefore, instead of using words like *rewards* (which focuses on feelings), Skinner talked about reinforcers and reinforcement in terms of "strengthening the response." Thus, reinforcement (and punishment) are always defined *after the fact*. If the rate of response increases *after* a supposed reinforcer is presented, then we can say the behavior has been *reinforced*. This may seem complicated, but the distinction is important. For example, men may buy women candy and flowers, believing that "all women love these things." However, some women hate candy (imagine that!), and some are allergic to flowers. Even avid candy and flower lovers aren't interested after a heavy meal or if they already have a lot of flowers. In both of these cases, the men were attempting to reinforce the women's feelings for them, but the women's reactions suggest that this is not what happened. Skinner would advise the men to watch the organisms' responses, *not* what they think the women should like or do.

As Table 16.1 shows, reinforcers can be grouped into two major classes:

1. *Primary and secondary reinforcers.* One of the chief methods for strengthening a response is with primary and secondary reinforcers. Through his research, Skinner found that food was an effective reinforcer for responses in rats but that humans responded according to primary or secondary reinforcers. Reinforcers such as food, water, and sex are called **primary reinforcers** because they normally satisfy an unlearned biological need. Reinforcers such as money, praise, attention, and material possessions that have no intrinsic value are called **secondary reinforcers**; the only power they have to reinforce behavior results from their learned value. A baby, for example, would find milk much more reinforcing than a hundred-dollar bill. Needless to say, by the time this baby has grown to adolescence, he or she will have learned to prefer the money. Among Westerners, money may be the most widely

B. F. Skinner and a typical Skinner box. *The rat in the box has been conditioned to receive a pellet of food as reinforcement for bar pressing.*

Reinforcement *Any action or event that increases the probability that a response will be repeated*

Punishment *Any action or event that decreases the likelihood that a response will be repeated*

Primary Reinforcers *Stimuli that increase the probability of a response because they satisfy a biological need, such as food, water, and sex*

Secondary Reinforcers *Stimuli that increase the probability of a response because of their learned value, such as money and material possessions*

TABLE 16.1 HOW REINFORCEMENT STRENGTHENS AND INCREASES BEHAVIORS

Positive Reinforcement (+; adds to and strengthens behavior)	Type of Reinforcer	Negative Reinforcement (−; takes away and strengthens behavior	Type of Reinforcer
You're hungry and eat a delicious hamburger.	Primary	The hamburger takes away your hunger pains.	Primary
Your boyfriend/girlfriend hugs you.	Primary	You take an aspirin for your headache, which takes away the pain.	Primary
You receive $200 as a bonus.	Secondary	After high sales, your boss says you won't have to work on weekends.	Secondary
You receive a good grade on your psychology exam.	Secondary	Professor says you won't have to take the final exam because you did so well on your unit exam.	Secondary

used secondary reinforcer because of its learned association with desirable commodities.

2. *Positive and negative reinforcement.* Adding or taking away relevant stimuli can also strengthen behavior. Suppose you tickle your baby and he smiles at you. His smile increases (or strengthens) the likelihood that you will tickle him again in the future. The smile itself is a *positive reinforcer*. The *process* whereby he "adds" his smile to the transaction and increases the likelihood that you will repeat the same tickling behavior is called **positive reinforcement**. On the other hand, suppose your baby is upset and crying, so you hug him and he stops crying. In this case, the removal of crying is a *negative reinforcer*, and the *process* is called **negative reinforcement** because it increases (or strengthens) the likelihood that you will hug him again in the future when he cries. Both responses to your behavior have been reinforced, and your behavioral tendencies have been strengthened.

(As a critical thinker, you may be wondering what's happening for the baby in this example. Assuming he likes being tickled, his smiling behavior will increase when he learns that his smile causes the parent to tickle him — *positive reinforcement*. In the second case, the baby learns that crying brings hugs from his parents, so his crying also will increase — *positive reinforcement*. Although this may seem like a potential problem, the baby soon will learn to talk and develop "better" ways to communicate.)

How can I keep from thinking of negative reinforcement as punishment? It is difficult to think of the word *negative* and not consider it as punishment. But it's important to remember that these two terms are actually completely opposite procedures. Reinforcement (either positive or negative) *strengthens a behavior*, whereas punishment *weakens a behavior*.

Our students also find it less confusing to think of positive and negative reinforcement in the mathematical sense (as shown in Table 16.1) rather than as personal values of good and bad. Personal values can get confusing because what's good for one person is bad for another. Again, this is why Skinner insisted we must only

Positive Reinforcement *The process of adding or presenting a stimulus that increases the likelihood of that response occurring again*

Negative Reinforcement *The process of taking away or removing a stimulus that increases the likelihood of that response occurring again*

TABLE 16.2 ESCAPE LEARNING AND AVOIDANCE LEARNING

Escape Learning	Avoidance Learning
A negative reinforcement that eliminates an aversive state of affairs that already exists	A negative reinforcement that prevents an expected aversive event from happening
Example: A parent begins to scold her child and the child runs from the room to escape; the child is negatively reinforced because the scolding stops when the child leaves the room	Example: A parent gets angry when a teenager comes home late, so the teen avoids the aversive confrontation by waiting until the parent is asleep to return home

look at the response. Instead of "good" or "bad," think of positive reinforcement as something being added (+) that increases the likelihood that the behavior will increase. If your boss compliments you on a job well done, the compliment is added (+) as a consequence to the good job you did, and your behavior is likely to increase. Similarly, if your baby awakens you in the morning and you bring her to bed with you and she stops crying, the taking away of the noise (–) is reinforcing, and your placing of the baby in your bed is likely to increase.

Researchers who study negative reinforcement have generally used two kinds of learning procedures: *escape learning* and *avoidance learning*. In a typical escape learning study, the animal learns that a response will end some kind of aversive (unpleasant) stimulus. For example, a rat might learn to escape a mild electric shock on the bottom of a cage by running to an area of the cage that is not electrified. This escape response leads to the removal of the aversive stimulus, so it is strengthened through negative reinforcement. In avoidance learning, the response the animal learns *prevents* the negative situation from occurring. The experimenter gives a signal (such as a light) that shock is forthcoming. In this case, the rat might learn to avoid the shock by running to the safe area of the cage as soon as the light comes on. Table 16.2 summarizes these concepts and offers additional (human) examples.

When I make myself study before I let myself go to the movies, is this escape learning? No, but it is an excellent strategy. You're actually using the **Premack principle**, named after psychologist David Premack, who suggested using any naturally occurring, high-frequency response to reinforce low-frequency responses. Recognizing that you love to go to movies, you intuitively tied your less-desirable, low-frequency activities (studying) to high-frequency behavior (going to the movies). You can use the Premack principle in other aspects of your college life, such as making yourself write 4 pages on your term paper or reading 20 pages before you allow yourself to call a friend or have a snack.

Should I use the Premack principle every time I want to go to the movies or just occasionally? The answer is complex and depends on your most desired outcome. To make this decision, you need to understand various *schedules of reinforcement,* or rules that determine when a response will be rewarded and when it will not (Purdy, Markham, Schwartz, & Gordon, 2001).

Schedules of Reinforcement

The term *schedule of reinforcement* refers to the rate or interval at which responses are reinforced (Gallistel & Gibbon, 2000). Although there are numerous schedules of reinforcement, they can be grouped into two types: *continuous* or *partial*. When

Premack principle *Using a response that has a high probability of occurrence to reinforce a response that has a lower probability of occurrence*

Continuous Reinforcement *Reinforcement in which every correct response is reinforced*

Partial (Intermittent) Reinforcement Schedule *Reinforcement in which some, but not all, correct responses are reinforced*

Skinner was training his animals, he found that learning was most rapid if the response is reinforced each time it occurs — a procedure called **continuous reinforcement.** However, real life seldom provides continuous reinforcement. You do not get an A each time you write a paper or a date each time you ask, but your behavior persists because your efforts are occasionally rewarded. Most everyday behavior is rewarded on a **partial (or intermittent) schedule of reinforcement,** which involves reinforcing only some responses, not all of them.

It is important to remember that continuous reinforcement leads to faster learning than does partial reinforcement. For example, if you are rewarded every time you blast an alien starship in a video game (*continuous reinforcement*), you will learn how to play faster than if you are rewarded for every third or fourth hit (*partial reinforcement*). However, although a continuous schedule of reinforcement leads to faster initial learning, it is *not* an efficient system for maintaining long-term behaviors. Imagine having to reward your children every morning for getting up, brushing their teeth, making their beds, dressing, and so on. You simply cannot reward someone constantly for every appropriate response. It is therefore important to move to a partial schedule of reinforcement once a task is well learned.

Why? Because under partial schedules, behavior is more resistant to extinction. Have you noticed that people spend long hours pushing buttons and pulling levers on slot machines in hopes of winning the jackpot? This high response rate and the compulsion to keep gambling in spite of significant losses are evidence of the strong resistance to extinction with partial schedules of reinforcement.

Four Forms of Partial Schedules of Reinforcement

Partial schedules of reinforcement are based on the number of responses between reinforcements (*ratio schedules*), or on the interval of time between reinforced responses (*interval schedules*). In addition, each type can be *fixed* or *variable*. There are, thus, four partial schedules of reinforcement: **fixed ratio, variable ratio, fixed interval,** and **variable interval.** Table 16.3 defines these terms and provides examples.

Fixed Ratio Schedule *A partial schedule of reinforcement in which a participant must make a certain number of responses before being reinforced*

Variable Ratio Schedule *A schedule of reinforcement in which the participant is reinforced, on the average, for making a specific number of responses but the number of required responses between reinforcement is varied*

Fixed Interval Schedule *A schedule of reinforcement in which a participant is reinforced for the first response after a specific period of time has elapsed*

Variable Interval Schedule *A schedule of reinforcement in which the participant is reinforced for the first response after a period of time has elapsed; this period of time varies from one reinforcement to the next*

How do I know which schedule to choose? The type of partial schedule selected depends on the type of behavior being studied and on the speed of learning desired (Neuringer, Deiss, & Olson, 2000). For example, suppose you want to

Continuous or partial reinforcement. Gumball machines provide continuous reinforcement, whereas roulette and other gambling games provide partial reinforcement.

TABLE 16.3 FOUR FORMS OF PARTIAL SCHEDULES OF REINFORCEMENT

	Definitions	Response Rates	Examples
Fixed ratio (FR)	Reinforced after a fixed number of responses	Produces a high rate of response but a brief dropoff just after reinforcement	In a laboratory, a rat receives a food pellet after pressing the bar 7 times Parents pay a child $10 after he washes 2 cars
Fixed interval (FI)	Reinforced for the first response after a specified time has elapsed	Responses tend to increase as the time for the next reinforcer is near but drop off after reinformencement and during interval	Rat's behavior is reinforced with a food pellet each time it presses a bar after 20 seconds has elapsed. You get a weekly paycheck
Variable ratio (VR)	Reinforced on an average number of responses, but the number varies	High response rates, no pause after reinforcement, and very resistant to extinction	Slot machines designed to pay out after an average number of responses (maybe every 10 times), but any one machine may pay out on the first response, then seventh, then the twentieth
Variable interval (VI)	Reinforced on a variable time interval	Relatively low, but steady rates because the animal or person cannot predict when reward will come	Rat's behavior reinforced with a food pellet after a response and a variable, unpredictable interval of time In a class with pop quizzes, you study at a slow but steady rate because you can't anticipate the next quiz

Figure 16.2 *Which is the best schedule of reinforcement?* Each of the different schedules produces its own unique pattern of response, and the best schedule depends on the specific task — see Table 16.3. Note that the "stars" on the lines represent the delivery of a reinforcer. (Adapted from Skinner, 1961.)

teach your dog to sit. Initially you reinforce your dog with a cookie every time he sits (continuous reinforcement). To save on your cookie bill and to make his training more resistant to extinction, you eventually switch to one of the partial reinforcement schedules, such as the *fixed ratio* schedule. You would then give your dog a cookie after he sat a certain number of times. The dog must make a fixed number of responses before he receives the reinforcement. As you can see in Figure 16.2, a fixed ratio leads to the highest overall response rate, but each of the four types of partial schedules has different advantages and disadvantages (Table 16.3).

Shaping

Each of the principles discussed above are important for maintaining behavior, but how do you teach something like playing the piano or a foreign language to someone who's never seen a piano or been exposed to another language? **Shaping** teaches a desired response by reinforcing, a series of successive steps leading to the final goal response. It is especially effective for teaching complex or novel behaviors. Skinner believed that shaping explains a wide variety of skills and abilities that each

Shaping *A procedure in which reinforcement is delivered for successive approximations of the desired response*

Operant conditioning in action.
*Momoko, a five-year-old female mon-
key, is famous in Japan for her water-
skiing, deep-sea diving, and other
amazing abilities. Can you imagine
how her trainers undoubtedly used
shaping to teach this type of behavior?*

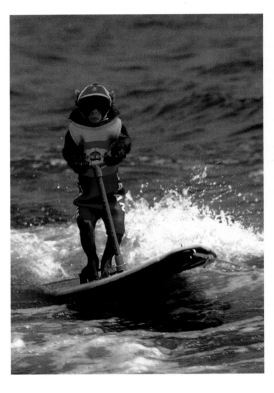

of us possess, from eating with a
fork, to playing a musical instrument, to driving a stick-shift car.

Parents, athletic coaches,
teachers, and animal trainers all
use shaping techniques. For example, if you want to shape a child to
make his bed, you could begin by
reinforcing when he first gets the
sheets and pillows on the bed. Over
time, you would stop reinforcing
that level of behavior and only reinforce when he gets the bedspread
on the bed and tucked over the pillows. Again, after a little time, you
would stop reinforcing until he gets
the bedspread on, tucked over the
pillows, and straight. Each step in
shaping, then, moves slightly
beyond the previously learned
behavior, allowing the person to
link the new step to the behavior
previously learned.

Weakening a Response

Now that you understand how to *strengthen* a response, we will examine ways to
weaken undesirable behaviors. Like reinforcement, punishment affects behavior,
but it has the opposite effect: it *decreases* the strength of the response — that is,
the likelihood that a behavior will be repeated again. Just as with reinforcement,
there are two kinds of punishment, *positive* and *negative* (Skinner, 1953; Gordon,
1989). Also as with reinforcement, remember to think in mathematical terms of
adding and taking away, rather than good and bad (Table 16.4).

Positive punishment is the addition of a stimulus that decreases (or weakens) the likelihood of the response occurring again. If your dog digs a hole every
time he sees a gopher mound, and you shout at him to decrease the digging, you
are applying positive punishment. **Negative punishment** is the taking away of a

Positive Punishment *The process of
adding or presenting a stimulus that
decreases the likelihood of that
response occurring again*

Negative Punishment *The process
of taking away or removing a stimulus
that decreases the likelihood of that
response occurring again*

TABLE 16.4 HOW PUNISHMENT WEAKENS AND DECREASES BEHAVIORS

Positive Punishment (+; adds to and weakens the behavior)	Negative Punishment (−; takes away and weakens the behavior)
You have to run 4 extra laps in your gym class because you were late.	You aren't allowed to join the gym class because you were late.
Your teacher asks you to give an oral report after you mention an interesting article in the school newspaper.	Your teacher reassigns you to another group because you were talking too much to your friend.
Your boss complains about your performance.	Your boss takes away your overtime pay because you finished all the work ahead of schedule.

stimulus that decreases (or weakens) the likelihood of the response occurring again. Parents use negative punishment when they take the car keys away from a teen who doesn't come home on time. Notice, as with reinforcement, that the concept is defined in terms of its effect (consequences) on behavior. Also, in both positive and negative punishment, the behavior has been punished and the behavioral tendencies have been weakened.

The "Tricky Business" of Punishment

When we discuss punishment, our students tend to think only of disciplinary procedures used by parents, teachers, and other authority figures. But from the psychological perspective (and the previous definitions), punishment is much more than parents giving a child a time-out for misbehaving or teachers giving demerits. Any process that adds or takes away something that causes the behavior to decrease is punishment. By this definition, if parents ignore all the A's on their child's report card and ask repeated questions about the B's and C's, they may unintentionally punish and weaken the likelihood of future A's. Dog owners who yell at their dogs for coming to them after being called several times are actually punishing the desired behavior — coming when called. Similarly, college administrators who take away "leftover" money from a department's budget because it wasn't spent by the end of the year are punishing desired behavior — saving money. (Yes, we did add this last example as a "subtle" message to our college administrators.)

As you can see, punishment is a tricky business. But an advantage of studying psychology is that you understand how positive and negative punishment (and positive and negative reinforcement) operate, and you can use this knowledge to become a better parent, teacher, and authority figure, as well as a better friend and lover. Punishment encompasses more than discipline, a difficult concept because of the way we use the terms *punish* and *discipline* in everyday language. To help you become a better disciplinarian, we offer the following general discussion and specific suggestions.

First of all, it's important to acknowledge that punishment plays a significant and unavoidable role in our social world. In his book *Walden Two* (1948), Skinner described a utopian world where reinforcers almost completely replaced punishment. Unfortunately, in our real world, reinforcement is not enough. Dangerous criminals must be stopped and possibly removed from society. Parents must stop their child from running into the street and their teenagers from drinking and driving. And teachers must stop disruptive students in the classroom and bullies on the playground.

There is a need for punishment at times, but it brings problems (Larzelere & Johnson, 2000; MacMillan, 2000). To be effective, punishment should be immediate and consistent. However, in the real world, this is extremely hard to do, and during the delay the behavior is likely to be reinforced on a partial schedule, which makes it highly resistant to extinction. Think about gambling. For almost everyone, it should be a *punishing* situation — on most occasions, you lose far more money than you win. However, the fact that you occasionally win keeps you "hanging in there." Furthermore, even when punishment immediately follows the misbehavior, the recipient may learn what *not* do but doesn't learn what he or she *should* do. Imagine trying to teach a child the word *dog* by only saying "*No!*" each time she said *dog* when it was inappropriate. The child (and you) would soon become very frustrated. It's much more efficient to teach someone by giving him or her clear examples of correct behavior. Punishment has several other serious side effects, as Table 16.5 shows.

TABLE 16.5 SIDE EFFECTS OF PUNISHMENT

1. *Passive aggressiveness.* Punishment often leads to frustration in the animal or person being punished, which can lead to anger and eventually aggression. But most of us have learned from experience that retaliatory aggression toward a punisher (especially one who is bigger and more powerful) is usually followed by more punishment. We therefore tend to control our impulse toward open aggression and instead resort to more subtle techniques, such as, showing up late or forgetting to mail a letter for someone. This is known as *passive aggressiveness* (McIlduff & Coghlan, 2000; Stormshak, Bierman, McMahon, & Lengua, 2000).

2. *Increased aggression.* Because punishment often produces a decrease in undesired behavior, at least for the moment, the punisher is in effect rewarded for applying punishment. Thus, a vicious circle may be established in which both people are actually being reinforced for inappropriate behavior — the punisher for punishing and the recipient for being fearful and submissive. This side effect partially explains the escalation of violence in spousal, child, and elder abuse despite immense pain and suffering (Larzelere & Johnson, 1999). In addition to fear and submissiveness, the recipient might also become depressed and/or respond with his or her own aggression.

3. *Avoidance behavior.* People and animals do not like to be punished, so they try to avoid the punisher. If every time you come home your parents or spouse starts yelling at you, you will delay coming home or find another place to go.

4. *Modeling.* Have you ever seen a parent spank or hit a child for hitting another child? The punishing parent may unintentionally serve as a "model" for the same behavior he or she is attempting to stop.

5. *Only temporary suppression of behavior.* Do you notice that car drivers quickly slow down when they see a police car but quickly resume their previous speed once the police officer is out of sight? Punishment generally suppresses the behavior only during the presence of the punishing person or circumstances.

6 *Learned helplessness.* Why do some people stay in abusive homes or marital situations? Research shows that if you repeatedly fail in your attempts to control your environment, you acquire a general sense of powerlessness or *learned helplessness* and may make no further attempts to escape (Alloy & Clements, 1998; Seligman, 1975).

Shared Terms for Both Classical and Operant Conditioning

In our earlier discussion of the principles of classical conditioning, you learned about *stimulus generalization, stimulus discrimination, extinction,* and *spontaneous recovery.* As you may have noticed in Table 15.1 at the beginning of Module 15, these same terms also are used in operant conditioning, and your previous learning will help you here. For example, just as 11-month-old Albert generalized his fear of rats to rabbits and Santa Claus masks, operantly conditioned responses also generalize. After learning the word for *Daddy* (through operant conditioning), children often use this same word for all adult men. This would be a form of *stimulus generalization* (and potential embarrassment to the parents). After parents explain the distinction, the child learns to differentiate (stimulus discrimination) and only call one man Daddy.

Now that you have completed your study of both reinforcement and punishment, check your understanding by filling in your own personal examples in the bottom box in the following figure:

In both classical and operant conditioning, *extinction* occurs when the original source of the learning is removed. In classical conditioning, the CR (Albert's fear of the rat) is extinguished if the CS (the rat) is repeatedly presented without the UCS (the loud noise). In operant conditioning, if the reinforcement (the rat's food pellets) is removed, the response (bar pressing) will gradually decline. Following extinction in either classical or operant conditioning, you also sometimes have *spontaneous recovery.* Just as the classically conditioned fear of rats may spontaneously return, the operantly conditioned bar pressing behaviors may reoccur.

One final comparison: In classical conditioning, we talked about *higher-order conditioning,* wherein a neutral stimulus (NS) is paired with a conditioned stimulus (CS), which is another stimulus that already produces a learned response. We said that if you wanted to demonstrate higher-order conditioning in Pavlov's dogs, you would first condition the dogs to salivate to the sound of the bell. Then you would pair the flash of light to the ringing of the bell. Eventually, the dog would salivate only to the flash of light.

A similar process, with a different name, also occurs in operant conditioning. If a rat learns that bar pressing produces food *only* when a light is flashing, the rat will soon learn to respond only when the light is flashing. The light has become a **discriminative stimulus**, which signals whether a response will pay off or not. We depend on discriminative stimuli many times every day. We pick up the phone only when it rings. We look for the *Women* or *Men* signs on bathroom doors. And children quickly learn to ask Grandma for toys.

Discriminative Stimulus *A cue that signals when a particular response is likely to be followed by a certain type of consequence*

After studying these basic operant conditioning principles, can you effectively apply them in your own life? The best method seems to be a combination of the major principles: Reinforce appropriate behavior, extinguish inappropriate behavior, and save punishment for the most extreme cases (such as a 2-year-old running into the street). Also, remember that you have grown up in a culture that considers reinforcement "bribery" and, ironically, stresses punishment. We encourage you to explore the technique of reinforcement — you'll find it very rewarding! Here are some further guidelines:

1. *Feedback.* When using both reinforcement and punishment, be sure to provide immediate and clear feedback to the person or animal whose behavior you wish to change. When using punishment, it is particularly important to make clear the desired response, because punishment is merely an indication that the response is undesirable. In other words, give the participant an alternative response to the punished one.

2. *Timing.* Reinforcers and punishers should be presented as close in time to the response as possible. The old policy of "wait till Father gets home" is obviously inappropriate for many reasons. In this case, it is because the delayed punishment is no longer associated with the inappropriate response. The same is true for reinforcement. If you're trying to lose weight, don't say you'll buy yourself a new wardrobe when you lose 30 pounds; reward yourself with a small treat (like a new blouse or shirt) after every few pounds.

3. *Consistency* To be effective, both reinforcement and punishment must be consistent. Have you ever seen a child screaming for candy in a supermarket? Parents often begin by saying "No," but when the child gets louder and throws a complete temper tantrum sometimes they give in and buy the candy. Although the parents are momentarily relieved (*negatively reinforced*) when the screaming stops, can you see how they're creating bigger problems in the long run? First, the child is being *positively reinforced* for the screaming and temper tantrum — and this behavior will increase. To make matters worse, the parents' inconsistency (saying "no" and then occasionally giving in) places candy begging on a *partial schedule of reinforcement,* which is highly resistant to extinction. Like a gambler who continues playing despite the odds, the child will continue the temper tantrums in hopes of the occasional payoff. Because effective punishment requires constant surveillance and *consistent* responses, it's almost impossible to be a "good punisher." It's best (and easiest) to use consistent reinforcement for good behavior and extinction for bad behavior. Praise the child for happy and cooperative behavior in the supermarket, and extinguish the temper tantrum by consistently refusing the request and ignoring the tantrum.

4. *Order of presentation.* As a teenager, did you ever promise to wash the family car or mow the grass on Saturday if they would just let you use the car on Friday night? Did your parents ever make you come home much earlier than your friends because they knew "that all teenagers get into trouble after midnight?" Can you see why the reward of using the car must come *after* the car wash or lawn mowing, and why punishment that comes *before* the behavior may create frustration and resentment? Both reinforcement and punishment should come *after* the behavior, never *before.*

Operant Conditioning in Real Life: Reinforcements Real and Accidental

Operant conditioning has many interesting applications in real life. Here we talk about *prejudice*, *biofeedback*, and *superstitious behavior*.

Prejudice

Recall the opening story and the three men who murdered James Byrd. What might have reinforced such a behavior? Could it have been attention, notoriety — something else? As you discovered earlier, people can learn prejudice through classical conditioning. They also learn prejudice through operant conditioning. For example, because demeaning others gains attention and sometimes approval from others, as well as increases one's self-esteem (at the expense of the victim), prejudice and discrimination are positively reinforced (Fein & Spencer, 1997). People also may have a single negative experience with a specific member of a group that they then generalize and apply to all members of the group (Vidmar, 1997) — an example of stimulus generalization.

But the men who killed James Byrd were sentenced to death or life imprisonment. Why would people do anything that they know could bring the death penalty? Punishment does suppress behavior, but as mentioned before, to be effective it must be consistent and immediate. Unfortunately, this seldom happens. To make matters worse, when punishment is inconsistent and the criminal gets away with one or more crimes, that behavior is put on a *partial (intermittent) schedule of reinforcement*. It is thus more likely to reoccur and become more resistant to *extinction*.

Biofeedback

In **biofeedback** (short for *biological feedback*, sometimes called *neurofeedback*), information about some biological function, such as heart rate, is conveyed to the individual through some type of signal. Sit quietly for a moment and try to determine your blood pressure. Is it high or low? Is it different from a few minutes ago? You can't tell, can you? Therefore, it is impossible for you to learn to control your blood pressure consciously. But if you were hooked up to a monitor that recorded, amplified, and displayed this information to you (biofeedback), you could learn to control it (Figure 16.3).

Biofeedback *A procedure for electronically recording, amplifying, and feeding back information about internal bodily changes that would normally be imperceptible (such as blood pressure); aids voluntary regulation of these changes*

Figure 16.3 *Biofeedback.* In biofeedback training, internal bodily processes (like blood pressure or muscle tension) are electronically recorded, amplified, and then reported back to the patient through headphones, signal lights, or other means. This information helps the person learn to control bodily processes not normally under voluntary control.

Superstition in everyday life. *Bingo players, like many other people, engage in special rituals and carry lucky charms, which they superstitiously believe will bring them good luck.*

Researchers have successfully used biofeedback techniques to treat hypertension and anxiety by lowering blood pressure and muscle tension (Lal et al., 1998; Nakao et al., 1997; Sarkar, Rathee, & Neera, 1999); epilepsy by changing brain wave patterns (Sterman, 1996); urinary incontinence by better pelvic muscle control (Sherman, Davis, & Wong, 1997); and headache by redirecting blood flow (Marcus, Scharff, & Turk, 1995; Kropp et al., 1997).

Biofeedback demonstrates several operant conditioning principles. Something is added (feedback) that increases the likelihood that the behavior will be repeated — *positive reinforcement*. The biofeedback itself is a *secondary reinforcer* because of the learned value of the relief from pain or other aversive stimuli (*primary reinforcer*). Finally, biofeedback involves *shaping*. The person watches a monitor screen (or other instrument) that provides graphs or numbers indicating their blood pressure (or other bodily states). Like a mirror, the biofeedback reflects back the results of the various strategies the participant uses to gain control. Through trial and error, the participant gets progressively better at lowering heart rate (or making other desired changes). Biofeedback techniques are limited, however, and so far, most successful when used in conjunction with other techniques, especially for pain control and stress management.

Superstitious Behavior

B. F. Skinner (1948, 1992) conducted a fascinating experiment to show how accidental reinforcement could lead to *superstitious behaviors*. He set the feeding mechanism on the cages of eight pigeons to feed them once every 15 seconds. No matter what the birds did, they were reinforced at 15-second intervals. Six of the pigeons acquired behaviors that they repeated over and over, even though the behaviors were not necessary to receive the food. For example, one pigeon kept turning in counterclockwise circles, and another kept making jerking movements with its head.

Why did the pigeons engage in such repetitive and unnecessary behavior? Recall that a *reinforcer* increases the probability that a response just performed will be

---

critical thinking ▶▶▶▶▶▶▶▶▶▶▶▶▶▶▶▶▶ Active Learning

Using Learning Principles to Succeed in College

Psychological theory and research have taught us that an active approach to learning is rewarded by better grades. Active learning means using the SQ4R (Survey, Question, Read, Recite, Review, and Write) study techniques discussed in the Tools for Student Success (pages 38–44). An active learner rises above old, easy patterns of behavior and applies new knowledge to everyday situations. When you transfer ideas or concepts you learn from class to

your personal life, your insight grows. Now that you have studied the principles of learning, use the following questions to help you apply your new knowledge to achieve your education goals and have an enjoyable college experience:

1. How can you positively reinforce yourself for studying, completing assignments, and attending class?

2. How might participating in club and campus activities reinforce your education commitment?

3. Compare the difference in the effort you spend studying for an exam when you get a high grade compared with your study effort when you get a low grade. How could you apply the Premack principle to your advantage in this situation?

4. When you take exams, are you anxious? How might this be a classically conditioned response? How could you use the principle of extinction to weaken this response?

repeated. Although Skinner was not using the food to reinforce any particular behavior, the pigeons associated the food with whatever behavior they were engaged in when the food was originally dropped into the cage. Thus, if the bird was circling counterclockwise when the food was presented, it would repeat that motion to receive more food.

Many people believe in superstitions and follow specific rituals (Table 16.6). Professional and Olympic-level athletes sometimes carry lucky charms or perform a particular ritual before every competition. Phil Esposito, a hockey player with the Boston Bruins and the New York Rangers for 18 years, always wore the same black turtleneck and drove through the same tollbooth on his way to a game. In the locker room, he put on all his clothes in the same order and laid out his equipment in exactly the same way he had for every other game. All this because once when he had behaved that way years before, he had been the team's high scorer. Alas, the power of accidental reinforcement.

TABLE 16.6 COMMON WESTERN SUPERSTITIONS

Behavior	Superstition
Wedding plans: *Why do brides wear something old and something borrowed?*	The something old is usually clothing that belongs to an older woman who is happily married. Thus, the bride will supposedly transfer that good fortune to herself. Something borrowed is often a relative's jewelry. This item should be golden, because gold represents the sun, which was once thought to be the source of life.
Spilling salt: *Why do some people throw a pinch of salt over their left shoulder?*	Years ago, people believed good spirits lived on the right side of the body and bad spirits on the left. When a man spilled salt, he believed his guardian spirit had caused the accident to warn him of evil nearby. At the time, salt was scarce and precious. Therefore, to bribe the spirits who were planning to harm him, he would quickly throw a pinch of salt over his left shoulder.
Boasting, making a prediction, or speaking of good fortune: *Why do some people knock on wood?*	Down through the ages, people have believed that trees were homes of gods, who were kind and generous if approached in the right way. A person who wanted to ask a favor of the tree god would touch the bark. After the favor was granted, the person would return to knock on the tree as a sign of thanks.

Check & Review

OPERANT CONDITIONING

In **operant conditioning**, people or animals learn by the *consequences* of their responses. Whether behavior is reinforced or punished (consequences) determines whether the response will occur again. Thorndike and Skinner are the two major contributors to operant conditioning. Thorndike's *law of effect* states rewarded behavior is more likely to recur. Skinner extended Thorndike's work to more complex behaviors but emphasized only external, observable behaviors.

Operant conditioning involves several important terms and principles. **Reinforcement** is any procedure that results in an increase in a response, whereas **punishment** is any procedure that results in a decrease. To strengthen a response, we use **primary reinforcers**, which satisfy an unlearned biological need (e.g., sex, thirst), and **secondary reinforcers**, which have learned value (e.g., money). **Positive reinforcement** (adding something) and **negative reinforcement** (taking something away) increase the likelihood the response will occur again. *Escape learning* and *avoidance learning* are two of the learning procedures used to study negative reinforcement. According to the **Premack**

principle, activities or behaviors that are more common or probable in one's life will act as reinforcers for activities that are less probable.

Continuous reinforcement rewards each correct response, whereas a **partial (intermittent) schedule** reinforces for some, not all, designated responses. The four partial reinforcement schedules are **variable ratio**, **variable interval**, **fixed ratio**, and **fixed interval**. Partial reinforcement schedules reinforce for some, but not all, responses. Complex behaviors can be trained through **shaping**, which refers to reinforcing successive approximations to the desired behavior.

To weaken a response, we use punishment, which decreases the likelihood of responding. **Positive punishment** (adding something) and **negative punishment** (taking something away) decrease the likelihood the response will occur again. Although some punishment is essential in social relations, it has serious side effects. To be effective, punishment must be immediate, consistent, and moderate.

Operant conditioning has several applications in real life. It helps explain prejudice, which is sometimes learned through positive reinforcement and stimulus gener-

alization. **Biofeedback**, another application, is the feeding back of biological information, such as heart rate or blood pressure, which a person uses to control normally automatic functions of the body. The third major application, superstitions, involves behaviors that are continually repeated because they are believed to cause desired effects. In reality the behaviors are only accidentally related.

Questions

1. Define operant conditioning and explain how it differs from classical conditioning.
2. Negative punishment _____ and negative reinforcement _____ the likelihood the response will continue. (a) decreases, decreases; (b) increases, decreases; (c) decreases, increases; (d) increases, increases
3. Partial reinforcements schedules make responses more _____ to extinction.
4. Marshall wears the same necklace to every exam. Explain how his superstitious behavior might have developed.

Answers to Questions can be found in Appendix B.

ACTIVE LEARNING WORKSHEET   MODULE 16

ACROSS

3. Adding or presenting a stimulus that leads to a likely decrease in behavior.

8. Participant must make a certain number of responses before being reinforced.

14. Stimuli that increase the probability of a response because they satisfy a biological need.

15. Taking away or removing a stimulus that leads to a likely decrease in behavior.

DOWN

1. Cue signaling when a particular response is likely to be followed by a certain type of consequence.

2. Participant is reinforced for the first response after a specified period of time has elapsed.

3. Adding or presenting a stimulus that leads to a likely increase in behavior.

4. Reinforcement in which every correct response is reinforced.

5. Stimuli that increase the probability of a response because of their learned value.

6. Learning based on consequences.

7. Taking away or removing a stimulus that leads to a likely increase in behavior.

9. Using a response that has a high probability of occurrence to reinforce a response that has a lower probability of occurrence.

10. Electronically recording, amplifying, and feeding back information about internal bodily changes.

11. Reinforcement for successive approximations of the desired response.

12. Any action or event that decreases the likelihood that a response will be repeated.

13. Any action or event that increases the probability that a response will be repeated.

Answers can be found in Appendix B.

MODULE 17
COGNITIVE-SOCIAL LEARNING

How and when do we learn according to cognitive-social theory?

Cognitive-Social Theory *A theory of learning that emphasizes the role of thought and social learning in behavior*

Insight *A sudden flash of understanding that occurs during problem solving*

Is this insight? *Grande, one of Wolfgang Köhler's chimps, has just solved the problem of how to get the banana. Is this insight or trial and error?*

So far, we have examined learning processes that involve associations between a stimulus and an observable behavior. Some behaviorists believe almost all learning can be explained in such stimulus–response terms, but other psychologists feel there is more to learning than can be explained solely by operant and classical conditioning. **Cognitive-social theory** (also called *cognitive-social learning* or *cognitive-behavioral theory*) incorporates concepts of conditioning but emphasizes thought processes, or cognitions, and social learning. According to this view, people (as well as, rats, pigeons, and other animals) have attitudes, beliefs, expectations, motivations, and emotions that affect learning. Furthermore, both humans and nonhuman animals are capable of learning new behaviors through observation and imitation. We begin with a look at the *cognitive* part of cognitive-social theory, followed by an examination of the *social* aspects of learning.

Insight and Latent Learning: Where are the Reinforcers?

As you'll discover throughout this text, cognitive factors play a large role in human behavior and mental processes. Given that these factors are covered in several other modules (e.g., Learning, Memory, Thinking/Language/Intelligence), our discussion here is limited to the classic research of Wolfgang Köhler and Edward Tolman and their studies of *insight* and *latent learning*.

Köhler's Study of Insight

Although early behaviorists likened the mind to a "black box," whose workings could not be observed directly, German psychologist Wolfgang Köhler wanted to look inside the box. He believed there was more to learning — especially learning to solve a complex problem — than responding to stimuli in a trial-and-error fashion. In several experiments conducted during World War I, Köhler posed several different types of problems to chimpanzees and apes to see how they learned to solve them. For example, in one experiment, he placed a banana just outside the reach of a caged chimpanzee. To reach the banana, the chimp would have to use a stick placed near the cage to extend its reach. The chimp did not solve this problem in the random trial-and-error fashion of Thorndike's cats or Skinner's rats and pigeons. Köhler noticed that he seemed to sit and think about the situation for a while. Then, in a flash of **insight** (a sudden understanding), the chimp picked up the stick and maneuvered the banana within its grasp (Kohler, 1925).

Another of Köhler's chimps, an intelligent fellow named Sultan, was put in a similar situation. But this time there were two sticks available to him and the banana was placed even farther away, too far to reach with a single stick. Sultan seemingly lost interest in the banana, but continued to play with the sticks. When he later discovered that the two sticks could be interlocked, he instantly used the now longer stick to pull the banana within grasp. Köhler designated this type of learning *insight learning,* because some internal mental event that we can only describe as "insight" went on between the presentation of the banana and the use of the stick to retrieve it.

Tolman's Study of Latent Learning

Although previous researchers suggested that rats learned mazes through trial-and-error and rewards, Edward C. Tolman (1898–1956) believed they underestimated the rat's cognitive processes and cognitive learning. He noted that rats placed in experimental mazes seemed to pause at certain intersections—almost as if they were *deciding* which route to take. When allowed to roam aimlessly in a maze with no food reward at the end, the rats also seemed to develop a **cognitive map,** or mental representation of the maze.

To test the idea of cognitive learning, Tolman allowed one group of rats to explore a maze in an aimless fashion with no reinforcement, a second group was always reinforced with food whenever they reached the end of the maze, and a third group was not rewarded initially (during the first 10 days of the trial), but starting on day 11 they found food at the end of the maze. As expected from simple operant conditioning, the first and third groups were slow to learn the maze; whereas the second group that had reinforcement showed fast, steady improvement. Also as expected, when the third group started receiving reinforcement (on the 11th day), the rats' learning of the maze quickly matched the performance of the group that had been reinforced every time (Tolman & Honzik, 1930). For Tolman, this was significant. It proved that the nonreinforced rats had been learning during their aimless wandering, but that their hidden, **latent learning** only showed up when there was a reason to display it (the food reward).

Cognitive learning is not limited to rats. If a new log is placed in its territory, a chipmunk will explore it for a time, but soon move on if no food is found. When a predator comes into the same territory, the chipmunk heads directly for and hides beneath the log. Similarly, as a child you may have casually ridden a bike around your neighborhood with no particular reason or destination in mind, and only demonstrated your hidden knowledge of the area when your dad was searching for the closest mailbox. The fact that Tolman's nonreinforced rats quickly caught up to the reinforced ones, that the chipmunk knew about the hiding place under the log, that you knew the location of the mailbox, and recent experimental evidence (Burgdorf, Knutson, & Panksepp, 2000) all provide clear evidece of latent learning and the existence of internal, cognitive maps.

Cognitive Map *A mental image of a three-dimensional space that person or animal has navigated*

Latent Learning *Learning that occurs in the absence of a reward and remains hidden until there is some incentive to demonstrate it.*

Observational Learning: Watching the Consequences of Others' Behavior

In addition to cognitive processes (such as insight and latent learning), observation and imitation also play important roles in learning. When you want to know how to act at a party, what do you do? If you want to learn how to give a speech, what is the best way? We learn these behaviors by observing others — thus the name *observational learning* (or *social learning*). When we learn by imitating someone, it is called *modeling.*

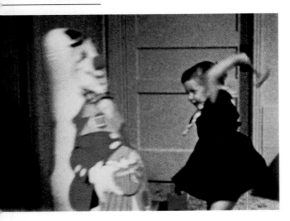

Bandura's classic Bobo doll study.
This child watched while an adult hit the Bobo doll and then imitated the behavior.

Albert Bandura (born in 1925) and others have demonstrated the importance of observation and modeling. In one experiment, one of three groups of children viewed a film of an adult acting aggressively toward a Bobo doll (hitting, punching, and kicking) (Bandura & Walters, 1963). Later, the children were given the opportunity to play in the same room with the same toys. The children who had seen the film were much more aggressive with the toys than were children who had not seen it. They had learned how to act in a particular situation by observing another person in that situation.

According to Bandura, four processes are involved in learning through observation; we must

1. Attend (or pay attention) to the model
2. Remember the modeled behavior
3. Be able to put into practice what was observed (for instance, we wouldn't be able to imitate someone riding a bike if we were paralyzed)
4. Decide whether we want to repeat the modeled behavior, on the basis of whether the model was reinforced or punished and/or on the basis of our esteem for the model

We can see these processes at work when we apply them to the children in Bandura's experiment. They paid attention to and remembered the aggressive behavior of the models, and were able to physically perform the modeled behaviors. Most of the children also decided to imitate the observed behaviors.

Applications of Cognitive-Social Learning: We See, We Do?

We use cognitive-social learning in many ways in our everyday lives, yet two of the most powerful areas of learning are frequently overlooked: **prejudice** and **media influences**.

Prejudice

Did the three men who murdered James Byrd learn some of their hatred and prejudice through observational learning? Family and friends of Bill King say that he was pleasant and quiet until he began serving an 8-year prison sentence for burglary (Galloway, 1999). It's also interesting to speculate what King might have learned from an uncle who was convicted of murdering a gay traveling salesman a number of years earlier, or what he might have observed during his active membership with the KKK (Associated Press, 1999).

In addition to what we learn from family, friends, and group memberships, the media also encourage some types of prejudice. Experimental and correlational research clearly show that when children watch TV, go to movies, and read books and magazines that portray minorities and women in demeaning and stereotypical roles, they learn to expect these behaviors and to accept them as "natural." Exposure of this kind initiates and reinforces the learning of prejudice (Dovidio, Brigham, Johnson, & Gaertner, 1995).

Media Influences

Observational learning also can teach us what to buy. Because most of us are well aware of the media's influence on children's food and toy preferences, let's consider adult behavior. For instance, when a TV commercial shows children enjoying a particular cereal and beaming at their mom in gratitude (and Mom is smiling back), the parents in the audience learn that they will be rewarded with happy children for buying a particular brand or will be punished (with children who won't eat) for buying a different brand. In other words, the consumer is rewarded vicariously and the purchasing behavior is reinforced (Solomon & Englis, 1994).

Unfortunately, both children and adults also may be learning violence through observational learning and the media. Correlational evidence from more than 50 studies indicates that observing violent behavior is related to performing violent behavior (Huesmann & Moise, 1996). As a critical thinker, you may be automatically noting that correlation is not causation. However, over 100 *experimental* studies have shown a causal link between observing violence and later performing it (Primavera & Herron, 1996).

What about video games? How do they affect behavior? Researchers are just beginning to study these questions. For example, psychologists Craig Anderson and Karen Dill (2000) have found that students who played more violent video games in junior high and high school also engage in more aggressive behaviors. Furthermore, when these researchers experimentally assigned 210 students to first play either a violent or a nonviolent video game and later allowed them to punish their opponent with a loud sound blast, those who played the violent game punished the opponent not only for a longer period of time but also with greater intensity. The researchers hypothesize that video games are more likely to model aggressive behavior because, unlike TV and other media, they are interactive, engrossing, and require the player to identify with the aggressor.

Video games and aggression. According-ing to research, these young boys iden-tify with the aggressor and may be more likely to imitate this behavior (Anderson & Dill, 2000). What do you think? Do video games affect your behavior or that of your friends?

GENDER & CULTURAL DIVERSITY

Scaffolding as a Teaching Technique in Different Cultures

Learning in the real world is often a combination of classical conditioning, operant conditioning, and observational learning. This is especially evident in informal situations in which an individual acquires new skills under the supervision of a master teacher. The ideal process used by teachers in these situations is known as *scaffolding* (Wood, Bruner, & Ross, 1976).

Scaffolding enables a student to accomplish tasks that would be impossible without the greater skill and knowledge of the teacher. In most cases, scaffolding is a combination of shaping and modeling, where the teacher selectively reinforces successes of the student and models more difficult parts of the task. Patricia Marks Greenfield (1984) has described two very different examples of scaffolding from two diverse cultures, language learning in Los Angeles and learning to weave in Zinacantán, Mexico. Although the cultures, tasks, and ages of the learners are quite different, the scaffolding process is very similar.

The Los Angeles study focused on the process by which children learn the meaning of adult-initiated offers, such as "Do you want a cookie?" or "Do you want to go for a ride?" Greenfield defines a successful offer in terms of its organizational structure: The offer must be presented to the child; the child must acknowledge the offer; and some object, action, or information must be transmitted from the adult to the child. Therefore, in a successful offer of a piggyback ride, the mother makes a verbal offer, the child acknowledges the offer in some way (by indicating he or she wants it), and the mother gives the child the ride.

When the child's verbal skills are not developed enough to comprehend a verbal offer, the mother uses a scaffolding process. She uses nonverbal cues as the scaffold and models the correct verbal response. In this way, the mother shapes the response of the child capable of making a verbal response and models appropriate behavior for the child who has not yet acquired the necessary verbal skills. Thus, it is through the scaffolding process that mothers help children learn verbal and non-verbal language involved in accepting offers of things they want.

Scaffolding as a form of learning. *This young Zinacanteco girl is learning to weave through the process of scaffolding.*

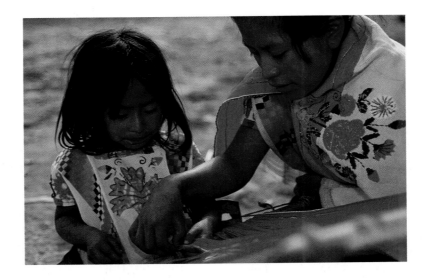

Weaving, of course, is not as universal as language, but the scaffolding process is similar. Weaving is an important part of the culture of the Zinacantecos, who live in the highlands of southern Mexico. Greenfield videotaped 14 girls at different levels of learning to weave. The weaving skills of the girls varied considerably, but the researchers were unable to distinguish between the final products of the girls because of the widespread use of scaffolding. The inexperienced girls were constantly monitored by experienced teachers. Each girl was allowed to complete what she was able to do with ease, whereas a more experienced teacher took over during the more difficult parts. Thus, no matter what the skill level of the novice weaver, she was able to produce a final product equal to the other weavers because of the scaffolding process. The experienced weaver created the scaffold by reinforcing correct weaving technique and modeling more difficult technique. For the first-time weavers, the teachers took over 53 percent of the time, during which the new weavers watched the teacher approximately 87 percent of the time. Although both the tasks and the cultures are different, the scaffolding processes are similar. First, the scaffold is adapted to the skill level of the learner so that learners are able to accomplish tasks they cannot accomplish on their own. Second, the amount of scaffolding and intervention by the parent or teacher decrease as the skill level of the learner increases. Third, scaffolding always involves a combination of shaping and modeling. Finally, in both situations the teachers appear oblivious of their teaching methods or of the fact that they are teaching at all. Most of the Zinacanteco women believe that girls learn to weave by themselves, and it is a common belief in Western culture that children learn to talk by themselves.

Check & Review

COGNITIVE-SOCIAL LEARNING

Cognitive-social theory incorporates concepts of conditioning but emphasizes thought processes, or cognitions, and social learning. According to this perspective, people learn through insight, latent learning, observation, and modeling.

Wolfgang Köhler, in working with chimpanzees, demonstrated that learning could occur with a sudden flash of **insight**. Tolman demonstrated that **latent learning** takes place in the absence of reward and remains hidden until some future time when it can be retrieved as needed. A **cognitive map** is a mental image of an area that a person or animal has navigated.

According to Albert Bandura, observational learning is the process of learning how to do something by watching others and performing the same behavior in the future. To imitate the behavior of others, we must pay attention, remember, be able to reproduce the behavior, and be motivated by some reinforcement.

Cognitive-social theory helps explain prejudice and media influences. People often learn their prejudices by imitating and modeling the behavior they see in friends, family, and the media. The media affect our purchasing behaviors as well as our aggressive tendencies. Video games may have a particularly strong influence.

Questions

1. _____ were influential in early studies of cognitive learning. (a) William James and Ivan Pavlov; (b) B. F. Skinner and Edward Thorndike; (c) Wolfgang Köhler and Edward Tolman; (d) Albert Bandura and R. H. Walters.

2. Learning that occurs in the absence of a reward and remains hidden until some future time when it can be retrieved is called _____.

3. Mental images of an area that a person or animal has navigated are known as _____.

4. Bandura's observational learning studies focused on how _____. (a) rats learn cognitive maps through exploration; (b) children learn aggressive behaviors by observing aggressive models; (c) cats learn problem solving through trial-and-error; (d) chimpanzees learn problem solving through reasoning

Answers to Questions can be found in Appendix B.

ACTIVE LEARNING WORKSHEET   MODULE 17

Enter the correct letter from Column A in the blank space in Column B, and then double-check your answers with those in Appendix B.

Column A	Column B
a. Albert Bandura	1.___ Mental image of a three-dimensional space.
b. Anderson and Dill	2.___ Insight learning.
c. Wolfgang Kohler	3.___ Emphasizes thinking and social learning.
d. Scaffolding	4.___ Cognitive maps and latent learning.
e. Insight	5.___ Hidden learning.
f. Cognitive-social theory	6.___ Combines shaping and modeling.
g. Edward C. Tolman	7.___ Studied weaving and language learning.
h. Latent learning	8.___ A sudden flash of understanding.
i. Cognitive map	9.___ Bobo dolls and observational learning.
j. Patricia Greenfield	10.___ Violent video games and aggression.

NEUROSCIENCE AND EVOLUTION

As you recall, learning is defined as *a relatively permanent change in behavior as a result of practice or experience.* For this change in behavior to persist over time, lasting biological changes must occur within the organism. In this section, we will examine the neurological changes that occur during and after learning. We also will explore the evolutionary advantages of learning.

Neuroscience and Learning: Changes in the Biochemistry and the Brain

Research conducted on humans and other animals indicates that learning involves at least two important biological changes:

1. Biochemistry. Neurological research confirms that learning results in alterations in synaptic transmission at specific sites. Because millions of neurons may be activated during an instance of classical conditioning in humans, researchers often use a small sea snail called *Aplysia.* This particular animal has fewer neurons than any vertebrate, and their neurons are often large (up to 1 mm in diameter) and therefore easier to study.

When disturbed by a squirt of water, the Aplysia will protectively withdraw its gill. If the squirt continues, the gill withdrawal diminishes (the snail "habituates" – see Module 12). During classical conditioning experiments, the snail repeatedly receives a small electric shock just after being squirted. The Aplysia learns to associate the squirt with the coming shock, and the withdrawal response to the squirt alone becomes stronger. Kandel and his colleagues have shown that this type of learning in the Aplysia coincides with an increase or decrease in the release of specific neurotransmitters by presynaptic and postsynaptic neurons (Bailey & Kandel, 1995; Kandel & Schwartz, 1982; Martinez & Derrick, 1996).

2. The Brain's Role in Learning. What happens within the brain when something is learned? An impressive series of experiments focused on changes within a structure at the base of the brain known as the cerebellum (Krupa, Thompson, & Thompson, 1993; Steinmetz, 1998; Thompson, 1989, 1992). Studying classical conditioning of blinking in rabbits, they presented first a tone (CS) and then a puff of air (UCS) to the cornea of the rabbit's eye. At first the rabbit would blink at the air puff but not at the tone. After repeated pairings, classical conditioning occurred, and the rabbit blinked at the tone also. The researchers' who recorded activity in various brain cells' found that when a microscopic spot in the cerebellum was destroyed, the rabbit continued to blink in response to the puff of air but not the tone. This research tells us that the cerebellum is involved in some types of classical conditioning. It does *not* mean that the cerebellum is the key to all learning. Other forms of learning create different pathways and involve additional areas of the brain — as you will discover in the following Research Highlight.

Evolution and Learning: Biological Preparedness and Instinctive Drift

So far, we have emphasized the learned aspects of behavior, but humans and other animals also are born with certain biological abilities that help ensure their survival. When your fingers touch a hot object, you immediately pull your hand away. When a foreign object approaches your eye, you automatically blink. These simple *reflexes* involve making a specific automatic reaction to a particular stimulus. In addition to

Taste aversion. Coyotes find sheep a readily available source of food, but if they are conditioned to develop a taste aversion to sheep, they will avoid them and seek other food.

Scanning the Brain for Learning

Researchers have long used PET and fMRI brain scans to study various structures in the brain. Now they're also using this highly sophisticated technology to scan for learning activity. In Norway, Kenneth Hugdahl (1998) paired a tone (NS) with a shock to the wrist (UCS) and used PET scans to determine which brain areas were activated during the acquisition of a conditioned response. He recorded significant brain activation in certain right hemisphere frontal lobe areas. In another study, participants were presented with either neutral words (no conditioning) or with threat-related words (higher-order conditioning) (Maddock & Buonocore, 1997). When the fMRI images were compared for the two different conditions, researchers found that the threat words activated a different part of the cerebral cortex than the neutral words.

In addition to these studies, other research has shown that classical conditioning activates other areas of the brain, including the thalamus, hippocampus, hypothalamus, amygdala, and cortex (Furmark, Fischer, Wik, Larsson, & Fredrikson, 1997; Schreurs, Shi, Pineda, & Buck, 2000; Steinmetz, 2000). As you can see, learning involves complex processes and numerous brain structures that are not yet well understood (Purdy, Markham, Schwartz, & Gordon, 2001).

reflexes, many species also have a second set of adaptive responses called *instincts,* or species-specific behaviors. For example, the weaverbird is known to tie a particular grass knot to hold its nest together. But even when these birds are raised in total isolation for several generations, they will still tie the same knot.

Although these inborn, innate abilities are important to our evolutionary survival, they are inadequate for coping with a constantly changing environment. Reflexively withdrawing your fingers from a hot object is certainly to your advantage. But what if you saw a sign showing that the hot object was an unusual door handle, which would allow you to escape a burning building? There are numerous important stimuli in the environment that require a flexible approach to unusual stimuli. Only through learning are we are able to react to spoken words, to written symbols, and other important environmental stimuli. From an evolutionary perspective, *learning* is an adaptation that enables organisms to survive and prosper in a constantly changing world. In this section, we will explore several evolutionary advantages to learning, as well as the limits imposed by an organism's biological heritage.

Classical Conditioning and Biological Preparedness

Years ago, a former student, named Rebecca, was unwrapping her favorite candy bar as she walked to class. After taking the first horrible bite, she stopped eating and looked questioningly at the candy, which was making small movements in her hand. The sight of the small, wriggling maggots filling the candy bar left an immediate and permanent impact. Are you surprised that many years later she still feels nauseous just thinking about this candy bar? Rebecca's response is called a *taste aversion,* and it may have an evolutionary purpose.

Several interesting studies have been done with taste aversion and its link to **biological preparedness,** the idea that an organism is innately predisposed to form associations between certain stimuli and responses. Garcia and his colleagues (1966) produced taste aversion in lab rats by pairing flavored water (NS) and a drug (UCS) that produced gastrointestinal distress (UCR). After being conditioned and recovering from the illness, the rats refused to drink the flavored water (CS) because of the conditioned taste aversion. But, remarkably, Garcia discovered that only certain neutral stimuli could produce the nausea. Pairings of a noise (NS) or a shock (NS) with the nausea-producing drug (UCS) produced no taste aversion. This finding called into question Pavlov's belief that any NS could be conditioned. Garcia suggested that when we are sick to our stomachs, we have a natural, evolutionary tendency to attribute it to food or drink. Being *biologically prepared* to quickly asso-

Biological Preparedness *The idea that an organism is innately predisposed to form associations between certain stimuli and responses* ciate nausea with food or drink is adaptive because it helps us avoid that food or drink in the future (Elkins, 1991; Kalat, 1985; Schafe et al., 2000).

Garcia's findings on taste aversion are important for two reasons: First, identifying exceptions to classical conditioning led to a better understanding of biological preparedness. And second, he and his colleagues used their basic research to help solve an economic problem for western ranchers. Coyotes were killing sheep, and the ranchers wanted to kill all coyotes. But this "solution" would have created a larger ecological problem because coyotes eat rabbits and small rodents. In a form of applied research, Garcia and his colleagues used classical conditioning to teach the coyotes not to eat sheep (Gustavson & Garcia, 1974). The researchers began by lacing freshly killed sheep with a chemical that causes extreme nausea and vomiting in coyotes that eat the tainted meat. The conditioning worked so well that the coyotes would run away from the mere sight and smell of sheep. This research has since been applied many times in the wild and in the laboratory with coyotes and with wolves (Gustavson, Kelly, Sweeney, & Garcia, 1976; Ziegler, Gustavson, Holzer, & Gruber, 1983).

Operant Conditioning and Instinctive Drift

Just as later research found that biological preparedness affects classical conditioning, researchers also have found that an animal's natural behavior pattern can interfere with operant conditioning. For example, the Brelands (1961) tried to teach a chicken to play baseball. Through shaping and reinforcement, the chicken first learned to pull a loop that activated a swinging bat, and then learned to actually hit the ball. But instead of running to first base, it would chase the ball as through it were food. Regardless of the lack of reinforcement for chasing the ball, the chicken's natural behavior took precedence. This biological constraint is known as **instinctive drift,** when an animal's learned responses tend to shift (or *drift*) toward innate response patterns.

Instinctive Drift *A biological constraint that occurs when an animal's learned responses shifts (or drifts) toward innate response patterns*

Although animals can be operantly conditioned to perform a variety of novel behaviors (like hitting a baseball), these studies show that reinforcement alone does not determine behavior. Rather, there is a biological tendency in species to favor natural inborn behaviors. Learning theorists initially believed that the fundamental laws of conditioning would apply to almost all species and all behaviors, but recent findings have identified several limits (such as biological preparedness and instinctive drift) that limit the generality of conditioning principles. As you discovered in Module 2, scientific inquiry is a constantly changing and evolving process.

A Final Note

We began this section with the story of James Byrd because prejudice is a worthy

Those who won't forget. Ross Byrd, left, and Renee Mullins, children of murder victim James Byrd, leaving the Jasper County Courthouse after John "Bill" King was convicted of capital murder.

(but unusual) topic and his story deserved retelling. Although the death of James Byrd shocked many Americans into facing the terrible hatred and racism that still exists in our country, unfortunately his death (like others) is too quickly forgotten. As you have discovered, however, little (if anything) about prejudice is biologically driven. It is *learned.* The good news is that *what we learn we can change* — through retraining, counseling, and self-reflection.

Check & Review

NEUROSCIENCE AND EVOLUTION

Learning and conditioning produce relatively permanent changes in biochemistry and various parts of the brain. But not all behaviors are learned. At least some behavior is *innate,* or inborn, in the form of either reflexes or instincts. It appears that all animals are programmed to engage in certain innate behaviors that have evolutionary survival benefits.

Through **biological preparedness** an organism is innately predisposed to form associations between certain stimuli and responses. Taste aversions are classically conditioned associations of food to illness that are rapidly learned, often in a single pairing, and reflect a protective survival mechanism for a species. Findings on **instinctive drift** show there are biological constraints on operant conditioning.

Questions

1. Research on classical conditioning of the eyeblink response in rabbits shows that the _____ is an important brain structure for learning. (a) hippocampus; (b) brainstem; (c) corpus callosum; (d) cerebellum.
2. How did Garcia condition a taste aversion in coyotes?
3. What is biological preparedness?
4. _____ occurs when an animal's learned responses tend to shift toward innate response patterns.

Answers to Questions can be found in Appendix B.

ACTIVE LEARNING WORKSHEET   MODULE 18

Circle either "T" for true or "F" for false, and then compare your answers with those in Appendix B.

1. Researchers use small snails (Aplysia) to study neuronal activity during learning because they have fewer and larger neurons than humans. T or F

2. Classical conditioning studies of the eyeblink response in rabbits shows that the corpus callosum is an important brain structure for learning. T or F

3. According to evolutionary psychologists, learning is an adaptation that enables humans to survive and prosper in a constantly changing world.

4. Biological preparedness suggests we would be most likely to develop a classically conditioned aversion to rats over snakes. T or F

5. Garcia and his colleagues taught coyotes to avoid sheep by pairing a nausea-inducing drug with freshly killed sheep meat that was later eaten by the coyotes. T or F

Visual Summary for Modules 15, 16, 17, and 18 ●─●─●─

Classical Conditioning

Understanding Classical Conditioning

Pioneers: Pavlov and Watson
Process: Involuntary
1) Before conditioning, originally **neutral stimulus (NS)** causes no relevant response, while **unconditioned stimulus (UCS)** causes **unconditioned response (UCR)**.
2) During conditioning, NS is paired with UCS that elicits the UCR.
3) After conditioning, previous NS becomes **conditioned stimulus (CS)**, which now causes a **conditioned response (CR)** or **conditioned emotional response (CER)**.

Principles of Classical Conditioning

- **Stimulus generalization**: Stimuli similar to original CS elicit CR.
- **Stimulus discrimination**: Only the CS elicits the CR.
- **Extinction**: Gradual suppression of a learned behavior by repeatedly presenting the CS without the UCS.
- **Spontaneous recovery**: Voluntary reappearance of a previously extinguished CR.
- **Higher order conditioning**: The NS is paired with the CS to which the organism has already been conditioned.

Classical Conditioning in Real Life

- *Prejudice*: Negative perceptions of others that are acquired through classical conditioning processes.
- *Phobias*: Irrational fears that are developed through association of a feared object with the UCS.
- *Medical treatments*: Using nausea producing drugs, alcoholics learn to pair alcohol (CS) with nausea (CR).
- *Advertising*: Products (NS) are repeatedly paired with pleasant images (UCS) until they become a CS.

Operant Conditioning

Understanding Operant Conditioning

Pioneers: Thorndike and Skinner
Process: Voluntary
People or animals learn through consequences of their behavior. When responses are reinforced, they are likely to increase; when punished, they are likely to decrease.

Principles of Operant Conditioning

- *Strengthening a response occurs through*:
1) Primary and secondary reinforcers: **Primary reinforcers**, like food, satisfy a biological need, whereas the value of **secondary reinforcers**, like money, is learned.
2) Positive and negative reinforcement: **Positive reinforcement** is adding something that increases the likelihood of the response, whereas **negative reinforcement** involves taking away something that increases the likelihood of the response.

Additional concepts:

In a **continuous schedule of reinforcement** every correct response is reinforced, whereas in a **partial (or intermittent) schedule** only some responses are reinforced. Partial schedules include **fixed ratio, variable ratio, fixed interval**, and **variable interval**.

Shaping involves reinforcement for successive approximations of the desired response.

Operant Conditioning (cont).

- *Weakening a response* occurs through:
  1) **Positive punishment** is adding something that decreases the likelihood of the reponse.
  2) **Negative punishment** involves taking away something that decreases the likelihood of the response.

Operant Conditioning in Real Life

- *Prejudice*: Negative perceptions of others that are acquired through operant conditioning processes.
- *Biofeedback*: "Feeding back" biological information (heart rate or blood pressure) to learn to control normally automatic body functions.
- *Superstitious behavior*: Develops from accidental rewarding of specific behaviors.

Cognitive-Social Learning

Insight and Latent Learning

- *Kohler*: Learning can occur with a sudden flash of understanding (**insight**).
- *Tolman*: Learning can happen without reinforcement and remain hidden until needed (**latent learning**). After navigating their environments people and animals create **cognitive maps**.

Cognitive-Social Learning

- *Bandura*: Learning occurs by observing others who serve as models.

Applications

- *Prejudice*: Learned by imitating and modeling prejudiced behavior of others.
- *Media influences*: Consumerism and aggressive behaviors are learned through watching media models.

Neuroscience and Evolution

Learning and conditioning produce relatively permanent changes in neural connections and various parts of the brain. Evolutionary theorists believe some behavior is unlearned (e.g., reflexes or instincts), and that learning and conditioning are further adaptations that enable organisms to survive and prosper in a constantly changing world.

Memory

My fellow Americans,

I have recently been told that I am one of the millions of Americans who will be afflicted with Alzheimer's disease. Upon learning this news, Nancy and I had to decide whether as private citizens we would keep this a private matter or whether we would make this news known in a public way. In the past, Nancy suffered from breast cancer and I had my cancer surgeries. We found through our open disclosures we were able to raise public awareness.

Ronald Reagan

So wrote Ronald Reagan, fortieth president of the United States, in an open letter to the people of the United States in November 1994, weeks after being diagnosed with Alzheimer's disease.

In 1953, a patient referred to as H. M. had portions of his temporal lobes surgically removed in an attempt to control severe epileptic seizures. The surgery was successful in reducing the severity and number of seizures, but his long-term memory processes were profoundly disrupted. Today, almost 50 years after the operation, H. M. still can't recognize the room where he lives, the people who care for him, or the scientists who have studied him for decades. He spends his days in an always-unfamiliar nursing home, often reading the same books and magazines over and over, each time as though it were the first. He thinks he is much younger than he is, and no longer recognizes a photograph of his own face.

Former President Ronald Reagan and H. M. both suffer from biological (or organic) causes of memory failure, but these are not the only reasons for trouble. Consider the following psychologically induced memory problem:

At the age of 14, Elizabeth's mother drowned. The details surrounding the death were always rather vague for Elizabeth, but she did remember her mother's tiptoed visit the evening before her death, the quick hug and whispered "I love you." At a family reunion some 30 years later, a relative told Elizabeth that she had been the one to find her mother's drowned body. Despite her initial shock and denial, over the next few days the memories slowly started coming back:

Elizabeth Loftus

I could see myself, a thin, dark-haired girl, looking into the flickering blue-and-white pool. My mother, dressed in her nightgown, is floating face down. I start screaming. I remember the police cars, their lights flashing, and the stretcher with the clean, white blanket tucked in around the edges of the body. The memory had been there all along, but I just couldn't reach it"

Loftus & Ketcham, 1994, p. 45

Imagine being a former president of the United States. What would it be like to discover you will slowly and inevitably lose your memory to Alzheimer's disease? Would you prefer to be H. M. — existing only in the present moment, unable to learn and form new memories? Can you imagine why a child might forget the details surrounding her mother's drowning? But what if the relative was wrong? Could Elizabeth create a *false memory* of finding her mother's body?

In this section, you will discover several amazing stories, facts, and theories about memory and learn how to use this information in your everyday life. Along the way, you will learn that our memory is *not* a gigantic library or storehouse of facts available for later retrieval. It is also *not* a video recorder or movie camera that accurately records and stores our everyday experiences. It is a highly selective and constructive process subject to serious errors and distortion.

On the other hand, our memories are also highly functional and biologically well adapted for everyday life. Every moment of the day, we rather automatically filter and sort through a barrage of information and then select, retain, and recover information essential to our survival.

Module 19 presents a brief overview of the three most popular theories and models that help explain "What is memory?" Module 20 explores several factors and theories that help answer "Why do we forget?" Module 20 also examines both common and unusual problems with memory, including amnesia, brain traumas, repressed memories, and eyewitness testimony. The module concludes with a summary of the research and examine some techniques that help improve memory.

MODULE 19
WHAT IS MEMORY?

Memory *An internal record or representation of some prior event or experience; also a set of mental processes that receives, encodes, stores, organizes, alters, and retrieves information over time*

> What are the three major approaches that help explain memory?

Memory is most often defined as "an internal record or representation of some prior event or experience" (Purdy, Markham, Schwartz, & Gordon, 2001, p. 9). Remember, however, that this internal record is fallible. It may be composed of less detail (or more) than the actual event or experience. Recognizing the problems and frailties of memory, we have sprinkled memory improvement suggestions throughout this module and the next. Our first tip: *organization*. When you want to learn and remember a large amount of information, you must organize it into meaningful patterns or categories. To provide an example, we have summarized and organized this module to create Table 19.1. Like a map that helps you plan your trip, note how this overview gives you "the big picture" and helps you master and remember the important details.

Each of the approaches shown in Table 19.1 and discussed in the upcoming section offers a slightly different but overlapping perspective on the way memory operates and is organized. They also offer you, the reader, a greater understanding of how your memory works — and when it fails. (Specific techniques for improving memory are summarized at the end of Module 20.) Let's begin with the first major approach.

Traditional Three-Stage Memory Model: The Need for Differing Storage Times

Since the late 1960s, one of the most widely used models in memory research has been the *traditional three-stage memory model* or the *three-box model* (Atkinson &

TABLE 19.1 AN OVERVIEW OF THREE COMMON MEMORY MODELS

Traditional three-stage memory model	This model suggests humans need to store information for different lengths of time. The first stage, *sensory memory*, holds information just long enough to select items worthy of further processing. The second stage, *short-term memory* (STM), allows time for brief sorting and organizing of information to send on to relatively permanent storage. The third stage, *long-term memory* (LTM), is a relatively permanent storehouse of all our memories.
Encoding, storage, and retrieval approach	Memory is seen as a *process*, with a variety of control mechanisms operating at each point in the process. At the beginning of the process (*encoding*), we select certain incoming environmental stimuli and translate (encode) them into neural messages the brain can understand. During storage, we select and organize specific information to save in "files" for permanent storage. At the final point in the process (*retrieval*), we search these files and bring back the necessary data.
Biological approach	This approach explains memory by looking at biological changes in the synapses that occur during encoding and storage and at where memories are located when retrieval is required.

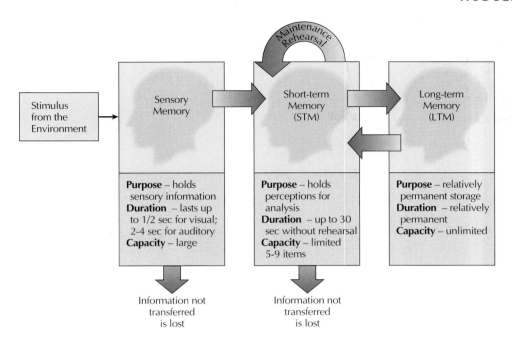

Figure 19.1 *Traditional three-stage memory model.* Each "box" represents a separate memory system that differs in duration, capacity, and function. When information is not transferred from sensory memory or short-term memory, it is assumed to be lost. Information stored in long-term memory can be retrieved and sent back to short-term memory for use.

Shiffrin, 1968; Healy & McNamara, 1996). According to this model, we need different storage "boxes" or stages to house information for various lengths of time. The first stage holds information for exceedingly short intervals, the second retains information for approximately 30 seconds or less (unless renewed), and the third stage provides relatively permanent storage. Because information must pass through each of these stages to get to the next, they are often depicted as three boxes with directional arrows indicating the flow of information (Figure 19.1). Each of these three stages (*sensory*, *short-term*, and *long-term*) has a somewhat different purpose, duration, and capacity.

Sensory Memory

Everything we see, hear, touch, taste, and smell must first enter our **sensory memory**, a very brief storage of sensory information. The *purpose* of sensory memory is to retain a relatively exact image of each sensory experience just long enough to locate and focus on relevant bits of information and transfer them on to the next stage of memory. The *duration* of sensory memory varies according to the specific sense. For visual information, known as *iconic memory*, the visual icon (or image) lasts about one-half of a second. Auditory information (what we hear) is held in sensory memory about the same length of time as visual information, one-quarter of a second, but a weaker "echo," or *echoic memory*, can last up to 2 to 4 seconds (Lu, Williamson, & Kaufman, 1992; Neisser, 1967).

How can such brief sensory messages be measured in a laboratory? One of the earliest researchers, George Sperling (1960), designed a clever experiment that briefly showed people visual arrays of 12 letters arranged in rows (Figure 19.2). Sperling rapidly flashed this three-letter–by–four-letter matrix on a screen. Immediately after the letters flashed off, he asked the participants to recall the letters. Participants generally recalled only 4 or 5 letters but insisted they had seen more letters before the memory slipped away. To test this possibility, Sperling devised a "partial report" experiment. Rather than reporting everything from the display, he asked participants to report the first row of letters if they heard a high tone, the second row if they heard a medium tone, and the third row when they heard a low tone.

Sensory Memory The first stage of memory in which a relatively exact image of each sensory experience is held briefly until it can be further processed; its capacity is relatively large, but its duration is restricted to a few seconds

Figure 19.2 *Experiments with sensory memory.* When George Sperling flashed an arrangement of letters like these for $1/20$ of a second, most people could only recall 4 or 5 (of 12). But when instructed to report the top, middle, or bottom row, depending on whether they heard a high, medium, or low tone, they reported almost all the letters correctly. Apparently, all 12 letters are held in sensory memory right after viewing them, but only those that are immediately attended to (with the tone) are noted and processed.

Short-Term Memory (STM) *The second stage of memory that contains information a person is consciously thinking about or working with; its capacity is limited to five to nine items and its duration is about 30 seconds*

Maintenance Rehearsal *The process of repeating the contents of short-term memory over and over to maintain it in short-term memory*

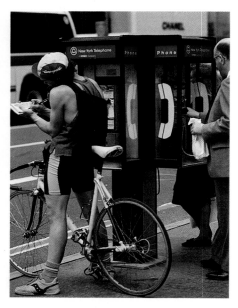

Short-term memory and maintenance rehearsal. *When you look up a telephone number, you can rehearse it over and over to keep it in short-term memory; however, you might not remember the number after you dial unless you stored it in long-term memory.*

Whatever row or column the participants were asked to recall, they were able to name the letters without any trouble, which indicates that they had memory access to all letters in the matrix for at least a few thousandths of a second. This suggests, then, that all objects in the visual field are available in sensory memory if they can be attended to quickly.

From this and other studies, early researchers assumed that sensory memory had an unlimited capacity. However, later research suggests that sensory memory does have its limits and that the stored images are fuzzier than was once thought (Best, 1999). Bear in mind, too, that all senses — taste, touch, smell, and hearing, as well as vision — have a sensory memory.

Short-Term Memory

Just as sensory memory maintains environmental stimuli only long enough to decide whether to send it on, the second stage, **short-term memory** (STM), only temporarily stores and processes the sensory image until it decides whether to send it along to the third stage. Although they share a similar *purpose*, STM does not store *duplicates* of sensory information but rather an end product of perceptual analyses. When your sensory memory registers the sound of your professor's voice, it holds the actual auditory information for a few seconds. If you decide the voice needs further processing, you send it along to STM. While being transferred from sensory memory, the voice is converted into a larger, more inclusive type of message capable of being analyzed and interpreted during short-term memory. If your STM decides the information is important (or may be on a test), it organizes and sends this information along to relatively permanent storage, called long-term memory (LTM).

The *duration* and *capacity* of STM are relatively limited. STM holds a restricted amount of new information, five to nine items, for up to 30 seconds, by most estimates, although some researchers extend the time to a few minutes (Best, 1999; Kareev, 2000). As with sensory memory, information in STM either is transferred quickly into the next stage (LTM) or it decays and is lost.

How can I increase the duration and capacity of my STM? Look back to the memory model in Figure 19.1 and note the looping arrow at the top labeled "maintenance rehearsal." You can extend STM almost indefinitely by consciously repeating the information over and over again, a process called **maintenance rehearsal**. You are using maintenance rehearsal when you look up a phone number and repeat it over and over until you dial the number. It is like juggling a set of plates; the plates stay in perfect shape as long as you keep juggling them. Once you stop, however, the plates fall and are destroyed (or the memory is lost).

If you'd like a simple demonstration of the duration of visual, *iconic memory*, hold your hand about 12 inches in front of you. Stare at it for a few seconds and then close your eyes. Note how the image, or *icon*, of your hand lingers for a fraction of a second. To appreciate (and remember) *echoic memory*, think about times when someone interrupted while you were deeply absorbed in a task. Did you sometimes ask "What?" yet find you could still answer their question without a repeat? Now you know why. If we divert our attention from the absorbing task quickly enough, we can "hear again" the echo of what was said.

To extend the *capacity* of STM, you can use **chunking**, a process of grouping separate pieces of information into units (or *chunks*) (Glassman, 1999; Miller, 1956). Have you noticed that numbers on credit cards, your Social Security identification, and telephone number are all grouped into three or four units separated by hyphens? This is because most people find it easier to remember numbers in chunks like *(760) 744–1129* rather than as a string of single digits. Similarly, in reading-improvement courses, students are taught to chunk groups of words into phrases so that fewer eye movements are required and the brain can process the phrases as units rather than as individual words.

Expert chess players also use chunking to organize the information on a game board into meaningful patterns or units. Researchers have found that novice players who look at a standard chessboard with the pieces arranged in a typical play position can remember the positions of only a few pieces. Expert chess players generally remember all the positions (Chase & Simon, 1973; Gobert, 1998). To the expert players, these seemingly randomly arranged pieces form meaningful patterns. Just as you group the letters of this sentence into meaningful words and remember them long enough to understand the meaning, expert chess players group the chess pieces into patterns (or chunks) that can be easily recalled.

If I have room for five to nine units or chunks, why doesn't chunking help me remember even three or four names during introductions? The limited capacity and brief duration of STM both work against you in this situation. Instead of concentrating on the name of someone you meet for the first time, you sometimes use all your short-term memory capacity wondering how you look and thinking about what to say. You might even fill STM space worrying about the fact that you have already forgotten his or her name! People who are good at remembering names repeat the name of each person out loud or silently to keep it entered in STM (maintenance rehearsal). They also make sure that other thoughts don't intrude until they have tested their ability to remember the name. Note that maintenance rehearsal keeps the name available only while you're actively rehearsing. If you want to really learn that name, you will need to transfer it into long-term memory.

Short-Term Memory as a "Working Memory"

Most current researchers (Baddeley, 1992, 2000; Cantor & Engle, 1993) prefer to think of STM as a three-part *working memory* (Figure 19.3):

1. Visuospatial sketchpad. This component is the visual workspace that allows us to temporarily hold and manipulate visual images and spatial information (Best, 1999; Friedman & Miyake, 2000). Mentally rearranging the furniture in your home requires activation of the visuospatial sketchpad.

2. Central executive. This component works as a supervisor that integrates and manages information from the phonological loop and the visuospatial sketchpad, as well as other material retrieved from LTM. It also coordinates material used during reasoning and decision making. When you mentally weigh the pros and cons of different movies to view, you are using the central executive.

3. Phonological rehearsal loop. This is the component responsible for holding and manipulating material related to speech, words, and numbers (Best, 1999; Gathercole & Pickering, 2000; Jiang et al., 2000). Suppose you're a waitperson (without a notepad) and you have the following orders from a table of diners: "I want the breakfast special with two scrambled eggs, orange juice, and coffee." "Give me the ham, very well done, with the stack of pancakes, and nothing to drink." "I'll have oatmeal without the raisins, dry toast, coffee, and grapefruit juice." Thanks to your phonological loop, and your use of maintenance rehearsal, you can keep these directions in working memory until you reach the kitchen and pass them along to the chef.

Chess as a type of chunking. *World-class chess players such as Garry Kasparov are able to remember groups of pieces by chunking them into meaningful patterns.*

Chunking *The process of grouping information into units to store more information in short-term memory*

Figure 19.3 Working memory as a central executive. According to this model, working memory serves as a central executive that coordinates the visuospatial sketchpad and the phonological loop.

Problems with short-term memory?
When being introduced to several peo-
ple at a party, you will be more apt to
remember the person's name if you
repeat it several times, and focus solely
on the person rather than other inter-
fering factors.

Long-Term Memory (LTM) *The*
third stage of memory that functions as
storage of information for long periods
of time; its capacity is limitless and its
duration is relatively permanent

Long-Term Memory

The *purpose* of the third stage, **long-term memory** (LTM), is to serve as a storehouse for information that must be kept for long periods of time. Once information is transferred from STM, it is organized and integrated with other information in LTM. It remains there until we need to retrieve it. Then it is sent back to STM for our use.

Compared to the sensory memory and short-term memory, long-term memory has unlimited *capacity* and *duration* (Klatzky, 1984). Although it may seem that lots of information gets lost in your long-term memory storehouse, your problem is more likely a result of poor organization. During the transfer of information from STM to LTM, incoming information is "tagged" or filed, hopefully in the appropriate place. If information is improperly stored, it creates major delays and problems during retrieval. The better you label and arrange things (whether it's your CD collection, your bills, or your memory), the more likely they will be accurately stored and readily available for retrieval. Organization is the key.

Admittedly, organization takes time and work. But you'll be happy to know that some memory organization and filing actually goes on while you sleep. Researchers have found that recent additions to LTM are partially reviewed, improved, and systematically catalogued during REM (rapid-eye-movement) sleep (Hennevin, Hars, Maho, & Bloch, 1995). Other research shows that sleep itself improves memory (Koulack, 1997; Plihal & Born, 1999).

What about tapes suggesting you can learn new skills like foreign languages while you sleep? Do they work? In one early study, participants' brain waves were recorded while they listened to tapes as they slept. Afterward, they were asked questions about the information they heard. Participants who listened to the tapes while in a drowsy state could answer 50 percent of the questions. Listeners in a transition state between drowsiness and light sleep could answer 5 percent of the questions. Listeners who were fully asleep did not remember any information (Simon & Emmons, 1956).

Learning a foreign language or anything else requires proper transfer and storage of information, which demands an alert, attentive mind. Even being slightly drowsy affects your ability to process and store information, thus the importance of staying alert while studying. It's easy to begin nodding off when you're reading a long textbook assignment. But if you're doing *active reading* (see Tools for Student Success Module 4), you'll stay alert and be more likely to remember what you read.

Encoding, Storage, and Retrieval: The Processes of Memory

The traditional three-stage memory model remains the leading approach because it offers a convenient way to organize the major findings of memory. However, later research has helped clarify several missing elements. The second approach adds to the three-stage model a focus on the memory *process* — how information is changed as it moves through the following operations: *encoding*, *storage*, and *retrieval*. Each of these three processes represents a different function that is somewhat analogous to those of a computer (Figure 19.4).

How do you remember the date of your next exam in psychology, the five items you need to buy at the grocery store, or your first romantic kiss? To remember any piece of information, you must first get it into your brain (**encoding**), then you must retain it (**storage**), and later you will need to recover it (**retrieval**). To input data into a computer, you begin by typing letters and numbers on the keyboard, which the computer translates into its own electronic language. In a similar fashion, your brain *encodes* sensory information (sound, visual image, and other senses) into a neural code (language) it can understand and use. Once information is encoded, it must be *stored*. Whereas computer memories are stored on a disk or hard drive, your human memories are stored in the brain. Finally, to retrieve information from either the computer or brain, you must search and locate the appropriate "files" and then bring the information up on the computer monitor or to your conscious awareness where it can be used.

Encoding *The process of translating information into neural codes (language) that will be retained in memory*

Storage *The process of retaining neural coded information over time*

Retrieval *The process of recovering information from memory storage*

Parallel Distributed Processing Approach

Like all analogies, this "memory as computer" model has its limits. Human memories are often fuzzy and fragile compared to the literal, "hard" data stored on a computer disk or hard drive. Critics of both the traditional three-stage model and the encoding, storage, and retrieval approach suggest that the human brain does not operate like a computer. A computer processes instructions and data *sequentially*; units of information follow one after another in a logical, orderly fashion.

Figure 19.4 *Memory as a computer.* The encoding, storage, and retrieval model uses a computer metaphor to explain the three basic functions of our memory system. Similar to a computer, incoming information is first *encoded* (typed on a keyboard and translated into computer language), stored on a disk or the hard drive, and later retrieved and brought to the computer screen to be used.

Human and computers. Even in jokes, our memory system is thought of in computer terms

"I forgot to make a back-up copy of my brain, so everything I learned last semester was lost."

Human memory, however, occurs *simultaneously*, through the action of multiple networks.

Because of these differences between computers and humans, some cognitive scientists prefer the **parallel distributed processing approach** (PDP), or *connectionist model*, of memory (McClelland, 1995; Sartori & Umilta, 2000). As the name implies, instead of recognizing patterns as a sequence of information bits (like a computer), our brain and memory processes perform multiple, *parallel* operations all at one time. In addition, memory is spread out, or *distributed*, throughout an entire network of processing units (nodes in the network). If you're swimming in the ocean and see a large fin nearby, your brain does not conduct a complete search of all fish with fins before urging you to begin a rush to the beach. Instead, you conduct a mental *parallel* search, noting the color of the fish, the fin, and the potential danger all at the same time. Because the processes are parallel, you can quickly process the information — and possibly avoid being eaten by the shark!

Parallel Distributed Processing Approach *A model of memory in which knowledge is represented as connections among interacting processing units, distributed in a vast network, and all operating in parallel*

Parallel distributing processing (PDP). According to PDP research, our memory system is like a telephone company simultaneously directing and processing a multitude of calls.

The PDP model of how memory works represents the most recent shift in theories of memory. As we just noted, survival in our environment requires instantaneous information processing. The PDP model allows a faster response time, and it also seems consistent with neurological information of brain activity and the parallel processing used when we recognize patterns. Therefore, the PDP approach may soon become the standard model for explaining memory.

Check & Review

THREE-STAGE MEMORY MODEL AND ENCODING, STORAGE, AND RETRIEVAL

The traditional three-stage memory model proposes that information must pass through each of three stages before being stored: *sensory memory*, *short-term memory*, and *long-term memory*. **Sensory memory** preserves a brief replica of sensory information. It has a large capacity and information lasts between 2 to 4 seconds. Selected information is sent to short-term memory. **Short-term memory** (STM), also called *working memory*, involves memory for current thoughts. Short-term memory can hold five to nine items for about 30 seconds before they are forgotten. Information can be stored longer than 30 seconds through **maintenance rehearsal**, and the capacity of STM can be increased with **chunking**. **Long-term memory** (LTM) is relatively permanent memory storage with an unlimited capacity.

The encoding, storage, and retrieval approach sees memory as a *process*. It uses similarities between human memory and a computer. Like typing on a keyboard, **encoding** translates information into neural codes that match the brain's language. **Storage** retains neural coded information over time, like saving material on the computer's hard drive or a disk. **Retrieval** gets information out of LTM storage and sends it to STM to be used, whereas the computer retrieves information and displays it on the monitor.

The **parallel distributed processing** (PDP), or *connectionist*, model explains that contents of our memory are represented as a vast number of interconnected units and modules distributed throughout a huge network, all operating in parallel — simultaneously.

Questions

1. According to the three-stage memory model, information must first enter _____, then transfer to _____ and then to _____ to be retained in our memory system.
   (a) sensory memory; short-term memory; permanent memory;
   (b) short-term memory; sensory memory; long-term memory;
   (c) sensory memory; short-term memory; long-term memory;
   (d) working memory; short-term memory; permanent memory

2. Maintenance rehearsal allows us to keep information in _____ memory longer than the typical 30 seconds.
   (a) short-term; (b) long-term; (c) sensory; (d) permanent

3. Explain how the encoding, storage, and retrieval approach to human memory is analogous to the workings of a computer.

4. How does the PDP approach explain memory?

Answers to Questions can be found in Appendix B.

Integrating the Two Major Approaches: Three-Stage Memory Model Meets Encoding, Storage, and Retrieval

Memory researchers continue to debate the merits and limits of the several models of memory. Given the durability of the *three-stage memory model* and the additional information provided by the *encoding*, *storage*, and *retrieval* approach, most psychologists currently emphasize an integration of these two models (Figure 19.5). In this section, we will show how an integration of the two major memory models provides a convenient way to organize the major findings on memory, as well as providing a good accounting for those findings. Let's start with encoding.

Integrating Encoding with the Three-Stage Memory Model

When we encode information, we are translating or recording it into a form the brain can recognize and use. As you can see in Figure 19.5, we first encode information when we transfer it from sensory memory to STM. We also perform a second type of encoding during the transfer from STM to LTM.

Figure 19.5 *The "Integrated Model"* This diagram shows how the traditional three-stage memory model can be incorporated with the encoding, storage, and retrieval approach. Note that encoding and storage take place, to some degree, in all three stages, whereas retrieval occurs only from long-term memory to short-term memory.

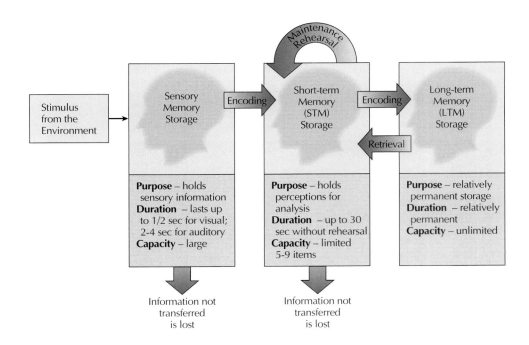

Although we cannot directly observe or measure how encoding occurs, the best guess is that storage codes are primarily *verbal* or *sensory*. To remember your most romantic kiss, you encode (or translate the experience) into a verbal description, "It was a wonderful, exciting moment that happened as we were…" But how would you encode the sight of his or her face, the sound of his or her laughter, or the smell of his or her skin? Sometimes words are inadequate, so we encode sensory impressions — smells, sounds, and visual images. There is truth to the saying that a picture (or smell or sound) is worth a thousand words. Finally, some memories are also encoded according to movement or action. This so-called "muscle" or kinesthetic memory explains why you also have a memory of how it felt to kiss this person. Driving a stick shift car, using a spoon or chopsticks to eat, or typing on a keyboard all seem to be coded verbally and pictorially, but they also involve your muscle memory.

Research findings related to encoding and the three-stage model can be integrated and grouped under two major strategies: *organization* and *rehearsal*:

1. Organization. As we discovered earlier, organization is one of the most important elements in memory. It is particularly important during encoding. Two of the most important forms of organization during encoding are *chunking* for STM and *hierarchies* for LTM. To extend the capacity of short-term memory (5 9 units), we discussed how to organize the information into chunks. To encode information for LTM, we need to organize these chunks into *hierarchies*, arranging a number of elements of information into a few broad concepts that are further divided and subdivided.

Do you recall how Module 6 organized the large body of information about the nervous system into a hierarchy with smaller and smaller units or chunks? Look at Figure 19.6. Note how the hierarchy for the nervous system is similar to our newly created hierarchy for the current information. Can you see how arranging the information into such hierarchies helps make them more understandable and *memorable*? This is the reason we use so many hierarchies throughout this text (in the form of diagrams and tables). If you want to improve your memory in this and other courses, study these carefully.

Better yet, try making your own hierarchies when studying for exams. Although this may sound difficult, keep in mind that you already possess all the basic skills.

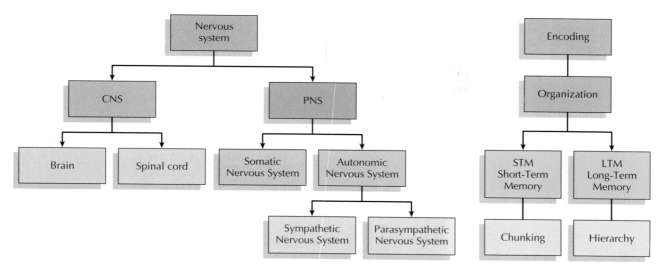

Figure 19.6 *Hierachies are a natural part of LTM.* Just as the diagram of the nervous system helped organize the material in Chapter 2, a similar diagram of the current information on memory helps you order and arrange the various terms. Encoding, storage, and retrieval in LTM are all improved through the use of hierarchies.

Think back to the first day you walked around your college campus. You probably felt overwhelmed by all the buildings, sidewalks, and parking lots, and needed a map just to find your classes. After being on campus for a while, however, the map was discarded because you "naturally" organized all the information into personally meaningful chunks (science building, library, cafeteria) that were further organized into an overall personal hierarchy. Try using these same skills to arrange the large assortment of facts and concepts required for a typical college exam.

2. Rehearsal. Because information is normally kept in STM for only about 30 seconds, encoding is very important. As we learned earlier, if you need to hold information longer than 30 seconds, you can do a type of juggling act called *maintenance rehearsal*, where you simply keep repeating it over and over. This type of *shallow processing* is normally enough for some information that you don't need in long-term storage. But if you've ever tried simple maintenance rehearsal to study for exams, you unfortunately discovered that it doesn't work. Storage in LTM requires *deep processing*, or **elaborative rehearsal**, in which new information is actively reviewed and related to information already in LTM.

According to Fergus Craik and Robert Lockhart's *levels-of-processing approach* (1972), a deeper analysis of meaning enables us to remember information better because we store it in LTM more efficiently. Have you noticed that older students in college classes often receive better grades? Although there are many reasons for this, their longer life and greater store of experiences provide them with more LTM information available for elaborative rehearsal.

If you're a younger student or an older student just returning to college, you may have to work a little harder at *elaborative rehearsal* in your college courses. You can improve this ability and process information at a deeper level by

• *Generating new, personal examples of the concept.* If you can't easily tag information to what you already know, create your own example. To encode and store the term *echoic memory*, look for examples of this in other people or yourself. Make a mental note when it happens and store the example with the term *echoic memory*.

Elaborative Rehearsal *An encoding technique of associating new information with already stored knowledge in long-term memory; (also known as deeper levels of processing)*

- *Expanding (or elaborating on) the information.* To store the term *long-term memory* in your actual LTM, think about what it would be like if you could store information for only 30 seconds. Picture the life of H. M. (the man introduced in the opening vignette). The more you elaborate on the term, the more likely you are to remember it.

- *Actively exploring and questioning new information.* Think about the term *iconic memory.* Ask yourself, "Why did they use this term?" Look up the term *icon* in the dictionary and you'll learn that *icon* is from the Greek word for image or likeness.

- *Trying to find meaningfulness.* When you meet people at a party, don't just maintenance-rehearse their name. Ask about their favorite TV shows, their career plans, political beliefs, or anything else that requires deeper analysis. You'll be much more likely to remember their name.

Integrating Storage with the Three-Stage Memory Model

As we discovered earlier, both sensory memory and STM store a very limited amount of information for a brief period of time. Our most important and valuable storehouse is that of LTM. Given that LTM is virtually unlimited in duration and capacity, we obviously collect a vast amount of information over a lifetime. How do we store it? Once again, organization is the key. As you can see in Figure 19.7 and Table 19.2, LTM appears to be composed of several interacting systems and subsystems — the brain's built-in *hierarchy.* At the top of the hierarchy, you can see that LTM is divided into two major systems — *explicit/declarative memory* and *implicit/nondeclarative memory.*

Explicit/Declarative Memory *The subsystem within long-term memory that stores facts, information, and personal life experiences (also called explicit memory or declarative memory)*

Semantic Memory *The subpart of explicit/declarative memory that stores general knowledge; a mental encyclopedia or dictionary*

1. *Explicit/declarative memory* Explicit *memory* refers to intentional learning or conscious knowledge. It is *memory with awareness.* Remembering your Social Security number, your first kiss, the name of your first-grade teacher, and the name of your current psychology professor are all examples of explicit memories. This type of memory is sometimes referred to as *declarative memory,* because, if asked, you consciously know the information and can "declare" it. When people think of memory, they often are referring to declarative memory (Best, 1999; Hayne, Boniface, & Barr, 2000).

Explit/declarative memory can be further subdivided into two parts — *semantic memory* and *episodic memory.* **Semantic memory** is memory for general knowledge, rules, events, objective facts, and information. It is our internal men-

Figure 19.7 *A Hierarchy for Long-Term Memory.* Taking time to study and memorize the separate systems and subsystems for long-term memory can improve your understanding and mastery of this material because it involves *elaborative rehearsal* or a *deeper level of processing.*

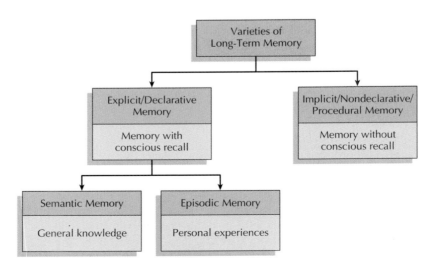

TABLE 19.2 LONG-TERM MEMORY (LTM)

Categories and Subcategories	Definition	Examples
Explicit (declarative) memory	Memory with awareness	Explicit memories of life events and facts
Semantic memory	General knowledge of rules, facts, and events; personal encyclopedia of information	Add *s* to make plurals. There are 3 feet in a yard. There are 12 months in a year.
Episodic memory	Personally experienced events; a cumulative record of the episodes of a person's life	Your high school graduation The birth of your first child
Implicit (nondeclarative or procedural) memory	Memory without awareness	Implicit memories of skills and procedures
Procedural memory	How to perform skills, operations, and actions; memories of perfected motor skills	How to drive a car How to brush your teeth How to ride a bike

tal dictionary or encyclopedia of stored knowledge. If you read and remember terms like *semantic*, *episodic*, *explicit/declarative*, and *implicit/nondeclarative*, it is because you have stored them in your semantic memory. Our **episodic memory** is somewhat like a mental diary (Best, 1999; Tulving, 1985). It records the episodes in our life — our first day in school, the people we have known, the places we have visited, and all the personal experiences we have had throughout our lifetime.

2. *Implicit/nondeclarative/procedural memory* *Implicit memory* refers to unintentional learning or unconscious knowledge. It is *memory without awareness*. It consists of motor skills, habits, and simple classically conditioned responses (Squire, Knowlton, & Musen, 1993). This type of memory is also sometimes called *nondeclarative memory* because it includes procedures involved in well-perfected skills and habits outside our conscious awareness, such as driving a car or eating with utensils (Best, 1999; Fernandez-Ruiz & Diaz, 1999).

Associated with implicit/nondeclarative/procedural memory is a phenomenon known as **priming**, where prior presentation of information subsequently makes it easier to recall related items — even when we have no conscious memory of the original information (Toth & Reingold, 1996). In a typical priming research experiment, the researcher flashes a word or symbol on a computer screen so briefly that it is not consciously perceived. When participants are later exposed to a group of unrelated stimuli and asked whether they recognize any item, they are more likely to identify the previously flashed stimuli — even though they deny having seen it before. This indicates that *priming* has taken place.

Integrating Retrieval with the Three-Stage Memory Model

So far, we've discussed how encoding and storage can be integrated with the three-stage memory model. In this section, we will examine *retrieval*, the process of accessing stored information, and how it also can be integrated with the three-stage

Episodic Memory *The subpart of explicit/declarative memory that stores memories of personally experienced events; a mental diary of a person's life*

Implicit/Nondeclarative Procedural Memory *The subsystem within long-term memory that consists of skills acquired through repetitive practice, habits, and simple classically conditioned responses (also called implicit memory, nondeclarative memory, or procedural memory*

Priming *The process by which an earlier encounter with a stimulus (such as a word or picture) increases the likelihood of that stimulus or a related stimulus being remembered at a later time*

One way to remember each of these various systems and subsystems is to encode them in your long-term memory (LTM) using *elaborative rehearsal* or a *deeper level of processing*. Our chapter opening incident included the story of former President Ronald Reagan's unfortunate experiences with Alzheimer's disease and the story of H. M. Try your hand at elaborative rehearsal by filling in the following blanks with the name of the correct subdivision of LTM.

1. When President Reagan couldn't remember the events and experiences surrounding his acting role in the film *Prisoners of War,* he was experiencing the fading of his _____ memory.
2. Later, it became apparent that Reagan's _____ memory was failing when he couldn't remember facts, such as the names of influential friends, like his secretary of state (Reagan & Reagan, 2000).

3. Most recently, Reagan's _____ memory has been affected, which makes everyday skills such as dressing and eating difficult.
4. After his operation, H. M. could not tell the researchers the day of the week, the year, or even about his last meal. His _____ memory was lacking.
5. Because his _____ memory remained intact, H. M. could acquire new manual or problem-solving skills, such as playing tennis.
6. When tested under specialized conditions that do not require conscious remembering, H. M. can approach or even match the performance of normal participants. This suggests that his _____ memory is intact.

Answers: *1. episodic;   2. semantic;   3. procedural;   4. declarative;   5. procedural;   6. implicit/nondeclarative.*

Retrieval Cue *A clue or prompt that helps stimulate recall and retrieval of a stored piece of information from long-term memory*

Recognition *Process of matching a specific retrieval cue to an appropriate item in long-term memory*

Recall *Process of using a very general retrieval cue to search the contents of long-term memory*

model. To do this, we examine four related areas of research: retrieval cues, recognition, recall, and the encoding specificity principle.

A **retrieval cue** is a stimulus that can begin a retrieval process from LTM (Klatzky, 1984). There are basically two types of retrieval cues—either specific or general. When you retrieve a memory using a specific cue, it is called **recognition**. When you use a general cue, it is called **recall**.

If you pick out a particular face you have previously seen from a police lineup, you use *recognition* to check the specific cue (the face) against your LTM contents to see if something matches (Figure 19.8). If, on the other hand, you remember someone's name from a description of that person (a general cue), you are using *recall*, which is a much more difficult task (Bransford, 1979). During recall, you use a general cue to generate a list of material associated with that cue and then search

Figure 19.8 *Recognition memory.* Results from a study of recognition memory in which participants were asked to identify pictures of their high school classmates. As you can see, both name recognition and picture recognition remain high, whereas recall memory would be expected to drop significantly over time.

through LTM to find something that matches the cue (Best, 1999, p. 143). This general cue often isn't enough to locate a single piece of information because the list of possible matches is often quite large. Therefore, the more specific the cue, the more likely you are to retrieve the needed information from your memory.

Most essay tests require *recall*. The questions provide only relatively general cues that ask you to dredge up and organize your memories on a particular topic. In contrast, multiple-choice questions primarily require *recognition*. Because you are given specific alternatives to match with your memories, recognition is easier and usually leads to more success in retrieving memories. (Tip for student success: While students are taking a test, most professors permit questions regarding clarification on difficult items. Their answers may provide additional retrieval cues.)

If retrieval is so difficult, why do we remember questions that we got wrong on an exam, even when we're trying to forget? Research has shown that interrupted tasks are better recalled than completed tasks, a phenomenon known as the **Zeigarnik effect** (House, & McIntosh, 2000; Munroe & Gauvain, 2001; Zeigarnik, 1927). Your frustration over the incorrect items creates a type of arousal that apparently facilitates retrieval. One of the best ways to prevent this unwanted retrieval is to complete the task by looking up the correct answer immediately after the exam. This will also improve your later performance on similar questions.

One of the best ways to improve retrieval is to recreate the original learning conditions. The ease of retrieval depends on the match between the way information is encoded and later retrieved; this is known as the **encoding specificity principle** (Tulving & Thompson, 1973). Three important research findings are related to this principle that may help improve your academic success:

- *Context and retrieval.* Have you noticed that you do better on a test when you take it in the same seat and classroom where you originally studied the material? This happens because the location is a retrieval cue to the material you studied. Godden and Baddeley (1975) demonstrated how context affects learning and memory in a clever study some years ago. They had underwater divers learn a list of 40 words either on land or underwater. The divers had better recall for lists they had encoded underwater when they were underwater at retrieval; conversely, lists encoded above water were better recalled above water. This can be one reason why we feel confident about material while studying at home yet still have trouble recalling it at school later.

- *Mood congruence.* Have you ever become so anxious during an exam that you had trouble remembering material you thought you knew well? When you are sad, do you tend to think of the same things as when you were sad in the past? When you are angry, do you tend to remember other situations that made you angry? The idea that a given mood tends to evoke memories that are consistent with that mood is called *mood congruence*.

  Research shows that people remember something better if their emotional states are the same at the time when they learn something and during the time when they try to retrieve it (Kenealy, 1997). If you suffer from test anxiety, you might try decreasing your anxiety during the exam by taking deep breaths and reassuring yourself. In addition, you might want to artificially increase your anxiety level while studying by reminding yourself of the importance of good grades or your long-range career plans. By lowering your test anxiety and upping your study anxiety, you create a better balance or match between your exam mood and your study mood. This should improve your retrieval.

- *State-dependent retrieval.* Research has also shown that if you learn something while under the influence of a drug, such as caffeine, you will remember it more easily when you take that drug again than at other times (Baddeley, 1998). Some students have found that drinking a cup of coffee while studying and before an exam does improve their performance. However, this study does *not* mean that

Zeigarnik Effect *Process whereby interrupted tasks are better recalled than completed tasks*

Encoding Specificity Principle *Retrieval of information is improved when conditions of recovery are similar to the conditions when information was encoded*

you should drink alcohol as you study and then again during exams! In fact, alcohol and most other drugs impair memory, as well as create serious health and social problems.

Biological Perspective: Memory's Effect on the Brain and Nervous System

Our two previous models of memory emphasize how information is processed into memories. In this section, we will focus our attention on the biological aspects of memory. It is obvious that something physical must happen in the brain and nervous system when we learn something new. (How else could we later recall and use this information?) In this section, we will first look at neuronal and synaptic changes that occur with memory. Then we will discuss hormonal influences on memory. Finally, in the Research Highlight we explore the anatomy of memory — where memory is located in the brain.

Neuronal and Synaptic Changes in Memory

One of the earliest researchers to study the biochemistry of memory was Donald Hebb (1949, 1955, 1966). After measuring the electrical activity of the brain during learning, Hebb suggested that neurons fire in *reverberating circuits* — that is, a set of neurons fires over and over during the STM process. Structural changes in the synapses from the reverberating circuits do not happen instantaneously. They take time. Before short-term memories can be converted into long-term memories, they must go through a general process called **consolidation**. The consolidation period can be compared to writing your name in freshly poured cement. When the cement dries and sets, your name is there to stay. In the meantime, until the cement is set, it is vulnerable to damage. This can explain why people suffering head injuries, such as a concussion from a traffic accident, often have trouble remembering the events just before the injury. The "cement" for those potential long-term memories was still wet and not fully consolidated.

Consolidation *A hypothetical process explaining the gradual conversion of information into long-term memories*

The research by Hebb and others has suggested a two-stage model for memory consolidation (McGaugh, 2000). The first stage involves STM and the reverberating circuits. During the second stage, information from STM is transferred to LTM where a permanent change occurs in the nervous system.

What causes this change? As you may recall from earlier modules, learning modifies the brain's neural networks. As a response is learned, specific neural pathways are established that become progressively more excitable and responsive. While you are learning to play tennis, for example, the repeated practice builds neural "pathways" that make it easier and easier to get the ball over the net. This prolonged strengthening of potential neural firing is called **long-term potentiation** (LTP). There are at least two ways that LTP can happen:

Long-Term Potentiation *A long-lasting increase in the strength of synaptic responsiveness believed to be a biological mechanism for learning and memory*

1. *Repeated stimulation of a synapse can strengthen the synapse by stimulating the dendrites to grow more spines* (Barinaga, 1999). This then would result in more synapses, more receptor sites, and more sensitivity. These structural changes were first demonstrated when rats placed in enriched environments grew more sprouts on their dendrites compared with those of rats raised in deprived environments (Rosenzweig, Benet, & Diamond, 1972).

2. *The ability of a particular neuron to release its neurotransmitters can be increased or decreased.* Support comes from *Aplysia*, sea slugs, which can be classically conditioned to reflexively withdraw their gills when squirted with water. After the conditioning occurs, the slugs release more neurotransmitters at certain synapses, and these synapses become more efficient at transmitting signals (see

Improving memory through genetic engineering. Scientists have created mice with an added gene, which so improved their memory they were named "Doogie" after the boy genius on the television show, Doogie Howser, M.D. This "Doogie" mouse stands on an object used in one of their standard learning and memory tests.

Module 15). Further evidence comes from researchers at Princeton University who have created mice with an added gene with additional receptors for a neurotransmitter named NMDA (N-methyl-D-aspartate). These genetic mutant "smart mice" performed significantly better on memory tasks than normal mice did (Tang et al, 1999; Tsien et al., 2000). In fact, they were so far superior that the researchers named them Doogie after the boy genius on the TV show *Doogie Howser, M.D.*

Obviously, it is difficult to generalize from sea slugs and mice. However, research on LTP in humans also has been widely supportive (Kikusui, Aoyagi, & Kaneko, 2000; Sutherland & McNaughton, 2000). Furthermore, research shows that drugs that block LTP interfere with learning and memory (Maren, 1999). As you may have noticed, people often have trouble remembering events of a previous evening after a night of heavy drinking.

Hormonal Changes and Memory

In addition to neuronal changes with memory, emotion also has a significant effect on memory (Cahill & McGaugh, 1998; McGaugh, 1992, 2000). When stressed or excited, we naturally produce hormones that arouse the body — the inner part of the adrenal glands sends out two hormones, epinephrine and norepinephrine. Can you see why heightened emotions might enhance memory? To survive, an animal or a person must remember exactly how they got into a dangerous situation and how they got out of it. The naturally produced surge of hormones apparently alerts our brains to "pay attention and remember!"

The power of hormones on memory can be seen in the common phenomenon known as *flashbulb memories* — a vivid image of circumstances associated with sur-

How does a sea slug learn and remember? After repeated squirting with water, followed by a mild shock, the sea slug, Aplysia, responds by releasing more neurotransmitters at certain synapses, which allows the circuit to communicate more efficiently. Similar structural changes in human synapses help explain how we also learn and remember.

Flashbulb Memories. Can you recognize the unintended benefit of studying psychology? You gain greater appreciation for Gary Larson cartoons!

THE FAR SIDE® BY GARY LARSON

© 1993 FarWorks, Inc. All Rights Reserved/Dist. by Creators Syndicate

More facts of nature: All forest animals, to this very day, remember exactly where they were and what they were doing when they heard that Bambi's mother had been shot.

prising or strongly emotional events (Brown & Kulik, 1977). Do you remember the moment of your high school graduation or your first romantic kiss? Is this memory so clear that it seems like a flashbulb went off, capturing every detail of the event in your memory? Assassinations (JFK, Bobby Kennedy, Martin Luther King, Jr.), disasters (*Challenger* explosion, Mount St. Helens's eruption, tragic events involving famous figures (the death of Princess Diana), and, of course, horrific, terroristic attacks like the one on the World Trade Center and the Pentagon have lasting effects on memory. We secrete fight-or-flight hormones when we initially hear of the event and replay these events in our minds again and again, which makes for stronger memories.

Despite their intensity, flashbulb memories are not as accurate as you might think (Schmolck, Buffalo, & Squire, 2000). For example, in a study of flashbulb memories after the space shuttle *Challenger* explosion, Jeffrey Gutkin (1989) reported significant memory changes over a 3-year period following the disaster. Thus, not even flashbulb memories are immune to alteration. It is also important to note the limits to "hormonally induced memory." If you've ever become so anxious that you "blanked out" during an exam or while giving a speech, you understand that emotions can also interfere with both the formation and retrieval of memories.

RESEARCH HIGHLIGHT

Looking for Memory in All the Right Places

So far, our discussion has focused on the formation of memories as a result of neural changes or hormonal influences. But where is memory stored? What parts of the brain are involved? One of the first scientists to explore this idea was Karl Lashley (1890–1958). Believing that memory was *localized*, or stored in a specific brain area, Lashley began with a standard learning maze experiment for rats. Once the maze was learned, he surgically removed tiny portions of the rats' cortex and then retested their memory of the maze. After 3 decades of frustrating research, Lashley found that rats were still able to run the maze regardless of

©2001 The New Yorker Collection. Robert Mankoff from cartoonbank.com. All Rights Reserved.

the area of cortex he removed (Lashley, 1929, 1950). Lashley joked, "I sometimes feel in reviewing the evidence on localization of the memory trace, the necessary conclusion is that learning is not possible" (1950, p. 477). Failing to locate a single brain site for memory, Lashley ulti-

mately decided memories were not localized. Instead, they were *distributed* throughout the cortex. Later research suggests that Lashley was both right and wrong: Memory tends to be localized *and* distributed throughout the brain — not just the cortex.

Since Lashley's time, the brain structures involved in long-term memory (LTM) have been under investigation for many years. Today, research techniques are so advanced that we can experimentally induce and measure memory-related brain changes as they occur — on-the-spot reporting! For example, James Brewer and his colleagues (1998) used functional magnetic resonance imaging (fMRI) to locate areas of the brain responsible for encoding memories of pictures. They showed 96 pictures of indoor and outdoor scenes to participants while scanning their brains, then later tested them on their ability to recall those pictures. Brewer and his colleagues identified the right prefrontal cortex and the parahippocampal cortex as the most active during the encoding of the pictures.

Keep in mind, however, that several brain regions are involved in memory (Figure 19.9). For example, some researchers believe memories are *consolidated* in the hippocampal region of the brain and then sent on to be stored in other areas (Gluck & Myers, 1997). This helps explains why H. M. (described in this chapter's introductory incident) found it impossible to form new memories. This area was removed as part of his temporal lobe surgery.

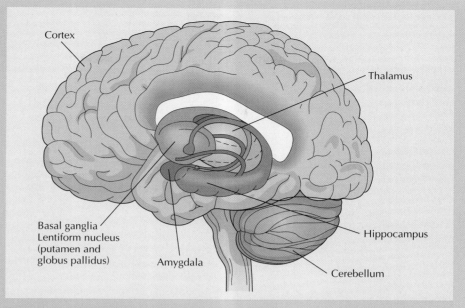

Figure 19.9 *Brain and memory formation*. Damage to any one of these areas can affect encoding, storage, and retrieval of memories.

Brain Area	Known or Suspected Relationship to Memory	Sources
Amygdala	Emotional memory and memory consolidation	McCaugh, 2000; Spanis, Bianchin, Izquierdo, & McGaugh, 1999
Basal Ganglia and Cerebellum	Creation and storage of implicit/nondeclarative memories (such as skills, habits, and simple classical conditioned responses)	Baddeley et al., 2000; Hazeltine, Grafton, & Ivry, 1997; Jog, Kubota, Connolly, Hillegaart, & Graybiel, 1999; Steinmetz, 1998
Hippocampal Formation (Hippocampus and Surrounding Area)	Memory recognition; explicit, spatial, episodic memory; and consolidation of declarative long-term memory	Chou et al., 1990; Eichenbaum. 1999; Fernandez et al., 1999
Thalamus	Formation of new memories and working memory	Bloom & Lazerson, 1988; Johnson & Ojemann, 2001; Manoach et al., 2000).
Cortical Areas: Motor, Parahippocampal, and Prefrontal Cortex; Regions of Occipital and Temporal Lobes	Encoding of explicit/declarative memories; storage of episodic and semantic memories; skill learning; priming	Abel et al., 2000; Gabrieli, Brewer, & Poldrack, 1998; Romo, Brody, Hernandez & Lemus, 1999; Wagner et al., 1998

Check & Review

INTEGRATION MODEL AND BIOLOGICAL PERSPECTIVE

Most psychologists currently emphasize an integration of the traditional *three-stage memory model* and the *encoding, storage, and retrieval approach.*

We first encode information when we transfer it from sensory memory to short-term memory, and then again during the transfer from STM to LTM. Organization and rehearsal are important to successful encoding. To improve encoding during STM, we can use the organizational method of *chunking* or the rehearsal key of *maintenance rehearsal.* During LTM, we can use the organizational strategy of creating *hierarchies* and the rehearsal key of *elaborative rehearsal.*

Storage in LTM is divided into two major systems—**explicit/declarative** and **implicit/nondeclarative/procedural** memory. Explit/declarative memory can be further subdivided into two parts—**semantic** and **episodic** memory.

Retrieval from LTM relies on **retrieval cues** (**recognition** and **recall**) and the **encoding specificity principle.**

The biological perspective of memory focuses on changes in neurons and hormones, as well as on searching for the locations of memory in the brain. Hebb's original idea that memory traces consist of specific neural circuits is supported by research on **long-term potentiation** (LTP). When we are stressed or excited, we naturally produce hormones that may enhance memory. Memory tends to be localized *and* distributed throughout the brain — not just in the cortex.

Questions

1. What is the difference between semantic and episodic memory?

2. Taking a multiple-choice test requires _____, whereas essay tests involve _____.

3. Circuits of neurons that fire over and over during STM are called _____. (a) reverberating circuits; (b) coding sequences; (c) electrically active units; (d) consolidation pathways.

4. Describe the two processes involved in LTP.

Answers to Questions can be found in Appendix B.

MODULE 19   ACTIVE LEARNING WORKSHEET

ACROSS

2. An encoding technique of associating new information with already stored knowledge in LTM.

11. Earlier encounter with a stimulus that increases the likelihood of that stimulus being later remembered.

12. Translation of information into neural codes that will be retained in memory.

13. A hypothetical process explaining the gradual conversion of information into LTM.

15. Process of using a very general retrieval cue to search the contents of LTM.

16. An internal record or representation of some prior event or experience.

17. First stage of memory where a relatively exact image of each sensory experience is held briefly until it can be further processed.

18. Second stage of memory containing information a person is consciously thinking about or working with.

19. Long-term memories for the performance of skills or actions.

DOWN

1. A long-lasting increase in the strength of synaptic responsiveness believed to be a biological mechanism for learning and memory.

3. Third stage of memory that stores information for long periods of time.

4. Subpart of explicit/declarative memory that stores general knowledge.

5. Grouping information into units in order to store more information in STM.

6. Process of retaining neural coded information over time.

7. Repeating contents of STM over and over to maintain it in STM.

8. Process of recovering information out of memory storage.

9. Clue or prompt stimulating recall and retrieval of information from LTM.

10. Subpart of explicit/declarative memory that stores memories of personally experienced events.

14. Process of matching a specific retrieval cue to an appropriate item in LTM.

Answers can be found in Appendix B.

MODULE 20
MEMORY FAILURES

What causes forgetting? How do we prevent forgetting of important information?

> Memory is what makes you wonder what you've forgotten.
>
> Anonymous

It may surprise you to learn that forgetting is essential to the proper functioning of memory. Think about what your life would be like if you couldn't forget. Your LTM would be filled with meaningless data, such as what you ate for breakfast every morning of your life. Although you might enjoy reliving the intense joy of previous happy experiences, think of the incredible pain and sorrow you would continuously endure if you couldn't escape through forgetting. Forgetting unnecessary or painful information, then, is essential to our lives. But what about those times when forgetting is an inconvenience or even dangerous? What causes forgetting? How can we prevent forgetting of important information?

Why Do We Forget: Factors Explaining Forgetting

These questions have been important issues in psychology ever since Hermann Ebbinghaus, a pioneer memory researcher who often used himself as his only subject, first introduced the experimental study of learning and forgetting in 1885. To measure memory performance, he calculated how long it took for him to learn a list of *nonsense syllables*. For his trials, Ebbinghaus chose three-letter nonsense syllables such as *SIB* and *RAL* because they were equally difficult to learn. Furthermore, nonsense syllables don't have the meanings and associations that words do, thus avoiding the complications of previous learning.

After Ebbinghaus memorized lists of nonsense syllables until he knew them perfectly, he retested his memory at regular intervals. He found that 1 hour after he knew a list perfectly, he remembered only 44 percent of the syllables. A day later, he recalled 35 percent, and a week later only 21 percent. Figure 20.1 presents his famous, and depressing, "forgetting curve."

Do we forget everything this fast? If you were to forget textbook materials and lecture notes this rapidly, you would be able to pass a test only if you took it immediately after studying the material. An hour later, you would fail the test because you would remember less than half of what you had studied. Keep in mind, however, that the forgetting curve in Figure 20.1 applies to meaningless nonsense syllables. Meaningful material is much less likely to be forgotten. The material you study for a test can be retained much longer if you make an effort to make it meaningful. But meaningful or not, you will still forget some of what you have studied.

On a more cheerful note, after some time passed and he had forgotten the list, Ebbinghaus also calculated the time it took to relearn the same list. He found that relearning a list took less time than the initial learning period; this is known as **relearning** (or the *savings method*). Ebbinghaus's research suggests that we often retain some memory for things we have learned, even when we seem to have forgotten them completely. This finding should be encouraging to you if you studied a foreign language years ago but are no longer proficient in recalling or recognizing the vocabulary. You could expect to relearn the material more rapidly the second time.

Relearning *Learning material a second time, which usually takes less time than original learning (also called the savings method)*

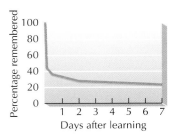

Figure 20.1 *Ebbinghaus's forgetting curve.* This graph dramatizes how rapidly nonsense syllables are forgotten, especially in the first few hours after learning.

Since Ebbinghaus's original research, scientists have discovered numerous factors that contribute to forgetting — which may have important implications for your life as a student. Two of the most important are the *serial position effect* and *spacing of practice*:

1. Serial position effect. When study participants are given lists of words to learn and are allowed to recall them in any order they choose, they remember the words at the beginning (*primacy effect*) and the end of the list (*recency effect*) better than those in the middle, which are quite often forgotten (Jones & Roediger, 1995) (Figure 20.2). The general term, including both the primacy effect and recency effect, is known as the **serial position effect**.

The reasons for this effect are complex, but it does help explain why material at the beginning and end of a chapter in a text is better remembered than that in the middle, or why you remember the first people you meet at a party and the last. It also has interesting applications for your employment success. If a potential employer calls to set up an interview, you can increase their memory for you and your application by asking to be either the first or last candidate.

2. Spacing of practice. Despite their best intentions, students often study in ways that encourage forgetting. In addition to studying in noisy places where attention is easily diverted and interference is maximized, they often try to memorize too much at one time by "cramming" the night before an exam. As the Tools for Student Success section in Module 4 emphasized, the single most important key to improving grades may be *distributed study*. **Distributed practice** refers to spacing your learning periods, with rest periods between sessions. Cramming is called **massed practice** because the time spent learning is massed into long, unbroken intervals. John Donovan and David Radosevich (1999) compared 63 separate studies and found that distributed practice produced superior memory and learning compared with massed practice. Unfortunately, research shows that most students study right before the test (Taraban, Maki, & Rynearson, 1999).

Figure 20.2 *The serial position effect.* If you try to recall a list of similar items, you'll tend to remember the first and last items best.

Serial Position Effect *The phenomenon of remembering the material at the beginning and the end of a list better than the material in the middle*

Distributed Practice *A learning technique in which practice sessions are interspersed with rest periods*

Massed Practice *A learning technique in which time spent learning is massed into long, unbroken intervals (also known as cramming)*

Massed versus distributed practice. Cramming for an examination is an attempt to learn too much at one time and is therefore less effective than spacing out study time into several sessions.

GENDER & CULTURAL DIVERSITY

Cultural Differences in Memory and Forgetting

How do you remember the dates for all your quizzes, exams, and assignments in college? What memory aids do you use if you need to buy 15 items at the supermarket? Most people from industrialized societies rely on written shopping lists, calendars, books, notepads, or computers to store information and prevent forgetting. Can you imagine living in a culture without these aids? What would it be like if you had to rely solely on your memory to store and retrieve all your past, current, and future information? Would you develop better memory skills if you didn't have the ability to write things down? Do people raised in preliterate societies with rich oral traditions develop better memory skills than do people raised in literate societies?

Ross and Millson (1970) designed a cross-cultural study to answer these questions. They compared American and Ghanaian college students' abilities to remember stories that were read aloud. Students listened to the stories without taking notes and without being told they would be tested. Two weeks later, all students were asked to write down as much as they could remember. As you might expect, the Ghanaian students had better recall than the Americans. Their superior performance was attributed to their culture's long oral tradition, which requires developing greater skill in encoding oral information (Matsumoto, 2000).

Does this mean that cultures with an oral tradition have better memories? As you may remember, a core requirement for scientific research is *replication* and the generation of related hypotheses and studies. In this case, when other researchers tested nonliterate African participants with lists of words instead of stories, they did *not* perform better (Cole, Gray, Glick, & Sharp, 1971). However, when both educated Africans and uneducated Africans were compared for mem-

Culture and memory. *In many societies, tribal leaders pass down vital information through stories related orally. Because of this rich oral tradition, children living in these cultures have better memories for information related through stories than do other children*

ory of lists of words, the educated Africans performed very well (Scribner, 1979). This suggests that formal schooling helps develop memory strategies for things like lists of words, which preliterate participants may see as unrelated and meaningless.

Wagner (1982) conducted a study with Moroccan and Mexican urban and rural children that helps explain the effect of formal schooling. Participants were presented with seven cards placed facedown in front of them, one at a time. They were then shown a card and asked to point out which of the seven cards was its duplicate. Everyone, regardless of culture or amount of schooling, was able to recall the latest cards presented (the *recency effect*). However, the amount of schooling significantly affected overall recall and the ability to recall the earliest cards presented (*primacy effect*).

Wagner suggests that the primacy effect depends on *rehearsal* — the silent repetition of things you're trying to remember — and that this strategy is strongly related to schooling. As a child in a typical classroom, you were expected to memorize letters, numbers, multiplication tables, and a host of other basic facts. This type of formal schooling provides years of practice in memorization and in applying these skills in test situations. According to Wagner, memory has two parts: a "hardware" section that does not change across cultures and a "software" part that develops particular strategies for remembering, which are learned.

In summary, research indicates that the "software" (or programming) part of memory is affected by culture. In cultures in which communication relies on oral tradition, people develop good strategies for remembering orally presented stories. In cultures in which formal schooling is the rule, people learn memory strategies that help them remember lists of items. From these studies, we can conclude that across cultures, people tend to remember information that matters to them, and they develop memory skills to match the demands of their environment.

Theories of Forgetting

Five major theories have been offered to explain why forgetting occurs: *decay, interference, motivated forgetting, encoding failure,* and *retrieval failure.* Each theory focuses on a different stage of the memory process or on a particular type of problem in processing information. (Study tip: If you want to remember the five theories, think of how forgetting involves memories that grow "dimmer," and note that the first letters of each theory has almost the same spelling — *D-I-M-E-R*.)

1) Decay Theory

Decay theory is based on the commonsense assumption that memory, like all biological processes, deteriorates as time passes. If memory is processed and stored in a physical form — for example, in a network of neurons — the fidelity of the representation could be expected to decrease over time. It is well documented that skills and memory are degraded if they are not used for a long period of time (Arthur, Bennett, Stanush, & McNelly, 1998). However, experimental support for decay theory is difficult to obtain. As we discovered in Module 12 when we discussed extrasensory perception, how do you prove something does *not* exist?

2) Interference Theory

Perhaps the most widely accepted theory, known as *interference theory,* suggests forgetting is caused by one memory competing with or trying to replace another memory (Anderson, Bjork, & Bjork, 1994; Conway & Pleydell-Pearce, 2000; Parkes & White 2000). Interference is particularly strong among memories for similar events or having similar retrieval cues.

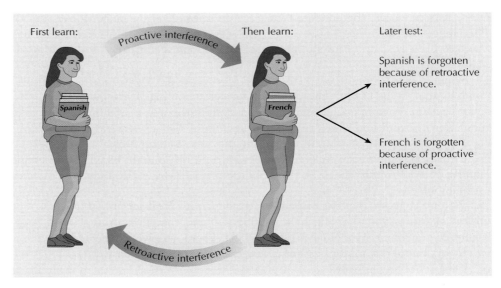

First learn:

Proactive interference

Then learn:

Later test:

Spanish is forgotten because of retroactive interference.

French is forgotten because of proactive interference.

Retroactive interference

Figure 20.3 *Types of interference.* (a) Retroactive (backward) interference occurs when new information causes forgetting of old material (*new interferes with the old*), and (b) proactive (forward-acting) interference occurs when old information causes forgetting of new material (*old interferes with the new*).

Proactive Interference *Forgetting in which old information interferes with remembering new information; forward-acting memory interference*

Retroactive Interference *Forgetting in which new information interferes with remembering old information; backward-acting interference*

There are two types of interference, *retroactive* and *proactive* (Figure 20.3). When new information leads to forgetting of previous material, it is called **retroactive interference** (acting backward in time). Learning your new phone number causes forgetting of your old phone number. Conversely, when old information leads to forgetting of new information, it is called **proactive interference** (acting forward in time). Old information (like the Spanish you learned in high school) may interfere with your ability to learn and remember your new college course in French.

3) Motivated Forgetting Theory

A third theory of forgetting focuses on our sometimes unconscious wish to forget something unpleasant. According to the *motivated forgetting theory*, we forget for a reason, which leads to inhibition of retrieval. Forgetting the name of an instructor who gave you a low grade, your dental appointment, or that embarrassing speech you made in eighth grade are all examples of motivated forgetting.

People obviously try to inhibit unpleasant or anxiety-producing thoughts or feelings. According to Freudian theory (Module 35), when they do this consciously, telling themselves not to worry about an upcoming final exam, it is called *suppression*. When they do it unconsciously, it is called *repression*. Sigmund Freud claimed that people repressed painful memories to avoid anxiety. If this is the case, appropriate therapy might overcome the repressive mechanisms and cause the repressed memory to be recovered. Memories of child abuse, sexual assault, war atrocities, and so on may create such painful experiences that the individual is highly motivated to forget them. The controversy surrounding repressed memories is discussed later in this module.

4) Encoding Failure

Whose head is on a U.S. penny? What is written at the top of a penny? Despite having seen a real penny thousands of times in your life, most of us have diffi-

Figure 20.4 *Encoding failure.* Can you identify a drawing of a real penny among fakes?

culty recognizing the details (Figure 20.4). Although the U.S. penny has eight distinguishing characteristics (Lincoln's head, the date it was minted, which way Lincoln is facing, and so on), the average person can only remember three (Nickerson & Adams, 1979). This is a great example of *encoding failure.* Unless we are coin collectors, we have likely never encoded the details of a penny. Our sensory memory certainly received the information and passed it along (encoded it) to STM. But during STM, we probably decided there was no need to remember the precise details of the penny, so we did not encode it and pass it on for storage in LTM.

5) Retrieval Failure Theory

Anyone who has ever "blanked out" during an exam or a conversation only to remember the "forgotten" information later has had a firsthand experience with the *retrieval failure* (or *cue-dependent*) *theory of forgetting.* According to this theory, memories stored in LTM are never really forgotten; they are just momentarily inaccessible as a result of such things as interference, faulty cues, or emotional states.

As you might imagine, it is difficult to distinguish retrieval failure from encoding failure. In fact, most memory failures are probably due to poor encoding, rather than retrieval failure (Howe & O'Sullivan, 1997). An experiment designed to find out why parents are so poor at reporting when and if their children received vaccinations illustrates this point. In this experiment, parents were asked immediately after their child's medical visit if the child had a vaccination during that visit (Lee et al., 1999). The same parents were asked the same question 10 weeks later. The researchers found that the parents were equally bad on both surveys. It appears that the reason for the forgetting is poor encoding, not retrieval failure. Retrieval failure would have caused the 10-week memories to be much worse than the immediate memories.

One of the most common experiences of retrieval *failure* is the **tip-of-the-tongue (TOT) phenomenon** — the feeling that at any second, a word or event you are trying to remember will pop out from the "tip of your tongue" (Brown & McNeill, 1966; Read & Bruce, 1982). Even though you can't say the word, you can often tell how many syllables it has, the beginning and ending letters, or what it rhymes with.

Tip-of-the-Tongue Phenomenon
A retrieval failure that involves a sensation of knowing that specific information is stored in long-term memory but of being temporarily unable to retrieve it

Check & Review

WHY DO WE FORGET?

Hermann Ebbinghaus was one of the first researchers to extensively study forgetting. His famous "curve of forgetting" shows that it occurs most rapidly immediately after learning. However, Ebbinghaus also showed that **relearning** usually takes less time than original learning. Two important factors in forgetting are the **serial position effect** (in which material at the beginning and end of the list is remembered better than material in the middle) and spacing of practice (in which **distributed practice** is found to be superior to **massed practice**).

The decay theory of forgetting simply states that memory, like all biological processes, deteriorates as time passes. The interference theory of forgetting suggests memories are forgotten because of either proactive or retroactive interference.

Proactive interference occurs when old information interferes with newly learned information. **Retroactive interference** occurs when new information interferes with previously learned information. The motivated forgetting theory states that people forget things that are painful, threatening, or embarrassing. Some material is forgotten because it was never encoded from short-term memory to long-term memory (LTM). Other forgetting occurs because of retrieval failure; information stored in LTM is not forgotten but may at times be inaccessible.

Questions

1. When taking an exam, students often do better with items taken from the first and last of the chapters covered by the exam. This demonstrates the (a) superiority of distributed practice; (b) Zeigarnik effect; (c) state-dependent effect; (d) serial position effect.

2. How would you study for a test using distributed practice? Using massed practice?

3. Which theory of forgetting is being described in each of the following examples?
   a. You are very nervous about having to introduce all the people at a party, and you forget a good friend's name.
   b. You meet a friend you haven't seen for 25 years and you cannot remember his name.
   c. You were molested as a child and have completely forgotten the incident.

Answers to Questions can be found in Appendix B.

Problems with Memory: Multiple Factors

What are the key memory problems?

What happens when people abruptly lose all memory of their past in cases of amnesia, or slowly lose it with Alzheimer's? Imagine a total loss of memory. With no memories of the past and no way to make new memories, there would be no way to use our previous skills or to learn new ones. We wouldn't know each other, nor would we know ourselves. In fact, our very survival would be in question. In this section, we will discuss the serious personal and social issues associated with memory problems. We begin with organically caused problems (including injury, disease, and amnesia). We then discuss problems with the constructive nature of memory — how we sometimes alter, distort, and create our personal memories.

Organic Causes

Some memory problems are the result of injury and disease (organic pathology). When people are in serious accidents or suffer strokes or other events that cause trauma to the brain, memory loss or deterioration can occur. Disease also can alter the physiology of the brain and nervous system and thereby affect memory processes. As we explore organic causes of memory problems, we will focus our attention on *brain injury* and *Alzheimer's disease*.

The Injured Brain

Have you ever wondered why health professionals are so insistent about participants' always wearing a helmet during most sports activities? *Traumatic brain injury* happens when the skull makes a sudden collision with another object. The compression, twisting, and distortion of the brain inside the skull often cause serious and sometimes permanent damage to the brain. The frontal and temporal lobes often take the heaviest hit because they directly impact against the bony ridges inside the skull. In the United States, traumatic brain injury is the leading cause of neurological disorders among Americans ages 15 to 25. These injuries most commonly result from car accidents, falls, blows, and gunshot wounds

What happens to our memory when we have a serious head injury or trauma? Forgetting as a result of brain injury or trauma is called *amnesia*. In **retrograde amnesia**, the patient loses memory for events that occurred *before* the accident yet has no trouble remembering things that happened afterward. Conversely, **anterograde amnesia** is a loss of memory for events that occur *after* an accident. Anterograde amnesia may result from a surgical injury or from diseases, such as chronic alcoholism. H. M. (the man introduced at the start of this section) suffers from both forms of amnesia. He has trouble remembering events that happened the last several years before the operation (*retrograde amnesia*). Also, for years after the operation, he thought the year was 1953 and that he was only 27 (*anterograde amnesia*). In most cases, retrograde amnesia is temporary and most patients recover slowly over time. Unfortunately, anterograde amnesia is usually permanent — as is the case with H. M.

Alzheimer's Disease

Alzheimer's disease (AD) is a progressive mental deterioration that occurs most commonly in old age. The most noticeable early symptoms are disturbances in memory, beginning with typical incidents of forgetfulness that everyone experiences from time to time. With AD, the forgetfulness progresses until, in the final stages, the person fails to recognize loved ones, needs total nursing care, and ultimately, dies. Not all types of memory are affected equally. One of the major differences between normal memory loss and memory loss due to AD is the latter's extreme decrease in episodic declarative memory (Collette, Van der Linden, & Salmon, 1999; Salmon, Butters, & Chan, 1999).

Autopsies of the brain of people with AD show unusual *tangles* (structures formed from degenerating cell bodies) and *plaques* (structures formed from degenerating axons and dendrites). Hereditary AD runs in families and generally strikes its victims between the ages of 45 and 55. Some experts believe the cause of AD is primarily genetic, but others think genetic makeup may make some people more susceptible to environmental triggers (Cowley, 2000; Mattila et al., 1998; Vickers et al., 2000).

Retrograde Amnesia *Difficulty in remembering previously learned material*

Anterograde Amnesia *The inability to form new memories*

Alzheimer's [ALLS-high-merz] Disease *A progressive mental deterioration that occurs most commonly in old age and is characterized by severe memory loss*

(a)   (b)

The effect of Alzheimer's disease on the brain. *Note the high amount of red and yellow color (signs of brain activity) in the positron emission tomography scans of the normal brain on the left, and the reduced activity in the brain of the Alzheimer's disease patient on the right. The loss is most significant in the temporal and parietal lobes, which indicates that these areas are particularly important for storing memories.*

Constructive Processes

Now that we've discussed organic causes of memory problems, you may want to try this short memory test before we continue discussing additional sources of errors in memory:

> Below is a series of words. Take a moment to carefully read through the entire list, then cover it and write down all the words you can recall in 2 minutes. Now, compare your recalled words with the original list.

Bed	Awake	Tired	Dream	Wake	Snooze	Snore
Rest	Blanket	Doze	Slumber	Nap	Peace	Yawn
Drowsy	Nurse	Sick	Lawyer	Medicine	Health	Hospital
Dentist	Physician	Patient	Stethoscope	Curse	Clinic	Surgeon

Number of correctly recalled words:
21 to 28 words = excellent memory
16 to 20 words = better than most
12 to 15 words = average
8 to 11 words = below average
7 or fewer = you might need a nap

How did you do? Do you have a good or excellent memory? Did you recall seeing the words *sleep* and *doctor*? If so, you have constructed a false memory. Look back over the list. These words were not there, yet over 65 percent of students will believe they saw these words. Why? The answers are found throughout this module. As we form new memories and sort through the old, we fill in missing pieces, we make "corrections," and rearrange information to make it logically consistent. Thus, the memory that we eventually retrieve is affected not just by the actual direct experiences we have had with the stimulus but also by our guesses and inferences about its meaning as well. You falsely remembered *sleep* and *doctor* because they were logically consistent. As we mentioned at the opening, memory is *not* a faithful duplicate of an event; it is a **constructive process** where we actively shape and build on information as it is encoded and retrieved.

When we encode information, we *construct* a mental representation (not an exact recording). Think about a recent, important lecture from your psychology instructor that you (hopefully) encoded for storage in LTM. You obviously did not record a word-for-word copy of the lecture. You summarized, augmented, and tied it in with related memories you have in LTM. Similarly, when we retrieve information, we *reconstruct* the previously *constructed* memories, thus introducing another set of potential errors. If you need to retrieve the stored lecture from your LTM, you repeat the general ideas or facts that were said, while leaving out seemingly unimportant elements or misremembering the details.

Constructive Process *The active organizing and shaping of information as we encode and retrieve it, which can result in errors and distortions*

Why isn't the original version stored in long-term memory? In addition to general constructive processes that occur during encoding and retrieval, there are three more specific types of construction errors: *source amnesia,* the *sleeper effect,* and the *misinformation effect*:

1. *Source amnesia.* We sometimes imagine or dream about something and later aren't sure whether it really happened. You might mistakenly recall that you heard the lecture information from a friend during shared study times or read it in the text, rather than from your psychology professor. This is known as **source amnesia,** which occurs when the true source of the memory is forgotten (Leichtman & Ceci, 1995).

2. *Sleeper effect.* Because of source amnesia, we also tend to confuse reliable information with the unreliable. This is particularly true with the passage of time.

Source Amnesia *Attributing to a wrong source an event that we have experienced, heard about, read about, or imagined (also called source confusion or source misattribution)*

Research on the **sleeper effect** finds that when we first hear something from an unreliable source we tend to disregard that information in favor of a more reliable source. However, over time, the source of the information is forgotten and the unreliable information is no longer discounted (Underwood & Pezdek, 1998). This sleeper effect can be a significant problem when reliable and unreliable information are intermixed. As a critical thinker, can you see why advertisers of shoddy services or products might benefit from "channel surfing?" What happens to the LTM of the television viewer who skips from news programs to cable talk shows to infomercials? Can you see how a movie star who offers an opinion about a weight-loss diet might later be remembered as a dietary expert?

3. *Misinformation effect*. Have you ever heard a story about your sibling or a friend and then later confused it as your own? As we discovered in the earlier discussion of flashbulb memories, people often misremember details about their own experiences and those of others. This type of incorporating other, outside information into your own memory is known as the **misinformation effect.**

As a critical thinker, see if you can identify *source amnesia* and the *misinformation effect* in this childhood memory experienced by the famous cognitive and developmental psychologist Jean Piaget (1951):

> One of my first memories would date, if it were true, from my second year. I can still see, most clearly, the following scene, in which I believed until I was about fifteen. I was sitting in my pram, which my nurse was pushing in the Champs-Élysées, when a man tried to kidnap me. I was held in by the strap fastened round me while my nurse bravely tried to stand between the thief and me. She received various scratches, and I can still see vaguely those on her face. Then a crowd gathered, a policeman with a short cloak and a white baton came up, and the man took to his heels. I can still see the whole scene, and can even place it near the tube station. When I was about fifteen, my parents received a letter from my former nurse saying that she had been converted to the Salvation Army. She wanted to confess her past faults, and in particular to return the watch she had been given as a reward on this occasion. She had made up the whole story, faking the scratches. I, therefore, must have heard, as a child, the account of this story, which my parents believed, and projected it into the past in the form of a visual memory, which was a memory of a memory, but false. [pp. 187–188].

How did you do? Did you identify *source amnesia* when Piaget falsely attributed his memory to his own experience rather than to his nursemaid's made-up story? Did you note how he incorporated her faked scratches into his own memory of actually seeing the scratches at the time of the "attempted kidnapping?" This would be part of the *misinformation effect*. Because Piaget's parents probably trusted the nursemaid and considered her information reliable, the *sleeper effect* was not a factor in this false memory.

Eyewitness Testimony and Repressed Memories

Misremembering the source for a new weight-loss product and Piaget's memory of being saved by a kind nursemaid may be relatively harmless memory problems. But what if the police had mistakenly arrested and convicted an innocent man because of Piaget's nursemaid's false claim? In this section, we will discuss two areas of memory problems that have profound legal and social implications: *eyewitness testimony* and *repressed memories*.

Eyewitness Testimony

You know the old saying "Seeing is believing." But can we really trust what we see — or *think* we see? In the past, one of the best forms of trial evidence a lawyer could have was an eyewitness, yet numerous research studies have identified several prob-

Sleeper Effect *The tendency to initially discount information from an unreliable source but later consider it more trustworthy because the source is forgotten*

Misinformation Effect *A memory error that results from incorporating outside information into one's own memory of an event (also known as suggestibility)* lems with eyewitness testimony (Bidrose & Goodman, 2000; Johnson & Seifert, 1994; Loftus, 2000; Wells et al., 2000).

In one eyewitness study, participants were shown a film of a car driving through the countryside. Members of one group were asked to estimate how fast the car was going when it passed the barn. Participants in the other group who saw the same film were also asked to estimate the car's speed, but a barn was not mentioned. When all participants were later asked if they saw a barn in the film, six times as many in the group given the misinformation about the barn reported having seen it, even though it never appeared in the film (Loftus, 1982).

It is impossible to determine how often eyewitnesses are mistaken in their recollections of events, but experimental evidence indicates that the error rate might be disturbingly high. For example, in an experiment at the University of Nebraska, participants watched people committing a staged crime. About an hour later, they were asked to pick out suspects from mug shots, and a week later, from a lineup. None of the participants in the staged crime appeared in the mug shots or lineups, yet 20 percent of the eyewitnesses identified innocent people in the mug shots, and 8 percent identified innocent people in the lineup (Brown, Deffenbacher, & Sturgill, 1977).

How could the research participants have been so mistaken? Several properties of memory could combine to create the type of mistaken identity that occurred at the lineup stage. First, we know that seeing a mug shot would lead to familiarity, which might lead to false recognition during the later lineup. Next, we know that memory is constructive, so the participants might have constructed an inaccurate memory of the crime situation using memories instilled by the mug shots.

These problems are so well established and important that judges now allow expert testimony on the unreliability of eyewitness testimony and routinely instruct jurors on its limits (Durham & Dane, 1999; Ramirez, Zemba, & Geiselman, 1996). If you serve as a member of a jury or listen to accounts of crimes in the news, remind yourself of these problems. Also keep in mind that research participants in eyewitness studies generally report their inaccurate memories with great self-assurance and strong conviction (Migueles & Garcia-Bajos, 1999). Eyewitnesses to actual crimes may similarly identify — with equally high confidence — an innocent person.

Repressed Memories

Do you recall the opening story of Elizabeth, who suddenly remembered a childhood scene of finding her mother's drowned body? This is a true story of Elizabeth Loftus, one of the leading experts in repressed memory research. The recovery of the memory, although painful, also brought great relief. "I started putting everything into place. Maybe that's why I'm such a workaholic." It also seemed to explain why she had always been fascinated by the topic of memory and had spent so many years on its research.

After all this resolution and relief, however, her brother called to say there had been a mistake! The relative who told Elizabeth that she had been the one to discover her mother's body later remembered it had actually been Aunt Pearl, not Elizabeth Loftus. Other relatives also confirmed that it was Aunt Pearl. Even though Loftus is an expert on memory distortions and false memories, she was not immune to the problems of memory construction.

As we've seen throughout this module, our memories are frequently faulty, and researchers have demonstrated that it is relatively easy to create false memories (Blagrove & Akehurst, 2000; Human & Kleinknecht, 1999; Loftus, 1993, 1997, 2000). Seeing the words *sleep* and *doctor* in the previous list, Piaget's kidnapping memory, the eyewitness participants who later recalled a nonexistent barn, and Loftus's memory of finding her mother's body are all examples of false memories.

So what about repressed memories? Can people recover true childhood memories? *Repression*, which was mentioned earlier as a part of motivated forgetting, is the supposed unconscious coping mechanism by which anxiety-provoking thoughts are prevented from reaching consciousness. Therefore, thoughts or memories that are extremely frightening to a person, such as memories of childhood sexual abuse, might be repressed. According to some therapists, these memories exist in a hidden corner of the person's brain, but they're normally inaccessible because of the pain they would causes if brought to conscious awareness (Bertram & Widener, 1999). In most cases, therapy would be necessary to unlock these hidden memories (Davies, 1996).

As you might imagine, this is a complex and controversial topic in psychology. No one doubts that some memories are forgotten and later recovered. When cued by a remark or experience, many people recover memories of long-forgotten events — a childhood trip to Disneyland, the move from one house to another, or details surrounding a painful event. What is questioned is the concept of *repressed memories* of painful experiences (*especially childhood sexual abuse*), and their storage in the unconscious mind (Loftus & Polage, 1999). Critics suggest that most people who have witnessed or experienced a violent crime, or are adult survivors of childhood sexual abuse, have intense, persistent memories. They have trouble forgetting, not remembering.

Some critics also wonder whether therapists retrieve actual memories or inadvertently create false memories. Just as a scientist's *experimenter bias* might unintentionally influence participants' responses, clinicians who sincerely believe their client may have been abused as a child may unintentionally influence their client's recall of information. If the clinician mentions possible abuse, the client's own constructive processes may lead him or her to create a false memory.

Remember how Loftus used her relative's suggestion that she found her mother's body to create her own detailed false memory? As a critical thinker, can you see how clients might respond similarly to their therapists' suggestions? Even though the clinician suggests only the possibility of abuse, the client might start to think about movies and books portraying other people's experiences and incorporate this information into his or her own memory (the *misinformation effect*), might forget where they heard these stories (*source amnesia*), and over time might forget these originally unreliable sources and see them as reliable (the *sleeper effect*).

Thus, the question "Are recovered memories true or false?" may be impossible to answer. As we've noted before, research clearly demonstrates that *all* our memories are imperfect constructions during encoding and reconstructions during retrieval. Attempting to label some memories as "true" and others as "false" may be misleading and oversimplifying.

The so-called repressed memory debate, however, has grown increasingly bitter, and research on both sides is hotly contested (Lindsay, 1998). This is not just an "academic debate." It has serious implications because civil lawsuits and criminal prosecutions are sometimes based on recovered memories of childhood sexual abuse, and family bonds are sometimes irreparably damaged by false accusations. It is dangerous to trust memory — recovered or repressed — to provide accurate recollections of the past. Researchers are currently seeking more information about the mechanisms underlying delayed remembering. (For more information about this research and the continuing controversy, call or write the American Psychological Association in Washington, D.C. Ask for the pamphlet "Questions and Answers about Memories of Childhood Abuse." Also check the *Psychology in Action* website.)

We will return to this hotly debated issue of repressed memories in Module 41. In the meantime, it is important to remember that child sexual abuse is a fact,

Exploring Your Memories

Reflective thinking is the ability to review and analyze your own mental processes — to "think about thinking." Reflective thinking is an important component of critical thinking. It allows you to objectively examine your thoughts and cognitive strategies and evaluate their appropriateness and accuracy. In the context of this module, we could employ reflective thinking to evaluate the processes used in recalling memories.

To practice reflective thinking:

1. Take out a sheet of paper and write down all you can remember about the first day of your introductory psychology course. What did you do from the minute you entered the room that day? What did the professor say or do?

Write down only the things you can remember in vivid detail, not those you "think" you remember.

2. Now compare your memories with your classmates'. Are your memories exactly the same? Are some personal and some shared? Do you remember only the ordinary first-day happenings, or do you remember any unusual occurrences? Do you remember any feelings or emotions? What do you remember that your classmates do not? Do additional memories come flooding back when triggered by others' recollections?

3. Take time to reflect on how your memories were stored and organized in your brain, on the basis of comparisons you made in the previous item. Most

people do not remember things in vivid detail. Most often, memories are more general, allowing you to fill in the details according to how you "think" the memory should have been rather than providing all the details for you. Is this true in your case?

4. Finally, try to recall an older memory, a vivid memory from your childhood. Write down as much detail as you can and then try to evaluate which part of that memory is likely to be factual and which part is reconstructed. You may find it necessary to ask your parents or old friends to verify the accuracy of these memories. But it is unlikely that even your most vivid childhood memories are a perfectly accurate representation of the past.

not a disputed issue, and we must be careful not to ridicule or condemn people who recover true memories of abuse. In the same spirit, we must protect the innocent from wrongful accusations that come from false memories. We look forward to a time when we can justly balance the rights of the victim with those of the accused.

Check & Review

PROBLEMS WITH MEMORY

Some memory problems are the result of injury and disease (organic pathology). Forgetting as a result of serious brain injuries or trauma is called *amnesia*. In **retrograde amnesia**, memory for events that occurred *before* the accident is lost. In **anterograde amnesia**, memory for events that occur *after* an accident is lost. **Alzheimer's disease** is a progressive mental deterioration and severe memory loss occurring most commonly in old age.

Memories are not exact duplicates. We actively shape and build on information as

it is encoded, stored, and retrieved. There are three major errors that occur during the constructive processes of memory: **source amnesia,** the **sleeper effect** and the **misinformation effect.** Two areas of memory problems that have profound legal and social implications are *eyewitness testimony* and *repressed memories*.

Questions

1. Forgetting that results from brain damage or trauma is called _____.

2. Ralph couldn't remember anything that happened to him between the time he

fell through the floor of his tree house and found himself in the hospital. His lack of memory for the interval between the events is called _____ amnesia. (a) retroactive; (b) proactive; (c) anterograde; (d) retrograde

3. Explain the difference between source amnesia, the sleeper effect, and the misinformation effect.

4. Why is eyewitness testimony not considered reliable in a court of law?

Answers to Questions can be found in Appendix B.

Improving Memory: Using Memory Research to Remember More

After reading about all the problems and dangers associated with memory, you'll be glad to know that our memories are normally quite accurate and serve us well in most situations. Our memories have evolved to encode, store, and retrieve information vital to our survival. While working to secure our food and shelter, we constantly search and monitor our potentially dangerous environment. Even while sleeping, we process and store important memories.

Evolutionarily speaking, our memories are adaptive and quite remarkable. However, when faced with tasks like remembering precise details in a college text, the faces and names of potential clients, or where we left our house keys, our brains are simply not well equipped. The beauty of the human brain is that we can recognize such limits and develop appropriate coping mechanisms. Just as our ancestors domesticated wild horses and cattle to overcome the physical limits of the human body, we can develop ways to improve our memory for fine detail. The field of psychology provides numerous helpful theories and concepts for improving memory, and concrete suggestions are sprinkled throughout this text. In this section, we will briefly summarize the most effective memory enhancement techniques. Then we close with a discussion of the "seven sins of forgetting," a topic with further tips for improving memory.

Specific Tips for Memory Enhancement

Everyone can improve his or her memory. The harder you work at it, the better your memory will become. Below, we have summarized key points from this module that you can put into practice to improve your memory. (You might also recognize several points that were presented earlier in Tools for Student Success in Module 4.)

- *Pay attention and reduce interference.* If you really want to remember something, you must pay attention to it. So when you're in class, focus on the instructor and sit away from people who might distract you. When you study, choose a place with a minimum of distractions. Also, try to avoid studying topics that are closely related (such as French and Spanish) on the same night or even within the same academic year.

- *Use rehearsal techniques.* Remember that the duration of STM is about 30 seconds, so to lengthen this time use *maintenance rehearsal*. To effectively encode memory into LTM, use *elaborative rehearsal*, which involves thinking about the material and relating it to other information that has already been stored. Hopefully, you've noticed that we formally define each key term immediately in the text, in the margin, and in the glossary at the back of the book. We also give a brief explanation and one or two examples for each of these terms. When you're studying this text, use these tools to help your elaborative rehearsal, while also making up your own examples. The more elaborate the encoding of information, the more memorable it will be.

- *Improve your organization.* This may be most important key to a good memory. Because the capacity of STM is around seven items, you can expand the capacity of STM by *chunking* (organizing) information into seven or fewer groups. To improve your LTM, create *hierarchies* that organize the material in meaningful patterns. The tables in this book and the visual summaries at the end of each section are examples of hierarchies that help you organize material. Be sure to study them carefully — and make up your own whenever possible.

- *Counteract the serial position effect.* Because we tend to remember information that occurs at the beginning or end of a sequence, spend extra time with the information in the middle. When reading or reviewing the text, start at different places — sometimes at the second section, sometimes at the fourth.

- *Manage your time.* Study on a regular basis and avoid cramming. *Distributed* (spaced) learning sessions are more efficient than *massed practice* (cramming). In other words, five separate half-hour sessions tend to produce better consolidation and retention than one session of $2^1/_2$ hours. When you learn something new, take the time to associate it with what you already know. By doing this, you'll be cataloguing the new information so that you can retrieve it easily. Also, get plenty of sleep, for two reasons: (1) we don't remember information acquired when we're drowsy as well as we do when we're alert and (2) during REM sleep we process and store most of the new information we acquired when awake.

- *Use the encoding specificity principle.* When we form memories, we store them with links to the way we thought about it at the time. Therefore, the closer the retrieval cues are to the original encoding situation the better the retrieval. Because you encode a lot of material during class time, avoid "early takes" or makeup exams generally scheduled in other classrooms. The *context* will be different and your retrieval may suffer. Similarly, when you take a test, try to remain calm and reinstate the psychological and physiological state that you were in when you originally learned the material. According to the *mood congruence* effect, you will recall more if the mood of your test taking matches the mood of the original learning. Also, according to the *state-dependent memory* research, if you normally drink a cup of coffee while studying, you might want to have a cup of coffee before your exam. (Remember: Caffeine is the only drug that could be recommended as a possible study aid.)

- *Employ self-monitoring and overlearning.* Whenever you are studying a text, you should periodically test your understanding of the material. This is why we build in the Check & Review sections throughout this text. Stopping to read these reviews and completing the short quiz section will provide personal feedback on your mastery of the material. Even when you are studying a single sentence, you need to monitor your understanding. Poor readers tend to read at the same speed for both easy and difficult material. Good readers tend to recognize when they are having difficulty and they slow down or repeat difficult sentences.

  When you finish reading a module or prepare to end a study session, do an additional monitoring of your understanding. If you evaluate your learning only immediately after reading the material, you will overestimate your understanding (because the information is still in STM). If you delay making your judgment (for at least a few minutes), your evaluation will be more accurate (Weaver & Kelemen, 1997). The best way to ensure your full understanding of material (and success on an exam) is through *overlearning* — studying information even after you think you already know it. Don't just study until you *think* you know it; work hard until you *know* you know it!

Mnemonic [nih-MON-ik] Device
A memory-improvement technique based on encoding items in a special way

- *Use mnemonic devices.* We saved this technique for last. **Mnemonic devices** (derived from the Greek word for "memory") are memory aids (or tricks) based on encoding items in a special way. As we mentioned at the beginning of this section, some memory experts use these mnemonics to perform amazing feats of recall. However, our experience as educators has been that simple mnemonics can be helpful with shopping lists and some academic tasks, but spending too much time on mnemonics may be more trouble than it's worth. Our students do better with the well-researched principles discussed in this module and reviewed above.

  If you would like to try some of the most popular mnemonic techniques, they are listed below:

  - The *method of loci* was developed by early Greek and Roman orators to keep track of the parts of their long speeches. *Loci* is the Latin word for "physical places." Orators would imagine the parts of their speeches attached to places inside a building or, if they were outside, in a courtyard. For example, if an opening point in a speech was the concept of *justice*, they might visualize a courtroom placed in the first corner of their garden to remind them of this point. As they mentally walked around their garden during their speech, they would encounter each of the points to be made in their appropriate order.

- To use the *peg-word* mnemonic, you first need to memorize a set of 10 visual images that you can use as pegs or markers on which to hang ideas. The easiest system of peg-words is to learn 10 items that rhyme with the numbers they stand for (e.g., *one in a bun, two in a shoe, three in a tree*, and so on). When you can mentally produce the peg-word image for each number, you are ready to use the images as pegs to hold the items of any list. Try it with items you might want to buy on your next trip to the grocery store: milk, eggs, bread, and razor blades. Visualize the first item (milk) with a bun, the second (eggs) with a shoe, and so on. Imagine a soggy bun in a bowl of milk. Imagine a giant shoe stepping on a carton of eggs, slices of bread hanging on a tree, and a giant razor blade as a door, complete with doorknob.

- The *substitute word* method is useful for when you are learning many new and complicated terms. For example, to remember some of the terms associated with the brain, break the word to be remembered into parts or use words that sound similar that can be visualized. The word *occipital* can be converted into *ox, sip it, tall*. Then create a vivid image. (You might visualize an ox on stilts sipping something through a straw.) Try a similar strategy with *parietal* (*pear, eye, it all*).

- The *method of word associations* is a mnemonic device that creates verbal associations for items to be learned. If you're taking a physics course and must remember the colors of the spectrum, think of a man's name: *Roy G. Biv* (Red, Orange, Yellow, Green, Blue, Indigo, Violet). Or, to recall the names of the Great Lakes for a geography course, think of *HOMES on a great lake* (Huron, Ontario, Michigan, Erie, Superior).

Seven Sins

Daniel Schacter (1999) from Harvard University wrote an interesting article entitled "The Seven Sins of Memory: Insights from Psychology and Cognitive Neuroscience." The first three sins are types of *forgetting*, the second three involve memory *distortions*, and the last sin is *persistence*. A brief discussion of these seven sins helps summarize this module and Module 19 (a form of *elaborative rehearsal*), as well as providing additional tips for memory improvement.

Three Sins of Forgetting

People forget because of three sins: *transience*, *absentmindedness*, and *blocking*. *Transience* means that not all memories are permanent. Even memories that are well encoded at the beginning may eventually be lost. Memory is especially likely to be lost if it is not used over time — "use it or lose it." Using information stored in your LTM creates interconnections and associations with other memories, builds better retrieval cues, and helps prevent storage decay.

Memories are also forgotten because we did not pay attention or take the time to encode the memory well in the first place. *Absentmindedness* at the time of encoding is a significant source of memory loss. You sit in your psychology class, but your mind wanders to other topics during the lecture. If you want to remember the lecture, you have to keep your mind and your attention focused on the lecture. Sit in the front of the room, ask questions, participate in the discussions, and look directly at the instructor. If you do not encode the memory, you cannot retrieve it at a later date.

Blocking occurs when something has been well encoded and retained in memory but cannot be retrieved. Although blocking normally has negative connotations, there are times when it is very helpful. Being unable to retrieve undesirable memories of abuse or the details surrounding the death of a loved one might allow people to better cope with tragedies and unpleasant life events. Elizabeth Loftus's inability to remember the details of her mother's death may be an example of blocking.

Three Sins of Distortion

Our memories are also faulty because of the three sins of distortion — *misattribution*, *suggestibility*, and *bias*. When we incorrectly identify the time, place, or person responsible for a memory, we've committed the sin of *misattribution*. This can happen in several ways:

- We can correctly remember an item or event from our past and misattribute it to an incorrect source.
- We may believe what we're writing or saying is our own creative idea, when in fact we've unintentionally "borrowed" material from others.
- We can recall a real event but believe that it is a fantasy.
- We can recall a fantasy event as real.

(Study tip: Recall that *misattribution* is another term for *source amnesia*, which we discussed earlier as a problem with LTM. To help your *elaborative rehearsal* and retention of this material, think about how it helps explain faulty eyewitness testimony, former President Reagan's confusion over his acting roles and actual historical events, some forms of plagiarism, as well as some cases of false memories.)

Suggestibility is the sin of incorporating information suggested by someone else into our own memory. This can easily happen because of misleading questions, comments, or direct suggestions — particularly at the time of retrieval. A witness can falsely remember a suspect's face after being questioned in a leading manner, and a therapist's comment about "possible signs of sexual assault" may later become a client's false memory. Therefore, it is important for parents, police, and therapists not to attempt to clarify memories with leading questions, comments, or suggestions during recall. (Study tip: Note that *suggestibility* is just another term for the *misinformation effect* discussed earlier as a problem with LTM.)

Memory *bias* occurs when current knowledge and beliefs distort our memory of the past. Most people believe that their beliefs and attitudes have not changed much over time, yet during a divorce, couples tend to only remember the bad things about their marriage. In contrast, couples celebrating their fiftieth wedding anniversary seem to remember "always being in love."

Final Sin of Persistence

And finally, sometimes our memories are better than we would like. Traumatic and extremely emotional events can cause memories to persist even when we would like to forget. This sin of *persistence* is especially noticeable in patients with post-traumatic stress disorder (PTSD). PTSD occurs when a person is exposed to an extremely emotional event or a life-threatening event that evokes extreme horror or helplessness. This results in nightmares, flashbacks, and an inability to forget the event. The extreme emotional memory that accompanies PTSD may lead to impaired social and mental functioning. (Study tip: Can you see that *persistence* is just another form of *mood congruence* discussed earlier as part of the *encoding specificity principle*? Persistence may reflect the fact that we tend to remember more negative memories when we're depressed than when we're happy.)

Memory problems. *According to the "sin of persistence," some memories persevere even when they cause tremendous pain and suffering.*

Some of these "seven sins of memory," such as persistence, may be evolutionary adaptations that have helped humans survive. Whatever the reason for these "sins," knowing about them can help us. As we have seen throughout this module, our memories are remarkable — yet highly fickle. Recognizing these limits will make us better jurors in the courtroom or consumers of daily news reports when we assess accounts of "eyewitness testimony" and "repressed memories." Knowing the frailties of memory might similarly improve our skills as students, teachers, friends, and, perhaps most importantly, as critical thinkers.

An intellectual is someone whose mind watches itself.

Albert Camus

Check & Review

IMPROVING MEMORY

This module offers concrete strategies for improving memory. These include paying attention and reducing interference, using rehearsal techniques (both maintenance and elaborative rehearsal), improving your organization (by chunking and creating hierarchies), counteracting the serial position effect, managing your time, using the encoding specificity principle, employing self-monitoring and overlearning, and using **mnemonic devices**.

According to Daniel Schacter, there are seven sins that affect memory and forgetting. The first three sins are types of *forgetting*, the second three involve memory *distortions*, and the last sin is *persistence*.

Questions

1. How can maintenance rehearsal and elaborative rehearsal improve your memory?

2. Explain how you can overcome the serial position effect while studying.

3. The best way to ensure your full understanding of material (and success on an exam) is through _____.

4. Which mnemonic device is being described in each of the following situations?
   a. You remember items to bring to a meeting by visualizing them in association with a previously learned sequence.
   b. You remember a speech for your communications class by forming visual images of the parts of your speech and associating them with areas in the classroom.
   c. You remember errands you need to run by making up the rhyme "First go to the store, then get books galore. Get my ring and then some gas, and the cleaners at the last."
   d. You remember a new acquaintance's name, Paul Barrington, by linking it to words that can be visualized: *pall-bearing town.*

Answers to Questions can be found in Appendix B.

MODULE 20 ACTIVE LEARNING WORKSHEET

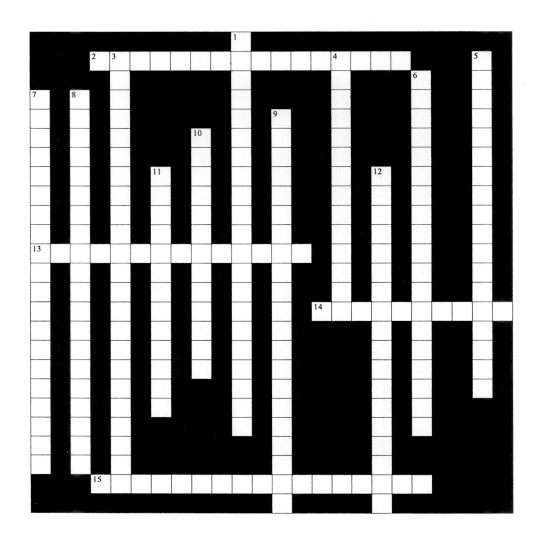

ACROSS

2. Long-term memories for the performance of skills or actions.

13. Learning occurring during long, unbroken intervals.

14. Learning material a second time.

15. Difficulty in remembering previously learned material.

DOWN

1. Forgetting because old information interferes with new information.

3. Forgetting because new information interferes with old information.

4. Memory improvement technique based on encoding items in a special way.

5. The inability to form new memories.

6. Learning occurring when practice sessions are interspersed with rest periods.

7. Memory error due to incorporating outside information into one's own memory of an event.

8. Remembering material at the beginning and the end of a list better than material in the middle.

9. Organizing and shaping of information during encoding and retrieval that may result in errors and distortions.

10. Attributing to a wrong source an event that has been experienced, heard about, read about, or imagined.

11. Initial tendency to discount information from an unreliable source, but later considering it trustworthier because the source is forgotten.

12. Progressive mental deterioration and memory loss occurring most commonly in old age.

Answers can be found in Appendix B.

Visual Summary for Modules 19 and 20 ----

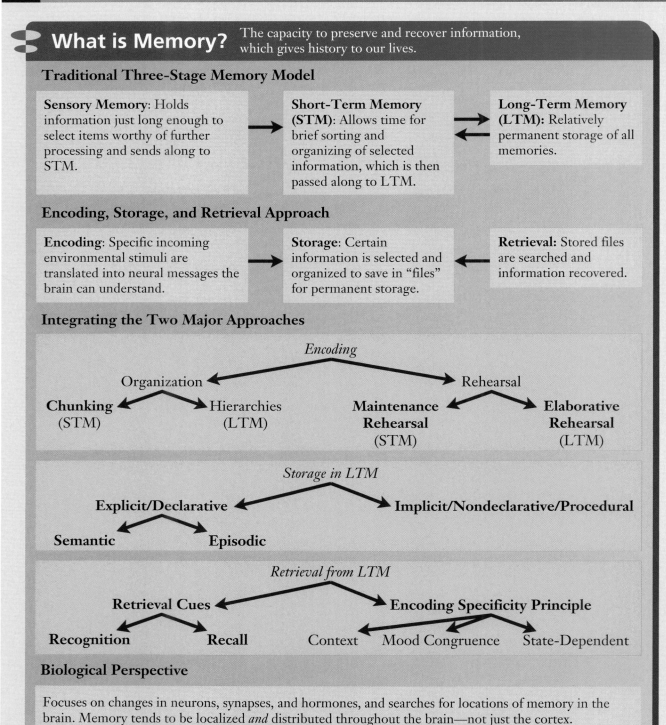

What is Memory?
The capacity to preserve and recover information, which gives history to our lives.

Traditional Three-Stage Memory Model

Sensory Memory: Holds information just long enough to select items worthy of further processing and sends along to STM.

Short-Term Memory (STM): Allows time for brief sorting and organizing of selected information, which is then passed along to LTM.

Long-Term Memory (LTM): Relatively permanent storage of all memories.

Encoding, Storage, and Retrieval Approach

Encoding: Specific incoming environmental stimuli are translated into neural messages the brain can understand.

Storage: Certain information is selected and organized to save in "files" for permanent storage.

Retrieval: Stored files are searched and information recovered.

Integrating the Two Major Approaches

Encoding

Organization → **Chunking** (STM) / **Hierarchies** (LTM)

Rehearsal → **Maintenance Rehearsal** (STM) / **Elaborative Rehearsal** (LTM)

Storage in LTM

Explicit/Declarative ← → **Implicit/Nondeclarative/Procedural**

Semantic / **Episodic**

Retrieval from LTM

Retrieval Cues ← → **Encoding Specificity Principle**

Recognition / **Recall**

Context — Mood Congruence — State-Dependent

Biological Perspective

Focuses on changes in neurons, synapses, and hormones, and searches for locations of memory in the brain. Memory tends to be localized *and* distributed throughout the brain—not just the cortex.

Why Do We Forget?

Research Findings

- Ebbinghaus: Found that forgetting occurs most rapidly immediately after learning, but **relearning** usually takes less time than original learning.
- **Serial position effect**: Material at the beginning and end of the list is remembered better than material in the middle.
- Spacing of practice: **Distributed practice** is better than **massed practice**.

Theories of Forgetting

Decay	Memory deteriorates over time.
Interference	Memories forgotten due to **proactive interference** (old information interferes with new) or **retroactive interference** (new information interferes with old).
Motivated Forgetting	Painful, threatening, or embarrassing memories are forgotten.
Encoding Failure	Material from STM to LTM was never successfully encoded.
Retrieval Failure	Information is not forgotten, just temporarily inaccessible.

Problems with Memory

Organic Causes

- *Brain injuries or trauma*: **Retrograde amnesia**, memory is lost for events that occurred before an accident , **Anterograde amnesia** memory is lost for events that occur after an accident.
- *Disease*: **Alzheimer's disease** is a progressive mental deterioration and severe memory loss occurring most commonly in old age.

Constructive Processes

Memory is a **constuctive process** that can have at least 3 major errors:
1) **Source amnesia** where we attribute memories to a wrong source.
2) **Sleeper effect** where we confuse reliable information with unreliable.
3) **Misinformation effect** where we incorporate outside information as our own.

Improving Memory

Specific Tips

- Pay attention and reduce interference.
- Use rehearsal techniques (maintenance for STM and elaborative for LTM).
- Improve organization (chunking for STM and hierarchies for LTM).
- Counteract the serial position effect.
- Time management (distributed versus massed practice).
- Use the encoding specificity principle (including context, mood congruence, and state-dependent retrieval).
- Employ self-monitoring and overlearning.
- Use **mnemonic devices** (method of loci, peg-word, substitute word , and method of word associations).

Thinking, Language, and Intelligence

Are you familiar with this very popular TV game show? Contestants must correctly answer 15 questions to win $1,000,000. After hearing each question, players can answer on their own or elect to use one of their limited number of lifeline helpers: polling the audience, asking a friend over the phone, or having the possible answers narrowed from four to two. They can also choose to quit at any time and walk away with their current winnings.

Who Wants To Be A Millionaire? *John Carpenter was the first contestant to win the million dollars. He's pictured here with the show's host, Regis Philbin.*

Were you watching the program when John Carpenter had successfully answered the $500,000 question and was one correct answer away from the million dollars? With only one lifeline remaining and the pressure mounting, the game show host, Regis Philbin, asked the $1,000,000 question: "Which of these U.S. presidents appeared on the television series Laugh-In? (a) Lyndon Johnson, (b) Richard Nixon, (c) Jimmy Carter, (d) Gerald Ford." While using his final remaining lifeline to call his father, John surprised everyone by announcing that he didn't need help from his father; he wanted to call him only so that his father would be on the line while he announced his final answer — Richard Nixon. With this answer, John Carpenter became the first contestant to win $1,000,000. Although the million-dollar question may seem easy, John also answered very difficult questions and even earned the title of "fastest finger" (honoring how quickly he answered the questions). Do you consider John Carpenter intelligent?

What about the famous case of the "wild child" known as Genie? From the age of 20 months until authorities rescued her at age 13 years, Genie had been kept locked in a tiny, windowless room in solitary confinement. By day, she was kept naked and tied to a chair with nothing to do and no one to talk to. At night, she was put in a kind of straitjacket and "caged" in a covered crib. Genie's abusive father forbade anyone to speak to her for the entire 13 years and refused to have a radio or TV in the home. If Genie made any noise, her father would beat her while he barked and growled like a dog. After she was discovered at age 13, linguists and psychologists worked with her intensively for many years, but she never progressed much beyond sentences like "Genie, go" (Curtiss, 1977; Rymer, 1993). With her limited language skills, would you say Genie is intelligent?

What about Thomas, a child who attended school for only 3 months? Despite his lack of formal education and progressive deafness throughout his life, Thomas patented over 1,000 inventions — more than any other single individual in history. His insatiable curiosity led him to study fields ranging from metallurgy to plastics, and long hours of tinkering produced momentous discoveries, including the phonograph, the kinetoscope for motion pictures, and the carbon transmitter for telephones. He has been called the "greatest inventor in American history" (Israel, 1998), yet some have said he was a "technologist rather than a scientist, adding little to original scientific knowledge" (Baldwin, 2001). Did you recognize this as the story of Thomas Edison, the famous inventor of the light bulb? Would you consider him intelligent?

Thomas Edison with his most famous invention — the light bulb.

Inventing the light bulb or winning a million dollars in a competitive game show obviously requires a large repertoire of thinking processes and intellectual agility. But doesn't Genie's survival also require some form of intelligence? To be intelligent, you must be aware and possess the capacity to learn. But awareness requires thinking, or the mental processing of information. And to express this thinking and intelligence, you need language.

The three topics of this unit — thinking, language, and intelligence — are often studied together under the larger umbrella of **cognition**, the mental activities of acquiring, storing, retrieving, and using knowledge. In a real sense, we discuss cognition throughout the text, because psychology is "the scientific study of behavior and *mental processes*." In this first module, however, we will explore cognitive processes in some depth — we will "think about our thinking."

Cognition *The mental activities involved in acquiring, storing, retrieving, and using knowledge*

THINKING

The term *thinking* has several meanings. For example, unsuccessful contestants on the *Who Wants To Be a Millionaire?* game might complain that they "needed more time to think of the right answer," that their particular question was confusing, or that they simply "couldn't think." As you can see, *thinking* involves problem solving and judgment, as well as long-term memory (LTM). Every time you use information and mentally act on it by forming ideas, reasoning, solving problems, drawing conclusions, expressing thoughts, and comprehending the thoughts of others, you are thinking. We begin this section by exploring how our brains perform the basic (but seemingly magical) act of thinking. Next, we examine the building blocks of thought, images, and concepts. Then, we discuss the mental processes and barriers to problem solving and creativity.

What is thinking and how does the brain do it?

The Thinking Brain: Making Connections

Thought processes are distributed throughout the brain in networks of neurons, much like a tightly interwoven galaxy of shooting stars. Like other psychological functions, however, thought processes are also localized. In some instances, especially during problem solving or decision making, our brains are active in a special processing area — the prefrontal cortex. It associates complex ideas, makes plans, forms and initiates attention, and allocates our attention as well. This is also the area involved in multitasking behavior, such as washing the dishes while also talking to your family or friends and simultaneously listening for the doorbell (Koechlin, Basso, Pietrini, Panzer, & Grafman, 1999).

The prefrontal cortex also links to other areas of the brain to synthesize information from several senses, as well as to the limbic system, which is the center of our emotions. As you recall from Modules 5 and 6, Phineas Gage, the railroad foreman whose brain was pierced by an iron rod, suffered damage to his prefrontal cortex. Like Gage, patients with damage to this region can solve problems, manipulate information in working memory, and generally have little trouble recalling events from the recent or distant past. However, they do have difficulty controlling their emotions and in making connections between their feelings and thoughts (Damasio, 1999). Interestingly, when other areas of the prefrontal cortex are damaged, the person may experience little or no emotion, and they also have significant problems in thinking and decision making (Bechara, Damasio, Damasio, & Lee, 1999; Damasio, 1994). In sum, whether it is because of links to emotion or the processing of complex ideas, regions of the prefrontal cortex may be the part of the brain most actively involved with thought.

Cognitive Building Blocks: The Foundation of Thought

What are the building blocks of thought?

Thinking involves three basic building blocks — *mental images*, *concepts*, and *language*. When you're thinking about your sweetheart, you may have a mental image of him or her in your mind. You might also think in terms of concepts or categories, such as *woman*, *man*, *strong*, *happy*. And you may have in mind linguistic statements such as "I wish I could be with him or her right now instead of reading this text." (Study tip: Keep in mind the *law of effect* from Module 16 — *rewarded behaviors are more likely to recur.* If you want to improve your study habits, use "time with your sweetheart" as reinforcement *after* you finish studying.) In this section, we will discuss the role of images and concepts in thinking. Language will be considered in a later section.

Mental Images

Stop for a moment and think about a warm, sandy ocean beach. Do you see tall palms swaying in the wind? Can you smell the salty ocean water and hear the laughter of the children playing in the surf? What you've just created in your mind's eye is a **mental image**, a mental representation of a sensory experience. As you noticed, mental imagery is not limited to the visual sense — you also experience auditory, olfactory, tactile, motor, and gustatory imagery (McKellar, 1972).

Where is this mental image located? According to research, we all have a fixed-size mental space (similar to the screen of a computer monitor) where we mentally visualize and manipulate our sensory images (Brewer & Pani, 1996; Kosslyn, 1987). In fact, some of our most creative moments come when we're forming mental images and manipulating them. Albert Einstein said that his first insight into relativity theory occurred when he pictured a beam of light and imagined himself chasing after it at its own speed.

Mental Images *The mind's representation of a sensory experience, including visual, auditory, gustatory, motor, olfactory, and tactile elements (e.g., visualizing a train and hearing its whistle)*

Mental imagery. *Can you imagine what this mountain climber is visualizing in his "mind's eye?" Constant use of mental imagery is critical to his success.*

TRY THIS Yourself

Look at the four geometrical patterns below. Can you see why the two forms in (a) are the same but the two forms in (b) are different? Solution to this problem requires mental manipulation of the patterns. (Those of you who are familiar with the computer game *Tetris* might find this puzzle rather simple. Others might want to turn to Appendix B for an explanation of the answer.)

(a)

(b)

Concept *A mental category that groups objects, events, activities, or ideas that share similar characteristics (e.g., the concept of river groups together the Nile, the Amazon, and the Mississippi because they share the common characteristic of being a large stream of water that empties into an ocean or lake)*

Concepts

In addition to mental images, our thinking also involves **concepts** — mental representations of a group or category. We form concepts by grouping objects, events, activities, or ideas that share similar characteristics (Smith, 1995). Our mental concept of *car* represents a large group of objects that share similar characteristics (vehicles with four wheels, seating space for at least one person, and a generally predictable shape). We also form concepts for ideas, such as *honesty, intelligence,* or *pornography.* These ideas, however, are often our own individual constructions that may or may not be shared by others. Therefore, it's generally harder to communicate about honesty than about a car.

Concepts are an essential part of thinking and communication because they simplify and organize information. Imagine being Genie, the "wild child" described at the beginning of this section. If you had been confined to a small, windowless room your entire life, how would you process the world around you without the use of concepts? Normally, when you see a new object or encounter a new situation, you relate it to your existing conceptual structure and categorize it according to where it fits. For example, if you see a rectangular box with moving pictures and sound and people are staring at it, you safely assume it is a TV set. Even though you've never encountered this specific brand before, you understand the concept of *TV set.* But if you were Genie, how would you process a TV set, a telephone, or even a bathroom? Without concepts, each object, event, and activity would be one of a kind. Can you see why she might have had difficulty adjusting to this world and learning language?

How do we learn concepts? There are at least three major methods: *artificial concepts, natural concepts,* and *hierarchies:*

1. Artificial concepts. Some of our concepts arise out of logical rules or definitions. For example, consider the concept of *triangle,* a geometric figure with three sides and three angles. Using this definition, we would group together and classify all three-sided geometric forms as triangles. If any of the defining features were missing, we would not include the object in the concept of triangle. These concepts are called *artificial* (or *formal*) because the rules for inclusion are so sharply defined. Artificial concepts are often found in the sciences and other academic disciplines. As we will see in the upcoming discussion of language, for example, psychologists (and other scientists) have created specific rules for what is labeled "language" and what is labeled "communication."

2. Natural concepts. In real life, however, we seldom use such precise, logical definitions. For example, when we see a small animal, we don't immediately turn to our *artificial concept* of *bird* — warm-blooded animals that fly, have wings, and lay eggs. Instead, we use *natural concepts,* known as **prototypes.** A prototype is essentially a "best example" or most typical example of that concept (Rosch, 1973). Most of us have a model bird, or prototype, in mind — such as a robin or a sparrow — that captures for us the essence of "birdness." When we develop a prototype in our mind, we abstract out the most important common features from the definition — most birds have wings, fly, and lay eggs — and then choose one or two prototypes (robin or sparrow) that fit these characteristics.

Prototypes provide a mental shortcut that helps us quickly and efficiently classify information. However, when confronted with a new item, like *penguin,* we cannot use our prototype robin. In this case, we need time to review our artificial concept (the definition of *bird*). Because the penguin doesn't fly, it takes longer to classify. For most of us, our prototype robin is a "birdier bird."

Prototype *A typical, highly representative example that serves as a model on which other examples are based or judged (e.g., baseball is a prototype of the concept of sports)*

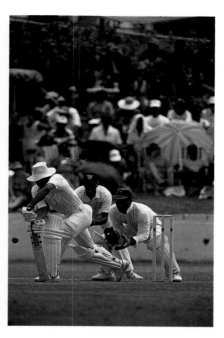

Is this your prototype for a sport? Most Americans readily recognize baseball as a prototype for sports. However, if you are from Bermuda where most people watch or play cricket, you would have a different sports prototype.

3. Hierarchies. When an object fits into more than one category (for example, a bird is also an animal), we tend to organize these concepts into successive ranks, or *hierarchies*, with specific concepts grouped as subcategories within broader concepts. Note in Figure 21.1 (a) how the top (superordinate) category of *animals* is very broad and includes lots of members, the midlevel categories of *bird* and *dog*, are more specific but still rather general, and the lowest (subordinate) categories of *parakeet* and *poodle* are the most specific.

Interestingly, research shows that we first learn and most commonly use the middle categories, which are called *basic-level* concepts (Rosch, 1978). For example, children tend to learn *bird* or *dog* before they learn superordinate concepts like *animals* or subordinate concepts like *parakeet* and *poodle*. Even when we as adults are shown a picture of a parakeet, we first classify it as a bird before thinking of the concepts of *animal* or *parakeet*.

As you learned in Module 19, organization and hierarchies are essential to efficient encoding and storage in LTM. If children did not build a mental hierarchy of *animal*, *bird*, and *parakeet*, they would have a terrible time trying to label or memorize the definition of each. You may have a similar problem if you attempted to simply memorize a long list of Key Terms from a textbook. It's much easier to master a large amount of material when it's organized into a hierarchy. This is one of the main reasons we include so many tables throughout this text and the visual summaries at the end of each section. It is even better if you develop your own hierarchies. For example, to help you master the material in this section, you could create a hierarchy similar to Figure 21.1b.

(a)

(b)

Figure 21.1 *Can hierarchies improve both thinking and exam scores?* (a) When we think, we naturally organize concepts according to superordinate and subordinate classes. We organize *concepts*, like *animals* or *birds*, with the most general concept at the top and the most specific at the bottom, and research shows we use the middle, *basic level* when initially categorizing objects and later add the upper and lower levels. Although they may look complicated, hierarchies significantly reduce the time and effort necessary for learning. For example, when you learn that all animals have mitochondria in their cells, you don't have to relearn that fact each time you learn a new animal species. (b) Hierarchies can be generated from almost any set of interrelated facts and can be used to provide a similar savings in time and effort. For example, instead of focusing on and attempting to memorize the key terms of *concepts*, *mental images*, and *prototype*, you should begin by making a hierarchy of how these terms are interrelated. Once you have this "big picture," it speeds up your mastery of the material, which translates into better exam scores.

Check & Review

THE THINKING BRAIN AND COGNITIVE BUILDING BLOCKS

Cognition, or thinking, is defined as mental activities involved in acquiring, storing, retrieving, and using knowledge. Thought processes are distributed throughout the brain in neural networks. Almost the entire cerebral cortex is activated when thinking involves forming mental representations. During problem solving and decision making, our thoughts are localized for special processing within the frontal lobes.

The prefrontal cortex links to other areas of the brain to synthesize information from several senses. It is also connected to the limbic system. Without connecting thoughts to feelings, solving problems and making decisions would be difficult.

The three basic building blocks of cognition are mental images, concepts, and lan-

guage. **Mental images** are mental representations of a sensory experience, including visual, auditory, gustatory, motor, olfactory, or tactile elements. **Concepts** are mental categories that group objects, events, activities, or ideas that share similar characteristics. (Language is discussed in a later section.)

There are three ways we learn concepts: (1) *Artificial concepts* are formed by logical, specific rules or characteristics. (2) *Natural concepts* are formed by experience in everyday life. When we are confronted with a new item, we compare it with the **prototype** (most typical) of that concept. (3) Concepts are generally organized into *hierarchies*. We most frequently use the middle, basic-level concepts, when first learning material.

Questions

1. All of the following are examples of concepts EXCEPT _____. (a) trees; (b) tools; (c) blue; (d) umbrellas

2. How do we learn concepts?

3. When asked to describe the shape and color of an apple, you probably rely on a _____.

4. For most psychologists, language is a formal _____, whereas the public generally uses fuzzy _____. (a) definition, descriptions; (b) artificial concept, natural concepts; (c) mental image, concepts; (d) superordinate concept, basic-level concepts

Answers to Questions can be found in Appendix B.

Solving Problems: Three Steps to the Goal

Several years ago in Los Angeles, a 12-foot-high tractor-trailer rig tried to pass under a bridge 11 feet 6 inches high. As you might expect, the truck got stuck, unable to move forward or back, thus causing a huge traffic jam. After hours of towing, tugging, and pushing, the police and transportation workers were stumped. About this time, a young boy happened upon the scene and asked, "Why don't you let some air out of the tires?" It was a simple, creative suggestion — and it worked.

Our everyday lives are filled with problems, some easier to solve than others. For example, figuring a way to make coffee without a filter is much easier than rescuing 118 Russian navy seamen trapped inside a submarine at the bottom of the Barents Sea. In all cases, though, problem solving requires moving from a *given state* (the problem) to a *goal state* (the solution), a process that usually involves three steps (Bourne, Dominowski, & Loftus, 1979).

Step 1: *Preparation.* Using the introductory story of the *Millionaire* contestants, there are at least three separate components to successful preparation:

- *Identifying given facts.* Contestants probably watched every program and carefully memorized the rules for the game.

- *Separating relevant from irrelevant facts.* Contestants might have tried to identify patterns in the questions. For example, if they noticed that many questions focused on historical facts and rarely on great literature, they might have reviewed history because it was relevant and didn't spend much time on facts about great literature.

- *Defining the ultimate goal.* This part of the preparation stage was easy for the contestants: They all wanted to win as much money as possible and they hoped for the full million dollars! But defining the goal isn't always this easy. The adults in the "stuck truck" problem thought the goal was to pull or push the truck from under the bridge. Only when the child defined the goal as freeing the truck did a solution present itself. Solving a problem often depends on how broadly we define the goal.

Step 2: *Production.* During the *production step*, the problem solver produces possible solutions, called *hypotheses.* There are at least two major approaches to generating hypotheses — *algorithms* and *heuristics*:

- An **algorithm** is a step-by-step procedure that, if appropriate to the problem, will always produce the solution. Math problems are ideal for demonstrating algorithms: An algorithm for solving the problem 2×10 is $2 + 2 + 2 + 2 + 2 + 2 + 2 + 2 + 2 + 2$. Algorithms will eventually lead to the correct answer, but for complex problems they may take a long time. Given the limited time allowed for finding solutions during the *Millionaire* game show, the contestants were unlikely to use algorithms. However, they are an excellent way to balance your checkbook or compute your grade point average. Computers are especially well suited for algorithms because they can quickly perform millions of calculations and logical operations in a step-by-step solution to a problem.

- A **heuristic** is a simple rule of thumb, or educated guess, resulting from watching others or developed from direct experience with similar problems. *Millionaire* contestants who decide to quit and protect their previous winnings might have watched previous contestants and developed a heuristic called "quit while you're ahead." Unlike algorithms, which generally require a lot of time, heuristics provide shortcuts to solutions because they examine only the options most likely to produce a solution. However, heuristics are error prone and do not guarantee a solution — they work most of the time, but not always.

How do we solve problems?

A failure of problem solving? On August 12, 2000, the Russian nuclear submarine "Kursk" sank as a result of a torpedo room explosion and all 118 men perished. Would faster or better problem solving have saved them?

Algorithm *A problem-solving strategy that guarantees a solution if correctly applied; it involves a step-by-step procedure, and as such, is particularly suited to use by a computer for math problems*

Heuristic *Problem-solving strategies, or rules of thumb, used as shortcuts to complex solutions, which generally, but not always, lead to a solution.*

TRY THIS
Yourself

Practice your newfound understanding of the steps in solving problems with this classic thinking problem (Bartlett, 1958). Your task is to determine the numerals 0 through 9 that are represented by letters, with each letter representing a separate, distinct number. You get one hint before you start: D = 5.

$$
\begin{array}{r}
\text{D O N A L D} \\
+\ \text{G E R A L D} \\
\hline
\text{R O B E R T}
\end{array}
$$

Did you try solving this problem with an algorithm? If so, you probably wasted a lot of time. There are 362,880 possible com-

binations of letters and numbers. At the rate of one combination per minute, 8 hours per day, 5 days a week, 52 weeks a year, it would take nearly 3 years to try all the possible combinations.

A heuristic approach is much easier and quicker. If you successfully solved the problem, you probably used the "creating subgoals" heuristic. You employed previous knowledge of arithmetic to set subgoals, such as determining what number T represents (if D = 5, then D + D = 10, so T = 0, with a carryover of 1 into the tens column). The complete answer is at the end of the next Check & Review section.

Several heuristics are particularly helpful in college, including (1) *means–end analysis*, (2) *working backward*, and (3) *creating subgoals* (Table 21.1). Successful college students seem to be particularly good at breaking down a solution into subgoals. When you're faced with a heavy schedule of exams and term papers, try creating subgoals to make the problem more manageable and increase the likelihood of reaching the overarching solution — a college degree.

Step 3: *Evaluation.* Once the hypotheses are generated, they must be evaluated to see if they meet the criteria defined in step 1. If one or more of the hypotheses meet the criteria, the problem is solved. If not, then you must return to the production stage and produce more possible solutions. Keep in mind, however, that "action must follow solution." Once the little boy solved the "stuck truck" problem, someone had to follow through and actually let some air out of the tires. Similarly, once you use the "means–end analysis" heuristic (Table 21.1) to solve your problem (getting an A in your psychology course), you must follow through and implement the necessary solution — more and improved study time.

Barriers to Problem Solving

Do you find that you can solve some problems easily yet seem to have a mental block when it comes to others? You're not alone; we all encounter barriers that prevent us from effectively solving problems. Three of the most common barriers are *mental sets*, *functional fixedness*, and *confirmation bias*:

1. Mental sets. Like the police and transportation workers who were trying to pull or shove the truck that was stuck under the bridge, have you ever persisted in attacking problems using the same or similar solutions that have worked in the past? This is known as a **mental set**. Although pulling and shoving obviously works sometimes, in this instance the old solution created a mental barrier to new, and possibly more effective, solutions (such as deflating the tires). The habit (or *mental set*) of working arithmetic problems from the right (ones) column to the left also explains why most people fail to see the solution to the DONALD + GERALD problem. Similarly, mental sets block some college students from using the SQ4R (Survey, Question, Read,

Mental Set *A mental barrier to problem solving that occurs when people apply only methods that have worked in the past rather than trying innovative ones*

TABLE 21.1 PROBLEM-SOLVING HEURISTICS

Problem-Solving Heuristics	Description	Example
Means–end analysis	The problem solver determines what measure would reduce the difference between the given state and the goal. Once the means to reach the goal are determined, the problem is solved.	You want an A in your psychology course. You ask your professor for suggestions, you interview several A students to compare and contrast their study habits, you assess your own study habits, and then determine the specific means (the number of hours and which study techniques) required to meet your end goal of an A.
Working backward	An approach that starts with the solution, a known condition, and works backward through the problem. Once the search has revealed the steps to be taken, the problem is solved.	Deciding you want to be an experimental psychologist, you ask your psychology professor and career counselor to recommend courses, graduate and undergraduate colleges and universities, areas to emphasize, and so on. Then you write the recommended college(s) requesting information on their admission policies and standards. You then plan your current college courses accordingly and work hard to meet (or exceed) the admission standards.
Creating subgoals	Large, complex problems are broken down into a series of small subgoals. These subgoals then serve as a series of stepping-stones that can be taken one at a time to reach the original large goal.	To write a successful college term paper, you choose a topic, go to the library and Internet to locate information related to the topic, organize the information, write an outline, write the paper, review the paper, rewrite, rewrite again, and submit the final paper on or before the due date.

Figure 21.2 *The nine-dot problem.* Draw no more than four lines that run through all nine dots on this page without lifting your pencil from the paper. (See Figure 21.3 on the next page for the solution.)

Figure 21.4 *Overcoming functional fixedness.* Can you use these supplies to mount the candle on a wall so that it can be lit in a normal way?

Recite, Review, and wRite) method or other study techniques described in the Tools for Student Success (Module 4). Their reliance on past study habits blocks them from considering newer and more efficient strategies. If we try to be flexible in our thinking, we can offset the natural tendency toward mental sets. To practice your flexibility, try the nine-dot problem in Figure 21.2.

2. Functional fixedness. The tendency to view objects as functioning only in the usual or customary way is known as **functional fixedness**. Suppose you wanted to make coffee in your automatic coffee maker but were out of filters. Would you dig through the trash looking for an old, dirty filter without thinking of using paper towels? What if you were given the objects shown in Figure 21.4 and asked to mount the candle on the wall so that it could be easily lit in the normal fashion, with no danger of toppling (Duncker, 1945)? How would you do this? Think about it before you read on.

Functional Fixedness *A barrier to problem solving that occurs when people are unable to recognize novel uses for an object because they are so familiar with its common use*

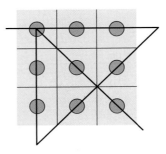

Figure 21.3 *Solution to the nine-dot problem.* People find this puzzle difficult because they see the arrangement of dots as a square. This *mental set* limits possible solutions because they "naturally" assume they can't go out of the boundaries of the square.

Figure 21.5 *The solution to the candle problem in Figure 21.4.* Use the tacks to mount the matchbox tray to the wall. Stand the candle on the tray and light the candle.

The solution is to empty the box, use the tacks to attach it to the wall, light the candle, drop some melted wax on the bottom of the box, then set the candle in the dripped wax (Figure 21.5). In the original test, research participants had a much more difficult time solving the problem when the box was filled with matches than when it was presented with the matches separately. In the former situation, the participants saw the box as only a container for matches and overlooked it as a useful item in itself. When you use a table knife instead of a screwdriver to tighten a screw, you have overcome functional fixedness.

3. *Confirmation bias.* Have you noticed how politicians frequently accept opinion polls that support their political views and ignore those that don't? Have you caught yourself agreeing with psychological theories that support your personal biases and discounting conflicting theories? This inclination to seek out evidence that confirms our own hypotheses, while at the same time discounting or overlooking contradictory evidence is known as **confirmation bias** (Nickerson, 1998). This phenomenon was first demonstrated by British researcher Peter Wason (1968) with the following test:

Confirmation Bias *The tendency to seek out and pay attention to information that confirms existing positions or beliefs while at the same time ignoring contradictory information*

Can you guess the rule?	2	4	6

Wason asked participants to guess the rule that applied to this same three-numbered set. Before submitting their rule, participants were also asked to generate additional sets of numbers that conformed to their hypothesized rule. The participants generated sets, such as (4, 6, 8) or (1, 3, 5). These sets reflected their commonly shared (but unspoken) guess that the rule was "numbers increasing by two." (Is this the same rule you generated?)

Each time the participants presented their list of numbers, Wason assured them their set of numbers conformed to the rule. However, when Wason later informed them that the rule "numbers increasing by 2" was incorrect, they were very frustrated. The actual rule was "numbers in increasing order of magnitude." (Did you guess the correct rule?) The barrier to solving this problem was that participants searched only for confirming information and failed to look for evidence that would disprove their hypothesis. If they had proposed a series, such as 1, 3, 4 instead, they would have discovered that their initial hypothesis was incorrect and they could have easily discovered the correct rule.

critical thinking ▸▸▸▸▸▸▸▸▸▸▸▸▸▸▸▸▸▸▸▸▸ Active Learning

Solving Problems in College Life

Critical thinking requires adaptive, flexible approaches to thinking and problem solving. Given that your success in college requires overcoming a number of problems in both school and life, the following exercise offers practice in critical thinking, new insights into common college-related problems, and a quick review of terms and concepts discussed in this section.

Before you begin, you may want to review the major problem-solving approaches we discussed — *algorithms* (step-by-step procedures that guarantee solu-

tions) and *heuristics* (generating possible solutions based on previous knowledge and experience). See Table 21.1 for three specific heuristics: *means–end analysis*, *working backward*, and *creating subgoals*.

Below, you will find two problems. For each problem, answer the following questions:

1. What was your first step in approaching the problem?

2. Which problem-solving approach did you select and why?

3. Did you consider potential obstacles, such as mental sets, functional fixed-

ness, and confirmation bias during the problem-solving process?

Problem 1   It is the end of the semester and you have a paper due Friday. Thursday afternoon, after studying for an exam, you turn on your computer to print your paper and can't find the file on your computer. How will you find the file?

Problem 2   The financial aid office has refused to give you your student loan until you verify how much money you made last year. You need to find your pay stubs to verify income.

If I leave an especially difficult problem alone for a while and return to it later, I sometimes find the answer just pops into my mind. Why is that? Some problems require a period of **incubation**, or time out, to allow the facts and possibilities to come into better focus. Wolfgang Kohler (1925) observed incubation in his chimpanzee Sultan. As described in Module 17, Sultan was presented with a banana that was out of reach and only two sticks at his disposal. Initially, the chimp was stumped. After a few weeks' incubation, however, the solution came to him in a flash of "insight." He fitted the two sticks together and successfully reached the banana.

Incubation *A period of time during which active searching for a problem's solution is set aside; this is sometimes necessary for a successful solution of the problem*

Check & Review

SOLVING PROBLEMS

Problem solving entails three steps: *preparation*, *production*, and *evaluation*. During the preparation stage, we identify given facts, separate relevant from irrelevant facts, and define the ultimate goal.

During the production stage, we generate possible situations, called hypotheses. We typically generate hypotheses by using **algorithms** and **heuristics**. Algorithms, as problem-solving strategies, are guaranteed to lead to a solution eventually, but they are not practical in many situations. Heuristics, or simplified rules of thumb that are based on experience, are much faster but do not guarantee a solution. Three common heuristics are *means–end analysis*, *working backward*, and *creating subgoals*.

The evaluation step in problem solving involves judging the hypotheses generated

during step two (production stage) against the criteria established in step one (preparation stage).

Three major barriers to successful problem solving are **mental sets**, **functional fixedness**, and **confirmation bias**. Some problems require a period of **incubation**, or time out, before a solution is apparent.

Questions

1. List and describe the three stages of problem solving.

2. Rosa is shopping in a new supermarket and wants to find a specific type of mustard. Which problem-solving strategy would be most efficient? (a) algorithm; (b) heuristic; (c) instinct; (d) mental set.

3. Before a new product arrives in the store, a manufacturer goes through several stages, including designing, building, testing a prototype, setting up a production line, and so on. This approach is called (a) working backward; (b) means–end analysis; (c) divergent thinking; (d) creating subgoals.

4. What are three barriers to problem solving, and how might incubation be useful in overcoming these obstacles?

Answers to Questions can be found in Appendix B.

Solution to the DONALD + GERALD = ROBERT problem:

```
    5 2 6 4 8 5
  + 1 9 7 4 8 5
    7 2 3 9 7 0
```

Creativity: Finding Unique Solutions

What is creativity, and how is it measured?

Creativity *The generation of ideas that are original, novel, and useful*

Divergent Thinking *Thinking that produces many alternatives or ideas; a major element of creativity (e.g., finding as many uses as possible for a paper clip)*

Convergent Thinking *Conventional thinking; thinking directed toward a single correct answer (e.g., standard academic tests generally require convergent thinking)*

Are you a creative person? Like most students, you may think of only painters, dancers, and composers as creative and may fail to recognize examples of your own creativity. Even when doing ordinary tasks, such as taking notes in class, you are being somewhat creative — unless you're copying the lecture verbatim. Similarly, if you've ever tightened a screw with a penny or used a magazine to splint a broken arm, you've found creative solutions to problems. All of us, to a greater or lesser degree, exhibit a certain amount of creativity in some aspects of life. Whether a solution or performance is considered creative often depends on its need and usefulness at the time (Weisberg, 1993). Definitions of creativity vary among psychologists and between cultures, but it is generally agreed that **creativity** is the ability to produce valued outcomes in a novel way (Bink & Marsh, 2000; Boden, 2000).

Measuring Creativity

Creative thought is associated with three special characteristics: *originality, fluency,* and *flexibility.* As you can see in Table 21.2, Thomas Edison's invention of the ligh bulb offers a prime example of each of these characteristics. In addition to the three characteristics of creativity, there is a distinct type of thinking that is related to creativity, called **divergent thinking**, where many possibilities are developed from a single starting point (Baer, 1994). The opposite of divergent thinking is **convergent thinking**, or *conventional thinking.* In this case, lines of thinking converge (come together) on the answer, and we select a single correct solution from among several alternatives. You used convergence in the DONALD + GERALD problem to find the one correct number represented by each letter.

Divergent thinking is the type of thinking most often associated with creativity and is thus the focus of most tests of creativity. In the *Unusual Uses Test,* the person is asked to think of as many uses as possible for an object (such as "How many ways can you use a brick?"). In the *Anagrams Test,* people are asked to reorder the letters in a word to make as many new words as possible. A type of anagram test is found in the following six groups of letters. Try rearranging these letters in these words to make new words, and then decide what they share in common. (Answers are listed after the Check & Review for this section.)

1. grevenidt _____
2. neleecitlgn _____
3. ytliibxilef _____
4. ptoyropet _____
5. yvitcearti _____
6. niubcaiotn _____

TABLE 21.2 THREE ELEMENTS OF CREATIVE THINKING

	Explanations	Thomas Edison Examples
Originality	Seeing unique or different solutions to a problem	After noting that electricity passing through a conductor produced a glowing red or white heat, Edison imagined capturing this light for practical uses.
Fluency	Generating a large number of possible solutions	Edison tried literally hundreds of different materials to find one that would heat to the point of glowing white heat without burning up.
Flexibility	Shifting with ease from one type of problem-solving strategy to another	When he couldn't find a long-lasting material, he thought of heating it in a vacuum — thereby creating the first lightbulb.

TABLE 21.3 RESOURCES OF CREATIVE PEOPLE

Intellectual Ability	Knowledge	Thinking Style	Personality	Motivation	Environment
Enough intelligence to see problems in a new light	Sufficient basic knowledge of the problem to effectively evaluate possible solutions	Pursue their own novel ideas and can distinguish between the worthy and worthless	Willing to grow and change, take risks, and work to overcome obstacles	Sufficient motivation to accomplish the task; internal rather than external motivation is best	Creative people need to work in an environment that supports creativity

Researching Creativity

Some researchers view creativity as a special talent or ability and therefore look for common personality traits among people they define as creative (Guilford, 1967; Jausovec & Jausovec, 2000). Other researchers explain the distinction between creative and noncreative people in terms of cognitive processes. That is, creative and noncreative people differ in life experiences, how they encode information, how they store it, and in what information they generate to solve problems (Bink & Marsh, 2000; Cooper, 2000; Jacoby, Levy, & Steinbach, 1992).

According to Sternberg and Lubart's *investment theory* (1992, 1999), creative people are willing to "buy low and sell high" in the realm of ideas. They buy low by championing ideas that they feel have potential but that most people think are worthless or worth very little. Once their creative ideas are supported and highly valued, they "sell high" and move on to another unpopular but promising idea.

Investment theory also suggests that creativity requires the coming together of six different but interrelated resources: intellectual ability, knowledge, thinking style, personality, motivation, and environment (Goertz, 2000; Sternberg & Lubart, 1999). These resources are summarized in Table 21.3. One way to improve your personal creativity is to study this list and then strengthen yourself in those areas that you think need improvement.

Do you want to test your creativity? Try the following. (See Figure 21.6 for the solution.)

1. In five minutes, see how many words you can make out of the following word.
   HIPPOPOTAMUS

2. In five minutes, list all the things you can do with a paper clip.

3. Find 10 coins and arrange them in the configuration shown here. By moving only two coins, form two rows that each contain 6 coins.

Check & Review

CREATIVITY

Creativity is the generation of ideas that are original, novel, and useful. Creative thinking involves *originality, fluency,* and *flexibility.* **Divergent thinking**, trying to generate as many solutions as possible, is a special type of thinking involved in creativity. In contrast, **convergent thinking**, or conventional thinking, works toward a single solution to a problem and is not related to creativity.

The investment theory of creativity proposes that creative people "buy low" by pursuing promising but unpopular ideas and "sell high" by developing the ideas until they are widely accepted. It also proposes that creativity depends on six specific resources: intellectual ability, knowledge, thinking style, personality, motivation, and environment.

Questions

1. Which of the following items would MOST likely appear on a test measuring creativity? (a) How long is the Ohio River? (b) What are the primary colors? (c) List all the uses of a pot. (d) Who was the first governor of New York?

2. Identify the type of thinking for each of these examples.
   a. You create numerous excuses ("reasons") for not studying.
   b. On a test, you must select one correct answer for each question.
   c. You make a list of ways to save money.

3. According to investment theory, what are the six resources necessary for creativity?

4. As a music teacher, you would like your students to create their own songs. Should you offer a prize as an incentive for the most creative song? Why or why not?

Answers to Questions can be found in Appendix B.

Solutions to the Anagrams Test
1. divergent
2. intelligence
3. flexibility
4. prototype
5. creativity
6. incubation
The answers are key terms found in this module.

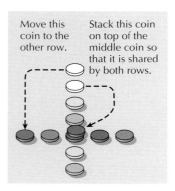

Move this coin to the other row.

Stack this coin on top of the middle coin so that it is shared by both rows.

Figure 21.6 *Coin problem solution.* Stack one coin on top of the middle coin so that it shares both the row and the column.

ACTIVE LEARNING WORKSHEET MODULE 21

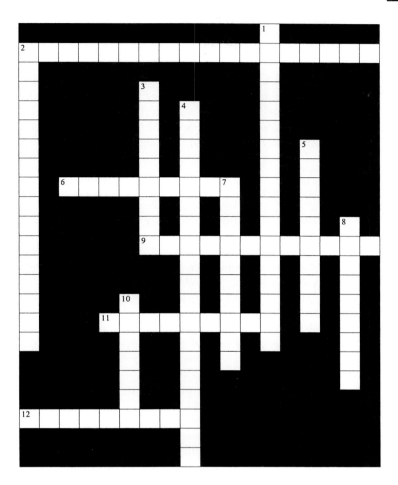

ACROSS

2. Conventional thinking directed toward a single correct answer.

6. Problem-solving strategies used as shortcuts to complex solutions.

9. Mind's representation of a sensory experience.

11. Mental activities involved in acquiring, storing, retrieving, and using knowledge.

12. Typical, highly representative example serving as a model on which other examples are based or judged.

DOWN

1. Thinking that produces many alternatives or ideas.

2. Paying attention to information that confirms existing positions or beliefs, while ignoring contradictory information.

3. Trying out all possible solutions to a problem in a systematic manner.

4. Being unable to recognize novel uses due to previous familiarity with common use.

5. A setting aside of active problem solving that sometimes leads to successful resolution.

7. Generating ideas that are original, novel, and useful.

8. Applying only methods that have worked in the past versus trying innovative ones.

10. Mental category that groups objects, events, activities, or ideas that share similar characteristics.

Answers can be found in Appendix B.

MODULE 22
LANGUAGE

What is language, and how is it related to thinking?

Any discussion of human thought processes must include a discussion of language. As mentioned earlier, language (along with mental images and concepts) is a foundation or building block of thinking. Language enables us to mentally manipulate symbols, thereby expanding our thinking. Most importantly, whether it's spoken, written, or signed, language allows us to communicate our thoughts, ideas, and feelings.

Characteristics of Language: Structure and Production

What is language? Do beavers slapping their tails, birds singing their songs, and ants laying their trails use language? Not according to a strict scientific definition. As we discussed earlier, scientists develop precise definitions and restrictions for certain *artificial concepts*. Psychologists, linguists, and other scientists define *language* as a form of communication whereby we put together sounds and symbols according to specified rules.

Beavers, birds, and ants obviously communicate. Even amoebae seem to send and receive crude messages chemically by discharging small amounts of carbon dioxide. However, this type of communication is believed to be simple, ritualistic, and bound by a limited repertoire of sounds or movements that are performed whenever a certain stimulus evokes them. In short, it is *instinctive* behavior.

Human language, on the other hand, is largely *learned* — passed on from parent to child, teacher to student, friend to friend. Despite the complexity of communication patterns among some nonhuman animals, these patterns differ significantly from human patterns of language. For example, because animal call systems are primarily instinctive, they are inflexible — each call almost always has the same form and conveys the same meaning. In contrast, once the rules of a language are learned, humans use them in creative and complex ways to convey their thoughts and feelings to others.

Building Blocks of Language

To produce language, we first build words using *phonemes* and *morphemes*. Then we string words into sentences using rules of *grammar* (*syntax* and *semantics*) (Table 22.1):

1. *Phonemes.* The basic building blocks of language are sounds of speech called **phonemes**. These basic speech sounds make up every language. The English language has about 40 or so phonemes. Each one has distinctive features, such as variations in sound (like the letter *a* in *am* and *ape*) or unvoiced versus voiced components (when we say *s*, we simply hiss; when we say *z*, we do the same but add the voice).

2. *Morphemes.* Phonemes are combined to form the second building block of language, morphemes. **Morphemes** are the smallest *meaningful* units of language. Morphemes are divided into two types: (a) *content morphemes*, which hold the basic meaning of a word, such as *cat*, and (b) *function morphemes*, which are prefixes and suffixes, such as *un-*, *dis-*, *-able*, and *-ing*. Function morphemes add additional meaning to the word.

3. *Grammar.* Phonemes, morphemes, words, and phrases are joined together by the third building block of language, the rules of **grammar**. Grammatical rules gov-

Phoneme [FOE-neem] *The most basic unit of speech; an individual speech sound*

Morpheme [MOR-feem] *The smallest meaningful unit of language, formed from a combination of phonemes*

Grammar *The rules of a language that specify how phonemes, morphemes, words, and phrases should be combined to meaningfully express thoughts*

TABLE 22.1 BUILDING BLOCKS OF LANGUAGE

Blocks	Description	Example
Phonemes	The smallest units of sound that make up every language	*p* in pansy; *ng* in sting
Morphemes	The smallest units that carry meaning; they are created by combining phonemes (*Function morphemes* are prefixes and suffixes. *Content morphemes* are root words.)	*unthinkable = un•think•able* (prefix = *un*, root word = *think*, suffix = *able*)
Grammar	A system of rules (syntax and semantics) used to generate acceptable language that enables us to communicate with and understand others	*I enjoy my psychology class.* versus *I my class psychology enjoy.*
Syntax	A system of rules for putting words in order	*I am happy.* versus *Happy I am.*
Semantics	A system of using words to create meaning	*I went out on a limb for you.* versus *Humans have several limbs.*

ern how to combine phonemes into morphemes and words, how to use various classes of words (nouns, verbs, etc.) and their inflections (plurals, verb tenses, etc.), and how to choose and order words to form meaningful sentences. Grammar is made up of two components, syntax and semantics.

- **Syntax.** The grammatical rules for ordering words in sentences are known as rules of **syntax**. By the time we are able to read, our syntactical sense is so highly developed that even a sentence composed of nonsense words sounds as if it makes sense, as long as it follows proper syntax, as in Lewis Carroll's poem, "Jabberwocky":

'Twas brillig, and the slithy toves

Did gyre and gimble in the wabe...

The word arrangement follows the rules of English syntax so well that we feel we know what Carroll is talking about.

Syntax varies from language to language. In English, for example, the verb is usually the second element in a sentence ("He *has driven* to New York"). But in German, the main verb often comes at the very end of a sentence (German word order would be "He *has* to New York *driven*"). English speakers always put the adjective before the noun ("my *precious* love"), but Italian, speakers sometimes place the adjective before and sometimes after, depending on the intended meaning: *Una carrisima amore* means "a very dear, precious love," whereas *un' amore carrisima* means "a very expensive love," one that costs a lot to keep kindled!

- **Semantics.** The choosing of words according to the meaning we want to convey is known as **semantics**. When we add *-ed* to the word *walk*, it refers to walking in the past. If we want to refer to a baby sheep, we use the word *lamb*, not the word *limb*, which means something entirely different. Actually, *limb* has

Syntax *The grammatical rules that specify in what order the words and phrases should be arranged in a sentence to convey meaning*

Semantics *Meaning or the study of meaning derived from morphemes, words, and sentences* several meanings, so we must depend on context to know whether the speaker is referring to an arm or a leg or to one of the larger branches of a tree. Then there is the expression "to go out on a limb," which means not that someone literally climbs a tree but rather that someone takes a risk. Meaning thus depends on many factors, including word choice, context, and whether the intent is literal or figurative, to name just a few.

How do children learn such complex rules? The linguist Noam Chomsky (1957, 1965) proposed that humans are born with an innate mental grammar, an ability to put words together in a meaningful way. Chomsky also proposed that every sentence we generate has two grammatical structures, a *surface structure* and a *deep structure*. The surface structure consists of the words that are spoken or written (or signed). *Deep structure* refers to the underlying meaning of the sentence. For example, the sentence "Terry made the coffee" can be rewritten as "The coffee was made by Terry." Although the surface structure changed, the deep structure remains the same.

As it turns out, both children and adults tend to focus on and remember the deep structure of a sentence rather than its surface structure. In a study by Sachs (1967), participants read a passage and were interrupted at various intervals and asked whether a certain sentence had appeared earlier in the passage. In some cases, the sentences were repeated verbatim, but in others, either the meaning or the syntax was slightly changed. When tested immediately, participants recognized changes in the sentence, but when tested after some time had elapsed, they noticed only when the meaning had changed. Thus, we tend to remember the meaning of sentences, though we might not remember the exact words used to convey that meaning. As a critical thinker, can you see why this might be to our evolutionary advantage and part of a child's built-in innate capacity?

Language and Thought: A Complex Interaction

Our cognitive processes and language are intricately related. Does the fact that you speak English versus Spanish — or Chinese versus Swahili — mean that you reason, think, and perceive the world differently? According to linguist Benjamin Whorf (1956), the language that a person speaks largely determines the nature of that person's thoughts. Whorf's *linguistic relativity* hypothesis suggests that our vocabulary determines how we perceive and categorize the world around us. As proof, Whorf offered a now classic example: Because Eskimos [Inuits] have many words to describe different kinds of snow (*apikak* for "first snow falling," *pukak* for "snow for drinking water," and so on), their richer vocabulary supposedly enables them to perceive and think about snow differently from English speakers, who have only one word — *snow*. People who speak different languages have different conceptions of the world around them.

Whorf's hypothesis is certainly intriguing, but most research does not support it. For one thing, he apparently exaggerated the number of Inuit words for snow (Pullum, 1991) and ignored the fact that English speakers have terms like *slush*, *sleet*, *hard pack*, *powder*, and so on. More importantly, Eleanor Rosch (1973) found counterevidence for Whorf's hypothesis when she experimentally tested his ideas with the Dani tribe in New Guinea. Although the Dani language has only two color names, one indicating cool, dark colors and the other warm, bright colors, Rosch found that the Dani could discriminate among color hues just as well as people speaking languages with multiple names for colors. In other words, although it may be easier to express a particular idea in one language than in another, language does not necessarily determine how or what we think.

Whorf apparently went too far with his theory that language *determines* thought, but there is no doubt that language *influences* thought (Lillard, 1998). For example, what happens when people speak two or more languages? Studies have found that people who are bilingual report feeling a different sense of self, depending on the language they are using (Matsumoto, 2000). When using Chinese, they found they tended to behave in ways appropriate to Chinese cultural norms, but when speaking English, they tended to adopt Western norms.

The influence of language on thought is also readily apparent in our word choice. For example, when companies want to alter workers' perceptions, they don't *fire* employees; rather, employees are *outplaced*, *dehired*, or *nonrenewed*. Similarly, the military uses terms like *preemptive strike* to cover the fact that they attacked first and *tactical redeployment* to refer to a retreat of troops. Our choice of words also has had some embarrassing and financial consequences for North American businesses. When Pepsi-Cola used its "Come alive with Pepsi" slogan in Japan, they later learned that it translated as "Pepsi brings your dead ancestors back from the grave." Words evoke different images and value judgments. Our words, therefore, *influence* not only our thinking but also the thinking of those who hear them.

Animals and Language: Can We Talk to the Animals?

Heated controversies exist over whether animals use language or can be taught to use language. Without question, animals communicate. Most species send warnings, signal sexual interest, share location of food sources, and so on. The question is this: Are animals capable of mastering the rich complexity of human language?

One of the earliest attempts to answer this question came from psychologists Winthrop and Luella Kellogg (1933), who raised a baby chimpanzee for several years alongside their son of about the same age. Although the chimp learned a few rudimentary, communicative gestures, she never uttered sounds that resembled language. Other early animal language researchers concluded, however, that the Kelloggs probably failed simply because apes do not have the necessary anatomical structure to vocalize that humans do.

Subsequent studies focused on teaching apes nonvocal languages. One of the most successful was a study by Beatrice and Allen Gardner (1969), who recognized the manual dexterity of chimpanzees and their ability to imitate gestures. The Gardners used American Sign Language (ASL), a language used by many deaf people, with a chimp named Washoe. Their success story speaks for itself. By the time Washoe was 4 years old, she had learned 132 signs and was able to combine them into simple sentences such as: "Hurry, gimme toothbrush" and "Please tickle more."

Since the Gardners' success with Washoe, several other language projects have been conducted with apes (Itakura, 1992; Savage-Rumbaugh, 1990). David Premack (1976) taught a chimp named Sarah to "read" and "write" by arranging plastic symbols on a magnetic board. She learned not only to use the plastic symbols but also to follow certain grammatical rules in communicating with her trainers.

Another well-known study was conducted with a chimp named Lana. She learned to push symbols on a computer to get things she wanted, such as food, a drink, a tickle from her trainers, and her curtains opened (Rumbaugh et al., 1974). And, of course, there is the famous gorilla Koko. Researcher Penny Patterson (1981) reportedly taught Koko over 600 signs in ASL.

A number of language studies have also been done with dolphins. Communication with dolphins is by means of hand signals or audible commands. The commands may be spoken by trainers or generated by computer and transmitted through an underwater speaker system. In one typical study, dolphins were given commands made up of two- to five-word sentences, such as "Big ball — square — return," which meant they should go get the big ball, put it in the floating square, and return to the trainer (Herman, Richards, & Woltz, 1984).

Is Koko using language? Researcher Francine (Penny) Patterson taught a gorilla named Koko to communicate through American Sign Language. At first she rewarded Koko with pieces of fruit if she made any sign that remotely resembled the correct one. Gradually, she reinforced only those gestures that were formed correctly. Today Koko reportedly knows over 600 signs and continues to learn new ones.

RESEARCH HIGHLIGHT

Language and the Brain

In some respects, the brain appears naturally "prewired" to learn language. At birth, the language areas of the temporal cortex are larger in the left than the right hemisphere, and the neurons in the left hemisphere are sensitive to speech sounds. Our neurological understanding of language is just beginning to unfold, but a number of studies provide insight into language and its development.

Functional magnetic resonance imaging (fMRI) studies, for example, indicate that areas of the brain may be organized differently depending on the age at which language is learned. When bilingual individuals learn both languages in childhood, a single region of *Broca's area* is used to produce complex sentences. But when people learn a second language during adolescence, two different regions of *Broca's area* are used (Kim et al., 1997), and the right hemisphere seems to be used more than if the language is learned during childhood (Barinaga, 2000). Finally, recent information suggests that two separate areas of the brain

are involved in the processing and production of language. *Broca's area* is involved in both speech production and language production, whereas the *supramarginal gyrus* (located in the parietal lobe) combines word meaning with the production of words (Crosson et al., 2001; Grodzinsky, 2000).

Although the brain may seem prepared to learn language, cognitive neuroscientists, linguists, and psychologists debate whether language is inborn and if we have sensitive periods for language acquisition (Plomin & Dale, 2000; Ramus, Hauser, Miller, Morris, & Mehler, 2000). (The *sensitive period hypothesis* suggests that humans most easily learn language between birth and puberty, the time when the brain is becoming increasingly specialized. If learning does not occur during this special time, it may be impossible to later "catch up.")

Genie's case provides an excellent example of the importance of sensitive periods for language development. When first discovered at age 13, she was almost completely silent. Because her father severely punished her for making any vocal sounds, Genie did not sob when she cried nor speak when in a fit of rage. She under-

stood only a few "word phrases" such as *stopit* and *nomore* (Rymer, 1993). After 8 months of training, Genie had a vocabulary of more than 200 words and was putting together 2-word sentences. However, her language development did not continue in the usual explosive pattern of normal children. According to last reports, Genie's adult language skills are limited to those of a typical 2- or 3-year-old (Harris, 1995). This is a conversation between Genie and her foster mother, when Genie was 18:

GENIE: At school is washing car.
MOTHER: Whose car did you wash?
GENIE: People car.
MOTHER: How many cars did you wash?
GENIE: Two car. [Curtiss, 1977, p. 28]

Despite years of intensive training, brain scans showed that Genie's left hemisphere remained virtually unresponsive. This suggests that her isolation during critical language-learning years may have failed to trigger innate brain mechanisms, and the cortical tissue normally committed to language may have functionally atrophied.

The interesting part of this experiment was that the commands varied in syntax and content, both of which altered meaning. For example, the next command might be "Square — big ball — return," which meant the dolphin should go to the square first, then get the big ball, then return to the trainer with the ball. Or the command might refer to one of the other objects floating in the pool, thereby changing its content: "Triangle — little ball — square," which required the dolphin to discriminate among various shapes and various sizes of balls to carry out the command. The study demonstrated that dolphins could carry out a great variety of commands that varied in both content and syntax.

Evaluating Animal Language Studies

Although these ape and dolphin studies seem impressive, psychologists nevertheless do not agree on the interpretation of the findings. Most psychologists believe that nonhuman animals communicate at some level, but compared with humans, animals express a severely limited repertoire of ideas. The average length of sentences produced and understood by humans is also significantly greater than the two- to five-word sentences used by other animals. Moreover, critics claim that apes and dolphins are unable to learn the rules of grammar and syntax that humans use to convey subtle differences in meaning. They question whether animals can use language in ways that are considered creative or unique and point out that they do not express the concept of time (*tomorrow, last week*), request information (*How do birds fly?*), comment on the feelings of others (*Penny is sad*), express similarities (*That cloud looks like a tree*), or propose possibilities (*The cat might sit on my lap*) (Jackendoff, 1994).

Finally, some critics raise the issue of operant conditioning (Module 16). They claim that animals do not have a conceptual understanding of the complex signs and symbols of language; those who do engage in simple human language are merely imitating symbols to receive rewards. In short, animals are not really trying to communicate but are simply performing operantly conditioned responses (Jackendoff, 1994; Savage-Rumbaugh, 1990; Terrace, 1979).

On the other hand, proponents of animal language are quick to point out that chimpanzees and gorillas can use language creatively and have even coined some words of their own. For example, Washoe called a refrigerator "open eat drink" and a swan a "water bird" (Gardner & Gardner, 1971). Koko signed "finger bracelet" to describe a ring and "eye hat" to describe a mask (Patterson & Linden, 1981). Proponents also argue that, as demonstrated by the dolphin studies, animals can be taught to understand basic rules of sentence structure.

Still, the fact remains that the gap between language as spoken and understood by humans and that generated and understood by other animals is considerable. All the evidence seems to suggest that animals can learn language at a rudimentary level, but that this language is less complex, creative, and rule-laden than any language used by humans. (As a critical thinker, have you ever thought about an opposite approach to animal language research? Why don't humans learn animal language? Could humans be taught to comprehend and use chimpanzee communication systems, for example?)

Check & Review

LANGUAGE

Human language is a creative form of communication consisting of symbols put together according to a set of rules. The three building blocks of language are **phonemes, morphemes,** and **grammar**. Phonemes are the basic speech sounds; they are combined to form morphemes, the smallest meaningful units of language. Phonemes, morphemes, words, and phrases are put together by rules of grammar (**syntax** and **semantics**). *Syntax* refers to the grammatical rules for ordering words in sentences; *semantics* refers to meaning in language.

Noam Chomsky believes that humans are born with an ability to put words together in a meaningful way. Also, according to Chomsky, every sentence has both a *surface structure* (the words themselves) and a *deep structure* (the actual meaning).

According to Benjamin Whorf's *linguistic relativity hypothesis*, language shapes thought. Generally, Whorf's hypothesis is not supported. However, our choice of vocabulary can influence our mental imagery and social perceptions.

The most successful animal language studies have been done with apes using American Sign Language. Dolphins have also been taught to comprehend sentences that vary in syntax and meaning. Some psychologists believe that animals can truly learn human language, but others suggest that the animals are merely responding to rewards.

Questions

1. The basic speech sounds /ch/ and /v/ are known as _____; the smallest meaningful units of language, such as *book*, *pre-*, and *-ing*, are known as _____.

2. Explain what Chomsky meant by the terms *surface* and *deep* structure.

3. What is Whorf's *linguistic relativity hypothesis*?

4. Human language differs from the communication of other animals in that it is (a) used more creatively to express thoughts and ideas; (b) the expression of an innate capability; (c) essential for thought; (d) composed of sounds.

Answers to Questions can be found in Appendix B.

MODULE 22   ACTIVE LEARNING WORKSHEET

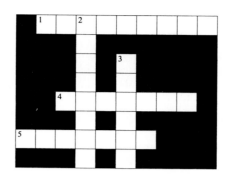

ACROSS

1. Meaning or the study of meaning derived from morphemes, words, and sentences.

4. The most basic unit of speech; an individual speech sound.

5. Rules of a language specifying how phonemes, morphemes, words, and phrases should be combined to meaningfully express thoughts.

DOWN

2. Smallest meaningful unit of language, formed from a combination of phonemes.

3. Grammatical rules specifying in what order the words and phrases should be arranged in a sentence in order to convey meaning.

Answers can be found in Appendix B.

MODULE 23
INTELLIGENCE

Millions of people watched when John Carpenter faced his final challenge on *Who Wants To Be A Millionaire*? As the studio lights glared down, he sat poised ready to answer the questions. Does this game show test for intelligence? Are Genie and Thomas Edison intelligent? What is intelligence? Are there different types of intelligence?

What is intelligence, and how can it be measured?

The Nature of Intelligence: Is it Real?

The term **intelligence** is commonly defined in psychology as the general capacity to profit from experience, to acquire knowledge, and adapt to changes in the environment. Although we use the term *intelligence* in our everyday conversation and assume we all share the same definition, we don't. Even among psychologists there is considerable debate over its definition and appropriate methods for measurement. However, there is one area of agreement — it is not a *thing*. It has no mass and it occupies no space. When people talk about intelligence as though it were a concrete, tangible object, they commit an error in reasoning, known as *reification*. Like consciousness, learning, memory, or personality, intelligence is nothing more than a useful *hypothethical, abstract construct*. As you will see later, it is estimated, rather arbitrarily, by scores on intelligence tests. Practically speaking, intelligence is what intelligence tests measure.

Intelligence *The general capacity to profit from experience, to acquire knowledge, and adapt to changes in the environment*

Intelligence is also socially constructed, and its definition varies according to the characteristics and skills valued in that culture (Sternberg & Kaufman, 1998). In fact, many languages have no word that corresponds to our notion of intelligence. The closest Mandarin word is a Chinese character meaning "good brain and talented" (Matsumoto, 2000), which is commonly associated with traits like imitation, effort, and social responsibility (Keats, 1982).

Because of the difficulty in identifying and defining intelligence, it remains a complex and controversial topic. For most Western psychologists, modern research on intelligence has centered on two unresolved questions:

- What is the basis for intelligence? Does it depend more on nature or nurture?

- What are the properties of intelligence? Is it a single general ability or several distinct kinds of abilities (intelligences)?

We will discuss several theories that attempt to answer these questions, beginning with Charles Spearman's early theory of *general intelligence*.

Intelligence as a Single Ability

In the early years of intelligence testing, psychologists viewed intelligence as innate, a broad mental ability that included all the cognitive functions. Charles Spearman (1923) proposed that intelligence is a single factor, which he termed *general intelligence* (g). He based his theory on his observation that high scores on separate tests of mental abilities, such as spatial and reasoning ability, tend to correlate with each other. Thus, Spearman believed g underlies all intellectual behavior, including reasoning, solving problems, and performing well in all areas of cognition. On the basis of Spearman's work, standardized tests were widely used in the military, schools, and business to measure this general intelligence (Lubinski & Dawis, 1992).

Multiple intelligences. *Most psychologists agree that there are many forms of intelligence.*

Paul Greengard, Arvid Carlsson, and Eric R. Kandel

Condoleezza Rice

Oprah Winfrey

Gao Xingjian

Celine Dion

Ricky Martin

Venus and Serena Williams

Julie Payette

Intelligence as Multiple Abilities

About a decade later, L. L. Thurstone (1938) proposed seven primary mental abilities: verbal comprehension, word fluency, numerical fluency, spatial visualization, associative memory, perceptual speed, and reasoning. He felt that Spearman's g had little, if any value. Naturally, at the time, Thurstone's view was rather radical. Many years later, J. P. Guilford (1967) expanded on this number and proposed that as many as 120 factors were involved in the structure of the intellect.

Intelligence Again as a Single Ability

About the same time that Guilford was working, Raymond Cattell (1963, 1971) reanalyzed Thurstone's data and argued against the idea of multiple intelligences. He proposed that a single g does exist, but that there are two types of g:

1. Fluid intelligence (gf) refers to reasoning abilities, memory, and speed of information processing. If you were asked to solve analogies or remember a long set of numbers, you would be relying on your fluid intelligence. Being relatively independent of education and experience, it reflects an inherited predisposition, and like other biological capacities it declines with advancing age (Burns, Nettelbeck, & Cooper, 2000; Schaie, 1993, 1994).

2. Crystallized intelligence (gc) refers to knowledge and skills gained through experience and education (Facon & Facon-Bollengier, 1999). You would rely on your crystallized intelligence if you were asked to explain the President's social security policy or the difference between a "bear" or "bull" stock market. Crystallized intelligence tends to increase over the life span, which explains why physicians, teachers, musicians, politicians, and people in many other occupations can continue working well into old age.

Recent findings show increased frontal lobe activity during very complex tasks, which helps support the idea of g (Duncan & Owen, 2000). Recall, however, that correlation does not necessarily imply causation and that other explanations are equally possible. Moreover, other studies find that more intelligent people are likely to show less, not more frontal lobe activation, possibly because tasks are not as challenging to them as to those less intelligent (Haier et al., 1993; Sternberg, 1999). All in all, the debate concerning g continues.

A Return to Multiple Intelligences

Many contemporary cognitive theorists see a relationship among diverse mental abilities and point out that some people excel in specific areas of intelligence more than in other areas. So perhaps, as suggested by Thurstone and Guilford, mental abilities actually are distinct from one another.

Gardner's theory of multiple intelligences. One cognitive theorist, Howard Gardner, has proposed a *theory of multiple intelligences* (Figure 23.1). Using his own stringent criteria, Gardner (1983, 1998) has identified the eight distinct intelligences shown in Table 23.1. According to Gardner (1991), people come to know their world through these eight intelligences. Also, people have different *profiles of intelligence* because they are stronger in some areas than others, and they use their intelligences differently to learn new material, perform tasks, and solve problems.

Gardner's theory has wide-reaching implications for intelligence testing and for education. Gardner (1986) maintains that intelligence testing should consist of assessing a person's strengths rather than coming up with a single "IQ score." He also challenges our education system to present material in a variety of learning modes rather than the traditional linguistic and logical–mathematical and to develop multiple means of assessment rather than the traditional paper-and-pencil method.

Fluid Intelligence *Aspects of intelligence, including reasoning abilities, memory, and speed of information processing, that tend to decline slowly as people age*

Crystallized Intelligence *Knowledge and skills gained through experience and education that tend to increase over the life span*

Figure 23.1 *Gardner's Theory of Multiple Intelligences.* Howard Gardner believes there are independent forms of intelligence and that the value of these intelligences may change according to culture.

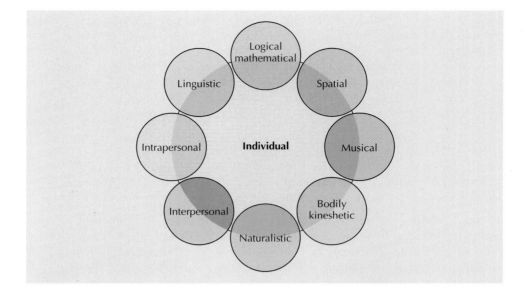

TABLE 23.1 GARDNER'S MULTIPLE INTELLIGENCES

Linguistic:	Spatial:	Bodily–kinesthetic:	Intrapersonal:	Logical–mathematical:	Musical:	Interpersonal:	Naturalistic:
language, such as speaking, reading a book, writing a story	mental maps, such as figuring out how to pack multiple presents in a box or how to draw a floor plan	body movement, such as dancing, hitting a baseball, or skiing	understanding oneself, such as setting achievable goals or recognizing self-defeating emotions	problem solving or scientific analysis, such as following a logical proof or solving a mathematical problem	musical skills, such as singing a song or playing the piano	social skills, such as talking with other people	Being attuned to nature, such as noticing seasonal patterns or using environmentally safe products

Sternberg's triarchic (three-part) theory of successful intelligence. On the basis of findings from information processing research, Robert Sternberg (1985) developed what he called a *triarchic theory of successful intelligence* (Figure 23.2). Sternberg argued that even more important than the outward products of intelligence such as correct answers on an intelligence test are the thinking processes we use to arrive at the answers and that theories of intelligence should account for these processes.

The *triarchic theory* proposes three aspects of intelligence: (1) analytic intelligence, (2) creative intelligence, and (3) practical intelligence (Frensch & Sternberg, 1990; Sternberg, 1999). People tend to have a stronger aptitude for one or more of these aspects of intelligence. Table 23.2 briefly describes each aspect.

The value of Sternberg's theory of intelligence is that he emphasizes the process underlying thinking rather than just the end product, and he stresses the importance of applying mental abilities to real-world situations rather than testing mental abilities in isolation. Recently, Sternberg (1998) introduced the term *successful intelligence* to describe the ability to adapt to, shape, and select environments in order to accomplish personal and societal goals. Gardner and Sternberg differ on a number of points in their theories, but they agree that intelligence involves multiple abilities. In fact, in modern times, most cognitive Scientists believe that, for most people, intelligence is a "very general mental ability" (Arvey et al., 1994).

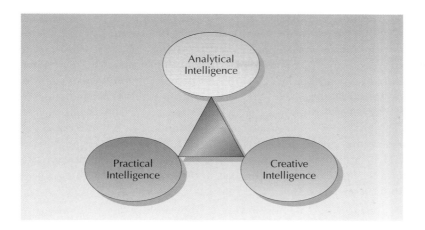

Figure 23.2 *Sternberg's triarchic (three-part) theory of successful intelligence.* According to Robert Sternberg's model, there are three separate and different aspects of intelligence. Each of these components is learned, not the result of genetics. Therefore, each can be strengthened or improved.

TABLE 23.2 STERNBERG'S TRIARCHIC THEORY OF SUCCESSFUL INTELLIGENCE

	Analytical Intelligence	Creative Intelligence	Practical Intelligence
Sample Skills	Good at analysis, evaluation, judgment, and comparison skills	Good at invention, discovery, coping with novelty, and imagination skills	Good at application, implementation, execution, and utilization skills
Methods of Assessment	These skills are assessed by any of the intelligence or scholastic aptitude tests. Questions ask about meanings of words based on context and how to solve number-series problems.	These skills are assessed in many ways, including open-ended tasks, such as designing an invention, writing a short story, drawing a piece of art, creating an adverstisement, or solving a scientific problem requiring insight.	Although these skills are more difficult to assess, they can be measured by asking for solutions to practical and personal problems.

Test Construction: What Makes a Good Test?

Think back to the questions we asked at the very beginning of our discussion of intelligence: Does the Millionaire game show test for intelligence? Are Genie and Thomas Edison intelligent? As you can see, intelligence is difficult to define and measure. But did you know that college admission officers, scholarship committees, and employers might have used scores from your own intelligence tests in their selection of you as a student or employee? How good are these tests? Are they good predictors of student and employee success? To answer these questions, we first need to introduce three general principles of psychological testing: *standardization,* *reliability,* and *validity.*

Standardization *The process of establishing the norms and uniform procedures for giving and scoring a test*

1. *Standardization.* To be useful, intelligence tests (as well as personality, aptitude, and most other tests) must be *standardized*. The term **standardization** has two meanings as it applies to testing (Groth-Marnat, 1990). First, every test must have *norms*, or average scores. To develop norms, the test is given to a *representative sample* — a large sample of diverse people who resemble those for whom the test was intended. Norms determine whether an individual's particular score is considered high, low, or average in comparison to the representative sample. Second, *testing procedures* must be standardized. Uniform conditions must exist for taking, giving, and scoring the test. All test takers must get the same instructions, questions, and time limits, and those who administer the test must know exactly how to explain the test and must follow specific, objective standards in their scoring.

Reliability *A measure of the consistency and stability of test scores when the test is readministered*

2. *Reliability.* Imagine having a stopwatch or oven temperature guide that gave different readings each time you measured. Obviously, every measuring device (including tests) must be consistent. That is, repeated measurements should produce reasonably similar findings. This stability, or **reliability,** of a test is usually determined by retesting to determine whether test scores have changed significantly (Groth-Marnat, 1990, p. 10). Retesting can be by the *test-retest method,* comparing participants' scores on two separate administrations of a test, or with the *split-half method,* splitting a test into two equivalent parts and comparing the degree of similarity between the two halves (e.g., whether scores from odd and even questions agree).

Validity *The ability of a test to measure what it was designed to measure*

3. *Validity.* The third important principle of test construction is **validity,** the ability of a test to measure what it is designed to measure (Groth-Marnat, 1990, p. 14). There are several types of validity. The most important is *criterion-related validity,* or the accuracy with which test scores can be used to predict another variable of interest, termed the *criterion.* Criterion-related validity is expressed as the *correlation* between the test score and the criterion. (A correlation is a standard measure of how two variables are related.) A high correlation indicates the two variables are closely related, and low or zero correlation indicates there is little or no relationship between them. If two variables are highly correlated, then one variable can be used to predict the other. Thus, if a test is valid, its scores will be useful in predicting people's behavior in some other specified situation, such as using intelligence test scores to predict grades in college.

Can you see why a test that is standardized and reliable, but *not* valid, is worthless? Suppose you are giving someone a test for skin sensitivity. Such a test may be easy to standardize (the instructions specify the exact points on the body to apply the test agent), and it may be reliable (similar results are obtained on each retest), but it would certainly not be valid for predicting college grades.

Although validity is central to a test's success, it is also the core issue in one of the oldest debates in psychology. What are we actually measuring on intelligence tests? If we say we are testing for intelligence but measure only mathematical ability, aren't we by default defining mathematical ability as intelligence? What happens if we only ask questions about acquired knowledge? People with less formal schooling would then be judged as less intelligent. The upcoming section on the origins of intelligence tests will help prepare you for the end-of-module Gender & Cultural Diversity, which explores the current controversy surrounding intelligence tests.

Check & Review

THE NATURE OF INTELLIGENCE AND TEST CONSTRUCTION

Today, **intelligence** is commonly defined as the general capacity to profit from experience, to acquire knowledge, and adapt to changes in the environment. However, there are several theorists who have defined it differently: Spearman viewed intelligence as "g," a general intelligence; Thurstone saw it as seven distinct mental abilities; Guilford believed it was composed of 120 or more separate abilities; and Cattell viewed it as two types of "g," which he called **fluid intelligence** and **crystallized intelligence.**

In addition to these early theorists, Gardner's theory of multiple intelligences identifies eight types of intelligence. He believes that both teaching and assessing should take into account people's learning styles and cognitive strengths. Sternberg's triarchic theory of successful intelligence emphasizes the thinking process rather than the end product (the answer). The Triarchic Theory of Successful Intelligence

identifies three aspects of intelligence: analytical, creative, and practical intelligences.

For any test to be useful, it must be standardized, reliable, and valid. **Standardization** refers to (a) giving a test to a large number of people in order to determine norms and (b) using identical procedures in administering a test so that everyone takes the test under exactly the same testing conditions. **Reliability** refers to the stability of test scores over time. **Validity** refers to how well the test measures what it is intended to measure.

Questions

1. The g factor originally proposed by Charles Spearman is best defined as (a) skill in the use of language as a tool for thought; (b) general intelligence; (c) the ability to adapt to the environment; (d) the type of intelligence we call common sense.

2. What is the difference between fluid and crystallized intelligences?

3. Explain Sternberg's triarchic theory of successful intelligence.

4. Identify which testing principle — standardization, reliability, or validity — is being described in each of the following statements:
   a. This ensures that if the same person takes the same test 2 weeks after taking it the first time, her score will not significantly change.
   b. This ensures that a test or other measurement instrument actually measures what it purports to measure.
   c. This ensures that the test has been given to large numbers of people to determine which scores are average, above average, and below average — in short, which scores are representative of the general population.

Answers to Questions can be found in Appendix B.

Assessing Intelligence: The Development of the IQ Test

There are many different kinds of IQ tests, and each approaches the measurement of intelligence from a slightly different perspective. Most, however, attempt to measure abilities that allow the test to be a valid predictor of academic performance. In other words, most IQ tests are designed to predict grades in school. To see how that's done, let's take a look at the most commonly used IQ tests.

Individual IQ Tests

The first IQ test to be widely used in the United States was the Stanford–Binet Intelligence Scale. It was loosely based on the very first IQ tests developed in France around the turn of the last century by Alfred Binet. In the United States, Lewis Terman (1916) developed the Stanford–Binet (at Stanford University) to test the intellectual ability of U.S.-born children ages 3 to 16. The test is revised periodically — the latest revision was done in 1985. The test items are administered individually (one test-giver and one test-taker) and consist of such tasks as copying geometric designs, identifying similarities, and repeating a sequence of numbers.

In the original version of the Stanford–Binet, results were expressed in terms of a mental age. For example, if a 7-year-old's score equaled that of an average 8-year-old, the child was considered to have a mental age of eight, as measured by the test. To determine the child's **intelligence quotient (IQ)**, mental age was divided by the child's chronological age (actual age in years) and multiplied by 100, as follows:

Intelligence Quotient (IQ) *A score on a test that is intended to measure verbal and quantitative abilities*

Figure 23.3 *The distribution of scores on the Stanford–Binet Intelligence Test.* Notice that over two-thirds of the people taking the test, 68.26 percent, have an IQ within the normal range.

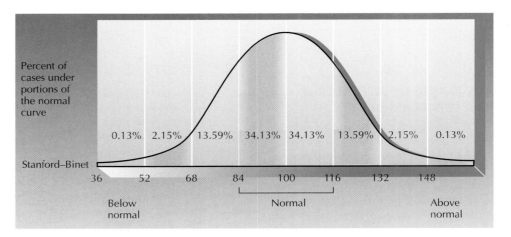

$$IQ = \frac{MA}{CA} \times 100 = \frac{8}{7} \times 100 = 1.14 \times 100 = 114$$

Thus, a 7-year-old with a mental age of 8 would have an IQ of 114. A "normal" child should have a mental age equal to his or her chronological age. (*Normal* in this case refers to the norms or statistics used to standardize the test.)

Today, most intelligence tests, including the Stanford–Binet, no longer compute an IQ. Instead, the test scores are expressed as a comparison of a single person's score to a national sample of similar-aged people. These deviation IQs are computed on the basis of how far the person's score on the test deviates from the national average. On a standardized IQ test such as the Stanford–Binet, the majority of people score within one standard deviation (16 points) above or one standard deviation below the national average, which is 100 points. Figure 23.3 illustrates the typical distribution curve of scores on the Stanford–Binet: The majority (68 percent) of the children taking the test score within the normal range, whereas approximately 16 percent score above 116 and approximately 16 percent score below 84. Even though the actual IQ is no longer calculated, the term *IQ* remains as a shorthand expression for intelligence test scores.

The Wechsler Tests

David Wechsler (pronounced "WEX-ler") developed the most widely used intelligence test, the Wechsler Adult Intelligence Scale (WAIS), in the early 1900s. He later created a similar test for school-age children, the Wechsler Intelligence Scale for Children, third edition (WISC-III; Table 23.3), and one for preschool children, the Wechsler Preschool and Primary Scale (WPPSI).

Like the Stanford–Binet, the Wechsler tests yield an overall intelligence score, but they have separate *verbal* (such as, vocabulary, comprehension, knowledge of general information) and *performance* scores (such as arranging pictures to tell a story, arranging blocks to match a given pattern). Wechsler's approach has three advantages: (1) The WAIS was specifically designed for adults — not children. (2) Different abilities can be evaluated either separately or together. (3) People who are unable to speak or understand English can still be tested. The verbal portion of the test doesn't have to be administered, because each subtest yields its own score.

Have intelligence scores gone up or down over the years? A comparison of intelligence scores over the years indicates that IQ scores increase from one generation to the next, and this increase is found in over 20 different countries (Flynn, 1987, 1999, 2000; Neisser, 1998). Fluid intelligence scores, typically measured with

TABLE 23.3 SUBTESTS OF THE WISC-III

Verbal Subtests	Example[a]
Information	How many senators are elected from each state?
Similarities	How are computers and books alike?
Arithmetic	If one baseball card costs three cents, how much will five baseball cards cost?
Vocabulary	Define *lamp*.
Comprehension	What should you do if you accidentally break a friend's toy?

Performance Subtests	Example[a]

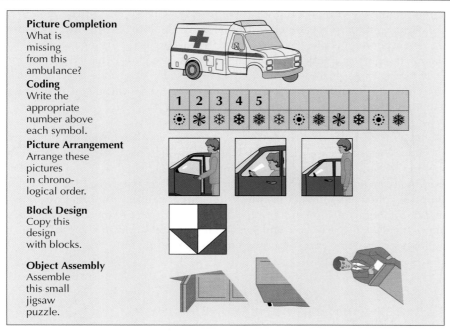

Picture Completion
What is missing from this ambulance?

Coding
Write the appropriate number above each symbol.

Picture Arrangement
Arrange these pictures in chronological order.

Block Design
Copy this design with blocks.

Object Assembly
Assemble this small jigsaw puzzle.

[a] These examples are similar to those used on the actual test.

problem-solving tasks, have increased about 15 points per generation, whereas crystallized intelligence scores, generally assessed by vocabulary and math skills, have increased about 9 points per generation.

The explanation is unclear, but there are at least three possible contributors to this phenomenon, which is termed the *Flynn effect*: (1) the level of public education has increased, (2) people have become more proficient test-takers, and (3) people benefit from better nutrition. James Flynn (1999, 2000) believes such increases may reflect the fact that intelligence tests aren't actually measuring intelligence but rather some weak link to intelligence.

Differences in Intelligence

If you want to judge the validity of any test (academic, intelligence, personality, and so on), one of the best methods is to compare people who score at the extremes. Students who get an A on a major exam should clearly have more information than those who fail. As you will see, the validity of IQ tests is somewhat supported by the fact that individuals who score at the lowest level on standard IQ tests *do* have clear differences in intellectual abilities compared to those who score at the top.

Tests versus GPA. *Although group aptitude tests such as the SAT and ACT are used extensively by colleges and universities in their admissions procedures, high school grade point average is a better predictor of college grades.*

Mental retardation. According to clinical standards, the label *mentally retarded* is applied when someone is significantly below average in general intellectual functioning (IQ less than 70), along with deficits in adaptive functioning (such as communicating with others, living independently, social or occupational functioning, and maintaining safety and health) (American Psychiatric Association, 2000). Mental retardation (like most aspects of human behavior) is on a continuum that ranges from mildly to severely retarded. As you can see in Table 23.4, less than 1 to 3 percent of the general population would be classified as mentally retarded, and of this group, 85 percent are only *mildly* retarded.

Children classified as mildly retarded are not easily distinguished from their classmates until they've been in school for several years. Once they leave academic settings, their mental limits are less noticeable, and many become self-supporting, integrated members of the community. Even those who are part of the moderately retarded group can learn vocational skills that allow them to live in supervised group homes. Furthermore, people can be retarded in most areas yet average or even gifted in others. The most dramatic examples are *savants*, mentally retarded or disturbed people who excel in a specific area, such as rapid calculation, memory, or musical ability. In the movie *Rain Man*, Dustin Hoffman portrayed a savant with exceptional mathematical ability.

What causes mental retardation? Some forms of retardation stem from genetic causes, as is the case with *Down syndrome*, which results from an extra chromosome in the body's cells, and *phenylketonuria* (PKU), which is a metabolic disorder resulting from an inherited enzyme deficiency. If detected early, PKU is treatable by minimizing phenylalanine in the child's diet. Other causes of retardation are environmental, including alcohol and other drug abuse during pregnancy, extreme deprivation or neglect in early life, and postnatal accidents that damage parts of the brain. However, in many cases, there is no known cause.

TABLE 23.4 DEGREES OF MENTAL RETARDATION

Level of Retardation	IQ Scores	Percent of Mentally Retarded Population	Characteristics
Mild	50–70	85	Usually able to become self-sufficient: may marry, have families, and secure full-time jobs in unskilled occupations
Moderate	35–49	10	Able to perform simple unskilled tasks; may contribute to a certain extent to their livelihood
Severe	20–34	3–4	Able to follow daily routines, but with continual supervision; with training, may learn basic communication skills
Profound	below 20	1–2	Able to perform only the most rudimentary behaviors, such as walking, feeding themselves, and saying a few phrases

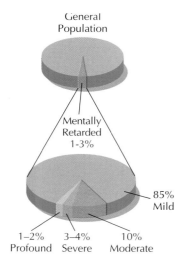

General Population

Mentally Retarded 1-3%

85% Mild

1–2% Profound   3–4% Severe   10% Moderate

An unusual form of intelligence. In the movie Rain Man, Dustin Hoffman portrayed a savant with exceptional mathematical ability.

Mental Giftedness

At the other end of the intelligence spectrum, we have people with especially high IQs (typically defined as being in the top 1 or 2 percent). Have you ever wondered what happens to people with such superior intellectual abilities?

In 1921, Lewis Terman conducted a long-term study of over 1,500 people, age 3 to 28, who scored 135 or better on IQ tests to see how intelligence relates to occupational and social success. By 1950, when their average age was 40, the number of "Terman Kids [a name bestowed by Terman] who became research scientists, engineers, physicians, lawyers, or college teachers, or who were highly successful in business and other fields, was many times the number a random group would have provided" (Terman, 1954, p. 41; Leslie, 2000).

On the other hand, not every member of the group was successful, and there were some notable failures. Nor did a high IQ guarantee a life of wealth or social stature. The members who were the most successful tended to have extraordinary motivation and someone at home or school who was especially encouraging (Goleman, 1980). But, in some respects, they were like others their age in the general public of average intelligence. They became alcoholics, got divorced, and committed suicide at close to the national rate (Leslie, 2000). A high IQ is no guarantee for success in every endeavor. It only offers more intellectual opportunities.

Explaining Differences in Intelligence: Brain, Genes, and the Environment

Some people are mentally gifted, some are mentally retarded, and most are somewhere in between. To explain these differences, we need to look at the brain, genes, and the environment.

How do biology, genetics, and the environment influence intelligence?

The Brain's Influence on Intelligence

A basic tenet of neuroscience is that all mental activity (including intelligence) results from neural activity in the brain. There are three major questions that have guided neuroscience research on intelligence:

1. *Does a bigger brain mean greater intelligence?* It makes logical sense. After all, humans have relatively large brains, and as a species we are more intelligent than dogs, which have smaller brains. Some animals, such as whales and dolphins, do have larger brains than humans, but the brains of humans are larger in relation to the size of our bodies. Since the early 1800s, researchers have asked whether "bigger is better" and modern studies using magnetic resonance imaging (MRI) have found a significant correlation between brain size (adjusted for body size) and intelligence (Andreasen et al., 1993; Rushton & Ankney, 1996). On the other hand, anatomical studies of Einstein's brain found that it was not heavier or larger than normal (Witelson, Kigar, & Harvey, 1999). Some areas were in fact smaller than average, but the area of the brain responsible for processing mathematical and spatial information (the lower region of the parietal lobe) was 15 percent larger. Rather than focusing on brain size, therefore, most of the recent research on the biology of intelligence has focused on the concept of brain functioning.

2. *Is a faster brain more intelligent?* The public seems to think so. As mentioned earlier, the winner of the first million dollars, John Carpenter, also earned the title "fastest finger" in honor of his speedy response. Neuroscientists have found that a faster response time is indeed related to higher intelligence (Bowling & Mackenzie, 1996; Deary & Stough, 1996, 1997). A standard experiment flashes simple images like the one in Figure 23.4 and participants must inspect them quickly and make an accurate decision. As simple as it may seem, those participants who respond most quickly also tend to score highest on intelligence tests.

3. *Does a smart brain work harder?* PET scans measure brain activity by recording the amount of radioactive glucose used in different parts of the brain. (A more active area of the brain uses more glucose than a less active area). Surprisingly, Haier and his research team (1988, 1995) found that areas of the brain involved in problem solving showed *less* activity in people of high intelligence than in people of lower intelligence when given the same problem-solving tasks.

Genetic and Environmental Influences on Intelligence

Like the central tenet of neuroscience (that all behavior is linked to the brain and nervous system), a similar, repeated theme of this text (and most areas of psychology) is that nature and nurture play interacting, *inseparable* roles. In the case of intelligence, any similarities between family members might be due to heredity (family members share similar genetic material) and/or environmental factors (family members share similar living arrangements).

One of the most popular ways to study the relative effects of genetics versus the environment is to use monozygotic (identical, one-egg) twins. Such studies have found significant heredity influences for personality, psychopathology, and intelligence (Andreasen, 2000; Phelps, Davis, & Schartz, 1997; Plomin, DeFries, McClearn, & Rutter, 1997; Plomin, 1999).

Perhaps the most important and most extensive of all twin studies is the Minnesota Study of Twins, which began in 1979 and continues today. For more than two decades, researchers from the University of Minnesota have been studying identical twins that grew up in different homes (Bouchard, 1994, 1999; Bouchard, McGue, Hur, & Horn, 1998; Wright, 1998). Each set of these "reared apart" twins was separated and adopted by different families early in life and reunited only as adults. Because each twin has identical genetic material but was raised in a dif-

(a)

(b)

Figure 23.4 *A test for intelligence?* Which "leg" of the drawing in (a) is longer, the right or the left? Although the answer seems simple, researchers have found that when images like these are flashed for a few milliseconds on a computer screen, the amount of time people need to make correct judgments may reveal something about their intelligence. The second figure (b) appears immediately after figure (a) to block or "mask" the lingering afterimage.

Do intelligent brains work harder? The PET scans in the left column are from a person with a tested low IQ, whereas the scans on the right are from someone with a high IQ. Note that when solving problems, the brain on the left is more active. (Red and yellow indicate more brain activity.) Contrary to popular opinion, this research suggests that lower IQ brains actually work harder than higher IQ brains.

ferent family, researchers have a unique natural experiment that can be used to distinguish the effects of genetics from the effects of the environment. When the IQ data were collected and the statistics computed, researchers found that genetic factors appear to play a surprisingly large role in the IQ score of monozygotic twins reared apart.

How would you critique these findings? First, adoption agencies tend to look for similar criteria in their choice of adoptive parents. Therefore, the homes of these "reared apart" twins were actually quite similar. In addition, these twins also shared the same nine-month prenatal environment, which also might have influenced their intelligence.

Identical twins reared apart. Jerry Levy and Mark Newman, twins separated at birth, first met each other as adults at a firefighter's annual convention.

What about the famous reunited "Jim twins" that had the same name and almost the same personality? This is one of the most widely publicized cases of the entire Minnesota study. These two children were separated 37 days after their birth and reared with no contact until 38 years later. Despite this lifelong separation, James Lewis and James Springer both had divorced and remarried women named Betty, had undergone police training, loved carpentry, vacationed at the same beach each summer, and had named their firstborn sons James Allan and James Alan (Holden, 1980). This is only a short list of their incredible similarities.

Heredity undoubtedly plays an important role, but can you think of other explanations? One study of unrelated pairs of students of the same age and gender found a striking number of similarities (Wright et al., 1984). People of the same age apparently share a common historical time that influences large aspects of their personality. In addition, do you recall our earlier discussion of the *confirmation bias* (the tendency to seek out and pay attention to information that confirms our existing positions or beliefs, while ignoring contradictory data)? Imagine suddenly finding your long lost identical twin. Wouldn't you be highly excited and thrilled with all your similarities and disinclined to note the differences?

As you can see, the research is inconclusive. Although heredity equips each of us with innate intellectual capacities, the environment significantly influences whether a person will reach his or her full intellectual potential. For example, early malnutrition can cause retarded brain development, which in turn affects the child's curiosity, responsiveness to the environment, and motivation for learning — all of which can lower the child's IQ (Ricciuti, 1993). We are reminded once again that nature and nurture are inseparable.

GENDER & CULTURAL DIVERSITY

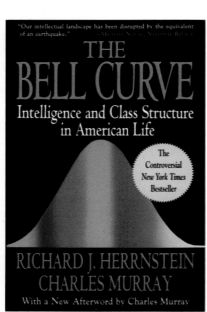

The Bell Curve, Stereotype Threat, and IQ Tests

As mentioned earlier, one of the most hotly debated and controversial issues in psychology has to do with the accuracy of intelligence tests and what group differences in test scores really mean. In 1969, Arthur Jensen began a heated debate when he argued that intelligence is largely genetic in origin and that, therefore, genetic factors are "strongly implicated" as the cause of ethnic differences in intelligence. A book by Richard J. Herrnstein and Charles Murray entitled *The Bell Curve: Intelligence and Class Structure in American Life* reignited this debate in 1994 when the authors claimed that African Americans score below average in IQ because of their "genetic heritage."

Psychologists have responded to these claims with several points:

- Some ethnic minority children do score differently on IQ tests (Blanton, 2001; Herrnstein & Murray, 1994; Rushton & Davison, 2000). In the United States, Asian American children score slightly higher on standardized IQ tests than European American children, who in turn score higher than African American, Latino, or Native American children (Brody, 1992; Lynn, 1995; Williams & Ceci, 1997).

- Members of every ethnic group can be found to have scores at all levels of the IQ scale, the bell curves of all groups show considerable overlap, and IQ scores and intelligence have their greatest relevance in terms of individuals, not groups (Garcia & Stafford, 2000; Myerson, Rank, Raines, & Schnitzler, 1998; Reifman, 2000). For example, many individual African Americans receive higher IQ scores than many individual white Americans. Most importantly, even if a trait is primarily genetic (which does not appear to be the case with intelligence), group differences can still be wholly due to the environment (Figure 23.5).

- Lack of cultural exposure to the concepts required on IQ tests can result in lowered IQ scores. Therefore, the tests may not be an accurate measure of true capability — they may be culturally biased (Blanton, 2001; Domino, 2000; Greenfield, 1997; Naglieri & Ronning, 2000).

- Group differences in IQ may have more to do with socioeconomic differences than ethnicity (McLoyd, 1998; Reifman, 2000). African Americans and most other minorities are far more likely than whites to live in poverty. The environmental effects of poverty, such as poor prenatal care, poorly funded schools, lack of textbooks and other resources, clearly influence intellectual development (Neisser et al., 1996).

- IQ does have a substantial genetic component, and racial and ethnic differences may reflect underlying hereditary differences (Plomin & DeFries, 1998; Plomin, 1999; Sternberg & Kaufman, 1998).

    Note, however, that race and ethnicity, like intelligence itself, are almost impossible to define. For example, depending on the definition that you use, there are between 3 and 300 races, and no race is pure in a biological sense (Beutler et al., 1996; Yee, Fairchild, Weizmann, & Wyatt, 1993).

- Intelligence is not a fixed characteristic. As we discovered earlier, research on the so-called *Flynn effect* shows there has been overall increase in IQ since the early 1900s, and this is far too short a time for genetics to have played a role. (Flynn, 1987, 1998, 1999; Neisser, 1998). Furthermore, there has been a steady increase in the verbal ability scores of African Americans over time and a slight decline for white Americans (Huang & Hauser, 1998).

- Differences in IQ scores also reflect motivational and language factors. For example, in some ethnic groups, a child who excels in school is ridiculed for trying to be different from his or her classmates (Pearson, 1995). Moreover, children grow up speaking the language of their culture and the dialect of their neighborhood. If this language or dialect does not match the education system of which they are a part or the IQ test they take, they are obviously disadvantaged (Tanner-Halverson, Burden, & Sabers, 1993).

- Finally, as we've seen earlier, there are multiple intelligences, and traditional IQ tests do not measure many of them (Gardner, 1999; Sternberg & Kaufman, 1998).

As you can see, there is no clear answer to this debate. The good news is that Herrnstein and Murray's controversial book has provoked more thought and scientific research than any other book on a psychological topic since the 1980s. Perhaps one of the most exciting areas of research spawned by this debate is the idea of **stereotype threats**, which can significantly depress the test performance of people in a wide variety of stereotyped groups (Brown & Josephs, 1999; Inzlicht & Ben-Zeev, 2000; Niemann, 2001).

The central thesis of *stereotype threat* is that an individual's performance on an IQ test depends in part on the individual's expectations about how he or she will do. And these expectations are often shaped by cultural stereotypes about the abilities of an individual's particular age, ethnicity, gender, or socioeconomic class. For example, if the dominant cultural stereotype says, "you can't teach old dogs new tricks" or "women aren't good at math," you can imagine how this might affect many older individuals and women when they take an IQ test.

Claude Steele and Joshua Aronson (1995) first revealed stereotype threat in an experiment at Stanford University. They recruited African American and white students to take a *performance exam* and informed them that their individual intellectual abilities would be examined. Participants were matched on ability levels prior to the exam, and the exam was composed of questions similar to the Graduate Records Exam (GRE). The results revealed that the African American students performed well below the white students. However, when the researchers repeated the same procedure and told students it was a *laboratory task* instead of a performance exam, there was no difference in African American scores and white scores.

Differences <u>within</u> groups are due entirely to genetics (the seed).

SEED

Poor soil   Fertile soil

Differences <u>between</u> groups are due <u>entirely</u> to environment (the soil).

Figure 23.5 *If plants could talk!* Note that even when you begin with the exact same package of seeds (genetic inheritance), the average height of corn plants in the fertile soil will be greater than those in the poor soil (environmental influences). The same is true for intelligence. Therefore, no conclusions can be drawn about possible genetic contributions.

Stereotype Threat *A psychological predicament in which a person experiences doubt about his or her performance, owing to negative stereotypes about his or her group's abilities*

What explains the difference in results? Subsequent work by Steele and others shows that stereotype threat occurs because members of the stereotyped groups doubt their own abilities (Steele, 1992, 1997). Simply being aware that you are not expected to do well lowers your score — you unintentionally fulfill the negative "self-fulfilling prophecy." Members fear that they will be evaluated in terms of the stereotype, and this worry translates into anxiety, which in turn lowers both the speed and accuracy of their responses to test questions. On the other hand, some individuals cope by "disidentifying," saying to themselves, "The test scores have no influence on how I feel about myself" (Major, Spencer, Schmader, Wolfe, & Crocker, 1998). Unfortunately, this attitude also decreases performance because of the lessened motivation.

Studies show that stereotype threat affects the test performance of many groups, including African Americans, women, Native Americans, low-income people, elderly people, and white male athletes (Brown & Josephs, 1999; Croizet & Claire, 1998; Inzlicht & Ben-Zeev, 2000; Niemann, 2001; Steele & Aronson, 1995). This research helps explain some group differences in intelligence and achievement tests. Employers, educators, and clinicians routinely use such tests for many purposes. Yet there is more to intelligence (and achievement) than what is measured by an exam. Relying solely on these tests to make critical decisions affecting individual lives is not warranted and possibly even unethical.

A Final Note

Think back to the questions we asked at the very beginning of our discussion of intelligence: Does the Millionaire game show test for intelligence? Are Genie and Thomas Edison intelligent? How would you answer these questions now? Before answering, let's update our story of Genie. Her life, as you might have guessed, does not have a happy Hollywood ending. Genie's tale is a heartbreaking account of the lasting scars from a disastrous childhood. At the time of her rescue, at age 13, Genie's intellectual performance was at the level of a normal 1-year-old. Over the years, she was given thousands of hours of special training and rehabilitation, and by the age of 19 she could use public transportation and was adapting well to her foster home and special classes at school (Rymer, 1993).

Genie was far from normal, however. Her intelligence scores were still close to the cutoff for mental retardation, and, as noted earlier, her language skills were similar to those of a 2- or 3-year-old. To make matters worse, she was also subjected to a series of foster home placements — one of which was abusive. At last report, Genie was living in a home for mentally retarded adults (Rymer, 1993).

Check & Review

ASSESSING INTELLIGENCE/ EXPLAINING DIFFERENCES IN INTELLIGENCE

Intelligence quotient (IQ) tests do not, and are not intended to, measure overall intelligence. Rather, they are designed to measure verbal and quantitative abilities needed for school success. Several individual IQ tests are in common use. The Stanford–Binet measures primarily verbal abilities of children ages 3 to 16. The Wechsler tests, consisting of three separate tests for three distinct age levels, measure both verbal and nonverbal abilities. People with IQs of 70 and below are identified as mentally retarded, whereas people with IQs of 135 and above are identified as gifted.

Most neuroscientists believe that all mental activity results from neural activity in the brain. Their research on intelligence has focused on three major questions: 1) Does a bigger brain mean greater intelligence? (Answer: "not necessarily.") 2) Is a faster brain more intelligent? (Answer: "a qualified yes." And 3) Does a smart brain work harder? (Answer: "No, the smarter brain is more efficient.")

According to the Minnesota Study of Twins Reared Apart, heredity and environment are important, inseparable factors in intellectual development. Heredity equips each of us with innate capacities, but environment significantly influences whether an individual will reach full potential.

Questions

1. Is IQ a true measure of intellectual ability? Why or why not?

2. What are the major differences between the Stanford–Binet and the Wechsler Intelligence Scales?

3. The more efficient brain uses fewer _____ to solve problems than a less efficient brain. (a) parts of the brain; (b) neurotransmitters; (c) synapses, (d) energy resources

4. Which is more important in determining intelligence — heredity or environment?

Answers to Questions can be found in Appendix B.

ACTIVE LEARNING WORKSHEET   MODULE 23

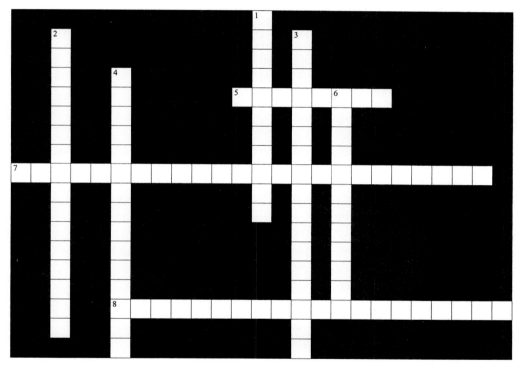

ACROSS

5. Ability of a test to measure what it was designed to measure.

7. Knowledge and learning gained over the course of life through an interaction between fluid intelligence and environmental experience.

8. Score on a test intended to measure verbal and quantitative abilities.

DOWN

1. Measure of the consistency and stability of test scores when the test is readministered.

2. Psychological predicament in which a person experiences doubt about his or her performance, due to negative stereotypes about his or her group's abilities.

3. Capacity for acquiring new knowledge and solving new problems partially determined by biological and genetic factors.

4. Establishing norms and uniform procedures for giving and scoring a test.

6. General capacity to profit from experience, to acquire knowledge, and adapt to changes in the environment.

Answers can be found in Appendix B.

Visual Summary for Modules 21, 22, and 23

Thinking

The Thinking Brain

Thought processes are distributed throughout the brain, but during problem solving and decision making, they are localized in the prefrontal cortex, which is directly connected to the emotional area of the brain—the limbic system. Without this connection, thinking and emotions are disrupted.

Cognitive Building Blocks

1) **Mental images**: Mind's representation of a sensory experience.

2) **Concepts**: Mental representations of a group or category that share similar characteristics. How do we learn concepts? They arise out of logical rules and definitions (artificial concepts), we create natural categories or concepts (**prototypes**), and we organize them into successive ranks (hierarchies).

3) Language: Method of communication.

Solving Problems

Step 1: Preparation	*Step 2: Production*	*Step 2: Evaluation*
• Identify given facts • Separate relevant facts • Define ultimate goal	Create hypotheses using **algorithms** and **heuristics** (means-end analysis, working backward, creating subgoals).	Judge the hypotheses from Step 2 against criteria from Step 1.

Barriers to problems solving: **Mental sets**, **functional fixedness**, and **confirmation bias**. **Incubation**, or time out, may help overcome these barriers.

Creativity

• *Elements of creativity*: Originality, fluency, and flexibility.
• *Measuring creativity*: Assess **divergent thinking** versus **convergent thinking**.
• *Researching creativity*: Investment theory finds creativity is a combination of intellectual ability, knowledge, thinking style, personality, motivation, and environment.

Language

Human language is a creative form of communication consisting of symbols put together according to a set of rules.

Characteristics of Language

Language is produced from words using **phonemes** (basic speech sounds) and **morphemes** (the smallest meaningful units of a language). The words are strung together into sentences using rules of **grammar—syntax** (the grammatical rules for ordering words) and **semantics** (meaning in language). Chomsky believes humans have an innate ability to put words together in a meaningful way, and that every sentence has both a *surface structure* (the words themselves) and a *deep structure* (the actual meaning).

Language (cont).

Language and Thought

According to Whorf's *linguistic relativity hypothesis*, language shapes thought. This theory is generally not supported, but choice of vocabulary can influence mental imagery and social perceptions.

Animals and Language

Apes, dolphins, and other animals have been taught to communicate with humans. Whether they are demonstrating creative language, or merely responding to rewards, is a topic of ongoing debate.

Intelligence

The Nature of Intelligence

Intelligence is the general capacity to profit from experience, to acquire knowledge, and adapt to environmental changes.

Competing theories and definitions:
- Spearman→Intelligence is "g," a general intelligence.
- Thurstone→Intelligence is seven distinct mental abilities.
- Guiliford→Intelligence is composed of 120 or more separate abilities.
- Cattell→Intelligence is two types of "g" (**fluid intelligence** and **crystallized intelligence**).
- Gardner→There are eight types of intelligence.
- Sternberg→Triarchic theory of intelligence (analytical, creative, and practical).

Test Construction

Elements of a useful test:
1) **Standardization**: Test is given to many people to establish norms and identical administrative procedures are used.
2) **Reliability**: The scores are stable over time.
3) **Validity**: The test measures what it is intended to measure.

Assessing Intelligence

Intelligence quotient (IQ) tests do not, and are not intended to, measure overall intelligence. Instead, they are designed to measure verbal and quantitative abilities needed for school success.

- *Stanford–Binet* measures verbal abilities of children ages 3 to 16.
- *Wechsler* measures verbal and nonverbal abilities of three distinct age levels.
- IQs of 70 and below are identified as mentally retarded, whereas IQs of 135 and above are identified as gifted.

Explaining Differences in Intelligence

- Neuroscientists ask: 1) Does a bigger brain mean greater intelligence? Not necessarily. 2) Is a faster brain more intelligent? A qualified yes. 3) Does a smart brain work harder? No, the smarter brain is more efficient.
- The Minnesota Study of Twins Reared Apart found heredity and environment are important, inseparable factors in intellectual development.

Life Span Development I

On April 13, 1997, Tiger Woods won the Masters Championship golf tournament in Augusta, Georgia. What makes this noteworthy? Consider that he was the youngest golfer ever to win the Masters and that he won with the lowest score (270) and by the largest margin ever (12 strokes). This accomplishment was also a first for a player of African or Asian heritage at the Masters — a tournament that had its first African American player only two decades earlier (Lace, 1999; Rosaforte, 2000).

On October 29, 1998, John Glenn spent nine days in the space shuttle Discovery. What makes this exceptional? Consider that he is the oldest human to travel in space and that 36 years earlier, in 1962, he was the first U.S. astronaut to orbit the earth. Moreover, in the years between these two historic flights, he served four terms as a senator from Ohio (Cole, 2000).

The accomplishments of Tiger Woods and John Glenn illustrate not only our need to rethink stereotypes about youth, minorities, and older adults but also the importance of understanding how people grow and develop throughout the entire life span. In this section and the next, we will explore the field of **developmental psychology**, the study of age-related changes in behavior and abilities throughout the life span, from conception to death (Table 24.1).

To emphasize that development is an ongoing, lifelong *process*, we will take a topical approach (as opposed to a chronological approach, which arbitrarily divides study into two periods, childhood–adolescence and adulthood).

Thus, in Modules 24, 25, and 26, we will trace physical, language, social–emotional, and cognitive development — one at a time — from conception to death.

Then, in Modules 27 and 28, we will explore moral development, personality development, and special issues related to death and dying, again, one topic at a time. The topical approach allows us to see how any one aspect of development affects an individual over the entire life span.

Developmental Psychology *The branch of psychology that describes, explains, predicts, and sometimes aims to modify age-related behaviors from conception to death; this field emphasizes maturation, early experiences, and various stages in development*

MODULE 24

STUDYING DEVELOPMENT AND PHYSICAL DEVELOPMENT

How is research in developmental psychology different from research in other areas of psychology?

Maturation *Biological growth processes that enable orderly changes in behavior, relatively uninfluenced by the environment*

Critical Period *A period of special sensitivity to specific types of learning that shapes the capacity for future development*

In all fields of psychology, certain theoretical issues seem to guide the basic direction of research. First, we look at what those issues are in human development, next we will look at how developmental psychologists do research, and then we explore the physical changes that occur over the life span.

Theoretical Issues: Ongoing Debates

The three most important issues or questions in human development are *nature versus nurture, continuity versus stages,* and *stability versus change.*

1. *Nature or nurture.* The issue of "nature versus nurture" has been with us since the beginning of psychology. Even the ancient Greeks had the same debate — Plato arguing for innate knowledge and abilities, and Aristotle, for learning through the five senses. Early philosophers proposed that at birth our minds are a tabula rasa (or blank slate) and that the environment determines what messages are written on the slate.

According to the nature position, human behavior and development are governed by automatic, genetically predetermined signals in a process known as **maturation**. Just as a flower unfolds in accord with its genetic blueprint, we humans crawl before we walk and walk before we run. Furthermore, there is an optimal period shortly after birth, one of several **critical periods**, when an organism's exposure to certain stimuli or experiences produces proper development.

Naturists would therefore say that Tiger Woods's achievements primarily reflect his innate athletic abilities. They would point out that Tiger shot 48 for nine holes at age three, was featured in Golf Digest at age five, and won the Optimist International Junior tournament six times before age 15. On the other side of the debate, those who hold an extreme nurturist position would argue that development occurs by learning through observation and experience. Nurturists would point to the close teaching and strong encouragement from his father and other family members as the major contributors to Tiger's exceptional accomplishments.

TABLE 24.1 LIFE SPAN DEVELOPMENT

Stage	Approximate Age
Prenatal	Conception to birth
Infancy	Birth to 18 months
Early childhood	18 months to 6 years
Middle childhood	6–12 years
Adolescence	12–20 years
Young adulthood	20–45 years
Middle adulthood	45–60 years
Later adulthood	60 years to death

2. *Continuity or stages.* Continuity proponents say development is continuous, with new abilities, skills, and knowledge gradually added at a relatively uniform pace. The continuity model, then, suggests that adult thinking and intelligence differ quantitatively from a child's. We simply have more math skills or verbal skills, for example. Stage theorists, on the other hand, believe development occurs at different rates, alternating between periods of little change and periods of abrupt, rapid change. In this group of modules and the next, we will discuss several stage theories: Piaget's theory of cognitive development, Erikson's psychosocial theory of personality development, and Kohlberg's theory of moral development.

3. *Stability or change.* Have you generally maintained your personal characteristics as you matured from infant to adult (stability)? Or does your current personality bear little resemblance to the personality you displayed during infancy (change)? Psychologists who emphasize stability in development hold that measurements of personality taken during childhood are important predictors of adult personality (Caspi, 2000; McCrae et al., 2000). Of course, psychologists who emphasize change disagree.

Which of these positions is more correct? Most psychologists do not take a hard line either way. Rather, they prefer an *interactionist perspective.* In the *nature or nurture* debate, for example, psychologists generally believe that development emerges from each individual's unique genetic predisposition and from individual experiences in the environment (Gottlieb, 2000; Maccoby, 2000). Similarly, the *continuity versus stage* question is not a matter of "either-or." Physical development and motor skills, for example, are believed to be primarily continuous in nature, whereas cognitive skills usually develop in discrete stages. Finally, research on *stability versus change* also shows that the answer is somewhere in the middle: Some traits are stable, whereas others vary greatly across the life span.

We will return to these three questions several times. Now we turn our attention to another aspect of studying development — how developmental psychologists collect their information.

Research Methods: Two Basic Approaches

To study development, psychologists use either a *cross-sectional* or *longitudinal* method. The **cross-sectional method** examines individuals of various ages (20, 40, 60, and 80 years) at one point in time — and gives information about age differences. The **longitudinal method** follows a single individual or group of individuals (for example, only 20-year-olds) over an extended period of time and gives information about age changes (Figure 24.1).

Imagine you are a developmental psychologist interested in studying intelligence in adults. Which method would you choose — cross-sectional or longitudinal? Before you decide, note the different research results shown in Figure 24.2.

Researchers suggest that the different results may reflect a central problem with cross-sectional studies. They often confuse genuine age differences with *cohort effects,* differences that result from specific histories of the age group studied (Elder, 1998). The decline in intelligence found in cross-sectional research might reflect early educational experiences rather than a true effect of aging. We cannot tell. Age effects and cohort effects are hopelessly tangled.

Longitudinal studies also have their limits. They are expensive in terms of time and money, and their results are restricted in *generalizability.* Because participants

Cross-Sectional Method *A technique of data collection that measures individuals of various ages at one point in time and gives information about age differences*

Longitudinal Method *A data collection technique that measures a single individual or group of individuals over an extended period and gives information about age changes*

Figure 24.1 *Cross-sectional versus longitudinal research.* Note that cross-sectional research uses different participants and is interested in age-related differences, whereas longitudinal research studies the same participants over time to find age-related changes.

often drop out or move away during the extended test period, the experimenter may end up with a self-selected sample that differs from the general population in important ways. As you can see in Table 24.2, each method of research has its own strengths and weaknesses. Keep these differences in mind when you read the findings of developmental research.

Before leaving the topic of research, let's examine the unique contributions cultural psychologists have made to the field of developmental studies.

Figure 24.2 Cross-sectional studies have historically shown that intelligence reaches its peak in early adulthood and then gradually declines. Longitudinal studies have found that a marked decline in intelligence does not begin until about age 60 (Schaie, 1994). How would you explain the differences? (Adapted from Schaie, 1994, with permission.)

TABLE 24.2 ADVANTAGES AND DISADVANTAGES OF CROSS-SECTIONAL AND LONGITUDINAL RESEARCH DESIGNS

	Cross-Sectional	Longitudinal
Advantages	Gives information about age differences Quick Less expensive Typically larger sample	Gives information about age changes Increased reliability More in-depth information per participant
Disadvantages	Cohort effects Restricted generalizability (measures behaviors at only one point in time)	More expensive Time consuming Restricted generalizability (typically smaller sample and dropouts over time)

GENDER & CULTURAL DIVERSITY

Cultural Psychology's Guidelines for Developmental Research

How would you answer the following question: "If you wanted to predict how a human child anywhere in the world was going to grow up, what his or her behavior was going to be like as an adult, and you could have only one fact about that child, what fact would you choose to have?"

According to cultural psychologists like Patricia Greenfield (1994, 2000), the answer to this question should be "culture." Yet developmental psychology has traditionally studied people (children, adolescents, and adults) with little attention to the sociocultural context (Brislin, 2000; Valsiner, 2000). In recent times, however, psychologists are paying increasing attention to the following points:

1. ***Culture may be the most important determinant of development.*** If a child grows up in an individualistic/independent culture (such as North America or most of western Europe), we can predict this child will probably be competitive and question authority as an adult. Were this same child reared in a collectivist/interdependent culture (common in Africa, Asia, and Latin America), she or he would most likely grow up to be cooperative and respectful of elders (Delgado-Gaitan, 1994; Segall, Dasen, Berry, & Portinga, 1990).

2. ***Human development, like most areas of psychology, cannot be studied outside its sociocultural context.*** In parts of Korea, most teenagers see a strict, authoritarian style of parenting as a sign of love and concern (Kim & Choi, 1995). Korean American and Korean Canadian teenagers, however, see the same behavior as a sign of rejection. Thus, rather than studying specific behaviors, such as "authoritarian parenting styles," researchers in child development suggest that children should be studied only within their *developmental niche* (Harkness & Super, 1996). A developmental niche has three components: the physical and social contexts in which the child lives, the culturally determined rearing and educational practices, and the psychological characteristics of the parents (Bugental & Johnston, 2000).

3. ***Each culture's ethnotheories are important determinants of behavior.*** Within every culture, people have a prevailing set of ideas and beliefs that attempts to explain the world around them (an *ethnotheory*) (Rosenthal & Roer-Strier, 2001). In the area of child development, for example, cultures have specific ethnotheories about how children should be trained. As a critical thinker, you can anticipate that differing ethnotheories can lead to problems between cultures. Even the very idea of "critical thinking" is part of our North American ethnotheory regarding education. And it, too, can produce culture clashes.

If you would like a personal demonstration of the invisibility of culture, try this simple experiment: The next time you walk into an elevator, don't turn around. Remain facing the rear wall. Watch how others respond when you don't turn around, or if you stand right next to them rather than walk to the other side of the elevator. Our North American culture has rules that prescribe the "proper" way to ride in an elevator, and people become very uncomfortable when these rules are violated.

Cultural influences on development. How might these two groups differ in their physical, social–emotional, cognitive, and personality development?

Concha Delgado-Gaitan (1994) has found that Mexican immigrants from a rural background have a difficult time adjusting to North American schools, which teach children to question authority and think for themselves. In their culture of origin, these children are trained to respect their elders, be good listeners, and participate in conversation only when solicited. Children who argue with adults are reminded not to be *malcriados* (naughty or disrespectful).

4. ***Culture is largely invisible to its participants.*** Culture consists of ideals, values, and assumptions that are widely shared among a given group and that guide specific behaviors (Brislin, 2000). Precisely because these ideals and values are widely shared, they are seldom discussed or directly examined. We take our culture for granted, operating within it, although being almost unaware of it.

Check & Review

STUDYING DEVELOPMENT

Developmental psychology is concerned with describing, explaining, predicting, and sometimes modifying age-related behaviors across the entire life span. Three important research issues are *nature or nurture, continuity or stages,* and *stability or change.*

Researchers in developmental psychology generally do **cross-sectional** (different participants of various ages at one point in time) or **longitudinal studies** (same participants over an extended period). Each method has advantages and disadvantages.

Cultural psychologists suggest that developmental researchers keep the following points in mind:

• Culture is the most important determinant of development.
• Human development cannot be studied outside its sociocultural context.
• Each culture's ethnotheories are important determinants of behavior.
• Culture is largely invisible to its participants.

Questions

1. Briefly define *developmental psychology.*

2. What three major questions are studied in developmental psychology?

3. Differences in age groups that reflect factors unique to a specific age group are called _____ effects. (a) generational; (b) social–environmental; (c) operational; (d) cohort

4. _____ studies are the most time-efficient method, whereas _____ studies provide the most in-depth information per participant. (a) Correlational, experimental; (b) Fast-track, follow-up; (c) Cross-sectional, longitudinal; (d) Cohort-sequential, cohort-intensive

Answers to Questions can be found in Appendix B.

Physical Development: Conception to Death

Perhaps the most obvious aspects of development are physical growth and changes in body proportions and size. In this section, we will look at two separate periods of life: prenatal and early childhood (characterized by rapid change) and adolescence and adulthood (a time of both dramatic and gradual physical change).

Prenatal and Early Childhood

Do you remember being a young child and feeling it would "take forever to grow up?" Contrary to a child's sense of time, the early years of development are a time of rapid and unparalleled change. In fact, if you continued to develop at the same rapid rate that marks the first 2 years of life, you would weigh several tons and be over 12 feet tall as an adult! Thankfully, physical development slows, yet it is important to note that change continues until the very moment of death.

Prenatal Physical Development Your prenatal development began at *conception*, when your mother's egg, or ovum, united with your father's *sperm* cell. At that time, you were a single cell barely $1/175$ of an inch in diameter — smaller than the period at the end of this sentence (Figure 24.3). This new cell, called a *zygote*, then began a process of rapid cell division that resulted in a multimillion-celled infant (you) some 9 months later.

The vast changes that occur during the 9 months of a full-term pregnancy are usually divided into three stages (Figure 24.4). The **germinal period** begins with fertilization and ends with implantation of the rapidly dividing mass of cells (the zygote) in the wall of the uterus. The outer portion of the zygote forms part of the placenta and umbilical cord, whereas the inner portion becomes the *embryo*. The **embryonic period**, the second stage, begins after implantation and lasts through the eighth week. During this time, the embryo's major organ systems begin to develop. The final stage is the **fetal period**, from the end of the second month until birth. During this period, the *fetus* continues to grow and the organs begin to function. Prenatal growth, as well as growth the first few years after birth, is *proximodistal* (near to far), with the head and upper body developing before the lower body.

Hazards to Prenatal Development During pregnancy, the placenta (connected to the embryo and fetus by the umbilical cord) serves as the link for food and excretion of wastes, and it screens out some, but not all, harmful substances. Environ-

> What are the major physical changes that occur throughout the life span?

Germinal Period *The first stage of pregnancy (conception to 2 weeks) characterized by rapid cell division*

Embryonic Period *The second stage of pregnancy (from uterine implantation through the eighth week), characterized by development of major body organs and systems*

Fetal Period *The third, and final, stage of prenatal development (eight weeks to birth), characterized by rapid weight gain in the fetus and the fine detailing of body organs and systems*

Figure 24.3 *The moment of conception.* (a) Note the large number of sperm surrounding the ovum. (b) Although a "joint effort" is required to break through the outer coating, only one sperm will actually fertilize the egg.

(a)   (b)

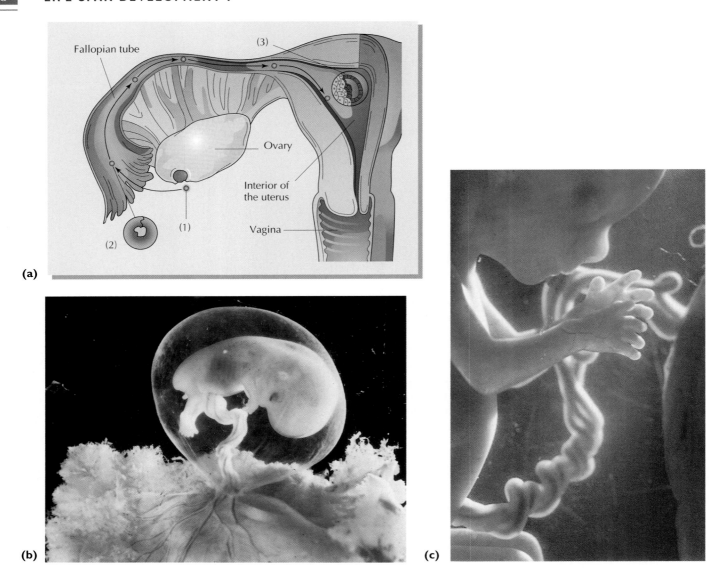

Figure 24.4 (*a*) *From ovulation to implantation.* After discharge from either the left or right ovary (number 1 on the diagram), the ovum travels to the opening of the fallopian tube. If fertilization occurs (2), it normally takes place in the first third of the fallopian tube. The fertilized ovum is referred to as a *zygote*. When the zygote reaches the uterus, it implants itself in the wall of the uterus (3) and begins to grow tendril-like structures that intertwine with the rich supply of blood vessels located there. After *implantation*, the organism is known as an *embryo*. (*b*) *Embryonic period.* This stage occurs from implantation to 8 weeks. At 8 weeks, the major organ systems have become well differentiated. Note that at this stage, the head grows at a faster rate than other parts of the body. (*c*) *Fetal stage.* This is the period from the end of the second month to birth. At four months all the actual body parts and organs are established. The fetal stage is primarily a time for increased growth and "fine detailing."

mental hazards such as X-rays or toxic waste, drugs, and diseases such as rubella can cross the *placental barrier* (Table 24.3). These influences generally have their most devastating effect during the first 3 months of pregnancy — making this a *critical period* in development.

The pregnant mother obviously plays a primary role in prenatal development, because her health directly influences the child she is carrying. Furthermore, almost everything she ingests can cross the placental barrier (a better term might

TABLE 24.3 SAMPLE ENVIRONMENTAL CONDITIONS THAT ENDANGER THE CHILD

Maternal Factors	Possible Effects on Embryo, Fetus, Newborn, or Young Child
Malnutrition	Low birth weight, malformations, less-developed brain, greater vulnerability to disease
Stress exposure	Low birth weight, hyperactivity, irritability, feeding difficulties
Exposure to X-rays	Malformations, cancer
Legal and illegal drugs	
Thalidomide	Hearing defects, deformed limbs, death
Androgens	Masculinization of female fetus
Diethylstilbestrol	Uterine and vaginal abnormalities in female fetus, possible carcinogenesis in male and female fetus, infertility
Analgesics	Respiratory depression
Aspirin in large doses	Respiratory depression
Tetracycline	Inhibition of bone growth, discolored teeth
Streptomycin	Hearing loss
Narcotics	Growth deficiency, withdrawal syndrome, central nervous system and respiratory depression, death
Nicotine	Low birth weight, increased fetal heart rate, premature birth, increased risk of spontaneous abortion, fetal death
Alcohol	Fetal alcohol syndrome (growth deficiency, developmental lag, mental retardation); increased risk of spontaneous abortion, fetal death, attention deficits in childhood
Cocaine	Increased risk of spontaneous abortion, withdrawal syndrome, erratic emotions in infants
Marijuana	Increased tremors and startles among newborns and poorer verbal and memory development at 4 years of age
Diseases	
German measles (rubella)	Blindness, deafness, mental retardation, heart malformation
Herpes, AIDS (acquired immunodeficiency syndrome), other STDs (sexually transmitted diseases)	Brain infection, death, spontaneous abortion, premature birth, mental retardation
Toxoplasmosis	Miscarriage, mental retardation, low birth weight, malformations

Fetal alcohol syndrome. This child was born with fetal alcohol syndrome (FAS). Note the wide-set eyes and thin upper lip. These subtle facial abnormalities, as well as defective limbs and heart, result from the mother's heavy alcohol consumption during pregnancy. Many children with FAS are also below average in intelligence.

Sources: Abadinsky, 2001; Butler, Joel, & Jeffries, 2000; Doweiko, 1999; Rybacki & Long, 1999; Watson, Mednick, Huttunen, & Wang, 1999.

AMERICAN CANCER SOCIETY

Why start life under a cloud?

be *placental sieve*). However, the father also plays a role — other than just fertilization. Environmentally, the father's smoking may pollute the air the mother breathes, and genetically, he may transmit heritable diseases. In addition, recent research suggests alcohol, opiates, cocaine, various gases, lead, pesticides, and industrial chemicals can all damage sperm (Pollard, 2000; Raloff, 1999).

Perhaps the most important, and generally avoidable, danger to the developing fetus comes from drugs — both legal and illegal (Abadinsky, 2001; Butler, Joel, & Jeffries, 2000; Pollard, 2000). Nicotine and alcohol are two major **teratogens**, environmental substances that can cause birth defects. Mothers who smoke tobacco have significantly higher rates of premature births, low-birth-weight infants, and fetal deaths (American Cancer Society, 2000; Day, Richardson, Goldschmidt, & Cornelius, 2000; Windham, Hopkins, Fenster, & Swan, 2000). Smoking during pregnancy has also been linked to lower IQ scores for children (Bower, 1999).

Alcohol also readily crosses the placenta, affects fetal development, and can result in a neurotoxic syndrome called **fetal alcohol syndrome** (FAS). Prenatal exposure to alcohol can cause facial abnormalities and stunted growth. But the most disabling features of FAS are neurobehavioral problems, ranging from hyperactivity and learning disabilities to mental retardation, depression, and psychoses. Recent research suggests that these problems may be due to widespread neuron death and reduced brain mass caused by alcohol's effect on two important brain neurotransmitters, glutamate and GABA (gamma aminobutyric acid) (Ikonomidou et al., 2000).

Teratogen [TER-ah-toh-jen] *An external, environmental agent that can cross the placental barrier and disrupt development, causing minor or severe birth defects; the term comes from the Greek word teras, meaning "malformation"*

Fetal Alcohol Syndrome (FAS) *A combination of birth defects, including organ deformities and mental, motor, and/or growth retardation, that results from maternal alcohol abuse*

Early Childhood Physical Development Although Shakespeare described newborns as capable of only "mewling and puking in the nurse's arms," they are actually capable of much more. In this section, we will explore three areas of change in early childhood: *brain, motor,* and *sensory/perceptual development.*

1. *Brain development.* The brain and other parts of the nervous system grow faster than any other part of the body during both prenatal development and the first 2 years of life. A newborn's brain is one-fourth its full adult size and will grow to about 75 percent of its adult weight and size by the age of 2 years. At age 5 years, the child's brain is nine-tenths its full adult weight (Figure 24.5).

Figure 24.5 *Body proportions.* Notice how body proportions change as we grow older. At birth, an infant's head is one-fourth their body's size, whereas in adulthood, the head is one-eighth.

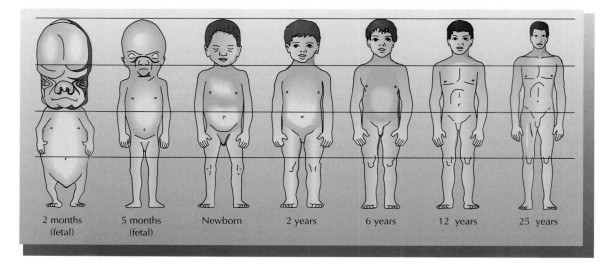

| 2 months (fetal) | 5 months (fetal) | Newborn | 2 years | 6 years | 12 years | 25 years |

It is generally believed that the newborn's brain contains most of the neurons it will ever have. Further brain development and learning occur primarily because neurons grow in size and because the number of axons and dendrites, as well as the extent of their connections, increases (DiPietro, 2000). The brain reaches its full adult weight by about age 16, but *myelination*, the accumulation of fatty tissue coating the axons of nerve cells, continues until early adulthood. Given that myelin increases the speed of neural impulses, the speed of information processing shows a corresponding increase. In addition, synaptic connections in the frontal lobes and other parts of the brain continue growing and changing throughout the entire life span.

2. *Motor development.* Compared to the hidden, internal changes in brain development, the orderly emergence of active movement skills, known as *motor development*, is easily observed and measured. The newborn's first motor abilities are limited to *reflexes,* involuntary responses to stimulation. For example, the rooting reflex occurs when something touches a baby's cheek: The infant will automatically turn its head, open its mouth, and root for a nipple.

In addition to simple reflexes, the infant soon begins to show voluntary control over movements of various body parts. As you can see in Figure 24.6, a helpless newborn that cannot even lift her head is soon transformed into an active toddler capable of crawling, walking, and climbing.

3. *Sensory and perceptual development.* At birth, a newborn can smell most odors and distinguish between sweet, salty, and bitter tastes. Breastfed newborns also recognize and show preference for the odor and taste of their mother's milk over another mother's (DiPietro, 2000). The newborn's sense of touch and pain is also highly developed, as evidenced by reactions to heel pricks for blood testing and circumcision (Williamson, 1997).

The sense of vision, however, is poorly developed. At birth, a newborn is estimated to have vision between 20/200 and 20/600 (Haith & Benson, 1998). If you have normal 20/20 vision, you can imagine what the infant's visual life is like. The level of detail you see at 200 or 600 feet is what they see at 20 feet. Within the first

Maturation and motor development. Some Hopi Indian infants spend a great portion of their first year of life being carried in a cradleboard, rather than crawling and walking freely on the ground. Yet by age one, their motor skills are very similar to those of infants who have not been restrained in this fashion (Dennis & Dennis, 1940).

Chin up — 2.2 mo.
Rolls over — 2.8 mo.
Sits with support — 2.9 mo.
Sits alone — 5.5 mo.
Stands holding furniture — 5.8 mo.
Walks holding on — 9.2 mo.
Stands alone — 11.5 mo.
Walks alone — 12.1 mo.
Walks up steps — 17.1 mo.

Figure 24.6 *Milestones in motor development.* In the typical progression of motor abilities, "chin up" occurs at age 2.2 months and walking up stairs at 17.1 months. However, no two children are exactly alike; all follow their own individual timetable for physical development. (Adapted from Frankenburg et al., 1992, with permission.)

Figure 24.7 *Can a fetus learn before birth?* This father apparently thinks so. He is using a special device called a "pregaphone" to talk to his baby.

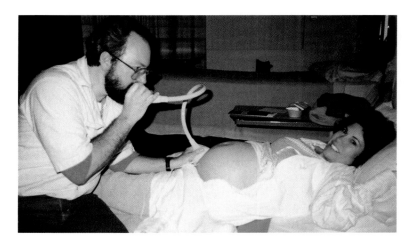

few months, vision quickly improves, and by six months, it is 20/100 or better. At 2 years, visual acuity reaches a near-adult level of 20/20 (Courage & Adams, 1990).

One of the most interesting findings in infant sensory and perceptual research concerns hearing. Not only can the newborn hear quite well at birth (Matlin & Foley, 1997) but also, during the last few months in the womb, the fetus can apparently hear sounds outside the mother's body (Vaughan, 1996). This raises the interesting possibility of fetal learning, and some doctors have advocated special stimulation for the fetus as a way of increasing intelligence, creativity, and general alertness (e.g., Van de Carr & Lehrer, 1997). Devices such as the "pregaphone" have been specially designed to help eager parents talk to their babies before birth (Figure 24.7).

Studies on possible fetal learning have found that newborn infants easily recognize their own mother's voice over that of a stranger. They also show preferences for children's stories (such as *The Cat in the Hat* or *The King, the Mice, and the Cheese*) that were read to them while they were still in the womb (DeCasper & Fifer, 1980; DeCasper & Spence, 1986; Trotter, 1987). On the other hand, some experts caution that too much or the wrong kind of stimulation before birth can be stressful for both the mother and fetus (Diamond & Hopson, 1998). They suggest that the fetus gets what it needs without any special stimulation.

How can scientists measure perceptual abilities and preferences in such young babies? Newborns and infants obviously cannot talk or follow directions, so researchers have had to create ingenious experiments to evaluate their perceptual skills. One of the earliest experimenters, Robert Fantz (1956, 1963), designed a "looking chamber" in which infants lie on their backs and look at visual stimuli (Figure 24.8).

Researchers also use newborns' heart rate and innate abilities, such as the sucking reflex, to study how they learn and how their perceptual abilities develop. To study the sense of smell, researchers measure changes in the newborns' heart rates when different odors are presented. Presumably, if they can smell one odor but not the other, their heart rate will change in the presence of the first but not the second. From research such as this, we now know that the senses develop very early in life.

Adolescence and Adulthood

Whereas the adolescent years are marked by dramatic changes in appearance and physical capacity, middle age and later adulthood are times of gradual physical changes. We begin with a look at adolescence.

Figure 24.8 *Fantz's "looking chamber."* Using this specially designed testing apparatus, Fantz and his colleagues measured the length of time infants stared at various stimuli. They found that infants preferred complex rather than simple patterns and pictures of faces rather than nonfaces.

Adolescence Think back for a moment to your teen years. Were you concerned about the physical changes you were going through? Did you worry about how you differed from your classmates? Changes in height and weight, breast development and menstruation for girls, and a deepening voice and beard growth for boys are important milestones for adolescents. **Puberty**, the period of life when a person becomes capable of reproduction, is a major physical milestone for everyone. It is a clear biological signal of the end of childhood.

Although commonly associated with puberty, *adolescence* is the loosely defined psychological period of development between childhood and adulthood. In the United States, it roughly corresponds to the teenage years. It is important to recognize that adolescence, like childhood, is not a universal concept. Some nonindustrialized countries have no need for such a slow transition, and children simply assume adult responsibilities as soon as possible.

The clearest and most dramatic physical sign of puberty is the *growth spurt,* characterized by rapid increases in height, weight, and skeletal growth (Figure 24.9), and significant changes in reproductive structures and sexual characteristics. Maturation and hormone secretion cause rapid development of the ovaries, uterus, and vagina and the onset of menstruation (*menarche*) in the adolescent female. In the adolescent male, the testes, scrotum, and penis develop, and he undergoes *spermarche* (the first ejaculation). The ovaries and testes in turn produce hormones that lead to the development of *secondary sex characteristics,* such as the growth of pubic hair, deepening of the voice, growth of facial hair, growth of breasts, and so on (Figure 24.10).

Once the large and obvious pubertal changes have occurred, further age-related physical changes are less dramatic. Other than some modest increase in height and muscular development during the late teens and early twenties, most individuals experience only minor physical changes until middle age.

Middle Age For women, *menopause,* the cessation of the menstrual cycle, which occurs somewhere between ages 45 and 55, is the second most important life milestone in physical development. The decreased production of estrogen (the dominant female hormone) produces certain physical changes. However, the popular belief that menopause (or "the change of life") causes serious psychological mood swings, loss of sexual interest, and depression is *not* supported by current research (Morrison & Tweedy, 2000; Stewart & Ostrove, 1998).

Puberty *The period in life when sex organs mature and sexual reproduction becomes possible; puberty generally begins for girls around ages 10 to 12, and for boys, about 2 years later*

Figure 24.9 *Adolescent growth spurt.* Note the gender differences in height gain during puberty. Most girls are about 2 years ahead of boys in their growth spurt and therefore are taller than most boys between the ages of 10 and 14.

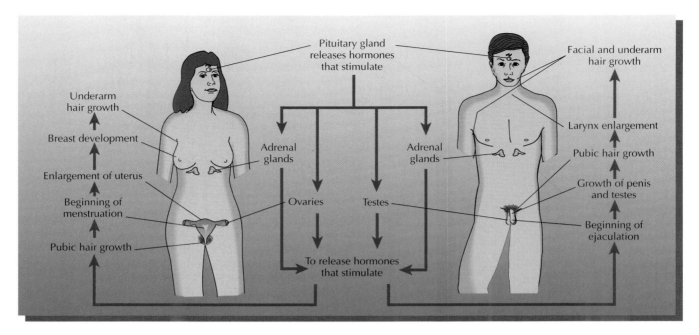

Figure 24.10 *Secondary sex characteristics.* Complex physical changes in puberty result primarily from hormones secreted from the ovaries and testes, the pituitary gland in the brain, and adrenal glands near the kidneys.

Beginning in middle adulthood, men experience a gradual decline in the production of sperm and testosterone (the dominant male hormone), although they may remain capable of reproduction into their eighties or nineties. Physical changes such as unexpected weight gain, decline in sexual responsiveness, loss of muscle strength, and graying or loss of hair may lead some men (and women as well) to feel depressed and to question their life progress. They often see these alterations as a biological signal of aging and mortality (Powell, 1998). Such physical and psychological changes in men are known as the *male climacteric*.

Late Adulthood

After middle age, most physical changes in development are gradual and occur in the heart and arteries and sensory receptors. For example, cardiac output (the volume of blood pumped by the heart each minute) decreases, whereas blood pressure increases due to the thickening and stiffening of arterial walls. Visual acuity and depth perception decline, hearing acuity lessens, especially for high-frequency sounds, and smell sensitivity decreases (Atchley & Kramer, 2000; Medina, 1996).

This all sounds depressing. Can anything be done about it? Television, magazines, movies, and advertisements generally portray aging as a time of graying hair, balding pates, sagging parts, poor vision and hearing, and, of course, no sex life. Recent research, however, shows that getting old may be better than we think. For example, a group of Dutch scientists (Lamberts, van den Beld, & van der Lely, 1997) believe the loss of muscle strength and physical frailty commonly seen in people as they age is neither inevitable nor irreversible. Their research suggests that hormone replacement treatment for both men and women can greatly offset the effects of osteoporosis, heart disease, Alzheimer's disease, and several

a Maya Angelou delivered a poem for President Clinton's Inauguration.
b Sojourner Truth received in White House by President Abe Lincoln for her work as an abolitionist and advocate of women's rights.
c Galileo Galilei made his last astronomical discoveries.
d Senator John H.Glenn, Jr. becomes the world's oldest space traveler.
e Dr. Rita Levi-Montalcini shared the 1986 Nobel Prize for physiology and medicine.
f Grandma Moses, who first began to paint in her seventies, gave her first one-person show.
g Ralph Vaughan Williams debuted his *9th Symphony*.
h Gloria Stuart in her *Titanic* acting comeback becomes Hollywood's oldest Oscar nominee.
i Philosopher Bertrand Russell published his autobiography.

Figure 24.11 *Achievement in later years.* Note the high level of productivity among some of the world's most famous figures late in their lifetime.

other age-related diseases. Scientists do caution, however, that hormone replacement therapy is still controversial and that more studies are needed on long-term risks and benefits.

What about people who have inherited genetic tendencies toward Alzheimer's disease and other serious diseases of old age? There's good news on this front, too. Scientists Caleb Finch and Rudolf Tanzi (1997) have found that genes have a "relatively minor effect" on our well-being in later years. They discovered that lifestyle and environmental factors (like exercise and good nutrition) "may profoundly influence the outcomes of aging." As we discovered in the section opener's description of John Glenn, for many individuals the later years of life are their most productive (Figure 24.11).

If we set aside contributions from *secondary aging* (changes resulting from disease, disuse, or neglect), we are left with studies of *primary aging* (gradual, inevitable age-related changes in physical and mental processes). There are two main theories explaining primary aging and death — programmed theory and damage theory (Cristofalo, 1996; Medina, 1996; Wallace, 1997).

According to the *programmed theory,* aging is genetically controlled. Once the ovum is fertilized, the program for aging and death is set and begins to run. Researcher Leonard Hayflick (1977, 1996) found that human cells seem to have a built-in life span. After about 50 doublings of laboratory-cultured cells, they cease to divide — they have reached the *Hayflick limit.*

The other explanation of primary aging is *damage theory,* which proposes that an accumulation of damage to cells and organs over the years ultimately causes death. Whichever theory is correct, human beings appear to have a maximum life span of about 110 to 120 years. Although we can try to control secondary aging in an attempt to reach that maximum, so far we have no means to postpone primary aging.

Use it or lose it? Research shows exercise may be the most important factor in maintaining mental and physical abilities throughout the life span.

Check & Review

PHYSICAL DEVELOPMENT

The prenatal period of development consists of three major stages: the **germinal**, **embryonic**, and **fetal**. Fetal development can be affected by environmental influences. Poor prenatal nutrition is a leading cause of birth defects, and most prescription and over-the-counter drugs are potentially **teratogenic** (capable of producing birth defects). Doctors advise pregnant women to avoid all unnecessary drugs, especially nicotine and alcohol.

During the prenatal period and the first year of life, the brain and nervous system grow faster than any other part of the body. Early motor development (crawling, standing, and walking) is largely the result of maturation. The sensory and perceptual abilities of newborns are relatively well developed.

At **puberty**, the adolescent becomes capable of reproduction and experiences a sharp increase in height, weight, and skeletal growth because of the pubertal growth spurt. Both men and women experience bodily changes in middle age. Many changes in women are related to the hormonal effects of menopause; similar psychological changes in men are called the male climacteric.

Although many of the changes associated with physical aging (such as decreases in cardiac output and visual acuity) are the result of primary aging, others are the result of abuse, disuse, and disease — secondary aging. Physical aging may be genetically built in from the moment of conception (programmed theory), or it may result from the body's inability to repair damage (damage theory).

Questions

1. What are the three stages of prenatal development?

2. Teratogens are _____ that can cause birth defects. (a) DNA fragments; (b) environmental agents; (c) recessive genes; (d) dominant genes

3. The period of life when an individual first becomes capable of reproduction is known as _____. (a) the age of fertility; (b) adolescence; (c) puberty; (d) the adolescent climacteric

4. What is the difference between primary and secondary aging?

Answers to Questions can be found in Appendix B.

ACTIVE LEARNING WORKSHEET   MODULE 24

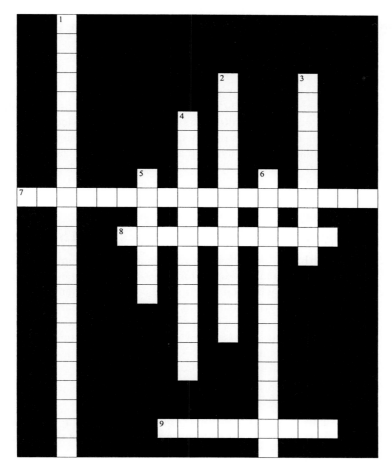

ACROSS

7. Data collection technique measuring a single individual or group of individuals over an extended period and producing information about age changes.

8. Third stage of prenatal development (eight weeks to birth).

9. External, environmental agent that can cross the placental barrier and cause minor or severe birth defects.

DOWN

1. Branch of psychology that studies age-related behaviors from conception to death.

2. Period of special sensitivity to specific types of learning.

3. Biological growth processes that enable orderly changes in behavior and are relativel uninfluenced by the environment.

4. First stage of pregnancy (conception to two weeks).

5. Period in life when sex organs mature and sexual reproduction becomes possible.

6. Second stage of pregnancy (from uterine implantation through the eighth week).

Answers can be found in Appendix B.

MODULE 25
LANGUAGE AND SOCIAL-EMOTIONAL DEVELOPMENT

What makes humans unique? Some believe it is our complex language, which allows us to label and organize the world around us, to communicate with others, and to transmit our entire civilization's accumulated knowledge from one generation to the next. Others think it is our social nature. The human infant is the most dependent of all animals, and all babies in all cultures do best when they develop intense bonds with their caregivers. But how do humans develop language? What happens if infants do not attach to those who care for them? How do parenting styles affect a child's personality? These are questions we will explore in this module.

How do children develop language?

Language Development: Stages and Theories

From birth, the child has a multitude of ways to communicate. Through such non-verbal means as facial expressions, eye contact, and body gestures, babies only hours old begin to "teach" their parents and caregivers when and how they want to be held, fed, and played with. As early as the late 1800s, Charles Darwin proposed that most emotional expressions, such as smiles, frowns, and looks of disgust, are universal and innate (Figure 25.1). Darwin's contention is supported by the fact that children who are born blind and deaf exhibit the same facial expressions for emotions that sighted and hearing children do.

Stages of Language Development

Eventually, children also communicate verbally. The first, *prelinguistic stage* begins with the newborn baby's reflexive cry. Within a short time, crying becomes more purposeful. At least three distinct patterns have been identified: the basic hunger cry, the anger cry, and the pain cry (Wolff, 1969). Although many child-care texts suggest that each of these cries can be easily identified and responded to by the primary caregivers, most parents find that they must learn through a process of trial and error what actions will satisfy their child.

At about age 2 to 3 months, babies begin **cooing**, producing vowel-like sounds ("ooooh" and "aaaah"). Around ages 4 to 5 months they start **babbling**, adding con-

Cooing *Vowel-like sounds infants produce beginning around age 2 to 3 months*

Babbling *Vowel/consonant combinations that infants begin to produce at about age 4 to 6 months*

Figure 25.1 *Early nonverbal communication.* Can you identify these emotions? Infants as young as 2.5 months at age can express several basic emotions, including interest, joy, anger, and sadness.

sonants to their vowels ("bahbahbah" and "dahdahdah"). Some parents mark babbling as the beginning of language and consider their child's vocalizations as "words," even though the child typically does not associate a "word" with a specific object or person, and despite the fact that all children the world over babble in the same fashion.

The true *linguistic stage* begins toward the end of the first year of life, when babbling begins to sound more like the language of the child's home and when the child seems to understand that sound is related to meaning. At the beginning of this stage, the child is generally limited to a single-utterance vocabulary such as "mama," "go," "juice," or "up." Children manage to get a lot of mileage out of these singular utterances: "Mama" can be used to mean, "I want you to come and get me," "I'm hurt," and "I don't like this stranger." However, their vocabulary more than doubles once they begin to express themselves by joining words into short phrases such as "Go bye-bye," "Daddy milk," and "No night-night!"

At this age, children sometimes overextend the words they use. **Overextension** is using words to include objects that do not fit the word's meaning. For example, having learned the word *doggie*, a child often overextends the word to include all small, furry animals (e.g., kittens, bunnies).

Around age 2 years, most children are creating short but intelligible sentences by linking several words. However, they leave out nonessential, connecting words: "Me want cookie;" "Grandma go bye-bye?" This pattern is called **telegraphic speech** because, like telegrams of days gone by, children's speech includes only words directly relevant to meaning, and nothing more.

While increasing their vocabulary at a phenomenal rate during these early years, children are also acquiring a wide variety of rules for grammar, such as adding *-ed* to indicate the past tense and *s* to form plurals. They also make mistakes, however, because they **overgeneralize**, or *overuse* the basic rules of grammar. This results in novel sentences like "I goed to the zoo" and "Two mans." (Study tip: If you're having difficulty differentiating between *overextension* and *overgeneralization*, remember the *g* in *overgeneralize* as a cue that this term applies to problems with *grammar*.)

By age 5 years most children have mastered the basic rules of grammar and typically use about 2,000 words. (Many foreign-language instructors consider this level of mastery adequate for getting by in any given culture.) Past this point, vocabulary and grammar acquisition gradually improve throughout the entire life span.

Theories of Language Development

What motivates children to develop language? Some theorists believe language capability is innate, whereas others claim it is learned through imitation and reinforcement (the nature-versus-nurture controversy again). Although there are staunch supporters of both sides, most psychologists find neither of these extreme positions satisfactory. Most believe that language acquisition is a combination of both nature and nurture — the interactionist position (Casti, 2000; Gottlieb, 2000).

According to the nativist position, language acquisition is primarily a matter of maturation. The most famous advocate of this viewpoint, Noam Chomsky (1968, 1980), suggests that children are born "prewired" to learn language. They possess a type of **language acquisition device** (LAD) that needs only minimal exposure to adult speech to unlock its potential. The LAD enables the child to analyze language and unconsciously extract the basic rules of grammar.

To support his viewpoint, Chomsky points to the fact that children all over the world go through similar stages in language development at about the same age and in a pattern that parallels motor development. He also cites the facts that babbling is the same in all cultures and that deaf babies babble just like hearing babies.

Although the nativist position enjoys considerable support, it fails to adequately explain individual differences. Why does one child learn rules for English, for exam-

Overextension *A child's tendency to define a word too broadly, to include objects that do not fit the word's meaning*

Telegraphic Speech *The two- or three-word sentences of young children that contain only the most necessary words*

Overgeneralize *A common error in language acquisition where the child overuses the basic rules of grammar; the rules for past tense and plurals are extended to irregular forms (e.g., they may say mans instead of men.)*

Language Acquisition Device (LAD) *In Noam Chomsky's view, the child's inborn brain capacity to analyze language and unconsciously understand essential grammatical rules* ple, whereas another learns rules for Spanish? The "nurturists" can explain individual differences and distinct languages. From their perspective, children learn language through a complex system of rewards, punishments, and imitation. Any vocalization attempt ("mah" or "dah") from the young infant is quickly rewarded with smiles and other forms of encouragement. When the infant later babbles "mama" or "dada," proud parents respond even more enthusiastically. (As a critical thinker, can you see how these parents are unknowingly using a type of *shaping* — a term we discussed in Module 16?)

Check & Review

LANGUAGE DEVELOPMENT

Children go through two stages in their acquisition of language: prelinguistic (crying, **cooing**, **babbling**) and linguistic (which includes single utterances, **telegraphic speech**, and the acquisition of rules of grammar).

Nativists believe that language is an inborn capacity and develops primarily by maturation. Noam Chomsky suggests that humans possess a **language acquisition device** (LAD) that needs only minimal environmental input. Nurturists emphasize the role of the environment and suggest that language development results from rewards, punishments, and imitating models.

Questions

1. How is "cooing" different from "babbling"?
2. Children make errors like "mouses" and "goed" versus "mice" and "went" because they _____ the rules of grammar. (a) ignore; (b) haven't learned; (c) overextend; (d) overgeneralize
3. Noam Chomsky believes we possess an inborn ability to learn language known as a _____. (a) telegraphic understanding device (TUD); (b) language acquisition device (LAD); (c) language and grammar translator (LGT); (d) overgeneralized neural net (ONN)
4. Compare and contrast the nature versus the nurture position on language development.

Answers to Questions can be found in Appendix B.

Social–Emotional Development: Attachment and Parenting Styles

The poet John Donne wrote, "No man is an island, entire of itself." In addition to physical and language development, developmental psychologists are very interested in social–emotional development. That is, they study how human beings become *entire* with the help of other human beings. Two of the most important topics in social–emotional development are those of *attachment* and *parenting styles*.

Attachment and The Importance of Early Bonds

An infant arrives in the world with a multitude of behaviors that encourage a strong bond of attachment with primary caregivers. **Attachment** can be defined as an active, intense, enduring emotional relationship that is specific to two people. Although most research has focused on the attachment between mother and child, fathers, grandparents, and other caretakers may also form attachment bonds with an infant.

In studying attachment behavior, researchers are often divided along the lines of the now-familiar nature-versus-nurture debate. Those who advocate the innate or biological position cite John Bowlby's work (1969, 1989, 2000). He proposed that newborn infants are biologically equipped with verbal and nonverbal behaviors (such as crying, clinging, smiling) and with "following" behaviors (such as crawling and walking after the caregiver) that serve to elicit certain instinctive nurturing responses from the caregiver. The biological argument for attachment is also supported by Konrad Lorenz's (1937) studies of **imprinting**. Lorenz's studies

Attachment *An active, intense, emotional relationship between two people that endures over time*

Imprinting *An innate or instinctual form of learning in which the young of certain species follow and become attached to large moving objects (usually their mothers)*

demonstrated how baby geese attach to, and then follow, the first large moving object they see during a certain critical period in their development.

Feeding or Contact Comfort? According to Freud, infants become attached to the caregiver that provides oral pleasure (Module 35). But is there scientific evidence to support Freud's claim? In what is now a classic experiment, Harry Harlow and Robert Zimmerman (1959) set out to experimentally investigate the variables that might affect attachment. They started by creating two types of wire-framed *surrogate* (substitute) "mother" monkeys: one covered by soft terry cloth and one left uncovered. The infant monkeys were fed by either the cloth or the wire mother and had access to both mothers (Figure 25.2).

Harlow and Zimmerman found those monkeys who were "reared" by a cloth mother spent significant amounts of time clinging to the soft material of their surrogate mother. They also developed greater emotional security and curiosity than did monkeys assigned to the wire mother. Monkeys who were given free choice of both mothers also showed strong attachment behaviors toward the cloth mother — even when the wire-framed mother provided all food!

Further evidence of the importance of contact comfort came from later research by Harlow and Harlow (1966), in which monkey babies were exposed to various forms of rejection. Some of the "mothers" contained metal spikes that would suddenly protrude from the cloth covering and push the babies away; others had air jets that would sometimes blow the babies away. Nevertheless, the infant monkeys waited until the rejection was over and then clung to the cloth mother as tightly as before.

On the basis of these and related findings, Harlow concluded that what he called *contact comfort,* the pleasurable tactile sensations provided by a soft and cuddly "parent," is a powerful contributor to attachment. The satisfaction of other physical needs, such as food, is not enough.

Is contact comfort similarly important between human mothers and infants? Several studies suggest that it may be. Touching and massaging premature infants, for example, produce significant physical and emotional benefits (de Roiste & Bushnell, 1996; Drummond, 1998). Touch elicits positive emotions and attention from almost all babies (Pelaez-Nogueras, Gewirtz, Field, & Cigales, 1996). Mothers around the world tend to kiss, nuzzle, nurse, comfort, clean, and respond to their children with lots of physical contact.

Japanese mothers and their children are rarely separated during the first months of life. They touch their infants to communicate with them, breast-feed, carry them around on their backs, and take baths with them. Japanese infants do not even sleep in separate beds (Matsumoto, 2000). Mayan children sleep alongside their mothers for several years. If a new baby comes along, the older child moves to a bed in the same room or shares a bed with another family member (Morelli, Oppenheim, Rogoff, & Goldsmith, 1992).

In short, attachment seems to depend, at least in part, on the hugging, cuddling, and caresses babies naturally receive from their mothers. We use the word *mother* because almost all research in this area has focused on mothers and their infants. However, research also shows the same results apply to fathers and other caregivers (Lopez, Melendez, & Rice, 2000; Peters & Day, 2000; van IJzendoorn & De Wolff, 1997).

What happens if a child does not form an attachment? Researchers have investigated this question in two ways: They have looked at children and adults who spent their early years in institutions without the stimulation and love of a regular caregiver or who lived at home but were physically isolated under abusive conditions (Zeanah, 2000).

Figure 25.2 *Contact comfort and attachment.* Harlow and Zimmerman found that infant monkeys spent more time on the terry-cloth-covered "mother," even when it was the wire "mother" that provided food. They concluded that contact comfort, rather than feeding, was the most important determinant of a monkey's attachment to its caregiver.

Imprinting and attachment. These ducklings are following scientist Konrad Lorenz because they instinctually form a strong attachment to the first large moving object they see. Usually it is the mother duck, but in this case it was Lorenz.

Is contact comfort biological? When nestled next to a hen or held in a person's cupped hands, chicks will almost immediately "relax" and close their eyes.

Infants raised in impersonal or abusive surroundings suffer from a number of problems. They seldom cry, coo, or babble; they become rigid when picked up; and they have few language skills. As for their social–emotional development, they tend to form shallow or anxious relationships. Some appear forlorn, withdrawn, and uninterested in their caretakers, whereas others seem insatiable in their need for affection (Zeanah, 2000). They also tend to show intellectual, physical, and perceptual retardation; increased susceptibility to infection; and neurotic "rocking" and isolation behaviors; in some cases, they die from lack of attachment (Belsky & Cassidy, 1994; Bowlby, 1973, 1982, 2000; Spitz & Wolf, 1946).

Levels of Attachment Although most children are never exposed to extreme institutional conditions, Mary Ainsworth and her colleagues (1967, 1978) have found significant differences in the typical level of attachment between infants and their mothers. Moreover, *level of attachment* affects long-term behaviors. Using a method called the *strange situation procedure*, a researcher observes infants in the presence or absence of their mother and a stranger. Ainsworth found that children could be divided into three groups: *securely attached, avoidant,* and *anxious/ambivalent.*

1. *Securely attached* (65%). When exposed to the stranger, the infant seeks closeness and contact with the mother, uses the mother as a safe base from which to explore, shows moderate distress on separation, and is happy when the mother returns.

2. *Avoidant* (25%). The infant does not seek closeness or contact with the mother, treats the mother much like a stranger, and rarely cries when the mother leaves the room.

3. *Anxious/Ambivalent* (10%). The infant becomes very upset as the mother leaves the room and when she returns seeks close contact, then squirms angrily to get away.

Ainsworth found that infants with a secure attachment style have caregivers that are sensitive and responsive to their signals of distress, happiness, and fatigue (Ainsworth et al., 1967, 1978; van IJzendoorn & DeWolff, 1997). On the other hand, avoidant infants had caregivers that were aloof and distant, and anxious/ambivalent infants had inconsistent caregivers that alternated between strong affection and indifference.

Can you see why infants who are securely attached generally develop feelings of emotional security and trust in others? Or why avoidant infants learn to avoid others and suppress their attachment needs, whereas anxious/ambivalent infants tend to be temperamental and anxious that others will not return their affection? It is not surprising that follow-up studies found securely attached children were the most sociable, enthusiastic, cooperative, persistent, curious, and competent (Goldberg, 2000; Jacobsen & Hofmann, 1997).

Evaluating Attachment Theories Although Hazan and Shaver's research and similar studies are consistent with infant attachment theory, the results are correlational rather than experimental. And as you know from Module 2, it is always risky to infer causation from correlation. Accordingly, the relationship between romantic love style and early infant attachment is subject to several alternative causal explanations. Further research is necessary before we fully understand the link between infant attachment and adult intimate relationships.

Also, be aware that early attachment experiences may predict the future but do not determine it. Despite the significance of the initial infant–parent attachment bond, we are capable of learning new social skills and different attitudes toward relationships in our later interactions with peers, close friends, lovers, and spouses. Unlike diamonds, attachment styles are not necessarily forever.

Friendship and attachment. These 50-year-old women have remained close friends since kindergarten. Despite heavy schedules, they get together at least once a year for a "summer reunion."

RESEARCH HIGHLIGHT

Romantic Love and Attachment

If you've been around young children, you've probably noticed how often they share toys and discoveries with a parent and seem much happier when a parent is near. You've probably also thought how cute and sweet it is when infants and parents coo and share baby talk with each other. But have you noticed that these very same behaviors often occur between you and your adult romantic partner?

Intrigued by these parallels, several researchers have studied the relationship between an infant's attachment to a parent figure and an adult's love for a romantic partner (Bachman & Zakahi, 2000; Klohnen & Bera, 1998). In one study, Cindy Hazan and Phillip Shaver (1987, 1994) discovered that adults who had an avoidant pattern in infancy are uncomfortable with intimacy as adults. They find it hard to trust others, difficult to self-disclose, and rarely report finding "true love" (Cooper, Shaver, & Collins, 1998; Fraley & Shaver, 1997). Anxious/ambivalent adults also have difficulty with intimate relationships, but unlike avoidants, they tend to be obsessed with their romantic partners, fearing their intense love will not be reciprocated. Individuals who are securely attached as infants easily become close to others, expect intimate relationships to endure, and perceive others as generally trustworthy.

Would you like to test your own attachment style? Thinking of your current and past romantic relationships, place a check next to those statements that best describe your feelings.

1. I find it relatively easy to get close to others and am comfortable depending on them and having them depend on me. I don't often worry about being abandoned or about someone getting too close.
2. I am somewhat uncomfortable being close. I find it difficult to trust partners completely or to allow myself to depend on them. I am nervous when anyone gets close, and love partners often want me to be more intimate than is comfortable for me.
3. I find that others are reluctant to get as close as I would like. I often worry that my partner doesn't really love me or won't stay with me. I want to merge completely with another person, and this desire sometimes scares people away.

According to research, 55 percent of adults agree with item 1 (*secure attachment*), 25 percent choose number 2 (*avoidant attachment*), and 20 percent choose item 3 (*anxious/ambivalent attachment*) (adapted from Fraley & Shaver, 1997; Hazan & Shaver, 1987; Shaver & Hazan, 1994). Note that the percentages for these adult attachment styles are roughly equivalent to the percentages for infant–parent attachment.

What your responses to this test may mean is that avoidant and anxious/ambivalent adults have developed intimacy patterns

The importance of attachment. Researchers have found that the degree and quality of attachments you formed as an infant may carry over to your adult romantic relationships.

from their early childhood experiences that frustrate, if not destroy, adult love relationships. The avoidant lover may block intimacy by being emotionally aloof and distant, whereas the anxious/ambivalent lover may smother intimacy by being possessive and emotionally demanding.

As you may expect, the securely attached lover has intimacy patterns that foster long-term relationships and is the most desired partner by the majority of adults, regardless of their own attachment styles (Klohnen & Bera, 1998; Pietromonaco & Carnelley, 1994). Studies of adult attachment are significant because they suggest our earliest bonding experiences may have lasting effects. Bowlby (1979), in fact, believed attachment behaviors "characterize human beings from the cradle to the grave" (p. 129).

Parenting Styles

How much of our personality comes from the way our parents treat us as we are growing up? Researchers since the 1920s have studied the effects of different methods of child rearing on children's behavior, development, and mental health. Recent studies done by Diana Baumrind (1980, 1995) found that parenting styles could be reliably divided into three broad patterns: *authoritarian, permissive,* and *authoritative.*

1. ***Authoritarian.*** These parents value unquestioning obedience and mature responsibility from their children, while remaining aloof and detached. An authoritarian parent might say, "Don't ask questions. Just do it my way or else." Children of authoritarian parents are easily upset, moody, aggressive, and generally have poor communication skills.

Are fathers important? Although overlooked in the past, the father's role in a child's development is now a topic of active research.

2. Permissive. Permissive parents come in two styles: (a) *permissive-indifferent,* the parent who sets few limits and provides little in the way of attention, interest, or emotional support, and (b) *permissive-indulgent,* the parent who is highly involved but places few demands or controls on the child. Children of permissive-indifferent parents have poor self-control (becoming demanding and disobedient) and poor social skills. Children of permissive-indulgent parents often fail to learn respect for others and tend to be impulsive, immature, and out of control.

3. Authoritative. These parents are caring and sensitive toward their children, but they also set firm limits and enforce them, while encouraging increasing responsibility. As you might expect, children do best under the authoritative parents. They become self-reliant, self-controlled, and high achieving. They also seem more content, friendly, and socially competent in their dealings with others (Baumrind, 1995; Parke & Buriel, 1998).

Evaluating Baumrind's Research Before you conclude that the authoritative pattern is the only way to raise successful children, you should know that many children raised in the other styles also become caring, cooperative adults. Criticism of Baumrind's findings generally falls into three areas: *child temperament, child expectations,* and *parental warmth:*

1. Child temperament. Results may reflect the child's unique temperament and reactions to parental efforts rather than the parenting style per se (Clarke-Stewart, Fitzpatrick, Allhusen, & Goldberg, 2000; McCrae et al., 2000). That is, the parents of mature and competent children may have developed the authoritative style because of the child's behavior rather than vice versa.

2. Child expectations. Cultural research suggests that a child's expectations of how parents should behave also plays an important role in parenting styles (Brislin, 2000; Valsiner, 2000). As we discovered at the beginning of Module 24, adolescents in Korea expect strong parental control and interpret it as a sign of love and deep concern. Adolescents in North America, however, would interpret the same behavior as a sign of parental hostility and rejection.

3. Parental warmth. Cross-cultural studies suggest that the most important variable in parenting styles and child development might be the degree of warmth versus rejection parents feel toward their children. On the basis of analyses of over 100 societies, Rohner (1986) concluded that universally, parental rejection adversely affects a child. The neglect and indifference shown by rejecting parents tend to produce hostile, aggressive children who have a difficult time establishing and maintaining close relationships. These children are also more likely to develop psychological problems that require professional intervention (Brook, Richter, and Whiteman, 2000; Giancola, 2000).

Do fathers differ from mothers in their parenting style? Until recently, the father's role in discipline and child care was largely ignored. But as more fathers have begun to take an active role in child rearing, there has been a corresponding increase in research. From these studies, we now know that fathers are absorbed with, excited about, and responsive to their newborns and that there are few differences in the way children form attachments to either parent (Biller, 1993; Lamb, 1996). After infancy, the father becomes increasingly involved with his children, yet he still spends less overall time in direct child care than the mother does (Demo, 1992; Hewlett, 1992). But fathers are just as responsive, nurturing, and competent as mothers when they do assume child-care responsibilities.

Check & Review

SOCIAL-EMOTIONAL DEVELOPMENT

Nativists believe that **attachment** is innate, whereas nurturists believe it is learned. The Harlow and Zimmerman experiments with monkeys raised by cloth or wire surrogate mothers found that contact comfort might be the most important factor in attachment.

Infants who fail to form attachments may suffer serious effects. When attachments are formed, they may differ in level or degree. Research on securely attached, avoidant, and anxious/ambivalent children found significant differences in behaviors that may persist into adulthood.

Parenting styles fall into three major categories: authoritarian, permissive, and authoritative. Critics suggest that a child's unique temperament, their expectations of parents, and the degree of warmth versus rejection from parents may be the three most important variables in parenting styles.

Questions

1. According to Harlow and Zimmerman's research with cloth and wire surrogate mothers, _____ is the most important variable for attachment. (a) availability of food; (b) contact comfort; (c) caregiver and infant bonding; (d) imprinting

2. List the three types of attachment reported by Mary Ainsworth.

3. Using Hazan and Shaver's research on adult attachment styles, match the following adults with their probable type of infant attachment:

____ 1. Mary is nervous around attractive partners and complains that lovers often want her to be more intimate than she finds comfortable.

____ 2. Bob complains that lovers are often reluctant to get as close as he would like.

____ 3. Rashelle finds it relatively easy to get close to others and seldom worries about being abandoned.

(a) avoidant; (b) secure; (c) anxious/ambivalent

4. Briefly summarize Baumrind's three parenting styles.

Answers to Questions can be found in Appendix B.

ACTIVE LEARNING WORKSHEET   MODULE 25

Enter the correct letter from Column A in the blank space in Column B, and then doublecheck your answers with those in Appendix B.

Column A
a. Telegraphic Speech
b. Babbling
c. Overextension
d. Attachment
e. Overgeneralize
f. Imprinting
g. Cooing
h. Authoritarian
i. Authoritative
j. Language Acquisition Device (LAD)

Column B
1. ___ Caring and sensitive, but sets firm limits.
2. ___ Innate attachment to large moving objects.
3. ___ Calling all men "Daddy."
4. ___ Values unquestioning obedience.
5. ___ Vowel-consonants, such as "ma-ma-ma-ma."
6. ___ Intense, enduring bond between two people.
7. ___ Vowel-like sounds, such as "ee-ee-ee-ee."
8. ___ Asking, "Dada go bye-bye?"
9. ___ Saying "foots" instead of "feet."
10. ___ Innate capacity to acquire language and grammar.

MODULE 26
COGNITIVE DEVELOPMENT

How does cognition, or the way we think about the world, change during the life cycle?

The following fan letter was written to Shari Lewis (1963), a children's television performer, about her puppet Lamb Chop:

> Dear Shari:
>
> All my friends say Lamb Chop isn't really a little girl that talks. She is just a puppet you made out of a sock. I don't care even if it's true. I like the way Lamb Chop talks. If I send you one of my socks will you teach it how to talk and send it back?
>
> Randi

Randi's understanding of fantasy and reality is certainly different from an adult's. Just as a child's body and physical abilities change, his or her way of knowing and perceiving the world also grows and changes. This seems intuitively obvious, but early psychologists — with one exception — focused on physical, emotional, language, and personality development. The one major exception was Jean Piaget (pronounced Pee-ahzhay).

Piaget demonstrated that a child's intellect is fundamentally different from an adult's (Flavell, 1999; Papert, 1999). He showed that an infant begins at a cognitively "primitive" level and that intellectual growth progresses in distinct stages, motivated by an innate need to know. Piaget's theory, developed in the 1920s and 1930s, has proven so comprehensive and insightful that it remains the major force in the cognitive area of developmental psychology today.

To appreciate Piaget's contributions, we need to consider three major concepts: schemas, assimilation, and accommodation. **Schemas** are the most basic units of intellect. They act as patterns that organize our interactions with the environment, like architect's drawings or builder's blueprints.

In the first few weeks of life, for example, the infant apparently has several schemas based on the innate reflexes of sucking, grasping, and so on. These schemas are primarily motor and may be little more than stimulus-and-response mechanisms — the nipple is presented and the baby sucks. Soon, however, other schemas emerge. The infant develops a more detailed schema for eating solid food, a different schema for the concepts of "mother" and "father," and so on. It is important to recognize that schemas, our tools for learning about the world, are enlarged and changed throughout our lives (Leahy and Harris, 1997). For example, a computer user previously accustomed to DOS (disk operating system, a text-based format) would need to develop new schemas in order to work with Windows (a graphic user interface).

Assimilation and accommodation are the two major processes by which schemas grow and change over time. **Assimilation** is the process of taking in new information that easily fits into an existing schema. For instance, infants use their sucking schema not only in sucking nipples but also in sucking blankets or fingers.

Accommodation occurs when new information or stimuli cannot be assimilated and new schemas are developed or when old schemas are changed to adapt to the new features. An infant's first attempt to eat solid food with a spoon is a good example of accommodation. When the spoon first enters her mouth, the child attempts to assimilate it by using the previously successful sucking schema — shaping lips and tongue around the spoon as around a nipple. After repeated trials, she accommodates by adjusting her lips and tongue in a way that moves the food off the spoon and into her mouth.

Schema *Cognitive structures or patterns consisting of a number of organized ideas that grow and differentiate with experience*

Assimilation *The process of responding to a new situation in the same manner that is used in a familiar situation*

Accommodation *The process of adjusting existing ways of thinking (reworking schemas) to encompass new information, ideas, or objects*

Study the "impossible figure" below. Now take out a piece of paper and try to draw the same figure (without tracing!). Students with artistic training generally find it relatively easy to reproduce, whereas the rest of us find it "impossible." This is because we lack the necessary artistic *schema* and cannot *assimilate* what we see. With practice and training, we could *accommodate* the new information and easily draw the figure.

Stages of Cognitive Development: Birth to Adolescence

As a result of assimilation, accommodation, and the corresponding changes in schemas, a child's cognitive abilities undergo an orderly series of increasingly complex changes. When enough changes have occurred, the individual experiences a large developmental shift in his or her point of view. Piaget called these developmental shifts cognitive stages in development (Table 26.1).

According to Piaget, all children go through the same four cognitive stages at approximately the same age, regardless of the culture in which they live. No stage can be skipped, because skills acquired at earlier stages are essential to mastery at later stages. Let's take a closer look at these four stages: sensorimotor, preoperational, concrete operational, and formal operational.

The Sensorimotor Stage

During the **sensorimotor stage**, lasting from birth until "significant" language acquisition (about age 2 years), children explore the world and develop their schemas primarily through their senses and motor activities — hence the term *sensorimotor*.

One important concept acquired during this stage is **object permanence**. At birth and for the next 3 or 4 months, children lack object permanence. They seem to have no schemas for objects that disappear from their vision — out of sight is truly out of mind (Figure 26.1).

Preoperational Stage

During the **preoperational stage** (roughly ages 2 to 7 years), language advances significantly, and the child begins to think *symbolically* — using symbols, such as

Sensorimotor Stage *The first of Piaget's stages (birth to approximately age two years), in which cognitive development takes place by exploring the world via sensory perceptions and motor skills*

Object Permanence *A Piagetian term for an infant's understanding that objects (or people) continue to exist even when they cannot be seen, heard, or touched directly*

Preoperational Stage *The second of Piaget's stages (roughly ages 2 to 7 years), characterized by the ability to employ significant language and to think symbolically, but the child lacks operations (reversible mental processes), and thinking is egocentric and animistic*

Can you guess this child's stage of cognitive development? Can you see why this stage is called "sensorimotor"?

Figure 26.1 *Object permanence.*
According to Piaget, young infants lack *object permanence* — an understanding that objects continue to exist even when they cannot directly be seen, heard, or touched. The baby in these pictures seems to believe the toy no longer exists once it is blocked by the screen.

Egocentrism *The inability to consider another's point of view, which Piaget considered a hallmark of the preoperational stage*

THE FAMILY CIRCUS®   By Bil Keane

"Look what I can do, Grandma!"

Reprinted with special permission of King Features Syndicate.

TABLE 26.1 PIAGET'S FOUR STAGES OF COGNITIVE DEVELOPMENT

Birth to 2 years	**Sensorimotor** Abilities: Uses senses and motor skills to explore and develop cognitively. Limits: Beginning of stage lacks *object permanence* (understanding things continue to exist even when not seen, heard, or felt).
Ages 2–7 years	**Preoperational** Abilities: Has significant language and thinks symbolically. Limits: • Cannot perform "operations." • *Egocentric* thinking (inability to consider another's point of view). • *Animistic* thinking (believing all things are living).
Ages 7–11 years	**Concrete Operational** Abilities: • Can perform "operation" on concrete objects. • Understands *conservation* (realizing thoughts and changes in shape or appearance can be reversed). Limits: Cannot think abstractly and hypothetically.
Ages 11 years and up	**Formal Operational** Abilities: Can think abstractly and hypothetically. Limits: *Adolescent egocentrism* at the beginning of this stage, with related problems of the *personal fable* and *imaginary audience*.

words, to represent concepts. On the other hand, there are also three major "problems" or limits to the child's thinking:

1. *Cannot perform operations.* Piaget labeled this period "preoperational" because the child lacks *operations*, reversible mental processes. For instance, if a preoperational boy who has a brother is asked, "Do you have a brother?" He will easily respond, "Yes." However, when asked, "Does your brother have a brother?" he will answer, "No!" To understand that his brother has a brother, he must be able to *reverse* the concept of "having a brother."

2. *Egocentric thinking.* Children at this stage have difficulty understanding that there are points of view other than their own. **Egocentrism** refers to the preoperational child's limited ability to distinguish between his or her own perspective and someone else's. The preschooler who moves in front of you to get a better view of the TV or repeatedly asks questions while you are talking on the telephone is demonstrating egocentrism. They assume that others see, hear, feel, and think exactly as they do. Consider the following telephone conversation between a 3-year-old, who is at home, and her mother, who is at work:

Mother: Emma is that you?

Emma: (Nods silently).

Mother: Emma, is Daddy there? Can I speak to him?

Emma: (Twice nods silently).

Egocentric preoperational children fail to understand that the phone caller cannot see their nodding head.

3. *Animistic thinking.* Children in the preoperational stage believe that objects such as the sun, trees, clouds, and bars of soap have motives, feelings, and intentions (for example, "dark clouds are angry" and "soap sinks to the bottom of the bathtub because it is tired"). *Animism* refers to the belief that all things are living (or animated). Our earlier example of Randi's letter asking puppeteer Shari Lewis to teach her sock to talk like Lamb Chop is also an example of animistic thinking.

Can't preoperational children be taught how to use operations and to avoid egocentric and animistic thinking? Although some researchers have reported success in accelerating the preoperational stage, Piaget did not believe in pushing children ahead of their own developmental schedule. He believed children should be allowed to grow at their own pace, with minimal adult interference (Elkind, 1981, 2000, 2001). In fact, Piaget thought Americans were particularly guilty of pushing children, calling American childhood the "Great American Kid Race."

Concrete Operational Stage

Between the approximate ages of 7 and 11 years, children are in the **concrete operational stage**. During this stage many important thinking skills emerge. Unlike the preoperational stage, concrete operational children are able to perform operations on *concrete* objects. Because they understand the concept of *reversibility,* they recognize that certain physical attributes (such as volume) remain unchanged although the outward appearance is altered, a process known as **conservation**.

If you know children in the preoperational or concrete operational stages, you may enjoy testing their grasp of conservation by trying some of the experiments shown in Table 26.2. The equipment is easily obtained, and you will find their responses fascinating. Keep in mind that this should be done as a game. Do not allow the child to feel that he or she is failing a test or making a mistake.

Formal Operational Stage

The final period in Piaget's theory is the **formal operational stage**, which typically begins around age 11 years. In this stage, children begin to apply their operations to abstract concepts, in addition to concrete objects. They also become capable of hypothetical thinking ("What if?"), which allows systematic formulation and testing of concepts.

Adolescents considering part-time jobs, for example, may think about possible conflicts with school and friends, the number of hours they want to work, and the kind of work they are qualified for before they start filling out applications. Formal operational thinking also allows the adolescent to construct a well-reasoned argument based on hypothetical concepts and logical processes. Consider the following argument:

1. If you hit a glass with a feather, the glass will break.
2. You hit the glass with a feather.

What is the logical conclusion? The correct answer, "The glass will break," is contrary to fact and direct experience. Therefore, the child in the concrete operational stage would have difficulty with this task, whereas the formal operational thinker understands that this problem is about abstractions that need not correspond to the real world.

Problems with Early Formal Operational Thinking

Along with the benefits of this cognitive style come several problems. Adolescents in the early stages of the formal operational period demonstrate a type of *egocentrism* different from that of the preoperational child. Although adolescents do recognize that others have unique thoughts and perspectives, they often fail to differentiate between what others are thinking and their own thoughts. This *adolescent egocentrism* has two characteristics that may affect social interactions as well as problem solving:

Test for conservation. *Using Piaget's research method, a child is first shown two equal-sized glasses filled with the same amount of water. The child then pours one of the glasses of water into a taller, thinner glass, and is asked if they both still contain the same amount of water. A preoperational child will say the taller glass has "more" because he or she lacks the cognitive ability known as* conservation

Concrete Operational Stage *The third of Piaget's stages of cognitive development (roughly ages 7 to 11 years); the child can perform mental operations on concrete objects and understands reversibility and conservation*

Conservation *The ability to recognize that a given quantity, weight, or volume remains constant despite changes in shape, length, or position*

Formal Operational Stage *Piaget's fourth stage of cognitive development (around age 11 years and beyond), characterized by abstract and hypothetical thinking*

T A B L E 2 6 . 2 ADDITIONAL TESTS FOR CONSERVATION

Type of Conservation	Step 1 of Experiment	Experimenter then . . .	Child is asked conservation question	Average age at which concept is grasped
Length	Center two sticks of equal length. Child agrees that they are of equal length.	... moves stick over.	*Which stick is longer?* Preconserving child will say that one of the sticks is longer. Conserving child will say that they are both the same length.	6–7
Substance amount	Center two identical clay balls. Child acknowledges that the two have equal amounts of clay.	... rolls out one of the balls.	*Do the two pieces have the same amount of clay?* Preconserving child will say that the long piece has more clay. Conserving child will say that the two pieces have the same amount of clay.	6–7
Area	Center two identical sheets of cardboard with wooden blocks placed on them in identical positions. Child acknowledges that the same amount of space is left open on each piece of cardboard.	... scatters the blocks on one piece of cardboard.	*Do the two pieces of cardboard have the same amount of open space?* Preconserving child will say that the cardboard with scattered blocks has less open space. Conserving child will say that both pieces have the same amount of open space.	8–10
Volume	Center two balls of clay in two identical glasses with an equal amount of water. Child acknowledges that they displace equal amounts of water.	... changes the shape of one of the balls.	*Do the two pieces of clay displace the same amount of water?* Preconserving child will say that the longer piece displaces more water. Conserving child will say that both pieces displace the same amount of water.	10–12

This is a sample of experiments used to test Piaget's different types of convervation. Try them with children of various ages. Do they fit the stages as described by Piaget?

1. *Personal fable.* As a result of their unique form of egocentrism, adolescents may conclude they alone are having certain insights or difficulties and that no one else could understand or sympathize. David Elkind (1967, 2000, 2001) described this as the formation of a *personal fable,* an intense investment in their own thoughts and feelings, and a belief that these thoughts are unique. One student in our class remembered being very upset in junior high when her mother tried to comfort her over the loss of an important relationship. "I felt like she couldn't possibly know how it felt — no one could. I couldn't believe that anyone had ever suffered like this or that things would ever get better."

Several forms of risk taking, such as engaging in sexual intercourse without contraception, driving dangerously, and experimenting with drugs, also seem to arise from the personal fable (Coley & Chase-Lansdale, 1998; Greene, Rubin, Hale, & Walters, 1996). The adolescent has a sense of uniqueness, invulnerability, and immortality. They recognize the dangers of these activities, but the rules don't seem to apply to them.

2. *Imaginary audience.* In early adolescence, people tend to believe they are the center of others' thoughts and attentions, instead of considering that everyone is equally wrapped up in his or her own concerns and plans. In other words, adolescents picture all eyes focused on their behaviors. Elkind referred to this as the *imaginary audience.* This may explain what seems like extreme forms of self-consciousness and concern for physical appearance ("Everyone knows I don't know the answer"; "They're noticing how fat I am and this awful haircut").

If the imaginary audience results from an inability to differentiate the self from others, the personal fable is a product of differentiating too much. Thankfully, these two forms of adolescent egocentrism tend to decrease during later stages of the formal operational period.

Personal fable in action? Can you see how this type of risk-taking behavior may reflect the personal fable — an adolescent's tendency to believe he or she is unique and special and that dangers don't apply to them?

Assessing Piaget's Theory: Criticisms and Contributions

As influential as Piaget's account of cognitive development has been, it has received significant criticisms. Let's look briefly at two major areas of concern: underestimated abilities and underestimated genetic and cultural influences.

critical thinking

Active Learning

Applying Your Knowledge of Piaget

One of the most important behavioral components in critical thinking is applying what you learn to new situations. If you can use new knowledge in different contexts, you have mastered it. Demonstrate your understanding of Piaget's theories by applying what you have learned to the following situations.

A young mother is encouraging her son to try another bite of chicken and rice, which he clearly doesn't like. The child is quietly whining, until the mother spreads the food around to cool it. He then becomes hysterical. What upset the child? Identify the cognitive stage of the child.

Last month Janie's mom could easily substitute a stuffed toy animal for a noisy toy, and Janie would continue happily playing. Now she cries and reaches for the noisy toy even when it is out of sight. What cognitive changes have occurred? Identify Janie's cognitive stage of development.

Tom is deeply upset when his parents forbid him to ride motorcycles. He refuses to believe this is risky behavior. Explain Tom's refusal from a Piagetian perspective, and label his stage of cognitive development.

An aunt gives her two nephews three cookies and tells them to share. The older child takes two cookies for himself and offers his brother the other cookie broken in half. Both children are happy with this arrangement. Label each child's stage of cognitive development.

Answers appear in Appendix B.

Contrary to Piaget's belief, children in the preoperational stage are not completely egocentric. They can occasionally take the perspective of another — like the children in this photo.

Underestimated Abilities

Research shows that Piaget may have underestimated young children's cognitive development. For example, researchers report that very young infants have a basic concept of how objects move, are aware that objects continue to exist even when screened from view, can recognize speech sounds, and even understand the concept of addition (Haith & Benson, 1998).

Research on infant imitation of facial expression also raises questions about Piaget's estimates of early infant cognition. In a series of well-known studies, Meltzoff and Moore (1977, 1985, 1994) found that newborns could imitate such facial movements as tongue protrusion, mouth opening, and lip pursing (Figure 26.2). At age 9 months, infants will imitate facial actions a full day after seeing them (Heimann & Meltzoff, 1996).

Underestimated Genetic and Cultural Influences

Piaget's model, like other stage theories, has also been criticized for not sufficiently taking into account genetic and cultural differences (Matusov & Hayes, 2000; Matsumoto, 2000; Plomin & Rutter, 1998). During Piaget's time, the genetic influences on cognitive abilities were poorly understood, but as you know from earlier discussions in this text, there has been rapid explosion of information in this field in the last few years. In addition, formal education and specific cultural experiences can also significantly affect cognitive development. Consider the following example from a researcher attempting to test the formal operational skills of a farmer in Liberia (Scribner, 1977):

> Researcher: All Kpelle men are rice farmers. Mr. Smith is not a rice farmer. Is he a Kpelle man?
>
> Kpelle farmer: I don't know the man. I have not laid eyes on the man myself.

Figure 26.2 *Infant imitation.* When an adult models a facial expression, even very young infants will respond with a similar expression. Is this true imitation or a simple stimulus–response reflex?

Instead of reasoning in the "logical" way of Piaget's formal operational stage, the Kpelle farmer reasoned according to his specific cultural and educational training, which apparently emphasized personal knowledge. Not knowing Mr. Smith, the Kpelle farmer did not feel qualified to comment on him. Thus, Piaget's theory may have underestimated the effect of culture on a person's cognitive functioning.

Despite criticisms, Piaget's contributions to psychology are enormous. As one scholar put it, "assessing the impact of Piaget on developmental psychology is like assessing the impact of Shakespeare on English literature or Aristotle on philosophy — impossible" (cited in Beilin, 1992, p. 191).

Information Processing: A Computer Model of Cognition

An alternative to Piaget's theory of cognitive development is the *information processing model*, which compares the workings of the mind to a computer and studies how information is received, encoded, stored, organized, retrieved, and used by people of different ages. This model offers important insights into two major areas of cognition: attention and memory.

Attention

Attention refers to focusing awareness on a narrowed range of stimuli. Infants pay attention to their environment for only short periods of time. Even toddlers, who can pay attention for longer periods, are easily distracted. When watching TV, for example, 2-year-olds talk more to other people, play more with toys, and look around the room more than 4-year-olds do. As children get older, their attention spans improve and they learn to discriminate between what is and what is not important to concentrate on at any given time (Bjorklund, 1995).

Memory

After children attend to information and take it into their information processing system, they must remember it. Attention determines what information enters the "computer," whereas memory determines what information is saved.

Like attention, memory skills also improve gradually throughout childhood and adolescence (Hayne, Boniface, & Barr, 2000; Richards, 1997). Two-year-olds can repeat back about two digits immediately after hearing them, but 10-year-olds can repeat about six. Improvement comes as children acquire strategies during the school years for storing and retrieving information. For example, they learn to rehearse or repeat information over and over, to use mnemonics (like "i before e except after c"), and to organize their information in ways that facilitate retrieval.

As people grow older, their use of information processing strategies and overall memory continue to change. Did you know that *fluid intelligence* (requiring speed or rapid learning) tends to decrease with age, whereas *crystallized intelligence* (knowledge and information gained over the life span) continues to increase until advanced old age? Despite concerns about "keeping up with 18-year-olds," older returning students often do as well as or better than their younger counterparts in college classes. This superior performance in older adult students is due in part to their generally greater academic motivation, but it also reflects the importance of prior knowledge. Cognitive psychologists have demonstrated that the more people know, the easier it is for them to lay down new memories (Chi & Glaser, 1985; Leahy & Harris, 1997). Older students, for instance, generally find this section development easier to master than do younger students. Their interactions with children and greater knowledge about life changes create a framework on which to hang new information.

In summary, the more you know, the more you learn. Thus, having a college degree and stimulating occupation may help you stay mentally sharp in your later years (Mayr & Kliegl, 2000; Powell, 1998).

Haven't studies also shown decreases in older adults' memory capabilities? This type of decrease may reflect problems with cross-sectional versus longitudinal

Age and intelligence. Although many people believe intelligence declines with age, research suggests that this is largely a myth.

research. In addition, earlier studies often asked participants to memorize simple lists of words or paired association tasks, which older people often find meaningless and uninteresting. When the information is meaningful, an older person's rich web of existing knowledge helps him or her remember it (Graf, 1990).

The public and most researchers have long thought aging is accompanied by widespread death of neurons in the brain. Although this decline does happen with degenerative disorders like Alzheimer's disease, this is no longer believed to be a part of normal aging. It is also important to remember that age-related memory problems are not on a continuum with Alzheimer's disease (Wilson et al., 2000). That is, normal forgetfulness "does not reflect a predisposition" for serious dementia.

Aging does seem to take its toll on *speed* of information processing, however (Miller & Vernon, 1997). For example, decreased speed of processing may reflect problems with *encoding* (putting information into long-term storage) and *retrieval* (getting information out of storage) (Finkel & Pedersen, 2000; Mayr & Kliegl, 2000). If memory is like a filing system, older people may have more filing cabinets, and it may take them longer to initially file and later retrieve information.

In summary, many psychologists have criticized earlier studies of memory deficits in the elderly. Although mental speed declines with age, general information processing and much of memory ability is largely unaffected by the aging process (Baltes, Staudinger, & Lindenberger, 1999; D'Esposito & Weksler, 2000). Contrary to popular stereotypes of frail and forgetful elderly, growing old, for most of us, will probably be better than expected — and, of course, far better than the alternative!

Check & Review

COGNITIVE DEVELOPMENT

Jean Piaget's theories of cognitive development are based on the concept of **schemas**, mental patterns or blueprints used to interpret the world. Sometimes existing schemas can be used "as is" and information is **assimilated**; on other occasions, existing schemas must be modified, which calls for **accommodation**.

According to Piaget, cognitive development occurs in an invariant sequence of four stages: **sensorimotor** (birth to 2 years), **preoperational** (between 2 and 7 years), **concrete operational** (between 7 and 11 years), and **formal operational** (age 11 years and up).

In the sensorimotor stage, children acquire **object permanence**. During the preoperational stage, children are better equipped to use symbols, but their thinking is limited by their lack of operations, **egocentrism**, and animism.

In the concrete operational stage, children learn to perform operations (to think about concrete things while not actually doing them). They understand the principles of conservation and reversibility. During the formal operational stage, the adolescent is able to think abstractly and deal with hypothetical situations but again is prone to egotism.

Although Piaget has been criticized for underestimating abilities and genetic and cultural influences, he remains one of the most respected psychologists in modern times.

Psychologists who explain cognitive development in terms of the information processing model have found this model especially useful in explaining attention and memory changes across the life span. In contrast to pessimistic early studies, recent research is much more encouraging about age-related changes in information processing.

Questions

1. _____ was one of the first scientists to prove that a child's cognitive processes are fundamentally different from an adult's. (a) Baumrind; (b) Beck; (c) Piaget; (d) Elkind

2. _____ occurs when existing schemas are used to interpret new information, whereas _____ involves changes and adaptations of the schemas. (a) adaptation; accommodation; (b) adaptation; reversibility; (c) egocentrism; postschematization; (d) assimilation; accommodation

3. Match the Piagetian stage with the relevant concept:

_____ 1. Egocentrism, animism

_____ 2. Object permanence

_____ 3. Abstract and hypothetical thinking

_____ 4. Conservation, reversibility

_____ 5. Personal fable, imaginary audience

   a. Sensorimotor
   b. Preoperational
   c. Concrete operational
   d. Formal operational

4. How does the information processing model explain some memory problems in older adults?

Answers to Questions can be found in Appendix B.

ACTIVE LEARNING WORKSHEET MODULE 26

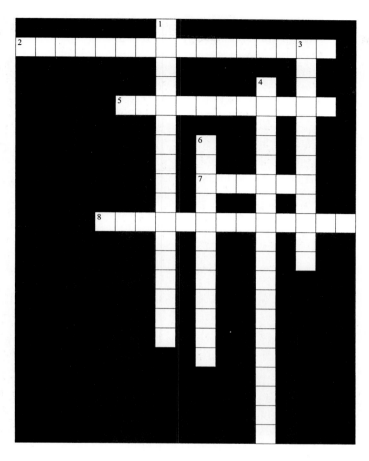

ACROSS

2. Piagetian term for an infant's understanding that objects (or people) continue to exist even when they cannot directly be seen, heard, or touched.

5. Inability to consider another's point of view.

7. Cognitive structures that grow and differentiate with experience.

8. Reworking schemas to encompass new information, ideas, or objects.

DOWN

1. Piaget's first stage where cognitive development occurs through exploration via sensory perceptions and motor skills.

3. Ability to recognize that a given quantity, weight, or volume remains constant despite changes in shape, length, or position.

4. Piaget's second stage where a child gains significant language and thinks symbolically, but lacks operations and thinking is egocentric and animistic.

6. Responding to a new situation in the same manner that is used in a familiar situation.

Answers can be found in Appendix B.

Visual Summary for Modules 24, 25, and 26

Studying Development

Developmental Psychology: concerned with describing, explaining, predicting, and modifying age-related behaviors from conception to death.

Theoretical Issues

Research Methods

Key Issues:
- Nature vs. Nurture
- Continuity vs. Stages
- Stability vs. Change

Cross–sectional: Different participants, various ages, one point in time. Major problem: cohort effects (a given generation may be affected by specific cultural/historical events).

Longitudinal: Same participants, extended period. Major problem: expensive, time consuming

Physical Development

Prenatal and Newborn

Three Major Stages: **germinal, embryonic,** and **fetal. Teratogens:** Environmental agents capable of producing birth defects.

Newborn and Early Childhood

Sensory and perceptual abilities are relatively well developed in newborns. Motor development comes with **maturation.**

Adolescence

Adolescence: Psychological period between childhood and adulthood.

Puberty: When sex organs become capable of reproduction.

Secondary sex characteristics: Hormonally induced changes (pubic hair, breasts, beards).

Adulthood

Menopause: Cessation of menstruation. Male climacteric: Physical and psychological changes in midlife. Primary aging: Inevitable, biological changes with age. Secondary aging: Accelerated aging due to disease, disuse, or abuse. Explanations of primary aging: *Programmed theory* (genetically built-in) and *wear-and-tear theory* (body's inability to repair damage).

Language Development

Stages

- *Prelinguistic:* Crying → **cooing** (vowel sounds) → **babbling** (vowel/consonant combinations).
- *Linguistic:* One-word utterances → **telegraphic speech** (omits unnecessary, connecting words) → grammatical speech.
- Problems: **Overextension** (e.g., "bunnies" called "dogs") and **overgeneralization** (e.g., "foots," "goed").

Theories

- *Nature:* Language results from maturation. Chomsky's innate **language acquisition device (LAD).**
- *Nurture:* Environment and rewards/punishments explain language.

Social-Emotional Development

Attachment

- Infant attachment: **Imprinting:** Attaching to first large moving object. Harlow's experiments found "contact comfort" very important to **attachment**. Infants who do not attach may suffer serious, lasting effects.
- Adult attachment: Patterns of infant attachment (secure, avoidant, and anxious/ambivalent) may carry over into adult romantic attachments.

Parenting Styles

There are three major categories (authoritarian, permissive, and authoritative), but critics suggest that a child's unique temperament, expectations of parents, and degree of warmth versus rejection from parents may be the most important determinants of parenting styles.

Cognitive Development

Piaget's Major Concepts:

- **Schema:** Cognitive structure for organizing ideas.
- **Assimilation:** Adding new information to an existing schema.
- **Accommodation:** Revising schemas to account for new information.

Four Stages	Abilities	Limits
Sensorimotor (Birth to 2 years)	Uses senses and motor skills to explore and develop cognitively.	Beginning of stage infant lacks **object permanence** (understanding things continue to exist even when not seen, heard, or felt).
Preoperational (Ages 2 to 7)	Has significant language and thinks symbolically.	• Cannot perform "operations." • **Egocentric** thinking (inability to consider another's point of view). • Animistic thinking (believing all things are living).
Concrete Operational (Ages 7 to 11)	• Can perform "operations" on concrete objects. • Understands **conservation** (realizing changes in shape or appearance can be reversed).	Cannot think abstractly and hypothetically.
Formal Operational (11 and up)	Can think abstractly and hypothetically.	Adolescent egocentrism at the beginning of this stage, with related problems of the *personal fable* and *imaginary audience*.

Information Processing Model: Process of taking in, remembering or forgetting, and using information. Major concepts: The mind is like a computer. Focuses on quantitative changes vs. Piaget's qualitative changes.

Life Span Development II

In Europe, a woman was near death from a special kind of cancer. There was one drug that doctors thought might save her. It was a form of radium that a druggist in the same town had recently discovered. The drug was expensive to make, but the druggist was charging 10 times what the drug cost him to make. He paid $200 for the radium and charged $2,000 for a small dose of the drug.

The sick woman's husband, Heinz, went to everyone he knew to borrow the money, but he could get together only about $1,000, which is half of what it cost. He told the druggist that his wife was dying and asked him to sell it cheaper or let him pay later. But the druggist said, "No, I

discovered the drug, and I'm going to make money from it." So Heinz got desperate and broke into the man's store to steal the drug for his wife.
Kohlberg, 1964, pp. 18–19

Was Heinz morally right to steal the drug? What do you consider moral behavior? Is morality "in the eye of the beholder," and everyone simply argues for his or her own self-interest? Or are there universal truths and principles? Whatever your answer, your ability to think, reason, and respond to Heinz's dilemma demonstrates another type of development that is very important to psychology: moral development.

As we discussed in the introduction to Modules 24, 25, and 26, developmental psychology is devoted to the study of age-related changes in behavior and abilities from conception to death. In this section, we continue our study of development with a focus on moral development, personality development, and special issues related to bereavement and death.

MORAL AND PERSONALITY DEVELOPMENT

What is moral behavior? Do our judgments change over time? Does a child's personality at two predict his or her personality at 20, 40, or 80 years of age? These are questions we'll explore in this section.

Moral Development: Kohlberg's Research

Developmental psychologists have traditionally examined morality from a developmental stage perspective. That is, they study how moral thoughts, feelings, and behaviors change over the life span (Eisenberg, 2000). One of the most influential researchers in moral development was Lawrence Kohlberg (1927–1987). He presented what he called "moral stories" like the Heinz dilemma to people of all ages, and on the basis of his findings, he developed a model of moral development (1964, 1984).

What is the right answer to Heinz's dilemma? Kohlberg was interested not in whether participants judged Heinz right or wrong but in the reasons they gave for their decision. On the basis of participants' responses, Kohlberg proposed three broad levels in the evolution of moral reasoning, each composed of two distinct stages (Table 27.1). Individuals at each stage and level may or may not support Heinz's stealing of the drug, but for different reasons.

Like Piaget's stages of cognitive development, Kohlberg believed his stages of moral development were *universal* and *invariant*. That is, they supposedly exist in all cultures, and everyone goes through each of the stages in a predictable fashion. The age trends that are noticed tend to be rather broad:

Preconventional Level *Lawrence Kohlberg's first level of moral development, characterized by moral judgments based on fear of punishment or desire for pleasure*

1. ***Preconventional level*** (stages 1 and 2 — birth to adolescence). At this level, moral judgment is *self-centered*. What is right is what one can get away with or what is personally satisfying. This level is called *preconventional* because children have not accepted society's (conventional) rule-making processes.

- During stage 1 (punishment-and-obedience orientation), the child conforms to rules made by authority figures so he or she can avoid punishment. Interestingly, goodness or badness also depends on the magnitude of the consequences. Thus, a 5-year-old will often say that *accidentally* breaking 15 cups is "badder" and should receive more punishment than *intentionally* breaking 1 cup.

- During stage 2 (instrumental-exchange orientation), moral reasoning reflects some concern for others, but it is ultimately motivated by the hope of benefit in return. "You scratch my back and I'll scratch yours" is the guiding philosophy.

Conventional Level *Lawrence Kohlberg's second level of moral development, where moral judgments are based on compliance with the rules and values of society*

2. ***Conventional level*** (stages 3 and 4 — adolescence and young adulthood). During this time, moral reasoning advances from being self-centered to *other-centered*. The individual accepts and internalizes *conventional* societal values.

- At stage 3 ("good child" orientation) the primary moral concern is with being nice and gaining approval. People are also judged by their intentions and motives — "His heart was in the right place."

- During stage 4 (law-and-order orientation), rules and laws are valued because they maintain a social order that is worth preserving. Stage 4 individuals understand that if everyone violated laws, even with good intentions, there would be

TABLE 27.1 KOHLBERG'S STAGES OF MORAL DEVELOPMENT

Name of Stage	Moral Reasoning	Heinz's Dilemma Responses	
		Pro	Con
Preconventional level			
Stage 1: punishment–obedience orientation	Morality is what you can get away with	If you let your wife die, you will get in trouble. You'll be blamed for not spending the money to save her and there'll be an investigation of you and the druggist for your wife's death.	You shouldn't steal the drug, because you'll be caught and sent to jail. If you do get away, your conscience would bother you thinking how the police will catch up with you at any minute.
Stage 2: instrumental–exchange orientation	Obey rules to obtain rewards or favors	If you do happen to get caught, you could give the drug back and you wouldn't get much of a sentence. It wouldn't bother you much to serve, a little jail term if you had your wife when you got out.	You may not get much of a jail term if you steal the drug, but your wife will probably die before you get out, so it won't do you much good. If your wife dies, you shouldn't blame yourself; it isn't your fault she has cancer.
Conventional level			
Stage 3: good child orientation	Obey rules to get approval	No one will think you're bad if you steal the drug, but your family will think you're an inhuman husband if you don't. If you let your wife die, you'll never be able to look anybody in the face again.	It isn't just the druggist who will think you're a criminal; everyone else will, too. After you steal it, you'll feel bad thinking how you've brought dishonor on your family and yourself, and you won't be able to face anyone again.
Stage 4: law-and-order orientation	Obey laws because they maintain the social order	If you have any sense of honor, you won't let your wife die just because you're afraid to do the only thing that will save her. You'll always feel guilty that you caused her death if you don't do your duty to her.	You're desperate and you may not know you're doing wrong when you steal the drug. But you'll know you did wrong after you're sent to jail. You'll always feel guilty for breaking the law.
Postconventional level			
Stage 5: social-contract orientation	Moral reasoning reflects belief in democratically accepted laws	You'll lose other people's respect, not gain it, if you don't steal. If you let your wife die, it would be out of fear, not out of reasoning it out. So you'd lose self-respect and probably the respect of others, too.	You would lose your standing and respect in the community and violate the law. You'd lose respect for yourself if you're carried away by emotion and forget the long-range point of view.
Stage 6: universal ethics orientation	Moral reasoning reflects individual conscience	If you don't steal the drug and let your wife die, you'll always condemn yourself for it afterward. You wouldn't be blamed and you would have lived up to the outside rule of the law, but you wouldn't have lived up to your own standards of conscience.	If you stole the drug, you wouldn't be blamed by other people, but you'd condemn yourself because you wouldn't have lived up to your own conscience and standards of honesty.

Sources: Kohlberg (1966, 1969), Rest, Turiel, & Kohlberg (1969).

"DON'T YOU REALIZE, JASON, THAT WHEN YOU THROW FURNITURE OUT THE WINDOW AND TIE YOUR SISTER TO A TREE, YOU MAKE MOMMY AND DADDY VERY SAD?"

© Sidney Harris

chaos. Thus, doing one's duty and respecting law and order are highly valued. According to Kohlberg, stage 4 is the highest level attained by most adolescents and adults.

Postconventional Level *Lawrence Kohlberg's highest level of moral development, which occurs when individuals develop personal standards for right and wrong*

3. ***Postconventional level*** (stages 5 and 6 — adulthood). This level advances beyond conventional societal rules that suggest authority and laws must be obeyed automatically. Instead, morality is guided by higher principles of human conduct, such as those described in the U.S. Constitution or the Ten Commandments.

- During stage 5 (social-contract orientation), individuals appreciate the underlying purposes served by laws. Furthermore, they believe laws should be derived from a democratic consensus so that they express the will of the majority or maximize social welfare.

- At stage 6 (universal-ethics orientation), "right" is determined by universal ethical principles that *all* religions or moral authorities might view as compelling or fair, such as nonviolence, human dignity, freedom, and equality. Thus, Mohandas Gandhi, Martin Luther King, Jr., and Nelson Mandela intentionally violated laws that they considered unjust because they did not treat all people equally. Few individuals actually achieve stage 6 (about 1 or 2 percent of those tested worldwide), and Kohlberg found it difficult to separate stages 5 and 6. Thus, in time, he combined the stages (Kohlberg, 1981).

Moral Behavior

Are the people who achieve higher stages on Kohlberg's scale really more moral than others, or do they just "talk a good game"? Although we might assume that moral reasoning would lead to moral behavior, there is considerable debate over whether Kohlberg's stages accurately predict an individual's actions. Some studies show a positive correlation between higher stages of reasoning and higher levels of moral behavior (Bond, Felter, & Ross, 2000; Borba, 2001; Rest, Narvaez, Bebeau, &

Thoma, 1999), but others have found that the pressures of the situation are better predictors of moral behavior (Bandura, 1986, 1991; Bruggeman & Hart, 1996).

In addition to the questionable relationship between moral reasoning and behavior, Kohlberg's model has also been criticized as politically biased (favoring liberals over conservatives), culturally biased (favoring Western ideals of what is morally "advanced"), and gender biased (favoring males over females). The last two points are the focus of our next section.

GENDER & CULTURAL DIVERSITY

Insights into Morality

There are two basic questions that guide developmental researchers: "nature or nurture?" and "continuity or stages?" Cross-cultural research on morality confirms that children in different cultures do conform to Kohlberg's model and generally progress sequentially from his first level, the preconventional, to his second, the conventional (Snarey, 1985, 1995; Rest, Narvaez, Bebeau, & Thoma, 1999). Thus, the *nature* and *stage* sides of these two basic questions seem to be supported by cross-cultural studies.

At the same time, cultural *differences* suggest that nurture, or culture, also determines morality. For example, cross-cultural comparisons of responses to Heinz's moral dilemma show that Europeans and Americans tend to consider whether they like or identify with the victim in questions of morality. In contrast, Hindu Indians consider social responsibility and personal concerns two separate issues (Miller & Bersoff, 1998). Researchers suggest that the difference reflects the Indians' broader sense of social responsibility.

In India, Papua New Guinea, China, and Israeli kibbutzim, rather than choosing between the rights of the individual and the rights of society (as the top levels of Kohlberg's model require), most people seek a compromise solution that accommodates both interests (Killen & Hart, 1999; Miller & Bersoff, 1998). Thus, Kohlberg's standard for judging the highest level of morality (the postconventional) may be more applicable to cultures that value individualism over community and interpersonal relationships.

Researcher Carol Gilligan has also criticized Kohlberg's gender bias (Mandel & Midler, 2000). Initially, Gilligan believed male and female values reflected two basic approaches to moral reasoning — *justice* versus *caring* (Gilligan, 1977, 1990, 1993; Hoffman, 2000). In the **justice perspective**, the person is seen as standing alone, and the focus is on the rights of the individual. The **care perspective**, on the other hand, stresses concern for others, and the person is viewed in terms of his or her relationship with others. Gilligan suggested Kohlberg emphasizes the justice perspective and underplays the care perspective in his studies of moral development.

In the case of Heinz, for example, arguing that Heinz should steal the drug because saving a life is more important than obeying laws is demonstrating a justice orientation, according to Gilligan. On the other hand, arguing that Heinz should steal the drug because he has an obligation to help someone he loves reflects a care orientation, in Gilligan's view.

Recent research supports Gilligan's idea that people have at least two forms of moral reasoning, but most studies have found few if any gender differences in level or type of moral reasoning (Hoffman, 2000; Jaffee & Hyde, 2000; Wark & Krebs, 1996). Both sexes typically use both care and justice orientations. Gilligan has therefore modified her initial position: Each of us has within ourselves two "voices" of morality — and both voices are valid (Gilligan & Attanucci, 1988).

Justice Perspective *Carol Gilligan's term for an approach to moral reasoning that emphasizes individual rights and views people as differentiated and standing alone*

Care Perspective *Carol Gilligan's term for an approach to moral reasoning that emphasizes interpersonal responsibility and interconnectedness with others*

Gilligan versus Kohlberg. *According to Carol Gilligan, women score "lower" on Lawrence Kohlberg's stages of moral development because they are socialized to assume more responsibility for the care of others.*

Check & Review

MORAL DEVELOPMENT

According to Lawrence Kohlberg, morality progresses through three levels, and each level consists of two stages. At the **preconventional level,** morality is self-centered. What is right is what one can get away with (Stage 1) or what is personally satisfying (Stage 2). **Conventional level** morality is based on a need for approval (Stage 3) and obedience to laws because they maintain the social order (Stage 4). **Postconventional level** morality comes from adhering to the social contract (Stage 5) and the individual's own principles and universal values (Stage 6).

Kohlberg's theory has been criticized for being politically, culturally, and gender biased. Carol Gilligan has suggested that women tend to take a **care perspective** in their moral reasoning, whereas men favor a **justice perspective.** Research shows that in real-life situations, not hypothetical situations, both sexes typically use both the justice and care orientations.

Questions

1. According to Kohlberg's theory of morality, self-interest and avoiding punishment are characteristic of the _____ level, personal standards or universal principles characterize the _____ level, and gaining approval or following the rules describes the _____ level.

2. Calvin would like to wear baggy, torn jeans and a nose ring, but he is concerned that others will disapprove. Calvin is at Kohlberg's _____ level of morality. (a) conformity; (b) approval seeking; (c) conventional; (d) preconventional

3. Five-year-old Tyler believes "bad things are what you get punished for." Tyler is at Kohlberg's _____ level of morality. (a) concrete; (b) preconventional; (c) postconventional; (d) punishment-oriented

4. How is Kohlberg's theory culturally and gender biased?

Answers to Questions can be found in Appendix B.

Life Span Personality Development: Temperament and Psychosocial Theories

> How does personality change from infancy to old age?

Temperament *A basic, inborn disposition that appears shortly after birth and characterizes an individual's style of approaching people and situations*

What were you like as an infant? Do your parents say you were an "easy" baby or a "difficult" baby? Are these early differences in personality related to later adult traits? In this section, we explore Stella Thomas and Alexander Chess's temperament theory and Erik Erikson's psychosocial theory.

Thomas and Chess's Temperament Theory

From the moment you were born, you differed from other infants in characteristic ways. As an infant, did you lie quietly and seem oblivious to loud noises? Or did you tend to kick and scream and respond immediately to every sound? Did you respond warmly to people, or did you fuss, fret, and withdraw? Your answers to these questions would help determine what developmental psychologists call **temperament,** the basic, natural disposition of an individual.

As you might imagine, there is considerable controversy over the essential dimensions of temperament. One of the earliest and most influential theories came from the work of psychiatrists Stella Thomas and Alexander Chess (Thomas & Chess, 1977, 1987, 1991). Thomas and Chess found that approximately 65 percent of the babies they observed could be reliably separated into three categories:

1. Easy children. These were children who were happy most of the time, relaxed and agreeable, and adjusted easily to new situations (approximately 40 percent).

2. Difficult children. These were children who were moody, easily frustrated, tense, and overreactive to most situations (approximately 10 percent).

3. Slow-to-warm-up children. These were children who showed mild responses, were somewhat shy and withdrawn, and needed time to adjust to new experiences or people (approximately 15 percent).

Follow-up studies found that certain aspects of an infant's basic temperamental styles tend to be consistent and enduring throughout early childhood and even adulthood (Caspi, 2000; Kagan, 1995, 1998; McCrae et al., 2000). That is not to say every shy, cautious infant ends up a shy adult. Many events take place between infancy and adulthood that shape an individual's development.

One of the most influential factors in early personality development is *goodness of fit* between a child's nature and the social and environmental setting (Eccles et al., 1999; Solomon, 2000; Thompson, 1998). For example, a slow-to-warm-up child does best if allowed time to adjust to new situations, whereas a difficult child thrives in a structured, understanding environment but not in an inconsistent, intolerant home. Alexander Thomas, the pioneer of temperament research, thinks parents should work with their child's temperament, rather than trying to change it. Goodness of fit is another example of how nature and nurture interact (Gottlieb, 2000; Maccoby, 2000).

Erikson's Psychosocial Theory

Erik Erikson (1902–1994) used Freud's notion of inborn biological forces as the basis for his theory of personality. But unlike Freud, Erikson continued his stage theory beyond adolescence all the way to mature adulthood (65 and older) (see Table 27.2). Erikson believed that Freud underestimated the power of social and cultural influences on human behavior and developed his theory, called **psychosocial stages** of development, in contrast to Freud's *psychosexual stages* (Module 35). Erikson identified eight stages in life, each characterized by a specific conflict or tension that the person must resolve.

Erikson's First Stage In Erikson's first stage (birth to approximately 12 months), the major tension is *trust versus mistrust*. When and how the infant's needs are met determine whether the infant decides the world is a good and satisfying place to live or a source of pain, frustration, and uncertainty.

Stages 2 to 4 The second stage, *autonomy versus shame and doubt* (ages 1 to 3 years), is a time for developing self-awareness and independence. During the "terrible twos," toddlers continually assert their wills — "no, no" and "me, me." Parents who handle these beginning attempts at independence with patience and good-humored encouragement help their toddlers develop a sense of autonomy. Conversely, if the parents are ridiculing, impatient, or controlling, the child develops feelings of shame and doubt.

During the third stage, *initiative versus guilt* (ages 3 to 6 years), the major conflict is between a child's desire to initiate activities and the guilt that comes from unwanted or unexpected consequences. If loving adults provide an environment that encourages the ever-increasing need for independence and opportunities for interaction with other children, the child will predominantly develop feelings of power and initiative rather than guilt and doubt.

During the fourth stage, *industry versus inferiority* (age 6 years through puberty), children develop a sense of industry, or competency, as they begin to practice skills they will use for a lifetime in productive work. How the external world reacts to a child's successes and failures determines whether she or he develops feelings of competency and industriousness or feelings of insecurity and inferiority.

Stages 5 and 6 Erikson's fifth stage is the period of *identity versus role confusion*. Erikson believed each individual's personal identity develops from a period of serious questioning and intense soul searching. During this **identity crisis**, adolescents attempt to discover who they are, what their skills are, and what kinds of roles

Psychosocial Stages *Erik Erikson's theory that individuals pass through eight developmental stages and that adult personality reflects how the distinct challenges or crises at each stage are resolved*

Identity Crisis *According to Erik Erikson, a period of inner conflict during which an individual examines his or her life and values and makes decisions about life roles*

TABLE 27.2   ERIKSON'S EIGHT STAGES

	Approximate Age	Psychosocial Crisis	Description
Erikson's first stage	Infancy (0–1)	Trust versus mistrust	Infants learn to trust that their needs will be met by the world, especially by the mother; if not, mistrust develops.
	Early childhood (1–3)	Autonomy versus shame and doubt	Children learn to exercise will, to make choices, to control themselves; if not, they become uncertain and doubt that they can do things by themselves.
	Play age (3–6)	Initiative versus guilt	Children learn to initiate activities and enjoy their accomplishments, acquiring direction and purpose; if they are not allowed initiative, they feel guilty for their attempts at independence.
Erikson's second stage	School age (6–12)	Industry versus inferiority	Children develop a sense of industry and curiosity and are eager to learn; if not, they feel inferior and lose interest in the tasks before them.
	Adolescence (12–20)	Identity versus role confusion	Adolescents come to see themselves as unique and integrated persons with an ideology; if not, they become confused about what they want out of life.
Erikson's sixth stage	Young adulthood (20–30)	Intimacy versus isolation	Young people become able to commit themselves to another person; if not, they develop a sense of isolation and feel they have no one in the world but themselves.
	Adulthood (30–65)	Generativity versus stagnation	Adults are willing to have and care for children, to devote themselves to their work and the common good; if not, they become self-centered and inactive.
Erikson's eighth stage	Mature (65+)	Ego integrity versus despair	Older people enter a period of reflection, becoming assured that their lives have been meaningful, and they grow ready to face death with acceptance and dignity; if not, they despair for their unaccomplished goals, failures, and ill-spent lives.

Source: Adapted from Clarke-Stewart, A., Friedman, S., and Koch, J., 1985. *Child development: A topical approach.* Copyright © 1985 by John Wiley & Sons, Inc. Reprinted by permission of John Wiley & Sons, Inc.

they are best suited to play for the rest of their lives. Failure to resolve the identity crisis may be related to a lack of stable identity, delinquency, or difficulty in maintaining close personal relationships in later life.

Once a firm sense of identity is established, Erikson believes the individual (now in young adulthood) is ready to meet the challenges of *intimacy versus isolation*, stage 6 of development. If close bonds are formed, a basic feeling of intimacy with others will result. If not, the individual may avoid interpersonal commitments and experience feelings of isolation. Erikson's model for stages 5 and 6 suggests that if we are to have close, loving relationships with others, we must first learn who we are and how to be independent.

Erikson's Last Two Stages In the seventh stage, *generativity versus stagnation* (*middle age*), the individual expands feelings of love and concern beyond the immediate family group to include all of society. If this expansion and effort do not occur, an individual stagnates, becoming concerned with only material possessions and personal well-being.

In the final years of life, adults enter the period of *ego integrity versus despair*, stage 8. Those who have been successful in resolving their earlier psychosocial crises will tend to look back on their lives with feelings of accomplishment and satisfaction. Those who resolved their earlier crises in a negative way or who lived fruitless, self-centered lives may deeply regret lost opportunities or become despondent because they realize it is too late to start over.

(Study tip: If you're having difficulty remembering Erikson's eight stages, try this mnemonic device based on the peg-word system from Module 20: *One is a bun, trust no one. Two is a shoe, shame on you. Three is a tree, I feel so guilty. Four is a door, I feel inferior. Five is a hive, I'm a busy bee working on my identity. Six are sticks, pick them up alone, I am working on my isolation. Seven is heaven, filled with stagnation? Eight is a gate, is it too late for integrity?* This study tip was adapted from one developed by Professor Eggleston of McKendree College in Illinois.)

Evaluating Erikson's Theory Many psychologists agree with Erikson's general idea that psychosocial conflicts, which are based on interpersonal and environmental interactions, do contribute to personality development (Bugental & Goodnow, 1998; Friedman & Coles, 1999). However, Erikson also has his critics. The labels Erikson uses to describe the eight stages may not be entirely appropriate cross-culturally. For example, in individualistic cultures, *autonomy* is highly preferable to *shame and doubt*, but in collectivist cultures, the preferred resolution might be

critical thinking

Active Learning

Applying Erikson's Stages to Your Own Life

Two important components of critical thinking are applying knowledge to new situations and clarifying personal values. Can you see evidence of Erik Erikson's stages in your friends and family? Perhaps more importantly, can you see how these stages apply to your own life? Answering the following questions will improve your understanding of Erikson's theory and help develop your critical thinking.

1. What Eriksonian stage are you now in? Does the description of that stage seem valid to you?

2. How have you resolved the crises you have already gone through? Is your personality affected by a negative resolution at one of the earlier stages?

3. If you found it difficult to identify your current stage, it may be because you are a woman or were raised in a collectivist culture. How might gender and culture affect the development and resolution of various Eriksonian stages?

dependence or *merging relations* (Matsumoto, 2000). In addition, it is difficult to squeeze an entire lifetime of development into one comprehensive theory.

Despite their limits, Erikson's stages have greatly contributed to the study of North American and European psychosocial development. Moreover, Erikson was among the first theorists to suggest that development continues past adolescence, and his theory encouraged further research.

Myths of Development Until recently, most psychologists characterized adolescence as a time of *storm and stress* — great emotional turbulence and psychological strain. Research within the last 20 years, however, has found that storm and stress is largely a myth: Adolescence is no stormier than any other life transition. And, contrary to Erikson's predicted need for psychological separation from parents in order to establish identity, most teenagers of both sexes remain close to their parents and admire them (Diener & Diener, 1996; Lerner & Galambos, 1998).

Numerous other beliefs about age-related crises have not been supported by research either. For example, the popular idea of a *midlife crisis* began largely as the result of Gail Sheehy's national best seller *Passages* (1976). Sheehy drew on the theories of Daniel Levinson (1977, 1996) and psychiatrist Roger Gould (1975), as well as her own interviews, and reported a "predictable crisis" at about age 35 for women and 40 for men. Although middle age is typically a time of reexamining one's values and lifetime goals (Smart & Peterson, 1997), Sheehy's book led many people to automatically expect a midlife crisis with drastic changes in personality and behavior. Research suggests that a severe reaction or crisis may actually be quite rare and not typical of what most people experience during middle age (Benazzi, 2000; McCrae & Costa, 1990; Stewart & Ostrove, 1998).

It is also a myth that when the last child leaves home, most parents experience an *empty nest syndrome* — a painful separation and time of depression for the mother, the father, or both parents. Again, however, research suggests that the empty nest syndrome may be an exaggeration of the pain experienced by a few individuals and an effort to downplay positive reactions (White & Rogers, 1997; Whyte, 1992). For example, one major benefit of the empty nest is an increase in marital satisfaction (Figure 27.1). Furthermore, parent–child relationships do continue once the child leaves home. As one mother said, "The empty nest is surrounded by telephone wires" (Troll, Miller, & Atchley, 1979).

Figure 27.1 *Life span marital satisfaction.* Do you believe children make a marriage happy or that parents experience a depressing empty nest syndrome when they later leave home? Research shows that the highest levels of conflict actually occur during the childbearing years and that the lowest levels are before children are born and after they leave home (Mackey & O'Brien, 1998, p. 132).

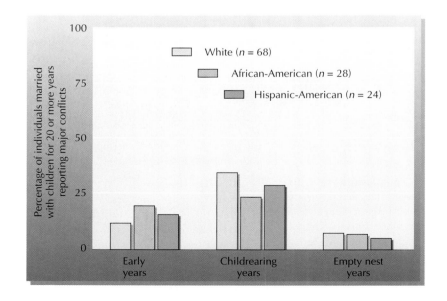

Check & Review

PERSONALITY DEVELOPMENT OVER THE LIFE SPAN

Stella Thomas and Alexander Chess emphasize the genetic component of certain traits (such as sociability) and the fact that babies often exhibit differences in **temperament** shortly after birth.

Erik Erikson expanded on Freud's ideas to develop eight **psychosocial stages** of development that cover the entire life span. The four stages that occur during childhood are trust versus mistrust, autonomy versus shame and doubt, initiative versus guilt, and industry versus inferiority.

Erikson believes the major psychosocial **identity crisis of** adolescence is the search for identity versus role confusion. During young adulthood, the individual's task is to establish intimacy over isolation, and during middle adulthood, the person must deal with generativity versus stagnation. At the end of life, the older adult must establish ego integrity or face overwhelming despair at the realization of lost opportunities.

Research shows that adolescent storm and stress, the midlife crisis, and the empty nest syndrome may be exaggerated accounts of a few people's experiences and not that of most people.

Questions

1. An infant's inborn disposition is known as _____. (a) personality; (b) reflexes; (c) temperament; (d) traits

2. Briefly describe Thomas and Chess's temperament theory.

3. Erikson suggests that problems in adulthood are sometimes related to unsuccessful resolution of one of his eight stages. For each of the following individuals, identify the most likely "problem" stage:

   a. Marcos has trouble keeping friends and jobs because he continually asks for guarantees and reassurance of his worth.

   b. Ann has attended several colleges without picking a major, has taken several vocational training programs, and has had numerous jobs over the last 10 years.

   c. Teresa is reluctant to apply for a promotion even though her coworkers have encouraged her to do so. She worries that she will be taking jobs from others and questions her worth.

   d. George continually obsesses over the value of his life. He regrets that he never married or had children and feels very lonely.

4. Discuss the text's three common myths of development.

Answers to Questions can be found in Appendix B.

MODULE 27   ACTIVE LEARNING WORKSHEET

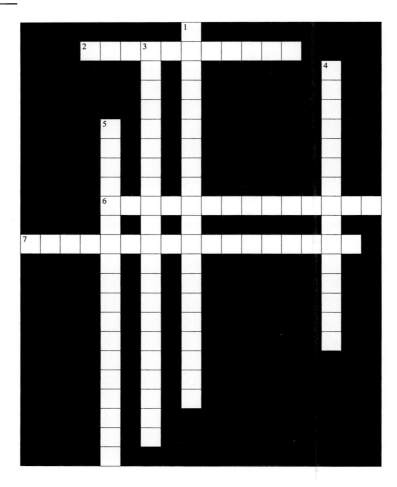

ACROSS

2. Inborn disposition appearing shortly after birth that characterizes ways of approaching people and situations.

6. Erikson's term for the period of inner conflict when individuals examine their life and values and make decisions about life roles.

7. Kohlberg's second level of moral development where judgments are based on compliance with the rules and values of society.

DOWN

1. Kohlberg's first level of moral development, characterized by moral judgments based on fear of punishment or desire for pleasure.

3. Kohlberg's highest level of moral development where individuals develop personal standards for right and wrong.

4. Gilligan's term that emphasizes interpersonal responsibility and interconnectedness with others.

5. Gilligan's term that emphasizes individual rights and views people as differentiated and standing alone.

Answers can be found in Appendix B.

MODULE 28
ADDITIONAL INFLUENCES ON DEVELOPMENT

Theorists like Erikson and Thomas and Chess offer important insights into general personality development. But what about family violence, teen pregnancy, divorce, occupational choice, bereavement, and death? How do they influence development? We will explore these questions in this module.

Families: Their Effect on Personality

Our families exert an enormous influence on our development, but not always for the best. Family violence, teen pregnancy, and divorce — the topics we discuss in this section — can have long-lasting, damaging effects on individual development.

Family Violence

Families can be warm and loving, but they can also be cruel and abusive. It is difficult to measure family violence because it usually occurs in private, and out of shame, powerlessness, or fear of reprisal, victims are reluctant to report it. Nevertheless, every year millions of domestic violence, child abuse, and elderly abuse cases are reported to police and service agencies (Fantuzzo & Mohr, 1999; McCloskey & Bailey, 2000; Wolfe, 1999).

What causes family violence? Violence occurs more often in families experiencing marital conflict, substance abuse, mental disorders, and economic stress (Melchert, 2000; Niehoff, 1999; Reppucci, Woolard, & Fried, 1999). It is important to remember that abuse and violence occur at all socioeconomic levels. However, abuse and violence occur more frequently in families disrupted by unemployment or other financial distress.

In addition to financial problems, many parents are socially isolated and lack good communication and parenting skills. Their anxiety and frustration may explode into spouse, child, and elderly abuse. In fact, one of the clearest identifiers of abuse potential is *impulsivity*. Parents who abuse their children, their spouses, or elderly parents seem to lack impulse control, especially when stressed. They also respond

Families and personality. Does this remind you of your own family? How did your father, mother, and siblings affect your own personality development?

to stress with more intense emotions and greater arousal (Cicchetti & Toth, 1998). This impulsivity is related not only to psychosocial factors like economic stress and social isolation but also to possible biological influences.

Biologically, three regions of the brain are closely related to the expression and control of aggression: the amygdala, the prefrontal cortex, and the hypothalamus (see Module 6 to review these regions). Interestingly, head injuries, strokes, dementia, schizophrenia, alcoholism, and abuse of stimulant drugs have all been linked to these three areas and to aggressive outbursts (Niehoff, 1999). Research also suggests that low levels of the neurotransmitter serotonin are associated with irritability, hypersensitivity to provocation, and impulsive rage (Oguendo & Mann, 2000; Volavka, 1999).

Is there anything that can be done to reduce this type of aggression? Treatment with antianxiety and serotonin-enhancing drugs like fluoxetine (Prozac) may lower the risk of some forms of impulsive violence. However, given the correlation between spousal, child, sibling, and elder abuse, and because violence affects other family members who are not victims or perpetrators, treatment generally includes the entire family (Briggs & Hawkins, 1999; Emery & Laumann-Billings, 1998).

Most professionals advocate two general approaches in dealing with family violence. *Primary programs* attempt to identify "vulnerable" families and prevent abuse by teaching parenting and marital skills, stress management, and impulse control. These programs also publicize the signs of abuse and encourage people to report suspected cases. *Secondary programs* attempt to rehabilitate families after abuse has occurred. They work to improve social services, establish self-help groups such as Parents Anonymous and AMAC (Adults Molested as Children), and provide individual and group psychotherapy for both victims and the abusers.

Teen Pregnancy

Another factor that may affect development is becoming a parent and starting a family at too early an age. The United States has one of the highest rates of teen pregnancy among major industrialized nations (Meschke, Bartholomae, & Zentall, 2000; Miller & Coyl, 2000). Ironically, today's rate is actually much lower than it has been throughout much of the twentieth century. For example, between 1960 and 1985, the rate of U.S. teen births was 89.1 per 1,000, compared to 52.3 per 1,000 in the mid-1990s (Ventura, Martin, Curtin, & Mathews, 1999).

With this decline, why is everyone so worried about teen pregnancies? Although the total rate has declined substantially, the percentage of *unwed teen births* has soared (Endersbe, 2000; Henshaw, 1998). The higher nonmarital rate is important because single-parent families headed by women are at great risk of poverty.

Pregnancy during adolescence also carries with it considerable health risk for both the mother and child, decreased chances of marital success, and lower education achievement (Endersbe, 2000; Fullerton, 1997; Roye & Balk, 1997). Pregnancy, in fact, is the most common reason for dropping out of high school. In view of these facts, is it any wonder that teen mothers also report one of the highest levels of depression (Figure 28.1)?

What can be done to reduce the number of teen pregnancies? Comprehensive *health-oriented services* seem to be the most promising avenue for decreasing the rate of pregnancy among high-risk teenagers (Coley & Chase-Lansdale, 1998). The Johns Hopkins Pregnancy Prevention Program, for example, provides complete medical care, contraceptive services, social services (such as counseling), and parenting education. This approach postponed the age of sexual activity onset, increased contraceptive use, reduced the frequency of sex, and reduced the actual

Figure 28.1 *Maternal age and satisfaction.* Note that the age of the mother directly relates to the percentage of reported feelings of sadness and tension.

pregnancy rate in the experimental group by 30 percent. During the same period, pregnancy rates in a comparison school rose by 58 percent (Hardy & Zabin, 1991).

The Teen Outreach Program is another success story. This program aims to enhance social development among adolescents through structured volunteer community service and classroom discussions of life choices, careers, and relationships (Allen, Philiber, Herrling, & Kupermine, 1997). Research shows that many teen pregnancies are due to poverty and the resulting perception that life options and choices are limited (Brewster, Billy, & Grady, 1993; Luker, 1996).

Most research and social programs (like the two described here) focus on economics: how money (or the lack of it) affects teen pregnancies. But researchers Rebekah Coley & Lindsay Chase-Lansdale (1998) suggest we should also be exploring the psychological consequences of early parenting. If adolescence is a time for solidifying identity and developing autonomy from parents, what happens with teen parents? What are the effects on a teen mother if she lives with her mother? What happens to the life span development of the "early" grandparents? What about the teen father? How does early fatherhood affect his course of development? And what about the child who is being raised by a teen mother or teen father or grandparent? How does this affect his or her development? Answers to these questions rest with the next generation of researchers (perhaps some of you who are reading this text).

The Impact of Divorce

> After years of advising other people on their personal problems, I was stunned by my own divorce. I only wish I had someone to write to for advice.
>
> Ann Landers

Although there has been a modest decline in the divorce rate since the 1970s, nearly one-half of marriages end in divorce in the United States (Hetherington, Bridges, & Insa-bella, 1998). Divorce has serious implications for both adult and child development (Lengua, Wolchik, Sandler, & West, 2000; Lopez, Melendez, & Rice, 2000). Both spouses generally experience emotional as well as practical difficulties and are at high risk for depression and physical health problems (Carbone, 2000; Davies & Cummings, 1998).

Some individuals appear to adapt well in the early stages of divorce but show effects at a later time (Hetherington & Stanley-Hagan, 1999; Wallerstein & Lewis, 1998; Whiteside & Becker, 2000). However, many problems assumed to be due to divorce are actually present before marital disruption (Carrere, Buehlman, Gottman, Coan, & Ruckstuhl, 2000; Sigelman, 1999). Thus, for some, divorce can be life enhancing. In a "healthy" divorce, ex-spouses must accomplish three tasks: *let go, develop new social ties,* and, when children are involved, *redefine parental roles* (Everett & Everett, 1994).

In addition to stresses on the divorcing couple, some research shows that children suffer both short-term and long-lasting effects. Compared with children in continuously intact two-parent families, children of divorce generally exhibit more behavioral problems, poorer self-concepts, more psychological problems, lower academic achievement, and more social difficulties (Hetherington & Stanley-Hagan, 1999; Melchert, 2000; Tein, Sandler, & Zautra, 2000; Wallerstein & Lewis, 1998). On the other hand, other research finds that children's psychological development is not affected by parental separation per se. Instead, it is related to mother's income, education, ethnicity, childrearing beliefs, depressive symptoms, and behavior (Clarke-Stewart, Vandell, McCartney, Owen, & Booth, 2000). Other researchers have suggested that children may also do better in homes without the constant tension and fighting of an unhappy, intact home (Emery, 1999).

Whether children become "winners" or "losers" in a divorce depends on the (1) individual attributes of the child, (2) qualities of the custodial family, (3) continued

If you want to estimate your personal chances for a happy marriage, consider the following points. Your chances for a successful marriage increase each time you answer *true*.

1. You and your partner are out of your teens and have known each other for at least 6 months.
2. Both sets of parents support the marriage, and neither set is divorced.
3. Neither you nor your partner is pregnant at the time of marriage.
4. You and your partner finished college and have a good income.
5. Both you and your partner think of one another as your best friend, and you both like one another as a person.
6. You were engaged before getting married and did not cohabit.
7. You agree on how to handle housework and child care.
8. You and your partner are religious and believe that marriage is sacred.
9. During conflicts, you and your partner communicate in an open, straightforward way and accept negative feedback without becoming overly defensive.

Source: Adapted from Gottman, 1998; Lauer & Lauer, 1992; Sigelman, 1999.

Resilience *A term referring to a child's good developmental outcome, sustained competence under stress, and recovery from trauma despite high-risk status*

involvement with noncustodial parents, and (4) resources and support systems available to the child and parents (Carbone, 2000; Gottman, 1998; Hetherington & Stanley-Hagan, 1999). If you or your parents are currently considering or going through divorce, you might want to keep these four factors in mind when making legal and other decisions about children.

RESEARCH HIGHLIGHT

Children Who Survive Despite the Odds

Children fortunate enough to grow up with days filled with play and discovery, nights that provide rest and security, and dedicated, loving parents usually turn out fine. But what about those who are raised in violent, impoverished, or neglectful situations? As we saw in the previous discussion of family violence, teen pregnancy, and divorce, a troubled childhood creates significantly higher risk of serious physical, emotional, and behavioral problems. There are exceptions to this rule, however. Some offspring of wonderful, loving parents have serious problems, and some children growing up amid major stressors are remarkably well adjusted.

What is it about children living in harsh circumstances that helps them survive and prosper — despite the odds? The answer holds great interest for both parents and society. Such *resilient* children can teach us

better ways to reduce risk, promote competence, and shift the course of development in more positive directions (Luthar, 1999; Masten, 1998). **Resilience** refers to good developmental outcomes, sustained competence under stress, and recovery from trauma despite high-risk status (Werner, 1995).

Resilience has been studied throughout the world in a variety of situations, including poverty, natural disasters, war, and family violence (e.g., Luthar, 1999; Taylor & Wang, 2000; Werner, 1995, 1999; Wright & Masten, 1997). Two researchers — Ann Masten at the University of Minnesota and Douglas Coatsworth at the University of Miami (1998) — identified several traits of the resilient child and the environmental circumstances that might account for the resilient child's success.

Most children who do well have (1) good intellectual functioning; (2) relationships with caring adults; and, as they grow older, (3) the ability to regulate their attention, emotions, and behavior. These traits

obviously overlap. Good intellectual functioning, for example, may help resilient children solve problems or protect themselves from adverse conditions as well as attract the interest of teachers who serve as nurturing adults. Their greater intellectual skills also may help them learn from their experiences and from the caring adults, so in later life they have better self-regulation skills.

In times of growing concern about homelessness, poverty, abuse, teen pregnancy, violence, and divorce, studies of successful children can be very important. On the other hand, there is no such thing as an invulnerable child. Masten and Coatsworth remind us that "if we allow the prevalence of known risk factors for development to rise while resources for children fall, we can expect the competence of individual children and the human capital of the nation to suffer" (Masten & Coatsworth, 1998, p. 216).

Did you grow up in a "high-risk" environment? Are you a resilient child? A 30-year longitudinal study of resilience (Werner, 1993, 1999) identified several environmental factors of high-risk children. Place a check mark by each risk factor that applies to your childhood:

_____ Born into chronic poverty

_____ Stressful fetal or birth conditions (e.g., prenatal hazards, low birth weight)

_____ Chronic discord in the family environment

_____ Parents divorced

_____ Mental illness in one or both parents

Two-thirds of the high-risk children who had experienced four or more of these factors by age 2 years later developed serious adjustment problems. But one-third of the children who also experienced four or more such risk factors were resilient. They developed into competent, confident, and caring adults.

Occupational Choices: The Effect of Work and Careers

Most working adults spend more time on the job than with their families. Erikson emphasized the importance of generativity to adult development — the need to accomplish something with one's life. Most people channel their accomplishment needs into their work.

How can I find a rewarding career that suits my personality and interests? Choosing an occupation is one of the most important decisions in our lives, and the task is becoming ever more complex as career options increase as a result of specialization. The *Dictionary of Occupational Titles*, a government publication, currently lists more than 200,000 job categories. One way to learn more about job categories and potential careers is to visit your college career center. Career counselors may suggest that you take vocational interest tests. (You can also try the online version of several vocational interest inventories — http://www.keirsey.com/cgi-bin/newkts.cgi).

Too often, career choices are made on the basis of income. Nearly 74 percent of college freshmen surveyed by the Higher Education Research Institute said that being "very well off financially" was "very important" or "essential." Seventy-one percent felt the same way about raising a family ("This year's freshmen," 1995). These young people no doubt expect to combine both family and work roles and "live the good life," but many will have to work long hours just to keep up with the rate of inflation. Given the decline in construction and many high-paying manufacturing jobs (which on the average pay three times the minimum wage), a college education is more important than ever in obtaining higher paying and more satisfying occupations.

Although they are still able to work, the large majority of men and women in the United States choose to retire sometime in their sixties. Like the midlife crisis and empty nest syndrome, the loss of self-esteem and depression that is commonly assumed to accompany retirement may be largely a myth. Life satisfaction after retirement appears to be most strongly related to good health, control over one's life, and participation in community services and social activities (Voltz, 2000; Whitbourne, 2000).

Although most researchers believe a fulfilling old age comes from remaining active and involved as long as possible, the **activity theory of aging**, some believe

Activity Theory *A theory of aging that suggests successful adjustment is fostered by a full and active commitment to life*

Disengagement versus activity.
Although disengagement theory suggests that older people naturally disengage and withdraw from life, activity theory argues that everyone should remain active and involved throughout the entire life span.

Disengagement Theory *A theory of aging suggesting that both the individual and society gradually and naturally pull away from each other in preparation for death*

successful aging is a natural and graceful withdrawal from life, the **disengagement theory** (Achenbaum & Bengtson, 1994; Voltz, 2000).

Although disengagement theory has been seriously questioned, it has stimulated important research. For example, studies have found that *selective* disengagement is one key to living fully throughout our entire adult life span (Carstensen, 1995; Schulz & Heckhausen, 1996). Beginning in early adulthood, we realize we cannot care deeply about 50 friends or work our best at 10 different pursuits. We must establish priorities. Gradually divesting ourselves of superfluous relationships and activities to focus on the most meaningful may be a healthy response at any age.

GENDER & CULTURAL DIVERSITY

Cultural Differences in Ageism

Physical decline is part of later life and causes emotional stress — although much less than most people think. A greater stress for the elderly, at least in the United States, is the **ageism** they encounter. In a society in which the old are seen as wise elders or keepers of valued traditions, the stress of aging is less than in a society in which they are seen as mentally slow and socially useless. In cultures like that in the United States in which youth, speed, and progress are strongly emphasized, a loss or decline in any of these qualities is deeply feared and denied (Powell, 1998).

Aren't there also cultures that honor their elderly? Yes, there are. In Japan, China, and in the United States, among African Americans and most tribes of Native Americans, the elderly are generally revered. Aging parents are respected for their wisdom and experience, are deferred to in family matters, and are expected to live with their children until they die (Klass, 2000; Martire, Stephens,

Ageism *Prejudice against people based on their age*

& Townsend, 2000). In Korea, for example, over 80 percent of the elderly are cared for by family members (Yoo & Sung, 1997). However, as these cultures become more urbanized and Westernized, often there is a corresponding decline in respect for the elderly.

Ageism in the United States

Between the extremes of being held in high or low esteem, there is considerable difference in the status and treatment of different subgroups of the elderly. In the United States, for example, studies show that older men have more social status, income, and sexual partners than do older women. Elderly women, on the other hand, have more friends and are more involved in family relationships but have lower status and income. Contrary to popular stereotype of the "rich old woman," elderly females represent one of the lowest income levels in North America (U.S. Bureau of the Census, 2001).

It is also interesting to look at ethnic differences in aging in the United States. Ethnic minority elderly, especially African Americans and Latinos, face problems related to both ageism and racism. They are more likely to become ill but less likely to receive treatment, and they are overrepresented among the elderly poor living below the poverty line (Contrada et al., 2000; Harrison & Gardiner, 1999; Markides, 1995).

Other research, however, reports that African Americans are more likely than Anglo-Americans to regard elderly persons with respect (Mui, 1992). Also, compared with whites, other ethnic groups often have a greater sense of community and may have stronger bonds of attachment, owing to their shared traits and experiences with prejudice. Ethnicity itself may therefore provide some benefits. "In addition to shielding them from majority attitudes, ethnicity provides the ethnic elderly with a source of esteem" (Fry, 1985, p. 233).

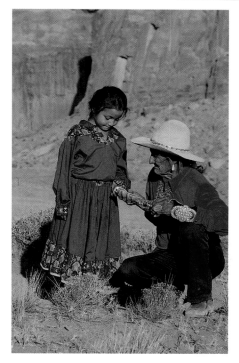

Elder respect. *Native Americans generally revere and respect the elder members of their tribe. How would aging be different if being old was an honor and blessing versus a dreaded process?*

Check & Review

ADDITIONAL INFLUENCES ON DEVELOPMENT

Family violence, teenage pregnancy, and divorce almost always have a negative effect on a child's development. **Resilient** children who survive abusive and stress-filled childhoods usually have good intellectual functioning; a relationship with a caring adult; and the ability to regulate their attention, emotions, and behavior.

The kind of work you do and the occupational choices you make can play a critical role in your life. One theory of successful aging, **activity theory**, says people should remain active and involved throughout the entire life span. The other major theory, **disengagement theory**, says the elderly naturally and gracefully withdraw from life because they welcome the relief from roles they can no longer fulfill. **Ageism** is an important stressor for the elderly, but in some cultures, the aged are revered.

Questions

1. Efforts to identify and prevent family violence are called _____ programs. (a) directive; (b) redirective; (c) primary; (d) secondary

2. The _____ theory of aging suggests that you should remain active and involved until death, whereas the _____ theory suggests that you should naturally and gracefully withdraw from life.

3. _____ is prejudice against people based on their age. (a) Ethnocentrism; (b) Elder abuse; (c) Ageism; (d) Disengagement

4. Explain how ethnicity may help the elderly overcome some problems of aging.

Answers to Questions can be found in Appendix B.

Are there predictable stages for grief and dying?

Bereavement and Death: The Ultimate Challenge

In this section, we will look at the four stages of grief and attitudes toward death and dying. We will then explore death itself as a final developmental crisis.

Grief

> What do I do now that you're gone? Well, when there's nothing else going on, which is quite often, I sit in a corner and I cry until I am too numbed to feel. Paralyzed motionless for a while, nothing moving inside or out. Then I think how much I miss you. Then I feel fear, pain, loneliness, desolation. Then I cry until I am too numbed to feel. Interesting pastime.
>
> PETER MCWILLIAMS, *HOW TO SURVIVE THE LOSS OF A LOVE*

Have you ever felt like this? If so, you are not alone. Bereavement and grief are an inevitable part of all our lives. Feelings of desolation, loneliness, and heartache, accompanied by painful memories, are common reactions to loss, disaster, or misfortune. Ironically, such painful emotions may serve a useful function. Evolutionary psychologists suggest that bereavement and grief may be adaptive mechanisms for both social animals and humans: The pain may motivate parents and children or mates to search for one another. Obvious signs of distress may also be adaptive because they bring the group to the aid of the bereaved individual.

What does it mean if someone seems emotionless after an important loss? Grieving is a complicated and personal process. Just as there is no right way to die, there is no right way to grieve (Koppel, 2000). People who restrain their grief may be following the rules for emotional display that prevail in their cultural group. Moreover, outward signs of strong emotion may be the most obvious expression of grief, but this is only one of four stages in the "normal" grieving process: numbness, yearning, disorganization/despair, and resolution (James & Friedman, 1998; Parkes, 1972, 1991).

In the initial phase of grief, *numbness*, bereaved individuals often seem dazed and may feel little emotion other than numbness or emptiness. They also may deny the death, insisting that a mistake has been made.

Next, individuals enter a stage of *yearning*, intense longing for the loved one, and pangs of guilt, anger, and resentment. The bereaved may also experience illusions: They "see" the deceased person in his or her favorite chair or in the face of a stranger, they have vivid dreams in which the deceased is still alive, or they feel the "presence" of the dead person. They also experience strong guilt feelings ("If only I had gotten her to a doctor sooner"; "I should have been more loving") and anger or resentment ("Why wasn't he more careful?"; "It isn't fair that I'm the one left behind").

Once the powerful feelings of yearning subside, the individual enters the *disorganization/despair* phase. Life seems to lose its meaning. The mourner feels list-

Grieving. Individuals vary in their emotional reactions to loss. There is no right or wrong way to grieve.

less, apathetic, and submissive. As time goes by, however, the survivor gradually begins to accept the loss both intellectually (the loss makes sense) and emotionally (memories are both pleasurable as well as painful). This acceptance, combined with building a new self-identity ("I am a single mother"; "We are no longer a couple"), characterizes the final state of grief — the *resolution or reorganization* stage.

Grief is obviously not the same for everyone. People vary in the stages of grief that they experience and the length of time for "recovery" (Davis, Nolen-Hoeksema, & Larson, 1998; Koppel, 2000). You can help people who are grieving by accepting their individual differences and recognizing that there is no perfect response. Simply say "I'm sorry," and then let the person talk if he or she wishes. Your quiet presence and caring is generally the best type of support.

When it comes to dealing with your own losses and grief, psychologists offer several techniques that you may find helpful (Holland, 1998; Napolitane, 1997; Wartik, 1996):

1. *Recognize the loss and allow yourself to grieve.* Despite feelings of acute loneliness, remember that loss is a part of everyone's life and accept comfort from others. Take care of yourself by avoiding unnecessary stress, getting plenty of rest, and giving yourself permission to enjoy life whenever possible.

2. *Set up a daily activity schedule.* One of the best ways to offset the lethargy and depression of grief is to force yourself to fill your time with useful activities (studying, washing your car, doing the laundry, and so on).

3. *Seek help.* Recognize that professional counseling may be necessary in cases of extreme or prolonged numbness, anger, guilt, or depression. (You will learn more about depression and therapy in Modules 39, 43, and 44.)

Attitudes Toward Death and Dying

Cultures around the world interpret and respond to death in widely different ways: "Funerals are the occasion for avoiding people or holding parties, for fighting or having sexual orgies, for weeping or laughing, in a thousand combinations" (Metcalf & Huntington, 1991, p. 62).

Similarly, subcultures within the United States also have different responses to death. Irish Americans are likely to believe the dead deserve a good send-off — a wake with food, drink, and jokes. On the other hand, African Americans traditionally regard funerals as a time for serious grief, demonstrated in some congregations by wailing and singing spirituals (Barley, 1997; Wartik, 1996). Most Japanese Americans, however, try to restrain their grief and smile so as not to burden others with their pain and to avoid the shame associated with losing emotional control (Cook & Dworkin, 1992).

Attitudes toward death and dying also vary with age. As adults, we understand death in terms of three basic concepts: (1) *permanence* — once a living thing dies, it cannot be brought back to life; (2) *universality* — all living things eventually die; (3) *nonfunctionality* — all living functions, including thought, movement, and vital signs, end at death.

Research shows that permanence, the notion that death cannot be reversed, is the first and most easily understood concept. Preschoolers seem to accept the fact that the dead person cannot get up again, perhaps because of their experiences with dead butterflies and beetles found while playing outside (Furman, 1990).

Understanding of universality comes slightly later, and by the age of 7 years, most children have mastered nonfunctionality and have an adultlike understanding of death. Although parents may fear that discussing death with young children will make them unduly anxious, children who are offered open, honest discussions of death have an easier time accepting it (Aspinall, 1996; Kastenbaum, 1999).

The Death Experience

Have you thought about your own death? Would you like to die suddenly and alone, or would you prefer to know ahead of time so you could plan your funeral and spend time saying good-bye to your family and friends? If you find thinking about these questions uncomfortable, it may be because most people in Western societies deny death. Unfortunately, avoiding thoughts and discussion of death and associating aging with death contribute to ageism (Atchley, 1997).

During the Middle Ages (from about the fifth century until the 1500s), people were expected to recognize when death was approaching so they could bid their farewells and die with dignity surrounded by loved ones (Aries, 1981). In recent times, Western societies have moved death out of the home and put it into the hospital and funeral parlor. Rather than personally caring for our dying family and friends, we have shifted responsibility to "experts" — physicians and morticians. We have made death a medical failure, rather than a natural part of the life cycle.

This avoidance of death and dying may be changing, though. Since the late 1990s, right-to-die and death-with-dignity advocates have been working to bring death out in the open, and mental health professionals have suggested that understanding the psychological processes of death and dying may play a significant role in good adjustment.

Confronting our own death is the last major crisis we face in life. What is it like? Is there a "best" way to prepare to die? Is there such a thing as a "good death"? After spending hundreds of hours at the bedsides of the terminally ill, Elisabeth Kübler-Ross developed her stage theory of the psychological processes surrounding death (1983, 1997, 1999).

On the basis of extensive interviews with patients, Kübler-Ross proposed that most people go through five sequential stages when facing death: *denial* of the terminal condition ("This can't be true; it's a mistake!"), *anger* ("Why me? It isn't fair!"), *bargaining* ("God, if you let me live, I'll dedicate my life to you!"), *depression* ("I'm losing everyone and everything I hold dear"), and finally *acceptance* ("I know that death is inevitable and my time is near").

Evaluating Kübler-Ross's Theory Critics of the stage theory of dying stress that each person's death is a unique experience and that emotions and reactions depend on the individual's personality, life situation, age, and so on (Dunn, 2000; Kastenbaum, 1999). Others worry that popularizing stage theory will cause further avoidance and stereotyping of the dying ("He's just in the anger stage right now"). In response, Kübler-Ross (1983, 1997, 1999) agrees that not all people go through the same stages in the same way and regrets that anyone would use her theory as a model for a "good death."

In spite of the potential abuses, Kübler-Ross's theory has given us valuable insights and spurred research into a long-neglected topic. **Thanatology**, the study of

Thanatology [THAN-uh-tall-uh-gee] *The study of death and dying. The term comes from thanatos, the Greek name for a mythical personification of death, and was borrowed by Freud to represent the death instinct*

death and dying, has become a major topic in human development. Thanks in part to thanatology research, the dying are being helped to die with dignity by the hospice movement, which has created special facilities and trained staff and volunteers to provide loving support for the terminally ill and their families (Smith & Smith, 1997).

> Healthy children will not fear life, if their parents have integrity enough not to fear death…
>
> Erik Erikson

Check & Review

BEREAVEMENT AND DEATH

Attitudes toward death and dying vary greatly across cultures and among age groups. Although adults understand the *permanence, universality,* and *nonfunctionality* of death, children often don't master these concepts until around age 7 years. Grief is a natural and painful reaction to a loss. For most people, grief consists of four major stages — *numbness, yearning, disorganization/despair,* and *resolution.* Elisabeth Kübler-Ross's theory of the five-stage process of dying (*denial, anger, bargaining, depression,* and *acceptance*) offers important insights into the last major crisis we face in life. The study of death and dying, **thanatology,** has become an important topic in human development.

Questions

1. Explain how an adult's understanding of death differs from a preschool child's.

2. Grieving people generally begin with the _____ stage and end with the _____ stage. (a) numbness, bargaining; (b) grief, anger; (c) yearning, acceptance; (d) numbness, resolution

3. Match the following statements with Elisabeth Kübler-Ross's five-stage theory of death and dying:

   ____ a. "I understand that I'm dying, but if I could just have a little more time…"

   ____ b. "I refuse to believe the doctors. I want a fourth opinion."

   ____ c. "I know my time is near. I'd better make plans for my spouse and children."

   ____ d. "Why me? I've been a good person."

   ____ e. "I'm losing everything. I'll never see my children again. Life is so hard."

4. The study of death and dying is known as _____ (a) gerontology; (b) ageism; (c) mortality; (d) thanatology

Answers to Questions can be found in Appendix B.

ACTIVE LEARNING WORKSHEET   MODULE 28

Enter the correct letter from Column A in the blank space in Column B, and then doublecheck your answers with those in Appendix B.

Column A

a. Resilience
b. Stages of grief
c. Disengagement theory
d. Ageism
e. Kubler-Ross
f. Teen pregnancy
g. Thanatology
h. Activity theory
i. Elderly females
j. Stages of death

Column B

1. ____ Most common reason females drop out of school.
2. ____ Prejudice based on age.
3. ____ Study of death and dying.
4. ____ Positive development despite harsh environment.
5. ____ Natural withdrawal in preparation for death.
6. ____ Denial, anger, bargaining, depression, acceptance.
7. ____ Advocates full, active commitment to life.
8. ____ Has one of the lowest incomes in North America.
9. ____ Proposed theory of 5 stages of impending death.
10. ____ Numbness, yearning, disorganization/despair, resolution.

Visual Summary for Modules 27 and 28

Moral Development

Kohlberg's Three Levels and Six Stages

Preconventional Morality	Conventional Morality	Postconventional Morality

Preconventional Morality

Stage 1: *Punishment-obedience orientation*. Morality is what you can get away with.

↓

Stage 2: *Instrumental-exchange orientation*. Obeys rules to obtain rewards or favors.

Conventional Morality

Stage 3: *Good-child orientation*. Obeys rules to get approval.

↓

Stage 4: *Law-and-order orientation*. Obeys laws because they maintain the social order.

Postconventional Morality

Stage 5: *Social-contract orientation*. Moral reasoning reflects belief in democratically established laws.

↓

Stage 6: *Universal ethics orientation*. Moral reasoning reflects individual conscience.

Criticisms of Kohlberg's theory: Politically, culturally, and gender biased. Gilligan says women take a **care perspective** in their moral reasoning and men a **justice perspective**. In fact, research shows both sexes typically use both perspectives.

Personality Development Over the Life Span

**Thomas & Chess'
Temperament Theory**

Temperament: Basic, inborn disposition. Three temperament styles: easy, difficult, and slow-to-warm-up. Styles seem consistent and enduring.

Erikson's
Eight **Psychosocial Stages**

Childhood: Trust vs. mistrust, autonomy vs. shame and doubt, initiative vs. guilt, industry vs. inferiority.
Adolescence: Identity vs. role confusion.
Young Adulthood: Intimacy vs. isolation.
Middle Adulthood: Generativity vs. stagnation.
Older Adult: Ego integrity vs. despair.

Additional Influences on Personality Development

Families

- Family violence, teenage pregnancies, and divorce can damage personality development.
- **Resilience** helps some children survive an abusive or stress-filled childhood.

Occupational Choices

Occupational choice is critically important because most people channel their accomplishment needs into their work.

Aging

Ageism: Prejudice against people based on their age. Two major theories of aging:

activity theory (should remain active).

disengagement theory (should gracefully withdraw).

 ## Bereavement and Death

Grief

Grief: A natural and painful reaction to a loss, consists of four major stages:

1) numbness → 2) yearning → 3) disorganization and despair → 4) resolution

Attitudes

Attitudes toward death and dying vary greatly across cultures and among age groups. Children generally don't fully understand the permanence, universality, and nonfunctionality of death until around age seven.

Death Experience

- Kübler-Ross proposes a five-stage process of dying (denial, anger, bargaining, depression, and acceptance).
- **Thanatology:** Study of death and dying.

Gender and Human Sexuality

Core Learning Objectives

As you read Modules 29 and 30, keep the following questions in mind and answer them in your own words.

► How are sex and gender defined, and how do we develop our gender roles? What are the major sex and gender differences between men and women?

► How do scientists study a sensitive topic like sex?

► How are men and women alike and different in sexual arousal and response? What is the latest research on sexual orientation?

► What factors contribute to sexual dysfunction and sexually transmitted infections?

It was an unusual circumcision. The identical twin boys were already 8 months old when their parents took them to the doctor to be circumcised. For many years in the United States, most male babies have had the foreskin of their penis removed during their first week of life, when it is assumed they will experience less pain. The most common procedure is cutting or pinching off the foreskin tissue. In this case, however, the doctor used an electrocautery device, which is used to burn off moles or small skin growths. The electrical current used for the first twin was too high, and the entire penis was accidentally ablated, or removed. (The parents did not let the physician try to circumcise the other twin.)

In anguish over the tragic accident, the parents sought advice from medical experts. Following discussions with John Money and other specialists at John Hopkins University, the parents and doctors made an unusual decision — the twin with the destroyed penis would be raised as a girl.

The first step in the reassignment process occurred at age 17 months, when the child's name was changed — Bruce became "Brenda" (Colapinto, 2000). Brenda was dressed in pink pants and frilly blouses and "her" hair was allowed to grow long. At 21 months, plastic surgery was performed to create external female genital structures. Further plastic surgery to create a vagina was planned for the beginning of adolescence, when the child's physical growth would be nearly complete. At this time she would also begin to take female hormones to complete the boy-to-girl transformation.

According to John Money (Money & Ehrhardt, 1972), the children's mother was surprised and pleased by the striking differences that developed in her two children. The case of "John/Joan" (pseudonyms) was reported in the medical literature as an unqualified success. By age three, the "female" twin wore nightgowns and dresses almost exclusively and liked bracelets and hair ribbons. During the preschool years, the girl reportedly preferred playing with "girl-type" toys and asked for a doll and carriage for Christmas. Her brother asked for a garage with cars, gas pumps, and tools. By age 6,

the brother was accustomed to defending his sister if he thought someone was threatening her. The daughter copied the mother in tidying and cleaning up the kitchen, whereas the boy did not. The mother agreed that she encouraged her daughter when she helped with the housework and expected the boy to be uninterested.

What first looked like a success was, in fact, a dismal failure. Follow-up studies report that the child never really adjusted to her assigned gender (Diamond & Sigmundson, 1997). In spite of being raised from infancy as a girl, she did not feel like a girl and avoided most female activities and interests. By age 14, she was so unhappy that she contemplated suicide. The father then tearfully explained what had happened earlier. For the child, "All of a sudden everything clicked. For the first time things made sense, and I understood who and what I was" (Thompson, 1997, p. 83).

What do you think about the parents' and experts' solution to this terrible accident? Is it possible that what makes some children prefer "girl-type" toys and clothes is how parents or others treat them? Or is biology the predictor of our gender-related behaviors? The concepts of sex, gender, attraction, and maleness and femaleness are not simple. You will learn more about "Brenda" and your own gender development and sexuality in the first part of Module 29. Then we introduce four pioneers in sex research and discuss cultural differences in sexual practices and attitudes. In the third section, we describe sexual arousal, response, and orientation. Finally, we look at sexual dysfunction and sexually transmitted infections, including AIDS (acquired immunodeficiency syndrome).

MODULE 29
SEX AND GENDER

Why is it that the first question most people ask after a baby is born is "Is it a girl or a boy?" What would life be like if there were no divisions according to maleness or femaleness? Would your career plans or friendship patterns change? These questions reflect the importance of *sex* and *gender* in our lives. This section begins with a look at the various ways sex and gender can be defined, followed by a discussion of gender role development and sex and gender differences.

Problems with Definition: What Is "Maleness" or "Femaleness"?

When people ask if a newborn is a girl or boy, they're typically thinking of standard biological differences as seen in Figure 29.1. But when they buy gifts for children, they frequently demonstrate their expectations of *femininity* ("She'll like this pretty doll") versus *masculinity* ("This fire truck is perfect for him"). In the case of the male twin who was reassigned as a female, do you still think of "her" as basically male? Is a man who cross-dresses female? The question of what is "male" and "female" can be confusing.

In recent years, researchers have come to use the term **sex** to refer to the biological elements of maleness and femaleness (such as having a penis or vagina), or physical activities (such as masturbation and intercourse). **Gender**, on the other hand, encompasses the psychological and sociocultural meanings added to biological maleness or femaleness (such as "Men should be aggressive" and "Women should be nurturing"). There are at least seven dimensions or elements of *sex* and two of *gender* (Table 29.1).

How are sex and gender defined, and how do we develop our gender roles? What are the major sex and gender differences between men and women?

Sex *Biological maleness and femaleness, including chromosomal sex, gonadal sex, hormonal sex, external genitals, and internal accessory organs; also, activities related to sexual behaviors, such as masturbation and intercourse*

Gender *The psychological and sociocultural meanings added to biological maleness or femaleness*

Figure 29.1 *Male and female internal and external systems.* (a) The internal and external sex organs of the male. (b) The internal and external sex organs of the female.

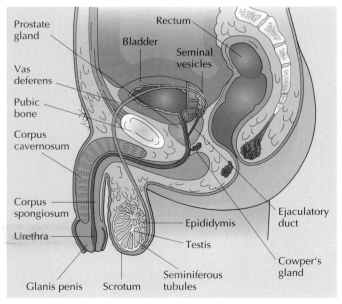

Prostate gland
Rectum
Bladder
Seminal vesicles
Vas deferens
Pubic bone
Corpus cavernosum
Corpus spongiosum
Urethra
Glanis penis
Scrotum
Epididymis
Testis
Seminiferous tubules
Ejaculatory duct
Cowper's gland

(a)

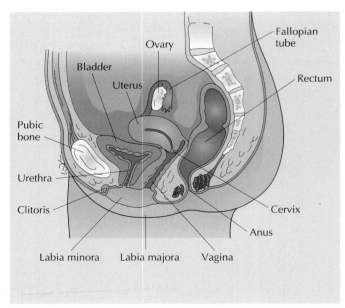

Ovary
Fallopian tube
Bladder
Uterus
Rectum
Pubic bone
Urethra
Clitoris
Cervix
Anus
Labia minora
Labia majora
Vagina

(b)

TABLE 29.1 DIMENSIONS OF SEX AND GENDER

	Male	Female
Sex Dimensions		
1. Chromosomes	XY	XX
2. Gonads	Testes	Ovaries
3. Hormones	Androgens	Estrogens
4. External genitals	Penis, scrotum	Labia majora, labia minora, clitoris, vaginal opening
5. Internal accessory organs	Prostate gland, seminal vesicles, vas deferens, ejaculatory duct, Cowper's gland	Vagina, uterus, fallopian tubes, cervix
6. Secondary sex characteristics	Beard, lower voice, wider shoulders, sperm emission	Breasts, wider hips, menstruation
7. Sexual orientation	Heterosexual, gay, bisexual	Heterosexual, lesbian, bisexual
Gender Dimensions		
8. Gender identity (self-definition)	Perceives self as male	Perceives self as female
9. Gender role (societal expectations)	Masculine ("Boys like trucks and sports")	Feminine ("Girls like dolls and clothes")

If you apply the dimensions of sex and gender that are presented in Table 29.1 to the case of the reassigned twin, you can see why it is a classic in the field of human sexuality. Although born a chromosomal male, the child's genital sex was first altered by the doctor who accidentally removed the penis and later by surgeons who created female genitals. The question was whether surgery, along with female hormones and "appropriate" gender role expectations of the parents, would be enough to create a stable female **gender identity**. Would the child accept the sex reassignment and identify herself as female?

At first, it appeared that Brenda's reassignment was successful, and psychology and sociology texts cited this case as evidence of the environment's predominant role in creating gender identity. As she entered adolescence, however, the early "success" began to be questioned. Her appearance and masculine gait led classmates to tease her and call her "cave woman." At this age, she also expressed thoughts of becoming a mechanic, and her fantasies reflected discomfort with her female role. She even tried urinating in a standing position. By age 14, she insisted she wanted to live as a boy (Diamond & Sigmundson, 1997).

Brenda was later surgically changed back to a man, with a new name, David. At age 25, he married a somewhat older woman and adopted her children. Although David now says, "I don't blame my parents," they still feel extremely guilty about their participation in the reassignment. David, his twin brother, and parents all suffered tremendously from the tragic accident and the no less tragic solution. The family members have since reconciled, but David is no longer in contact with the doctor, John Money.

[A similar botched circumcision occurred in 1985, exactly 20 years after David and his twin brother were born. Although David had announced his decision to live as a male 5 years earlier, "Baby Doe" was also surgically altered and reassigned as a female. The current status of this child is carefully guarded, but limited facts point to a similarly unhappy outcome (Colapinto, 2000). The consulting specialist was John Money.]

Gender Identity *How one psychologically perceives oneself as either male or female*

Why do some men cross-dress? *Those who are transvestites dress like women to release sexual tension and enjoy the other sex's gender role. Contrary to common believe, gay men seldom cross-dress.*

Sexual Orientation *An individual's primary erotic attraction can be toward members of the same sex (homosexual, gay or lesbian), both sexes (bisexual), or other sex (heterosexual)*

Gender Role *The societal expectations for normal and appropriate male and female behavior; when these expectations are based on exaggerated and biased beliefs about differences between the sexes and are rigidly applied to all members of each sex, they are known as gender role stereotypes*

The fact that David ultimately rejected his assigned female gender despite strong pressure from his family and doctors indicates that the most important factor in gender identity may be biological. A recent longitudinal study offers additional evidence of a biological link. Researchers at Johns Hopkins Hospital tracked the development of 27 normal boys, born without a penis, a rare defect known as *cloacal exstrophy.* Twenty-five of these boys were castrated at birth and raised as girls, yet researchers observed many signs of masculine behavior, including lots of "typical" male "rough-and-tumble" play. Fourteen of the children, currently ranging in age from 5 to 16 years, have recently rejected their female reassignment and declared themselves to be boys (Hettena, 2000).

In addition to the gender difficulties involved in David's case and the cases of the boys born without a penis, other gender problems may develop when a person expresses persistent discomfort about his or her gender and repeatedly expresses a wish to be a member of the other sex. This is known as *transsexualism* (having a gender identity opposite to biological sex). Although some may see the case of Brenda/Bruce/David as a form of transsexualism, "true" transsexuals are not the result of botched circumcisions. They are born chromosomally and anatomically one sex, but their **gender identity** is that of the other sex. Thus, an anatomically male transsexual feels he is the victim of a "birth defect" and often seeks corrective reassignment surgery (Bower, 2001). At one time, the number of men seeking reassignment was much higher than the number of women who wished to be men, but the ratio has narrowed considerably in recent years (Landen, Walinder, & Lundstrom, 1998).

Is a transsexual the same as a transvestite? No, *transvestism* involves individuals (almost exclusively men) who become sexually aroused or gratified by wearing the clothes stereotypical of the other sex (cross-dressing) (Allgeier & Allgeier, 2000). Transsexuals, however, feel that they are really members of the opposite sex imprisoned in the wrong body — their gender identity does not match their gonads, genitals, or internal accessory organs. Transsexuals may also cross-dress, but their motivation is to look like the "right" sex rather than to obtain sexual arousal. Transvestites can also be distinguished from female impersonators (who cross-dress to entertain) and from gay men who occasionally "go in drag" (cross-dress).

Are transvestites and transsexuals also homosexual? When a person is described as *homosexual*, it is because of a **sexual orientation** toward the same sex. (The preferred terms today are *gay* and *lesbian* rather than *homosexual*.) Transvestites are usually heterosexual (Bullough & Bullough, 1997). Transsexuality, on the other hand, has nothing to do with sexual orientation. In fact, a transsexual can be heterosexual, gay, lesbian, or *bisexual* (being sexually attracted to both males and females).

The confusion between homosexuality and transsexuality can be avoided if you remember that sexual orientation and gender identity are two different things. For example, a male transsexual's attraction to a male sex partner might appear to be a case of homosexuality. But after sex-change surgery, this same sexual orientation would logically be classified as heterosexual. Also, some male transsexuals are married to or sexually attracted to females before the sex-change operation and continue to prefer female partners after their bodies have been changed to females.

Gender Role Development: Two Major Theories

With a basic understanding of sexual orientation and problems with gender identity, let's look at **gender roles** — societal expectations for normal and appropriate female and male behavior. Gender roles influence our lives from the moment of birth (when we are wrapped in either a pink or blue blanket) until the moment of death (when we are buried in either a dress or a dark suit). By age two, children are well aware of gender roles. They recognize that boys "should" be strong, independent, aggressive, dominant, and achieving, whereas girls "should" be soft, dependent, passive, emotional, and "naturally" interested in children (Kimmel, 2000; Witt, 1997). The gender role expectations learned in childhood apparently influence us throughout our life.

How do we develop our gender roles? There are currently two major theories of gender role development: *social learning* and *cognitive developmental*.

Social Learning Theory

Social-learning theorists emphasize the power of the immediate situation and observable behaviors on gender role development. They suggest girls learn how to be "feminine" and boys learn how to be "masculine" in two major ways: (1) They receive rewards or punishments for specific gender role behaviors and (2) they watch and imitate the behavior of others — particularly the same-sex parent (Bandura, 1989, 2000; Leaper, Anderson, & Sanders, 1998; Ruble & Martin, 1998). A boy who puts on his father's tie or baseball cap wins big, indulgent smiles from his parents. But can you imagine what would happen if he put on his mother's nightgown or lipstick? Parents, teachers, and friends generally reward or punish behaviors according to traditional boy/girl gender role expectations. Thus, a child "socially learns" what it means to be male or female.

Cognitive Developmental Theory

Cognitive-developmental theorists acknowledge that social learning is part of gender development, but, they argue, the social learning model sees gender development as a passive process. Cognitive developmentalists point out that children also actively observe, interpret, and judge the world around them (Bem, 1981, 1993; Liben & Signorella, 1993; Welch-Ross & Schmidt, 1996). As children process this information, they create internal rules governing correct behaviors for boys versus girls. On the basis of these rules, they form *gender schemas* (mental images) of how they should act. (Recall from the discussion of Piaget in Module 26 that a schema is a cognitive structure, a network of associations, that guides perception.)

Thus, a little boy plays with fire trucks and building blocks because his parents smiled approvingly in the past and because he has seen more boys than girls playing

Early gender role conditioning. What are the long-term effects of this type of gender role training on young boys and girls?

with these toys. But his internal thought processes also contribute to his choice of "masculine" toys; he realizes he is a boy, and he has learned that boys "should" prefer fire trucks to dishes and dolls.

Sex and Gender Differences: Nature Versus Nurture

Now that we have looked at the different dimensions of sex and gender and examined gender role development, let's turn our attention to sex and gender differences between males and females.

Sex Differences

Physical anatomy is the most obvious biological difference between males and females. We differ in our secondary sex characteristics (facial hair, breasts, and so on), our signs of reproductive capability (the menarche for girls and the ejaculation of sperm for boys), and our physical reactions to middle age or the end of reproduction (the female menopause and male climacteric). The average man is also taller, heavier, and stronger than the average woman, but he is also more likely to be bald and color-blind.

There are also important functional and structural differences in the brains of human females and males. These differences result, at least in part, from prenatal sex differentiation and are most apparent in the *hypothalamus, corpus callosum,* and *cerebral hemispheres* (Diamond & Sigmundson, 1997; Dorion et al., 2000; Gur et al., 1995; Reiner, 1997). During puberty, a female's hypothalamus directs her pituitary gland to release hormones in a cyclic fashion, known as the menstrual cycle, whereas the male's hypothalamus directs a *relatively* steady production of sex hormones. Researchers have also documented differences in the cerebral hemispheres of men and women that may account for differences in verbal and spatial skills (Castle, 2000; Joseph, 2000; Shaywitz, 1996; Wisniewski, 1998).

Gender Differences

Do you think there are inborn psychological differences between women and men? Do you believe that women are more emotional and more concerned with aesthetics, whereas men are naturally more aggressive and competitive? Scientists have researched questions such as these; their major findings on gender differences are summarized in Table 29.2. In this section, we will focus on two of their most important findings — regarding cognitive abilities and aggression. We will also explore one way to minimize gender differences, through androgyny.

1. *Cognitive abilities.* For many years, researchers have noted that females tend to score higher on tests of verbal skills, whereas males score higher on math and visuospatial tests (Gallagher et al., 2000; Ruble & Martin, 1998). As mentioned earlier, some researchers suggest that these differences may reflect biology — that is, structural differences in the cerebral hemispheres, hormones, or in the degree of hemispheric specialization.

One very strong argument against such a biological model, however, is that cognitive gender differences have dramatically declined in recent years (Brown & Josephs, 1999; Halpern, 1997, 2000). By comparing a large number of studies, Hyde and her colleagues (1988, 1990) found a significant reduction in male–female differences in verbal ability scores and math scores. The major exception in this trend of vanishing gender differences is found in a small segment of the population, the brightest of the bright. Males in this group tend to score significantly higher in SAT math scores.

2. *Aggression.* One of the clearest and most consistent findings in gender studies is greater physical aggressiveness in males. From an early age, boys are more likely to

TABLE 29.2   RESEARCH-SUPPORTED SEX AND GENDER DIFFERENCES

Type of Behavior	More Often Shown by Men	More Often Shown by Women
Sexual	Begin masturbating sooner in life cycle and have higher overall occurrence rates. Start sexual life earlier and have first orgasm through masturbation. Are more likely to recognize their own sexual arousal. Experience more orgasm consistency in their sexual relations.	Begin masturbating later in life cycle and have lower overall occurrence rates. Start sexual life later and have first orgasm from partner stimulation. Are less likely to recognize their own sexual arousal. Experience less orgasm consistency in their sexual relations.
Touching	Are touched, kissed, and cuddled less by parents. Exchange less physical contact with other men and respond more negatively to being touched. More likely to initiate both casual and intimate touch.	Are touched, kissed, and cuddled more by parents. Exchange more physical contact with other women and respond more positively to being touched. Less likely to initiate either casual or intimate touch.
Friendship	Have larger number of friends and express friendship by shared activities.	Have smaller number of friends and express friendship by shared communication about self.
Personality	Are more aggressive from a very early age. Are more self-confident of future success. Attribute success to internal factors and failures to external factors. Achievement is task oriented; motives are mastery and competition. Are more self-validating Have higher self-esteem.	Are less aggressive from a very early age. Are less self-confident of future success. Attribute success to external factors and failures to internal factors. Achievement is socially directed with emphasis on self-improvement; have higher work motives. Are more dependent on others for self-validation Have lower self-esteem.
Cognitive Abilities	Are slightly superior in mathematics and visospatial skills.	Are slightly superior in grammar, spelling, and related verbal skills.

Sources: Allgeier & Allgeier, 2000; Baldwin & Baldwin, 1997; Crooks & Bauer, 1999; Hyde & Plant, 1995.

engage in mock fighting and rough-and-tumble play (Hettena, 2000; Niehoff, 1999; Reed & Brown, 2001). As adults, they are also more likely to commit aggressive crimes. But gender differences are clearer for physical aggression (like hitting) than for other forms of aggression (Zurbriggen, 2000). Although early research suggested females were more likely to engage in more indirect and relational forms of aggression, such as spreading rumors, ignoring, or excluding someone (Bjorkquist, 1994; Crick, 1996). But later research has not found such clear differences (Pakaslahti & Keltikangas-Jaervinen, 2000; Richardson & Green, 1999).

What causes these gender differences in aggression? Nativists generally cite biological factors. For example, several studies have linked the male gonadal hormone testosterone to aggressive behavior (Boyd, 2000; Dabbs & Dabbs, 2000; Sanchez-Martin et al., 2000). Other studies have found that men have lower levels of serotonin, a neurotransmitter found to be inversely related to aggression (Berman, Tracy, & Coccaro, 1997; Holtzworth-Munroe, 2000). In addition, studies on identical twins find that genetic factors account for about 50 percent of aggressive behavior (Cadoret, Leve, & Devor, 1997; Segal & Bouchard, 2000).

Nurturists typically point to environmental pressures that encourage "sex-appropriate" behaviors and skills. For example, children's picture books, video games, and TV programs and commercials frequently present women and men in stereotypical gender roles — men as pilots and doctors, women as moms and nurses (Dietz, 1998; Kimmel, 2000).

What if we don't like this part of gender roles? What can we do?

Androgyny

Androgyny [an-DRAW-juh-nee]
Combining characteristics considered typically male (e.g., assertive, athletic) with characteristics considered typically female (e.g., yielding, nurturant); from the Greek andro, meaning "male", and gyn, meaning "female."

One way to overcome gender role stereotypes is to encourage **androgyny**, expressing both the "masculine" and "feminine" traits found in each individual. Rather than limiting themselves to rigid gender-appropriate behaviors, androgynous men and women can be assertive and aggressive when necessary, but also gentle and nurturing.

Although some people think *androgyny* is a new term for asexuality or transsexualism, the idea of androgyny has a long history referring to positive combinations of gender roles, like the yin and yang of traditional Chinese religions. Carl Jung (1946, 1959), an early psychoanalyst, described a woman's natural masculine traits and impulses as her "animus" and feminine traits and impulses in a man as his "anima." Jung believed we must draw on both our masculine and feminine natures to become fully functioning adults.

Using personality tests and other similar measures, modern researchers have found that masculine and androgynous individuals generally have higher self-esteem, are more socially competent and motivated to achieve, and exhibit better overall mental health (Gianakos, 2000; Courtenay, 2000; Stake, 1997). It seems that androgyny and masculinity are adaptive for both sexes.

How can you explain this? The most likely explanation is that traditional masculine characteristics (analytical, independent) are more highly valued than traditional feminine traits (affectionate, cheerful). In fact, when college students in 14 different countries were asked to describe their "current self" and their "ideal self," the ideal self-descriptions for both men and women contained more masculine qualities than feminine (Williams & Best, 1990).

This shared preference for male traits also explains why extensive observation of children on school playgrounds has found that boys who engage in feminine activities (like skipping rope or playing jacks) lose status. The reverse of this is not true for girls (Leaper, 2000). Even as adults, it is more difficult for males to express so-called female traits like nurturance and sensitivity than for women to adopt traditionally

Androgeny in action. *Combining the traits of both genders helps many couples meet the demands of modern life.*

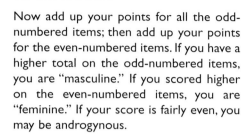

TRY THIS *Yourself*

Would you like to see how androgynous you are? Social psychologist Sandra Bem (1974, 1993) developed a personality measure that has been widely used in research. You can take this version of Bem's test by rating yourself on the following items. Give yourself a number between 1 (never or almost never true) and 7 (always or almost always true):

1. _____ Analytical
2. _____ Affectionate
3. _____ Competitive
4. _____ Compassionate
5. _____ Aggressive

6. _____ Cheerful
7. _____ Independent
8. _____ Gentle
9. _____ Athletic
10. _____ Sensitive

Now add up your points for all the odd-numbered items; then add up your points for the even-numbered items. If you have a higher total on the odd-numbered items, you are "masculine." If you scored higher on the even-numbered items, you are "feminine." If your score is fairly even, you may be androgynous.

male traits of assertiveness and independence (Kimmel, 2000; Christensen, Hebl, Rothgerber, & Wood, 1997). In short, most societies prefer "tomboys" over "sissies."

Recent studies show that gender roles in our society are becoming less rigidly defined (Kimmel, 2000; Loo & Thorpe, 1998). Asian American and Mexican American groups show some of the largest changes toward androgyny, and African Americans remain among the most androgynous of all ethnic groups (Espin, 1993; Harris, 1996; Huang & Ying, 1989).

But in spite of positive trends in gender roles, behavior in some areas — especially dating — is difficult to understand. Although most couples still follow the unspoken gender rule that men should make the first approach, how does the man know if the woman is interested? Researchers have found some very interesting answers; see the accompanying Research Highlight.

Check & Review

SEX AND GENDER

The term **sex** is differentiated along seven dimensions: chromosomal sex, gonadal sex, hormonal sex, external genitals, internal accessory organs, secondary sex characteristics, and sexual orientation. **Gender**, on the other hand, is differentiated according to **gender identity** and **gender role**. Transsexualism is a problem with gender identity; trans-

vestism is cross-dressing for sexual arousal. **Sexual orientation** (gay, lesbian, bisexual, or heterosexual) is unrelated to both transsexualism and transvestism. There are two main theories of gender role development: Social-learning theorists focus on rewards, punishments, and imitation, whereas cognitive-developmental theorists emphasize the active, thinking processes of the individual.

Studies of male and female sex differences find several obvious physical differences, such as height, body build, and reproductive organs. There are also important functional and structural sex differences in the brains of human females and males. Looking at gender differences, studies find some differences (such as in aggression and verbal skills), but the cause of these differences (either nature or nurture) is still being debated.

Questions

1. Match the following dimensions of gender with their appropriate meaning:

_____ Chromosomal sex

_____ Gender identity

_____ Gonadal sex

_____ Gender role

_____ Hormonal sex

_____ Secondary sex characteristics

_____ External genitals

_____ Sexual orientation

_____ Internal accessory organs

a. Ovaries and testes

b. XX and XY

c. Estrogens and androgens

d. One's perception of oneself as male or female

e. Breasts, beards, menstruation

f. Uterus, vagina, prostate gland, vas deferens

g. Labia majora, clitoris, penis, scrotum

h. Homosexual, bisexual, heterosexual

i. Differing societal expectations for appropriate male and female behavior

2. Individuals who have the genitals and secondary sex characteristics of one sex but feel as if they belong to the other sex are known as _____. (a) transvestites; (b) heterosexuals; (c) gays or lesbians; (d) transsexuals

3. Briefly summarize the two major theories of gender role development.

4. A combination of both male and female personality traits is called _____. (a) heterosexuality; (b) homosexuality; (c) transsexualism; (d) androgyny

Answers to Questions can be found in Appendix B.

RESEARCH HIGHLIGHT

The Art and Science of Flirting

Pretend for the moment that you are watching a man (Tom) and woman (Kaleesha) at a singles bar. As Tom approaches the table, Kaleesha sits up straighter, smiles, and touches her hair. Tom asks her to dance, and Kaleesha quickly nods and stands up while smoothing her skirt. During the dance, she smiles and sometimes glances at him from under her lashes. When the dance finishes, Kaleesha waits for Tom to escort her back to her chair. She motions him to sit in the adjacent chair and they engage in a lively conversation. Kaleesha allows her leg to graze his briefly. When Tom reaches for popcorn from the basket in front of Kaleesha, she playfully pulls it away. This surprises Tom and he frowns at Kaleesha. She quickly turns away and starts talking to her friends. Despite his repeated attempts to talk to her, Kaleesha ignores him.

What happened? Did you recognize Kaleesha's sexual signals? Did you understand why she turned away at the end? If so, you are skilled in the art and science of flirting. If not, you may be very interested in the work of Monica Moore at the Uni-

versity of Missouri (1998). As a scientist interested in describing and understanding flirting and the role it plays in human courtship, Moore has observed and recorded many scenes — in singles bars and shopping malls — like the one with Tom and Kaleesha. Although she prefers the term *nonverbal courtship signaling*, what Moore and her colleagues have spent thousands of hours secretly observing is flirting behavior.

From these naturalistic observations, we know a great deal more about what works and doesn't work in courtship. First of all, though both men and women flirt, women generally initiate a courtship. The woman signals her interest with glances that may be brief and darting, or direct and sustained. Often she smiles at the same time she gestures with her hands — often with an open or extended palm. Primping (adjusting clothing or patting hair) is also common. A flirting woman will also make herself more noticeable by sitting straighter, with stomach pulled in and breasts pushed out.

Once contact is made and the couple is dancing or sitting at a table, the woman increases the level of flirting. She orients her body toward his, whispers in his ear, and frequently nods and smiles in response to his conversation. Most significant, she touches the man or allows the man to touch her. Like Kaleesha with Tom, allowing her leg to graze his is a powerful indication of her interest.

Women also use play behaviors to flirt. They tease, mock-hit, and tell jokes, not only to inject humor but also to test the man's receptivity to humor. As in the case of Tom's reaction to the popcorn tease, when a man doesn't appreciate the playfulness, a woman often uses rejection signals to cool or end the relationship. Other studies confirm Moore's description of women's nonverbal sexual signaling (Lott, 2000).

Now that you know what to look for, watch for flirting behavior in others — or perhaps in your own life. According to Moore and other researchers, flirting may be the single most important thing a woman can do to increase her attractiveness. Because the burden of making the first approach is usually the man's, men are understandably cautious and welcome a woman who clearly signals her interest.

Two cautions are in order, however. First, signaling interest does not mean that the woman is ready to have sex with the man. She flirts because she wants to get to know the man better; later, she'll decide whether she wants to develop a relationship (Allgeier & Allgeier, 2000). Second, Moore reminds women to "use their enhanced flirting skills only when genuinely interested" (1997, p. 69). Being aware of sexual signals can benefit both men and women, but flirting should be reserved for times when you genuinely want to attract or keep the attention of a particular partner.

ACTIVE LEARNING WORKSHEET   MODULE 29

Fill-in the missing blanks, and then check your answers with those in Appendix B.

1. A transsexual has trouble with his or her _____, whereas a transvestite _____.

2. When asked on a form to identify your "sex," the questioner wants to know_____, whereas "gender" refers to _____.

3. Gender identity refers to _____, whereas gender role encompasses _____.

4. For females, the first sign of reproductive capacity is _____, and the first sign for males is _____.

5. Expressing both masculine and feminine traits is known as _____.

MODULE 30

SEXUAL BEHAVIOR AND PROBLEMS

How do scientists study a sensitive topic like sex?

Sex is used and abused in many ways: as a theme in literature, movies, and music; to satisfy sexual desires; to gain love and acceptance from partners and peer groups; as a way of expressing love or commitment in a relationship; as a way of ending relationships through affairs with others; to dominate or hurt others; and, perhaps most conspicuously, to sell products. In this module, we explore sexual behaviors and some of their associated problems.

The Study of Human Sexuality: History, Research, and Culture

People have probably always been interested in understanding their sexuality, but cultural forces have often suppressed and controlled this interest. During the nineteenth century, for example, polite society avoided mention of all parts of the body covered by clothing. The breast of chickens became known as "white meat," female patients were examined by male doctors in totally dark rooms, and some people even covered piano legs for the sake of propriety (Allen, 2000; Gay, 1983; Money, 1985a).

During this same Victorian period, medical experts warned that masturbation led to blindness, impotence, acne, and insanity (Allen, 2000; Michael, Gagnon, Laumann, & Kolata, 1994). Believing a bland diet helped suppress sexual desire, Dr. John Harvey Kellogg and Sylvester Graham developed the original Kellogg's Corn Flakes and Graham crackers and marketed them as foods that would discourage masturbation (Money, Prakasam, & Joshi, 1991). One of the most serious concerns of many doctors was nocturnal emissions (wet dreams), which were believed to cause brain damage and death. Special devices were even marketed for men to wear at night to prevent sexual arousal (Figure 30.1).

TRY THIS
Yourself

Before we begin our study of human sexuality, try this quiz. The answers are at the bottom, and expanded explanations are found throughout this module.

Which of the following statements are true and which are false?

1. The breakfast cereal Kellogg's Corn Flakes was originally developed to discourage masturbation.
2. Nocturnal emissions and masturbation are signs of abnormal sexual adjustment.
3. The American Academy of Pediatrics (AAP) no longer recommends routine circumcision for male babies.
4. The American Psychiatric Association and the American Psychological Association (APA) consider homosexuality a type of mental illness.
5. Sexual skill and satisfaction are learned behaviors that can be increased through education and training.
6. If you're HIV positive (have human immunodeficiency virus) you cannot infect someone else; only if you have AIDS (acquired immunodeficiency syndrome) can you spread the disease.
7. Women cannot be raped against their will.

Answers: 1. T 2. F 3. T 4. F 5. T 6. F 7. F

In light of modern knowledge, it seems hard to understand these strange Victorian practices and outrageous myths about masturbation and nocturnal emissions. One of the first physicians to explore and question these beliefs was Havelock Ellis (1858–1939). When he first heard of the dangers of nocturnal emissions, Ellis was frightened — he had personal experience with the problem. His fear led him to frantically search the medical literature, but instead of a cure, he found predictions of gruesome illness and eventual death. He was so upset, he contemplated suicide.

Ellis eventually decided he could give meaning to his life by keeping a detailed diary of his deterioration. He planned to dedicate the book to science when he died, but after several months of careful observation, he realized the books were wrong. He wasn't dying. He wasn't even sick. Angry that he had been so misinformed by the "experts," he spent the rest of his life developing reliable and accurate sex information. Today, Havelock Ellis is acknowledged as one of the most important early pioneers in the field of sex research.

The second major contributor to sex research was Alfred Kinsey and his colleagues (1948, 1953). Kinsey and his coworkers personally interviewed over 18,000 participants, asking detailed questions about their sexual activities and preferences. Given that most research participants were young, single, urban, white, and middle class, Kinsey's sampling and methodology were heavily criticized. But Kinsey's work is still widely respected, and his data are frequently used as a *baseline* for modern research. In recent years, hundreds of similar sex surveys and interviews have been conducted on such topics as contraception, abortion, premarital sex, and rape (Brannigan, Allgeier, & Allgeier, 1998; Janus & Janus, 1993; Laumann, Gagnon, Michael, & Michaels, 1994). By comparing Kinsey's data to the responses found in later surveys, we can see how sexual practices have changed over the years.

In addition to surveys, interviews, and case studies, some researchers have employed direct laboratory experimentation and observational methods. To document the physiological changes involved in sexual arousal and response, William Masters and Virginia Johnson (1961, 1966, 1970) and their research colleagues enlisted several hundred male and female volunteers. Using intricate physiological measuring devices, the researchers carefully monitored participants' bodily responses as they masturbated or engaged in sexual intercourse. Masters and Johnson's research findings are hailed as a major contribution to our knowledge of sexual physiology. Some of their results are discussed in later sections.

Figure 30.1 *Victorian sexual practice.* During the nineteenth century, men were encouraged to wear spiked rings around their penises at night to avoid nocturnal emissions (wet dreams). If the man had an erection, the spikes would cause pain and awaken him.

GENDER & CULTURAL DIVERSITY

A Cultural Look at Sexual Behaviors

Sex researchers interested in both universalities and variations in human sexual behavior conduct cross-cultural studies of sexual practices, techniques, and attitudes (Bhugra, 2000; Beach, 1977; Brislin, 1993, 2000; Mackay, 2001). Their studies of different societies put sex in a broader perspective and help counteract *ethnocentrism*, the tendency people have to judge their own cultural practices as "normal" and preferable to those of other groups.

For example, do you know that kissing is unpopular in Japan and unknown among some cultures in Africa and South America? Do you find it strange that Apinaye women in Brazil often bite off pieces of their mate's eyebrows as a natural part of sexual foreplay (Goldstein, 1976)? Does it surprise you that members of Tiwi society, off the northern coast of Australia, believe that young girls will not develop breasts or menstruate unless they first experience intercourse (Goodall, 1971)? Did you know that the Sambia of New Guinea believe that

The first sex scientist. Havelock Ellis was one of the first sex researchers to celebrate eroticism and acknowledge female sexuality.

Circumcision and religion. *Although circumcision is an important part of some religions, it is relatively rare in most parts of the world.*

young boys must swallow semen to achieve manhood (Herdt, 1981)? And that adolescent boys in Mangaia, a small island in the South Pacific, routinely undergo superincision, a painful initiation rite in which the foreskin of the penis is slit and folded back (Marshall, 1971)? Table 30.1 gives other examples of cultural variation in sexuality.

Although other cultures' practices may seem unnatural and strange to us, we forget that our own sexual rituals may appear equally curious to others. If the description of the Mangaian practice of superincision bothered you, how do you feel about our culture's routine circumcision of infant boys? Before you object that infant circumcision in the United States is "entirely different" and "medically safe and necessary," you might want to consider the position now taken by the American Academy of Pediatrics (AAP). In 1999, they decided the previously reported medical benefits of circumcision were so statistically small that the procedure should *not* be routinely performed. The AAP does consider it legitimate for parents to take into account cultural, religious, and ethnic traditions in deciding whether to circumcise their sons.

If the controversy over infant male circumcision surprises you, so, too, may information about female genital mutilation. Throughout history and even today in parts of Africa, the Middle East, and Asia, young girls undergo several types of genital mutilation: circumcision (removal of the clitoral hood), *clitoridectomy* (removal of the clitoris), and *genital infibulation* (removal of the clitoris and labia and stitching together of the remaining tissue to allow only a small opening for urine and menstrual flow (McConville, 1998; Barstow, 1999; Stewart, 1997). In most countries, the surgeries are performed on girls between ages 4 and 10 and often without anesthesia or antiseptic conditions (Abusharaf, 1998). The young girls suffer numerous health problems because of these practices — the most serious from genital infibulation. Risks include severe pain, bleeding, chronic infection, and

TABLE 30.1   SEXUAL BEHAVIORS ACROSS CULTURES

	Childhood Sexuality	Adult Sexuality
Mangaia (Polynesian Island)	Children readily exposed to sex. Adolescents are given direct instruction in techniques for pleasuring their sexual partners, and both boys and girls are encouraged to have many partners.	After marriage, three orgasms per night are not uncommon for men, and they are encouraged to "give" three orgasms to their female partner for every one of their own. Adults practice a wide range of sexual behaviors.
Yolngu (Island Near Australia)	Permissive attitude toward childhood sexuality. Parents soothe infants by stroking their genitals. Nudity accepted from infancy through old age.	Men can have many wives and are generally happy with their sex life. Women are given no choice in marital partner and little power in the home. Women are apathetic about sex, seldom orgasmic, and generally unhappy.
Inis Beag[a] (Irish Island)	Sexual expression is strongly discouraged. Children learn to abhor nudity and are given no information about sex. Young girls are often shocked by their first menstruation.	Little sex play before intercourse. Female orgasm is unknown or considered deviant. Numerous misconceptions about sex (e.g., intercourse can be debilitating, menopause causes insanity).

[a] Inis Beag is a pseudonym used to protect the privacy of this Irish island.

Sources: Crooks & Baur, 1999; Ford & Beach, 1951; Marshall, 1971; Money et al., 1991; Ortner & Whitehead, 1981.

menstrual difficulties. As adults, these women frequently experience serious child-birth complications or infertility (Ortiz, 1998).

What is the purpose of these procedures? The main objective is to ensure virginity before marriage (Orubuloge & Caldwell, 1997). Without these procedures, young girls are considered unmarriageable and without status. As you may imagine, these practices create serious culture clashes. For example, physicians in Western societies are currently being asked by immigrant parents to perform these operations on their daughters. What should the doctor do? Should this practice be forbidden? Or would this be another example of ethnocentrism?

As you can see, it is a complex issue. Canada was the first nation to recognize female genital mutilation as a basis for granting refugee status, and the United Nations has suspended its regular policy of nonintervention in the cultural practices of nations. The World Health Organization (WHO) and the United Nations International Children's Emergency Fund (UNICEF) have both issued statements opposing female genital mutilation and have developed programs to combat this and other harmful practices affecting the health and well-being of women and children.

Check & Review

THE STUDY OF HUMAN SEXUALITY

Although sex has always been an important part of human interest, motivation, and behavior, it received little scientific attention before the twentieth century. Havelock Ellis was among the first to study human sexuality despite the repression and secrecy of nineteenth-century Victorian times.

Alfred Kinsey and his colleagues were the first to conduct large-scale, systematic surveys and interviews of the sexual practices and preferences of Americans during the 1940s and 1950s. The research team of William Masters and Virginia Johnson pioneered the use of actual laboratory measurement and observation of human physiological response during sexual activity. Cultural studies are also important sources of scientific information on human sexuality.

Questions

1. During earlier times, it was believed that _____ led to blindness, impotence, acne, and insanity, whereas _____ caused brain damage and death. (a) female orgasms, male orgasms; (b) masturbation, nocturnal emissions; (c) menstruation, menopause; (d) oral sex, sodomy

2. Match the following researchers with their contributions to the study of human sexuality:

   a. Havelock Ellis   _____ Based his/their groundbreaking research into human sexuality on personal diaries

   b. William Masters   _____ Popularized the use of the survey method in
      and Virginia Johnson   studying human sexuality

   c. Alfred Kinsey   _____ Pioneered the use of direct observation and physiological measurement of bodily responses during sexual activities

3. What are the advantages of cultural studies in sex research?

4. Viewing one's own ethnic group (or culture) as central and "correct" and then judging the rest of the world according to this standard is known as _____. (a) standardization; (b) stereotyping; (c) discrimination; (d) ethnocentrism

Answers to Questions can be found in Appendix B:

What is the latest research on sexual orientation? How are men and women alike and different in sexual arousal and response?

Sexual Response Cycle *William Masters and Virginia Johnson's description of the bodily response to sexual arousal; the four stages are excitement, plateau, orgasm, and resolution*

Excitement Phase *First stage of the sexual response cycle, characterized by increasing levels of arousal and increased engorgement of the genitals.*

Plateau Phase *Second stage of the sexual response cycle, characterized by a leveling off of high arousal.*

Orgasm Phase *Third stage of the sexual response cycle when pleasurable sensations peak and orgasm occurs.*

Sexual Arousal and Response: Gender Differences and Similarities

Are women and men fundamentally alike in their sexual responses? Or are they unalterably different? What causes a gay or lesbian sexual orientation? What is sexual prejudice? These are some of the questions we will explore in this section.

To understand differences and similarities in male and female sexual behavior, it helps to begin with Masters and Johnson's (1966) four-stage **sexual response cycle** (Figure 30.2):

Stage 1: In the **excitement phase**, which can last from a few minutes to several hours, arousal is initiated through physical factors, such as touching or being touched, or through psychological factors, such as fantasy or erotic stimuli. During this stage, heart rate and respiration increase and blood flows to the pelvic region, causing engorgement of the penis and clitoris. Both males and females may have nipples becoming erect, and both may experience a *sex flush*, or reddening of the upper torso and face.

Stage 2: If stimulation continues, the **plateau phase** begins and heartbeat, respiration rate, and blood pressure stabilize or level off at a heightened rate. In the man, the penis becomes more engorged and erect while the testes swell and pull up closer to the body. In the woman, the clitoris pulls up under the clitoral hood and the entrance to the vagina contracts while the uterus rises slightly. This movement of the uterus causes the upper two-thirds of the vagina to balloon, or expand. As excitement reaches its peak, some fluid, which often contains sperm, may seep out of the opening of the penis and both sexes may experience a feeling that orgasm is imminent and inevitable.

Stage 3: During the **orgasm phase**, the individual experiences a highly intense and pleasurable release of tension. In the woman, muscles around the vagina

Figure 30.2 *Masters and Johnson's sexual response cycle.* One way to visualize (and remember) the four stages of the sexual response cycle is to compare it to diving off a high diving board. During the *excitement phase* (climbing up the ladder), both men and women become progressively more aroused and excited, resulting in penile and clitoral erection, and vaginal lubrication in women. In the *plateau phase* (walking across the diving board), sexual and physiological arousal "level off" at a heightened state. The *orgasm phase* (jumping off the diving board) involves rhythmic muscle contractions in both men and women and ejaculation of sperm in men. During the final *resolution phase* (resting and swimming back to shore), physiological responses return to normal.

squeeze the vaginal walls in and out and the uterus pulsates. Muscles at the base of the penis contract in the male, causing *ejaculation*, the discharge of semen or seminal fluid.

Stage 4: Both male and female bodies gradually return to their preexcitement state during the **resolution phase**. After one orgasm, most men enter a **refractory period**, during which further excitement to orgasm is considered impossible. Many women (and some men), however, are capable of multiple orgasms in fairly rapid succession.

Resolution Phase *Final stage of the sexual response cycle when the body returns to its unaroused state.*

Refractory Period *Phase following orgasm during which further orgasm is considered physiologically impossible.*

GENDER & CULTURAL DIVERSITY

Are There Evolutionary Advantages to *Female* Nonmonogamy?

In many ways, women and men are similar in their general sexual responses. But it is our differences that attract the most attention. For example, have you heard that men have more sexual drive, interest, and activity than women do? How do we explain these differences? There are two major perspectives — evolutionary and social role.

The *evolutionary perspective*, emphasizing genetic and biological forces, suggests that sexual differences (such as men having more sexual partners) evolved from ancient mating patterns that helped the species survive (Buss, 1989, 1999, 2000; Fischman, 2000; Low, 2000). According to this *sexual strategies theory* (SST), men have a greater interest in sex and multiple partners and are sexually jealous and controlling because these behaviors maximize their chances for reproduction. Women, on the other hand, seek a good protector and provider to increase their chances for survival, as well as their offspring's. Ultimately, both male and female strategies serve to pass along their genes and ensure the survival of the species.

Although the evolutionary perspective suggests that only men have a biological advantage to multiple sex partners, it is important to note that in at least 18 societies around the world it is *female nonmonogamy* (women having multiple sex partners) that offers survival value to women and children (Beckerman et al., 1999). People in these cultures believe in *partible paternity* (one child having more than one biological father), and pregnant women openly acknowledge their extramarital lovers as "secondary fathers."

Believing that multiple men contribute to the initial impregnation and later "building of the child" seems to benefit both the pregnant woman and her children. Among the Bari of Venezuela and Colombia, Beckerman and his colleagues found that pregnant women with lovers were less likely to miscarry, possibly because of courtship gifts that boosted their nutrition. In addition, 80 percent of children with "extra" fathers lived to age 15, in contrast to 64 percent of children with lone dads.

In contrast to the evolutionary perspective with its biological emphasis, the *social role approach* suggests that gender differences in sexual behavior result from the roles that men and women internalize from their society (Eagly, 1997). For instance, in traditional cultural divisions of labor, women are child bearers and homemakers whereas men are providers and protectors. But as women gain more reproductive freedom and educational opportunities, they also acquire more personal resources and status through means other than mates.

This hypothesis is directly supported by a recent reanalysis of Buss's original data collected from 37 cultures (Buss et al., 1990). Kasser and Sharma (1999) found that women did indeed prefer resource-rich men, but only when the women lived in cultures with little reproductive freedom and education equality. Therefore, say Kasser and Sharma, the conflict between the evolutionary and social role perspectives may be resolved by examining patriarchal cultural systems that limit women's choices.

If strong patriarchies existed during the Pleistocene epoch, enough time may have passed for psychological mechanisms to evolve in reaction to such environments (Smuts, 1995). If, however, patriarchy emerged only in the past 10,000 years, with the advent of agriculture (Miller & Fishkin, 1997), the time span is too short for evolutionary changes, and the social role explanation may be the best. Kasser and Sharma's theory is intriguing, but further research is necessary.

Sexual Orientation: Contrasting Theories and Myths

What causes homosexuality? What causes heterosexuality? Many have asked the first question, but few have asked the second. As a result, the roots of sexual orientation are poorly understood. However, research has identified several widespread myths and misconceptions about homosexuality (Bell, Weinberg, & Hammersmith, 1981; Fone, 2000; Golombok & Tasker, 1996; Lamberg, 1998; Parks, 1998). Every one of the following popular beliefs is false:

- *Seduction theory.* Gays and lesbians were seduced as children by adults of their own sex.

- *"By default" myth.* Gays and lesbians were unable to attract partners of the other sex or had unhappy heterosexual experiences.

- *Poor parenting theory.* Sons become gay because of domineering mothers and weak fathers, whereas daughters become lesbians because their fathers were their primary role model.

- *Modeling theory.* Children raised by gay and lesbian parents usually end up adopting their parents' sexual orientation.

It is important to remember that all of these popular beliefs have been shown to be *false* and that the causes of sexual orientation are still unknown. At this point, however, most studies suggest that genetics and biology play the dominant role in sexual orientation (Bailey, Dunne, Martin, 2000; Hamer & Copeland, 1999; Hershberger, 1997; LeVay, 1996; Williams et al., 2000).

For example, a genetic predisposition toward homosexuality is supported by studies on identical male and female twins, fraternal twins, and adopted siblings (Kirk, Bailey, Dunne, & Martin, 2000; Pillard & Bailey, 1995). These studies found that if one identical twin was gay, about 48 to 65 percent of the time so was the second twin. (Note that if the cause were totally genetic, the percentage would be 100.) The rate for fraternal twins was 26 to 30 percent and 6 to 11 percent for adopted brothers or sisters. Estimates of homosexuality in the general population run between 2 and 10 percent.

Some researchers have also hypothesized that prenatal hormone levels affect fetal brain development and sexual orientation. Animal experiments have found that administering male hormones prenatally can cause female sheep to engage in the mounting behavior associated with male sheep (Bagermihl, 1999). Because it is obviously unethical to experiment with human fetuses, we cannot come to any meaningful conclusions about the effect of hormones on fetal development. Furthermore, no well-controlled study has ever found a difference in adult hormone levels between heterosexuals and gays and lesbians (Banks & Gartrell, 1995; Le Vay, 1996).

The possibility of structural brain differences received support (and wide media attention) when Simon LeVay (1991, 1996) found that the front part of the hypothalamus (Figure 30.3) was smaller among gay men than among those he assumed were heterosexuals. Because we know the hypothalamus influences sexual behavior, LeVay's findings may help explain differences in sexual orientation. However, it is impossible to determine whether the brain differences were a cause or result of sexual orientation.

Although the origin of sexual orientation remains a mystery, the fact of being gay or lesbian brings certain difficulties and challenges. Gays and lesbians endure verbal and physical attacks; disrupted family and peer relationships; and high rates of anxiety, depression, and suicide (Fone, 2000; Herek, 2000; Lock & Steiner, 1999; Rottnek, 1999). Some of the hostility supposedly stems from an irrational fear of homosexuality in oneself or others, which Martin Weinberg labeled *homophobia* in the late 1960s. However, this term is too limited and not scientifically acceptable: It implies that antigay attitudes are limited to individual irrationality and pathology. Psychologist Gregory Herek (2000) proposes the term **sexual prejudice** instead, to emphasize multiple causes and to allow researchers to draw on the rich scientific research on prejudice.

Despite the acknowledgment in 1973 by both the American Psychiatric Association and the American Psychological Association that homosexuality is not a mental illness, it continues to be a divisive societal issue in the United States. Seeing *sexual prejudice* as a socially reinforced phenomenon rather than an individual pathology, coupled with political action by gays and lesbians, may help fight discrimination and hate crimes.

Figure 30.3 *The hypothalamus and sexual orientation.* Researcher Simon LeVay found that an area of the hypothalamus was smaller among gay men compared to the same area in men he assumed were heterosexual.

Sexual Prejudice *Negative attitudes toward an individual because of her or his sexual orientation*

Hate crimes. *The vicious beating and muder of Mattew Shepard in 1998 is a tragic reminder of the costs of sexual prejudice.*

Fighting back against sexual prejudice. These protesters are working to increase public awareness of and acceptance of different sexual orientations.

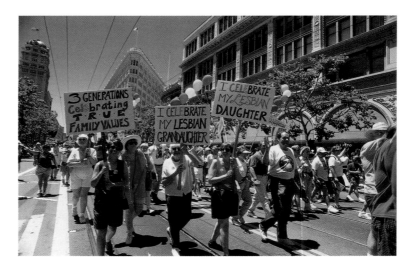

Check & Review

SEXUAL BEHAVIOR

William Masters and Virginia Johnson identified a four-stage **sexual response cycle** during sexual activity — *excitement*, *plateau*, *orgasm*, and *resolution*. There are numerous similarities and differences between the sexes in this cycle, but differences are the focus of most research. According to the *evolutionary perspective*, men engage in more sexual behaviors with more sexual partners because it helps the species survive. The *social role approach* suggests this difference results from traditional cultural divisions of labor.

Although researchers have identified several myths concerning the causes of homosexuality, the origins remain a puzzle. In recent studies, the genetic and biological explanation has gained the strongest sup-

port. Despite increased understanding, sexual orientation remains a divisive issue in the United States.

Questions

1. Briefly describe the four stages of Masters and Johnson's sexual response cycle.

2. How do the evolutionary and social role perspectives explain male and female differences in sexual behavior?

3. The genetic influence on sexual orientation has been supported by research reporting that_____.

   a. among identical twins, if one brother is gay, the other brother has a 52 percent chance of also being gay

   b. gay men have fewer chromosomal pairs than straight men, whereas

lesbians have larger areas of the hypothalamus than straight women

   c. among adoptive pairs of brothers, if one brother is gay, the other brother has an increased chance of also being gay

   d. parenting style influences adult sexual orientation for men but not for women

4. A homosexual orientation appears to be the result of_____.

   a. seduction during childhood or adolescence by an older homosexual

   b. a family background that includes a dominant mother and a passive, detached father

   c. a hormonal imbalance

   d. unknown factors

Answers to Questions can be found in Appendix B.

What factors contribute to sexual dysfunction and sexually transmitted diseases?

Sexual Dysfuntion: The Role of Biology and Learning

When we are functioning well sexually, we tend to take this part of our lives for granted. But what happens when things don't go smoothly? What causes normal sexual functioning to stop for some people and never begin for others? What are the major diseases that can be spread through sexual behavior? We will explore these questions in the following section.

There are many forms of **sexual dysfunction**, or difficulty in sexual functioning, and their causes are complex (Table 30.2). In this section, we will discuss how biology and learning both contribute to sexual problems.

Sexual Dysfunction *Impairment of the normal physiological processes of arousal and orgasm*

Biological Factors

Although many people may consider it unromantic, a large part of sexual arousal and behavior is clearly the result of biological processes (Meston, 2000). *Erectile*

T A B L E   3 0 . 2   THE MAJOR MALE AND FEMALE SEXUAL DYSFUNCTIONS

Type of Dysfunction	Description	Causes
Male		
Erectile dysfunction (impotence)	Inability to have or maintain an erection firm enough for intercourse	Physical — diabetes, circulatory conditions, heart disease, drugs, extreme fatigue, alcohol consumption, hormone deficiencies
Primary erectile dysfunction	The man has never been able to have sexual intercourse	Psychological — performance anxiety, guilt, difficulty in expressing desires to partner,
Secondary erectile dysfunction	Erection problems occurring in at least 25 percent of sexual encounters	severe antisexual upbringing
Premature ejaculation	The rapid ejaculation that is beyond the man's control, and his partner is nonorgasmic in at least 50 percent of their intercourse episodes	Almost always psychological — the man has learned to ejaculate quickly due to guilt, fear of discovery while masturbating, hurried experiences in cars or motels, and so on
Both male and female		
Dyspareunia	Painful intercourse more frequent in women but also occurs in men	Primarily physical — irritations, infections, or disorders of the internal or external genitals
Inhibited sexual desire (sexual apathy)	Lack of willingness to participate in sexual relations due to disinterest	Physical — hormone deficiencies, alcoholism, drugs, chronic illness Psychological — depression, prior sex trauma, relationship problems, anxiety
Sexual aversion	Lack of participation in sex due to overwhelming fear or anxiety	Psychological — severe parental sex attitudes, prior sex trauma, partner pressure, gender indentity confusion
Female		
Orgasmic dysfunction (anorgasmia, frigidity)	Inability or difficulty in reaching orgasm	Physical — chronic illness, diabetes, extreme fatigue, drugs, alcohol consumption, hormone deficiencies, pelvic disorders, lack of appropriate or adequate stimulation
Primary orgasmic dysfunction	The woman has never had an orgasm	Psychological — fear of evaluation, poor body image, relationship problems, guilt, anxiety, severe antisexual upbringing, difficulty in expressing desires to partner, prior sexual trauma, childhood sexual abuse
Secondary orgasmic dysfunction	The woman was regularly orgasmic at one time, but no longer is	
Situational orgasmic dysfunction	Orgasms occur only under certain circumstances	
Vaginismus	The muscles around the outer one-third of the vagina have involuntary spasms, and penile insertion is impossible or difficult and painful	Primarily psychological — the woman has learned to associate pain or fear with intercourse, owing to prior sexual trauma, severe antisexual upbringing, guilt

Sources: Adapted from Allgeier & Allgeier, 2000; Crooks & Baur, 1999; Masters et al., 1995.

dysfunction (the inability to get or maintain an erection firm enough for intercourse) and *orgasmic dysfunction* (the inability to respond to sexual stimulation to the point of orgasm) often reflect medical conditions such as diabetes, alcoholism, hormonal deficiencies, circulatory problems, and reactions to certain prescription and nonprescription drugs. Hormones also affect sexual drives and behaviors. Testosterone has a clear effect on sexual desire in both men and women, but otherwise, the precise role of hormones in human sexual behavior is not well understood.

In addition to problems resulting from medical conditions, sexual responsiveness can be affected by inappropriate activation of the spinal cord and sympathetic nervous system. Some aspects of human behavior are reflexive, that is, unlearned, automatic, and occurring without conscious effort or motivation, and sexual arousal for both men and women is partially reflexive. Just as a puff of air produces an automatic closing of the eye, certain stimuli, such as stroking of the genitals, can lead to automatic arousal. In both situations, nerve impulses from the receptor site travel to the spinal cord, which responds by sending messages to target organs or glands. Normally the blood flow into organs and tissues through the arteries is balanced by an equal outflow through the veins. During sexual arousal, however, the arteries dilate beyond the capacity of the veins to carry the blood away. This results in erection of the penis in men and an engorged clitoris and surrounding tissue in women.

If this is so automatic, why do some people have difficulty getting aroused? Unlike simple reflexes such as the eye blink, negative thoughts or high emotional states may block sexual arousal. Recall from Module 6 now the autonomic nervous system (ANS) is intricately involved in emotional (and sexual) responses. The ANS is composed of two subsystems: the sympathetic, which prepares the body for "fight or flight," and the parasympathetic, which maintains bodily processes at a steady, even balance. The parasympathetic branch is dominant during sexual arousal (the body must be relaxed to allow blood flow to the genital area), and the sympathetic branch is dominant during ejaculation and orgasm.

Problems with arousal are sometimes explained by the fact that strong emotions, like fear or anxiety, place the individual in sympathetic dominance, which blocks the initial arousal. Fear and anxiety also explain why young women often have difficulty with sexual arousal. The secretive and forbidden conditions of many early sexual experiences create strong anxieties and fear of discovery, fear of loss of respect, and fear of unwanted pregnancy. Many women discover that they need locked doors, committed relationships, and reliable birth control to enjoy sexual relations.

What about men? Men often have difficulty with arousal if they drink too much alcohol or are simply fatigued. Some men also experience **performance anxiety**, in which they fear they may not meet their partner's or their own expectations, and this anxiety creates problems with arousal. These same factors affect female arousal, and many men also share women's desire for privacy, commitment, and freedom from pregnancy concerns.

The Role of Learning

Our bodies may be biologically prepared to become aroused and respond to erotic stimulation, but learning also plays a role. As we have just seen, fear of evaluation or of the consequences of sexual activity and performance anxiety are all learned, psychological factors that contribute to both male and female sexual dysfunction. *Gender role training*, the *double standard*, and *sexual scripts* are also important contributors.

Gender role socialization begins at birth and significantly influences all aspects of our life, as the story of "Brenda/David" from the beginning of this section shows.

Performance Anxiety *A fear that one will be unable to meet the expectations, of oneself or one's partner, for sexual "performance"*

"Now, that's product placement!"

Can you imagine how traditional male gender roles — being dominant, aggressive, independent — could lead to different kinds of sexual thoughts and behaviors than traditional female gender roles — being submissive, passive, and dependent? These gender role differences have led to a **double standard**, where men are generally encouraged to explore their sexuality and bring a certain level of sexual knowledge into the relationship, whereas women are expected to stop male advances and refrain from sexual activity until marriage.

Although overt examples of the double standard are less evident in modern times, covert or hidden traces of this belief still cause many problems. After examining the gender differences in Table 30.3, can you see how items like men wanting women to "initiate sex more often" or women wanting men "to talk more lovingly" might be related to the double standard?

Double Standard *The beliefs, values, and norms that subtly encourage male sexuality and discourage female sexuality*

T A B L E 3 0 . 3 **WHAT MEN AND WOMEN WISH THEY HAD MORE OF IN THEIR SEXUAL RELATIONSHIPS**

Dating Couples	
Men wish Their Partners Would:	**Women Wish Their Partners Would:**
Be more experimental	Talk more lovingly
Initiate sex more often	Be more seductive
Try more oral-genital sex	Be warmer and more involved
Give more instructions	Give more instructions
Be warmer and more involved	Be more complimentary

Married Couples	
Men Wish Their Partners Would:	**Women Wish Their Partners Would:**
Be more seductive	Talk more lovingly
Initiate sex more often	Be more seductive
Be more experimental	Be more complimentary
Be wilder and sexier	Be more experimental
Give more instructions	Give more instructions
	Be warmer and more involved

Source: Based on Hatfield & Rapson, 1996, p. 142.

Sexual Scripts *Socially dictated descriptions of the sequences of behavior that are considered appropriate in sexual interactions*

In addition to gender role training and the double standard, we also learn explicit **sexual scripts** that teach us "what to do, when, where, how, and with whom" (Gagnon, 1990). During the 1950s, societal messages said the "best" sex was at night, in a darkened room, with a man on top and a woman on the bottom. Today, the messages are more bold and varied, partly because of media portrayals. Compare, for example, the sexual scripts portrayed in Figure 30.4.

Sexual scripts, gender roles, and the double standard may all be less rigid today, but a major difficulty remains. Many people and sexual behaviors do not fit society's scripts and expectations. Furthermore, we often "unconsciously" internalize societal messages and then fail to realize how they affect our values and behaviors. For example, modern men and women generally say they want equality, yet both may feel more comfortable if the woman is a virgin and the man has had many partners. Sex therapy encourages partners to examine and sometimes modify inappropriate sexual scripts, gender roles, and beliefs in the double standard.

How do therapists work with sex problems? Clinicians usually begin with interviews and examinations to determine whether the problem is organic, psycho-

Figure 30.4 *Changing sexual scripts.* In the 1950s and 60s, television and movies generally showed only married couples sleeping in long pajamas in separate twin beds. Contrast this with today's common portrayal of unmarried couples with minimal clothing "actively engaged" on one bed. Also compare the clothes and body postures in beach scenes from 1960 and today.

TABLE 30.4 SEXUAL EFFECTS OF COMMONLY ABUSED AND ILLICIT DRUGS

Drugs	Effects
Alcohol	Chronic abuse causes hormonal alterations (reduces size of testes and suppresses hormonal function) and permanently damages the circulatory and nervous systems
Tobacco	Decreases the frequency and duration of erections and vaginal lubrication
Cocaine	Causes erectile dysfunction, inhibits orgasm, and lowers sperm count
Amphetamines	High doses and chronic use result in inhibition of orgasm and decrease in erection and lubrication
Barbiturates	Cause decreased desire, erectile disorders, and delayed orgasm
Marijuana	Reduces testosterone levels and decreases sexual desire

Source: Abadinsky, 2001; Doweiko, 1999; Julien, 2000.

logical, or, more likely, a combination of both (Knoll & Abrams, 1998; Lefebvre, 1997). Organic causes of sexual dysfunction include medical conditions (such as diabetes mellitus), medications (such as antidepressants), and drugs (such as alcohol and tobacco — see Table 30.4). Erectile disorders are the problems most likely to have an organic component. In 1998, a medical treatment for erectile problems, *Viagra*, quickly became the fastest-selling prescription drug in U.S. history. Other medications for both men and women are currently being tested (Becker et al., 1998; Mann, 1998).

Years ago, the major psychological treatment for sexual dysfunction was long-term psychoanalysis, based on the assumption that sexual problems resulted from deep-seated personality conflicts that originated in childhood. During the 1950s and 1960s, behavior therapy was introduced; it was based on the idea that sexual dysfunction was learned. (See Module 44 for a more complete description of both psychoanalysis and behavior therapy). It wasn't until the early 1970s and the publication of Masters and Johnson's *Human Sexual Inadequacy* that sex therapy gained national recognition. Because the model that Masters and Johnson developed is still popular and used by many sex therapists, we will use it as our example of how sex therapy is conducted.

Masters and Johnson's Sex Therapy Program

Masters and Johnson's approach is founded on four major principles:

1. A relationship focus. Unlike forms of therapy that focus on the individual, Masters and Johnson's sex therapy focuses on the relationship between two people. To counteract any blaming tendencies, each partner is considered fully involved and affected by sexual problems. Both partners are taught positive communication and conflict resolution skills.

2. An integration of physiological and psychosocial factors. Because medication and many physical disorders can cause or aggravate sexual dysfunctions, Masters and Johnson emphasize the importance of medical histories and exams. They also explore psychosocial factors, such as how the couple first learned about sex and their current attitudes, gender role training, and sexual scripts.

3. An emphasis on cognitive factors. Recognizing that many problems result from fears of performance and *spectatoring* (mentally watching and evaluating responses

Experiments in sex? William Masters and Virginia Johnson were the first researchers to use direct laboratory experimentation and observation to study human sexuality.

TRY THIS
Yourself

If you would like to improve your own or your children's current or future sexual functioning, sex therapists would recommend the following:

- *Begin sex education as early as possible.* Children should be given positive feelings about their bodies and an opportunity to discuss sexuality in an open, honest fashion.
- *Avoid goal- or performance-oriented approaches.* Therapists often remind clients that there really is no "right" way to have sex. When couples or indi-

viduals attempt to judge or evaluate their sexual lives or to live up to others' expectations, they risk making sex a *job* rather than pleasure.

- *Communicate openly with your partner.* Mind reading belongs onstage, not in the bedroom. Partners need to tell each other what feels good and what doesn't, and sexual problems should be openly discussed without blame, anger, or defensiveness. If the problem does not improve within a reasonable time, consider professional therapy.

---

during sexual activities), couples are discouraged from goal setting and judging sex in terms of success or failure.

4. *An emphasis on specific behavioral techniques.* Couples are seen in an intensive 2-week counseling program. They explore their sexual values and misconceptions and practice specific behavioral exercises. "Homework assignments" usually begin with a *sensate focus* exercise in which each partner takes turns gently caressing the other and communicating what is pleasurable. There are no goal or performance demands. Later exercises and assignments are tailored to the couple's particular sex problem.

Sexually Transmitted Infections: The Special Problem of AIDS

Early sex education and open communication between partners are not only important for full sexual functioning; they are also key to avoiding and controlling sexually transmitted infections (STIs), formerly called sexually transmitted diseases (STDs), venereal disease (VD), or social diseases. *STI* is the term used to describe the disorders caused by more than 25 infectious organisms transmitted through sexual activity.

Each year, millions of North Americans contract one or more STIs, and more than two-thirds of them are under age 35 (CDC, 2000; Gilbert & Alexander, 1998; Loay & Loay, 2000). Also, as Figure 30.5 shows, women are at much greater risk than men of contracting major STIs. It is extremely important for sexually active people to get medical diagnosis and treatment for any suspicious symptoms and to inform their partners. If left untreated, many STIs can cause severe problems, including infertility, ectopic pregnancy, cancer, and even death.

The good news is that most STIs are readily cured in their early stages. See Table 30.5 for an overview of the signs and symptoms of the most common STIs. As you read through this table, remember that many infected people are *asymptomatic,* meaning lacking obvious symptoms. You can have one or more of the diseases without knowing it, and it is often impossible to tell if a sexual partner is infectious.

Although STIs such as genital warts and chlamydial infections have reached epidemic proportions, **AIDS (acquired immunodeficiency syndrome)** has received the largest share of public attention. AIDS results from infection with *human*

AIDS (Acquired Immunodeficiency Syndrome) *A catastrophic illness in which human immunodeficiency viruses (HIVs) destroy the immune system's ability to fight disease, leaving the body vulnerable to a variety of opportunistic infections and cancers*

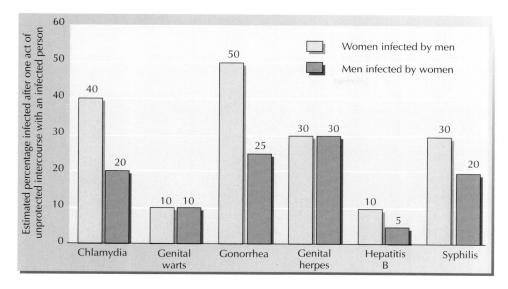

Figure 30.5 *Male–female differences in susceptibility to sexually transmitted infections (STIs).* These percentages represent the chances of infection for men and women after a single act of intercourse with an infected partner. Note that women are at much greater risk than men for four of these six STIs. This is partly because female genitals are more internal.

immunodeficiency virus (HIV). A standard blood test can determine if someone is **HIV positive**, which means the individual has been infected by one or more of the HIV viruses. Being infected with the HIV virus, however, is not the same as having AIDS. AIDS is the final stage of the HIV infection process.

In the beginning of the infection process, the HIV virus replicates rapidly. It is important to know that newly infected individuals are 100 to 1,000 times more infectious than they are throughout the remainder of the disease (Royce, Sena, Cates, & Cohen, 1997). This is especially troubling because most infected people are likely to remain symptom free for months or even years, yet during this time, they can spread the disease to others — primarily through sexual contact.

HIV Positive *Being infected by the human immunodeficiency virus (HIV)*

What Have You Got Against A Condom?

The simple act of putting on a condom can save your life, if they're used properly and every time you have sex. For more information about AIDS and condoms, call 1-800-342-AIDS.

AMERICA RESPONDS TO AIDS

TABLE 30.5 COMMON SEXUALLY TRANSMITTED INFECTIONS (STIs)

Danger Signs	Could Be	Complications
Male Signs Unusual discharge from penis Soreness inside penis	Chlamydia Gonorrhea Nongonococcal urethritis (NGU)	Untreated gonorrhea can cause prostatitis, sterility, arthritis, and heart trouble. Repeated infections can cause partial or complete blockage of penis or cause abscesses in the genital area or elsewhere.
Female Signs Unusual vaginal discharge Out-of-cycle abdominal pain Unusual vaginal bleeding	Chlamydia Gonorrhea Monilia (yeast) Trichomoniasis Vaginitis	Untreated gonorrhea or chlamydia can cause pelvic inflammatory disease (PID), which can resemble appendicitis. PID causes severe pain, fever, and sterility. Untreated gonorrhea in the birth canal can cause blindness in the newborn

Signs for Both Sexes
 	
Painful intercourse
Diarrhea
Painless sore on penis or vagina
Painful sore or blisters on or
   around genital area
Rash on hands and feet or entire
   body
Painful urination
Small, pink cauliflower growths on
   or around sex organs
Intense itching
Flulike feeling
Swollen glands in groin
Sore throat
	Acquired immunodeficiency
	   syndrome (AIDS)
	Crabs
	Genital warts
	Hepatitis
	Herpes
	Scabies
	Syphilis
		Untreated syphilis can cause brain and other organ damage, paralysis, blindness, heart disease, or death. The most severe complication of herpes genitalis is infection of the newborn during birth. Can be fatal to the baby. Presently, there is no demonstrated cure for herpes. (Refer to text of this module for more information on AIDS.)

You may have an STI without any of the danger signs but still acquire the complications. Seek medical attention if you suspect that you have come in contact with any of the infections! Follow all medical recommendations. This may include returning for a checkup to make sure you are no longer infected. Take only medications prescribed by your doctor, and take all of them as directed. Don't share them.

Sources: Adapted from Allgeier & Allgeier, 2000; Crooks & Baur, 1999; Kelley & Byrne, 1998.

As the initial HIV infection advances to AIDS, the virus progressively destroys the body's natural defenses against disease and infection. The victim's body becomes increasingly vulnerable to opportunistic infections and cancers that would not be a threat if the immune system were functioning normally. The virus may also attack the brain and spinal cord, creating severe neurological deterioration. The official term *full-blown AIDS* includes anyone infected with HIV who also has a CD4 count of 200 cells per cubic millimeter of blood or less. (The HIV virus destroys CD4 lymphocytes, also called T-cells, which coordinate the immune system's response to disease.)

AIDS is considered one of the most catastrophic diseases of our time. An estimated 1 million people in the United States and 31 million people worldwide are infected with HIV (Crooks & Baur, 1999). Recent advances in the treatment of AIDS have increased the survival time of victims, but for almost everyone, AIDS remains an ultimately fatal disorder, and some researchers doubt that a 100 percent effective vaccine will ever be developed. Despite the severity of this disease, there are signs of public complacency due to the false notion that drugs can now cure AIDS and to a reduced emphasis on prevention and education (Boyce, 2001; Vanable, Ostrow, McKirnan, Taywaditep, & Hope, 2000).

Reflecting cutbacks in AIDS education, myths are widespread. For instance, many people still believe AIDS can be transmitted through casual contact, such as a sneeze, handshake, sharing drinking glasses or towels, social kissing, sweat, or tears. Some also think it is dangerous to donate blood, and others are paranoid about gays, because male homosexuals were the first highly visible victims. All of these are false beliefs.

Infection by HIV spreads only by direct contact with bodily fluids — primarily blood, semen, and vaginal secretions. Blood *donors* are at *no* risk whatsoever. Furthermore, AIDS is not limited to the homosexual community. In fact, the AIDS epidemic is now spreading most quickly among heterosexuals, women, African Americans, Hispanics, and children (CDC, 2000).

Protecting Yourself Against AIDS and Other STIs

The best hope for curtailing the HIV/AIDS epidemic is through education and behavioral change. The following "safer sex" suggestions are not intended to be moralistic — but only to help reduce your chances of contracting both HIV/AIDS and other STIs:

1. Remain abstinent or have sex with one mutually faithful, uninfected partner. Be selective about sexual partners and postpone physical intimacy until laboratory tests verify that you are both free of STIs.

2. Do not use intravenous illicit drugs or have sex with someone who does. If you use intravenous drugs, do not share needles or syringes. If you must share, use bleach to clean and sterilize your needles and syringes.

critical thinking

Active Learning

Rape Myths and Rape Prevention

Sexuality can be a source of vitality and tender bonding, but it can also be traumatizing if one of the partners is unwilling. Rape is "oral, anal, or vaginal penetration forced on an unconsenting or unwilling victim" (Denney & Quadagno, 1998). As clear-cut as the definition seems, many people misunderstand what constitutes rape. To test your own knowledge, answer true or false to the following:

1. Women cannot be raped against their will.

2. A man cannot be raped by a woman.

3. If you are going to be raped, you might as well relax and enjoy it.

4. All women secretly want to be raped.

5. Male sexuality is biologically overpowering and beyond a man's control.

As you might have expected, all of these statements are false. Tragically, however, these myths are believed by a large number of men and women (Drieschner & Lange, 1999; Hall & Barongan, 1997; Reppucci, Woolard, & Fried, 1999). Using your critical thinking skills, can you explain how each of the following factors might contribute to rape myths?

• Gender role conditioning

• The double standard

• Media portrayals

• Lack of information

If you would like to compare your answers to ours or would like specific information regarding rape prevention, see Appendix B.

3. Avoid contact with blood, vaginal secretions, or semen. Using latex condoms and a spermicide containing nonoxynol 9 is the best way to avoid contact.

4. Avoid anal intercourse, with or without a condom. This is the riskiest of all sexual behaviors.

5. Do not have sex if you or your partner are impaired by alcohol or other drugs. The same is true for your friends. "Friends don't let friends drive [or have sex] drunk."

Check & Review

SEXUAL PROBLEMS

Many people experience **sexual dysfunction**. They often fail to recognize the role of biology in both sexual arousal and response. Ejaculation and orgasm are partially reflexive. And the parasympathetic nervous system must be dominant for sexual arousal, whereas the sympathetic nervous system must dominate for orgasm to occur. Several aspects of sexual arousal and response are also learned. Early *gender role training*, the **double standard**, and **sexual scripts** teach us what to consider the "best" sex.

Many sexual problems can be helped with sex therapy. William Masters and Virginia Johnson emphasize the couple's rela-tionship, combined physiological and psychosocial factors, cognitions, and specific behavioral techniques. Professional sex therapists offer important guidelines for everyone: Sex education should be early and positive, avoid a goal or performance orientation, and keep communication open.

The most publicized sexually transmitted infection (STI) is **AIDS (acquired immunodeficiency syndrome)**. Although AIDS is transmitted only through sexual contact or exposure to infected bodily fluids, many people have irrational fears of contagion. At the same time, an estimated 1 million North Americans are **HIV positive** and therefore carriers.

Questions

1. Briefly explain the roles of the sympathetic and parasympathetic nervous systems in sexual response.

2. Sexual learning that includes "what to do, when, where, how, and with whom" is known as _____. (a) appropriate sexual behavior; (b) sexual norms; (c) sexual scripts; (d) sexual gender roles

3. What are the four principles of Masters and Johnson's sex therapy program?

4. What are five "safer sex" ways to reduce the chances of AIDS and other STIs?

Answers to Questions can be found in Appendix B.

ACTIVE LEARNING WORKSHEET   MODULE 30

ACROSS

6. First stage of the sexual response cycle characterized by increasing levels of arousal and increased engorgement of the genitals.

7. Third stage of the sexual response cycle where pleasurable sensations peak and orgasm occurs.

9. STI where the human immunodeficiency virus (HIV) destroys the immune system's ability to fight disease, thus increasing chances for opportunistic infections and cancers.

10. Masters and Johnson's description of the bodily response to sexual arousal.

11. Phase following orgasm where further orgasm is considered impossible.

12. Final stage of the sexual response cycle where the body returns to nonaroused state.

DOWN

1. Fear of being unable to meet expectations for sexual "performance" of one's self or one's partner.

2. Socially dictated sequences of behavior considered appropriate in sexual interactions.

3. Beliefs, values, and norms that subtly encourage male sexuality and discourage female sexuality.

4. Negative attitudes toward an individual because of her or his sexual orientation.

5. Impairment of the normal physiological processes of arousal and orgasm.

8. Second stage of the sexual response cycle, characterized by a leveling off of high arousal.

Answers can be found in Appendix B.

Visual Summary for Modules 29 and 30

Sex and Gender

Definitions

Sex: Biological dimensions of maleness or femaleness, and physical activities (such as intercourse).

Gender: Psychological and sociocultural meanings of maleness and femaleness.

Gender Role Development

Gender role: Social expectations for appropriate male and female behavior.
Two major theories:

Social learning (reward, punishment, and imitation).

Cognitive Developmental (active thinking processes).

Sex and Gender Differences

Sex differences: Physical differences (like height) and brain differences (function and structure).

Gender differences: Females tend to score somewhat higher in verbal skills. Males score somewhat higher in math and are more physically aggressive.

Androgyny: Combination of masculine and feminine personality traits.

Study of Human Sexuality

Havelock Ellis

Based his research on personal diaries.

Kinsey & Colleagues

Popularized the use of surveys and interviews.

Masters and Johnson

Used direct observation and measurement of human sexual response.

Cultural Studies

Provide insight into universalities and variations in sexual behavior across cultures.

Sexual Behavior

Sexual Arousal and Response

Masters and Johnson´s **sexual response cycle: excitement, plateau, orgasm,** and **resolution.** There are numerous similarities of the sexes in this cycle, but differences are the focus of most research. According to the *evolutionary perspective*, males engage in more sexual behaviors with more sexual partners because it helps the species survive. The *social role approach* suggests this difference results from traditional cultural divisions of labor.

Sexual Orientation

Two major theories

Genetic/biological (genetic, prenatal biasing of the brain, and brain differences).

Psychosocial ("disturbed family," inability to attract opposite sex, and seduction—all unsupported by research).

Sexual Problems

Sexual Dysfunctions

Possible causes:

Biological: Anxiety blocks arousal. Parasympathetic nervous system must dominate for sexual arousal to occur, whereas sympathetic nervous system must dominate for orgasm to happen.

Psychological:

- Negative gender role training
- Unrealistic **sexual scripts**
- **Double standard** encourages male sexuality but discourages female's
- **Performance anxiety**, fearing one will not meet partner's sex expectations

Treatment: Masters and Johnson emphasize couple's relationship, combined physiological and psychosocial factors, cognitions, and specific behavioral techniques.

Sexually Transmitted Infections (STIs)

Most publicized STI is **AIDS.** AIDS transmitted only through sexual contact or exposure to infected bodily fluids, but irrational fears of contagion persist. An estimated one million in the U.S. are **HIV positive** and therefore carriers.

Motivation and Emotion

Core Learning Objectives

As you read Modules 31 and 32, keep the following questions in mind and answer them in your own words:

▶ Why do we feel hungry, search for stimulation, and need to achieve?

▶ Are we motivated by biological or by psychosocial factors? Or both?

▶ What major concepts do I need to know to understand emotion?

▶ How are emotional states produced?

D. HARMS

When Wilt Chamberlain died in October 1999, he left a hole in the heart of his many fans and in the world of professional sports. His list of awards was impressive: 2 NBA championships, scoring the most points in a season (4,029), setting the record for career rebounds (23,924), 7 straight scoring titles, 11 rebound titles, and setting an NBA record by scoring 100 points in a single game against the New York Knicks (Rosenblatt, 1999).

But perhaps his most important accomplishments were leading the league in assists and never fouling out of a game. These feats speak volumes. In a world of professional sports where players attack their opponents, teammates, fans, and referees, Wilt Chamberlain made a graceful difference. He almost never got into a fight. When opposing players tripped and fell, he picked them up. He was over 7 feet tall and dominated the game, but not once did he foul out. Chamberlain appreciated the importance of civility and sportsmanship. This "gentle giant" is missed.

Wilt Chamberlain

Coach Bobby Knight is another well-known sports figure with an impressive list of accomplishments. Knight was one of the most successful coaches in college basketball, but his success was based on intimidation and boorish behavior. Obscenity-filled shouting matches and frequent temper tantrums were used to psychologically terrorize his players as well as college administrators, who continued to give him "just one more chance."

What a contrast. Chamberlain controlled his strength and temper, supported his teammates, and respected his opponents, whereas Knight bullied and abused his players, opponents, coaches, referees, administrators, reporters, and anyone else who just happened to be there (Walton, 2000). Indiana University imposed a "zero tolerance" on Coach Knight's behavior in May 2000. But a few months later, Knight allegedly grabbed and twisted the arm of a student and cursed him for not calling him "Mr. Knight" or "Coach Knight" (Leo, 2000). Apparently, this was the last straw. Indiana University fired Coach Knight on September 10, 2000.

Bobby Knight

What motivated Chamberlain to rise to the top of the extremely competitive sports world? Why did Coach Knight continue to explode, despite promises to control his temper and the risk to his coaching position? What makes him so angry? Research in *motivation* and *emotion* attempts to answer such "what" and "why" questions and to explain emotional states such as anger.

Motivation refers to the process of activating, maintaining, and directing behavior toward a particular goal. **Emotion**, on the other hand, refers to subjective feelings or affective responses. In other words, motivation energizes and directs behavior, whereas emotion is the "feeling" response.

Motivation and emotion overlap. If you saw your loved one in the arms of another, you might experience a wide variety of emotions (jealousy, fear, sadness, and anger), and differing motives may determine how you act in the situation. Your desire for revenge might lead you to look for another partner, whereas your need for love and belonging might motivate you to look for ways to explain the behavior and protect your relationship. There is considerable overlap not only between motivation and emotion but also among motivation, emotion, and most areas of psychology. Moreover, recent advances in neuroscience and cognitive science have made the study of motivation and emotion one of the hot topics in science today (Cacioppo & Gardner, 1999; Damasio, 1999). In Modules 31 and 32, we will discuss some of the most recent and exciting findings, as well as classic studies in the field.

Motivation *Factors within an individual (such as needs, desires, and interests) that activate, maintain, and direct behavior toward a goal*

Emotion *An individual's feelings or affective responses that include cognitions (thoughts, beliefs, and expectations), physiological arousal (heart pounding), and behavioral expressions (frowns, smiles, running, and so on)*

UNDERSTANDING AND THEORIES OF MOTIVATION

Research in motivation attempts to answer the "why" questions about human and animal behavior. Why do you spend hours playing a new computer game instead of studying for a major exam? Why do salmon swim upstream to spawn? Human behavior comes from many different motives, some of which have been discussed already. For example, the sleep motive and the need for alternate states of consciousness were covered in Modules 13 and 14, and sexual motivation was discussed in Modules 29 and 30. Aggression, altruism, and interpersonal attraction will be discussed in Modules 47 and 48. Here, we will focus on three basic motives: hunger and eating, arousal, and achievement. We will also look at the major biological and psychological theories that best explain general motivation — or why we do what we do.

Why do we feel hungry, search for stimulation, and need to achieve?

Hunger and Eating: The Interaction of Both Internal and External Factors

What causes hunger? Is it your growling stomach? Or is it the sight of a juicy hamburger or the smell of a freshly baked cinnamon roll? Although hunger is obviously an internal, biological need, external, environmental forces also heavily influence it. Let's examine some of the major players in hunger.

The Stomach

Walter B. Cannon and A. L. Washburn (1912) conducted one of the earliest experiments exploring the internal factors in hunger. In this study, Washburn swallowed a balloon and then inflated it in his stomach. His stomach contractions and subjective reports of hunger feelings were then simultaneously recorded (Figure 31.1).

Figure 31.1 *Cannon and Washburn's technique for measuring hunger.* As a participant in his own study, Washburn swallowed a special balloon designed to detect stomach movement. His stomach movements were automatically recorded on graph paper attached to a rotating drum. At the same time, whenever Washburn experienced "hunger pangs," he would press a key that made a recording on the same graph paper. The two recordings (stomach movements and hunger sensations) were then compard. Finding that Washburn's stomach contractions occurred at the same time as his feelings of hunger led these early researchers to conclude that stomach movements caused hunger. Later research altered this conclusion.

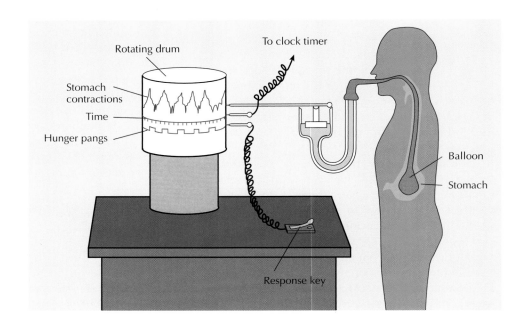

Because each time Washburn reported having stomach pangs (or "growling") the balloon also contracted, the researchers concluded that stomach movement caused the sensation of hunger.

What do you think was wrong with this study? Researchers must always control for the possibility of *extraneous variables*, factors that contribute irrelevant data and confuse the results. In this case, it was later found that an empty stomach is relatively inactive and that the stomach contractions experienced by Washburn were an experimental artifact — something resulting from the presence of the balloon. Washburn's stomach had been tricked into thinking it was full and was responding by trying to digest the balloon. Sensory input from the stomach is not essential for feeling hungry, as dieters have learned when they try to "trick" their stomachs into feeling full by eating large quantities of carrots and celery and drinking lots of water.

Does this mean there is no connection between the stomach and feeling hungry? Not necessarily. Specialized pressure receptors in the stomach walls do signal fullness or a feeling of emptiness (Woods, Schwartz, Baskin, & Seeley, 2000). However, animals and humans without stomachs continue to experience hunger and satiety (a feeling of fullness), so other factors must be involved.

Blood Chemistry

Research suggests that the level of glucose (sugar) in the blood may be a central factor in hunger (Woods, Schwartz, Baskin, & Seeley, 2000). When you've just finished a meal, your glucose level is high and you lose interest in food. Early research suggested low glucose does contribute to hunger, but people with diabetes can have high glucose levels and still be hungry. How could that be explained? Because it is not the *level* of glucose that affects feelings of hunger or satiety but the *uptake* of glucose (Franken, 1998).

Thus, in addition to glucose, the body needs *insulin* (a hormone secreted by the pancreas) to uptake or extract glucose from the blood. In nondiabetic people, both glucose and insulin are normally available after food is eaten and hunger feelings are satisfied. When diabetics take insulin, their cells can then use the glucose from food, and they stop feeling hungry.

The Brain

A part of the brain known as the *hypothalamus* has centers that regulate eating, drinking, and body temperature. In fact, one area of the hypothalamus, the *lateral hypothalamus* (LH), stimulates eating and another area, the *ventromedial hypothalamus* (VMH), creates feelings of satiation and signals the animal to stop eating. When the VMH area is destroyed in rats, they overeat to the point of extreme obesity (Figure 31.2). When the LH area is destroyed, animals may starve to death if they are not force-fed. (In time, LH-damaged rats will resume eating, but their weight stays well below normal.) Humans with tumors in the LH or VMH area show similar extreme weight loss or gain.

But the LH and VMH areas are not simple on–off switches for eating. For example, lesions to the VMH make animals picky eaters — they reject food that doesn't taste good. Lesions also increase the secretion of insulin, which may in turn cause overeating (Challem, Berkson, Smith, & Berkson, 2000). Lesions to the VMH may also raise the **set point**, or natural weight level. A higher set point may increase hunger, making the animal eat more (Woods, Seeley, Porte, & Schwartz, 1998). In contrast, when the LH is lesioned, the animal experiences a decrease in hunger and a lowered set point.

In sum, internal factors such as structures in the hypothalamus (the LH and VMH), blood chemistry (glucose and insulin), and signals from the stomach all

Set Point *An organism's personal homeostatic level for a particular body weight that results from factors such as early feeding experiences and heredity*

Figure 31.2 *How the brain affects eating.* (a) This diagram shows a rat's brain with the front half cut away. Note the positions of the ventromedial hypothalamus (VMH) and the lateral hypothalamus (LH). (b) The ventromedial area of the hypothalamus of the rat on the left was destroyed, which led to a tripling of body weight. Compare his size to that of the normal rat on the right.

Lateral hypothalamus

Pituitary   Ventromedial hypothalamus

(a)   (b)

seem to play important roles in hunger and eating. Other internal factors have also been researched, including other areas of the brain, genetics, and the presence or absence of certain neurotransmitters (DeFalco et al., 2001; Tai, Lau, Ho, Fak, & Tan, 2000; Woods, Schwartz, Baskin, & Seeley, 2000).

Cultural Factors

One of the most important *external* influences on when, what, where, and why we eat is cultural conditioning (Rozin, 1996). North Americans, for example, tend to eat their evening meal around 6 P.M., whereas people in Spain and South America tend to eat around 10 P.M. When it comes to *what* we eat, have you ever eaten rat, dog, or horsemeat? If you are a typical North American, this might sound repulsive to you, yet most Hindus would feel a similar revulsion at the thought of eating meat from cows.

Hunger is a complex psychological motive controlled by interacting internal and external factors. For instance, although innate biological factors may explain the basic need to eat (babies will reflexively turn and nurse when the nipple is placed near their mouth), learning through classical conditioning may be a major factor in specific, goal-oriented eating and drinking behaviors (Hall, Arnold, & Myers, 2000). Similarly, we are born with internal biological preferences for sweet and high-fat foods, but the manufacture and wide availability of snack foods in our external world exploit this inborn preference.

Is there any way to counteract these internal and external factors and successfully lose weight? Most cases of obesity result from consuming more calories than the body can metabolize, or burn up. Therefore, the safest and most reliable way to lose weight is to follow a sensible diet and to exercise regularly (Migliore, 2000; Wadden et al., 1997).

At the same time, weight is more than a simple function of caloric intake and energy expenditure. We all know some people who can eat anything they want and still not add pounds. Research suggests that these "naturally" thin people may be faster at digesting food or have a higher metabolic rate or lower set point (Bouchard, 1996, 1997; Migliore, 2000). Adoption and twin studies also suggest that each of these factors may result from inherited genes. Adoptive children of all weights (ranging from very thin to very obese) tend to resemble their biological parents more than their adoptive parents in body size (Hewitt, 1997). The causes of obesity are complex. Simplistic answers, like willpower or genetics, are appealing, but obesity occurs for a variety of reasons, including many that are outside an individual's control (Hill & Peters, 1998; Woods, Schwartz, Baskin, & Seeley, 2000).

Before we leave this topic, the role of biology in weight regulation should be put in perspective. Obesity is a major cause of morbidity (disease) and mortality (death) (American Heart Association, 2000). Overstating the role of genetics and biology may discourage lifestyle changes that could ultimately improve health. On the other hand, vast numbers of individuals operate on destructive cycles of diets and relapses, followed by guilt, depression, and new rounds of dieting. Recent research finds this type of "yo-yo dieting" can also significantly increase the risk of gallstones (Horowitz, 1999; U.S. Department of Public Health, 2000). According to Brownell and Rodin (1994b), "dieting clearly has costs and, for some, has the potential for benefit... Hence, it is important to distinguish dieting in individuals who are not overweight from those whose weight increases medical or psychosocial risks" (p.781).

Anorexia Nervosa and Bulimia Nervosa

Two serious eating disorders that demonstrate the potential dangers of dieting are **anorexia nervosa** (self-starvation and extreme weight loss) and **bulimia nervosa** (intense, recurring episodes of binge eating followed by purging through vomiting or taking laxatives). Contrary to myth, these eating disorders are not restricted to females from upper-middle-class backgrounds. They are found in all socioeconomic levels, and a few men also develop eating disorders, although the incidence is rare compared with that for women (Brooks, Taylor, Hardy, & Lass, 2000; Hewitt, Coren, & Steel, 2001).

Anorexia nervosa is characterized by an overwhelming fear of becoming obese, disturbed body image, and the use of dangerous measures to lose weight. The fear of fatness does not diminish even with radical and obvious weight loss, and the body image is so distorted that even a skeletal body is perceived as fat. Many people with anorexia nervosa not only refuse to eat but also take up extreme exercise regimens — hours of cycling or running or constant walking. The extreme malnutrition often leads to bone fractures and osteoporosis. Menstruation in women often ceases, and brain computed tomography (CT) scans show enlarged ventricles (cavities) and widened grooves. Such signs generally indicate loss of brain tissue (Wentz, Gillberg, Gillberg, & Rastam, 2000). A significant percentage of individuals with anorexia nervosa ultimately die of the disorder (Gordon, 2000).

Occasionally the person suffering from anorexia nervosa succumbs to the desire to eat and gorges on food, then vomits or takes laxatives. This type of bingeing and purging is also characteristic of bulimia nervosa, which is much more common than anorexia nervosa (Greeno, Wing, & Shiffman, 2000). Individuals suffering from bulimia nervosa are not just impulsive eaters; they also show impulsivity in other areas, sometimes by petty shoplifting or alcohol abuse (Dansky, Brewerton, & Kilpatrick, 2000; Narduzzi & Jackson, 2000). The vomiting associated with bulimia nervosa causes eroded tooth enamel and tooth loss, severe damage to the throat and stomach, cardiac arrhythmias, metabolic deficiencies, and serious digestive disorders.

What causes anorexia nervosa and bulimia nervosa? There are almost as many causes as there are victims. Some theories focus on physical causes such as hypothalamic disorders, low levels of various neurotransmitters, and genetic or hormonal disorders. Other theories emphasize psychological or social factors, such as a need for perfectionism, a perceived loss of control, destructive thought patterns, depression, dysfunctional families, distorted body image, and sexual abuse (Gordon, 2000; Richter, 2001; Robert-McComb, 2001; Wade, Bulik, Sullivan, Neale, & Kendler, 2000).

Anorexia Nervosa *An eating disorder, seen mostly in adolescent and young adult females, in which a severe loss of weight results from an obsessive fear of obesity and self-imposed starvation*

Bulimia Nervosa *An eating disorder in which enormous quantities of food are consumed (binges), followed by purging through vomiting or taking laxatives*

Culture and Eating Disorders

Culture and the media also play important roles in eating disorders (Anastasio, Rose, & Chapman, 1999; Davis, Dionne, & Shuster, 2001). A number of cross-cultural studies have found important differences in perceptions and stereotypes about eating, thinness, and obesity. For instance, Asian and African Americans report fewer eating and dieting disorders and greater body satisfaction than do European Americans (Akan & Grilo, 1995), and Mexican students report less concern about their own weight and more acceptance of fat people than do North American students (Crandall & Martinez, 1996).

Although social pressures for thinness certainly contribute to the development of eating disorders, it is interesting to note that anorexia nervosa has also been found in nonindustrialized areas like the Caribbean island of Curaçao (Riva, Marachi, & Molinari, 2000). On that island, being overweight is socially acceptable and the average woman is considerably heavier than women in North America are, yet some women still have anorexia nervosa. This research suggests that both culture and biology help explain eating disorders. Regardless of the causes, it is important to recognize the symptoms of anorexia and bulimia (Table 31.1) and seek therapy if the symptoms apply to you. There is no question that both disorders are serious and require treatment.

TABLE 31.1 *DSM-IV-TR*[a] **SYMPTOMS OF ANOREXIA NERVOSA AND BULIMIA NERVOSA**

Symptoms of Anorexia Nervosa
- Body weight below 85% of normal for one's height and age
- Intense fear of becoming fat or gaining weight, even though underweight
- Disturbance in one's body image or perceived weight
- Self-evaluation is unduly influenced by body weight
- Denial of seriousness of abnormally low body weight
- Absence of menstrual periods
- Purging behavior (vomiting or misuse of laxatives or diuretics)

Symptoms of Bulimia Nervosa
- Normal or above-normal weight
- Recurring binge eating
- Eating within an hour or two an amount of food that is much larger than most people would consume
- Feeling a lack of control over eating
- Purging behavior (vomiting or misuse of laxatives or diuretics)
- Excessive exercise to prevent weight gain
- Fasting to prevent weight gain
- Self-evaluation is unduly influenced by body weight

The extreme thinness of popular television stars like Lara Flynn Boyle may contribute to anorexia and bulimia.

[a] *DSM-IV-TR = Diagnostic and Statistical Manual of Mental Disorders*, fourth edition, revised.

(a)

(b)

Figure 31.3 *Arousal-seeking behavior.* (a) Monkeys will work very hard at opening latches for the sheer pleasure of satisfying their curiosity. (b) The arousal motive is also seen in young children, who are fascinated by ordinary household objects.

Arousal: The Need for Stimulation

Another biological motive that influences us is *arousal*, which refers to a general state of alertness and mental and physical activation. Although the hunger motive obviously affects behavior, we are less likely to recognize that all living organisms also need a certain degree of stimulation. According to the *arousal motive* theory, there is an ideal or optimal level of arousal that organisms are motivated to achieve and maintain.

The need for sensory stimulation begins shortly after birth. For example, infants show a marked preference for complex versus simple visual stimuli. Adults also pay more attention, and for a longer period of time, to complex and changing stimuli. Similarly, research with monkeys shows they will perform various tasks for the simple "reward" of a brief look around the laboratory (Butler, 1954). As can be seen in Figure 31.3, they will also learn to open latches for the sheer pleasure of curiosity and manipulation (Harlow, Harlow, & Meyer, 1950).

When arousal is too low or too high, performance is diminished, as shown in Figure 31.4. This inverted U-shape curve, so-named because the graph looks like an upside-down letter *U,* also demonstrates that performance is maximized when arousal is at an "optimum" level. Have you noticed this effect while taking exams? When underaroused, your mind wanders, causing you to make careless errors (like filling in the space for option A on a multiple-choice exam when you meant to fill in B). When overaroused, you may become so anxious that you can't remember what you studied. (This kind of forgetting is explained in part by the fact that overarousal seems to interfere with retrieving information from long-term memory [LTM].)

If you do become overly aroused on exam day, you may want to take a class in study skills or test anxiety. You can also try these basic study tips:

Step 1: *Prepare in advance.* Improve your reading, note taking, and study skills by reviewing and practicing the advice in Tools for Student Success in Module 4. The single most important cure for test anxiety is advance preparation and *hard work.* If you are well prepared, you will feel calmer and more in control.

- Read your textbook using the SQ4R (Survey, Question, Read, Recite, Review, and wRite) method.
- Practice good time management and distribute your study time; don't cram the night before.
- Actively listen during lectures and take detailed, and summarizing notes.
- Follow the general strategies for test taking mentioned in Module 4.

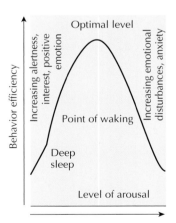

Figure 31.4 *Optimal level of arousal.* Our need for stimulation (the arousal motive) suggests that behavior efficiency increases as we move from deep sleep to increased alertness. However, there is a point at which we become too aroused and performance declines.

Step 2: *Learn to cope with the anxiety.* As you just learned, performance is best at a moderate level of arousal. A few butterflies before and during exams are okay and to be expected, but too much anxiety can interfere with concentration and cripple your performance. To achieve the right balance of arousal, try the following:

- Replace anxiety with relaxed feelings. Practice the relaxation response described in Module 10, on page 121.
- Desensitize yourself to the test situation. See Module 44, page 581.
- Exercise regularly. This is a great stress reliever and promotes deeper and more restful sleep.

Sensation Seeking

Each of us is motivated to achieve an optimal level of arousal, but how do we explain people who seem to have an extreme need for stimulation? What motivates people who hang-glide over deep canyons or go whitewater rafting down dangerous rivers? According to research, these "high sensation seekers" may be biologically "prewired" to need a higher level of stimulation (Zuckerman, 1979, 2000).

TRY THIS
Yourself

Before we continue, circle the choice, A or B, that *best* describes you in each of the following items:

1. A I would like a job that requires a lot of traveling.
   B I would prefer a job in one location.
2. A I am invigorated by a brisk, cold day.
   B I can't wait to get indoors on a cold day.
3. A I get bored seeing the same old faces.
   B I like the comfortable familiarity of everyday friends.
4. A I would prefer living in an ideal society where everyone is safe, secure, and happy.
   B I would have preferred living in the unsettled days of our history.
5. A I sometimes like to do things that are a little frightening.
   B A sensible person avoids activities that are dangerous.
6. A I would not like to be hypnotized.
   B I would like to have the experience of being hypnotized.
7. A The most important goal of life is to live it to the fullest and experience as much as possible.
   B The most important goal of life is to find peace and happiness.
8. A I would like to try parachute jumping.
   B I would never want to try jumping out of a plane, with or without a parachute.
9. A I enter cold water gradually, giving myself time to get used to it.
   B I like to dive or jump right into the ocean or a cold pool.
10. A When I go on a vacation, I prefer the comfort of a good room and bed.
    B When I go on a vacation, I prefer the change of camping out.
11. A I prefer people who are emotionally expressive even if they are a bit unstable.
    B I prefer people who are calm and even-tempered.
12. A A good painting should shock or jolt the senses.
    B A good painting should convey a feeling of peace and security.
13. A People who ride motorcycles must have some kind of unconscious need to hurt themselves.
    B I would like to drive or ride on a motorcycle.

Scoring

Count 1 point for each of the following items that you have circled: 1A, 2A, 3A, 4B, 5A, 6B, 7A, 8A, 9B, 10B, 11A, 12A, 13B. Add up your total and compare it with the norms below:

0–3: very low need for sensation seeking

4–5: low

6–9: average

10–11: high

12–13: very high

Source: Zuckerman, M. (1978, February). The search for high sensation, *Psychology Today,* pp. 38–46. Copyright © 1978 by the American Psychological Association. Reprinted by permission.

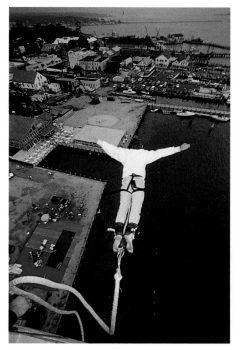

High sensation-seeking? *Would you be willing to try bungee jumping? If not, are you a low sensation-seeker on Zuckerman's scale?*

Research based on longer versions of Zuckerman's scale suggest four distinct factors that characterize sensation seeking (Franken, 1998; Johnson & Cropsey, 2000): (1) thrill and adventure seeking (skydiving, driving fast, or trying to beat a train), (2) experience seeking (travel, unusual friends, drug experimentation), (3) disinhibition ("letting loose"), and (4) susceptibility to boredom (lower tolerance for repetition and sameness).

If you scored very high or very low on this test, you might have problems in relationships with individuals who score toward the other extreme. Zuckerman warns that this is true not just between partners or spouses but also between parent and child and therapist and patient. There might also be job difficulties for a high-sensation seeker with a routine clerical or assembly line job or a low-sensation seeker with a highly challenging and variable occupation.

Achievement: The Need for Success

Do you wonder what motivated Wilt Chamberlain to achieve such success in basketball or why Coach Bobby Knight drove his players so mercilessly? What about someone like Thomas Edison? Inventing the lightbulb would have been achievement enough for any person, but Edison also received patents for the microphone, the phonograph, and over a thousand other inventions. Even as a child, he spent hours doing experiments and figuring out how things work. What drove Edison?

The key to understanding Wilt Chamberlain, Bobby Knight, and Thomas Edison lies in what psychologist Henry Murray (1938) identified as a high need for achievement (nAch), or **achievement motivation**, a desire for significant accomplishment. Before you continue reading, complete the Critical Thinking/Active Learning exercise that follows this section. It gives you an opportunity to test your own need for achievement.

Achievement Motivation *The need for success, for doing better than others, and for mastering challenging tasks; the desire to excel, especially in competition with others*

Characteristics of Achievers

How do individuals with a high nAch differ from other people? Researchers have identified several distinguishing traits in these people (McClelland, 1958, 1987, 1993; Mueller & Dweck, 1998; Wigfield & Eccles, 2000).

1. *Preference for moderately difficult tasks.* People high in nAch avoid tasks that are too easy because they offer little challenge or satisfaction. They also avoid extremely difficult tasks because the probability of success is too low. In a ring-toss game, for instance, they often stand at an intermediate distance from the target.

2. *Competitiveness.* High achievement–oriented people are more attracted to careers and tasks that involve competition and an opportunity to excel.

3. *Preference for clear goals with competent feedback.* High achievement–oriented people tend to prefer tasks with a clear outcome and situations in which they can receive feedback on their performance. They also prefer criticism from a harsh but competent evaluator to one who is friendlier but less competent.

4. *Responsibility.* People with high nAch prefer being personally responsible for a project. When they are directly responsible, they can feel satisfied when the task is well done.

5. *Persistence.* High achievement–oriented people are more likely to persist at a task when it becomes difficult. When participants were given an unsolvable task, 47 percent of the high-nAch individuals persisted until time was called. On the other hand, only 2 percent of those who were low on achievement motivation persisted.

6. *More accomplished.* People who have high nAch scores do achieve more than others. They do better on exams, earn better grades in high school and college, and excel in their chosen professions.

What causes some people to be more achievement oriented than others? Achievement orientation appears to be largely learned in early childhood, primarily through interactions with parents. Highly motivated children tend to have parents who encourage independence and frequently reward successes (Maehr & Urdan, 1999). The culture that we are born and raised in also affects achievement needs (Lubinski & Benbow, 2000). Events and themes in children's literature, for example, often contain subtle messages about what the culture values. In North American and Western European cultures, many children's stories are about persistence and the value of hard work. A study by Richard de Charms and Gerald Moeller (1962) found a significant correlation between the achievement themes in children's literature and the actual industrial accomplishments of various countries. Conversely, can you see how gambling and the lottery — both based on luck of the draw — might lower a person's nAch?

Intrinsic and Extrinsic Motivation and Achievement

Having some understanding of the characteristics of high achievers, let's look at two forms of motivation that affect achievement — *intrinsic* and *extrinsic*. **Intrinsic motivation** comes from within the individual. The person engages in an activity for its own sake or for internal satisfaction, with no ulterior purpose or need for an external reward. Some researchers believe this self-motivation comes from an innate need (e.g., Ryan & Deci, 2000). In contrast, **extrinsic motivation** stems from obvious external rewards or avoidance of punishment and is learned through interaction with the environment. Participation in sports and hobbies, like swimming or playing a guitar, is usually intrinsically motivated. Working at a boring job and going to the dentist come from extrinsic motivation. In most people's mind, "play" is intrinsic and "work" is extrinsic.

What do you think would happen if you were suddenly given extrinsic rewards (money, praise, or other incentives) for your current "play" activities? Studies have found that people who are paid or rewarded for something they had previously done for the sheer fun of it often lose enjoyment and interest in the task (Hennessey & Amabile, 1998; Kohn, 2000). One of the earliest experiments to demonstrate this effect involved preschool children who liked to draw (Lepper, Greene, & Nisbett, 1973). The children were all given artist's paper and felt-tipped pens, and one group was promised a "Good Player" certificate with a gold seal and ribbon for their drawings. A second group was asked to draw and then received an unexpected reward when they were done. A third group received no promise of a certificate and no reward was given. A few weeks later, these same children were placed in a situation in which they could draw if they wanted to, and the amount of time they spent drawing was recorded.

A prime example of intrinsic motivation. *Vincent van Gogh only sold one painting during his entire lifetime, yet he was one of the most prolific nineteenth century artists. How would you explain his motivtion?*

Intrinsic Motivation *Motivation that comes from personal enjoyment of a task or activity, rather than from external rewards or fear of punishment*

Extrinsic Motivation *Motivation based on obvious external rewards or threats of punishment, rather than on factors within the individual or the behavior itself*

critical thinking ▷▷▷▷▷▷▷▷▷▷▷▷▷▷▷▷▷▷▷▷▷

Measuring Your Own Need for Achievement

Are you interested in measuring your own need for achievement? If so, try the following:

Test I

On the basis of how you feel in *most* situations, answer the following questions honestly with a yes or no:

_____1. If offered a choice of tasks, would you pick one that is moderately difficult rather than one that is very difficult or easy?

_____2. Do you enjoy tasks more if you compete against others?

_____3. Do you prefer tasks that have clear, defineable goals and measurable outcomes?

_____4. Do you like receiving feedback about how well you are doing when you are working on a project?

_____5. Would you rather receive criticism from a harsh but competent evaluator than from one who is friendlier but less competent?

_____6. Do you prefer tasks where you are personally responsible for the outcome?

_____7. When working on a difficult task, do you persist even when you encounter roadblocks?

_____8. Do you typically receive high performance evaluations (e.g., receiving top honors or special recognition in sports, clubs, and other activities)?

Test 2

The Thematic Apperception Test (TAT) consists of a series of ambiguous pictures such as the one shown in Figure 31.5. The TAT is one of the most common methods for measuring achievement motivation. Look closely at the two women in the figure and write a short story answering the following questions:

1. What is happening in this picture, and what led up to it?

2. Who are the people in this picture, and how do they feel?

3. What is going to happen in the next few moments, and in a few weeks?

Scoring

Test I: Give yourself I point for each time you answered yes to the eight questions. On the basis of the characteristics of achievers discussed in the text, people with a higher number of yes answers tend to be high in achievement motivation.

Test 2: Give yourself I point each time any of the following is mentioned: (1) defining a problem, (2) solving a problem, (3) obstructions to solving a problem, (4) techniques that can help overcome the

Figure 31.5 *Measuring achievement.* This card is one of several from the Thematic Apperception Test (TAT). The strength of an individual's need for achievement is measured by the stories he or she tells about the TAT photos.

problem, (5) anticipation of success or resolution of the problem. The higher your score on this test, the higher your overall need for achievement.

The higher your score on both tests, the higher your overall need for achievement. Compare your scores with those of your friends and classmates.

What do you think happened? As Figure 31.6 shows, offers of a "Good Player" certificate greatly undermined the children's subsequent interest in drawing.

How can we explain the results of these studies? Apparently, the critical factor in enjoyment of a task is how we interpret our motivation to ourselves. When we perform a task for no apparent reason, we use internal, personal reasons ("I like it"; "It's fun"). But when extrinsic rewards are added, the explanation shifts to external, impersonal reasons ("I did it for the money"; "I did it to please the boss"). This shift generally decreases enjoyment and negatively affects performance.

But doesn't getting a raise or receiving a gold medal increase enjoyment and productivity? Not all extrinsic motivation is bad (Covington, 1999, 2000). The

(a)

(b)

Figure 31.6 *Intrinsic versus extrinsic motivation.* (a) As shown in this graph, children who were given *no* reward spent more free time drawing. (Source: Lepper, Greene, & Nisbett, 1973.) (b) These children are obviously having fun, yet few adults fingerpaint. Is this because we're too busy or because we were given grades, praise, or other extrinsic rewards that destroyed our early intrinsic motivation?

problem seems to lie in how extrinsic rewards are used: (1) to inform versus to control or (2) as a treat versus external pressure. First of all, research finds extrinsic rewards do not reduce intrinsic interest if they are based on competency (Deci, 1995). In fact, they may intensify the desire to do well again. Thus, getting a raise or gold medal can inform us and provide valuable feedback about our performance, which may increase enjoyment. On the other hand, if rewards are used to control, like giving children money or privileges for good grades, intrinsic motivation declines.

Second, research with children shows that when extrinsic rewards are perceived as a simple, "no strings attached" treat, their interest in creative tasks increases. As you can see in Figure 31.7, the reverse is true, however, if they see the reward as an external pressure to be creative (Eisenberger & Armeli, 1997).

Figure 31.7 *Motivation is in the eye of the beholder.* Do rewards increase motivation or are they seen as coercion or bribery? It depends. Note how a controlling reward and external pressure both lead to extrinsic motivation, whereas an informing reward and "no strings" treat produce intrinsic motivation.

TRY THIS
Yourself

Intrinsic–extrinsic motivation has important implications for raising children, running a business, or even studying this text. Consider the following guidelines for increasing motivation:

1. *Limit concrete extrinsic rewards.* In general, it is almost always better to use the least possible extrinsic reward and for the shortest possible time period. When children are first learning to play a musical instrument, it may help to provide small rewards until they gain a certain level of mastery. But once the child is working happily or practicing for the sheer joy of it, it is best to leave him or her alone. Similarly, if you're trying to increase your study time, begin by rewarding yourself for every significant improvement, but don't interrupt yourself with a reward when you're handling a difficult assignment easily. Save rewards for when you need them. We should emphasize, too, that we're speaking primarily of *concrete* rewards. In contrast, praise and positive feedback generally increase intrinsic motivation (Carton, 1996; Eisenberger & Cameron, 1996).

2. *Reward competency.* Use extrinsic rewards to provide feedback for competency or outstanding performance, rather than for simply engaging in the behavior. Schools might enhance intrinsic motivation by giving medals or privileges to students with no absences, rather than giving money for attendance. Similarly, reward yourself with a movie or call to a friend after you've studied *hard* for your scheduled time period or done particularly well on an exam. Don't reward yourself for half-hearted attempts.

3. *Emphasize intrinsic reasons for behaviors.* Rather than thinking about whom you'll impress with good grades or all the great jobs you'll get when you finish college, focus instead on personally satisfying, intrinsic reasons. Think about how exciting it is to learn new things or the value of becoming an educated person and a critical thinker.

Obviously, not all college classes or all aspects of our lives can be intrinsically interesting. Nor should they be. We all have to do many worthwhile things that are obviously extrinsically motivated —

going to the dentist, cleaning the house, and studying for exams. It's a good idea, therefore, to save your external reinforcers for the times you're having trouble motivating yourself to do an undesirable task, and avoid "wasting" rewards on well-established intrinsic activities. In other words, "Don't sweat the intrinsic stuff" and "Save rewards for a rainy day."

Check & Review

UNDERSTANDING MOTIVATION

Motivation is the study of the "whys" of behavior, whereas **emotion** is the study of feelings. Because motivated behaviors are often closely related to emotions, these two topics are frequently studied together. A wide variety of motives are discussed throughout this text. In this module, we focus on hunger, arousal, and **achievement motivation**.

Both internal (stomach, blood chemistry, the brain) and external (cultural conditioning) factors affect hunger and eating. A large number of people have eating disorders. Obesity seems to result from biological factors, such as the individual's genetic inheritance, and from psychological factors. **Anorexia nervosa** (extreme weight loss due to self-imposed starvation) and **bulimia nervosa** (excessive consumption of food followed by purging) are both related to an intense fear of obesity.

According to the arousal motive, people seek an optimal level of arousal that maximizes their performance. There are, however, individual differences in this need. According to Zuckerman, high-sensation seekers are biologically "prewired" to need a higher level of stimulation, whereas the reverse is true for low-sensation seekers. Achievement involves the need for success, for doing better than others, and for mastering challenging tasks. Research with **intrinsic** versus **extrinsic motivation** shows that extrinsic rewards can lower interest and achievement motivation.

Questions

1. Compare and contrast motivation and emotion.

2. What are the major internal and external factors that control hunger and eating behavior?

3. The _____ motive causes us to look for a certain amount of novelty and complexity from our environment for no apparent reason. (a) sensory; (b) social; (c) drive; (d) arousal

4. _____ refers to the desire to perform an act for its own sake, whereas _____ refers to the desire to perform an act because of external rewards or the avoidance of punishment. (a) Personal motivation, external motivation; (b) Internal drive, external drive; (c) Intrinsic motivation, extrinsic motivation; (d) Individual drive, social drive

Answers to Questions can be found in Appendix B.

Are we motivated by biological or by psychosocial factors? Or both?

General Theories of Motivation: Biological, Psychosocial, and Interactionism

Think back to the introductory stories about Wilt Chamberlain and Bobby Knight while reading the following section. See if you can identify which theory best explains both of their behaviors. We will explore five separate theories that fall into three general categories — biological, psychosocial, and interactionism (Table 31.2).

Biological Theories

Many theories of motivation are biologically based — that is, they look for inborn processes that control and direct behavior. Among these biologically oriented theories are *instinct* and *drive* theories.

Instinct Theories In the earliest days of psychology, researchers like William McDougall (1908) proposed that humans had numerous "instincts," such as repulsion, curiosity, and self-assertiveness. Other researchers later added their favorite "instincts," and by the 1920s, the list became so long it was virtually meaningless.

TABLE 31.2 FIVE THEORIES OF MOTIVATION

Theory	View
Biological Theories	
Instinct	Motivation results from behaviors that are unlearned, uniform in expression, and universal in a species.
Drive-reduction	Motivation begins with a physiological need (a lack or deficiency) that elicits a psychological energy (drive) directed toward behavior that will satisfy the original need.
Psychosocial Theories	
Incentive	Motivation results from environmental stimuli that "pull" the organisms in certain directions.
Cognitive	Motivation reflects thought processes (such as attributions and expectancies) in goal-directed behaviors.
Interactionism	
Maslow's hierarchy of needs	Lower motives (such as physiological and saftey needs) must be satisfied before advancing to higher needs (such as belonging and self-esteem).

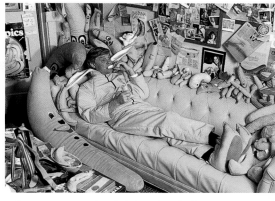

What motivates this behavior? *Which theory best explains this man's love for and collection of banana paraphernalia?*

One early researcher found listings for over 10,000 human instincts (Bernard, 1924).

In addition to producing a never-ending list, the label *instinct* led to circular explanations. Have you ever heard someone say that men are just naturally or instinctually aggressive, or that all women have a maternal instinct? When asked for evidence of these instincts, the person (like the researchers did in McDougall's time) most likely points to examples of male aggression or female nurturing. Thus, the explanation of the behavior is the behavior: "They act that way because they naturally act that way." Circular reasoning, however, is not acceptable to science.

In recent years, a branch of biology called *sociobiology* has revived the case for **instincts**. These are rigid and fixed motor response patterns that are not learned, are characteristic of a species, and have an inherited, genetic foundation established in the course of evolution. Instinctual behaviors are obvious in many animals: birds build nests and salmon swim upstream to spawn. But sociobiologists such as Edward O. Wilson (1975, 1978) believe humans also have instincts, like competition or aggression, which are genetically transmitted from one generation to another.

Drive-Reduction Theory In the 1930s, the concepts of drive and drive reduction began to replace the theory of instincts. According to **drive-reduction theory** (Hull, 1952; Spence, 1951), all living organisms have certain biological *needs* (such as food, water, and oxygen) that must be met if they are to survive. When these needs are unmet, a state of tension (known as a *drive*) is created, and the organism is motivated to reduce it. When we are deprived of food, our biological need creates a state of tension, in this case the hunger *drive*, and we are motivated to find food.

Drive-reduction theory is based largely on the biological concept of *homeostasis* — a state of balance or stability in the body's internal environment. Body temperature, blood sugar, oxygen level, and water balance are all normally maintained in a state of equilibrium. When this balance is disrupted, a need arises (a drive is created), and we are motivated to restore homeostasis. Drive-reduction theory and homeostasis are summarized in Figure 31.8.

Instincts *Behavioral patterns that are (1) unlearned, (2) always expressed in the same way, and (3) universal in a species*

Drive-Reduction Theory *The theory that motivation begins with a physiological need (a lack or deficiency) that elicits a psychological energy or drive directed toward behavior that will satisfy the original need; once the need is met, a state of balance (homeostasis) is restored and motivation decreases*

Instincts? *Nurturing of the young are instinctual behaviors for many species.*

Figure 31.8 *Drive-reduction theory.* Homeostasis, the body's natural tendency to maintain a state of internal balance, is the foundation of drive-reduction theory. When you need food or water, for example, the imbalance creates a drive that motivates you to search for food or water. When the balance is restored, your motivation (to seek food or water) is also decreased.

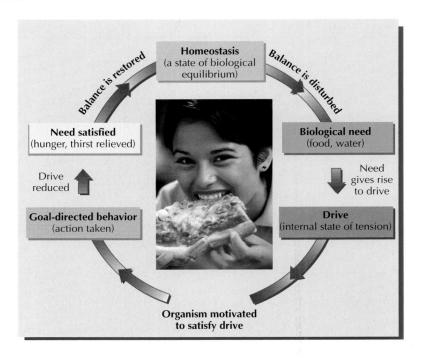

Psychosocial Theories

Instinct and drive-reduction theories explain some motivations but not all. Why, for example, do we continue to eat after our biological need is completely satisfied? Or why does someone work overtime when his or her salary is sufficient to meet all basic biological needs? These questions are better answered by psychosocial theories that emphasize incentives and cognition.

Incentive Theory *The theory that motivation results from environmental stimuli that "pull" the organism in certain directions, as opposed to internal needs that drive or "push" the organism*

Incentive Theory Although drive theory says internal factors *push* people in certain directions, **incentive theory** says external stimuli *pull* people (Bolles, 1970, 1975; Pfaffmann, 1982). Certain characteristics of external stimuli motivate an individual to act to obtain desirable goals or avoid undesirable events. People initially eat because their hunger "pushes" them, but they continue to eat because the sight of apple pie or ice cream "pulls" them. Many *incentives* drew Wilt Chamberlain to basketball, including fame, status, large financial rewards, and the simple joy of playing the game. But cognitive factors might have provided even more compelling motivation.

Cognitive Theories If you receive a high grade in your psychology course, you can interpret that grade in several ways: You earned it because you really studied; you "lucked out"; the textbook was exceptionally interesting and helpful (our preferred interpretation!). According to the cognitive perspective, motivation is directly affected by *attributions*, or how we interpret or think about our own and others' actions. Researchers have found that people who attribute their successes to personal ability and effort tend to work harder toward their goals than people who attribute their successes to luck (Weiner, 1972, 1982).

Expectancies are also important to motivation (Higgins, 1997). Your anticipated grade on a test affects your willingness to study — "If I can get an A in the course, then I will study very hard" — just as your expectancies regarding promotions at work affect your willingness to work overtime for no pay.

Interactionism As we've seen throughout this text, research in psychology generally emphasizes either biological or psychosocial factors (nature or nurture), but in the final analysis, *interactionism* almost always wins. Theories of motivation are no exception. One researcher who recognized this interactionism and developed a theory that accounts for both biological and psychosocial needs in motivation was Abraham Maslow (1954, 1970, 1999). Maslow believed that we all have numerous needs that compete for fulfillment but that some needs are more important than others. For example, your need for a good grade in psychology may compete with demands from other classes, but your need for food and shelter is more important than how you do in college.

As Figure 31.9 shows, Maslow's **hierarchy of needs** *prioritizes* needs, with survival needs at the bottom and social, spiritual needs at the top. Maslow's theory is usually depicted as a pyramid to emphasize that human motivation rests on a foundation of basic biological needs that must be satisfied for survival before higher-level needs can be addressed. As a humanistic psychologist, Maslow also believed that we all have a compelling need to "move up" — to grow, improve ourselves, and ultimately become "self-actualized." (We'll revisit Maslow and other humanistic perspectives in later modules.)

Maslow's hierarchy of needs seems intuitively correct — a starving person would first look for food, then worry about safety, then seek love and friendship, and so on. This prioritizing and the concept of *self-actualization* are important contributions to the study of motivation (Leclerk, Lefrancois, Dube, Hebert, & Gaulin, 1998; Rowan, 1998). But critics argue that parts of Maslow's theory are poorly researched. People sometimes seek to satisfy higher-level needs even when lower-level needs have not been met (Geller, 1982; Neher, 1991; Williams & Page, 1989).

In some nonindustrialized societies, for example, people may be living in a war zone, subsisting on very little food, and suffering from injury and disease (in other

Hierarchy of Needs *Maslow's theory of motivation, that some motives (such as physiological and safety needs) have to be satisfied before an individual can attend to higher needs (such as belonging and self-actualiztion)*

Figure 31.9 *Maslow's hierarchy of needs.* According to Maslow, basic physical necessities must be satisfied before higher-growth needs can be addressed.

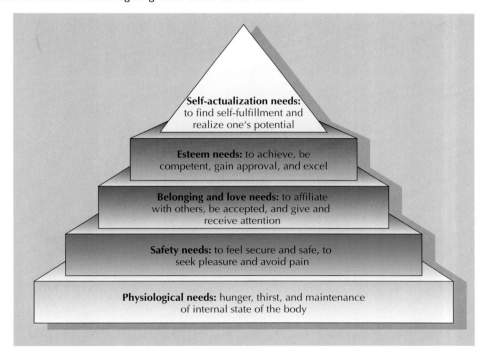

Self-actualization needs: to find self-fulfillment and realize one's potential

Esteem needs: to achieve, be competent, gain approval, and excel

Belonging and love needs: to affiliate with others, be accepted, and give and receive attention

Safety needs: to feel secure and safe, to seek pleasure and avoid pain

Physiological needs: hunger, thirst, and maintenance of internal state of the body words, not fulfilling Maslow's two most basic needs), yet still seek strong social ties and high self-esteem. During the famine and war in Somalia, many parents sacrificed their own lives to carry starving children hundreds of miles to food distribution centers, and parents at the centers often banded together to share the limited supplies. Because Maslow argued that each individual's own lower needs must be at least partially met before higher needs can influence behavior, these examples "stand Maslow's need hierarchy on its head" (Neher, 1991, p. 97). Although we're normally motivated to fulfill basic needs first, in certain circumstances we can bypass these lower stages and pursue higher-level needs.

Check & Review

GENERAL THEORIES OF MOTIVATION

There are three approaches to explaining motivation: biological (including **instinct** theory and **drive-reduction theory**) psychosocial (including **incentive** and cognitive), and interactionist (Maslow's **hierarchy of needs**).

Instinct theories emphasize inborn, genetic components in motivation. Drive-reduction theory suggests that internal tensions (produced by the body's demand for homeostasis) "push" the organism toward satisfying basic needs. According to **incentive** theory, motivation results from the "pull" of external environmental stimuli. Cognitive theories emphasize the importance of attributions and expectations. Maslow's hierarchy of needs or motives incorporates both biological and psychosocial theories. He believed that basic survival needs must be satisfied before a person can attempt to satisfy higher needs. Critics question the importance of sequentially working upward through these steps.

Questions

1. Define *instinct* and *homeostasis*.
2. Match the following examples with their appropriate theory of motivation: (a) instinct; (b) drive-reduction; (c) incentive; (d) cognitive; (e) Maslow's hierarchy of needs

   _____ i. Joining a club because you want to be accepted by others

   _____ ii. Two animals fighting because of their inherited, evolutionary desire for survival

   _____ iii. Eating to reduce hunger

   _____ iv. Studying hard for an exam because you expect that studying will result in a good grade

   _____ v. Eating because the pie looks so delicious

3. _____ theories emphasize the importance of attributions and expectancies in motivated behaviors. (a) Attribution; (b) Motivational; (c) Achievement; (d) Cognitive

4. According to _____ theory, basic survival and security needs must be satisfied before one can move on to such higher needs as self-actualization. (a) evolutionary; (b) instinct; (c) Maslow's; (d) Weiner's

Answers to Questions can be found in Appendix B.

ACTIVE LEARNING WORKSHEET   MODULE 31

ACROSS

1. Motivation based on external rewards or threats of punishment.

6. Behavioral patterns that are unlearned, always expressed in the same way, and universal.

10. Individual's feelings or affective responses.

11. Factors within an individual that activate, maintain, and direct behavior.

12. Theory that motivation begins with a physiological need that elicits a psychological energy directed toward behavior that will satisfy the original need.

DOWN

2. Motivation that comes from personal enjoyment of a task or activity.

3. Need for success, for doing better than others, and for mastering challenging tasks.

4. Eating disorder in which enormous quantities of food are consumed, followed by purging through vomiting or taking laxatives.

5. Maslow's theory that certain motives must be satisfied before an individual can advance to higher needs.

7. An organism's personal homeostatic level for a particular body weight.

8. Theory suggesting motivation results from environmental stimuli that "pull" the organism in certain directions.

9. Severe loss of weight resulting from an obsessive fear of obesity and self-imposed starvation.

Answers can be found in Appendix B.

MODULE 32
UNDERSTANDING AND THEORIES OF EMOTION

What major concepts do I need to know in order to understand emotion?

We have reviewed the major theoretical explanations for motivation and specific motives like hunger, eating, arousal, and achievement. But as we mentioned at the beginning of this section, motivation is inextricably linked to emotion. In this module, we will explore the three basic components of all emotions and then look at controversies surrounding the polygraph (or "lie detector") test and the concept of emotional intelligence (EQ).

Components of Emotion: Three Basic Ingredients

Emotions play an important role in our lives. They color our dreams, memories, and perceptions, and when they are disturbed they contribute significantly to psychological disorders. But what do we mean by the term *emotion*? In everyday usage, we describe emotions in terms of feeling states — Wilt Chamberlain "felt thrilled" when he set the NBA record against the New York Knicks, Bobby Knight frequently "felt angry" when coaching, and you "feel happy" watching a good basketball game. Psychologists define and study emotions according to their three basic components (cognitive, physiological, and behavioral).

The Cognitive Component

Our thoughts, beliefs, and expectations help determine the type and intensity of our emotional responses. Or, as Shakespeare wrote in *Hamlet*, "There is nothing either good or bad, but thinking makes it so." Consequently, emotional reactions are very individual: What you experience as intensely pleasurable may be boring or aversive for another.

To study the cognitive component of emotions, psychologists typically use self-report techniques such as paper-and-pencil tests, surveys, and interviews. But our cognitions or thoughts about our own and others' emotions are typically difficult to describe and scientifically measure. Individuals differ in their ability to monitor and report on their emotional states. In addition, some people may lie or hide their feelings because of social expectations or as an attempt to please the experimenter. Furthermore, it is often impractical or unethical to artificially create emotions in a laboratory. How can we ethically create strong emotions like anger in a research participant just to study his or her emotional reactions? Finally, memories of emotions are not foolproof. You may remember that trip to Yellowstone as the "best family camping trip ever," whereas your brother or sister may remember it as the "worst." Our individual needs, experiences, and personal interpretations all affect the accuracy of our memories.

The Physiological Component

Internal physical changes occur in our bodies whenever we experience an emotion. Imagine walking alone on a dark street in a dangerous part of town. You suddenly see someone jump from behind a stack of boxes and start running toward you. How do you respond? Like most of us, you would undoubtedly interpret the situation as threatening and would run. Your predominant emotion, fear, would involve several physiological reactions, including increased heart rate and blood pressure, dilated pupils, perspiration, dry mouth, rapid or irregular breathing, increased blood sugar, trembling, decreased gastrointestinal motility, and piloerection (goose bumps). Such physiological reactions are controlled by certain brain structures and by the autonomic branch of the nervous system (ANS).

The brain. The brain's reticular formation, limbic system, and cerebral cortex play important roles in emotion. Each of these structures plays a complex and interwoven role. There is some evidence that emotional reactions, such as Coach Knight's anger at his players, begin with the brainstem's reticular formation, which is responsible for general arousal and motor control (Davidson, 1999; Rosenzweig, Leiman, & Breedlove, 1999).

Situated above the reticular formation, limbic structures (in particular, the *hypothalamus* and *amygdala*) (Figure 32.1) are also involved in recognizing and controlling emotions, particularly during times of attack, defense, and retreat — the fight-or-flight response (Anderson & Phelps, 2000; Dimberg, Thunberg, & Elmehed, 2000; LeDoux, 1996). For example, electrical stimulation of parts of the limbic system can produce a "sham rage" that turns a docile cat into a hissing, slashing animal (Morris et al., 1996). Stimulating adjacent areas can cause the same animal to purr and lick your fingers. (The rage is called sham because it occurs in the absence of provocation and disappears immediately.)

The third part of the brain directly involved in emotions is the cerebral cortex, the outermost layer of the brain that serves as our body's ultimate control and information processing center. Recall from Modules 5 and 6 that when a 13-pound tamping rod slammed through Phineas Gage's cortex, he could no longer monitor and control his emotions. Recordings of brain activity show that negative emotions are primarily processed in the right hemisphere, whereas positive emotions are processed in the left (Davidson, 1984, 1992). This may explain why we sometimes feel happy and sad at the same time.

Some sensory information travels directly to the limbic system before the cortex can interpret or intervene in the response. Have you ever jumped at a noise on a dark street before you knew whether it was a real threat or just someone's cat? This shortcut from the unexplained noise directly to fear may sometimes embarrass us, but it also protects us from danger. Interestingly, the fact that some neural pathways involved in emotion bypass the cortex also helps explain why people with anxiety disorders often feel afraid without knowing why (Damasio, 1999; LeDoux, 1996).

The autonomic nervous system. As important as the brain is to emotion, it is the ANS that produces the obvious signs of arousal (increased heart rate, fast, shallow breathing, trembling, and so on). These largely automatic responses result from interconnections between the ANS and various glands and muscles (Figure 32.2).

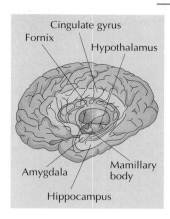

Figure 32.1 ***Brain areas involved in emotion.*** The limbic system consists of several subcortical structures that form a border (or limbus) around the brainstem. (The red structure in the center is the thalamus.)

Sympathetic		Parasympathetic
Pupils dilated	**Eyes**	Pupils constricted
Dry	**Mouth**	Salivating
Goose bumps, perspiration	**Skin**	No goose bumps
Respiration increased	**Lungs**	Respiration normal
Increased rate	**Heart**	Decreased rate
Increased epinephrine and norepinephrine	**Adrenal glands**	Decreased epinephrine and norepinephrine
Decreased motility	**Digestion**	Increased motility

Figure 32.2 ***Emotion and the autonomic nervous system.*** During emotional arousal, the sympathetic branch of the autonomic nervous system (in connection with the brain) prepares the body for fight or flight. Note that digestion and reproductive functions are inhibited during sympathetic dominance — neither is important when you are preparing to attack or run from an enemy. The parasympathetic system is responsible for returning the body to its prearoused state.

Gestures and communication. Can you interpret the emotions of each of these people?

The ANS has two major subdivisions: the *sympathetic nervous system* and the *parasympathetic nervous system*. When you are emotionally aroused, the sympathetic branch increases heart rate, respiration, and so on (the fight-or-flight response). When you are relaxed and resting, the parasympathetic branch reverses these effects. The combined action of both systems allows you to respond to emotional arousal and then return to a more relaxed state.

Where does adrenaline fit into this picture? Adrenaline, or, more properly, *epinephrine*, is a hormone secreted from the adrenal glands at the direction of the hypothalamus. Whereas the sympathetic nervous system is almost instantaneously "turned on" along with the limbic system and frontal lobes, epinephrine and another adrenal hormone, norepinephrine, keep the system under sympathetic control until the emergency is over. The damaging effects of prolonged and excessive sympathetic arousal due to stress are discussed in Module 9.

Behavioral Component

Having examined the cognitive and physiological components of emotions, we now turn our attention to how emotions are expressed — the behavioral component. Emotional expression is a powerful form of communication. An infant's smile can create instant bonding, a cry of "fire" can cause crowds to panic, and a sobbing friend can elicit heartbreaking empathy. Though we can talk about our emotions, we more often express them nonverbally through facial expressions, gestures, body position, use of touch, eye gaze, and tone of voice.

Facial expressions may be the most important form of emotional communication, and researchers have developed very sensitive measurement techniques allowing them to detect subtleties of feeling and differentiate honest expressions from fake ones. Perhaps most interesting is the difference between the "social smile" and the "Duchenne smile," the latter is named after French anatomist Duchenne de Boulogne, who first described it in 1862.

In a false, social smile, our voluntary cheek muscles are pulled back, but our eyes are unsmiling. Smiles of real pleasure, on the other hand, use the muscles not only around the cheeks but also around the eyes (Figure 32.3). According to Duchenne de Boulogne, the eye muscle "does not obey the will" and "is put in play only by the sweet emotions of the soul" (cited in Goode, Schrof, & Burke, 1991, p. 127). Studies found that people who show a Duchenne, or real, smile and laughter elicit more positive responses from strangers and enjoyed better interpersonal relationships and personal adjustment (Keltner & Bonanno, 1997; Keltner, Kring, & Bonanno, 1999).

Figure 32.3 *Duchenne smile.* Which smile looks most sincere? Do you know why? (a) A smile of real joy is referred to as a Duchenne smile. Note how the muscles around the eyes also contract. (b) In a social smile, however, only the muscles around the mouth contract.

GENDER & CULTURAL DIVERSITY

How Culture and Evolution Affect Emotional Expression

Where do our emotions come from? Do they differ from one culture to the next, or are they the same? Are they a product of our evolutionary past? As you might suspect, researchers have found several answers to these questions.

Cultural Similarities

All people of all cultures have feelings and emotions, and all must learn to deal with them (Matsumoto, 2000). But are these emotions the same across all cultures? Given the seemingly vast array of emotions within our own culture, it may surprise you to learn that some researchers believe all our feelings can be condensed into 7 to 10 *culturally universal* emotions. Table 32.1 presents four theorists's findings; note the strong similarities among the four lists.

How do these theorists explain emotions not on the list, such as love? They would say that love, like many other emotions, is simply a combination of primary emotions with variation in intensity. Robert Plutchik (1984, 1994, 2000) suggested that primary emotions, such as fear, acceptance, and joy, are like colors on a color wheel that combine to form secondary emotions, such as love, submission, awe, and optimism (Figure 32.4).

Cultural differences in emotional expression. Iranian men commonly greet one another with a kiss, whereas men in North America generally shake hands or pat one another's shoulders.

TABLE 32.1 THE BASIC HUMAN EMOTIONS

Carroll Izard	Paul Ekman and Wallace Friesen	Robert Plutchik	Silvan Tomkins
Fear	Fear	Fear	Fear
Anger	Anger	Anger	Anger
Disgust	Disgust	Disgust	Disgust
Surprise	Surprise	Surprise	Surprise
Joy	Happiness	Joy	Enjoyment
Shame	—	—	Shame
Contempt	Contempt	—	Contempt
Sadness	Sadness	Sadness	—
Interest	—	Anticipation	Interest
Guilt	—	—	—
—	—	Acceptance	—
—	—	—	Distress

Identifying emotions. Using Plutchik's color wheel, can you identify the primary or secondary emotions of each of these four individuals?

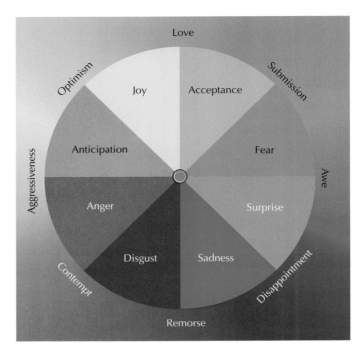

Figure 32.4 *Plutchik's wheel of emotions.* The inner circle represents the eight primary emotions that seem to exist in all cultures. Emotions in the inner circle combine to form secondary emotions located outside the circle. For example, joy and acceptance combine to form love. Robert Plutchik also found that emotions that lie next to each other are more alike than those located farther apart.

In addition to all cultures' sharing the same basic emotions, some researchers believe each of these emotions is expressed and recognized in essentially the same way in all cultures. They point to research that finds people from very different cultures display remarkably similar facial expressions when experiencing particular emotions (Biehl et al., 1997; Ekman, 1993; Ekman & Friesen, 1971; Keating et al., 1981). Moreover, whether respondents are from Western or non-Western societies, they can reliably identify at least six basic emotions: happiness, surprise, anger, sadness, fear, and disgust (Buck, 1984; Matsumoto, 1992, 2000). In other words, across cultures, a frown is recognized as a sign of displeasure, and a smile as a sign of pleasure (Figure 32.5).

Cultural Differences

How do we explain cultural *differences* in emotions? Although we all seem to share reasonably similar facial expressions for some emotions, each culture has its own *display rules* governing how, when, and where to express emotions (Ekman, 1993; Scherer & Wallbott, 1994). For instance, parents pass along their culture's specific display rules when they respond angrily to some emotions in their children, by being sympathetic to others, and on occasion by simply ignoring them. In this way, children learn which emotions they may express in certain situations and which emotions they are expected to control.

There are almost as many variations in display rules as there are cultures in the world. In Japanese culture, for instance, children learn to conceal negative emotions with a stoic expression or polite smile (Dresser, 1996). Young males in the Masai culture are similarly expected to conceal their emotions in public, but by appearing stern and stony-faced (Keating, 1994).

Public physical contact is also governed by display rules. North Americans and Asians are generally not touch-oriented, and only the closest family and

Figure 32.5 *Cultural comparisons of emotion.* To investigate whether emotional facial expressions are universal or culturally learned, Paul Ekman traveled to remote areas of New Guinea. There, he found that members of the Fore tribe could easily identify the emotions on a Westerner's face (top line of photos). He also found that American college students had no difficulty identifying similar expressions in the Fore (bottom line of photos).

friends might hug in greeting or farewell. In contrast, Latin Americans and Middle Easterners often embrace and hold hands as a sign of casual friendship (Axtell, 1998).

The Role of Evolution

Cross-cultural studies of emotional expression tend to support the innate, evolutionary perspective. The idea of universal facial expressions makes adaptive sense because they signal others about our current emotional state (Ekman & Keltner, 1997). Studies with infants also point to an evolutionary basis for emotions. For example, did you know that infants only a few hours old show distinct expressions of emotions that closely match adult facial expressions (Field, Woodson, Greenberg, & Cohen, 1982)? Or that all infants, even those born deaf and blind, show similar facial expressions in similar situations (Eibl-Eibesfeldt, 1980b; Feldman, 1982)? This collective evidence points to a strong biological, evolutionary basis for emotional expression and decoding.

The evolutionary theory of emotion was first advanced by Charles Darwin in 1872. In his classic book, *The Expression of the Emotions in Man and Animals*, Darwin proposed that emotions evolved in different species as a part of survival and natural selection. For example, fear helps animals avoid danger, whereas anger and aggression encourage fighting for mates and necessary resources. Modern evolution theory further suggests that basic emotions (such as fear and anger) originate in the limbic system. Given that higher brain areas (the cortex) developed later than the subcortical limbic system, evolution theory proposes that basic emotions evolved before thought.

The Polygraph: Do "Lie Detector" Tests Really Work?

Having studied the three basic components of all emotions (cognitive, physiological, and behavioral), we can now explore an important controversy related to these components — the *polygraph* (or so-called lie detector) test.

Polygraph *Instrument that measures emotional arousal through heart rate, respiration rate, blood pressure, and skin conductivity; these measurements are taken while a participant is asked questions designed to determine his or her credibility.*

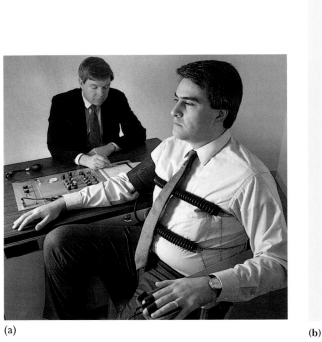

(a)

(b)

Figure 32.6 *Polygraph tests.* (a) During the administration of a polygraph — or lie detector — test, tapes around the individual's chest measure breathing rate, a cuff monitors blood pressure, and finger electrodes measure sweating, or galvanic skin response (GSR). (b) Polygraph printouts are used to detect lying or dishonesty in employees or suspected criminals. Note the sharp rise in the GSR to the question "Have you ever taken money from this bank?" Before concluding that this response indicates the individual is lying, remember that research has found error rates ranging between 25 and 75 percent!

Do you believe John and Patsy Ramsey killed their daughter? Would you be more or less convinced if they took a polygraph test? Many people like the idea that the polygraph can accurately detect when someone is lying. But can it? The polygraph is based on the theory that when people lie, they feel guilty and anxious. These feelings then supposedly activate their sympathetic nervous system, the activity of which is shown on the polygraph machine.

The polygraph does in fact measure sympathetic nervous system arousal (Figure 32.6). But research shows that lying is only loosely related to anxiety and guilt. Some people become nervous when telling the truth, whereas others remain calm when deliberately lying. Furthermore, a polygraph cannot tell *which* emotion is being felt (nervousness, excitement, sexual arousal, etc.) or whether a response is due to emotional arousal or something else, such as physical exercise.

For all these reasons, most judges, psychologists, and other scientists have serious reservations about using polygraphs as lie detectors (Lykken, 1998). Although proponents contend that polygraph tests are 90 percent or more accurate, actual tests show error rates ranging between 25 and 75 percent. Thus, although people say the innocent have nothing to fear from a polygraph test, the research suggests otherwise (Faigman, Kaye, Saks, & Sanders, 1997; Iacono & Lykken, 1997; Lykken, 1998).

Is there any way to make the polygraph reliable? One suggestion is to use "guilty knowledge" questions — that is, questions based on specific information that only a guilty person would know (such as the time a robbery was committed). The idea is that a guilty person would recognize these specific cues and respond in a different way than a nonguilty person (Lykken, 1984, 1988). Expanding on this idea, Bashore and Rapp (1993) developed a polygraph that measures brain wave patterns associated with lying. Other psychologists have suggested using computers and statistical analyses to improve polygraph reliability and validity (Saxe & Ben-Shakhar, 1999).

But even with improvements, many psychologists and others still strongly object to using polygraphs to establish guilt or innocence (Iacono & Lykken, 1997). In fact, scientific controversy and public concern led the U.S. Congress to pass a bill that severely restricts the use of polygraphs in the courts, in government, and in private industry.

Emotional Intelligence (EQ): Are You Emotionally Smart?

You've heard of IQ, the intelligence quotient, but what do you know about EQ — emotional intelligence? According to Daniel Goleman (1995, 2000), **emotional intelligence** (EQ) involves knowing and managing one's emotions, empathizing with others, and maintaining satisfying relationships. In other words, an emotionally intelligent person successfully combines the three components of emotions (cognitive, physiological, and behavioral).

Goleman argued that high EQ explains why people of modest IQ are often more successful than people with much higher IQ scores. He believes that traditional measures of human intelligence ignore a crucial range of abilities that characterize people who excel in real life: self-awareness, impulse control, persistence, zeal and self-motivation, empathy, and social deftness.

Goleman also suggests that many societal problems, such as domestic abuse and youth violence, can be attributed to a lack of EQ. Therefore, EQ should be fostered in everyone. Parents can help their children develop EQ by encouraging them to identify their emotions and understand how these feelings can be changed and how they are connected to their actions (Bar-On & Parker, 2000; Kuebli, 1999). Schools that have instituted Goleman's ideas say students show not just "more positive attitudes about ways to get along with people, but also improvements in critical thinking skills" (Mitchell, Sachs, & Tu, 1997 p. 62).

Critics fear that a handy term like *EQ* invites misuse, but their strongest reaction is to Goleman's proposals for teaching EQ. For example, Paul McHugh, director of psychiatry at Johns Hopkins University, suggests that Goleman is "presuming that someone has the key to the right emotions to be taught to children. We don't even know the right emotions to be taught to adults" (cited in Gibbs, 1995, p. 68).

EQ is a controversial concept, but most researchers are happy that the subject of emotion is being taken seriously. Further research will increase our understanding of emotion and perhaps even reveal the ultimate value of Goleman's theory.

Emotional Intelligence *According to Daniel Goleman, the ability to know and manage one's emotions, empathize with others, and maintain satisfying relationships.*

Developing emotional intelligence. Adults can help children identify and understand their own emotions, as well as how to change them.

Check & Review

UNDERSTANDING EMOTION

All emotions have three basic components: cognitive (thoughts, beliefs, and expectations), physiological (increased heart rate, respiration rate, and so on), and behavioral (facial expressions and bodily gestures). Self-report techniques, such as paper-and-pencil tests, surveys, and interviews, are used to study the cognitive component of emotions.

Studies of the physiological component of emotion find that most emotions involve a general, nonspecific arousal of the nervous system. This arousal involves the reticular formation, limbic system, and cerebral cortex of the brain. The most obvious signs of arousal (trembling, increased heart rate, sweating, and so on) result from activation of the sympathetic nervous system, a subdivision of the autonomic nervous system. The parasympathetic system restores the body to the status quo.

The behavioral component of emotions refers to how we express our emotions, including facial expressions. Most psychologists believe that emotions result from a complex interplay between evolution and culture. Studies have identified 7 to 10 basic emotions that may be universal — experienced and expressed in similar ways across almost all cultures. Display rules for emotional expression differ across cultures.

A **polygraph** measures changes in emotional arousal (increased heart rate, blood pressure, and so on), but research shows it is a poor "lie detector." **Emotional intelligence** (EQ) involves managing one's emotions, empathizing with others, and maintaining satisfying relationships.

Questions

1. Identify the following examples with the appropriate emotional component: (a) cognitive; (b) physiological; (c) behavioral

    _____ i. Increased heart rate

    _____ ii. Crying during a sad movie

    _____ iii. Believing crying is inappropriate for men

    _____ iv. Shouting during a soccer match

2. When people are emotionally aroused, the _____ branch of the _____ nervous system works to increase heart rate and blood pressure and to activate other crisis responses.

3. The polygraph, or lie detector, measures primarily the _____ component of emotions. (a) physiological; (b) articulatory; (c) cognitive; (d) subjective

4. Knowing and managing one's emotions, empathizing with others, and maintaining satisfying relationships are the key factors in _____. (a) self-actualization; (b) emotional intelligence; (c) emotional metacognition; (d) empathic IQ

Answers to Questions can be found in Appendix B.

How are emotional states produced?

James–Lange Theory *The theory that emotion is the perception of one's own bodily reactions and that each emotion is physiologically distinct*

General Theories of Emotion: Explaining Our Feelings

Researchers generally agree on *what* constitutes an emotion (cognitive, physiological, and behavioral), but there is less agreement on *how* we become emotional. The major theories are the James–Lange theory, Cannon–Bard theory, facial feedback hypothesis, and Schachter's two-factor theory. As you read about the different theories, you will find it helpful to refer to Figure 32.7.

James–Lange Theory

According to ideas originated by psychologist William James and later expanded by physiologist Carl Lange, emotions depend on feedback from the body. In other words, contrary to popular opinion, which says we cry because we're sad, James wrote: "We feel sorry because we cry, angry because we strike, afraid because we tremble" (James, 1890).

Why would I tremble unless I first felt afraid? According to the **James–Lange theory**, your bodily response of trembling is a reaction to a specific stimulus such as seeing a large snake in the wilderness. In other words, you perceive an event, your body reacts, and then you interpret the bodily changes as a specific emotion (Figure 32.7a). It is your perception of autonomic arousal (palpitating heart, sinking stomach, flushed cheeks), your actions (running, yelling), and changes in your facial expression (crying, smiling, frowning) that produce what we refer to as emotions. In short, bodily changes cause emotion. If there are no changes, there is no emotion.

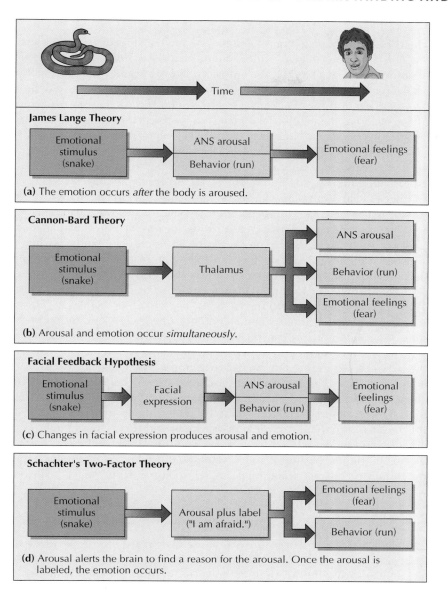

Figure 32.7 *Four major theories of emotion.* (a) In the James–Lange theory, the emotion occurs *after* the body is aroused. (b) In the Cannon–Bard theory, arousal and emotion occur *simultaneously.* (c) The facial-feedback hypothesis proposes that changes in facial expression produce arousal and emotions. (d) In Schachter's two-factor theory, arousal causes the brain to find a reason for the arousal; once the arousal is labeled, the emotion occurs.

Cannon–Bard Theory

Whereas the James–Lange theory argues that each emotion has its own distinct physiological reaction, the **Cannon–Bard theory** holds that all emotions are physiologically similar. Walter Cannon (1927) and Philip Bard (1934) proposed that during perception of the emotion-provoking stimuli (seeing the spider) the thalamus sends *simultaneous* messages to both the general body and the cerebral cortex (Figure 32.7b). Messages to the cortex produce the *experience* of emotion (fear), whereas messages to the autonomic nervous system produce bodily changes (heart palpitations, running, widening eyes, and open mouth).

A major point in the Cannon–Bard theory is that the body's response is not a necessary or even major factor in emotion. Cannon supported his position with several experiments in which animals were surgically prevented from experiencing physiological arousal. Yet, these surgically altered animals still showed observable behaviors (like growling and defensive postures) that might be labeled emotional reactions (Cannon, Lewis, & Britton, 1927).

Cannon–Bard Theory *The theory that the thalamus responds to emotion-arousing stimuli by sending messages simultaneously to the cerebral cortex and the autonomic nervous system; in this view, all emotions are physiologically similar*

Facial Feedback Hypothesis

The third major explanation of emotion — the facial feedback hypothesis — arose in reaction to James–Lange and Cannon–Bard. According to the **facial feedback hypothesis**, facial changes not only correlate with and intensify emotions but also *cause* or initiate the emotion itself (Adelman & Zajonc, 1989; Laird & Bressler, 1992). Contractions of the various facial muscles send specific messages to the brain, identifying each basic emotion. Like James, these researchers suggest that we don't smile because we are happy but rather that we feel happy because we smile (Figure 32.7c).

The facial feedback hypothesis also supports Darwin's (1872) evolutionary theory that freely expressing an emotion intensifies it, whereas suppressing outward expression diminishes it. Interestingly, recent research suggests that even watching another's facial expressions causes an automatic, *reciprocal* change in our own facial muscles (Dimberg & Thunberg, 1998). When people are exposed to pictures of angry faces, for example, the eyebrow muscles involved in frowning are activated. In contrast, the smile muscles show a significant increase in activity when participants are shown photos of a happy face. In follow-up research using "subliminal perception" techniques, scientists have shown that this automatic, matching response occurs even *without* the participant's attention or conscious awareness (Dimberg, Thunberg, & Elmehed, 2000).

This automatic, innate, and sometimes unconscious imitation of facial expressions that match others' expressions has important implications. Have you ever felt depressed after listening to a friend's problems? Your unconscious facial mimicry of the person's sad expression may create similar physiological reactions in your own body. This theory has applications for therapists who constantly work with depressed clients and for actors who simulate emotions for their livelihood. Studies also show that "happy workers are more productive than unhappy workers" (Cote, 1999). Does this mean that unhappy coworkers or a constantly angry boss might affect the happiness (and productivity) of the general workforce? If Darwin was right that expressing an emotion intensifies it and if watching it produces a matching response, maybe we should reconsider traditional advice to "express our anger." Maybe we should express only our positive emotions?

Facial Feedback Hypothesis *The proposal that movements of the facial muscles produce or intensify emotional reactions*

Schachter's Two-Factor Theory

Although previous theories provide some insight into the experience of emotions, they give little attention to the role of cognition and interpretation. According to **Schachter's two-factor theory**, however, emotions depend on two factors: (1) physical arousal and (2) cognitive labeling of that arousal. Schachter thus agrees

Schachter's Two-Factor Theory *The theory that emotional experience results from physical arousal and cognitive labeling (or interpretation) of that arousal*

Testing the facial feedback hypothesis. Hold a pen or pencil between your teeth with your mouth closed, as shown in the left photo. Spend about 15 to 30 seconds in this position. How do you feel? Now hold the pencil between your teeth with your mouth open and your teeth showing, as in the right photo. During the next 15 to 30 seconds, pay attention to your feelings. According to research, pleasant feelings are more likely when teeth are showing. Can you explain why? (Adapted from Strack, Martin, & Stepper, 1988.)

with James–Lange that our experience of an emotion comes from an awareness of our bodily arousal, but he also agrees with Cannon–Bard that emotions are physiologically similar. He reconciles the two theories by proposing that we look to *external* rather than *internal* cues to differentiate and label our emotions. If we cry at a wedding, for example, we interpret our emotion as joy or happiness, but if we cry at a funeral, we label our emotion sadness (Figure 32.7d).

In Schachter and Singer's classic study (1962), participants were given shots of epinephrine and told it was a type of vitamin. Their subsequent arousal and labeling were then investigated (Figure 32.8). One group of participants was *correctly* informed about the expected effects (hand tremors, excitement, and heart palpitations), and a second group was *misinformed* and told to expect itching, numbness, and headache. A third, *uninformed*, group was told nothing about the possible effects.

Following the injection, each participant was placed in a room with a *confederate* (a "stooge" who was part of the experiment but who pretended to be a fellow volunteer). The confederate was told to act happy and cheerful (throwing paper airplanes around the room and shooting wads of paper into the wastebasket) or unhappy and angry (complaining and expressing general dissatisfaction with the entire experiment).

The results of the study confirmed the experimental hypothesis: Participants who did not have an appropriate cognitive label for their emotional arousal (the misinformed group and the uninformed group) tended to look to the situation for an explanation. Thus, those placed with a happy confederate became happy, whereas those with an unhappy confederate became unhappy. Participants in the correctly informed group, on the other hand, knew their physiological arousal was the result of the shot, so their emotions were generally unaffected by the confederate.

Which theory is correct? As you may imagine, each theory has its limitations. For example, the James–Lange theory fails to acknowledge that physical arousal can occur without emotional experience (e.g., when we exercise). This theory also requires

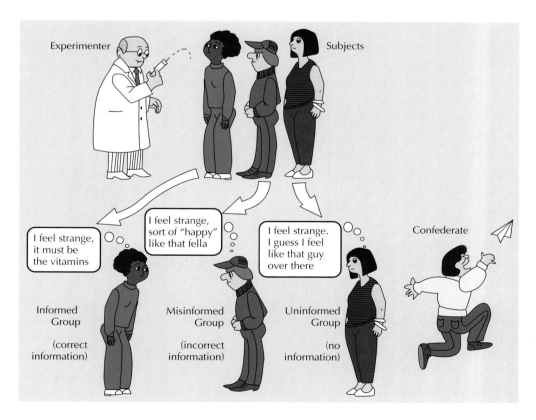

Figure 32.8 *Schachter's two-factor theory.* A comparison of informed, misinformed, and uninformed participants in Schachter and Singer's classic experiment demonstrates the importance of cognitive labels in emotions.

*"I don't sing because I am happy.
I am happy because I sing."*

Psychology in action. *Can you identify which of the four major theories of emotion best explains this bird's behavior? Drawing by Franscino; © 1991, The New Yorker Magazine, Inc.*

a distinctly different pattern of arousal for each emotion. Otherwise, how do we know whether we are sad, happy, or mad? Although research has found subtle differences in positron emission tomography (PET) scan studies of the brain and general physical arousal with basic emotions, such as happiness, fear, and anger (Lane, Reiman, Ahern, & Schwartz, 1997; Levenson, 1992), most people are not aware of these slight variations. Thus, there must be other explanations for why we experience emotion.

The Cannon–Bard theory (that the cortex and autonomic nervous system receive simultaneous messages from the thalamus) has received experimental support. For instance, victims of spinal cord damage still experience emotions — often more intensely than before their injuries (Bermond, Fasotti, Nieuwenhuyse, & Schuerman, 1991). Instead of the thalamus, however, other research shows that it is the limbic system, hypothalamus, and prefrontal cortex that are most important in emotional experience (Davidson, 1999; Jansen, Nguyen, Karpitskiy, Mettenleiter, & Loewy, 1995).

Research on the facial-feedback hypothesis has found a distinctive physiological response for basic emotions such as fear, sadness, and anger — thus partially confirming James–Lange's initial position (Dimberg, Thunberg, & Elmehed, 2000; Wehrle, Kaiser, Schmidt, & Scherer, 2000). Facial feedback does seem to contribute to the intensity of our subjective emotional experience and our overall moods. Thus, if you want to change a bad mood or intensify a particularly good emotion, adopt the appropriate facial expression. Try smiling when you're sad and extend the smiles when you're happy.

Finally, Schachter's two-factor theory emphasizes the importance of cognitive processes in emotions but fails to explain why we take an immediate liking to some people and not to others. Research shows that some neural pathways involved in emotion bypass the cortex and go directly to the limbic system. Recall our earlier example of jumping at a strange sound in the dark and then a second later using the

RESEARCH HIGHLIGHT

Are Abused Children More Alert to Negative Emotions?

Child abuse has been a tragic part of human history since the beginning of time. Only in modern times have we attempted to scientifically research its causes, treatment, and effects. Seth Pollak at the University of Wisconsin–Madison and his colleagues at the University of Rochester (1997) recently conducted an interesting study of children's responses to parental abuse.

A sample of 23 abused and 21 nonabused children, ranging in age from 7.1 to 11.4 years, were presented with black-and-white slides of the same adult female posing a happy, angry, or neutral expression. All children were asked to press a button when presented with the angry versus neutral face or the happy versus neutral face. Using electrodes attached to the children's scalp, researchers measured changes in brain electrical activity as the children viewed the happy, angry, and neutral faces.

As expected, both groups of children exhibited the strongest brain activity response to the happy and angry faces, and the weakest response to the neutral face. But the two groups differed in the strength of their response to the happy and angry faces. Although the nonabused children responded equally to the happy and angry faces, the abused children were most alert and responsive to the angry face.

This physiological research supports earlier behavioral observations. For example, in contrast to nonabused children, physically abused infants exhibit negative emotional expressions earlier and more frequently (Gaensbauer & Hiatt, 1984; Sroufe, 1979).

By extending behavioral investigations to include cognitive and physiological processes, Pollak and his colleagues may help clarify the developmental mechanisms that place maltreated children at risk for maladaptive development. For example, the abused child's heightened reactivity to anger may reflect more efficient and adaptive cognitive organization in a stressful, threatening environment.

However, this greater sensitivity toward negative emotions can create difficulties when abused children interact with others in normal situations (Rogosch, Cicchetti, & Aber, 1995). It may explain why maltreated children often have difficulty in responding to distress and why they react with hostile gestures to other children (Klimes-Dougan & Kistner, 1990; Main & George, 1985). Using earlier studies and the findings of Pollak and his colleagues, future researchers may be able to develop programs to help maltreated children and their parents.

cortex to interpret what it was. This and other evidence suggests that emotions can take place without conscious cognitive processes (Damasio, 1999; Dimberg, Thunberg, & Elmehed, 2000; LeDoux, 1992, 1996).

In sum, certain basic emotions are associated with subtle differences in arousal. These differences can be produced by changes in facial expressions or by organs controlling the autonomic nervous system. In addition, "simple" emotions (likes, dislikes, fears, and anger) do not initially require conscious cognitive processes. This allows a quick, automatic emotional response that can later be modified by cortical processes. On the other hand, "complex" emotions (jealously, grief, depression, embarrassment, love) seem to require cognitive elements.

Check & Review

GENERAL THEORIES OF EMOTION

There are four major theories to explain what causes emotion. According to the **James–Lange theory**, we interpret the way we feel on the basis of physical sensations, such as increased heart rate and trembling. The **Cannon–Bard theory** suggests feelings are created from independent and simultaneous stimulation of both the cortex and the autonomic nervous system.

According to the **facial feedback hypothesis**, facial movements elicit specific emotions. **Schachter's two-factor**

theory suggests that emotions depend on two factors — physical arousal and a cognitive labeling of the arousal. In other words, people notice what is going on around them, as well as their own bodily responses, and then label the emotion accordingly.

Questions

1. Briefly summarize the four major theories of emotion.

2. We see a bear in the woods, our hearts race as we begin to run, and then we experience fear. This is best explained by the _____ theory. (a) James–Lange; (b) Cannon–Bard; (c) facial feedback hypothesis; (d) Schacter's two-factor

3. According to _____, bodily arousal must be labeled or interpreted for an emotional experience to occur. (a) the Cannon–Bard theory; (b) the James–Lange theory; (c) the facial feedback hypothesis; (d) Schacter's two-factor theory

4. The Cannon–Bard theory of emotion suggests bodily arousal and emotional experience occur _____.

Answers to Questions can be found in Appendix B.

ACTIVE LEARNING WORKSHEET MODULE 32

Enter the correct letter from Column A in the blank space in Column B, and then doublecheck your answers with those in Appendix B.

Column A

a. Robert Plutchik

b. Polygraph

c. Display rules

d. James–Lange theory

e. Daniel Goleman

f. Schachter's 2-factor theory

g. Facial-feedback hypothesis

h. Cannon–Bard theory

i. Emotional intelligence

j. Emotion's behavioral component

Column B

1. ___ May explain modest IQ person's superior success.

2. ___ Facial expressions, gestures, body posture.

3. ___ Arousal and emotion occur simultaneously.

4. ___ Changes in facial expression produce emotion.

5. ___ Emotion occurs after bodily arousal.

6. ___ Emotion results from arousal and labeling.

7. ___ Developed theory of emotional intelligence.

8. ___ Measures emotional arousal.

9. ___ Cultural guidelines for expressing emotion.

10. ___ Suggests primary emotions combine to form secondary emotions.

Visual Summary for Modules 31 and 32

Understanding Motivation

Motivation: study of the "whys" of behavior, **emotion:** study of feelings.

Hunger and Eating

• Both *internal* (stomach, blood chemistry, brain) and *external* (cultural conditioning) factors.
• Eating disorders due to combination of both biological and psychological factors:

1) Obesity: Being significantly above the recommended weight level.

2) Anorexia nervosa: Extreme weight loss due to self-imposed starvation.

3) Bulimia nervosa: Excessive consumption of food followed by purging.

Arousal

Arousal motive: People seek *optimal level* of *arousal* that maximizes their performance. High sensation seekers are biologically "prewired" to need a higher level of stimulation.

Achievement

Achievement motivation: Need for success, doing better than others, and mastering challenging tasks. **Intrinsic** vs. **extrinsic motivation** research shows extrinsic rewards can lower interest and achievement motivation.

General Theories of Motivation

Biological Theories

• **Instinct theories:** Inborn, genetic component to motivation.

• **Drive-reduction theory:** Internal tensions (produced by body's demand for *homeostasis*) "push" organism to satisfy basic needs.

Psychosocial Theories

• **Incentive theory:** "Pull" of external environmental stimuli.

• *Cognitive theories:* Emphasize thoughts, attributions, and expectations in setting and meeting goals..

Interactionism

Maslow's **hierarchy of needs:** Basic physiological and survival needs must be met before higher needs, such as esteem and self-actualization

Understanding Emotion

Three Basic Components

Cognitive (thoughts, beliefs, and expectations)	Physiological (heart rate, respiration rate, etc.)	Behavioral (facial expressions and body movements)
Self-report techinques (paper-and-pencil tests, surveys, and interviews) are used to study this component.	Emotions are a general, nonspecific arousal of nervous system, involving cerebral cortex, limbic system, and reticular formation. Obvious signs of arousal: activation of *sympathetic nervous system. Parasympathetic nervous system* restores body to "status quo."	Seven to ten basic, *universal* emotions suggest emotions that may be innate; however, display rules differ across cultures and between men and women.

- **Polygraph**: Measures changes in emotional arousal but is not valid for measuring guilt or innocence.
- **Emotional intelligence (EQ)**: Knowing and managing emotions, empathizing, and maintaining satisfying relationships.

General Theories of Emotion

Four Theories

James-Lange	Cannon-Bard	Facial Feedback	Schachter's Two-Factor
Feelings are interpreted from physical sensations (increased heart rate, trembling, and so on).	Feelings are created from independent and simultaneous stimulation of both cortex and autonomic nervous system.	Facial muscles elicit specific emotions.	Emotions depend on two factors—physical arousal and cognitive labeling of the arousal.

Personality

Consider the following personality description. How well does it describe you?

> You have a strong need for other people to like you and admire you. You have a tendency to be critical of yourself. You have a great deal of unused capacity that you have not turned to your advantage. Although you have some personality weaknesses, you are generally able to compensate for them. You pride yourself on being an independent thinker and do not accept other opinions without satisfactory proof. Disciplined and self-controlled outside, you tend to be worried and insecure inside. At times, you have serious doubts whether you have made the right decision or done the right thing.

Adapted from Ulrich, Stachnik, & Stainton, 1963
What do you think? Does this sound like you? When this same personality description was given to research participants and they were told that it was written specifically for them on the basis of previous psychological tests, a high percentage reported that the description was "very accurate." Surprisingly, even when participants were informed that this was a made-up assessment based on generalized information, most still believed the description fit them better than a bona fide personality profile developed from scientifically designed tests (Hyman, 1981). You may be even more surprised to find that about 78 percent of women and 70 percent of men read newspaper horoscopes, and many of them believe these horoscopes are so correct that they were written especially for them (Halpern, 1998).

Back in the 1800s, if you wanted to have your personality assessed, you would go to a *phrenologist*. This highly respected person would carefully measure your skull, examine the bumps on your head, and then give you a psychological profile of your unique qualities and characteristics. Phrenologists used a *phrenology* chart to determine which personality traits were associated with bumps on different areas of the skull. Today, some people consult fortune-tellers, horoscope columns in the newspaper, tarot cards, and even fortune cookies in Chinese restaurants.

Why are so many people attracted to such nonscientific methods? For one thing, we think these fortune-tellers and pseudotests have somehow tapped into our unique selves. Actually, however, the traits they supposedly reveal are generalizations shared by almost everyone. Furthermore, the traits are generally positive and flattering — or at least neutral. (Would we like tests revealing that we are "irritable, selfish, and emotionally unstable"?) In Module 33, rather than these nonscientific methods, we will focus on research based methods used by psychologists to assess personality.

Before we begin, we need to define *personality*. For most people, "personality" is a relatively simple, everyday concept, as in "He's got a great (or lousy) personality." But for psychologists, personality is an inherently complicated topic, and there are numerous definitions. One of the most widely accepted models defines **personality** as an individual's unique and relatively stable pattern of thoughts, feelings, and actions. Personality describes you as a *person*: how you are different from other people and what patterns of behavior are typical of you. You might qualify as an "extrovert," for example, if you are talkative and outgoing most of the time, or as "conscientious" if you are responsible and self-disciplined most of the time.

Unlike pseudopsychologies presented in supermarket tabloids and newspaper horoscopes, personality theorists focus on empirical studies — the *science* of personality. In line with the basic goals of psychology presented in Module 1, they seek to (1) *describe* individual differences in personality, (2) *explain* how those differences come about, and (3) *predict* individual behavior based on personality findings. Before describing, explaining, or predicting personality, we must *assess* or measure it. Therefore, the first module in this section is personality assessment. We then discuss four major theories: trait, psychoanalytic/psychodynamic, humanistic, social/cognitive, and biological.

Personality An individual's relatively stable and enduring pattern of thoughts, feelings, and actions

Personality and bumps on the head? Franz Gall, founder of phrenology, believed that personality could be measured by reading bumps on the skull. Note that terms like sublimity (ability to squelch natural impulses, especially sexual) and ideality (ability to live by high ideals) probably reflect personality traits important in the 1800s. Can you imagine what traits might be measured if we still believed in phrenology? Would we create terms like suppressity (withholding of natural impulses, especially sexual) and computericity (ability to live in the Information Age)?

MODULE 33
PERSONALITY ASSESSMENT

How do psychologists measure personality?

Throughout history, people have sought information about their own and others' personalities. Modern research has produced various methods for assessing personality, which are used by clinical and counseling psychologists, psychiatrists, and other helping professionals in the diagnosis of patients and to assess progress in therapy. Personality assessment is also used for educational and vocational counseling and by industries and businesses to aid in hiring decisions.

How We Measure Personality: Do You See What I See?

Like a detective solving a mystery, modern psychologists typically use numerous methods and a complete *battery* (or series) of tests to fully *assess* personality. This assortment of measures can be grouped in a few broad categories: *interviews*, *observations*, *objective tests*, and *projective tests*.

Interviews

We all use informal "interviews" to get to know other people. When first meeting someone, we ask about their jobs, college major, family, and hobbies or interests. Psychologists also use interviews — both *structured* and *unstructured*. Unstructured interviews are often used for job and college selection and for diagnosing psychological problems. In an unstructured format, interviewers get impressions and pursue hunches or let a person expand on information that promises to disclose personality characteristics. The interviewee has a chance to explain unique qualifications in his or her own words. Structured interviews, on the other hand, ask specific questions and follow a set of procedures so that the person being evaluated can be evaluated more objectively. The results of a structured interview are often charted on a rating scale to standardize the evaluations and make comparisons easier.

Observation

In addition to structured and unstructured interviews, psychologists also use direct behavioral observation to assess personality. Most of us enjoy "people watching," but observation as an assessment procedure is a very sophisticated technique. The psychologist looks for examples of specific behaviors and follows a careful set of evaluation guidelines. For instance, a psychologist might arrange to observe a troubled client's interactions with his or her family. Does the client become agitated by the presence of certain family members and not others? Does he or she become passive and withdrawn when asked a direct question? Through careful observation, the psychologist gains valuable insights into the client's personality.

Objective Tests

Objective personality tests, or *inventories*, are standardized questionnaires that require written responses, typically to multiple-choice or true–false items. Answers to these questions help people to describe themselves — to "self-report." They are considered "objective" tests because they have a limited number of possible responses to items and empirical standards for constructing test items and scoring. Given that objective tests can be administered to a large number of people in a relatively short period of time and evaluated in a standardized fashion, they are by far the most widely used method for assessing personality.

You have been introduced to several self-report personality tests in this textbook. There was the androgyny scale in Module 29, for example, the sensation – seeking scale in Module 31, and the locus of control scale in Module 36. The complete versions of these tests measure one specific personality trait and are used primarily in research. Often, however, psychologists in clinical, counseling, and industrial settings are interested in assessing a range of personality traits all at once. To do this, they generally use *multitrait* (or *multiphasic*) inventories.

Many multitrait tests have been developed, including the Sixteen Personality Factors Questionnaire (16PF) discussed later. The most widely researched and clinically used multitrait test is the **Minnesota Multiphasic Personality Inventory** (MMPI) — or its revision, the MMPI-2 (Butcher, 2000; Butcher & Rouse, 1996). The test consists of over 500 statements that participants respond to with *True*, *False*, or *Cannot say*. The following are examples of the kinds of statements found on the MMPI:

My stomach frequently bothers me.

I have enemies that really wish to harm me.

I sometimes hear things that other people can't hear.

I would like to be a mechanic.

I have never indulged in any unusual sex practices.

Why are some of these questions about really unusual, abnormal behavior? Although there are many "normal" questions on the full MMPI, the test is designed primarily for clinical and counseling psychologists to diagnose psychological disorders. Table 33.1 shows how MMPI test items are grouped into 10 *clinical scales*, each measuring a different disorder. Depressed people, for example, tend to score higher on one group of questions, whereas people with schizophrenia score higher on a different group. Each group of items is called a *scale*. There are also four *validity scales* designed to reflect the extent to which respondents distort their answers, do not understand the items, or are being uncooperative. Research has found that the validity scales effectively detect "pseudopatients" who were asked to fake psy-

Minnesota Multiphasic Personality Inventory *The most widely researched and clinically used self-report personality test (called the MMPI; the revised version is called the MMPI-2)*

TABLE 33.1 SUBSCALES OF THE MMPI-2[A]

Name of Subscale	Typical Interpretations of High Scores
Clinical Scales	
1. Hypochondriasis	Numerous physical complaints
2. Depression	Seriously depressed and pessimistic
3. Hysteria	Suggestible, immature, self-centered, demanding
4. Psychopathic deviancy	Rebellious, nonconformist
5. Masculinity/femininity	Interests like those of other sex
6. Paranoia	Suspicious and resentful of others
7. Psychasthenia	Fearful, agitated, brooding
8. Schizophrenia	Withdrawn, reclusive, bizarre thinking
9. Mania	Distractible, impulsive, dramatic
10. Social introversion	Shy, introverted, self-effacing
Validity Scales	
1. L (lie)	Denial of common problems, "saintliness," presenting a false picture
2. F (confusion)	Validity of profile is doubtful
3. K (defensiveness)	Minimizes social and emotional complaints
4. ? (cannot say)	Number of items left unanswered

chological disturbances or try to appear more psychologically healthy (Bagby, Rogers, & Buis 1994).

Are these tests the same as career inventories? Personality tests, like the MMPI, are often confused with other self-report tests called *vocational interest tests* that help people make career decisions. For example, the *Strong Vocational Interest Blank* asks whether you would rather write, illustrate, print, or sell a book or whether you'd prefer the work of a salesperson or teacher. This self-report test compares the things you like to do to the responses of people in various occupational groups.

Given your vocational interest test profile, along with your scores on *aptitude tests* (which measure potential abilities) and *achievement tests* (which measure what you have already learned), a counselor can help you identify the types of jobs that best suit you. Most colleges have career counseling centers where you can take vocational interest tests to guide you in your career decisions.

Projective Techniques

Unlike objective tests, **projective tests** use ambiguous, unstructured stimuli, such as inkblots, which can be perceived in many ways. As the name implies, *projective* tests supposedly allow each person to *project* his or her own unconscious conflicts, psychological defenses, motives, and personality traits onto the test materials. Because respondents are unable (or unwilling) to express their true feelings if asked directly, the ambiguous stimuli reportedly provide an indirect, "psychological x-ray" of important unconscious processes. Two of the most widely used projective tests are the *Rorschach Inkblot Test* and the *Thematic Apperception Test* (TAT).

The most widely used projective test is the **Rorschach Inkblot Test**, introduced in 1921 by Swiss psychiatrist Hermann Rorschach. It consists of ten inkblots originally developed by spilling ink on paper and folding the paper in half (Figure 33.1). You report what you see in each card and the clinician records your responses verbatim while also observing your gestures and reactions. The clinician later interprets your answers as indications of your unconscious feelings and conflicts. If you report seeing a bear in one of the inkblots, for example, the interpretation might be that you have a strong degree of emotional control (Meloy, Acklin, Gacono, Murray, & Peterson, 1997).

Created by personality researcher Henry Murray in 1938, the **Thematic Apperception Test** (TAT) is another of the most frequently used projective tests. It consists of a series of black-and-white ambiguous pictures, such as Figure 33.2. As mentioned in Module 31, the TAT is frequently used to measure achievement

Projective Tests *Psychological tests using ambiguous stimuli, such as inkblots or drawings; the ambiguity of the stimuli reportedly allows the test taker to project his or her true, unconscious conflicts, motives, psychological defenses, and personality traits onto the test material*

Rorschach [ROAR-shock] Inkblot Test *A projective test that presents a set of 10 cards with symmetrical abstract patterns, known as inkblots, and respondents describe what they "see" in the image; their response is thought to be a projection of unconscious processes*

Thematic Apperception Test (TAT) *A projective test that shows a series of ambiguous black-and-white pictures and asks the test taker to create a story related to each; the responses presumably reflect a projection of unconscious processes*

Figure 33.1 *The Rorschach Inkblot Test.* Individuals are shown 10 inkblots like this, one at a time, and asked to report what figures or objects they see in each of them. Their responses are believed to reflect unconscious parts of their personality that they *project* onto the ambiguous stimuli. Thus, the Rorschach is known as a *projective* test. (Reproduced with permission.)

motivation, as well as for personality assessment. If you were taking this test, you would be asked to create a story about the picture, including what the characters are feeling and how the story turns out. As with the Rorschach, your responses reportedly reflect your unconscious needs and conflicts. For example, a person who sees a picture of a young girl looking at mannequins in a store window might create a story with angry references to the girl's parents. The clinician might infer that the test taker has hidden resentments toward his or her own parents (Davison & Neale, 2001).

Figure 33.2 *The Thematic Apperception Test (TAT).* Like the Rorschach, the TAT is a projective test designed to reveal unconscious parts of the personality. Participants are asked to talk about what led up to the pictured situation, what is happening now, and how the story will end. (Reproduced with permission.)

Are Personality Measurements Accurate? Evaluating the Methods

What do you think of these interpretations of the projective tests? Do they accurately reflect true personality? Let's evaluate each of the various methods of personality assessment, beginning with interviews and observations:

- *Interviews and observations.* Both of these methods can provide valuable insights to personality, but they are time consuming and therefore expensive. Furthermore, just as football fans can disagree over the relative merits of the same quarterback, raters of personality tests frequently disagree in their evaluations of the same individual. Interviews and observations also involve unnatural settings, and as we saw in Module 2, the very presence of an observer can alter the behavior that is being studied.

- *Objective tests.* Tests like the MMPI-2 provide specific, objective information about a broad range of personality traits in a relatively short period of time; however, accuracy largely depends on cooperative and truthful respondents. Thus, objective, self-report inventories are subject to three major criticisms:

  1. *Deliberate deception and social desirability bias.* Some items on self-report inventories are easy to "see through," so respondents may intentionally, or unintentionally, fake particular personality traits. In addition, some respondents want to look good and will answer questions in ways that they perceive as *socially desirable.*

  2. *Diagnostic difficulties.* When self-report inventories are used for diagnosis, overlapping items sometimes make it difficult to pinpoint a diagnosis (Graham, 1991). In addition, clients with severe disorders sometimes score within the normal range, and normal clients may score within the elevated range (Cronbach, 1990).

  3. *Cultural bias and inappropriate use.* Some critics think that the standards for "normalcy" on objective, self-report tests fail to recognize the impact of culture. For example, respondents from Latino cultures, such as Mexican, Puerto Rican, and Argentinian, on average tend to score differently than respondents from majority cultures on the masculinity–femininity scale on the MMPI-2 (Lucio-Gomez, Ampudia-Rueda, Duran-Patino, Gallegos-Mejia, & Leon-Guzman, 1999) The fact that these groups score higher on traditional gender roles reflects their cultural training more than individual personality traits.

critical thinking

Why Are Pseudo Personality Tests So Popular?

Throughout this text, we have emphasized the value of critical thinking, which requires that we recognize *our personal biases and analyze data for value and content.* By carefully evaluating the evidence and credibility of the source, critical thinkers recognize appeals to emotions and faulty logic. When we look at the various problems with pseudo personality evaluations like the one in our introductory incident, we can identify at least three different logical fallacies: the Barnum effect, the fallacy of positive instances, and the self-serving bias.

The Barnum Effect

The first reason we often accept pseudo personality descriptions and horoscope predictions is that we think they are accurate. We tend to believe these tests have somehow tapped into our unique selves, when in fact they are ambiguous, broad statements that fit just about anyone. Being so readily disposed to accept such generalizations is known as the *Barnum effect* — after P. T. Barnum, the legendary

circus promoter who said, "Always have a little something for everyone" and "There's a sucker born every minute." Reread the bogus personality profile in the introductory incident. Can you see how "You have a strong need for other people to like you and admire you" fits almost everyone? Do you know anyone who doesn't "at times have serious doubts whether [they've] made the right decision or done the right thing"?

The Fallacy of Positive Instances

Now look again at the personality profile and count the number of times both sides of a personality trait are given ("You have a strong need for other people to like you" and "You pride yourself on being an independent thinker.") According to the *fallacy of positive instances,* we tend to notice and remember events that confirm our expectations and ignore those that are nonconfirming. If we see ourselves as independent thinkers, for example, we ignore the "needing to be liked by others" part. Similarly, horoscope readers easily find "Sagittarius characteristics" in a Sagittarius horoscope but fail to notice when Sagit-

tarius predictions miss or when the same traits appear for Scorpios or Leos.

The Self-Serving Bias

Now check the overall tone of the personality description. Note how the traits are generally positive and flattering — or at least neutral. According to the *self-serving bias,* we tend to prefer information that maintains a positive self-image (Brown & Rogers, 1991; Gifford & Hine, 1997). In fact, research shows that the more favorable a personality description, the more people believe it, and the more likely they are to believe it is unique to themselves (Guastello, Guastello, & Craft, 1989). (The self-serving bias might also explain why people prefer pseudo personality tests to bona fide tests — they're generally more flattering.)

Taken together, these three logical fallacies help explain the belief in "pop psych" personality tests and newspaper horoscopes. They offer "something for everyone" (the Barnum effect); we pay attention only to what confirms our expectations (the fallacy of positive instances); and we like flattering descriptions (the self-serving bias).

- *Projective tests.* Although projective tests are extremely time consuming to administer and interpret, their proponents suggest that because they have no right or wrong answers, respondents are less able to deliberately fake their responses. In addition, because these tests are unstructured, respondents may be more willing to talk about sensitive, anxiety-laden topics. Critics point out, however, that the reliability and validity of projective tests is among the lowest of all tests of personality (Lilienfeld, Wood, & Garb, 2000). As you may know, the two most important measures of a good test are *reliability* (Are the results consistent?) and *validity* (Does the test measure what it's designed to measure?). One problem with the Rorschach, in particular, is that interpreting clients' responses depends in large part on the subjective judgment of the examiner, and some examiners are simply more experienced or skilled than others. Also, there are problems with *interrater reliability.* Two examiners may interpret the same response in very different ways.

As you can see, each of these methods has its limits. However, psychologists typically combine results from various methods to create a full picture of individual personality. Having seen how personality is measured and evaluated, we now turn our attention to the major theories that describe, explain, and predict personality.

Check & Review

PERSONALITY ASSESSMENT

Personality is defined as an individual's relatively stable and enduring pattern of thoughts, emotions, and actions. Psychologists assess, describe, explain, and predict personality according to different theoretical orientations.

Psychologists use four basic methods to measure or assess personality: interviews, observations, objective tests, and projective techniques. Objective tests, such as the **Minnesota Multiphasic Personality Inventory** (MMPI-2), use paper-and-pencil questionnaires or inventories, which provide objective standardized information about a large number of personality traits. However, they are limited by respondents' deliberate deception and social desirability bias, diagnostic difficulties, and inappropriate use.

Projective tests, such as the **Rorschach Inkblot Test** or the **Thematic Apperception Test** (TAT), ask test takers to respond to ambiguous stimuli. Although these tests reportedly provide insight into unconscious elements of personality, they have low reliability and validity.

Questions

1. Match each personality test with its description:

   (a) a projective test using inkblots;

   (b) an objective, self-report, paper-and-pencil personality test;

   (c) a projective test using drawings of ambiguous human situations

   _____ i. MMPI-2

   _____ ii. Rorschach

   _____ iii. TAT

2. Two important criteria for evaluating the usefulness of tests used to assess personality are _____. (a) concurrence and prediction; (b) reliability and validity; (c) consistency and correlation; (d) diagnosis and prognosis

3. Describe the three logical fallacies that encourage acceptance of pseudo personality tests and horoscopes.

Answers to Questions can be found in Appendix B.

ACTIVE LEARNING WORKSHEET   MODULE 33

Circle either "T" for true or "F" for false, and then compare your answers with those in Appendix B.

1. The Rorschach is the most widely used self-report, objective personality test. T or F

2. The MMPI uses black and white photos of ambiguous stimuli to test personality. T or F

3. Noticing and remembering events that confirm our expectations and ignoring nonconfirming events is known as the *fallacy of positive instances.* T or F

4. Compared to projective tests, objective personality tests generally have higher reliability and validity scores. T or F

5. Projective tests use ambiguous stimuli to allow expression of unconscious feelings and motives. T or F

Trait *A relatively stable and consistent characteristic that can be used to describe someone*

MODULE 34
TRAIT THEORIES

How would you describe your two or three best friends? Would you say they are funny, loyal, and good-natured? Or adventuresome and trustworthy? The terms you use to describe other people (and yourself) are called **traits**, relatively stable and consistent personal characteristics. Trait theorists are interested in first discovering how people differ (which key traits best describe them) and then in measuring how much they differ (the degree of variation in traits within the individual and among individuals).

Early Trait Theorists: Allport, Cattell, and Eysenck

As you may imagine, identifying and measuring essential traits sounds much easier than it actually is. Every individual differs from every other in a great number of different ways. An early study of dictionary terms found almost 18,000 words that could be used to describe personality; of these, about 4,500 were considered to fit the researchers' definition of personality *traits* (Allport & Odbert, 1936).

Faced with this enormous list of potential traits, Gordon Allport (1937) believed the best way to understand personality was to study an individual and then arrange his or her unique personality traits into a hierarchy. The most important and pervasive traits were listed at the top and the least important at the bottom.

Factor Analysis *A statistical procedure used to determine the most basic units or factors in a large array of data*

Later psychologists reduced the wide array of possible personality traits with a statistical technique called **factor analysis**. Raymond Cattell (1950, 1965, 1990) condensed the list of traits to 30 to 35 basic characteristics. Cattell developed many personality tests — the best known is the 16PF, referred to earlier.

Five-Factor Model (FFM) *A trait theory that explains personality in terms of a Big Five model — openness, conscientiousness, extraversion, agreeableness, and neuroticism*

Hans Eysenck (1967, 1982, 1990) reduced the list even further. He described personality as a relationship between three basic types of traits — extraversion–introversion (E), neuroticism (N), and psychotism (P). These dimensions are assessed with the *Eysenck Personality Questionnaire*.

The "Big Five" Model: Five Basic Personality Traits

Factor analysis was also used to develop the most talked about modern trait theory — **five-factor model** (FFM) (McCrae & Costa, 1990, 1997, 1999; McCrae et al., 2000). Combining all the previous research findings and the long list of possible personality traits, researchers discovered that several traits came up repeatedly, even when different tests were used. These five major dimensions of personality, often dubbed the Big Five, are described below. (You can easily remember the five factors by noting that together, the first letters of each of the Big Five traits spell the word *ocean*.)

1. (O) Openness. People who rate high in this factor are original, imaginative, curious, open to new ideas, artistic, and interested in cultural pursuits. Low scorers tend to be conventional, down-to-earth, narrower in their interests, and not artistic.

2. (C) Conscientiousness. This factor ranges from responsible, self-disciplined, organized, and achieving at the high end to irresponsible, careless, impulsive, lazy, and undependable at the other.

3. (E) Extraversion. This factor contrasts people who are sociable, outgoing, talkative, fun loving, and affectionate at the high end with introverted individuals who tend to be withdrawn, quiet, passive, and reserved.

Gordon Allport (1897–1967). *As a trait theorist, Allport believed personality consisted of a limited number of attributes, which could be arranged into a hierarchy with the most important at the top and the least important at the bottom.*

Study the following figure based on Raymond Cattell's factor analysis findings. Note how Cattell's 16 source traits exist on a continuum with extremes at either end, such as *reserved* and *less intelligent* at the far left and *outgoing* and *more intelligent* at the far right. Average falls somewhere in the middle.

Take a pen and make a dot on the line (from 1 to 10) that represents your own degree of reservation versus outgoingness. Then make a dot for yourself on the other 15 traits. (While making judgments of your traits, try to avoid the self-serving bias described in the previous Critical Thinking/Active Learning exercise.)

Finally, connect the dots. How does your personality profile compare with the profiles of creative artists, airline pilots, and writers?

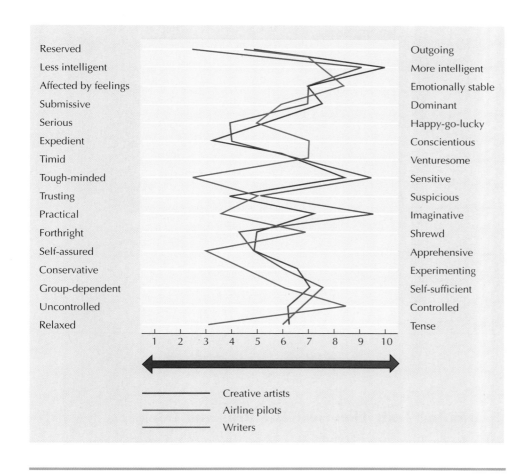

4. *(A) Agreeableness.* Individuals who score high on this factor are good-natured, warm, gentle, cooperative, trusting, and helpful, whereas low scorers are irritable, argumentative, ruthless, suspicious, uncooperative, and vindictive.

5. *(N) Neuroticism (or emotional stability).* People high on neuroticism are emotionally unstable and prone to insecurity, anxiety, guilt, worry, and moodiness. People at the other end are emotionally stable, calm, even-tempered, easygoing, and relaxed.

Use the following figure to plot your own Big Five profile by placing a dot on each line to indicate your degree of openness, conscientiousness, and so on. Do the same for a current or previous love partner. How do your scores compare? Now look at Table 34.1, which reports the characteristics most valued in potential mates. David Buss and his colleagues (1989, 1999) surveyed over 10,000 men and women from 37 different countries and found a surprising level of agreement. Moreover, most elements of the Big Five factors are found at the top of the table. Both men and women prefer dependability (conscientiousness), emotional stability (low neuroticism), pleasing disposition (agreeableness), and sociability (extraversion) to the alternatives.

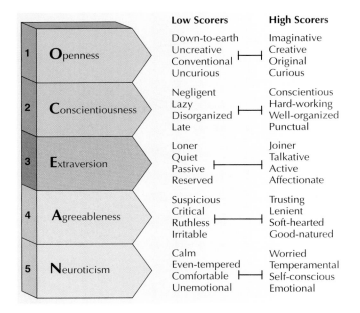

Evaluating Trait Theories: The Pros and Cons

According to Buss (1991, 1999), the strong correlation between his survey findings and the Big Five model reflects an evolutionary advantage to people who are more open, conscientious, extroverted, agreeable, and not neurotic. The evolutionary perspective is also confirmed by cross-cultural studies (McCrae et al., 2000; Paunonen & Ashton, 1998; Salgado, 1997) and comparative studies with chimpanzees and other species (see the accompanying Research Highlight).

Taken together, these studies suggest that the Big 5 (FFM) model may be a biologically based human universal (MacDonald, 1998). This model is the first to achieve the major goal of trait theory — to describe and organize personality characteristics using the fewest number of traits. Critics argue, however, that the great variation seen in personalities cannot be accounted for by only five traits and that the Big Five model fails to offer *causal* explanations for these traits (Digman, 1997; Matsumoto, 2000).

TABLE 34.1 THE IMPORTANCE OF VARIOUS TRAITS IN MATE SELECTION THROUGHOUT THE WORLD

Men's Ranking of Various Traits[a]	Women's Ranking of Various Traits[a]
1. Mutual attraction — love	1. Mutual attraction — love
2. Dependable character	2. Dependable character
3. Emotional stability and maturity	3. Emotional stability and maturity
4. Pleasing disposition	4. Pleasing disposition
5. Good health	5. Education and intelligence
6. Education and intelligence	6. Sociability
7. Sociability	7. Good health
8. Desire for home and children	8. Desire for home and children
9. Refinement, neatness	9. Ambition and industriousness
10. Good looks	10. Refinement, neatness
11. Ambition and industriousness	11. Similar education
12. Good cook and housekeeper	12. Good financial prospect
13. Good financial prospect	13. Good looks
14. Similar education	14. Favorable social status or rating
15. Favorable social status or rating	15. Good cook and housekeeper
16. Chastity (no previous experience in sexual intercourse)	16. Similar religious background
17. Similar religious background	17. Similar political background
18. Similar political background	18. Chastity (no previous experience in sexual intercourse)

[a] The lower the number, the more important men and women throughout the world consider this trait to be (on the average).

Source: Based on Buss et al., (1990), p. 19.

Trait theories, in general, are subject to three major criticisms:

1. *Lack of explanation.* Trait approaches are good at *describing* people but do little to *explain* why they develop certain traits and why traits sometimes change (Digman, 1997).

2. *Stability versus change.* Although trait theorists have documented a high level of personality stability after age 30 (Figure 34.1), most theories don't identify which characteristics last a lifetime and which are transient.

Figure 34.1 *Will this marriage survive?* It helps if both parties are over age 30. According to long-term studies of personality (McCrae et al., 2000), most changes in personality occur during childhood, adolescence, and young adulthood. After age 30, most traits are relatively fixed and changes after that point are few and small. Thus, people who marry after age 30 may have a more successful marriage because their personalities are more stable.

RESEARCH HIGHLIGHT

Do Animals Have Personality?

"It was exactly 33 years ago that I first met one of my oldest and dearest friends. To this day, the most outstanding aspect of her personality remains a quality I noticed the very first time I laid eyes on her: She is one of the most caring and compassionate people I know. She's also a chimpanzee" (Fouts, 2000, p. 68).

These are the words of a famous and highly respected comparative psychologist, Dr. Roger Fouts. What do you think? Do animals have personality? Roger Fouts proposes that "like us, chimps are highly intelligent, cooperative and sometimes violent primates who nurture family bonds, adopt orphans, mourn the death of mothers, practice self-medication, struggle for power and wage war. And that only makes sense, because the chimp brain and the human brain both evolved from the same brain — that of our common ape ancestor" (Fouts, 2000, p. 68). Other scientists, however, are generally reluctant to ascribe personality traits, emotions, and cognitions to animals, despite the often-cited statistic that humans have 98.4 percent of the same DNA as chimps.

Noting that previous studies on animal personality were scattered across multiple disciplines and various journals, researchers Samuel Gosling and Oliver John attempted to integrate this fragmented literature and summarize what is known about animal personality. They carefully reviewed 19 factor analytic personality studies of 12 different species: guppies, octopi, rats, dogs, cats, pigs, donkeys, hyenas, vervet monkeys, rhesus monkeys, gorillas, and chimpanzees. To integrate the diverse, multispecies information, Gosling and John used the human five-factor model (FFM) discussed earlier. Interestingly, three human FFM dimensions — extraversion, neuroticism, and agreeableness — showed the strongest cross-

Do animals have personality? Recent research has found that some species of animals demonstrate reliable personality traits similar to the Big 5 factors found in human personality.

species generality. How these personality traits are manifested, however, depends on the species. Although a human who scores low on extraversion "stays at home on Saturday night, or tries to blend into a corner at a large party, the [similarly low scoring] octopus stays in its protective den during feedings and attempts to hide itself by changing color or releasing ink into the water" (Gosling & John, 1999, p. 70).

One nonhuman dimension was also found important for describing animal personality — *dominance*. In adult humans, dominance is part of the extroversion dimension, but it has a wider range of personality implications in animals. Gosling and John explain that unlike most species, humans have multiple dominance hierarchies. The class bully may dominate on the schoolyard, the academically gifted may dominate the classroom, and the artist may win prizes for his or her creations.

Sex differences are another area where cross-species studies provide important information. For example, research on the human FFM consistently shows that women score higher on neuroticism than men (i.e., being more emotional and prone to worry) (Hrebickva, Cermak, & Osecka, 2000; McCrae et al., 1999). However, Gosling and John found a reversal of gen-

der differences among hyenas. It was the male hyenas that were most neurotic — being more high-strung, fearful, and nervous (Figure 34.2). They explain that among hyenas, the female is larger and more dominant than the male, and the hyena clan is matrilineal, with the mother recognized as the head of the family. Thus, it may be that sex differences in personality are related to the *ecological niches* (the place or function within the ecosystem) occupied by the two sexes in a species.

According to Gosling and John, comparative studies of animals not only provide insight into the existence of animal personality but also offer a fresh perspective on the interplay between social and biological forces in human personality. As Roger Fouts suggested, "In the past few decades, scientific evidence on chimps and other nonhuman primates has poured in to support one basic fact: We have much more in common with apes than most people care to believe" (Fouts, 2000, p. 68).

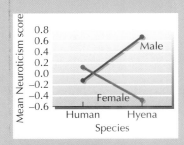

Figure 34.2 *Sex differences in standard (z) scores for neuroticism among humans and hyenas.* The ratings for hyenas are from Gosling (1998); the humans (n = 100) were described by peers on the same rating scales used for hyenas.

3. Situational determinants. Some personality theorists challenge the entire trait approach on the basis that it cannot be predicted. For example, in a classic study of children's honesty, May, Hartshorne, & Welty (1928) found children might lie at school but not at home, or might cheat on a test but not in an athletic event.

Extending the idea that behavior might be *situational*, in 1968, Walter Mischel published a landmark book in the field of personality, *Personality and Assessment.* Rather than seeing personality as the consistent, internal traits of an individual, Mischel thought that people respond to factors and conditions in the external environment. In other words, behavior — and thus personality — is determined almost entirely by the situations in which people find themselves. People are honest or dishonest, for example, not because of their internal personality but because of external rewards or threats of punishment.

Mischel's research findings were persuasive, and many joined his camp. Others, however, held out for the existence of stable traits that cause individuals to behave consistently in a wide range of settings. For years, a heated debate — known as "trait versus situationism" or the "person–situation controversy" — existed in psychology. After 2 decades of continuing debate and research, the consensus seems to be that situational pressures affect our relatively stable personality traits (Johnson, 1997; Mischel & Shoda, 1999). As you can see, this is another example of *interactionism* — a common theme in psychology.

Walter Mischel emphasized the power of the situation, or environment, in determining personality. In other words, honesty depends on the threat of detection or potential reward; it is not an internal personality trait.

Check & Review

TRAIT THEORIES

Trait theorists believe personality consists of relatively stable and consistent characteristics. Early theorists like Gordon Allport, Raymond Cattell, and Hans Eysenck used **factor analysis** to identify the smallest possible number of **traits**. More recently, researchers identified a **five-factor model** (FFM), which can be used to describe most individuals. The Big Five traits are openness, conscientiousness, extraversion, agreeableness, and neuroticism.

General trait theories are subject to three major criticisms: *lack of explanation* (they fail to *explain* why people develop certain traits and why traits sometimes change), *stability versus change* (personality appears stable after age 30, but current theories do not identify which characteristics endure and which are transient), and *situational determinants* (trait theories underestimate the influence of environmental influences).

Questions

1. A relatively stable and consistent characteristic that can be used to describe someone is known as a(n) _____. (a) character; (b) trait; (c) temperament; (d) personality.

2. Match the following personality descriptions with their corresponding Big Five personality factor: (a) openness; (b) conscientiousness; (c) introversion; (d) agreeableness; (e) neuroticism

    _____ i. Tending toward insecurity, anxiety, guilt, worry, and moodiness

    _____ ii. Being imaginative, curious, open to new ideas, and interested in cultural pursuits

    _____ iii. Being responsible, self-disciplined, organized, and high achieving

    _____ iv. Tending to be withdrawn, quiet, passive, and reserved

    _____ v. Being good-natured, warm, gentle, cooperative, trusting, and helpful

3. Trait theories of personality have been criticized for all but one of the following reasons. (a) they fail to explain why people develop their traits; (b) they do not include a large number of central traits; (c) they fail to identify which traits last and which are transient; (d) they fail to consider situational determinants of personality.

Answers to Questions can be found in Appendix B.

MODULE 34   ACTIVE LEARNING WORKSHEET

"What's My Trait?"

Using labels from the five-factor model (openness, conscientiousness, extraversion, agreeableness, or neuroticism), identify the major personality trait being expressed in the following sentences:

1. "I enjoy meeting new people and having a fun time."

2. "My employers always like me because they can count on me to show up on time, get my work done properly, and complete whatever task I say I will perform."

3. "New intellectual experiences and ideas are a real treat for me. I like to meet new people and explore new ideas and opinions."

4. "I generally trust others and have a tendency to be compassionate and cooperative."

5. "I am highly anxious, insecure, moody, and often emotionally unstable."

Answers can be found in Appendix B.

MODULE 35

PSYCHOANALYTIC/PSYCHODYNAMIC THEORIES

In contrast to trait theories that *describe* personality as it exists, psychoanalytic (or *psychodynamic*) theories of personality attempt to *explain* individual differences by examining how unconscious mental forces interplay with thoughts, feelings, and behavior. The founding father of psychoanalytic theory is Sigmund Freud. We will examine Freud's theories in some detail and then briefly discuss three of his most influential followers — Alfred Adler, Carl Jung, and Karen Horney.

Freud's Psychoanalytic Theory: The Power of the Unconscious

Who is the most well known figure in all of psychology? Most people immediately name Sigmund Freud. Even before you studied psychology, you probably came across his name in other courses. Freud's theories have been applied in the fields of anthropology, sociology, religion, medicine, art, and literature. Working from about 1890 until he died in 1939, Freud developed a theory of personality that has been one of the most influential and, at the same time, most controversial, in all of science (Gay, 1999; Taylor, 1999).

In discussing Freud's theory, we will focus on four of his most basic and debatable concepts: levels of consciousness, personality structure, defense mechanisms, and psychosexual stages of development.

Levels of Consciousness

What would you think if you heard a flight attendant say, "It's been a real job serving you ... I mean joy!"? From a Freudian perspective, this little slip of the tongue

What is Freud's psychoanalytic theory, and how did his followers build on his theory?

Freud and his famous couch. *Sigmund Freud (1856–1939) is one of the most influential personality theorists. He also developed a major form of therapy (known as psychoanalysis), and treated many patients in the office pictured here.*

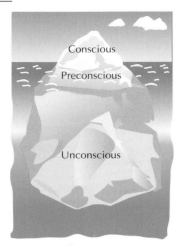

Figure 35.1 Freud's three levels of consciousness. The tip of the iceberg is comparable to the conscious mind, open to easy inspection. Directly below the conscious mind lies the preconscious; its contents can be viewed with a little extra effort. The large base of the iceberg is like the unconscious mind, completely hidden from personal inspection. For example, at this moment your conscious mind is focusing on this text, whereas your preconscious may include feelings of hunger and tiredness and thoughts of where you might go for lunch. Your unconscious might contain feelings of hostility toward your parents, repressed sexual desires, aggressive impulses, and irrational thoughts and feelings.

Conscious *In Freudian terms, thoughts or information that a person is currently aware of or is remembering*

Preconscious *Freud's term for thoughts or information that one can become aware of easily*

Unconscious *Freud's term for thoughts, motives, impulses, or desires that lie beyond a person's normal awareness but that can be made available through psychoanalysis*

"Good morning, beheaded—uh, I mean beloved.
Drawing by Dana Fradon © 1979 The New Yorker Magazine, Inc.

Is this an exmple of a Freudian slip?

(known as a *Freudian slip*) reflects the flight attendant's true, unconscious feelings. Freud believed the unconscious is hidden from our personal awareness but still has an enormous impact on our behavior — and reveals itself despite our intentions.

What exactly is the unconscious? Freud called the mind the *psyche* and believed the unconscious was one of three levels of awareness or consciousness (Figure 35.1). Using the analogy of an iceberg, the first level of awareness, the **conscious**, can be compared to the part of the iceberg above water. This part of the mind consists of all thoughts, feelings, and actions that we are actively aware of at any moment.

Immediately below the conscious realm, and the water's surface, is the somewhat larger **preconscious**. The preconscious includes mental activities not part of our current thoughts but able to be readily brought to mind. The third level, the **unconscious**, lies below the preconscious and forms the bulk of the psyche. According to Freud, the unconscious stores our primitive, instinctual motives, plus anxiety-laden memories and emotions that are prevented from entering the conscious mind.

Just as the enormous mass of iceberg below the surface destroyed the ocean liner *Titanic*, the unconscious may similarly damage our psychological lives. Freud believed most psychological disorders originate from repressed (hidden) memories and instincts (sexual and aggressive) stored in the unconscious.

To treat these disorders, Freud developed *psychoanalysis* — a type of therapy discussed in Module 44. As you can imagine, Freud's concepts of the conscious, preconscious, and unconscious mind, as well as his techniques for uncovering hidden, unconscious motives, are difficult to study scientifically. They have, therefore, been the subjects of great debate in psychology.

Personality Structure

In addition to proposing that the mind functions at three levels of awareness, Freud thought personality was composed of three mental structures: *id, ego,* and *superego.*

He believed that each resides, fully or partially, in the unconscious (Figure 35.2) and that each accounts for a different aspect of personality. (Keep in mind that the id, ego, and superego are mental concepts — or hypothetical constructs. They are not physical structures you could see if you dissected a human brain.)

The **id** is made up of innate, biological instincts and urges. Like a child, the id is immature, impulsive, and irrational. The id is also totally unconscious and serves as the reservoir of mental energy. When its primitive drives build up, the id seeks immediate gratification to relieve the tension. Thus, the id functions according to what Freud called the **pleasure principle**, the immediate and uninhibited seeking of pleasure and the avoidance of discomfort.

Because it is such a primitive and completely unconscious part of the psyche, the id operates without any consideration for logic or reality. The id can, however, obtain partial gratification for its instinctual energy by forming mental images of desired objects. Freud called this *wish fulfillment*. These mental images are the basis of many daydreams, fantasies, and dreams according to Freud.

If the id were the only part of the psyche, we might seek pleasure and avoid pain in immediate and dangerously impulsive ways, because this is what the id often urges us to do. However, Freud also postulated that the other two parts of the psyche — the ego and the superego — control and channel the id's potentially destructive energy.

The **ego** is the second part of the psyche to develop. It is capable of planning, problem solving, reasoning, and controlling the id. In Freud's system, the ego corresponds to the self — our conscious identity of ourselves as persons. Unlike the id, which lies entirely in the unconscious, the ego resides primarily in the conscious and preconscious.

One of the ego's tasks is to channel and release the id's energy in ways that are consistent with the external environment. Thus, the ego is responsible for delaying gratification when necessary. Contrary to the id's *pleasure principle*, the ego operates on the **reality principle**, because it has the ability to understand and deal with objects and events in the external environment.

Freud used the example of a rider and his horse to illustrate the relationship of the ego and id:

> In its relation to the id [the ego] is like a man on horseback, who has to hold in check the superior strength of the horse... Often a rider, if he is not to be parted from his horse, is obliged to guide it where it wants to go; so in the same way the ego is in the habit of transforming the id's will into action as if it were its own.
>
> Freud 1923/1961; p. 25

The final part of the psyche to develop is the **superego**. It originates as part of the ego but separates from it to become an overseer or moral censor for the psyche. The separation of the superego occurs when the child learns the rules and values of the parents and society. The superego is a set of ethical standards or rules for behavior that resides primarily in the preconscious and unconscious. It has two parts, the conscience and the ego-ideal. The *conscience* is a group of social prohibitions, similar to a penal code or legal statutes. It lists the things we should not do. The *ego-*

Figure 35.2 *Freud's personality structure.* According to Freud, personality is composed of three structures — the id, ego, and superego. The id operates on the pleasure principle, the ego operates on the reality principle, and the superego is guided by the conscience and ego-ideal. Note how the ego is primarily conscious and preconscious, whereas the id is entirely unconscious.

Id *According to Freud, the source of instinctual energy, which works on the pleasure principle and is concerned with immediate gratification*

Pleasure Principle *In Freud's theory, the principle on which the id operates — that immediate pleasure is the sole motivation for behavior*

Ego *In Freud's theory, the rational part of the psyche that deals with reality and attempts to control the impulses of the id while also satisfying the social approval and self-esteem needs of the superego*

Reality Principle *According to Freud, the principle on which the conscious ego operates as it tries to meet the demands of the unconscious id and the realities of the environment*

Superego *In psychoanalytic theory, the part of the personality that incorporates parental and societal standards for morality*

Freudian theory in action? *Can you imagine what the id, ego, and superego of this man and woman might be saying during this flirtation?*

Repression *Freud's first and most basic defense mechanism, which blocks unacceptable impulses from coming into awareness*

Psychosexual Stages *In psychoanalytic theory, five developmental periods during which particular kinds of pleasures must be gratified if personality development is to proceed normally*

ideal is a list of things we should do to feel proud of ourselves. The superego might be thought of as operating on the *morality principle*, because violating the rules of either the conscience or ego-ideal results in feelings of guilt.

The superego constantly strives for perfection and is therefore as unrealistic as the id. So now, the job of the ego becomes much more complicated. Not only must the ego find objects and events that satisfy the id, but these same objects and events also must not violate the standards of the superego. For this reason, the ego is often referred to as the "executive" of the personality — managing, organizing, and directing behavior.

Defense Mechanisms

When the ego fails to satisfy both the id and the superego, anxiety slips into conscious awareness. Anxiety is uncomfortable, so people try to rid themselves of it any way they can. One common way to ward off anxiety is with defense mechanisms. *Defense mechanisms* are strategies the ego unconsciously uses to reduce anxiety by distorting our perceptions of reality.

Although Freud described many kinds of defense mechanisms, he believed repression was the most important. **Repression** is the mechanism by which the ego prevents the most anxiety-provoking thoughts (in other words, the most unacceptable thoughts) from entering consciousness. It is the first and most basic form of anxiety reduction.

In recent years, repression has become a popular — and controversial — topic because of the number of lawsuits brought by adults who claim *repressed memories* of childhood sexual abuse. As we discussed in Module 20, however, it is difficult to determine the authenticity of such memories. Repression and several other Freudian defense mechanisms (all of which are unconscious) are presented in Table 35.1.

I see people using defense mechanisms all the time. Is this bad? Although defense mechanisms do twist the truth and distort reality, research supports Freud's belief that some misrepresentation seems to be necessary for our psychological well-being (Newman Duff, & Baumeister, 1997; Taylor & Armor, 1996). During a gruesome surgery, for example, physicians and nurses may *intellectualize* the procedure as an unconscious way of dealing with their personal anxieties. By focusing on highly objective technical aspects of the situation, they do not become emotionally overwhelmed by the potentially tragic situations they often encounter. Most psychologists agree that using defense mechanisms can be healthy as long as it does not become extreme.

Psychosexual Stages of Development

Freud believed that experiences during early childhood were important predictors of later adult personality. Anxieties arising from harsh parenting or other unfavorable early experiences, he believed, would reveal themselves as negative personality traits in adulthood.

Beginning at birth, strong biological urges residing within the id supposedly push all children through five universal **psychosexual stages** during the first 12 or so years of life. The term *psychosexual* reflects Freud's emphasis on *infantile sexuality* — his belief that children experience sexual feelings from birth (although in different forms from those of adolescents or adults). Four of his stages are named for the area of the body (or *erogenous zone*) that corresponds to the primary source of pleasure at these stages — the mouth, anus, phallus, and genitals (Table 35.2).

At each psychosexual stage, the id's impulses and social demands come into conflict. Therefore, if a child's needs are not met or are overindulged at one partic-

TABLE 35.1 SAMPLE PSYCHOLOGICAL DEFENSE MECHANISMS

Defense Mechanism	Description	Example
Repression	Preventing painful or dangerous thoughts from entering consciousness	Forgetting the details of your parent's painful death.
Sublimation	Working off unmet desires or unacceptable impulses in activities that are constructive	Rechanneling sexual desires into art, music, sports, hobbies
Denial	Protecting oneself from an unpleasant reality by refusing to perceive it	Alcoholics refusing to admit their addiction
Rationalization	Substituting socially acceptable reasons for thoughts or actions based on unacceptable motives	Justifying cheating on an exam by saying "everyone else does it"
Intellectualization	Ignoring the emotional aspects of a painful experience by focusing on abstract thoughts, words, or ideas	Emotionless discussion of your divorce while ignoring underlying pain
Projection	Transferring unacceptable motives or impulses to others	Becoming unreasonably jealous of your mate while denying your own attraction to others
Reaction formation	Refusing to acknowledge unacceptable urges, thoughts, or feelings by exaggerating the opposite state	Promoting a petition against adult bookstores even though you are secretly fascinated by pornography
Regression	Responding to a threatening situation in a way appropriate to an earlier age or level of development	Throwing a temper tantrum when a friend doesn't want to do what you'd like
Displacement	Substituting a less threatening object for the original object of impulse	Yelling at a coworker after being crriticized by your boss

ular stage, the child may *fixate* and a part of the personality will remain stuck at that stage. Even when individuals successfully pass through one or more of the five stages, they may at times of stress return (or *regress*) to a stage at which earlier needs were badly frustrated or overgratified.

During the first *oral stage* (birth to 12 to 18 months), the erogenous zone is the mouth and the infant receives satisfaction through sucking, eating, biting, and so on. Because the infant is highly dependent on parents and caregivers to provide opportunities for oral gratification, fixation at this stage can easily occur. According to Freud, if the mother overindulges her infant's oral needs, the child may fixate and as an adult become gullible ("swallowing" anything), dependent, and passive. The underindulged child, however, will develop into an aggressive, sadistic person who exploits others. Orally fixated adults may also orient their life around their mouth — overeating, becoming alcoholic, smoking, talking a great deal, and so on.

TABLE 35.2 FREUD'S FIVE STAGES OF PSYCHOSEXUAL DEVELOPMENT

Stage	Approximate Age	Erogenous Zone	Key Conflict or Developmental Task	Effects of Fixation or Regression on Adult Personality
Oral	0–18 months	Mouth	Weaning (from breast or bottle)	Gullibility, dependency, excessive pleasure from eating, drinking, and other oral activities
Anal	18 months–3 years	Anus	Toilet training	Excessive orderliness, cleanliness, and stubbornness (anal retentive) or extreme messiness, destructiveness, and rebelliousness (anal expulsive)
Phallic	3–6 years	Genitals	Overcoming the Oedipal complex (by identifying with same-sex parent)	Castration anxiety and struggles with authority figures (males), penis envy and flirtatiousness (females), preoccupation with attracting mates (both sexes)
Latency	6 years–puberty	None	Interacting with same-sex peers	Being asexual
Genital	Puberty to adult	Genitals	Establishing intimate relationships with the opposite sex	_____

Oedipus [ED-uh-puss] Complex *A period of conflict during the phallic stage, when children are sexually attracted to the opposite-sex parent and hostile toward the same-sex parent*

During the *anal stage* (between 12 to 18 months and 3 years), the erogenous zone shifts to the anus and the child receives satisfaction by having and retaining bowel movements. Because this is also the time when most parents begin toilet training, the child's desire to control his or her own bowel movements often leads to strong conflict. Adults who are fixated at this stage may display an *anal-retentive* personality and be highly controlled and compulsively neat. Or they may be very messy, disorderly, rebellious, and destructive — the *anal-expulsive* personality.

During the *phallic stage* (between 3 and 6 years), the major center of pleasure is the genitals. Masturbation and "playing doctor" with other children is common during this time. According to Freud, a 3- to 6-year-old boy develops an unconscious sexual longing for his mother and jealousy and hatred for the rival father. This attraction creates a conflict Freud called the **Oedipus complex**, after Oedipus, the legendary Greek king who unwittingly killed his father and married his mother. The young boy eventually experiences guilt and fears of punishment from the rival father, perhaps by castration. This *castration anxiety* and the Oedipus conflict are resolved when the boy represses his sexual feelings for his mother, gives up his rivalry with his father, and begins to *identify* with him instead. If this stage is not resolved completely or positively, the boy supposedly grows up resenting his father and generalizes this feeling to all authority figures.

Although Freud admitted that he was unsure about the development of young girls, he believed they did develop a special attachment to their father. Unlike the

Does art imitate life? Or does art imitate Freud? *According to Freudian interpretation, Shakespeare's* Hamlet *(upper left) portrayed unconscious Oedipal feelings — a young boy's wish to kill his father and marry his mother. similarly, the psychiatrist at the end of the movie* Psycho *(top middle) explained the famous murder scene in the shower as a result of "Oedipal problems." On the other hand,* Beauty and the Beast *(top right), and* The Little Mermaid *(bottom left) might tap into the young girl's desire for her father and rivalry with her mother. In each of these films, the mother is absent and the young girl has her father all to herself. What about* American Beauty *(bottom right)? How might Freud interpret Kevin Spacey's sexual fantasies about his teenage daughter's best friend?*

young boy who develops castration anxiety, however, the young girl discovers that she lacks a penis. This supposedly causes her to develop *penis envy* and hostile feelings toward the mother, who is blamed for the anatomical "deficiency." The conflict is resolved when the little girl suppresses her desire for her father, gives up her rivalry with her mother, and identifies with her instead.

Freud did not believe that most young girls ever really overcome penis envy or fully identify with their mothers. Consequently, he suggested women generally have a lower level of morality than men. (You are undoubtedly surprised or outraged by this statement, but remember that Freud's theories are very controversial — some more than others.)

Following the phallic stage is the *latency stage* (from age 6 years to puberty), in which children repress sexual thoughts and engage in nonsexual activities, such as developing social and intellectual skills. The task of this stage is to develop successful interactions with same-sex peers and refinement of appropriate gender roles.

With the beginning of adolescence comes the *genital stage*. The genitals are again erogenous zones, and the individual seeks to fulfill his or her sexual desires through emotional attachment to members of the opposite sex. Unsuccessful outcomes at this stage lead to participation in sexual relationships based only on lustful desires, not on respect and commitment. How a person meets the conflicts of this stage depends on how conflicts in the previous stages were resolved. If the person is fixated at an earlier stage, there will be little energy available for the needs of this stage. However, people who have successfully negotiated the earlier stages can now derive primary satisfaction through heterosexual mating outside the family.

Neo-Freudian/Psychodynamic Theories: Revising Freud's Ideas

Some initial followers later rebelled and proposed theories of their own; they became known as *neo-Freudians*. Although many neo-Freudians accepted Freud's emphasis on the unconscious, they believed he paid inadequate attention to social and cultural forces. Three of Freud's most influential followers were Alfred Adler, Carl Jung, and Karen Horney.

Adler's Individual Psychology

Alfred Adler (1870–1937) was the first to leave Freud's inner circle. He developed a theory he called *individual psychology*. Instead of seeing behavior as motivated by unconscious forces, he believed it is purposeful and goal-directed. That is, unlike Freud, he felt that consciousness is the center of personality. He believed that each of us has the capacity to choose and to create. According to Adler (1964), our goals in life provide the source of our motivation — especially those goals that aim to obtain security and overcome feelings of inferiority. Adler believed that almost everyone suffers from an **inferiority complex**, deep feelings of inadequacy that arise from childhood.

Alfred Adler (1870–1937). Although initially trained by Freud, Adler developed his own theories (such as the inferiority complex*) and later broke away to establish Adlerian psychotherapy and* individual psychology.

Inferiority Complex *Alfred Adler's idea that feelings of inferiority develop from early childhood experiences of helplessness and incompetence*

TRY THIS
Yourself

Adler's theory is popular in some circles for his emphasis on family constellation or birth order on the formation of personality. Are you a firstborn, second-born, the youngest, or an only child? Check the following Adlerian descriptions to see if your birth order reflects your adult personality.

Firstborns. Adler thought firstborns enjoy a temporary position of privilege and great parental attention. But with the arrival of the second child, the older child is "dethroned." As adults, firstborns tend to be independent and may seek to regain attention through achievements. On the other hand, firstborns can become insecure, cautious, and defensive adults.

Second-borns. Because second-borns live in the shadow of the older sibling, feelings of inferiority are intensified. This supposedly engenders a sense of restlessness and a continual striving to outdo others. The result can be high achievement, or on the negative side, a desire to dominate others. (It's interesting that Adler was a second-born child.)

The youngest child. Being the baby of the family, the youngest child is the most pampered and most likely to be dependent on others. The youngest child can look to older siblings as models for achievement and superiority, but always being younger, weaker, and less experienced can be discouraging.

The only child. Spending a lot of time around adults without siblings can contribute to a higher level of intellectual ability and academic success. Only children as adults may also become timid, passive, and withdrawn, and need to be pampered.

Adler's descriptions are rather vague and somewhat contradictory. A great deal of research on birth order was conducted during the 1960s and 1970s, but birth order effects turned out to be weaker and less consistent than Adler expected (Parker, 1998). However, recent research has revived the earlier interest and support (Paulhus, Trapnell, & Chen, 1999; Rodgers, Cleveland, van den Oord, & Rowe, 2000; Sulloway, 2000).

Why are inferiority feelings so common? In Adler's view, we have inferiority feelings because we begin life as completely helpless infants. Every young child feels small, incompetent, and helpless when dealing with skilled adults. These early feelings of inadequacy result in a *will-to-power* that causes children to strive to develop superiority over others or, more positively, to develop their full potential and gain mastery and control in their lives. Thus, the childhood inferiority complex can lead to negative adult traits of dominance, aggression, and envy, or positive traits such as self-mastery and creativity (Adler, 1964, 1998).

Adler also suggested that the *will-to-power* could be positively expressed through *social interest* — identifying with others and cooperating with them for the social good. In stressing social interest and the positive outcomes of inferiority feelings, Adlerian theory is more optimistic than Freudian theory.

Jung's Analytic Psychology

Another early dissenter, Carl Jung (pronounced "yoong"), developed *analytical psychology*. Like Freud, Jung (1875–1961) emphasized unconscious processes, but he also believed the unconscious contains positive and spiritual motives as well as sexual and aggressive forces.

Jung also thought we have two forms of unconscious mind, the *personal unconscious* and the *collective unconscious*. The personal unconscious is created from our individual experiences, whereas the **collective unconscious** is identical in each person and is inherited (Jung, 1936/1969). The collective unconscious consists of primitive images and patterns of thought, feeling, and behavior that Jung called **archetypes**. In other words, the collective unconscious is the ancestral memory of the human race and therefore explains the similarities in religion, art, symbolism, and dream imagery across cultures (Figure 35.3).

Because of archetypal patterns in the collective unconscious, we perceive and react in certain predictable ways. One set of archetypes refers to gender roles. Jung claimed that both males and females have patterns for feminine aspects of personality (*anima*) and masculine aspects (*animus*). The anima and animus within allow each of us to express both masculine and feminine personality traits and to understand and relate to the other sex.

Carl Jung (1875–1961). An initial follower of Freud, Jung later became a neo-Freudian who is credited with the development of analytical psychology *and with identifying the* collective unconscious *and* archetypes.

Collective Unconscious *Carl Jung's concept of an inherited unconscious that all humans share*

Archetypes *According to Carl Jung, the images or patterns of thoughts, feelings, and behavior that reside in the collective unconscious*

Figure 35.3 *The collective unconscious.* According to Jung, humans around the world and throughout history tend to share basic images that are stored in the collective unconscious. Note the symbol of the snake in this early Australian aboriginal bark painting, the ancient Egyptiian tomb painting, and the 15th century European painting.

GENDER & CULTURAL DIVERSITY

Horney, Freud, and Penis Envy

Karen Horney (pronounced "HORN-eye") was trained as a Freudian psychoanalyst in Germany and came to the United States in 1934. One of her major contributions was a creative blending of Freudian, Adlerian, and Jungian theory. She altered or rejected certain ideas of each theorist and added concepts of her own (Horney, 1939, 1945).

Horney strongly disagreed with Freud that differences in men and women were biologically based. She thought most of his ideas about female personality reflected male biases and misunderstanding. Instead of "biology is destiny," Horney contended that male–female differences were largely the result of social and cultural factors. Freud's concept of penis envy, for example, reflected women's feelings of cultural inferiority, not biological inferiority.

> The wish to be a man ... may be the expression of a wish for all those qualities or privileges which in our culture are regarded as masculine, such as strength, courage, independence, success, sexual freedom, and right to choose a partner.
>
> Horney, 1926/1967, p. 108

Horney suggested that the term *penis envy* be replaced by *power envy*. She also countered that some men develop womb envy — the desire to bear and nurse children. Horney emphasized that each sex has attributes and powers that are admired by the other and the neither should be seen as inferior or superior. Though Freud's theories have been criticized by a number of recent researchers for their male bias, Horney was one of the first to describe the problem.

Horney is also known for her theories of personality development. Compared to Freud's belief that fixation at any stage of psychosexual development (oral, anal, and so forth) was the strongest influence on adult personality, Horney believed it was the child's relationship to the parents that most influenced adult personality.

According to Horney, we all search for security in one of three basic and distinct ways. We can move toward people (by seeking affection and acceptance from others); we can move away (by striving for independence, privacy, and self-reliance); or we can move against people (by trying to gain control and power over others). Emotional health requires a balance among these three styles. Exaggerating or overusing one constitutes a neurotic, or emotionally unhealthy, response.

Stop for a moment and try to recapture your earliest childhood feelings and experiences. If as a child, you felt alone and isolated in a hostile environment and your needs were not met by nurturing parents, Horney believed you would experience extreme feelings of helplessness and insecurity. How people respond to this **basic anxiety** — a major concept in Horney's theory — greatly determines emotional health.

Evaluating Psychoanalytic Theories: Five Criticisms

Freud and his psychoanalytic theories have been enormously influential, but as we said at the onset, his theories have also been the subject of great debate. Five major criticisms are presented here:

1. *Difficult to test.* From a scientific point of view, a major problem with psychoanalytic theory is that most of its concepts cannot be empirically tested (Gay, 2000; Lilienfeld, 1999; Macmillan, 1997). How do you conduct an experiment on the id?

Basic Anxiety *According to Karen Horney, the feelings of helplessness and insecurity that adults experience because as children they felt alone and isolated in a hostile environment*

Karen Horney (1885–1952). One of the few women who were trained by Freud, Horney disagreed with his emphasis on biological determinants of personality. She believed penis envy *should be called* power envy *because it resulted from women's lower social status. Horney is also remembered for the concept of* basic anxiety.

Or on unconscious conflicts? Scientific standards require testable hypotheses and operational definitions.

2. *Overemphasis on biology and unconscious forces.* Like many of the neo-Freudians, modern psychologists believe that Freud overemphasized biological determinants and did not give sufficient attention to learning and culture in shaping behavior. In particular, the psychoanalytic belief that "anatomy is destiny" completely ignores the power of culture to create differences between men and women.

3. *Inadequate evidence.* Freud based his theories almost exclusively on the case histories of his patients. His data, therefore, were all subjective, leading critics today to wonder if Freud saw what he expected to see and ignored the rest. (Do you recognize this as the "fallacy of positive instances" described in the previous Module's Critical Thinking/Active Learning exercise?)

Moreover, Freud's patients were almost exclusively upper-class Viennese women who sought his help because they had serious adjustment problems. Such a small and selective sample may mean that his theory describes only disturbed personality development in upper-class Viennese women at the turn of the century.

4. *Sexism.* Many psychologists reject Freud's theories as misogynistic, or derogatory toward women. First, there is the concept of penis envy, which, as you read earlier, Karen Horney, and others since, have refuted. Second, Freud rejected his patients' reports of childhood sexual abuse when colleagues ridiculed him for taking them seriously. His revised position was that the women were expressing unconscious wishes and fantasies. Given our knowledge now of the high rate of rape and incest throughout history, it's entirely possible that Freud was right in initially trusting his patients and wrong to retreat (Masson, 1984, 1992).

5. *Lack of cross-cultural support.* The Freudian concepts that ought to be most easily supported empirically — the biological determinants of personality — are generally not borne out by cross-cultural studies (Crews, 1997).

Today there are few Freudian purists left. Modern psychodynamic theorists and psychoanalysts employ only some of his theories and techniques. Instead, they use empirical methods and research findings to reformulate and refine traditional Freudian theories and methods of assessment (Westen, 1998).

There are many legitimate criticisms of Freud. But even so, many psychologists argue that, wrong as he was on many counts, Freud still ranks as one of the giants of psychology (Breger, 2000; Taylor, 1999). He should be credited and remembered for at least four reasons: (1) the emphasis on the unconscious and its influence on behavior; (2) the conflict among the id, ego, and superego and the resulting defense mechanisms; (3) the development of an influential form of therapy, *psychoanalysis*; and (4) the sheer magnitude of his theory.

In reference to this last point, it is hard to overstate Freud's impact on Western intellectual history. He attempted to explain dreams, religion, social groupings, family dynamics, neurosis, psychosis, humor, the arts, and literature. It's easy to criticize Freud if you don't remember that he began his work at the start of the twentieth century and lacked the benefit of modern research findings and technology. To criticize his theory without historical perspective is to criticize the Wright brothers for their crude plane design. We can only imagine how our current theories will look 100 years from now.

Today, Freud's legacy lives on in our thinking and artistic imagination. Often without realizing the source, we talk about unconscious motives, oral fixations, and repression. We accuse people of being anal or egomaniacs. Right or wrong, Freud has a lasting place among the pioneers in psychology.

Freud and his daughter. *Despite criticisms of sexism, psychoanalysis was one of the few areas where women gained prominent positions in the early 20th century. Here Freud is walking with his daughter, Anna Freud (1895–1982), who also became an influential psychoanalyst.*

Check & Review

PSYCHOANALYTIC/PSYCHODYNAMIC THEORIES

Sigmund Freud founded the psychoanalytic approach to personality, which emphasizes the power of the unconscious. The mind (or psyche) reportedly functions on three levels (**conscious**, **preconscious**, and **unconscious**), and the personality has three distinct structures (**id, ego**, and **superego**). The ego struggles to meet the demands of the id and superego, and when these demands are in conflict, the ego may resort to defense mechanisms to relieve anxiety. According to Freud, all human beings pass through five **psychosexual stages**: oral, anal, phallic, latency, and genital. How specific conflicts at each of these stages are resolved is important to personality development.

Three influential followers of Freud who broke with him were Alfred Adler, Carl Jung, and Karen Horney. Known as neo-Freudians, they emphasized different issues. Adler emphasized the **inferiority complex** and the compensating *will-to-power*. Jung introduced the **collective unconscious** and **archetypes**. Horney stressed the importance of **basic anxiety** and refuted Freud's idea of *penis envy*, replacing it with *power envy*.

Critics of the psychoanalytic approach, especially Freud's theories, argue that it is difficult to test, overemphasizes biology and unconscious forces, has inadequate empirical support, is sexist, and lacks cross-cultural support. Despite these criticisms, Freud remains a notable pioneer in psychology.

Questions

1. Using the analogy of an iceberg, explain Freud's three levels of consciousness.

2. The _____ operates on the pleasure principle, seeking immediate gratification. The _____ operates on the reality principle, and the _____ contains the conscience and ego-ideal, which provide moral guidance for the ego. (a) psyche, ego, id; (b) id, ego, superego; (c) conscious, preconscious, unconscious; (d) oral stage; anal stage; phallic stage

3. Briefly describe Freud's five psychosexual stages.

4. Match the following concepts with the appropriate theorist, Adler, Jung, or Horney:

   a. inferiority complex: _____

   b. power envy: _____

   c. collective unconscious: _____

   d. basic anxiety: _____

Answers to Questions can be found in Appendix B.

ACTIVE LEARNING WORKSHEET MODULE 35

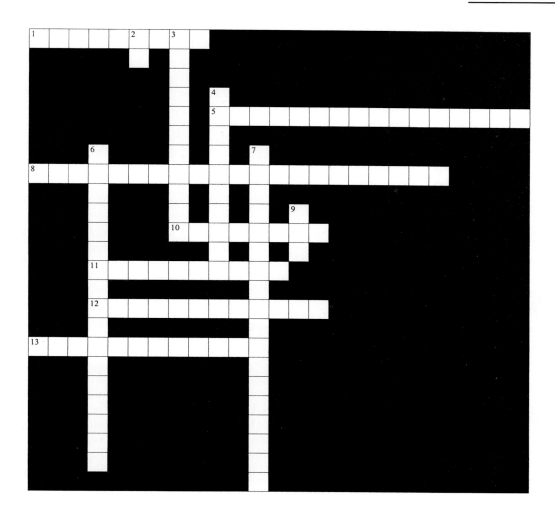

ACROSS

1. Thoughts or information that a person is currently aware of or is remembering.

5. Operating principle for the conscious ego.

8. Jung's concept of an inherited unconscious that all humans share.

10. Part of the personality that incorporates parental and societal standards for morality.

11. Basic defense mechanism that blocks unacceptable impulses from coming into awareness.

12. Thoughts or information that one can become aware of easily.

13. Horney's term for feelings of helplessness and insecurity.

DOWN

2. Source of instinctual energy concerned with immediate gratification.

3. Thoughts, motives, or desires beyond a person's normal awareness.

4. Jungian images or patterns that reside in the collective unconscious.

6. Operating principle for the unconscious id.

7. Adlerian idea that feelings of inferiority develop from early childhood experiences of helplessness and incompetence.

9. Freudian name for the rational part of the psyche.

Answers can be found in Appendix B.

MODULE 36
OTHER MAJOR THEORIES

In Module 34, we discovered the trait perspective, which seeks to describe and classify important elements of personality. The psychoanalytic/psychodynamic perspective in Module 35 emphasized unconscious processes. In this module, we explore two additional perspectives — humanistic and social/cognitive.

Humanistic Theories: Rogers and Maslow

Humanistic theories approach the study of personality from the "inside out," emphasizing internal experiences — feelings and thoughts — and the individual's own feelings of basic worth. From a humanistic perspective, people are naturally good (or, at worst, neutral), and they possess a positive drive toward self-fulfillment.

According to this view, each individual's personality is created out of his or her unique way of perceiving and interpreting the world. Behavior is controlled by the individual's perception of reality, not by traits, unconscious impulses, or rewards and punishments. To fully understand another human being you must know how he or she perceives the world. Humanistic psychology was developed largely through the writings of Carl Rogers and Abraham Maslow.

Rogers' Self-Concept Theory

To humanistic psychologist Carl Rogers (1902–1987), the most important component of personality is the *self*, the part of experience that a person comes to identify early in life as "I" or "me." Today, Rogerians (followers of Rogers) use the term **self-concept** to refer to all the information and beliefs you have as an individual regarding your own nature, unique qualities, and typical behaviors. Rogers was very concerned with the match between a person's self-concept and his or her actual experiences with life. He believed poor mental health and maladjustment developed from an incongruence or disparity between the self-concept and actual life experiences (Figure 36.1).

Mental Health, Congruence, and Self-Esteem
According to Rogers, there is an intimate connection between mental health, congruence, and *self-esteem* — how we feel about ourselves. If our self-concept is congruent (or matches) with our life experiences, we have high self-esteem and generally good mental health.

These three states (mental health, congruence, and self-esteem) are also part of our innate, biological capacities. Each of us is born into the world with an innate need to survive, grow, and enhance ourselves. We naturally approach and value people and experiences that enhance our growth and fulfillment and avoid those that do not. Therefore, Rogers believed we can — and should — trust our own internal feelings to guide us toward mental health and happiness.

If everyone has an inborn, positive drive toward self-fulfillment, why do some people have low self-esteem and poor mental health? Rogers believed these states generally result from early

Why we help others. Humanistic approaches to personality emphasize the positive nature of humans and our innate potential for goodness.

Self-Concept *In Carl Rogers's theory, all the information and beliefs individuals have about their own nature, qualities, and behavior*

Figure 36.1 Self-concept and adjustment. According to Carl Rogers, mental health is related to the degree of congruence (or match) between our self-concept and life experiences. If our self-concept is reasonably consistent with actual life experiences, our "self" is said to be congruent and we are well adjusted. The reverse is true when there is little overlap and incongruity.

Congruence

Experience

Self-concept

Well-adjusted individual
Considerable overlap between self-concept and experience

Incongruence

Self-concept   Experience

Poorly adjusted individual
Little overlap between self-concept and experience

> What do humanistic theorists believe about personality?

childhood experiences with parents and other adults who make their love *conditional*. That is, children learn that their acceptance is contingent on behaving in certain ways and expressing only certain feelings. When affection and love seem conditional, children block out the existence of negative impulses and feelings (which others label as "bad"), and their self-concepts and self-esteem become distorted. If a child is angry and hits his younger brother, for example, some parents might punish the older child or deny his anger, saying, "Nice children don't hit their brothers; they love them!" To gain parental approval, the child has to block out his true feelings of anger, which damages his self-esteem. He is obviously not "nice," because he *did* hit his sibling and he felt anger toward his brother instead of love.

Unconditional Positive Regard To help a child develop to fullest potential, adults need to create an atmosphere of **unconditional positive regard** — a setting in which children realize that they will be accepted no matter what they say or do. According to child expert Thomas Gordon:

> Acceptance is like the fertile soil that permits a tiny seed to develop into the lovely flower it is capable of becoming. The soil only enables the seed to become the flower. It releases the capacity of the seed to grow, but the capacity is entirely within the seed. As with the seed, a child contains entirely within the organism the capacity to develop. Acceptance is like the soil — it merely enables the child to actualize his potential.

> Gordon, 1975, p. 31

Does unconditional positive regard and acceptance mean that we should allow people to do whatever they please? Humanistic psychology is often misinterpreted in this way. Actually, however, humanists separate the value of the person from his or her behaviors. They accept the person's positive nature while discouraging specific self-destructive or hostile behaviors. Hitting a playmate or grabbing a toy is contrary to the child's positive nature as well as offensive to others. Such actions indicate that the child has not learned effective ways to behave. Humanistic psychologists believe in guiding children to control their behavior so they can develop a healthy self-concept and healthy relationships with others.

Maslow's Search for Self-Actualization

Like Rogers, Abraham Maslow believed there is a basic goodness to human nature and a natural tendency toward self-actualization. He saw personality as the expression of this tendency.

What exactly is self-actualization? According to Maslow, **self-actualization** is the inborn drive to develop all one's talents and capacities. It involves understanding one's own potential, accepting oneself and others as unique individuals, and taking a problem-centered approach to life situations (Maslow, 1970). Self-actualization is an ongoing process of growth rather than an end product or accomplishment — such as winning a trophy or graduating from college. Table 36.1 summarizes the characteristics of self-actualized people.

Maslow believed that only a few, rare individuals, such as Abraham Lincoln, Albert Einstein, Mohandas Gandhi, and Eleanor Roosevelt, become fully self-actualized. However, he saw self-actualization as part of every person's basic hierarchy of needs. (See Module 31 for a full discussion of Maslow's hierarchy of needs.)

Carl Rogers (1902–1987). *As a founder of humanistic psychology, Rogers emphasized the importance of the self-concept. He believed our personality and individual self-esteem are heavily influenced by early childhood experiences, such as whether we receive unconditional positive regard from our adult caregivers.*

Unconditional Positive Regard
Carl Rogers's term for how we should behave toward someone to increase his or her self-esteem; positive behavior shown toward a person with no contingencies attached

Self-Actualization *According to Abraham Maslow, an innate tendency toward growth that motivates all human behavior and results in the full realization of a person's highest potential*

TABLE 36.1 CHARACTERISTICS OF SELF-ACTUALIZED PEOPLE

Christopher Reeve

Oprah Winfrey

1. Perceive reality clearly and are comfortable with uncertainty
2. Accept themselves and others for what they are
3. Spontaneous in behavior, motivated by the attempt to develop their own style
4. Problem-centered rather than self-centered, focusing on accomplishing unselfish tasks
5. Enjoy solitude and make decisions privately
6. Maintain an inner serenity in unpleasant circumstances and when dealing with social pressures
7. Have a continued freshness of appreciation rather than taking things for granted
8. Have peak experiences, or feelings of transcendence and intense joy in basic experiences of life
9. Affectionately identify with other people
10. Establish deep, satisfying interpersonal relationships with a few, rather than many, people
11. Are democratic and unprejudiced in dealing with others
12. Are strongly ethical in behavior as well as attitudes
13. Have a spontaneous, nonhostile sense of humor
14. Are creative
15. Resist enculturation, although not purposely unconventional

Source: Maslow (1970, 1999).

Evaluating Humanistic Theories

Humanistic psychology was extremely popular during the 1960s and 1970s. It was a refreshing new perspective on personality after the negative determinism of the psychoanalytic approach and the mechanism of learning theories. Although this early popularity has declined, many humanistic ideas have been incorporated into approaches for counseling and psychotherapy (Wertz, 1998).

At the same time, humanistic theories have also been criticized. Three of the most important criticisms are:

1. Naive assumptions. Critics suggest the humanists are unrealistic, romantic, and even naive about human nature. Are all people as inherently good as they say? Our continuing history of murders, warfare, and other acts of aggression suggests otherwise.

2. Poor testability and inadequate evidence. Like many psychoanalytic terms and concepts, humanistic concepts such as unconditional positive regard and self-actualization are difficult to operationally define and scientifically test.

3. Narrowness. Like trait theories, humanistic theories have been criticized for merely *describing* personality — rather than *explaining* it. For example, where does the motivation for self-actualization come from? To say that it is an "inborn drive" doesn't satisfy those who favor experimental research and hard data as the way to learn about personality.

Check & Review

HUMANISTIC THEORIES

Humanistic theories emphasize internal experiences, thoughts, and feelings that create the individual's **self-concept**. Carl Rogers emphasized the concepts of *self-esteem* and **unconditional positive regard**. Abraham Maslow emphasized the potential for **self-actualization**. Critics of the humanistic approach argue that these theories are based on naive assumptions and are not scientifically testable or well supported by empirical evidence. In addi-

tion, their focus on description, rather than explanation, makes them narrow.

Questions

1. If you took the _____ approach to personality, you would emphasize internal experiences, like feelings and thoughts, and the basic worth of the individual. (a) humanistic; (b) psychodynamic; (c) personalistic; (d) motivational

2. Rogers thought that _____ is necessary for a child's uniqueness and posi-

tive self-concept to unfold naturally. (a) permissive parenting; (b) a challenging environment; (c) unconditional positive regard; (d) a friendly neighborhood

3. Abraham Maslow's belief that all people are motivated toward personal growth and development is known as _____.

4. What are three major criticisms of humanistic theories?

Answers to Questions can be found in Appendix B.

Social/Cognitive Perspective: Bandura and Rotter

According to the social/cognitive perspective, each of us has a unique personality because of our individual history of interactions with the environment, and because we *think* about the world and interpret what happens to us (Cervone & Shoda, 1999). Furthermore, our interpretations are distinctive because of our previous experiences. Two of the most influential social-cognitive theorists are Albert Bandura and Julian Rotter.

What is the social/cognitive perspective on personality?

Bandura's Approach

Although Albert Bandura is perhaps best known for his work on observational learning or social learning, he has also played a major role in reintroducing thought processes into personality theory. Cognition is central to his concept of **self-efficacy**, which refers to a person's learned expectation of success (Bandura, 1997, 1999, 2000).

How do you generally perceive your ability to select, influence, and control the circumstances of your life? According to Bandura, if you have a strong sense of self-efficacy, you believe you can generally succeed, regardless of past failures and current obstacles. This belief will in turn affect the challenges you accept and the effort you expend in reaching goals.

Doesn't such a belief also affect how others respond to you and thereby affect your chances for success? Precisely! This type of mutual interaction and influence is a core part of another major concept of Bandura's — **reciprocal determinism**. According to Bandura, our cognitions (or thoughts), behaviors, and the environment are interdependent and interactive (Figure 36.2). Thus, a cognition ("I can succeed") will affect behaviors ("I will ask for a promotion"), which in turn will affect the environment ("I can become an executive"), which then affects cognitions ("I am a success"), and so on.

Rotter's Perspective

Julian Rotter's theory is similar to Bandura's in suggesting that learning creates *cognitive expectancies* that guide behavior and influence the environment (Rotter, 1954, 1990). According to Rotter, your behavior or personality is determined by (1) what you *expect* to happen following a specific action and (2) the *reinforcement value* attached to specific outcomes — that is, the degree to which you prefer one reinforcer to another.

Self-Efficacy *According to Albert Bandura, a person's learned beliefs that he or she is capable of producing desired results, such as mastering new skills and achieving personal goals*

Reciprocal Determinism *Albert Bandura's belief that an individual's cognitions and behaviors and the learning environment interact to produce personality*

Figure 36.2 *Albert Bandura's theory of reciprocal determinism.* According to Bandura, thoughts (or cognitions), behavior, and the environment all interact to produce personality.

LOW SELF-ESTEEM

To understand your personality and behavior, for instance, Rotter would want to know your expectancies and what you see as the source of life's rewards and punishments. To secure this information, Rotter would use personality tests that measure your internal versus external *locus of control*. Rotter's tests ask people to respond "true" or "false" to a series of statements, such as "People get ahead in this world primarily by luck and connections rather than by hard work and perseverance," or "When someone doesn't like you, there is little you can do about it."

As you may suspect, *externals* think environment and external forces have primary control over their lives, whereas *internals* think they can control events in their lives through their own efforts. Numerous studies have found that having an internal locus of control is positively associated with higher psychological functioning and better mental health (Frazier & Waid, 1999; Hans, 2000; Wen, Wang, Zhao, & Sun, 2000).

Evaluating Social/Cognitive Theory

The social/cognitive perspective holds several attractions. First, it emphasizes how the environment affects, and is affected by, individuals. Secondly, it meets most standards for scientific research. It offers testable, objective hypotheses and operationally defined terms and relies on empirical data for its basic principles (Lin, 1998; Stajkovic & Luthans, 1998). Critics, however, believe social/cognitive theory is too narrow. It has been criticized for ignoring unconscious, emotional, and developmental aspects of personality (Carducci, 1998; Westen, 1998).

Both Bandura's and Rotter's theories emphasize cognition and social learning, but they are a long way from a strict behavior theory, which suggests that only environmental forces control behavior. They are also a long way from the biological theories that say inborn, innate qualities determine behavior and personality. Biological theories are the topic of our next section.

Check & Review

SOCIAL/COGNITIVE PERSPECTIVE

Social/cognitive theorists emphasize the importance of external events and mental processes: how we interpret and respond to external events. Albert Bandura's social-cognitive approach focuses on **self-efficacy** and **reciprocal determinism**, whereas Julian Rotter emphasizes an internal or external *locus of control*.

Social/cognitive theory is credited for its attention to environmental influences and its scientific standards. However, it has been criticized for its narrow focus and lack of attention to unconscious, emotional, and developmental components of personality.

Questions

1. The social/cognitive approach to personality is most likely to analyze _____.

2. According to _____, thoughts (or cognitions), behavior, and the environment all interact to produce personality. (a) reciprocal determinism; (b) interactionism; (c) confluence theory; (d) reverberating circuits theory

3. According to Bandura, _____ involves a person's belief about whether he or she can successfully engage in behaviors related to personal goals. (a) self-actualization; (b) self-esteem; (c) self-efficacy, (d) self-congruence

4. People with an _____ expect the environment and external forces to control events, whereas those with an _____ believe in personal control.

Answers to Questions can be found in Appendix B.

Biological Theories: The Brain, Neurochemistry and Genetics

As you were growing up, you probably heard comments such as "You're just like your father" or "You're so much like your mother." Does this mean that biological factors you inherited from your parents were the major contributors to your personality? *Biological theories* of personality focus on the brain, neurochemistry, and genetics. We begin our study with the brain. We conclude this module with a discussion of how all theories of personality ultimately *interact*.

> How does biology contribute to personality?

The Brain

The nineteenth-century phrenologists described at the beginning of this section read bumps on the skull because they believed specific areas of the brain controlled particular personality traits. Today we know that brain structures are not palpable on the skull surface, but, interestingly, modern biological research does suggest that certain brain areas may contribute to some personality traits.

Tellegen (1985), for example, proposes that extroversion and introversion are associated with particular areas of the brain, and research seems to support him. For instance, sociability (or extroversion) is associated with increased electroencephalographic (EEG) activity in the left frontal lobes of the brain, whereas shyness (introversion) shows greater EEG activity in the right frontal lobes (Schmidt, 1999).

A major limitation to research on brain structures and personality is the difficulty identifying which structures are uniquely connected with particular personality traits. Lesioning one structure tends to have wide-ranging effects. Neurochemistry seems to offer more precise data on biological bases of personality. Jerome Kagan (1998), a major personality researcher, believes that most biologically based personality differences rest "on differences in neurochemistry rather than anatomy" (p. 59).

Neurochemistry

Do you enjoy skydiving and taking risks in general? Neurochemistry may explain why. Research has found a consistent relationship between sensation seeking and monoamine oxidase (MAO), an enzyme that regulates levels of neurotransmitters such as dopamine (Zuckerman, 1994, 2000). Dopamine also seems to be correlated with extroversion (Depue & Collins, 1999; Ekelund, Lichtermann, Jarvelin, & Peltonen, 1999).

How can traits like sensation seeking and extroversion be related to neurochemistry? Studies suggest that high-sensation seekers and extroverts tend to have lower levels of physiological arousal than introverts (Brown & Schmidt, 2000; Dellu, Mayo, Piazza, Le Moal, & Simon, 1993). Their lower arousal apparently motivates them to seek out situations that will elevate their arousal. Moreover, it is believed

Are people born "shy?" Researchers have found that shyness seems to be innate and that it is one of the most stable, lifelong personality traits across the lifespan.

that a lower threshold is inherited. In other words, personality traits like sensation seeking and extroversion may be inherited.

Genetics

> Heredity is what sets the parents of a teenager wondering about each other.
>
> Laurence J. Peter

Psychologists have only recently recognized the importance and influence of genetic factors in personality (Borkenau, Riemann, Angleitner, & Spinath, 2001; Plomin & Crabbe, 2000; Wright, 1998). This relatively new area, called *behavioral genetics*, attempts to determine the extent to which behavioral differences among people are due to genetics as opposed to environment.

To measure genetic influence, researchers rely mostly on two kinds of data. First, they compare similarities between identical twins and fraternal twins. For example, studies of the heritability of the Big Five personality traits range from 0.40 to about 0.60 (Bouchard, 1997; Eysenck, 1967, 1991; Loehlin et al., 1998; Rowe, 1997). These correlations suggest that genetic factors contribute about 40 to 50 percent of personality.

Second, researchers compare the personalities of parents, their biological children, and their adopted children. Studies of the Big Five traits of extraversion and neuroticism find that parents' traits correlate moderately with those of their biological children and hardly at all with those of their adopted children (Bouchard, 1997; Jang et al., 1998; Loehlin et al., 1998).

Overall, studies show a strong influence of hereditary factors on personality. At the same time, researchers are careful not to overemphasize the genetic basis (Maccoby, 2000). Some believe the importance of the unshared environment (aspects of the environment that differ from one individual to another, even within a family) has been overlooked (Saudino, 1997). Others fear that research on "genetic determinism" could be misused to "prove" that an ethnic or racial group is inferior, that male dominance is natural, or that social progress is impossible. There is no doubt that genetics studies have produced exciting and controversial results, but it is also clear that more research is necessary before we have a cohesive biological theory of personality.

Interactionism

When it comes to personality, no one theory is more correct than another. Each provides a different perspective and offers different insights into how a person develops the distinctive set of characteristics we call "personality." In fact, instead of adhering to any one theory, many psychologists believe in *interactionism*, the idea that several factors overlap in their contributions to personality (Figure 36.3). Even some psychologists who have done major research in one area of personality theory lean toward interactionism (Cervone & Shoda, 1999; Mischel & Shoda, 1999).

Hans Eysenck (1990), a leading trait theorist and interactionist, believes certain traits (like introversion and extraversion) may reflect inherited patterns of cortical arousal, as well as social learning, cognitive processes, and the environment. Can you see how someone with an introverted personality, and therefore a higher level of cortical arousal, might try to avoid excessive stimulation by seeking friends and jobs with low stimulation levels?

Eysenck's work exemplifies how trait, biological, and social/cognitive theories can be combined to provide better insight into personality. This trend toward integration and interactionism is reflected in a growing number of books and articles, and in decreased polarization on certain issues, such as the "either–or" debate between trait theorists and situational determinists discussed earlier.

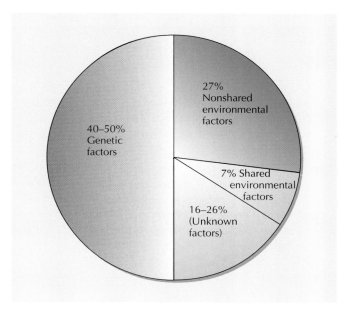

Figure 36.3 *Multiple influences on personality.* Researchers have concluded that personality can be broken down into four major factors: *genetics*, inherited traits (40 to 50 percent); *nonshared environmental factors*, or how each individual's genetic factors react and adjust to his or her particular environment (27 percent); *shared environmental factors*, involving parental patterns and shared family experiences (7 percent); and *error*, unidentified factors or problems with testing (16 to 26 percent) (Bouchard, 1997; Plomin, 1997; Talbot, Duberstein, King, Cox, & Giles, 2000; Wright, 1998).

GENDER & CULTURAL DIVERSITY

Cultural Concepts of Self

Up to this point, we have examined only Western theories of personality. The concept of self is central to each of these theories. Personality is seen as a composition of individual parts (traits and motives), and the self is a bounded individual — separate and autonomous from others (Gardner, Gabriel, & Lee, 1999; Matsumoto, 2000). Can you see how the *conscious, preconscious, unconscious, id, ego, superego, inferiority complex, basic anxiety, self-concept, self-esteem,* and *self-actualization* all assume a unique self composed of discrete traits, motives, and abilities? Our Western perspective reflects an *individualistic* perspective.

In *collectivist* cultures, however, the self is inherently linked to others. For example, in Asia, people are described not by a set of enduring traits but in terms of social relationships (Markus & Kitayama, 1998). The person is defined and understood primarily by looking at his or her place in the social unit. Relatedness, connectedness, and interdependence are valued, as opposed to separateness, independence, and individualism.

If you are North American or Western European, you may find the concept of a self defined in terms of others almost contradictory. A core selfhood seems intuitively obvious to you. Recognizing that this is not the case in collectivist cultures and among some minorities may prevent misunderstanding. For example, North Americans generally define *sincerity* as behaving in accordance with one's inner feelings, whereas Japanese see it as behavior that conforms to a person's role expectations (carrying out one's duties) (Yamada, 1997). Can you see how Japanese behavior might appear insincere to a North American and vice versa?

Understanding how the individualistic perspective differs from that in collectivist cultures may improve global relations. It also points out limits and biases in our current Western personality theories and the need for continued cross-cultural research.

Check & Review

BIOLOGICAL THEORIES

Biological theories emphasize brain structures, neurochemistry, and inherited genetic components of personality. Research on specific traits such as extroversion and sensation seeking support the biological approach. The interactionist approach suggests that the major theories overlap, and each contributes to our understanding of personality. Most theories of personality are biased toward Western, individualistic cultures and their perception of the "self." Recognizing and understanding this bias helps keep our study of personality in perspective.

Questions

1. _____ theories emphasize the importance of genetics in the development of personality. (a) Evolutionary; (b) Phenomenological; (c) Genological; (d) Biological

2. What concerns people about genetic explanations for personality?

3. The _____ approach represents a blending of several theories of personality. (a) unification; (b) association; (c) interactionist; (d) phenomenological

4. Explain how the Western concept of the self reflects an individualistic culture versus a collectivist culture.

Answers to Questions can be found in Appendix B.

ACTIVE LEARNING WORKSHEET MODULE 36

Enter the correct letter from Column A in the blank space in Column B, and then doublecheck your answers with those in Appendix B.

Column A

a. Rogers

b. Maslow

c. Bandura

d. Self-Actualization

e. Rotter

f. Tellegen

g. Behavioral Genetics

h. Individualistic Perspective

i. Reciprocal Determinism

j. Unconditional Positive
   Regard

Column B

1. ___ Cognitions, behaviors, and environment interact.

2. ___ Positive behavior with no contingencies.

3. ___ Self-concept.

4. ___ Locus of control.

5. ___ Studies genetic influences versus environment.

6. ___ Emphasizes the self.

7. ___ Associates personality with areas of the brain.

8. ___ Self-efficacy.

9. ___ Realization of highest potential.

10. ___ Created hierarchy of needs.

Visual Summary for Modules 33, 34, 35, and 36 ●-●-●-●

Personality   Personality: Unique, relatively stable pattern of thoughts, emotions, and actions.

Personality Assessment Psychologists use four methods to measure personality:

Interviews: Can be either structured or unstructured.

Observations: Psychologist uses direct behavioral observation with set of evaluation guidelines.

Objective Tests (such as the **MMPI-2**) ask test-takers to self-report on paper-and-pencil questionnaires or inventories. These tests provide objective standardized information about a large number of personality traits, but they have their limits, including deliberate deception, social desirability bias, diagnostic difficulties and inappropriate use.

Projective Tests [such as the **Rorschach "inkblot"** or **Thematic Apperception Test (TAT)**] ask test-takers to respond to ambiguous stimuli. Though these tests are said to provide insight into unconsious elements of the personality, they are not very reliable or valid.

Reliability and **validity** are the major criteria for evaluating the accuracy of personality tests.

Major Personality Theories and Assessment Techniques

Theorists and Key Concepts	Determinants of Personality	Methods of Assessment
Trait *Early theorists* • Allport: Arranged **traits** in hierarchy. • Cattell (16PF) and Eysenck (Personality Questionnaire): Used **factor analysis** to reduce number of traits. *Modern theory* • **Five-factor model** (FFM): Openness, conscientiousness, extraversion, agreeableness, and neuroticism.	Heredity and environment combine to create personality traits.	Objective (self-report) inventories (e.g., MMPI), observation.

Major Personality Theories and Assessment Techniques (cont.)

Theorist and Key Concepts	Determinants of Personality	Methods of Assessment
Psychoanalytic/Psychodynamic *Freud* • Levels of Consciousness—**conscious, preconscious,** and **unconscious.** • Personality Structure—**id (pleasure principle), ego (reality principle), superego** (morality principle). • Defense Mechanisms—**repression** and others. • **Psychosexual Stages**—oral, anal, phallic (**Oedipus complex**), latency, and genital. *NeoFreudians* • Adler—individual psychology, **inferiority complex,** and will-to-power. • Jung—analytical psychology, **collective unconscious,** and **archetypes.** • Horney—power envy vs. penis envy and **basic anxiety.**	Unconscious conflicts between id, ego and superego lead to defense mechanisms.	Interviews and projective tests: Rorschach inkblot test, Thematic Apperception Test (TAT).
Humanistic *Phenomenological perspective* • Rogers—**self-concept,** self-esteem, and **unconditional positive regard.** • Maslow—**self-actualization.**	Individual's subjective experience of reality.	Interviews, objective (self-report) inventories.
Social/Cognitive • Bandura—**self-efficacy** and **reciprocal determinism.** • Rotter—cognitive expectancies and locus of control.	Interaction between cognition and environment.	Observation, objective (self-report) inventories.
Biological • Brain structures like the frontal lobes may play a role. • Neurochemistry (dopamine, MAO, and others) may play a role. • Genetic factors also contribute to personality.	Brain, neurochemistry, genetics.	Animal studies and biological techniques

Interactionism: Major theories overlap and each contributes to our understanding of personality. Cultural comparisons find most theories biased toward Western, individualistic cultures that emphasize the "self."

Psychological Disorders

Mary's troubles first began in adolescence. She began to miss curfew, was frequently truant, and her grades declined sharply. During family counseling sessions, it was discovered that Mary also had been promiscuous and had prostituted herself several times to get drug money. She revealed a history of drug abuse, including "everything I can get my hands on." Mary also had ongoing problems with her peers. She quickly fell in love and overly idealized new friends. But when they quickly (and inevitably) disappointed her, she would angrily cast them aside. This pattern of poor grades, cutting classes, and unstable relationships continued throughout high school, two years of college, and a series of clerical jobs. Mary's problems, coupled with a preoccupation with inflicting pain on herself (by cutting and burning) and persistent thoughts of suicide, eventually led to her admittance to a psychiatric hospital at age 26.
Davison & Neale, 2001, p. 358

Jim is a third-year medical student. Over the last few weeks he has been noticing that older men appear to be frightened of him when he passes them on the street. Recently, he has become convinced that he is actually the director of the Central Intelligence Agency and that these men are secret agents of a hostile nation. Jim has found confirmatory evidence for his idea in the fact that a helicopter flies over his house every day at 8:00 A.M. and at 4:30 P.M. Surely, this surveil-

lance is part of the plot to assassinate him.
Bernheim & Lewine, 1979, p. 4

Ken Bianchi, the "Hillside Strangler," terrorized the Los Angeles area for more than a year. Working with his cousin, Angelo Buono, Bianchi used phony police badges to lure victims into his car or home where they were later raped, systematically tortured, and then murdered. Bianchi and Buono killed 10 women aged 12 to 28. Bianchi killed two more after moving to Washington State. After one of the longest trials in Los Angeles history, Bianchi was sentenced to life in prison. Presiding Judge Ronald M. George stated: "If ever there was a case where the death penalty was appropriate, this is that case. Angelo Buono and Kenneth Bianchi … abducted children and young women, torturing, raping and, finally, depriving their family and friends of them forever as they slowly squeezed out of their victims their last breath of air and their promise of a future life. And for what? The momentary, sadistic thrill of enjoying a brief perverted sexual satisfaction and the venting of their hatred of women."
Magid & McKelvey, 1987, pp. 15–18

Each of these individuals has a severe psychological problem, and each case raises interesting questions. What caused Mary's unstable relationships and suicidal thoughts, Jim's paranoia, and Ken's cold-blooded murders? Was there something in their early backgrounds to explain their later behaviors? Is there something medically wrong with them?

What about less severe forms of abnormal behavior? Is a person who dreams of airplane crashes and refuses to fly mentally ill? Does a compulsively neat student who types all his lecture notes and refuses to write in any textbook need a psychiatric examination? What is the difference between being eccentric and disordered?

In answer to these and other questions, this section begins with a look at ways psychological disorders are identified, explained, and classified. Then we explore five main categories of psychological disorders (anxiety, schizophrenia, mood disorders, dissociative disorders, and personality disorders). Modules in this section focus on describing and explaining the causes of abnormal behavior; the following set of modules explores their treatment.

Before we begin, we'd like to warn you about a common problem associated with studying psychological disorders. Reading about abnormal behavior and symptoms of mental disorders can sometimes result in a psychological version of *medical student's disease*, the tendency that medical students have to see in themselves the symptoms of whatever disease they are currently studying.

While reading about anxiety disorders, for example, you may think about how you felt when you had to give a speech in class. Or you may recall "blanking out" when introduced to an attractive stranger and may wonder if you have a *social phobia*. You focus on these isolated events and forget the rest of the picture — those times when you didn't behave this way and the fact that most people have similar experiences. On the other hand, psychological disorders are widespread, and most of us will encounter one or more of these disorders in our lifetime — either personally or with our family or friends. If you have serious concerns about yourself or others, we encourage you to talk to your instructor or a counselor.

MODULE 37

STUDYING PSYCHOLOGICAL DISORDERS

How do psychologists identify, explain, and classify abnormal behavior?

Abnormal Behavior *Patterns of emotion, thought, and action considered pathological (diseased or disordered) for one or more of these reasons: statistical infrequency, disability or dysfunction, personal distress, or violation of norms*

Would this behavior be considered abnormal? *Although it is not statistically "normal" to be such a collector and lover of piercing, the term abnormal behavior is generally restricted to behavior that is considered pathological (diseased or disordered).*

As the introductory cases show, mental disorders vary from person to person and in their severity. Also, like personality, consciousness, and intelligence, *abnormal behavior* is difficult to define. In this section, we will explore how psychologists attempt to identify, explain, and classify abnormal behavior.

Identifying Abnormal Behavior: Four Basic Standards

One widely accepted definition of **abnormal behavior** is patterns of emotion, thought, and action considered pathological (diseased or disordered) for one or more of the following reasons: statistical infrequency, disability or dysfunction, personal distress, or violation of norms (adapted from Davison & Neale, 2001). As we will see, each criterion has merit and captures some part of what might be the full definition. However, keep in mind that no *single* criterion is adequate for identifying abnormal behavior.

1. *Statistical infrequency.* One way to judge whether a person's behavior is abnormal is to compare the *frequency* of his or her behavior to that of others. Believing that others are plotting against you is statistically abnormal and is usually diagnosed as a *delusion of persecution*. However, as you read in Module 23, intelligence is believed to be distributed along a normal, bell-shaped curve, and individuals with an intelligence quotient (IQ) above 132 are statistically infrequent, or "abnormal." Yet having great intelligence — or great athletic ability or artistic skill — is *not* classified as abnormal by the public (or by psychologists). All in all, then, we cannot use statistical frequency as the sole criterion in determining what is normal versus abnormal (Figure 37.1).

2. *Disability or dysfunction.* An alternative to the statistical infrequency model is the disability or dysfunction model. According to this view, people are considered abnormal if their emotions, thoughts, or actions interfere with their ability to function in their own lives and within society. Disability or dysfunction is the primary criterion for identifying abnormal drug use. If the use of alcohol (or any other drug) interferes with a person's normal social or occupational functioning, the person may be diagnosed with a *substance-related disorder*.

3. *Personal distress.* Rather than rely on objective statistical measures or evidence of disability, for some disorders mental health professionals prefer to use an individual's own judgment of his or her level of functioning. For example, someone who drinks heavily every day may realize it is unhealthy and wish to stop. Thus, the personal distress model would help identify this behavior as abnormal. On the other hand, many people with true *alcohol-dependence disorders* deny they have a problem. Also, some serious psychological disorders cause little or no emotional discomfort. A serial killer, for instance, can torture someone without feeling remorse or guilt. The personal distress model by itself, then, is not sufficient for identifying all forms of abnormal behavior.

4. *Violation of norms.* The fourth approach to identifying abnormal behavior is based on *social norms*, cultural rules that guide behavior in particular situations. Behavior that violates social norms and threatens others can be considered abnormal. Being in such a highly excited state that you forget to pay the rent but pass out $20 bills to strangers is a violation of norms. This type of behavior is common among individuals who are diagnosed with *bipolar disorder*.

A major problem with this criterion, however, is that cultural diversity can affect what people consider a *violation* of norms (Lopez & Guarnaccia, 2000). The impact of culture on behavior is an important issue we have addressed throughout this text. As for culture and abnormal behavior, consider this: During the early years of marriage, the Lepcha of the southeastern Himalayas normally have sex five to nine times a night. Dani newlyweds of New Guinea, on the other hand, wait an average of 2 years before they have sex (cited in Crooks & Baur, 1999; Laumann, Paik, & Rosen, 1999). A Dani couple in New Guinea who behaved like most Americans and a married couple in the United States who waited 2 years before they had sex might be judged abnormal by their respective cultures.

Thus, abnormal behavior is often *culturally relative* — understandable only in terms of the culture in which it occurs. In addition, there are also *culture-bound* disorders that are unique and found only in particular cultures, and *culture-general* symptoms that are found in all cultures (Green, 1999; Lopez & Guarnaccia, 2000). These terms are discussed in the next section.

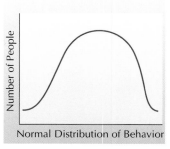

Figure 37.1 *Normal distribution.* When psychologists study behaviors such as intelligence, they often find that people are distributed along a "bell-shaped" curve. That is, a small number of people are found at the two ends of the curve, whereas most people cluster around the center.

GENDER & CULTURAL DIVERSITY

A Cultural Look at Disorders

Among the Chippewa, Cree, and Montagnais-Naskapi Indians in Canada, there is a disorder called *windigo* — or *wiitiko* — *psychosis*, which is characterized by delusions (irrational beliefs) and cannibalistic impulses. Believing the spirit of a *windigo*, or cannibal giant with heart and entrails of ice, has possessed them, victims become severely depressed (Barnouw, 1985). As the malady begins, the individual typically experiences loss of appetite, diarrhea, vomiting, and insomnia and may see the people around him or her turning into beavers or other edible animals.

In later stages, the victim becomes obsessed with cannibalistic thoughts. Family members often seek help from a shaman, a folk healer who uses special incantations and ceremonies to remove the spell of the *windigo* spirit. If they fail to seek help in time, the victim may attack and kill loved ones in order to devour their flesh (Berreman, 1971). As Table 37.1 shows, *windigo* psychosis is only one of many unique — or culture-bound — mental disorders that have been reported around the world.

Why do cultures develop such unique problems?

In the case of *windigo* psychosis, one explanation is that the disorder developed after fur trade competition depleted game that the Canadian tribes used for food, leading to widespread famine (Bishop, 1974). Facing starvation could have led to cannibalism and the subsequent "creation" of a *windigo* spirit. Belief in spirit possession is a common feature of many cultures, and in this case, people may have used it to explain a socially and psychologically abhorrent behavior, cannibalism (Faddiman, 1997).

Some researchers question the famine explanation for *windigo* psychosis and even the idea of culture-bound disorders (Dana, 1998; Hoek, Van Harten, Van Hoeken, & Susser, 1998). However, there is little doubt that some mental disorders are at least somewhat culture-bound (Guarnaccia & Rogler, 1999; Helms & Cook, 1999; Lopez & Guarnaccia, 2000).

Robert Nishimoto (1988) has found several culture-bound and culture-general symptoms that are useful in diagnosing disorders. Using the Langer (1962) index of psychiatric symptoms, Nishimoto gathered data from three diverse groups, Anglo-

TABLE 37.1 EXAMPLES OF CULTURE-BOUND DISORDERS

Culture	Disorder	Symptoms
Puerto Rican and other Latin cultures	*Ataque de nervios* ("attack of nerves")	Trembling, heart palpitations, and seizurelike episodes often associated with the death of a loved one, accidents, or family conflict
Southeast Asian, Malaysian, Indonesian, Thai	Running amok	Wild, out-of-control, aggressive behaviors and attempts to injure or kill others
West Africa	Brain fog	"Brain tiredness," a mental and physical response to the challenges of schooling
Ethiopia	Possession by the "Zar"	Involuntary movements, mutism, and incomprehensible language
South Chinese and Vietnamese	*Koro*	Belief that the penis is retracting into the abdomen and that when it is fully retracted, death will result; attempts to prevent the supposed retraction may lead to severe physical damage
Westerners	Anorexia nervosa	Occurs primarily among young women; preoccupied with thinness, they exercise excessively and refuse to eat; death can result

Sources: Davison & Neale, 2001; *Diagnostic and Statistical Manual of Mental Disorders*, 4th ed., 2000; Guarnaccia & Rogler, 1999; Matsumoto, 2000.

Americans in Nebraska, Vietnamese Chinese in Hong Kong, and Mexicans living in Texas and Mexico. (The Langer index is a screening instrument widely used to identify psychological disorders that disrupt everyday functioning but do not require institutionalization). When asked to think about their lives, respondents who needed professional help all named one or more of the same 12 symptoms (Table 37.2).

In addition to the culture-general symptoms (such as "nervousness" or "trouble sleeping"), Nishimoto also found culture-bound symptoms. For example, the Vietnamese Chinese reported "fullness in head," the Mexican respondents had "problems with my memory," and the Anglo-Americans reported "shortness of breath" and "headaches." Apparently people *learn* to express their problems in ways acceptable to others in the same culture (Brislin, 1997, 2000; Widiger & Sankis, 2000). In other words, most Americans learn that headaches are a common response to stress, whereas Mexicans learn that others will understand their complaints about memory. As you may imagine, it is very important that mental health professionals who work with culturally diverse populations understand that culturally general and culturally bound symptoms exist and what these are for any population.

TABLE 37.2 TWELVE CULTURE-GENERAL SYMPTOMS OF MENTAL HEALTH DIFFICULTIES

Nervous	Trouble sleeping	Low spirits
Weak all over	Personal worries	Restless
Feel apart, alone	Can't get along	Hot all over
Worry all the time	Can't do anything worthwhile	Nothing turns out right

Source: Adapted from Brislin, 1993, 2000.

An early "treatment" for abnormal behavior? During the Stone Age, many believed that demon possession was a primary cause of mental disorders, and one treatment was to bore holes in the skull to allow evil spirits to escape.

Culture obviously affects definitions of abnormality, but our concept of what is abnormal also changes over time. Our next section examines historical views of abnormality.

Explaining Abnormality: From Superstition to Science

Over the ages, popular views of the causes of abnormal behavior have changed. In prehistoric times, people believed both good and evil spirits made them see strange things and behave in unusual ways. During the Stone Age, for example, it was believed that demons could *possess* a person's body and soul and that the only treatment was *trephining*. In this operation, stone instruments were used to bore a hole in the skull to allow the evil spirit to escape.

The *demonological model* of abnormality persisted until the fourth century B.C., when the Greek physician Hippocrates suggested a physical basis for behavior disorders. According to this early **medical model**, problems such as epilepsy and depression were seen not as punishments from angry spirits but as results of disease of the brain or body.

Medical Model *Perspective that assumes diseases have physical causes that can be diagnosed, treated, and possibly cured; using this perspective, abnormal behaviors also have physical causes that can be diagnosed by their symptoms and treated and cured through therapy, including drugs and hospitalization*

The Middle Ages

During the Middle Ages (from about the fifth to the fifteenth century A.D.), supernatural explanations for abnormal behavior again dominated. This time, the Devil was the evil spirit believed to possess people, and the afflicted person was treated with a religious practice known as *exorcism*. Exorcism involved prayer, fasting, noise-

Witchcraft or mental illness? During the 15th century, some people who may have been suffering from mental disorders were accused of witchcraft and tortured or hung.

An early "Catch 22." In the Middle Ages, "dunking tests" were used to determine whether people who behaved abnormally were possessed by demons. Individuals who did not drown while being dunked were believed to be guilty of possession and then punished (usually by hanging). Those who did drown were judged to be innocent.

Psychiatry *The specialized branch of medicine dealing with the diagnosis, treatment, and prevention of mental disorder*

making, beating, and drinking terrible-tasting brews. The idea was to make the body so uncomfortable it would be uninhabitable by the Devil.

During the fifteenth century, people became even more obsessed with the Devil. Not only could you be possessed but you could also *choose* to consort with the Devil. These "willing people" (usually women) were called witches and were tortured, imprisoned for life, or executed. A church manual published in 1484 called *Malleus Maleficarum* ("The Witches' Hammer") described the characteristics of witches, which included sudden loss of reason, delusions, and hallucinations. Given these symptoms, some of the accused witches might have been mentally disturbed.

Asylums

As the Middle Ages ended, advances were made in the treatment of mental disorders. By the fifteenth and sixteenth centuries, specialized hospitals, or asylums, began to appear in Europe. Initially designed to provide quiet retreats from the world and to "protect" society (Alexander & Selesnick, 1966), the asylums unfortunately became overcrowded, inhumane "jails."

Improvement came in 1792 when Philippe Pinel, a French physician, was put in charge of a Parisian asylum where the inmates were shackled to the walls of unlighted and unheated cells. Pinel removed inmates from the dungeons and insisted they be treated humanely. Many inmates improved so dramatically they could be released. Pinel's belief that abnormal behavior was caused by "sick" minds soon became the accepted way of viewing people who had previously been feared and punished for their abnormality. Thus, his idea that disturbed individuals had an underlying *physical illness* resurrected the medical model first conceptualized by Hippocrates.

Modern Times

Pinel's medical model eventually gave rise to the modern specialty of **psychiatry**, in which disorders are diagnosed as physical illnesses and treatments are prescribed. Unfortunately, when we assume that a mental "disease" exists and label people "mentally ill," we sometimes increase rather than alleviate their problems. One of the most outspoken critics of the medical model is psychiatrist Thomas Szasz (1960, 1987, 1995). Szasz believes the medical model encourages people to believe they have no responsibility for their actions and that they can find solutions in drugs, hospitalization, or surgery. He contends that mental illness is a "myth" used to label individuals who are peculiar or offensive to others. The medical model does not acknowledge that labels are created in a particular social and cultural context. Furthermore, labels can become self-perpetuating; that is, the person begins behaving according to the diagnosed disorder.

A famous study done by David Rosenhan of Stanford University illustrates problems with diagnostic labels (Rosenhan, 1973). Rosenhan and several colleagues presented themselves to a local mental hospital and complained of hearing voices (a classic symptom of schizophrenia). Although they had no other complaints, they were admitted to the hospital with a diagnosis of schizophrenia. After admission, they stopped their claims of hearing voices and behaved in their normal fashion. The purpose? Rosenhan wanted to see how long it would take the doctors and hospital staff to recognize they were not mentally ill. Surprisingly, none of the pseudopatients was ever recognized as a phony. Once they were inside a mental ward with a label of "schizophrenia," staff members saw only what they expected to see. Interestingly, real patients were not so easily fooled. They were the first to realize that the psychologists were not really mentally ill.

Rosenhan's study offers important insights into problems with labeling mental illness (Hock, 1998). But as you remember from Module 2, the scientific method

TABLE 37.3 FIVE MAJOR PSYCHOLOGICAL PERSPECTIVES ON ABNORMAL BEHAVIOR

Perspective	General Explanation for Abnormal Behavior
Psychoanalytic	Unconscious conflicts
Humanistic	Blocked personal growth
Learning	Inappropriate conditioning or modeling
Cognitive	Faulty thinking
Biological	Problems with neurotransmitters, genes, or brain

requires operational definitions, control groups, single- and double-blind procedures, and replication. Unfortunately, none of these standards were met in the Rosenhan study. Despite its limits, the study does increase our awareness of the dangers of diagnostic labels in mental illness.

Today, the medical model remains a founding principle of psychiatry, and diagnosis and treatment of mental disorders continue to be based on the concept of mental *illness*. In contrast, psychology offers a multifaceted approach to explaining abnormal behavior. Each of the five major perspectives in psychology — psychoanalytic, learning, humanistic, cognitive, and biological — offers alternative explanations. Table 37.3 summarizes these perspectives.

Classifying Abnormal Behaviors: The *Diagnostic and Statistical Manual IV-TR*

Now that we have *identified* and *explained* abnormal behavior from a historical standpoint, we also need a clear and reliable system for *classifying* the wide range of disorders. Just as physicians need agreed-on terms for identifying one set of signs and symptoms as cancer and another as heart disease, psychologists and psychiatrists need agreed-on terms for distinguishing Mary's disruptive behaviors and broken relationships, as described in the opening vignette, from Jim's paranoia. Without a uniform system for classifying and clearly describing psychological disorders, scientific research on them would be almost impossible and communication among mental health professionals would be seriously impaired. Fortunately, mental health specialists do share a uniform classification system, the **Diagnostic and Statistical Manual of Mental Disorders**, fourth edition, text revision (**DSM-IV-TR**) (American Psychiatric Association, 2000), which was developed in coordination with the tenth edition of the World Health Organization's *International Classification of Diseases (ICD-10)*.

Published by the American Psychiatric Association, the *DSM-IV-TR* is much more than a professional reference book for mental health professionals. It has an extraordinary impact on what we learn, diagnose, and treat in the mental health field. For example, the *DSM-IV-TR* serves as the information base for textbooks in psychiatry, psychology, and other mental health fields. In addition, health professionals are often required to use its diagnostic numbers (that match disorders) to get paid by insurance companies. Now, let's examine this *DSM-IV-TR* more closely.

Diagnostic and Statistical Manual of Mental Disorders (DSM-IV-TR) *A classification system, developed by the American Psychiatric Association, used to describe abnormal behaviors; the IV-TR indicates it is the text revision (TR) of the fourth major revision (IV).*

Understanding the DSM

The *DSM-IV-TR* categorizes abnormal behaviors according to major similarities and differences in the way disturbed people behave. For example, the category *mood disorders* includes problems of emotional disturbance (such as depression) and lists the common symptoms associated with subcategories like *major depressive disorders* and *bipolar disorders.*

The *DSM-IV-TR* also carefully describes each disorder, including typical patterns of behavior, thought, and emotion; typical age of onset; predisposing factors; prevalence of the disorder; and cultural issues that help therapists make a diagnosis. This manual does not attempt to explain the causes of disorders or their treatment. It is strictly *descriptive.*

The first edition of the *Diagnostic and Statistical Manual,* now known as *DSM-I,* was published in 1952, the second edition in 1968, and the third edition, *DSM-III,* in 1980. A revised version of *DSM-III* (*DSM-III-R*) was published in 1987. The fourth edition, *DSM-IV,* was published in 1994. A special revised fourth edition, *DSM-IV-TR,* was published in 2000.

Why do they need to keep changing the manual? The major reason for the *DSM* revisions is to incorporate the large volume of new scientific information since the previous edition. Generally, each revision has expanded the list of disorders and changed the descriptions and categories to reflect both the latest in scientific research and changes in the way abnormal behaviors are viewed within our social context (Coolidge & Segal, 1998; Smart & Smart, 1997). For example, the use of the terms **neurosis** and **psychosis** as categories of disorders was significantly revised in *DSM-IV.* In previous editions, *neurosis* was used to describe Freud's idea of the causes of anxiety disorders. He believed anxiety could be felt and expressed directly (through phobias, obsessions, compulsions) or that the unconscious could convert it into bodily complaints (somatoform disorders). But one way or another, all neurotic conditions were believed to reflect repressed anxiety.

Mental health professionals came to feel that Freud's emphasis on unconscious processes was too limiting and the category too large to be maximally useful. In the *DSM-IV,* conditions previously grouped under neurosis were redistributed as anxiety disorders, somatoform disorders, and dissociative disorders. Despite these changes, the term *neurosis* continues as a part of everyday language, and clinicians still use it occasionally when discussing disordered behavior presumed to be due to underlying anxiety.

As with neurosis, the conditions grouped under *psychosis* have been redistributed. Individuals with a psychosis suffer extreme mental disruption and loss of contact with reality. They often have trouble meeting ordinary demands of life, making hospitalization necessary. Schizophrenia, some mood disorders, and some disorders due to medical conditions are recognized as psychoses. Though these disorders are now listed as separate categories, the term *psychosis* is still listed in the *DSM-IV-TR* because it is useful in distinguishing between the most severe mental disorders, where the individual loses contact with reality, and the less disruptive disorders.

What about the term insanity? Where does it fit in? **Insanity** is a legal term indicating that a person cannot be held responsible for his or her actions because of mental illness (Slovenko, 1995). In a criminal case, when a defendant is found not guilty by reason of insanity, that person is considered not responsible for the criminal conduct because a judge or jury determined that mental illness made the defendant unable to appreciate the criminality of the act. In a civil case, a person judged insane is believed to be incapable of conducting his or her affairs in a competent manner. In both criminal and civil cases, the individual may under certain circumstances be involuntarily committed to treatment facilities. The standards and problems of forced treatment and commitment are discussed in Module 45. Keep in mind, however, that despite the enormous amount of attention given to the insanity

Neurosis *A large group of disorders characterized by unrealistic anxiety and other associated problems*

Psychosis *Serious mental disorders characterized by loss of contact with reality and extreme mental disruption; because daily functioning is often impaired, psychotic individuals are more likely to need hospitalization*

Insanity *A legal term for people with a mental disorder that implies a lack of responsibility for their behavior and an inability to manage their affairs*

plea, it is pleaded in less than 1 percent of all cases that reach trial and is rarely successful (Silver, 1995).

The DSM-IV-TR and Modern Times

As a result of continuing scientific research and clinical practice, the current *DSM-IV-TR* is organized according to five major dimensions, called *axes*, which serve as guidelines for making decisions about symptoms (Table 37.4). Disorders are *diagnosed* along Axis I and II. Axis I describes *state disorders* (the patient's current condition, or "state"), whereas Axis II describes *trait disorders* (enduring problems that seem to be an integral part of the self, rather than something a person acquires). Examples of Axis I disorders are anxiety, substance abuse, and depression. Axis II lists long-running personality disturbances (like antisocial personality disorder) and mental retardation.

The other three axes are used to record important supplemental information. Axis III lists medical conditions that may be important to the person's psychopathology (such as diabetes or hypothyroidism, which can affect mood). Axis IV is reserved for psychosocial and environmental stressors that could be contributing to emotional problems (such as job or housing troubles or the death of a family member). Axis V evaluates a person's overall level of functioning, on a scale from 1 (serious attempt at suicide or complete inability to take care of oneself) to 100 (happy, productive, with many interests).

The current *DSM-IV-TR* also contains descriptions of hundreds of disorders grouped into 17 major categories (Table 37.5). Owing to space limitations, this text discusses only 5 of the 17 categories. We explore three of the most common categories — anxiety disorders, mood disorders, and schizophrenia. We also examine the less common, but fascinating, dissociative and personality disorders. Before going on, it is important to note that the *DSM-IV-TR* classifies disorders that people have, *not the people themselves*. To reflect this important distinction, this text (like the *DSM-IV-TR*) avoids the use of terms such as *schizophrenic*. Instead, we use the term *a person with schizophrenia*.

TABLE 37.4 FIVE AXES OF *DSM-IV-TR*[a]

Axis	Description
Axis I: clinical disorders	Symptoms that cause distress or significantly impair social or occupational functioning (such as anxiety disorders, depression)
Axis II: personality disorders and mental retardation	Chronic and enduring problems that generally persist throughout life and impair interpersonal or occupational functioning
Axis III: general medical condition	Physical disorders that may be relevant to understanding or treating a psychological disorder
Axis IV: psychosocial and environmental problems	Problems (such as interpersonal stressors and negative life events) that may affect the diagnosis, treatment, and prognosis of psychological disorders
Axis V: global assessment of functioning	The individual's overall level of functioning in social, occupational, and leisure activities

[a] *Diagnostic Manual of Mental Disorders*, fourth edition, text revision.

Source: Adapted from *DSM-IV-TR*, American Psychiatric Association, Washington, D.C., 2000.

TABLE 37.5 MAIN CATEGORIES OF MENTAL DISORDERS AND THEIR DESCRIPTIONS IN *DSM-IV-TR*[a]

1. Disorders usually first diagnosed in infancy, childhood, or early adolescence: mental retardation, bedwetting, etc.
2. Delirium, dementia, amnestic and other cognitive disorders: problems caused by Alzheimer's, human immunodeficiency virus (acquired immunodeficiency syndrome), Parkinson's, etc.
3. Mental disorders due to a general medical condition not elsewhere classified: problems caused by physical deterioration of the brain due to disease, drugs, etc.

4. Substance-related disorders: problems caused by dependence on alcohol, cocaine, tobacco, and so forth
5. Schizophrenia and other psychotic disorders: a group of disorders characterized by major disturbances in perception, language and thought, emotion, and behavior[b]
6. Mood disorders: problems associated with severe disturbances of mood, such as depression, mania, or alternating episodes of both[b]
7. Anxiety disorders: problems associated with severe anxiety, such as phobias, obsessive-compulsive disorder, and post-traumatic stress disorder[b]

8. Somatoform disorders: problems related to unusual preoccupation with physical health or physical symptoms with no physical cause
9. Factitious disorders: disorders that the individual adopts to satisfy some economic or psychological need

10. Dissociative disorders: disorders in which the normal integration of consciousness, memory, or identity is suddenly and temporarily altered, such as amnesia and dissociative identity disorder[b]

11. Sexual and gender identity disorders: problems related to unsatisfactory sexual activity, finding unusual objects or situations arousing, gender identity problems, and so forth
12. Eating disorders: problems related to food, such as anorexia nervosa, bulimia nervosa, and so forth
13. Sleep disorders: serious disturbances of sleep, such as insomnia, sleep terrors, or hypersomnia
14. Impulse control disorders not elsewhere classified: problems related to kleptomania, pathological gambling, pyromania, and so forth
15. Adjustment disorders: problems related to specific stressors such as divorce, family discord, economic concerns, and so forth

16. Personality disorders: problems related to lifelong behavior patterns such as self-centeredness, overdependency, and antisocial behaviors[b]

17. Other conditions that may be a focus of clinical attention: problems related to physical or sexual abuse, relational problems, occupational problems, and so forth

[a] *Diagnostic Manual of Mental Disorders*, fourth edition, text revision.

[b] Disorders discussed in this chapter.

Source: American Psychiatric Association, 2000.

substance-related disorders

mood disorders

anxiety disorders

Evaluating the DSM-IV-TR

The *DSM-IV* has been praised for carefully and completely describing symptoms, standardizing diagnosis and treatment, facilitating communication among professionals and between professionals and patients, and serving as a valuable educational tool. Critics, on the other hand, suggest it relies too heavily on the medical model and unfairly labels people (Dana, 1998; Roelcke, 1997; Sarbin, 1997). The *DSM-IV* has also been criticized for its possible culture bias. Although it does provide a culture-specific section and a glossary of culture-bound syndromes, the classification of most disorders still reflects a Western European and American perspective (Dana, 1998; Matsumoto, 2000; Smart & Smart, 1997). (Although the 2000 version, *DSM-IV-TR*, is too new for full evaluation, the praise and criticisms of *DSM-IV* should also apply because its changes were confined primarily to updated research.)

Despite its faults, many consider this fourth revision of the *DSM* the most advanced, scientifically based classification system ever developed (Barlow & Durand, 2001; First, Pincus, & Frances, 1999; Nathan & Langenbucher, 1999). As Winston Churchill said about democracy, it is "the worst system devised by the wit of man, except for all the others."

Check & Review

STUDYING PSYCHOLOGICAL DISORDERS

Abnormal behavior refers to patterns of emotion, thought, and action considered pathological for one or more of these reasons: statistical infrequency, disability or dysfunction, personal distress, or violation of norms.

In ancient times, people commonly believed that demons were the cause of abnormal behavior. The **medical model**, which emphasizes diseases and illness, later replaced this demonological model. During the Middle Ages, demonology returned and exorcisms were used to treat abnormal behavior. Toward the close of the Middle Ages, the medical model returned in the form of hospitals known as asylums. Although the medical model still dominates modern times, critics suggest it overlooks the importance of psychological fac-

tors, such as unconscious conflicts, inappropriate learning, faulty cognitive processes, and negative self-concepts.

The *Diagnostic and Statistical Manual of Mental Disorders (DSM-IV-TR)* categorizes disorders according to major similarities and differences in the way disturbed people behave. *DSM-IV-TR* classification provides detailed descriptions of symptoms, which in turn allow standardized diagnosis and treatment, and improved communication among professionals and between professionals and patients.

The *DSM* has been criticized for not paying sufficient attention to cultural factors, for continuing to support the medical model, and for labeling people. Misdiagnosis also occurs, and the label *mentally ill* can lead to social and economic discrimination.

Questions

1. What are the four major standards for identifying abnormal behavior?

2. In early treatment of abnormal behavior, _____ was used to allow evil spirits to escape, whereas _____ was designed to make the body so uncomfortable it would be uninhabitable by the devil. (a) purging, fasting; (b) trephining, exorcism; (c) demonology, hydrotherapy; (d) the medical model, the dunking test

3. Briefly define *neurosis*, *psychosis*, and *insanity*.

4. What are the chief advantages and disadvantages of the *DSM* system of classifying mental disorders?

Answers to Questions can be found in Appendix B.

MODULE 37   ACTIVE LEARNING WORKSHEET

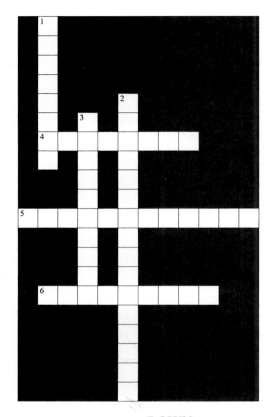

ACROSS

4. Legal term implying a lack of responsibility for behavior and an inability to manage one's affairs.

5. Perspective that assumes diseases have physical causes.

6. Loss of contact with reality and extreme mental disruption.

DOWN

1. Group of disorders characterized by unrealistic anxiety.

2. Patterns of emotion, thought, and action considered pathological.

3. Branch of medicine that deals with the diagnosis, treatment, and prevention of mental disorders.

Answers can be found in Appendix B.

MODULE 38
ANXIETY DISORDERS

Maria, A 25-year-old legal secretary, was about to leave her office one evening when she was suddenly overwhelmed by intense feelings of anxiety. Believing that something dreadful was going to happen to her, she became flushed and found it difficult to breathe — almost as though she were choking. She stumbled outside for some fresh air and the feelings gradually subsided. As Maria later described her terror, "It could not be worse if I were hanging by my fingertips from the wing of a plane in flight. The feeling of impending doom was just as real and frightening."

Fishman & Sheehan, 1985; p. 26

What are anxiety disorders and what causes them?

Maria and other people with an **anxiety disorder** share one central defining characteristic — unreasonable, often paralyzing, anxiety or fear. They feel threatened, ineffective, unhappy, and insecure in a world that seems dangerous and hostile. Anxiety disorders are the most frequently occurring category of mental disorders in the general population, and they are found about twice as often in women as men (Margolis & Swartz, 2001; National Institute of Mental Health, 1999).

Anxiety Disorder *Type of abnormal behavior characterized by unrealistic, irrational fear*

Unreasonable Anxiety: Five Major Anxiety Disorders

Symptoms of anxiety, such as rapid breathing, dry mouth, and increased heart rate, plague all of us during final exams, first dates, and visits to the dentist. But some people experience unreasonable anxiety that is so intense and chronic it seriously disrupts their lives. We will consider five major types of anxiety disorders: *generalized anxiety disorder*, *panic disorder* (Maria's diagnosis), *phobia*, *obsessive-compulsive disorder*, and *post-traumatic stress disorder*. Although we discuss these disorders separately, it is important to remember that people with one anxiety disorder often have others (Barlow, Esler, & Vitali, 1998).

Generalized Anxiety Disorder

Generalized anxiety disorder is a common chronic problem that affects twice as many women as men and leads to considerable impairment (Brawman-Mintzer & Lydiard, 1996, 1997). As the name implies, **generalized anxiety disorder** is characterized by long-lasting anxiety that is not focused on any particular object or situation. In other words, it is *unspecific* or *free-floating*. People with this disorder feel afraid of *something* but are unable to articulate the specific fear. They fret constantly and have a hard time controlling their worries. Because of persistent muscle tension and autonomic fear reactions, they may develop headaches, heart palpitations, dizziness, and insomnia. These physical complaints, combined with the intense, long-term anxiety, make it difficult to cope with normal daily activities.

Generalized Anxiety Disorder *Type of anxiety disorder characterized by chronic, uncontrollable, and excessive worry; the anxiety is not focused on any particular object or situation*

Panic Disorder

Panic disorder is even more troubling than generalized anxiety disorder. In **panic disorder**, the person suffers sudden but brief *attacks* of intense apprehension that cause trembling and shaking, dizziness, and difficulty breathing. Maria's sense of being "suddenly overwhelmed by intense feelings of anxiety" and feeling like she was choking are characteristic of panic attacks. The American Psychiatric Association (2000) defines a *panic attack* as fear or discomfort that arises abruptly and peaks in 10 minutes or less. Although panic attacks seem to occur out of nowhere, they generally happen after frightening experiences, prolonged stress, and even exercise. Many people

Panic Disorder *Type of anxiety disorder characterized by sudden and inexplicable attacks of intense fear; symptoms include difficulty breathing, heart palpitations, dizziness, trembling, terror, and feelings of impending doom*

who have occasional panic attacks interpret them correctly—as a result of a passing crisis or stress. Unfortunately, others begin to worry excessively and some may even quit jobs or refuse to leave home to avoid future attacks. It is labeled *panic disorder* when several apparently spontaneous panic attacks lead to a persistent concern about future attacks. A common complication of panic disorder is *agoraphobia*—anxiety about being in a place or situation where escape is difficult or embarrassing (Craske, 2000; Gorman, 2000). Phobias are the topic of our next section.

Phobia

Phobia *Type of anxiety disorder characterized by intense, irrational fear and avoidance of a specific object or situation*

Phobias involve a strong, irrational fear and avoidance of an object or situation. The person knows the fear is irrational, yet the anxiety remains. Phobic disorders differ from generalized anxiety disorders and panic disorders because there is a specific stimulus or situation that elicits the strong fear response. Imagine how it would feel to be so frightened by a spider that you would try to jump out of a speeding car to get away from it. This is how a person suffering from phobia might feel.

People with phobias have especially powerful imaginations, so they vividly anticipate terrifying consequences from encountering such feared objects as knives, bridges, blood, enclosed places, or certain animals. These individuals recognize their fears are excessive and unreasonable but are generally unable to control their anxiety.

In addition to *specific phobias*, such as fears of knives, rats, or spiders, there is another category of phobias known as *social phobias*. Individuals with this disorder experience intense fear of being negatively evaluated by others or of being publicly embarrassed because of impulsive acts. Almost everyone experiences "stage fright" when speaking or performing in front of a group. But people with social phobias become so anxious that performance is out of the question. In fact, their fear of public scrutiny and potential humiliation becomes so pervasive that normal life is impossible (den Boer, 2000; Margolis & Swartz, 2001).

A related Japanese social phobia is *taijin kyofusho* (TKS), which loosely translates as "fear of people." But it is not a fear that people will criticize you, as in the American disorder. The Japanese disorder is a morbid dread that you will do something to embarrass others. TKS does not exist in Western cultures (Kleinknecht, Dinnel, & Kleinknecht, 1997). In the United States, "we don't think of the fear of embarrassing other people as a psychological syndrome" (cited in Goleman, 1995, p. C-3). But it is so common in Japan that TKS treatment centers, like weight clinics in the United States, are on almost every corner. The difference between Western social phobias and TKS exemplifies again how individualist cultures (like ours) emphasize the individual, whereas collectivist cultures (like Japan) focus on others.

Obsessive-Compulsive Disorder

Obsessive-Compulsive Disorder *Type of anxiety disorder characterized by intrusive thoughts (obsessions), urges to perform repetitive, ritualistic behaviors (compulsions), or both*

Do you remember the movie As Good As It Gets? The main character, portrayed by Jack Nicholson, was endlessly counting, checking locks, and repeatedly washing his hands in a seemingly senseless, ritualistic pattern. What's drives this behavior? The answer is **obsessive-compulsive disorder** (OCD), which involves persistent, unwanted thoughts (*obsessions*), irresistible urges to perform an act or repeated ritual (*compulsions*), or both. In adults, this disorder is equally common in men and women, however it is more prevalent among boys when the onset is in childhood (American Psychiatric Association, 2000).

Consider the case of billionaire Howard Hughes:

Due to his unreasonable fear of germs, he made people who worked with him wear white gloves, sometimes several pairs, when handling documents he would later touch. When newspapers were brought to him, they had to be in stacks of three so he could slide the middle one out by grasping it with Kleenex. To escape contami-

As good as it gets. In this film, Jack Nicholson portrays a character struggling with obsessive-compulsive disorder.

nation by dust, he ordered that masking tape be put around the doors and windows of his cars and houses.

FOWLER (1986)

I sometimes find myself worrying about germs and what others might have touched. Would this be considered an obsessive-compulsive disorder? Many people have obsessive thoughts or find they occasionally check stove burners, count steps, or clean their homes and offices past the point of normal standards. People even casually refer to this as "being OC" or "anal." The difference between an OCD and milder forms of obsession and compulsion is that with OCD the repetitive thoughts and ritualistic actions become *uncontrollable* and seriously interfere with a person's life.

For example, a woman with OCD who worries obsessively about germs might compulsively wash her hands hundreds of times a day until they are raw and bleeding. A man might each night check the lights, locks, oven, and furnace 10 times in a ritualistic pattern before he can go to sleep. Most sufferers of OCD do not enjoy these rituals and realize that their actions are senseless. But when they try to stop the behavior, they experience mounting anxiety that is relieved only by giving in to the urges. They simply cannot stop themselves.

Concerned family and friends generally understand that the person cannot stop their obsessions and compulsions, but they also may feel irritated, confused, and resentful. As with other psychological disorders, therapists may recommend family counseling as well as individual therapies.

Post-traumatic Stress Disorder

The essential feature of **post-traumatic stress disorder** (PTSD) is severe anxiety that develops after experiencing a traumatic event (such as rape, natural disaster, war), learning about a violent or unexpected death of a family member, or even being a witness or bystander to violence (American Psychiatric Association, 2000; Brewin, Andrews, Rose, & Kirk, 1999). Symptoms include feelings of terror and helplessness during the trauma and recurrent flashbacks, nightmares, impaired concentration,

Post-traumatic Stress Disorder (PTSD) *Type of anxiety disorder following exposure to a life-threatening or other extreme event that evoked great horror or helplessness; it is characterized by flashbacks, nightmares, and impaired functioning*

and/or emotional numbing afterward. Symptoms may continue for years after the event itself.

Although PTSD has received much attention, there is considerable controversy over its prevalence and diagnosis (Keane, Taylor, & Penk, 1997). Some experts believe the largest single group of PTSD sufferers is female sexual assault and abuse victims (New & Berliner, 2000; Seedat & Stein, 2000). Kilpatrick et al. (1985) surveyed more than 2,000 adult women who had experienced various traumas, such as rape, sexual molestation, robbery, and aggravated assault. The women were asked if they had thought about suicide after the trauma, attempted suicide, or had a nervous breakdown. (*Nervous breakdown* is a lay term for severe psychological upset, but it has no official clinical meaning.) The crime with the most significant emotional impact was rape. Forty-four percent of rape victims reported suicidal thoughts, and 19.2 percent had attempted suicide.

Causes of Anxiety Disorders: Multiple Roots

The causes of anxiety disorders is a matter of considerable debate, but recent research has focused primarily on the roles of learning, biology, and cognitive processes.

Learning

The learning perspective on anxiety disorders suggests that phobias and other reactions are the result of conditioning (both classical and operant conditioning) and social learning (both modeling and imitation) (Chorpita & Barlow, 1998; King, Clowes-Hollins, & Ollendick, 1997). (See Module 16 for a review of these terms.)

During classical conditioning, for example, a stimulus that is originally neutral (e.g., the office building in Maria's case) becomes paired with a frightening event (the sudden panic attack) so that it becomes a conditioned stimulus that elicits anxiety. After this kind of classical conditioning, the phobia is typically maintained through operant conditioning. Maria begins to avoid the anxiety-producing stimulus (her office) because avoiding the stimulus reduces the unpleasant feelings of anxiety (a process known as negative reinforcement) (Figure 38.1).

Figure 38.1 *Explaining Maria's phobia.* According to the learning perspective, Maria's phobia (described in the introduction) developed as a result of classical and operant conditioning. In classical conditioning terms, the initial panic attack was paired with the office building where she worked, and a conditioned response (CR) of fear and anxiety developed. Maria's phobia was maintained through operant conditioning — avoiding the office led to reduced fear, which in turn reinforced her phobia. CS-conditioned stimulus; UCS-unconditioned stimulus.

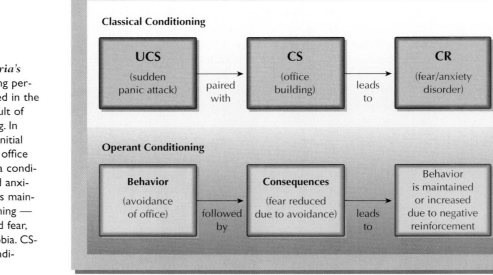

Social-learning theorists propose that some phobias are the result of modeling and imitation. Vulnerability for PTSD, for example, tends to increase when an immediate family member suffers from depression (American Psychiatric Association, 2000). Also, can you see how overprotective, fearful parents may make their children more prone to developing phobias and other anxiety disorders? Howard Hughes's mother, for instance, was extremely protective and worried constantly about his physical health.

Phobias may also develop vicariously (in an indirect, secondhand way). For example, one research team showed videotapes to four groups of rhesus monkeys (Cook & Mineka, 1989). The tapes were spliced together in a special way to show another monkey apparently experiencing extreme fear of a toy snake, a toy rabbit, a toy crocodile, and flowers. The "viewing" monkeys were later afraid of the toy snake and crocodile but not of the toy rabbit or flowers, which suggests that phobias have both a learned and biological component.

Vicarious phobias. Monkeys who watch artificially created videotapes of other monkeys being afraid of either a toy snake, toy rabbit, toy crocodile, or flowers will develop their own set of phobias. The fact that the viewing monkeys only develop fears of snakes and crocodiles demonstrates that phobias are both learned and biological.

Biology

The fact that the rhesus monkeys selectively learned their phobias may mean that we have an evolutionary predisposition to fear what was dangerous to our ancestors, such as snakes and crocodiles (Cartwright, 2000). Recent studies show that anxiety disorders may also have a genetic predisposition or may result from disrupted biochemistry or unusual brain activity (American Psychiatric Association, 2000; Bryant & Harvey, 1998; Fones, Manfro, & Pollack, 1998). For example, twin and family studies shows that some individuals with panic disorder seem to be genetically predisposed toward an overreaction of the autonomic nervous system (Kendler, Karkowski, & Prescott, 1999; Schmidt, Lerew, & Jackson, 1999). These people apparently respond more quickly and intensely to stressful stimuli than others. Stress and arousal also seems to play a role in panic attacks. For example, drugs such as caffeine or nicotine or even hyperventilation (breathing deeper and faster than normal) can trigger an attack, which also suggests a biochemical disturbance (Breslau & Klein, 1999; Yudolfsky & Silver, 1987).

Cognitive Processes

Cognitive approaches to anxiety disorders focus on the distorted thinking that causes people to magnify ordinary threats and failures. Most people are anxious in a public speaking situation, but those who are socially phobic are excessively concerned about others' evaluation, hypersensitive to any criticism, and obsessively worried about potential mistakes. This intense self-preoccupation not only intensifies the social anxiety but also leads socially phobic people to think they have failed — even when they have been successful. As you will see in Module 44, changing the thinking patterns of anxious people can greatly lessen their fears (Margolis & Swartz, 2001).

Check & Review

ANXIETY DISORDERS

People with **anxiety disorders** have persistent feelings of threat in facing everyday problems. **Phobias** are exaggerated fears of specific objects or situations, such as agoraphobia, a fear of being in open spaces. In **generalized anxiety disorders**, there is a persistent free-floating anxiety. In **panic disorder**, anxiety is concentrated into brief or lengthy episodes of panic attacks. In **obsessive-compulsive disorder**, persistent anxiety-arousing thoughts (obsessions) are relieved by ritualistic actions (compulsions) such as hand washing. In **post-traumatic stress disorder** (PTSD), a person who has experienced an overwhelming trauma, such as rape, has recurrent maladaptive emotional reactions, such as exaggerated startle responses, sleep disturbances, and flashbacks.

Three common explanations for anxiety disorders are learning, biology, and cognitive processes. Learning theorists suggest anxiety disorders result from classical and operant conditioning, as well as modeling and imitation, whereas the biological perspective emphasizes genetic predisposition, brain abnormalities, and biochemistry. The cognitive approach proposes that distorted thinking causes an amplification of ordinary threats.

Questions

1. Match the descriptions below with the following specific forms of anxiety disorder: (a) generalized anxiety disorder; (b) panic disorder; (c) phobia; (d) obsessive-compulsive disorder (OCD); (e) post-traumatic stress disorder (PTSD)

_____ i. Develops from an overwhelming, traumatic event

_____ ii. Characterized by severe attacks of extreme anxiety

_____ iii. Long-term anxiety that is not focused on any particular object or situation

_____ iv. Characterized by irrational fear of an object or situation

_____ v. Characterized by intrusive thoughts and urges to perform repetitive, ritualistic behaviors

2. How do learning theorists and social-learning theorists explain anxiety disorders?

3. Researchers believe that anxiety disorders are probably due to some combination of _____.

Answers to Review Questions can be found in Appendix B.

MODULE 38   ACTIVE LEARNING WORKSHEET

Complete the following, and then double-check your answers with those in Appendix B.

1. _____ is characterized by chronic, free-floating worry; whereas, _____ is exemplified by sudden and inexplicable attacks of anxiety.

2. _____ involve a strong, irrational fear of a specific object or situation, and _____ is anxiety about being somewhere where escape is difficult or embarrassing.

3. Irresistible urges to perform an act or ritual are known as _____; whereas _____ involve persistent, unwanted thoughts.

4. _____ develops after a traumatic event; whereas, _____ is a lay term for severe psychological upset.

5. The fact that rhesus monkeys selectively learn specific phobias suggests an _____ to fear what was dangerous to our ancestors.

MODULE 39
MOOD DISORDERS

Ann had been divorced for eight months when she called a psychologist for an emergency appointment. Although her husband had verbally and physically abused her for years, she had had mixed feelings about staying in the marriage. She had anticipated feeling good after the divorce, but she became increasingly depressed. She had trouble sleeping, had little appetite, felt very fatigued, and showed no interest in her usual activities. She stayed home from work for two days because she "just didn't feel like going in." Late one afternoon she went straight to bed, leaving her two small children to fend for themselves. Then, the night before calling for an emergency therapy appointment, she took five sleeping tablets and a couple of stiff drinks. As she said, "I don't think I wanted to kill myself; I just wanted to forget everything for a while."

Meyer & Salmon, 1988; p. 312

Ann's case is a good example of a *mood disorder* (also known as an *affective disorder*). This category encompasses not only excessive sadness like Ann's but also unreasonable elation and hyperactivity.

> **When do disturbances in mood become abnormal?**

Understanding Mood Disorders: Major Depressive Disorder and Bipolar Disorder

As the name implies, mood disorders are characterized by extreme disturbances in emotional states. There are two main types of mood disorders — *major depressive disorder* and *bipolar disorder*.

Major Depressive Disorder

Depression has been recorded as far back as ancient Egypt, when the condition was called melancholia and was treated by priests. Most everyone feels "blue" sometimes, especially following the loss of a job, end of a relationship, or death of a loved one. People suffering from **major depressive disorder**, however, may experience a lasting and continuously depressed mood without a clear trigger or precipitating event. In addition, their sadness is far more intense, interfering with their basic ability to function, feel pleasure, or maintain interest in life (Margolis & Swartz, 2001).

Clinically depressed people are so deeply sad and discouraged that they often have trouble sleeping, are likely to lose (or gain) weight, and may feel so fatigued that they cannot go to work or school or even comb their hair and brush their teeth. They may sleep both day and night, have problems concentrating, and feel so profoundly sad and guilty that they consider suicide. These feelings are without apparent cause and may be so severe that the individual loses contact with reality. As in the case of Ann, depressed individuals have a hard time thinking clearly or recognizing their own problems, but family or friends who recognize the symptoms can encourage them to seek professional help.

Major Depressive Disorder *A diagnostic term, from the Diagnostic and Statistical Manual of Mental Disorders, fourth edition, text revision, for individuals experiencing a long-lasting depressed mood that interferes with the ability to function, feel pleasure, or maintain interest in life; the feelings are without apparent cause and excessive to the given situation*

Bipolar Disorder

When depression ends, most people return to a "normal" emotional level. Some people, however, rebound to the opposite state, known as *mania*. In **bipolar disorder**, the person experiences periods of depression, *mania* (an excessive and unreasonable state of over-excitement and impulsive behavior), and normal moods (Figure 39.1).

Bipolar Disorder *A diagnostic term in the DSM-IV-TR, for individuals who experience episodes of mania or of both mania and depression; excessive and unreasonable elation and hyperactivity characterize manic episodes*

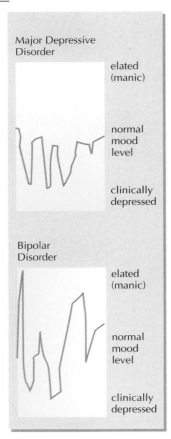

Figure 39.1 *Mood disorders.* If major depressive disorders and bipolar disorders were depicted on a graph, they might look something like this.

During a manic episode, the person is overly excited, extremely active, and distractible. The person exhibits an unrealistically high self-esteem and an inflated sense of importance or even delusions of grandeur. He or she often makes elaborate plans for becoming rich and famous. The individual is hyperactive and may not sleep for days at a time yet does not become fatigued. Thinking is speeded up and can change abruptly to new topics, showing "rapid flight of ideas." Speech is also rapid ("pressured speech"), and it is difficult to get a word in edgewise. Poor judgment is common: A person may give away valuable possessions or go on wild spending sprees.

Manic episodes may last a few days to a few months and generally end abruptly. The person's previous manic mood, rapid thinking and speaking style, and hyperactivity are reversed, and the following depressive episode generally lasts three times as long as the manic episode. The lifetime risk for bipolar disorder is low — somewhere between 0.5 and 1.6 percent — but it can be one of the most debilitating and lethal disorders, with a suicide rate between 10 and 20 percent (Goodwin & Ghaemi, 1998; MacKinnon, Jamison, & DePaulo, 1997).

Causes of Mood Disorders: Biological versus Psychosocial Factors

Numerous studies and theories attempt to explain major depressive disorder and bipolar disorder. Most can be categorized as either biological or psychosocial.

Biological Factors

Biological factors play a significant role in both major depression and bipolar disorder. Recent research shows the left frontal lobe, which is active during positive emotions, is inactive during depressive episodes (Davidson, 1999). Other research has identified a small area in the prefrontal cortex that may trigger both the sadness of depression and the mania of bipolar disorders (Liotti & Mayberg, 2001; Steffens & Krishnan, 1998).

Several lines of research also suggest that depression and mania may be caused by imbalances of the neurotransmitters norepinephrine and serotonin (Bellivier et al., 1998; Mann et al., 2000). This makes sense because these same neurotransmitters are involved in the capacity to be aroused or energized and in the control of other functions affected by depression such as sleep cycles and hunger. Moreover, drugs that alter the activity of these neurotransmitters also decrease the symptoms of depression (and hence are called *antidepressants*). The drug *lithium* reduces or prevents manic episodes by preventing norepinephrine and serotonin sensitive neurons from being overstimulated (Chuang, 1998).

There also is evidence that major depressive disorders, as well as bipolar disorders, may be inherited (Dubovsky & Buzan, 1999; Meltzer, 2000). For example, when one identical twin has a mood disorder, there is about a 50 percent chance that the other twin will also develop the illness (Margolis & Swartz, 2001). It is important to remember, however, that relatives generally have similar environments, as well as similar genes.

Psychosocial Theories

Psychosocial theories of depression focus on disturbances in the person's interpersonal relationships, thought processes, self-concept, and learning history (Agid et al., 1999; Rice & Mirzadeh, 2000). The psychoanalytic explanation sees depression as anger turned inward against oneself when an important relationship or attachment is lost. Anger is assumed to come from feelings of rejection or withdrawal of affection, especially when a loved one dies. The humanistic school says depression results when a person's self-concept is overly demanding or when positive growth is blocked.

The **learned helplessness** theory of depression, developed by Martin Seligman (1975, 1994), is an outgrowth of research on avoidance learning in animals. Seligman has demonstrated that when animals or humans are subjected to pain that they cannot escape; they develop a sense of helplessness or resignation and thereafter do not attempt to escape painful experiences. In other words, the perception that one is unable to change things for the better leads to depression. Seligman also suggests that our general societal emphasis on individualism and diminished involvement with others makes us particularly vulnerable to depression.

The learned helplessness theory may also involve a cognitive element, known as *attribution*, or the explanations people assign to their own and other's behavior. Once someone perceives that his or her behaviors are unrelated to outcomes (learned helplessness), depression is likely to occur. This is particularly true if the person attributes failure to causes that are *internal* ("my own weakness"), *stable* ("this weakness is long-standing and unchanging"), and *global* ("this weakness is a problem in lots of settings") (Barlow, 1999; Gotlieb & Abramson, 1999).

Learned Helplessness *In Martin Seligman's theory, a state of helplessness or resignation in which people or animals learn that escape from something painful is impossible and depression results*

GENDER & CULTURAL DIVERSITY

Gender, Culture, and Depression

Research shows certain symptoms of depression seem to exist across cultures: (1) frequent and intense sad affect, (2) decreased enjoyment, (3) anxiety, (4) difficulty in concentrating, and (5) lack of energy (Green, 1999; World Health Organization, 2000). On the other hand, there is evidence of some culture-specific symptoms. For example, feelings of guilt are found more often in North America and Europe. In China, *somatization* (converting depression into bodily complaints) is more frequent than in other parts of the world (Helms & Cook, 1999).

Not only does culture have an impact on depression but so does gender. It is widely accepted that women are more likely than men to suffer depressive symptoms. In North America, the rate of clinical (or severe) depression for women is two to three times the rate for men, and this ratio holds true in several other countries as well (Desai & Jann, 2000; Nolen-Hoeksema, Larson, & Grayson, 2000).

Why Are Women More Depressed?

Studies suggest the higher rate of female depression may be due to both biological factors (hormones and genes) and environmental stressors (poverty, discrimination, unhappy marriages, and sexual or physical abuse) (Culbertson, 1997; Desai & Jann, 2000; Schmidt, Fava, Robinson, & Judge, 2000). Other researchers suggest that thinking patterns and socialization processes for men and women reinforce certain behaviors that predispose women toward depression (Alloy et al., 1999; Nolen-Hoeksema, Larson, & Grayson, 2000). Women are encouraged toward passivity, dependence, and emotional sensitivity, whereas men are socialized toward activity, independence, and suppression of emotions. Because depression is related to lack of activity, low energy, and feelings of helplessness, it is not surprising that women may be more depressed than men. The greater degree of aggression found in men may also mean that they act out their depression rather than withdrawing or blaming themselves. Finally, the higher level of substance abuse among men may also mask underlying depression.

Suicide: Ending Your Own Life

Whatever the causes of depression, one of the major dangers associated with it is the increased risk of suicide. Severely depressed people often become suicidal because they feel hopeless and helpless.

TRY THIS
Yourself

Decide whether each of the following is true or false:

1. People who talk about suicide are not likely to commit suicide.
2. Suicide usually takes place with little or no warning.
3. Suicidal people are fully intent on dying.
4. Children of parents who attempt suicide are at greater risk of committing suicide.
5. Suicidal people remain so forever.
6. Men are more likely than women to actually kill themselves by suicide.
7. When a suicidal person has been severely depressed and seems to be "snapping out of it," the danger of suicide decreases substantially.
8. Only depressed people commit suicide.
9. Thinking about suicide is rare.
10. Asking a depressed person about suicide will push him or her over the edge and cause a suicidal act that would not otherwise have occurred.

Now let's look at the experts' answers to these questions (Bostwick & Pankratz, 2000; Davison & Neale, 2001; Garland & Zigler, 1999; Jamison & Baldessarini, 1999; Oquendo & Mann, 2000):

1. *and* 2. **False.** About 90 percent of people who are suicidal talk about their intentions. They may say, "If something happens to me, I want you to…" or "Life just isn't worth living." They also leave behavioral clues, such as giving away valued possessions, withdrawing from family and friends, and losing interest in favorite activities.

3. **False.** Only about 3 to 5 percent of suicidal people truly intend to die. Most are just unsure about how to go on living. They cannot see their problems objectively enough to realize that they have alternative courses of action. They often gamble with death, arranging it so that fate or others will save them. Moreover, once the suicidal crisis passes, they are generally grateful to be alive.

4. **True.** Children of parents who attempt or commit suicide are at much greater risk of following in their footsteps. As Schneidman (1969) puts it, "The person who commits suicide puts his psychological skeleton in the survivor's emotional closet" (p. 22).

5. **False.** People who want to kill themselves are usually suicidal only for a limited period.

6. **True.** Although women are much more likely to attempt suicide, men are more likely to actually commit suicide. Men are more likely to use stronger methods, such as guns versus pills.

7. **False.** When people are first coming out of a depression, they are actually at greater risk because they now have the energy to actually commit suicide.

8. **False.** Although suicide rates are highest for people with major depressive disorders, suicide is also the leading cause of premature death in people who suffer from schizophrenia. Suicide is also a major cause of death in people with anxiety disorders and alcohol and other substance-related disorders. Suicide is not limited to people with depression. Poor physical health, serious illness, substance abuse (particularly alcohol), loneliness, unemployment, and even natural disasters may push many over the edge.

9. **False.** Estimates from various studies find that 40 to 80 percent of the general public has thought about committing suicide at least once in their lives.

10. **False.** Because society often considers suicide a terrible, shameful act, asking directly about it can give the person permission to talk. In fact, *not asking* might lead to further isolation and depression.

How can you tell if someone is suicidal? If you believe someone is contemplating suicide, act on your beliefs. Stay with the person if there is any immediate danger, and encourage him or her to talk to you rather than withdraw. Show the person that

you care, but do not give false reassurances that "everything will be okay." This type of response makes the suicidal person feel *more* alienated. Instead, openly ask if the person is feeling hopeless and suicidal. Do not be afraid to discuss suicide with people who feel depressed or hopeless, fearing that you will just put ideas into their heads. The reality is that people who are left alone or who are told they can't be serious about suicide often attempt it.

If you suspect someone is suicidal, it is vitally important that you help the person obtain counseling. Most cities have suicide prevention centers with 24-hour hotlines or walk-in centers that provide emergency counseling. Also, share your suspicions with parents, friends, or others who can help in a suicidal crisis. To save a life, you may have to betray a secret when someone confides in you.

More than 2,000 American teens will end their life this year (Time, May 15, 2000, Vol.155, No. 20)

Warning Signs

- **Significant changes in a teen's eating or sleeping patterns**
- **Decline in school performance**
- **Dramatic change in personality or appearance**
- **Drug or alcohol abuse**
- **Obsession with death**
- **Withdrawal from friends, family and regular activities**
- **Profound guilt or hopelessness**
- **"Cleaning house" by giving away favorite possessions**

Check & Review

MOOD DISORDERS

Mood disorders are disturbances of affect (emotion) that may include psychotic distortions of reality. In **major depressive disorder**, individuals experience a long-lasting depressed mood, feelings of worthlessness, and loss of interest in most activities. The feelings are without apparent cause and the individual may lose contact with reality. In **bipolar disorder**, episodes of mania and depression alternate with normal periods. During the manic episode, speech and thinking are rapid, and the person may experience delusions of grandeur and act impulsively.

Biological theories of mood disorders emphasize disruptions in neurotransmitters (especially dopamine and serotonin).

There is also evidence of a genetic predisposition for both major depression and bipolar disorder.

Psychosocial theories of mood disorders emphasize disturbed interpersonal relationships, faulty thinking, poor self-concept, and maladaptive learning. **Learned helplessness** theory suggests that depression results from repeatedly failing to escape from a source of stress. Suicide is a serious problem associated with depression, but we can reduce the risk by becoming involved and showing concern.

Questions

1. The two main types of mood disorders are _____. (a) major depression, bipolar disorder; (b) mania, depression; (c) SAD, MAD; (d) learned helplessness, suicide

2. A major difference between major depressive disorder and bipolar disorder is that only in bipolar disorders do people have _____. (a) hallucinations or delusions; (b) depression; (c) manic episodes; (d) a biochemical imbalance

3. What is Martin Seligman's learned helplessness theory of depression?

4. Briefly explain why women are diagnosed with depression more often than men are.

Answers to Questions can be found in Appendix B.

MODULE 39   ACTIVE LEARNING WORKSHEET

Circle either "T" for true or "F" for false, and then compare your answers with those in Appendix B.

1 . Long-lasting depression that interferes with ability to function, feel pleasure, or maintain interest in life is known as major mood dysfunction. T or F

2 . In bipolar disorder, the person alternates between depression and mania. T or F

3 . Both depression and mania may be caused by imbalances of norepinephrine and serotonin. T or F

4 . When one identical twin has a mood disorder, there is about a 20 % chance that the other twin will also develop the illness. T or F

5 . People who believe their behavior is unrelated to life outcomes are less likely to become depressed. T or F

MODULE 40
SCHIZOPHRENIA

What are the symptoms and causes of schizophrenia?

Imagine for the moment that your daughter has just left for college and you hear voices inside your head shouting, "You'll never see her again! You have been a bad mother! She'll die." Or what if you saw dinosaurs on the street and live animals in your refrigerator? These are actual experiences that have plagued Mrs. T for almost 3 decades (Gershon & Rieder, 1993).

Mrs. T suffers from **schizophrenia**, a disorder characterized by major disturbances in perception, language, thought, emotion, and behavior. All the disorders we have considered so far cause considerable distress, but most sufferers can still function in daily life. Schizophrenia, however, is a form of *psychosis*, a term describing general lack of contact with reality. People with schizophrenia have serious problems caring for themselves, relating to others, and holding a job. In extreme cases, because they lack contact with reality, people with schizophrenia may require institutional or custodial care. To make matters worse, substance abuse rates are very high, perhaps reflecting an attempt to self-medicate (Batel, 2000; Green, 2000).

Schizophrenia is generally considered the most serious and severe form of mental disturbance. According to statistics, 1 of every 100 people develops schizophrenia and approximately half of all people admitted to mental hospitals are diagnosed with schizophrenia (Gottesman, 1991; Kendler, Gallagher, Abelson, & Kessler, 1996; Regier et al., 1993). The disorder usually emerges between the late teens and the mid-thirties and only rarely prior to adolescence or after age 45 (American Psychiatric Association, 2000).

Is schizophrenia the same as "split personality?" No. Schizophrenia means "split mind," but when Eugen Bleuler coined the term in 1911, he was referring to the fragmenting of thought processes and emotions found in schizophrenic disorders (Neale, Oltmanns, & Winters, 1983). Unfortunately, "split mind" and "split personality" are often confused by the general public. One study of college freshmen found that 64 percent thought having multiple personalities was a common symptom of schizophrenia (Torrey, 1998). But as you will read later, *multiple personality disorder* (now known as *dissociative identity disorder*) is the rare condition of having more than one distinct personality. Schizophrenia is a much more common — and altogether different — type of psychological disorder. What are the symptoms of schizophrenia? What are its causes? And how does it differ cross-culturally?

Symptoms of Schizophrenia: Five Areas of Disturbance

Schizophrenia is characterized by psychological disturbances in five areas: perception, language, thought, affect (or emotions), and behavior.

Perceptual Symptoms

The senses of people with schizophrenia may be either enhanced (as in the case of Mrs. T) or blunted. The filtering and selection processes that allow most people to concentrate on whatever they choose are impaired, and sensory stimulation is jumbled and distorted. One patient reported:

> When people are talking, I just get scraps of it. If it is just one person who is speaking, that's not so bad, but if others join in then I can't pick it up at all. I just can't

Schizophrenia *Group of psychotic disorders involving major disturbances in perception, language, thought, emotion, and behavior; the individual withdraws from people and reality, often into a fantasy life of delusions and hallucinations*

Symptoms of schizophrenia? Disorganized thoughts, emotions, and perceptions are sometimes reflected in the artwork of people suffering from schizophrenia.

get in tune with the conversation. It makes me feel all open — as if things are closing in on me and I have lost control.

McGhie and Chapman, 1961, p. 106

Hallucinations *Sensory perceptions that occur without an external stimulus*

People with schizophrenia also experience **hallucinations** — they perceive things without external stimuli. Hallucinations can occur in any of the senses (visual, tactile, olfactory), but auditory hallucinations (hearing voices and sounds) are most common in schizophrenia. As with Mrs. T, people with schizophrenia often hear voices speaking their thoughts aloud, commenting on their behavior, or telling them what to do. The voices seem to come from inside their own heads or from an external source such as an animal, telephone wires, or a TV set.

On rare occasions, people with schizophrenia will hurt others in response to their distorted internal experiences or the voices they hear. Unfortunately, these cases receive undue media attention and create exaggerated fears of "mental patients." In reality, a person with schizophrenia is most likely self-destructive and at greater risk of suicide than of violence toward others.

Language and Thought Disturbances

For people with schizophrenia, words lose their usual meanings and associations, logic is impaired, and thoughts are disorganized and bizarre. For example, a patient with schizophrenia gave this explanation for the meaning of the proverb "People who live in glass houses shouldn't throw stones":

> People who live in glass houses shouldn't forget people who live in stone houses and shouldn't throw glass.

When language and thought disturbances are mild, an individual with schizophrenia jumps from topic to topic. In more severe disturbances, phrases and words are jumbled together (referred to as *word salad*), and the person creates artificial words (*neologisms*). Table 40.1 presents examples of these language variations.

Delusions *Mistaken beliefs maintained in spite of strong evidence to the contrary*

The most common thought disturbances experienced by people with schizophrenia are distorted beliefs called **delusions**. In contrast to mistaken beliefs that we all experience from time to time, such as thoughts that a friend is trying to avoid us or that our parents' divorce was our fault, delusions are mistaken beliefs maintained in spite of strong evidence to the contrary.

TABLE 40.1 LANGUAGE VARIATIONS IN SCHIZOPHRENIA

Language Variation	Examples
Word salad	"The same children are sent of a rose, sweet-smelling perfume that gives us peace and parts and whole." "The sad, kind, and peaceful valleys of the mind come beckoning under rivers."
Neologisms	"Splisters" (combination of *splinters* and *blisters*) "Smever" (combination of *smart* and *clever*)

Mrs. T held the *paranoid delusion* that others were talking about her. In *delusions of grandeur*, people believe they are someone very important, perhaps Jesus Christ or the queen of England. In *delusions of persecution*, individuals believe they are the target of a plot to harm them, as was the case with Jim in our introduction, who believed secret agents were trying to assassinate him. In *delusions of reference*, unrelated events are given special significance, as when a person believes a radio program or newspaper article is giving him or her a special message.

Emotional Disturbances

Changes in emotion, or affect, usually occur in schizophrenia. In some cases, emotions are exaggerated and fluctuate rapidly in inappropriate ways. For example, a person may become extremely fearful, guilty, or euphoric for no reason. In other cases, emotions may become blunted or decreased in intensity. Some people with schizophrenia have *flattened affect* — almost no emotional response of any kind.

Behavioral Disturbances

Disturbances in behavior may take the form of unusual actions that have special meaning. One patient shook his head rhythmically from side to side to try to shake the excess thoughts out of his mind. Another massaged his head repeatedly "to help clear it" of unwanted thoughts. In other cases, the affected person may grimace and display unusual mannerisms. These movements, however, may also be side effects of the medication used to treat the disorder.

People with schizophrenia may become *cataleptic* and assume an uncomfortable, nearly immobile stance for an extended period. A few people with schizophrenia also have a symptom called *waxy flexibility*, a tendency to maintain whatever posture is imposed on them.

The abnormal behaviors of individuals with schizophrenia are often related to disturbances in their perceptions, thoughts, and feelings. For example, experiencing a flood of sensory stimuli or overwhelming confusion, a person with schizophrenia will often withdraw from social contacts and refuse to communicate.

Types of Schizophrenia: Recent Methods of Classification

For many years, researchers divided schizophrenia into *paranoid*, *catatonic*, *disorganized*, *undifferentiated*, and *residual* subtypes (Table 40.2). Although these terms are still used in the *DSM-IV-TR* (and sometimes by the public), critics say that they have little value in clinical practice and research. They contend that this classification does not differentiate in terms of prognosis (prediction for recovery), etiology

TABLE 40.2 SUBTYPES OF SCHIZOPHRENIA

Paranoid	Dominated by delusions (persecution and grandeur) and hallucinations (hearing voices)
Catatonic	Marked by motor disturbances (immobility or wild activity) and echo speech (repeating the speech of others)
Disorganized	Characterized by incoherent speech, flat or exaggerated emotions, and social withdrawal.
Undifferentiated	Meets the criteria for schizophrenia but is not any of the above subtypes
Residual	No longer meets the full criteria for schizophrenia but still shows some symptoms

(cause), or response to treatment, and that the undifferentiated type is a catchall for difficult diagnostic cases (American Psychiatric Association, 2000).

For all these reasons, Nancy Andreasen and others (Andreasen, 2000; Andreasen, Flaum, Swayze, Tyrrell, & Arndt, 1990; Toomey, Faraone, Simpson, & Tsuang, 1998) propose an alternative classification system of two groups instead of four:

1. *Positive symptoms* involve *additions* or exaggerations of normal thought processes and behaviors, including bizarre delusions, hallucinations, and disorganized speech

2. *Negative symptoms* involve the *loss* or absence of normal thought processes and behaviors, including impaired attention, limited or toneless speech, flattened emotions, and social withdrawal

(Study tip: If you're having difficulty understanding the distinction between positive and negative symptoms of schizophrenia, think back to what you learned regarding positive and negative reinforcement and punishment. *Positive* means "the addition of," whereas *negative* refers to the "removal or loss of.")

"That's the doctor who is treating me for paranoia. I don't trust him."

In addition to these two groups, the latest *DSM-IV-TR* suggests adding another dimension to reflect *disorganization of behavior.* One advantage of either a two- or three-dimension model is that they both acknowledge that schizophrenia is more than one disorder and that it has multiple causes.

Causes of Schizophrenia: Nature and Nurture Theories

There are several theories that attempt to explain schizophrenia. Biological theories emphasize physical changes in the nervous system based on abnormal brain functioning or inherited predisposition. Psychosocial theories focus on stressful experiences and disturbed family interactions.

Biological Theories

An enormous amount of scientific research exists concerning possible biological factors in schizophrenia. Most of this research is in three areas: genetics, neurotransmitters, and brain function:

1. *Genetics.* Genetics undoubtedly plays a primary role in the development of schizophrenia. Although researchers are beginning to identify specific genes related to schizophrenia, most genetic studies have focused on twin and adoption research (Bailer et al., 2000; Gershon et al., 1998; Petronis, 2000). By most estimates, heritability is around 50 percent. However, one study of both identical and fraternal twins found an estimated heritability of 83 percent (Cannon, Kaprio, Lonnquvist, Huttunen, & Koskenvuo, 1998). Figure 40.1 shows the risk of developing schizophrenia in people with differing degrees of relatedness to a person with schizophre-

Figure 40.1 *Genetics and schizophrenia.* Your lifetime risk of developing schizophrenia depends, in part, on how closely you are genetically related to someone with schizophrenia. As you evaluate the statistics, bear in mind that the risk in the general population is a little less than I percent (the bottom line on the graph). Risk increases with the degree of genetic relatedness.

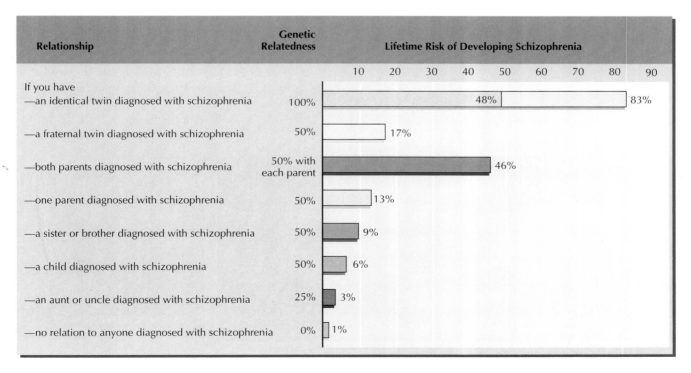

nia. As expected, the risk increases with genetic similarity; that is, people who share more genes are more likely to develop the disorder. For example, if one identical twin develops schizophrenia, the other twin has a 48 to 83 percent chance of also developing schizophrenia (Berrettini, 2000; Cannon, Kaprio, Lonnqvist, Huttunen, & Koskenvuo, 1998). But if one sibling develops schizophrenia, the chances of the other sibling developing it are only 9 percent. If you compare these percentages with the risk for the general population (which is around 1 percent), you can appreciate the role of genetics in schizophrenia.

2. *Neurotransmitters.* Precisely how genetic inheritance produces schizophrenia is unclear. The most widely held view implicates a dopamine imbalance (Gelman, 1999; Schwartz, Diaz, Pilon, & Sokoloff, 2000). According to the **dopamine hypothesis**, an overactivity of certain dopamine neurons in the brain causes schizophrenia. This hypothesis is based on two important observations:

> **Dopamine Hypothesis** *A theory suggesting that schizophrenia is caused by an overactivity of dopamine neurons in a specific region of the brain*

- Large doses of amphetamines increase the amount of dopamine and can produce the positive symptoms of schizophrenia (such as delusions of persecution) in people with no history of psychological disorders. Low doses of amphetamines worsen symptoms in people who have schizophrenia. Moreover, an amphetamine-induced psychosis is more likely to occur in individuals who have a genetic predisposition but no signs of active schizophrenia.
- Drugs effective in treating schizophrenia, such as chlorpromazine, block the effects of dopamine in the brain. The result is a reduction or elimination of positive symptoms such as hallucinations.

3. *Brain function.* The third major biological theory for schizophrenia involves possible brain damage. For example, researchers have found larger cerebral ventricles (cavities that contain cerebrospinal fluid) in some people with schizophrenia (Zipursky, Lambe, Kapur, & Mikulis, 1998). In Figure 40.2a, the enlarged ventricles of one patient with schizophrenia are clearly shown through the technique of magnetic resonance imaging (MRI). (Enlarged cerebral ventricles were found in the brain of John Hinkley Jr., the man who attempted to assassinate President Ronald Reagan.) Keep in mind, however, it could be the case either that the disease itself may result in brain damage or that the damage may cause or worsen the schizophrenia.

Figure 40.2 *Two views of schizophrenia.* (a) A three-dimensional magnetic resonance image (MRI) shows structural changes in the shrunken hippocampus (yellow) and enlarged, fluid-filled ventricles (gray) of the brain of a patient with schizophrenia (far left). Compare these regions to the brain of a person without schizophrenia (center). (b) These position emission tomography (PET) scans show variations in the brain activity of normal individuals, people with major depressive disorder, and individuals with schizophrenia. Levels of brain activity correspond to the colors and numbers at the far right of the photo. Higher numbers and warmer colors indicate increased activity.

(a)   (b)

Another technique, positron emission tomography (PET) (Figure 40.2b), shows that some people with chronic schizophrenia tend to have a lower level of activity in the frontal and temporal lobes. Because the frontal and temporal lobes are involved in language, attention and memory, damage here might explain the thought and language disturbances that characterize schizophrenia (Buchanan, Vlader, Barta, & Pearlson, 1998; Hazlett et al., 2000).

Some research suggests that prenatal viral infections, birth complications, immune responses, and maternal malnutrition play a role in schizophrenia (Cannon et al., 2000; Jablensky, 1999; Torrey & Yolken, 2000).

Psychosocial Theories

We can understand the degree to which psychosocial factors contribute to the development of schizophrenia by looking at genetic statistics for *identical twins*. Remembering that these children share *identical genes*, what would be the percentage chance that both twins would develop schizophrenia if the disorder were completely hereditary? If you guessed 100 percent, you're doing great. Because the rate is actually only 48 to 83 percent, nongenetic factors must contribute the remaining percentage. Other biological factors (such as neurotransmitters and brain structure) may take up part of the "leftover" percentage, but most psychologists believe there are at least two possible nonbiological contributors: stress and family communication.

1. Stress. In most theories of schizophrenia, stress plays an essential role in triggering schizophrenic episodes (Jansen, Wied, & Kahn, 2000; Torrey & Yolken, 1998, 2000). According to the *diathesis-stress model* of schizophrenia, a person inherits a predisposition toward schizophrenia and then experiences more stress than he or she can handle, which triggers a schizophrenic episode. Research also suggests that stress may be associated with patient relapse.

2. Family communication. Some investigators suggest that communication disorders in parents and family members may be a predisposing factor for schizophrenia. Such disorders include unintelligible speech; vague, fragmented communications; and contradictory messages. In these families, the child might withdraw into a private world and thereby set the stage for later schizophrenia.

Family communication patterns also can negatively affect patients with schizophrenia after hospitalization. In several studies researchers evaluated *expressed emotion* (EE) — levels of criticism and hostility aimed at the family member with schizophrenia and emotional overinvolvement in his or her life. They found greater relapse and worsening of symptoms among hospitalized patients who go home to high-EE families (Hooley, & Hiller, 2000; Lefley, 2000).

In sum, there is strong evidence linking schizophrenia to biological factors — genetics, neurotransmitters, and brain function — as well as evidence for nonbiological, psychosocial factors. The most recent research suggests a combination of both biology and environment (McDonald & Murray, 2000; Meltzer, 2000).

Evaluating the Theories

Critics of the dopamine hypothesis and the brain damage theory argue that they fit only some cases of schizophrenia. Moreover, with both theories, it is difficult to determine cause and effect. That is, does overactivity in dopamine neurons cause schizophrenia, or does schizophrenia cause overactivity of dopamine neurons? Similarly, does brain damage cause schizophrenia, or does schizophrenia cause brain damage? Or is there a third, as yet unknown, factor? Genetic predisposition may be the strongest factor, but as we pointed out, the highest correlation, found in identical twins, is still not 100 percent.

Figure 40.3 *Interacting factors in schizophrenia.* Research shows that schizophrenia may have various causes. Most probably, biological factors interact with psychosocial factors to produce the symptoms (Meltzer, 2000).

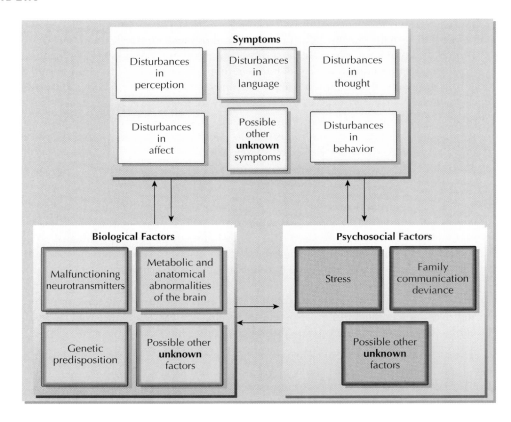

The disturbed-communication theories are also hotly debated, and research is equally inconclusive. This uncertainty points to the fact that schizophrenia is probably a combination of interacting (known and unknown) factors (Meltzer, 2000; Torrey & Yolken, 1998, 2000) (Figure 40.3).

GENDER & CULTURAL DIVERSITY

Culture and Schizophrenia

At the beginning of this section, we discussed how some researchers believe that certain mental disorders may be culturally universal; schizophrenia is a prime example. Culturally general symptoms of schizophrenia include delusions, thinking aloud, incoherent speech, difficulty forming emotional ties with others, poor rapport with others, and poor self-insight.

In contrast to these cultural *commonalties*, schizophrenia *differs* across cultures in four important ways:

1. **Prevalence.** Although schizophrenia is one of the more common disorders in the world, the reported incidence within any given culture varies. For example, comparisons of gender differences in Norway found that men tend to develop it 3 to 4 years earlier than women, have more and longer hospitalizations, and have poorer social functioning (Raesaenen, Pakaslahti, Syvaelahti, Jones, & Isohanni, 2000). It is unclear whether these differences result from an actual difference in prevalence of the disorder or from differences in definition, diagnosis, or reporting (Kleinman & Cohen, 1997; Lefley, 2000).

2. **Form.** The form or major mode of expression of schizophrenia also varies across cultures. In Nigeria, for example, the major symptom of schizophrenia is intense

suspicion of others, accompanied by bizarre thoughts of personal danger (Katz et al., 1988). However, in Western nations the major symptom is auditory hallucinations. Interestingly, the sources of auditory hallucinations have changed with technological advances. In the 1920s, the voices that people heard came from the radio; in the 1950s, they came from TV; in the 1960s, it was satellites in outer space; and in the 1970s and 1980s, they often came from microwave ovens (Brislin, 2000).

3. **Onset.** As we discussed, some theories suggest that stress may trigger the onset of schizophrenia. Research conducted in nine different sites in Asia, Europe, South America, and the United States supports the relationship between stress and schizophrenia (Benes, 1997; Torrey & Yolken, 1998). Some stressors were shared by many cultures, such as the unexpected death of a spouse or loss of a job, but others were culturally specific, such as feeling possessed by evil forces or being the victim of witchcraft.

4. **Prognosis.** The *prognosis*, or prediction for recovery, from schizophrenia also varies among cultures. Given the advanced treatment facilities and wider availability of trained professionals and drugs in industrialized nations, it may surprise you to learn that the prognosis for people with schizophrenia is better in nonindustrialized societies. This may be because the core symptoms of schizophrenia (poor rapport with others, incoherent speech, etc.) make it more difficult to survive in highly industrialized countries. In addition, individualism is highly encouraged in most industrialized nations, and families and other support groups are less likely to feel responsible for relatives and friends with schizophrenia (Brislin, 2000; Lefley, 2000).

The four culturally specific factors (prevalence, form, onset, and prognosis) support an environmental or psychosocial explanation of schizophrenia. On the other hand, the large number of culturally general symptoms and the fact that schizophrenia is found in almost every society support biological explanations. In sum, then, cultural studies suggest both nature and nurture are important in explaining schizophrenia.

Check & Review

SCHIZOPHRENIA

Schizophrenia is a serious psychotic mental disorder that afflicts approximately 1 of every 100 people. The five major symptoms are disturbances in perception (impaired filtering and selection, **hallucinations**), language (*word salad*, *neologisms*), thought (impaired logic, **delusions**), emotion (either exaggerated or blunted emotions), and behavior (social withdrawal, bizarre mannerisms, *catalepsy*, *waxy flexibility*).

Schizophrenic symptoms can be divided into a two-dimensioned classification system: *Addition* or exaggeration of normal thought processes and behaviors (e.g., delusions and hallucinations) is classified as *positive symptoms*, whereas loss or absence of normal thought processes and behaviors (e.g., toneless voice and flat emotions) is classified as *negative symptoms*.

Biological theories of the causes of schizophrenia propose genetics (people inherit a predisposition), disruptions in neurotransmitters (the **dopamine hypothesis**), and brain function (such as enlarged ventricles and lower levels of activity in the frontal and temporal lobes). Psychosocial theories of schizophrenia focus on stress and disturbed family communication.

Schizophrenia is the most culturally universal mental disorder in the world. Many symptoms are culturally general (such as delusions), but significant differences also exist across cultures in prevalence, form, onset, and prognosis.

Questions

1. _____ refers to "split mind," whereas _____ refers to "split personality." (a) Psychosis, neurosis; (b) Insanity, multiple personalities; (c) Schizophrenia, dissociative identity disorder; (d) Paranoia, borderline

2. Schizophrenia is also a form of _____, a term describing general lack of contact with reality.

3. Perceptions for which there are no appropriate external stimuli are called _____, and the most common type among people suffering from schizophrenia is _____. (a) hallucinations, auditory; (b) hallucinations, visual; (c) delusions, auditory; (d) delusions, visual

4. List three possible biological and two nonbiological, or psychosocial, causes of schizophrenia.

Answers to Questions can be found in Appendix B.

MODULE 40 ACTIVE LEARNING WORKSHEET

"Name That Symptom"

Schizophrenia is characterized by disturbances in perception, language, thought, affect, and behavior. Identify the type of disturbance in each of the following statements:

1. "I hear voices that tell me what to do."

2. "I become extremely fearful or euphoric for no apparent reason."

3. "My body may assume an uncomfortable, nearly immobile stance for an extended period."

4. "I believe secret agents are trying to assassinate me."

5. "I create new words and sometimes jumble them together."

Answers can be found in Appendix B.

MODULE 41

OTHER DISORDERS

We have now discussed anxiety, schizophrenia, and mood disorders. In this section, we will briefly describe two additional disorders — dissociative and personality disorders.

Dissociative Disorders: When the Personality Splits Apart

The most dramatic and popularized cases of psychological disorders are **dissociative disorders**. There are several types of dissociative disorders, but all involve a splitting apart (a *dis*-association) of significant aspects of experience from memory or consciousness. Individuals dissociate from the core of their personality by failing to recall or identify past experience (*dissociative amnesia*), leaving home and wandering off (*dissociative fugue*), losing the sense of reality and feeling estranged from the self (*depersonalization disorder*), or by developing completely separate personalities (*dissociative identity disorder*, previously known as *multiple personality disorder*).

Why would someone react this way? We've all had the experience of driving somewhere, arriving at our destination, and then realizing we don't remember a single detail of the drive. This is a very mild form of dissociation. To understand what a dissociative disorder might be like, imagine witnessing a loved one's death in a horrible car accident. Can you see how your mind might cope with the severe emotional pain by blocking out all memory of the event? Putnam (1992) described a heart-wrenching example of a dissociative disorder in a young girl who saw both her parents blown to bits in a minefield, and then tried to carefully piece their bodies back together, bit by bit.

The major problem underlying all dissociative disorders is the need to escape. A history of extreme trauma, usually sexual abuse, is found in nearly all cases (Dickinson, deGruy, Dickinson, & Candib, 1999; Scroppo, Drob, Weinberger, & Eagle, 1998). By developing amnesia, running away, or creating separate personalities, the individual is able to cope with the ongoing trauma or memories of the abuse. Unlike most psychological disorders, environmental variables are the primary cause, with little or no genetic influence (Waller & Ross, 1997).

Dissociative Identity Disorder

The most severe dissociative disorder is **dissociative identity disorder** (DID), previously known as multiple personality disorder (MPD), in which at least two separate and distinct personalities exist within the same person. Each personality has unique memories, behaviors, and social relationships. Transition from one personality to another occurs suddenly and is often associated with psychological stress. Usually the original personality has no knowledge or awareness of the existence of the alternate subpersonalities, but all of "them" may be aware of lost periods of time. Often, the alternate personalities are very different from the original personality and may be of the other sex, a different race, another age, or even another species (such as a dog or lion). The disorder is diagnosed more among women than men. Women also tend to have more identities, averaging 15 or more, compared with men, who average 8 (American Psychiatric Association, 2000).

The book and movie *Sybil* portrayed one of the best known cases of DID — that of Sybil Dorsett, a Midwestern schoolteacher with 16 personalities that took turns controlling her body. Instead of thinking of herself as one person who behaved differently at times, Sybil had lapses of memory when she became

How are dissociative disorders and personality disorders identified?

Dissociative Disorder *Stress-related disorder characterized by amnesia, fugue, or multiple personality; in all cases, though, the person is trying to escape from the memory of a painful experience*

Dissociative Identity Disorder (DID) *A dissociative disorder characterized by the presence of two or more distinct personality systems in the same individual; previously known as multiple personality disorder*

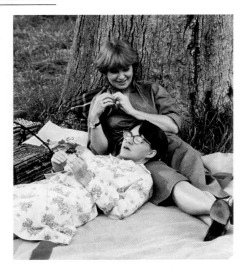

Sally Field won an Emmy Award for her sensitive portrayal of a woman suffering from dissociative identity disorder (DID), in the TV drama Sybil. *Joanne Woodward portrayed the psychiatrist who guided her back to mental health. Although this drama was based on a real-life patient, experts have recently questioned the validity of the case and the diagnosis of DID (Miller & Kantrowitz, 1999).*

"another person." When she was "Peggy Lou," she was aggressive and capable of anger; as "Vickie," she was a confident and sophisticated woman who knew of the other personalities.

What caused Sybil to develop these other personalities? Severe trauma in childhood is considered a primary cause of dissociative disorders (Draijer & Langeland, 1999; Lewis, Yeager, Swica, Pincus, & Lewis, 1997). Sybil's mother reportedly sexually tortured and emotionally abused her throughout her entire childhood. Before she was a year old, her mother began tying her up in various ways and, on occasion, suspending her from the ceiling. Imagine a small child in a situation like this. The child has no way of knowing that such parenting is unusual or wrong. In fact, Sybil's mother was widely respected in the community.

What can the child do? Sybil escaped by fantasizing that what she was experiencing was happening to another imaginary person. Finding that this method helped blunt the physical and emotional pain, she continued resorting to these imaginary personalities. Eventually the dissociation from ordinary consciousness to the imagined personalities became complete, and Sybil's original personality no longer recognized the existence of these "alters." Breaking down the "amnesiac walls" between the various personalities is a primary goal in the treatment of DIDs.

DID is a controversial diagnosis. As you remember from Module 20, there is considerable debate about whether repressed memories, particularly of childhood sexual abuse, are real or not. Some researchers and mental health professionals even question whether DIDs actually exist. They suggest that many cases are faked and that others result from an unconscious effort to please the therapist (Lilienfeld et al., 1999; Loftus, 1997; Powell & Gee, 1999). These skeptics also believe that therapists may be unintentionally encouraging and thereby over-reporting the incidence of multiple personalities.

Even the authenticity of "Sybil" is now being questioned (Miller & Kantrowitz, 1999). The real-life patient, Shirley Ardell Mason, died in 1998, and some experts are now disputing the original diagnosis of her condition. They suggest that Shirley was highly hypnotizable and suggestible and that her therapist, Cornelia Wilbur, unintentionally "suggested" the existence of multiple personalities.

On the other side of the debate are psychologists who not only accept the validity of multiple personality but also believe the condition is underdiagnosed (Spiegel & Maldonado, 1999). Consistent with this view, DID cases have been documented in many cultures around the world and there has been a rise in the number of reported cases (American Psychiatric Association, 2000). (However, this may reflect a growing public awareness of the disorder.)

The stakes in this controversy over childhood memories and dissociation are very high. On the one hand, research has clearly shown that various well-established psychological processes *can* create false memories. If careless therapists inadvertently create such memories in their patients, the mistaken accusations can irreversibly damage families and even lead to imprisonment of the accused "perpetrators."

On the other hand, evidence also shows that early traumatic experiences *can* cause selective dissociative amnesia (Gleaves, 1996; Spiegel, 1995). Moreover, a childhood history of extreme trauma, usually sexual abuse, is found in almost all cases of DID (Draijer & Langeland, 1999; Lewis et al., 1997). If these people are not believed and do not receive therapy, they are likely to experience lifelong suffering, and their perpetrators will escape legal responsibility.

Obviously, enormous harm can be done to innocent people on each side of the debate. Advocates on both sides agree that research must proceed as quickly as possible to clarify and resolve this debate (Kihlstrom, 1997; Pope, 1997).

Personality Disorders: The Antisocial and Borderline

People are diagnosed as having a **personality disorder** if they have inflexible and maladaptive personality traits that cause significant social or occupational problems. There are several types of personality disorders included in this category in *DSM-IV-TR*, but here we will focus on the best-known type, *antisocial personality disorder*, and the most commonly diagnosed, *borderline personality disorder*.

Antisocial Personality Disorder

The term **antisocial personality** is used interchangeably with the terms *sociopath* and *psychopath*. These labels describe behavior so far outside the usual ethical and legal standards of society that many consider it the most serious of all mental disorders. Although it would seem that such people would wind up in jail, many sociopaths avoid problems with the law and harm people in less dramatic ways as con artists, ruthless businesspeople, and "crooked" politicians.

Symptoms

Ken Bianchi, who was introduced at the beginning of this section, had the four hallmarks of an antisocial personality disorder: egocentrism, lack of conscience, impulsive behavior, and superficial charm (American Psychiatric Association, 2000). *Egocentrism* refers to a preoccupation with one's own concerns and insensitivity to the needs of others. Dr. Robert Hare described individuals with an antisocial personality disorder as "social predators who charm, manipulate, and ruthlessly plow their way through life, leaving a broad trail of broken hearts, shattered expectations, and empty wallets. Completely lacking in conscience and empathy, they selfishly take what they want and do as they please, violating social norms and expectations without the slightest sense of guilt or regret" (Hare, 1993, p. xi).

Individuals with antisocial personality disorder tend to have long histories of violating the rights of others and do not experience anxiety, guilt, or feelings of remorse, even when they cause great suffering (Anderson, Bechara, Damasio, Tranel, & Damasio, 1999; Rice, 1997). They are usually serene and poised when confronted with their destructive behavior and feel contempt for anyone they are able to manipulate.

Unlike most adults who have learned to sacrifice immediate gratification for the sake of long-range goals, these individuals act on their impulses, without giving thought to the consequences. They change jobs and relationships suddenly and often have a history of truancy from school and being expelled for destructive behavior. Even after repeated punishment, they seem to lack insight into the connection between their behavior and its consequences.

Interestingly enough, people with antisocial personalities can be quite charming and persuasive, and they have remarkably good insight into the needs and weaknesses of other people. Even while exploiting someone, they generally inspire feelings of trust. Ken Bianchi (the mass murderer described in our introductory incident) was so good at charming others that he convinced a woman whom he knew only casually to give him an alibi for some of the killings. Bianchi had been charged with several murders and was behind bars when he persuaded her to help him (Magid & McKelvey, 1987).

Causes

Although the causes of antisocial personality disorder are not completely understood, research supports both nature and nurture explanations, and a combination of the two is most likely. Evidence for biological causes comes from twin and adop-

Personality Disorders *A category in the Diagnostic and Statistical Manual of Mental Disorders, fourth edition, text revision, that describes individuals with inflexible, maladaptive personality traits; the best-known type is the antisocial personality*

Antisocial Personality *Personality disorder characterized by egocentrism, lack of conscience, impulsive behavior, and manipulation of others*

Antisocial personality?
Armstrong, a forme
USS Nimitz, li
nary exami
Wendy
De

tive studies that suggest a possible genetic predisposition (Bock & Goode, 1996; Jang, Vernon, & Livesley, 2000). Other studies have found abnormal autonomic activity during stress and reduced gray matter in the frontal lobes (Raine, Lencz, Bihrle, LaCasse, & Colletti, 2000).

Evidence also exists for environmental or psychological causes. Studies have found a high correlation between parenting styles and inappropriate modeling, and antisocial personalities (Farrington 2000; Wootton, Frick, Shelton, & Silverton, 1997). People with antisocial personality often come from homes characterized by emotional deprivation, harsh and inconsistent disciplinary practices, and antisocial behaviors on the part of parents. Still other studies show a strong interaction between both heredity and environment (Paris, 2000; Rutler, 1997).

Borderline Personality Disorder

Borderline Personality Disorder (BPD) *A personality disorder characterized by impulsivity and instability in mood, relationships, and self-image*

Of all the personality disorders, **borderline personality disorder** (BPD) is the most commonly diagnosed (Rutter, 2000). The core features of this disorder are impulsivity and instability in mood, relationships, and self-image. Although "borderline" sounds like it might be a relatively minor disorder, our introductory story of Mary illustrates the serious problems associated with this disorder. People with BPD experience extreme difficulties in relationships and engage in destructive, impulsive behaviors, like Mary's sexual promiscuity and self-mutilation. Others have problems with drinking, gambling, and eating sprees, which also are self-damaging and potentially lethal (Skodol, Oldham, & Gallaher, 1999; Trull, Sher, Minks-Brown, Durbin, & Burr, 2000). Subject to chronic feelings of depression, emptiness, and intense fear of abandonment, they often attempt suicide and engage in self-mutilating behavior, such as slicing into their forearms or legs with a razor blade (Pinto, Dhavale, Nair, Patil, & Dewan, 2000; Soloff, Lynch, Kelly, Malone, & Mann, 2000).

Have you known someone who fits Mary's description? If so, you know that being a friend, lover, or parent to someone like Mary can be extremely difficult. They can be exciting, friendly, and totally charming one moment, and angry, argumentative, irritable, and sarcastic the next. They also tend to see themselves and everyone else in absolutes — perfect or worthless (Mason & Kreger, 1998). Partly because of their fragile identity, they constantly seek reassurance from others and may quickly erupt in anger at the slightest sign of disapproval or rejection. A simple gesture, missed appointment, or wrong turn of phrase can trigger an angry outburst, even in public situations that would embarrass most people. People with BPD typically have a string of broken friendships, divorces, and lost jobs.

Causes of BPD

People with BPD frequently have a childhood history of neglect; emotional deprivation; and physical, sexual, or emotional abuse (Bailey & Shriver, 1999; Johnson, Smailes, Cohen, Brown, & Bernstein, 2000). BPD also tends to run in families, and some data suggest impaired functioning of the frontal lobes, which controls impulsive behaviors (Nigg & Goldsmith, 1994; Torgersen, 2000; Van Reekum, Conway, Gansler, & White, 1993).

Can anything be done to help these people? Prognosis is not favorable. In one study, seven years after treatment about 50 percent of the original group still had the disorder (Links, Heslegrave, & van Reekum, 1998). Because these people have such an intense emptiness and chronic fear of abandonment, they go from friend to friend, lover to lover, and therapist to therapist looking for someone to "complete" them. Given their troublesome personality traits, however, friends, lovers, and therapists often do "abandon" them — thus deepening their insecurities.

RESEARCH HIGHLIGHT

Alcohol Problems and Comorbidity

Alcohol use disorders (AUDs), which include alcohol abuse and alcohol dependence, may be the Western world's most serious drug problem. In addition to creating massive social and personal difficulties, AUDs also overlap with almost all other mental disorders — including anxiety disorders, mood disorders, schizophrenia, and personality disorders (Green, 2000; Kirchner, Owen, Nordquist, & Fischer, 1998; Sher, 2000). This combination of disorders is known as **comorbidity**, or *dual diagnosis*.

What Causes This Type of Overlap Between Disorders?

Perhaps the most influential hypothesis is that of self-medication — individuals drink to reduce their symptoms (Batel, 2000; Green, 2000). Research also shows a high genetic correlation between AUDs and other conditions (Heath, 2000). On the other hand, several environmental variables also predict AUDs and comorbid conditions in adolescence, including reduced parental monitoring, distance from teachers, selective socialization with deviant peers, and disaffiliation with peers (Costello, 2000). Although it may seem contradictory to have both genetic and environmental explanations, we see once again that nature and nurture interact. Researchers suggest that the interaction might result from an alcohol-abusing youth's tendency to seek out deviant peers or that the same genes that contribute to a mother's lax monitoring might also contribute to her child's early experimentation with alcohol (Sher, 2000).

The high cost of alcohol abuse. Children of alcoholic parents are at much greater risk of also abusing alcohol and developing related disorders. Is this because of a genetic predisposition, modeling by the parents, or the emotional devastation of growing up with an alcoholic parent?

Regardless of the causes or correlates of AUDs and comorbid conditions, it is critical that patients, family members, and clinicians recognize and deal with comorbidity if treatment is to be effective. For example, AUDs often accompany serious depression, and simply stopping drinking is not the only solution (though certainly an important first step). Similarly, people suffering from schizophrenia are far more likely to relapse into psychosis, require hospitalization, neglect their medications, commit acts of violence, and kill themselves when they also suffer from AUDs (Batel, 2000; Green, 2000). Recognizing this pattern and potential danger, many individual and group programs that treat schizophrenia now also include methods used in drug abuse treatment.

To sum up, people who suffer from AUDs are at great risk of also experiencing at least one or more other mental disorders. Understanding this *comorbidity* is of great importance to the suffering individual and his or her family. It is also important from a broad social perspective. The pain and destruction experienced by so many people results in enormous costs to society. But as you will see in the next set of modules, there are many forms of successful therapy that offer hope for everyone.

Comorbidity *The co-occurrence of two or more disorders in the same person at the same time, as when a person suffers from both depression and alcoholism*

critical thinking ▶▶▶▶▶▶▶▶▶▶▶▶▶▶▶ Active Learning

Testing Your Knowledge of Abnormal Behavior

Applying abstract terminology is an important component of critical thinking. Test your understanding of the six major diagnostic cate-gories of psychological disorders by matching the disorders on the left with the diagnostic categories on the right.

Answers can be found in Appendix B.

Description of Disorder

1. Julie mistakenly believes she has lots of money and is making plans to take all her friends on a trip around the world. She has not slept for days. Last month, she could not get out of bed and talked of suicide.
2. Steve is exceptionally charming and impulsive and apparently feels no remorse or guilt when he causes great harm to others.
3. Chris believes he is president of the United States and hears voices saying the world is ending.
4. Each day, Kelly repeatedly checks and rechecks all stove burners and locks throughout her house and washes her hands hundreds of times.
5. Lee has repeated bouts of uncontrollable drinking, frequently misses his Monday-morning college classes, and was recently fired for drinking on the job.
6. Susan wandered off and was later found living under a new name, with no memory of her previous life.

Possible Diagnosis

a. Anxiety disorder

b. Schizophrenia

c. Mood disorder

d. Dissociative disorder

e. Personality disorder

f. Substance-related disorder

Check & Review

OTHER DISORDERS

In **dissociative disorders**, critical ele-ments of personality split apart. This split is manifested in failing to recall or identify past experiences (*dissociative amnesia*), by leaving home and wandering off (*dissocia-tive fugue*), or by developing completely separate personalities (**dissociative iden-tity disorder** [DID]). Environmental vari-ables are the primary cause of dissociative disorders (e.g., a history of extreme trauma like sexual abuse).

Personality disorders involve inflexi-ble, maladaptive personality traits. The best-known type is the **antisocial per-sonality**, characterized by egocentrism, lack of guilt, impulsivity, and superficial charm. Research suggests this disorder may be related to defects in brain waves, genetic inheritance, or disturbed family relationships. **Borderline personality disorder** (BPD) is the most commonly diagnosed personality disorder. It is charac-terized by impulsivity and instability in mood, relationships, and self-image.

Questions

1. The major underlying problem for all dissociative disorders is the psycholog-ical need to escape from _____.

2. What is DID?

3. A *sociopath* or a *psychopath* would be diagnosed as a(n) _____ personality in the *Diagnostic and Statistical Manual of Mental Disorders*, fourth edition, text revision.

4. One possible biological cause of BPD is _____. (a) childhood history of neglect; (b) emotional deprivation; (c) impaired functioning of the frontal lobes; (d) all of these options.

Answers to Questions can be found in Appendix B.

ACTIVE LEARNING WORKSHEET   MODULE 41

"Name That Disorder"

Given the limited information below, complete each statement with the correct diagnostic label (dissociative identity disorder, antisocial personality, borderline personality disorder, alcohol use disorder).

1. "I am very charming, yet I feel little or no remorse for my dangerous and destructive behaviors."

2. "I suffer from a long list of broken relationships and often engage in impulsive behaviors like drinking, gambling, and sexual promiscuity."

3. "I tend to overuse alcohol and I am at increased risk of one or more other mental disorders."

4. "I have several distinct and separate personalities within my one body."

5. "Even when I've suffered repeated punishments, I seem to lack insight into the connection between my behavior and its consequences."

Answers can be found in Appendix B.

Visual Summary for Modules 37, 38, 39, 40, and 41

 ## Studying Psychological Disorders

Identifying Abnormal Behavior

Abnormal behavior: Pattern of emotion, thought, and action considered pathological for one of four reasons (statistical infrequency, disability or dysfunction, personal distress, or violation of norms).

Explaining Abnormality

| Prehistoric— demon model; treated with *trephining* in the Stone Ages. | → | 4th century B.C.—**medical model;** Hippocrates suggests physical causes. | → | Middle Ages— demon model; treated with exorcism, torture, imprisonment, execution. | → | 18th century— Pinel reintroduces medical model and humane asylums. | → | Modern times— medical model persists (e.g., **psychiatry**). |

Classifying Abnormal Behavior

The Diagnostic and Statistical Manual of Mental Disorders (DSM–IV–TR) categorizes disorders according to major similarities and differences and provides detailed descriptions of symptoms.
• Benefits: Standardized diagnosis and treatment, improved communication among professionals and between professionals and patients.
• Problems: Insufficient attention to cultural factors, supports medical model, and labels. Misdiagnosis also occurs, and labeling someone "mentally ill" can lead to social and economic discrimination.

Major Categories of Psychological Disorders

General Description, Examples, and Symptoms

Anxiety Disorders
Anxiety disorders: persistent feelings of threat in facing everyday problems.
• **Phobias:** Exaggerated fears of specific objects or situations.
• **Generalized anxiety disorder:** Persistent free-floating anxiety.
• **Panic disorder:** Anxiety concentrated into brief or lengthy episodes of panic attacks.
• **Obsessive-compulsive disorder (OCD):** Persistent anxiety arousing thoughts (obsessions) are relieved by ritualistic actions (compulsions) such as hand washing.
• **Post-traumatic stress disorder (PTSD):** After a traumatic event (rape, war), a person experiences flashbacks, sleep disturbances, an exaggerated startle response, etc. that may last for years.

Possible Causes

Learning theorists: Classical and operant conditioning, as well as modeling and imitation.

Biological perspective: Genetic predisposition, brain abnormalities, and biochemistry.

The cognitive approach: Distorted thinking that amplifies ordinary threats.

Major Categories of Psychological Disorders (cont.)

General Description, Examples, and Symptoms

Mood Disorders
Mood disorders are disturbances of affect (emotion) that may include psychotic distortions of reality. Two types:

- **Major depressive disorder:** Long-lasting depressed mood, feelings of worthlessness, and loss of interest in most activities. Feelings are without apparent cause and person may lose contact with reality.

- **Bipolar disorder:** Episodes of mania and depression alternate with normal periods. During manic episode, speech and thinking are rapid, and the person may experience delusions of grandeur and act impulsively.

- *Depression* involves several culture-general symptoms, such as feelings of sadness and loss of enjoyment in daily activities.
- Women more likely than men to suffer depressive symptoms in many countries.
- Suicide is a serious problem associated with depression, but risk can be reduced by others showing concern.

Schizophrenia
Schizophrenia: serious psychotic mental disorder afflicting approximately one out of every 100 people.
Five major symptoms: Disturbances in
1) Perception (impaired filtering and selection, **hallucinations**).
2) Language (word salad, neologisms).
3) Thought (impaired logic, **delusions**).
4) Emotion (either exaggerated or blunted emotions).
5) Behavior (social withdrawal, bizarre mannerisms, catalepsy, waxy flexibility).
Two-type classification system:

Positive symptoms—distorted or excessive mental activity (e.g., delusions and hallucinations).

Negative symptoms—behavioral deficits (e.g., toneless voice, flattened emotions).

Culture: Schizophrenia is the world's most culturally universal mental disorder with many symptoms culturally general (such as delusions). However, significant differences exist in prevalence, form, onset, and prognosis.

Other Disorders
Dissociative disorders: Critical parts of personality split apart. This split is manifested in failing to recall or identify past experiences (dissociative amnesia), by leaving home and wandering off (dissociative fugue), or by developing completely separate personalities (**dissociative identity disorder [DID]** or multiple-personality disorder). Although DID is believed to be rare, a few well-publicized cases (like Sybil) have drawn attention to it.

Personality disorders involve inflexible, maladaptive personality traits.
- **Antisocial personality**, the best-known example, is characterized by egocentrism, lack of guilt, impulsivity, and superficial charm.
- **Borderline personality disorders (BPD),** the most commonly diagnosed personality disorder, is characterized by impulsivity and instability in mood, relationships, and self-image.

Possible Causes

Biological theories: Neurotransmitters (especially dopamine and serotonin) and genetic predisposition for both major depression and bipolar disorder.

Psychological theories: Disturbed interpersonal relationships, faulty thinking, poor self-concept, and maladaptive learning. **Learned helplessness** theory suggests depression results from repeatedly failing to escape from a source of stress.

Biological theories: Genetics (people inherit a predisposition), disruptions in neurotransmitters (**dopamine hypothesis**) and brain function (such as enlarged ventricles and lower levels of activity in the frontal and temporal lobes).

Psychosocial theories: Stress and disturbed family communication.

Environmental variables are the primary cause, little or no biological or genetic influence. Major problem: Need to escape. A history of extreme trauma, usually sexual abuse, found in nearly all cases.

Defects in brain waves, genetic inheritance, or disturbed family relationships.

Therapy

Core Learning Objectives

As you read Modules 42, 43, 44, and 45, keep the following questions in mind and answer them in your own words:

▶ What do all therapies have in common?
▶ What are the major biomedical therapies?
▶ What is Freudian psychoanalysis? Are there more modern forms of this therapy?
▶ What are the major cognitive therapies?
▶ What is different about humanistic therapies?
▶ How are learning principles used in behavior therapy?
▶ How is psychotherapy done in groups and families?
▶ What are some of the major issues in therapy?

id you see the latest version of the movie The House on Haunted Hill? *Do you remember the gruesome "therapy" scenes in the dark asylum? The movie begins with rapid-fire shots of doctors performing surgery without anesthesia, men and women screaming, and mass hysteria as the inmates revolt against the doctors and nurses. A fire starts amid the chaos, and the sadistic director of the asylum pulls a switch, locking down the entire building so that every-*

one inside, including himself, burns to death. "A sanitarium of horrors, overseen by a surgeon gone mad" is how the fake newsreel footage of the events describes the scene.

Compare this dimly lit, overcrowded insane asylum with the painfully

bright, clinical-looking, high-tech mental facility in Terminator 2: Judgment Day. *The leading character, played by Sarah Connor, is trapped inside and desperate to be released. When her case comes up for review, she tries (unsuccessfully) to convince the doctor that she is cured. She says that a nuclear holocaust is not forthcoming and that she no longer believes that cyborgs from the future have been sent back in time to kill her son John. (Of course, everyone who has seen the first film knows that what she is denying is true.)*

Consider, too, how mentally ill people themselves are generally portrayed: They are either cruel, sociopathic criminals (Hannibal Lecter, played by Anthony Hopkins, in Silence of the Lambs*) or helpless victims who will never be believed again after being labeled insane (Sarah Connor in* Terminator 2, *Bruce Willis in* Twelve Monkeys, *Jack Nicholson in* One Flew Over the Cuckoo's Nest, *and Winona Ryder in* Girl Interrupted*). And all of them are inescapably trapped in dark, horror-filled asylums or cold, clinical hospitals.*

hat's wrong with these films? Are they only "harmless entertainment," or do they perpetuate harmful stereotypes? According to the Surgeon General's Report on Mental Health released in December 1999, the shame and embarrassment caused by the stigma that surrounds a diagnosis of mental illness is the "most formidable obstacle to future progress in the arena of mental illness and health." Remarking on the film industry's distorted and largely negative portrayal of mental illness and its treatment, the Surgeon General also stated: "We want to help overcome the stereotypes, and help people realize that, just as things go wrong with the heart, the liver and the kidney, things can go wrong with the brain, and there should be no shame in that" (Adams, 2000).

The Surgeon General's report also found that nearly two-thirds of all people who have mental disorders avoid seeking treatment because of financial problems, limited access, lack of awareness, and other situations. At least a part of their resistance to therapy also may be due to Hollywood's negative and one-sided portrayals. This is unfortunate. As you will see, modern therapy can be very effective and prevent much needless suffering (Kopta, Lueger, Saunders, & Howard, 1999). In our coverage of modern forms of therapy, we hope to offset what you might have "learned" from Hollywood films with a balanced, factual presentation of the latest research. To begin, it's important to emphasize that not everyone who seeks professional help is suffering from mental illness. Although psychological disorders are

much more prevalent than most people realize, for a large number of people the major goal of therapy is to help with everyday problems in living, such as parent–child conflicts, unhappy marriages, death of a loved one, or adjustment to retirement. In addition, some people enter therapy for greater self-knowledge or personal fulfillment.

Numerous forms of therapy exist to serve varying needs. According to one expert (Kazdin, 1994), there may be over 400 approaches to treatment. To organize our discussion of these treatments, we will focus on two major approaches: (1) **biomedical therapies** that act directly on the patient's brain and nervous system and involve the use of drugs, electroconvulsive therapy (ECT), or psychosurgery, and (2) **psychotherapy**, a collection of various *psychological* therapeutic techniques employed to improve psychological functioning and promote adjustment to life. (*Therapy* is a general term including both biomedical therapies and psychotherapies.) The final module in this section concludes by exploring several issues in therapy: the ethics of forced institutionalization, effectiveness of therapy, therapy in the electronic age, and women and minorities as clients.

Biomedical Therapy *Therapy involving physiological interventions (drugs, electroconvulsive therapy, and psychosurgery) to reduce symptoms associated with psychological disorders*

Psychotherapy *A collection of various psychological techniques employed to improve psychological functioning and promote adjustment to life through understanding one's problems and modifying troubling feelings, behaviors, or relationships*

MODULE 42
THERAPY ESSENTIALS

What do all therapies have in common?

In its strictest sense, *therapy* refers only to techniques used by professionals (e.g., behavior modification, client-centered therapy, group therapy, and psychoanalysis). The professionals who do therapy include not only psychologists who specialize in mental disorders but also psychiatrists, psychiatric nurses, social workers, counselors, and members of the clergy with special training in pastoral counseling.

Here we will focus on the therapies used primarily by psychologists. The one exception is our discussion of *biomedical therapies* (drug treatments, ECT, and psychosurgery). Although psychiatrists and other medical professionals are generally the only ones who can prescribe biomedical techniques, they often work with psychologists to design the best treatment for their clients. It is also becoming clear that general psychotherapy and biomedical therapies overlap. When successful, they both alter brain functions (Gabbard, 1999). All major forms of therapy are designed to help the client in five specific areas (Figure 42.1). Depending on the individual therapist's training and the client's needs, one or more of these five areas may be emphasized more than the others.

1. *Disturbed thoughts.* Troubled individuals typically suffer some degree of confusion, destructive thought patterns, or blocked understanding of their problems. Therapists work to change these thoughts, provide new ideas or information, and guide individuals toward finding their own solutions to problems.

2. *Disturbed emotions.* People who seek therapy generally suffer from extreme emotional discomfort. By encouraging free expression of feelings and by providing a supportive environment, therapists help their clients replace feelings of despair or incompetence with hope and self-confidence.

3. *Disturbed behaviors.* Troubled individuals usually exhibit problem behaviors. Therapists help their clients eliminate troublesome behaviors and guide them toward lives that are more effective.

Figure 42.1 *The five most common goals of therapy.* Most therapies focus on one or more of these five goals. As you read about each therapy, see if you can identify which goal(s) would be of most interest to a psychoanalyst, a cognitive therapist, a behaviorist, a psychiatrist, and so on. It will help you differentiate between the approaches to therapy — and it might even help you on an exam on this chapter.

The public often misunderstands therapy. Before we begin our discussion, let's examine some common myths:

- **Myth:** *There is one best therapy.*
  Fact: Many problems can be treated equally well with all major forms of therapy.
- **Myth:** *Therapists can read minds.*
  Fact: Good therapists often seem to have an uncanny ability to understand how their clients are feeling and to know when someone is trying to avoid certain topics. This is not due to any special mind-reading ability; rather, it reflects their specialized training and daily experience working with troubled people.

- **Myth:** *People who go to therapists are crazy or just weak.*
  Fact: Most people seek counseling because of stress in their life or because they realize that therapy can improve their level of functioning. It is difficult to be objective about our own problems, and seeking therapy is a sign not only of wisdom but also of personal strength.
- **Myth:** *Only the rich can afford therapy.*
  Fact: Although therapy is expensive, there are many clinics and therapists who charge on a sliding scale based on the client's income. Some insurance plans also cover psychological services.

4. *Interpersonal and life situation difficulties.* Therapists help clients improve their relationships with family, friends, and coworkers. They also help them avoid or minimize sources of stress in their lives, such as job demands or family conflicts.

5. *Biomedical disturbances.* Troubled individuals sometimes suffer biological disruptions that directly cause or contribute to psychological difficulties (e.g., chemical imbalances that lead to depression). Therapists help relieve these problems primarily with drugs.

Although most therapists work with clients in several of these areas, the emphasis varies according to the therapist's training. Psychoanalysts and psychodynamic therapists, for example, generally emphasize unconscious thoughts and emotions. Cognitive therapists focus on their client's faulty thinking and belief patterns, whereas humanistic therapists attempt to alter the client's negative emotional responses. Behaviorists, as the name implies, focus on changing maladaptive behaviors. Therapists who use biomedical techniques attempt to change biological disorders.

It is important to note, however, that if you go to a counseling service seeking a "behaviorist" or "cognitive therapist," you will not find such a listing. These items simply refer to the theoretical background and framework that guide a clinician's thinking. Just as Democrats and Republicans approach political matters in different ways, behaviorists and cognitive therapists approach therapy differently. At the same time, just as Democrats and Republicans borrow ideas from one another, clinicians from different perspectives also share ideas and techniques.

Clinicians who regularly borrow freely from various theories are said to take an **eclectic approach** (Kopta, Lueger, Saunders, & Howard, 1999). Now, although you won't find a listing for behaviorists, you will find listings for psychologists, psychiatrists, social workers, and sometimes psychoanalysts and counselors. Therapists also usually list the degrees they hold, which generally indicate their professional training (Table 42.1).

Eclectic Approach *An approach to therapy in which the therapist combines techniques from various theories to find the appropriate treatment for the client*

TABLE 42.1 MAJOR TYPES OF THERAPISTS

1. **Clinical or counseling psychologists** are therapists who have an advanced degree such as a Ph.D. (doctor of philosophy), a Psy.D. (doctor of psychology), or Ed.D. (doctor of education). They have usually had 4 or more years of graduate education, including a supervised internship.

2. **Psychiatrists** are physicians (M.D.) who specialize in psychiatry after graduation from medical school and completing a year of internship. The 3-year residency program in psychiatry includes supervised practice in therapy techniques and training in the biological treatment of disorders. Because only psychiatrists are physicians, they tend to emphasize biomedical therapies.

3. **Psychoanalysts** are almost always psychiatrists with additional specialized training in the techniques of psychoanalysis. (The exceptions are people trained in analysis after completing other graduate education, such as social work.) During the specialized training period, students must themselves undergo psychoanalysis.

4. **Social workers** have obtained at least a master's degree in social work (MSW). During their graduate education, they are supervised in the treatment of clients in hospitals and outpatient settings. Social workers can also obtain a doctorate (DSW or Ph.D.) or specialize in specific types of therapy, becoming certified to practice as a licensed marriage, family, and child counselor (MFT) or a licensed clinical social worker (LCSW).

5. **Counselors** specialize in problems related to marriage, family, and child relations (MFT). They also deal with everyday adjustment problems, substance abuse, and career issues. They have obtained at least a master's degree in counseling (M.A.) and have had 2 or more years of graduate training.

Check & Review

THERAPY ESSENTIALS

Therapy is a general term for both biological and psychological treatments for mental disorders. There are numerous forms of therapy, but they all focus treatment on five basic areas of disturbance — thoughts, emotions, behaviors, interpersonal and life situations, and biomedical problems.

Questions

1. Using therapeutic techniques to improve psychological functioning and promote adjustment to life is known as _____. (a) eclectic therapy; (b) psychoanalysis/psychodynamic therapy; (c) psychotherapy; (d) counseling

2. Match the following therapists with their primary emphasis:

   _____ psychoanalysts   (a) faulty thinking and belief patterns
   _____ behaviorists   (b) unconscious thoughts and patterns
   _____ humanistic therapists (c) biological disorders
   _____ biomedical therapists (d) negative emotions
   _____ cognitive therapists   (e) maladaptive behaviors

3. What are the five major categories of therapists?

Answers to Questions can be found in Appendix B.

ACTIVE LEARNING WORKSHEET   MODULE 42

Completing the following exercise may help provide insight to your own life, as well as greater understanding of the material in this section.

1. Therapy has five common goals (or areas of attempted change). List them here:

   _____

   _____

   _____

2. Think of the most troublesome area of your life, and identify which of the five goals would be most beneficial for you to change, and why.

   _____

   _____

   _____

3. Considering the five major types of therapists (see Table 42.1), which therapist would be most appropriate for the problem you described above? Why?

   _____

   _____

   _____

MODULE 43
BIOMEDICAL THERAPIES

What are the major biomedical therapies?

Biomedical therapies are based on the premise that problem behaviors are caused, at least in part, by chemical imbalances or disturbed nervous system functioning. A physician rather than a psychologist must prescribe biomedical therapies, but psychologists work with patients receiving biomedical therapies and are frequently involved in research programs to evaluate their effectiveness. Despite Hollywood's persistent linking of mental illness with asylums and hospitals, today only people with the most severe and intractable disturbances are institutionalized and abuses like those portrayed in most films are virtually nonexistent. Most people with psychological disorders can be helped with drugs, psychotherapy, or a combination of the two. In this section, we will discuss three types of biomedical therapies, including drugs, ECT, and psychosurgery.

Drug Therapy: The Pharmacological Revolution

Drug Therapy *Use of chemicals (drugs) to treat physical and psychological disorders*

Since the 1950s, drug companies have developed an amazing variety of chemicals to treat abnormal behaviors. In some cases, **drug therapy** corrects a chemical imbalance. In these instances, using a drug is similar to administering insulin to people with diabetes, whose own bodies fail to manufacture enough. In other cases, drugs are used to relieve or suppress the symptoms of psychological disturbances even if the underlying cause is not thought to be biological. Psychiatric drugs are classified into four major categories: antianxiety, antipsychotic, mood stabilizer, and antidepressant. Table 43.1 gives examples of drugs in each category.

TABLE 43.1 DRUG THERAPY

Type of Drug	Psychological Disorder	Chemical Group	Generic Name	Brand Name
Antidepressant drug	Severe depression (with suicidal tendencies)	Tricyclic antidepressants	Imipramine Amitriptyline	Tofranil Elavil
		Monoamine oxidase inhibitors (MAOIs)	Phenelzine	Nardil
		Second-generation antidepressants	Tranylcypromine Fluoxetine	Parnate Prozac
Antianxiety drugs	Anxiety disorders	Benzodiazepines	Chlordiazepoxide Diazepam	Librium Valium
		Glycerol derivatives	Meprobamate	Miltown Equanil
Antipsychotic drugs	Schizophrenia	Phenothiazines	Chlorpromazine Fluphenazine Thioridazine	Thorazine Prolixin Mellaril
		Butyrophenones	Haloperidol	Haldol
		Dibenzodiazepine	Clozapine	Clozaril
Mood-stabilizer drugs	Bipolar disorder	Antimanic	Lithium carbonate	Lithonate Lithane Eskalith

Antianxiety Drugs

Antianxiety drugs (also known as "minor tranquilizers") create feelings of tranquility and calmness in addition to relieving muscle tension. These drugs have replaced sedatives (which had side effects of drowsiness and sleepiness) in the treatment of anxiety disorders. Antianxiety drugs, such as Valium and Xanax, lower the sympathetic activity of the brain — the crisis mode of operation — so that anxiety responses are diminished or prevented (Margolis & Swartz, 2001; Pollack, 2000).

Antianxiety Drugs Medications used to treat anxiety disorders

Antipsychotic Drugs

The medications used to treat schizophrenia and other acute psychotic states are called **antipsychotic drugs**, or *neuroleptics*. They are often referred to as "major tranquilizers," creating the impression they invariably have a strong calming or sedating effect. Some antipsychotic drugs, such as Haldol or Navane, do reduce hallucinations and delusions. But other antipsychotic drugs, such as Clozaril, energize and animate patients. The main effect of antipsychotic drugs is to diminish or eliminate psychotic symptoms, including hallucinations, delusions, withdrawal, and apathy. They are not designed to sedate the patient.

Antipsychotic Drugs Chemicals administered to diminish or eliminate hallucinations, delusions, withdrawal, and other symptoms of psychosis; also known as neuroleptics or major tranquilizers

How do these drugs work? The traditional antipsychotics, like Thorazine, appear to decrease activity at the dopamine synapses, which further supports the theory that excessive dopamine contributes to schizophrenia. Given the multiple types of dopamine receptors in different parts of the brain, the newer *atypical antipsychotics*, like Clozaril, may be more effective because they target specific dopamine receptors (as well as serotonin receptors) and avoid interfering with others (Roth, Willins, Kristiansen, & Kroeze, 1999).

Mood Stabilizer and Antidepressant Drugs

For people suffering from bipolar disorders, *mood-stabilizer* drugs such as lithium can help manic episodes and depression. Because lithium acts relatively slowly — it can be 3 or 4 weeks before it takes effect — its primary use is in preventing *future* episodes and helping to break the manic–depressive cycle. Lithium also has potentially serious side effects, but recent research also shows that it increases the volume of gray matter (the so-called thinking part of the brain) (Manji, Husseini, Moore, & Chen, 2000; Webb, Solomon, & Ryan, 2001).

People with severe depression are usually treated with one of four types of **antidepressant drugs**:

Antidepressant Drugs Drugs prescribed to treat depression, some anxiety disorders, and certain eating disorders (such as bulimia)

1. *Tricyclics* (named for their chemical structure that contains three rings), such as imipramine, act on multiple neurochemical pathways in the brain, including serotonin and catecholamines.

2. *Monoamine oxidase inhibitors* (MAOIs), such as phenelzine, block the enzyme *monoamine oxidase*. Because this enzyme inactivates serotonin and catecholamines, blocking it increases the availability of these helpful neurochemicals.

3. *Selective serotonin reuptake inhibitors* (SSRIs), such as Prozac or Zoloft, *work* like the tricyclics, but they *selectively* affect only serotonin. They are by far the most commonly prescribed antidepressants.

4. *Atypical antidepressants*, such as Wellbutrin, are a miscellaneous group of drugs used for patients who fail to respond to the other drugs or for people who experience certain side effects (like decreased sexual function) that are common to other antidepressants.

Electroconvulsive Therapy and Psychosurgery: Promising or Perilous?

Electroconvulsive Therapy (ECT)
A biomedical therapy based on passing electrical current through the brain; it is used almost exclusively to treat serious depression when drug therapy does not work

In **electroconvulsive therapy** (ECT), also known as *electroshock therapy* (EST), a current of moderate intensity is passed through the brain between two electrodes placed on the outside of the head (Figure 43.1). The electrical current is applied for less than a second, but it triggers widespread firing of neurons, also known as convulsions. The convulsions produce many changes in the central and peripheral nervous systems, including activation of the autonomic nervous system, increased secretion of various hormones and neurotransmitters, and changes in the blood–brain barrier.

During the early years of ECT, some patients received hundreds of treatments (Fink, 1999), but today most receive 12 or fewer treatments. Sometimes the electrical current is applied only to the right hemisphere, which causes less interference with verbal memories and left hemisphere functioning. Modern ECT is used only as a last resort because it produces major brain seizures and may cause varying degrees of memory loss. However, it also can be very effective in the treatment of severe depression when drug therapy has failed, and it is sometimes recommended for suicidal patients because it works faster than antidepressant drugs (Cloud, 2001; Prudic & Sackheim, 1999; Sylvester et al., 2000).

Psychosurgery *Operative procedures on the brain designed to relieve severe mental symptoms that have not responded to other forms of treatment*

The most extreme, and least used, biomedical therapy is **psychosurgery**, brain surgery to reduce psychological symptoms. (It is important to note that psychosurgery is *not* the same as brain surgery used to remove physical problems, such as a tumor or blood clot.) Attempts to change disturbed thinking and behavior by altering the brain have a long history. In Roman times, for example, it was believed that a sword wound to the head could relieve insanity. In 1936, a Portuguese neurologist, Egaz Moniz, treated uncontrollable psychotics by cutting the nerve fibers between the frontal lobes (where association areas for monitoring and planning behavior are found) and the thalamus and hypothalamus. Severing these connections decreases emotional response and the patient accepts frustrating circumstances with a "philosophical calm." Moniz was awarded the Nobel Prize in medicine in 1949 for developing this technique, called a **lobotomy** (Pressman, 1998; Valenstein, 1998).

Lobotomy *A brain operation in which the nerve pathways between the frontal lobes and the thalamus and hypothalamus are cut in hopes of treating psychological disorders*

Figure 43.1 *Electroconvulsive therapy (ECT).* During ECT, electrodes on the forehead apply electric current to the brain, creating a brief cortical seizure. Although ECT is controversial and may seem barbaric to you, for some severely depressed people it is the only hope and often very effective.

One Flew Over the Cuckoo's Nest. *In this film, the lead character, McMurphy (played by Jack Nicholson) is a persistent problem for the hospital staff. To punish and control him, the staff first used drug therapy, then ECT, and finally psychosurgery — a prefrontal lobotomy. Although this was a popular movie, it also deepened public fear and misconceptions about biomedical therapy.*

In the mid-1950s, when antipsychotic drugs came into use, psychosurgery virtually stopped. Recently, however, psychiatrists have been experimenting with a much more limited surgical procedure, called *cingulotomy*, where small, specific target areas are destroyed. On rare occasions, it is used in the treatment of severely debilitating cases of obsessive-compulsive disorder (OCD), depression, and anxiety (Da Costa, 1997; Fenton, 1998).

Evaluating Biomedical Therapies

Like all forms of therapy, the biomedical therapies have both proponents and critics. We will summarize the research in this area:

1. *Drug therapies.* There are several potential problems with drug therapy. First, although drugs may provide relief of symptoms, they seldom provide "cures" or long-term solutions. Researchers also are still learning about the long-term effects and potential interactions. Furthermore, not all patients are helped by these drugs, and some show only modest improvement. Some patients also develop tolerance to the drugs and become physically dependent. Withdrawal symptoms (such as convulsions and hallucinations) can occur if they suddenly stop taking the drugs. Overdosing with psychotherapeutic drugs intentionally (to get a stronger effect) or unintentionally (by combining them with other drugs, such as alcohol) can be fatal.

Controlling negative side effects is also an important issue with drug therapy. For example, reactions to antipsychotic drugs range from reduced alertness and drowsiness to symptoms similar to Parkinson's disease, including muscle rigidity, tremors, and an unusual shuffling gate (Butler, Joel, & Jeffries, 2000; Drummond, 2000). Recall from Module 14 that Parkinson's disease is related to a deficit in dopamine, and that the drug L-dopa (levodopa) increases dopamine and reduces the symptoms of Parkinson's. Because antipsychotic drugs work by reducing excess dopamine, you can see how prolonged use could eventually produce Parkinson-like symptoms. Anti-parkinsonian medications can reduce the side effects of antipsychotic drugs, but they have their own side effects, and their use is controversial.

One of the most serious side effects of antipsychotic drugs is a movement disorder called *tardive dyskinesia*, which develops in 15 to 20 percent of the patients. The symptoms generally appear after prolonged use (hence the term *tardive*, from the Latin root for "slow"). They include involuntary movements of the trunk and limbs (*dyskinesia*, meaning "disorder of movement") that can be severely disabling. Perhaps more characteristic are the facial and tongue motor disturbances. When students see films about schizophrenia, they often confuse the patient's sucking and smacking of their lips or lateral jaw movements as signs of the disorder rather than signs of tardive dyskinesia.

Like antipsychotic medications, mood-stabilizer and antidepressant drugs also have major and minor side effects. Antidepressants may cause dry mouth, fatigue, sexual dysfunction, weight gain, and memory difficulties, whereas mood-stabilizer drugs, such as lithium, can impair memory and cause weight gain. In excessive dosages, lithium can be fatal. Thus, as with other drug therapies, it is important to carefully monitor dosage level and patient reactions (Butler, Joel, & Jeffries, 2000).

What about herbal remedies like St.-John's-wort to treat depression? Recent controlled studies of herbal treatments, such as St.-John's-wort, kava, ginkgo, and valerian, suggest they may be effective and may have fewer side effects than traditional prescription medications (Woelk, 2000). Although these drugs are considered "natural" and therefore "safe," they can produce a number of potentially serious side effects. The quality and amounts of active ingredients vary according to the manufacturer, and the U.S. Food and Drug Administration (US FDA) does not regulate them. For all these reasons, researchers advise a wait-and-see approach (Beaubrun & Gray, 2000).

Despite the problems associated with psychotherapeutic drugs, they have led to revolutionary changes in mental health. Before the use of drugs, some patients were destined for a lifetime in psychiatric institutions. Today, most improve enough to return to their homes if they continue to take their medication to prevent relapse (Conley, Love, Kelly, & Bartko, 1999).

In sum, medication is an effective and often the most appropriate treatment for many psychological disorders. However, the fact that it is also cost-effective and *generally* fast acting has led to its overuse in some cases. For example, one report found that antidepressants are now prescribed roughly 50 percent of the time a patient walks into a psychiatrist's office (Olfson et al., 1998). Although this reflects in part the increased efficacy of the new medications, it also reflects the economics of health care. Because a psychiatrist can see five or six medication patients in an hour, versus the one person per hour generally seen by a psychotherapist, there is considerable financial incentive to favor drugs over therapy. Yet, most studies that have compared medication alone versus medication plus therapy have found the combination more effective (e.g., Pollack, 2000).

2. ECT and Psychosurgery. After nearly half a century of use of ECT, we do not fully understand why an ECT-induced convulsion alleviates depression. Partly because we cannot explain how it works, but also because it seems barbaric, ECT is a controversial treatment (Baldwin & Oxlad, 2000; Cloud, 2001). Unlike ECT portrayals in movies like *One Flew Over the Cuckoo's Nest* and *The Snake Pit*, patients show few, if any, visible reactions to the treatment, owing to modern muscle-relaxant drugs, which dramatically reduce muscle contractions during the seizure. Although most ECT patients are given an anesthetic such as sodium pentothal to block their memory of the treatment, some patients report that they find the treatment extremely aversive (Johnstone, 1999). However, many others find it life-saving.

Problems with ECT may become obsolete thanks to a recently developed similar treatment known as *repetitive transcranial magnetic stimulation* (rTMS). Unlike ECT, which passes a strong electric current directly through the brain, rTMS delivers a brief but powerful electric current through a coil of wire placed on the head.

The coil creates a strong magnetic field which is applied to certain areas in the brain. When used to treat depression, the coil is usually placed over the prefrontal cortex, a region linked to deeper parts of the brain that regulate mood. Treatment with rTMS appears to be almost as effective as ECT, but it has fewer side effects and does not require anesthesia (George et al., 2000; Klein et al. 1999).

Because all forms of psychosurgery have potentially serious or fatal side effects and complications, some critics suggest it should be banned altogether. Furthermore, the consequences are irreversible. For these reasons, psychosurgery is considered experimental and remains a highly controversial treatment.

We now turn our attention to those forms of therapy most commonly conducted by psychologists — *psychotherapy*.

Check & Review

BIOMEDICAL THERAPIES

Biomedical therapies use biological techniques to relieve psychological disorders. **Drug therapy** is the most common form by far. **Antianxiety drugs** (Valium, Xanax) are used to treat anxiety disorders, **antipsychotic drugs** (Haldol, Navane) treat the symptoms of schizophrenia, **antidepressants** (Prozac, Zoloft) treat depression, and mood stabilizers (lithium) can stabilize bipolar disorders. Although drug therapy has been responsible for major improvements in many disorders, there are also problems with dosage levels, side effects, and patient cooperation.

Electroconvulsive therapy (ECT) is used primarily to relieve serious depression when medication has not worked, but it is risky and considered a treatment of last resort. **Psychosurgeries**, such as a **lobotomy**, have been used in the past but are rarely used today.

Questions

1. The dramatic reduction in numbers of hospitalized patients today, as compared with past decades, is primarily attributable to _____. (a) biomedical therapy; (b) psychoanalysis; (c) psychosurgery; (d) drug therapy

2. What are the four major categories of psychiatric drugs?

3. The effectiveness of antipsychotic drugs is thought to result primarily from blockage of _____ receptors. (a) serotonin; (b) dopamine; (c) acetycholine; (d) epinephrine

4. ECT is used primarily to treat _____. (a) phobias; (b) conduct disorders; (c) depression; (d) schizophrenia

Answers to Questions can be found in Appendix B.

MODULE 43 ACTIVE LEARNING WORKSHEET

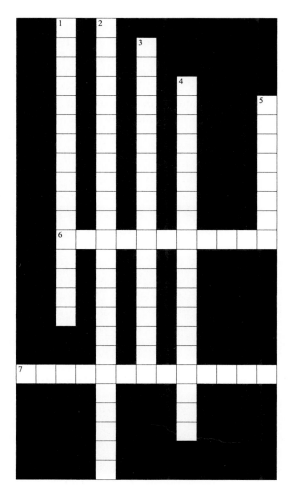

ACROSS

6. Use of chemicals to treat physical and psychological disorders.

7. Brain operation to relieve severe mental symptoms.

DOWN

1. Medications used to treat anxiety disorders.

2. Biomedical therapy that passes electrical current through the brain.

3. Chemicals administered to diminish or terminate symptoms of psychosis.

4. Drugs prescribed for depression, some anxiety disorders, and certain eating disorders.

5. Brain operation for psychological disorders that cuts nerve pathways between the frontal lobes and the thalamus and hypothalamus.

Answers can be found in Appendix B.

MODULE 44

PSYCHOTHERAPY

What do you think of when you hear the word *therapy*? When we ask our students this question, they usually describe a small, cluttered office with a sofa where patients recline and tell their secrets to a male therapist with a beard. Does this description match the one in your own mind? If so, it's probably due once again to Hollywood films. In most films, "therapy" is biomedical (drugs, ECT, and psychosurgery). When they do portray "talk therapy," they focus almost exclusively on a Freudian model, with a bearded therapist listening to a patient reclining on a couch (Figure 44.1). This stereotype has little to do with the realities of modern therapy, however. We begin our discussion of "real" therapy with traditional psychoanalysis (which does use a couch) and its modern counterpart, psychodynamic therapy. Then we explore cognitive, humanistic, and behavior therapies. We conclude with a look at group and family therapies.

Psychoanalysis/Psychodynamic Therapies: A Focus on the Unconscious

Why do psychoanalysts use couches in their form of therapy? Freud believed that the unconscious was more accessible when the patient reclined on a couch with only the ceiling to look at. He also felt the therapist should sit out of sight behind the patient. Freud wanted his patients to feel relaxed and nondefensive, almost as if they were talking to themselves rather than revealing information to another person. Traditional psychoanalysts still use a couch, but most modern forms of psychoanalysis do not.

The use of a couch is only one aspect of Freud's original therapy. Why not relax and recline on your own couch for the moment, and we'll describe the major goals and methods of psychoanalysis.

What is Freudian psychoanalysis? Are there more modern forms of this therapy?

Figure 44.1 *Stereotypes of therapy.* Movies often portray a simplistic view of Freudian style therapy. The patient reclines on a sofa and complains to a therapist who offers little or no direct intervention. In *Antz,* for example, the main character (Woody Allen) presents a lengthy, whining complaint about his boring ant life, while reclining on a sofa made of leaves. Can you see how these repeated, stereotypical portrayals could prejudice people against seeking therapy in real life? Unlike movie portrayals of therapy, most therapists conduct their sessions with both the therapist and client seated upright in chairs and facing one another, as you can see in the photo on the right.

Goals and Methods

Psychoanalysis *A system of therapy developed by Freud that seeks to bring unconscious conflicts, which usually date back to early childhood experiences, into consciousness; psychoanalysis is also Freud's theoretical school of thought, which emphasizes the study of unconscious processes*

Psychoanalysis means just what the name implies: A person's psyche (or mind) is analyzed. During psychoanalysis, the therapist (or psychoanalyst) works to bring unconscious conflicts, which are believed to date back to early childhood experiences, into consciousness. This traditional psychoanalysis is based on Sigmund Freud's central belief that abnormal behavior is caused by unconscious conflicts among the three parts of the psyche — the *id*, *ego*, and *superego*.

Recall from Module 35 that Freud believed primitive urges from the id, or overwhelming feelings of guilt from the superego, caused the ego to develop elaborate defense mechanisms and compulsive or self-defeating behaviors. During psychoanalysis, these unconscious conflicts are brought to consciousness. The patient comes to understand the reasons for his or her behavior and realizes that the childhood conditions under which the conflicts developed no longer exist. Once this realization (or *insight*) occurs, the conflicts can be resolved and the patient is free to develop more adaptive behavior patterns.

How can it change your behavior just to become aware of a conflict in your unconscious mind? Freud explained that becoming aware of a painful conflict permits a release of tension and anxiety. He observed that when his patients relived a traumatic incident, complete with disturbing emotions, the conflict seemed to lose its power to control the person's behavior. This emotional release, known as **catharsis**, frees up psychic energy previously devoted to id, ego, and superego conflicts. Healthier, less anxious living now becomes possible.

Catharsis *In psychoanalytic theory, the release of tension and anxiety through the reliving of a traumatic incident*

Gaining access into unconscious conflicts is not as simple as it sounds. The ego has strong defense mechanisms that block unconscious thoughts from coming to light. To gain insight into the unconscious, the ego must be tricked into relaxing its guard. The five major techniques for making the unconscious "conscious" are free association, dream analysis, analyzing resistance, analyzing transference, and interpretation.

1. *Free association.* Have you ever let your mind wander without attempting to monitor or control the direction of your thinking? If so, you might have noticed that some rather unexpected thoughts pop up. In the process of temporarily removing conscious censorship over thoughts — called **free association** — interesting and even bizarre connections seem to spring into awareness. (The term *free* does not mean uncaused — it only means free from conscious censorship and control.) In psychoanalysis, the patient is asked to report whatever comes to mind.

Free Association *In psychoanalysis, reporting whatever comes to mind without monitoring its contents — regardless of how painful, embarrassing, or irrelevant it may seem; Freud believed that the first thing to come to a patient's mind was often an important clue to what the unconscious mind wants to conceal*

2. *Dream analysis.* Similar to free association, dream analysis is a classic technique for observing unconscious processes. Freud called dreams "the royal road to the unconscious." Because the ego does not defend itself very well against unconscious conflicts during sleep, these conflicts are supposedly expressed in the form of dreams. Freud felt that dreams could be interpreted on two levels. On a superficial level, there is the *manifest content* of the dream, the immediate and conscious content of dreams. On a deeper level, dreams may be interpreted in terms of their *latent content*, the presumed true meaning hidden behind the manifest content. Thus, according to Freudian dream theory, a therapist might interpret a dream of riding a horse or driving a car (the manifest content) as a desire or concern about sexual intercourse (the latent content).

3. *Analyzing resistance.* When analyzing a patient's behavior and verbalizations, the analyst looks for examples of **resistance**, the defensive tendency of the unconscious to block (or *resist*) from consciousness, particularly threatening *repressed* materials. For example, if the patient is late or cancels an appointment, the analyst might think the patient's ego defenses are attempting to keep unconscious conflicts from being revealed. Similarly, if the patient pauses during significant points in conversation or changes topics suddenly, the analyst will try to find out what is causing the resistance by pursuing the topic that preceded the block.

Resistance *A stage in psychoanalysis when the patient avoids (resists) the analyst's attempts to bring threatening unconscious material to conscious awareness*

Although patients generally enter therapy to gain personal insight, they also exhibit resistance because it helps reduce anxiety. The closer the analyst comes to the source of the anxiety, the more the patient is motivated to run from it. To help you remember the concept of resistance, think of this classic joke about psychoanalysis: "If patients arrive on time for their appointment, they're compulsive; if they're early, they're dependent; and if late, they're resistant."

4. *Analyzing transference.* During psychoanalysis, the patient may displace (or "transfer") onto his or her relationship with the therapist feelings from an earlier stage in life, generally with the mother, father, or other important figures. This process is known as **transference**. Transference is assumed to have occurred if the patient becomes overly dependent on the analyst or falls in love and seeks to establish an intimate relationship. Rather than taking these reactions and emotions at face value, the analyst interprets them as evidence of unresolved attachments or conflicts in childhood or previous relationships. Transference is considered a valuable part of psychoanalysis because exposing repressed feelings offers the patient a chance to "work through" unconscious conflicts and gain insight into past and current relationships.

What happens if the patient really does fall in love with the therapist? Or vice versa? Just as the film industry inaccurately portrays therapy as always conducted on a couch, movies also frequently portray love affairs between patient and therapist. Although romance may enliven a movie, it is extremely destructive in a therapeutic setting (Dalenberg, 2000; Sloan, Edmond, Rubin, & Doughty, 1998). As expected, therapists must have their clients' trust, and they must uphold the highest standards of ethical behavior. Sex between patient and therapist is a serious breach of professional ethics, and in several states it is a criminal offense (Sloan, Edmond, Rubin, & Doughty, 1998).

5. *Interpretation.* The core of psychoanalytic therapy is **interpretation**. During psychoanalysis, the analyst listens closely and observes patterns and hidden meanings. At the right time, the therapist points out where resistance occurs and what free association, dream analysis, and transference reveal about impulses repressed in the unconscious. For instance, during therapy a man who has trouble with intimacy might look out the window and change the subject whenever anything touches on closeness or feelings. The analyst will attempt to interpret these defensive behaviors and help the patient recognize how he avoids the topic (Davison & Neale, 2001, p. 32).

Transference *In psychoanalysis, the patient may displace (or transfer) thoughts, feelings, fears, wishes, and conflicts from past relationships, particularly from childhood, onto new relationships, especially with the therapist*

Interpretation *A psychoanalyst's explanation of a patient's free associations, dreams, resistance, and transference; more generally, any statement by a therapist that presents a patient's problem in a new way*

"I dreamt I had a Harem, but they all wanted to talk about the relationship."

CALLAHAN

Cartoons and couches. *Have you noticed that most cartoons about therapy show a Freudian model with a patient reclining on a couch?*

Evaluation

Freud's theories of personality have been enormously influential, yet also the subject of heated debate. The same can be said of his method of therapy. Criticisms of psychoanalysis focus on two major points:

1. Limited applicability. Freud's methods were developed in the early 1900s for a particular clientele — upper-class Viennese people (primarily women). Although psychoanalysis has been refined over the years, critics say it still seems to suit only a select group of individuals. It is not only time consuming (often lasting several years with four to five sessions a week) and expensive, but it also does not work well with severe mental disorders, such as schizophrenia. This is logical because psychoanalysis is based on verbalization and rationality — the very abilities most significantly affected by serious disorders. Success appears to be best with less severe disorders, such as anxiety disorders, and with highly motivated, articulate patients. Critics jokingly proposed the acronym *YAVIS* to describe the perfect psychoanalysis patient: young, attractive, verbal, intelligent, and successful (Schofield, 1964). Even for a select group, however, critics suggest that spending years on a couch chasing unconscious conflicts from the past allows patients to escape from the responsibilities and problems of adult life — in effect, the patient becomes "couchridden."

2. Lack of scientific credibility. The goals of psychoanalysis are explicitly stated — to bring unconscious conflicts to conscious awareness. But how do you know when this goal has been achieved? If patients accept the analyst's interpretations of their conflicts, their "insights" may be nothing more than cooperation with the therapist's belief system. On the other hand, if patients refuse to accept the analyst's interpretations, the analyst may say they're exhibiting resistance. Moreover, the therapist can always explain away a failure. If patients get better, it's because of their insights. If they don't, then the insight was not real — it was only intellectually accepted. Such reasoning does not meet scientific standards. The ability to prove or disprove a theory is the foundation of the scientific approach.

How seriously should these criticisms be taken? Although psychoanalysts acknowledge that it is impossible to scientifically document certain aspects of their therapy, they insist that most patients benefit (Gabbard, 1999; Ward, 2000). Partially in response to criticism, however, more streamlined forms of psychoanalysis have been developed.

Modern Psychodynamic Therapy

Psychodynamic Therapy *A form of psychotherapy that emphasizes internal conflicts, motives, and unconscious forces*

In modern psychoanalytic therapies, known as **psychodynamic**, treatment is briefer (usually only one to two times a week), the patient is seen face to face (rather than reclining on a couch), and the therapist takes a more directive approach (rather than waiting for a gradual unveiling of the unconscious). Also, although contemporary psychodynamic therapists try to help clients gain insight into their early childhood experiences and unconscious roots of problems, they focus more attention on conscious processes and current problems. Such refinements have helped make psychoanalysis available to an increasing number of people and more effective in the short term (Book & Luborsky, 1998; Rutan & Stone, 2000).

Although no transcript of a single therapy session can actually convey what goes on, it can show how particular techniques are used. Following is an exchange between a patient (PT) and therapist (TH) (Shea, 1988, pp. 435–436). In the box on the next page, can you identify the psychodynamic and psychoanalytic techniques employed — free association, interpretation, dream analysis, resistance, and transference? If you want to compare your answers to ours, see Appendix B.

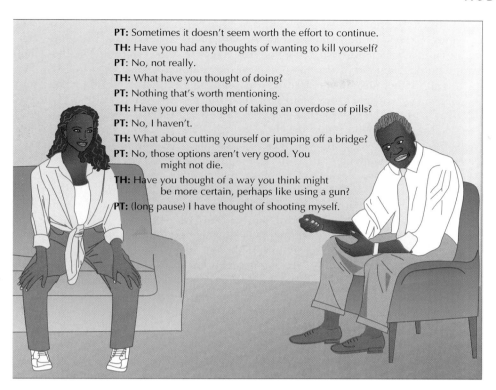

PT: Sometimes it doesn't seem worth the effort to continue.

TH: Have you had any thoughts of wanting to kill yourself?

PT: No, not really.

TH: What have you thought of doing?

PT: Nothing that's worth mentioning.

TH: Have you ever thought of taking an overdose of pills?

PT: No, I haven't.

TH: What about cutting yourself or jumping off a bridge?

PT: No, those options aren't very good. You might not die.

TH: Have you thought of a way you think might be more certain, perhaps like using a gun?

PT: (long pause) I have thought of shooting myself.

Check & Review

PSYCHOANALYSIS/PSYCHODYNAMIC THERAPIES

Sigmund Freud developed the psychoanalytic method of therapy to uncover unconscious conflicts and bring them into conscious awareness. The five major techniques of **psychoanalysis** are **free association**, **dream analysis**, analyzing **resistance**, analyzing **transference**, and **interpretation**. Like psychoanalytic theories of personality, psychoanalysis is the subject of great debate. It is primarily criticized for its limited availability (it is time-consuming, expensive, and suits only a small group of people) and its lack of sci-entific credibility. Modern **psychodynamic therapies** overcome some of these limitations.

Questions

1. The system of psychotherapy developed by Freud that seeks to bring unconscious conflicts into conscious awareness is known as _____. (a) transference; (b) cognitive restructuring; (c) psychoanalysis; (d) the "hot seat" technique

2. Which psychoanalytic technique best explains the following situations?

a. Mary is extremely angry with her therapist, who seems unresponsive and uncaring about her personal needs.

b. Although John is normally very punctual, he is frequently late for his therapy session.

3. What are the two major criticisms of psychoanalysis?

4. How does modern psychodynamic therapy differ from psychoanalysis?

Answers to Questions can be found in Appendix B.

Cognitive Therapies: A Focus on Faulty Thoughts and Beliefs

Cognitive therapy assumes that faulty thought processes and beliefs create problem behaviors and emotions. For example, a cognitive therapist would say that feelings of depression are created by such beliefs as "If I don't do everything perfectly, I am worthless" or "I'm helpless to change my life, so I'll never be happy." When people hold beliefs that are irrational, that are overly demanding, or that fail to match reality, their emotions and behaviors may become disturbed (Beck, 2000, 2001; Ellis, 1996, 2000).

What are the major cognitive therapies?

Cognitive Therapy *Therapy that focuses on faulty thought processes and beliefs to treat problem behaviors*

Cognitive therapists, like psychoanalysts, analyze a person's thought processes, believing that altering destructive thoughts will enable the person to live more effectively. Also like psychoanalysts, cognitive therapists assume that many of the beliefs that create problem behaviors operate at an unexamined level.

Cognitive therapists also agree with psychoanalysts that exploring an unexamined belief system can produce insight into the reasons for disturbed behaviors. However, instead of believing that a change in behavior occurs because of catharsis, cognitive therapists believe that insight into negative **self-talk**, the unrealistic things a person has been telling himself or herself, is most important. This insight allows the individual to challenge his or her thoughts, to directly change how he or she interprets events, and, ultimately, to change maladaptive behaviors. For example, the irrational statement "If I don't do everything perfectly, I am worthless" can be changed to more adaptive thoughts like "I can accept my limits" or "I can make constructive changes in my behavior." **Cognitive restructuring** is the name for this process of changing destructive thoughts or inappropriate interpretations.

Psychoanalysts focus primarily on childhood relationships within the patient's family, whereas cognitive therapists emphasize the way events and people both inside and outside the family influence beliefs. For example, going to college or boot camp, falling in love, or becoming a parent can change attitudes and beliefs in significant ways, and interactions with teachers, bosses, and friends can create disturbed as well as realistic ways of thinking.

Albert Ellis and Rational-Emotive Therapy

One of the best-known cognitive therapists is Albert Ellis, a former psychoanalytic therapist who developed his own approach, known as **rational-emotive therapy** (RET) (1961, 1997, 2000). Ellis calls RET an A-B-C approach, referring to the three steps involved in creating disturbed responses: (A) an activating event, which is some type of stimulus such as criticism from a boss or a failing grade; (B) the belief system, which is the person's interpretation of the activating experience; and (C) the emotional consequence the person experiences (Figure 44.2).

Ellis claims that unless we stop to think about our interpretation of events, we will automatically go from A (the activating event) to C (the emotional consequence).

Self-Talk *Internal dialogue; the things people say to themselves when they interpret events*

Cognitive Restructuring *The process in cognitive therapy by which the therapist and client work to change destructive ways of thinking*

Rational-Emotive Therapy (RET) *Cognitive therapy system developed by Albert Ellis that attempts to eliminate self-defeating beliefs through rational examination*

Figure 44.2 *The development of irrational misconceptions.* How do our thoughts and beliefs make us unhappy? According to Albert Ellis, our emotional reactions are produced by our interpretation of an event, not by the event itself. For example, if you receive a low exam score (activating event — A), you might feel sad and frustrated (emotional consequence — C). Although you might explain to yourself and others that your bad mood was a direct result of the low grade, Ellis would argue that the self-talk ("I'll never get through college," irrational belief — B) between the event and the feeling is actually what upset you. Furthermore, the bad mood causes you to ruminate on all the other bad things in your life, which maintains your negative emotional state. Ellis's theory explains why going for a jog or watching television can improve your mood — it breaks the vicious cycle.

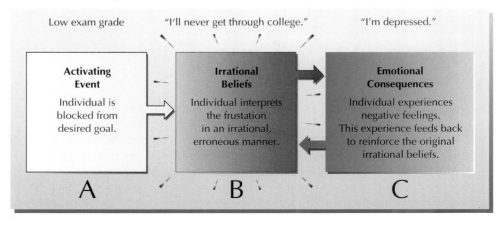

Low exam grade | "I'll never get through college." | "I'm depressed."

Activating Event
Individual is blocked from desired goal.

Irrational Beliefs
Individual interprets the frustation in an irrational, erroneous manner.

Emotional Consequences
Individual experiences negative feelings. This experience feeds back to reinforce the original irrational beliefs.

A   B   C

We fail to see that step B (the belief system) actually creates the subsequent emotion. Receiving a failing grade on an exam does not *cause* the emotion of depression. It is step B (the belief that "I'll never get through college") that is the culprit.

When he originally formulated his theory, Ellis emphasized a number of specific irrational beliefs resulting from his A-B-C model, such as "I must have love from everyone" and "I must be thoroughly competent." In recent years, however, he has shifted to a general concept of "demandingness" (Ellis, 1997, 2000; Kottler & Brown, 1999). When people *demand* certain "musts" and "shoulds" from themselves and others, they create emotional distress and behavioral dysfunction that often requires therapeutic intervention. For example, a divorced man whose wife left him for another man might engage in this self-talk: "I *must* be loved by everyone. She *should* not and *must* not reject me. I *demand* that she come back to me, or I'll get even."

Ellis believes that such unrealistic, unproductive self-talk, "demandingness," and "musturbation" generally goes unexamined unless the client is confronted directly. In therapy, Ellis often argues with clients, cajoling and teasing them, sometimes in very blunt language. Many clients are shocked by his bluntness — and by their own irrational beliefs. Once clients recognize their self-defeating thoughts, Ellis begins working with them on how to *behave* differently — to test out new beliefs and to learn better coping skills. Reflecting this increased attention to behavioral change, he renamed his therapy *rational-emotive behavior therapy* (REBT).

Aaron Beck and Cognitive-Behavior Therapy

Another well-known cognitive therapist is Aaron Beck (1976, 2000, 2001). Like Ellis, Beck believes that psychological problems result from illogical thinking and from destructive self-talk. But unlike Ellis and psychoanalysts who encourage the client to express thoughts and feelings to gain insight into the origins of maladaptive behaviors, Beck takes a much more active approach. He seeks to provide clients with experiences, both inside and outside the therapy session, that will alter their negative talk in a favorable way. The overall goal is to directly confront and change the behaviors associated with destructive cognitions — hence the term **cognitive-behavior therapy**.

Cognitive-Behavior Therapy
Aaron Beck's therapy that works to change not only destructive thoughts and beliefs but the associated behaviors as well

TRY THIS
Yourself

Although Albert Ellis believes that most people require the help of a therapist to see through their defenses and force them to challenge their self-defeating thoughts, you may be able to change some of your own irrational beliefs and responses with the following suggestions:

1. *Evaluate the consequences.* Emotions such as anger, anxiety, and depression often seem "natural," but they don't have to happen. Rather than perpetuating negative emotions by assuming they must be experienced, focus on whether your reactions make you more effective and enable you to solve your problems.
2. *Identify your belief system.* Find your irrational beliefs by asking yourself why you feel the particular emotions you do. Ellis believes that by confronting your beliefs, you can discover the irrational assumptions that are creating the problem consequences.
3. *Dispute the self-defeating beliefs.* Once you have identified an overly demanding or irrational belief, argue against it. For example, it is gratifying when people you cherish love you in return, but if they do not, continuing to pursue them or insisting that they must love you will only be self-defeating.
4. *Practice effective ways of thinking.* Continue to examine your emotional reactions to events and situations to create opportunities to dispute irrational beliefs and substitute realistic perceptions. Practice behaviors that are more effective by rehearsing them at home and imagining outcomes that are more successful.

One of the most successful applications of Beck's theory has been in the treatment of depression. Beck has identified several thinking patterns that he believes are associated with depression. These are among the most important:

1. Selective perception. Depression-prone people tend to focus selectively on negative events while ignoring positive events.

2. Overgeneralization. On the basis of limited information, depressed people overgeneralize and draw negative conclusions about their self-worth — for example, believing you are worthless because you lost a promotion or failed an exam.

3. Magnification. Depressed people tend to exaggerate the importance of undesirable events or personal shortcomings and see them as catastrophic and unchangeable.

4. All-or-nothing thinking. Depressed people see things in black-or-white categories. Everything is either totally good or bad, right or wrong, a success or a failure.

Beck's cognitive-behavior therapy works like this: To begin, clients are taught to recognize and keep track of their thoughts. Examples might be: "How come I'm the only one alone at this party" (selective perception) and "If I don't get straight A's, I'll never get a good job" (all-or-nothing thinking). Next, the therapist trains the client to develop ways to test these automatic thoughts against reality. For example, if the client believes that straight As are necessary for a certain job, the therapist needs to find only one instance of this not being the case to refute the belief. Obviously, the therapist chooses the tests carefully so that they do not confirm the client's negative beliefs but lead instead to positive outcomes.

This approach — identifying dysfunctional thoughts followed by active testing — helps depressed people discover that negative attitudes are largely a product of unrealistic or faulty thought processes. At this point, Beck introduces the second phase of therapy, persuading the client to actively pursue pleasurable activities. Depressed individuals often lose motivation, even for experiences they used to find enjoyable. Simultaneously taking an active rather than passive role and reconnecting with enjoyable experiences help in recovering from depression.

Evaluating Cognitive Therapies

Considerable evidence suggests that Beck's procedures are highly effective with depression, anxiety disorders, bulimia nervosa, anger management, addiction, and even some symptoms of schizophrenia (Beck, 2000, 2001; Haaga, Rabois, & Brody, 1999; McMullin, 2000; Tobin, 2000). Ellis's RET has had similar successes with a variety of disorders (Beal & DiGiuseppe, 1998; Ellis, 2000).

Both Beck and Ellis are criticized, however, for ignoring or denying the client's unconscious dynamics and minimizing the importance of the client's past (Butler, 2000). In addition, Ellis is criticized for "preaching an ethical system" (Davison & Neale, 2001, p. 505). By labeling his patients' beliefs "irrational" and insisting that they be replaced with "rational" thoughts, Ellis is imposing his own set of standards. Other critics suggest cognitive therapies are successful because they employ behavior techniques, not because they change the underlying cognitive structure (Bandura, 1969, 1997; Wright & Beck, 1999).

Humanistic Therapies: Blocked Personal Growth

Humanists believe human potential includes the freedom to become what one wants to be as well as the responsibility to make choices. **Humanistic therapy** therefore assumes that people with problems are suffering from a blockage or disruption of their normal growth potential. This blockage creates a defective self-concept. When obstacles are removed, the individual is free to become the self-accepting and genuine person everyone is capable of being.

What is different about humanistic therapies?

Humanistic Therapy *Therapy that helps individuals become creative and unique people through affective restructuring (emotional readjustment)*

Imagine for a minute how you feel when you are with someone who believes you are a good person with unlimited potential, a person whose "real self" is unique and valuable. These are the feelings that are nurtured in humanistic therapy approaches.

Carl Rogers and Client-Centered Therapy

One of the best-known humanistic therapists, Carl Rogers (1961, 1980), developed an approach that encourages people to actualize their potential and relate to others in genuine ways. His approach is referred to as **client-centered therapy**. Using the term *client* instead of *patient* was very significant to Rogers. He believed the label *patient* implied being sick or mentally ill, rather than responsible and competent. Treating people as clients emphasizes the fact that *they* are the ones in charge of the therapy and focuses on the equality of the therapist–client relationship.

Client-centered therapy, like psychoanalysis and cognitive therapies, explores thoughts and feelings to obtain insight into the causes for behaviors. For Rogerian therapists, however, the focus is on encouraging healthy emotional experiences. Clients are responsible for discovering their own maladaptive patterns, whereas the therapist provides an accepting atmosphere in which the client can freely explore important thoughts and feelings (Barrett-Lennard, 1999).

How does the therapist create such an atmosphere? Rogerian therapists create a therapeutic relationship by focusing on four important qualities of communication: empathy, unconditional positive regard, genuineness, and active listening.

1. **Empathy** is a sensitive understanding and sharing of another person's inner experience. When we put ourselves in other people's shoes, we enter their inner world, or phenomenological experience. Therapists watch body language and listen for subtle cues to help them understand the emotional experiences of clients. When clients express feelings verbally, they are encouraged to explore them further. The therapist uses open-ended statements such as "You found that upsetting" or "You haven't been able to decide what to do about this" rather than asking questions or offering explanations.

2. **Unconditional positive regard** is genuine caring for people based on their innate value as individuals. Because humanists believe human nature is positive and each

> **Client-Centered Therapy** *A type of psychotherapy developed by Carl Rogers that emphasizes the client's natural tendency to become healthy and productive; techniques include empathy, unconditional positive regard, genuineness, and active listening*

> **Empathy** *In Rogerian terms, an insightful awareness and ability to share another person's inner experience*

> **Unconditional Positive Regard** *According to Carl Rogers, the nonjudgmental attitude and genuine caring that the therapist should express toward the client*

"How would you feel if the mouse did that to you?"

Humanistic therapy? Can you identify the active listening technique satirized in this cartoon?

"It's no disgrace—somebody has to be plain vanilla."

person is unique, clients can be respected and cherished without having to prove themselves worthy of the therapist's esteem. Unconditional positive regard allows the therapist to trust that clients have the best answers for their own lives. To maintain a climate of unconditional positive regard, the therapist avoids making evaluative statements such as "That's good" and "You did the right thing," which give the idea that the therapist is judging them and that clients need to receive approval. Humanists believe that when people receive unconditional caring from others, they become better able to value themselves in a similar way.

3. Genuineness, or *authenticity*, is being aware of one's true inner thoughts and feelings and being able to share them honestly with others. When people are genuine, they are not artificial, defensive, or playing a role. If a Rogerian therapist were pleased with a client's progress, for example, he or she would feel free to share those feelings. When therapists are genuine with their clients, they believe their clients will in turn develop self-trust and honest self-expression.

4. Active listening involves reflecting, paraphrasing, and clarifying what the client says and means. To *reflect* is to hold a mirror in front of the person, enabling that person to see him- or herself. To *paraphrase* is to summarize in different words what the client is saying. To *clarify* is to check that both the speaker and listener are on the same wavelength.

For example, noticing the client's furrowed brow and clenched hands while he client is discussing his marital problems, the clinician might respond, "Sounds like you're angry with your wife and feeling pretty miserable right now." With this one statement, the clinician reflects the client's anger, paraphrases his complaint, and gives feedback to clarify the communication. By being an *active listener*, the clinician communicates that he or she is genuinely interested in what the client is saying.

Genuineness In Rogerian terms, authenticity or congruence; the awareness of one's true inner thoughts and feelings and being able to share them honestly with others

Active Listening According to Carl Rogers, the ability to listen with total attention to what another is saying; this involves reflecting, paraphrasing, and clarifying what the person says and means

Evaluation

Supporters say there is empirical evidence for humanistic assumptions (e.g., Bohart, O'Hara, & Leitner, 1998; Hayashi et al., 1998), but critics argue that the basic tenets of humanistic therapy, such as self-actualization and self-awareness, are difficult to test scientifically. Most of the research on the outcomes of humanistic therapy relies on client self-reports; however, people undergoing any type of therapy are motivated to justify their time and expense. In addition, research on specific therapeutic techniques, such as Rogerian "empathy" and "active listening" has had mixed results (Gottman, Coan, Carrere, & Swanson, 1998).

Would you like to check your understanding of empathy, unconditional positive regard, genuineness, and active listening? Identify the techniques being used in the following excerpt (Shea, 1988, pp. 32–33). Our choices are discussed in Appendix B.

THERAPIST (TH): What has it been like coming down to the emergency room today?

CLIENT (CL): Unsettling, to say the least. I feel very awkward here, sort of like I'm vulnerable. To be honest, I've had some horrible experiences with doctors. I don't like them.

TH: I see. Well, they scare the hell out of me, too (smiles, indicating the humor in his comment).

CL: (Chuckles) I thought you were a doctor.

TH: I am (pauses, smiles) — that's what's so scary.

CL: (Smiles and laughs)

TH: Tell me a little more about some of your unpleasant experiences with doctors, because I want to make sure I'm not doing anything that is upsetting to you. I don't want that to happen.

CL: Well, that's very nice to hear. My last doctor didn't give a hoot about what I said, and he only spoke in huge words.

In case you're wondering, this is an excerpt from an actual session — humor and informality can be an important part of the therapeutic process.

Check & Review

COGNITIVE AND HUMANISTIC THERAPIES

Cognitive therapy emphasizes the importance of faulty thought processes, beliefs, and negative **self-talk** in the creation of problem behaviors. Albert Ellis's **rational-emotive therapy** (RET) aims to replace a client's irrational beliefs with rational beliefs and accurate perceptions of the world. Aaron Beck's **cognitive-behavior therapy** takes a more active approach with clients by emphasizing changes in both thought processes and behavior.

Evaluations of cognitive therapies find Beck's procedures particularly effective for relieving depression; Ellis has had success with a variety of disorders. Both Beck and Ellis, however, are criticized for ignoring the importance of unconscious processes and the client's history. Some critics also attribute any success with cognitive therapies to the use of behavioral techniques.

Humanistic therapies are based on the premise that problems result when an individual's normal growth potential is blocked. In Carl Rogers's **client-centered therapy**, the therapist offers **empathy, unconditional positive regard, genuineness,** and **active listening** as means of facilitating personal growth. Humanistic therapies are difficult to evaluate scientifically, and research on specific therapeutic techniques has had mixed results.

Questions

1. Cognitive therapists assume that problem behaviors and emotions are caused by _____. (a) faulty thought processes and beliefs; (b) negative self-image; (c) incongruent belief systems; (d) lack of self-discipline

2. What are the three steps (the A-B-C) of Ellis's RET?

3. Beck identified four destructive thought patterns associated with depression (selective perception, overgeneralization, magnification, and all-or-nothing thinking). Using these terms, label the following thoughts:

_____ a. Mary left me, and I'll never fall in love again. I'll always be alone.

_____ b. My ex-spouse is an evil monster and our entire marriage was a sham.

4. Label each of the following Rogerian therapy techniques:

_____ a. A sensitive understanding and sharing of another's inner or phenomenological experience

_____ b. The honest sharing of inner thoughts and feelings

_____ c. A nonjudgmental and caring attitude toward another that does not have to be earned

Answers to Questions can be found in Appendix B.

How are learning principles used in behavior therapy?

Behavior Therapy *A group of techniques based on learning principles that are used to change maladaptive behaviors*

Behavior Therapies: Changing Maladaptive Behaviors

Have you ever understood why you were doing something you would rather not do but continued to do it anyway? Sometimes having insight into a problem does not automatically solve it. Take the example of Mrs. D, an agoraphobic woman who had not left her house for $3^1/_2$ years except with her husband. She had undergone $1^1/_2$ years of insight-based therapy and had become well aware of the causes of her problem, but she did not change her behavior. She finally sought the help of a behavior therapist, who, instead of working on her understanding of her problems or attempting to restructure her feelings, systematically trained her to behave differently. After less than 2 months, Mrs. D was able to leave her house and travel alone to appointments (Lazarus, 1971).

As this example shows, **behavior therapy** uses learning principles to change behaviors. Behavior therapists do not believe it is necessary to obtain insight or restructure feelings before changes in behavior can occur. The focus in this approach is on the problem behavior itself rather than on any underlying causes. That is not to say the person's feelings and interpretations are disregarded; they are just not emphasized. Behavior therapists believe that abnormal or maladaptive behaviors are learned in the same way that adaptive behaviors are learned. Thus, abnormal behaviors can also be "unlearned."

In behavior therapy, the therapist diagnoses the problem by listing the maladaptive behaviors that occur and the adaptive behaviors that are absent. The therapist then attempts to decrease the frequency of maladaptive behaviors and increase the frequency of adaptive behaviors. To accomplish this type of change, a behavior therapist draws on principles of classical conditioning, operant conditioning, and modeling (Sarafino, 2000).

Classical Conditioning Techniques

Behavior therapists use the principles of classical conditioning, derived from Pavlov's model for associating two stimulus events, to decrease maladaptive behavior by creating new associations to replace the faulty ones. We will explore two techniques based on these principles: systematic desensitization and aversion therapy.

© Sidney Harris

1. Systematic desensitization. Mrs. D's behavior therapist used *systematic desensitization*, a procedure developed by Joseph Wolpe (Wolpe & Plaud, 1997) to extinguish her agoraphobia. **Systematic desensitization** is a gradual process of associating a hierarchy of fear-evoking stimuli with deep relaxation. It is based on the opposite actions of the sympathetic and parasympathetic branches of the autonomic nervous system. Because the parasympathetic nerves control autonomic functions when we are relaxed and because the sympathetic nerves are dominant when we are anxious, it is physiologically impossible to be both relaxed and anxious at the same time. The goal, then, is to replace an anxiety response with a relaxation response when confronting the feared stimulus (Sturges & Sturges, 1998; Wolpe & Plaud, 1997).

Desensitization is a three-step process. First, a client is taught how to maintain a state of deep relaxation that is physiologically incompatible with an anxiety response. Next, the therapist and client construct a *hierarchy*, or ranked listing of 10 or so anxiety-arousing images (Figure 44.3). In the final step, the relaxed client mentally visualizes or physically experiences items at the bottom of the hierarchy and works his or her way to the most anxiety producing images at the top. If any image or situation begins to create anxiety, the client stops momentarily and returns to a state of complete relaxation. Eventually, the fear response is extinguished.

2. Aversion therapy. In sharp contrast to systematic desensitization, **aversion therapy** uses principles of classical conditioning to create anxiety rather than extinguish it. People who engage in excessive drinking, for example, build up a number of pleasurable associations. Because these pleasurable associations can-

Virtual reality therapy. Rather than mental imaging or actual physical experiences of a fearful situation, modern therapy can use the latest in computer technology — virtual reality headsets and data gloves. A client with a fear of heights, for example, can experience climbing a stepladder all the way to standing on the edge of a tall building, while never leaving the therapist's office.

Systematic Desensitization *In behavior therapy, a gradual process of extinguishing a learned fear (or phobia) by associating a hierarchy of fear-evoking stimuli with deep relaxation*

Aversion Therapy *Behavior therapy technique that pairs an aversive (unpleasant) stimulus with a maladaptive behavior*

Nearly everyone is somewhat anxious before an important exam. If you find this anxiety helpful and invigorating, skip ahead to the next section. However, if the days and evenings before a major exam are ruined by your anxiety and you sometimes "freeze up" while taking the test, you can benefit from an informal type of systematic desensitization.

Step 1: Review and practice the relaxation technique taught in Module 10.

Step 2: Create a 10-step "test taking" hierarchy — starting with the least anxiety arousing image (perhaps the day your instructor first mentions an upcoming

exam) and ending with actually taking the exam.

Step 3: Beginning with the least arousing image — hearing about the exam — picture yourself at each stage, while maintaining a calm, relaxed state. Work your way through all 10 steps. If you become anxious at any stage, stay there, repeating your relaxation technique until the anxiety diminishes.

Step 4: If you start to feel anxious the night before the exam, or even during the exam itself, remind yourself to relax. Take a few moments to shut your eyes and review how you worked through your hierarchy.

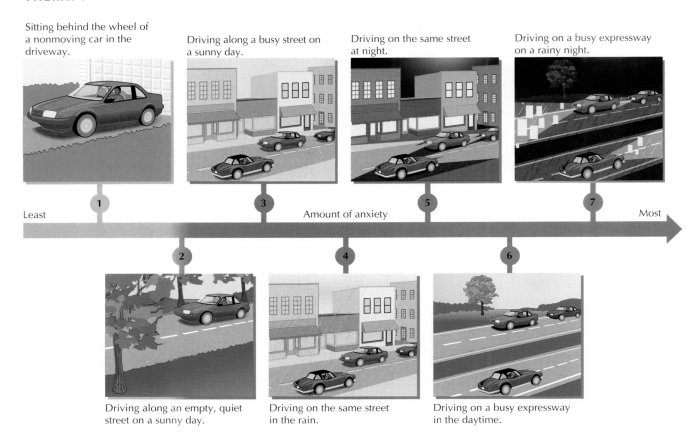

Sitting behind the wheel of a nonmoving car in the driveway.

Driving along a busy street on a sunny day.

Driving on the same street at night.

Driving on a busy expressway on a rainy night.

Least   1   Amount of anxiety   Most

2   4   6   3   5   7

Driving along an empty, quiet street on a sunny day.

Driving on the same street in the rain.

Driving on a busy expressway in the daytime.

Figure 44.3 *Sample hierarchy for a driving phobia.* During systematic desensitization, the client constructs a hierarchy, or ranked listing, of anxiety-arousing images or situations starting with one that produces very little anxiety and escalating to those that arouse extreme anxiety. To extinguish a driving phobia, the patient begins with images or actually sitting behind the wheel of a nonmoving car and ends with driving on a busy expressway.

not always be prevented, aversion therapy provides *negative associations* to compete with the pleasurable ones. Someone who wants to stop drinking, for example, could take a drug called Antabuse that causes vomiting whenever alcohol enters the system. When the new connection between alcohol and nausea has been classically conditioned, engaging in the once desirable habit will cause an immediate negative response (Figure 44.4). Although this treatment has had some limited,

Figure 44.4 *Aversion therapy for alcoholism.* Using the principles of classical conditioning, a nausea-producing drug (Antabuse) is paired with alcohol to create an aversion to drinking.

UCS (drug in alcohol)   UCR (nausea)   CS (alcohol)   CR (nausea)

temporary effect, it does not provide lasting relief (Seligman, 1994). Unlike a similar technique where coyotes quickly learned to avoid tainted sheep meat (Module 18), humans understand that the nausea is produced by the Antabuse and do not generalize their learning to the alcohol itself.

Operant Conditioning Techniques

Operant conditioning techniques use shaping and reinforcement to increase adaptive behaviors and punishment and extinction to decrease maladaptive behaviors.

Shaping and reinforcement. In behavior therapy, a behavior to be acquired is called the *target behavior*. Shaping — being rewarded for successive approximations of the target behavior — is one operant technique for eventually performing the target behavior. One of the most successful applications of shaping and reinforcement has been with autistic children. Children with *autism* do not communicate or interact normally with other people. Shaping has been used to develop their language skills. The child is first rewarded for any sounds and then later only for words and sentences.

Shaping is also used to help people acquire social skills. If you are painfully shy, for example, a clinician might first ask you to role-play simply saying hello to someone you find attractive. Then, you might practice behaviors that gradually lead you to suggest a get-together or date. During such *role-playing*, or *behavior rehearsal*, the clinician would give you feedback and reinforcement.

Behavior rehearsal is also the technique behind *assertiveness training*, which teaches people to stand up for themselves. Clients begin with simple situations and progress to practicing effective verbal responses and adaptive behaviors. In treating Mrs. D's agoraphobia, for example, her therapist used role playing to shape assertive behaviors such as standing up to her domineering father.

Adaptive behaviors can also be taught or increased with techniques that provide immediate reinforcement in the form of tokens (Sarafino, 2000). *Tokens* are secondary (conditioned) reinforcers, such as poker chips, "credit" cards, or other tangible objects that can be exchanged for primary rewards such as food, treats, watching TV, a private room, or outings. In an inpatient treatment facility, patients are sometimes rewarded with tokens and gradually shaped toward desirable activities such as taking medication, attending group therapy sessions, or taking part in recreational programs. Patients can also be "fined" for inappropriate behaviors by having tokens taken away.

Doesn't this approach depend too much on the tokens to have any lasting effect? Advocates point out that tokens help people acquire beneficial behaviors that become rewarding in themselves. A full-fledged behavior management program has a series of levels, each requiring increasingly complex behavior. For example, patients might at first be given tokens for merely attending group therapy sessions. Once this behavior is established, they would be rewarded only for actually participating in the sessions. Eventually, the tokens could be discontinued when the patient receives the reinforcement of being helped by participation in the therapy sessions. Tokens have been successfully used in a wide variety of settings, including hospitals, programs for delinquents, classrooms, and individual homes (Bower, 2000; Truchlicka, McLaughlin, & Swain, 1998).

Punishment and extinction. Although shaping and reinforcement can be used to *increase adaptive behaviors*, two other operant techniques — punishment and extinction — can be used to *decrease problem behaviors*. Punishment can be

Overcoming agoraphobia. *Behavior therapists would use shaping and reinforcement to treat this woman's agoraphobia.*

either positive (applying an aversive stimulus, such as a mild shock) or negative (removing a rewarding stimulus). Most behavioral techniques involve negative punishment. One of the most frequently used techniques (by both clinicians and parents) is *time out*. In time out, the person is physically removed from sources of rewards whenever he or she behaves inappropriately. The technique of *extinction*, or removing all rewards, also can be used to eliminate maladaptive behavior (Modules 15 and 16). When diagnosing problem behaviors, behavior therapists first identify how maladaptive behavior is being rewarded and then remove the rewards.

Modeling

Modeling Therapy *A type of behavior therapy that involves watching and imitating appropriate models that demonstrate desirable behaviors*

In addition to using classical and operant conditioning techniques, behavioral therapists also use **modeling therapy**, observing and imitating appropriate behaviors. By watching appropriate people perform desired behaviors, the client learns new behaviors. For example, Bandura and his colleagues (1969) asked clients with snake phobias to watch other (nonphobic) people handle snakes. After only 2 hours of exposure, over 92 percent of the phobic observers allowed a snake to crawl over their hands, arms, and neck. When the client combines live modeling with direct and gradual practice, it is called *participant modeling*.

Modeling is also part of social skills training and assertiveness training. Clients learn how to interview for a job by first watching the therapist role-play the part of the interviewee. The therapist models the appropriate language (assertively asking for a job), body posture, and so forth, and then asks the client to imitate the behavior and play the same role. Over the course of several sessions, the client becomes gradually desensitized to the anxiety of interviews and learns interview skills.

Evaluating Behavior Therapies

Research suggests behavior therapy based on classical and operant conditioning and modeling has been effective with various problems, including phobias, OCD, eating disorders, autism, mental retardation, and delinquency (Agras & Berkowitz, 1999; Sarafino, 2000; Sarkar, Rathee & Neera, 1999; Wolpe, 1997). Some patients have even returned to their homes and communities after years of institutionalization.

Critics of behavior therapy, however, raise important questions that fall into three major categories:

1. *Generalizability*. What happens after the treatment stops? Can the results be generalized? Critics argue that in the "real world" patients are not consistently reinforced, and their newly acquired behaviors may disappear. To deal with this possibility, behavior therapists work to gradually shape clients toward rewards that are typical of life outside the clinical setting.

2. *Symptom substitution*. Advocates of the psychoanalytic approach argue that behavior therapies simply substitute one symptom for another rather than resolving the underlying psychological problems. A person with a phobia about spiders, for example, may develop a new phobia. However, there is little evidence that symptom substitution actually occurs.

3. *Ethics*. Is it ethical for one person to control another's behavior? Are there some situations in which behavior therapy should not be used? In the movie *A Clockwork Orange*, people in positions of power used behavior modification principles to control the general population. Behaviorists reply that rewards and punishments already control our behaviors, and behavior therapy actually increases a person's freedom by making these controls overt. Also, say the behaviorists, behavior therapy increases self-control by teaching people how to change their own behavior and maintain these changes when they leave the clinical setting.

Check & Review

BEHAVIOR THERAPIES

Behavior therapies use learning principles to change maladaptive behaviors. Classical conditioning principles are used to change associations. In **systematic desensitization**, the client replaces anxiety with relaxation, and in **aversion therapy**, an aversive stimulus is paired with a maladaptive behavior. *Shaping, reinforcement, punishment,* and *extinction* are behavioral therapy techniques based on operant conditioning principles. In **modeling therapy**, clients watch and imitate positive role models.

Behavior therapies have been successful with a number of psychological disorders. But they are also criticized for lack of generalizability, the chance of symptom substitution, and the questionable ethics of controlling behavior.

Questions

1. A group of techniques based on learning principles that are used to change maladaptive behaviors is known as _____.

2. In behavior therapy, _____ techniques use shaping and reinforcement to increase adaptive behaviors and use punishment and extinction to decrease maladaptive behaviors. (a) classical conditioning; (b) modeling; (c) operant conditioning; (d) social learning

3. Describe how shaping can be used to develop desired behaviors.

4. What are the three criticisms of behavior therapy?

Answers to Questions can be found in Appendix B.

Group and Family Therapies: Healing Interpersonal Relationships

The therapies described thus far all consider the individual as the unit of analysis and treatment. In contrast, group and family therapies treat multiple individuals simultaneously. During sessions, therapists often apply psychoanalytic, cognitive, humanistic, and/or behavioral techniques. In this section, we will discuss both group and family therapies.

How is psychotherapy done in groups and families?

Group Therapy

Group therapy began as a response to the need for more therapists than were available and for a more economical form of therapy. What began as a practical and economic necessity, however, has become a preferred approach in its own right. In **group therapy**, multiple people meet together to work toward therapeutic goals. Typically, 8 to 10 people meet with a therapist on a regular basis, usually once a week for 2 hours. The therapist can work from any of the psychotherapeutic orientations we've previously discussed, and like individual therapy, members of the group talk about problems in their own lives. Unlike one-on-one therapies, however, the group members also gain from exploring *group process*, or the way members of the group interact with each other.

In addition to being less expensive than one-on-one therapy and providing insights from group processes, group therapy provides other advantages not found in individual therapy (Davison, Pennebaker, & Dickerson, 2000; Peterson & Halstead, 1998; White & Freeman, 2000).

1. Group support. During times of stress and emotional trouble, it is easy to imagine we are alone and that our problems are unique. Knowing that others have similar problems can be very reassuring. In addition, seeing others improve can be a source of hope and motivation.

2. Feedback and information. Because group members typically have comparable problems, they can learn from each other's mistakes and share insights. Furthermore, when a group member receives similar comments about his or her behavior

Group Therapy *Treatment method in which multiple people meet together to work toward therapeutic goals*

from several members of the group, the message may be more convincing than if it comes from a single therapist.

3. *Behavioral rehearsal.* Group members can role-play one another's employer, spouse, parents, children, or prospective dates. By playing and observing different roles in relationships, people gain insight into their problems and practice new social skills.

A variation on group therapy is the **self-help group**. Unlike other group therapy approaches, a professional does not guide these groups. They are simply groups of people who share a common problem and meet to give and receive support. For example, people who are learning to deal with painful life crises find support in organizations like AMAC (Adults Molested as Children), Formerly Employed, and Parents of Murdered Children. Individuals who need help with destructive lifestyles can find it in Alcoholics Anonymous, Debtors Anonymous; and Gamblers Anonymous. Some support groups use their shared pain for public service, like MADD (Mothers Against Drunk Driving). There are even groups for people in happy situations (New Parents, Parents of Twins) where the help may be more instructional than emotional.

Therapists often refer their patients to self-help groups to supplement individual therapy. Someone who has a problem with alcohol, for example, can find comfort and help with others who have "been there." They exchange useful information, share their coping strategies, and gain hope by seeing others overcome or successfully manage their shared problems. Research on self-help groups for alcoholism or obesity find they can be very effective — either alone or in addition to individual psychotherapy (Davison, Pennebaker, & Dickerson, 2000; Klein, 2000).

Self-Help Group Groups that are leaderless or guided by a nonprofessional, in which members assist each other in coping with a specific problem, as in Alcoholics Anonymous

Family Therapies

> Mental health problems do not affect three or four out of five persons but one out of one.
>
> Dr. William Menninger

Therapists have long known that dealing with an individual's problem may not be enough. Often, relationships within the family structure must be healed. Because a family is a system of interdependent parts, the problem of any one member unavoidably affects all the others (Barker, 2000; Carr, 2000; Lebow & Gurman, 1995). A teen's delinquency or a parent's drug problem affects each member of the family.

Sometimes the problems parents have with a child arise from conflicts in the marriage; other times a child's behavior creates distress in an otherwise well-functioning couple. The line between *marital* (or *couples*) *therapy* and *family therapy* is often blurred. Given that most married couples have children, our discussion will focus on **family therapy**, in which the primary aim is to change maladaptive family interaction patterns. All members of the family attend therapy sessions, though at times the therapist may also see family members individually or in twos or threes. (The therapist, incidentally, may take any orientation — behavioral, cognitive, etc.)

Many families initially come into therapy believing that one member is *the* cause of all their problems ("Johnny's delinquency" or "Mom's drinking"). However, family therapists generally find that this "identified patient" is the scapegoat (a person blamed for someone else's problems) for deeper disturbances. For example, instead of confronting their own problems with intimacy, the parents may focus all their attention and frustration on the delinquent child (Hanna &

Family Therapy A psychological treatment that attempts to change maladaptive interaction patterns among members of a family

Family therapy. Rather than one-on-one counseling, family therapists generally work with the entire family to improve communication and resolve conflicts.

Brown, 1999). It is usually necessary to change ways of interacting within the family system to promote the health of individual family members and the family as a whole.

Family therapy is also useful in treating a number of disorders and clinical problems. As we discussed in Module 40, schizophrenic patients are more likely to relapse if their family members express emotions, attitudes, and behaviors that involve criticism, hostility, or emotional overinvolvement (Butzlaff & Hooley, 1998; Linszen, et al., 1997). Family therapy can help family members modify their behavior toward the patient. It also seems to be the most favorable setting for the treatment of adolescent drug abuse (Lebow & Gurman, 1995).

Check & Review

GROUP AND FAMILY THERAPIES

In addition to being less expensive and more available than individual therapy, **group therapy** has three other advantages: It provides group support, feedback, information, and opportunities for behavior rehearsal. A variation on group therapy is the **self-help group** (like Alcoholics Anonymous), which is not guided by a professional.

The aim of **family therapy** is to change maladaptive family interaction patterns. Because a family is a system of interdependent parts, the problem of any one member unavoidably affects all the others.

Questions

1. In _____, multiple people meet together to work toward therapeutic goals. (a) encounter groups; (b) behavior therapy; (c) group therapy; (d) conjoint therapy

2. What are the three major advantages of group therapy?

3. Why do individual therapists often refer their patients to self-help groups?

4. _____ treats the family as a unit, and members work together to solve problems. (a) Aversion therapy; (b) Encounter groups; (c) Self-help groups; (d) Family therapy

Answers to Questions can be found in Appendix B.

Synthesizing Multiple Forms of Therapy

When first introduced to the various forms of therapy, many people decide one or two "make sense" and discard the others as worthless. But each approach has its strengths, and the ability to *synthesize* — combine various elements into meaningful patterns — is a valuable critical thinking skill.

Test your own abilities to synthesize, by reviewing each of the six major therapies (psychoanalysis, cognitive, humanistic, behavior, group, and biomedical) and then deciding how each therapy might treat the following problems:

Joe is 18 and deeply concerned that he might develop schizophrenia. Both his parents suffered from schizophrenia and close friends have complained about his "crazy thoughts" and depressed moods.

Ann is 35 and very depressed. She has been married for 10 years and always planned to have a large family. But her husband adamantly refuses to have children. Lately, she finds herself crying at odd times and feels so fatigued she often stays home from work.

Tim is 45 and dissatisfied with his work situation. His coworkers and manager avoid him and complain about his "difficult personality." This is Tim's fifth job in four years. He believes that others secretly envy his intelligence and are plotting against him.

ACTIVE LEARNING WORKSHEET   MODULE 44

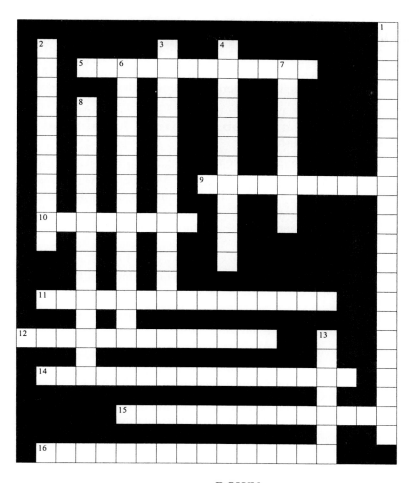

ACROSS

5. Displacement of unresolved conflicts from past relationships onto new relationships.

9. Avoidance of attempts to bring threatening unconscious material to conscious awareness.

10. Internal dialogue.

11. Reporting whatever comes to mind without monitoring the contents.

12. Attempts to change maladaptive interaction patterns among family members.

14. Therapy that emphasizes faulty thought processes and beliefs.

15. Therapist's statement that presents patient's problem in a new way.

16. Group of therapy techniques based on learning principles.

DOWN

1. Cognitive therapy process designed to change destructive ways of thinking.

2. Rogers' term for authenticity or congruence.

3. Freud's therapy that seeks to bring unconscious conflicts into consciousness.

4. Treatment where multiple people meet to work toward therapeutic goals.

6. Pairing an unpleasant stimulus with a maladaptive behavior.

7. Release of tension and anxiety through the reliving of a traumatic incident.

8. Listening with total attention to what another is saying.

13. Insightful awareness and ability to share another person's inner experience.

Answers can be found in Appendix B.

MODULE 45
ISSUES IN THERAPY

What are some of the major issues in therapy?

When is it appropriate to institutionalize people against their will? How do you choose a therapist? Is therapy effective? These are all major issues in therapy.

Institutionalization: Treating Chronic and Serious Mental Disorders

We all believe in the right to freedom, but when should people be protected from their own mental disorders? What about people who threaten suicide or are potentially violent? Despite Hollywood film portrayals, forced institutionalization of the mentally ill poses serious ethical problems and is generally reserved for only the most serious and life-threatening situations.

Involuntary Commitment

The legal grounds for involuntary commitment vary from state to state. But, generally, people can be sent to psychiatric hospitals if

- They are believed to be dangerous to themselves (usually suicidal) or dangerous to others (potentially violent)

- They are believed to be in serious need of treatment (indicated by bizarre behavior and loss of contact with reality)

- There is no reasonable, less restrictive alternative (Ruzovsky, 1984)

In emergencies, psychologists and other professionals can authorize temporary commitment for 24 to 72 hours. During this observation period, laboratory tests can be performed to rule out medical illnesses that could be causing the symptoms. The patient can also receive psychological testing, medication, and short-term therapy.

Deinstitutionalization

Although the courts have established stringent requirements for involuntary commitment, abuses do occur. In response to the potential for abuse, as well as to problems that come with long-term chronic institutionalization and the expense of

Deinstitutionalization. Keeping people locked in large mental institutions creates problems. But deinstitutionalization also creates problems because it forces many former patients onto the streeets with no home or medical care.

properly housing and caring for the mentally ill, many states have a policy of **dein-stitutionalization**, discharging as many patients from mental hospitals as possible and also discouraging admissions.

Although proponents hail deinstitutionalization as a humane and positive step, critics argue that thousands of patients are discharged without continuing provision for their protection. Many of these people end up living on the street with no shelter or means of support. It is important to note that although a sizable percentage of homeless people have mental disorders, the rise in homelessness is also due to such economic factors as increased unemployment, underemployment, and a shortage of low-income housing (Seager, 1998; Torrey, 1998).

What else can be done? Rather than returning patients to state hospitals, most clinicians suggest expanding and improving community care (Duckworth & Borus, 1999; Lamb & Weinberger, 1999). They recommend that general hospitals be equipped with special psychiatric units where acutely ill patients receive inpatient care. For less disturbed individuals and chronically ill patients, they recommend walk-in clinics, crisis intervention services, improved residential treatment facilities, and psychosocial and vocational rehabilitation. State hospitals would be reserved for the most unmanageable patients.

Community Mental Health Centers

Community mental health (CMH) centers are a prime example of alternative treatment to institutionalization. CMH centers provide outpatient services such as individual and group therapy and prevention programs. They also coordinate short-term inpatient care and programs for discharged mental patients, such as halfway houses and aftercare services. Psychiatrists, social workers, nurses, and volunteers who live in the neighborhood generally staff CMH centers.

As you can imagine, CMH centers and their support programs are enormously expensive. Investing in primary prevention programs could substantially reduce these costs. Instead of waiting until someone loses his or her job, home, and family, we could develop more intervention programs for high-risk individuals and offer short-term immediate services during crises.

Evaluating Therapy: Does It Work? How to Choose?

Have you ever thought about going to a therapist? If you've gone, was it helpful? In this section, we will discuss questions about the effectiveness of therapy and how to find a therapist.

Judging Effectiveness

Scientifically evaluating the effectiveness of therapy can be tricky. How can you trust the perception and self-report of clients or clinicians? Both have biases and a need to justify the time, effort, and expense of therapy.

To avoid these problems, psychologists use controlled research studies. Clients are randomly assigned to different forms of therapy or to control groups who receive no treatment. After therapy, clients are independently evaluated, and reports from friends and family members are collected. Until recently, these studies were simply compared. But with a new statistical technique called *meta-analysis*, years of such studies and similar research can be averaged together to produce a comprehensive report.

The good news, for both consumers and therapists, is that after years of controlled research and meta-analysis we have fairly clear evidence that therapy does work! Forty to 90 percent of people who receive treatment are better off than peo-

Deinstitutionalization *The policy of discharging as many people as possible from state hospitals and discouraging admissions*

Figure 45.1 *Duration of therapy.* In its 1995 annual survey, *Consumer Reports* magazine included a mental health section for the first time. According to the 7,000 respondents, long-term therapy (more than 2 years) is most effective. Effectiveness was based on (1) specific improvement (i.e., how much treatment helped with the problems that led to therapy), (2) satisfaction with the therapist, and (3) global improvement (i.e., how respondents felt at the time of the survey compared to when they began treatment).

ple who do not, and short-term treatments can be as effective as long-term (Kopta, Lueger, Saunders, & Howard, 1999; Kotkin, Daviet, & Gurin, 1996; Sanderson, 1995). Some therapies are more effective than others for specific problems. For example, phobias seem to respond best to systematic desensitization, and OCD can be significantly relieved with cognitive-behavior therapy accompanied by medication (see Seligman, 1994, for a review).

Control groups and random assignment are the standard scientific approach to measuring the effectiveness of therapy. However, a large-scale survey conducted by the popular magazine *Consumer Reports* (1995, November) may have added a new yardstick for measuring effectiveness. During its annual questionnaire on appliances and services, the magazine asked its 180,000 readers to fill out a separate mental health section if they had sought help (from friends, relatives, family doctor, clergy, support groups, or mental health professionals) in the previous 3 years. Approximately 7,000 of the respondents answered the mental health questions.

The *Consumer Reports* survey is important for at least two reasons: First, it provides interesting contradictions to the controlled studies research mentioned previously. For instance, the magazine study reported that no specific type of therapy, and therapy combined with medication, did better than any other for any disorder, and long-term therapy produced more improvement than did short-term treatments (Figure 45.1). Second, the study offers a legitimate research alternative. Surveys have certainly been done before now, but the *Consumer Reports* study had an unusually large sample and was developed in consultation with mental health experts.

As expected, the *Consumer Reports* study has been scientifically criticized for its lack of control groups, random assignment, and so on (e.g., Brock, Green, & Reich, 1998). In a type of catch-22, controlled studies are also questioned because they *do* have a control group. Is it ethical to assign troubled people to control groups in which they will receive either no treatment or restricted treatment?

Perhaps the most important finding of both the *Consumer Reports* study and previous controlled studies is that therapy does work. Most people get a lot better. Given that you might currently or someday be interested in therapy, this should be reassuring. A final helpful note from the *Consumer Reports* study is that active clients did better in treatment than passive recipients (Seligman, 1995). It was their idea to seek treatment, they checked around for therapists, they asked questions of the therapist, and they tried to be as open and cooperative as possible during therapy — doing their homework, keeping appointments, and asking for explanations and clarification.

Finding a Therapist

If you have time (and the money) to explore options, it is important to "shop around" for a therapist best suited to your specific goals. Consulting your psychology instructor or college counseling system for referrals can be an important first step. However, if you are in a crisis — suicidal thoughts, failing grades, or the victim of abuse — get help fast (Beutler, Shurkin, Bongar, & Gray, 2000; First, Pincus, Frances, 1999). Most communities have telephone hotlines that provide counseling on a 24-hour basis, and most colleges and universities have counseling centers that provide immediate, short-term therapy to students free of charge.

If you are encouraging someone to get therapy, you might offer to help locate a therapist and to go with them for their first visit. If he or she refuses help and the problem affects you, it is often a good idea to seek therapy yourself. You will gain insights and skills that will help you deal with the situation more effectively.

RESEARCH HIGHLIGHT

Therapy in the Electronic Age

I never think of the future. It comes soon enough.

Albert Einstein

As we've just seen in the previous section, research psychologists and therapists have been hard at work evaluating and improving current forms of traditional therapy, and, like Einstein, they may not have thought much about the future. But like it or not, the electronic age has arrived.

Today millions of people seek advice and "therapy" from radio call-in programs, telephone services with 900 numbers, and, now, websites for online therapy. The newest mental health therapy, called telehealth, has approximately 200 websites and between 350 and 1,000 online counselors offering counseling, group support chats, e-mail correspondence, private instant messages, and videoconferencing therapy (Davison, Pennebaker, & Dickerson, 2000; Kicklighter, 2000; Segal, 2000). These on-line counselors are psychologists, psychiatrists, social workers, licensed counselors, nonlicensed "helpers," and outright "quacks." Together, they treat an estimated 10,000 clients each week (Kicklighter, 2000).

As you might expect, many qualified therapists and academic institutions are concerned about this new form of therapy. They fear, among other things, that without a governing body to regulate this type of therapy, there are no checks and balances to protect the client from unethical and unsavory practices. However, many of these concerns were recently addressed by the formulation of 10 Interdisciplinary Principles for Professional Practice in Telehealth. According to these principles, psychologists would be required to follow the basic ethical policies of confidentiality, informed consent, and integrity as prescribed by the APA (American Psychological Association) Ethics Code (Reed, McLaughlin, & Milholland, 2000). Questions remain regarding interstate and international licensing conflicts for psychologists and the lack of consumer protection against those practicing without any license at all.

Why Would Anyone Want to Use an Online Counselor?

The Internet and other electronic forms of therapy may sometimes be more effective than traditional therapy. For example, Enid M. Hunkeler and her colleagues (2000) found that depressed patients who received standard care as well as weekly phone calls from health professionals were significantly more likely to show improvement in their depressive symptoms than were patients who did not receive such calls. In another study, Andrew Winzelberg and his colleagues (2000) evaluated an Internet-based program designed for college students with eating disorders and found a significant improvement in body image and a decrease in drive for thinness.

Studies have long shown that success rates for both physical and mental health are improved with increased contact between patients and their health care providers. Electronic forms of therapy may be the easiest and most cost-effective way of increasing this contact (Schopp, Johnstone, & Merrell, 2000). Online clients appreciate having increased access to their therapist, especially during times of crisis. Clients also tend to feel safer discussing sensitive topics in the privacy of their own homes.

On the other hand, critics claim that online therapy is a contradiction in terms — an oxymoron. They say psychotherapy is based on both verbal and nonverbal communication, and it's impossible for online therapists to adequately give therapeutic advice to clients without face-to-face contact. Others are concerned about sending private and confidential thoughts into unsecured cyberspace to a person who may not be a qualified therapist (e.g., Bloom, 1998). David Nickelson, director of technology policy and projects for the American Psychological Association (APA), advises people to first seek face-to-face therapy. "We still need research," Nickelson says, "and it may find that there are just some things therapists and their patients can't do over the Internet" *(http://www.apa.org/practice/pf/aug97/teleheal.html).*

GENDER & CULTURAL DIVERSITY

Cultural Variations and the Special Needs of Women in Therapy

All the therapies we have described in these modules are based on Western European and American culture. Does this mean they are unique? Or do our psychotherapists do some of the same things that, say, a native healer or witch doctor does? That is, are there cultural similarities in therapy? Conversely, are there fundamental cultural differences between therapies? Finally, there is the matter of women in therapy: Do women have special needs? Let's take up these issues one at a time.

Cultural Similarities

When we look at therapies in all cultures, we find certain key features are culturally similar (Helms & Cook, 1999; Jennings & Skovholt, 1999; Matsumoto, 2000; Corey, 2001b). Richard Brislin (1993) has summarized some of these features:

1. *Naming the problem.* One important step toward improving psychological functioning is labeling the problem. People often feel better just by knowing that others experience their problem and that the therapist has had experience with their particular problem.

2. *Qualities of the therapist.* Clients must feel the therapist is caring, competent, approachable, and concerned with finding solutions to their problem.

3. *Establishing credibility.* Word-of-mouth testimonials and status symbols (such as diplomas on the wall) establish the therapist's credibility. Among native healers, in lieu of diplomas, credibility may be established by having served as an apprentice to a revered healer.

4. *Placing the problem in a familiar framework.* If the client believes evil spirits cause psychological disorders, the therapist will direct treatment toward these spirits. Similarly, if the client believes in the importance of early childhood experiences and the unconscious mind, psychoanalysis will be the likely treatment of choice.

5. *Applying techniques to bring relief.* In all cultures, therapy involves action. Either the client or the therapist must do something. Moreover, what they do must fit the client's expectations. For example, the person who believes evil spirits possesses him or her expects the shaman to perform a ceremony to expel the demons. In the Western European and American model, clients expect to reveal their thoughts and feelings and provide background information. This "talk therapy" may also have biological or behavioral components, but people who seek therapy generally expect to talk about their problem.

6. *A special time and place.* The fact that therapy occurs outside the client's everyday experiences seems to be an important feature of all therapies. People apparently need to set aside a special time and go to a special place to concentrate on their problems.

Cultural Differences

Although there are basic similarities in therapies across cultures, there are also important differences. In the traditional Western European and American model, clients are encouraged toward self-awareness, self-fulfillment, self-actualization, and modifying self-behavior. The emphasis is on the "self" and on independence and control over one's life — qualities that are highly valued in individualistic cultures. When we look at therapies in collectivist cultures, however, the focus is on interdependence and accepting the realities of one's life (Sue & Sue, 1999).

Japanese *Naikan* therapy is a good example of a collectivist culture's approach to psychological disorders. In *Naikan* therapy, the patient sits quietly from 5:30 A.M. to 9 P.M. for 7 days and is visited by an interviewer every 90 minutes. During this time, the patient is instructed to look at his or her relationships with others from three perspectives: *care received* (recollect and examine the care and kindness you have received from others), *repayment* (recall what you have done to repay the care and kindness of others), and *troubles caused* (think about the troubles and worries you have caused others) (Berry, Poortinga, Segall, & Dasen, 1992).

The goals of *Naikan* therapy are to discover personal guilt for having been ungrateful and troublesome to others and to develop gratitude toward those who

Alternative therapies. In all cultures, therapy involves specific actions or treatments. In this photo, the therapist is using crystal healing, laying on of stones, and meditation.

have helped the patient. When these goals are attained, the person will have a better self-image and interpersonal attitude.

As you can see, there are pronounced differences between *Naikan* therapy goals and methods and the therapies we have described. Recognizing cultural differences is very important for building trust between therapists and clients and for effecting behavioral change. Clinicians who work with clients from different cultural backgrounds should learn about their clients' cultures as well as become more aware of their own cultural and ethnic-based values and beliefs (Fuertes & Gelso, 2001; Paniagua, 1998).

Women and Therapy

Not only must therapists be sensitive to their clients' cultural backgrounds but they must also be aware of gender differences. Within individualistic Western culture, men and women present different needs and problems to therapists. For example, compared with men, women are more comfortable and familiar with their emotions, have fewer negative attitudes toward therapy, and are more likely to seek psychological help (Komiya, Good, & Sherrod, 2000). Research has identified five major concerns related to women and psychotherapy (Desai & Jann, 2000; Holtzworth-Munroe, 2000; Reppucci, Woolard, & Fried, 1999; Yonkers et al., 1998):

1. *Rates of diagnosis and treatment of mental disorders.* Research has found that women are diagnosed and treated for mental illness at a much higher rate than men are. Is this because women are "sicker" than men as a group, because they are more willing to admit their problems, or because the categories for illness may be biased against women? More research is needed to answer this question.

2. *Stresses of poverty.* Poverty is an important contributor to stress, and stress is directly related to many psychological disorders. Therefore, women bring special challenges to the therapy situation because of their overrepresentation in the lowest economic groups.

3. *Stresses of multiple roles.* Women today are mothers, wives, homemakers, wage earners, students, and so on. The conflicting demands of their multiple roles often create special stresses.

4. *Stresses of aging.* Aging brings special concerns for women. They live longer than men do, but they also tend to be poorer, less educated, and have more serious

health problems. Elderly women also account for over 70 percent of the chronically mentally ill who live in nursing homes in the United States.

5. *Violence against women.* Rape, violent assault, incest, and sexual harassment all take a harsh toll on women's mental health. With the exception of violent assault, these forms of violence are much more likely to happen to women than to men. These violent acts may lead to depression, insomnia, post-traumatic stress disorders, eating disorders, and other problems.

These five areas of concern are important to therapists who treat women. Therapists must be sensitive to possible connections between clients' problems and their gender and/or culture. Rather than prescribing drugs to relieve depression in women, for example, it may be more appropriate for the therapist to explore ways to relieve the stresses of multiple roles or poverty.

Check & Review

ISSUES IN THERAPY

People believed to be mentally ill and dangerous to themselves or others can be involuntarily committed to mental hospitals for diagnosis and treatment. Abuses of involuntary commitments and other problems associated with state mental hospitals have led many states to practice **deinstitutionalization** — discharging as many patients as possible and discouraging admissions. Community services such as community mental health (CMH) centers try to cope with the problems of deinstitutionalization. Research on the effectiveness of psychotherapy has found that 40 to 80 percent of those who receive treatment are better off than those who do not receive treatment.

Therapies in all cultures share six culturally universal features: naming a problem, qualities of the therapist, establishing credibility, placing the problems in a familiar framework, applying techniques to bring relief, and a special time and place. Important cultural differences in therapies also exist. For example, therapies in individualistic cultures emphasize the self and control over one's life, whereas therapies in collectivist cultures emphasize interdependence. Japan's *Naikan* therapy is a good example of a collectivist culture's therapy.

Therapists must take five considerations into account when treating women clients: higher rate of diagnosis and treatment of mental disorders, stresses of poverty, stresses of multiple roles, stresses of aging, and violence against women.

Questions

1. The policy of discharging as many people as possible from state hospitals and discouraging admissions is called_____. (a) disengagement; (b) reinstitutionalization; (c) maladaptive restructuring; (d) deinstitutionalization

2. Name the six features of therapy that are culturally universal.

3. A Japanese therapy designed to help clients develop personal guilt for having been ungrateful and troublesome to others and to develop gratitude toward those who have helped them is known as_____. (a) *Kyoto* therapy; (b) *Okado* therapy; (c) *Naikan* therapy; (d) *Nissan* therapy

4. What are the five major concerns for women in therapy?

Answers to Questions can be found in Appendix B.

ACTIVE LEARNING WORKSHEET   MODULE 45

Completing the following exercise may help provide insight to your own or your friends' lives, as well as greater understanding of the material in this section.

1. Therapy has six features that are common across all cultures. List them here:

   _____

   _____

   _____

2. Of these six features, which element do you think is most beneficial in helping people change? Why?

   _____

   _____

   _____

3. Which is the least helpful? Why?

   _____

   _____

   _____

4. Considering the five major concerns related to women and psychotherapy, which area do you consider most important? Why?

   _____

   _____

   _____

Visual Summary for Modules 42, 43, 44, and 45 ••••

Major Forms of Psychotherapy

- **Psychotherapy:** Various approaches to improving psychological functioning and promoting adjustment to life.
- Therapy essentials: Five basic areas of disturbance -thoughts, emotions, behaviors, interpersonal and life situations, and biomedical.
- **Eclectic approach:** Borrows from all forms of therapy.

Description/ Major Goals	Techniques/Methods	Evaluation/Criticisms
Biomedical therapies: Use biological techniques to relieve psychological disorders.	**Drug therapy** is most common biomedical treatment. • **Antianxiety drugs** (Valium, Xanax) are used to treat anxiety disorders. • **Antipsychotic drugs** (Haldol, Navane) relieve symptoms of schizophrenia. • **Antidepressants** (Zoloft, Prozac) used to treat depression. • **Mood stabilizers** (lithium) help stabilize bipolar disorders. **Electroconvulsive therapy (ECT)** used primarily to relieve serious depression, when medication fails. **Psychosurgeries**, such as a **lobotomy**, are seldom used today.	• Drug therapy improves many disorders, but dosage levels, patient cooperation, and side effects, like tardive dyskinesia (a serious motor disturbance) are serious problems. • ECT and psychosurgery have been successful in treating certain disorders, but they're risky and considered a last resort.
Psychoanalysis/ psychodynamic therapies: Bring unconscious conflicts into conscious awareness.	Five major techniques: **Free association, dream analysis, resistance, transference,** and **interpretation.**	• Limited availability, time-consuming, expensive, unsuitable for many, and lack of scientific credibility. • Modern psychodynamic therapies overcome some of these limits.
Cognitive therapies: Analyze faulty thought processes, beliefs, and negative **self-talk,** and change these destructive thoughts with **cognitive restructuring.**	Ellis's **rational-emotive therapy (RET)** replaces irrational beliefs with rational beliefs and accurate perceptions of the world. Beck's **cognitive-behavior therapy** emphasizes change is necessary in both thought processes and behavior.	• Ellis has had success with a variety of disorders. Beck's procedures are particularly effective for relieving depression. • Criticized for ignoring unconscious processes and client's history, and success may be due to behavioral techniques.
Humanistic therapies: Work to facilitate personal growth.	Rogers' **client-centered therapy** offers **empathy, unconditional positive regard, genuineness,** and **active listening** to facilitate personal growth.	Difficult to evaluate scientifically, and research has had mixed results.

Major Forms of Psychotherapy (cont).

Description/Major Goals	Techniques/Methods	Evaluation/Criticisms
Behavior therapies: Use learning principles to eliminate maladaptive behaviors and substitute healthy ones.	Classical conditioning techniques include **systematic desensitization** (client replaces anxiety with relaxation) and **aversion therapy** (an aversive stimulus is paired with a maladaptive behavior). Operant conditioning techniques include shaping, reinforcement, punishment, extinction, and **modeling therapy** (clients watch and imitate positive role models).	• Behavior therapies are successful with a number of psychological disorders. • Criticized for lack of generalizability, symptom substitution, and questionable ethics of controlling behavior.
Group therapies: Several clients meet with one or more therapists to resolve personal problems.	Provide group support, feedback, information, and opportunities for behavior rehearsal. **Self-help groups** (like Alcoholics Anonymous) are sometimes considered group therapy, but professional therapists do not conduct them.	Less expensive and more available than individual therapy.
Family therapies: Work to change maladaptive family interaction patterns.	Sees family as a system of interdependent parts, therefore treats all members.	Less expensive and more available than individual therapy.

Issues in Therapy

Institutionalization

- People believed to be mentally ill and dangerous to themselves or others can be involuntarily committed to mental hospitals for diagnosis and treatment.
- Abuses of involuntary commitments and other problems led to **deinstitutionalization** — discharging as many patients as possible and discouraging admissions.
- Community services such as Community Mental Health (CMH) centers offset some problems of deinstitutionalization.

Seeking Therapy

- Forty to 80 percent of those who receive treatment are better off than those who do not.
- Take time to "shop around," but a crisis requires immediate help.
- If others' problems affect you, get help yourself.

Cultural Issues

- Common features of therapy in all cultures: naming a problem, qualities of the therapist, establishing credibility, placing the problems in a familiar framework, applying techniques to bring relief, and a special time and place.
- Differences in therapy between cultures: Individualistic cultures emphasize the "self" and control over one's life. Therapies in collectivist cultures, like Japan's Naikan therapy, emphasize interdependence.

Gender Issues

Higher rate of diagnosis and treatment of mental disorders, stresses of poverty, stresses of multiple roles, stresses of aging, and violence against women.

Social Psychology

Core Learning Objectives

As you read Modules 46, 47, and 48, keep the following questions in mind and answer them in your own words:

► How do our thoughts affect how we explain and judge others?

► What feelings are most important in our social interactions?

► How do our actions toward others affect their lives and our own?

Imagine you are one of several people responding to this ad. As you arrive at the Yale University laboratory, you are introduced to the experimenter and another participant in the study. The experimenter explains he is studying the effects of punishment on learning and memory. One of you will play the role of the learner and the other will be the teacher. You draw lots, and on your paper is written teacher. The experimenter leads you into a room where he straps the other participant — the "learner" — into an "electric chair" apparatus that looks escape-proof. The experimenter then applies electrode paste to the learner's wrist "to avoid blisters and burns" and attaches an electrode that is connected to a shock generator.

You, the "teacher," are shown into an adjacent room and asked to sit in front of this same shock generator, which is wired through the wall to the chair of the learner. As you can see in the photo on page 602, the shock machine consists of 30 switches representing successively higher levels of shock in 15-volt increments. Written labels appear below each group of levers, ranging from Slight Shock to Danger: Severe Shock, all the way to XXX. The experimenter explains it is your job to teach the learner a list of word pairs and to punish any errors by administering a shock. With each wrong answer, you are to give a shock one level higher on the shock generator. For example, at the first wrong response, you give a shock of 15 volts; at the second wrong response, 30 volts; and so on.

As the study begins, the learner seems to be having problems with the task. The responses are often wrong. Before long, you are inflicting shocks that must be extremely painful. Indeed, after you administer 150 volts, the learner begins to protest and demands, "Get me out of here. ...I refuse to go on."

You hesitate and wonder what to do. The experimenter asks you to continue. He insists that even if the learner refuses, you must keep increasing the shock levels. But the other person is obviously in pain. What should you do?

Actual participants in this series of studies suffered real conflict and distress when confronted with this problem. The following dialogue took place between the experimenter and one of the teachers (Milgram, 1974, pp. 73–74):

TEACHER: I can't stand it. I'm not going to kill that man in there. You hear him hollering?

EXPERIMENTER: As I told you before, the shocks may be painful, but [there is no permanent tissue damage].

LEARNER (screaming): Let me out of here, you have no right to keep me here. Let me out of here, let me out, my heart's starting to bother me, let me out! (Teacher shakes head, pats the table nervously.)

TEACHER: You see, he's hollering. Hear that? Gee, I don't know.

EXPERIMENTER: The experiment requires...

TEACHER (interrupting): I know it does, sir, but I mean — huh! He don't know what he's getting in for. He's up to 195 volts!

(Following this exchange, the teacher continues through 210 volts, 225 volts, 240 volts, 255 volts, and 270 volts, at which point the teacher, with evident relief, runs out of word-pair questions.)

EXPERIMENTER: You'll have to go back to the beginning of that page and go through them again until he's learned them all correctly.

TEACHER: Aw, no, I'm not going to kill that man. You mean I've got to keep going up with the scale? No, sir. He's hollering in there. I'm not going to give him 450 volts.

What do you think happened? Did the man continue? This particular teacher continued giving shocks — in spite of the learner's strong protests. He even continued after the learner refused to give any more answers.

As you might have guessed, this was not a study of punishment and learning. The psychologist who designed the study, Stanley Milgram, was actually investigating *obedience to authority*. Would participants see the experimenter as an authority figure and obey his prompts and commands to shock another human being?

Would you, or others you know, have followed the experimenter's demands in this same situation? In Milgram's public survey, less than 25 percent thought they would go beyond 150 volts. And not one respondent predicted they would go past the 300-volt level. Surprisingly, a full 65 *percent* of the teacher-participants obeyed completely — going all the way to the end of the scale. Even Milgram was surprised.

It is important to recognize that *no* participant-learner ever received an actual shock. The "learner" was an accomplice of the experimenter and simply *pretended* to be shocked. However, the "teachers" were true participants. They believed they were administering real shocks, and they sweated, trembled, stuttered, laughed nervously, and repeatedly protested that they did not want to hurt the learner. They were clearly upset. *But still they obeyed.*

Keep in mind that deception is an important part of some research projects, but Milgram's study could never be replicated today, owing to ethical concerns for the rights of participants. Although most participants *were* visibly upset by the experience, Milgram carefully debriefed everyone after the study and followed up with the participants for several months. Most "teachers" reported the experience as being personally informative and valuable.

Setting aside ethical concerns, one lasting benefit from Milgram's research might be its invaluable insight into human social behavior. Although many believe only "monsters" would have followed Hitler's commands to torture and kill millions of Jews during World War II, Milgram's research suggests otherwise. As philosopher Hannah Arendt has suggested, the horrifying, thing about the Nazis was not that they were so deviant but that they were so "terrifyingly normal."

Milgram's shock generator. Research participants were told to give increasing levels of shocks to someone they had watched being strapped down and connected to this machine. Note how the shock levels are clearly labeled, starting with *Slight Shock,* moving to *Very Strong Shock, Danger: Severe Shock,* and ultimately, *XXX.* How would you respond? Would you refuse from the beginning, or would you stop after a few shocks and complaints from the recipient? Would you go all the way to 450 volts?

TRY THIS
Yourself

Before we begin, test your understanding of social psychology and how it operates in everyday life by answering *true* or *false* to the following statements. Answers are at the end of this activity and expanded explanations are found throughout the following modules.

1. Groups generally make more conservative decisions than a single individual does.
2. Most people judge others more harshly than they judge themselves.
3. Looks are the primary factor in our initial feelings of attraction, liking, and romantic love.
4. Opposites attract.
5. Romantic love rarely lasts longer than 1 or 2 years.

6. The most effective way to change behavior is to first change the attitude.
7. Prejudice is the same as discrimination.
8. There are positive as well as negative forms of prejudice.
9. Watching a violent sports match or punching a pillow is a good way to release steam and reduce aggression.
10. People are more likely to help another individual when they are alone than when they are in a group.

Answers: 1. False 2. True 3. True 4. False 5. True 6. False 7. False 8. True 9. False 10. True

Our combination of confusion and fascination over social behaviors like those in Milgram's study is what draws many students and researchers to the field of **social psychology**. Social psychologists study how other people influence an individual's behavior (thoughts, feelings, and actions). They explore both the bizarre and the ordinary, from the mindless obedience of religious cults to prejudice, aggression, and attraction. Using the tools of science (experiments, surveys, case studies, self-report, and so on), they seek scientific answers to *social* questions.

Because almost everything we do is *social*, the subject matter is enormous and varied. We will therefore approach our study by looking at each component of the definition in turn. We begin by exploring topics related to *our thoughts about others* (attribution and attitudes). Next, we examine *our feelings toward others* by looking at prejudice, discrimination, and interpersonal attraction. (Prejudice and discrimination could also be discussed under thoughts or actions. But we consider it under feelings because negative emotions are the central defining characteristic of prejudice.) We conclude with a look at *our actions toward others* (social influence, group processes, aggression, and altruism).

Social Psychology *The branch of psychology that studies how other people influence an individual's behavior (thoughts, feelings, and actions)*

MODULE 46
OUR THOUGHTS ABOUT OTHERS

How could a mother brutalize and torture her child? Why would someone run into a burning building to rescue a stranger? Why did Chris stop going out with me? Trying to understand the world around us often means trying to understand other people's behavior. We look for reasons and explanations for others' behavior (the process of attribution). We also develop thoughts and beliefs (attitudes) about others.

Attribution: Explaining Other's Behavior

How do we explain people's obedience in Milgram's study? When we offer an explanation for behavior, we *attribute* it to something — "the participants were weak-willed," "the experimenter was intimidating," and so on. Psychologists use the term **attribution** to describe statements explaining why people do what they do.

Attribution *The principles people follow in making judgments about the causes of events, others' behavior, and their own behavior*

After studying how people explain others' behavior, Fritz Heider (1958) noted that most people begin with a basic question: Does the behavior stem mainly from internal *dispositions* or external *situations*? If you concluded that participants in Milgram's study acted because of their own personal characteristics, motives, and intentions, you would be making a *dispositional attribution*. On the other hand, if you decided they responded to situational demands and environmental pressures, you would be making a *situational attribution*.

The choice between disposition and situation is central to accurate judgments of why people do what they do. Unfortunately, our attributions are frequently marred by two major errors: the *fundamental attribution error* and the *self-serving bias*.

1. The fundamental attribution error — judging the behavior of others. When we recognize and take into account environmental influences on behavior, we generally make accurate attributions. However, given that people have enduring personality traits and a tendency to take cognitive shortcuts, we more often choose dispositional attributions — we blame the person. This bias toward personal, dispositional factors rather than environmental factors is so common in individualistic cultures that it is called the **fundamental attribution error** (FAE) (Nisbett, Peng, Choi, & Norenzayan, 2000; Susskind, Maurer, Thakkar, Hamilton, & Sherman, 1999).

Fundamental attribution error (FAE) *Misjudging the causes of others' behavior because of overestimating internal personal factors and underestimating external situational influences*

Social psychology in action. Can you imagine how Western television programs might affect the thoughts, feelings, and actions of these viewers?

PEANUTS; drawings by Charles Schulz; 1989 United Features Syndicate, Inc. Reprinted by permission of UFS, Inc.

Psychology in action. Can you see why this is an example of both the fundamental attribution error and the self-serving bias?

Noting that your instructor seems relaxed and talkative in front of the class, you would probably decide that he or she is an extroverted and outgoing person — a *dispositional attribution*. However, outside of class you may be surprised to find him or her shy and awkward on a one-on-one basis or at a party. Similarly, most students think participants in the Milgram study were "weak-willed" and that they would never act like that in the same situation. They blame the person (dispositional attribution) and overlook and underestimate the power of the environment (situational attribution).

Why do we tend to jump to internal, personal explanations? There are several possible explanations for why we tend to make dispositional rather than situational attributions. The most important reason may be that human personalities and behaviors are more salient (or noticeable) than situational factors. This **saliency bias** helps explain why we focus on participants in Milgram's study versus the situation

Saliency Bias *The tendency to focus on the most noticeable (salient) factors when explaining the causes of behavior*

TRY THIS
Yourself

One of the five individuals pictured below is a murderer who killed two people with a pickaxe, one is a rapist and serial killer, and another is an author of this text. Can you tell who is which? If you're in your critical thinking mode right now, you might be resisting this obvious setup and would argue that you can't make such judgments solely on the basis of appearance. However, research shows that we often do make such snap decisions about people — and that when we do, we rely on individual attitudes that reflect our specific life experiences and personal stereotypes (Stewart, Doan, Gingrich, & Smith, 1998). (If you want to check your guesses regarding the five photos, the answers are provided at the top of the following page).

Are you a good judge of character and personality? Which of these five individuals is a vicious serial killer, a murderer who died by lethal injection, or an author of this text? The answers appear on the following page.

Self-Serving Bias *A way of maintaining a positive self-image by taking credit for one's successes and emphasizing external causes for one's failures*

itself. It also explains why people often blame welfare recipients for their joblessness. This type of *blaming the victim* also reflects the fact that large situational factors leading to poverty and joblessness generally are not concrete and conspicuous.

2. *The self-serving bias — judging our own behavior.* When we judge others' behavior, we tend to emphasize internal personality factors over external situational causes. But when we explain our own behavior, we favor internal personal attributions for our *successes* and external environmental attributions for our *failures*. This **self-serving bias** is motivated by a desire to maintain our self-esteem, as well as a desire to look good to others (Campbell & Sedikides, 1999; Higgins & Bhatt, 2001; Louie, Curren, & Harich, 2000).

Students who do well on an exam, for instance, often take personal credit ("I really studied" or "I'm smart"). If they fail the test, however, they tend to blame the instructor, the textbook, or the "tricky" questions. Similarly, studies find both partners in divorced couples are more likely to see themselves as the victim, to rate themselves less responsible for the breakup, and as being more willing to reconcile (Gray & Silver, 1990).

Culture and Attributional Biases

Both the FAE and the self-serving bias may depend in part on cultural factors (Matsumoto, 2000). In most Western nations, people are more likely to make the FAE because of the cultural belief that individuals are responsible for their own actions. The FAE is much harder to demonstrate with Asian populations. In most Eastern countries, people are more group oriented and tend to be more aware of situational constraints on behavior (Nisbett, Peng, Choi, & Norenzayan, 2000; Norenzayan & Nisbett, 2000). If you were watching a baseball game in China and the umpire made a bad call, as a Westerner you would probably make a personality attribution ("He's a lousy umpire"), whereas a Chinese spectator would tend to make a situational attribution ("He's under pressure").

Like the FAE, the self-serving bias is also much less common in Eastern nations, where people do not define themselves as much in terms of their individual accomplishments. Self-esteem is not related to doing better than others. Rather, fitting in and not standing out from the group is stressed. As the Japanese proverb says, "The nail that sticks up gets pounded down."

This emphasis on group relations in Asian cultures is also true of many Native Americans in North America. For example, when the Wintun Native Americans originally described being with a close relation or intimate friend, they would not say, for example, "Linda and I," but rather, "Linda we" (Lee, 1950). This importance attached to community relations instead of individual *selfhood* often seems strange to contemporary Western, individualist societies. But it remains common in collectivist cultures (Markus & Kitayama, 1998).

Attitudes: Our Learned Predisposition Toward Others

Attitude *A learned predisposition to respond cognitively, affectively, and behaviorally to a particular object*

An **attitude** is a learned predisposition to respond cognitively, affectively, and behaviorally to a particular object in a particular way. The object can be anything from pizza to people, from diseases to drugs, from abortion to psychology.

Components of Attitudes

Social psychologists generally agree that an attitude has three components (Figure 46.1): cognitive, affective, and behavioral. The *cognitive component* consists of thoughts and beliefs, such as "Marijuana is a relatively safe drug" or "The dangers of marijuana are greatly underestimated." The *affective*, or *emotional*, *component* involves feelings, such as frustration that our legal system has not legalized marijuana yet or, conversely, that it seems to even consider legalization.

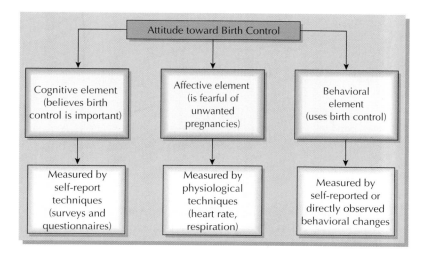

Figure 46.1 *Three components of all attitudes.* When social psychologists study attitudes, they measure each of the three components — cognitive, affective, and behavioral.

The *behavioral component* consists of a *predisposition* to act in certain ways toward an attitude object. For example, someone who held a positive attitude toward marijuana might write to textbook authors and publishers complaining that we are too critical in our discussion of drugs. Someone with a negative attitude, on the other hand, might write to complain that even the use of marijuana as an example could encourage its use. (Yes, we are speaking from experience. People do write just this type of letter, and we are glad to get the feedback.)

Attitude Change Through Cognitive Dissonance

You are not born with your attitudes — they are learned. From earliest childhood, you began forming your attitudes through direct experience (eating pizza) and through indirect observation (listening to your parents discuss social issues). Although attitudes begin in early childhood, they are not permanent. Politicians spend millions of dollars on campaigns because they know attitudes can be shaped and manipulated throughout the entire life span.

Although attitude change often involves deliberate efforts at persuasion, one of the most efficient methods is brought about by cognitive dissonance, a perceived discrepancy between an attitude and a behavior or between an attitude and a new piece of information (Albarracin & Wyer, 2000; Cook, 2000; Harmon-Jones, 2000; Shultz, Leveille, & Lepper, 1999). According to Leon Festinger (1957), who developed **cognitive dissonance theory**, this discrepancy leads to a state of psychological tension similar to anxiety. The tension, in turn, motivates the individual to change the attitude, the behavior, or the perception of the inconsistent information to eliminate the discrepancy and the accompanying tension (Figure 46.2).

Picture yourself in this situation. You, as an individual who strongly objects to racist and sexist remarks, must give a speech in favor of the Ku Klux Klan (KKK). How do you think this would affect your attitudes? Do you think you would feel more or less favorable toward the KKK afterward?

This is the type of question that led to a classic experiment conducted by Leon Festinger and J. Merrill Carlsmith (1959). Students selected as participants were given excruciatingly boring tasks for an hour. The experimenters told them that the aim of this procedure was to test their performance, but the actual purpose was to create a negative attitude toward the task. After finishing the task, participants were approached by the experimenter and asked for a favor. The experimenter asked if they would serve as research assistants and tell the next "participant" (who was really a confederate of the experiment) that the task was "very enjoyable" and "fun." Sometimes the person was offered $1 for helping and sometimes $20. After the person lied to the incoming participant and was paid, he or she was led to another room and asked about his or her true feelings toward the experimental tasks.

Cognitive Dissonance Theory
Leon Festinger's theory that tension results whenever people discover inconsistencies between their attitudes or between their attitudes and their behaviors; this tension drives people to make attitudinal changes that will restore harmony or consistency

Cognitive dissonance and the military. The more grueling and difficult the initiation or training, the more these recruits will come to like and appreciate the military life. Can you explain this according to cognitive dissonance theory?

Figure 46.2 *Cognitive dissonance theory.* When differences exist between our strongly held attitudes, or when there are large inconsistencies between our attitudes and behavior, we experience discomfort (*dissonance*) and a need to change either the attitude or behavior.

What happens when someone is coaxed into doing something (lying) that is inconsistent with his or her actual experience and attitude? You might expect that people who received $20 for lying would feel more positive toward the task than would those paid $1. In fact, just the reverse occurred.

Can you explain this? Cognitive dissonance theory is essentially a *drive-reduction theory* (Module 31), where an attitude change is reinforced by reduction of an uncomfortable emotional state (a drive). People have a strong need to feel that their attitudes are in sync with one another and that their attitudes and behavior are consistent. When this harmony is disrupted, people feel distressed. Festinger believed that this distress (*dissonance*), like the feeling of hunger, is unpleasant and that people are strongly motivated to reduce or eliminate it. To relieve the distress and restore balance, we must change either our attitude or behavior.

In the boring task experiment, participants faced a mismatch between their attitude toward the experiment ("That was boring") and their behavior ("I told another participant it was interesting"). To relieve the resulting tension, they changed their original attitude from boredom to "I enjoyed the task."

The reason that the "$1 participants" showed more attitude change was because they experienced a greater amount of cognitive dissonance than did the "$20 participants." Participants who received only $1 either had to change their attitude toward the task or acknowledge they had lied rather cheaply. Because they could not deny they had lied, they changed their attitude.

In contrast, participants who were paid $20 did not need to change their attitude as much because they could readily explain their behavior in terms of the payment ($20 was a considerable amount in the late 1950s). Being paid well for their actions helped relieve the logical inconsistency (the cognitive dissonance) between what they truly believed about the boring task and what they told others. In contrast, the participants who received $1 had *insufficient justification* for lying to another participant and had more motivation to change their attitude to "The task wasn't so boring after all."

Culture and Dissonance

The experience of cognitive dissonance may not be the same in other cultures. It may presume a particular way of thinking about and evaluating the self that is distinctively Western. As noted earlier, North Americans are highly individualistic and independent. Making a bad choice or decision has strong, negative effects on self-esteem and a greater motivation for attitude change.

Asians, on the other hand, tend to be much more collectivist and interdependent. Consequently, they feel more tension over a potential loss of connection with others than with a threat to their individual self-esteem. Research comparing Japanese and other Asian samples with Canadian and U.S. participants supports this position (Choi & Nisbett, 2000; Markus & Kitayama, 1998).

Check & Review

OUR THOUGHTS ABOUT OTHERS

We explain people's behavior (make **attributions**) by determining whether their actions resulted from internal factors (their own traits and motives) or external factors (the situation). Attribution is subject to several forms of error and bias. **Fundamental attribution error** is the tendency to overestimate internal personality influences when judging the behavior of others. When we explain our own behavior, however, we tend to attribute positive outcomes to internal factors and negative outcomes to external causes (**self-serving bias**).

Attitudes are learned predispositions toward a particular object. Three components of all attitudes are the cognitive responses (thoughts and beliefs), affective responses (feelings), and behavioral tendencies (predispositions to actions). We sometimes change our attitudes because of **cognitive dissonance**, a state of tension or anxiety we feel when two or more attitudes contradict each other or when our attitudes do not match our behaviors. This mismatch and resulting tension motivate us to change our attitude to restore balance.

Questions

1. The principles people follow in making judgments about the causes of events, others' behavior, and their own behavior are known as _____. (a) impression management; (b) stereotaxic determination; (c) attribution; (d) person perception

2. What is the fundamental attribution error?

3. After hearing about the "shocking" behavior of participants in Stanley Milgram's experiment, most people strongly believe they would have acted differently and easily remember instances in which they have refused to obey others. This may be an example of _____. (a) cognitive dissonance; (b) groupthink; (c) the illusion of invulnerability; (d) the self-serving bias

4. According to _____ theory, people are motivated to change their attitudes because of tension created by a mismatch between two or more competing attitudes or between their attitudes and behavior.

Answers to Questions can be found in Appendix B.

ACTIVE LEARNING WORKSHEET   MODULE 46

Circle either "T" for true or "F" for false, and then compare your answers with those in Appendix B.

1. The tendency to overestimate internal personality factors and underestimate external situational factors is known as the self-serving bias. T or F

2. The tendency to focus on the most noticeable factors when explaining the causes of behavior is known as the saliency bias. T or F

3. The fact that husbands and wives both think they're doing more than their share of household tasks is known as the fundamental attribution error. T or F

4. Both the fundamental attribution error and the self-serving bias are less common in Eastern nations. T or F

5. One of the most efficient ways to change attitudes is through the creation of cognitive dissonance. T or F

MODULE 47
OUR FEELINGS ABOUT OTHERS

What feelings are most important in our social interactions?

Prejudice *A generally negative attitude directed toward others because of their membership in a specific group; like all attitudes, prejudice involves cognitions (thoughts), affect (feelings), and behavioral tendencies*

Stereotype *A set of beliefs about the characteristics of people in a group that is generalized to all group members; also, the cognitive component of prejudice*

Discrimination *Negative behaviors directed at members of a group*

Having explored our thoughts about others (attribution and attitudes), we now turn our attention to our feelings about others. We begin by examining the negative feelings (and thoughts and actions) associated with *prejudice* and *discrimination*. We will then explore the generally positive feelings of *interpersonal attraction*.

Prejudice and Discrimination: It's the Feeling That Counts

Prejudice, which literally means *prejudgment*, is a generally *negative* attitude directed toward specific people solely because of their membership in an identified group. Positive forms of prejudice do exist, such as "all women love babies" or "African Americans are natural athletes."

However, most research and definitions of prejudice usually focus on the negative forms. (It is also interesting to note that even positive forms of prejudice harm the victims. For example, women might think there must be something wrong with them if they don't like being around babies, or African Americans might see athletics as their major way to achieve success.)

Prejudice is prejudgment of others on the basis of limited knowledge and limited contact. It biases us against others and limits our ability to accurately process information. Like all attitudes, prejudice is composed of three elements: (1) a *cognitive component* or **stereotype**, thoughts and beliefs held about people strictly because of their membership in a group; (2) an *affective component*, consisting of feelings and emotions associated with objects of prejudice; and (3) a *behavioral component*, consisting of predispositions to act in certain ways toward members of the group (discrimination).

Although the terms *prejudice* and *discrimination* are often used interchangeably, there is an important difference between them. *Prejudice* refers to an *attitude*, whereas **discrimination** refers to a *behavior* (Fiske, 1998). Discrimination often results from prejudice, but not always (Figure 47.1). People do not always act on their prejudices.

Major Sources of Prejudice and Discrimination

How do prejudice and discrimination originate? Why do they persist? As we explore these questions, you may find your values and beliefs challenged. Use this opportunity to apply your highest critical thinking skills to evaluate your attitudes. We begin with a look at the four most commonly cited sources of prejudice: learning, cognitive processes, economic and political competition, and displaced aggression.

1. *Learning* People learn prejudice in the same ways they learn their attitudes toward abortion, divorce, or pizza — through classical and operant conditioning and social learning (Modules 15, 16, and 17). When children watch TV and movies and read books and magazines that portray minorities and women in demeaning and stereotypical roles, they learn that such images must be acceptable. When children hear their parents, friends, and teachers expressing prejudice, they imitate them. Exposure of this kind initiates and reinforces the learning of prejudice (Dovidio, Brigham, Johnson, & Gaertner, 1995).

People also learn their prejudices through direct experience. They derogate others and experience a rise in their own self-esteem (Fein & Spencer, 1997). They receive attention and sometimes approval for expressing racist or sexist remarks. Also, they may have a single negative experience with a specific mem-

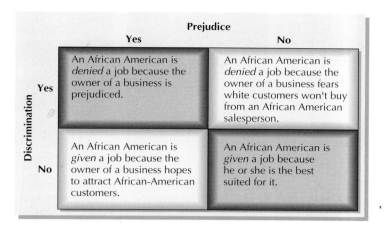

Figure 47.1 *Prejudice and discrimination.* Note how prejudice can exist without discrimination and vice versa. The only condition in this example without prejudice or discrimination is where someone is given a job simply because he or she is the best candidate.

ber of a group that they then generalize and apply to all members of the group (Vidmar, 1997).

2. Cognitive processes. According to some researchers, prejudice develops as a result of normal cognitive processes and everyday attempts to explain a complex social world (Devine & Monteith, 1999; Sherman & Bessenoff, 1999). Stereotypes (the cognitive component of prejudice) are a byproduct of how we cognitively simplify the world through categorization. Stereotyping allows people to make quick judgments about others, thus freeing their mental resources for other activities.

Just as a biologist classifies all living things into categories and mental health professionals classify mental disorders in the *DSM-IV-TR* (*Diagnostic and Statistical Manual of Mental Disorders,* fourth edition, revised; see Module 37), people use stereotypes to classify others by membership in a specific group ("jocks," "Mexicans," "chicks," and so on). Given that people generally classify themselves as part of the preferred group, they also create ingroups and outgroups.

An *ingroup* is any category that people see themselves belonging to, whereas an *outgroup* consists of all others. People tend to see ingroup members as being more attractive, having better personalities, and engaging in more socially accepted forms of behavior than outgroup members. In other words, cognitively, they practice **ingroup favoritism** (Mohr & Larsen, 1998; Perreault & Bourhis, 1999).

In addition to ingroup favoritism, people also tend to see more diversity among members of their own ingroup and less among the outgroup (Bartsch, Judd, Louw, Park, & Ryan, 1997; Hilton & Von Hippel, 1996). This "they all look alike to me" tendency is termed the **outgroup homogeneity effect**.

This outgroup homogeneity bias can be particularly dangerous. When members of minority groups are not perceived as varied and complex individuals who have the same needs and feelings as the dominant group, it is easier to perceive them as faceless objects and treat them in discriminatory ways. During the Vietnam War, for example, Asians were labeled "gooks" for whom "life is cheap." Facelessness made it easier to kill large numbers of Vietnamese civilians (Johnson, 1999).

3. Economic and political competition Still other theorists think prejudice develops out of competition for limited resources and is maintained because it offers significant economic and political advantages to the dominant group (Hughes & Dodge, 1997; Pettigrew, 1998). The competition for resources idea is supported by findings showing lower-class whites in the United States having more racist attitudes than higher-class whites. It may be that the upper class can afford to be less prejudiced because minorities represent less threat to their employment, status, and income. In addition, prejudice is maintained because it serves a function — protecting the interests of the dominant class. The stereotype that blacks are inferior to

Ingroup Favoritism *A cognitive process in prejudice whereby members of an ingroup are viewed in more favorable terms than members of an outgroup*

Outgroup Homogeneity Effect *A cognitive process in prejudice whereby members of the outgroup are judged as less individual, or diverse, than members of the ingroup*

(a)

(b)

(c)

Figure 47.2 *The price of prejudice.* Here are only a few examples of the atrocities associated with prejudice: (a) the Holocaust, when millions of Jews were exterminated by the Nazis; (b) slavery in the United States, where Africans were bought and sold as slaves; and (c) the relocation of Native Americans to reservations, which led to almost complete extermination. Can you think of other examples?

whites, for example, helps justify a social order in the United States where whites hold disproportionate power.

4. *Displaced aggression.* Have you ever wondered why lower-class groups tend to blame each other rather than the upper class or the class system itself? As you will see in the section on aggression, frustration often leads people to attack the source of frustration. But when the source is bigger and capable of retaliating, or when the cause of the frustration is ambiguous, people often displace their aggression on an alternative, nonthreatening target. The innocent victim of displaced aggression is known as a *scapegoat*. There is strong historical evidence for the power of scapegoating (Eilenberg & Wyman, 1998; Miller, 1998; Sidel, 1996). During the Great Depression of the 1930s, Hitler used Jews as scapegoats Germans could blame for their economic troubles. If it is true that a picture is worth a thousand words, then the photos in Figure 47.2 may serve as a small reminder of the atrocities resulting from prejudice and discrimination.

Reducing Prejudice and Discrimination

> Let's go hand in hand, not one before another.
>
> William Shakespeare

What can be done to combat prejudice? We will look at five approaches: cooperation, superordinate goals, increased contact, cognitive retraining, and cognitive dissonance.

1 and **2. *Cooperation and superordinate goals.*** Research shows that one of the best ways to combat prejudice is to encourage *cooperation* rather than *competition* (Brewer, 1996; Walker & Crogan, 1998). Muzafer Sherif and his colleagues (1966, 1998) conducted an ingenious study to show the role of competition in promoting prejudice. The researchers created strong feelings of ingroup and outgroup identification in a group of 11- and 12-year-old boys at a summer camp by physically separating the boys in different cabins and assigning different projects to each group, such as building a diving board or cooking out in the woods.

Once each group developed strong feelings of group identity and allegiance, the researchers set up a series of competitive games, including tug-of-war and touch football, and awarded desirable prizes to the winning teams. Because of this treatment, the groups began to pick fights, call each other names, and raid each other's camps — behaviors the researchers pointed to as evidence of the research-produced prejudice.

After using competition to create prejudice between the two groups, the researchers demonstrated how cooperation could be successfully used to eliminate it. They created "minicrises" and tasks that required expertise, labor, and cooperation from both groups, and prizes were awarded to all. The hostilities and prejudice between groups slowly began to dissipate, and by the end of the camp, the boys voted to return home in the same bus, and the self-chosen seating did not reflect the earlier camp divisions. Sherif's study showed not only the importance of cooperation as opposed to competition but also the importance of *superordinate goals* (the minicrises) in reducing prejudice (Der-Karabetian, Stephenson, & Poggi, 1996).

3. *Increased contact.* A third approach to reducing prejudice is *increasing contact between groups.* By interacting with members of other groups, prejudice can be reduced (Brewer & Brown, 1998; Dovidio, Gaertner, & Bachman, 2001; Pettigrew, 1998). But as you just discovered with Sherif's study of the boys at the summer camp, contact can sometimes increase prejudice. It works under only certain conditions: (1) close interaction (if minority students are "tracked" into vocational education courses and white students are primarily in college prep courses, they seldom interact and prejudice is increased), (2) interdependence (both groups must be involved in superordinate goals that require cooperation), and (3) equal status (everyone must be at the same level). Once people have positive experiences with a group, they tend to generalize to other groups (Pettigrew, 1998).

4. *Cognitive retraining.* One of the most recent strategies in prejudice reduction requires taking another's perspective or undoing associations of negative stereotypical traits (Galinsky & Moskowitz, 2000; Kawakami, Dovidio, Moll, Hermsen, & Russin, 2000). For example, in a computer training session, Kawakami and colleagues (2000) instructed participants to *try not to* think of cultural associations when they saw a photograph of an elderly person and to press a *no* button when they saw a photograph of an elderly person with a trait stereotypically associated (e.g., slow, weak) with elderly people. Conversely, they were instructed to press a *yes* button when they saw a photograph of an elderly person with a trait not normally associated with the elderly. After a number of trials, their response times became faster and faster, indicating they were undoing negative associations and learning positive ones. After the training, participants were less likely to activate any negative stereotype of elderly people in another activity, compared with others who did not participate in the training exercise.

People can also learn to be nonprejudiced if they are taught to selectively pay attention to *similarities* as opposed to *differences* (Phillips & Ziller, 1997). When we focus on how "black voters feel about affirmative action" or how Jewish people feel about "a Jewish candidate for vice president of the United States," we are indirectly encouraging stereotypes and ingroups versus outgroups. Can you see how this might also apply to gender? By emphasizing gender differences (*Men Are from Mars, Women Are from Venus*), we may be perpetuating gender stereotypes (Powlishta, 1999).

5. *Cognitive dissonance.* As mentioned earlier, prejudice is a type of attitude that has three basic components — affective (feelings), behavioral tendencies, and cognitive (thoughts). And one of the most efficient methods to change an attitude is through *cognitive dissonance*, a perceived discrepancy between an attitude and a behavior or between an attitude and a new piece of information (Albarracin & Wyer, 2000; Cook, 2000). As a critical thinker, can you see how recent social changes, such as school busing, integrated housing, and increased civil rights legislation, might create cognitive dissonance and a subsequent reduction in prejudice? Moreover, do you recognize how the four methods of reducing prejudice we just described also involve cognitive dissonance? Cooperation and superordinate goals, increased contact, and cognitive retraining all create discrepancy in the prejudiced person, which leads to tension that motivates them to change their attitudes — and prejudice.

Interpersonal Attraction: Liking and Loving Others

Stop for a moment and think about someone you like very much. Now picture someone you really dislike. Can you explain your feelings? Social psychologists use the term **interpersonal attraction** to refer to the degree of positive or negative feelings toward another. Attraction accounts for a variety of social experiences — admiration, liking, friendship, intimacy, lust, and love. In this section, we will discuss several factors that explain interpersonal attraction.

Interpersonal Attraction *The degree of positive or negative feelings toward another*

Three Key Factors in Attraction: Physical Attractiveness, Proximity, and Similarity

Social psychologists have found three compelling factors in interpersonal attraction — *physical attractiveness*, *proximity*, and *similarity*. Although physical attractiveness and proximity are more influential in the beginning stages of relationships, similarity is the single most important factor in maintaining a long-term relationship.

Physical Attractiveness. Can you remember what first attracted you to your best friend or romantic partner? Was it his or her warm personality, sharp intelligence, or great sense of humor? Or was it looks? Research consistently shows that *physical attractiveness* (size, shape, facial characteristics, and manner of dress) is one of the most important factors in our initial liking or loving of others (Frederick & Morrison, 1999; Langlois et al., 2000).

Like it or not, attractive individuals are seen by both men and women as more poised, interesting, cooperative, achieving, sociable, independent, intelligent, healthy, and sexually warm (Langlois et al., 2000; Mulford, Orbell, Shatto, & Stockard, 1998, Watkins & Johnston, 2000).

GENDER & CULTURAL DIVERSITY

Physical Attractiveness Across Cultures

If you found the previous list of advantages of physical attractiveness unnerving, you'll be even more surprised to know that some research also shows that judgments of attractiveness appear consistent across cultures, and that in 37 cultures around the world, women are judged more beautiful if they are youthful in appearance (Buss, 1989, 1994, 1999; Cartwright, 2000; Cunningham, Roberts, Barbee, Druen, & Wu, 1995; Langlois et al., 2000). For men, on the other hand, maturity and financial resources seem to be more important than appearance in attracting a mate. According to Buss (1994), "Men prefer to mate with beautiful young women, whereas women prefer to mate with men who have resources and social status" (p. 239).

How can this be so universally true? Evolutionary psychologists would suggest that this cross-cultural similarity in judgment of attractiveness reflects the fact that good looks generally indicate good health, sound genes, and high fertility. For example, facial and body symmetry appear to be key elements in attractiveness (Rhodes, Sumich, & Byatt, 1999; Zajonc, 1998) and symmetry seems to be correlated with genetic health. The fact that women prefer men with resources and social status also supports the evolutionary position. Because the responsibility of rearing and

Culture and attraction. Which of these women do you find most attractive? Can you see how your cultural background would train you to prefer one look over the others?

nurturing children more often falls on women's shoulders, men with greater resources will have more to invest in children.

In contrast to this seeming universal agreement on standards of attractiveness, there also is evidence that beauty is in "the eye of the beholder." What we judge as beautiful varies somewhat from era to era and culture to culture. For example, the Chinese once practiced foot binding because small feet were considered beautiful in women. All the toes except the big one were bent under a young girl's foot and into the sole. The physical distortion made it almost impossible for her to walk, and she suffered excruciating pain, chronic bleeding, and frequent infections throughout her life (Dworkin, 1974). Even in modern times, cultural demands for attractiveness encourage an increasing number of women (and men) to undergo expensive and often painful surgery to *increase* the size of their eyes, breasts, lips, chest, and penis and *decrease* the size of their nose, ears, chin, stomach, hips, and thighs (Atkins, 2000; Etcoff, 1999).

Given that only a small percentage of people are as attractive as Cameron Diaz or Denzel Washington or have the money (or inclination) for extensive cosmetic surgery, how do the rest of us ever find mates? The good news is that what people judge as "ideally attractive" may be quite different than what they eventually choose for a mate (Regan, 1998). According to the *matching hypothesis,* men and women of approximately equal physical attractiveness tend to select each other as partners. What people judge as "ideally attractive" may be quite different than what they ultimately choose for a mate (Reagan, 1998).

Proximity Attraction also depends on people being in the same place at the same time, making **proximity**, or geographic nearness, another major factor in attraction. A study of friendship in college dormitories found that the person next door was more often liked than the person two doors away, the person two doors away was liked more than someone three doors away, and so on (Priest & Sawyer, 1967).

Proximity promotes attraction largely because of *mere exposure.* Just as familiar people become more physically attractive over time, repeated exposure also increases overall liking (Seamon, McKenna, & Binder, 1998; Zajonc, 1998). This makes sense from an evolutionary point of view. Things we have seen before are less likely to pose a threat than novel stimuli. It also explains why modern advertisers tend to run highly redundant ad campaigns, with familiar faces and jingles (Zajonc, 1968, 1998). Repeated exposure increases our liking — and purchases.

We even like *ourselves* better when we see ourselves in a familiar way. When researchers showed college students pictures of themselves or reversed photos (the mirror image), students strongly preferred the reversed photos — that is, the image they were used to seeing in the mirror. Close friends of the same students preferred the true photos of their friend. They were used to seeing this image (Mita, Dermer,

Proximity *A key factor in attraction involving geographic, residential, and other forms of physical closeness*

Exposure and liking. According to the "mere exposure effect," this model would prefer the reversed photo on the left because this is the version she sees in the mirror. However, most people prefer the "normal" photo on the right because this is what is most familiar to the audience.

& Knight, 1977). (Can you see why people often complain that photos of themselves "never really look like" them?)

One caution. Repeated exposure to a *negative* stimulus can *decrease* attraction, as evidenced by the high number of negative political ads. Politicians have learned that repeatedly running an attack ad associating an opposing candidate with negative cues (like increased taxes) decreases the viewers' liking of the opponent. On the other hand, running ads showing themselves in a positive light (kissing babies, helping flood victims) helps builds positive associations and increased liking.

Similarity. Once we've had repeated opportunity to get to know someone through simple physical proximity, and assuming we find him or her attractive, we then need something to hold the relationship together over time. The major cementing factor for long-term relationships, whether liking or loving, is *similarity.* We tend to prefer, and stay with, people who are most like us, those who share our ethnic background, social class, interests, and attitudes (Akers, Jones, & Coyl, 1998; Herman, 1998). In other words, "Birds of a feather flock together."

What about the old saying "Opposites attract"? Although it does seem that these two pieces of common folklore are contradictory, the term *opposites* here probably refers to personality traits rather than to social background or values. An attraction to a seemingly opposite person is more often based on the recognition that in one or two important areas that person offers us something we lack (Dryer & Horowitz, 1997). If you are a talkative and outgoing person, for example, your friendship with a quiet and reserved individual may endure because each of you provides important resources for the other. Psychologists refer to this as **need complementarity**, as compared with the **need compatibility** represented by similarity.

Need Complementarity *The tendency to seek out and be attracted to people whose qualities we admire but personally lack*

Need Compatibility *A sharing of similar needs*

Opposites attract or similarity? Research shows that similarity is the single best predictor for long-term relationships. As shown here, however, many people ignore dissimilarities and hope that their chosen partner will change over time.

Reprinted with special permission of King Features Syndicate.

TABLE 47.1 SAMPLE ITEMS FROM RUBIN'S LIKING AND LOVING TEST

Love Scale
1. I feel that I can confide in _____ about virtually everything.
2. I would do almost anything for _____.
3. If I could never be with _____, I would feel miserable.

Liking Scale
1. I think that _____ is unusually well adjusted.
2. I would highly recommend _____ for a responsible job.
3. In my opinion, _____ is an exceptionally mature person.

Source: Rubin, Z. (1970). "Measurement of romantic love," *Journal of Personality and Social Psychology, 16,* 265–273. Copyright © 1970 by the American Psychological Association. Reprinted by permission of the author.

Loving Others

To complete our discussion of interpersonal attraction, we will explore three perspectives on the mystery of love: liking versus loving, romantic love, and companionate love.

Liking versus loving Because love relationships often develop from friendships and initial feelings of liking for one another, Zick Rubin (1970, 1992) developed two paper-and-pencil tests to explore the relationship between liking and loving (Table 47.1).

In spite of the apparent simplicity of Rubin's scales, they have proven to be useful indicators of both liking and loving. For example, Rubin hypothesized that "strong love" couples would spend more time gazing into one another's eyes than "weak love" couples. To test his hypothesis, while the couples were waiting for the experiment to begin, Rubin and his assistants secretly recorded the actual amount of eye contact between all couples. As predicted, couples who scored highest on the love scale also spent more time looking into one another's eyes. In addition, Rubin found that although both partners tended to match each other on their love scores, women liked their dating partners significantly more than they were liked in return.

How does love differ from liking on Rubin's scales? Rubin found that liking involves a favorable evaluation of another, as reflected in greater feelings of admiration and respect. He found not only that love is more intense than liking but also that love is composed of three basic elements:

- *Caring,* the desire to help the other person, particularly when help is needed

- *Attachment,* the need to be with the other person

- *Intimacy,* a sense of empathy and trust that comes from close communication and self-disclosure from another

Romantic Love When you think of romantic love, do you think of falling in love, a magical experience that puts you on cloud nine? **Romantic love**, also called *passionate love* or *limerence,* has been defined as "any intense attraction that involves the idealization of the other, within an erotic context, with the expectation of enduring for some time in the future" (Jankowiak, 1997, p. 8).

Romantic love has intrigued people throughout history, and its intense joys and sorrows have inspired countless poems, novels, movies, and songs around the world. A cross-cultural study by anthropologists William Jankowiak and Edward Fischer found romantic love in 147 of the 166 societies they studied. The researchers concluded that "romantic love constitutes a human universal, or at the least a near universal" (1992, p. 154).

Romantic Love *An intense feeling of attraction to another person, within an erotic context and with future expectations*

Problems with Romantic Love   Romantic love may be almost universal, but that hardly means it is problem free. First, romantic love is typically short lived. Even in the most devoted couples, the intense attraction and excitement generally begin to fade after 6 to 30 months (Hatfield & Rapson, 1996; Livingston, 1999). Although this research finding may disappoint you, as a critical thinker do you really think any emotion of this intensity could last forever? What would happen if other intense emotions, such as anger or joy, were eternal? Moreover, given the time consuming nature of romantic love, what would happen to other parts of our lives, such as school, career, and family?

Another major problem with romantic love is that it is largely based on mystery and fantasy. People fall in love with others not necessarily as they are but as they want them to be (Fletcher & Simpson, 2000; Levine & Markman, 2001). What happens to these illusions when we are faced with everyday interactions and long-term exposure? Our "beautiful princess" isn't supposed to snore, and our "knight in shining armor" doesn't look very knightly flossing his teeth. And, of course, no princess or knight would ever notice our shortcomings, let alone comment on them.

Is there any way to keep love alive?   If you mean romantic love, one of the best ways to fan the flames is through interference, or some form of frustration that keeps you from fulfilling your desire for the presence of your love. Researchers have found that interference (for example, the parents in Shakespeare's *Romeo and Juliet*) apparently increases the feelings of love (Driscoll, Davis, & Lipetz, 1972).

Romantic love in the media. *Do you remember the story of Snow White? After fleeing from a wicked stepmother and being rescued by seven dwarfs, she apparently dies from a poisoned apple and the dwarfs place her in a glass coffin in the middle of the forest. Prince Charming happens by on a horse, falls in love with her dead body, and is surprised when his kiss brings her back to life. The story ends as they ride off into the sunset to live "happily ever after." The rescuing of a damsel in distress followed by lifelong happiness is a common theme in childhood stories, as well as in modern day romance novels, movies, and love songs. Is this simple entertainment? Or could these early childhood stories and ongoing romantic messages create unrealistic expectations of real life and adult relationships?*

Because romantic love depends on uncertainty and fantasy, it can also be kept alive by situations in which we never really get to know the other person. This may explain why computer chat room romances or old high school flings have such a tug on our emotions. Because we never really get to test these relationships, we can always fantasize about what might have been.

One of the most constructive ways of keeping romantic love alive is to recognize its fragile nature and nurture it with carefully planned surprises, flirting and flattery, and special dinners and celebrations. In the long run, however, romantic love's most important function might be to keep us attached long enough to move on to companionate love.

Companionate Love. Companionate love is based on admiration and respect, combined with deep feelings of caring for the person and commitment to the relationship. Studies of close friendships show that satisfaction grows with time as we come to recognize the value of companionship and of having an intimate confidante (Kiraly, 2000; & Hazan, 1991). Companionate love, unlike romantic love, which is very short lived, seems to grow stronger with time and often lasts a lifetime (Figure 47.3).

Companionate love is what we feel for our best friends, and it can be the basis for a strong and lasting marriage. But finding and keeping a long-term relationship is no easy task. Many of our expectations for love are based on romantic fantasies and unconscious programming from fairy tales and TV shows in which everyone lives happily ever after. Therefore, we are often ill equipped to deal with the hassles and boredom that come with any long-term relationship. One tip for maintaining companionate love is to *overlook each other's faults.* Studies of both dating and married couples find that people report greater satisfaction with — and stay longer in — relationships where they have a somewhat idealized or unrealistically positive perception of their partner (Fletcher & Simpson, 2000; Murray & Holmes, 1997). This makes sense in light of research on cognitive dissonance (discussed earlier). Idealizing our mates allows us to believe we have a good deal — and hence avoids the cognitive dissonance that might naturally arise every time we saw an attractive alternative. As Benjamin Franklin put it, "Keep your eyes wide open before marriage, half shut afterwards."

Figure 47.3 *Love over the life span.* Romantic love is high in the beginning of a relationship but tends to diminish over time, with periodic resurgences or "spikes." Companionate love usually increases over time.

Companionate Love *A strong feeling of attraction to another person characterized by trust, caring, tolerance, and friendship; it is believed to provide an enduring basis for long-term relationships*

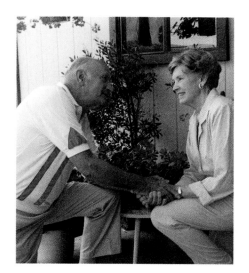

Companionate versus romantic love. *This couple just celebrated their 60th wedding anniversary. Unlike romantic love, which rarely lasts longer than 6 to 30 months, companionate love can last a lifetime.*

Check & Review

OUR FEELINGS ABOUT OTHERS

Prejudice is a generally negative attitude directed toward specific people solely because of their membership in a specific group. It contains all three components of attitudes (cognitive, affective, and behavioral). **Discrimination** is not the same as prejudice. It refers to the actual negative behavior directed at members of a group. People do not always act on their prejudices.

The four major sources of prejudice are learning (classical and operant conditioning and social learning), cognitive processes (categorization), economic and political competition, and displaced aggression (scapegoating). Cooperation, superordinate goals, increased contact, cognitive retraining, and cognitive dissonance reduction are five methods for reducing prejudice and discrimination.

Physical attractiveness is very important to **interpersonal attraction**. Physically attractive people are often perceived as more intelligent, sociable, and interesting than less attractive people. Standards for physical attractiveness vary across cultures and time. Physical **proximity** also increases one's attractiveness. If you live near someone or work alongside someone, you are more likely to like that person. Although people commonly believe that "opposites attract" (**need complementarity**), research shows that similarity (**need compatibility**) is a much more important factor in attraction.

Love can be defined in terms of caring, attachment, and intimacy. **Romantic love** is highly valued in our society, but because it is based on mystery and fantasy, it is hard to sustain. **Companionate love** relies on mutual trust, respect, and friendship and seems to grow stronger with time.

Questions

1. Explain how prejudice differs from discrimination.

2. Saying that members of another ethnic group "all look alike to me" may be an example of _____. (a) ingroup favoritism; (b) the outgroup homogeneity effect; (c) outgroup negativism; (d) ingroup bias

3. Cross-cultural research on physical attractiveness has found all but one of the following. (a) the Chinese once practiced foot binding because small feet were considered attractive in women; (b) in most male dominated societies, physical beauty is the most important attribute in a potential wife; (c) in most Eastern cultures, men prefer women with power and financial status over beauty; (d) for men, maturity and financial resources are more important than appearance in their ability to attract a mate

4. Compare the dangers associated with romantic love with the benefits of companionate love.

Answers to Questions can be found in Appendix B.

ACTIVE LEARNING WORKSHEET   MODULE 47

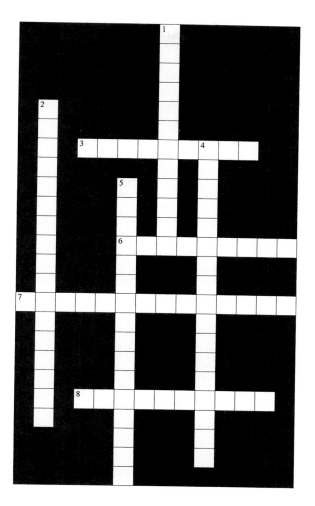

ACROSS

3. Key factor in attraction involving forms of physical closeness.

6. Generally negative attitude directed toward others because of their membership in a specific group.

7. Negative behaviors directed at members of a group.

8. Set of beliefs about the characteristics of people in a group generalized to all members.

DOWN

1. Intense feeling of attraction and erotic feelings toward another person.

2. Sharing of similar needs.

4. Viewing members of an ingroup more favorably.

5. A strong attraction to another involving trust, caring, tolerance, and friendship.

Answers can be found in Appendix B.

MODULE 48
OUR ACTIONS TOWARD OTHERS

How do our actions toward others affect their lives and our own?

Having just completed our whirlwind examination of how our thoughts and emotions influence others — and vice versa — we turn to topics associated with actions toward others. We begin with a look at social influence (conformity and obedience), and then continue with group processes (membership and decision making). We conclude by exploring two opposite kinds of behavior — aggression and altruism.

Social Influence: Conformity and Obedience

The society and culture into which we are born influence us from the moment of birth until the moment of death. Our culture teaches us to believe certain things, feel certain ways, and act in accordance with these beliefs and feelings. These influences are so strong and so much a part of who we are that we rarely recognize them. Just as a fish doesn't know it's in water, we are largely unaware of the strong impact cultural and social factors have on all our behaviors. In this section, we will discuss two kinds of *social influence*: conformity and obedience.

Conformity — Going Along with Others

Imagine for a moment that you have volunteered for a psychology experiment on perception. You find yourself seated around a table with six other students. You are all shown a card with three lines labeled A, B, and C, as in Figure 48.1. You are then asked to select the line that is closest in length to a fourth line, X. Each of you is asked to state your choice out loud, in order, around the table. At first, everyone agrees on the correct line, and the experiment seems pretty boring. On the third trial, however, the first participant gives what is obviously a wrong answer. You know that line B is correct, but he says line A. When the second, third, fourth, and fifth participants also say line A, you really start to wonder: "What's going on here? Are they blind? Or am I?"

Conformity *A type of social influence in which individuals change their behavior as a result of real or imagined group pressure*

What do you think you would do at this point in the experiment? Would you stick with your convictions and say line B, regardless of what the others have answered? Or would you go along with the group? In the original version of this experiment, conducted by Solomon Asch (1951), six participants were actually confederates of the experimenter, and seating was arranged so that the one participant who was the real subject was always in the next-to-last position. The six confederates had been instructed to respond incorrectly on the third trial and selected later trials as a way of testing the participant's degree of **conformity**, or changing one's behavior as a result of real or imagined group pressure.

How did Asch's participants respond? More than one-third conformed and agreed with the group's obviously incorrect choice. This level of conformity is particularly intriguing when it is compared with responses in the control group, which experienced no group pressure and chose correctly virtually 100 percent of the time.

Figure 48.1 *Solomon Asch's study of conformity.* Participants were shown four lines such as these and then asked which line (A, B, or C) was most similar to the one on the bottom (X).

Why would so many people conform? To the onlooker, conformity is often difficult to understand, and even the conformer sometimes has a hard time explaining his or her behavior. We can better understand Asch's participants and our own forms of conformity if we look at three factors: (1) *normative social influence*, (2) *informational social influence*, and (3) the role of *reference groups*.

© Sidney Harris

Normative social influence. The first factor, **normative social influence**, refers to conformity to group pressure out of a need for approval and acceptance by the group. A **norm** is an expected behavior that is adhered to by members of the group. Norms are society's definition of how we "should" behave. They are sometimes explicit, but most often, norms are quite subtle and implicit. Have you ever asked what others are wearing to the party or watched your neighbor's table manners to be sure you pick up the right fork? Such behavior reflects your desire to conform and the power of normative social influence.

An important norm in every culture has to do with *personal space* (Axtell, 1998; Hall, 1966, 1983; Sommer, 1969). If someone invades the invisible "personal bubble" that we like to maintain around our bodies, we generally feel very uncomfortable. Imagine yourself as the typical American traveling in several Middle Eastern countries. How would you respond when a local citizen answers your question while standing close enough to feel your breath? Most Americans, Canadians, and Northern Europeans feel very uncomfortable at this distance (unless talking with a lover), but most Middle Easterners like to be close enough to "read" one another's eyes. If you "naturally" back away during the conversation, the Middle Easterner might think you are cold and standoffish at the same time that you might consider him or her rude and intrusive.

Why do some people like to stand closer than others do? There are a number of possible explanations. First, culture and socialization have a lot to do with personal space. For reasons unknown, people from Mediterranean, Moslem, and Latin

Normative Social Influence *Conforming to group pressure out of a need for acceptance and approval*

Norm *Cultural rule of behavior that prescribes what is acceptable in a given situation*

TRY THIS
Yourself

If you want to personally experience the power of social norms, approach a fellow student on campus and ask for directions to the bookstore, library, or some other landmark. As you are talking, move toward the person until you invade his or her personal space. You should be close enough to almost touch toes. How does the person respond? How do you feel? Now repeat the process with another student, but this time try standing 5 to 6 feet away while asking directions. Which procedure was most difficult for you? Although most people think this will be a fun assignment, they often find it extremely difficult to willingly break our culture's unwritten norms for personal space.

The advantages of conformity. *What would happen to our everyday social functioning if MOST people did not conform?*

Informational Social Influence *Conforming to group pressure out of a need for direction and information*

Reference Groups *People to whom we conform (or with whom we go along) because we like and admire them and want to be like them*

Obedience *A type of social influence in which an individual follows direct commands, usually from someone in a position of authority*

American countries tend to maintain smaller interpersonal distances than do North Americans and Northern Europeans (Axtell, 1998; Steinhart, 1986). Children also tend to stand very close to others until they are socialized to recognize and maintain a greater personal distance. Second, certain relationships, situations, and personalities affect interpersonal distances. Friends stand closer than strangers, women tend to stand closer than men, and violent prisoners prefer approximately three times the personal space of nonviolent prisoners (Axtell, 1998; Gilmour & Walkey, 1981; Roques, Lambin, Jeunier, & Strayer, 1997).

Informational Social Influence Have you ever bought a specific brand of ski equipment or automobile simply because of a friend's recommendation? You conform not to gain their approval (normative social influence) but because you assume they have more information than you do. Conforming to group pressure out of a need for direction and information is considered the result of **informational social influence**. Participants in Asch's experiment might also have conformed for similar reasons. Totalitarian governments recognize the importance of information in social influence and generally maintain strict control over books and news reports within their country.

Reference groups The third major factor in conformity is the power of **reference groups** — those people we most admire, like, and want to resemble. Attractive actors and popular sports stars are paid millions of dollars to endorse certain products because advertisers know that we want to be as cool as Wesley Snipes or as beautiful as Jennifer Lopez. Of course, we also have more important reference groups in our lives — parents, friends, family, teachers, religious leaders, and so on.

Does this mean that all conformity is bad and even dangerous? Not at all. In fact, most people conform most of the time because it is in their best interests and everyone else's to do so (Henrich & Boyd, 1998). You stand in line at the bookstore instead of pushing ahead of everyone, and you expect others to wait their turn, too. Conformity allows social life to proceed with order and predictability.

Obedience — Going Along with a Command

A second form of social influence, **obedience**, involves going along with a direct command, usually from someone in a position of authority. Under orders from an experimenter, would you shock a man with a known heart condition who is screaming and asking to be released? Most people assume that few people would do so. But as you recall from Milgram's study described at the opening of this section, approximately two-thirds of the participants administered the full 450 volts. This happened even when the learner had stopped responding (screaming or otherwise) and was apparently either unconscious or dead (Milgram, 1963, 1974).

Even Milgram was surprised by the results of his study. When he polled a group of psychiatrists before the study began, they predicted that most people would refuse to go beyond 150 volts, and that less than 1 percent of those tested would "go all the way." Only someone who was "disturbed and sadistic" would obey to the fullest extent. But as you know, almost two-thirds of the participants, both men and women, of all ages and all walks of life, administered the highest voltage.

Factors in obedience. Personality researchers frequently debate the relative importance of the *person* as opposed to the *situation* in determining behavior. However, Milgram's research suggests when it comes to obedience, *situational factors* are most important. We will examine five of these factors:

1. *Power of authority.* People in positions of authority have an extraordinary — and often underestimated — power to elicit obedience. As Figure 48.2 shows, when an ordinary person instead of the experimenter gave the orders, obedience dropped significantly.

2. *Distance between the teacher and learner.* Look again at Figure 48.2. Note that when the learner was in the same room with the participant, only 40 percent obeyed fully. And when the teacher-participant was required to force the learner's hand down on a simulated "shock plate," only 30 percent obeyed. Can you see how these results relate to modern warfare? Think how much harder it might be to obey a military command to directly stab and kill one person, compared to the "ease" of dropping a bomb from a high-flying airplane that might kill thousands.

3. *Assignment of responsibility.* Research has also found that when participants are reminded that they will be held responsible for any harm to the victim, obedience is sharply reduced (Hamilton, 1978). Note the sharp contrast in Figure 48.2 between the one condition when participants were asked to just read the list of words while another teacher delivered the shock, compared with the second condition when the teacher was responsible for choosing the level of shock.

4. *Modeling/imitation.* Watching others also can have a tremendous impact on participant obedience. When two confederates (who were acting like "teachers") were instructed to either administer the maximum shock or to openly rebel and refuse to continue, actual participants copied either the obedient or the disobedient model (see again Figure 48.2).

Final Note

Milgram's research provides important insights into situational pressures that can lead normal people to engage in surprising levels of obedience. However, his study remains highly controversial (Berkowitz, 1999; Blass, 1999) and it would not be allowed under contemporary standards of research ethics.

Figure 48.2 *Participant's responses to different research conditions.* In addition to the original study of "teacher" versus "learner" described at the opening of this section (bar 1 on the graph), Milgram also wanted to see how participants would respond to authority when orders came from an ordinary person (bar 2), when there were varying distances between the teacher and learner (bars 3 and 4), when the teacher's level of responsibility varied (bars 5 and 6), and when teachers watched others quit or continue (bars 7 and 8).

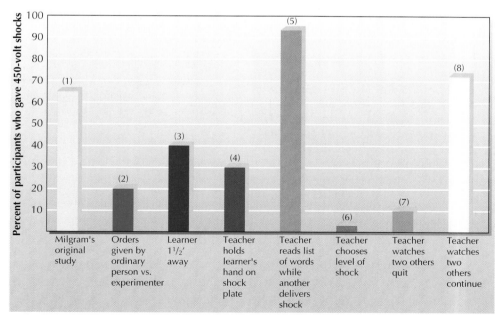

Perhaps the most important message is to recognize that obedience, like conformity, can be both good and bad. When police or firefighters order the crowd to step back away from the scene of the crime or the fire, it's important (and adaptive) to quickly obey. However, on some occasions we should not go along with the crowd (conformity) or cooperate with commands from authority (obedience).

It's also important to remember the power of modeling and a single act of rebellion. One of the most beautiful and historically important examples occurred in Alabama in 1955. Rosa Parks boarded a bus and as expected in those times she obediently sat in the back section marked "Negroes." When the bus became crowded, the driver told her to give up her seat to a white man. Surprisingly, Parks refused and was eventually forced off the bus by police and arrested. By refusing to obey, she gave impetus to the growing civil rights movement and the repeal of Jim Crow laws in the South. Her act of courage also inspires the rest of us to think about when it is good to obey authorities and when to disobey unethical demands from authorities.

Foot-in-the-Door Technique *A social influence technique in which a first, small request is used as a setup for later requests*

critical thinking

Active Learning

Would You Have Obeyed Milgram's Experimenters?

One common intellectual illusion that hinders critical thinking about obedience is the belief that only evil people do evil things or that evil announces itself. For example, the experimenter in Stanley Milgram's study looked and acted like a reasonable person who was simply carrying out a research project. Because he was not seen as personally corrupt and evil, the participants' normal moral guard was down and obedience was maximized.

This relaxed moral guard might also explain obedience to a highly respected military officer or the leader of a religious cult. One of the most infamous cult leaders, Jim Jones, was well known and highly revered for his kindness and "good works" — at least in the beginning. Perhaps because of their relaxed moral guard (combined with the five factors discussed earlier), in 1978 over 900 members of the People's Temple in Guyana committed mass suicide on Jones's order. People who resisted were murdered, but the vast majority took their lives willingly by drinking cyanide-laced Kool-Aid.

In addition, the gradual nature of many obedience situations may explain why so many people were willing to give the maximum shocks in Milgram's study. The initial

The foot-in-the door technique. If this homeowner allows the salesperson to give him a small gift (a "foot-in-the-door" technique), he's more likely to agree to buy something. *Can you explain why?*

mild level of shocks may have worked as a **foot-in-the-door technique**, in which a first, small request is used as a setup for later, larger requests. Once Milgram's participants complied with the initial request, they might have felt obligated to continue (Chartrand, Pinckert, & Burger, 1999; Sabini & Silver, 1993).

Take this opportunity to think critically about extreme forms of destructive obedience and the everyday examples that we encounter. Rank the following by placing a 1 next to the situation you believe is the most ethical act of obedience and a 3 next to the least ethical.

_____ Jane is 19 and wants to become a commercial artist. She is offered a scholarship to a good art school, but her parents strongly object to her career choice. After considerable pressure, she gives in and enrolls at the same engineering school her father attended.

_____ Tom is 45 and having serious doubts about his employer's shady business practices, such as double-billing the clients. Although he believes his boss is dishonest and unethical, he cooperates because he really needs the job.

_____ Mary is 20 and a senior in college. She desperately wants to get into a graduate program at a very prestigious school but is failing an important class. The instructor has suggested she could have an A in his course if she would sexually "cooperate." She agrees.

Having analyzed Jane's, Tom's, and Mary's responses, think of a situation in your own life in which you were unethically persuaded. Can you use what you have learned about conformity and obedience to clarify why you were persuaded — and perhaps prevent future problems?

Check & Review

SOCIAL INFLUENCE

The process of social influence teaches important cultural values and behaviors that are essential to successful social living. Two of the most important forms of social influence are conformity and obedience.

Conformity refers to changes in behavior in response to real or imagined pressure from others. People conform for approval and acceptance (**normative social influence**), out of a need for more information (**informational social influence**), and to match the behavior of those they admire and feel similar to (their **reference group**). Peo-ple also conform because it is often adap-tive to do so.

Obedience involves giving in to a com-mand from others. Stanley Milgram's study showed that a surprisingly large number of people would obey orders even when another human being is physically threat-ened. At least four factors increase or decrease obedience: the power of author-ity, distance between teacher and learner, assignment of responsibility, and model-ing/imitation.

Questions

1. Explain how conformity differs from obedience.

2. A social influence technique in which a first, small request is used as a setup for later requests is known as_____. (a) the lowball technique; (b) the foot-in-the-door technique; (c) infiltration technique; (d) ingratiation

3. Milgram's participants thought they were participating in an experiment designed to study the effect of_____. (a) obedi-ence to authority; (b) arousal on mem-ory; (c) punishment on learning; (d) elec-tric shock on brain-wave activity

4. What are the four factors that increase or decrease obedience?

Answers to Questions can be found in Appendix B.

Group Processes: Membership and Decision Making

Psychologists define a *group* as "two or more persons interacting with one another in such a manner that each person influences and is influenced by each other per-son" (Shaw, 1981, p. 8). In other words, a group consists of any collection of peo-ple who have some mutually recognized relationship with one another. A couple on their first date, a family, a class in psychology, and a basketball team are all con-sidered groups. On the other hand, people riding together in an elevator are not a group.

Group Membership

Have you ever been with friends and found yourself doing something that you might not have done alone? Or have you noticed that you behave differently with your friends than with your parents or with your employer or roommates? In each situa-tion, your behavior is largely the result of your group membership. Although we sel-dom recognize the power of such membership, social psychologists have identified several important ways that groups affect us. In this section we will explore, first, how the roles we assume influence behavior and, next, how group membership sometimes leads to deindividuation.

Roles in groups. Every person in a group is expected to play one or more *roles* — a set of behavioral patterns connected with particular social positions. Some roles are very specifically spelled out and regulated (police officer), whereas others are assumed through informal learning and inference (father). Have you ever wondered how these roles affect behavior? This question fascinated social psychologist Philip Zimbardo. In his famous study at Stanford University, 20 carefully screened, well-adjusted young college men were paid $15 a day for participating in a simulation of prison life (Haney, Banks, & Zimbardo, 1978; Zimbardo, 1993).

To appreciate Philip Zimbardo's prison study, pretend you are one of the 20 college students who volunteered to be a participant and that you were randomly assigned to play the role of "prisoner." You're watching TV at home when you unexpectedly hear a loud knock. When you open the door, several uniformed police officers take you outside, spread-eagle you against the police car, frisk you, and inform you that you are being arrested. At the police station, you are photographed, fingerprinted, and booked. You are then blindfolded and driven to your final destination — the "Stanford Prison." Here you are given an ID number in place of your name; deloused, and issued a shapeless gown to wear, a tight nylon cap to conceal your hair, and no underwear. All prisoners are in similar prisoner clothes; whereas participants who were assigned to be "guards" are outfitted with official-looking uniforms, billy clubs, and whistles. You and the other prisoners are locked in your cells, and the guards are given complete control. What do you think happens next?

Not even Zimbardo foresaw how the study would turn out. Although some guards were "good guys" who did little favors for the prisoners and others were "tough but fair," they all engaged in some abuse of power. They insisted that prisoners quickly obey all prison rules, as well as their own arbitrary punishments. The slightest disobedience was followed by degrading tasks (such as cleaning the toilet with bare hands) or the loss of "privileges" (such as eating, sleeping, and washing). Most prisoners initially responded to the bossing and punishment with good-humored acceptance. But as demands increased and abuses began, they became passive and depressed. Only one prisoner fought back with a hunger strike, which ended with a forced feeding by the guards.

Four prisoners had to be released within the first 4 days because of severe reactions, including uncontrollable sobbing, fits of rage, severe depression, and, in one case a psychosomatic rash over his entire body. Although the study was planned to last 2 weeks, it was stopped after only 6 days because of the alarming psychological changes in the participants. The guards were seriously abusing their power, and the traumatized prisoners were becoming more and more depressed and dehumanized.

Although this was not a true experiment in that it lacked control groups and clear measurements of the dependent variable, it offers insights into the potential *power of roles* on individual behavior. According to interviews conducted after the study, the students apparently became so absorbed in their roles they forgot they were volunteers in a university study (Zimbardo, Ebbeson, & Maslach, 1977). If this type of personality disintegration and abuse of power could be generated in a mere 6 days in a mock prison with fully informed *volunteers*, can you imagine what happens during life imprisonment, 6-year sentences, or even overnight jail stays?

Deindividuation *The increased arousal and reduced self-consciousness, inhibition, and personal responsibility that can occur when a person is part of a group, particularly when the members feel anonymous*

Deindividuation. Zimbardo's study shows that the roles we play as members of a group can have a powerful effect on behavior. Perhaps an even more extreme example of group effects occurs during **deindividuation**. To be deindividuated means that you feel less self-conscious, less inhibited, and less personally responsible as a member of a group than when you're alone. This is particularly likely under conditions of anonymity. Groups sometimes actively promote deindividuation as a way to increase allegiance and conformity.

Sometimes deindividuation can be positive. We all enjoy being swept along with a crowd's joyous celebration on New Year's Eve and the raucous cheering

Power corrupts. Zimbardo's prison study showed how the demands of roles and situations can produce dramatic changes in behavior.

and shouting during an exciting sports competition. Deindividuation also encourages increased helping behaviors and even heroism, as we will see later in this module. Unfortunately, deindividuation also helps explain angry mobs, rioters, and tragic consequences like gang rapes, lynchings, and hate crimes (Akert, 2000; Aronson, Wilson, & Akert, 1999; Green, Glaser, & Rich, 1998).

How does this happen? There are several possible explanations for deindividualization. But one of the most compelling is the fact that the presence of others tends to increase arousal and feelings of anonymity. For example, in one experiment, women who wore KKK-like disguises that completely covered their faces and bodies (see photo) delivered twice as much electric shock to a victim than did women who were not disguised and wore large nametags (Zimbardo, 1970). (As in all such experiments, the "victim" was a confederate who did not receive actual shocks.) It seems that *anonymity* is a powerful disinhibitor, which also helps explain why Halloween masks seem to increase vandalism and why most crimes and riots occur at night —

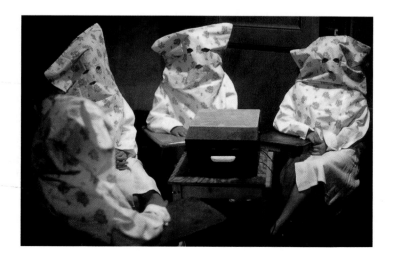

Deindividuation. When participants were covered with hoods and white coats, they delivered twice the amount of shock as those who were not covered. Can you see why anonymity, or deindividuation, may increase aggression and other forms of negative social behavior?

under the cover of darkness. It is important to emphasize, however, that not everyone in a crowd becomes deindividuated. Some people do resist and do maintain their personal values and beliefs.

Group Decision Making

Are two heads truly better than one? Do juries make better decisions than a judge does? Should managers assign important decisions to groups or to individuals? There are no simple answers to these questions. To formulate some response, we need to look not only at how group discussions affect individual opinions (group polarization) but also at how group membership affects access to accurate information (groupthink).

Group polarization. Most people assume that group decisions are more conservative, cautious, and "middle of the road" than individual decisions. But is this true? Initial investigations indicated that after discussing an issue, groups actually supported *riskier* decisions than decisions they made as individuals before the discussion (Stoner, 1961). Partly because it contradicted the common belief about group caution and moderation, this *risky shift* concept sparked a great deal of research.

Subsequent research shows that the risky shift phenomenon is only part of the picture in group decision making. Although some groups do, in fact, make riskier decisions, others become extremely conservative (Liu & Latane, 1998). Whether the final decision is risky or conservative depends primarily on the dominant preexisting tendencies of the group. That is, as individuals interact and discuss their opinions, their initial positions become more exaggerated. This movement toward one polar extreme or the other is known as **group polarization**.

Why does this happen? The tendency toward group polarization generally results from increased exposure to *persuasive arguments* (Liu & Latane, 1998). When people hear arguments from other people, they are exposed to new information. Because most informal, political, or business groups consist of like-minded individuals, the "new" information generally only reinforces the group's original opinion. Thus, the group's preexisting tendencies are strengthened by the group discussion.

Group Polarization *A group's movement toward either riskier or more conservative behavior, depending on the members' initial dominant tendency*

Groupthink *A condition that results when a highly cohesive group strives for agreement to the point of avoiding inconsistent information; the result is faulty decision making*

Juries and group polarization. Is group polarization a desirable part of jury deliberation? Yes and no. In an ideal world, attorneys from both sides present the facts of the case. Then, after careful deliberation, the jury moves from its initially neutral position toward the defendant to a more extreme position — either conviction or acquittal. In a not-so-ideal world, the quality of legal arguments from opposing sides may not be equal, the individual members of the jury may not be neutral at the start, and some jurors may unduly influence other jurors.

Groupthink. Group decision making may not only be affected by the tendency toward group polarization; another related and equally dangerous tendency is toward **groupthink**. Irving Janis (1972, 1989) defines *groupthink* as "a mode of thinking that people engage in when they are deeply involved in a cohesive in-group, and when the members' strivings for unanimity override their motivation to realistically appraise alternative courses of action" (p. 9). That is, when groups are strongly cohesive (a family, a panel of military advisers, an athletic team), they generally share a strong desire for agreement (to see themselves as one). This desire may lead them to ignore important information or points of view held by outsiders or critics (Vaughn, 1996).

Antecedent Conditions

1 A highly cohesive group of decision makers
2 Insulation of the group from outside influences
3 A directive leader
4 Lack of procedures to ensure careful consideration of the pros and cons of alternative actions
5 High stress from external threats with little hope of finding a better solution than that favored by the leader

Strong desire for group consensus—The groupthink tendency

Symptoms of Groupthink

1 Illusion of invulnerability
2 Belief in the morality of the group
3 Collective rationalizations
4 Stereotypes of outgroups
5 Self-censorship of doubts and dissenting opinions
6 Illusion of unanimity
7 Direct pressure on dissenters

Symptoms of Poor Decision Making

1 An incomplete survey of alternative courses of action
2 An incomplete survey of group objectives
3 Failure to examine risks of the preferred choice
4 Failure to reappraise rejected alternatives
5 Poor search for relevant information
6 Selective bias in processing information
7 Failure to develop contingency plans

Low probability of successful outcome

Figure 48.3 *Groupthink and marriage.* Few people realize that the decision to marry can be a form of groupthink. (Remember that a "group" can have as few as two members). While dating, the couple may show several of the antecedent conditions (top box): strong need for cohesiveness ("We agree on almost everything"), insulation from outside influences ("We do almost everything as a couple"), and failure to carefully consider the pros and cons of alternative actions. When planning for marriage, they also sometimes show symptoms of groupthink (middle box). These symptoms include: illusion of invulnerability ("We're different — we won't ever get divorced"), collective rationalizations ("Two can live more cheaply than one"), shared stereotypes of the outgroup ("Couples with problems just don't know how to communicate"), and avoidance of dissenters — anyone who doesn't fully support their decision to marry.

Presidential embarrassments, such as Franklin Roosevelt's failure to anticipate the attack on Pearl Harbor, John F. Kennedy's disastrous backing of the Bay of Pigs invasion of Cuba, Lyndon Johnson's escalation of the Vietnam War, Richard Nixon's cooperation with the Watergate cover-up, Ronald Reagan's Iran-Contra scandal, and Bill Clinton's impeachment have all been blamed on groupthink. It also seems to have contributed to the 1986 explosion of the space shuttle *Challenger* and the loss, in 1999, of the *Mars Climate Orbiter* (Esser, 1998; Janis, 1972, 1989; Raven, 1998).

As outlined in Figure 48.3, the process of groupthink begins with group members feeling a strong sense of cohesiveness and relative isolation from the judgments of qualified outsiders. Add a directive leader and little chance for debate, and you have the recipe for a potentially dangerous decision. During the actual discussion process, the members also come to believe they are invulnerable, tend to develop common rationalizations and stereotypes of the outgroup, and exert considerable pressure on anyone who dares to offer a dissenting opinion. Some members actually start to play the role of group "mindguards," working rather like bodyguards to isolate and protect the group from all differences in opinion.

Check & Review

GROUP PROCESSES

Groups differ from mere collections of people because group members share a mutually recognized relationship with one another. Group membership affects us through the roles we play. The importance of roles in determining and controlling behavior was dramatically demonstrated in Philip Zimbardo's Stanford Prison Study.

Group membership can also lead to **deindividuation**, in which a person becomes so caught up in the group's identity that individual self-awareness and responsibility are temporarily suspended.

Group polarization research shows that if most group members initially tend toward an extreme idea, the entire group will polarize in that direction. This is because the other, like-minded, members reinforce the dominant tendency. **Groupthink** is a dangerous type of thinking that occurs when a group's desire for agreement overrules its desire to critically evaluate information.

Questions

1. Zimbardo stopped his prison study before the end of the scheduled 2 weeks because _____.

2. The critical factor in deindividuation is _____. (a) loss of self-esteem; (b) anonymity; (c) identity diffusion; (d) group cohesiveness

3. What are the major symptoms of groupthink?

4. In a groupthink situation, the person who takes responsibility for seeing that dissenting opinions are not expressed is called the _____. (a) censor; (b) mindguard; (c) monitor; (d) whip

Answers to Questions can be found in Appendix B.

Aggression *Any behavior that is intended to harm someone*

Aggression: Explaining and Controlling It

Aggression is any form of behavior intended to harm or injure another living being that is motivated to avoid such treatment (Baron, 2000). Why do people act aggressively? We will explore a number of possible explanations for aggression — both *biological* and *psychosocial*. Then we will look at how aggression can be controlled or reduced.

Biological Factors in Aggression

1. Instincts. Because aggression has such a long history and is found among all cultures, many theorists believe humans are instinctively aggressive. After personally witnessing the massive death and destruction that occurred during World War I, Sigmund Freud stated that aggressive impulses are inborn. He argued that the drive for violence arises from a basic instinct and that, therefore, human aggression cannot be eliminated (Gay, 1999, 2000; Rohrlich, 1998).

Evolutionary psychologists and ethologists (scientists who study animal behavior) propose another instinct theory. They believe that aggression evolved because it contributes to survival of the fittest. Whereas Freud saw aggression as destructive and disruptive, ethologists believe aggression prevents overcrowding and allows the strongest animals to win mates and reproduce the species (Cartwright, 2000; Dabbs & Dabbs, 2000; Lorenz, 1981). Most social psychologists, however, reject both Freud's and the ethologists' view of instinct as the source of aggression.

2. Genes. Twin studies suggest that some individuals are genetically predisposed to have hostile, irritable temperaments and to engage in aggressive acts (Miles & Carey, 1997; Segal & Bouchard, 2000; Wasserman & Wachbroit, 2000.) Note, however, this does *not* mean that these people are doomed to behave aggressively. Aggression develops from a complex interaction of biology, social experience, and each individual's behavior.

3. The brain and nervous system. Electrical stimulation or severing specific parts of an animal's brain has a direct effect on aggression (Delgado, 1960; Delville, Mansour, & Ferris, 1996; Roberts & Nagel, 1996). Research with brain injuries and organic disorders has also identified possible aggression circuits in the brain — in particular, the hypothalamus, amygdala, and other parts of the brain (Davidson, Putnam, & Larson, 2000; Raine et al., 1998).

4. Substance abuse and other mental disorders. Substance abuse (particularly alcohol) within the general public is a major factor in most forms of aggression — child abuse, spousal assault, robberies, murders, stabbings, and so on (Casswell & Zhang, 1998; Goodwin, 2000; Shuntich, Loh, & Katz, 1998). Homicide rates are also higher among men with schizophrenia and antisocial disorders, particularly if they also abuse alcohol (Raesaenen et al., 1998; Tiihonen, Isohanni, Rasanen, Koiranen, & Moring, 1997).

5. Hormones and neurotransmitters. Several studies have linked the male gonadal hormone testosterone to aggressive behavior (Boyd, 2000; Dabbs & Dabbs, 2000; Sanchez-Martin et al., 2000). However, the relationship between human aggression and testosterone is complex. Testosterone seems to increase aggression and dominance, but dominance itself increases testosterone (Mazur & Booth, 1998). Violent behavior has also been linked with low levels of the neurotransmitters serotonin and GABA (gamma-aminobutyric acid) (Bernhardt, 1997; Brady, Myrick, & McElroy, 1998; LeMarquand et al., 1998; Manuck et al., 1998).

Psychosocial Factors in Aggression

1. Aversive stimuli. Research shows that aversive stimuli such as noise, heat, pain, insults, and foul odors can increase aggression (Anderson, Anderson, Dorr, DeNeve, & Flanagan, 2000; Berkowitz, 1990). Traffic congestion (road rage), cramped airlines (airplane rage), and excessive demands at work (office rage) all reflect another aversive stimuli — *frustration*. Being blocked short of a goal increases aggressive tendencies.

John Dollard and his colleagues (1939) noted this relationship between frustration and aggression more than half a century ago. According to the **frustration-aggression hypothesis**, frustration creates anger, which for some may lead to aggression. This does not mean that if you get mad at your boss, you necessarily punch him or her in the nose. You may displace your aggression and take out your anger on your family when you get home. Or you may turn your aggression toward yourself, becoming self-destructive or withdrawing, giving up, and getting depressed.

Frustration-Aggression Hypothesis *The idea that frustration — the blocking of a desired goal — creates anger, which may lead to aggression*

2. Culture and learning. As we discovered in Module 17, observational or social learning theory suggests that we learn by watching others. Thus, people raised in a culture with aggressive models will learn aggressive responses (Matsumoto, 2000). In Japan, for example, children are taught very early to value social harmony, and Japan has one of the lowest rates of violence in all industrialized nations (Nisbett, Peng, Choi, & Norenzayan, 2000; Zahn-Waxler, Friedman, Cole, Mizuta, & Himura, 1996). In contrast, the United States is one of the most violent nations, and our children grow up with numerous models for aggression, which they tend to imitate.

3. Media and video games. Despite protestations that violence in movies, TV, and video games is only entertainment, considerable evidence exists that the media can contribute to aggression in both children and adults (Anderson & Dill, 2000; Gilligan, 2000; Hogben, 1998; Zillman & Weaver, 1999). For example, the latest video games, such as *Doom, Mortal Kombat, Resident Evil,* and *Half-Life,* all feature realistic sound effects and gory depictions of "lifelike" violence, which may teach children that violence is exciting and acceptable. Obviously, most children who play violent video games and watch violent movies and TV shows do not go on to become dangerous killers. However, children do imitate what they see on TV [and, presumably, video games] and seem to internalize as a value that violence is acceptable behavior.

RESEARCH HIGHLIGHT

America's "Anger Epidemic"

Two supermarket shoppers get in a fist-fight over who should be first in a newly opened checkout lane.

A Continental Airlines flight returns to the Anchorage airport after a passenger allegedly throws a can of beer at a flight attendant and bites a pilot.

A father beats another father to death in an argument over rough play at their sons' hockey practice.

What do you think of these media reports? According to some experts, our nation is in the middle of an "anger epidemic," ranging from tantrums in supermarkets and on airplanes to deadly fights over a child's hockey practice (Gilligan, 2000; Peterson, 2000). Perhaps most disturbing is the increase in teen violence (Zanigel & Ressner, 2001).

One of the most dramatic examples of teen violence occurred on Tuesday, April 20, 1999, in Littelton, Colorado. On that infamous day, Eric Harris and Dylan Klebold shot and killed 12 fellow Columbine High School students and 1 teacher, wounded many others, and then turned the guns on themselves and committed suicide. Armed with a semiautomatic rifle, two sawed-off shotguns, a semiautomatic handgun, and dozens of homemade

bombs, these two young men joined a growing list of recent school shootings in the United States.

Although juvenile massacres are still an aberration, the slaughter at Columbine High "opened a sad national conversation about what turns two boys' souls into poison" (Gibbs, 1999, p. 25). What causes kids to gun down other kids? Can we identify high-risk children at early ages? Is aggressiveness a personality trait that is easily malleable or highly resistant to change?

These are the kinds of questions addressed by researchers Rolf Loeber and Magda Stouthamer-Loeber (1998) of the University of Pittsburgh. Noting that the numbers of juvenile perpetrators and victims have gradually increased over the past decades, these researchers also cite research demonstrating that highly aggressive children are at risk for adult crime, alcoholism, drug abuse, unemployment, divorce, and mental illness.

Research on juvenile antisocial behavior is voluminous, yet Loeber and Stouthamer-Loeber identify five major misconceptions and controversies that

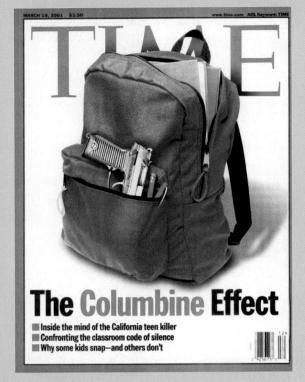

block our understanding of the problem and future research.

1. *Stability of childhood aggression.* Correlation studies give the impression that aggression is highly stable from childhood to adulthood (a review of the literature shows coefficients range from .63 to .92 — very high). In other

---

Could it be that aggressive children just tend to prefer violent television and videogames? Research suggests it is a two-way street. Laboratory studies, correlational research, and cross-cultural studies among children in five different countries (Australia, Finland, Israel, Poland, and the United States) have all found that exposure to TV violence did increase aggressiveness and that aggressive children tend to seek out violent programs (Aluja-Fabregat & Torrubia-Beltri, 1998; Singer, Slovak, Frierson, & York, 1998).

Controlling or Eliminating Aggression

Some therapists advise people to release aggressive impulses by engaging in harmless forms of aggression, such as vigorous exercise, punching a pillow, and watching competitive sports. But studies suggest that "draining the aggression reservoir" doesn't words, individuals who are aggressive as children are likely to be aggressive as adults. However, Loeber and Stouthamer-Loeber think we are stopping short of the real challenge, researching why some children *don't* go on to become aggressive adults. They cite studies showing that preschool boys commonly show aggressive behaviors and that aggression decreases from preschool to elementary school and from adolescence to adulthood. Knowing why some individuals outgrow aggression could greatly help mental health professionals intervene in high-risk cases.

2. *All serious aggression begins in early childhood.* Loeber and Stouthamer-Loeber suggest we need additional research into violent individuals without a history of early aggression. They go on to suggest three developmental types of aggressive individuals: (a) a life-course type (characterized by aggression in childhood that persists and worsens into adulthood), (b) a limited-duration type (individuals who outgrow aggression), and (c) a late-onset type (individuals without a history of aggression). This three-type classification could be more helpful to clinicians, probation officers, and others working with children.

3. *Controversy over single or multiple pathways.* Loeber and Stouthamer-Loeber suggest researchers should spend less time debating whether a single pathway or multiple pathways lead to antisocial behavior and violence. (By "pathways," they mean causes such as genes, culture, learning, or any of the other possible causes discussed at the beginning of this section). Instead, we should research multiple pathways because "casting a wide net" is more likely to produce results than looking at each possibility one at a time.

4. *Simple versus complex causes of aggression.* Loeber and Stouthamer-Loeber looked at three possible causes of aggression in children — family factors, physiology, and genetics. They report that a more complex relationship exists than was previously thought.

   Studies of family factors, for example, show a relationship exists between children who live with aggressive parents in a conflictual home atmosphere and children who commit personal or violent crimes, but not children who commit property crimes. Similarly, physiological studies link certain hormones (such as testosterone) and neurotransmitters (such as serotonin) to juvenile aggression, but not to property crimes. Genetic studies have produced conflicting results.

5. *Male and female aggression is not the same.* Loeber and Stouthamer-Loeber say the assumption that violence develops in much the same way in women and men is erroneous. Although few gender differences have been recorded in toddlerhood, beginning in preschool and throughout adulthood boys show more personal and physical aggression. Furthermore, several investigators have documented that women tend to use more indirect and verbal aggression and relational aggression (gossip and excluding peers) and are less likely to participate in group fighting, gang fighting, aggravated assault, sexual violence, and homicide. For these reasons, Loeber and Stouthamer-Loeber believe major gender differences exist in aggression, but at the same time, they stress that these variations are pieces of the bigger puzzle that must be addressed by future research.

Following the Columbine massacre, the media offered standard and all-too-familiar answers (violence on TV and in the movies, availability of guns, divorce, and "no-parent" households). But as Loeber and Stouthamer-Loeber document in their analysis of juvenile research studies, the problem is complex and we are a long way from answers.

---

really help (Bushman, Baumeister, & Stack, 1999). In fact, expressing an emotion, anger or otherwise, tends to intensify the feeling rather than reduce it.

A second approach, which does seem to effectively reduce or control aggression, is to introduce incompatible responses. Because certain emotional responses, such as empathy and humor, are incompatible with aggression, purposely making a joke or showing some sympathy for the other person's point of view can reduce anger and frustration (Harvey & Miceli, 1999; Kaukianen et al., 1999; Oshima, 2000).

A third approach to controlling aggression is to improve social and communication skills. Studies show that people with the most deficient communication skills account for a disproportionate share of the violence in society (Trump, 2000; Vance, Fernandez, & Biber, 1998). Unfortunately, little effort is made in our schools or families to teach basic communication skills or techniques for conflict resolution.

Altruism: Why We Help (and Don't Help) Others

After reading about prejudice, discrimination, and aggression, you will no doubt be relieved to discover that human beings also behave in positive ways. People help and support one another by donating blood, giving time and money to charities, helping stranded motorists, and so on. There are also times when people do not help.

Consider the following: In 1964, on Austin Street in Queens, New York, a woman named Kitty Genovese was stabbed to death as she returned to her apartment. Thirty-eight of her neighbors heard her screams and pleas for help: "Oh my God, he stabbed me! Please help me! Please help me!" and watched as she struggled to fight off her assailant. The lights in the windows of the observers' apartments apparently scared off the attacker, who left Kitty lying in the street, wounded but still alive. But when the neighbors turned off their lights and went back to bed, the attacker returned and stabbed her again. Kitty's screams once again awakened her neighbors and again the lights scared off her attacker. But the neighbors went back to bed a second time, and the murderer returned for a third and fatal attack.

Why did the neighbors keep going back to bed, and why didn't the police come? Throughout the entire series of attacks (which lasted for over 35 minutes), only 1 of the 38 neighbors belatedly called the police. Why didn't they respond immediately? More generally, under what conditions do people sometimes help and sometimes ignore others' pleas for help?

Why Do We Help?

Altruism *Actions designed to help others with no obvious benefit to the helper*

Altruism (or prosocial behavior) refers to actions designed to help others with no obvious benefit to oneself. Evolutionary theory suggests that altruism is an instinctual behavior that has evolved because it favors survival of one's genes (Bower, 2000; Cartwright, 2000; Ozinga, 2000; Wright, 1998). As evidence, these theorists cite altruistic acts among lower species (e.g., worker bees living for their mother, the queen) and the fact that altruism in humans is strongest toward one's own children and other relatives. Altruism protects not the individual but the individual's genes. By helping or even dying for your child or sibling, you increase the odds that your genes will be passed on to future generations.

Egoistic Model *The proposal that helping behavior is motivated by anticipated gain — later reciprocation, increased self-esteem, or avoidance of guilt and distress*

Other research suggests that helping may actually be a form of egoism or disguised self-interest. According to this **egoistic model**, helping is always motivated by some degree of anticipated gain. We help others because we hope for later reciprocation, because it makes us feel good about ourselves, or because it helps us avoid feelings of distress and guilt that loom if we don't help (Cialdini, 2001; Williams, Haber, Weaver, & Freeman, 1998).

Empathy-Altruism Hypothesis *The proposal that altruistic behavior is motivated by empathy for someone in need of help*

Opposing the egoistic model is the **empathy-altruism hypothesis** proposed by C. D. Batson and his colleagues (Batson, 1991, 1998; Batson et al., 1999). As Figure 48.4 shows, Batson thinks some altruism is motivated by simple, selfish concerns (the top part of the diagram), but in other situations, helping is truly selfless and motivated by concern for others (the bottom part of the diagram).

According to the empathy-altruism hypothesis, simply seeing another person's suffering or hearing of his or her need can create *empathy*, a subjective grasp of that person's feelings or experiences. When we feel empathic toward another, we focus on that person's distress, not our own, and are motivated to help the person for his or her own sake (Batson et al., 1999; Kahne, 1999). The ability to empathize may even be innate. Research with infants in the first few hours of life shows that they become distressed and cry at the sound of another infant's cries (Hay, 1994; Hoffman, 1993).

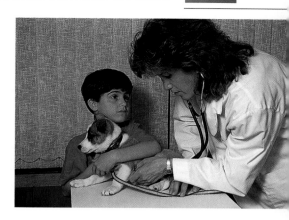

Figure 48.4 *Two major explanations for helping.* Do you think the egoistic or the empathy-altruism model is best shown in this photo? Would the young child be motivated to help his pet? Why? According to C. D. Batson and his colleagues, both models motivate helping. Can you explain this?

Why Don't We Help?

Many theories have been proposed to explain why people help, but few explain why we do not. How do we explain the Kitty Genovese tragedy? One of the most comprehensive explanations for helping or not helping comes from the research of Bibb Latane and John Darley (1970). They found that whether or not someone helps depends on a series of interconnected events and decisions. The potential helper must first *notice* what is happening, must then *interpret* the event as an emergency, must accept *personal responsibility* for helping, and then must *decide how to help* and actually initiate the helping behavior.

Where did the sequence break down for Kitty Genovese? Kitty's neighbors obviously noticed what was happening and interpreted it as an emergency. The first break in the helping sequence was in their willingness to accept personal responsibility. Newspaper interviews with each of the neighbors described a great deal of anguish, but each of them "naturally" assumed that someone else had already called the police. This is the **diffusion of responsibility** phenomenon — the tendency to assume that someone else will respond and act. It is ironic that if only one neighbor had seen Kitty's attack and known that there were no other witnesses, Kitty might still be alive today.

Diffusion of Responsibility *In groups of two or more, people tend to take less individual responsibility because they assume someone else will take action (or responsibility)*

How Can We Promote Helping?

The most obvious way to increase altruistic behavior is to clarify when help is needed. For example, if you notice a situation in which it seems unclear whether someone needs help, simply ask. On the other hand, if you are the one in need of help, look directly at anyone who may be watching and give specific directions, such as "Call the police."

Helping behaviors could also be encouraged through societal rewards. Some researchers suggest that states need to enact more laws that protect the helper from potential suits and punish people who fail to respond. Certain existing police programs, such as Crime Stoppers, actively recruit public compliance in reporting crime, give monetary rewards, and ensure anonymity. Such programs have apparently been highly effective in reducing crime.

A Final Note

As we close this final module, we sincerely hope that this introduction to psychology has encouraged you to see psychology not only as a science and academic discipline but also as a method for personal and social change. This may sound grandiose. However, if you accept the view that people are rational and behavior can be described, explained, predicted, and changed, then no problem is insurmountable. As you may remember, these are the four goals of psychology discussed in Module 1. We encourage you to share our belief in the transformative nature of psychology and to apply what you have learned from this text and course to your everyday life. We also invite you to continue your exploration of the subject through a career in psychology, or simply as part of your lifelong learning and personal growth.

Check & Review

AGGRESSION AND ALTRUISM

Aggression is any deliberate attempt to harm another living being who is motivated to avoid such treatment. Some researchers believe it is caused by biological factors, such as instincts, genes, the brain and nervous system, substance abuse and other mental disorders, and hormones and neurotransmitters. Other researchers emphasize psychosocial factors, such as aversive stimuli, culture and learning, and media and video games. Releasing aggressive feelings through violent acts or watching violence is not an effective way to reduce aggression. Introducing incompatible responses (such as humor) and teaching social and communication skills is more efficient.

Altruism refers to actions designed to help others with no obvious benefit to oneself. Evolutionary theorists believe altruism is innate and has survival value. Psychological explanations for altruism emphasize the **egoistic model**, which suggests that helping is motivated by anticipated gain, or the **empathy-altruism hypothesis**, which proposes that helping can also be activated when the helper feels empathy for the victim.

Whether or not someone helps depends on a series of interconnected events, starting with noticing the problem and ending with a decision to help. Some people don't help because of the ambiguity of many emergency situations or because of **diffusion of responsibility** (assuming someone else will respond). To increase the chances of altruism, we should reduce ambiguity, increase the rewards for helping, and decrease the costs.

Questions

1. What are the five major biological and three chief psychosocial factors that contribute to aggression?

2. According to research, which of the following does *not* reduce aggression? (a) channeling aggressive impulses into harmless activities; (b) introducing incompatible responses; (c) improving social and communications skill; (d) attacking the problem at a societal level

3. How do evolutionary theorists, the egoistic model, and the empathy-altruism hypothesis explain altruism?

4. Kitty Genovese's neighbors failed to respond to her cries for help because of the _____ phenomenon. (a) empathy-altruism; (b) egoistic model; (c) inhumanity of large cities; (d) diffusion of responsibility

Answers to Questions can be found in Appendix B.

ACTIVE LEARNING WORKSHEET   MODULE 48

ACROSS

3. Following direct commands, usually from some-one in a position of authority.

6. Changing behavior as a result of real or imagined group pressure.

7. Cultural rule prescribing acceptable behavior in a given situation.

8. Any behavior intended to harm another.

9. Faulty decision-making resulting from a highly cohesive group's attempt to maintain agreement and avoid inconsistent information.

10. Actions designed to help others with no obvious benefit to the helper.

DOWN

1. Group's movement toward either riskier or more conservative behavior, depending upon the mem-bers' initial dominant tendency.

2. People we follow because we like and admire them and want to be like them.

4. Increased arousal and reduced self-consciousness due to group membership.

5. Helping behavior motivated by anticipated gain.

Answers can be found in Appendix B.

Visual Summary for Modules 46, 47, and 48 ━ ━ ━ ━

Our Thoughts about Others

Social Psychology: Studies how other people influence an individual's behavior (thoughts, feelings, and actions).

Attribution

Attribution: Explaining others' behavior by deciding that their actions resulted from internal factors (their own traits and motives) or external factors (the situation).

Problems:

Fundamental attribution error: Tendency to overestimate internal personality influences and underestimate situational factors when judging behavior of others. Why? May be **saliency bias**, focusing on most noticeable (salient) factors.

Self-serving bias: Tendency to explain our own behavior by attributing positive outcomes to internal factors and negative outcomes to external causes.

Attitudes

Attitudes: Learned predispositions toward a particular object.

Three components of all attitudes:

Cognitive: thoughts and beliefs

Affective: feelings

Behavioral tendencies: predispositions to action

Cognitive dissonance theory: A state of tension experienced when people discover inconsistencies between their attitudes or between their attitudes and their behavior. This mismatch and resulting tension motivate attitude change to restore balance.

Our Feelings about Others

Prejudice and Discrimination

Prejudice: Generally negative attitude directed toward people solely because of their membership in a specific group. Contains all three components of attitudes—cognitive **(stereotype)**, affective, and behavioral (discrimination).
Discrimination: Refers to the actual negative behavior directed at members of a group. People do not always act on their prejudices.

Four major sources of prejudice:

Learning: Classical and operant conditioning and social learning

Cognitive processes: **Ingroup favoritism, outgroup homogeneity effect**

Economic and political competition

Displaced aggression: Scapegoating

Five methods for reducing prejudice and discrimination:
• Cooperation
• **Superordinate goals**
• Increased contact
• Cognitive retraining
• Cognitive dissonance

Our Feelings about Others (cont).

Interpersonal attraction: Degree of positive or negative feelings toward another. Three key factors:

Physical attractiveness is important to initial attraction, more important to men than women, yet standards of beauty vary across cultures and historically. Physically attractive people generally are considered more intelligent, sociable, and interesting.

Physical **proximity** increases attraction largely due to the *mere exposure effect.*

Although people commonly believe that "opposites attract" **(need complementarity)**, research shows **similarity (need compatibility)** is much more important.

- *Love:* Rubin defines it in terms of caring, attachment, and intimacy.
- **Romantic love** highly valued in our society, but it's based on mystery and fantasy; thus, hard to sustain.
- **Companionate love** relies on mutual trust, respect, and friendship and grows stronger with time.

Our Actions toward Others

Social Influence

Conformity: Changes in behavior in response to real or imagined pressure from others.

Four reasons we conform:

For approval and acceptance **(normative social influence).**

Need for more information **(informational social influence).**

To match behavior of those we admire and feel similar to **(reference group).**

We also conform because it is often adaptive to do so.

Obedience: Going along with a direct command. Milgram's experiment showed a large number of people will obey orders. Why?

Power of authority

Distance between teacher and learner

Assignment of responsibility

Modeling/imitation

Aggression

Aggression: Deliberate attempt to harm another living being who is motivated to avoid such treatment.
- *Biological causes*: Instincts, genes, the brain and nervous system, substance abuse and other mental disorders, hormones, and neurotransmitters.
- *Psychosocial causes*: Aversive stimuli, learning, media, and videogames.
- *Treatment*: Incompatible responses (like humor), social skills, and improved communication help reduce aggression, but releasing aggressive feeling through violent acts or watching violence are not helpful.

Group Processes

Groups are two or more people interacting and influencing one another's behavior.
- *Group membership* affects us through the roles we play, as demonstrated in Zimbardo's Stanford Prison Study, or through **deindividuation** (immersion in group identity leads to decreased self-awareness and personal responsibility).
- *Group decision making* is affected by two key factors:

Group polarization: If most group members initially tend toward an extreme idea, the entire group will move toward that extreme. Why? "Like-minded" members exposed to persuasive arguments that reinforce the dominant tendency.

Groupthink: Dangerous type of decision making where group's desire for agreement overrules its desire to critically evaluate information.

Altruism

Altruism: Actions designed to help others with no obvious benefit to oneself.
Why do we help?
- Evolutionary theorists believe altruism is innate and has survival value.
- Psychological explanations suggest helping is motivated by anticipated gain **(egoistic model)**, or when helper feels empathy for the victim **(empathy-altruism hypothesis)**.
Why don't we help?
- It depends on a series of interconnected events, starting with noticing the problem and ending with a decision to help.
- Many emergency situations are ambiguous.
- We assume others will respond **(diffusion of responsibility).**
How do we increase altruism?
- Reduce ambiguity by giving clear directions observers.
- Increase the rewards, while decreasing the costs.

Industrial/ Organizational Psychology

Core Learning Objectives

As you read Modules 49, 50, 51, and 52, keep the following questions in mind and answer them in your own words:

- How has I/O psychology evolved from the early 1900s to the present day?
- What is human factors psychology?
- Why is personnel psychology important?
- What does organizational psychology encompass?

*T*his is your first day as a car washer at an automobile dealership. Your boss points to a new, and very expensive, white car and tells you to clean and prepare it for delivery to a customer. He asks you to move it from the display lot to the washing facility in the back. You get the keys, unlock the door, get in, fasten your seatbelt, insert the key, and start the car. After shifting into reverse and turning around to check behind you, you begin backing up. Suddenly the car begins to accelerate. You jam on the brakes, but the car does not stop. You push even harder on the brake pedal, but the car goes faster and faster. You crash into another new car parked behind you. As your co-workers rush to help, you're physically okay, but you feel confused and shocked. Two very expensive cars are badly damaged.

How could this have happened? You were sure your foot was on the brake pedal, but the car kept accelerating out of control. Did the brakes malfunction? The transmission? The engine? Could you have made some terrible mistake?

Describing the accident, you assure the manager of the dealership you definitely had your foot on the brake the entire time. However, he insists the car was thoroughly inspected by a service technician just that morning, and the steer-

ing, brakes, engine controls, and computer were all functioning perfectly. To make matters worse, when the car was reinspected after the accident, the technician could find no mechanical or computer failure. How to solve this puzzle? Perhaps Sherlock Holmes suggested an answer when he said in *The Sign of the Four,* "When you have eliminated the impossible, whatever remains, however improbable, must be the truth"

(Doyle, 1889).

Assuming that the technician was competent and honest, a mechanical failure was unlikely. Most researchers who study unintended acceleration accidents believe they are the result of driver error, not a mechanical malfunction of the automobile (Vernoy and Tomerlin, 1989). As the car washer, you must have actually had your foot on the gas pedal when you thought it was on the brake. This phenomenon, called "unintended acceleration," is relatively rare, but it has resulted in several lawsuits against automobile manufacturers.

Industrial/Organizational (I/O) Psychology
The study of how individual behavior affects, and is affected by, the physical environment and the organizational culture of the workplace.

Anytime a person makes a movement or a decision, there is possibility of error. Most errors such as spilling your milk, hitting the wrong key on your word processor, or betting on the Buffalo Bills, do not result in serious physical injury or property damage. However, if a manager makes a wrong decision in filling a key job or a designer misreads the market for a new line of clothing, a company may lose profits because of lack of productivity or low sales. Similarly, if a worker hits the wrong button at a nuclear power plant, the mistake can damage expensive machinery, seriously damage the environment, and possibly kill or injure thousands of people.

Reducing human error in the workplace involves many factors, including equipment design, selection and training of personnel, design of the work environment, and organizational and decision-making strategies. **Industrial/Organizational (I/O) psychology** studies how individual behavior affects and is affected by the physical environment and the organizational culture of the workplace.

With the possible exception of sleeping, a person spends more time at work than at any other single activity. Thus, finding ways to make our jobs safer and more fulfilling is essential, and perhaps even urgent. You have undoubtedly heard of cases where disgruntled workers attack their bosses or co-workers in a fit of job-related rage. We even have a new term for this behavior, coined as a result of several well publicized cases involving postal workers: "going postal." Reducing the number of workers who "go postal" is one job of the I/O psychologist.

I/O psychologists are frequently employed by business, industry, and the government. Their focus is in three major areas: (1) *human factors psychology* (improving the design and function of machines and the work environment); (2) *personnel psychology* (recruitment, testing, training, placement, and evaluation of workers); and (3) *organizational psychology* (managerial style, worker motivation, and job satisfaction). (See Figure 17.1.) We discuss each of these major areas, but to set the stage we begin with a look at the historical development of I/O psychology.

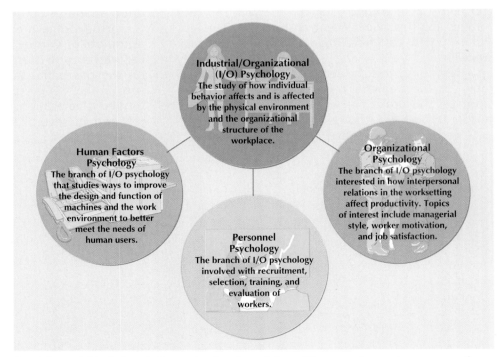

Specialties within industrial/organizational psychology. There are three primary areas of interest for I/O psychologists: human factors psychology, personnel psychology, and organizational psychology.

MODULE 49
THE DEVELOPMENT OF I/O PSYCHOLOGY

The formal study of psychology is relatively short, spanning a mere 125 years or so. The study of I/O psychology is even shorter, originating with the work of Walter Dill Scott, Frederick W. Taylor, and Hugo Munsterberg at the beginning of the twentieth century.

> How has I/O psychology evolved from the early 1900s to the present day?

The Beginnings: Applying Psychology to Sales and Worker Efficiency

On December 20, 1901, Walter Dill Scott, a psychology professor at Northwestern University, addressed a group of advertising professionals. In his talk, he proposed an interesting idea: Using psychological principles in the field of advertising. Instead of merely exhibiting a product and hoping that customers would realize their need for it, he thought advertisers could aggressively influence customers by *suggesting* they buy it or by *arguing* and *debating* the undeniable merits of the purchase. In other words, use persuasion and argumentation to *sell*.

Scott also proposed several other ideas, radical at the time, but taken for granted today. He suggested imitating other companies' successful products, advertising, and production policies; encouraging competition among companies producing similar goods; building loyalty between producers and suppliers; and creating specialized products for markets (Muchinsky, 1993).

Walter Dill Scott

Other Major Figures

Frederick W. Taylor, the next major figure in I/O psychology, emphasized the value of designing the work situation to increase worker output. He correctly surmised that if workers performed their jobs more efficiently, the company would increase profits and workers' wages would go up. In his book *The Principles of Scientific Management* (1911), Taylor formulated four principles for increasing the efficiency and profitability of any organization: (1) scientifically design work methods for greater efficiency; (2) select the best workers and train them in new methods; (3) develop a cooperative spirit between managers and workers; and (4) encourage cooperation between workers and management to improve the work environment.

A particular story is often told about Taylor's attempt to increase the efficiency of workers who shoveled heavy pig iron. Each man moved an average of 12.5 tons of pig iron per day, which to most of us, sounds like a lot. But by allowing the men to rest at scientifically determined periods, and designing new shovels to better match the material being moved, Taylor increased each man's output to 47 *tons* per day! This incredible increase in efficiency resulted in less fatigue and increased wages for the worker, and increased profit for the company (Muchinsky, 1993). Taylor was not a psychologist, but he is nevertheless considered one of the founders of human factors psychology.

Like Scott, Hugo Munsterberg was an early psychologist interested in applying psychology to the workplace. His book *Psychology and Industrial Efficiency* (1913) covered three topics: (1) selecting workers, (2) designing work situations, and (3) using psychology in sales. Munsterberg was most influential in the area of personnel selection and training, and his best known research was a study of streetcar operators, where he created laboratory simulation of an actual streetcar. This research allowed Munsterberg to develop personnel selection criteria and training procedures that eventually led to better street car operators (Muchinsky, 1993).

Frederick W. Taylor

Hugo Munsterberg

Although Scott, Taylor, and Munsterberg all demonstrated the importance of applying psychology in the workplace, for many people in industry it took World War I to give I/O psychology real respectability. At the beginning of the war, the American Psychological Association, led by President Robert Yerkes, approached Army officials and proposed that psychological testing be used to evaluate the mental ability of recruits. The results could then help establish criteria for assigning recruits to appropriate military jobs.

The Army agreed and Yerkes and a group of psychologists were assigned to develop the first group intelligence test, the *Army Alpha*. Finding that approximately 30 percent of the World War I recruits were functionally illiterate, they later developed the first nonverbal intelligence test, the *Army Beta*.

Walter Dill Scott, mentioned earlier for his advertising ideas, also contributed to the effort to classify and place soldiers in jobs according to their abilities. He is credited with developing job descriptions for over 500 military jobs. Although plans for complete testing of all recruits were never fully implemented, World War I saw a significant expansion of I/O psychology.

The Hawthorne Effect

During the period between World War I and World War II, I/O psychology continued to grow. Many companies added human resource departments for the first time, and a number of colleges and universities began to offer training in I/O psychology (Miner, 1992). Considerable research also was being conducted on advertising, personnel selection, and worker training, but the focus of most I/O research during this period was on testing. Rather than individual testing in the laboratory or in the military, however, workers were now tested in the workplace. In 1924, the most extensive—and by far the most famous—of these workplace projects was begun at the Hawthorne Works of the Western Electric Company, just outside Chicago.

In the original study, researchers from Harvard University installed lights of varying brightness levels in different workrooms where electrical equipment was assembled. The light in some rooms was intense, while as subdued as moonlight in others. The object was to study the relationship between worker efficiency and lighting. The results were quite surprising.

Psychologists, led by Robert Yerkes, developed the Army Alpha, *the first group IQ test. The* Army Alpha, *and later the* Army Beta, *were used to test and classify World War I recruits.*

The Western Electric Hawthorne Works was the site of a famous study of workplace behavior conducted between World War I and World War II.

Researchers found that worker productivity had little or nothing to do with the lighting level. Productivity improved under both *increased* and *decreased* brightness! Even more surprising, when the brightness level remained *unchanged*, productivity still increased. Simply knowing they were being used as research participants apparently improved worker performance. This is known as the **Hawthorne effect,** when people change their behavior because of the novelty of the research situation or because they know they are being observed.

You may have observed the Hawthorne effect in everyday life. When you walk down the sidewalk singing and suddenly notice other people looking at you, you probably stop singing. Similarly, students taking a test are less likely to cheat if they know the professor is watching them, and people are more likely to wash their hands after using a public restroom when others are watching. Little Leaguers also pay more attention to the game when the coach yells their name. In each of these cases, behavior is changed as a result of being observed.

Because of the remarkable findings from the lighting tests, the Hawthorne project was expanded to investigate many other topics, including pre-employment testing, interviewing techniques, and personnel counseling. Various studies continued for over 10 years, ending just as World War II was beginning. The major contribution of the Hawthorne studies was to document the fact that a worker's behavior was influenced not only by the physical setting, but also by social factors in the workplace. That is, the workplace is a social system as well as a system for producing goods and services.

Hawthorne Effect
The phenomenon that occurs when people change their behavior because of the novelty of the research situation or because they know they are being observed.

Try This Yourself

You can easily do a mini study on the Hawthorne effect. Choose a good friend—let's say your friend is a male—and (without his knowledge) observe him studying or watching television for about five minutes. Write down in detail what he is doing. Document how many times he looks up from his book, changes channels on the television, and so on.

At the end of five minutes, tell him you need to observe his behavior for five minutes as part of a psychology assignment. Now record the same behaviors. Does his behavior change? Does he look up from his studies more often? Less often? Does he do more or less "channel surfing" while watching television? If his behavior changes, you will have observed the *Hawthorne effect.* ∎

Modern Times: Expanding the Role of I/O Psychology

By the beginning of World War II, I/O psychology had begun to mature. Many companies now had personnel offices that routinely tested and placed employees. They also implemented scientifically designed worker-training programs to improve productivity. Researchers were beginning to conduct studies in human factors psychology, as machines in the workplace became more complicated.

Many of these advances were applied to the war effort. The first contribution from I/O psychology was the development of the *Army General Classification Test* (AGCT). The AGCT made it possible to classify new recruits into a few broad categories based on their ability to learn the duties and responsibilities of a soldier. Psychologists also helped develop situational stress tests to select and train candidates for military intelligence units (spies). In addition, they developed tests for selecting aircraft pilots and training them more rapidly and safely.

Human factors psychology also contributed greatly to the operational safety of airplanes by designing better control panels. For example, at the beginning of the war many planes and pilots were lost because, when preparing for landing, pilots tended to mistake the landing gear control for the wing flap control. Consequently, pilots tried to land planes with the wheels up or with the wing flaps in the wrong position, providing insufficient lift.

The human factors solution to this problem was simple: design the controls to correspond to their function. Consequently, they redesigned the landing gear controls to look and feel like wheels, and they redesigned the wing flap controls to look and feel like a wing. The result: greatly reduced landing errors! These World War II airplane design changes are still used on contemporary aircraft.

Early I/O psychology was, in effect, industrial psychology, focusing on worker efficiency and productivity. During World War II, however, personnel psychology had emerged as a major subspecialty, and many researchers began to shift their attention from the manufacturing floor to the executive management offices. They thereby created organizational psychology and put the "O" in I/O psychology. Organizational psychologists studied companies with the goal of improving administration and productivity.

The civil rights movement of the late 1950s and early 1960s culminated in the Civil Rights Act of 1964. Among other things, it mandated the creation of employment tests, training programs, and recruitment programs that were fair to all job applicants regardless of ethnicity, religion, or gender. Tests given to screen job appli-

This photograph of a World War II bomber cockpit shows how human factors psychologists made flying safer and easier. Notice how the controls for the landing gear are designed to look and feel like the function they perform. The landing gear controls are round like a wheel (as shown in box).

cants had to be valid predictors of job performance. For example, general IQ tests could no longer be used to screen applicants at the Telephone Company for the job of directory assistance operator; instead, the Telephone Company might administer a spelling and reading comprehension test.

The Civil Rights Act of 1964 also forced a radical change in corporate recruitment and hiring policies that resulted in opening many previously unobtainable jobs to ethnic minority and women job applicants. Hence, I/O psychology was now responsible not only to corporate management, but to the federal government as well.

In the next section we will introduce you to human factors psychology in which I/O psychologists study how to make humans and machines work together.

CHECK AND REVIEW

Development of I/O Psychology

Industrial/organizational (I/O) psychology is the study of how individual behavior affects and is affected by the physical environment and the organizational structure of the workplace. Major founding figures were Walter Dill Scott, Fredrick W. Taylor, and Hugo Munsterberg.

The personnel needs of World War I gave the I/O field respectability. Based on newly developed group IQ tests, Walter Dill Scott developed a program to place recruits in jobs that suited their abilities.

Among important I/O research findings during this period was a phenomenon termed the Hawthorne effect, when people change their behavior because of the novelty of a research situation or because they know that they are being observed.

World War II led to scientifically designed worker training programs to improve productivity for the war effort. After the war, many I/O psychologists turned their attention from the manufacturing floor to the executive management offices, thereby creating organizational psychology.

The Civil Rights Act of 1964 required I/O psychology to create employment tests, training programs, and recruitment programs that were fair to all job applicants regardless of ethnicity, religion, age, or gender.

QUESTIONS

1. Match the founders of I/O psychology (Scott, Taylor, Munsterberg) with their major contribution:
    (a)   Pioneered methods leading to improved personnel selection and training.
    (b)   Developed principles companies could use to increase worker efficiency and company profit.
    (c)   First to apply psychological principles to advertising

2. Hui-Ching is a consultant who is hired by a large law firm to study worker motivation and job satisfaction. Hui-Ching is part of which branch of I/O psychology? (a) consulting; (b) organizational; (c) personnel; (d) human factors.

3. The _____ occurs when a research participant changes his or her behaviors because they know they are being observed. (a) halo effect; (b) observational bias; (c) Hawthorne effect; (d) spectator bias.

4. How did the Civil Rights Act of 1964 influence I/O psychology?

Answers to Questions can be found in Appendix B.

MODULE 50
HUMAN FACTORS PSYCHOLOGY

How has I/O psychology evolved from the early 1900s to the present day?

Human Factors Psychology
The branch of I/O psychology that studies ways to improve the design and function of machines and the work environment to better meet the needs of human users.

Human–Machine System
An arrangement of people and machines, tools, and other devices that produce a product or service.

Displays
Devices such as gauges and video monitors that form the machine output in the human—machine system.

Controls
Devices such as wheels, levers, and knobs that are the input for the machine in the human–machine system.

An automatic teller machine (ATM) is obviously more complicated than a videocassette recorder (VCR). However, most people find it much easier to get $20 out of their local ATM than to program their VCR to record "Ally McBeal" on Monday night. Why is the more complicated machine easier to use? At least part of the answer is in human factors.

Human factors psychology is the branch of I/O psychology that studies ways to improve the design and function of machines and the work environment to better meet the needs of human users. Thousands of hours of human factors research went into making your ATM easy to use. To get your money, all you need is a plastic card, a personal identification number, and the ability to read a few simple commands. To program your VCR, however, you must read a 20-page booklet. In this case, human factors research has been largely ignored.

The Human–Machine System: How to Get People and Machines to Mix

The problem with machines is that ordinary people run them. It is not difficult for an engineer to design a machine that functions efficiently by itself or when operated by an engineer. The difficulty arises when someone other than an engineer and the machine must work together as one unit to become a *human–machine system* (Oborne, 1995). A **human–machine system** is an arrangement of people and machines, tools, and other devices that produce a product or service. The basic components of the human–machine system are illustrated in Figure 50.1.

As Figure 50.1 shows, the machine side of the system consists of **displays** (the machine output) and **controls** (the machine input). The human side of the system consists of sensory functions (the human input), cognitive functions, and motor functions (the human output). The machine's displays provide the sensory input for the human, and the human's motor responses provide the control input for the machine.

Why is it so much easier to use an ATM machine than to program your VCR? The answer comes from human factors research.

Figure 50.1 ***The human–machine system.*** In a human–machine system, a human and machine work as a unit to produce a product or service. The machine displays, such as gauges and video monitors, output information about the status of the machine to the sensory receptors of the human, which serve as the input for the human part of the system. Sensory information from the eyes or other sensory organs is processed by the brain of the human, and adjustments to the machine are communicated to the machine controls via the human's muscles and voice commands.

It is an interdependent system, where neither the human nor the machine can produce the product or service without the other.

Once the machine is running, the human needs the display data from the machine to determine whether corrections need to be made, and the machine needs the human to input the necessary corrections via the controls. In this way, machines can do the tedious precision tasks that are difficult for humans, and humans can do the cognitive tasks involving judgments and corrections that are impossible for the machine to do.

A driver and automobile are a good example of a human–machine system. The driver has the cognitive ability to guide the car to its intended destination, and the automobile has the power to move the driver at relatively great speeds over large distances. When you are driving, you and the car act as one unit, a human–machine system. You use your sensory systems to collect and monitor information about the operation of the machine. You read the speedometer, the tachometer, and other gauges; you listen and feel for (hopefully!) normal functioning of the engine, body, and tires; and you even use your sense of smell if a strange odor suggests a problem. Using this varied input, you adjust the machine by pressing harder on the accelerator, adding oil, or stopping to change a flat tire. Once in a while, the human–machine system fails to perform properly—the car runs out of gas, or you step on the accelerator instead of the brake pedal.

Human factors psychologists help design the controls and displays in automobiles.

Designers can make the human–machine system more reliable in two ways: They can better train the people using it, or they can modify the machine. Because modifying the machine is easier than modifying people (it is much easier to make a display larger than to make a person's vision more acute), human factors psychology generally focuses on improving the design of the controls and displays on machines. Improving the design of a machine translates to matching its displays and controls to human sensory and motor skills.

Displays: How the Machine Talks to You

Displays providing data about the machine's operation form the input for the human side of the human–machine system. Or, to put it simply, the machine talks to you through its displays; video monitors, gauges, bells, and blinking lights. A good display design must recognize how people sense and perceive their world, as well as how people think. Therefore, a human factors psychologist must have a thorough knowledge of human sensation, perception, and cognition.

Failure to understand the limits of human sensory capabilities can have disastrous results (Aberg and Rimmoe, 1998; Shappell and Wiegmann, 1997). If the beeping sound accompanying the lowering of a heavy motor cannot be heard above background noise, a dangerous accident might occur on the automotive assembly line. If a gauge has lettering that is too small to read, a machine could overheat, requiring costly repairs. If a warning light does not get the machine operator's attention, the nuclear reactor core could be damaged.

Suppose you are hired to monitor several machines in a factory. Your supervisor explains that the machines' display panel was designed so that an uninterrupted line of green lights indicates normal operation. If any component malfunctions, its corresponding light on the display panel turns red. When you notice a red light, you are told to refer to the manual and make the indicated adjustments to bring the machine back into proper working order.

But, you tell the supervisor, you are red/green color defective and cannot tell the difference between red and green lights. She smiles and tells you not to worry: Human factors psychologists helped design these machines. Because they were aware of color deficiencies, they made sure that the red warning lights would blink instead of remaining lit like the green lights, so that any sighted person would be sure to detect a malfunction. (Of course, the blink rate of the light must not be too slow or too fast. But that is a different perceptual/human factors problem.)

Control panels of large complicated machines, such as this automated can maker, use color-coded lights, dials, gauges, and displays to lessen the chance for human error.

In addition to knowing about human sensory abilities, human factors psychologists also need to be aware of the cognitive abilities and limits of the people who will be part of the human–machine system (Reinach et al., 1997; Sterns and Camp, 1998). Suppose you want to design a display that indicates speed of a car to the driver. You have the three options displayed in Figure 50.2. The first option, Figure 50.2a, is a typical circular speedometer scaled in one-mile-per-hour increments. The second option, a digital speedometer, also gives the reading in one-mile per hour increments (see Figure 50.2b). The third option, Figure 50.2c, is a continually changing bar graph that shows changes in increments of one mile per hour. Which one of these speedometers can be most quickly and accurately read by a typical driver? If you picked Figure 50.2b, you were right. People can read the exact speed more quickly and more accurately off a digital display than any other type.

But is speed the only information a speedometer is designed to display to a driver? The answer is no. Speedometers also give information about acceleration, the rate of change in speed. If you had to pick the speedometer that best indicates acceleration, you should choose the circular speedometer, Figure 50.2a because it takes very little cognitive processing to determine the direction of the needle's movement. Each of these types of speedometers has been tested in actual automobiles, but as human factors psychologists have found, the circular display is still the best design for relaying both speed and acceleration of the automobile.

Controls: How You Talk to the Machine

When someone decides to change a machine's functioning, they must input instructions via the machine controls. These controls can be as simple as a dial, a wheel, or a switch, or as complicated as a keyboard. The design of any control device must reflect the capabilities of both machine and human. If the machine demands input beyond the cognitive or motor abilities of the human, the system will fail or function at a suboptimal level. Human factors psychologists study variables like workers' strength, endurance, speed, and accuracy of movement.

Let's explore the topic of accuracy of movement. When you reach for a can of soda, you usually pick it up with no trouble. But once in a while, you bump and spill it. This is an example of a motor control error, an error everyone makes at one time or another—even Kobe Bryant misses a slam-dunk once in a while. Missing a shot in basketball is not life threatening, however. Hitting the wrong pedal in your car, could be.

As mentioned in the opening section, the most probable cause of unintended acceleration accidents was driver error. The driver, thinking he or she is stepping on the brake pedal, actually slams on the accelerator. Mark Vernoy and George Tomerlin (1989, 1990) investigated pedal errors in various types of cars using hundreds of licensed drivers as participants. They asked drivers to sit in cars, shift the transmission into park, reverse, or drive, step on the gas pedal, and step on the brake pedal. At an unexpected point in the experiment, participants were commanded to: "Stop! Step on the brake!"

The movement and placement of the participant's feet during this surprise braking were videotaped and later analyzed for errors. On several trials, participants failed to hit the brake, and hit the accelerator pedal instead. Thus, Vernoy and Tomerlin documented the role of human error in these instances of unintended acceleration. Because it is impossible to train a driver to be totally free from this type of pedal error, carmakers could modify the automobile controls to either reduce or eliminate this error.

Why not try to place the pedals as far apart as possible in order to minimize confusion between the brake and the gas? This is a possible solution, except increasing the distance between the pedals also increases the time needed to move the foot from the gas pedal to the brake. At 60 miles per hour, a delay of one-tenth of a second causes the car to travel an additional 8.8 feet before the brake is applied. Pedals that are farther apart might decrease pedal errors, but the overall number and severity of accidents might increase because the cars would take longer to stop.

Figure 50.2 ***Three different types of automobile speedometers.*** Which of these would be the easiest to read if you wanted to know only the speed of the automobile? Which of these would be the best if you wanted to know both the speed and acceleration of the automobile?

(a) Spatial Correspondence | Poorly designed | Well-designed
(b) Visibility | Poorly designed | Well-designed
(c) Shape Indicates Function | Landing gear | Landing flap

Figure 50.3 **Human factors design and the real world.** Well-designed appliances and machinery are easily understood and operated. (a) The controls for stovetops should be arranged in a pattern that corresponds to the placement of the burners. (b) In an automobile, gauges for fuel, oil, and speed should be easily visible to the driver. (c) Controls and knobs are easier and safer to use if their shape corresponds to their function.

What is the solution? Nearly all cases of severe unintended acceleration happen when people are *backing up* in a new or relatively unfamiliar car. If drivers first had to brake to unlock the transmission before they could shift into reverse, they would be less likely to mistake the brake pedal for the accelerator (Vernoy and Tomerlin, 1989). Such a simple correction would also have prevented the accident described in our chapter opener.

Figure 50.3 offers additional examples showing how a well-designed human–machine system can accomplish its task quickly, accurately, and safely.

 CHECK AND REVIEW

Human Factors Psychology

Human factors psychology is a branch of I/O psychology that studies ways to improve the design and function of machines and the work environment to better meet the needs of human users.

Researchers consider humans and the machines they use a human–machine system, an arrangement of people and machines, tools, and other devices that produce a product or service. The human side of the system consists of sensory functions (input) and cognitive and motor functions (output); the machine side consists of displays (output) and controls (input)

QUESTIONS

1. The improvement of the design and function of machines and the work environment to meet the needs of human users is studied by _____ psychology. (a) personnel; (b) human factors; (c) organizational; (d) technology.

2. When the human's motor responses provide the control input, while the machine's displays provide the sensory input, this is an example of _____.

3. What is the difference between a display and a control?

4. The keys of the first manual typewriters were not arranged alphabetically, but in a pattern that prevented fast typists from jamming the keys. This is an example of a good _____. (a) human-machine system; (b) operator/machine team; (c) man versus machine problem; (d) human factors analysis.

Answers to Questions can be found in Appendix B.

MODULE 51
PERSONNEL PSYCHOLOGY

Why is personnel psychology important?

At the beginning of this chapter, we said that with the possible exception of sleeping, a person spends more time at work than at any other single activity. Think about that again: In your lifetime, you will spend at least twice as much time at work as you will with your friends and family. In other words, the quality of your life is directly related to the satisfaction you receive from your work. The importance of your career choice cannot be overestimated. And just as you need a job that maximizes your skills and satisfaction, business and industry need employees who have the skills and motivation to maximize productivity.

Personnel psychology plays an important role in locating the "right person for the right job" (Smith and Sutherland, 1996). In addition to (1) recruitment and selection, personnel psychologists also become involved in (2) employee training, and (3) developing objective criteria for evaluating employee performance. In this section, we will discuss each of these three elements. We will also explore the special problem of sexual harassment.

Personnel Psychology
The branch of I/O psychology involved with recruiting, selecting, training, and evaluating workers.

Recruitment and Selection: Finding the Right Person for the Right Job

Personnel recruitment and selection begins with **job analysis,** a detailed description of the skills, knowledge, and activities required by a particular job (Borman et al., 1997). Let's apply this definition to something that may be of interest to you as a student—the work of college instructors. They are primarily responsible for education and research, while administration (president, deans, etc.) and support staff (office personnel, custodians, directors) assume responsibility for running the college (funding, buildings, and maintenance).

Job Analysis
A detailed description of the skills, knowledge, and activities required by a particular job.

While the knowledge, skills, and abilities necessary to perform as a successful college instructor vary according to academic discipline (psychology, math, physical education, etc.), all instructors share similar tasks: Teaching assigned classes, maintaining required office hours, preparing and grading exams and papers, attending department meetings, and serving on college committees. In addition, many colleges and universities expect professors to conduct research and to publish in professional journals.

If a college wanted to hire a new college instructor, they would begin with a job analysis like this, followed by the selection of a large, field of candidates. The next step—for any job—is to choose the one most qualified candidate. The number of candidates may be narrowed through applications, questionnaires, interviews, observations, standardized psychological tests, knowledge and skills tests, performance tests, and *biodata* (detailed biographical information).

Of all the selection devices, the interview continues to be the most popular—and to carry the most weight (Dipboye, 1992). Interviews can be *structured* or *unstructured*. Structured interviews involve a set of preplanned questions that are asked of every person who is interviewed and a standardized rating of the applicant's qualifications. This reduces several biases associated with unstructured interviews, which tend to be casual, short, and made up of random questions. As expected, structured interviews are much better predictors than unstructured interviews (Campion et al., 1999; Clarke et al., 1998; Rogers et al., 1997).

A personal interview involves questioning job applicants to learn their qualifications and to get an impression of their personalities (Borman et al., 1997). If you perform poorly at this stage, you are not likely to be hired, regardless of your experience, test scores, or letters of recommendation. Therefore, let's spend some time talking about interviewing.

Table 51.1   WHY MOST PEOPLE HATE BEING INTERVIEWED

Problems	
"First date" syndrome	In initial meetings with important, but unstated, outcomes both parties behave with artificial care and skill.
Nervousness	Applicants know they are being evaluated and compared to others, and they are typically in a "one-down" position (they need what the employer has to give). Thus, most interviewees are tense and anxious.
Subjectivity	When one person meets another, impressions tend to be formed immediately—sometimes due to nothing more than clothes or facial appearance. These first impressions are often resistant to change.

Source: Auerbach, 1996.

If you are asked to come in for an interview, you can expect a face-to-face meeting with one or more interviewers. They may be using the interview as an alternative or adjunct to the application form. Questions are designed to measure your attitudes ("Did you like your last job?" "Do you prefer working in groups or alone?"), job experiences ("What did you do in your last job?"), and personal background ("What was your college major?"). Interviewers also use this face-to-face meeting to assess your communication and interpersonal skills. Successful applicants are typically friendly (but not overly so), eager (but not desperate), and assertive (but not aggressive).

Is interviewing really that complicated? I'm getting nervous just reading about this. Most interviewees tend to be anxious, and that is perfectly normal (Table 51.1). But there are also reasons to look forward to interviews. First, interviews allow for longer and more detailed answers than application forms, and most people find it easier to talk than to write. In addition, both parties have the opportunity to ask questions and to clarify exactly what the job requires. In effect, you are interviewing the company as much as it is interviewing you.

Try This Yourself

If you would like to improve your interviewing skills, try the following:

1. *Research*   Before your interview, research the company, employer, supervisors, and all available positions. The information you gather can be invaluable in helping you respond to interview questions. Also, simply knowing the history and size of the company will show the interviewer that you are serious about your job search. Research can also help you decide if you really want to work for this company.

2. *Role playing*   Ask someone to help you practice playing both interviewer and interviewee. Encourage honest feedback about verbal and nonverbal habits that may affect your interview. For example, do you nervously jiggle your feet or avoid eye contact? Also, brainstorm ahead of time about potential questions and good responses.

3. *Personality*   Interviewers generally like friendly, eager, and assertive applicants. These are basic personality traits you've undoubtedly used before, when meeting new friends or on a first date, for example. Recognizing you've used these skills in the past, may help you relax in the interview and "be yourself."

(On the other side, if you become an interviewer, you can make the interview process more comfortable—and therefore more productive—in several ways. Most important, recognize that the applicant is tense. Begin by introducing yourself. Be relaxed and friendly, and briefly describe what the interview will be like. Tell how long it will take and what topics will be discussed. Finally, encourage the interviewee to ask questions.)

Employee Training: Objectives and Methods

After applicants are tested and interviewed and the best candidate is hired, the personnel psychologist helps train the new employee. Research shows training not only provides workers with appropriate skills for the assigned job, it also reduces frustration and stress (Aamodt, 1999; Saal and Knight, 1988).

Training typically begins with some form of *orientation*. Just as you may have had a college orientation designed to introduce the educational organization, new employees are usually given either a formal or informal introduction to the business setting. Pay close attention. The orientation is designed to "clue in" new employees. You are being taught the facts of organizational structure and operations as well as appropriate attitudes and allegiances.

Every organization has its shared pattern of thought and action, an **organizational culture.** This culture arises from each group's history and involves group identity, policies, and rituals. For example, organizations typically develop characteristic attitudes toward diversity, creativity, attention to detail, team versus individual orientation, and stability versus innovation (Hurley and Hult, 1998; Miller, 1998; Tesluk et al., 1997; Wilpert, 1995). Fitting into an organization means fitting into its culture.

Organizational Culture
A group's shared pattern of thought and action; a common perception held by the organization's members.

Personnel psychologists are also involved with training and upgrading skills for new and existing employees. Skill training can be technical and highly job specific. You might be taught how to sell or service the company's product, or how to operate the communication system and other machines. General training may also be offered for interpersonal skills, including effective listening, communication, and how to be a "team player."

One of the fastest growing areas of interpersonal skill development is diversity training, learning to work with individuals from various cultural backgrounds (Aamodt, 1999; Haggerty, 1993). Even the smallest of U.S. businesses may now compete globally and employees and managers need to adjust their style to conduct business all over the world.

Gender and Cultural Diversity

WHAT HAPPENS TO BUSINESS WHEN CULTURES CLASH?

As a tourist, have you ever unintentionally violated the cultural rules in a foreign country and been horribly embarrassed? As an international businessperson, you risk more than embarrassment: You might lose important business contacts, or even find yourself in serious legal trouble. Given our multicultural society and our expanding interactions with other nations, it is important to understand and appreciate diversity, and help prevent *culture clashes*. Consider this story from Richard Brislin (1993):

> Kiyoshi, a Japanese executive, was visiting an automobile plant in the American Midwest to explore a possible joint venture in manufacturing a new model of car. Hank, an executive at the plant, invited Kiyoshi and his wife to dinner at his house. They arrived at the agreed upon time of 6:00 P.M. and the group enjoyed pleasant conversation over soft drinks ("No one drinks hard liquor any more!" Hank thought). Dinner was served at 7:00 P.M. and dessert at about 8:15 P.M. After finishing their dessert, Kiyoshi and his wife quickly thanked Hank and then quickly left. Hank thought something was wrong, either with himself or with Kiyoshi's manners. What went wrong? Why did Kiyoshi and his wife leave so quickly? (p. 98)

You may be surprised to see how differing cultural expectations help explain this awkward and confusing *culture clash*. The norms in Hank's culture require guests to engage in pleasant conversation after dessert, and if people leave early it is consid-

Table 51.2   DOING BUSINESS IN CANADA

Canadian V-for-Victory gesture

Canadian beckoning and waving gestures

Appointments

French-speaking areas of Canada may be more casual about time, but, as a foreigner, it is always good manners to be prompt. While business lunches are popular in Canada, dinners have traditionally been social occasions—if business is discussed at all, it is at the end of the meal. This is changing, but to be safe, allow your Canadian counterpart to bring up business first.

Negotiating

Although styles are similar, many Canadians think U.S. business people "hype" their products. Never inflate your product's benefits. English and French are the official languages, but in Quebec there are very stringent rules—French is the only legal language in which to conduct business.

Gestures

To beckon someone wave all the fingers in a scooping motion with the palm facing up. To wave good-bye, move your entire hand, facing outward. The "V-for-victory" sign is done with the palm facing out—it may be taken as an insult when done with the palm inward.

Gifts

Business gifts should be modest—Canadians tend to frown on ostentation. When visiting a home, it is customary to take flowers, candy, or liquor.

French–Canadian homes may be divided into "public" rooms that visitors may enter and "private" rooms where visitors may enter only when asked. The kitchen is often a private room—do not enter unless asked.

Source: Adapted from *Kiss, Bow, or Shake Hands* by T. Morrison, W. A. Conaway, and G. A. Borden, 1994. Adams Media Corp.

ered an insult. However, in Kiyoshi and his wife's culture, remaining after dinner is a sign that you are still hungry, and the host would be expected to offer more food! If you think differences exist mainly between Eastern and Western cultures, see Table 51.2, which outlines small, subtle differences between very similar nations, the United States and Canada.

While some clashes between cultures are inevitable, there are ways to minimize misunderstandings (adapted from Brislin, 1993, Dresser, 1996):

1. *Examine your thought processes*   Because norms are generally covert and unexamined, it is easy to mistakenly assume that our rules for conducting business or social interactions are the same as others'. One way to prevent misunderstandings like Hank and Kiyoshi's, is to become aware of your own cultural rules, and then learn the norms of your business client's country.

2. *Adjust your behaviors to match the other culture*   If you are doing business in Quebec, for example, use French in your transactions or ask for a French-speaking assistant to translate for you. At the least, apologize for not knowing the official language. Adjusting your behavior demonstrates that you recognize diversity and respect the other person's culture. Even within the United States, it can be helpful to adjust your behavior. For example, many Native Americans prefer more silence in their communications than Anglo Americans, who usually interpret silence as a sign that interactions are not going well. An Anglo American who understands this cultural difference will refrain from rushing to fill any silence when doing business with a Native American.

3. *Recognize that culture clashes are emotionally stressful*   When people interact with unfamiliar people in unfamiliar circumstances, stress is inevitable. It is frustrating not to be able to easily communicate with others and to find that familiar ways of behaving do not work in other cultures. For example, in the United States during informal entertaining, dinner guests often gather in the kitchen while the host finishes preparing the food. After dinner, guests often help clear the table and perhaps even put leftovers in the refrigerator. In French-Canadian homes, however, the kitchen is generally considered a "private" room that guests should not enter. Simply recognizing that some culture clashes are inevitable, may help reduce your stress.

CHECK AND REVIEW

Recruiting, Selecting, and Training Employees

Personnel psychology involves recruiting, selecting, training, and evaluating workers. Recruitment begins with a job analysis, which is a detailed description of skills, knowledge, and activities required in a particular job. Interviews are the most popular method of choosing the most qualified candidate. Structured interviews are better predictors of future job performance than unstructured interviews.

Prepare for an interview by doing research on the company, role playing with a friend, and emphasizing desirable personality traits.

Employee training typically begins with an orientation program. One of the major unstated goals of orientation is transmitting the organizational culture—the group's shared pattern of thought and action.

QUESTIONS

1. The branch of I/O psychology involved with recruiting, selecting, training, and evaluating workers is known as _____psychology. (a) human factors; (b) engineering; (c) social; (d) personnel.

2. When choosing a candidate for a job, the _____ is the most popular and most heavily weighted of all selection devices.

3. What are the three basic personality traits that most appeal to interviewers?

4. A group's shared pattern of thought and action is known as _____. (a) the organizational culture; (b) personality/job-fit theory; (c) the Hawthorne effect; (d) the organizational structure.

Answers to Questions can be found in Appendix B.

Evaluating Workers: Measuring Job Performance

After an employee has been in a job for awhile, his or her performance is then evaluated. **Performance evaluation** is the formal procedure an organization uses to assess the multidimensional job performance of employees (Arvey and Murphy, 1998). Organizations use performance evaluations for a number of purposes. One of the most important is providing feedback to the employee on how the organization views his or her performance. Employees need to know when they are doing well (so they can keep on doing well), and when they are not (so they can change). Research shows that employees fare better when their work is evaluated, when reinforcers are closely related to job performance, and when criticism is delivered constructively (Baron, 1990; Locke and Latham, 1990).

Performance evaluations are also useful for identifying training and development needs. Does the employee need upgrading of skills or retraining? In addition, management uses performance evaluations for decisions on promotions, transfers, and termination.

Performance Evaluation
The formal procedure used by an organization to assess job performance of employees.

A performance evaluation may be *objective* or *subjective*. Objective measures include such things as the number of sales for a salesperson or the number of publications for a college instructor. Many jobs (like management and support services), however, do not have an easily identifiable and objective product, and in some cases objective measures may not be appropriate. For example, how do you identify the *product* of a college instructor? The effect of one college instructor on any one student is difficult to measure objectively. Furthermore, benefits from a college instructor or a college degree are sometimes years away.

Subjective measures avoid some of these problems (but introduce others, as you will shortly see). Subjective ratings by supervisors or others who are familiar with the employee's job performance are the most common form of performance evaluation. Despite their popularity, subjective methods suffer from serious rater biases and other human errors (Arvey and Murphy, 1998). One of the most widely researched problems is the tendency to rate individuals either too high or too low based on one outstanding trait, the **halo effect.** If a person is rated "exceptional" in one area, he or she tends to be rated "exceptional" in all areas. The same thing occurs when someone is rated "poor" in one area.

The halo effect is a significant problem. If a supervisor happens to value friendliness, will he or she overrate an employee who smiles a lot? Also, how can we differentiate between what might be termed a *legitimate* halo—an employee who *does* perform well on all dimensions—and bias caused by the undue influence of one characteristic? Preventing and minimizing the halo effect is a major research topic in personnel psychology (Larose and Standing, 1998; Murphy, Jako, and Anhalt, 1993; Solomonson and Lance, 1997).

To offset problems with the halo effect and other evaluation biases, some organizations have recently turned to "360-degree" performance measures, which include evaluations from supervisors, peers, subordinates, and even customers. These multisource measures are useful for both feedback and personnel decisions (Arvey and Murphy, 1998).

Organizations may also use specially designed rating scales, where the supervisor evaluates an employee in certain critical areas by assigning a numerical rating. As Figure 51.1 shows, your job as student could be evaluated with this type of rating

Halo Effect
The tendency to rate individuals either too high or too low based on one outstanding trait. The halo effect is a characteristic defect in rating scales.

"He's not a perfect boss, but he *does* give you plenty of feedback."

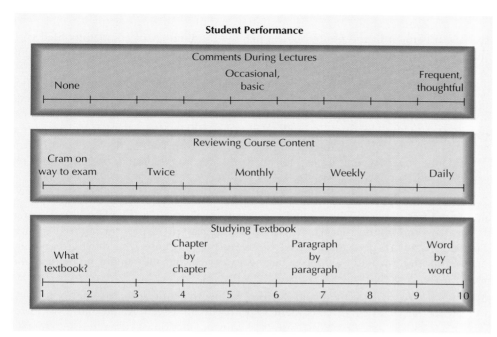

Student Performance

Comments During Lectures

None | Occasional, basic | Frequent, thoughtful

Reviewing Course Content

Cram on way to exam | Twice | Monthly | Weekly | Daily

Studying Textbook

What textbook? | Chapter by chapter | Paragraph by paragraph | Word by word

1   2   3   4   5   6   7   8   9   10

*Figure 51.1 **A possible rating scale for students.*** How would you score on this rating scale? Would you like this kind of performance evaluation or do you prefer the traditional rating scale, known as "grades"?

scale. The idea is that raters will be more accurate if they focus on specific *behaviors* rather than *traits*, such as friendliness.

Although rating scales are helpful, they also have drawbacks. As you know, some college instructors can be hard graders, while others may be easy. Supervisors in the work world can be similarly tough or lenient raters. In addition, research shows that supervisors like employees who perform well (Robbins and DeNisi, 1994), and that they do, in fact, give higher ratings to employees they like (Ferris et al., 1994).

Sexual Harassment: An Abuse of Power

What happens to the evaluation process when a supervisor says, "Let's go to the Holiday Inn and negotiate your raise"? Historically, personnel psychologists have been involved with recruitment and selection, training, and evaluation of workers; but today, they are also involved with problems of sexual harassment. The legal definition of **sexual harassment** is unwelcome sexual advances, requests for sexual favors, and other unwelcome verbal or physical conduct of a sexual nature.

A federal study defined three levels of sexual harassment: *less severe* (e.g., sexual teasing, suggestive gestures, sexual remarks), *severe* (e.g., pressure for dates or sexual favors, touching, letters, telephone calls), and *criminal* (sexual assault, attempted rape, and rape). The point is that any pattern of unwelcome sexual behavior may constitute sexual harassment (Egler, 1995). The suggestion to negotiate a raise at a motel was part of an actual court case, and the court ruled that this, and similar behavior, was sexual harassment. The plaintiff was awarded significant damages (Harris v. Forklift Systems, 1993; cited in Aamodt, 1999).

Sexual Harassment
Unwelcome sexual advances, requests for sexual favors, and other unwelcome verbal or physical conduct of a sexual nature.

Myths about Sexual Harassment

There are at least three major misconceptions about sexual harassment.

1.   "It's a minor problem." Law Professor Anita Hill's charge that Supreme Court Justice Clarence Thomas sexually harassed her, the U.S. Navy's Tailhook convention, and the Army's Aberdeen scandal all brought national attention to the issue of sexual harassment (Healy, 1998; Shenon, 1997). The most recent case to make the headlines was Paula Jones' sexual harassment lawsuit against President Clinton. Despite such high profile cases, most people still underestimate the prevalence of occupational

Paula Jones's suit against President Clinton brought renewed debate and attention to the topic of sexual harassment.

sexual harassment and consider it a minor issue. One measure of the prevalence of sexual harassment in the United States may be the number of complaints filed with the EEOC (Equal Employment Opportunity Commission), which rose from 6,000 in 1990 to 15,300 in 1996 (Kaufman, 1997).

In addition to these business settings, sexual harassment also seems to be a major problem in the academic world. A recent survey of more than 1,000 Canadian female students reported that over 23 percent had experienced at least one episode of sexual harassment in the last six months (Bagley et al., 1997). Power is misused to coerce students into sexual acts. Students comply with the perpetrator's demands out of fear of academic repercussions, a need for a letter of recommendation, or desire for a research or work opportunity (Riger, 1991).

2. "It's overreported." Contrary to misperceptions that charges of sexual harassment are often made for the slightest provocation, a survey by The Working Women United Institute found that when women were harassed 75 percent ignored the harassment. Only 18 percent reported the harassment! Those who did not complain believed nothing would be done. They also worried that they might be blamed and would suffer negative repercussions.

3. "It's an expression of sexual desire." While the harasser *may* sometimes be attracted to the victim, the harassment is primarily an assertion and abuse of power (Cleveland and Kerst, 1993). Because of the misperception of sexual desire, older or less attractive women who complain of sexual harassment are often ignored or ridiculed ("Don't flatter yourself"). On the other hand, when the victim is young and attractive she is accused of "inviting" a sexual approach. Like other victims of sexual abuse, those who are harassed are often accused of "asking for it."

Sexual harassment is a serious issue. Victims often face severe financial difficulties, such as unemployment, demotion, or loss of promotions if they resist the harassment. On a psychological level, victims also suffer various physical and psychological effects, including nervousness, loss of motivation, sleeplessness, guilt, shame, anger, depression, and helplessness (Charney and Russell, 1994; Rhode, 1997).

Harassment also affects business and academic institutions. It causes stress, poor work or academic performance, absenteeism, and high turnover. The cost of sexual harassment averages at least $6 million a year for a Fortune 500 company (Rhode, 1997).

Recent court cases awarding large sums of money to victims have increased the cost of sexual harassment. Title VII of the 1964 Civil Rights Act imposes liability on companies for sexual harassment and the U.S. Department of Education guidelines can deny federal funds to schools that do not take measures to remedy the situation (Scher, 1997).

Preventing Sexual Harassment

There are several, specific steps that can be taken to reduce the likelihood of sexual harassment and an organization's potential legal liability:

1. All complaints, no matter how trivial or farfetched they appear, must be investigated.

2. Complaints must be kept confidential to protect both the accused and the complainant.

3. Action must be taken to protect the complainant from possible retaliation by the accused.

4. Both the accused and complainant must be given due process, and results of the investigation must be communicated in writing to both parties.

5. The severity of any punishment must match the severity of the violation.

(*Based on:* Bloch, 1995; and Robinson et al., 1993)

What can the victim or target of sexual harassment do to stop the abuse?   Here are several suggestions (Crooks and Baur, 1999):

1. If a professor or an employer harasses you, make your objections clear. A firm "no" is an important first step.

2. Discuss the problem with fellow students or employees. Identifying other victims bolsters your case and provides social and emotional support

3. If the problem continues, keep a detailed record (noting times, dates, locations, possible witnesses, and precisely what was said or done). In addition, contact authorities on the campus or at work. You might begin by consulting another professor or supervisor, whom you trust, to help you determine the appropriate officials and channels for complaints.

4. If the harassment continues and your grievances are not acted upon, you may want to contact your state's civil rights commission and file a formal grievance. Current affirmative action regulations protect those who file harassment complaints from instructor retaliation and from job demotion or firing.

CHECK AND REVIEW

Evaluating Workers, Sexual Harassment

Performance evaluation is the formal procedure an organization uses to assess the job performance of employees. Evaluations can be objective or subjective.

The subjective method is the most popular, but the halo effect (the tendency to rate individuals too high or too low based on one outstanding trait) can create a major problem. To overcome the halo effect, some organizations use "360-degree" multisource measures and special rating scales.

Sexual harassment involves sexual advances, requests for sexual favors, and other unwelcome verbal or physical conduct of a sexual nature. Most sexual harassment is an assertion or abuse of power, not an expression of sexual desire. Victims of sexual harassment often suffer financial losses and psychological difficulties.

QUESTIONS

1. The formal procedure an organization uses to assess the job performance of employees is known as _____. (a) job analysis; (b) the Hawthorne effect; (c) performance evaluation; (d) knowledge and skills evaluation.

2. What are the two major functions of performance evaluations?

3. What is the halo effect?

4. Sexual harassment is primarily _____ and not an expression of sexual desire.

Answers to Questions can be found in Appendix B.

MODULE 52
ORGANIZATIONAL PSYCHOLOGY

When it comes to work, most people are social animals—they generally prefer to work with others. **Organizational psychologists** are interested in how interpersonal relations in the work setting affect productivity. In this section, we discuss three topics of special interest to organizational psychologists: managerial style, worker motivation, and job satisfaction.

What does organizational psychology encompass?

Organizational Psychology
The branch of I/O psychology interested in how interpersonal relations in the work setting affect productivity. Topics of interest include managerial style, worker motivation, and job satisfaction.

DILBERT. Reprinted by permission of United Features Syndicate, Inc.

Theory X
The proposal that employees dislike working, are lazy, avoid responsibility, and must be prodded or manipulated to perform.

Theory Y
The proposal that employees like to work, are industrious, seek responsibility, and can exercise self-direction.

Participative Decision Making
A decision-making model in which the people involved in implementing a decision are also involved in making it.

Quality Circles
A form of participative decision making involving regular meetings of supervisors and employees to discuss improvement of product or service.

Managerial Style: Theory X and Theory Y

Douglas McGregor (1960) identified two types of managers, each with very different assumptions about human nature—one negative and the other positive. **Theory X** managers believe that employees dislike work, are lazy, avoid responsibility, and must be prodded or manipulated into being productive. Therefore, they believe in close supervision and extrinsic rewards, such as work quotas, bonuses, and commissions to motivate their workers. **Theory Y** managers believe that employees like work, are industrious, seek responsibility, and can exercise self-direction. They do not believe employees need close supervision because they are self-motivated by intrinsic rewards, such as personal feelings of achievement and satisfaction.

Which style do you endorse? McGregor himself favored Theory Y. As business and industry come to recognize that a worker's self-esteem and satisfaction are important to job efficiency, Theory Y is becoming increasingly popular.

An essential part of Theory Y management is **participative decision making,** in which the people involved in implementing a decision are also involved in making it. Theory Y managers realize that participative decision making promotes teamwork and avoids an adversarial relationship between management and employees. In comparison, Theory X managers typically make all decisions and tell employees what to do. Studies support Theory Y. When workers are given a greater voice in how their work will be accomplished, both efficiency and job satisfaction are improved (Ali et al., 1997; Farson, 1996; Greller, 1998; Harrison and Pietri, 1997).

Quality circles are a well-known form of participative decision making in some countries. Employees and employers meet regularly to discuss quality problems, investigate causes, recommend solutions, and take corrective action. The concept of the quality circle originated in Japanese car assembly plants. At the end of the work day or work week, some of the workers from each line meet with their supervisors in a circle (implying equal contributions) to discuss ways to improve efficiency and employee satisfaction (Chaffins et al., 1998; Jewell, 1990; Matsui and Onglatco, 1990).

As implemented in the United States (Figure 52.1), both management and employees initially discuss company problems. Then the circle team members choose which problem to address, and generate and evaluate their own feedback. Management typically retains control over the final decision.

When the San Diego Zoo reorganized animal exhibits into separate, cage free areas that resemble natural habitats, they also instituted participative decision making. Employees formed teams that assumed responsibility for operating and maintaining specific exhibits. For example, the Tiger River exhibit pictured here is self-managed by a team of horticulturists, mammal and bird specialists, and maintenance and construction workers.

Figure 52.1 *A typical quality circle in the United States.* Note that management and employees begin by identifying problems. The quality circle (composed of employees) then selects which problem to work on, reviews it, and recommends solutions. Management reviews the solutions and makes the final decision. Most quality circles have been discontinued in the United States because management and employees tend to be more adversarial than loyal and trusting.

Do quality circles really work? Quality circles have not always worked well outside of Japan. In the United States, they seem to improve productivity, but have little or no effect on employee satisfaction, and have been mostly discontinued (Cotton, 1993). Their continued popularity in Japan may reflect Japanese organizational culture, which is based on lifetime employment, mutual respect between employer and employee, use of broad-based consensus to reach decisions, and fierce loyalty and devotion to the company by all employees (Chaffins et al., 1998; Ouchi, 1981). The U.S. organizational culture is quite different.

Worker Motivation: Goal-Setting, Equity, and Expectancy

Why do some workers put in long hours even when they are not being directly compensated, while others arrive late, do the minimum, and leave early if the boss isn't looking? You may have some answers after reading about personality differences and motivation and reinforcement in earlier chapters. In this section, we will explore three theories I/O psychologists have developed about what motivates workers: goal-setting theory, equity theory, and expectancy theory.

Goal-Setting Theory

Did your parents ever tell you to "just do your best?" What does this mean? How do you know when you have succeeded and can quit trying? Research on **goal-setting theory** suggests that setting *specific* and *difficult* goals leads to higher performance (Locke, 1968, 1996).

Goal-Setting Theory
The proposal that having specific and difficult goals leads to higher performance.

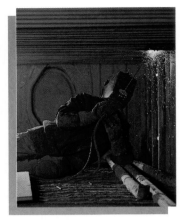

Under Detroit Edison's goals, measures, and targets (GMT) program, teams of employees define their joint and individual goals and performance measures. This photo shows a welder replacing boiler tubes at one of the company's power plants. Employees generated this cost-reduction project, which saved Detroit Edison $200,000 over the lowest bid from outside contractors. The savings were passed on to employees.

Equity Theory
The idea that individuals are driven by a need to maintain equilibrium or balance. In a work setting, employees prefer jobs in which the output is equal to the input. If imbalances occur, workers adjust their input, output, or their psychological perceptions.

Expectancy Theory
The idea that expectancy of outcomes, their desirability, and the effort needed to achieve them all determine worker motivation.

All things being equal, a person with specific goals will outperform someone without goals or with only a generalized "do my best" goal. For instance, when a sales representative commits to making 20 new contacts per week, he or she is setting a specific objective or goal. Also, the more difficult the goal (as long as it remains within reach), the greater the motivation. This theory enjoys wide support (Durham et al., 1997; Gilbourne and Taylor, 1998; Lee et al., 1997).

Equity theory

Have you ever worked for an employer who regularly asked for special favors, such as coming in on your day off? How would you respond if this same employer later refused to let you rearrange your lunch hour for a doctor's appointment? According to **equity theory,** we are strongly motivated to maintain a state of equilibrium or balance. We not only compare our contributions to that of our employer, we also compare our job's rewards and compensations with those of others (friends, neighbors, coworkers, colleagues in other organizations) and previous jobs (Beckett-Camarata et al., 1998; van Dierendonck et al., 1998; Wilpert, 1995).

If we compare our job contributions and job rewards and detect an imbalance (we're giving more than we're getting in return), we may quit or decrease our efforts in an effort to restore balance. If this doesn't work, we may change our psychological perceptions, by focusing on other compensations such as time off, ease of work, and so on. Balance is very important to workers, according to equity theory. If perceived *job input* (contributions) matches perceived *job outcome* (rewards), balance (or equity) is achieved and the worker goes home happy.

When an imbalance exists (the employer asks for extra consideration but is unwilling to return the favor), the worker is motivated to rebalance the relationship by altering inputs and outcomes or by psychologically adjusting his or her perception of the gains and losses. We can give the employer less, ask for more, or alter our thinking, e.g., "the boss would let me rearrange lunch if it were possible."

Expectancy Theory

One of the most popular theories of worker motivation is **expectancy theory,** the idea that workers perform in line with their expectancy of outcomes, the desirability of those outcomes, and the effort needed to achieve them. Before deciding to work hard (or not to work hard), individuals supposedly ask themselves three questions:

1. *What can I reasonably expect from my efforts?* If employees perceive that rewards such as salary increases, bonuses, and promotions are based on hard work, they will work hard. On the other hand, if workers believe rewards are based on factors such as seniority or politics, both motivation and morale will be extremely low.

2. *Do I really want the rewards offered by management?* If you've been working hard hoping for a salary increase, but are offered a promotion with increased responsibility and only a small bonus, you will obviously be disappointed. Similarly, if you had put in long hours hoping for a transfer to the West Coast office, but instead were offered the East Coast, you would be very disappointed. Managers should recognize that individual workers have different ideas of what is rewarding.

3. *If I give maximum effort, will it be reflected in my job evaluation?* For some employees, the answer is too often no. If you lack the training or necessary skill level for a particular job, you are unlikely to be a high performer, no matter how hard you try. On the other hand, some workers are qualified but their supervisors may be unfair or may not like them. Regardless of their efforts, these external situations may block them from getting a good evaluation.

Try This Yourself

If you are a manager interested in increasing worker motivation (or someday hope to be), here are three ways you (and your employees) can benefit from expectancy theory:

1. *Clarify the route to rewards.* Be sure that promotions, salary increases, and bonuses are based on clear, definable measures of performance. Communicate these measures to your employees and give them frequent feedback on their efforts.

2. *Personalize the payoffs.* Ensure the rewards you've chosen for good performance are meaningful or valued by your employees. Ask employees to help design payoffs that fit their personal goals and expectations.

3. *Reward maximum effort.* Begin by establishing a good fit between employees and their job assignments, and then ensure that employees are well trained. Once established in the work position, provide employees frequent evaluation on their work, including feedback on how their current performance level will affect their long-term job promotions and raises.

■

In sum, general knowledge of the three major worker motivation theories (goal-setting, equity, and expectancy) and implementation of this knowledge can help improve your own job performance and your management of others.

Job Satisfaction: What are the Important Factors?

What is the worst job you have ever had? What made it so bad? Was it the working conditions or low pay? Perhaps it was the work itself. Or maybe you just hated sitting at a desk for eight hours. Job satisfaction research is a high priority for I/O psychologists. In this section, we examine why managers should be concerned about employee job satisfaction (benefits to management and employees), and what factors determine worker satisfaction (personality/job factors).

Benefits to Management and Employees

Workers obviously prefer jobs that are rewarding and satisfying. But why should managers or business owners care if their employees are satisfied or not? According to research, there are several reasons:

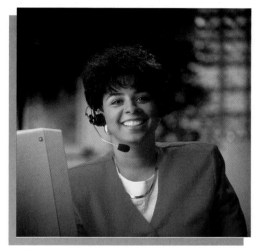

Why should employers care if workers are happy? Job satisfaction research shows important benefits to both employer and employee.

1. **Decreased resignations**   Dissatisfied workers are more likely to resign or be absent from work (Tharenou, 1993). Because turnover and absenteeism are expensive, managers generally try to reduce them (Hellman, 1997; O'Quin and LoTempio, 1998).

2. **Increased productivity**   Research shows that job satisfaction leads to increased productivity (Ostroff, 1992; Wilk and Redmon, 1998). Although some early studies questioned this assumption, (e.g., Brayfield and Crockett, 1988), when satisfaction and productivity data are gathered for the organization as a whole rather than at the individual level, Ostroff found that organizations with more satisfied employees tend to be more effective.

3. **Employee health**   Studies show that satisfied workers have less stress, less "burnout," and better physical and psychological health (Bhatt, 1997; Pearson, 1998; Siu et al., 1997; Tang, 1998). In addition, satisfaction on the job apparently carries over to the employee's life outside the office. Job satisfaction not only contributes to overall quality of life, but it may be a better predictor of length of life than physical condition or tobacco use (Judge and Watanabe, 1993).

Personality/Job Factors

Now that we know that job satisfaction is important to both employer and employee, how do we discover what determines job satisfaction? One of the most interesting

"All work and no play makes you a valued employee."

Personality-Job Fit Theory
This theory identifies six personality types and proposes that a "good fit" between personality type and occupation determines job satisfaction.

and influential answers comes from John Holland (1985, 1994). According to Holland's **personality-job fit theory,** a match (or "good-fit") between a person's personality and occupation is a major factor in job satisfaction.

Holland developed a *Self-Directed Search* questionnaire that scores each person on six personality types and then matches them with various occupations. By matching personality types to appropriate occupations, Holland believes workers will bring the right interests and abilities to a job's demands. This "good fit" match between personality and occupation ensures success on the job and a higher level of job satisfaction (people tend to like what they are good at). Studies generally support Holland's theory (Hesketh and Myors, 1997; Judge and Cable, 1997; Maurer and Tarulli, 1997; Young et al., 1998).

Try This Yourself

Would you like to know which occupations might best match your own personality? Choose which of the personality descriptions on the left that most closely describes you, and then check the column on the right that lists matching/congruent occupations.

Personality Characteristics	Holland's Six Types	Matching/Congruent Occupation
Shy, genuine, persistent, stable, conforming, practical	1. Realistic: Prefers physical activities that require skill, strength, and coordination	Mechanic, drill press operator, assembly-line worker, farmer
Analytical, original, curious, independent	2. Investigative: Prefers activities that involve thinking, organizing, and understanding	Biologist, economist, mathematician, news reporter
Sociable, friendly, cooperative, understanding	3. Social: Prefers activities that involve helping and developing others	Social worker, counselor, teacher, clinical psychologist

Personality Characteristics	Holland's Six Types	Matching/Congruent Occupation	Personality Characteristics	Holland's Six Types	Matching/Congruent Occupation
Conforming, efficient, practical, unimaginative, inflexible	4. Conventional: Prefers rule regulated, orderly, and unambiguous activities	Accountant, bank teller, file clerk, corporate manager	Self-confident, ambitious, energetic, domineering	6. Enterprising: Prefers verbal activities where there are opportunities to influence others and attain power	Lawyer, real estate agent, public relations specialist, small business manager
Imaginative, disorderly, idealistic, emotional, impractical	5. Artistic: Prefers ambiguous and unsystematic activities that allow creative expression	Painter, musician, writer, interior decorator			

(*Source:* Adapted from *You and Your Career* by J. L. Holland, 1985).

RESEARCH HIGHLIGHT

Job Satisfaction And Psychotherapy

Have you ever wondered about the work life of a psychotherapist? Is this a satisfying career? What are the most significant stressors and rewards? How do therapists cope when they have work-related problems?

Psychotherapy has always been a complex and demanding job, and earlier surveys documented numerous occupational hazards (Deutsch, 1985; Farber and Heifetz, 1981; Nash et al., 1984). These hazards could be categorized as (1) business-related problems (economic uncertainty, record keeping), (2) client-related issues (suicidal threats), (3) personal challenges of the psychotherapist (constant giving), (4) setting-related stressors (excessive workload), and (5) evaluation-related problems (difficulty evaluating client progress).

To add to this list, modern therapists also face problems from an increasingly litigious society and the expansion of managed care (Coster and Schwebel, 1997). With everyone more willing to sue these days, therapists must keep more detailed records. Expanded managed care creates even more paperwork, and its bureaucracy reduces the therapist's independence.

Which of these hazards is most stressful? Researchers Barbara Kramen-Kahn and Nancy Downing Hansen (1998) recently surveyed over 200 psychotherapists to identify their top occupational hazards, as well as, their personal coping strategies.

Their respondents rated business and economic demands and uncertainties, along with time and workload pressures as their top stressors. The most frequent coping methods were a sense of humor, freely consulting with other therapists, participating in leisure activities to balance work stresses, attending continuing education seminars, perceiving client problems as interesting, and using interpersonal supports.

Are there rewards in psychotherapy that offset the stress? According to the survey participants, the greatest rewards are seeing clients improve and grow, their own opportunities for self-growth, challenging and diverse tasks, and professional autonomy. It is interesting that female therapists reported greater occupational rewards and use of coping strategies than male therapists. Kramen-Kahn and Hansen suggest that this gender difference may reflect the fact that women are generally more relational than men (Jordan et al., 1991), and that therapy is an essentially relational occupation.

What can we learn from this research? Therapists should obviously try to reduce their perceived hazards, increase the rewards, and use more coping strategies. There is also a lesson for all of us in this research. Given the human tendency to react more strongly to (and perhaps have a longer memory for) aversive events—especially interpersonal ones (Rook, 1984), we might try to ignore the problems of our work and actively search for possible overlooked rewards. We could also emulate the therapists' most successful coping strategies. Developing a sense of humor and balancing work and leisure are important life skills for everyone.

CHECK AND REVIEW

Organizational Psychology

Organizational psychologists study how interpersonal relations affect productivity. Theory X managers take a negative approach, believing employees need close supervision and extrinsic rewards for motivation. Theory Y managers are positive and believe employees are self-motivated. Theory Y managers often use participative decision making, such as quality circles—groups of employees who meet regularly with supervisors to solve problems.

Goal setting is one major way to motivate workers; having specific and difficult goals improves performance. Equity theory says workers are motivated if they perceive that their job inputs match the perceived rewards. Expectancy theory, on the other hand, maintains that employees are motivated to work according to their expectancy of outcomes, the desirability of those outcomes, and the effort needed to achieve them.

Job satisfaction is important to both employer and employee. Employers gain because they save money (lower absenteeism and fewer resignations) and increase productivity. Employees gain because they are under less stress, enjoy better physical health, and have an improved overall quality and length of life.

According to personality-fit theory, job satisfaction results from a match between personality and occupation. Supportive colleagues, supportive working conditions, mentally challenging work, and equitable rewards are also important.

QUESTIONS

1. Briefly explain participative decision making, and why quality circles have been less successful in the United States than in Japan.

2. Identify the worker motivation theory that best explains the following situations:
   (a) Seong enjoys assignments that are difficult but attainable.
   (b) Denise avoids work and responsibility, but does not fear being fired because she is best friends with the boss and enjoys high seniority.
   (c) Juan, a salaried employee, feels he is being underpaid so he decides to cut back on his hours at work.

3. How does management benefit when employees have job satisfaction? What are the major benefits of job satisfaction to employees?

4. The theory that a match between a person's personality and occupation results in increased job satisfaction is known as _____. (a) expectancy theory; (b) the halo effect; (c) participative decision making; (d) personality job-fit theory.

Answers to Questions can be found in Appendix B.

Are You In The Right Job?

An important component of critical thinking is the ability to *define problems accurately*. By carefully identifying the problem in clear and concrete terms, critical thinkers prevent confusion and lay the foundation for gathering relevant information. For example, in choosing a career, first identify what you like and do not like about your current (and past) jobs. With this information in hand, you are then prepared to research jobs that will better suit your interests, needs, and abilities. To help your analysis, answer "Yes" or "No" to these questions:

_____ 1. Is there a sufficient amount of laughter and sociability in your workplace?

_____ 2. Does your boss notice and appreciate your work?

_____ 3. Is your boss understanding and friendly?

_____ 4. Are you embarrassed by the physical conditions of your workplace?

_____ 5. Do you feel safe and comfortable in your place of work?

_____ 6. Do you like the location of your job?

_____ 7. If you won the lottery and were guaranteed a lifetime income, would you feel truly sad if you also had to quit your job?

_____ 8. Do you watch the clock, daydream, take long lunches, and leave work as soon as possible?

_____ 9. Do you frequently feel stressed and overwhelmed by the demands of your job?

_____10. Compared to others with your qualifications, are you being paid what you are worth?

_____11. Are promotions made in a fair and just manner?

_____12. Given the demands of your job, are you fairly compensated for your work?

Now score your answers. Give yourself one point for each answer that matches the following: 1. No; 2. No; 3. No; 4. Yes; 5. No; 6. No; 7. No; 8. Yes; 9. Yes; 10. No; 11. No; 12. No.

The questions you just answered are based on four factors that research shows are conducive to job satisfaction: supportive colleagues, supportive working conditions, mentally challenging work, and equitable rewards (Robbins, 1996). Your total score reveals your overall level of dissatisfaction, while a look at specific questions can help identify which of these four factors is most important to your job satisfaction—and most lacking in your current job.

Supportive Colleagues (Items 1, 2, 3). For most employees, work fills important social needs. Therefore, having friendly and supportive colleagues and superiors leads to increased satisfaction.

Supportive Working Conditions (Items 4, 5, 6). Not surprisingly, studies find most employees prefer working in safe, clean, and relatively modern facilities. They also prefer jobs close to home.

Mentally Challenging Work (Items 7, 8, 9). Jobs with too little challenge create boredom and apathy, while too much challenge creates frustration and feelings of failure.

Equitable Rewards (Items 10, 11, 12). Employees want pay and promotions based on job demands, individual skill levels, and community pay standards.

KEY TERMS

Visual Summary for Modules 49, 50, 51, and 52

The Development of I/O Psychology

Industrial/Organizational (I/0) Psychology: studies how individual behavior affects and is affected by the physical environment and the organizational culture of the workplace.

The Beginnings

- Scott, Taylor, and Munsterberg were major founding contributors to I/0 psychology.

- World War I: Personnel needs gave **I/0** respectability. Based on newly developed group IQ tests, Scott developed a program to place recruits in jobs suiting their abilities.
  Hawthorne effect: people change their behavior because of the novelty of a research situation or because they know they're being observed.

Modern Times

- World War II: led to scientifically designed worker training programs to improve productivity for the war effort. After the war, many I/0 psychologists turned from manufacturing to management, thus creating *organizational psychology.*

- Civil Rights Act of 1964: **I/0** psychology's creation of employment tests, training programs, and recruitment programs that ignored ethnicity, religion, age, or gender.

Human Factors Psychology
Human factors psychology studies ways to improve the design and function of machines and the work environment to better meet the needs of human users.

Human-machine system: an arrangement of people and machines, tools, and other devices that produce a product or service. Human: sensory functions (input) and cognitive and motor functions (output). Machine: **displays** (output) and **controls** (input). The Human-Machine System:

Displays: Machines "talk" to human operators through their displays (video monitors, gauges, bells, and blinking lights).

Controls: Humans "talk" to machines by inputting instructions via machine controls (dial, wheel, switch, and keyboard).

Personnel Psychology
Personnel psychology: involved with recruiting, selecting, training, and evaluating workers.

Recruitment and Selection

Recruitment begins with a **job analysis,** a detailed description of the skills, knowledge, and activities required in a particular job. Selection often based on interviews. Structured (vs. unstructured) interviews are better predictors of future job performance. Prepare for an interview by doing research on the company, role playing, and emphasizing desirable personality traits.

Employee Training

Orientation programs transmit **organizational culture,** group's shared pattern of thought and action.

Personnel Psychology (cont.)

Evaluating Workers

Performance evaluation: formal procedure used to assess employee job performance. Evaluations can be objective or subjective. Subjective method most popular, but the **halo effect** (tendency to rate individuals too high or too low based on one outstanding trait) can be a problem. New techniques include "360-degree" multisource measures and special rating scales.

Sexual Harassment

Sexual harassment: sexual advances, requests for sexual favors, and other unwelcome verbal or physical conduct of a sexual nature. Most sexual harassment is an assertion or abuse of power, not sexual desire. Victims often suffer financial losses and psychological difficulties.

Organizational Psychology

Organizational psychology studies how interpersonal relations affect productivity.

Managerial Style: Two Theories

Theory X: negative approach (believing employees dislike work, thus need close supervision and extrinsic rewards for motivation).

Theory Y: positive approach (believing employees like work and are self-motivated).

Theory Y managers often use **participative decision making**, such as **quality circles**—groups of employees who meet regularly with supervisors to solve problems.

Worker Motivation: Three Major Theories

Goal setting theory: setting specific and difficult goals improves performance.

Equity theory: workers are better motivated if they perceive a balance between their job inputs and their perceived rewards.

Expectancy theory: employees perform according to the likely outcomes, the desirability of those outcomes, and the effort needed to achieve them.

Job Satisfaction: Importance of Job Satisfaction

Employees have less stress, better physical health, improved quality and length of life.

Employers save money from lower absenteeism, less turnover, increased productivity.

According to **personality-job fit theory**, job satisfaction comes from a match (or "good-fit") between personality and occupation.

Applying Psychology in the Workplace

Have you heard the tale about the "Tragedy of the Commons?" Ecologist Garret Hardin (1968) used this metaphor to illustrate how individual interests often conflict with group goals. When individual selfishness is combined with limited resources, the results can be disastrous for the group. Hardin derived the name of the tale from the centrally located pasture areas in old English towns where villagers were free to graze one or two animals. If their animals grazed on their own private pastures, villagers knew that overgrazing would destroy the grass and starve the animals. On the "commons," however, they showed no such restraint. Because each individual herder reasoned that adding their one extra cow wouldn't make a difference, the lush, grassy area soon became a worthless mud field—hence the Tragedy of the Commons.

This tale has obvious parallels to modern problems like global pollution and the escalation of nuclear arms. But what does this metaphor say about the nature of conflict? Is it always about competing interests? Is it always destructive? Does the individual have to sacrifice his or her own interests to avoid conflict? What does the tragedy of the commons teach us about the behavior of people in groups, their motivations, and the way they communicate with each other?

In answer to these and other questions, this section begins with an in-depth look at leadership. We then explore the topics of dealing with workplace motivation, groups in organizations, the communication process, and dealing with conflict. Along the way, you will discover that although conflict can be quite destructive, it also can be resolved and may lead to productive change. You will also learn what makes a good leader, how do they motivate themselves and others? How does communication help or hurt them and their organizations?

MODULE 53
LEADERSHIP

What Is Leadership?

Over the years, leadership has been defined in many different ways. Even today there are no single, universally accepted definitions of the terms *leadership* and *leader*. Spector (2000) defines a leader as "the one who is in charge." Tom Peters (1985), a best-selling author on leadership in organizations, states that a leader is a "cheerleader, enthusiast, nurturer of champions, hero finder, wanderer, dramatist, coach, and facilitator." True leaders are all this and more. They are also the visionaries who challenge the ordinary, create the dreams, and chart the course that others will follow. For our purposes, leadership can be defined as the use of interpersonal influence to inspire or persuade individuals or groups to support the goals and perform the tasks desired by the leader.

Why Is Leadership Important?

The study of what makes people effective leaders is important for several reasons. Think about various courses and jobs you have had and the quality of the teachers and bosses you've worked for. Did you perform well for teachers and managers whom you perceived as insensitive, incompetent, and uncaring? Or did you work harder for leaders who inspired you, who set a good example and performed their jobs competently, who made you feel that you were important and that your efforts were sincerely appreciated? Did you work hardest for those who recognized and rewarded your efforts?

Obviously, effective leadership has an important impact on work and academic life, but it may have an even greater effect on politics and global economics. The laws passed by political leaders and representatives, and the policy decisions of corporate executives, have daily and life-altering effects on everyone under their control–just ask the cavalrymen who fought for General Custer, the Germans who lived under Adolf Hitler, or the employees of Enron.

Can you see why psychologists are interested in the scientific study of leadership? The question of what causes us to choose some people, and not others, as leaders is an important topic in psychology. We are also interested in how certain people emerge as leaders within peer groups. Why do some leaders abuse power while others use it altruistically? How is it that cult leaders like Jim Jones or David Koresh, or a political leader like Osama Bin Laden, can persuade followers to willingly go to their own doom or kill thousands of other innocent people?

Industrial/organizational psychologists are particularly interested in leadership in the workplace. The productivity of workers on the job is strongly affected by the quality of leadership in management. Managers who are effective leaders can inspire workers to go well beyond the minimal level of performance that they might otherwise achieve.

Worker productivity is often linked to morale, absenteeism, and employee turnover, which in turn are linked to corporate profits. In today's international economy, competition is intense. Even small differences in worker productivity and performance can have large impacts on a company's profitability. To the extent that leadership affects worker productivity, it is important to understand how effective leaders operate so that companies can train managers and employees to be better leaders.

Leaders and Managers

A question that has long been debated is whether *leaders* are similar to or different from *managers*. On a general level, Bennis and Nanus (1985) have stated that "Managers are people who do things right. Leaders are people who do the right things." More specifically, John Kotter (1990) has identified 5 important differences between leaders and managers:

1. Leadership is visionary, intuitive, and often based on the personal abilities of the individual leader, whereas management is more formal, rational, and scientific, and is more dependent on the system than on any one individual within the system.

2. Leaders create a vision for others to follow, and often do not get deeply involved in the mechanics of how it is implemented, whereas managers are primarily responsible for implementing the vision.

3. Leaders use a variety of persuasive techniques to motivate and inspire people and gain the cooperation of those who must implement their vision. Managers give orders to implement policy.

4. Leaders push people to change things and start in new, often unpredictable directions, whereas managers typically work to maintain order, stability, and predictability (the status quo).

5. Leaders transform their organizations, while managers keep theirs on established paths.

Other investigators have explored how managers and leaders are perceived. They have found that while leaders are typically perceived as visionary, independent, flexible, and creative, managers are perceived as analyzing, rational, authoritative, and problem solving. Whereas leaders are typically seen as inspiring, people-oriented communicators who take charge when the going gets tough, managers are typically viewed as task-oriented, "by-the-book" followers who do what they're told, implement the orders of others, and try not to "rock the boat" (Capowski, 1994, Fagliano, 1997).

These differences tend to be overstated. Good leaders must be good managers themselves in order to get the detailed work accomplished that is necessary to implement their vision, or they must be able to recognize, hire, and motivate good

---

LEADERSHIP SKILLS FOR THE TWENTY-FIRST CENTURY

LEADER AS LEARNER

Contrary to popular perception, leaders are not people who are always certain of themselves and their direction. Rather, leaders are people who are open-minded learners. What's more, they are not afraid to let others see them in this light. In fact, creating an environment in which learning and its natural byproduct, mistakes, are okay can be a potent tool to unite a group and inspire creativity, risk-taking, and effort.

Today those who practice leadership must be open to learning about their colleagues and followers. That includes their differences in personality and work styles, their lifestyle as it affects their effort, and the interplay of such factors as age, race, religion, sexual orientation, and gender. No one can be expected to grasp all the implications of such a wide range of differences, so leaders especially must show they are willing and able to learn. But interpersonal skills in understanding group members do not stop with the leader. The leader must promote such understanding among group members themselves, so they can empower each other and call forth and recognize each other's contributions.

managers to get the job done. While it is helpful if an inspiring leader is also a good manager, and vice versa, many leaders are not good managers. Similarly, many effective managers are not necessarily good leaders. What is crucial is for leaders to recognize their strengths and weaknesses and hire subordinates whose strengths complement theirs and compensate for their weaknesses. So a leader who is a great philosophical or entrepreneurial visionary, but who has no patience for the detailed daily work necessary to balance a company's books or fill customers' orders, needs to hire managers and accountants whose strengths are in those areas. Otherwise the company will quickly go bankrupt (DuBrin, 2001).

Are Leaders Born or Made?

What causes an individual to emerge as a leader? Is leadership an inborn quality or something that is learned as one grows up?

Charisma and the Great Person Theory. The **great person theory** argues that leaders are born, not made. It holds that people who become great leaders inherit certain personality traits, such as extraversion and charisma, that cause them to rise to top political, military, and business positions. These people are likely to become successful leaders no matter when they are born or what circumstances they are born into. Thus, Napoleon, Abraham Lincoln, Catherine the Great, or Ghandi would have emerged as great leaders regardless of the time, location, or circumstances of their birth.

Trait theorists have offered some support for this approach by identifying several traits that may be universally linked to successful leadership. Robert House, for example, has done extensive research on the affects of *charisma*, or "personal magnetism" on leadership effectiveness. He defines charismatic leaders as those who by the sheer force of their personal abilities are capable of having profound and extraordinary effects on their followers. These leaders are extremely confident and are convinced that their beliefs are morally right. They have excellent communication skills, but they also lead by example. They make it clear that they have high expectations of their followers and confidence in them, which, in turn, builds up their confidence and their desire to achieve the leader's goals. House conducted a study of American presidents that found significant links between charisma and presidential effectiveness.

Charisma is not always a positive quality. The difference between a Martin Luther King, Jr. and an Adolph Hitler is that charismatic leaders like King tend to use their abilities to selflessly empower others, whereas leaders like Hitler tend to use their abilities to selfishly empower themselves. Moreover, charisma alone does not necessarily translate into good leadership. An employee-centered outlook, a wide range of interests, a sense of humor, warmth, an internal locus of control, and good written and verbal communication skills all appear to play a role in effective leadership.

Situational Theories. **Situational theorists** argue that no single personality trait is universally desirable or effective. In their view, leaders are more the result of environmental influences that produce the characteristics necessary to succeed in a certain situation than the result of any particular inherited trait or quality. These approaches focus more on how leaders behave in specific circumstances rather than what they are like as human beings. They argue that in another time and place, Hitler might have spent his life as an unknown house painter rather than becoming a powerful political leader. Hitler's rise to power can be attributed to the interaction of his personal style with the uniquely chaotic social and economic situation that prevailed in Germany after World War I. In a more stable, wealthier, and happier Germany, Hitler would never have attracted the following that he gathered in the 1930s. Contingency, behavioral, and cognitive theories have generally offered support for this viewpoint.

Can you see how the contrast between the great person and situational theories is another example of the nature-nurture debate introduced at the beginning of this text? And here too, as you've seen before, powerful arguments can be made for both sides. However, the debate is important to us now because if leadership is the result of inborn abilities, there is little that can be done to train people who do not have the "proper" inherited qualities to be effective leaders. It becomes more important to identify what inherited traits make people effective leaders, so that one can find and hire people with those characteristics, than to waste time on leadership training programs that are doomed to fail. On the other hand, if leaders are the products of environmental influences, it becomes crucial to identify what environmental factors influence the development of the characteristics that are essential to leadership. We can then set up training programs to develop those qualities in managers or others who seek to become leaders.

Training Leaders

In recent years many researchers have examined the question of whether and how people can be trained to be effective leaders. What characteristics or behaviors would be the focus of such training? Conger and Kanungo (1988) have identified 5 "charismatic skills" that they believe are central to individual development in programs that train leaders. These skills are:

1. **Sensitivity** to the most appropriate contexts for charisma, with an emphasis on critical evaluation and problem detection.

2. **Visioning,** with an emphasis on creative thinking to learn and think about profound change.

TRY THIS
Yourself

Do you have what it takes to become a great leader? Researchers have identified several behaviors and characteristics that are generally found in successful leaders (Schermerhorn, Hunt, & Osborne, 2000). In the following list, place a check beside each trait that you believe you currently possess. Then place a star beside any attribute that you would think you could develop in the coming years:

1. **Energy:** physical vitality: Others have discussed this in terms of enthusiasm for one's work.

2. **Tolerance for stress, frustration, and uncertainty:** emotional resilience and the ability to adjust to unclear or changing situations over which you do not always have control.

3. **Prosocial power motivation:** A high need for power exercised primarily for the benefit of others.

4. **Achievement orientation:** Need for achievement, desire to excel, drive for success, willingness to assume responsibility, concern for task objectives.

5. **Emotional maturity:** Well-adjusted, does not suffer from sever psychological disorders.

6. **Self-confidence:** General confidence in self and in the ability to perform the job of a leader. Effective leaders like to lead; they do not shy away from leadership responsibilities because of fear of failure or embarrassing themselves.

7. **Integrity:** Behavior consistent with espoused values: honest, ethical, trustworthy.

8. **Perseverance or tenacity:** Ability to overcome obstacles; strength of will.

9. **Cognitive ability, intelligence, social intelligence:** Ability to gather, integrate, and interpret information; problem-solving ability; understanding of social setting.

10. **Task-relevant knowledge:** Knowledge about the company, the industry , and technical aspects of the company's activities.

11. **Flexibility:** Ability to respond appropriately to changes in setting.

THREE PERSPECTIVES OF LEADERSHIP

Several common themes emerge from an analysis of this chapter's three perspectives on leadership (servant, transformational, and critical models).

1. Leadership is a relationship, as opposed to the property of an individual.
It is conducted with leaders and followers, and followers are essential parts of the equation. The role of the leader is to serve followers and to empower them to become leaders themselves.

2. Leadership entails change.
Both leaders and followers experience change, originating within themselves and then emanating outward to the community. Leadership requires critical reflection and analysis in order to determine whether the vision of change being pursued is inclusive or whether it excludes or diminishes some members of the community.

3. Leadership can be done by anyone, not only those who are designated as leaders.
Alternative perspectives on leadership gained credence because they more fully captured some aspects of our experience with leadership than did the conventional view. Because the alternative perspectives raised questions that could not be addressed by the industrial paradigm of leadership, they prompted the search for a new paradigm of leadership for the twenty-first century.

3. **Communication,** with an emphasis on working with oral and written linguistic skills.

4. **Impression management,** with an emphasis on improving appearance, body language, and verbal communication skills.

5. **Empowering,** with an emphasis on communicating high performance expectations, improving participation in decision making, loosening upbureaucratic constraints, setting meaningful goals, and establishing appropriate reward systems.

Other leadership training programs have focused on similar skills, particularly helping leaders develop "vision," or "visionary behavior," and better communication and impression-management skills. These training programs tend to emphasize a "hands on" workshop type of approach so that leaders must actually use the skills in which they are being trained, rather than merely reading or hearing about them in a book or lecture (Schermerhorn, 2001). Overall, the research evidence indicates that people can be trained in at least some leadership skills, and in a manner that can have a direct and positive impact on the job.

Leadership Philosophies and Styles

Leaders use differing styles to motivate others. Some are much more "take charge" and controlling whereas others are more likely to "let things take care of themselves." Some prefer a "do it yourself" style, whereas others are much more willing to delegate authority. Often the style leaders use to manage others depends on their beliefs about the nature of the people they are leading.

Leadership Philosophies

Douglas McGregor (1960) identified two underlying leadership philosophies that determine leadership styles: **theory X** and **theory Y.**

Theory X is the "traditional" leadership philosophy, dating back to the beginning of the twentieth century. It is based on management philosophies that were current in an era when most workers were unskilled laborers. It assumes that workers are essentially lazy and unmotivated, work only because they have to, will do no more than what is absolutely required, and need direction and even coercion to be productive. In many ways this philosophy is a reflection of the union-management conflicts that were common at the time. While theory X assumptions will probably always be true of some workers, whether they were ever true of the majority of workers is debatable. Unfortunately, managers who use a theory X may create a self-fulfilling prophecy. Because they assume the worst of workers and treat them accordingly, they may create a punishing atmosphere in which workers do little more than they have to because there are no incentives to do more than the minimum necessary to avoid punishment.

Today's corporate managers are more likely to follow the assumptions of theory Y. This approach assumes that work is a natural function of living and that most people like work. If they are treated with dignity and respect, they will try their best to do the job right, seek achievement and responsibility, and be creative and imaginative. The efforts by many managers to empower employees are a reflection of the emergence of theory Y values as the dominant values among today's corporate leaders. Managers who employ theory Y policies often find that these policies, too, can create a self-fulfilling prophecy. When it is clear that leaders expect workers to perform their best, and reward them for trying, workers often do make greater efforts, which are more likely to lead to the desired outcomes.

In recent years a third management philosophy, **theory Z,** has emerged (Ouchi, 1981). Theory Z is in many ways an extension of theory Y. It also argues for the empowerment of workers by assuming that workers want to be part of the decision-making process whenever possible. They will worker harder and have better morale if they feel that they are being listened to and that their ideas are being acted upon. Theory Z philosophy is part of why Japanese managers often wear the same uniforms, eat in the same cafeterias, and have their offices on the same floor as their subordinates. This creates an atmosphere in which everyone feels like they are "part of the family" and working together toward the same goal, in contrast to the traditional adversarial atmosphere that has so often existed between workers and managers in American companies. Theory Z also assumes that workers are more effective if they have long-term job security and won't be laid off or fired during economic downturns. This is why many Japanese companies promise workers lifetime employment. In recent years, however, some companies have not been able to follow though on these commitments; moreover, a lifetime job may also mean limited upward job mobility (Rathus, 2002).

Leadership Styles

The behavior of leaders is often described as a continuum ranging from autocratic/authoritarian leaders on one end to laissez-faire/free-reign leaders on the other. Generally, leadership styles have been categorized into three types along this continuum: Autocratic leaders, participative leaders, and laissez-faire leaders, with autocratic and participative leaders being the dominant leadership styles in the United States today.

Autocratic leaders have also been called "dictatorial" or "authoritarian" leaders because they tend to take a top-down approach to leadership. They are more likely to have an "if you want it done right, do it yourself" philosophy, and therefore they are less likely to delegate authority to subordinates. They are more likely than other leaders to lean toward the theory X view of workers. They look for strict obedience and tend to be more task-oriented than people-oriented. While this type of leadership allows for rapid decision-making and can be useful in a crisis or in working with truly unmotivated, unskilled workers, it is limited by the quality and competence of the leader. Even the best leaders can't think of everything, and since autocrats rarely solicit or listen to feedback or suggestions from

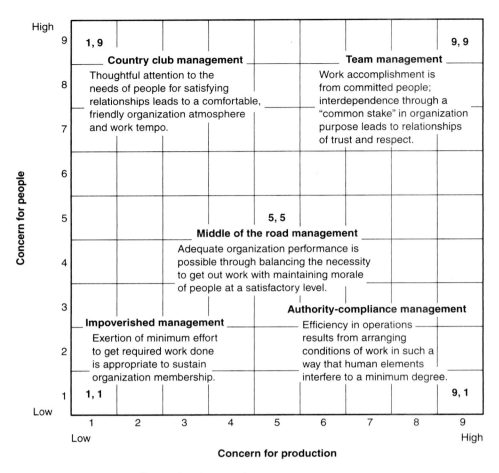

The Leadership Grid® Leadership Styles
Source: Leadership Dilemmas—Grid Solutions. p. 29, by Robert R. Blake, Ph.D. and Anne Adams McCanse. Copyright © 1991, by Robert R. Blake and the Estate of Jane S. Mouton, Austin, Texas. The Grid® designation is property of Scientific Methods, Inc. Gulf Publishing Company, Houston, Texas. Used with permission. All rights reserved.

subordinates, this type of leadership to some degree limits the pool of available ideas and can be abused by an autocratic leader who is selfish or corrupt. Finally, it can be demoralizing for intelligent, skilled, career-oriented workers who cannot grow and gain leadership experience in an "I'm not paying you to think" autocratic environment.

Participative leaders may actually use several somewhat different styles of leadership, with one common thread: they involve workers in the decision-making process. DuBrin (2001) discusses three subtypes of participative leaders: consultative leaders, consensus leaders, and democratic leaders. **Consultive leaders** will ask subordinates for input before making a decision, but retain the power to make the final decision by themselves. So while they will listen to the group, they are not bound to follow its suggestions. **Consensus leaders** seek input from all subordinates and try to reach a decision that is agreed to, at some level, by everyone. **Democratic leaders** delegate the final authority for making the decision to subordinates. They allow the group to discuss the issues and vote on them, and then they seek to do their best to implement the will of the majority.

Participative leaders tend to have a theory Y philosophy and use this approach to empower workers and make them feel valued. They tend to be more people-oriented than autocratic leaders, and they appreciate the ideas and opinions of their subordinates. This approach is generally viewed as more appropriate than the auto-cratic approach for most skilled, career-oriented workers, as it takes advantage of their training and expertise. As such, it is often the better approach with today's highly educated workers, who see the workplace not as "just a job" but as a source of growth and fulfillment.

Laissez-faire leaders prefer to let their subordinates manage themselves. They are likely to believe in a philosophy of hiring "the right people" and then trusting them to do the job right. They see themselves as facilitators whose pri-mary function is to coordinate the efforts of their subordinates rather than "man-age" them in the traditional sense of the word. This approach tends to be most effective with mature, professional, career-oriented workers who are highly disci-plined self-starters. The freedom of action they are granted under this approach can be highly motivating and can allow them to fully tap into their creativity and imagination to accomplish work-related goals. The major drawback of this approach is the potential for subordinates to abuse the freedom it offers them, which is why it is not usually the best approach to use with immature, unmoti-vated, or unskilled workers.

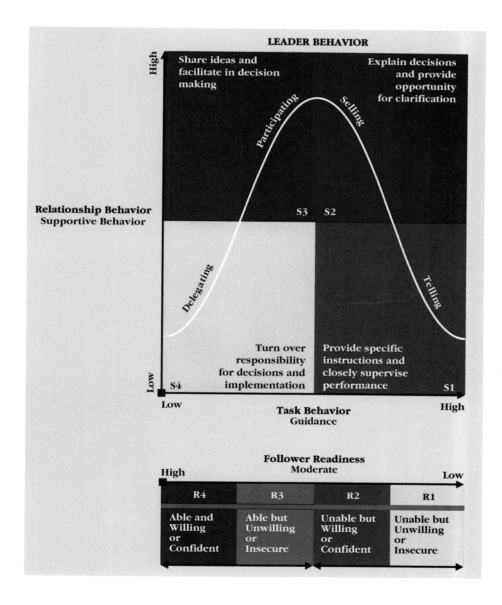

Hersey and Blanchard model of situational leadership.

Which Style of Leadership Is Best?

While most experts argue that the participative approach is most effective with most workers, there is no single approach that works well with all workers. Effective leaders and managers are flexible and may sometimes use all three approaches, depending on the situation and the particular subordinates with whom they are working.

Hershey and Blanchard's Situational Leadership Model. Hershey and Blanchard (1988) believe that the most appropriate style of leadership depends on the task and the readiness of the subordinate to follow the leader's directives. They argue that there is a preferred leadership style for each of four levels of follower readiness:

1. A "telling" style for followers who are low in readiness and either unable or unwilling to take responsibility for themselves. This is primarily an autocratic approach.

2. A "selling" style for followers who are low to moderate in readiness; this style combines direction with support for those who are unable to take responsibility yet willing to do so. This style thus combines elements of the participative and autocratic approaches.

3. A "participating" style for followers who are moderate to high in readiness and are able to take responsibility but unwilling to do so. This style focuses on offering support to enhance the follower's desire to perform the task. This is a classic participative approach.

4. A "delegating" style for followers who are high in readiness and both able and willing to perform the task. This is essentially a laissez-faire approach.

Leaders who use this or some other situational approach must have the perceptiveness and intellectual capacity to recognize the demands of the situation, the strengths and weaknesses of various employees, and the leadership style that is best suited for that particular combination of situation and employees.

Feidler's Cognitive Resource Theory. Fred Feidler argues that how directive, or autocratic, a leader should be depends on 4 situational contingencies:

1. The leader or subordinate group members' ability or competence.

2. The amount of stress experienced by the leader in the situation.

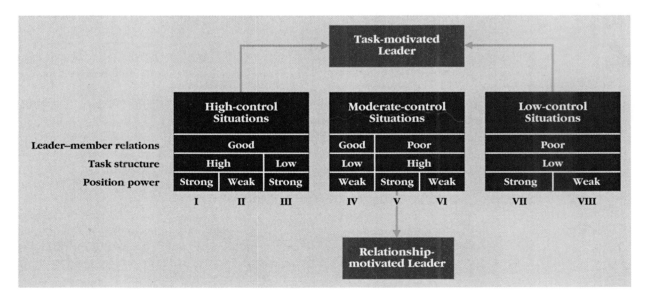

Predictions from Fiedler's contingency theory of leadership.

3. The leader and subordinates' levels of experience.

4. The level of subordinates' support for the leader.

A directive approach is most likely to be effective when the leader is competent, relaxed, and supported. A nondirective, or participative, approach is most likely to be effective when the leader is strongly supported by the group and the group members are highly skilled.

GENDER & CULTURAL DIVERSITY

Male/Female Differences in Leadership Styles

Do women differ significantly from men as leaders? There appears to be no simple answer to this question. Some researchers have concluded that they do, while others argue just as strongly that they do not. Historically, many people have accepted the common stereotypes in which men tend to use more autocratic, task-oriented, punishment-based management styles whereas women tend to use more participative, relationship-oriented, reward-based styles. However, these stereotypes are not consistently supported by research evidence. Some field studies have found men to be more autocratic and women more democratic in their management styles. Bass (1990) reported that women are more likely than men to be seen as charismatic and to combine criticism with constructive feedback. Rosener (1990), examining self-reports of male and female managers, found that men were more likely to use an autocratic, "take charge" style of leadership whereas women were more likely to emphasize interpersonal and communication skills. A meta-analysis by Eagly and Johnson (1990) found that in laboratory studies, men were rated higher in structure and women higher in consideration. However, field studies that evaluated actual leaders found no such differences. The researchers speculated that while women may be inclined to use a different supervision style than men, organizational settings do not allow them to do so. So in organizational settings women adopt leadership styles quite similar to those used by men.

What do these two women have in common? They were both leaders of their countries. Although the United States has never had a woman as president, other countries have had female leaders. Both Golda Meir of Israel (left) and Margaret Thatcher of the United Kingdom (right) were prime ministers of their countries.

Gur and Gur (in Schrage, 1999) have argued that biological differences between men and women lead to differing leadership styles. They reported that women are better than men at recognizing emotional cues, such as those expressed in nonverbal behavior, and subtleties in verbal communication. Thus, they are better at recognizing the feelings that underlie comments made by others and therefore are better able to relate to people and respond appropriately to their concerns.

Jan Grant's (1988) and Bernard Bass's (1990) reviews of the literature found no significant differences between the management styles of male and female managers. Whatever differences existed dwindled as the level of management increased. Several researchers have noted that as women move up the corporate ladder they increasingly use management styles that are stereotypically "male." Also, it is important to note that within-group differences in management style among men and women are substantially greater than between-group differences. So while there seem to be some male-female differences in leadership style, they are probably not as great as some have argued, and they become less noticeable at higher levels of management.

Leadership and Power

Why do some leaders seem especially powerful and able to overcome oppositions of all kinds? Many investigators have attempted to identify various sources of leader power and to explain how a leader's use of power affects subordinates. French and Raven (1959) identified 5 bases of leader power: legitimate, expert, referent, reward, and coercive. Let's examine each of these in detail.

1. **Legitimate power** is the power that comes with a job title or position. It is derived from the authority that accompanies a specific job title and the belief by subordinates they have a duty to obey the directives of someone with that title. Legitimate power is valid only to the degree to which employees respect the job title, accept the authority that comes with it, and fear some form of punishment if they fail to obey the leader's directives. As such, it can be nonexistent if subordinates do not respect the leader's authority or do not fear the consequences of failing to follow the leader's directives.

2. **Expert power** is the power a leader has because of his or her experience and expertise. People who are recognized as experts in an area that is crucial to a company's functioning may wield far more power than the legitimate power that comes with their job title. Many managers have learned, to their dismay, how much "expert" a secretary or administrative assistant has when he or she isn't there to keep everything running smoothly. It is not uncommon for these people to become "gatekeepers" who effectively control access to the manager and actually run the office. In many offices it is a standing joke that the most powerful person in the organization is the copy-machine repair person. This type of power is difficult to maintain in today's rapidly changing work environment because it requires constant updating to stay current and remain an expert, especially in technology-based companies.

3. Referent power is the power leaders attain from the strength of their personality and their interpersonal skills. Charisma is one type of referent power. Referent power typically depends on how much subordinates like the supervisor. Taking the time to develop close, supportive personal relationships with subordinates increases referent power, as does raising the status of the supervisor. This type of power can build powerful personal loyalty among subordinates, with the result that they will obey orders from the supervisor that they would never obey from anyone else. As such, this power can be easily abused by leaders who choose to take advantage of it or use it selfishly.

4. **Reward power** is the power leaders have to give rewards, such as promotions, pay raises, bonuses, and the like for compliance with their directives. This power typically increases as a leader's legitimate power increases. For example, an executive vice-president typically has more reward power than a low-level supervisor. While reward power can be very effective if it is used properly, if it is used inappropriately it can be perceived as bribery and lose its effectiveness.

5. **Coercive power** is the power to use punishment, or the threat of it, to shape the behavior of subordinates. It involves the use of disciplinary actions, fines, salary reductions, suspension, or even firing. Like other forms of   punishment, it is best used selectively and as a last resort. While coercive power can be an effective short-term measure to stop unacceptable behavior among subordinates, overreliance on it usually leads to resentment and lowers morale. Eventually it can be perceived as abusive, which leads to counterproductive employee behaviors, revenge, and higher employee turnover.

None of these types of power is inherently the best or the worst. Effective leaders use all five types of power, and each can be effective if used properly. Conversely, each can be counterproductive if used improperly. The key is knowing when and where each type is appropriate and likely to be most effective.

In summary, leadership is a complex issue involving a wide variety of factors. While certain personal characteristics may make it easier for some people to be effective leaders than others, situational factors, and the ability of the leader to accurately "read," understand, and adjust to those factors, are probably more important in most circumstances. There are many different leadership styles, and no one style works best with all subordinates, although participative styles tend to work better with most subordinates. There are also many different types of power that leaders can use to accomplish their goals, but as with leadership styles, the type of power that works best varies according to the individual subordinate and the demands of the situation. Researchers have not found consistent and significant differences between the management styles of men and women.

FIVE CHARISMATIC SKILLS

- Sensitivity to most appropriate contexts for charisma—Emphasis on critical evaluation and problem detection
- Visioning—Emphasis on creative thinking to learn and think about profound change
- Communication—Working with oral and written linguistic aspects
- Impression management—Emphasis on modeling, appearance, body language, and verbal skills
- Empowering—Emphasis on communicating high performance expectations, improving participation in decision making, loosening up bureaucratic constraints, setting meaningful goals, and establishing appropriate reward systems

---

Check & Review

LEADERSHIP

Leadership is the use of interpersonal influence to inspire or persuade individuals or groups to support the goals of and perform the tasks desired by the leader. To be effective, good leaders must also be good managers, but not all leaders are good managers or vice-versa. Leadership appears to involve a combination of inborn traits, and situational factors. Overall, the research evidence indicates that at least some leadership skills can be trained, and in a manner that can have a direct and positive impact on the job.

Researchers have identified three leadership philosophies and three fundamental styles used by leaders to motivate others.

No single style or philosophy is appropriate for all workers. However, the participative approach appears to be the most effective with most workers. There are five types of leader power. Each is effective when used appropriately, but can be counterproductive when used improperly.

Questions

1. Briefly explain five ways in which leaders differ from managers.
2. Identify the 5 "charismatic skills" named by Conger and Kanungo that they believe are central to individual development in programs that train leaders

3. _____ is the classic management theory, which assumes that workers are lazy and unmotivated and need direction from the top to be productive. _____ assumes that workers want to do a good job, and will be most productive when treated with dignity and respect. _____ focuses on workers' desires to be included in decision-making and for long-term job security.

4. _____ leaders take a "top-down" approach to management. _____ leaders involve workers in the decision-making process in a variety of ways. _____ leaders take a hands-off approach to leadership.

REFERENCES

Bass, B. *Bass & Stogdill's Handbook of Leadership: Theory, Research, & Managerial Applications (3rd Ed.)*, New York: The Free Press, 1990

Bennis, Warren, & Nanus, Burt. *"Leaders, The Strategies of Taking Charge."* Executive Summary, *Vol. 1, No. 4, June 1985, p. 2.*

Capowski, Genevieve, *"Anatomy of a Leader: Where Are the Leaders of Tomorrow?"* Management Review, *March 1994, p. 12.*

Conger, J., & Kanungo, R., *Charismatic Leadership: The Elusive Factor in Organizational Effectiveness*. San Fransisco: Jossey-Bass, 1988.

DuBrin, Andrew J., *Leadership: Research Findings, Practice, and Skills (3rd Ed.)*. New York: Houghton-Mifflin, 2001

Fagliano, David, *"Managers versus Leaders: A Corporate Fable."* Management Review, *November 1997, p. 5.*

Feidler, F., & Garcia, J. *New Approaches to Effective Leadership*, New York: Wiley & Sons, 1987.

French, J. R. P. Jr., & Raven, B. in Cartwright (Ed.), *Studies in Social Power*, Ann Arbor, Michigan: Institute for Social Research, 1959, pp. 150–167.

Grant, J. *"Women as Managers: What Can They Offer Organizations?"* Organizational Dynamics, Winter, 1988.

Hershey, P., & Blanchard, K. *Management of Organizational Behavior*. Englewood Cliffs, N. J.: Prentice Hall, 1988.

House, R. J., Spangler, W. D., & Woycke, J., *"Personality and Charisma in the U. S. Presidency,"* Administrative Science Quarterly, *Vol. 36 (1991), pp. 394–396.*

Kotter, John , *A Force for Change: How Leadership Differs from Management*. New York: The Free Press, 1990).

McGregor, D. M. *The Human Side of Enterprise*. New York: McGraw-Hill, 1960.

Ouchi, W. G. *Theory Z*. New York: Avon, 1981.

Peters, T., & Austin N. *A Passion for Excellence: The Leadership Difference*. New York: Random House, 1985, p. 256.

Rathus, S. & Nevid J. *Psychology and the Challenges of Life(8th Ed.)*. New York: John Wiley & Sons, 2002.

Schermerhorn, J., Hunt, J., & Osborn, R. *Organizational Behavior (7th Ed.)*. New York: John Wiley & Sons, 2000.

Schrage, M. *"Why Can't a Woman Be More Like a Man?"* Fortune, August 16, 1999, p. 184.

Spector, P. *Industrial and Organizational Psychology(2nd Ed.)*. New York: John Wiley & Sons, 2000.

MODULE 54
MOTIVATION IN THE WORKPLACE

What is Motivation?

Motivation refers to the process of activating, maintaining, and directing behavior toward a particular goal. In the workplace, motivation is important because it affects employees' focus, consistency, and level of effort—which obviously is crucial in today's highly competitive global economy.

But how do you motivate employees? We've all heard the old saying, "You can lead a horse to water, but you can't make 'em drink." This technically may be true, as all motivation ultimately comes from within—you can always choose *not* to respond to other people's efforts to motivate you. However, psychologists who study motivation have identified specific types of circumstances that tend to be motivating to most people most of the time, as well as types of situations that are highly stressful and unmotivating to most people. Clearly, it is important for managers and supervisors to recognize factors that tend to enhance or reduce motivation so that they can create work environments that have the greatest chance of maximizing worker performance and satisfaction.

Theories of workplace motivation can be divided into three broad categories: *reinforcement theories, content theories,* and *process theories.* In this module we will examine each of these groups of theories in detail. Before we begin, try the following exercise.

TRY THIS
Yourself

You may dream of becoming an influential business owner someday. How will you identify (and reward) workers who are highly motivated and change those who are not?

A first step is to note that the definition of motivation given earlier includes *inferred* forces within individuals that push them to behave in certain ways. Because motivation comes from within, it cannot be directly measured. We can never know for sure how motivated someone is, but we can *infer* it by observing how she or he behaves.

To improve your future skills as an employer, start by observing your present behavior as a student.

- Examine how you behave in a course when the subject really interests you and, because of your interest, you are motivated to learn more about it.

- Compare that behavior to your behavior in a course in which you have little or no interest in the subject and, hence, little motivation. What's different?

- What do you do in the first course that you do not do in the course in which you are unmotivated? How much effort and time do you spend on each? How often do you attend each? How many questions do you ask about the material you are learning in each course?

Did you notice that your differing levels of motivation were directly reflected in your behavior? Usually, when you are motivated you will attend class more regularly, do more "extra" activities, and put in more time and effort than when you are not motivated. Not surprisingly, you generally have an easier time getting good grades in the courses in which you feel highly motivated.

In the workplace, managers and supervisor infer worker motivation in the same way. So, rightly or wrongly, you are much more likely to be judged by your observable efforts than your underlying motivations. Knowing this, you can use your observations of your student behavior to improve your relationships with your current teachers and supervisors. (Don't try to use this information to create the impression of motivation when you are not really motivated. Most astute teachers and bosses recognize "kissing up" when they see it!)

Classical Conditioning	Stimulus		Behavior
Learning occurs through conditioned stimuli	A person: sees the boss smile and hears boss's criticisms	→	feels nervous grits teeth
	and later: sees the smile	→	feels nervous grits teeth

Operant Conditioning	Behavior		Consequence
Learning occurs through consequences of behavior	A person: works overtime	→	gets boss's praise
	and later: works overtime again		

Differences between classical and operant conditioning approaches.

Reinforcement Theories: Using Conditioning to Increase Worker Motivation

Reinforcement theories of motivation are based on the principles of *operant conditioning*, in which behavior is manipulated by controlling its consequences. As discussed in Module 16, a fundamental principle of operant conditioning is the *law of effect*, which states that behavior that results in pleasant consequences is more likely to be repeated and will increase in frequency. Conversely, behavior that results in unpleasant consequences is less likely to be repeated and will decrease in frequency or disappear (Thorndike, 1911).

In the workplace, the systematic reinforcement of desirable work behavior and the nonreinforcement, or punishment, of undesired work behavior is known as organizational behavior modification, or OB mod (Schermerhorn, 2000). In this section we will briefly review the major terms and key concepts of operant conditioning and discuss how OB mod programs have used these principles to help motivate employees and improve productivity and worker satisfaction.

Positive Reinforcement

As you may remember from Module 16, positive reinforcement is defined as "adding or presenting a stimulus that increases the likelihood of that response occurring again." In everyday practice, positive reinforcement frequently involves the use of *rewards* to increase desired behaviors. People often use the terms *reward* and *reinforcement* as if they were interchangeable, but this is not always true. A reward is a pleasant consequence for a behavior. A reinforcer is *anything* that increases the frequency of a desired behavior. To the extent that a reward increases the frequency of a desired behavior, it is also a reinforcer. But a reward does not always increase the frequency of the desired behavior.

© 1997 United Feature Syndicate, Inc.

Contrived Rewards: Some Direct Cost		Natural Rewards: No Direct Cost	
refreshments	promotion	smiles	recognition
piped-in music	trips	greetings	feedback
nice offices	company car	compliments	asking advice
cash bonuses	paid insurance	special jobs	
merit pay increases	stock options		
profit-sharing	gifts		
office parties	sport tickets		

A sample of extrinsic rewards allocated by managers.

For example, you can give a worker a pay raise as a reward for superior work behavior. Although the increase in pay may make the employee feel good, it does not guarantee that the employee's desired work behavior will increase in frequency. If the behavior does not become more frequent, the reward is not a reinforcer. Conversely, a reinforcer does not necessarily have to be something pleasant. A parent who spanks a child for misbehavior may see the spanking as punishment, hoping that it will decrease the frequency of the undesired behavior. But if the child is starved for attention, and the spanking becomes a source of attention—albeit painful attention—the child may engage in the undesired behavior *more* frequently as a means of getting attention. Ironically, the spanking has now become a reinforcer because it has increased the frequency of the unwanted behavior.

Not all rewards work equally well as positive reinforcers. Researchers have identified two major classes of workplace rewards: extrinsic rewards and intrinsic rewards. Generally, intrinsic rewards are more effective in producing long-term behavior change than extrinsic rewards. These are discussed more fully in Module 31.

> **WORK GUIDELINES FOR ALLOCATING EXTRINSIC REWARDS**
>
> 1. Clearly identify the desired behaviors.
> 2. Maintain an inventory of rewards that have the potential to serve as positive reinforcers.
> 3. Recognize individual differences in the rewards that will have positive value for each person.
> 4. Let each person know exactly what must be done to receive a desirable reward. Set clear target antecedents and give performance feedback.
> 5. Allocate rewards contingently and immediately upon the appearance of the desired behaviors.
> 6. Allocate rewards wisely in terms of scheduling the delivery of positive reinforcement.

Negative Reinforcement

Negative reinforcement involves "taking away or removing a stimulus that increases the likelihood of that response occurring again." It is often called *avoidance learning* because the person is motivated to *avoid* painful consequences by performing a specific behavior. Phobias (extreme, irrational fears) are often difficult to eliminate because the affected individual tends to *avoid* the object of his or her phobia. Such avoidance negatively reinforces the avoidance behavior. If you have a snake phobia, for example, even the thought of confronting a snake can arouse anxiety. Deliberately avoiding an encounter with a snake, such as walking away from the reptile house at the zoo rather than going into it, lowers that anxiety, thereby negatively reinforcing the avoidance behavior.

Studying for a test also can involve negative reinforcement. Ideally, grades are given as a form of positive reinforcement – you study for a test in the hopes of getting an A on the test, and the A serves as a reward, promoting further studying. What if you repeatedly study and still barely pass the test? After a while you may give up hope of ever getting an A, in which case the hope of getting an A can no longer serve as a positive reinforcer. But do you stop studying completely? Usually not. Why? Because you want to *avoid* failing the course. Your studying is a form of negative reinforcement. (As a critical thinker, can you see that most students study because it is both positively and negatively reinforcing? They want the A, *and* they want to *avoid* failure.)

Although negative reinforcement can be a very effective form of *avoidance learning*, as in the case of phobias, in the workplace it tends to be less effective than positive reinforcement. There are several reasons for this.

1. Negative reinforcement often produces only short-term changes in behavior. Imagine a supervisor (or parent) who constantly nags you to do something. How often will you respond to the nagging if that person is not directly observing you? Most workers will stop engaging in the behavior as soon as the nagging supervisor goes away, and will resume the behavior only when the person returns. Similarly, someone whose primary motivation to study is avoidance of low grades will put off studying until a test is imminent.

2. Negative reinforcement typically produces a consistent, but *minimal,* pattern of behavior. If you nag someone to do something, they may do just enough of it to keep you from nagging them, but typically will do no more than is absolutely necessary to get you to leave them alone. The student who studies in order to avoid failing will study no more than is necessary to pass the test.

3. Constant use of negative reinforcement can sometimes have unwanted effects such as sabotage or revenge. People obviously don't like being nagged all the time. In such a situation they may deliberately sabotage the behavior they are being nagged to perform. They seem to be saying, "If you're going to nag me all the time, I'll do what you want, but I'll deliberately do it so poorly that you'll wish you had done it yourself or that you'd left me alone." This is a form of "getting even." There are numerous reported cases of employees sabotaging products in the workplace as a way of getting even with managers who constantly nag them. Therefore, negative reinforcement is best used selectively, when positive reinforcement is not possible or has not worked, rather than as the primary method of changing behavior.

Punishment

Most OB mod programs focus on the use of reinforcement (both positive and negative) whenever possible because researchers have found that it generally has the greatest long-term effects with the fewest unwanted effects. They have found that while punishment may temporarily stop the undesired behavior, it often results in unwanted effects that can be as problematic as the undesired behavior itself (Larzelere & Johnson, 2000; MacMillan, 2000). Also, because people tend to punish when they are frustrated or angry, they often punish impulsively and in ways that make the punishment ineffective or that produce anger and resentment in those being punished (Chance, 1988; Skinner, 1953).

In spite of its problems, punishment can be appropriate in some situations. It is the only operant-conditioning strategy designed to decrease or eliminate behavior. In the workplace, researchers have found that appropriate punishment for poor performance can enhance worker performance without significantly reducing worker satisfaction. However, if the punishment is perceived to be capricious or arbitrary, it can significantly lower morale, worker satisfaction, and performance (Korukunda & Hunt, 1989). In this case, the effects of punishment may be neutralized by support from other workers. Such support can be reinforcing enough that the employee will tolerate the punishment and continue to engage in the undesired behavior (Schermerhorn, 2000).

For these reasons, most OB mod programs focus on the use of positive reinforcement to shape behavior, and most researchers advocate using punishment with caution and as a last resort rather than as the primary method for changing behavior. Most critics of punishment admit that it is sometimes necessary and that the threat of punishment can be a powerful deterrent to unwanted behavior. However, they note that when punishment is used, it is more effective when it is accompanied by reasoned explanations for the punishment and positive reinforcement for engaging in more desirable behaviors (Larzelere et al., 1996). When administered appropriately, it can be a decisive intervention that will stop unwanted behavior, at least in the short term.

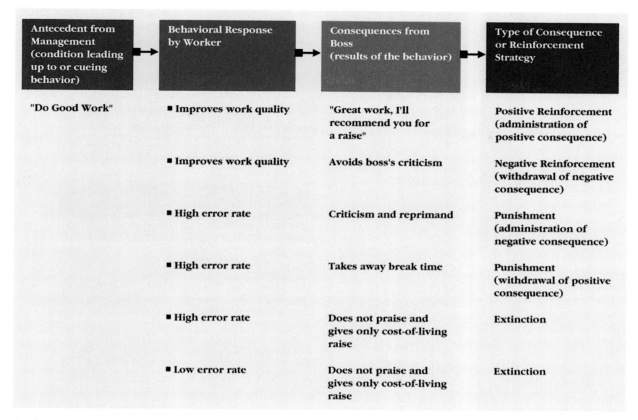

Antecedent from Management (condition leading up to or cueing behavior)	Behavioral Response by Worker	Consequences from Boss (results of the behavior)	Type of Consequence or Reinforcement Strategy
"Do Good Work"	▪ Improves work quality	"Great work, I'll recommend you for a raise"	Positive Reinforcement (administration of positive consequence)
	▪ Improves work quality	Avoids boss's criticism	Negative Reinforcement (withdrawal of negative consequence)
	▪ High error rate	Criticism and reprimand	Punishment (administration of negative consequence)
	▪ High error rate	Takes away break time	Punishment (withdrawal of positive consequence)
	▪ High error rate	Does not praise and gives only cost-of-living raise	Extinction
	▪ Low error rate	Does not praise and gives only cost-of-living raise	Extinction

Applying Reinforcement strategies.

Content Theories: Looking "Inside" to Increase Worker Motivation

Content theories of motivation suggest that people are motivated to engage in the behaviors that best satisfy their physical and psychological needs. If certain behaviors are required for a person's needs to be met, he or she is more likely to engage in those behaviors. In this section we will examine three major content theories: Maslow's hierarchy of needs, Herzberg's two-factor theory, and Holland's personality-job fit theory.

Maslow's Hierarchy of Needs

A classic content theory of motivation is Maslow's *hierarchy of needs* theory (see Module 31). Maslow argued that people have five distinct levels of needs, ranging from basic physiological needs at the bottom to higher-order psychological needs at the top. These needs are ranked in a hierarchy (often pictured as a pyramid). From bottom to top, the levels are physiological/survival needs, safety needs, belonging and love needs, esteem needs, and self-actualization needs.

People are motivated to satisfy the lower-order physiological and safety needs before satisfying higher-level needs. For example, you may have psychological needs to be popular and successful, but those needs will probably be set aside if you are starving to death. Your need for physical survival will be your first priority. Only when you have satisfied your basic survival needs will you begin focusing on safety, and only when you feel safe will you focus on higher-order needs such as belonging, esteem, or self-actualization.

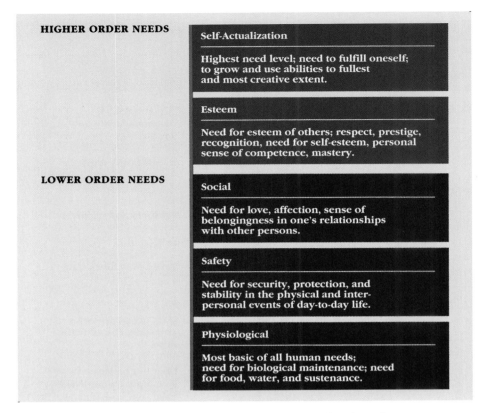

Higher order and lower order needs in Maslow's hierarchy of needs.

In the workplace, Maslow's theory has been very popular for years, largely because its straightforward five-step approach is easily understood and appears simple to implement. Unfortunately, research evidence has failed to support the existence of a rigid, five-level hierarchy of needs. To the extent that different levels of needs exist, they probably operate in a much more flexible manner than the rigid bottom-to-top model suggested by Maslow (Schermerhorn, 2000). Different people may be motivated by different things at different times. Moreover, while people may have a hierarchy of needs, there is no research evidence to support the notion that it is the same for each individual. For some people, esteem needs may be more important than belonging and love needs. Which needs are most important to an individual may also change from one day to another, and not necessarily in the manner predicted by Maslow. Porter (1963) reported evidence that as employees move up the corporate ladder, higher-order needs tend to become more important than lower-order needs. But research evidence does not support the notion that satisfying safety needs, for example, lessens their importance and increases the importance of belongingness and love needs (Hall & Nougaim, 1968). There is also evidence that levels of needs may not be consistent across cultures. In other words, what is highly valued by individuals in one culture may not be equally valued and would not show up in the same place on Maslow's hierarchy in other cultures (Lawler & Shuttle, 1973; Wahba & Bridwell, 1974).

While Maslow's theory may suffer from inflexibility, it is still useful in that it has made people aware of the fact that individuals differ in their needs and may have different needs at different times and at different points in their lives. To the extent that it is used as a "canned" approach that treats all employees as having similar needs, it will probably fail. However, to the extent that it motivates managers to try to learn the unique and specific needs of individual employees, it can still be helpful.

Herzberg's Two-Factor Theory

Frederick Herzberg began conducting studies of workers in the late 1950s. The results convinced him that motivation does not develop along a hierarchy or continuum as suggested by Maslow. In his view, work motivation results from the nature of the job itself, not from the conditions in which employees operate or from external rewards and punishments. Herzberg's theory of work motivation is known as the two-factor theory or the motivator-hygiene theory. In it, Herzberg identified two broad categories of needs, which he called *hygiene factors* and *motivator factors* (Herzberg, 1967, 1968).

Hygiene factors are sources of job dissatisfaction. Their presence does not satisfy or motivate people; it only prevents dissatisfaction. Their absence, on the other hand, can be a powerful source of dissatisfaction. Hygiene factors are more closely connected to the conditions in which people work than to the job itself. They include things such as salary; quality of supervision; relationships with coworkers, supervisors, and subordinates; having proper equipment and support to do the job; security; and organizational policies. **Motivator factors** are related to what people do on the job itself. Their presence increases job satisfaction. Their absence does not lead to dissatisfaction but to lack of satisfaction. They include achievement, recognition, responsibility, growth potential, and the nature of the work itself.

In Herzberg's theory, hygiene factors and motivator factors are independent dimensions. So changing the levels of one does not affect levels of the other. According to Herzberg, to be fully motivated, employees must have both hygiene and motivator factors.

Herzberg's theory is controversial on several levels. First, many critics contend that money is a motivator, not a hygiene factor. Herzberg's research convinced him that while low pay causes dissatisfaction, higher pay by itself does not improve satisfaction or motivate people. Others have argued that this varies from one individual to another, that under many circumstances money is a powerful motivator, and that Herzberg's research methods were flawed (Luthans, 1992). Second, others have charged that the theory is too inflexible to account for individual, professional, or

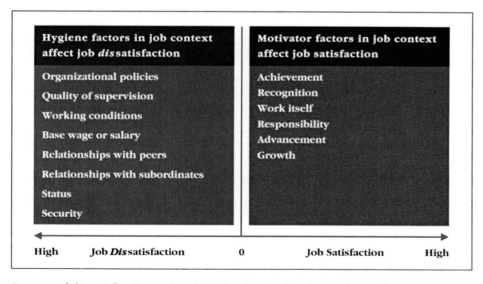

Sources of dissatisfaction and satisfaction in Herzberg's two-factor theory.

cultural differences among workers (House & Wigdor, 1967). Finally, critics contend that Herzberg's theory has not been supported by research and that most researchers consider it to be invalid (Locke & Henne, 1986).

Despite these criticisms, Herzberg's theory remains influential. His argument that "If you want people to do a good job, give them a good job to do" (Herzberg, 1968) has led researchers to focus on how best to provide meaningful work and has led to the development of job enrichment programs in many organizations (Spector, 2000).

Holland's Personality Job-Fit Theory

Have you ever worked at a job that you eventually left because it wasn't "right" for you? Even though you had the technical ability to do the work, you weren't comfortable because the people around you and the nature of the job didn't blend well with your personal style. John Holland (1997) would likely argue that you were in a fairly common situation and it was probably smart of you to leave. He believes that people are most satisfied and motivated if they are working at jobs whose demands are closely matched to their personality. On the basis of his research, he has identified six personality types and six matching work environments: realistic, investigative, artistic, social, enterprising, and conventional (see Module 56 for a full description of each).

According to Holland, few individuals are characterized by only one personality type. Each of us has different levels of each type. The two or three types in which we are highest are likely to be the best predictors of the career areas in which we will be most content. Some personality combinations lend themselves more easily to finding a satisfying career area than others. For example, someone who is high in the artistic and conventional personality types is likely to have more difficulty finding a job that satisfies both sets of needs than someone who is highest in the realistic and investigative types.

This is because there are many jobs that provide both physical and mental challenges and allow people to work with both their hands and their minds. There are far fewer jobs that provide both a structured, detailed oriented environment and a spontaneous, unstructured, highly creative environment. So for someone who is both artistic and conventional the solution may be to find a job that meets one set of needs and to satisfy the other needs through hobbies or other outside activities. Research findings have provided fairly strong support for Holland's approach.

Content theories have been criticized as simplistic and too rigid in their approach to motivation and worker satisfaction. Their apparent simplicity often leads to overconfidence on the part of supervisors, who then misapply them in the workplace. Since the theories do not directly link specific needs to motivated behavior, they must be interpreted by supervisors, and this can be challenging. Motivation is much more subtle and complex than any one of these theories implies. Overly simple interpretation and application of these theories can cause supervisors to assume that they know the needs of their subordinates, creating needless problems. Therefore, while useful, these theories must be applied flexibly and with some caution (Schermerhorn, 2000).

GENDER & CULTURAL DIVERSITY

Why Does a Woman Work?

(by Spencer Rathus and Jeffrey Nevid)

Sigmund Freud posed the famous question: What does a woman want? The question is "cute," but naively condescending. Guess what, Siggie, women are people, so the question should be "What do people want?" Answer that one and we'll give you a new cigar.

In more recent years, the question has been posed "Why do women work?" What are the possible answers? So that the family can afford a second car? So that the family can go on a vacation? To send the kids off to camp in the summer? Not according to a poll by Louis Harris and Associates (cited in Lewin, 1995a). These stereotypes are long outdated. Women no longer work to provide the family with a supplemental income. Women, like men, work to support the family. Or put it this way: Those who pose the second question – "Why do women work?" – are as naively condescending as Freud was. Women are people, and the proper question is: Why do people work?"

Perhaps we are more familiar with the high-powered mothers like Jane Pauley, Michelle Pfeiffer, even Hillary Rodham Clinton. These women either outearn their husbands or support their children on their own. But out of the spotlight the earning power of ordinary women has been growing by leaps and bounds. According to the Harris Poll, wives share about equally with their husbands in supporting their families. Nearly half of them—48%— reported that they provided at least half of their family's income. We're not talking vacation money here. We mean half of the mortgage, half of the clothing, half of the medical bills, even half of the new pairs of Nikes and the mountain bikes (Lewin, 1995a).

So why do most of us still think of women as primarily mothers. Why haven't we paid more attention to their new role as providers? Perhaps it is because working mothers continue to do what mothers were doing before they became such a, well, force in the workforce. That is, 9 of 10 working mothers still bear the primary responsibility for the children, the cooking, and the cleaning (Lewin, 1995a).

Are these mothers overburdened? Perhaps. The Harris survey found that working mothers are pressed for time. They are worried about not having enough time with their families and about balancing the demands of a work and a home life. Nevertheless, when they were asked whether they would like to surrender some of their responsiblities, 53% of working women said no. Even more ironic, full-time working mothers reported that they felt more likely to feel valued for their contributions at home than full-time homemakers were.

Despite their new earning power, working mothers are still primarily concerned about their children. When they were asked what made them feel successful at home, about one man and woman in four mentioned good relationships and spending time together. The next largest group of women (22%) reported good, well-adjusted, healthy children. But 20% of men mentioned money, or being able to afford things. Only 8% of men mentioned well-adjusted kids. Just 5% of the women mentioned money.

So mom is still "traditional"— if by tradition we mean doing what mom has been expected to do. She is still looking after the house and kids. But now she also pays half the bills.

Process Theories: What's the "Thinking" Behind Worker Motivation

Process theories examine the thought processes behind motivation. They are interested in *how* employees are motivated rather than in *what* specific needs motivate them. We will examine 4 well-known process theories: Vroom's expectancy theory, equity theory, self-efficacy theory, and goal-setting theory.

Victor Vroom's (1964) **expectancy theory** is the best known of the process theories. Vroom suggests that motivation results from a rational process that can be boiled down to a simple mathematical formula. He argues that workers make choices about how much effort they will give to a task based on a combination of self-confidence, trust that they will be rewarded, and desire for the reward. His theory is a useful way to predict when and why reinforcements will work to motivate people (Spector, 2001).

Key terms and managerial implications of Vroom's expectancy theory.

According to Vroom, motivation is affected by 3 conditions:

1. **Expectancy (self-confidence)**: the extent to which you believe that your efforts will attain an acceptable level of performance. In other words, your confidence in your ability to succeed at the required task. "Can I do it?"

2. **Instrumentality (trust)**: your belief that your efforts will be appropriately rewarded if you succeed at the desired task. "Will they really reward me as promised if I succeed?" or "Can I trust them?"

3. **Valence (desire)**: your belief that the rewards being offered are desirable and worth the effort necessary to achieve them. "Do I want what they're offering me to do this?"

Using these three concepts, Vroom argues that motivation is the result of expectancy times instrumentality times valence, or $M = E \times I \times V$. It is important to note that Vroom uses multiplication to link these concepts, not addition. What this implies is that if any of the three factors is zero, overall motivation will be zero even if the other two factors are very high. For example, you may be 100% confident that you can succeed at a task. You may also be 100% confident that your supervisor will reward you as promised if you succeed. But if you have no interest (valence) at all in the reward being offered, your motivation to complete the task will be zero until some alternative reward is made available. Similarly, you may want the reward being offered and know that you will get it if you succeed, but if you have no self-confidence (expectancy), your motivation will still be zero. (Perhaps include here Table 8.1 from Spector, page 183) While there have been many variations of Vroom's theory since it was originally published, all argue that for motivation to be high, all the component factors (expectancy, instrumentality, and valence) must be high.

Research has generally supported expectancy theory. In a meta-analysis of studies of expectancy theory, Van Eerde & Thiery (1996) found that work performance is related to expectancy, instrumentality, and valence individually as well as when multiplied together. The fact that expectancy theory allows for motivation to be calculated in a unique way for each individual gives it a degree of flexibility that is lacking in most content theories. As such, it can be applied across cultures and in a wide range of settings.

Equity Theory

Equity theory, first developed by J. Stacy Adams (1965), argues that people seek a state of balance or equilibrium (equity) in their dealings with others. According to this approach, we are most comfortable when our **inputs** (what we give at work or in a personal relationship) are balanced by **outcomes** (what we get back from work or a personal relationship). When there is perceived inequity, we feel uncomfortable. If we feel that we are giving more than we get back (**negative equity**), we tend to feel resentment and guilt. If we feel that we are getting back more than we have given (**positive equity**), we tend to feel guilty. When we have these feelings, we tend to engage in one or more of the following behaviors in order to restore a sense of equity in the relationship (Huseman & Hatfield, 1989).

1. **Reduce inputs:** Come to work late, do less work, do careless work, call in sick, take extended breaks and lunch hours, "forget" to carry out instructions, engage in sabotage.

2. **Increase outputs:** Ask for pay raises, promotions, increased job security, more benefits, job transfers, better working conditions.

3. **End the relationship:** Quit.

Researchers have found that workers who feel that they are overpaid will increase the quantity and quality of their work, whereas those who feel that they are underpaid will decrease the quality and quantity of their work (Adams, 1965). This is especially true when workers feel that they are underpaid (Schermerhorn, 2000). It is important to note that *actual* equity is less important than *perceived* equity. As a supervisor, you may have overwhelming objective evidence that workers are being treated equitably, but if those workers *perceive* that they are being shortchanged, they will act accordingly in spite of the objective evidence. In this regard, it is important for supervisors to communicate effectively with employees and co-workers to understand how they perceive the situation, rather than relying solely on objective data. Dealing with the perceptions of others so that they believe they are being treated equitably can be just as important as managing the actual equity in a given situation.

On the surface, maintaining a sense of equity may seem fairly simple, but in reality it can be very difficult to achieve. Huseman & Hatfield (1989) have offered three reasons for this:

1. **People often use the wrong psychological currency:** We give people what *we* would like to get rather than taking the time to find out what *they* really want. This can leave people feeling frustrated and resentful, even though we feel that we've been fair to them.

2. **Trust bankruptcy:** Most workers do not trust higher-level management because they have been "burned" by unkept promises in the past. Until managers can earn workers' trust, no efforts to achieve equity will be successful.

3. **Hidden expectations:** People often have desires and expectations that they do not openly communicate. However, they still expect others to meet these expectations. Unless an attempt is made to identify and negotiate these expectations, efforts to achieve a sense of equity will fail.

To manage these problems, Huseman and Hatfield (1989) have proposed a five-step model that they call the **equity power paradigm.** They argue that to achieve a sense of equity among workers, managers need to:

1. Use the **power of perspective:** Make a serious effort to understand the perceptions of others and help them understand your own perspective *before* problems arise.

2. Use the **power of positive expectations:** Let workers know that you have high expectations for them and confidence in them. Give them assignments in which they can succeed and do things to allow them to feel like winners. When people experience success, believe in themselves, and know that others believe in them, they will usually be happier and work harder.

STEPS FOR MANAGING THE EQUITY PROCESS

- Recognize that equity comparisons are inevitable in the workplace.
- Anticipate felt negative inequities when rewards are given.
- Communicate clear evaluations of any rewards given.
- Communicate an appraisal of performance on which the reward is based.
- Communicate comparison points appropriate in the situation.

3. Use the **power of goal setting**: People will usually work harder when they have specific, challenging, but attainable goals to meet.

4. Use the power of **performance feedback**: Workers perform better when they receive regular feedback about their efforts, especially constructive, positive feedback.

5. Use the power of **rewards**: People perform better when they are rewarded for their efforts and made to feel proud of their accomplishments.

There is substantial research evidence to support equity theory, although much of the research has been criticized because it has been conducted in laboratory settings rather than in the workplace. Locke & Henne (1986) found support for the belief that underpayment results in less effort, but they did not find evidence for the belief that overpayment increases effort. Greenburg (1990) found that factory workers were more likely to steal from the company after a pay cut. Iverson & Roy (1994) found that when employees felt shortchanged, their intentions to quit the job increased and they were more likely to begin looking for another job. Overall, the research suggests that supervisors are wise to do whatever they can to ensure that workers do not feel negative equity on the job. However, the research on positive equity is not nearly as supportive of the theory.

Self-Efficacy Theory

Do you believe in yourself? Do you feel that you can be effective or successful, if given a reasonable chance, in most situations? If so, then you have what Albert Bandura (1982) called **self-efficacy.** Bandura's concept of self-efficacy is very similar to Vroom's concept of expectancy, or what many people would call self-confidence. People who are high in self-efficacy have confidence that they can succeed and achieve goals, whereas those who are low in self-efficacy do not have confidence in their ability to accomplish tasks.

Self-efficacy theory argues that high levels of self-efficacy lead people to work harder to achieve goals. This extra effort increases their chances of success. Thus, high self-efficacy can lead to a self-fulfilling prophecy: If you believe that you will succeed, you are more likely to succeed, which further increases your sense of self-efficacy and your future efforts. This has been called the **Galatea effect** (Eden et al., 1993, 1995).

Conversely, low self-efficacy leads to less effort because people rarely give 100 percent when they believe they are going to fail. Less effort increases the chance of failure, which results in lower self-efficacy and even less effort in the future. In other words, people with low self-efficacy give up on themselves and, in the process, doom themselves to failure.

Self-efficacy theory has been widely researched, and the findings have been strongly supportive of the theory (Spector, 2000). Research results support Bandura's notions that increasing self-efficacy can improve performance and future self-efficacy. They also support Huseman and Hatfield's (1989) assertion that showing confidence in employees andproviding them with successful experiences will increase their confidence and work performance. The research also suggests that efforts to improve self-efficacy can be a useful and effective component of job training programs (Karl et al., 1993).

Goal-Setting Theory

In my years as a college professor, I have repeatedly noticed that the students who are most likely to succeed are not necessarily the ones with the highest IQ scores. They are more commonly the students who have challenging, specific, and well-defined goals for what they want out of their college education. These goals provide a focus for their efforts, and because they are focused, they are likely to work harder and more efficiently to achieve those goals than students who are not sure

An integrated model of individual motivation to work.

why they are in college other than to "get a degree." Researchers measuring work performance have found that this is also true in the workplace.

Goal-setting theory (Locke & Latham, 1990) claims that people's behavior is motivated by their internal intentions, objectives, or goals. The theory defines a *goal* as whatever a person consciously wants to obtain or achieve. Locke & Henne (1986) have identified four ways in which goals affect people's behavior:

1. Goals focus a person's attention and action on the behaviors that the person believes will achieve the goals.

2. Goals motivate people to try harder.

3. Goals increase persistence.

4. Goals motivate people to search for effective strategies to attain the goals.

To be effective, goals must be accepted by the employee, specific, based on measurable behaviors, challenging but attainable, and accompanied by behavioral feedback (Locke & Henne, 1986). Goal-setting theory has been widely studied and is strongly supported by research evidence. It is currently the most popular theory of motivation in industrial/organizational psychology (Spector, 2000).

To summarize, there is strong support for the effectiveness of reinforcement theories and process theories of motivation, especially self-efficacy and goal–setting theories. The evidence for the content theories is much weaker and indicates that they must be applied with caution. Perhaps the greatest challenge for supervisors is recognizing which theories best fit their particular work situation and are most likely be effective with their subordinates.

Check & Review

WORKPLACE MOTIVATION

Theories of workplace motivation can be divided into three categories: reinforcement theories, content theories, and process theories. Most Organizational Behavior Modification programs focus on the use of reinforcement whenever possible.

Content Theories of motivation suggest that people are motivated to engage in behaviors that best satisfy their physical and psychological needs. They have been criticized as being overly simplistic, and often too rigid in their approach to motivation and worker satisfaction. Process theories examine the thought processes behind motivation. There is strong support for the effectiveness of process theories of motivation, especially self-efficacy and goal–setting theories.

Questions

1. Identify each of the five levels of needs in Maslow's theory.

2. Herzberg identified two broad categories of needs he called _____ factors and _____ factors.

3. Identify and briefly explain each of the three conditions identified by Vroom as being important to workplace motivation.

4. Briefly describe each of the four ways that goals affect people's behavior.

REFERENCES

Adams, J. S. Inequality in Social Exchange. In L. Berkowitz (Ed.), *Advances in Experimental and Social Psychology*, New York: Academic Press.

Bandura, A. Self-Efficacy Mechanism in Human Agency. *American Psychologist*, 37, 1982, 122–147.

Bridwell, L. G., & Wahba, M. A. Maslow Reconsidered: A Review of Research on the Need Hierarchy Theory. *Academy of Management Proceedings*, 1974, 514–520.

Chance, P. *Learning and Behavior (2nd Ed.)*. Belmont, CA: Wadsworth, 1988.

Eden, D., & Aviram, A. Self-Efficacy Training to Speed Reemployment: Helping People to Help Themselves. *Journal of Applied Psychology*, 78, 1993, 352–360.

Eden, D., & Zuk, Y. Seasickness as a Self-Fulfilling Prophecy: Raising Self-Efficacy To Boost Performance at Sea. *Journal of Applied Psychology*, 80, 1995, 628–635.

Greenburg, J,. Employee Theft as a Reaction to Underpayment inequity: The Hidden Cost of Pay Cuts. *Journal of Applied Psychology*, 5, 1990, 561–568.

Hall, D. T. & Nougaim, K. E. An Examination of Maslow's Needs Hierarchy in an Organizational Setting. *Organizational Behavior and Human Performance*, 3,1968, 12–35.

Herzberg, F., Mausner, B., & Snyderman, B. B. *The Motivation to Work (2nd Ed.)*. New York: John Wiley & Sons, 1967.

Herzberg, F. One More Time: How Do You Motivate Employees? *Harvard Business Review*, 46, January/February, 1968, 53–62.

Holland, J. L. *Making Vocational Choices: A Theory of Vocational Personalities and Work Environment (3rd Ed.)*. Odessa, FL: Psychological Assessment Resources, 1997.

House, J. H., & Wigdor. L. A. Herzberg's Dual-Factor Theory of Job Satisfaction and Motivation: A Review of the Evidence and a Criticism. *Personnel Psychology*, 20, 1967, 369–389.

Huseman, R. C., & Hatfield, J. D., *Managing the Equity Factor ...or "After All I've Done for You..."*, Boston: Houghton-Mifflin, 1989.

Iverson, R. D., & Roy, P. A Causal Model of Behavioral Commitment: Evidence from a Study of Australian Blue-Collar Employees. *Journal of Management*, 20, 1994,15–41.

Karl, K. A., O'Leary-Kelly, A. M., & Martocchio, J. J. The Impact of Feedback and Self-Efficacy on Performance in Training. *Journal of Organizational Behavior*, 14, 1993, 379–394.

Korukunda, A. R., & Hunt, J. G. Pat on the Back Versus Kick in the Pants: An Application of Cognitive inference to the Study of Leader Reward and Punishment Behavior. *Group and Organizational Studies*, 14, 1989. 299–334.

Larzelare, R. E., Schneider, W. N., Larson, D. B., & Pike, P. L. The Effects of Discipline Responses in Delaying Toddler Misbehavior Recurrences. *Child & Family Behavior Therapy*, 18, 1996, 35–37.

Larzelere, R. E. & Johnson, B. Evaluations of the Effects of Sweden's spanking ban on Child Abuse Rates: A Literature Review. *Psychological Reports*, 85 (2), 2000, 381–392.

Lawler, E. E. III, & Shuttle, J. L. A Causal Correlation Test of the Need Hierarchy Concept. *Organizational Behavior and Human Performance*, 7, 1973, 265–287.

Lewin, T. Women Are Becoming Equal Providers. *The New York Times*, 1995a, p. a27.

Locke E. A., & Henne, D. Work Motivation Theories. In C. L. Cooper & I. T. Robertson (Eds.), *International Review of Industrial and Organizational Psychology*, Chichester, UK: John Wiley & Sons, 1986, 1–35.

Locke, E. A., & Latham, G. P. *A Theory of Goal-Setting & Task Performance*. Englewood Cliifs, N. J.: Prentice Hall, 1990.

Luthens, F. *Organizational Behavior (6th Ed.)*. New York: McGraw-Hill, 1992, 160.

MacMillan, H. L. Child Maltreatment: What We Know in the year 2000. *Canadian Journal of Psychiatry*, 45 (8), 2000, 702–709.

Porter, L. W. Job Attitudes in Management: II. Perceived Importance of Needs as a Function of Job Level. *Journal of Applied Psychology*, 47, 1963, 141–148.

Rathus, S. & Nevid J. *Psychology and the Challenges of Life (8th Ed.)*. New York: John Wiley & Sons, 2002.

Schermerhorn, J., Hunt, J., & Osborn, R. *Organizational Behavior (7th Ed.)*. New York: John Wiley & Sons, 2000.

Skinner, B. F. *Science and Human Behavior*. New York: MacMillan, 1953.

Spector, P. *Industrial and Organizational Psychology(2nd Ed.)*. New York: John Wiley & Sons, 2000.

Thorndike, E. L. *Animal Intelligence*, New York: MacMillan, 1911.

Van Eerde, W., & Thierry, H. Vroom's Expectancy Model and Work-Related Criteria: A Meta-Analysis. *Journal of Applied Psychology*, 81, 575–586, 1996.

Vroom, V. *Work and Motivation*. New York: John Wiley & Sons, 1964.

MODULE 55
GROUPS IN ORGANIZATIONS

In today's workplace, employers are constantly seeking new ways to cut costs, increase productivity, and improve customer service and employee satisfaction. One area that is receiving a great deal of attention is group dynamics. Many companies are organizing workers into cooperative work teams and groups in the hopes of achieving greater creativity and efficiency. Psychologists study group dynamics in order to understand what makes some groups effective and cohesive while others are inefficient and fragmented. In addition, psychologists are interested in how group dynamics affect individual behavior and vice versa. In this section we explore the various types of work groups, how they develop, their characteristics, and how they make decisions.

Types of Groups in Organizations

A **group** is a collection of two or more people who work and interact with one another to accomplish a task or achieve a goal. Its members are mutually dependent on one another, and they interact regularly to achieve their goals over a sustained period (Schermerhorn, 2000). A university department faculty is a work group, as faculty members interact with one another to accomplish the task of educating students within the department. The students, on the other hand, are not a work group because they do not regularly interact with one another to accomplish a task (although subsets of them do so at times) and do not have shared goals (Spector, 2000).

Groups Versus Teams

A **work team** is a specific type of group. Borrill & Unsworth (1998) have identified three qualities of a work team:

1. The actions of the individuals must be interdependent and coordinated.
2. Each member must have a particular, specified role.
3. The group must have common task, goals, and objectives.

So, for example, on an automotive design team, each member of the team is assigned a specific task as part of designing the car. One person might design the body while another works on the structural components, another on the passenger compartment, and so on. But the project can be properly completed only if each member of the team successfully completes her or his assigned task.

While a work team is always a group, not all groups are work teams. In many work groups, individuals interact informally and do not have specific assigned roles. Some management and faculty committees take this form. So do many campus clubs and organizations. While members interact and often work together toward a common goal, they do not necessarily have specific assigned roles, nor do they always act in a coordinated manner with other members.

Formal Versus Informal Groups

Work groups are commonly classified into two major categories: formal and informal . Organizations need both types of groups to accomplish their goals.

Formal groups are created by the organization for a specific organizational purpose. Gibson (1995) describes three types of formal groups:

HOW GROUPS CAN HELP ORGANIZATIONS

- Groups are good for people.
- Groups can improve creativity.
- Groups can make better decisions.
- Groups can increase commitments to decisions.
- Groups help control their members.
- Groups help offset large organization size.

1. **Functional groups**, also known as *task groups*. These are ongoing groups made up of members who interact regularly. A customer service department or a research department are examples.

2. **Project groups**. These are made up of individuals from different departments who have been brought together to achieve a common goal. After the goal is achieved, the group is disbanded.

3. **Committees**. These are made up of individuals who typically discuss policy or some other functional aspect of the organization. They may be either *standing committees*, which meet regularly for an extended period, or *ad hoc* committees, which are temporary and disband when their goal has been achieved.

The Internet has led to the development of a fourth type of formal group, the **virtual group**, whose members communicate electronically. Members of these groups may never meet face-to-face, but with computer and other technology they are often able to see each other (via web cams) and discuss issues (via chat rooms, computer-linked microphones, conference calls, and e-mail). With today's technology, members of virtual groups can accomplish almost anything that traditional groups can accomplish. Virtual groups can be very efficient in that their members to not have to physically move to a common site to accomplish the task. Members can operate from their own homes or multiple work locations and can interact with other members from thousands of miles away.

Informal groups are unofficial and are created spontaneously by employees themselves. Schermerhorn and colleagues (2000) have discussed two type of informal groups: **interest groups,** which are based on common interests, and **friendship groups**, which are based on personal relationships. Interest groups might consist of employees who share similar hobbies, religious beliefs, or job-related interests such as how a computer network is set up. Friendship groups consist of members who share a personal interest in each other beyond a common interest in a hobby or work task. Informal groups often improve people's abilities to get things done because they provide lines of communication that extend beyond the formal channels of communication offered by the organization. They also provide opportunities for people to help each other outside the normal work setting. They may also satisfy workers' social and affiliation needs, thereby lowering stress levels and allowing members to work more effectively.

Autonomous Work Groups

Autonomous work groups are used in many factories as an alternative to the traditional assembly line approach in which workers repeatedly assemble the same part and may never see the finished product. Members of such groups learn all aspects of how a product is built, and the group assembles the entire product. Workers are normally rotated regularly to reduce boredom and maintain proficiency in all aspects of assembling the product. Members of the group are trained to manage themselves and are provided with the necessary resources to accomplish their task, so they usually require little supervision. Since the group assembles the entire product, it is responsible for the quality of the product. This increased accountability helps ensure that every effort is made to produce a high-quality product with no defects. The primary drawbacks to autonomous work groups are the extra time and effort necessary for training members and the disruptions caused if members quit. Training replacements so that they can smoothly blend in with the group also requires extensive time and energy.

Research has generally supported the usefulness of autonomous work groups. Wall, Kemp, Jackson, and Clegg (1986) found that workers in autonomous work groups usually reported higher levels of job satisfaction than those in a traditional factory but were no more productive. Cordery, Nueller, and Smith (1991) and

Banker, Field, Schreoder, and Sinha (1996) also found higher levels of job satisfaction among autonomous work groups. However, Cohen and Ledford (1994) found that autonomous work groups performed better than traditional workers in non-manufacturing organizations.

Quality Circles

Quality circles have their origins in Japanese management but have been commonly used in all types of American business organizations since the 1980s. Quality circles are groups of employees who meet periodically to discuss workplace problems and possible solutions. Typically, they are composed of workers with similar jobs and provide a forum for discussion of safety, production, and quality control problems. In theory, quality circles motivate workers by allowing them to have input into the decision-making processes that affect their jobs. Such input increases workers' self-esteem by making them feel that they have some control over their work. They also inform workers about issues related to their jobs and provide a means of learning supervisors' and other workers' perspectives about job-related issues. Since workers are often more directly involved than managers in the manufacturing process or in working directly with customers, they are often in the best position to know about subtle problems with equipment or customer service. Thus, it is important for managers to provide a setting in which such issues can be openly and honestly discussed. Quality circles provide such an opportunity. Managers also like them because they are inexpensive and easy to implement and consume few resources (Spector, 2000).

Quality circles have been touted for years as an effective means of improving worker satisfaction and productivity; however, most of the evidence for their effectiveness is anecdotal. There have been few controlled studies of their effectiveness. To the extent that quality circles have been studied, the results have been mixed and have not been adequately replicated (Spector, 2000). Marks, Mirvis, Hackett, and Grady (1986) found that participants in quality circles were more productive and had lower rates of absenteeism than employees who did not participate. However, Van Fleet and Griffin (1989) concluded that too little research has been conducted on quality circles to allow any firm conclusions about how effective they are at improving employee productivity or job satisfaction.

Stages of Group Development

Groups, like people, pass through various stages of development or decline. How well a group functions can be largely affected by its developmental stage. Schermerhorn and colleagues (2000) describe five stages of group development: forming, storming, norming, performing, and adjourning.

The Forming Stage

During the *forming stage* of group development, the primary focus is the entry of members to the group and the establishment of rules to guide the group's functioning. Group members are curious about what the group's purpose is, what it has to offer them, what they are expected to contribute, and how they can contribute. They are also developing social bonds with other members and trying to learn the group's behavioral rules and norms.

The Storming Stage

The *storming stage* can be a stage of intense pressure and turmoil, and some groups do not survive this stage of development. This stage is characterized by high levels of tension, emotion, change, and sometimes hostility and infighting. During this

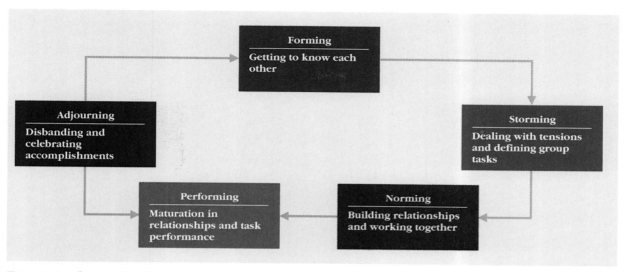

Five stages of group development.

stage, some members attempt to take charge of the group and impose their will on it. Such attempts are typically met by opposition from other members, who may have differing priorities or wish to lead the group themselves. In many ways, members are jockeying for position within the group's social and power structures. This maneuvering often leads to heated debates that eventually clarify the group's goals, expectations for group members, and obstacles preventing the accomplishment of those goals and expectations. It is during this stage that group members begin to understand each other's personal styles and how to accommodate each other while working toward a common goal. They often struggle to find a balance between satisfying their personal needs and trying to accomplish the group's goals.

The Norming Stage

During the *norming stage* of development, the group effectively comes together as a single, unified entity. In this stage, group members develop a sense of common purpose and harmony, to the point that dissenting viewpoints may be frowned upon or openly rejected. Unofficial norms of what is and is not acceptable become clearly established during this time. To many members, keeping the group unified and establishing a consensus among members may become more important than accomplishing the group's goals. The "good of the group" outweighs the "good of the individual" as well as almost every other consideration. It is also at this time that group decision-making is most vulnerable to error, as the desire for consensus may stifle legitimate opposition to ineffective or potentially harmful choices.

The Performing Stage

During the *performing stage,* the group finally emerges as a mature, stable, and tightly integrated functional unit. It is now more capable of accomplishing complex assignments and overcoming internal disagreements without damaging group effectiveness. By this stage, group communication, decision-making methods, and loyalty are operating at maximum efficiency. There is more tolerance for healthy dissension and alternative points of view, as most members feel secure in their positions within the group. Because of this, the group is flexible and capable of "changing gears" and adapting to a wide range of situations or demands.

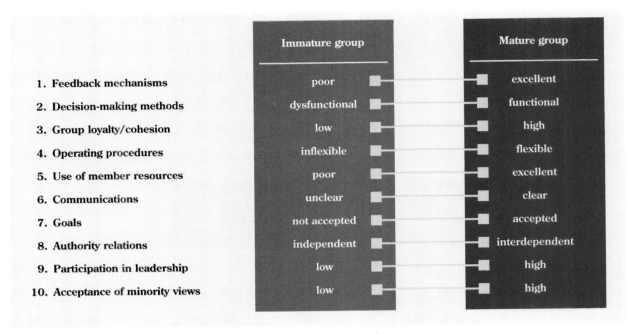

	Immature group	Mature group
1. Feedback mechanisms	poor	excellent
2. Decision-making methods	dysfunctional	functional
3. Group loyalty/cohesion	low	high
4. Operating procedures	inflexible	flexible
5. Use of member resources	poor	excellent
6. Communications	unclear	clear
7. Goals	not accepted	accepted
8. Authority relations	independent	interdependent
9. Participation in leadership	low	high
10. Acceptance of minority views	low	high

Ten criteria for measuring the maturity of a group.

The Adjourning Stage

The *adjourning stage* occurs when a group has accomplished its tasks and has to disband. This stage is the final stage of development for temporary work groups and committees. While this stage can be painful to some members, who have identified strongly with the group and bonded with other group members, it is essential for groups whose work is done to be able to disband successfully so that members can return to other job assignments. The ability to separate successfully after accomplishing its tasks can be viewed as a measure of the group's success.

Characteristics of Groups

Groups do not always function in the same way as individuals. Certain characteristics of groups can help or hinder their functioning. Understanding those characteristics is essential to understanding how groups work. Let's look, therefore, at some key characteristics of groups.

Roles

A **role** is the part someone plays, or how a person is expected to behave within a group. Different people have different functions within a group and therefore play different roles as the group carries out its tasks. Some play leading roles and help direct group activities, while others play support roles and help carry out group functions. Still others help play mediating roles to ensure that group members work well together. In effective work groups, each member's role is clearly defined and members know what their roles are and what is expected of them.

From an organizational perspective, there are two types of group roles: formal and informal. **Formal roles** are defined by one's job description. Thus, a vice president of a corporation has a certain role to play within the organization based on the duties and responsibilities assigned to the job title "vice president." A secretary has a different, but equally important, role to play based on the duties assigned to the job title "secretary."   In theory, the organization runs most smoothly when people perform their formal roles as expected.

Informal roles develop spontaneously from the personal interactions of members. Based on people's unique talents, interests, and abilities, they may invent roles or take on responsibilities "above and beyond" their formal roles within the group. For example, if a member happens to be very caring and empathic, he or she may become the group's "counselor," spending extra time helping members who are having personal difficulties.   Even though "counselor" is not a formal role defined by the job description, it may well become an important part of the role that individual plays within the group.   In some cases, the informal roles played by group members can become more important than their formal roles in the functioning of the group.

From an individual's standpoint, there are three types of roles within a group: perceived roles, expected roles, and enacted roles (Gibson, 1995). A **perceived role** is how you believe you *ought* to act within the group. It is what you expect from yourself, given your position in the group. An **expected role** is how other group members expect you to act within the group. An **enacted role** is how you *actually behave* within the group. Generally, you will have the fewest difficulties when your perceived, expected, and enacted roles are all very similar. Problems can develop when your perceived role is very different from your expected role—that is, you have very different expectations for yourself than other group members have for you. Problems can also develop when your enacted role is different from either your perceived role or your expected role – your actual behavior is different from the behavior you or others expect from you. And problems can occur when you are not sure how you are supposed to act within the group—you do not know what others in the group expect from you. This is called **role ambiguity**.

Finally, problems can occur when a person has to enact two mutually incompatible roles; this causes **role conflict**. Role conflict can occur when someone you supervise is also a friend. What happens if you have to discipline or fire that person? You are thrust into a role conflict. In your role as a friend, you do not want to cause the person pain or harm. But your role as their supervisor may force you to cause pain by firing him or her. This is not a pleasant situation. It is why many organizations bar employees from supervising relatives or anyone with whom they are emotionally involved, such as a romantic partner or spouse. The romantic relationship conflicts with the supervisory relationship and can make it difficult, if not impossible, to function effectively as the person's supervisor.

Norms

Norms are unwritten, and often unstated, rules of behavior that are accepted by members of the group. Norms affect what people expect from each other and how they behave within groups. They influence everything from expected work effort to how group members dress and even the language they use when conversing within the group. Some groups have much more restrictive norms than others.

As a group member, it is important to recognize what the group's norms are so that you do not unintentionally violate them. Violations of group norms may be overlooked at first or met with subtle hints that such behavior is "not how it's done" within the group, if it is clear that the violator was unaware of the norm. If violations continue, the violator will eventually be ostracized or even forced out of the

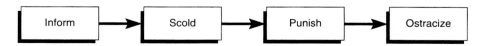

Norm violators are informed, scolded, punished, and then ostracized from the group.

group. Supervisors need to understand group norms because they can have a bigger impact on the behavior of group members than either supervisors or organizational expectations (Spector, 2000). Changing the behavior of individuals within a group may often involve changing the group norms under which they operate. This can be challenging at times, but it can be done. Sundstrum, DeMeuse, and Futrell (1990) found that goal setting was effective in getting groups to develop norms that were consistent with those desired by the organization.

Group Cohesiveness

A simple way to think about **cohesiveness** is to think of it as "stickiness." It is the mutual attraction and closeness that group members have toward each other and the group. It is a collection of psychological forces that hold a group together. Cohesiveness is crucial to group success. Members of highly cohesive groups tend to have higher morale, work harder, and be more productive than members of groups with low cohesiveness, regardless of their level of outside supervision (Gibson, 1995). They will strongly enforce group norms and find violation of those norms highly threatening. Members of cohesive groups are also highly supportive of one another and are more cooperative and friendly; this produces strong emotional and social bonds among group members.

However, cohesiveness can be a double-edged sword. How productive a highly cohesive group is depends on what the group's norms are. If a cohesive group establishes norms for low productivity, group members will support each other in low production. In this case, any member who works *too* hard might be criticized by the rest of the group for "trying to make everyone else look bad." Management efforts to improve productivity are likely to be met with a unified resistance, which can be very difficult to overcome. Therefore, in the workplace it is important for cohesive groups to have high productivity norms; otherwise cohesiveness can become an obstacle to effective performance.

Given the dual nature of group cohesiveness, it is not surprising that the findings of researchers studying the relationship between cohesiveness and productivity vary widely. Several studies have found that cohesive groups are more productive than less cohesive groups (Keller, 1986; Tziner & Vardi, 1983). Some studies have also found that members of highly cohesive groups have higher levels of satisfaction than members of groups with low cohesiveness (Colarelli & Boos, 1992; Keller,

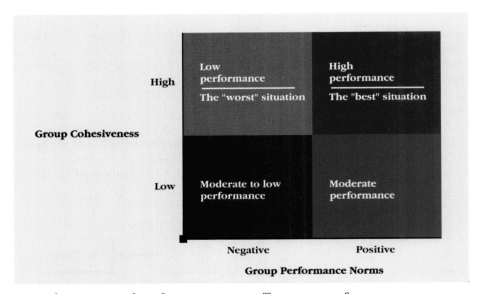

How cohesiveness and conformity to norms affect group performance.

How to Decrease Cohesion	TARGETS	How to Increase Cohesion
Create disagreement	Goals	Get agreement
Increase heterogeneity	Membership	Increase homogeneity
Restrict within team	Interactions	Enhance within team
Make team bigger	Size	Make team smaller
Focus within team	Competition	Focus on other teams
Reward individual results	Rewards	Reward team results
Open up to other teams	Location	Isolate from other teams
Disband the team	Duration	Keep team together

Ways to increase and decrease group cohesiveness.

1986).   However, other studies have found no relationship between cohesiveness and productivity (George & Bettenhousen, 1990; Greene, 1989).   These findings support the idea that while cohesiveness has a positive impact on group morale and loyalty, its effects on productivity depend primarily on the norms and goals of the group.

Group Size

A group's size can have dramatic effects on its functioning and cohesiveness. The ideal size for problem-solving groups appears to be about 5 to 7 people. In a smaller group, cohesiveness and communication may be very high, but group members may be forced to take on multiple tasks to accomplish group goals; this can lead to mistakes and miscommunications. As groups get larger, work can be allocated among members so that each member has fewer tasks to juggle. As a result, efficiency, performance, and morale increase. However, at a certain point—usually when group size exceeds 8 people—the drawbacks of increasing group size begin to outweigh the benefits.

In larger groups, cohesiveness suffers because people will split off into subgroups that may form their own norms and set their own agendas, which may or may not be in line with those of the larger group. Communication begins to deteriorate because it is harder for each individual to be heardwithin the group. This increases the chances that the group's ideas and decisions will be dominated by one or two aggressive or vocal members, even if their ideas are not the best. Effective but quiet members may get discouraged and stop trying to participate. In the workplace, as functional groups get larger, absenteeism and turnover tend to increase while satisfaction and morale decrease. In addition, from a practical standpoint, the larger a group gets, the more difficult it becomes to find a time and place for everyone to meet (Thomas & Fink, 1968).

Advantages of Working in Groups

There are several advantages to having people work together in groups as opposed to working separately as individuals. They are as follows:

1.   **Creativity.** Groups offer the potential for a much wider pool of ideas for accomplishing a task than any member of the group would come up with separately. As a result, groups are often more creative and innovative than individuals.

2. **Education.** Groups provide a setting in which members can share job skills and experiences and learn from one another.

3. **Synergy.** Groups may offer the potential for *synergy*, a condition in which is the whole is greater than the sum of its parts. In other words, members of a group working together can often accomplish more than any of them could as individuals. For example, four people working together can move an object that would be too heavy for any of them to move individually. They can also assemble complex items that could not be assembled by an individual working alone.

4. **Feedback.** Group members also provide immediate feedback on each other's ideas as well as ways of improving on those ideas that might not be thought of individually.

5. **Social support.** Group members provide social support for each other and may help meet individual members' emotional, security, and affiliation needs. As such, they may increase the morale and confidence levels of group members.

6. **Social facilitation.** Working in the presence of others can create emotional arousal, which improves work performance when the tasks are relatively simple and straightforward.

Disadvantages of Working in Groups

Working in groups has potential disadvantages as well. They are as follows:

1. **Social loafing.** People often work less hard in groups than they would as individuals. This can be due to *diffusion of responsibility*. If things don't get done, they can blame others, and they may count on others to do some of their work for them so that the group does not get into trouble.

2. **Social inhibition.** While working in the presence of others may improve performance on simple tasks, it can impair performance on more complex or unfamiliar tasks. This is especially true of people who are highly self-conscious.

3. **Conformity.** Group members are often placed under intense pressure to conform to group norms. This can stifle creativity and may cause highly productive people to lower their efforts when the group's performance norms are low.

4. **Inefficient use of time.** Groups may get so involved in the process of reaching a decision that they may take forever to do so. Often groups have so many meetings, conferences, and consultations, in an effort to achieve consensus, that they cannot get things done nearly as fast as one or two motivated individuals.

It is clear that working in groups is not the answer to all workplace problems. Groups are best used in situations that require teamwork, thoughtful discussion, and creative synergy. For supervisors to maximize group effectiveness, it is essential to identify the work situations that are best suited to group efforts, as well as those that can best be handled by individuals.

Group Decision-Making

Researchers have found that groups do not make decisions the same way individuals do. Sometimes this is beneficial, but it can have its drawbacks. In this section we examine how groups make decisions, some techniques that can improve group decision-making, and some problems associated with group decision-making.

How Groups Make Decisions

Edgar Schein (1988), an expert on group decision-making, has identified 6 methods used by groups to make decisions. They are as follows:

1. **Decision by lack of response.** In this method, several ideas are presented but are passed over with no discussion or evaluation. Finally an idea is chosen simply because it is the only one left. This is not usually the best way to make decisions, as there is no critical evaluation of each idea.

2. **Decision by authority rule.** In this method, the leader or person in authority makes the decision for the group. While this allows for quick decision-making, the quality of the decision is only as good as the quality of the leader and the information at his or her command.

3. **Decision by minority rule.** In this method, two or three powerful group members put forward an idea and then use social pressure or manipulation to get other members to support it. Usually there is little thoughtful discussion of the idea, so the decision is not necessarily a good one.

4. **Decision by majority rule.** In this method, a formal vote may be taken on each idea. The idea that gets the majority vote is chosen. This method is "democratic," but unless it is handled carefully it can result in a "tyranny of the majority," in which a narrow majority can continually impose its will on a large minority, ignoring their sensitivities and concerns. This can lead to underlying resentments that can lower the morale and performance of these members or even lead to open revolt if the perceived unfairness is severe enough.

5. **Decision by consensus.** In this method, options are discussed until there is a single option that is favored by most of the members and supported by the rest. This method allows for dissenters to express their opinions and compromises to be made so that the chosen option is agreeable to all. It tends to lower the level of resentment among those who initially opposed the option (as compared to majority rule), because they have been listened to and may have been able to make modifications in the chosen option.

6. **Decision by unanimity.** In this method, all group members agree completely on the chosen option. While ideally this is the perfect method for making a decision because everyone is satisfied, in reality it is almost impossible to achieve in most work situations. When it does occur, one must sometimes wonder how thoroughly all the alternative ideas were discussed or if there was some bias in how the ideas were presented.

GUIDELINES FOR GROUP CONSENSUS

1. Don't argue blindly; consider others' reactions to your points.
2. Don't change your mind just to reach quick agreement.
3. Avoid conflict reduction by voting, coin tossing, and bargaining.
4. Try to involve everyone in the decision process.
5. Allow disagreements to surface so that information and opinions can be deliberated.
6. Don't focus on winning versus losing; seek alternatives acceptable to all.
7. Discuss assumptions, listen carefully, and encourage participation by everyone.

Problems with Group Decision-making

Group decision making is not always superior to decision-making by individuals. There are several reasons for this. Some of the problems of working within groups also negatively affect group decision-making, such as the extra time it takes for groups to make decisions and the pressure for members to conform to group norms, which may prevent all options from being discussed openly. Other problems include minority domination, groupthink, and the "risky shift. "

Minority Domination

A constant danger in groups is the tendency of one or two very vocal or dominant members, or a dominant and very cohesive minority of members, to impose their will on a passive majority. These members may be effective at expressing their opinions and dominating group discussions, but this does not mean that their ideas are the best choices for the group. Often these dominant members intimidate the quieter and more introverted members into going along with their ideas. In the process, the other members' ideas are not heard or discussed. This type of domination can lead to abuse of power, poor decision-making, and resentment by other members, and may eventually fragment the group.

The decision that led to the *Challenger* disaster was likely caused by groupthink. (Moorhead, Ference, & Neck, 1991)

HOW TO AVOID GROUPTHINK

- Assign the role of critical evaluator to each group member.
- Have the leader avoid seeming partial to one course of action.
- Create subgroups to work on the same problem.
- Have group members discuss issues with outsiders and report back.
- Invite outside experts to observe and react to group processes.
- Assign someone to be a "devil's advocate" at each meeting.
- Write alternative scenarios for the intentions of competing groups.
- Hold "second-chance" meetings after consensus is apparently achieved.

Groupthink

Groupthink is the tendency of members of highly cohesive groups with strong leaders to go along with the majority of the group, even when they may know that the group's choice is a poor one. Fear of being criticized or ostracized by other members prevents them from expressing their doubts about the group's decisions or expressing alternative points of view. Often members will convince themselves that the group leaders "must know what they are doing," even when they know that the group is making a mistake. Because no one is willing to play "devil's advocate" and ask critical questions such as "What happens if this doesn't work?" the group plunges headlong into often risky and foolish choices. Researchers have noted several cases in which groupthink has led to disastrous results. These include President John F. Kennedy's decision to launch the Bay of Pigs invasion, President Lyndon B. Johnson's decision to escalate the war in Vietnam, the Watergate affair, NASA's decision to launch the *Challenger* space shuttle in freezing weather, and the Iran-Contra scandal during the Reagan administration (Janis, 1972; Moorhead, Ference, & Neck, 1991). One must wonder whether Osama Bin Laden and the leaders of Al Qaeda exhibited groupthink when planning the September 11, 2001, attacks on the World Trade Center and the Pentagon as, at this writing, those attacks seems to have resulted in disaster for them. Clearly, the consequences of the attacks were not what they anticipated, which is typical of most cases of groupthink.

The Risky Shift

Related to groupthink is the phenomenon of **risky shift**. This is the tendency of people in groups to take more chances and make riskier decisions than any of them would make as individuals. While this can lead groups to make more creative and innovative choices than individuals, it can also lead them to take foolish, irresponsible risks and make disastrous choices that responsible individuals would almost never make. The risky shift is often directly related to groupthink because in very cohesive groups, when risky options are presented by a dominant member or leader, no one will challenge them. Groups can produce a false sense of security in which members keep reassuring each other that "we can make this work" to the point that they underestimate the obstacles and overestimate their chances of success. There is also some diffusion of responsibility, with the result if things go wrong, members may feel that "it's not my fault" or "I was just following orders." This makes it easier to take chances that one would never take as an individual. It is believed that the risky shift was also involved in situations such as Watergate, the *Challenger* disaster, and the Iran-Contra scandal.

Improving Group Decision-making

Several techniques have been developed to improve group decision-making. In this section we will briefly examine three of them: brainstorming, the nominal group technique, and the Delphi technique.

Brainstorming is a technique designed to enhance group decision-making by generating a wider and more creative pool of ideas for members to choose from. In brainstorming, members are given a task and told to generate as many ideas as possible for accomplishing the task. Those ideas are to be presented to the group with no critical judgment or evaluation. In fact, members are often told, "The crazier the better." No one is allowed to criticize or judge anyone's ideas while they are being presented. This is to prevent people from "self-censoring" ideas that may sound absurd or impossible at first but, with more serious consideration turn out to be highly creative and workable. Only after all the ideas have been presented does the group go back and evaluate them.

Several factors can lead to groupthink. Of the four shown here, group cohesiveness seems unnecessary according to Aldag and Fuller (1993).

How the brainstorming is conducted may determine how successful it is. In the traditional method of brainstorming, people state their ideas out loud to the rest of the group. Unfortunately, shy or introverted group members may still feel uncomfortable expressing themselves in front of the group, and such sessions may result in two or three dominant, but not necessarily creative, members making all the suggestions. Researchers have failed to find evidence that this method of brainstorming is superior to individuals working alone (Gallupe, Bastianutti, & Cooper, 1991).

Another form of brainstorming, *electronic brainstorming*, involves asking group members to anonymously enter their ideas into a computer rather than verbally expressing them to the group. This anonymity may reduce the social anxiety felt by introverted members in traditional brainstorming techniques. It also allows people to enter their ideas into the computer immediately, rather than having to "wait their turn" to be heard in traditional brainstorming methods. Such waiting can cause some members to forget their ideas before they can be presented. Researchers have found that electronic brainstorming improves performance in an idea generation task compared to individuals working alone or traditional brainstorming techniques (Dennis & Valacich, 1993; Gallupe et al., 1991).

The Nominal Group Technique

The **nominal group technique** is often used when a group is too large to manage a brainstorming session or to enable members to participate in an open discussion of the issues. It involves breaking the group up into subgroups of 5 to 7 people each. Everyone in each of the subgroups is asked to write a response to a "nominal question" such as, "How can we improve productivity in this organization?" As in brainstorming, everyone is encouraged to come up with as many alternatives as possible and to be as creative as possible. Then the suggestions are read out loud, with no one allowed to criticize them. Questions are asked about each suggestion, for clarification, and a formal vote is held to determine which suggestions members favor most. The emphasis here is to make sure everyone is fully heard, but in a manageable way.

The Delphi Technique

The **Delphi technique** was developed by the Rand Corporation for use in situations in which group members are unable to meet face to face. It involves distributing a series of questionnaires to a panel of decision-makers, who submit their preliminary responses to a decision coordinator. The coordinator summarizes their responses and returns the summary, along with a follow-up questionnaire, to the panel. Members of the panel then revise their responses to answer the questions in the follow-up questionnaire and send them back to the decision coordinator. They continue this back-and-forth process until everyone agrees on a decision (Schermerhorn, 2000).

Check & Review

GROUPS IN ORGANIZATIONS

Work groups are commonly classified into two major categories: formal groups and informal groups. **Autonomous work groups** are used in many factories as an alternative to the traditional assembly line approach. groups grow, evolve, and pass through various stages of development or decline.

There are certain characteristics of groups that can help or hinder their functioning. From an organizational perspective, there are two types of group roles: formal roles and informal roles. From an individual's standpoint, there are three types of roles within a group: perceived roles, expected roles, and enacted roles.

Norms, cohesiveness, and size affect what people expect from each other and how they behave within groups.

Groups do not make decisions the same way individuals do. Sometimes this is beneficial, but it can have drawbacks. Brainstorming, the nominal group technique, and the Delphi technique are techniques that have been developed over the years to improve group decision-making.

Questions

1. Identify the five stages of development in groups.

2. A _____ role is how you believe you *ought* to act within the group. An _____ role is how other group members expect you to act within the group. An _____ role is how you *actually behave* within the group.

3. Identify the advantages and disadvantages to having people work together in groups as opposed to working separately as individuals.

4. _____ is the tendency of members in highly cohesive groups with strong leaders to go along with the majority of the group, even when they may know that the group choice is a poor one. Whereas, _____ is the tendency of people in groups to take more chances and make riskier decisions than any of them would make as individuals.

REFERENCES

Banker, R. D., Field, J. M., Schreoder, R. G., & Sinha, K. K. Impact of Work Teams on Manufacturing Performance: A Longitudinal Field Study. *Academy of Management Journal*, 39, 867–890.

Colarelli, S. M., & Boos, A. L., Sociometric and Ability-Based Assignment Work Groups: Some Implications for Personnel Selection. *Journal of Organizational Behavior*, 13, 1992, 187–196.

Cordery, J. L., Mueller, W. S., & Smith, L. M. Attitudinal and Behavioral Effects of Autonomous Group Working: A Longitudinal Field Study. *Academy of Management Journal*, 34, 1991, 464–476.

DuBrin, Andrew J., *Leadership: Research Findings, Practice, and Skills (3rd Ed.)*. New York: Houghton-Mifflin, 2001.

George, J. M., & Bettenhausen, K. Understanding Prosocial Behavior, Sales Performance, and Turnover: A Group Level Analysis in a Service Context. *Journal Of Applied Psychology*, 72, 1990, 698–709.

Gibson, J. W. *The SupervisoryChallenge (2nd Ed.)*. Englewood Cliffs, N.J.: Prentice Hall, 1995.

Greene, C. N. Cohesion and Productivity in Work Groups. *Small Group Behavior*, 20, 1989, 70–86.

Janis, I. L., *Victims of Groupthink*. Boston: Houghton-Mifflin, 1972.

Keller, R. T., Predictors of Performance of Project Groups in R & D Organizations. *Academy of Management Journal*, 29, 1986, 715–726.

Moorhead, G., Ference, R., & Neck, C. P. Group Decision Fiascoes Continue: Space Shuttle Challenger and a Revised Groupthink Framework. *Human Relations*, 44, 1991, 539–550

Rathus, S. & Nevid J. *Psychology and the Challenges of Life (8th Ed.)*. New York: John Wiley & Sons, 2002.

Schein, E. H. *Process Consultation*. New York: Addison-Wesley, 1988.

Schermerhorn, J., Hunt, J., & Osborn, R. *Organizational Behavior (7th Ed.)*. New York: John Wiley & Sons, 2000.

Spector, P. *Industrial and Organizational Psychology (2nd Ed.)*. New York: John Wiley & Sons, 2000.

Sundstrom, E., DeMeuse, K. P.,& Futrell, D. Work Teams Applications and Effectiveness. *American Psychologist*, 45, 1990, 120–133.

Thomas, E. J., & Fink, C. F. "Effects of Group Size," in Larry Cummings and William E. Scott (eds.) *Readings in Organizational and Human Performance*. Homewood, IL: Irwin, 1969, 394–408.

Tziner, A. & Vardi, Y. Ability as a Moderator Between Cohesiveness and Tank Crews Performance. *Journal of Occupational Behaviour*, 4, 1983, 137–143.

Wall, T. D., Kemp, N. J., Jackson, P. R., & Clegg, C. W., Outcomes of Autonomous Work Groups: A Long-Term Field Experiment. *Academy of Management Journal*, 29, 1986, 280–304.

MODULE 56
THE COMMUNICATION PROCESS

Effective communication has always been important in personal relationships, and in business it is becoming increasingly important to leaders and organizations. A recent Lucent Technologies report noted the following:

- 900 million voice-mail messages are exchanged every day
- 5 million e-mails are sent each minute
- 2.7 trillion e-mails are sent each year
- 100 million Internet users come on line each year
- Internet traffic doubles every 100 days

Is it any wonder that many observers call the present era the "information age"? Clearly, revolutionary changes are occurring in the ways in which we communicate, and our desire for more and more information seems insatiable. People seem to want to be "connected" all the time. How many times have you heard someone's cell phone ringing in the middle of a movie, concert, or other event? and think about the number of states that have banned or are considering banning the use of cell phones while driving. For organizations in today's "online" world, keeping up with these changes and finding ways to stay connected with customers can be critical to their survival. Yet many American businesses have encountered significant problems in their efforts to communicate with their employees and customers (Lowry & Reimus, 1996).

Leaders as well as organizations need to understand the communication process and communicate effectively. In a review of studies, Bass (1990) found substantial evidence that effective leadership is strongly related to effective verbal and nonverbal communication. The ability to "sell" a vision or a new idea, to persuade others to believe in a goal and do what is necessary to accomplish it, to listen to the ideas of subordinates and co-workers, and to give and seek appropriate feedback from others are all crucial to effective leadership. Having the most ingenious and visionary plan for a company's future is worthless if you cannot communicate it effectively.

This is just as true in personal relationships as it is in organizational settings. Communication patterns between spouses at the time of their marriage are a key predictor of marital satisfaction five years later (Markman, 1981). The ability to communicate effectively to resolve disputes has also been show to be strong predictors of marital satisfaction, even stronger than sex or childrearing problems (Snyder, 1979). So being an effective communicator is important in your personal as well as your professional life. In this chapter we examine how communication occurs, the dimensions and types of communication, persuasive communication, and ways to improve communication.

What Is Communication?

Communication is a process of sending and receiving a meaningful message. The key element of this definition is the idea that the message is *meaningful*. A meaningless message does not communicate anything (other than perhaps the sender's lack of ability to communicate effectively). To communicate, you must be able to send information in a way that is meaningful to the person receiving the message; otherwise you will have wasted your time and theirs. **Effective communication** occurs when the sender's *intended* meaning is identical to the receiver's *perceived* meaning. This is an ideal goal, but because communication is a complex process that involves many steps, it is not always possible to achieve.

A Basic Model of Communication

Gibson (1995) proposes a model interpersonal communication consisting of 6 steps: ideation, encoding, transmission, reception, decoding, and understanding. When we communicate effectively, the process flows smoothly. However problems can occur at each stage, and these problems can lead to serious misunderstandings and miscommunication if they are not promptly identified and corrected. If we examine each step specifically, it is easy to see how these problems can occur.

(It would be useful to have a graphic of this model here).

1. Ideation. This involves having an idea that you want to communicate. A major problem occurs at this stage if people do not clearly think through what they are trying to communicate. In that case the message is jumbled, vague, or unclear and the receiver cannot understand the point of the message. Another problem that can occur at this stage arises when you "speak before you think." In this case you start talking without having any idea what you are trying to say. This is a common problem for inexperienced public speakers, who are afraid that if they remain silent for more than a few seconds their audience will think they do not know what they are doing. So they start talking just to "fill time." Often the result is perceived as "rambling on" or even "babbling," which does nothing to enhance the speaker's credibility. The best communicators have a clear idea of what they are trying to communicate *before* they begin talking or writing.

2. Encoding. This is the process of converting an idea into words that make it understandable to others. A common problem here is insensitivity to the audience. When encoding, it is important to know your audience and what it can tolerate or understand. Sending a message full of technical terms to an audience of grade-school children is inappropriate because you are talking "over their heads." Conversely, talking to reasonably intelligent people in overly simplistic language can be perceived as insulting, condescending, or patronizing. The use of slang, colloquialisms, or inappropriate language results from poor encoding and can often be confusing or offensive to an audience.

Another problem at this stage is poor vocabulary. A broad and diverse vocabulary is very important to effective communication, because people do judge you by the words you use. If you only have simple words at your command, your ability to express or understand sophisticated and complex ideas will be limited. If you consistently use only grade-school vocabulary to express yourself, people will, perhaps inaccurately, perceive you as being ignorant. The broader your vocabulary, the easier it becomes to encode a wide range of ideas and concepts in a manner that is appropriate for your audience and will command their attention and respect.

3. Transmission. This is the actual written or spoken delivery of the message. Even excellent ideas that are beautifully encoded will be meaningless if they are not delivered in a manner that the receiver can understand. Problems at this stage can include written communication problems such as poor grammar or spelling, or verbal communication problems such as speaking too softly or too rapidly, speaking with a thick accent, repeatedly stammering or using words like "um" or "ah," or engaging in nonverbal behaviors that distract the receiver from the message. All of these can prevent the receiver from understanding the message, and good communicators take the extra time and effort necessary to minimize or eliminate these problems.

4. Reception. This is the process of actually hearing or seeing the words. Some problems that can occur at this stage include poor listening and not paying attention. No matter how well an idea is presented, if you are only "half listening" to the message, you probably will not remember it or understand it in a useful manner. Another problem that can arise at this stage takes the form of physical distractions such as other people talking and other background noise, which can be very distracting to listeners. Thus, it is important for effective communicators to try to create a setting that is conducive to good listening, just as it is important for receivers to develop good listening skills so that they can fully attend to the sender's message.

5. Decoding. This is the process by which the receiver translates the sender's words into meaningful ideas. A major problem at this stage is, again, poor vocabulary. If you do not understand the words in the sender's message, you will not be able to decode them effectively and the message will be meaningless to you. Building your vocabulary so that you can understand senders' ideas in the variety of work and personal situations in which you find yourself is essential to becoming an effective communicator.

6. Understanding. This is the process of putting the sender's ideas together into an integrated, meaningful message. This can be the most difficult step of all, because it is during this step that your own biases, experiences, and expectations come into play. How you interpret or understand someone else's message can be greatly affected by your personal feelings, biases, or prejudices toward the sender or the sender's viewpoint. A strong negative bias may cause you to unfairly disparage or ignore the sender's message. On the other hand, a strong positive bias may cause you to accept the sender's idea with little or no critical evaluation.

Given how many things there are that can go wrong in a simple communication, it is amazing that we communicate as well as we do. Even the best communicators often admit that they have to continuously work at communicating to remain effective at it. But with practice anyone can improve their communication skills, and the model just described offers a good starting point for those efforts.

Dimensions of Communication

Most models of communication, like the one just described, focus on the delivery of the words themselves. But communication, especially spoken communication, is more than just words. In fact, the words themselves often are not even the most important part of a communication. It turns out that the words we use are just one of three dimensions of communication that affect how a message is received and understood by others. Those dimensions are verbal, nonverbal, and contextual. In this section we describe each of these dimensions.

The Verbal Dimension

The **verbal dimension** of communication includes not only the words themselves but also the way the words are spoken, or **paralanguage**. Paralanguage includes the pace, pitch, and volume at which the words are spoken and the tone of voice and inflections used by the speaker. Mehrabian (1968) found that in the average verbal communication, only about 7 percent of the entire communication was contained in the words themselves. A much larger part of the communication, 38 percent, was contained in the paralanguage. If you think about it, this makes sense. Think about how someone's inflection or tone of voice affects how you perceive his or her messages. A subtle increase in pitch at the end of a sentence can imply a question, but it can also imply nervousness or insecurity. Contrast this to a sharp drop in pitch along with an increase in volume and a firmer tone at the end of the same sentence. These paralanguage cues convey confidence, control, and authority. Sarcasm is often difficult to convey in writing because it is almost entirely based on differences in pitch and tone rather than on the words. Telling someone "That was really smart!" as a compliment after the person has done something brilliant involves different inflections and tone than saying "That was really smart!" as a sarcastic comment after someone has done something foolish. The words are the same, but the meanings are opposite. Only the paralanguage allows us to know which is which.

The Nonverbal Dimension

Mehrabian (1947, 1968) found that the most important dimension in a typical communication is the **nonverbal dimension**. In the average communication, over half of the overall message and up to 90 percent of the emotional content is transmitted through nonverbal communication.　Nonverbal communication includes eye contact, facial expressions, **kinesics** (body language and gestures), and **proxemics** (the way people use space in communicating).

Nonverbal behavior often is more important than verbal behavior in understanding what someone is thinking or feeling. This occurs in part because a subtle gesture, wink, nod, or grin at just the right place in a message can completely change its meaning. Also, people often learn to be very good at lying or misleading people with their verbal behavior, but lying with nonverbal behavior is much more difficult. Thus, some people may lie very effectively with their words but reveal the lie with their body language. Counseling and clinical psychologists and many criminal investigators are trained to pay particular attention to clients' nonverbal behaviors because they can provide insight into the clients' genuine motives and emotions.

Researchers have found that when there is a conflict between verbal and nonverbal behavior, people will tend to pay more attention to the nonverbal behavior than to the verbal behavior (Graham et al., 1991). Just the existence of a conflict between verbal and nonverbal communications may lead someone to distrust the message and the person sending it. Thus, interviewers respond more favorably to job applicants who display positive nonverbal cues such as consistent eye contact and an erect posture than to applicants whose nonverbal cues include avoiding eye contact or slouching.

Eye contact is probably the most important nonverbal behavior. Age-old sayings such as "The eyes are the mirror of the soul" and "Liars never look you in the eye" may not always be true, but they reflect the importance people have placed on eye contact throughout history. Facial expressions often complement eye contact and are also very important in nonverbal communication. Caution must be used, however, in interpreting nonverbal behavior, especially when communicating with people from different cultural backgrounds. While in American culture lowering one's eyes may be a signal of guilt or shame, in Asian and Hispanic cultures it can be a sign of respect.

Another aspect of nonverbal behavior is proxemics, or personal space. There are two ways in which the use of space can be important. First, how space is used in an office can say to great deal to visitors. Placing a visitor's chair across a large desk from you tends to keep communications more formal than placing the chair at the side of the desk. Similarly, having a seating area away from the desk where both you and your visitors can converse comfortably creates a much more relaxed and informal atmosphere for conversing.

Second, how close to people you stand or sit when communicating with them can also affect the communication. Experts in proxemics have identified four distances that people in North America are most comfortable with when communicating with others, depending on the relationship between them.　**Intimate distance** ranges from touching to about 18 inches away. This distance is reserved for romantic partners, close family members, and intimate friends. Even then, we use this distance only in special situations like comforting, embracing, or cuddling. If others intrude into this space, we tend to become tense and instinctively try to increase our distance from them. **Personal distance** ranges from 18 inches to about 4 feet.

We prefer to maintain this distance when conversing informally with good friends or close co-workers. **Social distance** ranges from 4 to 12 feet. We prefer this distance when we are having formal conversations with supervisors, co-workers, subordinates, customers, or other people whom we do not know well, such as some acquaintances. Finally, **public distance** is 12 feet and beyond. This is where we prefer to keep people who are strangers or whom we have reason not to trust. This distance is typically used for communication in formal lectures and speeches or large, formal business meetings.

It is important to recognize these invisible zones, because intruding too closely can cause other people to feel pressured, intimidated, defensive, or generally uncomfortable. Staying too far away may make others wonder if we are angry at them or if they have done something wrong. There is evidence that these personal space norms differ between men and women (Kaya & Erkip, 1999) and among cultures (Remlind, Jones, & Brinkman, 1991; Baron & Byrne, 2000).

GENDER & CULTURAL DIVERSITY

Men's and women's communication styles and personal space needs differ in many ways. Given the different ways in which men and women use communication, it should not be surprising that sometimes they seem to "talk by" each other rather than "talk to" each other. Dubrin (1997, pp. 53–54) summarized the research findings on male-female differences in communication patterns as follows:

1. Women prefer to use conversation for building rapport.

2. Men prefer to use talk primarily as a means to preserve independence and status by displaying knowledge and skill.

3. Women are more likely than men to want empathy, not solutions, when they communicate.

4. Men prefer to work out their problems by themselves, whereas women prefer to talk out solutions with another person.

5. Women are more likely to compliment the work of a co-worker, whereas men are more likely to be critical.

6. Men tend to be more directive in their conversation, while women emphasize politeness.

7. Women tend to be more conciliatory when facing differences, while men become more intimidating.

8. Men are more interested than women in calling attention to their accomplishments or hogging recognition.

9. Men tend to dominate discussions during meetings.

In summarizing research findings about male-female differences in personal space, Rathus & Nevid (2002) report:

> Women interact at closer distances than men do. They also seek to keep more space between themselves and strangers of the other gender than men do. Men are made more uncomfortable by strangers who sit across from them whereas women are more likely to feel "invaded" by strangers who sit next to them. In libraries, men tend to pile books protectively in front of them. Women place books and coats in adjacent seats to discourage others from taking them (p. 356).

Men and women also differ in their use of touch while communicating. In the workplace, men are more likely to touch women than women are to touch men (Major, Schmidlin, & Williams, 1990). However, since people with high status and power are more likely to touch people of lower status and power than vice versa, the higher rate of males touching females may reflect power and status differences more than gender-based differences. This idea is bolstered by the finding that in social

"I am the boss!"   "I am the boss, but let's talk."   "Forget I'm the boss, let's talk."

Furniture placement and nonverbal communication in the office.

interactions women are more likely than men to touch other people (Stier & Hall, 1984).

The Contextual Dimension

The **contextual dimension** refers to the background, or setting, in which a communication occurs. Contextual factors include clothing, office location and decor, lighting, background noise, and technical equipment. These are important in "setting the stage" for effective communication and can often lend credibility to a message. For example, when you go to a lawyer's office, what do you expect to see? Law degrees hanging on the wall? A large mahogany desk? A bookshelf loaded with leather-bound law books? How would you expect the lawyer to be dressed? In an expensive, well-tailored suit? What would you think if you went to the same lawyer's office and you had to sit on a folding chair and discuss your case over a card table in a room decorated with no books or degrees, just comic book posters, with a lawyer dressed in a tie-dyed T-shirt underneath bib overalls? Even though the lawyer might be the same person, you probably would have much less confidence in winning your case in the "card table" scenario than in the "plush office" scenario.

In many situations the context can make or break the credibility of a message. Why is this so? We often have very specific expectations about what we should find in many situations. We expect lawyers to have offices with law degrees, books, and so on. We expect doctors to have medical degrees on their office walls and an examining table in the exam room, and to wear a stethoscope and a white medical coat.

Many clients coming in for therapy still expect psychologists to smoke a pipe, speak with an Austrian accent, and have them lie on a couch. When the setting for a communication is dramatically different from what we expect, it can cause us to be distracted from the sender's message and doubt its credibility. So making the contextual elements of a communication as consistent as possible with what the receiver expects to find can profoundly influence the impact and credibility of the message.

Types of Organizational Communication

There are two types of organizational communication: formal and informal. **Formal communication** refers to channels of communication that are established by the organization and follow the organizational structure or "chain of command." Sending memos or letters and holding pre-announced formal meetings are examples of formal communication. While formal communication is necessary to communicate official policies, schedules, assignments, and announcements, there are limits to what can be communicated through formal channels. Many people are hesitant to express themselves formally on some issues because of shyness or fear of retaliation, and will say nothing at all if formal communication is their only option. Much of what employees learn in an organization comes from networking outside the officially sanctioned communication channels.

Informal communication develops among the workers themselves and does not necessarily follow the organizational structure. It consists of casual conversations, personal notes, and e-mails exchanged by workers. Such communication can cut across departmental or hierarchical boundaries and the "red tape" that can limit formal communication.

One of the most common informal channels of communication is the **grapevine**, an informal network of friends and acquaintances within an organization who share information with each other. Most of the time, grapevines share information that is not transmitted through official channels, or they share people's reactions to official information. Grapevines provide a sense of security and involvement so that people feel that they are "on top of things" when important changes or events are occurring within the organization. They can be very efficient at transmitting information widely and quickly—much faster at times than formal communication. They help fill informational voids when management does not provide enough information to enable employees to feel secure about the organization.

The grapevine can be problematic when there is a lack of accurate information about major changes within an organization, people may start "hypothesizing" and spreading their hypotheses through the grapevines as rumors. If people are scared, they may imagine the worst and then spread rumors that assume that the "worst" is actually true. Rumors are difficult to refute once they get started and can be very destructive to workers' morale and performance.

Therefore, it is very important for organizations to provide employees with as much accurate information as possible, rather than making it available only to selected "insiders." Failure to disseminate accurate information can give rise to deeply felt distrust and resentment among subordinates. It is also important for organizations to pay close attention to the grapevine, as it can often serve as a barometer of employees' morale and their true feelings about organizational policies.

Directions of Communication

There are three directions of formal communication within an organization: upward, downward, and lateral. **Upward communication** involves the movement of information from employees to others higher in the chain of command. It often involves employees making suggestions to management about how to improve productivity or fix problems. It may also involve employees giving supervisors feedback about the practical effects of new policies or procedures, or employees asking for basic supplies and equipment. Upward communication is essential if upper management is to stay informed about the day-to-day needs of employees and customers.

Downward communication is the movement of information from executives and managers to supervisors and employees lower in the organizational hierarchy. This is the most frequently used type of formal communication; it is important because it allows lower-level employees to know what is going on "at the top." Downward communication is used to provide workers with information about the company's policies and procedures, future plans, and goals; reminders about current priorities; and feedback about performance and productivity; as well as to correct inaccurate rumors about organizational changes and policies. Lack of frequent and reliable downward communication is a frequent cause of frustration among workers, resulting in lack of trust toward management.

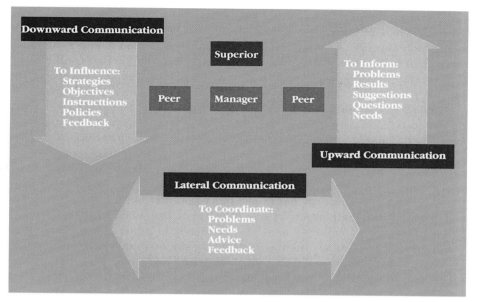

Directions for information flows in organizations.

Lateral communication occurs between employees at similar levels in the organization, such as two supervisors talking about personnel issues or two line workers sharing information about a piece of equipment. It is important because it enables departments and divisions within an organization to coordinate their efforts so that they do not work at cross-purposes. Cross-departmental task forces, project groups, and committees all use lateral communication to accomplish their goals. Lateral communication is increasingly important as businesses strive to reduce multiple layers of management in order to become more efficient.

Improving Communication

Effective communication doesn't just happen automatically. It develops through regular training, effort, and practice. There are many things that can become barriers to good communication if they are not monitored carefully. However, there are also many things you can do to improve your communication. In this section we examine some of the barriers to communication and some methods for enhancing communication skills.

Barriers to Communication

Barriers to communication are collectively described as **noise**. This term refers to anything that disrupts or interferes with communication. There are many types of noise, including physical distractions, selective perception, semantic problems, mixed messages, lack of feedback, status differences, and communication overload.

Physical Distractions. **Physical distractions** include noises, music, background conversations, interruptions, temperature, or other factors in the physical environment that interfere with a communication or prevent it from occurring. As such, they negatively influence the context in which a communication occurs. Even when they do not completely disrupt a communication, they can be so annoying that they change the entire tone of the communication. Many physical distractions can be prevented or minimized with a little forethought and consideration for the receiver.

Selective Perception. **Selective perception** is the tendency of people to focus on one part of a message and ignore the rest. Generally, once people have formed an opinion about someone or something, they will attend to information that confirms their beliefs and ignore, discount, or distort information that conflicts with them. For example, if you like someone, you will tend to see and remember the things that person does that confirm your belief that he or she is a good person. If the person does something that a good person would not do, you are likely to make excuses such as "She was just having a bad day" or "It wasn't his fault." On the other hand, if you do not like the person, you will remember all the bad things he or she does and ignore or discount the good behavior as "lucky" or "phony."

Selective perception can have a profound impact on communication, for when you do not like individuals, you will tend to hear only the parts of their messages that confirm that you are smart not to like them. You may not pay attention to any credible ideas or information they have to offer. If you like them, you may give their ideas too much credit and not examine them critically. Selective perception is often linked to prejudicial attitudes such as **racism**, **sexism**, or **ethnocentrism**. In these cases, individuals discount or distort any information from others who are members of groups toward which they are prejudiced.

The most insidious aspect of selective perception is that it often occurs automatically and unconsciously, so people usually do not realize they are doing it. They will not see that they are perceiving things in a biased and unfair manner and will often wonder why others can't see the "truth" as they see it. This is one of the reasons that prejudice can be so difficult to eliminate. However, by monitoring yourself and others you can learn to notice selective perception when it occurs, and not be seduced into letting it interfere with your efforts to communicate with others.

Semantic Problems. **Semantic problems** involve the use of words that do not accurately convey the meaning of the message to your audience. Confusing people by using overly complex words to explain a simple concept is a typical semantic problem. Another involves using emotionally charged words or labels to make a point, this may anger others or make them feel defensive. Name-calling is a good example of this. It hurts people's feelings and almost always changes the nature of the communication by forcing others to defend themselves.

A third semantic problem is using vague or ambiguous language that can be interpreted in many different ways. This is often unintentional, but it can cause the receiver to perceive the message much differently than the sender intended it to be perceived. Sometimes ambiguous language is used deliberately by senders who want to leave themselves "wiggle room" in case their message causes a negative reaction— "Oh, you must have misunderstood. I didn't mean it THAT way!" Either way, poor semantics can cause needless confusion and is easily corrected by stating your ideas clearly and encoding your message in a manner that is sensitive to your audience.

Mixed Messages. **Mixed messages** occur when a person's words simultaneously convey two conflicting messages or the words communicate the opposite of the person's body language or behavior. For example, in counseling it is not unusual to have clients say they are "fine" while they are looking downcast, with a tense, rigid, "closed" posture, and fidgeting constantly. Their nonverbal behavior clearly indicates that they are anything but "fine." Someone who tells a romantic partner "I love only you" while openly flirting with someone else is sending a mixed message. Another version of this is the romantic partner who says "Love me, but don't get too close!" A supervisor who tells an employee "You're working too hard and I want you to cut back," but then assigns the same employee to a new project that will require extensive overtime, is also sending a mixed message. Often people send mixed messages when they are conflicted themselves or are not sure how they feel about something. At other times they send mixed messages because they are saying what they believe they are supposed to say, but it is not what they really feel or believe.

Mixed messages can be very annoying as well as confusing. Generally, it is best to confront them openly, in a polite and respectful manner, when you become aware of them—"I'm not clear about what you're telling me here. I'm getting two different messages from you, and I'm not sure which one to pay attention to. These are the messages I'm perceiving ..."

Lack of Feedback. **Lack of feedback** occurs when the receiver of a communication fails to respond or provide any reaction to the communication. To be effective, communication must be a two-way street. Researchers have found that while two-way communication is more expensive and time-consuming than one-way communication (sending memos, giving orders, etc.), it is more accurate and effective in the long run (Schermerhorn et al, 2000). Allowing a receiver to provide you with feedback ensures that the message was understood accurately. It also gives the receiver an opportunity to express a reaction to the message and let you know possible problems that might result from carrying out the plans or orders conveyed in it.

Status Differences. **Status differences** can prevent free and open sharing of information between people with different ranks in the organizational hierarchy. Employees often fear telling managers anything that might get them into trouble or come back to "haunt" them on their annual evaluations. Too many times, and often with good reason, employees fear that if they tell managers something they don't want to hear, those managers will "shoot the messenger" rather than pay attention to the message. This results in supervisors not getting an accurate view of what is going on in the workplace, and it may allow serious problems to go unresolved and get progressively worse. On the management side, often the person with superior rank has a tendency to constantly give orders, and spend too little time listening to subordinates. Again, this results in management that is out of touch with workers and customers, which can have serious negative consequences for everyone involved. Therefore, it is important that managers establish an atmosphere in which subordinates are allowed to report problems without fear of retribution. It is also important for managers to openly solicit information from subordinates and listen to them.

Communication Overload. **Communication overload** is what happens when someone receives too much information to manage at one time. This problem has worsened as a result of the explosion of electronic methods of communication. From e-mail, voicemail, snail mail, and cell phones to instant messaging and the Internet, today's workers are often overwhelmed with information. Trying to sort through which messages have high priority and which ones do not, and what information is relevant and what isn't, adds to daily responsibilities and takes time away from other job duties. The cumulative effect is often increased job stress and a longer workday as people try desperately to keep up. Inevitably, some messages will be missed or forgotten, and this can cause further problems and stress.

Improving Communication

Just as there are many barriers to communication, there are also many ways to improve it. One of the most basic and effective ways to improve communication is to develop better listening skills. Americans have a reputation for being poor listeners (Gibson, 1995). We are often so busy trying to push our own agenda and "sell" ourselves to others that we fail to pay attention to what they are telling us. The costs to American business of poor listening are incalculable, and the problems it creates

GUIDELINES FOR ACTIVE LISTENING

1. Listen for content—try to hear exactly what is being said.
2. Listen for feelings—try to identify how the source feels about things.
3. Respond to feelings—let the source know that his or her feelings are recognized.
4. Note all cues—be sensitive to both verbal and nonverbal expressions.
5. Reflect back—repeat in your own words what you think you are hearing.

are endless (Hulbert, 1989; Nichols, 1957). For example, Pearce (1989) found that ideas get distorted by as much as 80 percent as they travel up and down an organizational chain of command. Much of this distortion is due to poor listening.

One method of improving listening skills is to use **active listening** techniques. Active listening means listening for underlying meanings and key elements of the sender's message. It involves paying attention to both the verbal and the nonverbal dimensions of a message. It requires that you look past context and delivery style and focus on content. It involves asking yourself, or the sender, questions about the message rather than passively and unquestioningly absorbing information. Simple questions like "Does this make sense?" "What evidence is there to support this claim?" "Is this statement biased?" or "Is there another point of view on this issue?" can make a world of difference in how you process information. The questions you raise through active listening can create a dialog rather than a monologue, and as stated earlier, two-way communication is generally more effective than one-way communication.

A variation of active listening is **empathic listening**. It involves using active listening to identify the underlying feelings or emotional content of someone's message, and trying to understand the situation from the other person's point of view. This can be particularly useful when combined with reflection (see "Try This Yourself"). For example, suppose someone tells you about a series of personal problems and you respond by saying, "If I were in your situation, I'd feel totally overwhelmed. How do you feel about all this?" or "It sounds as if you feel overwhelmed because so many things have gone wrong lately. What's it like for you to be struggling with so much?" This combines reflection with empathy and the questioning of active listening, and it opens the door to a deeper-level discussion of the person's situation.

With some practice, empathic listening can be a very powerful communication tool. It is particularly useful in dealing with individuals who are struggling with emotional problems or with people who are shy and have difficulty expressing themselves. It can also be a method of building trust in a relationship by showing your caring and concern for the other person's situation.

TRY THIS Yourself

Good listening does not develop naturally. It is a skill that can be practiced and learned. One simple technique that is commonly used by therapists to improve their listening skills is **reflection**. This involves acting like a mirror when you are receiving a communication. You listen for the essential meaning of the sender's message and then periodically reflect it back to the sender to make sure you have understood its meaning correctly. A simple way of doing this is to say "What I just heard you say was .... What I think you mean is ..." Other ways of reflecting that sound less stilted would be to simply say "Let me see if I understand. Do you mean ...?" or "I want to make sure I'm with you on this. Are you saying ...?" or "Let me make sure I'm clear about this. Are you telling me ..." There are innumerable ways to phrase a reflection, but the key is to reflect the essential meaning of the person's message.

Often people do not use reflection because they are afraid that the other person will think they are ignorant or somehow don't "get it." Actually, the opposite is usually true. People tend to see reflection as a sign of respect, caring, and a sincere effort to make sure you understand. The next time you are in a conversation in which it is important to correctly understand a complex message, occasionally try some simple reflection statements and see what impact they have on the conversation and on how well you understand the message.

Another way to improve communication is to create a **supportive climate** for communication. Gibb (1961) identified 6 ways of doing this:

1. Use descriptive speech rather than evaluative speech.
2. Take a collaborative approach to problem solving,
3. Communicate honestly and with spontaneity, rather than from a hidden agenda or strategy.
4. Demonstrate empathy.
5. Promote equality across and within levels of an organization.
6. Try to hear all sides of a debate rather than simply sticking to your own agenda.

A third way to improve communication is by providing effective **feedback**. This is the process through which you react to a sender's message by communicating back to the sender how you feel about the message. Feedback provides the sender with information about whether or not you understood the message. It can also let the sender know the impact of the message. Feedback can also be used to provide someone with an evaluation of how his or her behavior is affecting others or needs to be changed.

Not all feedback is helpful. Hurtful criticism given in the guise of feedback can be very destructive. Effective feedback has several characteristics:

1. **It is constructive, not destructive.** It is designed to help people build on their strengths and improve, not to humiliate them or tear them down to make yourself look good at their expense.

2. **It is specific and is given with clear examples.** Vague, general criticisms such as "You *always* let us down when we give you any responsibility" invite the response "Give me an example." If you don't have an appropriate example, your communication will not be effective.

3. **It focuses on specific behaviors that *can* be changed**, not on general traits or situations that the receiver cannot control. Saying "You are an idiot" may be a reflection of how you feel, but it does nothing to let the other person know what they are doing that leaves you feeling that they are "an idiot." Thus, they do not know what behaviors to change to stop being "an idiot" or if it is even possible to change. On the other hand, saying "When you criticize customers in front of other customers, I get very angry with you because it creates a very negative impression that may hurt our business" clearly states a behavior that is can be changed and lets the other person know the reason that you believe the behavior is a problem.

4. **It focuses on current behavior, not irrelevant past behavior.** If a person's current problem behavior is an extension or continuation of past problem behaviors, it might be appropriate to mention the long-term pattern of behavior when giving feedback. But criticizing someone about something that happened ages ago and can no longer be changed is inappropriate. Attacking irrelevant past behavior is a technique that some people use to win an argument or make the other person look bad. Effective feedback focuses on the "here and now," because that is all a person can control.

5. **It is given directly, privately, and in a spirit of trust and cooperation.** Giving feedback, especially negative feedback, in public can be embarrassing and force the receiver to go on the defensive to avoid public humiliation. This may defeat the purpose of the feedback and create needless problems.

6. **It is given at a time when the receiver is most ready to accept it** –in other words, don't "dump" it on someone when they are trying to cope with other crises or are clearly having a bad day.

> HOW TO GIVE CONSTRUCTIVE FEEDBACK
>
> - Give directly and in a spirit of mutual trust.
> - Be specific not general; use clear examples.
> - Give when receiver is most ready to accept.
> - Be accurate; check validity with others.
> - Focus on things the receiver can control.
> - Limit how much receiver gets at one time.

7. **It is given in limited doses.** Don't overwhelm someone with so much feedback that they can't possibly digest it all in one sitting. Be sensitive to what a person can handle.

Characteristics of Effective Communicators

Effective communicators are characterized by many of the characteristics discussed in this chapter. It is not any one thing they do that makes them effective; rather, it is the combination of many techniques used properly that allows them to communicate so well. Those characteristics include the following:

1. They think before they speak.
2. They are sensitive to their audience.
3. Their verbal and nonverbal behaviors are consistent with each other.
4. They appear confident, sincere, and enthusiastic in the way they deliver their message.
5. They are good listeners who use active and empathic listening techniques.
6. They encourage feedback and create a supportive climate for communication.

The Persuasive Communication

How many television advertisements do you see every week? More than you can count? How many of them do you remember? Probably not nearly as many as you have seen. How many of the ads you remember have inspired you to go out and buy the product being advertised? Probably only a small number. Each of those advertisements represents a particular form of communication known as **persuasive communication**, or a communication designed to change your attitudes, opinions, or behaviors in a predictable way desired by the sender. The fact that you do not remember all the television ads, and even fewer of them actually influenced your behavior, is a good indication that not all efforts at persuasion are equally effective. Since persuasive communication is such an important part of organizational communication, in this section we will look at a few of the factors that can affect it.

Characteristics of the Communicator and the Audience

Persuasive communicators are effective communicators. In addition, they have other qualities that enhance their ability to persuade others. You may have noticed that most of the celebrities on television commercials selling diet plans, weight loss devices, and exercise equipment do not look as if they need to use the equipment or diets they are selling. They are usually very attractive and in very good physical condition.

This is because, all things being equal, we are more likely to be persuaded by someone we perceive as physically and personally attractive than by someone we feel is unattractive (Petty et al., 1997). This is why the actors and actresses in most advertisements are young, healthy, and physically appealing.

We are also more likely to be persuaded by someone we perceive as an expert in a given field than by someone of low or questionable status (Petty et al., 1997). This is why advertisements that talk about what "doctors recommend" are so successful. In fact, just projecting an image of expertise can affect persuasiveness. Commercials in which a celebrity says, "I'm not a real doctor, but I play one on television" take advantage of the *perception* that the actor is a medical expert. Even though the actor is admitting that he or she has no real expertise on the subject, viewers will still buy the product.

We are more likely to be persuaded by someone with high social status, such as a sports hero or a Hollywood celebrity (Rathus & Nevid, 2000). This is why you see people like Britney Spears, Michael Jordan, and Tiger Woods in so many ads. Many people *identify* with celebrities and try to imitate them in ways that include using the products the celebrities appear to use. Advertisers take advantage of this tendency, using popular celebrities in advertisements in the hope that adoring fans will imitate what they see their heroes wearing or using.

Numerous researchers have found that we are more likely to be persuaded by people we believe are trustworthy (Petty et al., 1997). Surveys have repeatedly shown that the public trusts people in certain occupations, such as physicians, teachers, and librarians, more than used-car salespersons, lawyers, and politicians. Thus, people are more likely to be persuaded by someone from one of the more trusted occupations than one of the less trusted occupations—unless, of course, the particular politician or lawyer doing the persuading has established a reputation for being honest and trustworthy.

We are more likely to be persuaded by someone we believe is similar to us and shares our concerns (Petty et al., 1997). This is why some advertisers use actors and actresses who look like attractive versions of your next-door neighbors to sell products, especially household and yard-care products.

Finally, we are more likely to be persuaded by fast speakers than by slow speakers (Miller et al., 1976), especially if we are not paying full attention to the communication. It seems that when we are partially distracted, we are less able to refute the persuasive argument and become more vulnerable to its appeal (Allyn & Festinger, 1961; Romero et al., 1996).

The characteristics of the people receiving the persuasive message can be just as important to its effectiveness as the characteristics of the communicator. Researchers have found that people who are low in self-esteem and high in social anxiety are more likely to be persuaded than people who are high in self-esteem and low in social anxiety (Santee & Maslach, 1982). People with a weak attitude about a topic are much more easily swayed by a persuasive argument than those with a strong attitude about a topic (Petty & Krosnick, 1996). This may be why politicians spend so much time courting "independent" voters, who are less likely to have strongly liberal or conservative attitudes.

The setting in which a message is given and the mood of the person receiving the message can also affect the persuasiveness of a communication. People are more likely to be persuaded when they are relaxed and in a good mood. This tendency is enhanced when various aspects of the surrounding environment are calming and comfortable. Thus, the presence of pleasant background music and a pleasing decor can increase the chances that a persuasive message will succeed in its objectives. Apparently this occurs because when we are feeling relaxed and in a good mood we "let our guard down" and are less likely to evaluate a persuasive message critically (Forgas et al., 1997; Petty et al., 1997). Perhaps it is no accident that so many business transactions are conducted over lunch or dinner. An enjoyable meal in a pleasant setting can help relax people and put them in a good mood, making them more likely to respond positively to the sales pitch, which is always delivered toward the end of or after the meal.

Methods of Persuasion

There are many techniques that are commonly used to enhance the effectiveness of a persuasive communication. These include emotional appeal, repeated exposure, the foot-in the door technique, the door-in-the-face technique, lowballing, and the use of two-sided arguments.

Emotional Appeal. **Emotional appeal** involves attempting to arouse strong emotions in a person in order to make him or her more vulnerable to a persuasive communication. A person who is experiencing strong emotions is less likely to rationally evaluate a message and develop a logical counterargument. This makes the person more vulnerable to the persuasion effort. Researchers have found that persuasion efforts using emotional appeals can be very effective, particularly if the emotion being aroused is fear (Leventhal et al., 1965). However, people tend to respond most to fear messages that are linked to negative consequences that are perceived as immediate, relevant, likely to happen, and severe (Huseman & Hatfield, 1989). The more people perceive the consequence of a behavior as unlikely to happen any time soon, if at all, the less effective the attempt at scaring them into changing their behavior will be, even if the long-term consequences could be severe. This is why so many ads aimed at scaring teenagers into not smoking have failed. To most 15–year-olds who are inclined to smoke, the idea that if you smoke you *might* get lung cancer 20 or 30 years in the future is neither immediate nor relevant enough to deter them.

It is too far in the future and the danger is too remote and hypothetical to stop them from enjoying themselves now. In addition, the fact that they are doing something that others perceive as risky may enhance the attraction rather than increase their fear.

Repeated Exposure. Have you ever wondered why you may see the same commercial several times during a television program? This occurs because advertisers often use the technique of **repeated exposure**. The more you see or hear something, the more familiar with it you become. And the more familiar you are with something, the more likely it is that your attitude toward it will become more favorable.

By showing the same advertisement repeatedly, advertisers are hoping that you will be more likely to remember their product when you go shopping and that you will feel comfortable with it, making you more likely to buy it rather than competitors' products, with which you are less familiar.

The Foot-in-the-Door Technique. Another persuasion technique is the **foot-in-the-door technique**, which involves inducing compliance by initially making a small request and then following it with increasingly larger requests. As the person says yes to each request, it becomes more and more difficult to say no to the next request. This technique is commonly used by people involved in commission sales and telemarketing. They get their "foot-in-the-door" by asking for "just a minute of your time" to answer some simple survey questions. From there, the requests increase steadily. By the time you are finally presented with the sales pitch, you've gotten into the habit, or **response set**, of saying yes to the other person. You are now much more likely to agree to buy the product than you would have been had you been asked to buy it at the very beginning.

The Door-in-the-Face Technique. The opposite approach to the foot-in-the-door technique is the **door-in-the-face technique**. Here, you initially make a very intrusive request that is likely to be refused. If it *is* agreed to, all the better for you. However, if it is not agreed to, you follow it up with a less intrusive request, which is more likely to be agreed to because it seems so much more reasonable than the original request. Cialdini and colleagues (1975) found that people were almost 3 times as likely to agree to a request when it were preceded by a more intrusive request than when it was not preceded by another request at all.

Lowballing. **Lowballing** is a technique that is often used in sales. Here, the seller agrees to a deal on what appear to be favorable terms to the buyer. Once the buyer has committed to the deal, the seller finds an excuse to revise the terms in a way that is much less favorable to the buyer, knowing that since the buyer has already committed to the sale, it will now be difficult to back out of the deal. This technique is often used in negotiating the purchase of a car, and it is one of many reasons that car salespeople are neither respected nor trusted by the general public.

A variation of this technique is known as the **bait-and-switch technique.** In this method, a store advertises a basic model of an item, such as a stereo system, to get you into the store. Once you get there you find that they are "out of stock" on the advertised item, but they are willing to give you a "great deal" on a much more expensive system that has features you do not want or need. Since you are already there, you may be tempted to accept the new deal. Often it turns out that the new deal isn't a bargain after all, but by the time you figure this out it may be too late to do anything about it, and you are stuck with an overpriced system that you couldn't really afford.

Two-Sided Arguments.   A final persuasion technique is the use of **two-sided arguments**. In this technique, the communicator presents the other side's arguments in a way that looks fair-minded but is designed to show how flawed they are so that they can be easily refuted by the communicator's arguments. If people are forewarned of the other side's arguments in this way, they are less likely to be swayed by those arguments later on (Jacks & Devine, 2000).

Check & Review

THE COMMUNICATION PROCESS

Effective communication occurs when the sender's *intended* meaning is identical to the receiver's *perceived* meaning. Gibson (1995) describes a six-step model interpersonal communication. There are three dimensions in communication. These are the verbal dimension, the nonverbal dimension, and the contextual dimension. Experts in proxemics have identified four distances in North American culture that we are most comfortable with when communicating with others, depending on our relationship with them.

There are two types of organizational communication: formal communication and informal communication. There are also three directions of formal communi-cations within an organization: upward communication, downward communica-tion, and lateral communication.

Barriers to communication include physical distractions, selective perception, semantic problems, mixed messages, absence of feedback, status differences, and communi-cation overload. However, better listening, a supportive climate, and feedback can all improve communication.

Persuasive communication is a communication designed to change your attitudes, opinions, or behaviors in a pre-dictable way desired by the sender. The characteristics of the communicator, the audience, and the setting in which the communication occurs can all affect its persuasiveness.

Questions

1. The three dimensions of communica-tions are the _____ dimension, the _____ dimension, and the _____ dimension.
2. Briefly describe each of the four dis-tances in North American culture that we are most comfortable with when communicating with others.
3. Describe each of the 6 ways for creat-ing a supportive climate for communi-cation.
4. People who are _____ in self-esteem, _____ in social anxiety, and with a _____ attitude on an issue are more likely to be persuaded than others.

REFERENCES

Allyn & Festinger, 1961

Baron, R. A., & Byrne, D. *Social Psychology: Understanding Human Interaction* (9th *Ed.*). Boston: Allyn & Bacon, 2000.

Bass, B. M. *Bass and Stogdill's Handbook of Leadership: Theory, Research, and Manage-rial Applications* (3rd *Ed*). New York: The Free Press, 1990.

Cialdini, 1975.

DuBrin, Andrew J. *Human Relations: Interpersonal Job-Oriented Skills* (6th *Ed.*). Upper Saddle River, NJ: Prentice Hall, 1997.

DuBrin, Andrew J., *Leadership: Research Findings, Practice, and Skills* (3rd *Ed.*). New York: Houghton-Mifflin, 2001.

Forgas, J. P., Levinger, G., & Moylan, S. J. Feeling Good and Feeling Close: Affective Influ-ences on Perception of Intimate Relationships. *Personal Relationships*, *1*(2), 1994, 165–184.

Gibson, J. W. *The SupervisoryChallenge (2nd Ed.).* Englewood Cliffs, N.J.: Prentice Hall, 1995.

Graham, G. H., Unruh, J., & Jennings, P. The Impact of Nonverbal Communications in Orgainzations: A Survey of Perceptions. *The Journal of Business Communication*, 60, Winter, 1991.

Hulbert, J. E. Barriers to Effective Listening, *The Bulletin*, June 1989, 3.

Huseman, R. C., & Hatfield, J. D., *Managing the Equity Factor ...or "After All I've Done for You...",* Boston: Houghton-Mifflin, 1989.

Jacks, J. Z., & Devine, P. G. Attitude Importance, Forewarning of Message Content, and Resistance to Persuasion. *Basic and Applied Social Psychology*, 22 (1), 2000, 19–29.

Kaya, N., & Erkip, F. Invasion of Personal Space Under the Condition of Short-Term Crowding: A Case Study on an Automatic teller Machine. *Journal of Environmental Psychology*, 19(2), 1999, 183–189.

Leventhal, et. al., 1965.

Lowry, P., & Reimus, B. Ready, Aim, Communicate! *Management Review*, July, 1996, 40–43.

Lucent Technologies, *1998 Annual Report*

Major, B., Schmidlin, A. M., & Williams, L. *Journal of Personality and Social Psychology*, 58 (4), 1990, 634–643.rMalamuth, N.M. & Donnerstein, E. The Effects of Aggressive-Pornographic Mass Media Stimuli. *Advances in Experimental Social Psychology*, 15, 1982, 103–136.

Markman, H. J., Prediction of Marital Distress: A Five-Year Follow-Up. *Journal of Consulting and Clinical Psychology*, 49, 1981, 760–762.

Mehrabian, A. & Weiner, M., Decoding of Inconsistent Communications. *Journal of Personality and Social Psychology*, 6, 1947, 109–114.

Mehrabian, A. A Relationship of Attitude to Seated Posture Orientation, and Distance. *Journal of Personality and Social Psychology*, 10, 1968, 26–30.

Miller, 1976.

Nichols, R. G. Listening is a 10–Part Skill. *Nation's Business*, July 1957, 57.

Pearce, C. G. Doing Something abut Your Listening Ability. *Supervision Management*, March 1989, p. 26.

Petty, R. E., & Krosnik, 1996.

Petty, R. E., Wegener, D. T., & Fabrigar, L. R. Attitudes and Attitude Change. *Annual Review of Psychology*, 48, 1997, 609–647.

Rathus, S. & Nevid J. *Psychology and the Challenges of Life (8th Ed.).* New York: John Wiley & Sons, 2002.

Remlind, M. S., Jones, T. S., & Brinkman, H. Proxemics and Haptic Behavior in Three European Countries. *Journal of Nonverbal Behavior*, 15 (4), 1991, 215–232.

Romero, et. al. 1996.

Santee, R. T. & Maslach, C. To Agree or Not to Agree: Personal Dissent Amid Social Pressure to Conform. *Journal of Personality and Social Psychology*, 42, 1982, 690–700.

Schermerhorn, J., Hunt, J., & Osborn, R. *Organizational Behavior (7th Ed.).* New York: John Wiley & Sons, 2000.

Snyder, D. Multidimensional Assessment of Marital Satisfaction. *Journal of Marriage And the Family*, 41, 1979, 813–823.

Stier, D. S., & Hall, J. A. Gender Differences in Touch: An Empirical and Theoretical Review. *Journal of Personality and social Psychology*, 47(2), 1984, 440–459.

MODULE 57
DEALING WITH CONFLICT

Identifying Conflict: "Why can't we all just get along?"

There are many types and levels of conflict, and each has different causes and effects. However, there is one defining feature that is common to all conflict — *incompatible interests*. Business owners want the highest profit on their product, whereas the consumer wants the lowest price. The 2–year-old wants his mother's full attention, but she needs to drive the car safely.

Interestingly, conflicts sometimes develop when individuals or groups don't have real opposing interests but *believe* they do (e.g., Tjosvold & DeDreu, 1997). Employers and employees generally share the common goal of increased profits. However, if one side or both believes that the other side is preventing them from maximizing their earnings, conflict arises and will escalate. Employers may reduce salaries, eliminate certain positions, or reduce their work force. Employees may demand more pay or even threaten to strike and attempt to close the business entirely.

As these examples demonstrate, conflict is usually perceived negatively because it is generally associated with stress and discomfort. But it also has a positive side. Any organization (or personal relationship) that lacks conflict is lacking in passion and vitality. Conflict that is recognized and managed properly can stimulate renewed and improved human relations.

Levels and Types of Conflict

There are two kinds of conflict that occur in the workplace: intrapersonal conflict and interpersonal conflict. Intrapersonal Conflict

In module 9 we defined conflict as a negative emotional state caused by having to choose between two or more incompatible goals or impulses. We also identified three basic forms of conflict: approach-approach, avoidance-avoidance, and approach-avoidance. Can you see why these are all intrapersonal conflicts? They all occur within (*intra*) the person. There are two major types of interpersonal conflict: substantive and emotional (Schermerhorn et al., 2000). Substantive conflict involves disagreement over the goals to be pursued or the methods used to pursue those goals. Two workers disagreeing over how best to complete a job, or two managers arguing about what a department's first priority should be, are examples of substantive conflict. Since we are often faced with competing priorities in the workplace and there are usually many ways to accomplish a task, substantive conflicts are commonplace, and successful managers must learn to deal with them effectively.

In contrast to substantive conflict, emotional conflict occurs when feelings of anger, fear, mistrust, dislike, or resentment develop between two or more people (Walton, 1969). Emotional conflicts differ from substantive conflicts in that emotional conflicts are *personal* in nature and focus on the other individual involved in the conflict, whereas substantive conflicts are *impersonal* and focus on the task rather than on the other person. Emotional conflicts tend to be much more stressful and emotionally draining than substantive conflicts. They tend to be harder to "let go of" when you leave the job, and thus they create chronic stress that can detract from your personal life as well as your job performance. One of the difficulties with substantive conflicts is if they are deep enough and last long enough, one or more parties begin to take the conflict personally and it evolves into an emotional conflict.

Interpersonal Conflict

When two or more individuals have mutually incompatible goals or disagree on the methods for achieving stated goals, the result is **interpersonal conflict**. For example, when one person wants to hire outside consultants for advice on a project and another wants to set up an internal committee, or two managers have differing goals for an organization, you have conflict between (*inter*) individuals. Interpersonal conflict can also exist at the group level, when two or more departments in an organization argue over budget allocations, or even at the organizational level if different companies compete for the same customers' business.

Conflict and Competition

How does conflict differ from competition? They are sometimes difficult to distinguish because they often overlap. However, if you look closely, you will see that they each have unique characteristics. These differences are particularly clear when comparing competition with emotional conflict. First, competition tends to be *impersonal*, whereas emotional conflict is *personal*. The goal in competition is to win, not to hurt your competitors. Although your competitors may end up being hurt by losing, it is an unintended side effect, not a goal. And often, after a healthy competition, the winner will reach out and help the loser "pick up the pieces" so that they can work together or begin another competition with each other. In conflict, as it becomes personal and resentment develops, the goal is often as much to hurt or even destroy the opponent as it is to win. The pain inflicted on the opponent is deliberate, and the "winner" may take great pride and comfort at having hurt or destroyed the "loser." This *intention to hurt* is not a part of healthy competition and can cause long-term negative consequences that may make it difficult to "patch things up" and start over again.

Another difference is that in competition, there are usually agreed upon rules about how to win the contest. Whether out of mutual respect or fear of retribution, competitors generally stick to those rules, which helps to keep the contest impersonal. In conflict, as it becomes emotional, there is a tendency to throw out the rules and do whatever it takes to defeat the opponent, no matter who gets hurt. In such situations you feel justified in breaking the rules because of your resentment and hostility toward your competitors. They are often perceived as evil or dangerous and therefore as "getting what they deserve."

Competition is typically perceived as healthy and productive, because when conducted properly it can inspire people to be more creative and productive. Conversely, conflict is typically perceived as negative and counterproductive because it so often becomes emotional, personal, and destructive. In the process it may generate extreme stress, anger, and resentment that can last indefinitely, lower productivity, and even impair physical and emotional health.

The major drawbacks to competition emerge when people take it too seriously and make it personal. When people become so focused on winning that they start to "demonize" their opponents, they will often begin breaking the rules, turning the contest into a "cut-throat" competition—which almost always evolves into a personal conflict, with all its attendant problems. A key aspect of using competition successfully in the workplace is to enforce the rules, keep it impersonal, and prevent it from devolving into emotional conflict.

Causes of Conflict: Let Me Count The Ways

Conflict usually has its roots in several obvious and not so obvious factors, rather than a single, blatant cause. Although the causes of some conflicts are readily apparent, sorting out all the interrelated underlying causes can be difficult, if not impossible. Just look at how challenging it has been to sort out all the causes of the Israeli-

Palestinian conflict. Both sides have legitimate grievances, but in trying to resolve them the debate often becomes nothing more than an exercise in name-calling and finger-pointing, with each side blaming the other for "causing" the problem. As a result, nothing substantive gets done and the violence continues.

Recognizing the causes of conflict can be an important first step toward understanding the nature of the conflict and eventually resolving it. There are several common causes of conflict in the workplace. They include resource scarcity, role conflict, personality and value differences, goal differences, and discrimination and harassment.

Resource Scarcity

One of the most common causes of workplace conflict is competition for limited resources, also called **resource scarcity**. If there are not enough resources to meet demand, the competition for those resources can get quite intense and may escalate into full-fledged emotional conflict. For example, if there are limited funds available for pay raises, the competition to get the biggest share of those funds is often very personal and intense. Those who end up with small raises or no raises at all may feel cheated and resentful toward those who got larger raises and toward the managers who assigned the pay raises. These feelings of resentment may lead to personal animosity toward co-workers and supervisors as well as lower productivity, deliberately doing lower quality work, openly challenging management directives, or even quitting the job.

Role Conflict

Another common source of workplace conflict is **role conflict**. This occurs when a person is expected to carry out job duties or accomplish goals that are incompatible with each other. It often results from unclear communication of work expectations or from work assignments that demand too much from an employee to be accomplished in the time allowed. For example, ordering an employee to complete two separate tasks within a time frame that only allows for one task to be completed properly can cause role conflict. If only one task can be done properly, which one do you choose to carry out? Or do you superficially complete both of them, doing neither of them properly? Such conflicts can be very stressful.

Employees in customer service occupations sometimes find themselves in a role conflict in that they are serving two "masters" at once. They must meet the needs and demands of customers as best they can, but sometimes those needs and demands conflict with organizational policy and management directives. This is especially problematic when policies and directives are not clearly stated or are not flexible enough to cover a wide range of possible customer problems. In these conflicts, employees are often caught between the need to satisfy customers and the need to avoid getting in trouble with their supervisors, or between the need to please their supervisors and the need to avoid being berated by customers, who may complain to those supervisors. This kind of conflict is best characterized by the phrase "caught between a rock and a hard place."

Personality and Value Differences

Personality and value differences are a primary source of emotional conflict in the workplace. People differ greatly in the personal styles, values, interests, and work ethic they bring to their jobs. When these styles and values are incompatible with those of co-workers, they may create tension, resentment, and frustration. Someone who is very neat, meticulous, and well organized, for example, may have serious problems working regularly with someone who is disorganized and sloppy, even though both may do good-quality work. Similarly, someone who is very passive and deferential may have great difficulty working with someone who is very aggressive or abrasive.

Value differences can be difficult to resolve because people often find them offensive or threatening and will resist any effort to compromise their values. Differences in personal style can be equally difficult to resolve because often people cannot specify exactly which behaviors are bothering them. Saying that someone "rubs me the wrong way" is often an expression of this type of style difference, but such statements are too vague to be helpful in resolving the problem.

Differences in religious beliefs, age, and racial, ethnic or cultural background can amplify personality differences because of stereotypes about people with very different beliefs or from very different backgrounds. Such stereotypes may cause people to perceive selectively, or see what they want to see, when dealing with others. This, in turn, can reinforce negative stereotypes and exacerbate existing personality conflicts.

Goal Differences

Another source of workplace conflict is **goal differences.** These occur when two or more people or departments within an organization are simultaneously striving to accomplish incompatible goals, arguing over the goal toward which the organization should direct itself, or working to achieve their own goals at the expense of everyone else's. When a salesperson at a car dealership tries to "close the deal" by making promises to a customer that cannot be met by the service department, he or she has created a goal conflict. The salesperson's goal is to make the sale, but as a result of the unrealistic promises, the customer service department cannot achieve its goal of keeping the customer satisfied at a reasonable cost. This type of conflict can be very destructive because it can cause individuals or departments to work at cross-purposes in a way that breeds distrust and contempt. Hence, it is important that managers make sure everyone is "on the same page" regarding organizational goals, policies, and procedures, and that goal conflicts are resolved as quickly and equitably as possible.

Discrimination and Harassment

A final source of workplace conflict involves **discrimination** (discussed more fully in 47) and **harassment** (discussed more fully in module 45). In both, individuals are treated unfairly because of personal characteristics such as race, age, ethnicity, or gender. They are particularly bothersome because of the severe distress they can cause. They often force individuals to choose between their morals, self-respect, or safety, and their job. Since discrimination and harassment are prohibited by law, they can lead to legal action being taken against the organization that allows them to occur and fails to take immediate and effective corrective action. If left unchecked, harassment and discrimination cause emotional conflicts that are very deep and difficult to resolve, often resulting in other workers "taking sides" and creating new conflicts. It is therefore incumbent on organizations to establish well-defined policies on harassment and discrimination, to clearly state those policies, and to enforce them aggressively and consistently.

Positive Conflict: Is There Such a Thing?

As we mentioned at the beginning of this module, conflict does not always have to be destructive, or **dysfunctional.** Because conflict is a natural occurrence, it is important to try to find ways to resolve it that result in positive benefits to the organization and to the individuals involved. When a conflict is resolved beneficially, it is known as a **functional conflict.** How can conflict result in positive benefits? There are several ways:

1. **Conflict changes things.** Sometimes the only way a problem can be resolved is for someone to take a firm stand and resist someone else's goals. Passive resist-

---

WHEN TO USE CONFLICT MANAGEMENT STYLES

- Collaboration and problem solving is preferred to gain true conflict resolution when time and cost permit.
- Avoidance may be used when an issue is trivial or more important issues are pressing, or when people need to cool down temporarily and regain perspective.
- Authoritative command may be used when quick and decisive action is vital or when unpopular actions must be taken.
- Accommodation may be used when issues are more important to others than to yourself or when you want to build "credits" for use in later issues.
- Compromise may be used for temporary settlements to complex issues or to arrive at expedient solutions when time is limited.

ance, a form of nonviolent conflict, was used by Ghandi to help India gain independence from Great Britain. The 13 American colonies used violent resistance to gain independence from Britain. Workers launching a strike against unfair management practices have often been able to get those practices changed.

2. **Conflict "clears the air."** Sometimes people like a "good fight" or a "spirited discussion" because it motivates them to express themselves fully and honestly. It also can let you know where the other person stands. Such information can be helpful in resolving problems and preventing future disputes. It can lead to an understanding of why the other person feels the way he or she does, so that although you may still disagree, you can now disagree *respectfully*.

3. **Conflict can bring out the best in people.** Like competition, conflict often inspires people to be more creative and work harder than they otherwise would. It can become a test of character for some that forces them to "rise to the occasion" and bring out strengths they never knew they had. Resolving a conflict successfully can raiseone's confidence level and self-esteem.

4. **Conflict can unite people.** Sometimes conflict brings diverse groups of people together in an effort to solve mutual problems. Such alliances can sometimes result in long-term friendships that benefit everyoneinvolved. Similarly, successful resolution of a conflict can sometimes bring former combatants together with an increased understanding and respect for each other.

5. **Conflict can improve decision-making.** The potential for conflict can cause people to think more carefully about the choices they are making and be more sensitive to the impact of those choices on others. In groups, substantive conflict can help prevent problems such as risky shift and groupthink.

This does not mean that conflict is the *preferred* method of effecting change, making decisions, or uniting people. The potentially negative consequences of conflict often outweigh its potential benefits. However, sometimes there is no other way to resolve an issue, so conflict occasionally is necessary.

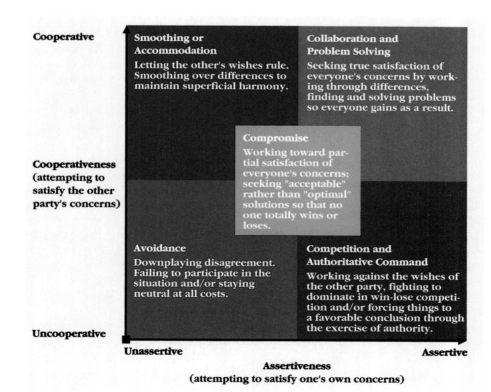

Five ways to manage conflict.

Conflict Resolution: Is There a Way When There's a Will?

There are numerous factors to consider when attempting to manage or resolve conflict. We have already discussed a few of them. Understanding the type of conflict you are dealing with is often the first step in finding a way to resolve it. Another factor is identifying the underlying causes of the conflict. This also can be helpful in that it may allow you to discover "hidden agendas" or other subtle factors contributing to the conflict that might prevent its resolution if they are not made public and discussed openly. Having clearly stated rules and policies regarding organizational goals and issues such as discrimination can be helpful in preventing some conflicts before they start and resolving others before they get out of hand.

Schermerhorn and colleagues (2000) have identified five approaches to conflict resolution that are commonly used in the workplace: avoidance, accommodation, compromise, authoritative command, and collaboration. No single strategy is effective in every situation, and some strategies cannot be implemented in some situations. No matter which approach is used, true resolution of problems will not occur until the underlying emotional and substantive issues are dealt with in a way that leaves no one feeling like a "loser" (Filley, 1975).

Avoidance

Avoidance involves pretending that a conflict does not exist. Usually the person avoiding conflict is hoping that, with patience and time, the conflict will resolve itself and disappear. Avoidance is generally considered an ineffective strategy because unless active steps are taken to resolve many problems, they progressively worsen to the point where they can no longer be avoided and may be much more difficult to resolve than if they had been confronted early. Avoidance can be the best approach when an issue is unimportant and does not justify the time and attention needed to resolve it. It can also be useful when people need to take time away from a problem for a while to calm down and gather their thoughts so that they can deal with the problem at a later time.

Accommodation

Accommodation is also known as **smoothing**. It involves focusing on areas of agreement between conflicting parties and downplaying or "smoothing over" areas of conflict or disagreement. This is not usually an effective strategy for resolving serious conflicts because it often leaves them simmering underneath a veneer of happiness and cooperation. Over the long term, these "hidden" conflicts can lead to underlying resentments that can undercut true cooperative effort and lead to other conflicts. Smoothing can still be useful when areas of conflict are minor and people agree on most major goals and objectives. In this case, smoothing can take the form of "agreeing to disagree" on the minor areas where conflict exists.

Compromise

Compromise involves the use of **negotiation** so that each party involved in the conflict gives up something that it values in order to obtain similar concessions from the other parties and achieve a reasonably fair settlement of the problem. Compromise can be frustrating because no one gets everything he or she wants, but each party can take some comfort in the fact that no one else got everything they wanted either. Compromise can be the best option when there is no perfect solution to a problem and each side feels that the compromise is the fairest and most workable option available. It can be used when there isn't enough time to resolve all the intricacies of a complex problem, or as a temporary solution for problems that cannot be resolved at a given time. However, it can sometimes result in "halfway" solutions that complicate matters even further, and there are some issues on which effective compromise is not possible.

Authoritative Command

Authoritative command is also known as imposing a solution. In this case a leader uses legitimate authority to dictate a solution that subordinates must follow. This approach often results in one or more parties in the conflict feeling that his or her needs have been ignored or neglected, and this creates resentment toward the leader. Moreover, this approach usually does not deal with the underlying causes of the conflict. Since these are left unresolved, it very often results in continuing low-level conflict occurring "below the radar screen" of the leader, and it can lead to higher-level conflicts in the future. However, authoritative command may be the best approach when quick or decisive actions are required, especially when those actions are unpopular.

Collaboration

Collaboration, or problem solving, occurs when all parties in the conflict recognize that there is a serious problem that must be dealt with, and put solving the problem ahead of their own interests. In this approach, time is taken to gather all relevant information, ensure that it is accurate, and discuss it thoroughly. Participants are given the opportunity to indicate what they consider the best overall solution to the problem.

This approach works best when all parties involved see a responsibility to be open and honest, and resolve the problem for everyone's good. The goal here is to arrive at a solution that acceptably achieves the goals of each party, or what is called a "win-win" solution. Although this is the ideal conflict resolution strategy, it isn't always possible to achieve. It often requires more time and effort than is available, and there are some situations in which, because of the nature of the conflicting parties' goals, it is not possible to achieve everyone's goals fully. Finally, there are conflicts in which the various parties are unwilling to set aside their own agendas and cooperate.

Assertiveness: Are You a Lion or a Mouse?

Do you remember the corny lightbulb joke from module 1—the one that asks how many psychologists it takes to change a lightbulb? The answer was "None. The lightbulb has to want to change itself." We repeat this joke now because we think it's funny (and we get to be the authors) and because it illustrates the power of assertiveness in dealing with conflict. Many attempts at conflict resolution fail because someone *doesn't want to change*. The beauty of our last method of con-

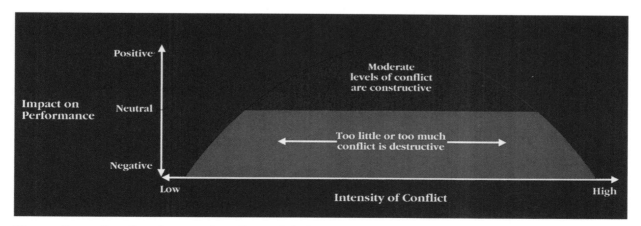

The two faces of conflict: functional conflict and dysfunctional conflict.

flict resolution, **assertiveness**, is that most of the power is in your own hands. Even if the other person (or lightbulb) doesn't want to change, you can change yourself.

When you are faced with potential conflict, you can choose among three possible behavioral options: You can be passive, assertive, or aggressive. **Passive behavior** involves failing to stand up for your rights even when you are fully justified in doing so. It often results in other people walking all over you and treating you like a doormat. Although passive individuals often "get along" with everyone, they are seldom respected by anyone and rarely achieve their goals. They are self-denying and self-inhibiting, experience low self-esteem, and feel hurt and anxiety ridden (Alberti & Emmons, 1974; Rathus & Nevid, 2002). Passive behavior may be an effective way of avoiding short-term problems, but its negative long-term effects are usually quite costly.

Aggressive behavior involves standing up for your rights no matter whom you hurt. It is designed to deny, humiliate, and deny the rights of others. It includes insults, threats, and even physical intimidation and attacks (Alberti & Emmons, 1974). Aggressive behavior is more likely than passive behavior to get you what you want in the short term. But, like passiveness, it, too, usually has negative long-term consequences. For example, others may initially give in to aggressive people and feel intimidated by them, yet they rarely like or respect them. Think about how much liking and respect you had for classroom or playground bullies when you were growing up. Also, aggressive behavior often provokes aggressive responses, which can easily escalate into violence. Moreover, chronic aggression often leads to feelings of guilt and low self-esteem in the aggressive person, unless he or she is completely insensitive to the reactions of others (Rathus & Nevid, 2002).

Assertive behavior strikes a balance between passive and aggressive behavior. It involves "a socially acceptable method of expressing personal rights" (Wolpe & Lazarus, 1976). In other words, it involves standing up for your rights while simultaneously respecting the rights of others. Many researchers have found that assertive individuals are more likely to achieve their goals and be liked and respected by others. They also tend to have higher levels of self-esteem, self-worth, and self-satisfaction because they have more control over their life choices and direction. Most important, they are more likely to resolve conflicts effectively.

Lazarus (1973) identified four types of assertive behavior:

1. The ability to say "no."
2. The ability to ask for favors or make requests.
3. The ability to express both positive and negative feelings.
4. The ability to initiate, continue, and terminate general conversations.

Someone who is competent in any one of these types of assertiveness may not be competent in the others. In other words, a person may be very skilled at saying "no" to requests from others but may not be able to ask for favors or make requests of others. All four types of assertiveness may be important in resolving various kinds of conflicts.

Keep in mind that assertive behavior doesn't guarantee that you will achieve your goals or force others to respect your rights. But it can definitely increase your chances of doing so. Even if you fail, you will know that you have tried, and this can help preserve your self-respect and the respect of others.

The Rathus Assertiveness Schedule

What about you? Do you enrich the pockets of every telemarketer, or do you say no? Do you stick up for your rights or do you allow others to walk all over you? Do you say what you feel or do you say what you think other people want you to say? Do you initiate relationships with attractive people, or do you shy away from them?

One way to gain insight into how assertive you are is to take the Rathus Assertiveness Schedule (Rathus, 1973). Once you have finished, turn to page XXX to find out how to calculate your score. A table will also allow you to compare your assertiveness with that of 1,400 students drawn from 35 college campuses across the United States.

Directions: Indicate how well each item describes you by using this code:

  3 = very much like me
  2 = rather like me
  1 = slightly like me
−1 = slightly unlike me
−2 = rather unlike me
−3 = very much unlike me

_____ 1. Most people seem to be more aggressive and assertive than I am.*

_____ 2. I have hesitated to make or accept dates because of "shyness."*

_____ 3. When the food served at a restaurant is not done to my satisfaction, I complain about it to the waiter or the waitress.

_____ 4. I am careful to avoid hurting other people's feelings, even when I feel I have been injured.*

_____ 5. If a salesperson has gone to considerable trouble to show me merchandise that is not quite suitable, I have a difficult time saying "No."*

_____ 6. When I am asked to do something, I insist upon knowing why.

_____ 7. There are times when I look for a good, vigorous argument.

_____ 8. I strive to get ahead as well as most people in my position.

_____ 9. To be honest, people take advantage of me.*

_____ 10. I enjoy starting conversations with new acquaintances and strangers.

_____ 11. I often don't know what to say to people who are sexually attractive to me.*

_____ 12. I will hesitate to make phone calls to business establishments and institutions.*

_____ 13. I would rather apply for a job, or for admission to a college by writing letters than by going through personal interviews.*

_____ 14. I find it embarrassing to return merchandise.*

_____ 15. If a close and respected relative were annoying me, I would smother my feelings rather than express my annoyance.*

_____ 16. I have avoided asking questions for fear of sounding stupid.*

_____ 17. During an argument I am sometimes afraid that I will get so upset that I will shake all over.*

_____ 18. If a famed and respected lecturer makes a comment which I think is incorrect, I have the audience hear my point of view as well.

_____ 19. I avoid arguing over prices with clerks and salespeople.*

_____ 20. When I have done something important or worthwhile, I manage to let others know about it.

_____ 21. I am open and frank about my feelings.

_____ 22. If someone has been spreading false and bad stories about me, I see him or her as soon as possible and "have a talk" about it.

_____ 23. I often have a hard time saying "No."*

_____ 24. I tend to bottle up my emotions

rather than make a scene.*

_____ 25. I complain about poor service in a restaurant or elsewhere.

_____ 26. When I am given a compliment, I sometimes just don't know what to say.*

_____ 27. If a couple near me in a theater or at a lecture were conversing rather loudly, I would ask them to be quiet or to take their con-

versation elsewhere.

_____ 28. Anyone attempting to push ahead of me in line is in for a good battle.

_____ 29. I am quick to express an opinion.

_____ 30. There are times when I just can't say anything.*

(Reprinted from Rathus & Nevid, 2002, pp. 134–135).

Check & Review

DEALING WITH CONFLICT

There is one defining feature that is common to all conflict—*incompatible interests*. There are two levels of conflict that occur in the workplace: *intrapersonal* conflict and *interpersonal* conflict.

While there are many similarities between conflict and competition, there are also several key differences that tend to result in competition being less destructive and more positively perceived than conflict. Conflict usually has its roots in several factors, rather than a single, obvious cause.

There are five conflict resolution approaches commonly used in the workplace. No single strategy is effective in every situation, and some strategies cannot be implemented in some situations. When you are faced with potential conflict there are three possible behavioral options from which to choose. You can be passive, assertive, or aggressive. Assertive individuals are more likely to achieve their goals and be well liked and respected by others.

Questions

1. Identify five common sources of conflict in the workplace.

2. Briefly explain five ways that conflict can be beneficial.

3. Identify the five conflict resolution approaches commonly used in the workplace.

4. Describe four types of assertive behavior.

REFERENCES

Alberti, R. E., & Emmons, M. L. *Your Perfect Right: A Guide to Assertive Behavior*. San Luis Obispo, CA: Impact, 1974.

Filley, A. C. *Interpersonal Conflict Resolution*. Gelenview, IL: Scott, Foresman, 1975.

Hardin, G. (1968). The tragedy of the commons. Science, 162, 1243–1248.

Lazarus, A. A. On Assertive Behavior: A Brief Note. *Behavior Therapy*, 4, 1973, 697–699.

Rathus, S. A. A 30–Item Schedule for Assessing Assertive Behavior. *Behavior Therapy*, 4, 1973, pp. 398–406.

Rathus, S. & Nevid J. *Psychology and the Challenges of Life(8th Ed.)*. New York: John Wiley & Sons, 2002.

Schermerhorn, J., Hunt, J., & Osborn, R. *Organizational Behavior (7th Ed.)*. New York: John Wiley & Sons, 2000.

Tjosvold, D., & DeDreu, C. (1997). Managing conflict in Dutch organizations: A test of the relevance of Deutsch's cooperation theory. Journal of Applied Social Psychology, 27, 2213–2227.

Walton, R. E. *Interpersonal Peacemaking: Confrontations and Third Party Consultations*. Reading, MA: Addison-Wesley, 1969.

Wolpe, J. & Lazarus, A. A. *Behavior Therapy Techniques*. New York: Pergamon Press, 1966.

Visual Summary for Modules 53, 54, 55, 56, and 57

Leadership

Traditional Three-Stage Memory Model

- Leaders are similar to, but also different from, managers. Leadership involves a combination of inborn traits (the *great person theory*) or environmental influences (*situational theories*).
- Programs that train leaders emphasize sensitivity, visioning, communication, impression management, and empowering.
- There are three major leadership philosophies:

Theory X
Workers are lazy and need direction/coercion

Theory Y
Workers are self-motivating and creative

Theory Z
Workers want to be part of decision

- The three fundamental styles of leadership exist along a continuum:

Autocratic ⟶ Participative ⟶ Laissez-faire

- There are five types of leadership power (legitimate, expert, referent, reward, and coercive), and each is effective if used appropriately.

Workplace Motivation

Reinforcement Theories	*Content Theories*	*Process Theories*
Employ law of effect, positive reinforcement, negative reinforcement, punishment	Use Maslow's hierarchy of needs, Herzberg's two-factor theory, and Holland's personality-job-fit theory	Employ Vroom's expectance theory, equity theory, self-efficacy theory, and goal-setting theory

Groups in Organizations

Work groups are commonly classified into two major categories: Formal groups and informal groups. **Autonomous work groups** are used in many factories as an alternative to the traditional assembly line approach. Groups grow, evolve, and pass through various stages of development or decline.

Stages of Group Development

Forming ➡ Storming ➡ Norming ➡ Performing ➡ Adjourning

There are two types of group roles, formal and informal, and there are three types of roles within a group: perceived roles, expected roles, and enacted roles. Norms, cohesiveness, and size affect what people expect from each other and how they behave within groups. Brainstorming, the nominal group technique, and the Delphi technique improve group decision-making.

The Communication Process

- Gibson proposed a six-step model of interpersonal communication—ideation, encoding, transmission, reception, decoding, and understanding.
- There are three key dimensions of communication—verbal, nonverbal, and contextual.
- Organizational communication can be formal or informal. Formal communication can go in three directions—upward, downward, and lateral.
- Barriers to communication include physical distractions, selective perception, semantic problems, mixed messages, absence of feedback, status differences, and communication overload. However, better listening, a supportive climate, and feedback can improve communication.
- Persuasive communication is designed to change attitudes, opinions, or behaviors in a predictable way desired by the sender. Characteristics of the communicator, audience, and setting all affect the degree of persuasion.

Dealing With Conflict

- There are two kinds of conflict in the workplace—intrapersonal and interpersonal. Interpersonal conflict can be substantive and/or emotional.
- Conflict and competition share many similarities, but competition is generally less destructive and more positively perceived.
- Common causes of conflict include resource scarcity, role conflict, personality and value differences, goal differences, discrimination and harassment.
- Conflict has positive benefits when it changes things, "clears the air," brings out the best in people, unites people, and improves decision-making.
- There are five major conflict resolution strategies—avoidance, accommodation, compromise, authoritative command, and collaboration. There also are three behavioral options—passive, assertive, or aggressive.

APPENDIX A

Answers to Review Questions, Try This Yourself, Active Learning Exercises, and Active Learning Worksheets

Module 1 Check & Review Page 10 1. scientific; behavior; mental processes. 2. The process of objectively evaluating, comparing, analyzing, and synthesizing information. Critical thinking has three components: *affective skills* (e.g., empathy and tolerance for ambiguity), *cognitive abilities* (e.g., independent thinking and synthesizing), and *behavioral traits* (e.g., delaying judgment and applying knowledge to new situations). 3. (a). *Description* tells "what" occurred. (b). An *explanation* tells "why" a behavior occurred. (c). *Prediction* specifies the conditions under which a behavior or event is likely to occur. (d). *Change* means applying psychological knowledge to prevent unwanted outcomes or bring about desired goals 4. (a). biopsychology or neuroscience, (b). developmental psychology, (c). cognitive psychology, (d). clinical and counseling psychology, (e). industrial/organizational psychology. *Module 1 Active Learning Worksheet Page 10* 1. c. 2. f. 3. a. 4. j. 5. h. 6. g. 7. i. 8. b. 9. e. 10. d.

Module 2 Check & Review Page 18 1. (a). literature review (b). formulating a testable hypothesis, (c). designing the study and collecting the data, (d). analyzing the data and accepting or rejecting the hypothesis, (e). publishing followed by replication and scientific review, and f). building further theory. 2. In an experiment, the experimenter manipulates and controls the variables, which allows them to isolate a single factor and examine the effect of that factor alone on a particular behavior. 3. c. 4. The two problems for researchers are experimenter bias and ethnocentrism, whereas the two problems for participants are sample bias and participant bias. To guard against **experimenter bias,** researchers employ blind observers, single-blind and **double-blind studies,** and **placebos.** To control for **ethnocentrism,** they use cross-cultural sampling. To offset participant problems with **sample bias,** researchers use random/representative sampling and **random assignment.** To control for participant bias, they rely on many of the same controls in place to prevent experimenter bias, such as double-blind studies. They also attempt to assure anonymity, confidentiality, and sometimes use deception. *Module 2 Check & Review Page 26* 1. **Naturalistic observation** studies and describes behavior in its natural habitat, surveys use interviews or questionnaires to obtain information on a sample of participants, and individual case studies conduct in-depth studies of a participant. 2. d. 3. b. 4. c. *Module 2 Active Learning Worksheet Page 27*

Module 3 Check & Review Page 36 1. experimental. 2. functionalists. 3. Freud's theories are controversial because of his non-scientific approach, emphasis on sexual and aggressive impulses, and possible sexist bias in his writings and theories. 4. a. *Module 3 Active Learning Worksheet Page 37* 1. Gestalt. 2. Behaviorism. 3. Psychoanalytic/Psychodynamic. 4. Cognitive psychology. 5. Evolutionary. 6. Neuroscience/biopsychology. 7. Humanistic. 8. Functionalism. 9. Sociocultural. 10. Eclectic.

Module 5 Check & Review Page 54 1. central; peripheral. 2. d. 3. d. 4. The sympathetic nervous system arouses the body and mobilizes energy stores to deal with emergencies, whereas the parasympathetic nervous system calms the body and conserves the energy stores. *Module 5 Check & Review Page 62* 1. Check your diagram with Figure 2.2. 2. c. 3. b. 4. Neurotransmitters and endorphins are manufactured and released at the synapse, where the messages are picked up and relayed by neighboring neurons.

Hormones are released from glands in the endocrine system directly into the bloodstream. *Module 5 Active Learning Worksheet Page 63*

Crossword answers: SYNAPSE; PERIPHERAL NERVOUS SYSTEM; NEUROSCIENCE; HORMONES; AXONS; MYELIN SHEATH; SYMPATHETIC NERVOUS SYSTEM; ACTION POTENTIALS; CENTRAL NERVOUS SYSTEM; SOMATIC; ENDORPHINS; NEURONS; DENDRITES; NERVOUS SYSTEM; NEUROTRANSMITTER; AUTONOMIC NERVOUS SYSTEM; GLIAL CELLS

Module 6 Check & Review Page 71 1. Electrical recording techniques implant electrodes into the brain or on its surface to study the brain's electrical activity, whereas electrical stimulation of the brain uses a weak electric current to stimulate specific areas or structures of the brain and then observe the response. 2. CT, PET, MRI, fMRI. 3. cerebellum. 4. b. *Module 6 Check & Review Page 80* 1. cerebral cortex. 2. occipital; temporal; frontal; parietal. 3. a. 4. c. *Module 6 Active Learning Worksheet Pages 82–83*

Crossword answers: LOCALIZATION OF FUNCTION; CEREBELLUM; ASSOCIATION AREAS; AMYGDALA; FRONTAL LOBES; BRAINSTEM; SPLIT-BRAIN; STEM CELL; CEREBRAL CORTEX; LATERALIZATION; LIMBIC SYSTEM; OCCIPITAL LOBE; THALAMUS; CORPUS CALLOSUM; PARIETAL LOBES; MEDULLA; RETICULAR FORMATION; NEUROPLASTICITY; PONS; NEUROGENESIS; TEMPORAL LOBES; HYPOTHALAMUS

Module 7 Check & Review Page 90 1. c. 2. Behavioral geneticists use twin studies, adoption studies, family studies, and genetic abnormalities. 3. Because natural selection favors animals whose concern for kin is proportional to their degree of biological relatedness, most people will devote more resources, protection, love and concern to close relatives, which helps ensure their genetic survival. 4. One possible answer is that in ancient societies men were the "hunters" and women "gatherers." The man's superiority on many spatial relationships and target-directed motor skills, may reflect demands of hunting, whereas activities such as gathering, child-rearing, and domestic tool construction and manipulation may have contributed to the woman's language superiority.

Module 8 Check & Review Page 100 1. It is the study of the relationship between psychological behavior and physical health and illness, with an emphasis on wellness and the prevention of illness. 2. contagious; noncontagious. 3. In addition to social pressures that encourage smoking, nicotine is a powerfully addictive drug and smokers learn to associate positive things with smoking. 4. d. *Module 8 Check & Review Page 103* 1. When a man consumes five or more alcoholic drinks in a row and a woman consumes four or more alcoholic drinks in a row. 2. Binge drinkers are just average drinkers — make it clear that binge drinking is not the norm; Binge drinking is harmless — binge drinking causes loss of control that can lead to injury, death, and exposure to sexually transmitted diseases; Okay to binge drink because administration ignores it — administrators must enforce rules; Binge drinking is just part of fraternity or sorority life — colleges must work within the Greek System to decrease binge drinking; Students see alumni drinking at sports and alumni events — all drinking rules must also apply to alumni. 3. chronic. 4. a. *Module 8 Active Learning Worksheet Page 103* 1. stress; immune system. 2. practitioners. 3. tobacco. 4. No, you cannot conclude that alcohol is the direct cause of birth defects because this is correlational research. There are other explanations, including; pregnant mothers who drink alcohol might be under additional stress, have less economic and social support, etc. 5. Increased attention to pain increases the perceived level. Therefore, your friend should avoid this topic and divert his grandmother's attention. *Module 8 Check & Review Page 109* 1. a. 2. a. 3. a blocked goal; conflict. 4. Choosing between apple pie or pumpkin pie is an example of an approach-approach conflict. Choosing between early morning or evening classes normally is an approach-avoidance conflict. Taking an exam when you're underprepared or not taking the exam and receiving an automatic F is an example of an avoidance-avoidance conflict.

Module 9 Check & Review Page 112 1. The sympathetic branch of the autonomic nervous system is activated, thereby increasing heart rate, blood pressure, etc. The parasympathetic branch of the autonomic nervous system is activated during low-stress conditions and it lowers heart rate and blood pressure, while increasing activity in the stomach and intestines. 2. alarm; resistance; exhaustion. 3. c. 4. They have probably experienced a lot of stress, and stress can suppress the immune system, making them vulnerable to cold and flu viruses. *Module 9 Check & Review Page 115* 1. epinephrine; cortisol. 2. b. 3. shotgun, target behavior. Answers will vary, but alternatives include a shotgun approach because it will change my whole Type A personality, or a target behavior approach because it will change only the behaviors that lead to a hostile attitude. 4. A hardy personality is based on three qualities:

a commitment to personal goals, control over life, and viewing change as a challenge rather than a threat. *Module 9 Active Learning Worksheet Page 116*

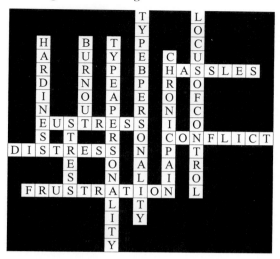

Module 10 Check & Review Page 122 1. emotion-focused, problem focused. 2. Rationalization and denial. Defense mechanisms alleviate anxiety but distort reality. 3. internal. 4. The six resources are health and energy, positive beliefs, social skills, social support, material resources, and personal control. Answers will vary depending on personality and individual life style.

Module 11 Check & Review Page 132 1. c. 2. absolute threshold. 3. The sensory receptors for smell adapt and send fewer messages to the brain. 4. b. *Module 11 Check & Review Page 140* 1. Compare your diagram to Figure 4.4.2. thinning and flattening, thickening and bulging, accommodation. 3. Compare your diagram to figure 4.8. 4. Place theory explains how we hear higher-pitched sounds, whereas frequency theory explains how we hear lower-pitched sounds. *Module 11 Check & Review Page 144* 1. b. 2. d. 3. kinesthetic. 4. d. *Module 11 Active Learning Worksheet Page 145*

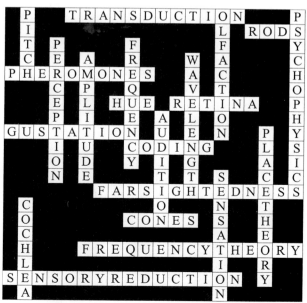

Module 12 Check & Review Pages 148–149 1. Illusions are false impressions of the physical world produced by actual physical distortions, hallucinations are sensory perceptions that occur without an external stimulus, and delusions are false beliefs. 2. feature detectors. 3. "Horizontal cats" reared in a horizontal world failed to develop potential feature detectors for vertical lines or objects. 4. c. *Module 12 Check & Review Page 154* 1. proximity, continuity, closure. 2. size constancy. 3. brightness constancy. 4. c. *Module 12 Check & Review Page 159* 1. c. 2. b. 3. color aftereffects, green rectangle. 4. The trichromatic system operates at the level of the retina, whereas the opponent-process system occurs at the level of the brain. *Module 12 Check & Review Page 163* 1. a. 2. a. 3. telepathy, clairvoyance, precognition, telekinesis. 4. usually cannot be replicated. *Module 12 Active Learning Worksheet Page 165*

Module 13 Check & Review Page 172 1. b. 2. They considered it too unscientific and not the proper focus of psychology. 3. focused, minimal. 4. d. *Module 13 Check & Review Page 179* 1. d. 2. b. 3. electroencephalograph (EEG). 4. a. *Module 13 Check & Review Pages 183–184* 1. Repair/restoration theory suggests we sleep to physically restore our mind and body, whereas evolutionary/circadian theory says that sleep evolved because it helped conserve energy and provided protection from predators. 2. Both men and women have dreams that reflect important life events, but women are more likely to dream of familiar people, household objects, and indoor events, whereas men dream about strangers, violence, sex, achievement, and outdoor events. All cultures dream about basic human needs and fears, but the Yir Yoront men dream of aggression from their mother's brother. Also, Americans dream of being naked in public, whereas cultures wearing few clothes do not dream of being naked. 3. d. 4. c. *Module 13 Check & Review Page 187* 1. insomnia. 2. sleep apnea. 3. night terrors. 4. narcolepsy.

Module 13 Active Learning Worksheet Pages 187–188

Module 14 Check & Review Page 201 1. c. 2. d. 3. Physical dependence refers to changes in the bodily processes that require continued use of the drug to prevent withdrawal symptoms, whereas psychological dependence refers to the mental desire or craving to achieve the effects produced by the drug. 4. Psychoactive drugs can alter the production, affect storage or release, alter the reception, and block the inactivation of neurotransmitters. *Module 14 Check & Review Page 206* 1. They may feel guilty or negative because they do not make a distinction between thought and behavior–thinking is not the same as doing. 2. Hypnosis requires the subject to make a conscious decision to relinquish some personal control of his or her consciousness. 3. d. 4. As a part of sacred rituals, for social interactions, and for individual rewards. *Module 14 Active Learning Worksheet Page 207*

Module 15 Check & Review Page 217 1. b. 2. conditioned stimulus, conditioned response. 3. d. 4. c. *Module 15 Check & Review Page 222* 1. You no longer respond to the sound of the fire alarm because your response has been extinguished, which occurs when the UCS is repeatedly withheld, and the association

between the CS and the UCS is broken. 2. d. 3. higher-order conditioning. 4. c. *Module 15 Active Learning Worksheet Page 223*

Module 16 Check & Review Page 238 1. Operant conditioning occurs when organisms learn by the consequences of their responses, whereas in classical conditioning organisms learn by pairing up associations. Operant conditioning is voluntary, whereas classical conditioning is involuntary. 2. c. 3. resistant. 4. Marshall's superstition may be wearing the same necklace to every exam because he believes it is helpful to his performance, although in reality wearing the necklace and previous good luck on exams were only accidentally related. *Module 16 Active Learning Worksheet Page 239*

Module 17 Check & Review Page 245 1. c. 2. latent learning. 3. cognitive maps. 4. b. *Module 17 Active Learning Worksheet Page 245* 1. i. 2. c. 3. f. 4. g. 5. h. 6. d. 7. j. 8. e. 9. a. 10. b.

Module 18 Check & Review Page 249 1. d. 2. Garcia and his colleagues laced freshly killed sheep with a chemical that caused nausea and vomiting in coyotes. After the coyotes ate the tainted meat and became ill, they avoided all sheep. 3. Biological preparedness refers to the fact that organisms are innately predisposed to form associations between certain stimuli and responses. 4. Instinctive drift. *Module 18 Active Learning Worksheet Page 249* 1. T. 2. F. 3. T. 4. F. 5. T.

Module 19 Check & Review Page 261 1. c. 2. a. 3. Encoding is comparable to typing on a keyboard, storage compares to the hard drive of the computer, and retrieval is analogous to the computer's retrieval of information and its display on the monitor. 4. According to the Parallel Distributed Processing (PDP), or *connectionist,* model, memory resembles a vast number of interconnected units and modules distributed throughout a huge network, all operating in parallel — simultaneously. *Module 19 Check & Review Page 272* 1. Semantic memory involves remembering facts and how they relate to one another, whereas episodic memory involves remembering where and when an event happened. 2. recognition, recall. 3. a. 4. Repeated stimulation of a synapse can strengthen the synapse by stimulating the dendrites to grow more spines, and the ability of a particular neuron to release its neurotransmitters can be increased or decreased. *Module 19 Active Learning Worksheet Pages 272–273*

Module 20 Check & Review Page 280 1. d. 2. Using distributed practice, you would space your study time into many learning periods with rest periods in between; using massed practice, you would "cram" all your learning into long, unbroken periods. 3. Retrieval failure theory, decay theory, motivated forgetting theory. *Module 20 Check & Review Page 286* 1. amnesia. 2. d. 3. Source amnesia occurs when the true source of the memory is forgotten. The sleeper effect refers to the initial tendency to discount information from an unreliable source, but later consider it more trustworthy because the source is forgotten. The misinformation effect results from incorporating outside information into one's own memory of an event. 4. Research shows that it is unreliable. *Module 20 Check & Review Page 291* 1. Given that the duration of short-term memory is about 30 seconds, to lengthen this time use *maintenance rehearsal,* which involves continuously repeating the material. To effectively encode memory into long-term memory, use *elaborative rehearsal,* which involves thinking about the material and relating it to other information that has already been stored. 2. Because we tend to remember information that falls at the beginning or end of a sequence, be sure to spend extra time with information in the middle of the chapter. 3. organization. 4. Peg-word system, method of loci, method of word associations, substitute word system. *Module 20 Active Learning Worksheet Pages 292–293.*

Module 21 Try This Yourself Page 299 The figures in b are not the same. To solve this problem, mentally rotate one of the objects and then compare the rotated image with the other object to see whether they matched or not. The figures in b were more difficult to solve because they required a greater degree of mental rotation. This is also true of real objects in physical space. It takes more time and energy to turn a cup 20 degrees to the right, than to turn it 150 degrees. *Module 21 Check & Review Page 302* 1. c. 2. There are at least three methods — artificial concepts, natural concepts, and hierarchies. 3. prototype. 4. b. *Module 21 Check & Review Page 307* 1. Preparation, in which we identify the facts, determine which ones are relevant, and define the goal; production, in which we propose possible solutions, or hypotheses; and evaluation, in which we determine whether the solutions meet the goal. 2. b. 3. d. 4. mental sets, functional fixedness, and confirmation bias. Incubation allows a "time out," which helps overcome each of these barriers. *Module 21 Check & Review Page 310* 1. c. 2. divergent, convergent, divergent. 3. intellectual ability, knowledge, thinking style, personality, motivation, and environment. 4. Probably not because people tend to be less creative when they are working for extrinsic rewards.

Module 21 Active Learning Worksheet Page 311

Crossword solution:
CONVERGENTTHINKING · CONFIRMATIONBIAS · ALGORITHM · FUNCTIONAL · DIVERGENTTHINKING · HEURISTIC · INCUBATION · MENTALSET · CREATIVITY · MENTALIMAGES · COGNITION · CONCEPT · FIXEDNESS · PROTOTYPE

Module 22 Check & Review Page 317 1. phonemes, morphemes. 2. The surface structure refers to the words in a sentence, whereas the deep structure is the actual meaning of the sentence. 3. Language shapes thought. 4. a. *Module 22 Active Learning Worksheet Page 318*

Crossword solution:
SEMANTICS · MORPHEME · SYNTAX · PHONEME · GRAMMAR

Module 23 Check & Review Page 325 1. b. 2. Fluid intelligence refers to reasoning abilities, memory, and speed of information processing, whereas crystallized intelligence refers to knowledge and skills gained through experience and education. 3. Sternberg proposed three aspects of intelligence — analytic, creative, and practical. 4. reliability, validity, standardization. *Module 23 Check & Review Pages 334–335* 1. No, an IQ test merely measures verbal and quantitative abilities and predicts school success. 2. The Stanford–Binet is a single test consisting of several sets of various age-level items, whereas the Wechsler consists of three separate tests; also the Stanford–Binet primarily measures verbal abilities, while the Wechsler measures both verbal and performance abilities. 3. d. 4. Both heredity and environment are important, interacting influences. *Module 23 Active Learning Worksheet Page 335*

Crossword solution:
STEREOTYPETHREAT · STANDARDIZATION · RELIABILITY · FLUIDINTELLIGENCE · VALIDITY · CRYSTALLIZEDINTELLIGENCE · INTELLIGENCE · INTELLIGENCEQUOTIENT

Module 24 Check & Review Page 344 1. Developmental psychology studies age-related changes in behaviors and abilities from conception to death. 2. nature or nurture, continuity or stages, stability or change. 3. d. 4. c. *Module 24 Check & Review Page 354* 1. The three major stages are the germinal period, the embryonic period, and the fetal period. 2. b. 3. c. 4. Primary aging is defined as the inevitable age-related biological changes in physical and mental processes, whereas secondary aging results from abuse, neglect, disuse, or disease. *Module 24 Active Learning Worksheet Page 355*

Crossword solution:
DEVELOPMENTALPSYCHOLOGY · CRITICALPERIOD · MATURATION · GERMINALPERIOD · LONGITUDINALMETHOD · PUBERTY · FETALPERIOD · EMBRYONICPERIOD · TERATOGEN

Module 25 Check & Review Page 358 1. Cooing is only vowel sounds ("eee"), while babbling adds consonants ("dadada"). 2. d. 3. b. 4. Nativists suggest language is inborn and develops primarily from maturation, while nurturists emphasize the environment and the role of rewards, punishments, and imitation of models. ***Module 25 Check & Review Page 363*** 1. b. 2. Securely attached, anxious-avoidant, and anxious-ambivalent; 3. 1a, 2c, 3b. 4. Authoritarian parents value unquestioning obedience and mature responsibility from their children. Permissive parents either set few limts and provide little attention (the permissive-indifferent), or they're highly involved but few demands (the permissive-indulgent). Authoritative parents are caring and sensitive, but also set firm limits and enforce them. ***Module 25 Active Learning Worksheet Page 363*** 1. i. 2. f. 3. c. 4. h. 5. b. 6. d. 7. g. 8. a. 9 e. 10. j.

Module 26 Active Learning Exercise Page 369 1. The child is upset because he thinks he now has MORE of the disliked food since the mother spread it around to cool it. He is in the preoperational stage and cannot conserve. 2. Janie has acquired object permanence. She is still in the sensorimotor stage. 3. Tom is upset because of his intense idealism and adolescent egocentrism. He is in the beginning part of the formal operational stage. 4. The older child is in the concrete operational (or formal operational) stage. The younger child is preoperational and cannot conserve, which allows him to be happy with one cookie broken into two pieces — he thinks he has "two cookies." ***Module 26 Check & Review Page 372*** 1. c. 2. d. 3. 1b, 2a, 3d, 4c, 5d. 4. Memory problems for older adults are primarily problems of encoding, taking more time to store the information, and retrieval, taking more time to find the information. ***Module 26 Active Learning Worksheet Page 373***

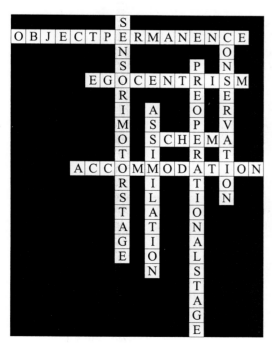

Module 27 Check & Review Page 382 1. Preconventional, post-conventional, conventional. 2. c. 3. b. 4. Kohlberg's theory is culturally biased toward individualism versus community and interpersonal relationships. His theory is gender biased because it supposedly favors the male's justice perspective over the female's care perspective. ***Module 27 Check & Review Page 387*** 1. c. 2. Thomas and Chess describe three categories of temperament — easy, difficult, and slow-to-warm-up — that seem to correlate with stable personality differences. 3. trust versus mistrust, identity versus role confusion, initiative versus guilt, ego integrity versus despair. 4. Research shows that beliefs about adolescent storm and stress, the midlife crisis, and the empty nest syndrome may be exaggerated accounts of a few people's experiences and not those of most people. ***Module 27 Active Learning Worksheet Page 388***

Module 28 Check & Review Page 395 1. c. 2. activity; disengagement. 3. c. 4. The social support may help reduce the losses that accompany aging. ***Module 28 Check & Review Page 399*** 1. Preschool children only understand the permanence of death, they do not yet comprehend the nonfunctionality or universality of death. 2. d. 3. a bargaining, b denial, c resolution, d anger, e despair. 4. d. ***Module 28 Active Learning Worksheet Page 399*** 1. f. 2. d. 3. g. 4. a. 5. c. 6. j. 7. h. 8. i. 9. e. 10. b.

Module 29 Check & Review Pages 411–412 1. Chromosomal sex b, gender identity d, gonadal sex a, gender role I, hormonal sex c, secondary sex characteristics e, external genitals g, sexual orientation h, internal accessory organs f. 2. d. 3. Social learning theory emphasizes learning through rewards, punishments, and imitation, while cognitive-developmental theory focuses on the active, thinking processes of the individual. 4. d. ***Module 29***

Active Learning Worksheet Page 413 1. gender identity; cross-dresses for sexual arousal and expression of other gender role. 2. your biological sex; your social role expectations based on masculinity or femininity. 3. self-definition of being male or female; societal expectations of normal and appropriate gender behavior. 4. cognitive abilities; aggression. 5. androgyny. *Module 30 Check & Review Page 418* 1. b. 2. Ellis based his research on personal diaries; Masters and Johnson pioneered the use of direct observation and measurement of bodily responses during sexual activities; Kinsey popularized the use of the survey method. 3. Cultural comparisons put sex in a broader perspective and help counteract ethnocentrism. 4. d.

Module 30 Check & Review Page 422 1. Masters and Johnson identified a four-stage sexual response cycle (excitement, plateau, orgasm, and resolution) that acknowledged both similarities and differences between the sexes. However differences are the focus of most research. 2. According to the evolutionary perspective, males engage in more sexual behaviors with more sexual partners because it helps the species survive. The social role perspective suggests this difference reflects a double standard, which subtly encourages male sexuality while discouraging female sexuality. 3. c. 4. d. *Module 30 Critical Thinking/Active Learning Exercise Page 431 Gender role conditioning* — A main part of traditional gender conditioning is the belief that women should be the "gate-keepers" for sexuality and men should be the "pursuers." This leads to the myth that male sexuality is overpowering and women are responsible for controlling the situation. *Double standard* — Female gender role also encourages passivity, and women are not taught how to aggressively defend themselves. People who believe the myth that women cannot be raped against their will generally overlook the fact that the female gender role encourages passivity and women are not taught how to aggressively defend themselves. *Media portrayals* — Novels and films typically portray a woman resisting her attacker and then melting into passionate responsiveness. This helps perpetuate the myth that women secretly want to be raped and the myth that she might as well "relax and enjoy it." *Lack of information* — The myth that women cannot be raped against their will overlooks the fact that most men are much stronger and much faster than most women, and a woman's clothing and shoes further hinder her ability to escape. The myth that women cannot rape men ignores the fact that men can have erections despite negative emotions while being raped. Furthermore, an erection is unnecessary, since many rapists (either male or female) often use foreign objects to rape their victims. The myth that all women secretly want to be raped overlooks the fact that if a woman fantasizes about being raped she remains in complete control, whereas in an actual rape she is completely powerless. Also, fantasies contain no threat of physical harm, while rape does.

Tips for Rape Prevention Sex educators and researchers suggest the following techniques for reducing stranger rape (the rape of a person by an unknown assailant) and acquaintance (or date) rape (committed by someone who is known to the victim) (Crooks & Baur, 1999; Denny & Quadagno, 1998). To avoid stranger rape: 1. Follow commonsense advice for avoiding all forms of crime: lock your car, park in lighted areas, install dead-bolt locks on your doors, don't open your door to strangers, don't hitchhike, etc. 2. Make yourself as strong as possible. Take a self-defense course, carry a loud whistle with you, and demonstrate self-confidence with your body language. Research shows that rapists tend to

select women who appear passive and weak (Richards et al., 1991). 3. During an attack, run away if you can, talk to the rapist as a way to stall, and/or attempt to alert others by screaming ("Help, rape, call the police") (Shotland & Stebbins, 1980). When all else fails, women should actively resist an attack, according to current research (Fischhoff, 1992; Furby & Fischhoff, 1992). Loud shouting, fighting back, and causing a scene may deter an attack. To prevent acquaintance rape: 1. Be careful on first dates — date in groups and in public places; avoid alcohol and other drugs (Gross & Billingham, 1998). 2. Be assertive and clear in your communication — say what you want and what you don't want. Accept a partner's refusal. If sexual coercion escalates, match the assailant's behavior with your own form of escalation — begin with firm refusals, get louder, threaten to call the police, begin shouting and use strong physical resistance. Don't be afraid to make a scene! *Module 30 Check & Review Page 432* 1. The parasympathetic branch of the autonomic nervous system dominates during sexual arousal, whereas the sympathetic branch dominates during ejaculation and orgasm. 2. c. 3. Relationship focus, integration of physiological and psychosocial factors, emphasis on cognitive factors, emphasis on specific behavioral techniques. 4. Remain abstinent or have sex with one mutually faithful, uninfected partner. Do not use IV drugs or have sex with someone who does. If you do use IV drugs, sterilize or don't share equipment. Avoid contact with blood, vaginal secretions, and semen. Avoid anal intercourse. Don't have sex if you or partner is impaired by drugs. *Module 30 Active Learning Worksheet Page 433*

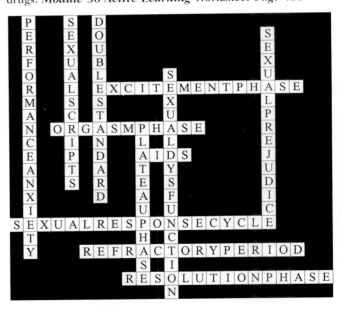

Module 31 Check & Review Page 450 1. Although these two terms often overlap and interact to influence behavior, motivation refers to internal factors that energize and direct behavior, whereas emotion refers to feelings or affective responses. 2. The major internal factors are the stomach, blood chemistry, and the brain; while the major external factors are cultural conditioning and visual stimuli. 3. d. 4. c. *Module 31 Check & Review Page 454* 1. An instinct is an unlearned, behavioral pattern that is uniform in expression and universal in a species. Homeostasis is the state of balance or stability in the body's internal environment. 2.

a2, b3, c5, d4, el. 3. d. 4.c. *Module 31 Active Learning Worksheet Page 455.*

specific crisis presented in each psychosexual stage (oral, anal, phallic, latency, and genital). 4. Adler, Horney, Jung, Horney. *Module 35 Active Learning Worksheet Page 499*

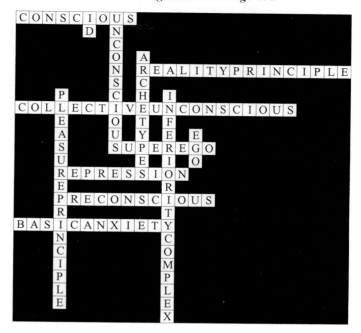

Module 32 Check & Review Page 464 1. a3, b1, c2 and c4 2. sympathetic, autonomic. 3. a. 4. b. *Module 32 Check & Review Page 469* 1. According to the **James-Lange theory,** emotions are based on physical sensations, such as increased heart rate and trembling, whereas the **Cannon-Bard theory** suggests feelings are created from independent and simultaneous stimulation of both the cortex and the autonomic nervous system. The **facial feedback hypothesis** suggests facial movements elicit specific emotions, **Schacter's two-factor theory** proposes that emotions depend on physical arousal and a cognitive labeling of the arousal. 2. a. 3. d. 4. simultaneously. *Module 32 Active Learning Worksheet Page 469* 1. i. 2. j. 3. h. 4. g. 5. d. 6. f. 7. e. 8. b. 9. c. 10. a.

Module 33 Check & Review Page 479 1. a2, b1, c3. 2. b. 3. 4. People accept pseudopersonality tests because they offer generalized statements that apply to almost everyone (Barnum effect), they notice and remember events that confirm predictions and ignore the misses (fallacy of positive instances), and they prefer information that maintains a positive self-image (self-serving bias). *Module 33 Active Learning Worksheet Page 479* 1. F. 2. F. 3. T. 4. T. 5. T.

Module 34 Check & Review Page 485 1. b. 2. a2, b3, c4, d5, el. 3. b. *Module 34 Active Learning Worksheet Page 486* 1. extraversion. 2. conscientiousness. 3. openness. 4. agreeableness. 5. neuroticism.

Module 35 Check & Review Page 498 1. The conscious is the tip of the iceberg and the highest level of awareness; the preconscious is just below the surface but can readily be brought to awareness; the unconscious is the large base of the iceberg and operates below the level of awareness. 2. b. 3. Freud believed an individual's adult personality reflected his or her resolution of the

Module 36 Check & Review Page 503 1. a. 2. c. 3. self-actualization. 4. Humanistic theories are criticized for their naive assumptions, poor testability and inadequate evidence, and narrowness in merely describing, not explaining, behavior. *Module 36 Check & Review Page 505* 1. How each individual thinks about the world and interprets experiences. 2. a. 3. c. 4. external locus of control, internal locus of control. *Module 36 Check & Review Page 508* 1. d. 2. Some researchers emphasize the importance of the unshared environment, while others fear that genetic determinism could be misused to "prove" certain ethnic groups are inferior, male dominance is natural, or that social progress is impossible. 3. c. 4. Western theories emphasize the "self" as separate and autonomous from others, while collectivist cultures see the self as inherently linked to others. *Module 36 Active Learning Worksheet Page 509* 1. i. 2. j. 3. a. 4. e. 5. g. 6. h. 7. f. 8. c. 9. d. 10. b.

Module 37 Check & Review Page 523 1. Statistical infrequency, disability or dysfunction, personal distress, and violation of norms. 2. b. 3. Early versions of the DSM used neurosis to refer to mental disorders related to anxiety, while psychosis is currently used to describe disorders characterized by loss of contact with reality and extreme mental disruption. Insanity is a legal term for people with a mental disorder that implies a lack of responsibility for behavior and an inability to manage their own affairs. 4. The chief advantages of the DSM is that it provides detailed descriptions of symptoms, which in turn allows standardized diagnosis and treatment, and improved communication among professionals and between professionals and patients. The major disadvantage is that the label "mental illness" can lead to social and economic discrimination. *Module 37 Active Learning Worksheet Page 524*

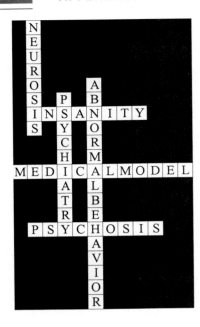

Module 38 Check & Review Page 530 1. a3, b2, c4, d5, e1. 2. Learning theorists most often believe anxiety disorders result from classical and operant conditioning, while social learning theorists argue that imitation and modeling are the cause. 3. Learning and biology. **Module 38 Active Learning Worksheet Page 530** 1. Generalized anxiety disorder; panic disorder. 2. Phobias; agoraphobia. 3. compulsions; obsessions. 4. Post-traumatic stress disorder; nervous breakdown. 5. inherited predisposition.

Module 39 Check & Review Page 535 1. a. 2. c. 3. Seligman believes the individual becomes resigned to pain and sadness and feels unable to change, which leads to depression. It may be due to biological causes (hormones and genes) as well as environmental stressors (poverty, discrimination, unhappy marriages, and sexual or physical abuse). **Module 39 Active Learning Worksheet Page 536** 1. F. 2. T. 3. T. 4. F. 5. F.

Module 40 Check & Review Page 545 1. c. 2. psychosis, 3. a. 4. Three biological causes might be malfunctioning neurotransmitters, brain abnormalities, and genetic predisposition. Two possible psychosocial causes of schizophrenia may be stress and family communication problems. **Module 40 Active Learning Worksheet Page 546** 1. perception. 2. affect. 3. behavior. 4. thought. 5. language.

Module 41 Check & Review Page 552 1. Stress. 2. Dissociative identity disorder (DID) refers to a dissociative disorder characterized by the presence of two or more distinct personality systems within the same individual. 3. Antisocial personality. 4. d. **Module 41 Critical Thinking/Active Learning Exercise Page 552** 1. c. 2. e. 3. b. 4. a. 5. f. 6. d. **Module 41 Active Learning Worksheet Page 553** 1. antisocial personality. 2. bor-

derline personality. 3. alcohol use disorder. 4. dissociative identity disorder. 5. antisocial personality.

Module 42 Check & Review Page 560 1. c. 2. b psychoanalysts, e behaviorists, d humanistic therapists, c biomedical therapists, a cognitive therapists. 3. clinical or counseling psychologists, psychiatrists, psychoanalysts, social workers, and counselors. **Module 42 Active Learning Worksheet Page 561** 1. disturbed thoughts, disturbed emotions, disturbed behaviors, interpersonal and life situation difficulties, biomedical disturbances. 2. and 3. Answers will vary according to individual life histories.

Module 43 Check & Review Page 567 1. d. 2. antianxiety, antipsychotic, antidepressant, and mood stabilizer. 3. b. 4. c. **Module 43 Active Learning Worksheet Page 568**

Module 44 Try This Yourself Page 573 The clearest technique being used in this example is resistance. **Module 44 Check & Review Page 573** 1. c. 2. Mary is exhibiting transference, reacting to her therapist as she apparently did to someone earlier in her life. John is exhibiting resistance, arriving late because he fears what his unconscious might reveal. 3. Limited applicability, lack of scientific credibility. 4. Psychodynamic therapy is briefer, face-to-face, more directive, and emphasizes current problems and conscious processes. **Module 44 Try This Yourself Page 579** All four techniques are shown in this example: empathy ("they scare the hell out of me too"), unconditional positive regard (therapist's acceptance and nonjudgmental attitude and caring about not wanting to do "anything that is upsetting" to the client), genuineness (the therapist's ability to laugh and make a joke at his or her own expense); and active listening (therapist demonstrated genuine interest in what the client was saying). *Module 44 Check & Review Page 579* 1. a. 2. The activating event, the belief system, the emotional consequence. 3. Magnification, all-or-nothing thinking. 4. Empathy, genuineness, unconditional positive regard. *Module 44 Check & Review Page 585* 1. behavior therapy. 2. c. 3. By rewarding successive approximations of a target behavior, the patient is "shaped" toward more adaptive behaviors. 4. Behavior therapy is criticized for lack of generalizability, symptom substitution, and questionable ethics. *Module 44 Check & Review Page 587* 1. c. 2. Group support, feedback and information, behavioral rehearsal. 3. Self-help groups are recommended as a supplement to individual therapy. 4. d. *Module 44 Active Learning Worksheet Page 589*

qualities of the therapist, establishing crediblity, placing the problem in a familiar framework, applying techniques to bring relief, a special time and place. 2., 3., & 4. Answers will vary according to individual responses.

Module 46 Check & Review Page 609 1. c. 2. When judging the causes of others' behaviors, a tendency to overestimate internal personality factors and underestimate external situational factors. 3. d. 4. Cognitive dissonance. *Module 46 Active Learning Worksheet Page 609* 1. F. 2. T. 3. F. 4. T. 5. T.

Module 47 Check & Review Page 620 1. Prejudice is an attitude with behavioral tendencies that may or may not be activated, whereas discrimination is actual negative behavior directed at members of an outgroup. 2. b. 3. c. 4. Romantic love is short lived (6 to 30 months) and largely based on mystery and fantasy, which leads to inevitable disappointment. Companionate love is long lasting and grows stronger with time. *Module 47 Active Learning Worksheet Page 621*

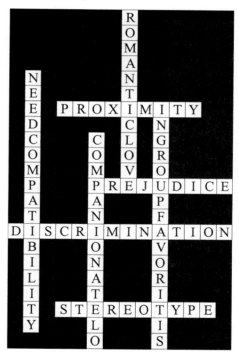

Module 45 Check & Review Page 596 1. d. 2. Naming the problem, qualities of the therapist, establishment of credibility, placing the problem in a familiar framework, applying techniques to bring relief, a special time and place. 3. c. 4. Rates of diagnosis and treatment of mental disorders, stresses of poverty, stresses of multiple roles, stresses of aging, violence against women. *Module 45 Active Learning Worksheet Page 597* 1. naming the problem,

Module 48 Check & Review Page 627 1. Conformity involves changing behavior in response to real or imagined pressure from others, whereas obedience involves giving in to a command from others. 2. b. 3. c. 4. the power of authority, distance between teacher and learner, assignment of responsibility, and modeling/imitation. *Module 48 Check & Review Page 632* 1. Guards and prisoners were abusing their roles. 2. b. 3. illusion of invulnerability, belief in the morality of the group, collective rationalizations, stereotypes of the outgroup, self-censorship of doubts and dissenting opinions, illusion of unanimity, and direct pressure on dissenters. 4. b. ***Module 48 Check & Review Page 638*** 1. The five major biological factors are instincts, genes, brain and nervous system, substance use and other mental disorders, hormones and neurotransmitters. The tree key psychosocial factors aversive stimuli, culture and learning, and media and video games. 2. a. 3. According to evolutionary theorists, altruism evolved because it favored overall genetic survival. The egoistic model says helping is motivated by anticipated gain for the helper, while the empathy–altruism hypothesis suggests helping is activated when the helper feels empathy for the victim. 4. d. ***Module 48 Active Learning Worksheet Page 639.***

Glossary

abnormal behavior Patterns of emotion, thought, and action considered pathological (diseased or disordered) for one or more of these reasons statistical infrequency, disability or dysfunction, personal distress, or violation of norms. *Page 514*

absolute threshold The smallest magnitude of a certain stimulus energy that can be detected. *Page 130*

accommodation In vision, the process by which the lens changes shape to focus light on the retina. The lens thins and flattens to focus on distant objects and thickens and bulges to focus a nearby object. *Page 135*

In cognition, the process of adjusting existing ways of thinking (reworking schemas) to encompass new information, ideas, or objects. *Page 364*

achievement motivation (nAch) The need for success, for doing better than others, and for mastering challenging tasks; the desire to excel, especially in competition with others. *Page 445*

acquired immunodeficiency syndrome See AIDS (acquired immunodeficiency syndrome). *Page 428*

action potential An electro-chemical impulse that carries information along the axon of a neuron. The action potential is generated when positively charged ions move in and out of channels in the axon's membrane. *Page 55*

activation–synthesis hypothesis The idea that dreams are by-products of random stimulation of brain cells. The brain attempts to combine (or synthesize) this spontaneous activity into coherent patterns, known as dreams. *Page 182*

active listening According to Carl Rogers, the ability to listen with total attention to what another is saying. This involves reflecting, paraphrasing, and clarifying what the person says and means. *Page 578*

activity theory A theory of aging that suggests successful adjustment is fostered by a full and active commitment to life. *Page 393*

ageism Prejudice against people on the basis of their age. *Page 394*

aggression Any behavior that is intended to harm someone. *Page 632*

agonist A chemical (or drug) that mimics the action of a specific neurotransmitter. *Page 197*

AIDS (acquired immunodeficiency syndrome) A catastrophic illness in which human immunodeficiency viruses destroy the immune system's ability to fight disease, leaving the body vulnerable to a variety of opportunistic infections and cancers. *Page 428*

algorithm A problem-solving strategy that guarantees a solution if correctly applied; it involves a step-by-step procedure, and as such, is particularly suited to use by a computer for math problems. *Page 303*

alternate states of consciousness (ASCs) A mental state other than ordinary waking consciousness, found during sleep, dreaming, use of psychoactive drugs, hypnosis, and so on. During ASCs, distinct changes typically occur in perception, emotion, memory, time sense, thinking, self-control, and suggestibility. *Page 169*

altruism Actions designed to help others, with no obvious benefit to the helper. *Page 636*

Alzheimer's [ALLS-high-merz] disease (AD) A progressive mental deterioration that occurs most commonly in old age. It is characterized by severe memory loss. *Page 253*

amplitude The height of a light or sound wave; pertaining to light, it refers to brightness. *Page 133*

amygdala [uh-MIG-dull-uh] An almond-shaped lower-level brain structure that is part of the limbic system and involved in emotion. *Page 68*

androgyny [an-DRAW-juh-nee] Combining characteristics considered typically male (e.g., assertive, athletic) with characteristics considered typically female (e.g., yielding, nurturant); from the Greek andro, meaning "male," and gyn, meaning "female." *Page 410*

anorexia nervosa An eating disorder, seen mostly in adolescent and young adult females, in which a severe loss of weight results from an obsessive fear of obesity and self-imposed starvation. *Page 441*

antagonist A chemical (or drug) that opposes or blocks the action of a neurotransmitter. *Page 197*

anterograde amnesia The inability to form new memories. *Page 281*

antianxiety drugs Medications used to treat anxiety disorders. *Page 192*

antidepressant drugs Drugs prescribed to treat depression, some anxiety disorders, and certain eating disorders (such as bulimia). *Page 532*

antipsychotic drugs Chemicals administered to diminish or terminate hallucinations, delusions, withdrawal, and other symptoms of psychosis; also known as neuroleptics or major tranquilizers. *Page 536*

antisocial personality Personality disorder characterized by egocentrism, lack of conscience, impulsive behavior, and manipulation of others. *Page 549*

anxiety disorder Type of abnormal behavior characterized by unrealistic, irrational fear. *Page 525*

applied research Research that uses the principles and discoveries of psychology for practical purposes, to solve real-world problems. *Page 6*

approach–approach conflict Conflict in which a person must choose between two or more alternatives that will lead to desirable results. *Page 107*

approach–avoidance conflict Conflict in which a person must choose between two or more alternatives that will lead to both desirable and undesirable results. *Page 107*

archetypes According to Carl Jung, the images or patterns of thoughts, feelings, and behavior that reside in the collective unconscious. *Page 495*

assimilation The process of responding to a new situation in the same manner that is used in a familiar situation. *Page 364*

association areas So-called quiet areas in the cerebral cortex involved in interpreting, integrating, and acting on information processed by other parts of the brain. *Page 74*

attachment An active, intense emotional relationship between two people that endures over time. *Page 358*

attitude A learned predisposition to respond cognitively, affectively, and behaviorally to a particular object. *Page 606*

attribution The principles people follow in making judgments about the causes of events, others' behavior, and their own behavior. *Page 452*

audition The sense of hearing. *Page 137*

automatic processes Mental activities requiring minimal attention; other ongoing activities are generally not affected. *Page 171*

autonomic nervous system (ANS) Subdivision of the peripheral nervous system that controls involuntary functions, such as heart rate and digestion. It is further subdivided into the sympathetic nervous system, which arouses, and the parasympathetic nervous system, which calms. *Page 52*

aversion therapy Behavior therapy technique that pairs an aversive (unpleasant) stimulus with a maladaptive behavior. *Page 581*

avoidance–avoidance conflict Conflict in which a person must choose between two or more alternatives that will each lead to undesirable results. *Page 107*

axon A long, tubelike structure that conveys impulses away from the neuron's cell body toward other neurons or to muscles or glands. *Page 55*

babbling Vowel–consonant combinations that infants begin to produce at about age 4 months. *Page 356*

basic anxiety According to Karen Horney, the feelings of helplessness and insecurity that adults experience because as children they felt alone and isolated in a hostile environment. *Page 496*

basic research Research conducted to study theoretical questions without trying to solve a specific problem. *Page 6*

behavior therapy A group of techniques based on learning principles that are used to change maladaptive behaviors. *Page 580*

behavioral genetics A new field that combines genetics and psychology to study genetic and environmental influences on behavior. *Page 84*

binocular cues Visual input from two eyes that allows perception of depth or distance. *Page 155*

biofeedback A procedure for electronically recording, amplifying, and feeding back information about internal bodily changes that would normally be imperceptible (such as blood pressure); aids voluntary regulation of these changes. *Page 235*

biological preparedness The idea that an organism is innately predisposed to form associations between certain stimuli. *Page 246*

biomedical therapy Therapy involving physiological interventions (drugs, electroconvulsive therapy, and psychosurgery) to reduce symptoms associated with psychological disorders. *Page 557*

bipolar disorder A diagnostic term in DSM-IV-TR (Diagnostic and Statistical Manual of Mental Disorders, fourth edition, text revision) for individuals who experience episodes of mania or of both mania and depression. Excessive and unreasonable elation and hyperactivity characterize manic episodes. *Page 514*

borderline personality disorder (BPD) A personality disorder characterized by impulsivity and instability in mood, relationships, and self-image. *Page 549*

bottom-up processing Information processing that begins "at the bottom" with raw sensory data that feed "up" to the brain; perceptual analysis that emphasizes characteristics of the stimulus itself rather than internal, cognitive processes. *Page 128*

brainstem An area at the base of the brain, in front of the cerebellum, that is responsible for automatic, survival functions. *Page 67*

bulimia nervosa An eating disorder involving consumption of enormous quantities of food (binges), followed by purging through vomiting or taking laxatives. *Page 441*

burnout A state of physical, emotional, and mental exhaustion attributable to long-term involvement in emotionally demanding situations. *Page 106*

Cannon–Bard theory The theory that the thalamus responds to emotion-arousing stimuli by sending messages simultaneously to the cerebral cortex and the autonomic nervous system. In this view, all emotions are physiologically similar. *Page 465*

care perspective Carol Gilligan's term for an approach to moral reasoning that emphasizes interpersonal responsibility and interconnectedness with others. *Page 381*

case study An in-depth study of a single research participant. *Page 20*

catharsis In psychoanalytic theory, the release of tension and anxiety through the reliving of a traumatic incident. *Page 570*

cell body The part of the neuron that contains the cell nucleus, as well as other structures that help the neuron carry out its functions. *Page 55*

central nervous system (CNS) The brain and spinal cord. *Page 50*

cerebellum [sehr-uh-BELL-um] Structure at the base of the brain, behind the brainstem, responsible for maintaining smooth movement, balance, and some aspects of perception and cognition. *Page 67*

cerebral cortex The bumpy, convoluted area on the outside surface of the two cerebral hemispheres that regulates most complex behavior, including receiving sensations, motor control, and higher mental processes. *Page 71*

chromosome Threadlike strands of DNA (deoxyribonucleic acid) molecules that carry genetic information. *Page 84*

chronic pain Continuous or recurrent pain over a period of 6 months or more. *Page 101*

chunking The process of grouping information into units to store more information in short-term memory. *Page 257*

circadian [ser-KAY-dee-an] rhythms Biological changes that occur on a 24-hour cycle; from circa, meaning "about," and dies, meaning "day." *Page 173*

classical conditioning A basic form of learning in which an organism involuntarily learns to associate stimuli. A previously neutral stimulus is paired with an unconditioned stimulus to elicit a conditioned response that is identical or very similar to the unconditioned response. (Also known as respondent or Pavlovian conditioning.) *Page 212*

client-centered therapy A type of psychotherapy developed by Carl Rogers that emphasizes the client's natural tendency to become healthy and productive; techniques include empathy, unconditional positive regard, genuineness, and active listening. *Page 577*

cochlea (KOK-lee-uh) The three-chambered, snail-shaped structure in the inner ear that contains the receptors for hearing. *Page 138*

coding The three-part process that converts a particular sensory input into a specific sensation. *Page 130*

cognition The mental activities involved in acquiring, storing, retrieving, and using knowledge. *Page 298*

cognitive-behavior therapy Aaron Beck's therapy that works to change not only destructive thoughts and beliefs but the associated behaviors as well. *Page 575*

cognitive dissonance theory Leon Festinger's theory that tension results whenever people discover inconsistencies among their attitudes or between their attitudes and their behaviors. This tension drives people to make attitudinal changes that will restore harmony or consistency. *Page 607*

cognitive-social theory A theory of learning that emphasizes the role of thought and social learning in behavior. *Page 240*

cognitive map A mental image of a three-dimensional space that a person or animal has navigated. *Page 241*

cognitive restructuring The process in cognitive therapy by which the therapist and client work to change destructive ways of thinking. *Page 574*

cognitive therapy Therapy that focuses on faulty thought processes and beliefs to treat problem behaviors. *Page 573*

collective unconscious Carl Jung's concept of an inherited unconscious that all humans share. *Page 495*

comorbidity The co-occurrence of two or more disorders in the same person at the same time, as when a person has both depression and alcoholism. *Page 551*

companionate love A strong feeling of attraction to another person characterized by trust, caring, tolerance, and friendship. It is believed to provide an enduring basis for long-term relationships. *Page 619*

concept A mental category that groups objects, events, activities, or ideas that share similar characteristics. For example, the concept of river groups together the Nile, Amazon, and Mississippi because they share the common characteristic of being a large stream of water that empties into an ocean or lake. *Page 300*

concrete operational stage The third of Jean Piaget's stages of cognitive development (roughly ages 7 to 11 years). The child can perform mental operations on concrete objects and understand reversibility and conservation. *Page 366*

conditioned emotional response (CER) Any classically conditioned emotional response to a previously neutral stimulus. *Page 216*

conditioned response (CR) A learned response to a previously neutral stimulus that has been associated with the stimulus. *Page 213*

conditioned stimulus (CS) A previously neutral stimulus that, through conditioning, now causes a classically conditioned response. *Page 213*

cones Visual receptors concentrated near the center of the retina that are responsible for color vision and fine detail. They are most sensitive in brightly lit conditions. *Page 136*

confirmation bias The tendency to seek out and pay attention to information that confirms existing positions or beliefs while ignoring or not considering contradictory information. *Page 306*

conflict A negative emotional state caused by having to choose between two or more incompatible goals or impulses. *Page 107*

conformity A type of social influence in which individuals change their behavior as a result of real or imagined group pressure. *Page 622*

conscious In Freudian terms, thoughts or information that a person is currently aware of or is remembering. *Page 488*

consciousness An organism's awareness of its own self and surroundings, according to Damasio. Consciousness is always about something. It concerns perceptions (of objects and events), thoughts (including verbal thought and mental images, such as dreams and daydreams), feelings, and actions, according to Farthing. *Page 169*

conservation The ability to recognize that a given quantity, weight, or volume remains constant despite changes in shape, length, or position. *Page 367*

consolidation A hypothetical process explaining the gradual conversion of information into long-term memories. *Page 268*

constructive processes The active organizing and shaping of information as we encode and retrieve it, which can result in errors and distortions. *Page 282*

continuous reinforcement Reinforcement in which every correct response is reinforced. *Page 227*

control group In a controlled experiment, the group of participants that receives a zero level of the independent variable and that is used to assess the effects of the independent variable or treatment. *Page 15*

controlled processes Mental activities found at one extreme of the continuum of awareness; they require focused attention and generally interfere with other ongoing activities. *Page 171*

conventional level Lawrence Kohlberg's second level of moral development, where moral judgments are based on compliance with the rules and values of society. *Page 378*

convergence A binocular depth cue in which the closer the object, the more the eyes converge, or turn inward. *Page 155*

convergent thinking Conventional thinking; thinking directed toward a single correct answer (e.g., standard academic tests generally require convergent thinking). *Page 308*

cooing Vowel-like sounds infants produce beginning at about age 2 months. *Page 356*

corpus callosum [**CORE-puss**] [**cah-LOW-sum**] Bundle of nerve fibers connecting the brain's left and right hemispheres. *Page 76*

correlational study A form of research that studies relationships between variables without the ability to infer causal relationships. Correlational studies describe how strongly two variables are related and whether they are positively, negatively, or not at all (zero) correlated. *Page 21*

creativity The generation of ideas that are original, novel, and useful. *Page 308*

critical period A period of special sensitivity to specific types of learning that shapes the capacity for future development. *Page 340*

critical thinking The process of objectively evaluating, comparing, analyzing, and synthesizing information. Critical thinking has three components affective skills (e.g., empathy and tolerance for ambiguity), cognitive abilities (e.g., independent thinking and synthesizing), and behavioral traits (e.g., delaying judgment and applying knowledge to new situations). *Page 4*

cross-sectional method A technique of data collection that measures individuals of various ages at one point in time and gives information about age differences. *Page 341*

crystallized intelligence Knowledge and skills gained through experience and education that tend to increase over the life span. *Page 321*

dark adaptation The process by which the eyes' rods and cones adjust to allow vision in dim light. *Page 137*

debriefing A necessary and important aspect of deception research in which the participants are informed after the research about the purpose of the study, the nature of the anticipated results, and any deceptions used. *Page 25*

defense mechanisms Unconscious strategies used to distort reality and relieve anxiety and guilt. *Page 117*

deindividuation The increased arousal and reduced self-consciousness, inhibition, and personal responsibility that can occur when a person is part of a group, particularly when the members feel anonymous. *Page 628*

deinstitutionalization The policy of discharging as many people as possible from state hospitals and discouraging admissions. *Page 590*

delusions Mistaken beliefs maintained in spite of strong evidence to the contrary. *Page 146*

dendrites Branching neuron structures that receive neural impulses from other neurons and convey impulses toward the cell body. *Page 54*

dependent variable (DV) The variable that is observed and measured for change in an experiment; thought to be affected by (or dependent on) the manipulation of the independent variable. *Page 15*

depressants Psychoactive drugs that act on the central nervous system to suppress or slow bodily processes and reduce overall responsiveness. *Page 191*

depth perception The process by which we organize perception in three dimensions — even though the images that strike the retina are two-dimensional — so that we can perceive distance. *Page 154*

designer drugs Illicitly manufactured variations on known recreational drugs. *Page 201*

developmental psychology The branch of psychology that describes, explains, predicts, and sometimes aims to modify age-related behaviors from conception to death. This field emphasizes maturation, early experiences, and various stages in development. *Page 8*

Diagnostic and Statistical Manual of Mental Disorders, fourth edition, text revision (DSM-IV-TR) A classification system, developed by the American Psychiatric Association, used to describe abnormal behaviors; the IV-TR indicates it is the text revision (TR) of the fourth major edition (IV). *Page 519*

difference threshold The smallest magnitude of difference in stimulus energy that a person can detect; also called the just-noticeable difference. *Page 130*

diffusion of responsibility In groups of two or more, people tend to take less individual responsibility because they assume someone else will take action (or responsibility). *Page 637*

discrimination Negative behaviors directed at members of a group. *Page 610*

discriminative stimulus A cue that signals when a particular response is likely to be followed by a certain type of consequence. *Page 233*

disengagement theory A theory of aging suggesting that both the individual and society gradually and naturally pull away from each other in preparation for the individual's death. *Page 394*

dissociative disorder Stress-related disorder characterized by amnesia, fugue, or multiple personality. In all cases, though, the person is trying to escape from the memory of a painful experience. *Page 547*

dissociative identity disorder (DID) A dissociative disorder characterized by the presence of two or more distinct personality systems in the same individual; previously known as multiple personality disorder. *Page 537*

distress Unpleasant, objectionable stress. *Page 104*

distributed practice A learning technique in which practice sessions are interspersed with rest periods. *Page 275*

divergent thinking Thinking that produces many alternatives or ideas; a major element of creativity (e.g., finding as many uses as possible for a paper clip). *Page 308*

dopamine hypothesis A theory suggesting that schizophrenia is caused by an overactivity of dopamine neurons in a specific region of the brain. *Page 542*

double-blind study A study in which neither the participant nor the experimenter knows which treatment is being given to the participant or to which group the participant has been assigned. *Page 16*

double standard The beliefs, values, and norms that subtly encourage male sexuality and discourage female sexuality. *Page 425*

drive-reduction theory The theory that motivation begins with a physiological need (a lack or deficiency) that elicits a psychological energy or drive directed toward behavior that will satisfy the original need. Once the need is met, a state of balance (homeostasis) is restored and motivation decreases. *Page 451*

drug abuse Drug taking that causes emotional or physical harm to the drug user or others. *Page 189*

drug therapy Use of chemicals (drugs) to treat physical and psychological disorders. *Page 562*

eclectic approach An approach to therapy in which the therapist combines techniques from various theories to find the appropriate treatment for the client. *Page 559*

ego In Sigmund Freud's theory, the rational part of the psyche that deals with reality and attempts to control the impulses of the id while also satisfying the social approval and self-esteem needs of the superego. *Page 489*

egocentrism The inability to consider another's point of view, which Jean Piaget considered a hallmark of the preoperational stage. *Page 366*

egoistic model The proposal that helping behavior is motivated by anticipated gain — later reciprocation, increased self-esteem, or avoidance of guilt and distress. *Page 636*

elaborative rehearsal An encoding technique of associating new information with already-stored knowledge in long-term memory. Also known as deeper levels of processing. *Page 263*

electroconvulsive therapy (ECT) A biomedical therapy based on passing electrical current through the brain. It is used almost exclusively to treat serious depression when drug therapy does not work. *Page 564*

embryonic period The second stage of pregnancy (from uterine implantation through the eighth week), characterized by development of major body organs and systems. *Page 345*

emotion-focused forms of coping Coping strategies based on changing one's perceptions of stressful situations. *Page 117*

emotion An individual's feelings or affective responses that include cognitions (thoughts, beliefs, and expectations), physiological arousal (heart pounding), and behavioral expressions (frowns, smiles, running, etc.). *Page 456*

emotional intelligence According to Daniel Goleman, the ability to know and manage one's emotions, empathize with others, and maintain satisfying relationships. *Page 463*

empathy In Rogerian terms, an insightful awareness and ability to share another person's inner experience. *Page 577*

empathy–altruism hypothesis The proposal that altruistic behavior is motivated by empathy for someone in need of help. *Page 636*

encoding The process of translating information into neural codes (language) that will be retained in memory. *Page 261*

encoding specificity principle The principle that retrieval of information is improved when conditions of recovery are similar to the conditions when information was encoded. *Page 267*

endocrine [EN-doh-krin] system A system of glands located throughout the body that secrete hormones into the bloodstream. *Page 61*

endorphins [en-DOR-fins] Chemical substances in the nervous system that are similar in structure and action to opiates and are involved in pain control, pleasure, and memory. *Page 61*

episodic memory The subpart of explicit/declarative memory that stores memories of personally experienced events; a mental diary of a person's life. *Page 264*

ethnocentrism The belief that behavior in your culture is typical of all cultures. Also, viewing one's own ethnic group (or culture) as central and "correct" and then judging the rest of the world according to this standard. *Page 16*

eustress Pleasant, desirable stress. *Page 104*

evolutionary psychology A branch of psychology that studies evolutionary principles, like natural selection and genetic mutations, which affect adaptation to the environment and help explain commonalities in behavior. *Page 87*

evolutionary/circadian theory The theory that sleep is a part of circadian rhythms and evolved as a means of conserving energy and protecting individuals from predators. *Page 180*

excitement phase First stage of the sexual response cycle, characterized by increasing levels of arousal and increased engorgement of the genitals. *Page 418*

experiment A carefully controlled scientific procedure conducted to determine whether certain variables manipulated by the experimenter have a causal effect on other variables. *Page 14*

experimental group In a controlled experiment, the group of participants that receives the independent variable. *Page 15*

experimenter bias The tendency of experimenters to influence the results of a research study in the expected direction. *Page 16*

explicit/declarative memory The subsystem within long-term memory that stores facts, information, and personal life experiences; also called explicit memory or declarative memory. *Page 264*

extinction The gradual suppression of a behavior or a response that occurs when a conditioned stimulus is repeatedly presented without the unconditioned stimulus with which it had been previously associated. *Page 218*

extraneous variables Variables that are not directly related to the hypothesis under study and that the experimenter does not actively attempt to control (e.g., time of day and heating of room). *Page 16*

extrasensory perception (ESP) Perceptual, or "psychic," abilities that supposedly go beyond the known senses, including telepathy, clairvoyance, precognition, and psychokinesis. *Page 162*

extrinsic motivation Motivation based on obvious external rewards or threats of punishment rather than on factors within the individual or the behavior itself. *Page 466*

facial feedback hypothesis The proposal that movements of the facial muscles produce or intensify emotional reactions. *Page 465*

factor analysis A statistical procedure used to determine the most basic units or factors in a large array of data. *Page 480*

family therapy A psychological treatment that attempts to change maladaptive interaction patterns among members of a family. *Page 586*

farsightedness (hyperopia) A visual acuity problem that results when the cornea and lens focus an image behind the retina. *Page 135*

feature detectors Specialized cells in the brain that respond only to certain sensory information. *Page 147*

fetal alcohol syndrome (FAS) A combination of birth defects, including organ deformities and mental, motor, and/or growth retardation, that results from maternal alcohol abuse. *Page 347*

fetal period The third, and final, stage of prenatal development (8 weeks to birth), characterized by rapid weight gain in the fetus and the fine detailing of fetal body organs and systems. *Page 345*

figure and ground A Gestalt law of perceptual organization stating that our perceptions consist of two aspects the figure, which stands out and has a definite contour or shape, and the ground, which is less distinct. *Page 149*

five-factor model (FFM) A trait theory that explains personality in terms of a "Big Five" model — openness, conscientiousness, extraversion, agreeableness, and neuroticism. *Page 480*

fixed-interval schedule A schedule of reinforcement in which a participant is reinforced for the first response after a specific period of time has elapsed. *Page 228*

fixed-ratio schedule A partial schedule of reinforcement in which a participant must make a certain number of responses before being reinforced. *Page 228*

fluid intelligence Aspects of intelligence, including reasoning abilities, memory, and speed of information processing, that tend to decline slowly as people age. *Page 321*

foot-in-the-door technique A social influence technique in which a first, small request is used as a "setup" for later requests. *Page 626*

formal operational stage Jean Piaget's fourth stage of cognitive development (around age 11 years and beyond) characterized by abstract and hypothetical thinking. *Page 366*

free association In psychoanalysis, reporting whatever comes to mind without monitoring its contents — regardless of how painful, embarrassing, or irrelevant it may seem. Sigmund Freud believed that the first thing to come to a patient's mind was often an important clue to what the unconscious mind wants to conceal. *Page 570*

frequency How often a light wave or sound wave cycles; that is, the number of complete wavelengths that pass a point in a given time (e.g., per second). *Page 133*

frequency theory Theory that explains how we hear lower-pitched sounds; hair cells on the basilar membrane of the cochlea bend and fire action potentials at the same rate as the frequency of the low sound. *Page 139*

frontal lobes Cortical lobes in the front of the brain, which govern motor control, speech production, and higher functions, such as thinking, personality, emotion, and memory. *Page 71*

frustration An unpleasant state of tension, anxiety, and heightened sympathetic activity resulting from a blocked goal. *Page 107*

frustration-aggression hypothesis The idea that frustration — the blocking of a desired goal — creates anger, which may lead to aggression. *Page 633*

functional fixedness A barrier to problem solving that occurs when people are unable to recognize novel uses for an object because they are so familiar with its common use. *Page 305*

fundamental attribution error (FAE) Misjudging the causes of others' behavior because of overestimating internal, personal factors and underestimating external, situational influences. *Page 604*

gate-control theory of pain The idea that pain sensations are processed and altered by mechanisms within the spinal cord. *Page 131*

gender The psychological and sociocultural meanings added to biological maleness or femaleness. *Page 404*

gender identity How one psychologically perceives oneself as either male or female. *Page 406*

gender role The societal expectations for normal and appropriate male and female behavior. When these expectations are based on exaggerated and biased beliefs about differences between the sexes and are rigidly applied to all members of each sex, they are known as gender role stereotypes. *Page 406*

gene A segment of DNA (deoxyribonucleic acid) that occupies a specific place on a particular chromosome and carries the code for hereditary transmission. *Page 84*

general adaptation syndrome (GAS) As described by Hans Selye, a generalized physiological reaction to severe stressors consisting of three phases the alarm reaction, the resistance phase, and the exhaustion phase. *Page 110*

generalized anxiety disorder Type of anxiety disorder characterized by chronic, uncontrollable, and excessive worry. The anxiety is not focused on any particular object or situation. *Page 525*

genuineness In Rogerian terms, authenticity or congruence; the awareness of one's true inner thoughts and feelings and being able to share them honestly with others. *Page 578*

germinal period The first stage of pregnancy (conception to 2 weeks) characterized by rapid cell division. *Page 345*

glial cells Nervous system cells that provide structural, nutritional, and other support for the neuron; also called glia or neuroglia. *Page 54*

grammar The rules of a language that specify how phonemes, morphemes, words, and phrases should be combined to meaningfully express thoughts. *Page 312*

group polarization A group's movement toward either riskier or more conservative behavior, depending on the members' initial dominant tendency. *Page 630*

group therapy Treatment method in which multiple people meet together to work toward therapeutic goals. *Page 585*

groupthink A condition that results when a highly cohesive group strives for agreement to the point of avoiding inconsistent information; the result is faulty decision making. *Page 630*

gustation The sense of taste. *Page 142*

habituation The tendency of the brain to ignore environmental factors that remain constant. *Page 148*

hallucinations Sensory perceptions that occur without an external stimulus. *Page 146*

hallucinogens [hal-LU-sin-oh-jenz] Drugs that produce sensory distortions or perceptual distortions. *Page 192*

hardiness A resilient personality characteristic based on three qualities a commitment to personal goals, control over life, and viewing change as a challenge rather than a threat. *Page 114*

hassles Little problems of daily living that are not significant in themselves, but they accumulate and sometimes become a major source of stress. *Page 106*

health psychology The study of the relationship between psychological behavior and physical health and illness, with an emphasis on wellness and the prevention of illness. *Page 96*

heritability The proportion of observed variance in a particular trait (such as intelligence) that can be attributed to inherited genetic factors in contrast to environmental ones. *Page 86*

heuristic Problem-solving strategies, or "rules of thumb," used as shortcuts to complex solutions, which generally, but not always, lead to a solution. *Page 303*

hierarchy of needs Abraham Maslow's theory of motivation that some motives (such as physiological and safety needs) have to be satisfied before an individual can attend to higher needs (such as belonging and self-actualization). *Page 453*

higher-order conditioning In classical conditioning, a procedure in which a neutral stimulus (NS) becomes a conditioned stimulus through association with an already established conditioned stimulus (CS); a NS is paired with a previous CS (CS1), which then becomes a secondary CS (CS2) and produces the same conditioned response as CS1. *Page 218*

HIV positive Being infected by the human immunodeficiency virus (HIV). *Page 429*

hormones Chemicals manufactured by endocrine glands and circulated in the bloodstream to produce bodily changes or maintain normal bodily functions. *Page 61*

hue The visual dimension seen as a particular color; determined by the length of a light wave. *Page 133*

humanistic therapy Therapy that helps individuals become creative and unique persons through affective restructuring (or emotional readjustment). *Page 576*

hypnosis An alternate state of heightened suggestibility characterized by relaxation and intense focus. *Page 202*

hypothalamus [high-poh-THAL-uh-muss] Small structure beneath the thalamus that maintains homeostasis and regulates emotions and drives, such as hunger, thirst, sex, and aggression. *Page 68*

hypothesis A statement of a predicted relationship between two or more variables. *Page 12*

id According to Sigmund Freud, the source of instinctual energy, which works on the pleasure principle and is concerned with immediate gratification. *Page 489*

identity crisis According to Erik Erikson, a period of inner conflict during which an individual examines his or her life and values and makes decisions about life roles. *Page 383*

illusion A false impression of the environment. *Page 146*

implicit/nondeclarative/procedural memory The subsystem within long-term memory that consists of skills acquired through repetitive practice, habits, and simple classically conditioned responses; also called implicit memory, nondeclarative memory, or procedural memory. *Page 264*

imprinting An innate or instinctual form of learning in which the young of certain species follow and become attached to large moving objects (usually their mothers). *Page 358*

incentive theory The theory that motivation results from environmental stimuli that "pull" the organism in certain directions, as opposed to internal needs that drive or "push" the organism. *Page 452*

incubation A period of time during which active searching for a problem's solution is set aside; this is sometimes necessary for a successful solution of the problem. *Page 307*

independent variable (IV) In an experiment, a variable that is manipulated by the experimenter to determine its causal effect on the dependent variable. *Page 15*

inferiority complex Alfred Adler's idea that feelings of inferiority develop from early childhood experiences of helplessness and incompetence. *Page 495*

informational social influence Conforming to group pressure out of a need for direction and information. *Page 624*

informed consent A participant's agreement to take part in a study after being told what to expect. *Page 24*

ingroup favoritism A cognitive process in prejudice whereby members of an ingroup are viewed in more favorable terms than members of an outgroup. *Page 611*

insanity A legal term for people with a mental disorder that implies a lack of responsibility for their behavior and an inability to manage their affairs. *Page 520*

insight A sudden flash of understanding that occurs during problem solving. *Page 240*

insomnia A sleep disorder in which a person has persistent problems in falling asleep or staying asleep or awakens too early. *Page 184*

instinctive drift A biological constraint that occurs when an animal's learned responses shifts (or drifts) toward innate response patterns. *Page 248*

instincts Behavioral patterns that are (1) unlearned, (2) always expressed in the same way, and (3) universal in a species. *Page 451*

intelligence The general capacity to profit from experience, to acquire knowledge, and adapt to changes in the environment. *Page 319*

intelligence quotient (IQ) A score on a test that is intended to measure verbal and quantitative abilities. *Page 325*

interaction A process in which multiple factors mutually influence the outcome — as in the interaction between heredity and environment. *Page 6*

interpersonal attraction The degree of positive or negative feelings toward another. *Page 614*

interpretation A psychoanalyst's explanation of a patient's free associations, dreams, resistance, and transference; more generally, any statement by a therapist that presents a patient's problem in a new way. *Page 571*

intrinsic motivation Motivation that comes from personal enjoyment of a task or activity, rather than from external rewards or fear of punishment. *Page 446*

James–Lange theory The theory that emotion is the perception of one's own bodily reactions and that each emotion is physiologically distinct. *Page 464*

justice perspective Carol Gilligan's term for an approach to moral reasoning that emphasizes individual rights and views people as differentiated and standing alone. *Page 381*

kinesthesis The sensory system that provides information on body posture and orientation. *Page 144*

language acquisition device (LAD) In Noam Chomsky's view, the child's inborn brain capacity to analyze language and unconsciously understand essential grammatical rules. *Page 357*

latent content The true, unconscious meaning of a dream, according to Freudian dream theory. *Page 570*

latent learning Learning that occurs in the absence of a reward and remains hidden until there is some incentive to demonstrate it. *Page 240*

lateralization Specialization of the left and right hemispheres of the brain for particular operations. *Page 75*

learned helplessness In Martin Seligman's theory, a state of helplessness or resignation in which people or animals learn that escape from something painful is impossible and depression results. *Page 232*

learning A relatively permanent change in behavior or behavioral potential as a result of practice or experience. *Page 210*

limbic system An interconnected group of brain structures involved with the arousal and regulation of emotion, motivation, memory, and learning. *Page 70*

lobotomy A brain operation in which the nerve pathways between the frontal lobes and the thalamus and hypothalamus are cut in hopes of treating psychological disorders. *Page 564*

localization of function Specialization of various parts of the brain for particular functions. *Page 67*

locus of control The belief that life's circumstances are under personal, internal control, or controlled by outside, external factors. *Page 120*

long-term memory (LTM) The third stage of memory that functions as storage of information for long periods of time; its capacity is limitless and its duration is relatively permanent. *Page 258*

long-term potentiation (LTP) A long-lasting increase in the strength of synaptic responsiveness believed to be a biological mechanism for learning and memory. *Page 268*

longitudinal method A data collection technique that measures a single individual or group of individuals over an extended period and gives information about age changes. *Page 341*

maintenance rehearsal The process of repeating the contents of short-term memory (STM) over and over to maintain it in STM. *Page 256*

major depressive disorder A DSM-IV-TR (Diagnostic and Statistical Manual of Mental Disorders, fourth edition, text revision) diagnostic term for individuals experiencing a long-lasting depressed mood that interferes with the ability to function, feel pleasure, or maintain interest in life. The feelings are without apparent cause and excessive to the given situation. *Page 531*

manifest content The surface content of a dream, containing dream symbols that distort and disguise the true meaning of the dream, according to Freudian dream theory. *Page 570*

massed practice A learning technique in which time spent learning is massed into long, unbroken intervals; also known as cramming. *Page 275*

maturation Biological growth processes that enable orderly changes in behavior, relatively uninfluenced by the environment. *Page 340*

medical model Perspective that assumes diseases have physical causes that can be diagnosed, treated, and possibly cured. Using this perspective, abnormal behaviors also have physical causes that can be diagnosed by their symptoms and treated and cured through therapy, including drugs, hospitalization, and so on. *Page 517*

meditation A group of techniques designed to focus attention and produce a heightened state of awareness. *Page 204*

medulla [muh-DULL-uh] Structure at the base of the brain stem responsible for automatic body functions such as breathing and heart rate. *Page 67*

memory An internal record or representation of some prior event or experience; also a set of mental processes that receives, encodes, stores, organizes, alters, and retrieves information over time. *Page 254*

mental images The mind's representation of a sensory experience, including visual, auditory, gustatory, motor, olfactory, or tactile elements (e.g., visualizing a train and hearing its whistle). *Page 299*

mental set A mental barrier to problem solving that occurs when people apply only methods that have worked in the past rather than trying innovative ones. *Page 304*

meta-analysis A statistical procedure for combining and analyzing data from many studies. *Page 13*

Minnesota Multiphasic Personality Inventory (MMPI-2) The most widely researched and clinically used self-report personality test; the revised version is called the MMPI-2. *Page 475*

misinformation effect A memory error that results from incorporating outside information into one's own memory of an event. (Also known as suggestibility.) *Page 283*

mnemonic [nih-MON-ik] device A memory-improvement technique based on encoding items in a special way. *Page 288*

modeling therapy A type of behavior therapy that involves watching and imitating appropriate models that demonstrate desirable behaviors. *Page 584*

monocular cues Visual input from a single eye alone that contributes to perception of depth or distance. *Page 155*

morpheme [MOR-feem] The smallest meaningful unit of language, formed from a combination of phonemes. *Page 312*

motivation Factors within an individual (such as needs, desires, and interests)

that activate, maintain, and direct behavior toward a goal. *Page 438*

myelin [MY-uh-lin] sheath A layer of fatty insulation wrapped around the axon of some neurons, which increases the rate at which nerve impulses travel along the axon. *Page 55*

narcolepsy [NAR-co-lep-see] A disease marked by sudden and irresistible onsets of sleep during normal waking hours; from narco, meaning "numbness," and lepsy, meaning "seizure". *Page 186*

natural selection The driving mechanism behind evolution that allows individuals with genetically influenced traits that are adaptive in a particular environment to stay alive and produce offspring. *Page 87*

naturalistic observation The systematic recording of observable behavior in the participant's natural state or habitat with little or no experimenter intervention. *Page 19*

nature–nurture controversy The long-standing dispute over the relative contributions of nature (heredity) and nurture (environment) to the development of behavior and mental processes. *Page 86*

nearsightedness (myopia) A visual acuity problem that occurs when the cornea and lens focus an image in front of the retina. *Page 135*

need compatibility A sharing of similar needs. *Page 616*

need complementarity The tendency to seek out and be attracted to people whose qualities we admire but personally lack. *Page 616*

negative punishment The process of taking away or removing a stimulus that decreases the likelihood of that response occurring again. *Page 230*

negative reinforcement The process of taking away or removing a stimulus that increases the likelihood of that response occurring again. *Page 226*

neurogenesis [new-roh-JEN-uh-sis] The division of nonneuronal cells to produce neurons. *Page 81*

neuron Individual nerve cell responsible for processing, storing, and transmitting information throughout the body. *Page 54*

neuroplasticity The brain's ability to reorganize and change its structure and function throughout the life span. *Page 81*

neuroscience An interdisciplinary field studying how biological processes, espe-

cially activity in the brain and nervous system, relate to behavior. *Page 49*

neurosis A large group of disorders characterized by unrealistic anxiety and other associated problems. *Page 520*

neurotransmitter Chemicals manufactured and released by neurons that alter activity in other neurons. *Page 57*

night terrors Abrupt awakenings from non-REM (non–rapid-eye-movement) sleep accompanied by intense physiological arousal and feelings of panic. *Page 186*

nightmares Anxiety-arousing dreams that generally occur near the end of the sleep cycle, during REM (rapid-eye-movement) sleep. *Page 186*

norm Cultural rule of behavior that prescribes what is acceptable in a given situation. *Page 623*

normative social influence Conforming to group pressure out of a need for acceptance and approval. *Page 623*

obedience A type of social influence in which an individual follows direct commands, usually from someone in a position of authority. *Page 624*

object permanence A Piagetian term for an infant's understanding that objects (or people) continue to exist even when they cannot be directly seen, heard, or touched. *Page 365*

obsessive-compulsive disorder (OCD) Type of anxiety disorder characterized by intrusive thoughts (obsessions) and urges to perform repetitive, ritualistic behaviors (compulsions). *Page 526*

occipital [ahk-SIP-uh-tuhl] lobes Cortical lobes at the back of the brain responsible for vision and visual perception. *Page 71*

Oedipus (ED-uh-puss) complex During the phallic stage, children are sexually attracted to the opposite-sex parent and hostile toward the same-sex parent. *Page 492*

olfaction The sense of smell. *Page 141*

operant conditioning Learning based on consequences. Behavior is strengthened if followed by reinforcement and diminished if followed by punishment. *Page 213*

operational definition A precise description of how the variables in a study will be observed and measured. For example, drug abuse might be defined as "the number of missed work days due to excessive use of an addictive substance." *Page 12*

opiates Drugs that are derived from opium and function as an analgesic or pain reliever. The word opium derives from the Greek word meaning "juice." *Page 192*

opponent-process theory The theory first proposed by Ewald Hering that color perception is based on three systems of color opposites — blue–yellow, red–green, and black–white. *Page 159*

orgasm phase Third stage of the sexual response cycle when pleasurable sensations peak and orgasm occurs. *Page 418*

outgroup homogeneity effect A cognitive process in prejudice whereby members of the outgroup are judged as less individual, or diverse, than members of the ingroup. *Page 611*

overextension A child's tendency to define a word too broadly to include objects that do not fit the word's meaning. *Page 357*

overgeneralize A common error in language acquisition in which the child overuses the basic rules of grammar. The rules for past tense and plurals are extended to irregular forms (e.g., they may say "mans" instead of "men.") *Page 357*

panic disorder Type of anxiety disorder characterized by sudden and inexplicable attacks of intense fear. Symptoms include difficulty breathing, heart palpitations, dizziness, trembling, terror, and feelings of impending doom. *Page 525*

parallel distributed processing (PDP) approach A model of memory in which knowledge is represented as connections among interacting processing units, distributed in a vast network, and all operating in parallel. *Page 259*

parasympathetic nervous system Subdivision of the autonomic nervous system responsible for calming the body. *Page 52*

parietal [puh-RYE-uh-tuhl] lobes Cortical lobes at the top of the brain where bodily sensations are interpreted. *Page 71*

partial (intermittent) reinforcement Reinforcement in which some, but not all, correct responses are reinforced. *Page 228*

perception The process of selecting, organizing, and interpreting sensory data into usable mental representations of the world. *Page 128*

perceptual constancy The tendency for the environment to be perceived as remaining the same even with changes in sensory input. *Page 152*

perceptual set A readiness to perceive in a particular manner on the basis of expectations. *Page 160*

performance anxiety A fear that one will be unable to meet the expectations for sexual "performance" of oneself or one's partner. *Page 424*

peripheral nervous system (PNS) All nerves and neurons outside the brain and spinal cord. Its major function is to connect the central nervous system to the rest of the body. *Page 51*

personality An individual's relatively stable and enduring pattern of thoughts, feelings, and actions. *Page 473*

personality disorders A DSM-IV-TR (Diagnostic and Statistical Manual of Mental Disorders, fourth edition, revised) category that describes individuals with inflexible, maladaptive personality traits. The best-known type is the antisocial personality. *Page 549*

pheromones **(FARE-oh-mones)** Airborne chemicals released from one individual that affect another individual's behavior, including recognition of family members, aggression, territorial marking, and sexual mating. *Page 142*

phobia Type of anxiety disorder characterized by intense, irrational fear and avoidance of a specific object or situation. *Page 526*

phoneme [FOH-neem] The most basic unit of speech; an individual speech sound. *Page 312*

physical dependence A condition in which bodily processes have been so modified by repeated use of a drug that continued use is required to prevent withdrawal symptoms. *Page 190*

pitch The highness or lowness of tones or sounds, depending on their frequency. *Page 137*

place theory Theory that explains how we hear higher-pitched sounds; different high-pitched sounds bend the basilar membrane hair cells at different locations in the cochlea. *Page 139*

placebo [pluh-SEE-boh] An inactive substance or fake treatment used as a control technique, usually in drug research, or given by a medical practitioner to a patient. *Page 16*

plateau phase Second stage of the sexual response cycle, characterized by a leveling off of high arousal. *Page 418*

pleasure principle In Freudian theory, the principle on which the id operates — that immediate pleasure is the sole motivation for behavior. *Page 489*

polygraph Instrument that measures emotional arousal through heart rate, respiration rate, blood pressure, and skin conductivity. These measurements are taken while a participant is asked questions designed to determine his or her credibility. *Page 461*

pons Structure at the top of the brainstem involved in respiration, movement, waking, sleep, and dreaming. *Page 67*

positive punishment The process of adding or presenting a stimulus that decreases the likelihood of that response occurring again. *Page 230*

positive reinforcement The process of adding or presenting a stimulus that increases the likelihood of that response occurring again. *Page 226*

postconventional level Lawrence Kohlberg's highest level of moral development, which occurs when individuals develop personal standards for right and wrong. *Page 379*

post-traumatic stress disorder (PTSD) Type of anxiety disorder following exposure to a life-threatening or other extreme event that evoked great horror or helplessness; it is characterized by flashbacks, nightmares, and impaired functioning. *Page 290*

preconscious Sigmund Freud's term for thoughts or information that one can become aware of easily. *Page 488*

preconventional level Lawrence Kohlberg's first level of moral development, characterized by moral judgments based on fear of punishment or desire for pleasure. *Page 378*

prejudice A generally negative attitude directed toward others because of their membership in a specific group. Like all attitudes, prejudice involves cognitions (thoughts), affect (feelings), and behavioral tendencies. *Page 610*

Premack principle Using a response that has a high probability of occurrence to reinforce a response that has a lower probability of occurrence. *Page 227*

preoperational stage The second of Jean Piaget's stages (roughly ages 2 to 7 years) characterized by the ability to employ significant language and to think symbolically. But the child lacks operations (reversible mental processes), and thinking is egocentric and animistic. *Page 365*

primary reinforcers Stimuli that increase the probability of a response because they satisfy a biological need, such as food, water, and sex. *Page 225*

priming The process by which an earlier encounter with a stimulus (such as a word or picture) increases the likelihood of that stimulus or a related stimulus being remembered at a later time. *Page 265*

proactive interference Forgetting in which old information interferes with remembering new information; forward-acting memory interference. *Page 278*

problem-focused forms of coping Coping strategies based on using problem-solving strategies to decrease or eliminate the source of stress. *Page 117*

projective tests Psychological tests using ambiguous stimuli, such as inkblots or drawings. The ambiguity of the stimuli reportedly allows the test taker to project his or her true unconscious conflicts, motives, psychological defenses, and personality traits onto the test material. *Page 476*

prototype A typical, highly representative example that serves as a model on which other examples are based or judged (e.g., baseball is a prototype of the concept of sports). *Page 300*

proximity A key factor in attraction involving geographic, residential, and other forms of physical closeness. *Page 615*

psychiatry The specialized branch of medicine dealing with the diagnosis, treatment, and prevention of mental disorder. *Page 518*

psychoactive drugs Chemicals that affect the nervous system and cause a change in behavior, mental processes, and conscious experience. *Page 189*

psychoanalysis A system of therapy developed by Sigmund Freud that seeks to bring unconscious conflicts, which usually date back to early childhood experiences, into consciousness. Psychoanalysis is also Freud's theoretical school of thought, which emphasizes the study of unconscious processes. *Page 570*

psychodynamic therapy A form of psychotherapy that emphasizes internal conflicts, motives, and unconscious forces. *Page 31*

psychological dependence A desire or craving to achieve the effects produced by a drug. *Page 190*

psychology The scientific study of behavior and mental processes. *Page 4*

psychoneuroimmunology [sigh-koh-NEW-ro-IM-you-NOLL-oh-gee] An interdisciplinary field that studies the effects of psychological factors on the immune system. *Page 111*

psychophysics The branch of psychology that studies the relation between attributes of the physical world and our psychological experience of them. *Page 130*

psychosexual stages In psychoanalytic theory, five developmental periods during which particular kinds of pleasures must be gratified if personality development is to proceed normally. *Page 490*

psychosis Serious mental disorders characterized by loss of contact with reality and extreme mental disruption. Because daily functioning is often impaired, psychotic individuals are more likely to need hospitalization. *Page 520*

psychosocial stages Erik Erikson's theory that individuals pass through eight developmental stages and that adult personality reflects how the distinct challenges or crises at each stage are resolved. *Page 382*

psychosurgery Operative procedures on the brain designed to relieve severe mental symptoms that have not responded to other forms of treatment. *Page 253*

psychotherapy A collection of various psychological techniques employed to improve psychological functioning and promote adjustment to life through understanding one's problems and modifying troubling feelings, behaviors, or relationships. *Page 557*

puberty The period in life when sex organs mature and sexual reproduction becomes possible. Puberty generally begins for girls between the ages of 10 and 12 years and for boys about 2 years later. *Page 351*

punishment Any action or event that decreases the likelihood that a response will be repeated. *Page 225*

random assignment Occurs when participant's chances of being assigned to each group in an experiment are equal, thereby ensuring that any later differences between people in the experimental and control conditions must be the result of the treatment. *Page 17*

rapid-eye-movement (REM) sleep A stage of sleep marked by rapid eye movements, high-frequency brain waves, and dreaming. *Page 177*

rational-emotive therapy (RET) Cognitive therapy system developed by Albert Ellis that attempts to eliminate self-defeating beliefs through rational examination. *Page 574*

reality principle According to Sigmund Freud, the principle on which the conscious ego operates as it tries to meet the demands of the unconscious id and the realities of the environment. *Page 489*

recall Process of using a very general retrieval cue to search the contents of long-term memory. *Page 266*

reciprocal determinism Albert Bandura's belief that an individual's cognitions and behaviors and the learning environment interact to produce personality. *Page 503*

recognition Process of matching a specific retrieval cue to an appropriate item in long-term memory. *Page 266*

reference groups People to whom we conform (or with whom we go along) because we like and admire them and want to be like them. *Page 624*

refractory period Phase following orgasm during which further orgasm is considered physiologically impossible. *Page 419*

reinforcement Any action or event that increases the probability that a response will be repeated. *Page 224*

relearning Learning material a second time, which usually takes less time than original learning; also called the savings method. *Page 274*

reliability A measure of the consistency and stability of test scores when the test is readministered. *Page 324*

repair/restoration theory The theory that sleep serves a recuperative function, allowing organisms to repair or replenish key factors in the brain or body that are depleted during daytime activities. *Page 180*

repression Sigmund Freud's first and most basic defense mechanism that blocks unacceptable impulses from coming into awareness. *Page 490*

resilience A term referring to a child's good developmental outcome, sustained competence under stress, and recovery from trauma despite high-risk status. *Page 392*

resistance A stage in psychoanalysis when the patient avoids (resists) the analyst's attempts to bring threatening unconscious material to conscious awareness. *Page 570*

resolution phase Final stage of the sexual response cycle when the body returns to its unaroused state. *Page 419*

reticular formation (RF) A diffuse set of neurons in the core of the brain stem that screens incoming information and arouses the cortex. *Page 67*

retina The light-sensitive inner surface of the back of the eye, which contains the receptor rods and cones plus other neurons that help in processing visual information. *Page 135*

retinal disparity A binocular cue to distance in which the separation of the eyes causes different images to fall on each retina. *Page 155*

retrieval The process of recovering information from memory storage. *Page 265*

retrieval cue A clue or prompt that helps stimulate recall and retrieval of a stored piece of information from long-term memory. *Page 266*

retroactive interference Forgetting in which new information interferes with remembering old information; backward-acting interference. *Page 278*

retrograde amnesia Difficulty in remembering previously learned material. *Page 281*

rods Visual receptors in the retina that detect black, white, and gray and are responsible for peripheral vision. They are most sensitive in dim light. *Page 136*

romantic love An intense feeling of attraction to another person, within an erotic context and with future expectations. *Page 617*

Rorschach [ROAR-shock] Inkblot Test A projective test that presents a set of 10 cards with symmetrical abstract patterns, known as inkblots, and respondents describe what they "see" in the image. Their response is thought to be a projection of unconscious processes. *Page 476*

saliency bias The tendency to focus on the most noticeable (salient) factors when explaining the causes of behavior. *Page 605*

sample bias The tendency for the sample of participants in a research study to be atypical of a larger population. *Page 17*

Schachter's two-factor theory The theory that emotional experience results from physical arousal and cognitive labeling (or interpretation) of that arousal. *Page 465*

schema Cognitive structures or patterns consisting of a number of organized ideas that grow and differentiate with experience. *Page 364*

schizophrenia Group of psychotic disorders involving major disturbances in perception, language, thought, emotion, and behavior. The individual withdraws from people and reality, often into a fantasy life of delusions and hallucinations. *Page 537*

secondary reinforcers Stimuli that increase the probability of a response because of their learned value, such as money and material possessions. *Page 225*

selective attention The process whereby the brain sorts out and attends to only the important messages from the senses. *Page 146*

self-actualization According to Abraham Maslow, an innate tendency toward growth that motivates all human behavior and results in the full realization of a person's highest potential. *Page 453*

self-concept In Rogerian theory, all the information and beliefs individuals have about their own nature, qualities, and behavior. *Page 507*

self-efficacy According to Albert Bandura, a person's learned beliefs that he or she is capable of producing desired results, such as mastering new skills and achieving personal goals. *Page 503*

self-help group Groups that are leaderless or guided by a nonprofessional, in which members assist each other in coping with a specific problem, as in Alcoholics Anonymous. *Page 586*

self-serving bias A way of maintaining a positive self-image by taking credit for one's successes and emphasizing external causes for one's failures. *Page 478*

self-talk Internal dialogue; the things people say to themselves when they interpret events. *Page 574*

semantic memory The subpart of explicit/declarative memory that stores general knowledge; a mental encyclopedia or dictionary. *Page 264*

semantics Meaning or the study of meaning derived from morphemes, words, and sentences. *Page 313*

semicircular canals Three arching structures in the inner ear that contain hair receptors that respond to head movements to provide information on balance. *Page 143*

sensation The process of receiving, translating, and transmitting raw sensory data from the external and internal environments to the brain. *Page 128*

sensorimotor stage The first of Jean Piaget's stages (birth to approximately age 2 years), in which cognitive development takes place by exploring the world via sensory perceptions and motor skills. *Page 365*

sensory adaptation A sensory phenomenon in which the perceived intensity of a repeated stimulus decreases over time. *Page 131*

sensory memory The first stage of memory, in which a relatively exact image of each sensory experience is held briefly until it can be further processed; its capacity is relatively large but its duration is restricted to a few seconds. *Page 255*

sensory reduction The process of filtering and analyzing incoming sensations that occur before a neural impulse is sent to the cortex. *Page 129*

serial position effect The phenomenon of remembering the material at the beginning and the end of a list better than the material in the middle. *Page 275*

set point An organism's personal homeostatic level for a particular body weight that results from factors such as early feeding experiences and heredity. *Page 439*

sex Biological maleness and femaleness, including chromosomal sex, gonadal sex, hormonal sex, external genitals, and internal accessory organs. Also, activities related to sexual behaviors, such as masturbation and intercourse. *Page 404*

sexual dysfunction Impairment of the normal physiological processes of arousal and orgasm. *Page 422*

sexual orientation An individual's primary erotic attraction can be toward members of the same sex (homosexual or gay or lesbian), both sexes (bisexual), or other sex (heterosexual). *Page 406*

sexual prejudice Negative attitudes toward an individual because of his or her sexual orientation. *Page 421*

sexual response cycle William Masters and Virginia Johnson's description of the bodily response to sexual arousal. The four stages are excitement, plateau, orgasm, and resolution. *Page 418*

sexual scripts Socially dictated descriptions of the sequences of behavior that are considered appropriate in sexual interactions. *Page 426*

shaping A procedure in which reinforcement is delivered for successive approximations of the desired response. *Page 229*

short-term memory (STM) The second stage of memory that contains information a person is consciously thinking about or working with; its capacity is limited to five to nine items and its duration is about 30 seconds. *Page 256*

sleep apnea A temporary cessation of breathing during sleep; one of the suspected causes of snoring, sudden infant death syndrome (SIDS), high blood pressure, and heart damage. *Page 185*

sleeper effect The initial tendency to discount information from an unreliable source but to later consider it more trustworthy because the source is forgotten. *Page 282*

social psychology The branch of psychology that studies how other people influence an individual's behavior (thoughts, feelings, and actions). *Page 603*

somatic nervous system (SNS) A subdivision of the peripheral nervous system that connects to sensory receptors and controls skeletal muscles. *Page 52*

source amnesia Attributing to a wrong source an event that we have experienced, heard about, read about, or imagined; also called source confusion or source misattribution. *Page 282*

split-brain A surgical separation of the brain's two hemispheres used medically to treat severe epilepsy. Split-brain patients provide data on the functions of the two hemispheres. *Page 76*

spontaneous recovery The reappearance of a previously extinguished response after a period of time without exposure to the conditioned stimulus. *Page 218*

standardization The process of establishing the norms and uniform procedures for giving and scoring a test. *Page 324*

stem cell Precursor (immature) cells that produce new specialized cells. A stem cell holds all the information it needs to make bone, blood, brain — any part of a human body — and can also copy itself to maintain a stock of stem cells. *Page 81*

stereotype (1) A set of beliefs about the characteristics of people in a group that is generalized to all group members or (2) the cognitive component of prejudice. *Page 610*

stereotype threat A psychological predicament in which a person experiences doubt about his or her performance, owing to negative stereotypes about his or her group's abilities. *Page 333*

stimulants Drugs that act on the brain and nervous system to increase their overall activity and general responsiveness. *Page 191*

stimulus discrimination The occurrence of a learned response to a specific stimulus but not to other, similar stimuli. *Page 217*

stimulus generalization The occurrence of a learned response not only to

the original stimulus but also to other similar stimuli. *Page 217*

storage The process of retaining neural coded information over time. *Page 264*

stress A nonspecific response of the body to any demand made on it; the arousal, both physical and mental, to situations or events that we perceive as threatening or challenging. *Page 104*

subliminal Pertaining to any stimulus presented below the threshold of conscious awareness. *Page 161*

superego In psychoanalytic theory, the part of the personality that incorporates parental and societal standards for morality. *Page 489*

survey Nonexperimental research technique that assesses behaviors and attitudes of a sample or population. *Page 19*

sympathetic nervous system Subdivision of the autonomic nervous system responsible for arousing the body and mobilizing its energy during times of stress; also called the fight-or-flight system. *Page 52*

synapse [SIN-aps] The junction between the axon tip of the sending neuron and the dendrite or cell body of the receiving neuron. *Page 57*

syntax The grammatical rules that specify in what order the words and phrases should be arranged in a sentence to convey meaning. *Page 313*

systematic desensitization In behavior therapy, a gradual process of extinguishing a learned fear (or phobia) by associating a hierarchy of fear-evoking stimuli with deep relaxation. *Page 581*

telegraphic speech The two- or three-word sentences of young children that contain only the most necessary words. *Page 357*

temperament A basic, inborn disposition that appears shortly after birth and characterizes an individual's style of approaching people and situations. *Page 382*

temporal lobes Cortical lobes above the ears involved in audition (hearing), language comprehension, memory, and some emotional control. *Page 71*

teratogen [TER-ah-toe-jen] An external, environmental agent that can cross the placental barrier and disrupt development, causing minor or severe birth defects; from the Greek word teras, meaning "malformation." *Page 348*

thalamus [THAL-uh-muss] A brain structure at the top of the brainstem that

relays sensory messages to the cerebral cortex. *Page 68*

thanatology [THAN-uh-tall-uh-jee] The study of death and dying. The term comes from Thanatos, the Greek name for a mythical personification of death, and was borrowed by Sigmund Freud to represent the death instinct. *Page 398*

Thematic Apperception Test (TAT) A projective test that shows a series of ambiguous black-and-white pictures and asking the test taker to create a story related to each. The responses presumably reflect a projection of unconscious processes. *Page 447*

theory A system of interrelated, accumulated research findings used to explain a set of observations and generate testable hypotheses. *Page 12*

tip-of-the-tongue (TOT) phenomenon A retrieval failure that involves a sensation of knowing that specific information is stored in long-term memory but being temporarily unable to retrieve it. *Page 279*

tolerance A decreased sensitivity to a drug brought about by its continuous use. *Page 190*

top-down processing Processing that starts "at the top" with the observer's thoughts, expectations, and knowledge and works down; perceptual analysis that emphasizes the perceiver's internal cognitive processes rather than being driven by characteristics of the outside stimuli. *Page 128*

trait A relatively stable and consistent characteristic that can be used to describe someone. *Page 480*

transduction The process by which a stimulus to a receptor is converted into neural impulses. *Page 129*

transference In psychoanalysis, the patient may displace (or transfer) thoughts, feelings, fears, wishes, and conflicts from past relationships, particularly from childhood, onto new relationships, especially with the therapist. *Page 571*

trichromatic theory The theory, first proposed by Thomas Young, stating that color perception results from mixing three distinct color systems — red, green, and blue. *Page 159*

type A personality Set of behavior characteristics that includes intense ambition, competition, drive, constant preoccupation with responsibilities, exaggerated time urgency, and a cynical, hostile outlook. *Page 114*

type B personality Set of behavior characteristics consistent with a calm, patient, relaxed attitude toward life. *Page 114*

unconditional positive regard According to Carl Rogers, the nonjudgmental attitude and genuine caring that the therapist should express toward the client to increase his or her self-esteem. *Page 501*

unconditioned response (UCR) The reflex response evoked by a stimulus without any learning required. *Page 213*

unconditioned stimulus (UCS) Any stimulus that causes a reflex or emotional response without any learning or conditioning. *Page 213*

unconscious Sigmund Freud's term for thoughts, motives, impulses, or desires that lie beyond a person's normal awareness but that can be made available through psychoanalysis. *Page 171*

validity The ability of a test to measure what it was designed to measure. *Page 323*

variable-interval schedule A schedule of reinforcement in which the participant is reinforced for the first response after a period of time has elapsed. This period of time varies from one reinforcement to the next. *Page 228*

variable-ratio schedule A schedule of reinforcement in which the participant is reinforced, on the average, for making a specific number of responses, but the number of required responses between reinforcements is varied. *Page 228*

wavelength The length of a light wave or sound wave, measured from the crest of one wave to the crest of the next. *Page 133*

withdrawal Discomfort and distress, including physical pain and intense cravings, experienced after stopping the use of addictive drugs. *Page 190*

Zeigarnik effect Process whereby interrupted tasks are better recalled than completed tasks. *Page 267*

Name Index

Subject Index